WRITTEN OUT
OF
TELEVISION

A TV Lover's Guide to Cast Changes
1945-1994

STEVEN LANCE

MADISON BOOKS

Lanham • New York • London

Copyright © 1996 by Madison Books

Published by Madison Books
4720 Boston Way
Lanham, Maryland 20706

3 Henrietta Street
London WC2E 8LU, England

Library of Congress Cataloging-in-Publication Data

Lance, Steven, 1953-
Written out of television : a tv lover's guide to cast changes
1945-1994 / Steven Lance.
p.   cm.
Includes bibliographical references and index.
1. Television programs—United States—Casting.
I. Title. PN1992.8.C36L36   1996   791.45' 75' 0973—dc20   95-47417   CIP

ISBN 1-56833-071-5 (paper : alk. paper)

Distributed by National Book Network

∞ ™ The paper used in this publication meets the minimum requirements
of American National Standard for Information Sciences — Permanence of
Paper for Printed Library Materials, ANSI Z39.48–1984.
Manufactured in the United States of America.

To Heidi, for her love American style that is more powerful than a locomotive, and for being the only person on this shining planet known as earth to understand me better than I do myself.

Research Assistant
Linda Rhodes

To tell these stories of those characters who have been written out of television, many entries contain segments of actual dialogue, which have been transcribed by the author from the broadcast episodes of the series which have aired on ABC, CBS, DuMont, Fox, NBC, PBS, the Family Channel, and programs produced for first-run syndication as follows: *The A-Team,* NBC; the *Adventures of Superman,* syndicated, ABC; *All in the Family,* CBS; *The Andy Griffith Show,* CBS; *The Ann Sothern Show,* CBS; *Anything but Love,* ABC; *The Beverly Hillbillies,* CBS; *Bewitched,* ABC; *Bonanza,* NBC; *Burke's Law,* ABC, CBS; *CHEERS,* NBC; *The Dick Van Dyke Show,* CBS; *Diff'rent Strokes,* NBC; *Family Ties,* NBC; *Geraldo,* Investigative News Group/syndicated; *Gilligan's Island,* CBS; *Good Sports,* CBS; *Good Times,* CBS; *Happy Days,* ABC; *Hazel,* NBC, CBS; *The Hogan Family,* NBC, CBS; *Hogan's Heroes,* CBS; *Home Improvement,* ABC; *The Honeymooners,* DuMont, CBS, ABC; *I Dream of Jeannie,* NBC; *I Love Lucy,* CBS; *In the Heat of the Night,* NBC; *The Invisible Man,* Official Films/CBS, NBC; *Isis,* CBS; *Land of the Lost,* NBC; *The Lone Ranger,* ABC; *Love & War,* ABC; *The Love Boat,* ABC; *M*A*S*H,* CBS; *The Many Loves of Dobie Gillis,* CBS; *Married . . . With Children,* Fox; *Maverick,* ABC, CBS, NBC; *Mission: Impossible,* CBS, ABC; *Mr. Ed,* CBS; *The Munsters,* CBS, NBC, syndicated; *My Three Sons,* ABC, CBS; *Newhart,* CBS; *Night Court,* NBC; *The Odd Couple,* CBS, ABC; *Pee-wee's Playhouse,* CBS; *Perry Mason,* CBS, NBC; *Remington Steele,* NBC; *Sanford and Son,* NBC; *Saved by the Bell,* NBC; *Sesame Street,* PBS; *The Torkelsons,* NBC; *Star Trek: The Next Generation,* Paramount/syndicated; *The Streets of San Francisco,* ABC, NBC; *Tarzan,* NBC, CBS; *Three's Company,* ABC; *The Untouchables,* ABC, Paramount/syndicated; *Valerie,* NBC, CBS; *Zorro,* ABC, Family Channel.

CONTENTS

Acknowledgments   xi

Introduction   xiii

Teaser   xv

The Encyclopedia   1

Bibliography   457

Index   461

About the Author   509

GUEST STARRING
(in order of appearance)

Robert Shayne
Henry Darrow
Don DeFore
Jane Milmore
Billy Van Zandt
Bob Elliott
Larry Harmon
Michael Ansara
Ralph Bellamy
Harold J. Stone
Viola Harris
Jack Larson
Roy Stuart
Ron DeFore
James Doohan
Paul Regina
Walter Koenig
James Keach
Edna Skinner
Al Lewis
Butch Patrick
Pat Priest
Vanessa Brown
Barry Sullivan
Roscoe Orman
Ward Saxton
Irish McCalla
Claude Kirchner
Ed McMahon
Denny Miller
Tom Amandes
Duncan Regehr
Michael Tylo
James Victor

SPECIAL GUEST APPEARANCES BY
(in alphabetical order)

Helen Bailey; Danton Burroughs/*Edgar Rice Burroughs, Inc.;* Marion DeFore; John Gertz/*Zorro Productions, Inc.;* Dean Hargrove/*Dean Hargrove Productions;* Timothy Hunter/*Television Index, Inc.;* Hasha Mintz; Susan Sackett; Elizabeth "Aunt Bette" Shayne; *Van Zandt and Milmore Productions;* Patrick J. White; Bill Yenne.

ACKNOWLEDGMENTS
(in alphabetical order)

Vince Acera, Rob Acampora, Claudia Ansorge, Jeff Arban, Charlie Barrett, Kathy Bassett, Aimee Bell, Robert W. Blihar, Karen Blythe, James Burnett, "Dr. Wayne" Calabretta, Mark B. Campbell, *Canal Plus of France, Stephen J. Cannell Productions, Carson Tonight, Inc., Christopher Crowe Productions,* Jim Clark, Mike Collins, Ed Cook, Wil Crosta, Roger M. Crowley, Pat Cruise, Jerry Digney, John Drinkwater, Michael B. Druxman, *Michael B. Druxman Public Relations,* Dr. John E. Durst, *Elliotland, Ellipse Programme, The Family Channel,* Conrad P. Felber, Ed Ferrara, Jan Fisher, Bill Flanagan, Rudolf Flesch, Chip Fortier, Dave Fontaine, Bob Fowler, *Fox Broadcasting Company,* Bruce Garrabrandt, David Garrison, *Gil Grant Productions, Goodman-Rosen Productions,* Susan G. Grey, *Guttman/Pam, Ltd.,* J. Miller Hahn, J.T. Harding, *Larry Harmon Pictures,* Susan Harmon, Dave Holland, Dr. Darren Holman, *Investigative News Group,* Madelyn Kelly, Rosamond Kiefer, Miles Krueger, Kimberly Last, Marci Lee, *The Lippin Group, Love & War Productions, Inc.,* Staci Lynne, Leonard Maltin, Jennifer Mann, Jackie Martling, Andrew Scott Marvel, Phil McFall, John S. Mac Gowan, *The Mac Gowan Agency, McMahon Communications, Inc.,* Dewey Mee, Rick Mitz, Kevin Murphy, My Family, Tova Navarra, *New World Television, The New York Times,* Jim Nolt, Bill O'Shaughnesy, James Robert Parish, *Paramount Pictures Paramount Television,* Wally Patrick, Fran & Mike Perano, Michael R. Pitts, Anthony S. Policastro, Ron Prager, Robin Pringle, Lou Quallenberg, *Lou Quallenberg Studios,* A.K. Quinn, *Radio Television Italiana,* Bob Reed, Jim Reme, Linda Rhodes, Larry Richards, Geraldo Rivera, Sibyl Roberts, Nathan Rosenhouse, Andrea "Andy" St. James, Karen Sanchez, Mike Sauter, Dr. John P. Shaffer, *SPY,* Lawrence R. Stein, Wally Stroby, Neil Sullivan, Neil Summers, Robert S. Susser, Esq., Stuart Tenzer, John & Verna Townsley, *Twentieth Television, The Two River Times, Universal Television,* John D. Van Pelt, Mary Van Zandt, Mark Voger, WHTG FM106.3, Bernard Weinraub, Earl Weirich, *The Westerner,* Kim Wilder, Dick Wolf, *Wolf Films,* Donna M. Worsdorfer, Zachary "Zack" The Wonder Dog Morris.

The Author gratefully wishes to thank the following people without whose help this book would not have been possible:

Vincent Terrace, who as an established author on the subject of television, has unselfishly shared his wealth of knowledge, experience, resources and time to help make *Written Out of Television* the most complete and accurate book on the subject ever published. It is also his dedication to preserving the history of televison that made it possible for this writer to wear the title "author."

Doug McClelland, the respected motion picture author who has given this author much more than the research assistance he provided on a seven-day-a-week, twenty-four-hour-a-day basis—and that is his encouragement and his friendship.

Donna St. Marie, my personal editor and friend, who after learning that editing this book was a much bigger job than it appeared, saw to it that this project was better than when she began.

And those two incredible young ladies, Staci Lynne and Marci Lee, whose unswerving devotion and understanding have proven them to be wise beyond their years.

INTRODUCTION

First, a word about my methodology. *Written Out of Television* is an encyclopedic examination of programs in which actors have been written out, from 1945 through the beginning of 1994. The research has not been limited to a specific category of television; this encyclopedia includes adventures, comedies, dramas, science fiction, Westerns, and children's programs that have aired in daytime and prime time, on networks, cable and in syndication.

The book is arranged alphabetically and each chapter covers the programs whose titles begin with the corresponding letter of the alphabet, excluding the words "A" and "The," in accordance with standard alphabetizing practices. Therefore the *Adventures of Superman* is found under letter "A" for *Adventures* and not "S" for *Superman.* Wherever there are conflicting titles there is a *(see:)* note under the alternative title. This way, if readers look up *Superman,* they will be referred to the *Adventures of Superman.*

Each entry includes the title of the program, the first and last broadcast dates, the network or networks on which the series aired, or the notation that the program was syndicated.

This is followed by the character's name, the actor who first played the character, and the dates during which the role was played by that actor.

Under that are the name(s) of the character(s) who replaced the one listed in the first entry, and the date or dates the actor played the role.

It is important to note that many of the replacement actors and characters listed may be from a later production of the same series; for example, the characters and cast from the two live action productions of *Zorro.* If a new actor played the same character in the same production of a series—for example, John Hart replacing Clayton Moore on *The Lone Ranger*—the "Replaced by" listing carries the same character name; that is, in this instance, The Lone Ranger.

If a new character replaced the old character, as when Colonel Sherman Potter replaced Lieutenant Colonel Henry Blake on *M*A*S*H,* Colonel Sherman Potter is listed on the "Replaced by" line, which is followed by the name of the actor who played him, Harry Morgan, as well as the first and last dates he played the part.

The "Replaced by" listing is repeated for as many times as the character was replaced in a series and subsequent productions of the series—even if they are produced years apart, as was *Zorro.*

Most entries begin with a synopsis of the program, which is followed by the stories of why and how each character was replaced. In many instances, entries include quotations by the cast members and production people, taken from interviews that were conducted exclusively for this work. The actors and actresses who were responsible for creating a piece of television history and have so graciously given of their time to speak and correspond with the author have been credited in the special acknowledgment page under the heading *GUEST STARRING.* Additional interviews with writers, producers and others closely related to series to which they have contributed, have been listed on the acknowledgment page under the heading *SPECIAL GUEST APPEARANCES BY.*

The length of each listing varies depending on the amount of verifiable information available for each program and actor discussed.

If an actor who was written out of a series in one entry was also written out of another series, the notation "(See Entry)" follows the name of the other series. However, if an actor or actress being written about appeared in another series included in *Written Out of Television,* but was not the actor or actress who was written out in that series, there is no notation to see the first entry.

All of the information presented herein has been meticulously researched and extensively cross-referenced—especially the spellings of the names of shows, characters and actors. More importantly, much of the information in this book has come from exclusive interviews with the actors, actresses, producers, writers and directors associated with the program. It also comes from viewing thousands of hours of episodes—some of which have not been seen in more than forty years. This is to assure readers of the most accurate and detailed information ever available, in one source, about the programs where actors have been written out.

These rarely-seen shows include episodes of *Captain Z-Ro, Captain Video, The Halls of Ivy, How to Marry a Millionaire, The Invisible Man, Isis, Johnny Jupiter, Land of the Lost, Life with Luigi, Mama, Meet Corliss Archer, My Friend Irma, Richard Diamond, Private Detective, The Roaring 20's, Route 66, Shazam!, SurfSide Six, The Thin Man, Tom Corbett, Space Cadet, Two Girls Named Smith, The Whirlybirds* and *Zorro.*

Many entries for *Written Out of Television* also include the names of other television series and motion pictures in which the actors and actresses being written about have appeared, to help make this a one-volume reference source. These secondary references, in most instances, carry the release dates of the motion pictures mentioned and the first and last air dates for the series.

If a date is not provided after an actor's or actress's credits, it is most likely because the series mentioned appears as a complete entry elsewhere in the book. The *(See Entry)* statement has been included to both help and encourage the reader to locate more information on an actor or actress who has been written out of another series. It is also used to avoid repeating information about an actor's career which appears elsewhere. To locate further information about anyone included in an entry, readers are encouraged to refer to the index.

Please keep in mind that this is not a complete directory of television programs and that every program ever broadcast is not included.

What have been included are those programs in which a character was replaced either by a new actor, or a new character was played by a different actor but performed the same function in the series. An example of this is from *Newhart,* which had the maid, Leslie Vanderkellen, replaced by her cousin, Stephanie Vanderkellen.

Not every listing contains the stars of the show. On *Hogan's Heroes,* for instance, the main stars—Bob Crane (Colonel Robert Hogan), Werner Klemperer (Colonel Wilhelm Klink) and John Banner (Sergeant Hans Schultz)—remained with the series from beginning to end. The characters examined in this instance are "Baker" and his replacement, "Kinchloe," and Colonel Klink's secretaries, Helga and Hilda.

Since it has very often been the practice to recast a series after a pilot has been shot, these changes have not been included in the "Replaced by" listing, though an entry may contain some mention of the change when this is pertinent.

Variety programs with repertory casts, such as *The Carol Burnett Show* and *Saturday Night Live,* as well as game shows such as *To Tell the Truth, Family Feud* and *Wheel of Fortune,* do not appear in this edition.

Motion pictures, television programs based on motion pictures and motion pictures based on television series all constitute a separate topic and are not treated in this book, but in a companion volume, *Written Out of The Movies.* Replacements of voice talent for animated cartoons have also been set aside for a later work, *Written Out of Cartoons.*

Television soap operas, daytime or evening, are not included, for two reasons. First, the sheer longevity of their runs warrants far more cast changes than the average television series. Second, these long-running dramas occupy a unique niche in television and should be treated separately.

Most of the photographs reproduced in *Written Out of Television* have come from *Personality Photos, Inc./*The Howard Frank Collection. A few others were graciously loaned to the author by *Larry Harmon Pictures, New World Television,* Edna Skinner and Helen Bailey.

In those frustrating instances where the information needed was either unavailable or unverifiable, the word "unknown" has been used—which brings me to my final point.

This book was not one of those overnight projects. I actually began the initial research in 1982 and have worked on it steadily on sunny days, weekends and holidays for the past twelve years. There were even some writing sessions that began and ended at the same time of day—twenty-four hours apart! All of this was to make *Written Out of Television* as accurate and complete as humanly possible. If I have not included your favorite show, it was not by design or intention.

I welcome your comments, corrections and notes on missing or inaccurate entries. Please include your sources and as much information as possible and send them to me care of the publisher.

The new information will be carefully cross-checked and, if it can be verified, included in subsequent editions, because as long as new shows are being produced, there are going to be actors and actresses who will be *Written Out of Television.*

Steven Lance
Thousand Oaks, CA

TEASER

Every day, millions of Americans allow dozens of strangers into their living rooms, dens and bedrooms—something not to be taken lightly. These strangers enter our homes through an electronic device known as a television set.

Consequently, television producers take great pains to avoid cast changes because they know that the viewing public may be unwilling to let yet another unfamiliar face into their homes—and that could cause a popular series to fail.

A change in cast is also dreaded, albeit unconsciously, by television viewers for fear that it will alter their extended family, which they have openly taken into their hearts and homes.

It is understood that the job of the casting director is to hire the cast. The trick, of course, is to assemble the "perfect cast," and that takes some doing.

In its simplest definition, a cast is a group of actors to whom parts are assigned. A good cast, however, demands much more of its members than just playing the parts that are assigned. A good cast works together more like a team than a group of individuals.

The perfect cast functions more like the cells of the human body, all working together for the common good of the individual (the show). Perhaps this is why so many observers of the television phenomenon use the word "chemistry" when describing the perfect relationships between cast members. It is this special chemistry between actors that helps bring a show to life.

To the viewer, a change in cast, of any cast member, once established, seems unthinkable. Consequently, every possible safeguard is taken to keep the original cast intact. Yet, with all these precautions, cast changes have happened on more than 375 programs involving more than 2,000 actors and to some programs, more than once. But no one seemed to notice—or did they?

Often it is the writer's task to determine what the viewer will and will not notice. Until the end of the 1969/1970 television season, Dick York was Darrin Stephens on *Bewitched.* The following season, Dick Sargent was Darrin Stephens. In this instance, the writers decided not to make any mention of this major cast change and the hit series continued uninterrupted until July 1, 1972.

On the other hand, when Hal Conklin was hired to take over the role of Dr. Pauli, Captain Video's electronic adversary, from Bram Nossen, who left the series due to exhaustion, it was explained to the space rangers viewing at home that the evil Dr. Pauli had undergone plastic surgery in a bold attempt to deceive the good Captain.

These are just two examples of actors taking over the roles of other actors in an established TV series—one explained, the other not—proving that there really is more than one right actor for every role. In fact, it is not unheard of for a change in cast to make an already successful show even more popular. A great example of this was the introductions of Colonel Potter (Harry Morgan), B.J. Hunnicut (Mike Farrell) and Charles Winchester, III (David Ogden Stiers) in TV's already hit series, *M*A*S*H.*

This is not a new phenomenon; it has proven successful in many continuous motion picture series. There have been, for instance, two Judge Hardys, four Charlie Chans, six James Bonds and nineteen screen Tarzans!

In recent years, TV series have spawned major motion pictures such as THE NUDE BOMB, a feature version of TV's *Get Smart* in which the producers of the film replaced the late Edward Platt with Dana Elcar as The Chief of CONTROL without damaging the integrity of the other characters.

Another popular series of motion pictures gave audiences the third actor to portray the man of steel in SUPERMAN, 1978; SUPERMAN II, 1980; SUPERMAN III 1983 and SUPERMAN IV: THE QUEST FOR PEACE. In each of these films the characters that had been brought to the screen twice before were again recast. There was a new Perry White, a new Lois Lane, a new Jimmy Olsen and, of course, a new Superman. But the one character from the *Adventures of Superman* (See Entry)—which is today even more popular than it was during the 1950s—which did not appear in the SUPERMAN movies was Clark Kent's police contact and best friend, Inspector William Henderson. Reflecting on playing a continuing character in a television series, actor Robert Shayne, who played Inspector Henderson on the *Adventures of Superman,* said: ''Never leave a series. It's a gift bestowed upon you to constantly create. What could be more fullfilling?''[1]

Why do actors leave successful television series? How are their replacements chosen and how are the changes explained to the audience? Read on—that's what *Written Out of Television* is all about.

---

1. Robert Shayne, in a letter to the author dated July 28, 1991.

Maybe you could hire the *A-Team* who in this first season publicity still starred George Peppard (seated) as Colonel John ''Hannibal'' Smith. Standing (left to right) behind Peppard are Dirk Benedict as Lieutenant Templeton ''Face'' Peck, Dwight Schultz as Captain ''Howling Mad'' Murdock, Melinda Culea as Amy A. Allen and Mr. T as Sergeant Bosco B.A. ''Bad Attitude'' Baracus.

THE A-TEAM

January 23, 1983–June 14, 1987.   NBC

Character:	Amy Amanda Allen
Played By:	Melinda Culea
Date(s):	January 23, 1983–May 8, 1984
Replaced by:	Tawnia Baker
Played by:	Marla Heasley
Date(s):	January 10, 1984–September 25, 1984
Character:	Colonel Lynch
Played by:	William Lucking
Date(s):	1983–1984
Replaced by:	Colonel Roderick Decker
Played by:	Lance LeGault
Date(s):	1983–1986
Replaced by:	Colonel Briggs
Played by:	Charles Napier
Date(s):	October 2, 1984
Replaced by:	Colonel Harlan ''Bull'' Fulbright
Played by:	Jack Ging
Date(s):	January 21, 1986–May 13, 1986

''In 1972, a crack commando unit was sent to prison by a military court for a crime they didn't commit! These men promptly escaped from a maximum security stockade to the Los Angeles Underground. Today, still wanted by the government, they survive as soldiers of fortune. If you have a problem—if no one else can help, and *if* you can find them, maybe you can hire—the A-Team!''

The members of the A-Team are Colonel John ''Hannibal'' Smith (George Peppard), Sergeant Bosco, ''B.A.'' Baracus (the ''B.A.'' stands for ''Bad Attitude'') (Mr. T), and Captain ''H.M.'' Murdock (the ''H.M'' stands for Howling Mad) (Dwight Schultz). The last member of the team is Lieutenant Templeton Peck, also known as ''Face'' or the ''Faceman.'' He was played throughout the series by Dirk Benedict, who took over the role from Tim Dunnigan, who appeared in the two-hour NBC pilot which aired on January 23, 1983.

George Peppard, already a well-known film and television actor, had played Thomas Banacek in the NBC series *Banacek,* which aired from September 13, 1972 to September 3, 1974.

Mr. T became a household name when he appeared as Clubber Lang in the 1982 action drama, ROCKY III.

In 1988, Tim Dunnigan played Davy Crockett (See Entry) and television science fiction fans may best remember Dirk Benedict as the Han Solo clone in the small screen's space adventure, *Battlestar Galactica* (See Entry).

The opening narration of every episode of *The A-Team* contains the phrase, ''Today, still wanted by the government . . .''

The government is after the A-Team for robbing the Bank of Hanoi during the Vietnam War in 1972. It is a crime they did not commit, but until they can clear their names they must live their lives as fugitives in the Los Angeles underground.

During the five-year run of *The A-Team,* ''The Government'' has been represented by three United States Army colonels and two generals, each of whom was charged with the responsibility of ''delivering'' the A-Team to their superiors.

The A-Team was originally hunted by Colonel Lynch, who began his mission in the pilot *The A-Team.* Lynch was played by William ''Bill'' Lucking, who played Oscar Kalahani, the foreman of the Paradise Ranch on the 1977 NBC adventure series, *Big Hawaii,* and has played cops and military officers ever since. He played Captain Potts in the three-part, eight-hour CBS miniseries, *The Blue and the Gray,* which aired from November 14 to 17, 1982, and soon afterward joined the cast of *The A-Team* as Colonel Lynch—a part he held for nearly two seasons. Following *The A-Team,* Lucking traded his army fatigues for a policeman's uniform for his role as Sergeant Mac McClellan in the short-lived ABC crime drama, *Jessie.*

In the episode, ''When You Comin' Back Range Rider?'' the A-Team was introduced to its next adversary, Colonel Roderick Decker, played to a tee by the gravel-voiced Lance LeGault. We first see Decker on an army firing range as a three-star U.S. Army general briefs him on the A-Team:

GENERAL:	These men have been wanted for over ten years. It's time we closed the file.
DECKER:	The case has been back-burnered for years, General. It's common knowledge Colonel Lynch has been waging his own ridiculous little vendetta.
GENERAL:	Precisely the reason that Colonel Lynch is now out and this matter is hanging fire. These three

soldiers were tried and convicted because of extreme political pressure at the time. Which is something that you should understand.

DECKER: (Firing off seven rounds in rapid succession at one of the targets.) Yes, sir.

GENERAL: They were practically forgotten about within a couple of years of their escape but Lynch keeps throwing balls down their alley. Now he's mushroomed this whole thing into what's considered to be a highly embarrassing series of situations.

The general continues by sharing a file on Lynch's snafus, via clips from previous episodes in which Lynch lost one military executive jet, five MP cars and allowed the A-Team to escape from a full-security military installation after it had been publicized that they had been captured.

The general concludes his discussion with Decker by telling him, ''Do what you have to do. Get me the A-Team.''

The first encounter comes when Decker crashes Face's (Dirk Benedict) fund raiser for his film project, THE BEAST OF THE YELLOW NIGHT, which is being held at the Hollywood Palladium. Hannibal has already checked out their latest client and is busy assembling the team for its next mission.

HANNIBAL: Now we need the job. This guy, Daniel Running Bear, needs our help. Go get Murdock. And keep your head down, I've got a feeling Lynch is outside this minute.

What happens instead is that Colonel Decker and his men burst into the room and begin their first chase scene, which starts out on foot and continues with a full two-minute automobile chase with Decker and his men in MP cars pursuing Hannibal and Face in a ''borrowed'' car.

When the A-Team is unable to shake Decker off its tail, Face asks, ''Who in the world is this guy? Sure isn't Lynch.'' Hannibal answers, ''I don't know. It's gonna be fun finding out, huh?''

Later in the episode, Colonel Decker and his men use an electronic homing device to track the A-Team to a warehouse located in Berth 57 at the Port of Los Angeles. Using a bullhorn, Decker announces himself to the A-Team:

DECKER: This is Colonel Decker of the U.S. Army. You are completely surrounded.

HANNIBAL: Ah, no kidding.

FACE: It's Colonel Decker. Did ya hear that?

AMY: Do you know this guy?

FACE: Everyone in Vietnam knew him. He's one of those guys who got the job done under any circumstances and he never lost any sleep over how he did it.

B.A.: Yeah, Hannibal and this guy mixed it up once in the Dune Club.

AMY: The Dune Club?

HANNIBAL: The Da Nang officers' open mess.

AMY: What? You didn't like the way he sugared his coffee?

HANNIBAL: No. I didn't like the way he blew up Cong hospitals like it was his favorite sport.

The A-Team having escaped, Decker utters his last line of the episode in his trademark deep guttural voice: ''Next time Hannibal Smith, next time.''

There were several next times, but unfortunately for Lance LeGault, Colonel Decker never did capture the A-Team. During the 1989 season of the syndicated science fiction series, *Star Trek: The Next Generation,* Lance LeGault had his features completely submerged beneath Klingon make-up. The only thing that could not be covered up was his distinctive voice.

The third military thorn in the A-Team's side was Colonel Briggs, who appeared in the October 2, 1984 episode as outlined in *TV Guide:* ''Yet another military nemesis (Charles Napier) takes the team in his sights while they help a small-town fire chief (Stepfanie Kramer) battle a rival engine company trying to force her out of business.''[2]

Hannibal first encounters Colonel Briggs in a wax museum where Mr. Lee (one of Hannibal's alter egos played under heavy makeup) has told his potential client, Annie Sanders, to meet him.

BRIGGS: Miss, if you're thinking about hiring the A-Team, I'm afraid you're out of luck. I'm Colonel Briggs, United States Army and the men you're looking for are federal fugitives wanted by the military.

Briggs stumbles around the museum trying to find Hannibal, looking in a suit of armor, pulling the hood off the executioner and releasing the guillotine. After he leaves, Hannibal stands up from behind the guillotine wearing a headless costume.

HANNIBAL: Colonel Briggs, huh? A new face on the block is always a welcome change. You've just found the A-Team, Miss Sanders.

Hannibal and Miss Sanders join the rest of the A-Team in the museum's workshop.

2. *TV Guide,* October 2, 1984.

HANNIBAL: Well, we were right. Decker's been replaced. Somebody else has got a shot at our golden gooses.

After some brief dialogue between Face and Murdock, Hannibal continues.

HANNIBAL: I hate to interrupt an artist, but the MP's just came out of the next room led by Decker's replacement, a Colonel Briggs.

There is some further discussion among the team before Colonel Briggs bursts into the studio firing weapons. The team hightails it out the back door and jumps into a black van being driven by B.A. Baracus.

B.A.: This guy's worse than Decker.

HANNIBAL: It's gonna be interesting. Go B.A.!

Colonel Briggs eventually does catch up with the A-Team and has a heart to heart with Colonel John ''Hannibal'' Smith.

BRIGGS: You do insane things, Smith. That's why I figured you'd come back here and try to help her [Annie Sanders]. What is with you? How could you give up 20 years of your life in a military prison to come back here?

HANNIBAL: That would require an understanding of the human condition. I'm surprised the thought crossed your mind, Briggs.

BRIGGS: Let me tell you something, Smith. All that garbage about Lynch and Decker admiring you and the others while they were chasing ya. That's stupid.

HANNIBAL: Yeah. What happened to Decker? Did they ship him to Alaska because he didn't catch us?

Decker's fate was never explained beyond this dialogue and Colonel Briggs' tenure lasted only one episode.

Charles Napier had previously appeared as Luthor Sprague in the short-lived NBC Western, *The Oregon Trail,* which aired from September 21, 1977 to October 26, 1977. Five years later, Napier turned up as Major Harrison in the CBS Civil War miniseries, *The Blue and the Gray,* which also featured Napier's predecessor, Bill Lucking, as Captain Potts.

Jack Ging, who played both Captain Stark in the *A-Team* episode, ''A Small and Deadly War,'' and Lieutenant Taggart of the U.S. Border Patrol in ''Bad Time on the Border,'' was reincarnated as General Harlan ''Bull'' Fulbright in ''The A-Team is Coming, The A-Team is Coming.''

We first see General Fulbright as he introduces himself to Lean of the S.I.A.

FULBRIGHT: Bull Fulbright.

LEAN: I'm Lean, S.I.A. In charge of special operations and covert anti-radical procedures, West Coast.

FULBRIGHT: Ah, well, what brings the company down here to my store?

LEAN: In the past twenty-four hours there's been a defection of a Russian ballerina that ended in a K.G.B. shootout and a dramatic rise in intelligence reports on the movements of radicals.

FULBRIGHT: Sounds to me like you had a very busy morning. I'm just dying to know how I fit into your Commie mumbo jumbo.

Lean then hands Fulbright an envelope containing what he calls ''routine surveillance photos'' that were shot in front of the Russian consulate.

FULBRIGHT: Smith and Peck.

LEAN: I thought that might pique your interest. It appears the A-Team has jumped sides and gone to work for the Russians.

FULBRIGHT: Traitors huh? I love it. There are some things, Lean, that never change. All right. From here on out it's shoot-to-kill. Thank you.

When Lean and Fulbright catch up with the A-Team, Hannibal Smith explains that they are working with Russians to prevent a Russian colonel from stealing an antimissile satellite and starting World War III.

Lean believes Smith's story and gives him the go-ahead to complete the mission with the aid of the U.S. government. Fulbright will only agree to work alongside the A-Team on the condition that they surrender to him when the mission is over. Reluctantly, Hannibal agrees. However, when the mission is completed Hannibal reneges on his agreement with Fulbright.

HANNIBAL: We'd give ourselves up General, but remember what Ulysses Grant once said. ''There are no promises in war, just stratagems.''

Fulbright, however, was prepared for Smith's actions and brought enough backup with him to capture the A-Team.

Inside the army military police van, Face laments, ''It's ironic, hey guys? Every time we try to serve our country we wind up behind bars.'' The camera cuts to the front seat of the van.

LEAN: So how does it feel to have the A-Team's duffel bag under your bunk?

FULBRIGHT: Piece of cake. I don't understand Decker's problem in trying to run these clowns down.

Of course, the A-Team escapes.

General Fulbright made his last appearance on the *A-Team* in a bittersweet episode, "The Sound of Thunder," which was written by the series' cocreator, Frank Lupo.

Fulbright contacts the A-Team on the pretense that Colonel Morrison, the one person who could clear them, was not killed during the war but is still alive and being held in a Vietnamese P.O.W. camp. Having their names cleared is so important that B.A., who has a phobia of flying, even agrees to make the trip by air.

Fulbright's real reason, however, is that he needs the team's help to get his son (born to his wartime girlfriend, Chin Tu) out of Vietnam and back to the United States.

Early on in the episode, The A-Team saves Fulbright's life by getting him to duck a sniper's machine-gun fire. After which he makes this faithful admission:

FULBRIGHT: I didn't have anyone else to turn to when I came to you guys. I figured well. If you're everything that you say you are, you'd take the mission. If you turned it down, I'd know what you really are.

FACE: Tough way to prove we're innocent.

FULBRIGHT: I want all of you to know one thing. As much as I wanted and needed you to go on this mission with me, I never really thought you were innocent . . . until now.

The twist is that Fulbright doesn't have a son, but a daughter Tia (Tia Carrere), and it is she who was trying to kill him because she resented his leaving Vietnam without her mother, Chin Tu.

Hannibal finally arranges a meeting between Fulbright and his daughter, but while waiting for the A-Team to return he is captured and tortured by an old Vietnamese adversary, Colonel Su. In an all-too-realistic scene which personified the horrors of the Vietnam War, the A-Team blows up Colonel Su and his soldiers, but not in time to prevent Su from shooting General Fulbright in the back.

In the most poignant scene of the series, a beaten, bloody and dying Fulbright, lying in Hannibal's arms in a helicopter poised for takeoff, painfully gives his last speech to his newly-found daughter and the A-Team.

FULBRIGHT: Oh, you're so pretty.

HANNIBAL: Not like her old man.

FULBRIGHT: Smith . . . you and your men . . . good soldiers. I'm glad we wound up on the same side.

Fulbright then gasped and died, making him the first of only two characters ever to die on *The A-Team*.[3]

Jack Ging was born near Alva, Oklahoma on November 30, 1931. In 1961, at the age of thirty, he joined the cast of the NBC Western, *Tales of Wells Fargo,* and played Dale Robertson's young assistant, Beau McCloud, through 1962. After leaving *The A-Team,* Jack Ging turned up as Lieutenant Ted Quinlan in another Stephen J. Cannell production, *Riptide.* Ging stayed with the series during the 1984–1985 season.

In *The A-Team* pilot, Melinda Culea was introduced as the fifth member of the team when she hired them to go to Mexico to rescue Al Massey, a fellow reporter on the *Los Angeles Courier-Express,* who was kidnaped by Jefe Valdez, played by Sergio Calderon.

Amy Allen was often treated as if she were a fifth wheel by the team's leader, Hannibal Smith, and there was very little substance to her role. The only change this character ever went through was having her shoulder-length brown hair bobbed.

In John Javna's book, *Cult TV,* he said that Melinda Culea left *The A-Team* because she didn't get along with George Peppard.

TV Guide reporter Tom Nolan spent a week with the *A-Team* in March of 1984. And it just so happened that the cast and crew were filming the episode "The Battle of Bel Air," the 1984 season opener that introduced the character Tawnia Baker, played by Marla Heasley. In that article, which appeared in the March 10, 1984, issue, Dwight Schultz (Howling Mad Murdock) spoke with Tom Nolan about Marla Heasley replacing Melinda Culea. "One former team member," writes Nolan, "the departed Melinda Culea, had been vocal about her dissatisfaction with her series role. What about her absence this year?"

"Well," Schultz answers in roundabout fashion, "The last thing I did in New York City was an off-Broadway play. It was tremendously successful. The reviews were the best I have ever received from the big three major critics. There were lots of rumors of it going on to Broadway.

"One day I picked up the paper and read that the show was indeed going on to Broadway—but with another actor, not me. I was shocked. Obviously something had been wrong, but I'll never know the reason I was replaced.

"And I think it's much the same case with Melinda. There were lots of little problems . . . but whatever happened in the offices over there, we'll never really know. They made the decision it was the best thing to replace her.

"But every actor is replaced at one point or another. That's what this business is about: replacing and being replaced . . . ."

The producers handled Amy Allen's leaving the series by explaining that she had been assigned to a new job as a foreign correspondent. Shortly after leaving "The A-Team," Melinda Culea landed the role of Terry Randolph in the ABC drama, *Glitter,* which aired from September 13, 1984 to December 27,

---

3. The other character who died on *The A-Team* was David McCallum in "The Say Uncle Affair." He was shot by, of all people, Robert Vaughn, who had co-starred with him on *The Man from U.N.C.L.E..*

1985. She had a guest-starring role as Alex Keaton's boss in an episode of the NBC situation comedy, *Family Ties,* and played Paula Vertosick on the CBS evening soap opera, *Knot's Landing.*

The next regular female member of the team was Tawnia Baker, played by the very sexy Marla Heasley. Before becoming a regular on *The A-Team,* Marla Heasley made a brief appearance as Charis in "Bad Time on the Border." Wearing a bikini, Ms. Heasley spoke a total of less than 40 words in a role which didn't amount to very much more than window dressing.

Her role as Tawnia Baker in "The Battle of Bel Air," however, was a little meatier. It opens inside Intermode World Wide Securities Data Center with Tawnia, another reporter on the *Los Angeles Courier-Express,* using one of Intermode's computers to uncover information about the A-Team. In the process, she discovers that Colonel Decker has scheduled an assault on the team later that morning and she goes to warn them that Decker is on the way.

When she arrives, the A-Team isn't convinced she's telling the truth, but before they can cross-examine her, Colonel Decker shows up and, in one sentence, explains what happened to Amy Allen.

DECKER: Miss Allen takes an overseas assignment and you don't waste any time replacing her, do ya?

After the A-Team escapes from Colonel Decker, Tawnia pleads her case with Hannibal Smith.

TAWNIA: I'm telling you, I am a reporter. I work for the *L.A. Courier-Express* and I know Amy Allen very well.

HANNIBAL: Which is very difficult for us to confirm on short notice, seeing that Amy's in Djakarta right now.

Tawnia then explains that Amy Allen's promotion was a direct result of her close association with the A-Team.

TAWNIA: Come on, you practically won her that foreign correspondent appointment.

HANNIBAL: Which you'd like us to do for you?

Tawnia continues her sales pitch.

TAWNIA: You could use someone who's not hot to work the outside for you like Amy used to.

Trying to make his offer appear as distasteful as possible, Face offers to spend some time alone with the beautiful Ms. Baker to find out if she really is on the level. Back at her apartment in more intimate surroundings, Tawnia tries to get an interview with Face for her newspaper, while at the same time making an obvious attempt to persuade him to let her join the A-Team.

TAWNIA: I thought you had a hard fast rule about fraternizing with members of the team.

FACE: Ah, but you're not a member of the team . . .

TAWNIA: (Finishing Face's sentence), Yet. But I'll bet you can see me as one.

In the show's epilogue, after an explosive helicopter chase, Tawnia makes her final bid for membership by recounting all of the assistance she gave to the A-Team on their mission to save the life of wealthy Arab oil magnate, Sheik Fatasi.

HANNIBAL: And you think all this buys you a locker in our gym? Sound familiar?

B.A.:   (Growls)

TAWNIA: You can't tell me Amy would have done any more than I did. I deserve the same chance she got.

There are some more exchanges of dialogue under which Colonel Decker's military police siren can be heard getting closer and closer.

HANNIBAL: See ya, Baker, and thanks.

TAWNIA: Hannibal, wait! Decker saw me with you. He'll haul me off to jail. You gotta let me come with you.

HANNIBAL: We'll give ya a lift.

TAWNIA: Great, we can kick this around on the way. Really get to know each other.

The team stops getting into the van and give Tawnia a stare of disbelief. The frame freezes and the theme music sneaks in along with the closing credits.

"Listen up! Word from the Los Angeles Underground (the last known address for the A-Team) is that the show's incumbent distaff regular, Marla Heasley, will not be back.

" 'We're just not going to try to integrate any more outsiders in the *A-Team*,' says coexecutive producer, Frank Lupo. Is this just male chauvinism? Lupo denies it: 'This has nothing to do with any supposed trouble between the guys and women, or with women performers.' "[4]

When it was decided to write Marla Heasley's character out

---

4. "Insider Grapevine," *TV Guide,* Vol. 32, No. 27, Issue #1632, July 7, 1984, p. 17.

of the series, she was fortunate enough to have her last appearance in "The Bend in the River," the two-hour 1984 third-season opener, which happens to be a particularly good episode.

In that episode, Barry Van Dyke plays Brian Lefcourt, the rich owner of the *L.A. Courier-Examiner,* who also holds a Ph.D. in archaeology. While searching for the treasure of the Peruvian Indians in the Amazon, Lefcourt is taken captive by a wonderfully disgusting river pirate who calls himself, "El Cajon." Face points out that cajon isn't a name, but a Spanish word which translates as "The Coffin." El Cajon is played by Sergio Calderon, the same character actor who played Jefe Valdez in *The A-Team* pilot.

Back in her apartment, Tawnia tells Hannibal and Face who Brian Lefcourt is and why she is so interested in finding him.

HANNIBAL: And you're engaged to this Brian Lefcourt?

TAWNIA: Pre-engaged. We gave each other these St. Christopher's [medals]. And when he got back from trying to find the lost treasure of Del Rio, we were going to be married.

In the end, El Cajon turns out not to be such a bad guy after all. He was just following the orders of a Neo-Nazi, Doyle, whom the A-Team trashes at the end of the episode.

In the epilogue, El Cajon marries Brian and Tawnia in a short ceremony he conducts in Spanish. Hannibal gives Tawnia away, Face and B.A. are her ushers and Murdock takes the imaginary wedding movies. After the ceremony, Tawnia hugs Hannibal.

TAWNIA: Face, Hannibal, I'll never forget you guys.

HANNIBAL: Felicitations, kid. Good having you around. Congratulations.

LEFCOURT: Thank you. Tawnia and I will write you and let you know how the excavations are going.

As it turned out, they never wrote and neither character was ever mentioned again.

Tawnia Baker was the last regular female member of the A-Team, although in the epilogue of "The Sound of Thunder," the dialogue suggested that General Fulbright's daughter, Tia, whom the A-Team had brought back to the States from Vietnam, might be joining them.

TIA: I will pay all of you for what you have done for me. You'll see, I won't be just an extra burden to you.

HANNIBAL: Tia, I don't think you understand something. We brought you out of Vietnam because you're . . . now you're . . . you're wanted, you're a criminal. You'd be hunted by the government. And that's our situation here.

There are some brief exchanges between the other member of the team before Tia answers.

TIA: What was my home for 20 years, no longer is. I don't belong here. I'm without papers, or proof of who my father is. If I am caught, what will happen to me?

HANNIBAL: (Takes a long pause.) Maybe you can stick with us until we figure something out.

Hannibal must have figured something out, because Tia was never seen or heard from again.

THE ABBOTT AND COSTELLO SHOW

1952–1954.   Syndicated

Character: Mrs. Bronson
Played by: Renie Riano
Date(s):   unknown

Replaced by: Mrs. Bronson
Played by: Sara Haden
Date(s):   unknown

"Heyyyyyyyyaaabeeeet!" was the familiar cry heard at the opening of *The Abbott and Costello Show.* These lovable stars of vaudeville, radio and motion pictures brought their clever repartee and slapstick humor to televion in 1952.

Bud Abbott and Lou Costello played themselves in all fifty-two episodes of the original *The Abbott and Costello Show,* which aired between 1952 and 1954 and ever since in syndication.

One of the boys' neighbors, however, was played by two actresses.

Renie Riano, who portrayed the first Mrs. Bronson, previously played Maggie in the JIGGS AND MAGGIE films, which were based on the comic strip, *Bringing Up Father.*

The second Mrs. Bronson was played by Sara Haden, who is best remembered as Aunt Millie in the popular ANDY HARDY film series.

ADAM 12

September 21, 1968–August 26, 1975.   NBC
September 29, 1990-September 1991   Syndicated

Character: Officer Pete Malloy
Played by: Martin Milner
Date(s):   September 21, 1968–August 26, 1975

Replaced by: Officer Gus Grant
Played by: Peter Parros
Date(s):   September 29, 1990–September 1991

Character:	Officer Jim Reed
Played by:	Kent McCord
Date(s):	September 21, 1968–August 26, 1975
Replaced by:	Officer Matt Doyle
Played by:	Ethan Wayne
Date(s):	September 29, 1990–September 1991

Character:	Sergeant MacDonald
Played by:	William Boyett
Date(s):	September 21, 1968–August 26, 1975
Replaced by:	Sergeant Harry Santos
Played by:	Miguel Fernandes
Date(s):	September 29, 1990–September 1991

Character:	Jean Reed
Played by:	Mikki Jamison
Date(s):	November 1, 1969
	February 14, 1970
Replaced by:	Jean Reed
Played by:	Kristin Nelson
Date(s):	February 18, 1975

Sixteen years after creating *Dragnet,* which dealt with the day-to-day activities of two Los Angeles detectives, producer Jack Webb created *Adam 12,* a police drama following the day-to-day activities of two Los Angeles police officers—sort of *Dragnet* on wheels.

The officers were Pete Malloy (Martin Milner) and rookie Jim Reed (Kent McCord) and each episode followed them during their shift where they encountered everything from domestic squabbles to drug stakeouts. Their commanding officer, Sergeant MacDonald, was played by William Boyett.

While Martin Milner had played Jimmy Clark from 1954 to 1955 on the ABC situation comedy, *The Stu Erwin Show* and Don Marshall on *The Life of Riley* from 1957 to 1958, audiences knew him best as the freewheeling Tod Stiles from the CBS adventure series, *Route 66* (See Entry).

Kent McCord, who was fifteen years younger than Milner, appeared in six episodes of Jack Webb's *Dragnet* before being cast in the co-starring role of Officer Jim Reed. Following his work on *Adam 12,* McCord appeared in episodes of *Marcus Welby, M.D.* and *Black Sheep Squadron* before landing the role of Captain Troy on the revamped *Battlestar Galactica* (See Entry).

Although much talked about, Officer Reed's wife, Jean, was seen only three times during the series run. In "A Sound Like Thunder," and "A Rare Occasion," she was played by Mikki Jamison. Jean Reed last appeared on *Adam 12* in the episode, "Lady's Night." Kristin (Harmon) Nelson, the real-life wife of actor/singer Rick Nelson, played Jean in this episode. Kristin appeared as herself on *The Adventures of Ozzie & Harriet,* from 1964 to 1966.

To add to the realism of the *Adam 12* stories, which are based on actual police cases, Jack Webb cast Shaaron Claridge, a police radio operator, to provide the voice for all of the show's radio calls that always begin with Malloy and Reed's patrol car ID, "One, Adam Twelve. One Adam Twelve." Shaaron, whose husband Frank Claridge is a motorcycle officer, worked the four-to-midnight shift at the Los Angeles police station in Van Nuys, California.

Seven seasons and 174 episodes later, *Adam 12* answered its last call for fourteen years. Then, in 1989, it was reactivated for an all-new, updated version of first-run episodes produced specifically for the syndication market. *Dragnet* was also revised for syndication at that time.

Accuracy and realism once again prevailed over the fictionalized chase scenes and gun play of its lesser cousins. In addition to the same disclaimer used in the new *Dragnet* (See Entry) series, about the characters and events being based on facts, the series employed Ron Ship of the L.A.P.D. as its technical adviser. The closing credits also thanked the L.A.P.D.: "We gratefully acknowledge the cooperation of the Los Angeles Police Department and the officers of Chief Daryl Gates and Commander Bill Booth."

The officers assigned to Adam Twelve were Gus Grant (Peter Parros) and Matt Doyle (Ethan Wayne). As in the original series, one was a senior officer, but the ages of the pair were much closer. Bachelor Grant only had eight months on Doyle, who was married.

Grant and Doyle took their orders from Sergeant Harry Santos (Miguel Fernandes). Like a mother, Santos cared passionately for the safety and well-being of his officers. (This was evident in his roll call speeches, which were reminiscent of those given by Sergeant Phil Esterhaus [Michael Conrad] on NBC's *Hill Street Blues.*) This caring was especially evident in the premiere episode during a conversation in which Sergeant Santos was updating Grant and Doyle on the activities of a police sniper.

SANTOS:	I don't know what's worse; having something happen, or waiting for something to happen.
DOYLE:	Sounds like my mother.
SANTOS:	(Bending over to speak into Doyle's ear) I am your mother.

The family broke up after fifty-two original episodes.

THE ADDAMS FAMILY

September 18, 1964–September 2, 1966.   ABC

Character:	Wednesday Addams
Played by:	Lisa Loring
Date(s):	September 18, 1964–September 2, 1966
Replaced by:	Wednesday Addams Jr.
Played by:	Jennifer Surprenant
Date(s):	October 30, 1977 (*Halloween with the New Addams Family.* NBC Special)

Character: Pugsley Addams
Played by: Ken Weatherwax
Date(s):   September 18, 1964–September 2, 1966

Replaced by: Pugsley Addams Jr.
Played by: Kenneth Marquis
Date(s):   October 30, 1977 (*Halloween with the New Addams Family.* NBC Special)

Character: Grandmama Addams
Played by: Blossom Rock
Date(s):   September 18, 1964–September 2, 1966

Replaced by: Grandmama Addams
Played by: Jane Rose
Date(s):   October 30, 1977 (*Halloween with the New Addams Family.* NBC Special)

Character: Cousin Itt
Played by: Felix Silla
Date(s):   February 5, 1965–September 2, 1966

Replaced by: Cousin Itt
Played by: Roger Arravo
Date(s):   (several episodes)

Character: Esther Frump
Played by: Margaret Hamilton
Date(s):   September 18, 1964–September 2, 1966

Replaced by: Esther Frump
Played by: Elvia Allman
Date(s):   October 30, 1977 (*Halloween with the New Addams Family.* NBC Special)

Character: Thing
Played by: Ted Cassidy
Date(s):   September 18, 1964–September 2, 1966

Replaced by: Thing
Played by: Jack Voglin
Date(s):   January 15, 1965
               January 22, 1965
               March 14, 1965
               April 16, 1965
               October 29, 1965
               November 5, 1965
               January 14, 1966
               March 4, 1966
               March 18, 1966

The Addams Family was virtually free of cast changes during its two-season run on ABC and only the actors who played the family long hair, Cousin Itt, and the dexterous dismembered hand, Thing, were temporarily replaced for a few episodes.

A hair-raising experience for Uncle Fester (Jackie Coogan, right) as Felix Silla (left), the midget actor who played Cousin Itt, takes a breath of fresh air in a posed shot from *The Addams Family.*

Cousin Itt, who was played by the same midget actor who later played the robot *Twiki* in the NBC science fiction series, *Buck Rogers in the 25th Century* (See Entry), was replaced by Roger Arravo.

Thing, the Addams's right hand—well . . . hand—(though occasionally seen as a lefty) was played by Ted Cassidy, the same actor who played Lurch, the towering butler with the guttural growl. There were, however, nine separate occasions when both Thing and Lurch were required for the same scene. In these instances it was the hand of *The Addams Family*'s Assistant Director Jack Voglin that doubled for Cassidy's.

There were a few minor cast changes in the NBC special, *Halloween with the New Addams Family.* These included Grandmama Addams and Esther Frump.

The original Grandmama Addams was played by Jeanette MacDonald's older sister, Blossom McDonald, who appeared in films during the 1930s and 1940s under the name of Marie Blake. In 1926, Blossom married Clarence W. Rock, but it wasn't until the 1960s that she legally changed her name to Blossom Rock.

Ms. Rock's speech was affected by a severe stroke suffered in the 1970s and this is what prevented her from reprising the role of Grandmama in the reunion special. Her replacement in the NBC special, *Halloween with the New Addams Family,* was

Jane Rose, who may be familiar to television audiences as "Mother" Audrey Dexter from *Phyllis.*

Jane Rose also played Mrs. Selby on the half-hour comedy pilot, *Co-Ed Fever,* CBS's answer to the successful film, ANIMAL HOUSE. *Co-Ed Fever* aired on February 4, 1979. Jane Rose died on June 29, 1979.

One of the new characters introduced in the Halloween special was Pancho Addams, Gomez's brother.

Even more interesting is the fact that there was some talk about reviving the series. Actor Henry Darrow said that "They had talked about replacing John Astin. It was unclear as to whether I was going to be Gomez or whether Pancho was going to step in. It wasn't clear, but it had been intimated that there might be a deal, but the producers were waiting to hear from John Astin who was doing the pilot for *Operation Petticoat* (See Entry), which did get picked up as a series.

"It was fun shooting and meeting Carolyn Jones, Ted Cassidy and Jackie Coogan because *The Addams Family* was one of those shows that I watched and totally enjoyed. I recall making a conscious effort to imitate some of John Astin's mannerisms when I was playing Pancho."[5]

During the regular series, Morticia's mother, Esther Frump, was played by everyone's favorite witch, Margaret Hamilton. Ms. Hamilton, who played the Wicked Witch of the West in the 1939 classic, THE WIZARD OF OZ, later played Cora, the Maxwell House Coffee spokeswoman, in a long-running series of television commercials. In those commercials, despite popular belief, Ms. Hamilton never said, "Drink Maxwell House Coffee—and that goes for your little dog, too!"

In the NBC special, *Halloween with the New Addams Family,* Margaret Hamilton was replaced by Elvia Allman, who had played another Cora on early televison—Cora Dithers, on the 1957 situation comedy *Blondie* (See Entry). Born in Spencer, North Carolina, in 1905, Ms. Allman worked extensively in radio and television and her long list of television credits include Selma Plout on *Petticoat Junction* and Elverna Bradshaw on *The Beverly Hillbillies.*

A pilot for a musical remake of *The Addams Family* was made in 1973, but never aired.

Eighteen years later, the Addamses returned—this time to the large screen in a 1991 motion picture titled, appropriately enough, THE ADDAMS FAMILY. This twenty-five-million-dollar Paramount picture, which was written by Caroline Thompson, Larry Wilson and Paul Rudnick and directed by Barry Sonnenfeld, was truer to the Charles Addams cartoons than the television series.

This theatrical version of THE ADDAMS FAMILY, starred Raul Julia, who admitted to incorporating some of John Astin's "rascally essence" for his portrayal of Gomez Addams. At the time of the film's release, Raul Julia was starring on Broadway in a revival of *Man of La Mancha.* He had previously played Michael Reisler in the 1978 crime drama, EYES OF LAURA MARS, and Valentin Arregui in the 1985 drama, KISS OF THE SPIDER WOMAN.

Morticia was brought back to life by Anjelica Huston, the daughter of legendary director John Huston. Starting out with a small part in her father's 1969 comedy, SINFUL DAVEY, she went on to win the Academy Award for her portrayal of Maerose Prizzi in the 1985 comedy, PRIZZI'S HONOR, which was also directed by John Huston.

Gomez's bald-headed brother, "Uncle Fester," was played by an actor who specialized in playing bizarre, evil and just slightly off-center characters, Christopher Lloyd. Since gaining national recognition as the burned-out cabbie, "Reverend Jim" Ignatowski on the ABC sitcom *Taxi,* he has played outlaw Butch Cavendish in the 1981 Western, THE LEGEND OF THE LONE RANGER, the Klingon, Kruge, in Paramount Pictures' 1984 science fiction film, STAR TREK III: THE SEARCH FOR SPOCK and Switchblade Sam in the 1993 big screen version of DENNIS THE MENACE.

Lloyd has also managed to build something of a small empire out of playing the eccentric time-traveling Dr. Emmett "Doc" Brown. He created the character in the 1985 box-office success, BACK TO THE FUTURE, and went on to reprise the role in both the 1989 and 1990 sequels, BACK TO THE FUTURE PART II and BACK TO THE FUTURE PART III, in addition to appearing in the live wraparounds for the CBS Saturday morning animated series *Back to the Future,* which debuted on September 14, 1991.

The Addams's faithful manservant, Lurch, was played by Carel Struycken, who first appeared as The Giant in the November 10, 1990 episode of the ABC evening soap opera, *Twin Peaks.*

Grandmama, whose name was changed to Granny, was played by Judith Malina, stone-faced Christina Ricci was Wednesday, and Jimmy Workman, Pugsley. Five-foot-tall John Franklin was the face (wherever that was) and the voice of Cousin Itt, and the right hand of magician Christopher Hart portrayed Thing. The cast was reunited for the 1993 sequel, THE ADDAMS FAMILY VALUES.

The Addams Family returned to Saturday morning television on September 12, 1992, in an all-new animated series that starred the voice talents of John Astin as Gomez, Nancy Linari as Morticia, Rip Taylor as Uncle Fester, Carol Channing as Granny Frump, Debi Derryberry as Wednesday, Jeannie Elias as Pugsley, Jim Cummings as Lurch and Pat Fraley as Cousin Itt. "Da-da-da-dum."

ADVENTURES IN PARADISE

October 5, 1959–April 1, 1962.   ABC

Character:	Oliver Kee
Played by:	Weaver Levy
Date(s):	October 5, 1959–May 9, 1960

Character:	Clay Baker
Played by:	James Holden
Date(s):	October 3, 1960–June 19, 1961

5. From an exclusive interview with Henry Darrow on January 19, 1991.

James Holden as Clay Baker perched on the deck of the Tiki in a publicity still from *Adventures in Paradise*.

Replaced by:	Chris Parker
Played by:	Guy Stockwell
Date(s):	October 1, 1961–April 1, 1962

Character:	Trader Penrose
Played by:	George Tobias
Date(s):	1960–1961

Replaced by:	Clay Baker
Played by:	James Holden
Date(s):	October 3, 1960–June 19, 1961

The "adventure" was based on the Tiki's Captain Adam Troy's (Gardner McKay) search for passengers and cargo. The "paradise" was the South Pacific. To outsiders, it may appear as though Captain Troy was a drifter, but he wasn't. He has his roots in Tahiti and hopes to return to the states when he has enough money saved to buy his dream—a ranch.

Oliver Kee, a Chinese American played by Weaver Levy, was Captain Adam Troy's friend and first mate when the series began in 1959. In 1960, James Holden joined the regular cast as Captain Troy's first mate, Clay Baker.

Two important cast changes were made the following season. Clay Baker went ashore and replaced Trader Penrose (George Tobias) as the manager of the Bali Miki Hotel and renamed it the Bali Miki Baker Hotel, which was actually a small inn where he also served as bartender—he did not leave the series.

Captain Troy, who was now left without a first mate, took on Chris Parker (Guy Stockwell).

It is interesting to note that Lon Chaney, Jr., who guest starred as Trader One Arm (so nicknamed because he had lost one arm to a shark) in the episode of October 12, 1959, "The Black Pearl," may have been the prototype for the Trader Penrose character.

Guy Stockwell was born in New York City on November 16, 1933, to stage actors Harry Stockwell and Betty Veronica. His younger brother is television and motion picture actor, Dean Stockwell. After *Adventures in Paradise,* Guy Stockwell joined Richard Boone, Robert Blake, Lloyd Bochner, Harry Morgan and others as a regular member of the dramatic series, *The Richard Boone Show,* which aired on CBS on Tuesday nights from September 24, 1963 to September 15, 1964. It was another New York City native (born in 1901), George Tobias who played Trader Penrose on *Adventures in Paradise.* He had been considered for the role of Jake on *The Goldbergs* (See Entry), but never took the part. From 1964 to 1972, Tobias played Abner Kravitz on the ABC comedy, *Bewitched.* George Tobias died on February 27, 1980.

ADVENTURES IN SHERWOOD FOREST *see:* THE ADVENTURES OF ROBIN HOOD

THE ADVENTURES OF CAPTAIN HARTZ

October 11, 1953–January 1, 1956.   ABC-NBC-Syndicated

Character:	Captain Hartz
Played by:	Philip Lord
Date(s):	October 11, 1953–1954

Replaced by:	Captain Hartz
Played by:	Tom Mercein
Date(s):	Fall 1954–February 1955

Replaced by:	Captain Hartz
Played by:	Ned Locke
Date(s):	February 1955–January 1, 1956

Since Hartz Mountain Pet Foods made foods and treats for pets, and knew that kids have pets, they produced an adventure show geared specifically to that young audience.

In the first of two formats, Phil Lord, as Captain Hartz, narrated films and related exciting stories about animals to his young companion, Bruce (Lindgren).

The second format for this early youth-oriented series featured a change of name locale, a change of costume and a change in cast.

Philip Lord, who had previously played the Judge in the NBC dramatic comedy, *Hawkins Falls, Population 6,200* (June 17 to October 12, 1950), was replaced as the Captain by Tom Mercein, with the series renamed, *Captain Hartz and His Pets.*

Suited up in a pilot's uniform, Captain Hartz set out in his plane to explore the mysterious jungles of the world. He returned with exotic animals which he shared with his nine-year-old friend, Brigid (Bazlen).

A new Captain and several new segments were added to the formula in February of 1955. Among the new features presented by Ned Locke, the third actor to play the adventuresome Captain Hartz, were visits by Robert Roudy and his trained panthers, zoologists and other guests who gave tips on the care and training of animals.

At the start of the 1955/1956 season, Jerry Garvey served as Captain Hartz's bright and inquisitive young co-star. Jerry was replaced in the fall by Buzz (Podewell), who during the same television season also helped out Mr. Wizard (Don Herbert) with his science experiments on NBC's *Watch Mr. Wizard*. Mr. Wizard's first assistant, Willie Watson (1951–1953), was played by Don Herbert's real-life next-door neighbor, Bruce Lindgren—"Gee!"

THE ADVENTURES OF ELLERY QUEEN

October 14, 1950–September 5, 1976.   Dumont-ABC-Syndicated-NBC

Character:	Ellery Queen
Played by:	Richard Hart
Date(s):	October 1950–Novermber 1950

Replaced by:	Ellery Queen
Played by:	Lee Bowman
Date(s):	December 1950–November 26, 1952

Replaced by:	Ellery Queen
Played by:	Hugh Marlowe
Date(s):	September 1954[6]

Replaced by:	Ellery Queen
Played by:	George Nader
Date(s):	September 26, 1958–February 20, 1959

Replaced by:	Ellery Queen
Played by:	Lee Phillips
Date(s):	February 27, 1959–June 5, 1959

Replaced by:	Ellery Queen
Played by:	Peter Lawford
Date(s):	November 14, 1971
	(*Ellery Queen: Don't Look Behind You*, pilot for *The Further Adventures of Ellery Queen*.)

Replaced by:	Ellery Queen
Played by:	Jim Hutton
Date(s):	September 11, 1975–September 19, 1976

Character:	Inspector Richard Queen
Played by:	Florenz Ames
Date(s):	1950–1954

Replaced by:	Inspector Richard Queen
Played by:	Les Tremayne
Date(s):	1958–February 20, 1959

Replaced by:	Inspector Richard Queen
Played by:	Harry Morgan
Date(s):	November 14, 1971
	(*Ellery Queen: Don't Look Behind You*, pilot for *The Further Adventures of Ellery Queen*.)

Replaced by:	Inspector Richard Queen
Played by:	David Wayne
Date(s):	September 11, 1975–September 19, 1976

Character:	Sergeant Velie
Played by:	Bill Zuckert
Date(s):	November 14, 1971
	(*Ellery Queen: Don't Look Behind You*, pilot for *The Further Adventures of Ellery Queen*.)

Replaced by:	Sergeant Velie
Played by:	Tom Reese
Date(s):	September 11, 1975–September 19, 1976

The son of a Manhattan police inspector, Ellery Queen was in many ways an Americanized Sherlock Holmes because he used his grey matter to solve crimes instead of his fists. Ellery Queen had been around for more than twenty years and appeared in a number of different media including novels, periodicals, radio and motion pictures before coming to television.

The first Ellery Queen novel, *The Roman Hat Mystery*, appeared in 1928, the creation of cousins Frederic Dannay and Manford B. Lee. Seven years later, the character had become popular enough to warrant the first Ellery Queen motion picture, THE SPANISH CAPE MYSTERY, which starred Donald Cook. Later films in the series subsequently starred Eddie Quillan, Ralph Bellamy and William Gargan. The quintessential Queen was played by Ralph Bellamy, who starred in four of the nine pictures in the series and later went on to star as Mike Barnett on *Man Against Crime* (See Entry).

Richard Hart was the first actor to portray Ellery Queen on television. In January 1951, after appearing only eleven times as one of America's best-known detectives, Richard Hart died of a sudden heart attack during a rehearsal in New York. The title of the episode he was rehearsing was "The Survivors' Club." Hart, who was born in 1914,[7] played the Witch Boy in the 1945 Broadway show, *Dark of the Moon*, and appeared in four motion pictures before taking on the role of Ellery Queen.

---

6. Some sources give 1955 as the year the syndicated *Adventures of Ellery Queen* were first broadcast.

7. Richard Hart's birth date is listed as "circa 1915" in *The Complete Directory for Prime Time TV Stars* by Tim Brooks. Ballantine Books, New York, 1987, p. 387.

In 1947, Richard Hart played William Ozanne in GREEN DOLPHIN STREET. That same year, he also played Jean Renaud in the MGM drama, DESIRE ME. In 1948, he played Robert S. Tasmin in another MGM drama, B.F.'S DAUGHTER. His last film role was Francois Barras in the 1949 adventure, REIGN OF TERROR, which was retitled, THE BLACK BOOK.

Because of the demands of live television, Richard Hart was replaced in less than twenty-four hours by Lee Bowman, a leading man in B-pictures who was not only the same age but looked a lot like Hart. He even sported a pencil-thin mustache. Bowman continued with the *Ellery Queen* series until it left the air in November, 1952.

Lee Bowman's most notable film role was that of singer and songwriter, Ken Conway, in the 1947 drama, SMASH-UP, THE STORY OF A WOMAN. Susan Hayward made her first major film appearance as Bowman's wife, Angie Evans.

In September, 1954, a syndicated series produced on film, *The New Adventures of Ellery Queen,* aired on local stations across the country. This version starred Hugh Marlowe in the title role. Marlowe was an excellent choice since he had been the first of four actors to play the detective on the *Ellery Queen* radio program, which ran from 1939 to 1947. He also looked very much like the character described in the Ellery Queen novels by Frederic Dannay and Manfred B. Lee.

Hugh Marlowe was born Hugh Herbert Hipple, in Philadelphia on January 30, 1911. He began his career in radio using his authoritative thick voice as an announcer before taking on acting roles. Prior to his becoming Ellery Queen on television, Huge Marlowe played Tom Stevens in the 1951 science fiction classic, THE DAY THE EARTH STOOD STILL.

Three seasons after the syndicated series left the air, NBC brought Ellery Queen back to live television in a new series called *The Further Adventures of Ellery Queen,* which first aired on September 26, 1958. One month later, on October 24, 1958, the title was changed to the more succinct, *Ellery Queen.* This version, which was broadcast in color, starred the handsome George Nader as television's fourth Ellery Queen.

In February, 1959, after only twenty episodes, production of *Ellery Queen* moved from Hollywood to New York and both George Nader and Les Tremayne (Inspector Richard Queen) left the cast.

Almost immediately following his departure from the series, George Nader landed the role of Dr. Glenn Barton in the NBC adventure series, *Man and the Challenge.* This show ran for nearly one year from September 12, 1959 to September 3, 1960, with a total of thirty-six episodes completed.

When production of *Ellery Queen* resumed in New York,

several important changes were made. First, a Brooklyn-born actor, Lee Phillips, assumed the title role and "played Ellery as a man of awareness and compassion, substantially closer to the original conception of the character in the novels."[8] Phillips also bore an uncanny resemblance to George Nader. In fact, Phillips looked more like Nader than Bowman looked like Hart.

The second change was that the program was produced on videotape instead of being broadcast live. And third, original scripts replaced adaptations from various mystery novels.

Shortly after completing the *Ellery Queen* series, Lee Phillips embarked on a successful new career directing television series such as *The Andy Griffith Show, The Dick Van Dyke Show* and *The Waltons.*

Ellery Queen returned to television in *Ellery Queen: Don't Look Behind You.* This failed pilot was aired as a made-for-television movie in 1971. Peter Lawford took on the title role, while Jack Webb's fifth partner and *M*A*S*H*'s (See Entry) second commanding officer of the 4077th, Harry Morgan, played Ellery's father, Inspector Richard Queen.

Although critics seemed to like Morgan as Queen's father, most agreed that teaming him with Lawford was ludicrous. In his book, *Movies Made for Television,* author Alvin Marill said that the pilot was "marred by the miscasting of too-suave Lawford in the leading role."[9] Ric Meyers' comments were even less flattering; he wrote, "Casting Lawford as Queen was like casting Al Pacino as Sherlock Holmes."[10] His photo caption below a still of Peter Lawford was even more scathing "The Ludicrous Queen: casting Peter Lawford made as much sense as having Chevy Chase play Sherlock Holmes."[11]

The producers must have agreed, because both actors were replaced for the second NBC pilot, *Ellery Queen,* which aired on March 23, 1975.[12] This pilot was later shown in syndication under the new title *Ellery Queen: Too Many Suspects.*

Jim Hutton took over the honors as Ellery Queen while the part of his father, Inspector Richard Queen, went to David Wayne.

" 'We auditioned a lot of actors for the part,' Richard Levinson recalled. 'But the network liked Jim [Hutton], and the head of television production at Universal liked Jim, and he was a very nice guy.' "[13]

Levinson, later reflecting on his selection of Jim Hutton for the role of Ellery Queen, said, "The guy we should have hired was Edward Hermann."[14] Herrmann, who was born in Washington, D.C. on July 21, 1943, played Richard Palmer in CBS's prime-time soap opera, *Beacon Hill.* In 1976, Herrmann played Franklin Roosevelt in the four-part ABC mini-series, *Eleanor and Franklin.*

In all, twenty-three[15] one-hour episodes of *Ellery Queen*

8. Nevins, Francis M., Jr. "Ellery Queen on the Small Screen," *The Golden Years of Radio & TV,* No. 1, Winter, 1983, p. 37.
9. Marill, Alvin H. *Movies Made for Television, The Telefeature and the Mini-Series, 1964–1986.* New York Zoetrope, Inc., New York, 1987, p. 121.
10. Meyers, Ric. *Murder On the Air, Television's Great Mystery Series.* The Mysterious Press, New York, 1989, p. 41.
11. *Ibid.,* p. 42.
12. Some sources give March 25, 1975 as the air date of the second *Ellery Queen* pilot.
13. Meyers, Ric, *op. cit.,* p. 44.
14. *Ibid.,* p. 46.
15. Some sources put the total number of *Ellery Queen* episodes at 26.

starring Jim Hutton were produced on film and aired on NBC from September 11, 1975 to September 19, 1976.

Jim Hutton was born in Binghamton, New York in 1933. The most famous of his nearly two dozen film roles was his portrayal of Sergeant Peterson in the 1968 John Wayne war drama, THE GREEN BERETS. Jim Hutton died of cancer, at the age of 44, on June 2, 1979.

The part of Ellery Queen's father, Inspector Richard Queen of the New York Police Department, was played by four actors during the various runs on television.

Veteran character actor, Florenz Ames, created the role of Inspector Queen on television and played opposite Richard Hart, Lee Bowman and Hugh Marlowe.

Florenz Ames played Silas Applegate in the twenty-part serial *The Hardy Boys and the Mystery of the Applegate Treasure.* These half-hour episodes were broadcast from January 7, 1957 through February 1, 1957 as part of *The Mickey Mouse Club.* From January 4 to September 27, 1957, Florenz Ames played J.C. Dithers, Dagwood Bumstead's boss, on the NBC comedy, *Blondie* (See Entry). In a later version of the *Blondie* series, the part of Mr. Dithers was played by Jim Backus.

When *Ellery Queen* was recast in 1958 for *The Further Adventures of Ellery Queen,* Florenz Ames was replaced by another distinguished character actor, Les Tremayne.

When the program first aired on NBC on September 26, 1958, Les Tremayne played Inspector Richard Queen opposite George Nader, but when production moved to New York, Les Tremayne left the show and the character of Inspector Richard Queen was dropped.

Les Tremayne was born in London, England on April 16, 1913.

During the 1930s and 1940s, Tremayne's rich tenor voice made him the ideal romantic lead in radio's *The First Nighter* and *Grand Hotel.* In 1950, he played Bill Herbert in the evening soap opera, *One Man's Family* (See Entry), but was later replaced by Walter Brooke, who stayed with the series until 1952. From September 7, 1974 to September 3, 1977, Les Tremayne played Mentor, Billy Batson's companion in the Saturday morning live action/animation adventure series, *Shazam!* opposite both Captain Marvels.

Character actor David Wayne replaced Harry Morgan as Inspector Richard Queen in the second NBC pilot, *Ellery Queen: Too Many Suspects.*

An article in the November 11, 1975 *TV Guide* says "Jim Hutton . . . [has] a part that suits him to a cup of old-fashioned tea. Equally inspired casting was David Wayne. His earnest professionalism as Ellery's father . . . makes him the perfect foil for his son's apparently aimless amateurism."[16]

In his article, "Ellery Queen on the Small Screen," Francis M. Nevins, Jr. wrote, "David Wayne was magnificently crusty as Inspector Queen. . . ."[17]

David Wayne, who has been described as little, wiry, impish and distinguished, was born Wayne McMeekan in Traverse City, Michigan on January 30, 1914. He starred as Pearson Norby in the 1955 situation comedy, *Norby,* one of the first television series to be filmed in color. Wayne played opposite Larry Hagman as the first Willard "Digger" Barnes during the 1978 season of the evening soap opera, *Dallas,* but was replaced the following season by Keenan Wynn.

When the first *Ellery Queen* pilot was produced in 1971, it featured Bill Zuckert as Richard Queen's aide, Sergeant Velie. Zuckert was replaced by Tom Reese in the second pilot and series that followed. Bill Zuckert's earlier television roles include Mr. Arthur Bradwell on *Mr. Novak,* a part he played from 1964 to 1965.

THE ADVENTURES OF OZZIE & HARRIET

October 3, 1952–September 3, 1966.   ABC

Character:	"Thorny" Thornberry
Played by:	Don DeFore
Date(s):	1952–1956
Replaced by:	Joe Randolph
Played by:	Lyle Talbot
Date(s):	1956–1966
Character:	Mr. Donald Kelly
Played by:	Joe Flynn
Date(s):	1961–1962
Replaced by:	Unknown
Played by:	Unknown
Date(s):	Unknown

The Adventures of Ozzie & Harriet began on radio in 1944 with actors portraying David and Ricky Nelson for the first four and one-half years. "At first he [Ozzie Nelson] refused to allow the boys to portray themselves, feeling that the experience of big-time radio was a bit too much for youngsters of 8 and 4 to handle."[18] Two juvenile actors, Tommy Bernard and Joel Davis, played David Nelson while Henry Blair played Ricky. On February 20, 1949, the actors were replaced by the real David and Ricky. Much to everyone's pleasure, they proved to have an innate sense of comedy timing.

Bea Benaderet played both the Nelson's housemaid, Gloria, and the domineering Mrs. Waddington on the initial radio broadcasts. Dink Trout played her husband, Roger Waddington. Ozzie Nelson replaced them both with less exaggerated and more believable characters.

Don DeFore, who played Ozzie and Harriet's next-door neighbor, "Thorny" Thornberry, on the television adaptation of the Nelson's radio program, was not a holdover from radio, as some sources have indicated. In fact, he didn't even know the

16. *TV Guide,* November 11, 1975.
17. Nevins, Francis M., Jr. "Ellery Queen on the Small Screen," *The Golden Years of Radio & TV,* No. 1, Winter 1983, p. 43.
18. Dunning, John. *Tune In Yesterday.* Prentice-Hall, 1976, p.10.

Nelsons back then, and has related the story of how they met and how that meeting may have led to his being asked to play their next-door neighbor on television.

As president of the Television Academy in 1951 and 1952, Don DeFore felt very strongly about giving the members a little something back for their original $15, and later $25, membership dues. His response was to throw what he called an ice cream box social, on the one-and-one-fifth-acre lawn of his home in Brentwood, California. The kicker was that DeFore didn't charge his guests a dime.

The gathering was attended by more than 900 members of the academy and included actors and actresses such as Gale Storm and Eddie Bracken. Also in attendance were Hollywood gossip columnists, Louella Parsons and Hedda Hopper; DeFore described the latter as "the gal who wore all the big hats."[19]

"In the following day's papers one quote read, 'Can you imagine a big box social of ice cream and cake at Don DeFore's home for the Television Academy. There was no charge and there was no alcohol,' "[20] recalled DeFore.

When Ozzie and Harriet Nelson arrived at the box social, Marion DeFore introduced them to her husband. She knew the Nelsons quite well because she was singing with an orchestra at the same time that Harriet was singing with Ozzie's band.

"I met them officially that afternoon," said DeFore, "so maybe that meeting and a further check-up on my background in pictures and on TV was possibly what interested them in me doing Thorny,"[21] he said modestly.

Don DeFore stayed with *The Adventures of Ozzie & Harriet* for four complete seasons before he was replaced. But he did not leave the series in 1956[22] to play Captain Skidmore in the Rock Hudson war drama, BATTLE HYMN, as some sources indicate.

Mrs. Marion DeFore recalled quite vividly the sequence of events leading up to her husband's being written out of *The Adventures of Ozzie & Harriet:* "The last day of filming of the *Ozzie & Harriet* fourth year product took place on or about May 4, 1956, and some time after lunch, Don called and asked, 'How'd I like to go to Africa?' At first, I was taken aback until he explained that two persons at NBC, Vice President John West and Shirley Thomas, both had asked him the same question. John West explained that a representative of a cerebral palsy organization in Johannesburg, South Africa, had come to Hollywood to work with Cerebral Palsy national president Dorothy Ritter, wife of singing cowboy star 'Tex' Ritter, to put together the entertainment for a review to take to Joburg. They'd firmed up Pat O'Brien, Zsa Zsa Gabor, Martha Tilton, 'Tex' Ritter, opera star Felix Knight [who had played Tom Tom in the 1934 Laurel and Hardy film, *BABES IN TOYLAND*], a stand-up comic John Hopkins and a classical dance team. John West told Don that he'd recommended him because of his excellent handling of the presidency of the National Television Academy and other master of ceremony

chores! Would Don consider accepting the job of the review's master of ceremonies? We had a week to give them an answer.

"Don, knowing that contract-wise 'Oz' [Nelson] would have to notify his agent if the company were to exercise his last year's option, semi-jokingly said to 'Oz,' 'If you plan on picking up my option for next year, I'd appreciate an increase in salary and a little better break on publicity.' Ozzie's reply was that the company had a good contract, including the fifth year. Don then told him, as he later related to me, 'Whether or not the option's picked up, my agent, Norman Brokaw, will be mailing the decision to me in Johannesburg, South Africa, where I'll be going to emcee a benefit review.'

"Some time later, while in Africa, Don received a letter from his William Morris agent, Norman Brokaw, explaining that the *Ozzie and Harriet* company spent so much time finding new sponsors that they ran out of time (allotted in the contract) to pick up his option for the fifth year.

"In retrospect, though semi-jokingly made, Don's remarks to 'Oz' might have been the reason Don was not asked to return to the role of 'Thorny.'

"We had taken our four kids with us to Africa, then on to Egypt, Greece, Italy, France, Norway and Denmark, where we visited my relatives. A week or so after our return to L.A., we invited Ozzie and Harriet to attend a baseball game with us. They picked us up in their limousine. Several times during the game, Ozzie, sitting next to me, Harriet next to Don, both expressed the same feelings! 'Oz' said to me, 'I can't tell you how much we miss Don on the show!' Harriet's comments to Don were practically the same.

"Now, one must realize that once an agent has negotiated a contract, only that agent, or another assigned from that office, can renegotiate any of its clauses. Therefore, even after these expressed glowing compliments from both Ozzie and Harriet, there was nothing Don could do or say—except I believe he did say, 'I sure miss doing the show!' Later, Don phoned his agent several times to find out if there was any attempt to negotiate his returning to the series—there was none!"[23]

DeFore returned to television as Hazel's first employer, George Baxter, in the situation comedy *Hazel* (See Entry).

The *Adventures of Ozzie & Harriet* television series actually came about after Aaron Rosenberg, who was at the time a producer at Universal Studios, expressed an interest in producing a feature film based on the successful *Ozzie & Harriet* radio program. Ozzie Nelson and his brother, Don, along with Bill Davenport, co-authored the screenplay for HERE COME THE NELSONS, which was filmed in August 1951. The film was released in February 1952 and was, for all intents and purposes, the pilot for the television series. In the film, the Nelson's neighbors, Joe and Clara Randolph, were played by Jim Backus and Ann Doran. Three years later, Backus and Doran played James Dean's parents in the classic Warner Bros. drama, REBEL WITHOUT A CAUSE.

19. From an exclusive telephone interview with Don DeFore on August 25, 1990.
20. *Ibid.*
21. *Ibid.*
22. Some sources give 1958 as the year Don DeFore left the cast of *The Adventures of Ozzie & Harriet.*
23. Mrs. Marion DeFore in a letter to the author dated September 16, 1990.

When Don DeFore left the series in 1956, Ozzie's old friends, the Randolphs, moved back into the neighborhood. Replacing the film's stars, Backus and Doran, were Lyle Talbot and Mary Jane Croft. Both actors remained with the series to the end.

When Talbot began work on *The Adventures of Ozzie & Harriet* in 1956, he was still playing Paul Fonda on *The Bob Cummings Show*. His role on *The Bob Cummings Show* ran from January 2, 1955 to September 15, 1959, overlapping his work on *The Adventures of Ozzie & Harriet*.

Mary Jane Croft, who began her career in radio during the 1940s, later replaced Vivian Vance as Lucille Ball's confederate on *The Lucy Show* (See Entry) in 1965 and *Here's Lucy* in 1968.

Joe Flynn played David and Ricky's boss, Mr. Donald Kelly, a partner in the Dobson and Kelly law firm where they worked. From 1961 to 1962, while playing Mr. Kelly on *The Adventures of Ozzie & Harriet,* Flynn was simultaneously playing Frank on *The Joey Bishop Show* and was a regular on *The Bob Newhart Show*.

Joe Flynn left *The Adventures of Ozzie & Harriet* in 1962 to star in the role he is best remembered for, Captain Wallace B. Binghamton in *McHale's Navy,* which aired from October 11, 1962 to August 30, 1966 on ABC.

Current information on *The Adventures of Ozzie & Harriet* indicates that Joe Flynn left the series to star in *McHale's Navy,* but it is unclear if his character was ever replaced on *Ozzie & Harriet*.

On September 10, 1972, NBC aired a pilot for an updated version of *The Adventures of Ozzie & Harriet* entitled *Ozzie's Girls*. In effect, the two coeds who rent David and Ricky's room are themselves replacements for David and Ricky even though they are not the daughters of Ozzie and Harriet. Susan Sennett played Susan Hamilton and Brenda Sykes was Jennifer MacKenzie in all twenty-four episodes of the syndicated program. During the short run of the series, only one change was made. Jennifer's name was changed to Brenda, which makes perfect sense since most of the characters on *The Adventures of Ozzie & Harriet* used the actors' real first names.

THE ADVENTURES OF RIN TIN TIN

October 15, 1954–August 28, 1959.   ABC

Just one month after Lassie pawed her way into television as *Jeff's Collie*, Rusty's German shepherd, Rin Tin Tin, followed in *The Adventures of Rin Tin Tin*. This was also a story about a boy and his dog—the difference being the location and time frame. Instead of being set on a farm in the present, *The Adventures of Rin Tin Tin* took place in Fort Apache, Arizona during the 1880s. The boy, Rusty (Lee Aaker), and his dog, Rin Tin Tin, were the only survivors of an Indian raid on their

Rin Tin Tin IV poses with photographs of his ancestors Rin Tin Tin I, II and III while the image of Rinty's owner and trainer, Lee Duncan, appears on the television screen.

wagon train and were taken in by Ripley "Rip" Masters (James L. Brown), a lieutenant serving in the 101st Cavalry.

Although no "human" actors were replaced during the series, three different German shepherds played Rin Tin Tin. Two of the dogs were direct descendants of the original Rin Tin Tin, who made his acting debut in the 1922 silent film, THE MAN FROM HELL'S RIVER.[24] He died on August 10, 1932.

Rin Tin Tin, Jr. starred in all twelve episodes of the 1935 serial, THE ADVENTURES OF REX AND RINTY. The third shepherd was the pup of Flame, Jr., who also appeared in feature films.

J.R., also known as Junior, was actually Rin Tin Tin IV, the great, great grandson of Rin Tin Tin. He was a very bright animal and did all of the close-up work. He shied away from horses though, after getting kicked by one while licking its face.

Hey You was the Rinty used for all of the fight scenes, which didn't include any close-ups because one of his eyes was clouded over. It is likely that this condition, known as a buphthalmic eye, may very well have been due to trauma caused by a deep scratch or tear in Hey You's cornea—perhaps the result of one of his fight scenes.[25]

The third canine look-alike worked with the horses and was also used in the long shots.

In 1975,[26] Stan Moger, the executive vice-president of SFM

---

24. Some sources give 1924.
25. Dr. Darren Holman, a licensed veterinarian practicing in Lakewood, New Jersey, explained that although trauma appears to be the most likely cause of Hey You's clouded eye, it may also have been the result of glaucoma, a cataract or nuclear sclerosis. Dr. Holman also suggested that it is possible that the condition may have been an anomaly from birth. This, of course, is only speculation based on the information available. A true diagnosis is not possible without having the dog examined by a veterinarian.
26. Some sources give 1976.

Media Services, New York, repackaged the 164 episodes of *The Adventures of Rin Tin Tin* for resyndication. Moger made several changes in the program in an effort to make it more appealing to today's audience. First, the black and white prints were sepia toned. Second, new color wraparound openings and closings were shot in Utah. These segments featured Lieutenant Rip Masters (James Brown) sharing his stories of the ten-year-old orphan, Rusty, and his dog Rin Tin Tin, with a group of kids who were supposedly in Arizona visiting Fort Apache.

Brown, who was born in Desdemona, Texas on March 22, 1920 and played Lieutenant Rip Masters in the original series, won the role over the more than 150 actors who auditioned for it. Prior to his six-year stint on *The Adventures of Rin Tin Tin*, James Brown played George Tracy in the 1942 action/adventure film THE FOREST RANGERS, and Pfc. Charlie Bass in the 1949 John Wayne war drama, SANDS OF IWO JIMA.

On Saturday, September 17, 1988, an updated version, titled *Rin Tin Tin K-9 Cop*, aired across the country at 7 p.m. on the CBN Family Channel, starring yet another descendant of the famed canine as mentioned in the promotional ad that ran in the October 1988 issue of *The Cable Guide:* "... this month we're celebrating the world premiere of *Rin Tin Tin, K-9 Cop.* This direct descendant of the original Rinty patrols an urban beat eager to take a bite out of crime." The listing, which appeared in *TV Guide,* read as follows:

CBN RIN TIN TIN K-9 COP—Adventure
   Debut: This updated version of the 1950s series features the highly intelligent dog aiding the police rather than the cavalry.

THE ADVENTURES OF ROBIN HOOD

September 26, 1955–September 22, 1958.   CBS

Character:	Maid Marian Fitzwater
Played by:	Bernadette O'Farrell
Date(s):	October 24, 1955--June 24, 1957

Replaced by:	Maid Marian Fitzwater
Played by:	Patricia Driscoll
Date(s):	October 14, 1957–June 30, 1958

Character:	Little John
Played by:	Archie Duncan
Date(s):	October 10, 1955–January 23, 1956

Replaced by:	Little John
Played by:	Rufus Cruikshank
Date(s):	January 30, 1956–June 30, 1958

Character:	Prince John
Played by:	Donald Pleasence
Date(s):	February 20, 1956–June 24, 1957

Replaced by:	Prince John
Played by:	Hubert Gregg
Date(s):	October 14, 1957–June 30, 1958

Television's first Robin Hood (Richard Greene, center) delivers a faggot of fire wood to Maid Marion (Patricia Driscoll, right) while the evil Sheriff of Nottingham (Alan Wheatley, left) contemplates his next move in *The Adventures of Robin Hood.*

Character:	Will Scarlet/Will of Winchester
Played by:	Ronald Howard
Date(s):	March 5, 1956–July 9, 1956

Replaced by:	Will Scarlet/Will of Winchester
Played by:	Paul Eddington
Date(s):	March 18, 1957–June 30, 1958

One of England's most enduring legends is Robin Hood, the green-garbed archer and swordsman of Sherwood Forest who, along with his loyal band of Merry Men, did his best to right wrong and redistribute wealth by stealing from the rich and giving to the poor. The story, which became the motion picture THE ADVENTURES OF ROBIN HOOD, was taken in large part from *Ivanhoe* by Sir Walter Scott. Until the summer of 1991, the most famous Robin Hood was Errol Flynn, who starred in that 1938 Warner Bros. adventure. A live-action clip of Errol Flynn as Robin Hood in this film appeared in the 1950 Bugs Bunny short, RABBIT HOOD.

For some reason there have been more satires of this heroic swashbuckling character than faithful adaptations. These include *Monty Python's Flying Circus*'s John Cleese as Dennis Moore, and Daffy Duck in the 1958 animated short, ROBIN HOOD DAFFY. On television there was Mel Brooks' short-lived situation comedy *When Things Were Rotten.* It ran for only thirteen episodes, which aired between September 10 to December 24th, 1975 and starred Dick Gautier as Robin Hood. Maid Marian was played by Misty Rowe, Friar Tuck by Dick Van Patten and Little John by David Sabin. The evil Sheriff of Nottingham was played by Henry Polic II.

On the set of *Zorro and Son*, Dick Gautier, the former Robin Hood gave some advice to Henry Darrow, who was playing

Zorro in the series. "Dick Gautier came over to me and said 'Hank, don't camp it up too much, because when we did *When Things Were Rotten,* we camped it up too much—made too much fun of the legend of Robin Hood and the show bombed."[27]

In the summer of 1993, producer Mel Brooks took another cheap shot at this classic hero in his big budget comedy, ROBIN HOOD, MEN IN TIGHTS.

The prince of thieves was played by Sean Connery in the 1976 adventure, ROBIN AND MARIAN. Connery's son, Jason, took over the role of Robin Hood from Michael Praed in *Robin of Sherwood,* which aired on cable's Showtime network from 1984 to 1986.

The big hype in 1991 was for the pending summer release of ROBIN HOOD: PRINCE OF THIEVES, starring Kevin Costner, but Fox television beat Warner Bros.' June premiere by a month, airing their ill-fated theatrical film, ROBIN HOOD, as a television movie. This last-minute switch made the cast of Fox's *Robin Hood* the third to have played the roles on television, with the film airing on May 13, 1991.

On the original television version, which was produced in England, Patricia Driscoll, who was born in Cork, Ireland in the early 1930s, replaced Bernadette O'Farrell in 1957 as Maid Marian Fitzwater. The film roles of Bernadette O'Farrell, who was born in 1926, include Mrs. Fagan in the 1947 drama, CAPTAIN BOYCOTT; Janie in the 1951 British comedy, LADY GODIVA RIDES AGAIN; and Jessie Bond in the 1953 musical comedy, THE GREAT GILBERT AND SULLIVAN.

Archie Duncan played Little John from 1955 to 1956 and was replaced by Rufus Cruikshank from 1956 to 1958. Prior to his being cast in the role for *The Adventures of Robin Hood,* Duncan portrayed Inspector Lestrade from 1954 to 1956 in the syndicated series, *Sherlock Holmes.* Archie Duncan was born in Glasgow, Scotland on May 26, 1914 and died at the age of sixty-five, on July 24, 1979.

The first actor to portray Prince John was a thirty-six-year-old, Donald Pleasence, who was born on October 5, 1919 in Worksop, England. Pleasence, who often portrays the heavy, appeared in more than thirty films and his roles include the forger, Colin Blythe, in the 1963 war film, THE GREAT ESCAPE. In 1966, he played Dr. Michaels in the science fiction film, FANTASTIC VOYAGE, and Himmler in the 1976 film, THE EAGLE HAS LANDED. In 1978, Donald Pleasence was nominated for an Emmy in the category, Outstanding Performance by a Supporting Actor in a Comedy or Drama Series, for his portrayal of Captain Vladimir Popov in the CBS drama, *The Defection of Simas Kudirka.* CBS aired this two-hour made-for-television movie on January 23, 1978.

Ronald Howard, the son of Leslie Howard, first played Will Scarlet beginning with the episode of March 3, 1956, "Will Scarlet," and ending with the episode, "The Prisoner," on July 9, 1956.

Paul Eddington became the new Scarlet on March 18, 1956 with the episode, "Fair Play," and last played the role in, "Farewell to Tuck," on June 30, 1958. Ronald Howard's first

film role was the Earl of Harpenden in the 1946 comedy, WHILE THE SUN SHINES. From 1954 to 1955 he played the title character in the *Sherlock Holmes* series opposite Archie Duncan.

THE ADVENTURES OF SUPERBOY

October 8, 1988–October 1992.   Syndicated

Character:	Superboy/Clark Kent
Played by:	John Haymes Newton
Date(s):	October 8, 1988–September 30, 1989
Replaced by:	Superboy/Clark Kent
Played by:	Gerard Christopher
Date(s):	October 7, 1989–October 1992
Character:	Lex Luthor
Played by:	Scott Wells
Date(s):	October 8, 1988–September 30, 1989
Replaced by:	Lex Luthor
Played by:	Sherman Howard
Date(s):	October 7, 1989–October 1992
Character:	Trevor Jenkins "T.J." White
Played by:	Jim Calvert
Date(s):	October 8, 1988–September 30, 1989
Replaced by:	Andy McAlister
Played by:	Ilan Mitchell-Smith
Date(s):	October 7, 1989–October 1992

Superboy first appeared in the April 1946 issue of *Adventure Comics,* but it took forty-two years; seventeen theatrical cartoons; two fifteen-chapter SUPERMAN serials; a feature film; a 104–episode *Superman* television series; a failed *Superboy* pilot; a number of *Superman* and *Superboy* animated Saturday morning cartoons; four big-budget SUPERMAN motion pictures; and a SUPERGIRL feature before the kid from Krypton made it to the small screen in his own weekly live-action television series.

The failed attempt was initiated in 1961 by Whitney Ellsworth, the second producer of the *Adventures of Superman.* Ellsworth, along with Leslie Bellem and Vernon E. Clark, wrote thirteen scripts for a spinoff series, *The Adventures of Superboy.* Allan Asherman, in an article that appeared in issue No. 2 of *The Amazing World of DC Comics,* speculated that the twelfth script, "Rajah's Ransom," was selected to be filmed as the pilot "because of the limited number of sets involved. The story also avoided any mention of Jonathan Kent, so there was one less part that had to be cast."[28]

The show opens with a cumbersome and tediously long

---

27. From an exclusive telephone interview with Henry Darrow on January 19, 1991.

28. Asherman, Allan. "The Adventures of Superboy," *The Amazing World of D.C. Comics,* Vol. 1, No. 2, September-October 1974. National Periodical Publications, Inc., New York, p. 11.

introduction that ran for a minute and seventeen seconds, as compared with the cohesive fifty-one-second introduction for the *Adventures of Superman* (See Entry). ''The program begins with a montage in outer space *Superman* viewers would have recognized, but director George Blair then cuts to Rockwell standing in limbo—his hands folded on his chest, his body slouched and his uniform in need of a two-dollar pressing. The music sounds like early Mantovani ground through a miracle Veg-O-Matic. The only redeeming quality is Rockwell's remarkable copy of Reeves's bored expression whenever some two-bit thug tries the old bullet-to-the-chest routine.''[29]

The announcer begins the opening narration with ''It's the Adventures of Superboy. Incredible boy of steel. Powerful, fearless, invulnerable. Only survivor of the doomed planet Krypton. . . .'' He goes on to explain how the child was sent to earth by his scientist father and adopted by Jonathan and Martha Kent. The narration concludes with ''. . . And now some years later, the child is young Clark Kent, a student at Smallville High School, where his meek, retiring manner hides an exciting secret known only to himself and his foster parents—the secret that Clark Kent is in reality, Superboy, champion of the oppressed, enemy of all evildoers, dedicated to the cause of truth and justice.''

To save money, a number of clips used in this introduction were taken from ''Superman on Earth,'' the first episode of the *Adventures of Superman*. This was fine for the shots of Krypton's governing council and even the close-up of the infant Kal-El (Superboy), but the newly created shot of the rocket shown on earth is much larger and of a completely different design from the one shown in the clips taken from the *Adventures of Superman*. The narrator also refers to Superboy's parents as Jonathan and Martha Kent, which were the names used in the *Superman* and *Superboy* comics, but in ''Superman on Earth'' the Kents were named Sarah and Eben. It was explained once by the editor of *Superman* comics that Sarah and Eben were the Kents' middle names.

It is evident that great pains were taken in the casting of John Rockwell in the dual role of Clark Kent/Superboy, for he did bear an uncanny resemblance to George Reeves. There are, in fact, several scenes in which Rockwell's mannerisms and appearance are almost indistinguishable from George Reeves'.

Once John Rockwell was cast, a number of actresses were tested opposite him for the role of Clark Kent's Smallville sweetheart, Lana Lang. The young actresses who auditioned included Trudy Ellison, Marla Ryan, Mary Ann Roberts and Bunny Henning. While Bunny Henning won the part of Lana, the other actresses were retained and cast in other roles. In Gary Grossman's book, *Superman Serial to Cereal*, historian David L. Miller is quoted on John Rockwell's performance as Superboy in ''Rajah's Ransom'': '' 'His takeoffs were just as good as things Reeves had done with his springboard,' says historian Miller. 'But the flying was horrendous. Ellsworth used four basic stock shots: a flight path across the country, one against Smallville, a forty-five degree angle up, and the same down. It

was basically a bad imitation of Superman flying; no dramatic music or theme, just dull, boring violin strings. The only consolation is a decent landing.' ''[30]

Just as in the *Adventures of Superman,* the boy of steel's adversaries in Whitney Ellsworth's *The Adventures of Superboy* were down-to-earth crooks. As a matter of fact, Shifty Barnes, one of the thugs in ''Rajah's Ransom,'' was played by Richard Reeves, who had also played heavies on the *Adventures of Superman*. Reeves (who is no relation to George) played Bad Luck Brannigan in ''No Holds Barred'' (1951); Frenchy in ''Jet Ace'' (1953) and Stacey Tracey in ''Olsen's Millions'' (1954).

The Salkinds (Alexander and Ilya), on the other hand, occasionally borrowed characters appearing in *Superman* magazine, such as Lex Luthor, the evil scientific genius brought to the screen by Gene Hackman in three of the four Christopher Reeve SUPERMAN films. In the *Superboy* series, the boy of steel faced another familiar adversary from the comics, Mr. Mxyzkptlk. The mischievous imp from the fifth dimension was brought to life by Michael J. Pollard, who had played C.W. Moss in the 1967 crime film, BONNIE AND CLYDE. He may also be remembered as Jahn in ''Miri,'' the October 27, 1966 episode of NBC's *Star Trek*.

During the first season of the syndicated *Superboy* series, the producers introduced an adolescent Lex Luthor, and cast Sherman Howard in the role. With the first and second episodes of the second season, Sherman Howard took over the dubious honors as Superboy's nemesis.

For the first season, Clark Kent/Superboy was played by John Haymes Newton.

The start of the second season marked a change in the program's title from *Superboy* to *The New Adventures of Superboy,* which more closely aligned with the nostalgia of the George Reeves series. Even more important than that the series had a new name and a new Lex Luthor, was that it had a new Superboy!

In a plotline that was almost identical to the one played out by another of television's superheroes, Captain Marvel (Jackson Bostwick) on *SHAZAM!* (See Entry), John Haymes Newton turned in his union suit over a contract dispute at the end of the series' first season.

Since *Superboy* was produced by Alexander and Ilya Salkind and not Whitney Ellsworth, it is more reasonable to compare this series with the SUPERMAN films produced by the Salkinds, which is exactly what Robert MacKenzie did in his October 21, 1989, review in *TV Guide:* ''When the Salkind family made the ''Superman'' movies, they got it right. . . . The first season of *Superboy,* the Salkinds' syndicated TV series, also got it right. John Haymes Newton played the role square as a post, Superboy as a cornfed kid from Kansas. Suited up, he was Clark cubed.

''This season, I detect efforts to make Superboy hipper. The role is now played by Gerard Christopher. . . , an older-looking East Coast type who plays the hero as a suave character, conscious of his good looks. He even smirks as he slips the comeuppance to the bad guys.''[31]

There is very little in print available about John Haymes

29. Grossman, Gary. *Superman Serial to Cereal*. Popular Library, New York, 1976, p. 169.
30. Grossman, Gary. *Superman Serial to Cereal*. Popular Library, New York, 1976, p. 170.
31. MacKenzie, Robert. ''Superboy.'' *TV Guide*, Vol. 37, No. 42, October 21, 1989, Issue #1908, p. 32.

Newton's portrayal of Superboy, but in February 1990, D.C. Comics released the first issue of *Superboy: The Comic Book* featuring a color still of television's Lana Lang and Superboy (Stacy Haiduk and Gerard Christopher). The promotional cover copy (borrowed from the closing credits of STAR TREK: THE MOTION PICTURE) read "The Adventure Continues! Based on the hit syndicated Action Series!!"

The changes in cast were also acknowledged on the editorial page. " *'The Adventure Continues.'* That's what the advertisements said about a year or so ago when 'Superboy: The Series' hit the syndication airwaves across America. That was 1988 and the series has come a long way and gone through several changes since its debut week in October of that year—not the least of which are several personnel changes; roommates come and go, as do leading actors in the role of Superboy/Clark Kent."[32]

The roommate the editors were referring to was T.J. White (Jim Calvert), a nerdish photographer who happened to be the son of Perry White, the editor-in-chief of *The Daily Planet,* a great metropolitan newspaper. There was no transition episode filmed, but John Moore did explain T.J.'s exit in "Big Man on Campus," in issue number 4 of *Superboy: The Comic Book.* At the end of that story, T.J., who since the first issue had been trying to make it as a stand-up comedian, was discovered by Ben Donnely, a reporter for a GBS (Galaxy Broadcasting System) affiliate. Donnely, on assignment for *Gary David's After Midnight Show,* was in Crescent County covering the story of a fraternity kid named Dodger, who was transformed into a fifty-foot giant by accidentally passing through a Gateway Lens developed by Dr. Kristova. Superboy had restored Dodger to normal size before Ben Donnely arrived, but he had a chance to catch T.J. disarming the giant with his stand-up routine. As T.J. packs his car for the move to Metropolis, he says good-bye to Clark and Lana and tells them if his stand-up career doesn't work out, he may call his dad about a job shooting pictures for the *Daily Planet.*

Like the comics, the series acknowledged its roots by using the names of Superman's creators, Jerry Siegel and Joe Shuster. The Siegel School of Journalism, for instance, was located on the campus of Shuster University.

Clark Kent's second-season raucous roommate was Andy McAlister (Ilan Mitchell-Smith).

Not counting infants, youngsters and adolescents appearing as Clark Kent/Superboy in portions of previous films and the television series, Gerard Christopher is the second actor to wear the famous red and blue costume on television. Gerard, the oldest of twelve children, was born in the Bronx, New York, and has appeared in more than sixty television commercials including spots for Chrysler and Coca-Cola. His other television work includes NBC's *Murphy's Law* and CBS's *True Confessions.*

During a promotional appearance on ABC's *Regis & Kathie Lee,* Regis Philbin asked Gerard Christopher (whom he kept calling Superboy) about his landing the part:

REGIS:	Now, you watched *Superman* when you were a kid, right?
GERARD:	Oh, yeah.
REGIS:	Did you pretend you were Superman?
GERARD:	I did. A lot of this I forgot about but—my mother reminds me. . . .
REGIS:	. . . A casting director who had met Gerard Christopher a few years earlier remembered him. And [he] was asked to read for the part when it became available.

Gerard Christopher, who looks very much like a young Christopher Reeve, in much the same manner that John Rockwell resembled George Reeves, has been told all along about the resemblance, as he explained to Regis:

GERARD:	When this came up, I kind of started thinking, maybe after all these years of people telling me I look like Chris Reeve, maybe finally it's going to pay off.

And, of course, it did, as verbalized by one viewer, Steve McCauley, in a letter that appeared in the sixth issue of *Superboy: The Comic Book.* "Speaking of the Show, I am really impressed with the cast. I love Stacy Haiduk [Lana Lang], and I think Gerard Christopher makes a fantastic Superboy! I thought John Haymes Newton did a great job in the role as well, and I worried when I heard he had left the show. It appears, though, that Gerard has settled into the wearing of the cape very nicely, thanks."[33]

Still, some readers of *Superboy: The Comic Book,* seemed to be confused by the recasting of Superboy on the television series, as can be seen in this letter from T.L. Durbin in the seventh issue: "On another matter, I am confused on how you are planning to portray Clark Kent in this book. Will it be done in the John Haymes Newton style, the Gerard Christopher style, or something different?"[34]

The cagey response given by the editor was, "Clark Kent will be portrayed in the Clark Kent style in this book."[35] And Superboy fans really couldn't ask for much more than that.

32. *Superboy 1.* D.C. Comics, Inc., New York 1989, Jenette Kahn, President & Editor-in-Chief.
33. *Superboy 2.* D.C. Comics, Inc., New York, 1989. Jenette Kahn, President & Editor-in-Chief.
34. *Superboy 7.* D.C. Comics, Inc., New York, 1990. Jenette Kahn, President & Editor-in-Chief.
35. *Ibid.*

ADVENTURES OF SUPERMAN

April 1, 1952–November 1957.   Syndicated
September 12, 1993   ABC

Character: Clark Kent/Superman
Played by: George Reeves
Date(s):   April 1, 1952–November 1957

Replaced by: Clark Kent/Superman
Played by: Dean Cain
Date(s):   September 12, 1993–

Character: Lois Lane
Played by: Phyllis Coates
Date(s):   1952–1953

Replaced by: Lois Lane
Played by: Noel Neill
Date(s):   1953–1957

Replaced by: Lois Lane
Played by: Teri Hatcher
Date(s):   September 12, 1993–

Character: Jimmy Olsen
Played by: Jack Larson
Date(s):   April 1, 1952–November 1957

Replaced by: Jimmy Olsen
Played by: Michael Landes
Date(s):   September 12, 1993–

Character: Perry White
Played by: John Hamilton
Date(s):   April 1, 1952–November 1957

Replaced by: Perry White
Played by: Lane Smith
Date(s):   September 12, 1993–

Character: Inspector William "Bill" Henderson
Played by: Robert Shayne
Date(s):   1952–1957

Replaced by: Deputy Inspector Hill
Played by: Marshall Reed
Date(s):   1952

Character: Uncle Oscar Quinn & Professor Twiddle

Played by: Sterling Holloway
Date(s):   1953–1954

Replaced by: Professor J.J. Pepperwinkle
Played by: Phillips (Phil) (Phipps) Tead
Date(s):   1955–1957

Character: Receptionist
Played by: Dani Nolan
Date(s):   1951

Replaced by: Miss Bachrach
Played by: Almira Sessons
Date(s):   1951

Replaced by: Receptionist
Played by: Aline Towne
Date(s):   1951

"The Adventures of Superman. Faster than a speeding bullet. More powerful than a locomotive. Able to leap tall buildings in a single bound—'Look, up in the sky,' 'it's a bird,' 'it's a plane,' 'it's Superman!'—Yes, it's Superman, strange visitor from another planet who came to earth with powers and abilities far beyond those mortal men. Superman, who can change the course of mighty rivers, bend steel in his bare hands—and who, disguised as Clark Kent, mild-mannered reporter for a great metropolitan newspaper, fights a never-ending battle for truth, justice and the American way."

The *Adventures of Superman* made its New York television premiere on ABC-TV at 6:15 in the evening of April 1, 1952. The unusual starting time was due to the fact that back in 1952 the evening news on ABC ran for only fifteen minutes.

It was natural for the producers of the *Adventures of Superman* to hire Phyllis Coates to portray the character of Lois Lane on television since she had already played the same part with George Reeves as the Man of Steel in the Lippert Pictures theatrical film, SUPERMAN AND THE MOLE MEN, released the previous year. During the second season, she says "I left the series to do a comedy pilot ["Here Comes Calvin"] for MCA with Jack Carson and Allen Jenkins."[36] The program aired on General Electric Theater on February 21, 1954, but failed to become a regular series.

Ms. Coates explained that her reason for leaving the *Adventures of Superman* was that "I wanted to do comedy and in those days we worked six days a week on *Superman* and I wanted to get out of it then."[37] Even though *Superman's* producer, Whitney Ellsworth, had offered to double Coates' salary, she still felt there would be more money, in the long run, on the new series.

In the 1954 NBC situation comedy, *The Duke,* Phyllis Coates landed the role of the Duke's girlfriend, Gloria. The short-lived half-hour series ran from July 2 to September 3, 1954 and aired on Friday nights from 8:00 to 8:30. Four months later, Phyllis

---

36. From a 1987 radio interview with Phyllis Coates on *The Alan Colmes Show,* which aired on WNBC-AM radio, New York.
37. *Ibid.*

Superman (George Reeves) silently watches the destruction of the world's deepest oil well and casing by the creatures from the center of the earth. This scene is from the conclusion of "Unknown People Part II" as Lois Lane (Phyllis Coates) vocalized their actions "It's almost as if they were saying 'You live your lives and we'll live ours.' "

Coates turned up as Nurse Madge Allen in another short-lived situation comedy, *Professional Father*. This show, which aired on CBS from January 9 to July 2, 1955, also starred Good Ol' Mr. Wilson, Joseph Kearns, as Madge's husband, Fred, and Beaver's mom, Barbara Billingsley, as Helen Wilson. *Professional Father* ran for a total of thirteen episodes.

Noel Neill took over the role of Lois Lane the following season. Ms. Neill actually created the character of Lois Lane in the fifteen-chapter 1948 Columbia serial SUPERMAN, opposite Kirk Alyn as the man of steel. She reprised the role in another fifteen installments in the 1950 serial ATOM MAN VS. SUPERMAN. Ms. Neill stayed with the *Superman* cast until the series ended production.

During the 1970s, Ms. Neill toured colleges and universities across the country offering a program that featured three *Superman* episodes, "The Tomb of Zaharan," "The Perils of Superman" and "All That Glitters." After the showing of these episodes she made a personal appearance. Noel Neill brought with her a copy of the script from the *Superman* episode, "Panic in the Sky," and asked for volunteers from the audience to come up on stage to read a scene with her. Some of the schools of higher learning included on this nationwide tour were the University of North Carolina, the University of Kentucky and Upsala College in East Orange, New Jersey.

In 1980, Noel Neill and the screen's first Superman, Kirk Alyn, filmed scenes in which they played young Lois Lane's parents in the 1978 motion picture, SUPERMAN. Unfortunately, the scenes were cut from the finished film. All that remains is a six-second glimpse of Neill and Alyn through the window of a passing train as young Clark Kent outruns the speeding locomotive on his way home from football practice. A couple of these scenes were restored when forty-nine minutes of outtakes were added for the version that aired on the ABC network.

As every fan of the *Adventures of Superman* knows, Clark

Kent's best friend and Superman's police contact was Inspector William J. Henderson, played throughout the series by Robert Shayne. However, in "The Human Bomb," the twenty-first episode of the series, which initially aired in 1952, Superman enlists the assistance of Police Deputy Inspector Hill, played by Marshall Reed.

Lois Lane, played in this episode by Phyllis Coates, is handcuffed to Bet-a-Million Butler (Trevor Bardette), and is forced to stand on a ledge outside the *Daily Planet* building, many stories above the ground. Butler's plan is to keep Superman in sight while a robbery is taking place at the Metropolis Museum.

Superman rearranges Clark Kent's office and sits in a chair he has positioned to allow the desk lamp to throw a shadow of his profile on the wall. He then has Perry White block Butler's view while Inspector Hill changes places with him. When White moves away it still looks as though Superman is sitting there.

It has been said that Robert Shayne was ill or away on vacation while this episode was being filmed, or that Marshall Reed was hired to replace him because Reed's profile more closely resembled Reeves', which was the key element in this episode. This, however, was not the case, as the ninety-year-old actor confessed.

"Robert Maxwell, who liked me very much, didn't believe all the crap going around about my blacklisting. He had to let me go for that episode and replace me with another actor, because Kellogg's didn't want me in it," [38] explained Shayne. It must be noted that Robert Shayne, like so many other actors, was completely innocent and not involved in any subversive activity and should never have been subpoenaed. Thanks to the convictions of Robert Maxwell, *Superman*'s producer and Shayne's good friend, he was able to return to the role of Inspector Henderson after missing only two episodes. This was because Maxwell threatened to walk off the series if Kellogg's, the show's sponsor, did not agree to let Shayne return. Kellogg's capitulated and Robert Shayne continued with the series until its end.

Jack Larson, the actor who played cub reporter, Jimmy Olsen, offered his recollections of the incident:

"He [Robert Shayne] was involved with a couple of groups who were helping feed poor people during the depression. Suddenly Bob was called up before the Senate investigating committee. We came to work one day and F.B.I. agents were at the stage doors of the old Selznick Studios, where we were shooting, and they had a subpoena for Bob. Everybody panicked and he was written out of the series. I give producer Bob [Robert] Maxwell a great deal of credit for displaying such fine and distinguished behavior when everyone else was running for cover and not knowing what to do. He brought Bob Shayne back after he was done testifying, without ever knowing if the show could have been banned because Bob was in it." [39]

Bette Shayne, Robert Shayne's wife, also recalled Larson's

defense of her husband: "I remember he said, 'You've got to be crazy. Bob Shayne is the greatest guy in the world. He's a family man and is on the board of trustees of the church. You've got to be nuts!' George Reeves and Phyllis Coates also came to Bob's defense.

"But Bob wouldn't run. A lot of his friends were going to Europe to avoid the ordeal. Bob said, 'I'm not guilty, I'm not going any place.' So we stayed right where we were.

"On Tuesday, September 11, 1951, during the first session of the 82nd Congress, Bob gave his testimony to the Committee on Un-American Activities, "Communist Infiltration of Hollywood Motion Pictures, Part IV." [40]

"In 1953, the subject was brought up again and *Superman*'s new producer, Whitney Ellsworth, said, 'No way! Bob Shayne stays even if we have to get another sponsor.' Kellogg's never mentioned it again," [41] concluded Shayne.

But before Robert Shayne's return, a second episode was filmed that featured Marshall Reed—"The Whistling Bird," the fifty-first show of the series. In Reed's only scene, which took place in Clark Kent's office, he is not referred to by name as he speaks to Kent while Lois Lane listens:

REED: I'm sorry, Mr. Kent, the Commission is doing everything it can. You've looked at our files yourself and my men are checking every possible lead. All we can do is just sit and wait.

The "Commission" Reed is referring to is the Federal Security Commission. His dialogue, however, suggests that he is once again representing the police, although he is never directly referred to as Inspector, or as Hill.

Marshall Reed was born on May 28, 1917 in Englewood, California. In addition to his two appearances on the *Adventures of Superman,* he appeared as Inspector Fred Asher, from 1954 to 1959, on the police drama *The Lineup* (See Entry).

Robert Shayne, a handsome and very successful character actor, explained how he got the part of Inspector Henderson on the *Adventures of Superman:* "One day my agent, Sam Armstrong, phoned me and said, 'Meet me at the RKO lot in Culver City, I have a possible job for you.' I said, 'What is it?' and he said, 'It's *Superman,*' and I said, 'The *Superman* series? Sure, lets go.'

"So I went over to the RKO lot with Sam and walked into the office of Bob [Robert] Maxwell and we had a very friendly chat, but I could tell that he was looking me over. He then asked me if I'd mind graying my hair a little because they wanted me to look older for the part. I answered, 'Certainly not. I don't mind you graying my hair. You can make my hair any color you want to!'

"He said, 'You'll be fine. I want you to play the part of Inspector Bill Henderson on the *Superman* series. Sam and I have discussed your salary and that's okay with me and I hope it's okay with you.' And that's the way it happened.

38. From an exclusive telephone interview with Robert Shayne on January 4, 1991.
39. From an exclusive telephone interview with Jack Larson on September 8, 1990.
40. From an exclusive telephone interview with Bette Shayne on January 4, 1991.
41. From an exclusive telephone interview with Robert Shayne on January 4, 1991.

"I enjoyed working with George Reeves very much. We were very compatible. We both had a sense of humor and we had fun. I would frequently come onto the stage in the morning and George would ask, 'Do you know your lines?' and I'd say, 'Sure,' because I had a photographic memory and had learned my lines the night before. So George would say, 'Well, lets go into my dressing room and learn them. So we'd go into his dressing room and run the lines of our scenes together so they would be letter perfect, because everything was done so fast."[42]

Of the ninety-seven major motion pictures in which Robert Shayne appeared, the one film in which he didn't put in an appearance, but probably should have, was the 1978 fantasy adventure, SUPERMAN. "I remember being quite miffed at not being asked to be in that,"[43] said Shayne, who paused for a moment before adding "I didn't see why I had to be left out."[44]

Nearly ten years after working on the *Adventures of Superman*, Robert Shayne replaced Edward G. Robinson, Jr. as the sound mixer on the NBC dramatic series, *Bracken's World* (See Entry).

At the age of ninety, Robert Shayne returned to television as Reggie, the blind newsstand vendor, on another comic book adventure series, *The Flash* (See Entry).

In 1953, the thirty-ninth episode of the *Adventures of Superman* featured a forty-three-year-old Sterling Holloway, the voice of many Disney animated characters including the Cheshire Cat and Winnie the Pooh.

Holloway played the part of a brilliant, but somewhat naive professor, lovingly referred to as Uncle Oscar. Superman simply called him "Uncle" in one scene from "The Machine that Could Plot Crimes." At the end of the season, Holloway appeared in another episode, "The Whistling Bird."

The second episode of the following season, "Through the Time Barrier," featured Sterling Holloway for the third and last time as the lovable scientist now renamed "Professor Twiddle." "Through the Time Barrier" was also the first episode of the series to be filmed in color.

The next time a lovable, but somewhat absent-minded professor was called for was in the 1955 episode, "Topsy Turvy." Character actor Phil Tead took over the honors of Professor Pepperwinkle. In "Topsy Turvy," Professor Pepperwinkle invents a machine that makes people think that everything is turned upside down. Tead continued in the role as Professor Pepperwinkle in the 1956 season when he invented a machine that could send people anywhere in the world via a telephone line in "The Phony Alibi."

Professor Pepperwinkle appeared three times during the 1957 season. In "The Big Forget" he invents an aerosol spray that obliterates the subject's immediate memory. In "The Gentle Monster" he builds a robot, Mr. McTavish, as a companion for himself. And in the series' last episode, "All That Glitters," Professor Pepperwinkle invents a machine that turns base metals, along with some unshelled peanuts, apple cider and platinum, into 24–karat gold.

It is a tribute to an actor, and to the writers who created this lovable character, that although Professor Pepperwinkle seemed to be around so much, he really only appeared in five of the 104 television episodes.

Phil Tead actually made his first appearance on the Superman television series a season before. In "The Seven Souvenirs," he plays Mr. J. Willy, proprietor of the Superman Souvenir Shop. Phil Tead, who appeared in many feature films, once played a subway rider in the "Loving Cup" episode of *I Love Lucy*. Coincidentally, the very next episode of *I Love Lucy* (See Entry), featured a guest appearance by George Reeves as Superman.

Over the course of the series, the *Daily Planet*'s receptionist was only seen three times and in each instance she was played by a different actress. In the premiere episode, "Superman on Earth," Perry White's unnamed receptionist was played by Dani Nolan, whose name does not appear in the closing credits. We know she's Perry's receptionist because that's what the nameplate on her desk says.

Five episodes later, in "A Night of Terror," Miss Bachrach was played by the highly excitable Almira Sessons. The third unnamed *Daily Planet* receptionist appeared in "The Human Bomb." She was played by Aline Towne, the same actress who played Superman's Kryptonian mother, Lara, in "Superman on Earth."

The three actors/characters who did remain constant throughout the series were George Reeves as Clark Kent/Superman, John Hamilton as *Daily Planet* editor, Perry White, and Jack Larson as cub reporter Jimmy Olsen. Larson says:

"I was offered another series by Bob Maxwell who had gone on to produce *Lassie*. The new series, *Waldo*, was about a rich young man whose family was trying to declare him insane because he lived with a chimpanzee.

"I was in New York at the time and ABC very much wanted me to leave the *Adventures of Superman* and do the *Waldo* pilot for them. Out of deference to Bob Maxwell, I did fly out to California to meet with them and the chimpanzees, but I didn't want to leave *Superman*. I have always felt that you should never leave a series. I didn't know that this would finish off my acting career because I was so typed as Jimmy.

"But I still feel today as I felt then, that audiences who tune in every week because they know you and love you as a particular character wouldn't forgive you if you suddenly decided to leave—for whatever reason. I think it leaves a bad taste in everybody's mouth.

"Even though I was offered a number of other parts, in addition to *Waldo*, I would never have left the *Superman* series. I think it's a mistake for any actor to leave a series. I think you should run with it to the end. If you do it, do it—do it to the end. If you're in it, go on with it!" concluded Larson emphatically.[45]

Jack Larson did, however, make guest appearances on single episodes of *The Dick Van Dyke Show* and *Gomer Pyle, U.S.M.C.* (See Entry).

More than forty years after the *Adventures of Superman*

42. From an exclusive telephone interview with Robert Shayne on January 4, 1991.
43. *Ibid.*
44. From an exclusive telephone interview with Robert Shayne on January 4, 1991.
45. From an exclusive telephone interview with Jack Larson on September 8, 1990.

made its debut on syndicated television, Lorimar Television risked an updated version of the classic series titled, *Lois and Clark: The New Adventures of Superman*. In the May 17–23, 1993, edition of *TV Pro-Log*, Editor and Publisher Timothy Hunter wrote "It's the old story, but with a 90s sensibility. Clark Kent (Dean Cain) is in love with Lois Lane (Teri Hatcher), but can't tell her he's Superman. And, Lois, a workaholic, is in love with Clark's alter ego, Superman. Together, Lois and Clark cover breaking news stories all over Metropolis."

The pilot for this updated version about the man of steel and Superman's girlfriend, Lois Lane, aired as a one-hour and forty-five-minute made-for-television movie that began with Clark Kent's arrival in Metropolis, ignoring the legend portion of the story which was the greater part of the first episode of the George Reeves series.

Besides the understandable updating of the characters, some liberties were taken with the origin story; most notably Pa Kent, who is alive and well and still living on the farm in Smallville where Clark visits for Sunday dinners. This is a major departure where in "Superman on Earth" and at the beginning of SUPERMAN: THE MOVIE, Pa Kent dies of a heart attack.

The other major rewriting of the Superman legend is the origin of his blue, red, and yellow costume. In all previous versions, Clark's mom stitched the world's most recognizable outfit from the swaddling blanket the infant Kal-El was wrapped in when he was rocketed to earth by his Kryptonian parents, Jor-El and Lara.

Here it was Clark's idea that he needed a secret identity and employs his mother to design his colorful disguise. The viewer is then treated to the suit's evolution in a cute section of the telefilm, as the young Kent tries on a number of costumes his mother has sewn that run the gamut from a carnival strongman through a series of superhero costumes that strongly resembly those worn by the Green Lantern, Captain America and the Flash.

The design they finally settle on is only missing the stylish "S" insignia.

CLARK: (Admiring the costume in the mirror) What do you think?

MA KENT: One thing's for sure, nobody's going to be looking at your face.

CLARK: Mom!

MA KENT: (Laughing out loud) Well, they don't call 'em tights for nothin'.

Still, Mrs. Kent isn't completely satisfied either—there's something missing, but what? That's when she opens up an old suitcase and pulls out the familiar red "S" on the triangular yellow field, explaining that it was found along with his blanket in the rocket that brought him to earth. And although young

Clark isn't completely sold on the red cape, his mother insists it adds just the right touch.

MA KENT: Your folks'd be proud of you . . . we sure are.

All well and good, but since the costume was sewn out of early yardgoods it's sure to stain, burn, and ultimately tear to shreds, which was addressed in the second episode. In the comics, Superman kept his costume clean by diving into a vat of acid that burned neither his skin, nor the Kryptonian fabric. Even on the *Adventures of Superman,* the costume could not be burned, or cut.

It is obvious that the basis for this series was not those thirty-minute episodes produced by Whitney Ellsworth, but the series of motion pictures produced by Alexander and Ilya Salkind. And in keeping with the premise of these films and even the *Adventures of Superboy* series, Lex Luthor was introduced as Superman's chief foil, instead of the lunkheaded crooks that populated the first series.

AFTERM*A*S*H

September 26, 1983–October 30, 1984.   CBS

Character:	Mildred Potter
Played by:	Barbara Townsend
Date(s):	September 26, 1983–March 12, 1984
Replaced by:	Mildred Potter
Played by:	Ann Pitoniak
Date(s):	September 25, 1984–October 30, 1984
Character:	Mike D'Angelo
Played by:	John Chappell
Date(s):	September 26, 1983–March 12, 1984
Replaced by:	Wally Wainwright
Played by:	Peter Michael Goetz
Date(s):	September 25, 1984–October 30, 1984

". . . of the 22 new shows to debut this fall, only two stand out as potential commercial hits (ABC's *Hotel* and CBS' *AfterM*A*S*H*).''[46] The latter lasted for only twenty-eight episodes.

There were actually five original characters who made the transition from the series *M*A*S*H* to *AfterM*A*S*H*. Three of them were series regulars: Colonel Sherman Potter (Harry Morgan), Corporal Max Klinger (Jamie Farr) and Father Francis Mulcahy (William Christopher). The fourth character was Soon-Lee, played by Rosalind Chao who was introduced in the last episode of *M*A*S*H*. In that two-and-one-half-hour special, which aired on February 28, 1983, Max Klinger falls in love with and marries Soon-Lee.

46. *TV Pro-Log: Television Programs and Production News.* TI-Volume 35, No. 48. Television Index Information Services, L.I., New York, August 1, 1983. Jerry Leichter, Editor and Publisher.

A publicity still from the October 24, 1983 episode of *AfterM*A*S*H* of Mildred and Sherman Potter (Barbara Townsend, left, and Harry Morgan, right) made up for a flashback sequence recalling their younger days when a number of crises require Sherman, Klinger (Jamie Farr) and Father Mulcahy (William Christopher) to work the night shift at the hospital, forcing Potter to miss an important dinner with his beloved Mildred.

In *AfterM*A*S*H,* Klinger has brought his new bride with him to Missouri, which is the setting for the series.

The fifth and final character who made the transition from *M*A*S*H* to *AfterM*A*S*H* was the love of Colonel Potter's life, Mildred, whom viewers knew only through Potter's words and the picture that sat upon his desk in *M*A*S*H.* I have thus far been unable to ascertain the name of the actress who appeared in that photograph.

On January 13, 1983, the *Baltimore Sun* ran an article, ''There will be spinoff life after *M*A*S*H,*'' which reported that ''Several other cast members have said they have no interest in any kind of spinoff.'' *The Sun* went on to say that actor Mike Farrell, who played B.J. Hunnicut, ''. . . said he had also been offered a spinoff. 'They wanted to know if I had any interest in continuing the character of B.J. and I said no.' ''

Speaking about roles which had not yet been cast, *TV Guide* wrote, ''. . . and most awaited of all, Sherman Potter's wife Mildred. (Ah, Mildred! How we've missed you . . .)'' The article, ''A New Hawkeye?'' appeared in the June 4, 1983 issue.

Before Barbara Townsend was cast, producer Burt Metcalfe described the character of Mildred Potter: ''Still to be cast is Colonel Potter's long-unseen wife Mildred, who executive producer Burt Metcalfe tantalizingly describes as 'a cross between Bess Truman and Gracie Allen.' ''[47] Ms. Townsend was replaced in the second season by Ann Pitoniak ''to make Mildred more of a Gracie Allen type.''[48]

Peter Michael Goetz replaced John Chappell as the more serious hospital administrator, Wally Wainwright. The first hospital administrator of the General John J. Pershing Veteran's Administration Hospital in River Bend, Missouri was Mike D'Angelo, played by John Chappell. John Chappell has appeared in more than one dozen mini-series and movies made for television in both major and minor roles.

Peter Michael Goetz, who took over the duties as hospital administrator during the second season, later played Chuck Cavanaugh in the CBS sitcom, *The Cavanaughs,* which aired from December 1, 1986, to March 9, 1987.

THE ALDRICH FAMILY

October 2, 1949–May 29, 1953.   NBC

Character:	Henry Aldrich
Played by:	Robert Casey
Date(s):	1949–1950

Replaced by:	Henry Aldrich
Played by:	Richard Tyler
Date(s):	1950–1951

Replaced by:	Henry Aldrich
Played by:	Henry Girard
Date(s):	1951–1952

Replaced by:	Henry Aldrich
Played by:	Kenneth Nelson
Date(s):	1952

Replaced by:	Henry Aldrich
Played by:	Bobby Ellis
Date(s):	1952–1953

Character:	Mrs. Alice Aldrich
Played by:	Lois Wilson
Date(s):	1949–1950

Replaced by:	Mrs. Alice Aldrich
Played by:	Nancy Carroll
Date(s):	1950–1951

Replaced by:	Mrs. Alice Aldrich
Played by:	Lois Wilson (returns to series)
Date(s):	1951

Replaced by:	Mrs. Alice Aldrich
Played by:	Barbara Robbins
Date(s):	1951–1953

47. *TV Guide.* ''Grapevine.'' Vol. 31, No. 26, June 25, 1983, Issue #1578, p. 25.
48. *TV Guide.* ''Grapevine.'' Vol. 32, No. 39, September 29, 1984, Issue #1644, p. 25.

Character:	Mary Aldrich
Played by:	Charita Bauer
Date(s):	1949–1950

Replaced by:	Mary Aldrich
Played by:	Mary Malone
Date(s):	1950–1952

Replaced by:	Mary Aldrich
Played by:	June Dayton
Date(s):	1952–1953

Character:	Homer Brown
Played by:	Jackie Kelk
Date(s):	1949–1951

Replaced by:	Homer Brown
Played by:	Robert Barry
Date(s):	1951–1952

Replaced by:	Homer Brown
Played by:	Jackie Grimes
Date(s):	1952–1953

Character:	Mr. Bradley
Played by:	Richard Midgley
Date(s):	1949

Replaced by:	Mr. Bradley
Played by:	Joseph Foley
Date(s):	1950–1953

Character:	Kathleen
Played by:	Marcia Henderson
Date(s):	1949–1953

Replaced by:	Eleanor
Played by:	Loretta Leversee
Date(s):	1952–1953

The Aldrich Family, which was supposed to represent the typical American household in the early 1950s, may be a better example of a typical American family in the nineties considering that there were five Henrys, four Alices and three Marys. There were also three Homer Browns and two Mr. Bradleys.

House Jameson played Henry's father, Sam, and was the only member of the television cast to remain with the series for its entire run. He was also one of three cast members who played the same role in the *Henry Aldrich* radio series. The other two actors were Jackie Kelk, who played Homer Brown from 1949 through 1951 and Leona Powers, who played Mrs. Bradley.

The first and third actors who played Henry Aldrich, Robert Casey and Henry Girard, left acting after their year in television. The other three actors do have other television credits.

Richard Tyler, the second Henry Aldrich, played Buck (Annette Funicello's boyfriend) on *The Danny Thomas Show* during the mid-1960s.

The fourth Henry Aldrich, Kenny (Kenneth) Nelson, was born in Rocky Mount, North Carolina on March 24, 1930. He played Ranger Colt on DuMont's hit adventure series of the 1950s, *Captain Video and His Video Rangers.* He also appeared on the CBS variety special, *Hooray for Love,* which aired on October 2, 1960. At the age of fifty-three, this juvenile actor of the 1950s and 1960s played the New York hotel manager on the ABC mini-series, *Lace,* which aired on February 26 and February 27, 1984.

The fifth and final Henry Aldrich was played by Bobby Ellis. Born in Chicago, Illinois in 1933, Ellis had played Corliss Archer's boyfriend, Dexter Franklin, in both the 1951 and 1954 versions of the situation comedy, *Meet Corliss Archer* (See Entry). He later played Ralph Granger, Ronnie Burns's friend on *The George Burns and Gracie Allen Show,* during the 1950s, and was Joe DePaw on *Love That Bob.* Bobby (Robert) Ellis also appeared in films during the late 1940s and 1950s.

Both the first and the third Mrs. Aldrich were played by the same actress—Lois Wilson.

Ms. Wilson played Helen Joyce in the 1932 Tom Mix Western, RIDER OF DEATH VALLEY, Laura Dodacker in the 1936 Cary Grant comedy, WEDDING PRESENT, and Miss Jamieson in the 1940 drama, NOBODY'S CHILDREN. The following year, she retired from films. Eight years later she turned to television and starred as Mrs. Alice Aldrich from 1949 to 1950. She also appeared on *Magnavox Theater* in 1950. Ms. Wilson was temporarily replaced by Nancy Carroll (a beautiful 1930s film star) during most of 1950/1951 season and then returned to the role to finish out the 1951 season. She died on January 8, 1983.

The fourth and final Mrs. Aldrich was played by Barbara Robbins until the series ended in 1953. On April 27, 1967, Barbara Robbins played Mrs. Fairfax in the CBS drama special, *Jane Eyre.*

In addition to the cast changes listed, the part of Henry's mother was actually recast one additional time. Actress Jean Muir was hired during the summer of 1950 to play Mrs. Aldrich for the upcoming 1950/1951 season, but was fired after it was discovered that her name was listed in *Red Channels,* the pamphlet put out by proponents of Senator Joseph McCarthy which listed actors and actresses who were suspected of being Communist sympathizers.

The program's sponsor, General Foods, and its advertising agency, Young and Rubicam, canceled the season's opening episode until Ms. Muir could be replaced.

Jean Muir later testified before a Congressional committee that she was not and had never been a Communist, but like so many others, her career had already been destroyed by the vicious accusations and the truth was of little consequence.

The first of the three actresses to play Mary Aldrich was Charita Bauer. Ms. Bauer may have stayed with the cast of *The Aldrich Family* for only a short time but she found a lifelong home with the cast of the daytime soap opera, *The Guiding Light,* as Bert, a part which began on radio in 1950 and continued on television from 1952 through 1984. In 1983, the Television Academy of Arts and Sciences presented her with a

Lifetime Achievement Award. Ms. Bauer, who was born in Newark, New Jersey on December 20, 1923, died at the age of sixty-two on February 28, 1985.

Charita Bauer was replaced on *The Aldrich Family* by Mary Malone, who had played Emily Kimbrough in the CBS situation comedy, *The Girls,* from January 1 to March 25, 1950.

The third Mary Aldrich was played by June Dayton, who was Patsy Hamilton in the CBS daytime serial, *The Brighter Day,* from January 4, 1954 to September 25, 1962. Ms. Dayton was also Beth March in the second of eight versions of Louisa May Alcott's novel, *Little Women.* This one aired on CBS on December 18 and December 25, 1950. In 1979, Ms. Dayton played a secretary in the first CBS pilot for *Captain America,* and June Cullen in the second.

The first of the three Homer Browns, Jackie Kelk, went on to star in his own series, *Young Mr. Bobbin,* in which he played eighteen-year-old Alexander Bobbin. This live NBC comedy series ran from August 26, 1951 to May 18, 1952.

The second of two Mr. Bradleys was played by Joseph Foley who was simultaneously playing Mr. Gabriel Gurney on the NBC situation comedy, *Mr. Peepers.*

In the case of Henry's girlfriends, the producers replaced Kathleen with Eleanor; however, instead of leaving the series, as is usually the case when a character is replaced, Marcia Henderson remained with the *Aldrich Family* cast until 1953.

The following year, Ms. Henderson joined the cast of *Dear Phoebe,* as Mickey Riley, a female sportswriter for the *Los Angeles Daily Blade.* The half-hour NBC situation comedy, which starred Peter Lawford as Bill Hastings, ran from September 10, 1954 to September 11, 1956.

ALIAS SMITH AND JONES

January 21, 1971–January 13, 1973.   ABC

Character:	Hannibal Heyes/Joshua Smith
Played by:	Peter Duel
Date(s):	January 21, 1971–February 10, 1972

Replaced by:	Hannibal Heyes/Joshua Smith
Played by:	Roger Davis
Date(s):	February 17, 1972–January 13, 1973

Character:	Narrator
Played by:	Roger Davis
Date(s):	January 21, 1971–February 10, 1972

Replaced by:	Narrator
Played by:	Ralph Story
Date(s):	February 17, 1972–January 13, 1973

Character:	Sheriff Lom Trevors
Played by:	James Drury
Date(s):	January 5, 1971

Replaced by:	Sheriff Lom Trevors
Played by:	Mike Road
Date(s):	January 21, 1971–January 13, 1973

Hannibal Heyes/"Joshua Smith" and Jed "Kid" Curry/"Thaddeus Jones" were the two notorious outlaws in this television knockoff of the popular 1969 motion picture, BUTCH CASSIDY AND THE SUNDANCE KID that starred Paul Newman and Robert Redford. The film duo, who never do go straight, were a little more larcenous than their television counterparts, who were to be granted a full pardon by the governor for their past crimes if they could keep their noses clean for one year.

Actor Peter Deuel, who later simplified the spelling of his name to Duel, starred as Hannibal Heyes from 1971 to 1972. Ben Murphy played Jones throughout the short run of the series.

On Thursday, December 30, 1971 at the age of 31, Peter Duel watched his then current episode of *Alias Smith and Jones* on television with his girlfriend, Diane Ray. Later that evening he watched a Los Angeles Lakers basketball game on television.

Shortly after 1:25 a.m. (now Friday, December 31, 1971), Duel joined Ray in the bedroom and said, "I'll see you later."[49] But he never did. Duel left the bedroom and went back into the living room. A few minutes later Ray heard a gun shot. When Ray ran to investigate "she found Duel sprawled beneath the still-decorated Christmas tree, his .38 caliber revolver nearby, a jagged bullet hole spilling blood from his right temple."[50]

With only a few episodes completed, Roger Davis, who had narrated the program's openings and closings, was chosen for the role of Hannibal Heyes "and a partially completed episode was finished with Davis redoing scenes already filmed by Duel."[51] Prior to *Alias Smith and Jones,* Davis had played the young and immature driver, Private Roger Gibson, in the 1962–1963 ABC war drama, *The Gallant Men,* and Mike in the 1963 NBC Western, *Redigo.*

When Davis took over the role of Heyes, Ralph Story was hired as the program's new narrator. In 1956 Story replaced Sonny Fox as the emcee of the highly successful quiz program *The $64,000 Challenge,* and continued with the program until its last broadcast on September 7, 1958 when it was forced off of the air as a result of the quiz show scandals precipitated by *Twenty-One* and *Dotto.*

James Drury, who is best known as *The Virginian,* played Sheriff Lom Trevors in the series pilot and a few episodes before turning over the part to Mike Road whose voice is perhaps more famous than his face due to his voice characterization of Race Bannon in Hanna-Barbera's animated adventure series, *Jonny Quest.*

49. Rovin, Jeff. *TV Babylon,* Signet, New York, April 1987, pp. 68–70.
50. *Ibid.,* p. 70.
51. Brooks, Tim and Marsh, Earle. *The Complete Directory to Prime Time Network TV Shows 1946–Present (Fourth Edition).* Ballantine Books, New York, 1988, p. 45.

Former narrator Roger Davis (left) as Hanibal Heyes/Joshua Smith, with Ben Murphy (right) as Jed ''Kid'' Curry/Thaddeus Jones on location in Moab, Utah from the second season of *Alias Smith and Jones*.

Whether it was because of the suicide of Peter Duel or the recasting of his role, *Alias Smith and Jones* ended prematurely in 1973, after completing only 48 episodes.

ALICE

August 31, 1976–March 19, 1985.   CBS

Character:	Florence Jean Castleberry (Flo)
Played by:	Polly Holliday
Date(s):	August 31, 1976–February 24, 1980
Replaced by:	Belle Dupree
Played by:	Diane Ladd
Date(s):	March 2, 1980–November 10, 1982
Replaced by:	Jolene Hunnicutt
Played by:	Celia Weston
Date(s):	October 4, 1981–March 19, 1985

To set the record straight, the television sitcom, *Alice*, is based on the 1975 motion picture, ALICE DOESN'T LIVE HERE ANYMORE, not the 1969 film, ALICE'S RESTAURANT, which was itself inspired by the Arlo Guthrie song of the same name.

The series, which shares the lives of three waitresses working at Mel's Diner, consisted of four main characters: Alice Hyatt (Linda Lavin); her son Tommy Hyatt (Philip McKeon); Mel Sharples, the owner of Mel's (Vic Tayback); and two other waitresses, Florence Jean Castleberry, known as ''Flo'' (Polly Holliday), and Vera Louise Gorman (Beth Howland).

Except for the part of Alice's son, Tommy, who was played by Alfred Lutter, all but one member of the original cast remained intact throughout the series. The exception was the part of the boisterous waitress from Cowtown, Texas, Flo, who was written out and replaced twice.

The original producer of *Alice,* Bruce Johnson, explained how Polly Holliday became Flo. ''Polly came in and read for us in New York when we were casting the show, and she just

Inside Mel's Diner, Mel Sharples (Vic Tayback, far right) slings another insult at the third cast of *Alice* featuring (left to right): Alice Hyatt (Linda Lavin), Vera Louise Gorman (Beth Howland) and Jolene Hunnicutt (Celia Weston).

knocked us out. We signed her on the spot."[52] That's a pretty big compliment to pay an actress who was reading for a role that had already been done by another actress.

The characterization of Flo was created by Diane Ladd in the motion picture, for which she earned an Oscar nomination for Best Supporting Actress, but Polly Holliday said she never saw the film. "I didn't want to take the chance that I'd be overawed by Ladd's performance. I didn't want to be influenced to the point where I might wind up doing the actress and not doing the role."[53]

Speculating on the possibility of a spinoff series, which materialized less than three years later, Polly Holliday said, "I'm not sure Flo could work as well on her own. And if she couldn't, I'd prefer to stay where I am. . . . I really don't need my own series to be happy."[54]

Happy or not, after four seasons of *Alice*, Polly Holliday left for her own spinoff series, *Flo*, which was a midseason replacement during the 1979/1980 season, premiering on March 24. Holliday once said, "I have every intention of making *Flo* work as a long-running series. But even if it doesn't succeed, I won't want to return to *Alice*. It's like leaving the nest. Once you do, you don't go back."[55]

But before she left *Alice* in 1980, Polly Holliday was nominated for an Emmy for Outstanding Continuing Performance by a Supporting Actor in a Comedy or Drama Series; she lost to *Rhoda*'s Julie Kavner. In 1979, Holliday was nominated

for Outstanding Supporting Actress in a Comedy Series, which she lost to *All in the Family's* Sally Struthers. But at the Golden Globe Awards that same year, *Alice* won for Best Television Show, Musical or Comedy and Linda Lavin won for Best Television Actress, Musical or Comedy. Polly Holliday won a Golden Globe Award for Best Supporting Actress and Vic Tayback won for Best Supporting Actor.

While still working on *Alice*, Polly Holliday played Mrs. Kirby in the 1979 CBS comedy special, *You Can't Take It With You*, which also starred another *Alice* regular, Beth Howland, as Essie. In October, 1982 Polly Holliday temporarily replaced Eileen Brennan in *Private Benjamin* (See Entry).

Beginning in the spring of 1980, Mississippi-born actress Diane Ladd joined the cast of *Alice* as Belle Dupree. Belle, who was from Mississippi, wrote Country-and-Western songs and had the same aggressive, no-nonsense personality displayed by her predecessor, Flo.

For the remainder of the TV series the part of the brash waitress, now Jolene Hunnicutt, was played by Celia Weston, who was born in Spartanburg, South Carolina. If Weston seemed natural in the comic part of a waitress, it may have been because she once worked as one in a Salem, North Carolina steak house.

In an appearance on *Live At Five*, which aired on New York's NBC-TV on January 7, 1983, Weston said of the difficulties of replacing an established character, "It's been a [tough] road to hoe, but it's coming about." Apparently it did come about, because Ms. Weston stayed with the series to its end, appearing in approximately the same number of episodes as Polly Holliday.

ALL IN THE FAMILY

January 12, 1971–September 16, 1979.   CBS
September 23, 1979–September 21, 1983

Character:	Henry Jefferson
Played by:	Mel Stewart
Date(s):	April 6, 1971–October 20, 1973
Replaced by:	George Jefferson
Played by:	Sherman Hemsley
Date(s):	October 20, 1973–January 11, 1975
Replaced by:	Frank Lorenzo
Played by:	Vincent Gardenia
Date(s):	September 15, 1973
Character:	Tommy Kelsey
Played by:	Brendon Dillon
Date(s):	November 20, 1971

52. Prelutsky, Burt. "Polly Holliday Flips her Wig. . . and becomes a brassy hash-slinger in *Alice.*" *TV Guide*, Vol. 25, No. 27, Issue #1266, July 2, 1977, p. 24. Radnor, Pennsylvania.
53. *Ibid.,* pp. 23–24.
54. *Ibid.,* p. 25.
55. Mitz, Rick. *The Great TV Sitcom Book.* Richard Marek Publishers, New York, 1980, p. 386.

Replaced by:	Tommy Kelsey
Played by:	Bob Hastings
Date(s):	December 4, 1971–March 12, 1977

Replaced by:	Tommy Kelsey
Played by:	Frank Maxwell
Date(s):	1977–1978

Character:	Joey Stivic
Played by:	Jason Draeger
Date(s):	1975–1978

Replaced by:	Joey Stivic
Played by:	Justin Draeger
Date(s):	1975–1978

Character:	Joey Stivic
Played by:	Corey Miller
Date(s):	unknown

Replaced by:	Joey Stivic
Played by:	Christopher Johnston
Date(s):	February 28, 1982

Replaced by:	Joey Stivic
Played by:	Christian Jacobs
Date(s):	September 26, 1982–September 21, 1983 (*Gloria* spinoff)

Character:	Louise Jefferson
Played by:	Isabel Sanford
Date(s):	March 2, 1971

Replaced by:	Irene Lorenzo
Played by:	Sada Thompson
Date(s):	(never appeared on air)

Replaced by:	Irene Lorenzo
Played by:	Betty Garrett
Date(s):	September 15, 1973–1975

Character:	Floyd Mills
Played by:	Marty Brill
Date(s):	March 3, 1979

Replaced by:	Floyd Mills
Played by:	Ben Slack
Date(s):	unknown

Producer Norman Lear was the one responsible for bringing the Bunkers, the first truly typical American family, to television. Critics like the *New York Times*' Cynthia Lowry, weren't enamored with the premiere of the series. She wrote: "... it was a half-hour of vulgarity and offensive dialogue. . . . The series concerns the family of Archie Bunker, a loud-mouthed, short-fused man whose bellowing is reminiscent of Jackie Gleason in the original *The Honeymooners,* but he is without Gleason's redeeming charm. His wife is a silly naive woman who wants peace at any price."[56]

Somehow, after we got past the shock of seeing ourselves on television, *All in the Family* went on to become one of television's most popular series, running for nine seasons before becoming *Archie Bunker's Place* on September 23, 1979.

Not only has the series been in syndication ever since, but during the summer of 1991 CBS aired six "classic" episodes as part of its Sunday evening lineup with on-air promos touting it as "The surprise hit of summer." Well, as Archie Bunker would have said, "Oh, what a surprise."

The initial cause of friction on the series was ignited by the next-door neighbors. But unlike Ed and Trixie Norton in *The Honeymooners,* these neighbors George and Louise Jefferson, their son Lionel, and Lionel's uncle, Henry Jefferson, were blacks!

There was much interaction between the Bunkers and Lionel and Louise (Mike Evans and Isabel Sanford) but, although he was mentioned a lot, George Jefferson wasn't seen until 1973. What viewers saw, instead, was George's brother, Henry, played by Mel Stewart.

This came out in this scene from "The First and Last Supper," in which Archie agreed to have dinner with the Jeffersons. The episode aired on April 6, 1971.

LOUISE:	Edith, I have a confession to make to you. This isn't my husband.
EDITH:	It isn't?
ARCHIE:	That's not your husband?
LOUISE:	No, George didn't want to have dinner with you either. And when I couldn't change his mind, I didn't know what to do. I was so embarrassed that I asked my brother-in-law, Henry, to come with me.
ARCHIE:	Your brother-in-law, Henry. Oh, what a lie.

Following his role as Henry Jefferson on *All in the Family,* Mel Stewart went on to work in five other situation comedies. These included Sargeant B.J. Bryant in CBS's *Roll Out* (October 5, 1973–January 4, 1974); Mr. Gibson in ABC's *On the Rocks* (September 11, 1975–May 17, 1976) and Tabitha's boss, Marvin Decker, at KXLA-TV in the short-lived *Bewitched* spinoff, *Tabitha* (See Entry). One of Stewart's more prominent

---

56. Lowry, Cynthia. "Situation Comedy Has Its Premiere." *New York Times,* January 13, 1971.

dramatic roles was Billy Melrose, on the Bruce Boxleitner/Kate Jackson adventure series, *Scarecrow and Mrs. King,* which aired on CBS from October 3, 1983 to September 10, 1987.

Then in 1973, Sherman Hemsley was hired to play George Jefferson, a role he continued to play until 1975, when he left *All in the Family* to star in his own spinoff, *The Jeffersons.*

On the January 11, 1975 episode of *All in the Family,* the Jeffersons bade the Bunkers farewell as they moved on up to their own series on CBS, which made its debut the following Saturday, January 18, 1975. *The Jeffersons* left CBS's Tuesday evening lineup on July 23, 1985. More than eleven years later, Sherman Hemsley returned to television as Deacon Ernest Frye in the successful NBC situation comedy, *Amen,* which premiered on September 27, 1986.

With the Jeffersons gone, Archie's new source of irritation was Frank and Irene Lorenzo, the Bunkers' new neighbors, who moved into the neighborhood in the September 15, 1973 episode, "We're Having a Heat Wave."

Vincent Gardenia, who played Frank Lorenzo, had already appeared as different characters in two previous episodes of the series: the March 2, 1971 episode, "Lionel Moves into the Neighborhood," and "The Bunkers and the Swingers," which aired on October 28, 1972. He had also appeared in the December 14, 1975 episode of *Kojak,* "Winner Takes Nothing," a pilot for a proposed spinoff series in which he played former New York City cop, Vincent La Guardia, working for the Las Vegas, Nevada police department. The episode of *Kojak* was well received, but the series commitment was shot down.

Betty Garrett, however, didn't start out as Irene. Sada Thompson, who won a Tony Award for *Twigs* and is best known to television audiences as Kate Lawrence, the mom on *Family,* was originally cast as Frank Lorenzo's wife. But before she actually began working on episodes, which were filmed in California, she quit the series, saying that she missed her family and the New York stage.

Speaking about the loss of Sada Thompson in *The Hollywood Reporter,* Norman Lear said, "Thank heavens she came to me early enough. Had we made a couple of shows with her it would have been impossible."

The neighborhood hangout was Kelsey's Bar which was originally run by Brendon Dillon as Kelsey. Bob Hastings, who replaced Dillon as Tommy Kelsey in 1973, is perhaps best known for his role as Lt. Elroy Carpenter in *McHale's Navy.*

Mike and Gloria's first child, a son, H. Joseph "Joey" Michael Stivic, was born on the December 22, 1975 episode of *All in the Family.* The infants hired to alternate playing the part were the nine-day-old twins, Jason and Justin Draeger, the sons of a police officer. The producers chose twins to play the role of a single infant because of the rules outlined in California's child labor law, twins allow the producers to get twice as much footage of the infant, while still working within the law.

On February 28, 1982, Gloria (Sally Struthers) returned from California to *All in the Family* with her son, Joey, (now played by Christopher Johnston), and explains that her husband, Mike (Rob Reiner), has run off to a commune with another woman. Even though Archie is willing to once again support his "little girl," Gloria asserts herself and tells Archie that she must become her own person.

Needless to say, Gloria not only becomes her own person, but her own spinoff. *Gloria* ran on CBS from September 26, 1982 to September 21, 1983. Gloria's now eight-year-old son, Joey (that's just about right if you calculate his age from his birth on *All in the Family* in December of 1975), was played by Christian Jacobs who had played Bruce Weston on *Maggie* from 1981 to 1982.

There were times when the producers of *All in the Family* thought that both Archie and Gloria would have to be written out of the series because of their highly-publicized salary strikes. At the beginning of the 1974/1975 season, Carroll O'Connor went out on strike and sued Tandem Productions for approximately $65,000 and contract clarification. It was also rumored that O'Connor wanted to have his name appear above the program's title. The writers had planned a four-part episode dealing with inflation, but were forced to come up with a scenario that explained Archie's absence. The storyline they came up with had Archie missing at a convention in Buffalo, New York. The series of four episodes was planned so that if O'Connor did not come to terms with the producers by the fourth episode, Archie could have been written out of the series by being killed at the convention.

The first actor to play Stephanie's father, Floyd Mills, was Marty Brill, who appeared from 1971 to 1973 as Bernie Davis on *The New Dick Van Dyke Show.*

ALMOST HOME *see: THE TORKELSONS*

THE ANDY GRIFFITH SHOW

October 3, 1960–September 16, 1968.   CBS

Character:	Sheriff Andy Taylor
Played by:	Andy Griffith
Date(s):	October 3, 1960–September 16, 1968
	April 13, 1986 (*Return to Mayberry,* NBC)

Replaced by:	Sam Jones
Played by:	Ken Berry
Date(s):	September 23, 1968–September 6, 1971

Character:	Deputy Barney P. Fife[57]
Played by:	Don Knotts
Date(s):	October 3, 1960–1965
	April 13, 1986 (*Return to Mayberry,* NBC)

---

57. The writers seemed to have some trouble deciding on Barney's middle name. In episode 25, "A Plaque for Mayberry," Barney's middle name is Oliver. In episode 82, "Class Reunion," his middle name is Milton. And in episode 103, "Opie's Ill-Gotten Gain," Barney had written "Barney P. Fife" in his old history book.

Andy Griffith as Sheriff Andy Taylor (left) exuding his trademark form of restrained patience with Barney's replacement, Deputy Warren Ferguson (Jack Burns, right) in *The Andy Griffith Show.*

Replaced by:	Deputy Warren Ferguson		Character:	Rose
Played by:	Jack Burns		Played by:	Mary Treen
Date(s):	October 11, 1965–January 31, 1966		Date(s):	February 15, 1960 (pilot)
Character:	Opie Taylor		Replaced by:	Aunt Bee
Played by:	Ronny Howard		Played by:	Frances Bavier
Date(s):	October 3, 1960–September 16, 1968		Date(s):	October 3, 1960–September 16, 1968
	April 13, 1986 (*Return to Mayberry,* NBC)			
Replaced by:	Mike Jones (*Mayberry R.F.D.*)		Replaced by:	Cousin Alice (*Mayberry R.F.D.*)
Played by:	Buddy Foster		Played by:	Alice Ghostley
Date(s):	September 23, 1968–September 6, 1971		Date(s):	October 5, 1970–September 6, 1971

Character: Gomer Pyle
Played by: Jim Nabors
Date(s):   December 24, 1962–May 18, 1964
                April 13, 1986 (*Return to Mayberry,* NBC)

Replaced by: Goober Pyle
Played by: George Lindsey
Date(s):   September 21, 1964–September 19, 1968
                April 13, 1986 (*Return to Mayberry,* NBC)

Character: Floyd
Played by: Walter Baldwin
Date(s):   December 26, 1960

Replaced by: Floyd Lawson
Played by: Howard McNear
Date(s):   January 2, 1961–April 10, 1967

Character: Mary Simpson
Played by: Julie Adams
Date(s):   March 19, 1962

Replaced by: Mary Simpson
Played by: Sue Ane Langdon
Date(s):   April 9, 1962

Replaced by: Irene Fairchild
Played by: Nina Shipman
Date(s):   March 14, 1966

Replaced by: Miss Ellie Walker
Played by: Elinor Donahue
Date(s):   September 1960–May 15, 1961

Replaced by: Peggy McMillan
Played by: Joanna Moore
Date(s):   October 8, 1962–December 3, 1962

Replaced by: Helen Crump
Played by: Aneta Corsaut
Date(s):   March 4, 1963–1968
                April 13, 1986 (*Return to Mayberry,* NBC)

Character: Miss Rosemary
Played by: Amzie Strickland
Date(s):   November 14, 1960

Replaced by: Hilda May
Played by: Florence MacMichael
Date(s):   December 12, 1960–February 20, 1961

Replaced by: Thelma Lou
Played by: Betty Lynn
Date(s):   March 6, 1961–January 10, 1966
                April 13, 1986 (*Return to Mayberry,* NBC)

Character: Will Hoople
Played by: Frank Cady
Date(s):   February 15, 1960 (pilot)

Replaced by: Otis Campbell
Played by: Hal Smith
Date(s):   1960–1967

Replaced by: Mayor Pike
Played by: Dick Elliot
Date(s):   January 2, 1961–January 22, 1962

Replaced by: Mayor Roy Stoner
Played by: Parley Baer
Date(s):   October 15, 1962–1963

Character: Ben Weaver
Played by: Will Wright
Date(s):   February 15, 1960
                December 19, 1960
                April 24, 1961
                March 5, 1962

Replaced by: Ben Weaver
Played by: Tol Avery
Date(s):   March 2, 1964

Replaced by: Ben Weaver
Played by: Jason Johnson
Date(s):   March 28, 1966

Character: Wally
Played by: Norman Leavitt
Date(s):   November 12, 1962
                January 14, 1963

Replaced by: Wally
Played by: Trevor Bardette
Date(s):   November 4, 1963

Replaced by: Wally
Played by: Cliff Norton
Date(s):   March 28, 1966
                December 25, 1967

Character: Dud Wash
Played by: Hoke Howell
Date(s):   March 18, 1963
                April 29, 1963

Replaced by: Dud Wash
Played by: Bob Denver
Date(s):   March 30, 1964

The Andy Griffith Show began as an episode of the *Danny Thomas Show,* ''Danny Meets Andy Griffith,'' which aired on February 15, 1960. In that episode, Danny Williams is arrested by Sheriff Andy Taylor for running a Stop sign in the town of Mayberry and, true to form, refuses to pay the one hundred dollar fine.

There are two very familiar faces present in this pilot and one missing. Present was Frances Bavier who played Henrietta Perkins, a citizen of Mayberry. It is obvious that Ms. Bavier endeared herself to the producers, because when the first full episode of *The Andy Griffith Show,* ''The New Housekeeper,'' aired on October 3, 1960, it was devoted to the introduction of her new character, Aunt Bee Taylor.

In that episode, Opie is having trouble accepting the fact that the housekeeper, Rose, has gotten married to Wilbur Pine and his Aunt Bee has come to live with him. So Opie decides to run away from home, but only after checking with his ''paw'' to see if its okay.

ANDY: Opie, why can't you put Rose out of your mind and make room for Aunt Bee? If you'll give her a chance, well, pretty soon you'll love Aunt Bee as much as you ever loved Rose.

OPIE: Aw pa, she can't do anything like Rose can. She can't fish or hunt frogs or play baseball with me like Rose did. Gosh.

Yep, you guessed it, Opie did give Aunt Bee a chance and both he and America fell in love with her. Aunt Bee stayed with the series through its transitional period to *Mayberry R.F.D.*

We know that young Opie Taylor was originally looked after by his Aunt Lucy because in the pilot for *The Andy Griffith Show,* Andy tells Opie, ''Now you go on home and tell Aunt Lucy I says give you a great big ol' bottle of pop, you hear.'' The audience, however, never gets to meet her.

Like the Taylors, the Joneses also had a housekeeper. Her name was Mrs. Fletcher and she left Sam's employ when the Venchenti family moved to Mayberry to work for him. That's also when Aunt Bee moved in with Sam and his son, Mike.

Two years later, on September 16, 1968, Frances Bavier left the series. ''ALICE GHOSTLEY, Esmeralda the witch in *Bewitched,* has been hired as KEN BERRY'S new housekeeper in *Mayberry R.F.D.* She replaces FRANCES BAVIER.''[58]

Ms. Ghostley played Cousin Alice, who moved in with Sam and Buddy Jones to keep house for them after serving a twenty-year hitch in the Army. Following *Mayberry R.F.D.,* Alice Ghostley went on to play Bertha, the saloon proprieter in the James Garner Western, *Nichols,* which aired on NBC from September 16, 1971 to August 1, 1972. Before setting up housekeeping on *Mayberry R.F.D.,* Alice Ghostley played Carter Nash's mother on the NBC superhero spoof, *Captain Nice,* which aired from January 9 to August 28, 1967. Ms.

Ghostley's film roles include Stephanie Crawford in the 1962 drama, TO KILL A MOCKINGBIRD, Mrs. Packard in the 1967 comedy, THE FLIM FLAM MAN, and Mrs. Murdock in Paramount's 1978 musical comedy, GREASE.

In 1967, the Academy of Television Arts and Sciences saw fit to honor Frances Bavier's portrayal of Aunt Bee Taylor with an Emmy for Outstanding Performance by an Actress in a Supporting Role in a Comedy.

Due to her poor health, Frances Bavier chose to be written out of the 1986 CBS special, *Return to Mayberry.* In a touching scene, we hear the voice of Aunt Bee (provided by an uncredited actress) as Andy pays his respects at the foot of her grave.

AUNT BEE: You know, Andy, all I ever wanted was for you and Opie to be good citizens and to treat people right. I know you will. You two boys are the button on the cap of kindness. Oh, and remember one green vegetable every day. One hot meal, six glasses of water and to sleep before midnight, that's important.

According to Phil McFall, the co-founder of the Nip It in the Bud! chapter of The Andy Griffith Show Rerun Watcher's Club, ''Frances Bavier has been a recluse here for some years now. She never leaves her house located in Siler City.''[59]

Randy Case, co-founder of the Nip It in the Bud! chapter, ''is also the editor of our hometown paper [*Messenger*]. He has tried, unsuccessfully, in the past to interview Miss B. The reason he was given was her poor health. This was also the reason she no longer pursues an acting career.''[60]

Frances Bavier was born in 1905 in New York City. Her early stage work included roles in *The Poor Nut, On Borrowed Time* and *Kiss and Tell.* She also played Mrs. Berkley in the 1951 science fiction film, THE DAY THE EARTH STOOD STILL. Three years later, Ms. Bavier joined the cast of the NBC sitcom, *It's a Great Life,* as Mrs. Amy Morgan. She stayed with this program from September 7, 1954 to June 3, 1956. Just prior to *The Andy Griffith Show,* Frances Bavier played Eve Arden's mother, Nora, in the CBS situation comedy, *The Eve Arden Show,* which ran from September 17, 1957 to March 25, 1958. Four years after leaving *Mayberry R.F.D.,* Ms. Bavier played the lady with the cat in the delightful canine comedy, BENJI. Frances Bavier died for real on December 8, 1989.

The other familiar face in the *Andy Griffith Show* pilot was Frank Cady, who played the town drunk, Will Hoople. Cady didn't continue with the series, but is known and loved by TV audiences as Sam Drucker, the proprietor of the General Store that served both *Petticoat Junction* and neighboring sitcom, *Green Acres.*

In 1960, a new town drunk, Otis Campbell, was introduced to the series. He was played by Hal Smith. Smith staggered in and out of episodes as Otis from 1960 through 1967, and returned

58. ''TV Teletype: Hollywood Joseph Finnigan Reports.'' *TV Guide,* Vol. 18, No. 25, Issue #898, June 13, 1970.

59. Phil McFall in a letter to the author dated February 27, 1989.

60. *Ibid.*

again as a reformed alcoholic and ice cream man in the 1986 TV movie, *Return to Mayberry.*

As a well-known voice talent for Disney animated features and Saturday morning cartoons, Hal Smith's voice is at least as well known as his face. Among the most durable characters voiced by Smith are those from Art Clokey's 1963 puppet animation series, *Davey and Goliath,* which was produced for the Lutheran church. Smith was the voice of Davey Hanson's dad, John, and of course, Goliath, Davey's dog. It may seem strange that the actor associated with the role of a town drunk would at the same time be a spokesman for the church, something he continues to do to this day as John ''Whit'' Whitaker, the owner of Whit's End in the inspirational radio dramas for kids, *Adventures in Odyssey.* Most recently, Hal Smith provided the voice for Owl in the live action/costumed production of *Winnie the Pooh,* being broadcast on the Disney Channel.

The owner of Mayberry's local department store, Ben Weaver, was quite the opposite of easygoing Sam Drucker. Ben Weaver was mean, ill-tempered, greedy and just downright nasty. *The Andy Griffith Show* pilot featured Will Wright as Ben Weaver. Beginning with the March 2, 1964 episode, ''The Shoplifters,'' Ben was played by Tol Avery, who was later replaced by Jason Johnson.

Missing from *The Andy Griffith Show* pilot was Don Knotts. ''I saw Andy's pilot on *The Danny Thomas Show* and noticed he didn't have a deputy. I learned Andy was on vacation in North Carolina, so I called him and said, 'It would be neat if you had a deputy.' He said, 'Yeah, that's a good idea. Why don't you talk to Sheldon Leonard.' ''[61]

After Knotts met with Leonard, the show's executive producer, he was signed to a five-year contract and Griffith's long-time friend and co-star from the *No Time for Sergeants* play and film, became Andy Taylor's cousin, Barney Fife.

Don Knotts left *The Andy Griffith Show* at the end of the 1964/1965 season to work in films at Universal, as a result of what may have been a lack of communication between himself and Andy Griffith. It seems that Griffith told Knotts that he planned on leaving *The Andy Griffith Show* at the end of the season. Not wanting to be out of work, Knotts discussed his options with all three networks and finally accepted a motion picture deal with Universal Studios. In 1966,[62] he starred as Luther Heggs in the Universal comedy/mystery, THE GHOST AND MR. CHICKEN, which also featured Mayberry's town drunk, Hal Smith, as yet another town drunk, Calver Weems.

Another source reports that Knotts left *The Andy Griffith Show* to star in *The Don Knotts Show.* But since that variety series didn't air until September 15, 1970, it seems unlikely that Knotts left to work on a show that was in development for five years.

It was explained on *The Andy Griffith Show* that Barney left Mayberry to take a job in state traffic with the Raleigh North Carolina police department, where he was later promoted to the position of ''staff detective.''

Don Knotts returned to reprise his role as Barney Fife on several occasions. In ''The Return of Barney Fife,'' which aired during the 1965/1966 season, Barney returns to Mayberry to attend his high school reunion, hoping to pick up where he left off with Thelma Lou, who makes her last appearance on the *Andy Griffith Show.* Barney doesn't get Thelma Lou, but Don Knotts does get an Emmy for Outstanding Performance by an Actor in a Supporting Role in a Comedy.

The week after Knotts appeared in ''The Return of Barney Fife,'' he appeared in ''The Legend of Barney Fife.'' In that episode, he gives his replacement, Warren, some assistance tracking down an escaped criminal (Frank Cady).

During the 1966/1967 season, Andy goes to Raleigh to visit Barney in ''A Visit to Barney Fife,'' and the following week ''Barney Comes to Mayberry'' for a vacation, and Knotts takes home his fourth Emmy Award for his portrayal of the excitable law enforcement officer.

Griffith explained how Jack Burns, the ''huh'' half of the comedy team, Burns and Schreiber, was hired as Don Knotts's replacement:

''We went to San Francisco to meet this very funny stand-up comedian. We thought his performance was fine and decided to make him Floyd's nephew [Warren Ferguson] on the show. So we put him on—and we said we were not replacing Don—but we *were* replacing Don and we were giving him Don Knotts material—and it didn't work.''[63]

Burns's first appearance as Deputy Warren Ferguson was in ''The Bazaar,'' the fifth episode of the 1965 season. He appeared in a dozen more episodes including ''A Warning from Warren,'' ''The Cannon,'' ''Girl-shy,'' ''Otis and the Artist'' and ''The Legend of Barney Fife.'' It was painfully obvious to Griffith, the producers and the audience that it was not possible to replace Don Knotts. Burns was let go just before Christmas, 1966 and no further replacements were hired.

While Jack Burns was working on *The Andy Griffith Show,* his stand-up partner Avery Schreiber, was playing the heavy ''heavy,'' Captain Mancini, in *My Mother the Car.*

The next regular role Jack Burns was seen in was that of Officer Rudy Colcheck in the ABC sitcom, *Getting Together.* The short-lived series, which starred Bobby Sherman, aired only fifteen episodes between September 18, 1971, and January 8, 1972. Jack Burns was also the voice of Ralph, the annoying neighbor in the adult animated series, *Wait Till Your Father Gets Home,* which starred Tom Bosley of *Happy Days,* as Harry Boyle. Among the many celebrities who voiced characters on the series was Don Knotts. Altogether, forty-eight half-hour episodes of this syndicated series were produced between 1972 and 1974.

Burns later became a writer for *The Kraft Music Hall, Hee Haw,* and *The Flip Wilson Show.* In addition to being the head writer on *Fridays,* the ABC late-night comedy clone of *Saturday Night Live,* Jack Burns appeared both on and off camera as the program's announcer. *Fridays* aired from April 11, 1980 to October 22, 1982.

61. Kelley, Richard. *The Andy Griffith Show.* John F. Blair, Publishers, Winston-Salem, N.C., 1988, p. 40.
62. *Halliwell's Film and Video Guide: 6th Edition.* Charles Scribner's Sons, New York, 1987, p. 395 gives 1965 as the release date of THE GHOST AND MR. CHICKEN.
63. Kelly, Richard. *The Andy Griffith Show.* John F. Blair, Publishers, Winston-Salem, N.C., 1988, p. 59.

Andy Griffith, who played Sheriff Andy Taylor from the pilot episode, decided to leave the series in 1968, after the series' eighth season, to work in films for Universal Pictures. Universal had given Griffith a five-year, ten-movie contract beginning with the 1969[64] release, ANGEL IN MY POCKET. In that film, Griffith played Reverend Samuel "Sam" Whitehead, the parson of Church of the Redeemer, a small-town parish in Wood Falls, Kansas. Jack Dodson, who had played Howard Sprague in later episodes of *The Andy Griffith Show*, appeared as Norman Gresham in the film. Shortly after the film's release, Griffith terminated his contract with Universal.

He returned to television as Andy Thompson in the dramatic comedy, *Headmaster,* which ran on CBS for a total of thirteen episodes. *Headmaster* was then replaced by *The New Andy Griffith Show,* which aired from January 8, 1971 to May 21, 1971. Thirteen episodes later, reruns of *Headmaster* aired in the same time slot.

His next regular role was Lew Vernor in the NBC "maxi-series," *Centennial.* Based on the novel by James A. Michener, the extended twelve-part series of two-hour movies ran from October 1, 1978 to October 25, 1980.

Real-life ex-test pilot, Ernest Truax, was the basis for Andy Griffith's homespun astronaut, Harry Broderick, in the adventure series, *Salvage I,* which aired on ABC from January 20 to November 11, 1979.

Since meting out justice seemed to be Griffith's strong point, the role of Atlanta defense attorney Benjamin L. Matlock was a natural progression from his Andy Taylor character. Don Knotts joined the cast of *Matlock* in "The Lemon," the first episode of the series' third season, which began on Tuesday, November 29, 1988. To hype the addition of Knotts to the cast, NBC ran a thirty-second promotional announcement which used Earle Hagen's whistling theme song from *The Andy Griffith Show,* under the first five seconds:

"Tonight, Matlock's back to solve a case with a familiar face. Andy Griffith and Don Knotts haven't been on a stakeout in twenty years. Now they've got to lock up a louse that's been leasing lemons? But when the salesman's dealt a deadly deal they may bury Andy. The dynamic duo do it again. Welcome to the season premiere of Matlock, next."

The character Knotts played, Leslie "Les" Calhoon, prefers to be called "Ace." It should be noted that both "Les" and "Ace" are single-syllable names like "Barn." And Knotts even called Griffith's character "Ben," just a letter away from his familiar "Anj."

A smooth transition from the *Andy Griffith Show* to *Mayberry R.F.D.* was made by having Andy Taylor marry Helen Crump on the very first episode of the new series which aired on September 23, 1968 at 9 p.m. E.S.T. Don Knotts even returned for another guest shot so that Andy's cousin and best friend, Barney Fife, could be best man at the wedding.

Executive producer, Sheldon Leonard, spoke about being written out of a TV series in Richard Kelly's book, *The Andy Griffith Show:* "I have lots of people leave my shows at one time or another. A show has to be built on the premise that everybody is replaceable, nobody is indispensable, with the exception of the star."[65]

Knotts proved Leonard correct not only by leaving *The Andy Griffith Show,* but by joining the cast of *Three's Company* in 1979 as the replacement for both Mr. and Mrs. Roper.

Ken Berry, who had achieved national recognition as Captain Wilton Parmenter in the 1965 ABC situation comedy, *F Troop,* managed to prove Sheldon Leonard wrong by successfully replacing Andy Griffith as the new star of the series.

His early work in television included the role of Woody during the 1960/1961 season of *The Ann Sothern Show,* but his biggest break after *Mayberry R.F.D.* came as a result of a recurring sketch, "Ed & Eunice," on *The Carol Burnett Show,* in which he played Vicki Lawrence's ambitionless son, Vinton Harper. Like the original "The Honeymooners" skit on *The Jackie Gleason Show,* "Ed & Eunice" became a regular series, which was renamed *Mama's Family.* The spinoff aired on NBC from January 22, 1983 to August 17, 1985, and in first-run syndication from September 1986 to September 1990.

Not surprisingly, farmer and councilman Sam Jones was also a widower who had a young son. It was also no great secret that Buddy Foster, who played Sam Jones' son, Mike, was to be the replacement for Opie Taylor in the *R.F.D.* series. Opie was played by Ronny Howard for the entire eight-year run of *The Andy Griffith Show.*

Born on March 1, 1954 in Duncan, Oklahoma, Ronny was only six years old when he uttered his first "paw," but he had been acting since he was two. In Baltimore, he appeared on stage with his parents, Rance and Jean, in a 1956 production of THE SEVEN YEAR ITCH. His early television appearances included *The Red Skelton Show, Playhouse 90, The Danny Thomas Show* and *Dennis the Menace.* Just prior to his long-running role on *The Andy Griffith Show,* Ronny Howard played Bob Smith in all thirty-nine episodes of the ABC dramatic comedy, *The Smith Family,* which aired from January 20, 1971 to June 14, 1972. One of Ronny Howard's most memorable early film roles was Winthrop Paroo, the little boy with the lisp in the 1962 musical comedy, THE MUSIC MAN. Twelve years later a humorous allusion was made about this part when Howard played Richie Cunningham in his own ABC situation comedy, *Happy Days.*

It occurred in an episode in which Richie's sister, Joanie (Erin Moran) got a part-time job at a movie theater to earn money for her own car. When her parents, Howard and Marion (Tom Bosley and Marion Ross) go down to the theater to bring their daughter back home, they discuss the poster from THE MUSIC MAN that is hanging on the wall.

MARION: I just love that little freckle-faced boy. He reminds me so much of Richie when he was younger.

---

64. Some sources give 1968 as the release date of ANGEL IN MY POCKET.
65. Kelly, Richard. *The Andy Griffith Show.* John F. Blair, Publishers, Winston-Salem, N.C., 1988, pp. 57–58.

HOWARD: (Looking closely at the still of the boy on the poster) Oh, you gotta be kidding sweetheart.

Today, Ron Howard, has made a career for himself on the other side of the camera as a highly respected director of films such as the 1984 comedy, SPLASH; the 1985 comedy fantasy film, COCOON, and its 1988 sequel, COCOON II; Steve Martin's 1989 comedy, PARENTHOOD; the 1991 adventure, BACKDRAFT; and the 1992 Irish-American romance, FAR AND AWAY.

When *The Andy Griffith Show* became *Mayberry R.F.D.*, it was 11-year-old Buddy Foster who replaced Ronny Howard as the son of the series' lead. Foster won the role of Mike Jones a year after he had played the part of Johnny Dow on the short-lived Western, *Hondo*.

Jim Nabors's character, Gomer Pyle, had become so popular that the producers felt that Nabors could carry a series of his own, so it was decided that Gomer Pyle would leave Mayberry to join the United States Marine Corps. A spinoff episode of *The Andy Griffith Show*, appropriately titled, *Gomer Pyle, U.S.M.C.*, was written, produced and directed by Aaron Ruben, who left *The Andy Griffith Show* the following season to produce the new series, which first aired on CBS on Friday, September 25, 1964. The highly successful series ended on September 9, 1970 after racking up an impressive 230 episodes in six seasons.

George Lindsey played Gomer Pyle's cousin, Goober Pyle, even though Sheriff Andy Taylor referred to him as Goober Beasley in the "TV or Not TV" episode which aired on March 1, 1965. In any event, Goober replaced his cousin Gomer at Wally's Filling Station when Gomer left for the Marines and his own series, *Gomer Pyle U.S.M.C.* (See Entry) in 1965. It should be noted, however, that George Lindsey made his first appearance on *The Andy Griffith Show*, as Goober, in "The Fun Girls" episode which aired on April 13, 1964.

Lindsey continued with "The Andy Griffith Show" right through the end of the *Mayberry R.F.D.* series. In 1972, Lindsey, who was born in Jasper, Alabama, became a regular on the hayseed comedy/variety show, *Hee Haw*, still wearing Goober's trademark KingPin hat.

Goober returned to the small screen on May 17, 1978 in his own CBS pilot, *Goober and the Trucker's Paradise*. The title song of the ill-fated *Andy Griffith Show* spinoff was written and performed by Ray Stevens, who achieved national attention with his humorous novelty records, *Ahab the Arab, Gitarzan* and *The Streak*, all of which are still quite popular and played regularly on the nationally syndicated radio program, *The Dr. Demento Show*.

It is not known who clipped the hair of the men of Mayberry from October 3 to December 19, 1960, because Floyd the barber didn't appear until December 26 of that year. When writer Arthur Stander titled the twelfth episode of series, "Stranger in Town," he could have had no way of knowing that the stranger would not turn out to be guest star William Lanteau as Ed Sawyer, but Floyd the barber. In that episode only, Floyd was played by Walter Baldwin, who was whisked away when he didn't cut it.

His replacement was Howard McNear as Floyd Colby, who gave his first haircut in the following week's episode, "Mayberry Goes Hollywood." The character's last name was soon changed, and so Howard McNear, as Floyd Lawson, went on to practice his tonsorial skills in Mayberry for seven seasons and nearly seventy-five shows.

Due to a debilitating stroke in 1963, Floyd's barbershop was left empty for the last half of the 1962/1963 season and all of the 1963/1964 season. Howard McNear returned to *The Andy Griffith Show* in "Barney's Bloodhound," which aired on October 26, 1964, and remained with the series until "Goober's Contest,"— the last episode of the 1966/1967 season. In the episodes following McNear's stroke he is often seen sitting. In scenes that required Floyd to stand behind the barber's chair, McNear was supported by a specially constructed brace.

Even though Howard McNear, who died on January 3, 1969, will always be remembered lovingly as Floyd the barber—not a bad epitaph—he had an extensive stage, film and television career. During the 1950s, Howard McNear played Doc in the radio version of *Gunsmoke*, which starred William Conrad as Matt Dillon and Parley Baer (Mayberry's Mayor Stoner) as Chester. His work on television includes episodes of *December Bride, I Love Lucy* and *The Many Loves of Dobie Gillis*. He even played a barber in a segment of *Leave It to Beaver*. He also played Mr. Hamish, a recurring regular on *The George Gobel Show*.

McNear's film roles include Congressman Parker in Irwin Allen's 1961 science fiction fantasy, VOYAGE TO THE BOTTOM OF THE SEA, Mr. Chapman in the 1961 Elvis Presley musical, BLUE HAWAII and Mr. Cimoli in the 1966 Jack Lemmon comedy, THE FORTUNE COOKIE.

Sheldon Leonard described the frustrations involved in the casting of a romantic interest for widower Andy Taylor. "Actually none of the women used during the first three years worked successfully with Griffith, including Elinor Donahue (as Ellie, the druggist) and Sue Ane Langdon (as Mary the county nurse). There were others brought in as well, but they lasted an even shorter time."[66]

Ellie Walker, often referred to as Miss Ellie, ran the drugstore and was Andy Taylor's first girlfriend. Before moving to Mayberry, actress Elinor Donahue played Betty Anderson on one of America's best loved television family shows, *Father Knows Best*. According to Griffith, not only didn't Ms. Donahue work out, but she herself asked him to be released from her contract.

After leaving the *Andy Griffith Show*, Elinor Donahue picked up another regular role, between 1972 and 1974, as Miriam Welby, the steady girlfriend of Felix Unger on TV's version of *The Odd Couple*. Then on November 10, 1967, she beamed aboard NBC's *Star Trek* for a guest appearance as Assistant Federation Commissioner, Nancy Hedford. Her most recent work is as Gladys Peterson, in Chris Elliott's Fox comedy, *Get a Life*, that premiered on September 23, 1990 and featured Chris's real-life dad, Bob, as his TV dad, Fred.

66. Kelly, Richard. *The Andy Griffith Show.* John F. Blair, Publishers. Winston-Salem, N.C., 1988, p. 54.

Don Knotts discussed Griffith's frustration with the casting of his romantic interest: "Each year Andy would say, 'I got to get another girl on this show.' I think he related to Aneta Corsaut (Helen Crump) the best."[67]

Knotts was right on the money because Helen Crump, played by Aneta Corsaut, replaced all of Andy Taylor's previous girlfriends—including Ellie Walker. She also holds the distinction of being the one who finally managed to drag Andy to the altar. Science fiction movie buffs may remember Aneta Corsaut as Jane Martin, the quiet and level-headed girlfriend of Steve McQueen in the 1958 science fiction classic, THE BLOB. Ms. Corsaut was also one of the original cast members of *The Andy Griffith Show* who appeared in *Return to Mayberry*.

There were two mayors of Mayberry. "They [Pike and Stoner] weren't enough to us to put on a continuing contract basis, and sometimes they were available and sometimes not. If they weren't available, we got somebody else."[68]

Andy, however, wasn't the only one in the show to "go a courtin'." Barney also had a couple of lady friends before settling down with his one and only true love, Thelma Lou (Betty Lynn), whom he first met in "Cyrano Andy." Twenty-five years later, Barney and Thelma Lou finally tied the knot when they were married at the end of the 1986 TV reunion movie, *Return to Mayberry*.

The first young lady to catch Deputy Fife's eye was Mayberry's dressmaker, Miss Rosemary (Amzie Strickland), who only appeared in the November 14, 1960 episode, "Andy the Matchmaker." For a short while after that, Barney courted Hilda May, who was played by Florence MacMichael, the actress who replaced Edna Skinner as the wife of the Post's new neighbors on *Mr. Ed* (See Entry).

Character actor Dick Elliot played Mayberry's first Mayor, Mayor Pike. Elliot worked in dozens of films and television programs including the *Adventures of Superman* in which he appeared as wrestling promoter Sam Bleaker in the 1951 episode, "No Holds Barred."

During the third season, another veteran character actor, Parley Baer, replaced Dick Elliot as the Mayor of Mayberry. Baer, who played Chester in the radio version of *Gunsmoke* from 1952 to 1961 played Darby from 1955 to 1961, on *The Adventures of Ozzie & Harriet*, which overlapped his work on radio. Three years after leaving the cast of *The Andy Griffith Show*, Parley Baer played Mr. Hamble in all seventeen episodes of Red Buttons' ABC comedy, *The Double Life of Henry Phyfe*, which ran from January 13 to September 18, 1966. In between he made occasional appearances on *The Addams Family* as the family's insurance agent, Arthur J. Henson.

With Don Rickles' return to television as Don Robinson in the CBS situation comedy, *The Don Rickles Show*, Parley Baer was there as Rickles' boss, Mr. Vanderpool, a partner in the New York advertising agency, Kingston, Cohen and Vanderpool, Inc. The short-lived series aired from January 14 to May 26, 1972.

Parley Baer's film roles include Boozer in the 1950 Western, COMANCHE TERRITORY; the head waiter in the 1952

Humphrey Bogart newspaper drama, DEADLINE U.S.A.; Mr. Kringelein in the 1962 musical biography, GYPSY; the police captain in the 1965 Tony Randall comedy, FLUFFY; and the circus owner in the 1966 children's film, THE AMAZING DOBERMANS.

ANDY'S GANG

September 23, 1950–June 28, 1958.   NBC

Character:	Smilin' Ed McConnell (host)
Played by:	Ed McConnell
Date(s):	August 26, 1950–April 23, 1955
Replaced by:	Andy Devine (host)
Played by:	Andy Devine
Date(s):	August 20, 1955–June 28, 1958
Character:	Froggy the Gremlin (rubber toy)
Played by:	Ed McConnell
Date(s):	August 26, 1950–April 23, 1955
Replaced by:	Froggy the Gremlin (rubber toy)
Played by:	Archie Presby
Date(s):	August 26, 1950–April 23, 1955
Replaced by:	Froggy the Gremlin (hand puppet)
Played by:	Frank Ferrin
Date(s):	August 20, 1955–December 31, 1960

Andy's Gang went through four title changes and two hosts before it actually became *Andy's Gang* with Andy Devine in 1955.

The weekly Saturday morning children's program that featured stories, music, songs, Midnight the cat, and Froggy the Gremlin also featured a filmed segment *Gunga, the East India Boy*. Although no actors or characters were replaced in the *Gunga* series (sometimes spelled Ghanga), Nino Marcel, the student from the University of Southern California who played Gunga, also played Little Fox, while Lou Krugman doubled as the Maharaja of Bakore and various villains.

The fun began as *The Buster Brown TV Show with Smilin' Ed McConnell and the Buster Brown Gang*, which aired on NBC from September 23, 1950 to August 4, 1951. This lengthy title was actually taken directly from the radio program. The "TV" was inserted to distinguish it from the radio version.

The show then moved from 5:30 in the afternoon on NBC to air at 9:30 on alternate Saturday mornings on CBS under the slightly abbreviated title *Smilin' Ed McConnell and his Gang*. This, however, was only the title in the *TV Guide* listing; the ad promoting the show read: "A Wow of a show! *The Buster Brown TV Show with Smilin' Ed McConnell and the Buster*

---

67. Kelly, Richard. *The Andy Griffith Show*. John F. Blair, Publishers. Winston-Salem, N.C., 1988, p. 55.
68. *Ibid.*, p. 53.

Brown Gang. A brand new kind of TV program! A top-notch children's show that's fun for every age!'' When the program moved to ABC late in 1953, its title was shortened to *Smilin' Ed's Gang,* the title McConnell began with on radio.

There is a great deal of conflicting information regarding the air dates of *Smilin' Ed's Gang.* The first original air dates are given as August 26 and September 23, 1950. The final air dates of *Smilin' Ed's Gang* appear as April 16 and August 13, 1955. Both of the latter dates refer to reruns because Smilin' Ed McConnell, who was born James Ed McConnell in 1892, was found dead on a cabin cruiser at Newport Beach, California on July 24, 1954. ''Smilin' Ed'' was sixty-two.[69]

As a result of McConnell's death, this successful children's program was nearly cancelled. Then, on October 9, 1954, Andy Devine, who was concurrently playing Wild Bill Hickok's loyal sidekick, Jingles, on both radio and television, also took over the reins of Smilin' Ed's program. The show, which was appropriately renamed *Andy's Gang,* returned to NBC on Saturday, August 20, 1955. Devine stayed with the program until it was canceled on June 28, 1958. It continued in reruns until December 31, 1960.

From December 5 to December 12, 1964, Andy Devine played Hap Gorman, an old-time marine carpenter, on the Ivan Tors family-oriented adventure series, *Flipper.*

Andy's mischievous foil on *Andy's Gang* was a puppet (actually just a rubber toy) named Froggy the Gremlin—Froggy for short. Froggy was originally played by Smilin' Ed McConnell. Whenever McConnell was required to sing a duet with the mischievous imp, the program's announcer, Archie Presby, provided the voice for the rubber frog.

On *Andy's Gang,* it wasn't the program's host who brought the rubber toy on a stick to life, but its producer and director, Frank Ferrin.

The confusion surrounding the conflicting air dates is the result of the program having been aired on all three networks in addition to being run in syndication.

ANNIE OAKLEY

January 1954–February 1957.   Syndicated-ABC

Character:	Tagg Oakley
Played by:	Billy Gray
Date(s):	January 9, 1954

Replaced by:	Tagg Oakley
Played by:	Jimmy Hawkins
Date(s):	January 1954

Character:	Marge Hardy
Played by:	Virginia Ann Lee
Date(s):	unknown

Replaced by:	Mary Farnsworth
Played by:	Wendy Drew
Date(s):	unknown

Replaced by:	Deborah Scott
Played by:	Nancy Hale
Date(s):	unknown

Character:	Tom Conrad
Played by:	Fess Parker
Date(s):	May 8, 1954

Replaced by:	Chet Osgood
Played by:	Stanley Andrews
Date(s):	unknown

Law and order were kept in Diablo County, Arizona by a fearless gunfighter who could outdraw any desperado. What was even more humiliating to these bellicose badmen was the fact that their adversary was a woman. Her name was Annie Oakley and she, along with her younger brother Tagg, kept the peace during the early 1900s. Using her remarkable sharpshooting skills, Annie Oakley always managed to subdue the bad guys without killing anyone—just like the Lone Ranger.

Annie and Tagg are orphans living with their uncle, Luke MacTavish, who was rarely seen on the series. The series was loosely based on the real-life Annie Oakley who was born Phoebe Anne Oakley Mozee in 1860 and performed in *Wild Bill's Wild West Show* from 1885 to 1902.

The title character was brought to life by Gail Davis, a latter-day Annie Oakley who could handle guns and ride and rope every bit as well as her alter ego. She even did most of her own stunts, although Donna Hall did double for her when dangerous stunts were required. Throughout the course of the series, Annie Oakley rode two different Golden Palominos. In the earlier episodes her horse was Target, and later on her mount's name was Daisy.

Cowboy star and producer Gene Autry originally hired Gail Davis to appear in nearly twenty of his motion pictures. Her roles included Dell Middler in Autry's 1951 Western, SILVER CANYON and Cathy Wheeler in his 1953 film, GOLDTOWN GHOST RIDERS. Ms. Davis also played a tomboy in several 1951 episodes of Gene Autry's syndicated Western, *The Range Rider.*

When *Annie Oakley* first went on the air it was titled *Annie Oakley and Tagg* and co-starred sixteen-year-old Billy Gray as Tagg, Annie's eleven-year-old brother. The ''Bull's Eye'' episode is the only recorded appearance of Gray in the series. A year before, he had appeared as Alan, an amateur photographer who managed to snap a still of Clark Kent changing into Superman. He may also be remembered as Bobby Benson, from the 1951 science fiction classic, THE DAY THE EARTH STOOD STILL, which also featured Superman's George Reeves as the newscaster. He is best known as James ''Bud''

---

69. James Ed McConnell was found dead on a cabin cruiser at Newport Beach, California on July 24, 1954. McConnell was 62. *Smilin' Ed's Gang* continued in reruns until the first airdate of *Andy's Gang,* which sources list as August 13 and August 20, 1955.

Anderson, Jr., Jim and Margaret's son on *Father Knows Best,* which aired from October 3, 1954 to April 5, 1963.

When Jimmy Hawkins joined the cast as Billy Gray's replacement, the title was shortened to *Annie Oakley.* Before becoming Annie Oakley's little brother, Jimmy Hawkins played Donald Ruggles on *The Ruggles.* He later played Jonathan Baylor on the CBS situation comedy, *Ichabod and Me,* which aired on Tuesday evenings from September 26, 1961 to September 18, 1962.

There were three school teachers who appeared at different times throughout the series. The first was Marge Hardy, played by Virginia Lee who later appeared as Lottie on *Banyon,* the NBC crime drama which aired from September 15, 1972 to January 12, 1973. She played Mailin on the afternoon soap opera, *General Hospital.* She was also one of two actresses to provide the voice for Suzie Chan in the animated cartoon, *The Amazing Chan and the Chan Clan,* which aired Saturday mornings on CBS from September 9, 1972 to September 22, 1974.

The second school teacher, Mary Farnsworth, was played by Wendy Drew, who for a short time during 1953 played Betty Hughes on DuMont's *Jimmy Hughes, Rookie Cop* (See Entry). A more lasting role came in 1956 when she became the first of two actresses to play Ellen Lowell Stewart on the CBS daytime soap opera, *As the World Turns.* She was replaced in 1960 by Patricia Bruder.

The third schoolmarm of Diablo County was Deborah Scott. She was portrayed by Nancy Hale who played Helen Carter, the second secretary on *The Whirlybirds* (See Entry).

Diablo, like most TV Western towns, had its own newspaper. Originally, it was the *Diablo Courier,* whose editor, Tom Conrad, was played by Fess Parker, who went on to achieve immortality as both *Davy Crockett* (See Entry) and *Daniel Boone* (See Entry).

The second editor of the town's tabloid, now the *Diablo Bugle,* was Chet Osgood. He was played by Stanley Andrews who, as "The Old Ranger," hosted *Death Valley Days* from 1952 to 1965. His replacement, the second of five, was Ronald Reagan. In 1938, as outlaw Mark Smith, Andrews went head-to-head with another Ranger, in the fifteen-part serial, THE LONE RANGER.

THE ANN SOTHERN SHOW

October 6, 1958–September 25, 1961.   CBS

Character:	Jason Macauley
Played by:	Ernest Truex
Date(s):	1958–1959

Replaced by:	James Aloysius Devery
Played by:	Don Porter
Date(s):	1959–1961

When Ann Sothern's *Private Secretary* series went off the air in 1957, Ms. Sothern sued the producers for more than $93,000 which she claimed was owed to her from the profits earned through the distribution rights of the program.

After she released control of the series, another producer tried to put it back on the air with Don Porter. The only hitch was that the producer was unable to find a suitable replacement for Ms. Sothern, so the project was dropped.

Then in 1958, Ms. Sothern created a new program, *The Ann Sothern Show,* which starred Ernest Truex as Jason Macauley, the manager of New York's posh Bartley House Hotel. She played Kathleen "Katy" O'Connor, the hotel's assistant manager.

It was obvious to Ms. Sothern and the producers that the show was in trouble. As a result, in mid-season, all of the cast members except Ann Tyrrell were fired. Don Porter, formerly Peter Sands, Sothern's boss on *Private Secretary,* was hired to play James Devery, the hotel's new manager.

The change in hotel managers was the basis for the episode which aired on March 9, 1959. It explained why Mr. Macauley was leaving, gave the cast a chance to say their goodbyes, and introduced the hotel's new manager, Mr. James Devery.

MACAULEY: In three days, Mrs. Macauley and I will swap the sidewalks of New York for the mudbanks of the Ganges.

KATY: Ganges? That's in India!

MACAULEY: Yes, the land of mystery, yoga, the Taj Mahal, dancing girls, Omar Khayyám, dancing girls . . .

KATY: Well now, just a minute, before you give the girls another encore, would you please enlighten me?

MACAULEY: Mr. Bartley wants me to assume the management of the Calcutta Bartley.

Katy then congratulates Macauley and he congratulates her, explaining that he has recommended her to Mr. Bartley for the position of hotel manager.

But Katy has her reservations about accepting the job and it takes not one, but two dream sequences to convince her. The first daydream places her in charge of the hotel where nine guests are stuck in an elevator, her secretary wants a promotion and she hasn't had a date with her boyfriend, David, in three years.

The second daydream, however, has her at a luncheon accepting the honor of "Woman of the Year." But just when she agrees to accept the position, Macauley reads her a telegram sent by Mr. Bartley that ends, "James Devery arriving Thursday to take over." In a scene reminiscent of Dorothy's leaving Oz, the cast assembles in the hotel's lobby to say their goodbyes, which must have been somewhat emotional for them, since Macauley and his wife, played by Reta Shaw, were actually leaving the show.

MACAULEY: I sure hate to leave this place.

KATY: Well, walk straight ahead, Mr. Macauley, and don't look back.

MACAULEY: Yeah. (Pulling his hat's brim down over his eyes.) Let's go, Flora.

Mr. and Mrs. Macauley then walk out of the door and the series.

One of Ernest Truex's later film roles was that of Claridge in the 1965 comedy, FLUFFY, which starred Tony Randall and featured one of *The Andy Griffith Show*'s mayors, Parley Baer. Truex later spent a year as Pop during the 1961 season of Harry Morgan's situation comedy, *Pete and Gladys.*

When Don Porter arrived at the Bartley House, the first thing the audience saw was his luggage tags, which read, ''JAMES DEVERY, CHICAGO, ILL.,'' but Porter was actually from Miami, Oklahoma. During this episode Katy calls Porter ''James Aloysius Devery,'' yet in the very next episode, Porter refers to himself as ''James Arlington Devery.'' Perhaps he was just tired from his long trip and forgot what his middle initial stood for.

Coming up with the names for the characters can be almost as important to a program's success as the actual casting. A close examination of opening and closing credits may offer some insight into this difficult process. In the case of *The Ann Sothern Show,* the names Aloysius and Arlington don't appear anywhere; however, the show's producer was Devery Freeman. Probably more than just a coincidence.

Four years after getting out of the hotel business, Don Porter tried his best to raise his teenage daughter, Gidget (See Entry), from 1965 to 1966.

ANYTHING BUT LOVE

March 7, 1989–February 12, 1992.   ABC
May 27, 1992-June 10, 1992   ABC

Character:	Norman Kiel
Played by:	Louis Giambalvo
Date(s):	March 7, 1989–August 29, 1989

Replaced by:	Catherine Hughes
Played by:	Ann Magnuson
Date(s):	September 27, 1989–February 12, 1992
	May 27, 1992
	June 3, 1992
	June 10, 1992

Character:	Brian Alquist
Played by:	Joseph Maher
Date(s):	September 27, 1989–September 5, 1990

Replaced by:	Mike Urbanek
Played by:	Bruce Weitz
Date(s):	February 6, 1991–February 12, 1992
	May 27, 1992
	June 3, 1992
	June 10, 1992

Due to submerged ratings in 1978, Jamie Lee Curtis was forced to abandon ship after playing Lieutenant Barbara Duran on the first version of ABC's *Operation Petticoat* (See Entry). Eleven years later, following a string of fairly successful movie roles, she surfaced as writer Hannah Miller in a new ABC situation comedy, *Anything But Love.* Her co-star was standup comedian Richard Lewis, whose neurotic gloom-and-doom comedic personality makes Woody Allen seem well adjusted.

The show's format can best be likened to a 90's *Mary Tyler Moore Show* with magazine *Chicago Monthly* (later *Chicago Weekly*) substituting for television station WJM. And instead of a blustery producer Lou Grant (Ed Asner), there is a blustery editor, Norman Kiel.

The rest of the newsroom staff consists of the usual sitcom mélange of goofballs along with a couple of sincere ''good friends'' thrown in.

But *Anything But Love* is not another cheap knockoff of a formerly successful series; its focus was very different. Instead of emphasizing the camaraderie and goings on in the newsroom (though there is some of that), it focuses on the relationship between Hannah Miller and senior writer Martin ''Marty'' Ezekiel Gold (Richard Lewis).

This new sitcom showed much promise from the start, although the producers knew that it still needed some fine tuning.

Billy Van Zandt and Jane Milmore were executive story editors on *Anything But Love* during its second season, and Jane Milmore explained the events leading up to the first cast changes on the show:

''They did six episodes that aired after *Roseanne* and they did very well. They decided to bring it back, but the network was very unhappy with Wendy Kout, the executive producer and creator of the series. So they brought in Peter Noah and he brought in a whole new staff who did some rewriting.''[70]

Van Zandt expanded on this adding, ''Peter is the one responsible for changing the concept, the casting and the direction the show was going to take—hence his 'developed by' credit at the opening of the show. That was the only reason he took the job—if he could do a major overhaul to correct what he thought was wrong—which he apparently interpreted as being too much like *The Mary Tyler Moore Show.* He felt that Louis Giambalvo as managing editor Norman Kiel, as good an actor as he is, created too much of a Mary Richards/ Lou Grant relationship and he wanted to explore something new.''[71]

''And Sandy Faison as Pamela Peyton-Finch, the senior writer, was too much like Mary Richards's friend, Phyllis Lindstrom (Cloris Leachman). They had no idea what to do

70. From an exclusive telephone interview with Jane Milmore on January 7, 1991.
71. From an exclusive telephone interview with Billy Van Zandt on January 7, 1991.

with her and she played a different character with the same name every week in a desperate attempt to find something that clicked. So they wrote her out along with Norman Kiel,"[72] said Van Zandt. "They also wrote out Bruce Kirby, who was playing Hannah's father, Leo, basically because it was too bizarre—he lived in a log cabin in Chicago!"[73] interjected Ms. Milmore.

Replacing Norman Kiel as the magazine's editor was Catherine Hughes. She was described to Hannah by Jules Bennett[74] (Richard Frank) who would shortly be named as Ms. Hughes' executive assistant in the September 27, 1989 episode, "Ch-Ch-Changes." Jules told Hannah, "The magazine has been bought. They fired Norman and they brought in this high-powered new editor from New York."

This was also the episode in which television columnist Brian Alquist was introduced. Catherine Hughes tells Hannah that Alquist is "the most highly regarded book and theater critic in London" and uses words like "erudite" and "intellectual" to describe him. Then she says that she's hired him as the magazine's television critic.

Van Zandt expanded on his explanation of Louis Giambalvo's replacement: "They brought in Ann Magnuson as Hannah's new boss, Catherine Hughes, and Peter [Noah] really had to fight the network to bring her in."[75]

Jane Milmore explained why Noah had such a difficult time with his casting choice: "When we filmed in front of an audience in August, before any episodes had aired, nobody really 'got' her character. Ann didn't play to the audience but to the camera, so the studio audience didn't laugh loud enough at her and the network people freaked out.

"It was amazing to watch the transformation once the show went on the air in September. Catherine became a really popular character and the live audiences responded quite differently to her. She began getting laughs where she hadn't before even though she wasn't doing anything different."[76] Ms. Milmore smiled and concluded, "And then, of course, the network shut up."[77]

Both Jane Milmore and Billy Van Zandt appeared on the series as staff writers. Van Zandt played Harold Stang and Ms. Milmore played Kelly Carroll; both were named after characters they created for a play they wrote called *Infidelities*. One of the reasons the producers were able to get Van Zandt and Milmore to work on the series was that they offered them roles. Van Zandt laughed when he told how because they were writers playing writers, "Half the time when Jane and I were in the background, we would be working on actual scripts for the next week's episode."[78]

Eventually, Van Zandt and Milmore bowed out of the series. He explained: "We came out here from New York to create our own shows and we wanted to work on an established show, which we did on *Newhart* (See Entry). And then we did *Anything But Love* because we wanted to work on a new show to learn what the network input would be. After thirteen shows we learned enough and the roles weren't exactly what they had promised us. We had several offers and accepted the one from Grant-Tribune that will allow us to create our own sitcoms. So we talked to Peter Noah and he was very gracious and let us out of our contracts."[79]

Their departure was taken advantage of by having Ms. Hughes, who was always correcting Harold's work, fire him right on the air for making some stupid suggestions. "And as I was slinking out the door, Joe [Joseph] Maher, who played Brian Alquist, had won the pool on the next one to be fired and he called me back into the room to pay up because I had apparently bet on myself,"[80] Van Zandt said.

The characters of Harold and Kelly were never replaced although Ms. Milmore did say that, at one time, they did consider replacing Kelly.

The show's cast was still being tweaked when the third season began on February 6, 1991. Joseph Maher left the show to resume his successful stage career. He also appeared as Bishop O'Hara in the 1992 Whoopie Goldberg comedy, SISTER ACT.

Executive Producer Peter Noah took responsibility for the departure of the Alquist character in the February 1, 1991 issue of *Entertainment Weekly,* saying, "As producers and writers, we didn't service that character in the right way."

As a replacement, the episode, "Say It Again, Han," included an introduction of an ex-*Hill Street Blues* cop, Bruce Weitz, as a no-nonsense "what you see is what you get" columnist, Mike Urbanek. Television audiences will remember Bruce Weitz as Detective Mick Belker from his work on the critically acclaimed police drama.

After being introduced to the assembled staff by Catherine Hughes, Urbanek used a series of pop culture examples to make his philosophy of journalism and life very clear to his new coworkers.

URBANEK: I'm not going to call it pasta if it's really spaghetti. . . . I don't care who killed Laura Palmer. . . . I neither know, nor do I want to discover what "Fahrvergnugen"[81] means . . . and woe to the man who tries to Fax with me.

72. *Ibid.*
73. From an exclusive telephone interview with Jane Milmore on January 7, 1991.
74. Billy Van Zandt said that the character of Jules Bennett was named after Constance and Joan Bennett.
75. From an exclusive telephone interview with Billy Van Zandt on January 7, 1991.
76. From an exclusive telephone interview with Jane Milmore on January 7, 1991.
77. *Ibid.*
78. From an exclusive telephone interview with Billy Van Zandt on January 7, 1991.
79. *Ibid.*
80. *Ibid.*
81. Driving pleasure.

Catherine (and the show's writers) took advantage of this opportunity to explain why the pompous English television critic, Brian Alquist, was no longer with the *Chicago Weekly*.

CATHERINE: And there is one final announcement. After a year spent reviewing American television, Brian Alquist, late last night, walked into Marshall Field's department store, marched to the electronics department and bashed in the entire bank of TV screens. He's presently in a tight white coat on his way home to Surrey.

APPLE'S WAY

February 10, 1974–January 12, 1975.   CBS

Character:	Patricia Apple
Played by:	Franny Michel
Date(s):	February 10, 1974–May 19, 1974

Replaced by:	Patricia Apple
Played by:	Kristy McNichol
Date(s):	September 15, 1974–January 12, 1975

Appleton, Iowa is the setting for this family drama about the Apple family, who escaped the daily pressures of life in Los Angeles, California and returned to the small community founded by George Apple's (Ronny Cox) ancestors. George and his wife Barbara (Lee McCain) were the parents of four children, one of whom was played by two different actresses.

Franny Michel, the first Patricia Apple, was born on September 8, 1961 in Brooklyn, New York. She played Patricia Apple for only one season before being replaced by Kristy McNichol.

Almost exactly a year younger than Ms. Michel, Kristy McNichol (whose screen credit spelled her name as Kristie) was born on September 11, 1962 in Los Angeles, California. She began acting in television commercials when she was only six years old, and at the age of nine appeared in *Love American Style*, among her other guest appearances. In September of 1974 she took over the role of Patricia Apple.

Kristy McNichol gained audience and critics' acclaim for her portrayal of Letitia ''Buddy'' Lawrence on the ABC drama, *Family*, for which she was nominated for four Emmy awards, winning two. She won the 1977 Emmy for Outstanding Continuing Performance by a Supporting Actress in a Drama Series. Two years later, she won the 1979 Emmy for Outstanding Supporting Actress in a Drama Series.

An all-grown-up Kristy co-starred as Barbara Weston, the daughter of widowed pediatrician Dr. Henry Weston (Richard Mulligan) in the warm situation comedy, *Empty Nest*, which premiered on NBC on September 8, 1988.

THE AQUANAUTS

September 14, 1960–September 27, 1961.   CBS

Character:	Drake Andrews
Played by:	Keith Larsen
Date(s):	September 14, 1960–January 18, 1961

Replaced by:	Mike Madison
Played by:	Ron Ely
Date(s):	January 25, 1961–September 27, 1961

When *The Aquanauts* began in 1960, Drake Andrews and Larry Lahr were two professional salvage divers based in Honolulu, Hawaii. They lasted for just one season, which consisted of only nineteen episodes.

The episode which aired on January 18, 1961 was the last in which diver Drake Andrews appeared. The following week, Lahr recruited Mike Madison (Ron Ely) as his assistant. From 1979 to 1981, Ron Ely replaced another actor—Bert Parks—in a long-standing role—as the host of the Miss America pageant.

Ron Ely's most famous television portrayal, however, did not call for a tie and tux. Wearing little more than a loincloth and a smile, Ron Ely holds the distinction as being the first actor to play the lord of the jungle in a *Tarzan* television series (See Entry). Ely later replaced Lloyd Bridges in an updated version of *Sea Hunt* (See Entry).

The title of the series, ''The Aquanauts,'' was replaced on February 15, 1961 with a new title, *Malibu Run*. But even after the format was revamped, the program ended a few months later after only a dozen more episodes.

Keith Larsen, who played Drake Andrews on the series before he was replaced by Ely, was the first of two actors to play Bart Adams in the 1950s CBS series, *The Hunter* (See Entry).

THE AVENGERS

March 28, 1966–September 15, 1969.   ABC

Character:	Mrs. Catherine Gale
Played by:	Honor Blackman
Date(s):	September 1962–September 1965

Replaced by:	Emma Peel
Played by:	Diana Rigg
Date(s):	September 1965–March 20, 1968

Replaced by:	Tara King
Played by:	Linda Thorson
Date(s):	March 20, 1968–May 26, 1969

Replaced by:	Purdy and Mike Gambit (*The New Avengers*)
Played by:	Joanna Lumley and Gareth Hunt
Date(s):	September 15, 1978–March 23, 1979

Before *The Avengers* first aired on ABC television in the United States, it had already been on British television for more than five years.

During the first of the program's five formats, from March 18, 1961 through September 1962, the main character of the series, Jonathan ''John'' Steed, played by Patrick Macnee, did not yet have a regular female associate and the series ended as a result of an actors' strike.

It resumed production in May of 1962 following the settle-

Diana Rigg (left) and Patrick Macnee (right) as the always stylish John Steed and Mrs. Emma Peel—*The Avengers*.

was produced in England from 1977 to 1981 and was syndicated in the United States in August of 1983.

At the beginning of the third format of *The Avengers,* which ran from September 1965 to March 20, 1968, Mrs. Gale resigns and Steed meets and befriends Mrs. Emma Peel, the beautiful widow of test pilot Peter Peel. Diana Rigg, who signed on as the replacement for Honor Blackman, was actually the first lady agent to which American TV viewers were treated.

In 1967 and 1968, Diana Rigg was nominated for an Emmy in the category, Outstanding Continued Performance by an Actor in a Leading Role in a Dramatic Series. She lost both times to *Mission Impossible's* Barbara Bain. Rigg stayed with *The Avengers* for only two years and was replaced by three other agents, yet it is her portrayal of the agent clad in black leather that will forever be recognized as the quintessential female "Avenger."

In an attempt to overcome a strong stereotype, she starred as Diana Smythe in her own situation comedy, "Diana." Unfortunately, this NBC series only ran for 15 episodes from September 10, 1973 to January 7, 1974 and she is still best remembered as Mrs. Peel. Diana Rigg, as Tracy Draco, became James Bond's wife in the 1969 Bond film, ON HER MAJESTY'S SECRET SERVICE, which also starred *Kojak's* Telly Savalas as Ernst Stavro Blofeld.

The fourth format of *The Avengers* series began on March 20, 1968. In the new storyline, Peter Peel, Emma's husband, is found alive in the Amazon and flown back to England. Emma Peel, who had believed her husband was killed in a plane crash, leaves Steed and the series, presumably to rejoin her husband.

Another shapely brunette, Canadian-born actress Linda Thorson, picked up where Diana Rigg left off as Ministry Agent Tara King. Her reign ended on May 26, 1969. On January 18, 1973, Ms. Thorson joined Barbara Feldon and Robert Powell as Toni, in the NBC thriller, *Lady Killer.*

Nearly seven years after *The Avengers* was canceled, an updated version, *The New Avengers,* returned in Britain. Two years later the series aired on *The CBS Late Movie.* That old stalwart of crime, Patrick Macnee, was back as John Steed, along with two younger agents, Purdy and Mike Gambit.

Agent Purdy was played by thirty-year-old actress Joanna Lumley, who did quite well in films following *The New Avengers.* She appeared in the 1969 James Bond spoof, SOME GIRLS DO, and followed up the same year with the role of the English girl in the real Bond film, ON HER MAJESTY'S SECRET SERVICE, which starred her predecessor, Diana Rigg, and George Lazenby as 007.

Gareth Hunt, who played Purdy's sidekick Mike Gambit, appeared as Kadem in the ABC television movie *The House on Garibaldi Street,* which aired on May 28, 1979.

ment of the strike and returned to the air in September with a completely new format which included Honor Blackman as a British Government Ministry agent, Mrs. Catherine Gale, a widow and Steed's glamorous associate.

By 1964 Blackman had become the star of the series and, according to one source, did not sign on for the fourth season of *The Avengers* to avoid being typecast. Another source says that Ms. Blackman left the successful television series so that she could accept the role of Pussy Galore, a pilot and martial arts expert, in the third James Bond film, GOLDFINGER, which was released in 1964.

Ms. Blackman returned to British television as Marian Nicholls, in the situation comedy, *Robin's Nest,* which was itself a spinoff of the British television series, *Man About the House,* the show that inspired *Three's Company. Robin's Nest*

B

BAA BAA BLACK SHEEP

September 21, 1976–September 1, 1978.   NBC

Character:	Lieutenant Robert ''Bob'' Boyle
Played by:	Jake Mitchell
Date(s):	September 21, 1976–March 22, 1977

Replaced by:	Lieutenant Robert ''Bob'' Boyle
Played by:	Larry Minetti
Date(s):	December 14, 1977–September 1, 1978

Adventure series with World War II pilots and planes generally fared better than this one by Stephen J. Cannell starring Robert Conrad as Major Gregory ''Pappy'' Boyington.

During the first season one of the squadron members, Lieutenant Boyle, was played by Jake Mitchell. Mitchell went on to play Charlie Bogart in the equally short-lived police drama, *Paris,* which aired on CBS from September 29, 1979 to January 15, 1980.

Even though *Baa Baa Black Sheep* was cancelled at the end of the 1976/1977 season, both the producer, Cannell, and the series star, Robert Conrad, began a lobbying effort with the network, which paid off when NBC needed a replacement for a couple of failed series in its 1977/1978 schedule.

When the series returned on December 14, 1977 it had been retitled *Black Sheep Squadron* and Jake Mitchell had been replaced by Larry Minetti as Lieutenant Boyle. Minetti later starred as Orville ''Rick'' Wright, who ran a Honolulu night-club on the successful detective drama, *Magnum, P.I.*

BABY BOOM

September 10, 1988–September 10, 1989.   NBC

Character:	Elizabeth Wiatt
Played by:	Michelle Kennedy (two-year-old twin)
Date(s):	September 10, 1988–September 10, 1989

Replaced by:	Elizabeth Wiatt
Played by:	Kristina Kennedy (two-year-old twin)
Date(s):	September 10, 1988–September 10, 1989

Character:	Helga Von Haupt
Played by:	Joy Behar
Date(s):	September 10, 1988–August 14, 1989

Replaced by:	Ofelia
Played by:	Camille Saviola
Date(s):	September 10, 1989

The NBC situation comedy, *Baby Boom,* starred Kate Jackson as J. C. Wiatt, a high-powered executive with no skill in the simple art of child rearing. The series, based on the 1987 motion picture of the same name, had an erratic schedule which began with a special premiere on September 10, 1988. The actual series premiered on November 2, 1988 and aired through January 4, 1989.

TV Guide then noted that the series was going on hiatus; other sources indicated that *Baby Boom* had been axed due to poor ratings. Two months later, NBC announced that the program would return with a change in cast.

The role of the nanny, Helga Von Haupt, played by Joy Behar, would be replaced by '' 'a hot-tempered Latin type,' played by Camille Saviola.''[1] The change took place on the episode which aired on September 10, 1989, as explained in the *TV Guide* listing: ''J.C. (Kate Jackson) has her hands full when Helga (Joy Behar) quits, Elizabeth gets sick, the doctor (Mark Lindsay Chapman) is cute, and the procession of unsuitable nannies seems never ending.''

During 1989, the series only aired three new episodes on July 13, August 14 and September 10. The final episode, which aired on January 4, was a repeat of the series opener. This brought the total number of episodes aired to ten.

The two-year old twins, Michelle and Kristina Kennedy, are the same twins who played Elizabeth, ''the baby'' in the feature film; they are also the only holdovers in the cast from the theatrical version.

Behind the scenes, Nancy Myers, the film's producer and co-writer, was the executive producer and co-writer for the series. Her writing partner was Charles Shyer, who co-wrote and directed the motion picture. Shyer also directed the series pilot.

1. *TV Pro-Log: Television Programs and Production News.* TI-Volume 41, No. 26. Television Index Information Services, L.I., New York. Timothy Hunter, Editor and Publisher. February 27–March 6, 1989, p. 2.

BABY TALK

March 8, 1991–July 3, 1992.   ABC

Character: Maggie Campbell
Played by: Julia Duffy
Date(s):   March 8, 1991–May 24, 1991

Replaced by: Maggie Campbell
Played by: Mary Page Keller
Date(s):   September 20, 1991–July 3, 1992

Character: Fogarty
Played by: William Hickey
Date(s):   March 8, 1991–May 24, 1991

Character: Howard
Played by: Lenny Wolpe
Date(s):   March 8, 1991–May 24, 1991

Replaced by: James Holbrook
Played by: Scott Baio
Date(s):   September 20, 1991–July 3, 1992

The television series *Baby Talk* is the offspring of the 1989 motion picture LOOK WHO'S TALKING which employed a comic device that was not too far afield from an early bit Sid Caesar used to do. The main difference was that while Caesar himself played the sarcastic baby, the film used a real infant on camera, with humorous observations and witticisms provided by the voice of Bruce Willis.

In the film, Kirstie Alley played Mollie, the unwed mother of Mikey, the adorable wisecracking baby who, at various ages, was played by Jason Schaller, Jaryd Waterhouse, Jacob Haines and Christopher Aydon. The basic premise has Mollie on the lookout for a suitable father for her son, who turns out to be a cab driver named James (John Travolta).

A year later, a stillborn sequel, LOOK WHO'S TALKING TOO, featuring the same main cast except for Lorne Sussman as Mikey, was delivered to theatergoers and had a lukewarm reception.

Television producer, Ed. Weinberger, however, saw life in these one-joke films and put *Baby Talk* into development as a weekly sitcom for ABC, starring Tony Danza as the voice of baby Mickey (not Mikey), who was played by Ryan and Paul Jessup, not Brandon and Justin Conkling as originally reported; and Connie Selleca as Maggie (not Mollie).

Right from the start the project was plagued with casting problems, as can be seen from the coverage given to the series in the industry newsletter, *TV Pro-Log.*

"Connie Selleca [who appeared in the first of two pilots] has left the cast of ABC's *Baby Talk* (Tuesdays, 8:30–9 p.m. NYT), apparently due to differences between her and executive producer Ed. Weinberger. Mr. Weinberger is looking for a replacement and would like to begin production on the series, based on the film LOOK WHO'S TALKING, by Tuesday, August 21."[2]

But finding a replacement for a new series isn't as easy as it looks. "Nobody was found to replace Connie Selleca in Columbia's *Baby Talk* (Tuesday's, 8:30–9 p.m. NYT), so ABC will fill the space with *Head of the Class* [See Entry], premiering September 11."[3]

The first replacement hired was Alison LaPlaca, who left after appearing in the second unaired pilot. Perhaps the producers should have renamed the series *Look Who's Walking.*

"No doubt you've already heard that Julia Duffy is taking Connie Selleca's place in ABC's *Baby Talk.* Ms. Selleca left due to creative differences between her and executive producer Ed. Weinberger. Production on *Baby Talk* was supposed to begin on Wednesday, August 22, but was postponed to August 29 because of the casting shakeup. *Baby Talk,* which has been replaced on the schedule by *Head of the Class* (Tuesday's 8:30–9 p.m. NYT), is now one of ABC's backups."[4]

Being hired to replace an established character was really nothing new for Julia Duffy. She is, of course, best known to television audiences as Stephanie Vanderkellen on *Newhart* (See Entry) where she replaced Jennifer Holmes as Leslie Vanderkellen.

The casting nightmares seemingly solved, the series went into production and aired on March 8, 1991. Twelve episodes later, the series was pulled from the schedule and went through a major revamping including changes in characters and locale.

"As you know, Julia Duffy has quit ABC's *Baby Talk* (Friday, 9:30–10 p.m. NYT) and will be moving over to CBS, where she will replace Delta Burke on *Designing Women* [See Entry] (Monday, 9:30–10 p.m. NYT). Ms. Duffy wasn't happy playing straight woman to a baby. You may remember that Connie Selleca, who was originally hired to play the mom, quit for the same reason. Well, the new Maggie Campbell is Mary Page Keller. If you don't know who that is, Ms. Keller starred for three seasons in Fox's series, *Duet.* This past season, she had the recurring role of Gina Giordano, sister of Libby Thacher (Patty LuPone), on ABC's *Life Goes On* (Sunday, 7–8 p.m. NYT). Production of new *Baby Talk* episodes will begin in August. . . .

". . . Michele Greene has joined the list of performers not returning to NBC's *L.A. Law* (Thursday, 10–11 p.m. NYT). According to Ms. Greene, 'It's time I started thinking about the

2. *TV Pro-Log: Television Programs and Production News.* TI-Volume 42, No. 51. Television Index Information Services, L.I., New York. Timothy Hunter, Editor and Publisher. August 20–26, 1990, p. 1,

3. *TV Pro-Log: Television Programs and Production News.* TI-Volume 42, No. 52. Television Index Information Services, L.I., New York. Timothy Hunter, Editor and Publisher. August 27– September 2, 1990, p. 4.

4. *TV Pro-Log: Television Programs and Production News.* TI-Volume 43, No. 2. Television Index Information Services, L.I., New York. Timothy Hunter, Editor and Publisher. September 10–16, 1990. p. 1.

next step in my career.' Michele Greene was approached about filling the lead in *Baby Talk,* but declined the opportunity.''[5]

The male presence during first season episodes were provided by two carpenters, Fogarty and Howard (Lenny Wolpe), who always seemed to be around, like *Murphy Brown*'s Eldin Bernecky (Robert Pastorelli). Fogarty was played by William Hickey, who starred as Stoney Stevenson in Kurt Vonnegut, Jr.'s time/space fantasy *Through Time and Timbuktu; or The Flight of Prometheus-5,* which first aired on PBS stations on March 13, 1972.

When the revamped series returned, Fogarty and Howard were gone and in their place was Scott Baio as Maggie's building superintendent, James Holbrook, a character a little closer to the one played by John Travolta in the film.

Fans of television's nostalgic 1950s sitcom, *Happy Days,* will remember Scott Baio as Fonzie's cousin, Chachi, who later loved Richie Cunningham's (Ron Howard) sister Joanie (Erin Moran) in their own short-lived spinoff.

Timothy Hunter, editor and publisher of *TV Pro-Log* summed up with a Mickeyesque line that might very well have been spoken by Tony Danza on the first show of the second season.

HUNTER:	''Replacing actresses must have gotten bothersome.''[6] (Mickey smiles into the camera. Freeze frame. Super credits).

BACHELOR FATHER

September 15, 1957–September 25, 1962.   CBS-NBC-ABC
September 1957–June 1959   CBS
June 1959–September 1961   NBC
October 1961–September 1962   ABC

Character:	Vickie
Played by:	Alice Backes
Date(s):	1957–1958
Replaced by:	Kitty Deveraux
Played by:	Shirley Mitchell
Date(s):	1958–1959
Character:	Kitty Deveraux
Played by:	Jane Nigh
Date(s):	(unknown)
Replaced by:	Kitty Marsh
Played by:	Sue Ane Langdon
Date(s):	1959–1961

Replaced by:	Connie
Played by:	Sally Mansfield
Date(s):	1961–1962
Character:	Ginger Farrell
Played by:	Bernadette Withers
Date(s):	September 15, 1957–September 25, 1962
Replaced by:	Ginger Loomis
Played by:	Bernadette Withers
Date(s):	September 15, 1957–September 25, 1962
Replaced by:	Ginger Mitchell
Played by:	Bernadette Withers
Date(s):	September 15, 1957–September 25, 1962
Character:	Louise Farrell,
Played by:	Catherine McLeod
Date(s):	September 15, 1957–
Replaced by:	Amy Loomis
Played by:	Florence MacMichael
Date(s):	1958
Character:	Adelaide Mitchell
Played by:	Evelyn Scott
Date(s):	1960
Character:	Bert Loomis
Played by:	Whit Bissell
Date(s):	1958
Replaced by:	Cal Mitchell
Played by:	Del Moore
Date(s):	1960

Bachelor Father began as a 1957 edition of *General Electric Theater* and first aired on CBS at 7:30 p.m. on September 15, 1957.

This, one of the favorite television families of the 1950s, was headed by wealthy Hollywood attorney and bachelor, Bentley Gregg, played by John Forsythe. The television family unit comprised Bentley Gregg, his orphaned niece Kelly (Noreen Corcoran), their indispensable houseboy, Peter Tong (Sammee Tong), and a large shaggy dog, Jasper.

What is fascinating, however, is how in a program that was supposed to portray a stable family environment, there could exist such utter chaos in the cast, from name changes to

5. *TV Pro-Log: Television Programs and Production News.* TI-Volume 43, No. 46. Television Index Information Services, L.I., New York. Timothy Hunter, Editor and Publisher. July 15–21, 1991. p. 2.
6. *TV Pro-Log: Television Programs and Production News.* TI-Volume 43, No. 48. Television Index Information Services, L.I., New York. Timothy Hunter, Editor and Publisher. July 29–August 4, 1991. p. 1.

character replacements. So hold on to the lapels of your white dinner jackets while we try to unravel this casting problem.

Bentley Gregg and his young niece Kelly were played throughout the series by John Forsythe and Noreen Corcoran.

Now, Kelly had a friend, as all young girls do. Her friend's name was Ginger Farrell and was played by Bernadette Withers for the entire series. In 1957, Ginger's mom was Louise Farrell, played by Catherine McLeod. So far, so good. Now here is where things get sticky.

In 1958 Ginger's last name was changed to Loomis and she had two new parents. Her mother, Amy Loomis, was played by Florence MacMichael, and her father, Bert Loomis, was played by Whit Bissell. Earlier in the series, Whit Bissell had played Steve Gibson, the father of one of Kelly's friends.

In 1960, Ginger's last name was changed to Mitchell and her new parents, Adelaide and Cal, were played by Evelyn Scott and Del Moore. Still another source states that the Mitchells were dropped from the series and replaced by yet another set of parents. Poor Ginger.

Meanwhile, Bentley Gregg, that stable, handsome, kind and wealthy Beverly Hills attorney, went through four different secretaries during the course of the series. Actually five, if you count the two actresses who played Kitty Deveraux. And all of these changes took place without explanations being made to the audience.

Mr. Gregg's first secretary was Vickie, played by Alice Backes. Vickie was replaced in 1958 by Kitty Deveraux, played by Shirley Mitchell, who went on to play Janet Colton on the situation comedy *Pete and Gladys* from 1960 to 1962.

The second Kitty Deveraux, and the third actress to sit in the secretarial chair, was Jane Nigh, who had played the third of five Lorelei Kilbournes in the 1950s drama, *Big Town*. The Kitty Deveraux character was then replaced by a new Kitty— Kitty Marsh, played by veteran actress Sue Ane Langdon.

Gregg's fourth secretary, Connie, was played by Sally Mansfield.

Bernadette Withers, who played Ginger throughout the series, joined the cast of the CBS situation comedy, *Peck's Bad Girl*, in 1959 while still portraying Kelly's friend.

Florence MacMichael, who played Ginger's second mom in 1958, played Mrs. Florence Pearson from 1960 to 1961 on the long-running sitcom, *My Three Sons*, though she may be more readily recognized as Winnie Kirkwood, the female half of the Posts' second set of next-door neighbors on the CBS situation comedy, *Mr. Ed* (See Entry).

Ginger's third mom, Adelaide Mitchell, was played by Evelyn Scott, who from 1965 through 1969 played Ada Jacks on *Peyton Place*.

The first of Ginger's dads (she actually only had two that we know of) was Bert Loomis, played by Whit Bissell.

This would make Ginger's mom either a divorcee or a widow, the latter being the most likely for a family program during the 1950s.

In 1960, Del Moore replaced Bissell as Ginger's new dad, Cal Mitchell. In 1963, following *Bachelor Father,* Del Moore worked for thirteen weeks as the announcer for *The Jerry Lewis Show.*

BARETTA

January 17, 1975–June 1, 1978.   ABC

Character:	Inspector Shiller
Played by:	Dana Elcar
Date(s):	January 17, 1975–July 1975
Replaced by:	Lt. Hal Brubaker
Played by:	Edward Grover
Date(s):	July 1975–June 1, 1978

Baretta is actually a reworked version of *Toma,* which starred Tony Musante as Detective David Toma, a dedicated undercover cop who often used unorthodox police procedures to break his cases. The hour-long ABC crime drama originally aired from October 4, 1973 to September 6, 1974.

Despite the fact that ABC had already renewed *Toma* for a second season, lead actor Tony Musante announced, to the surprise of everyone involved, that he would not return because of the rigorous demands of the weekly production schedule.

The producers' first plan was to bring *Toma* back with a new actor in the title role. The suggested title for the revamped version was *Toma Starring Robert Blake.* Producer Roy Huggins' first choice was *Baretta 690,* while the executives at ABC preferred *Johnny Baretta.* Robert Blake complained that *Johnny Baretta* sounded like the name of a pizza parlor. They finally agreed on the one-word title, *Baretta.*

When *Baretta* premiered on January 17, 1975, it made Robert Blake a star and won him the 1975 Golden Globe Award for Best Television Actor, Drama.

"Regulars on the show included Inspector Shiller, a master of the slow burn who was replaced by the more sympathetic Lieutenant Hal Brubaker in the second season."[7]

Lieutenant Brubaker was played by Edward Grover, who in 1976 replaced Tom Klunis as Walter Pace in the CBS daytime soap opera, *Search for Tomorrow,* and later played Mr. Bendarik on another CBS daytime drama, *Love of Life.*

Dana Elcar, Baretta's first boss, went on to replace Don Adams' boss, the Chief of Control in THE NUDE BOMB, the motion picture return of television's *Get Smart* (See Entry).

BARNABY JONES

January 28, 1973–September 4, 1980.   CBS

Character	Lieutenant Joe Taylor
Played by	Vince Howard
Date(s):	February 25, 1973–April 22, 1973
Replaced by:	Lieutenant John Biddle
Played by:	John Carter
Date(s):	December 16, 1973–April 3, 1980

7. Collins, Max Allan and Javna, John. *The Best of Crime and Detective TV.* Harmony Books, New York, 1988, pp 86–87.

Just a couple of years earlier, he was "shootin' at some food when up through the ground came a bubblin' crude." But, by 1973, he was shooting at some criminals.

The man doing all of this shooting was Buddy Ebsen, the actor initially hired for the Tin Woodsman in THE WIZARD OF OZ and famous to television audiences as Jed Clampett from the CBS sitcom, *The Beverly Hillbillies.* He took his gentle manner to the streets of Los Angeles, California as private detective Barnaby Jones.

Assisting him at Barnaby Jones Investigations was his daughter-in-law Betty Jones, and later, his cousin Jedidiah Romano ("J.R.") Jones. Betty was played by Lee Meriwether who, among her many credits, also has the distinction as being the third actress to play Catwoman on *Batman* (See Entry). Mark Shera took on the more strenuous duties as J.R. Jones.

At the LAPD Barnaby's police contacts were Lieutenants Taylor and Biddle. The first, Vince Howard as Lieutenant Joe Taylor, appeared in three episodes of *Barnaby Jones* during the first season before being replaced by John Carter as Lieutenant John Biddle.

John Carter played the recurring character of Lieutenant Biddle beginning with "The Secret of the Dunes," in December of the second season. He continued in guest-starring status until the fifth season, which began on October 7, 1976, when he was upgraded to a series regular.

BATMAN

January 12, 1966–March 14, 1968.   ABC

Character:	The Riddler
Played by:	Frank Gorshin
Date(s):	January 12, 1966 & January 13, 1966
	March 30, 1966 & March 31, 1966
	April 27, 1966 & April 28, 1966
	August 3, 1966 (BATMAN) September 21, 1967

Replaced by:	The Riddler
Played by:	John Astin
Date(s):	February 8, 1967 & February 9, 1967

Character:	Catwoman (Miss Kitka)
Played by:	Julie Newmar
Date(s):	March 16, 1966 & March 17, 1966
	September 14, 1966 & September 15, 1966
	December 14, 1966 & December 15, 1966
	December 28, 1966 & December 29, 1966
	January 19, 1967 & January 25, 1967
	February 22, 1967 & February 23, 1967

Replaced by:	Catwoman
Played by:	Eartha Kitt
Date(s):	December 14, 1967
	December 28, 1967 & January 4, 1968

Character:	Mr. Freeze
Played by:	George Sanders
Date(s):	February 2, 1966–February 3, 1966

Replaced by:	Mr. Freeze
Played by:	Otto Preminger
Date(s):	November 9, 1966 & November 10, 1966

Replaced by:	Mr. Freeze
Played by:	Eli Wallach
Date(s):	March 29, 1967 & March 30, 1967

William Dozier, the executive producer of *Batman,* had originally wanted Ty Hardin for the title role but he was unable to play the part because he was working on Westerns in Italy. Hardin's agent then offered Dozier one of his other clients, Adam West. West won the role as Gotham City's caped crusader over Lyle Waggoner, who had also been tested for the part. The network executives agreed with Dozier's selection and Adam West was fitted for his cowl and cape. The role of Robin, the Boy Wonder, went to Burt Ward.

When *Batman* premiered on January 12, 1966, his first adversary was The Riddler, played by actor, impressionist and comedian, Frank Gorshin. Gorshin explained how he landed the role of The Riddler in a *New York Times* article, "They Love to Be Mean to Batman," by George Gent. The article appeared on Sunday, May 1, 1966.

"Frank Gorshin says that when he was first approached to play The Riddler, he thought it was a joke. 'Then I discovered the show had a good script and agreed to do the role, but only on a show-to-show basis. Now I'm in love with the character.' "

After six appearances on the TV series and one in the 1966 BATMAN movie, Gorshin apparently fell out of love with the character, because on February 8 and 9, 1967 he was replaced by John Astin, who had played Gomez Addams in *The Addams Family* from 1964 to 1966.

On September 21, 1967, however, Gorshin was once again back in his green tights and purple mask because, according to Joel Eisner, "After the disappointing portrayal of The Riddler by John Astin, Gorshin was convinced to make this token appearance."[8]

Two more episodes were planned for The Riddler, "A Penny for Your Riddles" and "They're Worth a Lot More," but because Gorshin had already turned in his green leotard to pursue other roles, the episodes were rewritten and retitled for a new Bat Villain, The Puzzler, to be played by Maurice Evans. The new titles were "The Puzzles Are Coming" and "The Duo Is Slumming" and aired on December 21 and 22, 1966.

William Dozier mentioned that he had another choice for the part of Chief O'Hara, Batman's police contact in Gotham City, but settled for Stafford Repp, who had played Lieutenant Ralph Raines in *The Thin Man* from 1957 to 1958 and Brink on *The New Phil Silvers Show* from 1963 to 1964. Dozier did not mention who his first choice was.

Actor Malachi Throne, who played the "Bat Villain," False Face, in episodes seventeen and eighteen, was quoted about the

8. Eisner, Joel. *The Official Batman Batbook,* Contemporary Book, Inc., Chicago, 1986, p. 129.

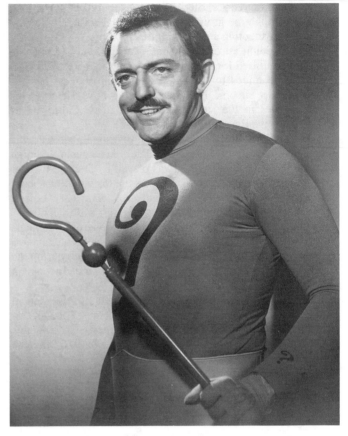

Riddle me this—How many times did Frank Gorshin (above) play the Riddler on *Batman?*

It's not easy being green. That's what John Astin (above) found out after appearing as the Riddler in only one episode of *Batman.*

casting of the part of Blaze, who was played by Myrna Fahey: "They were going to use Angie Dickinson for the part of Blaze, because everybody was dying to be on that show and play any part."[9]

Another of Dozier's second choices was Cesar Romero for the part of The Joker. His first choice was Jose Ferrer, of whom Dozier said, "He either didn't want to do it or couldn't't."[10]

The handsome Latin-American actor, Cesar Romero, played the part of The Joker without ever shaving off his trademark mustache, which was concealed under the heavy white make-up. Viewers with keen eyes, however, can still spot Romero's mustache in some closeups and publicity stills.

The first of the three Mr. Freezes was played by veteran actor George Sanders. Sanders appeared as Mr. Freeze in "Instant Freeze" and "Rats Like Cheese," which aired on February 2 and 3, 1966. Sanders was born on July 3, 1906 in St. Petersburg, Russia and had starred as John Garrick in the 1944 drama, THE LODGER. Sadly, on April 25, 1972, at age sixty-six, George

Sanders committed suicide. He left a note saying that he was bored.

When Mr. Freeze next appeared on *Batman* it was Otto Preminger who was squeezed into the temperature-controlled suit. Playing a guest villain on *Batman* had become something of a status symbol and everyone wanted to get into the act, as Malachi Throne pointed out. *Batman's* executive producer, William Dozier, explained how a phone call from Otto Preminger, a highly respected producer and director who hadn't acted in seventeen years, came to play Mr. Freeze. " 'Bill, I must do a *Batman.* If I don't do a *Batman,* my children won't let me come home.' "[11]

It seems safe to assume that Preminger was allowed to return home after his appearances as Mr. Freeze in the "Green Ice" and "Deep Freeze" episodes of *Batman* that aired on November 9 and 10, 1966.

In his two final appearances, Mr. Freeze was played by Eli Wallach in the third season episodes, "Ice Spy" and "The Duo

9. *Ibid.* p. 32.
10. *Ibid.*
11. *Ibid.,* p. 83.

Defy,'' which aired on March 29 and 30, 1967. Eli Wallach explained that because Otto Preminger was unavailable for these episodes, he was hired to play the role. He did so with a Premingeresque Austrian/American accent. Like Preminger, Wallach was also coaxed by his kids to appear on *Batman.*

Julie Newmar was living at Beekman Place in New York at the time she got the call to audition for Catwoman. The call came in on a Friday or Saturday, as she recalls, and she had to be in California on Monday. Her brother, a fan of *Batman,* was visiting from Harvard. Newmar told her brother, ''They want me to play Catwoman.' He said, 'Do it!' So I said, 'OK, I'll do it.' ''[12]

Newmar passed the audition and went on to play Catwoman in a dozen *Batman* episodes. She was also cast to play Catwoman in the 1966 BATMAN movie, but was unavailable when shooting began. Prior to playing Catwoman, Julie Newmar had played the robot, Rhoda Miller, in the CBS situation comedy, *My Living Doll.*

Lee Meriwether was one of six other actresses who read for the part of Catwoman in the 1966 BATMAN movie. She landed the role because during her audition she did things a cat would do, such as curling up in the chair and licking her hand as if it were a paw. She even purred a little.

According to *Batman* scriptwriter Stanley Ralph Ross, Eartha Kitt replaced Julie Newmar as Catwoman in the December 14, 1967 episode, ''Catwoman's Dressed to Kill,'' because Newmar was working on the film, MACKENNA'S GOLD, which was released in 1969 and starred two other ''Batman'' graduates, Burgess Meredith (the Penguin) and Eli Wallach.

Alan Napier, who played Bruce Wayne/Batman's trusty butler, Alfred Pennyworth, compared Eartha Kitt to Julie Newmar. ''Julie Newmar was the best Catwoman, but Eartha Kitt was kind of marvelous. She did complain a lot on the set though.''[13]

Lee Meriwether returned to the cast of *Batman* in March 1967, not as Catwoman but as Lisa Carson, the daughter of wealthy socialite John E. Carson in episodes 87 and 88, ''King Tut's Coup'' and ''Batman's Waterloo,'' which aired on March 8 and 9.

In the February 29, 1968 episode, ''The Joker's Flying Saucer,'' Marc Cavell, who had played Gray Hawk on the CBS situation comedy, *Pistols and Petticoats,* which aired from September 17, 1966 to August 19, 1967, was scheduled to play Verdigris (one of the Joker's henchmen dressed as a Martian). When the episode began production, though, Richard ''Dick'' Bakalyan played the part.

Precisely six months to the day after the cancellation of *Batman,* the characters returned to the little screen in an animated series, *The Batman/Superman Hour.* Produced by Filmation Studios, it featured the voice of former Superman actor, Bud Collyer, as the Caped Crusader in his final role before retirement. Syndicated radio and television host and voice-over actor, Casey Kasem, played the Boy Wonder.

When *Batman* went on the air in 1966, it took two of the top ten spots in the ratings, number five on Thursday and number

10 on Wednesday. In the Emmys for the 1965/1966 season, *Batman* was nominated for Outstanding Comedy Series, but lost to *The Dick Van Dyke Show. Batman's* first Riddler, Frank Gorshin, was nominated for an Emmy for Outstanding Performance by an Actor in a Supporting Role in a Comedy, but lost to Don Knotts. Sound engineers Richard Legrand, Ross Taylor, Harold Wooley and Ralph Hickey were each nominated for Individual Achievements in Sound Editing.

While Adam West remains the only actor to have played the dual role of millionaire Bruce Wayne/Batman on a live-action television series, Michael Keaton became the third actor to bring the character to the motion picture screen. The first actor to play the caped crusader was Lewis Wilson, who starred in Columbia Pictures' 1943 BATMAN serial. Robert Lowery (later to star on *Circus Boy*) donned the cowl and cape in 1948 for Columbia's second serial, BATMAN AND ROBIN.

When Warner Bros. brought BATMAN back to the wide screen in a $35 million budget motion picture released in 1989, Michael Keaton starred in the title role opposite Jack Nicholson as the Joker/Jack Napier, Pat Hingle as Commissioner Gordon and Michael Gough as Alfred.

The success of the first picture spawned another slick sequel, BATMAN RETURNS, which premiered on June 19, 1992. Keaton was back in the dual role of millionaire Bruce Wayne/ Batman and this time was pitted against Danny DeVito as the Penguin and Michelle Pfeiffer as Catwoman. The character of Robin did not appear in either of these films.

BATTLESTAR GALACTICA

September 17, 1978–August 17, 1980.   ABC

Character:	Boxey
Played by:	Noah Hathaway
Date(s):	September 17, 1978–April 29, 1979
Replaced by:	Captain Troy (Boxey as an adult)
Played by:	Kent McCord
Date(s):	January 27, 1980–February 10, 1980
	March 16, 1980-May 4, 1980
Character:	Dr. Zee
Played by:	Robbie Rist
Date(s):	January 27, 1980–February 10, 1980
Replaced by:	Dr. Zee
Played by:	Patrick Stuart
Date(s):	March 16, 1980–August 17, 1980

Battlestar Galactica, which was television's response to the phenomenal success of the 1977 motion picture STAR WARS, borrowed heavily not only from the content but also from the

12. Eisner, p. 35.
13. *Ibid.,* p. 145.

production team headed by John Dykstra, which was responsible for bringing the STAR WARS story to life.

The plot differed from STAR WARS in that the only thing the heroes of the series were trying to save were their necks, as they fled from the Evil Cylons. The mentor and brave leader of this wagontrain in space was Lorne Greene as Commander Adama. He is, of course, known to millions as the patriarch of the Ponderosa on *Bonanza.*

The two young leads were, without question, Luke Sky-walker and Han Solo clones in both character and physical appearance. Adama's son, Captain Apollo, was fashioned after Luke, while Lieutenant Starbuck was, pound-for-pound, Han Solo.

Apollo was played by Richard Hatch, who had played Inspector Dan Robbins on *The Streets of San Francisco* (See Entry). The more worldly Starbuck was played by Dirk Benedict, who went on to bigger fame as Templeton Peck in *The A-Team* (See Entry).

Battlestar Galactica was actually not one, but two different series. It first aired as *Battlestar Galactica* on September 17, 1978 and went off the air on April 29, 1979, after twenty episodes. Then, approximately nine months later, the series was replaced by a revamped version retitled, *Galactica 1980.* This version ran from January 27 to February 10 and from March 16 to May 4, 1980, racking up a total of nine additional episodes.

Since the two versions were so different it seems unreasonable and unfair to compare characters from the two versions and list them as replacements. There were, however, several changes in cast that should be examined.

During *Battlestar Galactica,* Apollo's adopted son, Boxey, was played by child actor Noah Hathaway. When the series resurfaced as *Galactica 1980,* the plot was advanced by thirty years and now young Boxey was an adult, Captain Troy, played by Kent McCord, who had been officer Jim Reed on the original *Adam 12* (See Entry).

Dr. Zee, the Galactica's fourteen-year-old scientific genius, was originally played by Robbie Rist, who had previously played Glendon Farrell from 1974 to 1975 on the NBC school drama, *Lucas Tanner.* He joined *The Brady Bunch* as Cousin Oliver in ''Two Petes in a Pod,'' which aired on February 8, 1974 and remained with the series for its final six episodes, the last of which aired on March 8, 1974. From 1976 to 1977, Robbie Rist played David Baxter, the eight-year-old adopted son of Ted and Georgette Baxter on *The Mary Tyler Moore Show.* He was replaced by juvenile actor Patrick Stuart, who should not be confused with the Patrick Stewart who commanded the next generation of space explorers on *Star Trek.*

THE BAXTERS

September 1979–1981.   Syndicated

Character:	Fred Baxter
Played by:	Larry Keith
Date(s):	September 1979–1980

Replaced by:	Jim Baxter
Played by:	Sean McCann
Date(s):	1980–1981

Character:	Nancy Baxter
Played by:	Anita Gillette
Date(s):	September 1979–1980

Replaced by:	Susan Baxter
Played by:	Terry Tweed
Date(s):	1980–1981

Character:	Naomi Baxter (age 19)
Played by:	Derin Altay
Date(s):	September 1979–1980

Replaced by:	Allison Baxter (age 19)
Played by:	Marianne McIsaac
Date(s):	1980–1981

Character:	Jonah Baxter (age 14)
Played by:	Chris Peterson
Date(s):	September 1979–1980

Replaced by:	Gregg Baxter (age 14)
Played by:	Sammy Snyders
Date(s):	1980–1981

Character:	Rachael Baxter (age 10)
Played by:	Terri Lynn Wood
Date(s):	September 1979–1980

Replaced by:	Lucy Baxter (age 10)
Played by:	Megan Follows
Date(s):	1980–1981

In 1977, ex-divinity student Hubert Jessup conceived and first produced *The Baxters* at WCVB-TV in Boston. The production was later taken over by Norman Lear, who was responsible for bringing ''thinking sitcoms'' like *All in the Family, The Jeffersons* and *Maude* to television. The format was very innovative: the first half of the program presented the middle-class Baxter family wrestling with one of the day's controversial topics, with no resolution. The second half of the program opened up discussions with a live studio audience who offered their suggestions for a solution to that week's dilemma.

Norman Lear produced *The Baxters* for only one season in Hollywood and left because the program did not receive the audience he had expected. *The Baxters* was then taken over by the original producers and moved to Toronto with a complete change in cast. The producers also changed the first names of all of the characters and the profession of Fred Baxter (now Jim Baxter) from an insurance salesman to a school teacher.

The first Baxter family consisted of Larry Keith as Fred and

Anita Gillette as his wife, Nancy. Their nineteen-year-old daughter, Naomi, was played by Derin Altay, fourteen-year-old son, Jonah, by Chris Peterson; and ten-year-old daughter, Rachael, by Terri Lynn Wood.

Soap opera viewers may remember Larry Keith as Nick Davis from *All My Children* or Lefty Burns from *Another World*. Anita Gillette appeared as Dr. Emily Hanover from 1982 to 1983 on Jack Klugman's police drama, *Quincy, M.E.,* which aired on NBC from October 3, 1976 to September 5, 1983.

The oldest of the Baxter's children, Naomi, was played by Derin Altay, who had played Ascha Luckett in the NBC three-part miniseries, *The Awakening Land,* which aired from February 19 to 21, 1978. Naomi's younger sister, Rachael, was played by Terri Lynn Wood, who had appeared as Terri in the 1976 ABC holiday special, *Christmas in Disneyland.*

The Canadian cast starred Sean McCann as Jim Baxter and Terry Tweed as his wife, Susan. McCann later starred as Lieutenant Jim Hogan on the CBS police drama, *Night Heat,* which premiered on January 31, 1985.

The youngest actor from the Canadian troupe was Megan Follows, who four years later starred as Didi Crane on the short-lived situation comedy, *Domestic Life.* The series, produced by that wild and crazy guy, Steve Martin, aired on CBS from January 4 to September 11, 1984.

BAYWATCH

September 22, 1989–August 26, 1990.   NBC
September 23, 1991–   Syndicated

Character:	Hobie Buchannon
Played by:	Brandon Call
Date(s):	September 22, 1989–August 26, 1990

Replaced by:	Hobie Buchannon
Played by:	Jeremy K. Jackson
Date(s):	September 23, 1991–

Character:	Shauni McClain
Played by:	Erika Eleniak
Date(s):	September 22, 1989–September 26, 1992

Replaced by:	Roberta "Summer" Quinn
Played by:	Nicole Eggert
Date(s):	September 26, 1992–September 20, 1994

Character:	Eddie Kramer
Played by:	Billy Warlock
Date(s):	September 22, 1989–September 26, 1992

Replaced by:	Matt Brody
Played by:	David Charvet
Date(s):	September 26, 1992–

Character:	Captain Don Thorpe
Played by:	Monte Markham
Date(s):	September 22, 1989–September 19, 1992

Character:	Lieutenant Ben Edwards
Played by:	Richard Jaeckel
Date(s):	September 23, 1991–September 19, 1992

Replaced by:	Lieutenant Stephanie Holden
Played by:	Alexandra Paul
Date(s):	October 3, 1992–

There's something very special about the lure of the beach in the summer. It's exhilarating, it's romantic and it triggers images of vacations and nice days away from the daily pressures and the J-O-B. It's also a great way to include gratuitous shots of bikini-clad bathers. No doubt, NBC took all of these factors into consideration when they created *Baywatch,* a weekly adventure series about Los Angeles County lifeguards working out of Baywatch. But *Baywatch* frequently followed stories that took the action off the beach.

The series began as *Baywatch: Panic at Malibu Pier,* a two-hour made-for-television movie that aired on NBC on April 23, 1989. In this pilot film, as in all pilots, the leading characters are introduced. Heading up the cast is David Hasselhoff as Mitch Buchannon, a Baywatch lifeguard who has just been promoted to Lieutenant and is supposed to spend his time managing the lifeguards and calling the shots in rescue operations. Of course, underneath the tailored uniform and "crab stompers" (lifeguard slang for hard-soled shoes) is a dedicated lifeguard ready to dive in—literally, as he did in the film when a riptide dragged a number of bathers out to sea.

Under Hasselhoff, who spent half of the 1980s as Michael Knight on *Knight Rider* (See Entry), were Parker Stevenson as Craig Pomeroy, Billy Warlock as Eddie Kramer, and Shawn Weatherly as Jill Riley, who was killed by a shark in the March 2, 1990 episode, "Shark Derby."

Overseeing the station house was Captain Don Thorpe, who was joined in 1991 by Lieutenant Ben Edwards. Captain Thorpe was played by Monte Markham, who starred as the title character in the 1973 revival of *Perry Mason* (See Entry). He appeared as Clint Ogden in the 1981 season of the CBS evening soap opera, *Dallas,* and as Lieutenant Mason Harnett in "Say It with Bullets," the January 17, 1984 episode of *The A-Team.*

Richard Jaeckel, who played Lieutenant Ben Edwards, has been working in television since the early 1950s and is remembered for a number of roles. These include Lieutenant Pete McNeil in *Banyon,* the NBC detective drama that aired from September 15, 1972 to January 12, 1973; Klinger in the Andy Griffith adventure series, *Salvage I,* which aired on ABC from January 20 to November 11, 1979; and Lieutenant Martin Quirk on *Spenser: For Hire,* the Robert Urich detective series that aired on ABC from September 20, 1985 to September 3, 1988.

As great as things may sound, life's not a beach for Mitch, who is recently divorced and locked in a custody battle with his ex-wife, Gayle (Wendie Malick). The couple's son, Hobie, was played by juvenile actor Brandon Call until the series ended its network run in August 1990.

Baywatch received CPR when it went back into production for first-run syndication, with only one change in cast—Hobie. It seems Brandon Call lost visitation rights to the series and was replaced by Jeremy K. Jackson without a word being said.

Some major changes in cast occurred after a season of successful syndicated episodes. The first to go were Shauni and Eddie, who moved to Australia to start a family in the September 26, 1992 episode, "River of No Return," after they learned that Shauni was pregnant by Eddie.

Billy Warlock, who played Eddie, came to *Baywatch* after a stint as Flip Phillips during the 1982/1983 season of ABC's nostalgic sitcom, *Happy Days*. He left the beaches of Southern California for the streets of Vancouver, British Columbia, to co-star as Matt Matheson, one of three foster brothers who are members of the special crime unit known as *The Hat Squad*. The tense hour-long police drama from Stephen J. Cannell Productions ran on CBS from September 16, 1992 to January 23, 1993.

Shauni was replaced by Summer Quinn, a lifeguard in training who became a full-fledged lifeguard two episodes later. Her love interest and Eddie's replacement was Matt Brody (David Charvet).

Playing Summer was Nicole Eggert, who in 1987 joined the cast of *Charles in Charge* (See Entry) as Jamie Powell.

Detractors of the series may cite an overabundance of bikini beach bimbos, but the odds were evened when Alexandra Paul joined the cast as Lieutenant Stephanie Holden—replacement for both Captain Thorpe (Monte Markham) and Lieutenant Edwards (Richard Jaeckel)—proving that one woman could in fact do the work of two men.

BEAUTY AND THE BEAST

September 25, 1987–August 4, 1990.   CBS

Character:	Assistant D.A. Catherine "Cathy" Chandler
Played by:	Linda Hamilton
Date(s):	September 25, 1987–December 12, 1989
Replaced by:	Diana Bennett
Played by:	Jo Anderson
Date(s):	December, 13 1989–August 4, 1990

The timeless story of *Beauty and the Beast* has been translated to film a number of times. Perhaps the best screen adaptation of the classic fairy tale by Mme. Leprince de Beaumont, first published in 1757, was the 1947 production written and co-directed by the French poet and writer, Jean Cocteau. A rather abysmal attempt at copying Cocteau's work made it to theaters in 1963. That was even an injustice to makeup artist Jack Pierce, who fashioned the beast's makeup on the one he had created for Lon Chaney, Jr.'s Wolf Man.

Thirteen years later George C. Scott won an Emmy Award nomination for his portrayal of the beast in the ninety-minute NBC adaptation that aired on December 3, 1976.

The most recent screen incarnation was the 1992 Academy Award-winning animated feature released by Walt Disney studios on November 22, 1991. It starred Robby Benson as the voice of the Beast and Paige O'Hara as the voice of Belle, née Beauty.

All three of these versions were based on the original fairy tale which told of a merchant who inadvertently picks a rose from the garden of what he believed to be a deserted castle. It turns out that the castle was the home of a beast who sentences the merchant to death. But the merchant's beautiful daughter fearlessly offers to trade places with her father. She is spared when the Beast falls hopelessly in love with her.

The CBS dramatic fantasy shares only the name and spirit of the fairy tale and of the above productions, for this is a story set in modern-day New York. Beauty is Catherine Chandler (Linda Hamilton), a wealthy debutante and corporate attorney working for her dad's firm. Shortly after walking out on an important social gathering, Cathy, who is trying to hail a cab, is mistaken for a Carol Stabler, thrown into a van, beaten up and slashed by a couple of thugs working for Martin "Marty" Belmont and dumped into Central Park, where she is left to die.

We then see her limp and lifeless body taken away by a shadowy figure who carries her down through a series of what look like subway tunnels. When Cathy regains consciousness she finds her entire head, except for her mouth, wrapped in bandages. She's scared, but a calm resonant voice, from the only character in the series to call her Catherine, reassures her that she is out of danger and encourages her to rest. This dark figure feeds her, cares for her and even reads *Great Expectations* to help her pass the time.

Catherine slowly regains her strength and, frustrated by being in the dark, removes her bandages to reveal hideous long scars across her forehead and cheeks. She finds a mirror and looks at herself for the first time since the brutal attack. "Oh god . . . no," she whispers out loud to herself. That is when Vincent, unannounced, appears from behind her. She catches a glimpse of his face in the mirror and is frightened by his lion-like countenance. She begins to scream as she turns around to throw the mirror at him, evoking a fierce growl. Vincent then turns and leaves, and Catherine falls back in a chair and weeps.

Later Vincent returns.

VINCENT: I've never regretted what I am (PAUSES) . . . until now.

CATHERINE: How? How did this happen to you?

VINCENT: I don't know how. I have ideas. I'll never know. I was born and I survived.

What is known is that Vincent, the Beast, was a baby who had been abandoned and left to die. He was found and brought to Jacob "Father" Wells (Roy Dotrice) in the "Tunnel World." He was named Vincent, because he was discovered near St. Vincent's Hospital.

Having recovered from her injuries, it is time for Catherine to return to "The World Above." Vincent leads Catherine through the maze of underground tunnels right to the basement of her own apartment building. Before they part, Catherine promises to keep Vincent's existence a secret, hugs him warmly for all he has done, and asks, rhetorically, "What can I say to you?"

The scene fades to black, then into an operating room where Catherine is undergoing plastic surgery to remove her scars. In recovery, as the anesthesia wears off, Catherine is heard calling out to Vincent (Ron Perlman).

Eight months later, Catherine leaves her dad's law firm to take a job in the investigative bureau of the New York City District Attorney's office. She also hires a trainer, Isaac Stubbs (Ron O'Neil), to teach her the art of self defense—not fancy martial arts, just down-and-dirty New York City street fighting, as he puts it. This, however, is not the last of Vincent, for he possesses empathic powers enabling him to feel what others are feeling, much in the same way as Gem (Kathryn Hays) did in the 1968 *Star Trek* episode, "The Empath."

VINCENT: I can't forget her. I'm still connected. I can feel what she's feeling . . . thinking . . . when she's frightened . . . when she's happy or sad.

As a consequence, Vincent is tormented—torn between his love of Catherine and the very real possibility that should he seek her out he may be discovered, captured or even killed.

Beauty and the Beast, which featured fantastic sets, great makeup, beautiful cinematography and a compelling music score, took a turn for the worse when Linda Hamilton announced that she was pregnant and would be leaving the series. Preparing for the ultimate transition, Catherine and Vincent are permitted to consummate their relationship so that Ms. Hamilton could be pregnant in the storyline as well.

The plot takes a dark turn when a power-hungry criminal named Gabriel (Stephen McHattie) kidnaps Catherine, keeping her alive just long enough to have her baby, whom he named Julian and called "Julie." Gabriel, a cold and horribly cruel man who admitted to killing his first love and later his own father, orders the doctor working for him to kill Catherine with a lethal injection of morphine. The remainder of the storyline has Vincent seeking his son and waiting to unleash his vengeance against Gabriel. Aiding him in this matter is an investigator named Diana Bennett, who finds out the truth about him, Catherine and the underground.

" 'When we returned for the third season,' [Co-Supervising Producer George R.] Martin details, 'we knew Linda was leaving and had several decisions to make. Should we introduce a new female lead? Well, obviously you do have to introduce a new female lead. Do you recast Catherine, or do you somehow get rid of the character and introduce a new one? . . . We didn't think that recasting would work. It was probably the safest choice, although it's very seldom been done successfully in prime time television.' "[14]

The choice made by Martin and the staff was to kill off the character of Catherine and introduce Diana Bennett (Jo Anderson) as the new female lead. " 'Diana *had* to be different,

otherwise you've just got a second-rate Catherine,' interjects Martin. 'We wanted a whole different dynamic, and a relationship with Vincent that would not duplicate Catherine's by any means but would take us to new places and give us new possibilities we had not seen before. We were extraordinarily fortunate in our casting. I think Jo Anderson was just sensational and the character was really terrific.' "[15]

Diana Bennett, a top-notch investigator, was hired by Catherine's boss, Deputy District Attorney Joe Maxwell (Jay Acavone), to track down the person responsible for murdering Catherine. On paper it all sounded wonderful, but the harsh reality of the situation was that that unknown element between actors in a series, referred to as "chemistry," simply did not exist between Ron Perlman and Jo Anderson.

Reflecting on the other option open to the producers, that of recasting the role of Catherine, George Martin candidly pointed out that "Recasting Catherine, I think, would have produced a failure just as quickly, but a less interesting one."[16]

The climatic scene from "Invictus," the final episode of *Beauty and the Beast,* has Vincent breaking free from his cell moments before his infant son is to be smothered with a pillow by the demented Gabriel. Vincent smashes through the door to the nursery and claws the murderous kidnapper, tearing three long, deep gashes down the left side of his face and sending him reeling across the room. But Vincent is prevented from finishing Gabriel off by Diana, who bursts into the room and insists that he take his child safely back to the Tunnel World before he is discovered. There is a short exchange between Gabriel and Diana that neatly ties up the storyline.

GABRIEL: I'll have the child back. In the end, I always win.

DIANA: Not this time Gabriel. This is Catherine Chandler's gun. (Diana Raises the gun, cocks the trigger, and fires point-blank—killing Gabriel.)

Though the killing is unethical, illegal and raises some strong moral questions, the death of Gabriel does in fact bring a fairly satisfying ending to the story and the series.

BEN CASEY

October 2, 1961–March 21, 1966.   ABC

Character:	Dr. David Zorba
Played by:	Sam Jaffe
Date(s):	October 2, 1961–1965

Replaced by:	Dr. Daniel Niles Freeland
Played by:	Franchot Tone
Date(s):	September 13, 1965–March 21, 1966

14. Gross, Edward. *Above and Below: A Guide to "Beauty and the Beast."* Image Publishing, New York, 1990, p. 98.
15. *Ibid.,* p. 99.
16. *Ibid.,* p. 108.

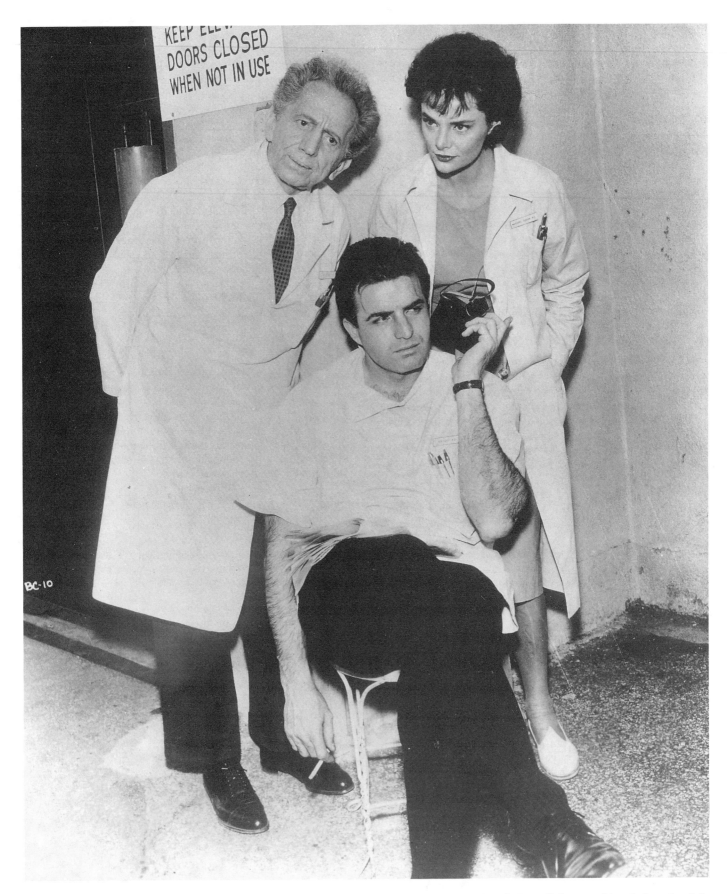

He may have played a brilliant neurosurgeon on *Ben Casey,* but that didn't stop actor Vince Edwards (seated) from smoking during a break in filming in this unusual posed candid that featured co-stars Sam Jaffe as Dr. David Zorba (left) and Bettye Ackerman as Dr. Maggie Graham (right).

57   BENJI, ZAX AND THE ALIEN PRINCE

Ben Casey was a landmark television medical drama about Dr. Ben Casey (Vince Edwards), the chief resident of neurosurgery at California's County General Hospital. "It went on in the autumn of 1961; by spring of this year it was in the Top 10 of a national rating service, claiming a weekly audience of 32,000,000."[17] Vince Edwards, who played Dr. Ben Casey in the pilot, stuck with the series for its entire run.

The wizened chief of neurosurgery was Dr. Zorba, played by Sam Jaffe in his most famous television role. He was later replaced by Franchot Tone. But before Dr. Zorba's replacement, a situation arose that could have resulted in the replacement of the series' lead. The creator of the series, Jim Moser, had said, "We'd tested dozens of actors in Hollywood and New York. Then one day Vince came in. He had the build, he had the look. All I thought was, if only he can act!"[18]

By the end of the 1961/1962 season, *Ben Casey* had climbed from number nineteen to number seven in the ratings, just behind *The Andy Griffith Show,* and ahead of *The Danny Thomas Show, The Dick Van Dyke Show* and *Gunsmoke.*

It may have been this jump in the ratings that gave Vince Edwards the confidence to, in Gehman's words, "make unusually high demands,"[19] which would have given him a higher salary than any other actor in a dramatic series was getting at the time. Gehman concluded his article by asking *Ben Casey's* number two executive, Matthew Rapf (who later produced *Kojak*), "... what would happen if Edwards did not sign."

Rapf nervously said that Moser would replace him. " 'Other stars have been replaced in series. William Bendix became *Riley* after Jackie Gleason was through enjoying *The Life of* him, John McIntire replaced the late Ward Bond on *Wagon Train* (See Entry). How many mothers has that kid on *Lassie* had? How many Lassies have there been?'

" 'Do you think it will hurt the series if Edwards goes?' I asked Matthew Rapf.

He trembled like a man facing a *Ben Casey* operation.

" 'I think it would take us a while to build back up without him, but I think we could do it.' "[20]

Sam Jaffe, the frail-looking character actor with a Larry Fine haircut, played the role of Dr. Zorba, with which he is most often identified, until the beginning of the 1965/1966 season, when he was discharged as the chief of neurosurgery and replaced by Franchot Tone as Dr. Niles Freeland.

Tone, a handsome actor, appeared in dozens of motion pictures between 1932 and 1968. One of his most outstanding performances was as Jimmy Davis in the 1937 Spencer Tracy drama, THEY GAVE HIM A GUN.

In 1962, *Ben Casey* was nominated for an Emmy for Outstanding Program Achievement in the field of Drama, but lost to *The Defenders.* That same year, Sam Jaffe was nominated for Outstanding Performance in a Supporting Role by an Actor, but lost to Don Knotts. Vince Edwards lost to E.G.

Marshall of *The Defenders,* for Outstanding Continued Performance by an Actor in a Series (Lead).

BENJI, ZAX AND THE ALIEN PRINCE

September 17, 1983–September 1, 1984.   CBS

Character:	Darah
Played by:	Angie Bolling
Date(s):	September 17, 1983–unknown

Replaced by:	Darah
Played by:	Anna Holbrook
Date(s):	unknown

Character:	Khyber
Played by:	Joe Rainer
Date(s):	September 17, 1983–unknown

Replaced by:	Khyber
Played by:	Dallas Miles
Date(s):	unknown

Benji may have been hunted in the 1987 motion picture, but in this Saturday morning children's adventure series it's the lovable stray who is responsible for protecting the alien Prince Ubi (Chris Burton) and his droid Zax from their outerworldly adversaries, Darah and her aid Khyber.

When CBS first beamed this series in America's homes, Angie Bolling and Joe Rainer were playing the alien antagonists, but by the time *Benji, Zax and the Alien Prince* left the air, the roles had been taken over by Anna Holbrook and Dallas Miles.

BENSON

September 13, 1979–August 30, 1986.   ABC

Character:	John Taylor
Played by:	Lewis J. Stadlen
Date(s):	September 13, 1979–March 27, 1980

Replaced by:	Clayton Endicott III
Played by:	René Auberjonois
Date(s):	October 31, 1980–August 30, 1986

Character:	Marcy Hill
Played by:	Caroline McWilliams
Date(s):	September 13, 1979–November 27, 1981

---

17. Gehman, Richard. "TV Guide Views 'Ben Casey' Caseyitis. How the epidemic started and why it spread," *TV Guide,* 1962, in Harris, Jay S. *TV Guide: The First 25 Years.* Simon and Schuster, New York, 1978, pp. 63–65.
18. *Ibid.,* pp. 63–65.
19. *Ibid.,* pp. 63–65.
20. *Ibid.*

Replaced by: Denise Stevens Downey
Played by: Didi Conn
Date(s):   November 27, 1981–August 30, 1986

If you are wondering how it is possible to make fun of soap operas, which are already caricatures of themselves, try to catch a rerun of the ABC spoof, *Soap,* which after a shaky start managed to last for ninety-three epsodes over a five-year period from September 13, 1977 to April 20, 1981. It starred Katherine Helmond as Jessica Tate, Robert Mandan as her husband Chester, Richard Mulligan as Burt Campbell, and Billy Crystal as Jodie Dallas.

It was the typical soap opera saga of two (very confused) families—one wealthy, one not. The Tates were, the Campbells weren't. And it was one of the supporting characters, the Tates' faithful butler, Benson DuBois, played by Robert Guillaume, who stood out so far above the others that he was given his own series. He was replaced by Roscoe Lee Browne as the Tates' new butler, Sanders. Gillaume was undoubtedly singled out for this honor when he won the 1978/1979 Emmy for Best Supporting Actor in a Comedy Series.

The reason given for Benson's departure from the Tate household was his agreement to assist Jessica's (Katherine Helmond) cousin, Governor Gene Gatling (James Noble), in his household affairs. He winds up extending his services and helping the honest but inept governor in handling his political responsibilities as well.

John Taylor, always addressed by his last name, was the Governor's less-than-helpful political aide. He was played by David Hedison in the pilot episode and thereafter by Lewis J. Stadlen. Hedison is best known to televison audiences as Commander Lee Crane on *Voyage to the Bottom of the Sea.* Stadlen was essentially a stage actor with a reputation for his portrayal of Groucho Marx in the Broadway play, *Minnie's Boys.*

In 1980, the character of Taylor was replaced by Clayton Endicott III, the governor's chief of staff, played by René Auberjonois. Auberjonois, as the shape shifter Odo, later served Commander Benjamin Sisko (Avery Brooks) as the security officer aboard the syndicated science fiction *Star Trek: Deep Space Nine,* which made its debut on January 4, 1993.

When *Benson* was spun off from *Soap,* Caroline McWilliams, who played Sally on that series from 1978 to 1979, tagged along, but as a new character, Marcy Hill, the governor's secretary. From 1969 to 1975 Ms. McWilliams had appeared as Janet Mason on the real daytime soap opera, *The Guiding Light.*

Caroline McWilliams left *Benson* during the early part of the 1981/1982 season when Benson was appointed the state budget director. Her replacement was Didi Conn, who picked up the slack as Benson's secretary, Denise Stevens Downey. Television audiences may remember Conn as Helen on Danny Thomas's situation comedy, *The Practice,* which aired on CBS from January 30, 1976 to January 26, 1977. To moviegoers she's Frenchy from the 1978 musical comedy, GREASE, and its 1982 sequel, GREASE 2.

THE BEULAH SHOW

October 3, 1950[21]–September 22, 1953.   ABC

Character: Beulah
Played by: Ethel Waters
Date(s):   October 3, 1950–1951

Replaced by: Beulah
Played by: Hattie McDaniel
Date(s):   Summer 1951

Replaced by: Beulah
Played by: Louise Beavers
Date(s):   April 1952–September 22, 1953

Replaced by: Beulah
Played by: Lillian Randolph
Date(s):   1953–1954

Character: Harry Henderson
Played by: William Post, Jr.
Date(s):   October 3, 1950–April 1952

Replaced by: Harry Henderson
Played by: David Bruce
Date(s):   April 1952–September 22, 1953

Character: Alice Henderson
Played by: Ginger Jones
Date(s):   October 3, 1950–April 1952

Replaced by: Alice Henderson
Played by: Jane Frazee
Date(s):   April 1952–September 22, 1953

Character: Donnie Henderson
Played by: Clifford Sales
Date(s):   October 3, 1950–April 1952

Replaced by: Donnie Henderson
Played by: Stuffy Singer
Date(s):   April 1952–September 22, 1953

Character: Bill Jackson
Played by: Percy (Bud) Harris
Date(s):   October 3, 1950–April 1952

---

21. Some sources give October 10, 1950 as the first official air date.

Replaced by: Bill Jackson
Played by: Dooley Wilson
Date(s):   1952–April 1952

Replaced by: Bill Jackson
Played by: Ernest Whitman
Date(s):   April 1952–September 22, 1953

Character: Oriole
Played by: Butterfly McQueen
Date(s):   October 3, 1950–1951

Replaced by: Oriole
Played by: Ruby Dandridge
Date(s):   1951–September 22, 1953

The Beulah Show is about a black maid working for a white New York attorney, Harry Henderson, and his wife, Alice. This popular television series was based on the supporting character that first appeared on the popular radio program, *Fibber McGee and Molly,* in 1944, and a year later as its own series which ran through 1950.

When *Beulah* premiered on radio in 1945, the first Beulah was played by its creator, Marlin Hunt, who, incidentally, was a white male. Hunt had played the part on radio since 1939 on *Hometown Unincorporated.* By 1943, Beulah was a regular part of *That's Life,* which led to the opening of the *Fibber McGee and Molly* show.

Hunt died in 1946 and was replaced for a few months by another white actor, Bob Corley. Corley was eventually replaced by Hattie McDaniel.

On television there were actually three actresses who appeared in the title role. The first to play Beulah on television was Ethel Waters, who played Granny Dysey Johnson in the 1949 Darryl F. Zanuck drama, PINKY. Television's second Beulah was played by radio's third—Hattie McDaniel, who had won an Academy Award for her portrayal of Mammy in the 1939 classic, GONE WITH THE WIND.

There were apparently several reasons why Ms. Waters gave up the role of Beulah. First, "Ethel cited 'pressing commitments' elsewhere upon the completion of her first-fifteen week cycle of TV's *Beulah.*"[22] Second, Ms. Waters said she was also interested in doing some motion pictures and Broadway shows, but her schedule didn't give Ethel the time she needed to travel to New York. Her decision may also have been precipitated by the fact that the NAACP was examining *Beulah* in an effort to prevent a return of the stereotyped Negro characterizations, and Ms. Waters did not wish to repeat an earlier run-in she had had with the organization.

The producers decided to replace Ethel Waters with Hattie McDaniel, who was then playing the role on radio. The logistics were worked out so that Ms. McDaniel could film *Beulah* during the summer while the radio series was on hiatus.

Ms. Waters had brought her radio co-stars with her, which is why Ruby Dandridge and Ernest Whitman replaced Butterfly McQueen and Dooley Wilson when Hattie McDaniel came on board.

On August 18, 1951, two weeks before she was scheduled to begin taping the radio series, Hattie McDaniel was ordered to bed by her physician, Dr. Edward Stratton. The diagnoses ran from exhaustion and a painful boil under her left arm, to a stroke and diabetes. The final opinion was that Ms. McDaniel had suffered a heart attack, and the search was on for a new Beulah.

Before long, Hattie McDaniel's old friend, Louise Beavers, replaced her as television's new Beulah. Speaking about black maid stereotypes, in a June 29, 1974 *TV Guide* interview, Esther Rolle (Florida on both *Maude* [See Entry] and *Good Times* [See Entry]) said, "Louise Beavers of *Beulah* wasn't allowed to be real. Because she had feelings of her own they replaced her."

Ms. Beavers is well remembered for her role as Gussie, the Blandings' cheerful housekeeper in the 1948 comedy, MR. BLANDINGS BUILDS HIS DREAM HOUSE. At the end of that film, it's Gussie who saves Jim Blandings' (Cary Grant) job by coining the advertising slogan, "If you ain't eatin' Wham, you ain't eatin' ham."

Louise Beavers turned the role over to Lillian Randolph in 1953 and when Randolph quit in 1954, the series was cancelled. Ms. Randolph was later the first actress to play Bill Cosby's mom, Rose Kincaid, on *The Bill Cosby Show* (See Entry).

Beulah's best friend was Oriole, originally played by Butterfly McQueen, who endeared herself to moviegoers as the squeaky-voiced Prissy in the 1939 classic, GONE WITH THE WIND.

In 1951, Ruby Dandridge took over the Oriole role. Eight years later, Ms. Dandridge played the Banks' maid, Delilah, on the situation comedy, *Father of the Bride.* The series aired on CBS from September 29, 1961 to September 14, 1962.

In addition to Beulah, most of the other major characters were replaced with new actors in April 1952.

William Post, Jr., who had been playing the part of Harry Henderson, a New York attorney and Beulah's employer, was replaced by David Bruce, who played the title character in the 1950 adventure film, YOUNG DANIEL BOONE. His wife, Alice, who was originally played by Ginger Jones, was replaced by Jane Frazee, a singer and leading lady who had appeared in many minor musicals during the 1940s and was immortalized in the October 1, 1955 *Honeymooners* episode, "TV or Not TV." While looking through the TV listings in the evening paper Ralph comes across a fictitious RHYTHM film created by the writers Marvin Marx and Walter Stone.

RALPH: Hey, here's a movie. RHYTHM ON ICE with Kay Baker, Jane Frazee, Buddy Ebsen, Jerry Colonna and Frankie Darro.

NORTON: Hey, hey. Hey, that's a neat picture Ralph. That Jane Frazee can skate, hey.

---

22. Jackson, Carlton. *Hattie, The Life of Hattie McDaniel.* Madison Books, Lanham, MD, 1990, p 137.

Dooley Wilson replaced Percy (Bud) Harris as Bill Jackson, Beulah's incorrigible boyfriend. Bill Jackson may have been Wilson's only major television role, but he is remembered fondly by film buffs as the piano player, Sam, who played and sang "As Time Goes By" in the 1942 Humphrey Bogart classic, CASABLANCA. Incidentally, Wilson was a drummer but could not play the piano; the piano music was dubbed in the film.

The third actor to play Bill Jackson was Ernest Whitman who played Jim Europe in the 1943 musical, *Stormy Weather*.

Audiences stopped "bawling" for Beulah on September 22, 1953.

THE BEVERLY HILLBILLIES

September 26, 1962–September 7, 1971.   CBS

Character: Daisy "Granny" Moses
Played by: Irene Ryan
Date(s):   September 26, 1962–September 7, 1971

Replaced by: Granny's Maw
Played by: Imogene Coca
Date(s):   October 6, 1981
                  (*The Return of the Beverly Hillbillies*)

Character: Jethro Bodine
Played by: Max Baer, Jr.
Date(s):   September 26, 1962–September 7, 1971

Replaced by: Jethro Bodine
Played by: Ray Young
Date(s):   October 6, 1981
                  (*The Return of the Beverly Hillbillies*)

Character: Milburn Drysdale
Played by: Raymond Bailey
Date(s):   September 26, 1962–September 7, 1971

Replaced by: Charles David "C.D." Medford
Played by: Werner Klemperer
Date(s):   October 6, 1981
                  (*The Return of the Beverly Hillbillies*)

The Beverly Hillbillies was a story about a man named Jed, a poor mountaineer who barely kept his family fed. Then one day, he was shootin' at some food, an' up thru the ground came a bubblin' crude (oil). The first thing you know, Ol' Jed's a millionaire, so he loaded up the truck and they moved to Beverly—Hills that is.

Paul Henning, the creator of *The Beverly Hillbillies,* took a chance in 1981 and produced what is referred to in the industry as an extension or reunion episode. Whatever you call it, the purpose is to reunite the cast (and often the crew) of a successful television series to cash in on the nostalgia, and at the same time

test the waters for a return of the series. The original title for this extension episode was, *The Beverly Hillbillies Solving the Energy Crisis,* but it was retitled, *The Return of the Beverly Hillbillies.*

It had been ten years since the cancellation of the original series and not only were Buddy Ebsen (Uncle Jed Clampett), Donna Douglas (Elly May Clampett) and Max Baer, Jr. (Jethro Bodine) a little older, but two members of the original cast, Irene Ryan (Granny) and Raymond Bailey (Mr. Drysdale) had died.

Almost as important to a series as its original cast are its familiar sets. This presented another obstacle since the sets, which cost more than one hundred thousand dollars in 1961, would have been too costly to duplicate twenty years later, especially for what would most likely be a single use. Even the truck was gone—donated by Paul Henning to the Ralph Foster Museum at the School of the Ozarks in Branson, Missouri. Still, these stumbling blocks did not deter Henning, although many TV critics seem to feel they should have.

Irene Ryan created the role of Granny in 1961 after beating out buxom Bea Benaderet, who had asked producer Paul Henning to let her audition for the role. Benaderet, however, was hired to play Cousin Pearl.

Two years after *The Beverly Hillbillies,* Irene Ryan won a Tony Award nomination for her role as Bertha, another type of grandmother, in Bob Fosse's musical, *Pippin.* Sadly, Irene Ryan died of a brain tumor on Thursday, April 26, 1973, following a stroke suffered during a performance of the play several weeks earlier. She was seventy-one.

This meant that a replacement for Granny, or for the Granny character, had to be found. The producers chose the latter course and hired veteran comedienne Imogene Coca to play Granny's 104-year-old "Maw." Nancy Kulp, who played Miss Jane Hathaway in both the series and the return, thought Ms. Coca was miscast.

The audience was brought up to date through a reflective voice-over by Miss Hathaway, who, as the movie opens, is seen serenely riding an old plow horse past a picturesque forest lake in search of Jed Clampett's cabin.

MISS HATHAWAY: Ah yes, I know, the last time we saw Mr. Clampett he was living in a magnificent mansion in Beverly Hills. But after Granny went to her reward, as they say, he divided his enormous fortune between Elly May and Jethro and moved back to his beloved hills.

Later on in the story, Jed tells Miss Jane that Granny's Maw is still alive and that she is the only one who still knows the secret recipe for Granny's "White Lightnin'," which had been passed down from daughter to daughter. This was necessary for the development of the storyline, which centered around Miss Jane's belief that Granny's moonshine (med'cine or tonic to Granny's Maw) could replace conventional petroleum-based fuels and solve the energy crisis.

The producers, in the meantime, had another crisis of their own: how to replace Raymond Bailey, who died of a heart attack on April 15, 1980. Bailey, who played the Clampett's

Taking a rest outside their mountain cabin in the Missouri Ozarks are *Beverly Hillbillies* (left to right) Ellie May Clampett (Donna Douglas), Granny Moses (Irene Ryan), Jethro Bodine (Max Baer, Jr.) and Jed Clampett (Buddy Ebsen).

banker and neighbor, Milburn Drysdale, was seventy-four years old when he died.

The solution was to have Mr. Drysdale's secretary, Miss Hathaway, leave the Commerce Bank of Beverly Hills and go to work for another employer. That employer was the Energy Department in Washington, D.C. and her new boss was C.D. Medford, played by Werner Klemperer. Klemperer had already earned his place in television history as Colonel Wilhelm Klink in the CBS situation comedy, *Hogan's Heroes.*

The script was written to take place around Jed Clampett's cabin back in the Ozarks, which neatly eliminated the need for the mansion, the bank and the truck.

Everything was now set, until Max Baer, Jr. decided not to become involved with the project. "He said yes originally to Paul [Henning] when he was approached about the part. He kept saying yes, but when it got close to filming Paul could not get hold of Max. He was dodging Paul. Finally Paul sent someone to see Max, and Max refused the part at the last minute, so they found this other guy who looked a little like Jethro, but wasn't a seasoned actor. He did what he could."[23]

Max Baer, Jr. said that "I'm too old to play Jethro. I'm a man, not a boy. I'm almost as old as Buddy was when he played Jed. . . . It's not charming for a forty-year-old man to play an idiot. It's not charming at forty. It's charming at eighteen. . . . And I don't want to play Jethro for the rest of my life."[24] And he didn't.

BEWITCHED

September 17, 1964–July 1, 1972.   ABC

Character:	Darrin Stephens
Played by:	Dick York
Date(s):	September 17, 1964–1969

Replaced by:	Darrin Stephens
Played by:	Dick Sargent
Date(s):	September 18, 1969–July 1, 1972

23. Cox, Stephen. *The Beverly Hillbillies,* Contemporary Books, Inc., Chicago, 1988, p. 115.
24. *Ibid.,* pp. 88–89.

Dick York as the definitive Darrin Stephens (left) snuggles close to his *Bewitched* wife Samantha "Sam" (Elizabeth Montgomery, center) and their daughter Tabitha (Erin Murphy, front) as Endora (Agnes Moorehead, right), Darrin's witch of a mother-in-law, horns in on this family portrait.

A bewitching change in cast as Dick Sargent (left) takes over the role of Darrin Stephens. Seated next to Darrin are Elizabeth Montgomery (center) and Erin Murphy (bottom right) as his wife Samantha and daughter Tabitha. Standing behind the Stephens are Maurice Evans (left) and Agnes Moorehead (right) as Samantha's parents, Maurice and Endora.

Character:	Louise Tate
Played by:	Irene Vernon
Date(s):	1964–1966

Replaced by:	Louise Tate
Played by:	Kasey Rogers
Date(s):	September 2, 1966–July 1, 1972

Character:	Gladys Kravitz
Played by:	Alice Pearce
Date(s):	1964–1966

Replaced by:	Gladys Kravitz
Played by:	Sandra Gould
Date(s):	October 20, 1966–July 1, 1972

Character:	Frank Stephens
Played by:	Robert F. Simon
Date(s):	unknown

Replaced by:	Frank Stephens
Played by:	Roy Roberts
Date(s):	unknown

Character:	Aunt Hagatha
Played by:	Ysabel MacCloskey
Date(s):	unknown

Replaced by:	Aunt Hagatha
Played by:	Reta Shaw
Date(s):	unknown

Character:	Betty
Played by:	Marcia Wallace
Date(s):	unknown

Replaced by:	Betty
Played by:	Samantha Scott
Date(s):	unknown

Replaced by:	Betty
Played by:	Jean Blake
Date(s):	unknown

Replaced by:	Betty
Played by:	Samantha Hathaway
Date(s):	unknown

Character:	Howard McMann
Played by:	Leon Ames
Date(s):	February 12, 1970

Replaced by:	Howard McMann
Played by:	Gilbert Roland
Date(s):	unknown

Character:	Tabitha Stephens
Played by:	Heidi Gentry
Date(s):	January 13, 1966

Replaced by:	Tabitha Stephens
Played by:	Laura Gentry
Date(s):	January 13, 1966

Replaced by:	Tabitha Stephens
Played by:	Tamar Young
Date(s):	January 20, 1966–August 25, 1966

Replaced by:	Tabitha Stephens
Played by:	Julie Young
Date(s):	January 20, 1966–August 25, 1966

Replaced by:	Tabitha Stephens
Played by:	Erin Murphy
Date(s):	September 16, 1966–July 1, 1972

Replaced by:	Tabitha Stephens
Played by:	Diane Murphy
Date(s):	September 16, 1966–unknown

Character:	Adam Stephens
Played by:	David Lawrence
Date(s):	October 16, 1969–July 1, 1972

Replaced by:	Adam Stephens
Played by:	Greg Lawrence
Date(s):	October 16, 1969–July 1, 1972

"Once upon a time, there was a typical American girl, who happened to bump into a typical red-blooded American boy. And she bumped into him. . . and bumped into him. So they decided they better sit down and talk this over before they had an accident. They became good friends. They found they had a lot of interests in common—radio, television, trains. And when the boy found the girl attractive, desirable, irresistible, he did what any red-blooded American boy would do. He asked her to marry him.

"They had a typical wedding. Went on a typical honeymoon in a typical bridal suite. Except, it so happens that this girl is a witch."[25]

The girl was Samantha, played by Elizabeth Montgomery. The boy was Darrin Stephens, played by Dick York—but only for the first five seasons.

Darrin was a respected vice president at McMann & Tate Advertising and really loved "Sam," as he affectionately called his new bride. But unlike the rest of us, who would love to have a spouse with supernatural powers to make life easier and more fun, Darrin was painfully honest and made his wife—who was a good witch, not a bad witch—promise to give up using witchcraft. But old habits are hard to break, as Samantha proved at the end of the first episode when Darrin left her in the kitchen to clean up. She considered doing it the mortal way and then gave in to her bewitching instincts—waved her hands and, *voila,* there was a tidy kitchen, to which she exclaimed, "Maybe I can taper off."

Bewitched made television history on September 18, 1969 with what may very well be the most famous incident of a lead character being written out of a series. Dick York was replaced by Dick Sargent. According to published sources, here is how it happened.

While working on the 1959 Gary Cooper drama, THEY CAME TO CORDURA, Dick York, who played Private Renziehausen, sustained a serious back injury in which he "tore all the muscles from [his] spine."[26]

A more detailed explanation appeared in "Darrin's Double Features," Chapter six of *The Bewitched Book* by Herbie J. Pilato.

"When Dick York was filming THEY CAME TO CORDURA with Gary Cooper in 1959, York and several other

---

25. Voice-over transcribed from the first episode of *Bewitched.*
26. Javna, John. *Cult TV: A Viewer's Guide to the Shows America Can't Live Without.* St. Martin's Press, New York, 1985, p. 119.

actors were doing a scene that required them to lift a railroad handcar. At one point, the director yelled 'Cut!' and everyone but York let go. The car fell on him, wrenching his spine and tearing the muscles around it. His pain continued on *Bewitched,* later escalating, and he had to be replaced by Dick Sargent as Darrin in 1969.''[27]

In addition to his spine injury, which became a degenerative condition, York later developed emphysema and lived with pain every day for nearly ten years. He was said to have become addicted to drugs and alcohol. In 1969 the pain became debilitating and forced him to be written out of fourteen episodes. York returned to continue the role until the fifth season, when he suffered a seizure during filming that nearly paralyzed him. He was rushed to the hospital and never returned to the series.

"My physical condition was rapidly deteriorating, my children and I were becoming virtual strangers, and the atmosphere on the set of *Bewitched* was extremely unpleasant. I left in an ambulance writhing in pain, but I never missed the show, nor have I ever regretted the decision to leave.''[28]

On the air, there weren't any explanations, or jokes made about Darrin looking a little different, but it was mentioned in the *TV Guide* listing: "Dick Sargent takes over the role of Darrin and the Stephenses await another baby as the series' sixth season begins.''[29]

But the replacement is still the most talked about of any actor who has ever been written out of television. It was used in a gag when Sarah Chalke was introduced as the new Becky on ABC's *Roseanne* (See Entry), and even pondered by that cable television genius, Wayne Campbell (Mike Myers), in the 1992 motion picture, WAYNE'S WORLD:

WAYNE: I mean there was two Darrin Stephens, right?
          Dick York, Dick Sargent—shee, ha, ha—right
          . . . as if we wouldn't notice. Oh, hold on . . .
          Dick York, Dick Sargent, Sergeant York—
          wow, that's weird.

" 'We toyed with the idea of having Endora change Darrin's looks,' says Bill Asher, 'but then we'd have a wall between Endora and Samantha.' And as Elizabeth adds, 'Samantha would never have put up with that. It wouldn't have been fair to the characters or the actors—and the audience would have hated it.'

"Of the York-Sargent exchange, she notes, 'This kind of thing [replacing actors] happens all the time . . . on soap operas . . . in theater, and the audiences aren't stupid. They're certainly smarter than any network executive gives them credit for.''[30]

Sargent did bear a close resemblance to his predecessor, but the producers still put in the extra effort to update the series' animated intro with a new caricature of Darrin.

Sargent, who was originally considered for the role of Darrin, apparently wasn't aware of York's health problems at the time he took over. "I don't know why York quit the show. I just thank God that he did.''[31] Before *Bewitched,* Dick Sargent played Terrance Ward on the ABC situation comedy, *The Tammy Grimes Show.*

Coincidentally, Tammy Grimes, a stage actress, was originally asked to play Samantha Stephens, but she didn't like the script and turned the role down in order to pursue another project; it was *The Tammy Grimes Show.* This was an unfortunate decision for Ms. Grimes because, of the ten episodes produced, only four actually aired between September 8 and 29, 1966. *Bewitched,* on the other hand, produced and aired 254 episodes during its eight-season run.

Every good sitcom has its wacky next door neighbors and *Bewitched* was no exception. Abner and Gladys Kravitz were the Stephens' next-door neighbors, for the entire series, and are also the most likely models for the Tanners' neighbors, the Ochmoneks, on *ALF.* Gladys Kravitz was a nosy neighbor— perhaps television's nosiest until Raquel Ochmonek (Liz Sheridan) came along on *ALF.*

Alice Pearce came to television after a long career on stage and in films. Most notably was her portrayal of Lucy Schmeeler, the chronic sneezer, in both the play and the motion picture ON THE TOWN. Gladys Kravitz was her last role. She died on March 3, 1966 while still working on the series.

Ms. Pearce was replaced by Sandra Gould, who continued with the role until the series left the air.

The part of Darrin's dad was also played by two actors. The first was Robert F. Simon, who replaced David White as Peter Parker's boss, J. Jonah Jameson, in *The Amazing Spider-Man.* White, of course, played Darrin's boss, Larry Tate, the "Tate" in "McMann & Tate."

Simon was later replaced, not by David White but by Roy Roberts, who played John Cushing from 1964 to 1967 on *The Beverly Hillbillies.*

Howard McMann, the less seen partner of the advertising agency for which Darrin worked, appeared only twice during the course of the series and was played by a different actor on each occasion. In "What Makes Darrin Run?" McMann was played by Leon Ames, who replaced Larry Keating as the Posts' next-door neighbors on *Mr. Ed* (See Entry). The second and last time Howard McMann apeared he was played by Gilbert Roland who among his many roles, had played El Cuchillo on *Zorro* (See Entry).

Samantha's Aunt Hagatha was played by both Ysabel MacCloskey and Reta Shaw. Shaw had played Mrs. Macauley on *The Ann Sothern Show* (See Entry) and replaced Bub on *My Three Sons* (See Entry).

Still another lovable relative of Samantha's was Esmerelda,

27. Pilato, Herbie J. *The Bewitched Book: The Cosmic Companion to TV's Most Magical Supernatural Comedy.* Dell Publishing Group, Inc., New York, 1992, p. 47.

28. Lamparski, Richard. *Whatever became of . . . ? all new eleventh series.* Crown Publishers, New York. 1989. p. 197.

29. *TV Guide,* Vol. 17, No. 37, Issue #859, September 13, 1969.

30. Pilato, Herbie J. *The Bewitched Book: The Cosmic Companion to TV's Most Magical Supernatural Comedy.* Dell Publishing Group, Inc., New York, 1992, p. 47.

31. Mitz, Rick. *The Great TV Sitcom Book,* Richard Marek Publishers, New York, 1980, p. 218.

who popped into the series in 1969 in the guise of Alice Ghostley (what a great name for a witch), who later played Aunt Alice on *The Andy Griffith Show* (See Entry) spinoff, *Mayberry R.F.D.*

Whether or not Esmerelda was meant to be a direct replacement for Aunt Clara, who was played by the delightfully daffy Marion Lorne from September 17, 1964 to 1968, she did serve much the same function as a sort of maid and babysitter.

Darrin's secretary, Betty, was played by four different actresses during the series, the first of whom was Marcia Wallace. She went on to play receptionist Carol Kester Bondurant on *The Bob Newhart Show* from 1972 to 1978 and provided the voice for Mrs. Karbapple, Bart's school teacher on *The Simpsons,* which premiered on Fox on December 17, 1989.

The Stephens' first child, Tabitha, was born on the January 13, 1966 episode of *Bewitched.* She was played by the twins Heidi and Laura Gentry in that episode only. The reason twins were used is because of a California child labor law that doesn't allow a child under the age of six to work for more than two hours a day. Producers, therefore, prefer to use twins because it doubles the time they are able to put the youngsters before the cameras.

The remainder of the episodes for the 1965/1966 season called for slightly older babies and so Heidi and Laura were replaced by Tamar and Julie Young. The twins were replaced one last time at the beginning of the following season by Erin and Diane Murphy, who were two years old at the time they began. Eventually Diane dropped out and Erin handled the role on her own until the series ended in 1972.

In just five years, this cute little tot grew into a beautiful young lady with her own spinoff series, but what did you expect from a witch? That series was *Tabitha* and its star, Lisa Hartman, became the eighth actress to play the bewitching offspring of Darrin and Samantha Stephens. This is because in the first of two pilots for the series, which aired on April 24, 1976, Liberty Williams starred in the title role.

Tabitha, which aired on ABC from November 12, 1977 to August 25, 1978, was set in a television newsroom that was not unlike the newsroom of *The Mary Tyler Moore Show.* The station was KXLA-TV in Los Angeles and Tabitha Stephens worked as a production assistant on *The Paul Thurston Show.*

Thurston, a handsome Ted Baxter-type, was played by an even younger and handsomer Robert Urich, who went on to fame as Dan Tanna on the ABC series, *VEGA$.* Mel Stewart, who had played Henry Jefferson on *All in the Family* (See Entry), was their boss and the producer of *The Paul Thurston Show.*

Also grown up was Tabitha's brother, Adam. Born on Dick Sargent's fifth episode of the *Bewitched* series and played alternately by twins David and Greg Lawrence, he was now being played by David Ankrum. Since another actor, Bruce Kimmel, did the role of Adam in the *Tabitha* pilot with Liberty Williams, David Ankrum became the fourth actor to play the young warlock.

But even all of this powerful witchcraft wasn't enough to save the series from the ABC executives; they twitched their noses after only twelve episodes and made the series vanish for good.

BIG JOHN, LITTLE JOHN

September 11, 1976–September 3, 1977.   NBC

Character:	"Big" John Martin
Played by:	Herb Edelman
Date(s):	September 11, 1976–September 3, 1977

Replaced by:	"Little" John Martin
Played by:	Robbie Rist
Date(s):	September 11, 1976–September 3, 1977

Producer Sherwood Schwartz, who gave us *It's About Time, Gilligan's Island* and *The Brady Bunch,* tried to buck the Saturday morning cartoon syndrome with this clever live-action program created for younger viewers.

The premise is simple. John Martin, a forty-five-year-old teacher at Madison Junior High School, periodically changes from an adult to a twelve-year-old boy. These unplanned and uncontrollable transformations are the result of a sip of water he took from a lost fountain of youth he discovered while vacationing in the Ponce de Leon National Park in Florida.

When he's Big John, he's played by Herb Edelman and when he's Little John, he's played by Robbie Rist.

Prior to this Saturday morning stint, Edelman had played Bert Gramus in the CBS comedy, *The Good Guys,* opposite *Gilligan's Islanders* Bob Denver and Jim Backus though he may best be remembered by audiences as Murray the cop in the 1968 motion picture, THE ODD COUPLE.

Juvenile actor Robbie Rist later went on to become the first of two Dr. Zees in the science fiction series, *Galactica 1980* (See Entry).

BIG TOP *see:* SUPER CIRCUS

BIG TOWN

October 5, 1950–October 2, 1956.   CBS-DuMONT-NBC

Character:	Steve Wilson
Played by:	Patrick McVey
Date(s):	1950–1954

Replaced by:	Steve Wilson
Played by:	Mark Stevens
Date(s):	1954–1956

Character:	Lorelei Kilbourne
Played by:	Mary K. Wells
Date(s):	1950–1951

Replaced by:	Lorelei Kilbourne
Played by:	Julie Stevens
Date(s):	1951–1952

Replaced by:	Lorelei Kilbourne
Played by:	Jane Nigh
Date(s):	1952–1953

Replaced by:	Lorelei Kilbourne
Played by:	Beverly Tyler
Date(s):	1953–1954

Replaced by:	Lorelei Kilbourne
Played by:	Trudy Wroe
Date(s):	1954–1955

Replaced by:	Diane Walker
Played by:	Doe Avedon
Date(s):	Fall 1955

Based on a radio series which ran from 1937 to 1948, *Big Town* was one of television's early crime dramas. The program's lead was Steve Wilson, a crime reporter and ex-managing editor of *The Illustrated Press* who was first played by Patrick McVey, who went on to play Lieutenant Colonel Hayes in the 1957 syndicated Western, *Boots and Saddles: The Story of the Fifth Cavalry.*

Big Town moved from CBS to DuMont in the fall of 1954 and McVey was replaced by Mark Stevens. Stevens had just completed work as the fourth Martin Kane in the NBC detective drama, *Martin Kane, Private Eye* (See Entry). Stevens also took over as the producer and director of the series, which gave him the creative control to restore Wilson to the position of managing editor.

When the series began on television Steve Wilson's romantic interest was Lorelei Kilbourne, originally played by Mary K. Wells who appeared on a number of daytime soap operas. In 1956 she became the second of three actresses to take on the role of Ellie Crown on *The Love of Life.* Two years later Ms. Wells played Louise Cole on *As the World Turns,* which she followed with another Louise—Grimsley Capice, which she played on *The Edge of Night* from from 1961 to 1970.

During the series run at least four other actresses played the role of Lorelei Kilbourne. Some sources indicate that a sixth actress, Margaret Hayes, played Lorelei from 1950 to 1951. These sources also suggest a different order for these actresses: Margaret Hayes, 1951; Mary K. Wells, 1951 to 1953; Jane Nigh, 1951 to 1953; Beverly Tyler, 1953; Trudy Wroe, 1954; and Julie Stevens, 1954 to 1955.

In the fall of 1955, Lorelei Kilbourne was written out of the series and Doe Avedon was added to the cast as reporter[32] Diane Walker—Steve Wilson's new romantic interest.

THE BILL COSBY SHOW

September 14, 1969–August 31, 1971. NBC

Character:	Rose Kincaid
Played by:	Lillian Randolph
Date(s):	September 14, 1969–1970

Replaced by:	Rose Kincaid
Played by:	Beah Richards
Date(s):	1970–August 31, 1971

Character:	Verna Kincaid
Played by:	De De Young
Date(s):	1969

Replaced by:	Verna Kincaid
Played by:	Olga James
Date(s):	1969–August 31, 1971

The multi-talented comedian and actor, Bill Cosby, having already established himself in a weekly adventure series, moved into a realm with which he was more at home with, the situation comedy.

The adventure series was *I Spy,* which teamed Robert Culp as Kelly Robinson and Bill Cosby as Alexander ''Scotty'' Scott, a couple of government agents. For three seasons straight, 1965/1966, 1966/1967 and 1967/1968, Bill Cosby won the Emmy Award in the category of Outstanding Continued Performance by an Actor in a Leading Role in a Dramatic Series, beating out his co-star all three times.

The Bill Cosby Show, set in a middle-class neighborhood of Los Angeles, California, pitted Cosby not against international spies, but against the daily problems of life. As Chet Kincaid, the physical education instructor and coach of the Richard Allen Holmes High School, Cosby used his gentle sense of humor to deal with domestic and professional life.

A classic episode had Mr. Kincaid dealing with the use of foul language by members of the basketball team. His solution was to shout out the names of foods, like ''peanut butter'' and ''marshmallows,'' instead of the stronger expletives.

Chet lived at home with his brother, Brian (Lee Weaver) and his sister-in-law, Verna (Olga James). The Kincaids lived with their mother Rose, who was played by two actresses. The first was Lillian Randolph, who was the fourth actress to play the Henderson's housekeeper on *Beulah* (See Entry). The other actress to play Mrs. Kincaid was Beah Richards, who turned in a moving and Emmy-worthy performance as Minnie in the hour-long special episode of *Designing Women* that aired on January 1, 1990.

BILLY *see:* HEAD OF THE CLASS

B.J. AND THE BEAR

February 10, 1979–August 1, 1981. NBC

Replaced by:	Barbara Sue McAllister
Played by:	Jo Ann Harris
Date(s):	February 10, 1979
	December 1, 1979

Character:	Barbara Sue McAllister
Played by:	Kitty Ruth
Date(s):	unknown

---

32. Some sources give Diane Walker's profession as a commercial artist, not a reporter.

Like the Bandit character Burt Reynolds played in the 1977 comedy, SMOKEY AND THE BANDIT B.J. McKay (Greg Evigan) was a trucker who would haul any legal load—anywhere (for just $1.50 a mile). And just as Bandit had his Sheriff Buford T. Justice (Jackie Gleason) on his butt, B.J. was hounded by one Sheriff Elroy P. Lobo (Claude Akins). That, however, is where the similarites end, because instead of riding with an attractive lady like Sally Field's Carrie, B.J. chose to hit the open road with his pet chimpanzee, Bear—well, there's no accounting for taste.

B.J. did, however, have a female friend in Orly County, Georgia. Her name was Barbara Sue McAllister and she was played by Jo Ann Harris in the ninety-minute pilot, "Odyssey of the Shady Truth." Ten months later she reprised her role in "B.J.'s Sweetheart," which also starred one-time James Bond, George Lazenby. Ms. Harris was later replaced by Kitty Ruth.

Greg Evigan, who starred in the title role, went on to co-star as Joey Harris in the sensitive NBC situation comedy, *My Two Dads*.

Lobo, the corrupt Orly County, Georgia sheriff mentioned earlier was played by Claude Akins, whose second role on televison was the crook, Ace Miller who tried to steal Perry White's (John Hamilton) formula for extracting U^{183} from seawater in "Peril by Sea," a 1955 episode of the *Adventures of Superman*. From there he built up an impressive list of credits which include episodes of *I Love Lucy*, *Wagon Train*, *The Untouchables* and *The Twilight Zone*.

He was finally given his own series *Movin' On*, in which he himself played a trucker—Sonny Pruitt. The weekly adventure aired on NBC from September 12, 1974 to September 14, 1976.

But it was his work on *B.J. and the Bear* that elevated him to television star status and earned him his own spinoffs—*The Misadventures of Sheriff Lobo* and *Lobo* (See Entry).

He later had a recurring role as Ethan Cragg on *Murder, She Wrote* (See Entry), and was replaced by William Windom as Doctor Hazlitt.

BLAKE'S SEVEN

1977–1981.   Syndicated

Character:	Roj Blake	
Played by:	Gareth Thomas	
Date(s):	1977–unknown	
Replaced by:	Kerr Avon	
Played by:	Paul Darrow	
Date(s):	1980	
Character:	Commander Travis	
Played by:	Stephen Greif	
Date(s):	1977–unknown	
Replaced by:	Commander Travis	
Played by:	Brian Croucher	
Date(s):	unknown	

While *Star Trek*'s United Federation of Planets depicted a united earth at peace with many of its galactic neighbors, the Federation of the BBC produced *Blake's Seven* where ruthless dictators controlled the inhabitants of our small blue planet making freedom a capital offense.

The series, which was set on earth, a radioactive wasteland in the third century of the second calendar (whenever that is), where its inhabitants live in dome-enclosed cities.

Roj Blake, played by Gareth Thomas, is the hero of the series, which was produced as four thirteen-episode segments, and has sworn to free the human race from the oppression of the Federation.

The other members of the original seven were Jenna Stannis (Sally Knyvette), Kerr Avon (Paul Darrow), Cally (Jan Chappell), Vila Restal (Michael Keating), Olag Gan (David Jackson) and Zen (Peter Tuddenham).

But unlike the continuing cast of the original *Star Trek*, who could never be killed, members of Blake's Seven were not immortals.

Gan was killed off in "The Web," the fifth episode of the series and both Jenna and Blake vaporized in "Star One," the last episode of the second series.

In "Aftermath," the first episode of the third series, computer genius, Kerr Avon, assumed Blake's role as leader of the resistance force. Joining him was Commander Travis who was played at first by Stephen Greif and later by Brian Croucher.

Blake's Seven, which was created by Terry Nation, who is credited with the inspiration for Dr. Who's Daleks, which aired on PBS stations beginning in 1986, was actually produced in England between 1977 and 1981. In all, a total of fifty-two episodes were produced.

BLONDIE

January 4, 1957–September 27, 1957.   NBC
September 26, 1968–January 9, 1969   CBS

Character:	Blondie Bumstead	
Played by:	Pamela Britton	
Date(s):	January 4, 1957–September 27, 1957	
Replaced by:	Blondie Bumstead	
Played by:	Patricia Harty	
Date(s):	September 26, 1968–January 9, 1969	
Character:	Dagwood Bumstead	
Played by:	Arthur Lake	
Date(s):	January 4, 1957–September 27, 1957	
Replaced by:	Dagwood Bumstead	
Played by:	Will Hutchins	
Date(s):	September 26, 1968–January 9, 1969	
Character:	Cookie Bumstead	
Played by:	Ann Barnes	
Date(s):	January 4, 1957–September 27, 1957	

Replaced by:	Cookie Bumstead
Played by:	Pamelyn Ferdin
Date(s):	September 26, 1968–January 9, 1969

Character:	Alexander Bumstead
Played by:	Stuffy Singer
Date(s):	January 4, 1957–September 27, 1957

Replaced by:	Alexander Bumstead
Played by:	Peter Robbins
Date(s):	September 26, 1968–January 9, 1969

Character:	Julius C. Dithers
Played by:	Florenz Ames
Date(s):	January 4, 1957–September 27, 1957

Replaced by:	Julius C. Dithers
Played by:	Jim Backus
Date(s):	September 26, 1968–January 9, 1969

Character:	Cora Dithers
Played by:	Lela Bliss
Date(s):	January 4, 1957–unknown

Replaced by:	Cora Dithers
Played by:	Elvia Allman
Date(s):	unknown–September 27, 1957

Replaced by:	Cora Dithers
Played by:	Henny Backus
Date(s):	September 26, 1968–January 9, 1969

Character:	Harriet Woodley
Played by:	Lois Collier
Date(s):	January 4, 1957–unknown

Replaced by:	Harriet Woodley
Played by:	Hollis Irving
Date(s):	unknown–January 9, 1969

Replaced by:	Tootsie Woodley
Played by:	Bobbi Jordan
Date(s):	September 26, 1968–January 9, 1969

Character:	Mr. Beasley
Played by:	Lucien Littlefield
Date(s):	January 4, 1957–September 27, 1957

Replaced by:	Mr. Beasley
Played by:	Bryan O'Byrne
Date(s):	September 26, 1968–January 9, 1969

The short-lived situation comedy, *Blondie,* was based on the comic strip by Chic Young that was syndicated in 1930. That strip spawned a radio series that ran from 1939 to 1951 and twenty-eight motion pictures released from 1938 to 1950.

When *Blondie* came to television, Arthur Lake, who had played Dagwood Bumstead in both previous versions, continued the role he created. His wife, Blondie, however, was now played by Pamela Britton, not by Penny Singleton, who had played the character briefly on radio and in all of the motion pictures. She was also the voice of Jane in the 1990 motion picture and all of the television episodes of *The Jetsons.*

There were two unaired pilots for the series. The first, produced in 1952, featured Jeff Donnell as Blondie and John Harvey as Dagwood. Two years later, a second pilot cast Pamela Britton as Blondie and Hal LeRoy (a remarkable Arthur Lake look-alike) as her long suffering husband, Dagwood. The other members of the cast were Stuffy Singer as Alexander, Mimi Gibson as Cookie, Robert Burton as J.C. Dithers, Isabel Winters as Cora Dithers and Robin Raymond as Tootsie Woodley. Except for the differences in cast, this version was almost identical with the 1957 series; it even featured the same house number and the same background music.

The cast of the 1957 *Blondie* series was fairly stable, only two actors being replaced. Elvia Allman replaced Lela Bliss as Cora Dithers and Hollis Irving replaced Lois Collier as Harriet Woodley.

While Hollis Irving had played Aunt Phoebe in the ABC situation comedy, *Margie,* which aired from October 12, 1961 to August 31, 1962, Elvia Allman replaced Margaret Hamilton as Esther Frump on *The Addams Family* (See Entry).

CBS made an attempt to bring the series back during the 1968/1969 season with an all new cast that included Patricia Harty as Blondie, Will Hutchins as Dagwood and Jim Backus as Mr. Dithers.

Using her new professional name, Trisha Hart, Patricia Harty co-starred as Bob Crane's wife, Ellie Wilcox, on the situation comedy, *The Bob Crane Show,* which aired from March 6 to June 19, 1975. She later co-starred as Susan MacLane in *Herbie the Love Bug,* the short-lived TV adaptation of the popular Disney movie. The series aired on CBS from March 17 to April 14, 1982.

The new Dagwood was Will Hutchins, already well known to television viewers as Tom "Sugarfoot" Brewster in the ABC Western, *Sugarfoot,* which aired from September 17, 1957 to July 3, 1961. And Jim Backus, who played Dagwood's boss, Mr. Dithers, is well known to television viewers as Thurston Howell, III, one of the castaways on *Gilligan's Island* (See Entry).

THE BLUE ANGELS

Produced 1960.   Syndicated

Character:	Commander Arthur Richards
Played by:	Dennis Cross
Date(s):	1960 (episodes 1–12)

Replaced by:	Commander Donovan
Played by:	Morgan Jones
Date(s):	1960 (episodes 13–39)

Sam Gallau, who made a career of producing television programs based on the United States Navy, such as *Behind Closed Doors* and *Navy Log*, produced a syndicated series in 1960 based on the activities of the Navy's precision jet pilots, The Blue Angels.

The leader of this elite group of flyers was Commander Arthur Richards, who was played by Dennis Cross in the first dozen episodes. Thereafter, the leader of the squadron was Commander Donovan, played by Morgan Jones. Jones later appeared as Colonel Nesvig in the unsold science fiction pilot, *Assignment Earth*, that aired as an episode of *Star Trek* on March 29, 1968.

THE BLUE KNIGHT

December 17, 1975–October 27, 1976.   CBS

Character:	William A. "Bumper" Morgan
Played by:	William Holden
Date(s):	November 13, 1973–November 16, 1973 (A four-part miniseries.)

Replaced by:	William A. "Bumper" Morgan
Played by:	George Kennedy
Date(s):	December 17, 1975–October 27, 1976

Character:	Detective Charley Bronski
Played by:	Sam Elliott
Date(s):	November 13, 1973–November 16, 1973 (A four-part miniseries.)

Replaced by:	Detective Charley Bronski
Played by:	Alex Rocco
Date(s):	May 9, 1975

Academy Award-winning leading man, William Holden, made his dramatic television debut as Patrolman Bumper Morgan in the NBC mini-series, *The Blue Knight*. The role earned him a 1973/1974 season Emmy award for Best Lead Actor in a Limited Series. This four-hour, four-part, made-for-television movie was based on the best-selling novel by ex-cop Joseph Wambaugh, who had a small role in the film as the desk sergeant.

Even with an Emmy in hand, William Holden preferred not to work in series television and the role was taken over by George Kennedy. Kennedy, all six-foot-four of him, played Bumper Morgan in the pilot which aired on May 9, 1975 and in the subsequent series.

The part of Detective Bronski, played by Sam Elliott in the mini-series, was portrayed by Alex Rocco in the pilot. The character was dropped before the series premiered.

While Sam Elliott was known for his series role on *Mission Impossible* as Doug, Alex Rocco gained his highest visibility as

Al Floss, the slimy entertainment agent on *The Famous Teddy Z*, which premiered on CBS's schedule on September 18, 1989.

THE BOB AND RAY SHOW

November 26, 1951–September 28, 1953.   NBC

Character:	Mary Backstayge
Played by:	Cloris Leachman
Date(s):	1952

Replaced by:	Mary Backstayge
Played by:	Audrey Meadows
Date(s)	Spring 1953–September 28, 1953

Bob and Ray were the undisputed masters of understatement, dishing out their unique brand of humor that is in some ways reminiscent of the dry British wit of playwright Harold Pinter. But Bob and Ray were much more than understatement. They could take an idea and stretch it further than any one else without ever losing its plausibility.

They began their careers in Boston on radio station WHDH and created a host of satirical and offbeat characters such as Mister Science, Fred Falvy the do-it-yourselfer, Komodo Dragon Expert Doctor Daryll Dexter, and crack broadcast journalists David Chetley and Wally Ballou. Wally Ballou, whose first name incidentally is Wallace, is thought of by most radio listeners as Lee Ballou because his newscasts were always cut into after he had already begun his introduction.

The team also spoofed radio soap operas such as *One Man's Family* and *Mary Noble, Backstage Wife*. The Bob and Ray versions were *One Fella's Family* and *Mary Backstayge, Noble Wife*. Some of these lovable characters were brought to television in a show appropriately titled, *The Bob and Ray Show*.

Audiences were continually confounded by which one was Bob and which one was Ray. To clear up the confusion, Bob was Bob Elliott and Ray was Ray Goulding. If that doesn't clear things up, just remember their own helpful hint: "Bob over here, Ray over there," and if you can keep that straight, you'll never mix them up again.

You, may, however, be inclined to be confused about the actress who played Mary Backstayge. Was it Ray Goulding, Audrey Meadows, Cloris Leachman, Madeline Kahn or Natalie Attired? If you guessed the first four, you were right. Natalie never played Mary Backstayge.

The Bob, of Bob and Ray, began his explanation by first setting the record straight about actors who have been "written out of television." "There was no other Bob and Ray,"[33] he said in his familiar deadpan delivery and nasal voice.

Ms. Meadows joined the team in 1951 for their first foray into television, playing the title role in the Bob and Ray soap opera spoof, *The Life and Loves of Linda Lovely*. According to Bob Elliott, getting the job was simplicity itself. "Our manager, John Moses, had seen her appear in something and he suggested

---

33. From an exclusive telephone interview with Bob Elliott on December 22, 1990.

that she would be good. We had a meeting with Audrey and hired her on the spot.

"We weren't going to give her any lines. On radio, Ray did all of the women's voices, but he didn't want to do it in drag on TV; that's why we got a girl, because we figured, 'we've got to have a female on the show.' So we said we won't let her talk, we'll invent business for her. And one of the things we said was, 'Why don't we have her roller skate into and out of the scene?' In fact, among the questions we asked Audrey during the interview was, 'Can you roller skate?' and she said, 'Sure.' She said she could do anything, dance, sing—and she could. So for two weeks, whenever she was in the scene, we had her roller skate in and out, but then that got a little tired. Within three or four weeks we had to start using her with lines and she was great. She could ad-lib—and did, because the show's weren't really scripted."[34]

During that time, Audrey Meadows was also starring in *Top Banana* on Broadway. "Then she left to go with [Jackie] Gleason and we continued with Cloris Leachman,"[35] said Bob Elliott. When Ms. Meadows left to play Alice Kramden on *The Honeymooners* (See Entry), it was once again Bob and Ray's agent who was responsible for suggesting Cloris Leachman as her replacement. But Ms. Leachman didn't play Linda Lovely. Instead, she became the first actress to play the title role in another of the Bob and Ray soap spoofs, *Mary Backstayge, Noble Wife.* Cloris Leachman only stayed with this role for the 1952 season, after which Audrey Meadows rejoined Bob and Ray and took over the role of Mary Backstayge.

When Bob Elliott, who wrote the book on nonchalance, was asked if they found it in any way difficult to have a recurring character like Mary Backstayge played first by one actress, then replaced by another, and then have the first actress return, he answered very succinctly, "It just wasn't that big a deal."[36]

One person who did think that it was a big deal was Dick Cavett, who brought *Mary Backstayge, Noble Wife* back to television for a week during *This Morning,* his first talk show, which aired on ABC from April 1, 1968 to January 24, 1969. In that version, Mary Backstayge was played by Madeline Kahn, making her the third actress to play that beloved character.

Bob and Ray returned to New York radio during the 1970s when they hosted a daily afternoon drive-time show on WOR-AM. They guest-starred with the original female cast members of *Saturday Night Live* in an NBC special, *Bob & Ray & Jane, Laraine & Gilda,* which aired on October 24, 1981 and appeared on Broadway in *Bob and Ray: The Two and Only.*

Their books include *From Approximately Coast to Coast . . . It's the Bob and Ray Show,* published in 1983 by Atheneum, and *The New! Improved! Bob and Ray Book,* published in 1985 by G.P. Putnam's Sons.

Ray Goulding died of kidney failure on March 24, 1990 after a twelve-year-long bout with the affliction.

On September 23, 1990, Bob Elliott who years before had produced a son, Chris, returned to television as Fred Peterson, Chris Peterson's (Chris Elliott) father on the outrageous Fox situation comedy, *Get a Life.*

And never forget Bob and Ray's closing reminder: "This is Ray Goulding reminding you to write if you get work. Bob Elliott reminding you to hang by your thumbs."

THE BOB CUMMINGS SHOW

January 2, 1955–September 15, 1959.   NBC-CBS-NBC

Character:	Francine Williams
Played by:	Diane Jergens
Date(s):	January 2, 1955–1956

Replaced by:	Olive Sturgess
Played by:	Carol Henning
Date(s):	1956–1957

In his most famous television role, Bob Cummings played Bob Collins, a professional photographer and ladies' man (and not necessarily in that order). Dwayne Hickman played Bob's nephew, Chuck McDonald, who also had a girlfriend . . . or two. The first woman to garner Chuck's attention was Francine Williams. She was played by Diane Jergens, who had played one of the agents on the syndicated Spy series, *Counterthrust,* which was syndicated in 1958.

The second beauty to become the focus of Chuck's attention was Olive Sturgess, who was played by Carol Henning.

BONANZA

September 12, 1959–January 16, 1973.   NBC
November 28, 1993   NBC

Character:	Ben Cartwright
Played by:	Lorne Greene
Date(s):	September 12, 1959–January 16, 1973

Replaced by:	Bronk Evans
Played by:	Ben Johnson
Date(s):	November 28, 1993

Character:	Little Joe Cartwright
Played by:	Michael Landon
Date(s):	September 12, 1959–January 16, 1973

Replaced by:	Benjamin "Benj" Cartwright
Played by:	Michael Landon, Jr.
Date(s):	November 28, 1993

Character:	Eric "Hoss" Cartwright

---

34. *Ibid.*
35. *Ibid.*
36. *Ibid.*

Played by: Dan Blocker
Date(s):   September 12, 1959–1972

Replaced by: Josh Overton
Played by: Brian Leckner
Date(s):   November 28, 1993

Character: Adam Cartwright
Played by: Pernell Roberts
Date(s):   September 12, 1959–May 23, 1965

Replaced by: Candy
Played by: David Canary
Date(s):   September 17, 1967–1970
                  1972–1973

Replaced by: Dusty Rhodes
Played by: Lou Frizzel
Date(s):   1970–1972

Replaced by: Jamie Hunter
Played by: Mitch Vogel
Date(s):   1970–1973

Replaced by: Adam "A.C." Cartwright
Played by: Alistair MacDougall
Date(s):   November 28, 1993

Character: Hop Sing
Played by: Victor Sen Yung
Date(s):   September 12, 1959–January 16, 1973

Replaced by: Buckshot
Played by: Jack Elam
Date(s):   November 28, 1993

Character: Elizabeth Stoddard
Played by: Geraldine Brooks
Date(s):   May 27, 1961

Replaced by: Inger
Played by: Inga Swenson
Date(s):   April 15, 1962

Replaced by: Marie DeMarne
Played by: Felicia Farr
Date(s):   February 10, 1963

Essentially the story of the Cartwright family was about a widower, his three sons, and their struggle with day-to-day life during the mid-1800s and the operation of their ranch, the Ponderosa, in Virginia City, Nevada.

Each of Ben Cartwright's (Lorne Greene) three sons—Adam (Pernell Roberts), Hoss (Dan Blocker) and Little Joe (Michael Landon)—are, according to the storyline, half-brothers. This was the result of their father having been married three times. Each marriage ends with the birth of a son and the tragic death of his wife as depicted in three flashback episodes titled "Elizabeth My Love," "Inger My Love," and "Marie My Love."

Adam's mother was Elizabeth Stoddard, a Bostonian woman and Ben Cartwright's long-time fiancée. Cartwright was the first mate on a ship and had a dream to travel west. After their marriage they settle in New England where Ben starts a ship chandler's business. A year later, Elizabeth gives birth to Adam and dies.

Ben sells his business, heads west and settles in St. Joseph, Missouri. Eight years later he marries a Scandinavian girl, Inger, and continues his westward journey with a wagon train he has organized. While traveling through Nevada, Inger gives birth to Ben's second son, Eric, and names him "Hoss," after her father and brother, Eric Hoss. It was also explained that Hoss was a Norwegian word meaning "big friendly man," and although this is appropriate, it is puzzling how she knew that's how her infant would grow up. Tragically, Inger is killed during an attack by Indians.

Ben abandons his dream of traveling to California and settles in Virginia City, Nevada, where he establishes a huge ranch, the Ponderosa, named after the Ponderosa Pines that were growing on the Comstock Lode timberlands. The actual size of the ranch has been reported as being 100,000 acres, 600,000 acres and 1,000 square miles. To set the record straight, the following dialogue from the first scene of the first episode is offered:

BEN: Look at it Adam. Feast thine eyes on a sight that approaches heaven itself.

ADAM: But you never seen, or been to heaven, paw.

BEN: But heaven is gonna have to go some to beat the thousand square miles of the Ponderosa.

In the final flashback episode of the Cartwright tragic nuptial trilogy, "Marie My Love," Ben must travel to New Orleans' French Quarter to see Marie DeMarne, the widow of a ranch hand who died while saving his life. Naturally, Ben falls in love with Marie and she blesses him with a third son, "Little" Joe. Sadly, but not surprisingly, Marie is thrown by a horse and dies.

Ben was then left on his own to raise his three sons and run the Ponderosa, which he did right through the end of the 1964/1965 season. It was then that Pernell Roberts, who was disgruntled with a role he had grown tired of, left the series. Roberts' role was written out of the series and it wasn't until the beginning of the 1967/1968 season that a replacement, of sorts, was cast. A wanderer, Mr. Canady (Candy for short), was hired as the ranch foreman and, for all intents and purposes, became a member of the Cartwright family.

Actor David Canary, who played Candy, left the series in 1970 and two new characters joined the Cartwrights. Dusty Rhodes, played by Lou Frizzel and Jamie Hunter, played by Mitch Vogel. Frizzel, stayed with the series until 1972, the

Standing among the ponderosa pines on the 1,000 square-mile Ponderosa ranch are (left to right) Little Joe Cartwright (Michael Landon), Eric "Hoss" Cartwright (Dan Blocker), Adam Cartwright (Lorne Greene), and ranch hand Candy (David Canary).

same year Candy returned to the series. Vogel stayed through 1973.

Fifteen years later a syndicated made-for-television movie, *Bonanza: The Next Generation,* aired as a pilot for a new series which didn't feature any of the original cast. It did, however, star some of their offspring.

John Ireland starred as the late Ben Cartwright's seafaring brother. Michael Landon, Jr. played Little Joe's son and Gillian Greene, Lorne Greene's daughter, was introduced as a love interest.

On November 28, 1993, twenty years after *Bonanza* went off the air, and five years after the syndicated TV movie, NBC offered Ponderosa-starved viewers, *Bonanza—The Return,* a two-hour telefilm that took great care to woo Bonanza fans and attract younger viewers.

Their approach began with casting the sons of two of the original cast members for the made-for-television movie. Michael Landon, Jr. played Little Joe's son Benjamin "Benj" Cartwright, a sharp Boston attorney, named after his grandfather. Dan Blocker's son, Dirk, was cast as Walter Finster, a journalist from the east who traveled to Virginia City to do a story on "real" cowboys. Although the second-generation Blocker, albeit smaller and balding, did resemble his dad, the producers opted for Brian Leckner, who looked even more like Blocker than Dirk, to become Hoss's son, Josh.

Continuity with the original series was achieved by casting veteran Western actor Ben Johnson as Bronk Evans, the new head of the Ponderosa through the clever use of a flashback clip from "Top Hand," the January 17, 1971 *Bonanza* episode, which featured Johnson in his third and last guest appearance on the series.

These changes were unavoidable as Lorne Greene, Dan Blocker and Michael Landon had all died. The one original cast member still living was Pernell Roberts, who was written out by having his character Adam Cartwright stuck in Australia recovering from a relapse of malaria, and unable to travel. Enter Australian actor, Alistair MacDougall, as Adam "A.C." Cartwright, Jr.

The new cast was rounded out with Jack Elam as Buckshot, chief cook and bottlewasher for the Cartwright clan, replacing the legendary Hop Sing, Victor Sen Yung. And although Jack Elam only appeared on the original series twice, his continued presence on TV Westerns since 1954, leaves one with the impression that he has always been with the Cartwrights.

The cast also includes Linda Gray as the saloon owner, Richard Roundtree as Jacob, a ranch hand and close friend of the family and Dean Stockwell in the role of the movie's heavy, Augustus Brandenberg.

Set in 1905, the television movie opens with Bronk paying his respects at Ben Cartwright's grave. The stone carried the markings "Born 1815" "Died 1899." The simple plotline has millionaire Augustus Brandenburg out to buy the Ponderosa from the surviving Cartwrights. His plan (which he denies but which everyone knows) is to clear-cut the timber and strip mine the soil. The Cartwrights are naturally opposed to the sale and

exploitation of their land and use every means possible to stop him.

Though very basic, it was strong enough to drive this entertaining telefilm on for two full hours, leaving the door open for further films or even a series revival—which for television viewers would be a real bonanza.

BONINO

September 12, 1953–December 26, 1953.   NBC

Character:	Jerry
Played by:	Chet Allen
Date(s):	September 12, 1953–November 14, 1953

Replaced by:	Jerry
Played by:	Donald Harris
Date(s):	November 21, 1953–December 26, 1953

Babbo Bonino, one of television's first single parents, was faced with the challenge of raising his six children, whom he hardly knows, having spent little time with his family while touring as a concert singer.

Ezio Pinza, the Luciano Pavarotti of the day, starred in the title role in this live situation comedy.

Chet Allen, who briefly played Bonino's twenty-year-old son, Jerry, later played Slats on the NBC adventure series, *Troubleshooters,* which ran from September 11, 1959 to June 17, 1960. He was replaced by Donald Harris.

Another of Bonino's four sons was played by Conrad Janis, who was also in his twenties at the time. Some twenty-five years later and sans much of his hair, he would himself play Frederick McConnell, an adoptive father of sorts to Mork from Ork on the ABC sitcom *Mork & Mindy.*

BOZO

January 23, 1949–present.   Syndicated

Replaced by:	Bozo*
Played by:	Bill Britten
Date(s):	1957–unknown
	(WPIX, New York)

Replaced by:	Bozo*
Played by:	Don Allen
Date(s):	mid 1950s
	(KRON/NBC, San Francisco)

Replaced by:	Bozo*
Played by:	Willard Scott
Date(s):	1958–unknown
	(Washington, D.C.)

---

* NOTE: The actors listed as having played Bozo are not truly replacements for each other, as they each were playing the same character on various television stations, often simultaneously.

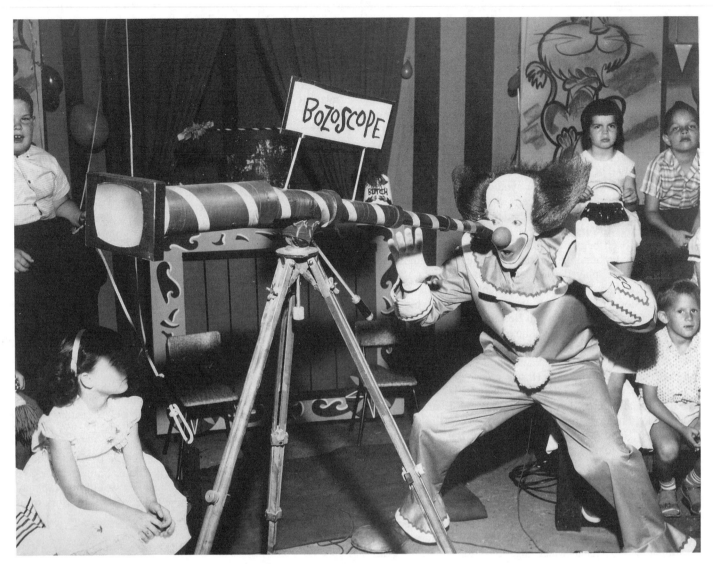

Don Allen (San Francisco) playing Bozo on an early KRON-TV/NBC broadcast in the Bay Area.

Replaced by:	Bozo*
Played by:	Frank Avruch
Date(s):	1958–1970
	(Fall 1966. Syndicated version taped at WHDH, Boston)

Replaced by:	Bozo*
Played by:	Vance Colvig
Date(s):	1959–1966
	(KTLA, Los Angeles)

Replaced by:	Bozo*
Played by:	Johnny Mountain
Date(s):	1960s–unknown

Replaced by:	Bozo*
Played by:	Bob Bell
Date(s):	1961–August 1984
	(WGN, Chicago)

Replaced by:	Bozo*
Played by:	Dick Richards
Date(s):	August 1, 1965–Present
	(WZZM, Grand Rapids, Michigan)

Replaced by:	Bozo*
Played by:	Art Cervi
Date(s):	1966–1976
	(Detroit, Michigan
	CKOW-TV Windsor, Canada)

Larry Harmon, the original Bozo, blows out the candles at a Los Angeles function in front of the Mayor's office to kick off his 1984 bid for the presidency of the United States, using the campaign slogan ''Put the Real Bozo in the White House.'' The campaign, which was launched to help register voters, garnered Harmon hundreds of thousands of write-in votes.

Replaced by:	Bozo*
Played by:	Joey D'Auria
Date(s):	August 1984–present
	(WGN, Chicago)

Bozo the Clown has been entertaining the kid in all of us for more than forty-five years and there's no sign of his letting up.

The original Bozo recording character was created in 1946 by Capitol Records as a storytelling personality, Bozo the Capitol Clown, for a series of 78 rpm record readers. That is, each record came with a storybook that could be followed along by young readers with the help of Bozo the Capitol Clown who would tell them when to turn the page.

The voice of Bozo was provided by Pinto Colvig, who was the first of two actors to supply the voice for Popeye's nemesis, Bluto, as well as for Walt Disney's Goofy.

The one name, however, that is synonymous with Bozo is Larry Harmon. Harmon was an actor whose roles in more than seventy-five motion pictures include the leader of the mounted circus band in ANNIE GET YOUR GUN, 1950; the bugler in THE RED BADGE OF COURAGE, 1951; and the bandleader in the 1951 musical, ROYAL WEDDING. As the drummer on the boat, he performed the dancing drum routine with Fred Astaire.

Larry Harmon's association with Bozo began in 1949 when he beat out more than 200 other hopefuls to become the second voice on the Capitol records and the first to play the clown on television.

''They auditioned just about everyone in Hollywood because

they wanted a younger actor to bridge the gap into the new medium—television."[37] said Larry Harmon. Among those turned down were Hal March, Stan Freberg, and Ray Bolger.

"I created the look and the feeling of the Bozo character for the 1950 television pilot, *Pinky Talks Back,* which was a half-hour live-action film. Pinky, by the way, was an elephant," chuckled Harmon.

"That look," Harmon went on to explain, "included Bozo's costume, makeup, and huge bright orange cantilevered wig made from yak's hair,[38] as well as his walk and now famous laugh."

"Up until that time, Pinto [Colvig] had been doing a voice very similar to the one he later gave to Walt Disney's Goofy. It was very much like Mortimer Snerd's, which was not unlike the original voice Bob Smith had given to Howdy Doody [(See Entry)]."

"Unfortunately the pilot for *The Bozo Show,* which was produced by Elmo Williams and directed by Les Goodwins, never aired because the sponsors and the advertising agencies said 'Film will never work. The show has to be done live!' But how wrong they were."[39] said Harmon.

The Bozo records, which had netted $20 million for Capitol Records, began to lose their popularity because of the advent of television in the mid-1950s. That's when Larry Harmon, the thirty-one-year-old Bozopreneur, changed the direction of his life in the early fifties by purchasing all rights to the Bozo character and officially became *the first* TV Bozo.

Larry Harmon Pictures Corporation produced 156 *Bozo* cartoons featuring the redheaded clown and his little pal Butch and an array of other recurring characters including Elvis the dog, Wacko Wolf, Professor Tweedyfoofer, Sniffer, Slippery Bly, Big Shorty and Short Biggie, all voiced by Harmon! These cartoons, which varied in length from between five to seven minutes, premiered on WPIX, New York in 1957, and were integrated into all of Larry Harmon's licensed *Bozo* programs which were hosted by live actors as the Bozo character. "I created a show where I could go to each station and clone a local actor to be the star of *Bozo's Big Top* and *Bozo's Circus,* which are today known as, *The Bozo Show, Bozo's Circus,* and *Bozo's Big Top.* You might say that I was the first clown who ever cloned another clown, who became a clone while he was clowning around while he was actually being a clone."[40] laughed Harmon in that familiar Bozo laugh.

In 1959 Larry Harmon recruited Pinto's son, Vance Colvig, to play Bozo on KTLA-TV, Los Angeles, a show which ran until 1966. Vance was also the voice of Hanna-Barbera's Chopper the Bulldog in a series of *Yakky Doodle* cartoons produced by Hanna-Barbera between 1961 and 1963.

Over on the east coast, *Bozo the Clown* was airing on WPIX-TV, New York. This incarnation starred Bill Britten, who was formerly Johnny Jellybean on WABC-TV's *Time for Fun.* Meanwhile, *Bozo's Circus* began airing in 1961 on WGN, Chicago and starred forty-three-year-old announcer, Bob Bell as Bozo.

In the fall of 1966, Larry Harmon added 130 half-hour canned programs taped at WHDH in Boston with Frank Avruch in the title role. This was done in addition to the live shows. "I wanted to enhance *Bozodom* by bringing *Bozo* to the stations that couldn't afford to produce live shows of their own—both in this country and around the world,"[41] said Harmon.

The thirty-minute program featured all of the original elements which made Bozo so popular. These included a live studio audience, games, contests, prizes, circus acts, comedy routines and, of course, the *Bozo* cartoons.

One of Harmon's other Bozo "brainy brainstorms" was an educational program titled *Bozo's Place.* "I wanted to do *Bozo's Place* to bring education to young people with warmth and humor. The educational aspects were based on conceptual orientation, with each program addressing a different concept, such as 'high and low' and 'short and tall.' We produced a pilot in 1970 for a number of specific sponsors who not only thought the concept was terrific—and it was—but assured me that they would back an entertainment show with an educational slant. Then, at the last minute, they had a change of heart and we had no choice but to shelve the pilot for another day . . . another year,"[42] said Harmon with great optimism.

Another educational program, *Bozo's Window on the World,* was designed to explore countries of the world through filmed vignettes. Segments shot for the first thirteen half-hour programs included trips to China, Thailand, and the jungles of New Guinea—with real cannibals! "I also (as Bozo) trained with the astronauts in zero-gravity, went through training for the New York fire department and even learned how to milk cobras for their venom which is used in pain killers for cancer patients. Some of the segments did air on one or another of our *Bozo* shows, but the program never materialized as a series as planned.

"I wrote 130 segments for everywhere in the world and someday hope to go back and finish the rest of them."[43] said Harmon.

During its peak in the 1960s, Bozo appeared on all 183 stations broadcasting in the United States. "Anywhere there was a television station and an antenna, there was a live *Bozo* show,"[44] said Harmon proudly. He also managed to *Bozo-ize* sixty other stations in forty-six countries, which brought the total number of *Bozo* programs on the air to 243! "We had live

---

37. Larry Harmon in an exclusive interview with the author on July 10, 1992.
38. Yak's hair was also used by Universal's Jack Pierce to create the original Wolf Man make-up on Lon Chaney, Jr. in the 1941 horror film.
39. Larry Harmon in an exclusive interview with the author on July 10, 1992.
40. *Ibid.*
41. *Ibid.*
42. *Ibid.*
43. *Ibid.*
44. *Ibid.*

Bozo shows on from Bangor, Maine to Bangkok, Thailand,"[45] quipped Harmon.

Then in August 1984, after twenty-three years of doing shtick on WGN's *The Bozo Show* (originally *Bozo's Circus*), sixty-two-year-old Bob Bell passed on his size 83 AAA shoes, rubber nose, white grease paint and yak-hair wig to thirty-one-year-old Joey D'Auria, an experienced stage and television performer who had lived in Los Angeles since 1978.

To celebrate Bozo's thirty-second anniversary on television in 1989, Larry Harmon donated his original Bozo costume to the Smithsonian Institution in Washington, D.C. The blue costume, with red and white trim, is on display in the museum's community life exhibition, right next to Irving Berlin's piano.

One final note of interest is that in October 1989, Larry Harmon trained Bob McCone, the 200th actor to portray "The World's Most Famous Clown," for an all new sixty-minute *Bozo Show,* which aired on WGBS-TV, channel 57, in Philadelphia.

These, of course, are only a few of the Bozos who have graced our TV screens for the last thirty-six years. So to the rest of those wonderful clowns who were not mentioned, I would like to personally extend a warm Bozo *Hoop-Dee-Doo, Dee-Doo-Doo-Doo and Howdy-Do To You!*

BRACKEN'S WORLD

September 19, 1969–December 25, 1970.   NBC

Character:	Sylvia Caldwell
Played by:	Eleanor Parker
Date(s):	September 19, 1969–January 9, 1970

Replaced by:	Ann Frazer
Played by:	Bettye Ackerman
Date(s):	January 16, 1970–December 25, 1970

Character:	John Bracken
Played by:	Warren Stevens
Date(s):	September 19, 1969–March 27, 1970

Replaced by:	John Bracken
Played by:	Leslie Nielsen
Date(s):	September 18, 1970–December 25, 1970

Character:	Sound Mixer
Played by:	Edward G. Robinson, Jr.
Date(s):	September 19, 1969–March 6, 1970

Replaced by:	Sound Mixer
Played by:	Robert Shayne
Date(s):	March 13, 1970–December 25, 1970

John Bracken's glamourous executive secretary, Sylvia Caldwell (Eleanor Parker), the woman behind the scenes of *Bracken's World.*

The real sound stages and back lots of the 20th Century-Fox studios doubled as Century Studios in this drama about the motion picture business and the powerful studio head, John Bracken.

Eleanor Parker, who played John Bracken's executive secretary, quit the show after appearing in only sixteen episodes, because "It was supposed be a repertory show, with just the contracted players appearing every week. But then to bolster it, they used guest stars. That left me answering telephones and scolding 'children.' This was not the concept I had accepted when I signed for it."[46] Ms. Parker was replaced by Bettye Ackerman, who from 1961 to 1968 appeared as Dr. Maggie Graham opposite her husband, Sam Jaffe, who starred as Dr. Zorba on the ABC medical drama, *Ben Casey* (See Entry).

During the planning stages of the series, Spencer Tracy had shown an interest in playing the role of John Bracken, but when it was decided that Bracken would not be seen on camera the part was not shown to Tracy.

When the series first went on the air, the voice of John Bracken was supplied by Warren Stevens, who played Lt. "Doc" Ostrow in the 1956 science fiction film, FORBIDDEN

45. *Ibid.*
46. McClelland, Doug. *Eleanor Parker: Woman of a Thousand Faces,* Scarecrow Press, Metuchen, N.J., 1989, p. 19.

PLANET. At the start of the second season, Warren Stevens was replaced by his FORBIDDEN PLANET co-star, Leslie Nielsen, who played Commander J.J. Adams in the film. Nielsen, who appeared on camera as John Bracken, later went on to star in the comedies, AIRPLANE! and THE NAKED GUN, the latter of which was based on his hilarious but short-lived television series, *Police Squad!*

The part of the studio's sound mixer was first played by Edward G. Robinson, Jr., the son of one of Hollywood's favorite bad guys. The role was later taken over by Robert Shayne, who is best remembered for his role as Clark Kent's best friend, Inspector William J. Henderson, on the *Adventures of Superman* (See Entry).

Following standard casting procedure, Robert Shayne's agent spoke to the people at *Bracken's World* and set up an interview for his client. "He called me and I went over to the Twentieth Century Fox lot to interview for the part. They liked my looks, so they hired me. I didn't know that another actor had played the sound mixer before me, so I just did it the way I thought it should be played. I would never try to imitate another actor."[47]

This was Robert Shayne's last regular role on television for twenty years until he returned as Reggie, Central City's blind newspaper vendor in the CBS adventure series, *The Flash.*

THE BRADY BUNCH

September 26, 1969–August 30, 1974.   ABC

Character:	Marcia Brady
Played by:	Maureen McCormick
Date(s):	September 26, 1969–August 30, 1974

Replaced by:	Marcia Brady
Played by:	Leah Ayres
Date(s):	February 9, 1990–March 9, 1990

Character:	Jan Brady
Played by:	Eve Plumb
Date(s):	September 26, 1969–August 30, 1974

Replaced by:	Jan Brady
Played by:	Geri Reischl
Date(s):	January 23, 1977–May 25, 1977
	(*The Brady Bunch Hour.* ABC)

Character:	Cindy Brady
Played by:	Susan Olsen
Date(s):	September 26, 1969–August 30, 1974

Replaced by:	Cindy Brady
Played by:	Jennifer Runyon
Date(s):	December 18, 1988
	(*A Very Brady Christmas,* TV movie)

"Here's the story of a lovely lady . . ." If you grew up anytime during the late 1960s and early 1970s, you probably not only recognize these words as the lyrics from the opening credits of *The Brady Bunch,* but can most likely sing the rest of the theme from memory.

Chances are that at one time or another you wished that you could either be one of the Brady kids or, at the very least, go over to their house to play. If you were a little older, you may have wished that you could date one of the Bradys. But one thing is certain, we all loved *The Brady Bunch.*

The Brady Bunch was about two single-parent families who became one when this fella Michael Brady (Robert Reed) marries this lovely lady Carol Martin (Florence Henderson). The series, which ran for nearly five years, went into reruns in 1973, spawned an animated series, four reunion shows and a new series, *The Bradys.*

In *The Brady Bunch Hour,* the family moves to a beach house in southern California to star in their own variety series. All of the original cast members were there except Eve Plumb, who relinquished her role as Jan Brady to Geri Reischl, who in 1974 had appeared as Annie in the low-budget horror film, I DISMEMBER MAMA. This, the first of the reunions, ran from February 23 to May 25, 1977 and only racked up nine episodes.

When *The Brady Girls Get Married* in 1981 we were there all three nights for the double wedding on February 6, 13, and 20. The good news for *Brady Bunch* fans was that the entire cast was back intact for the wedding of the two oldest Brady girls, Marcia and Jan.

Two weeks later, the newlyweds turned up with their husbands and an occasional appearance by Florence Henderson, the girls' mom, Carol Brady, and Ann B. Davis, the Brady's loyal housekeeper, Alice Nelson. Maureen McCormick was back as Marcia and Eve Plumb was back as Jan. This installment of seven more episodes ran from March 6 to April 17, 1981.

While the original series was still in production during 1972, the animated series, *The Brady Kids,* also went into production. Filmation did the animation and all six *Brady Bunch* kids provided the voices for their cartoon counterparts. The program ran on Saturday mornings on ABC from September 16, 1972 to August 31, 1974—just one day longer than the evening series.

In 1988, "CBS has announced what we've all been waiting for . . . production has begun on *A Very Brady Christmas,* the Yuletide reunion of *The Brady Bunch.* Everyone will be there with the exception of Susan Olsen who portrayed Cindy on the series. Jennifer Runyon will be taking her place."[48]

Susan Olsen explained that she wasn't able to work on the

---

47. From an exclusive telephone interview with Robert Shayne on January 4, 1991.

48. *TV Pro-Log: Television Programs and Production News.* TI-Volume 41, No. 5. Television Index Information Services, L.I., New York, Jerry Leichter, Editor and Publisher, October 3–9, 1988. p. 3.

The cast of *The Brady Bunch,* the quintessential television family for the seventies, (back row, left to right): Greg Brady (Barry Williams), Mike Brady (Robert Reed); (center row, left to right): Jan Brady (Eve Plumb), Cindy Brady (Susan Olsen), Peter Brady (Christopher Knight); (front row, left to right): Alice Nelson (Ann B. Davis), Carol Brady (Florence Henderson), Bobby Brady (Mike Lookinland), Marcia Brady (Maureen McCormick).

underway to bring back *The Brady Bunch* as a regular series, and a two-hour pilot was in production even as the rebroadcast of the 1988 Christmas special aired on December 22, 1989.

The new problem was that even though Eve Plumb had returned to the role of Jan, and Susan Olsen had returned as her sister, Cindy, the original family would still not be intact, because Maureen McCormick, Marcia Brady, decided to drop out.

Several members of the cast apeared on the ABC morning talk program, *Sally Jessy Raphael,* on Friday, February 23, 1990, to talk about their careers and the new series. When a member of the audience asked why Maureen McCormick did not return, Susan Olsen explained, ''She's on to doing other things. I guess she figured that it's time to move on.'' Florence Henderson interrupted, ''She just had a baby, too.'' Ms. Plumb continued, ''And she just had a baby. And she's working now on . . . I think it's a series, it's a project with Blake Edwards, so I'm really very happy for her.''

The role of Marcia Brady was therefore played by Leah Ayres, who played Valerie Bryson from 1981 to 1983 on the ABC daytime soap opera, *The Edge of Night.* For the balance of 1983, Ms. Ayres played Linda Bowman on the ABC situation comedy, *9 to 5.*

The February 5, 1989 episode of NBC's situation comedy, *Day By Day,* gave us the opportunity to live vicariously with the Bradys though Ross Harper's (Christopher Daniel Barnes) daydream that he is the ''lost'' Brady, Chuck. Six members of the original cast, including Maureen McCormick as Marcia, reprised their roles. Also featured were Florence Henderson and Robert Reed as Carol and Michael Brady, Christopher Knight as Peter, Michael Lookinland as Bobby, and Ann B. Davis as Alice.

Eight weeks before the TV movie *The Bradys* aired, audiences were treated to another guest appearance by Florence Henderson and Robert Reed on ABC's bewitching comedy, *Free Spirit.* They played a couple filing for divorce, but who (not surprisingly) still really loved each other.

The *TV Guide* ad touting the two-hour preview of *The Bradys* said ''America's Favorite Family is all grown up and back on TV!''[50]

The program, which was listed in *TV Guide* as a comedy-drama, was both well written and well-produced and could be more easily compared with *Eight Is Enough* than with the original *Brady Bunch.* The TV movie aired on CBS from 8 to 10 p.m. on Friday, February 9, 1990.

The storyline vacillated between the introduction of new family members and the rehabilitation of Bobby Brady (Mike Lookinland). Bobby, you see, had been paralyzed from the waist down in an automobile accident he suffered while racing in the Nashville 500 at the beginning of the show.

The movie ended with Bobby, still wheelchair bound, marrying his girlfriend, Tracy (Martha Quinn, the MTV VJ). The ceremony was officiated by one of America's most beloved parsons, Dabbs Greer, who, twenty years earlier, had officiated

special because she had her very own Brady wedding to attend and had already made her honeymoon plans. She also hinted that she was approached by the producers, but couldn't come to terms on salary. She had reportedly asked for somewhere between $30 and $50 thousand. ''They looked in the kitty and they said, 'Hey, let's replace somebody. . . .' I had a honeymoon to go on and they had a budget. It's a lot cheaper to replace somebody . . . I wasn't fooled.''[49]

Even without Ms. Olsen the two-hour made-for-television movie swept the ratings and earned the distinction of being the second highest rated movie for the entire 1988/1989 season. Who knows, if Ms. Olsen had been there, it might have hit number one.

With the success of *A Very Brady Christmas,* plans got

49. Taken from an interview with Susan Olsen on *The Howard Stern Show,* WXRK-FM, Infinity Broadcasting, New York.
50. *TV Guide.* Vo. 38, No. 5. February 3, 1990. Issue # 1923. Philadelphia edition.

at the wedding of Mike and Carol Brady, which was shown in a brief flashback. Dabbs Greer had played Reverend Robert Alden on the NBC adventure/drama, *Little House on the Prairie,* which aired from September 11, 1974 to March 21, 1983.

Although Maureen McCormick was the only member of the original cast not to return, the producers in no way reduced her part. In fact, Leah Ayres, Ms. McCormick's replacement, received as much—or more—air time as any of the original Brady girls.

The hour-long weekly series began airing the following Friday, February 16, at 8 p.m. It should be noted that this is the same time slot the original *Brady Bunch* occupied during most of its run on ABC. CBS aired the final episode of this five-part limited series on March 9, 1990. And ''that's the way they all remained the Brady Bunch.''

THE BROTHERS

October 2, 1956–September 7, 1958.   CBS

Character:	Barbara
Played by:	Barbara Billingsley
Date(s):	October 2, 1956–unknown

Replaced by:	Dr. Margaret Kleeb
Played by:	Ann Morriss
Date(s):	1956–September 7, 1958

Character:	Captain Sam Box
Played by:	Frank Orth
Date(s):	1956

Replaced by:	Captain Sam Box
Played by:	Howard McNear
Date(s):	1956–1957

Back in 1956, just before *Leave It to Beaver,* one of America's favorite moms, Barbara Billingsley, played Barbara, the girl-friend of Harvey Box, who was played by Gale Gordon in this series about two brothers who chipped in to buy a San Francisco photography studio.

Ms. Billingsley left the series, undoubtedly thankfully, to play June Cleaver. She was replaced by Ann Morriss, who played Dr. Margaret Kleeb for the remainder of the series.

Captain Sam Box was first played by character actor Frank Orth, who had played Inspector Faraday from 1951 to 1953 on the syndicated detective drama, *Boston Blackie.* Howard McNear, who took over the role from Orth, went on to become everyone's favorite barber, Floyd, on *The Andy Griffith Show* (See Entry) where one of the directors was Bob Sweeney, the actor who played Harvey's brother, Gilmore Box.

BUCK ROGERS IN THE 25TH CENTURY

April 15, 1950–January 30, 1951.   ABC
September 20, 1979–April 16, 1981   NBC

Character:	Captain Buck Rogers
Played by:	Kem Dibbs
Date(s):	April 15, 1950–September 1950

Replaced by:	Buck Rogers
Played by:	Robert Pastene
Date(s):	September 1950–January 30, 1951

Replaced by:	Captain William ''Buck'' Rogers
Played by:	Gil Gerard
Date(s):	September 20, 1979–April 16, 1981

Character:	Lieutenant Wilma Deering
Played by:	Lou Prentis
Date(s):	April 15, 1950–January 30, 1951

Replaced by:	Colonel Wilma Deering
Played by:	Erin Gray
Date(s):	September 20, 1979–April 16, 1981

Character:	Dr. Huer
Played by:	Harry Sothern
Date(s):	April 15, 1950–January 30, 1951

Replaced by:	Dr. Elias Huer
Played by:	Tim O'Connor
Date(s):	September 20, 1979–September 13, 1980

Replaced by:	Dr. Goodfellow
Played by:	Wilfred Hyde-White
Date(s):	January 1981–April 16, 1981

Character:	Twiki
Played by:	Mel Blanc (voice only)
Date(s):	September 20, 1979–April 16, 1981

Replaced by:	Twiki
Played by:	Bob Elyea (voice only)
Date(s):	1981 (temporary replacement)

Replaced by:	Twiki
Played by:	Patti Maloney
Dates(s):	unknown (temporary replacement)

Character: Kane
Played by: Henry Silva
Date(s):   September 20, 1979 (pilot)

Replaced by: Kane
Played by: Michael Ansara
Date(s):   November 29, 1979–April 3, 1980

Character: Tigerman
Played by: Duke Butler
Date(s):   unknown

Replaced by: Tigerman
Played by: H.B. Haggerty
Date(s):   unknown–September 13, 1980

The fantastic science fiction adventures of Buck Rogers were launched in a 1928 edition of *Amazing Stories* magazine and soon followed by a syndicated newspaper comic strip that debuted on January 7, 1929. It wasn't long before this popular strip, written by Philip Nowlan and illustrated by Dick Calkins, was adapted for radio. *Buck Rogers in the 25th Century* aired on CBS from 1932 to 1939 and then moved to the Mutual network where it continued until 1947.

Radio's first Buck Rogers was Curtis Arnall. Over the years he was replaced by three other actors, Matt Crowley, Carl Frank and John Larkin.

There was an attempt to bring these futuristic adventures to television in 1949 with Earl Hammond and Eva Marie Saint as Buck Rogers and Wilma Deering, but the pilot they filmed was never aired.

When Captain Rogers did make the move to live television in 1950, he was played by Kem Dibbs. Six months later, Dibbs was replaced by Robert Pastene, at which time the series was moved to Tuesdays. Just five months later the series was cancelled by ABC.

Two attempts were made to return Buck Rogers and his companions to the small screen. In April 1959 a revised series consisting of thirty-nine episodes was planned, but never produced. NBC commissioned a script and hired a production team in the spring of 1977, but the project was temporarily put on hold.

Then in January 1988, after a couple of false starts, Gil Gerard was asked to play "Captain Rogers" and sent a script to review. "I had the idea that *Buck Rogers* was comic book and I just didn't want to get involved with it. I turned it down without reading it . . . twice." [51]

The script was then sent to Gerard's agent, who read it and passed it on to his client. Gerard liked it and soon afterward began negotiations with the producers. "It's a dynamic script. It has a lot of good stuff in it. The humor of the character appealed

The 1981 cast of *Buck Rogers in the 25th Century* takes a break from saving the universe to pose for this publicity still featuring (clockwise) Erin Gray as Colonel Wilma Deering, Gil Gerard as Captain William "Buck" Rogers, Wilfred Hyde-White as Dr. Goodfellow, and Felix Silla as the robot, Twiki.

to me especially. And he is vulnerable—not afraid to show that he's confused. He's strong, but he can show weakness. He's a human being—not some super-plastic figure without feelings." [52]

The explanation used to get Captain Rogers from 1987 to 2491 was given by William Conrad in the opening narration of each week's episode: "The year is 1987 and NASA launches the last of America's deep space probes. In a freak mishap, Ranger Three and its pilot, Captain William 'Buck' Rogers, are blown out of their trajectory into an orbit which freezes his life support systems and returns Buck Rogers to Earth—500 years in the future."

The set-up used in the live series wasn't nearly as dramatic. While surveying an abandoned mine, Rogers, a young Air Force veteran was rendered unconcious by a mysterious gas.

51. *Starlog* Number 19, O'Quinn Studios, Inc., New York. February 1979.
52. Ibid.

When he awoke, it was the year 2430—400 years in the future. He didn't travel as far into the future as the later Buck Rogers, but then again, the writers weren't paid as much in 1950 either.

In the 1950s series, the beautiful Wilma Deering, a member of the Space General's staff, was played by Lou Prentis. The Wilma Deering of the 1980s, a colonel in charge of the earth's defenses, was played by Erin Gray, who played Kate Summers Stratton on *Silver Spoons,* the NBC situation comedy that ran from September 25, 1982 to September 7, 1986.

The brilliant scientist, Dr. Huer, who was played by Harry Sothern in the early television series, was now being portrayed more elegantly by Tim O'Connor, who had played Elliott Carson on *Peyton Place* from September 15, 1964 to 1968. One of Tim O'Connor's most recent appearances was in "Nobody Expects the Spanish Inquisition," the February 13, 1991 episode of *Doogie Howser, M.D.,* in which he played Doogie's grandfather, Don O'Brien.

September 13, 1981 marked the end of the first season and the first version of the series. When the program returned for its brief second season on January, 13, 1981, several major changes had taken place.

Dr. Huer, the head of earth's Defense Directorate, was gone and in his place were several new characters, the scientist, Dr. Goodfellow being the closest thing to a replacement. Dr. Goodfellow was played by Wilfred Hyde-White, who had just completed his role as Emerson Marshall on the situation comedy, *The Associates,* which ran on ABC from September 23, 1979 to April 17, 1980.

Buck's sidekick was Twiki, a three-foot-tall robot whose voice was provided by the immortal Mel Blanc, except for a short time during 1981 when Blanc was replaced by Bob Elyea. Inside the costume was Felix Silla, the same midget actor who played Cousin Itt on *The Addams Family* (See Entry). One source says that Felix Silla actually provided Twiki's voice for the first two or three episodes of *Buck Rogers in the 25th Century.*

Killer Kane, the evil Princess Ardala's henchman, was played for the first part of 1979 by Henry Silva. Silva had played Maximilian in the 1960 Jerry Lewis comedy, CINDERFELLA, and Chunjim in the 1962 Frank Sinatra war drama, THE MANCHURIAN CANDIDATE. For the remainder of 1979 through 1980, the part of Killer Kane was played by Michael Ansara, who is best known as Cochise, the chief of the Apache Indians, in the Western, *Broken Arrow.* The reason for Silva's departure was, according to industry rumors, a result of an impasse over salary demands.

Michael Ansara, the actor who replaced him, had also heard the same rumors:

"The thing I heard, and this is only hearsay, is that he demanded too much money. He was asking for money up in the stratosphere somewhere. I don't want to say anything negative about him, but I guess as all actors do when they have been in a successful series, they start shooting for the moon. He probably asked for way too much money and they decided to replace him.

"Universal called my agent and asked, 'Would he like to do the part?' [He referring to Ansara.] They sent me a script which I read and said, 'It looks like fun.' I had played Kang, the Klingon, in an episode of *Star Trek*[53] and because Kang and Kane were somewhat similar characters I said, 'Hey, it might be fun,' so I took it—and it was fun. I really enjoyed that series.[54]

The Kang of the eighties had an opportunity to work with the Buck Rogers of the thirties in the 1956 Western, GUN BROTHERS. In that film, Larry "Buster" Crabbe starred as Chad while Michael Ansara co-starred as Shawnee. Speaking about the man who laid the foundation for this updated retelling of the futuristic space adventure, Michael Ansara said, "He looked great and was wonderful to work with, but I don't relate his doing that [*Buck Rogers*] serial with the series we did."[55] Ardala's bodyguard, Tigerman, was played by both Duke Butler and H.B. Haggerty.

BURKE'S LAW

September 20, 1963–January 12, 1966.   ABC
January 7, 1994–   CBS

Character:	Amos Burke
Played by:	Dick Powell
Date(s):	September 26, 1961

Replaced by:	Captain Amos Burke
Played by:	Gene Barry
Date(s):	September 20, 1963–January 12, 1966
	January 7, 1994–

Character:	Detective Tim Tilson
Played by:	Gary Conway
Date(s):	September 20, 1963–August 31, 1965

Character:	Detective Sergeant Les Hart
Played by:	Regis Toomey
Date(s):	August 31, 1965

Replaced by:	Peter Burke
Played by:	Peter Barton
Date(s):	January 7, 1993–

Character:	Sergeant Ames
Played by:	Eileen O'Neill
Date(s):	1964–January 12, 1966

---

53. From an exclusive telephone interview with Michael Ansara on January 15, 1991.
54. *Ibid.*
55. *Ibid.*

Replaced by: Lily Morgan
Played by: Bever-Leigh Danfield
Date(s):   January 7, 1994

Character: Henry
Played by: Leon Lontoc
Date(s):   September 15, 1965–January 12, 1966

Replaced by: Henry
Played by: Danny Kamekona
Date(s):   January 7, 1993–

In 1963 Captain Amos Burke dashed the old adage by proving you could do it on a cop's salary. Well, actually it wasn't his salary that allowed the Los Angeles chief of detectives to live in a mansion located at 109 North Milbourne and be chauffeured to the crime scene in his own RollsRoyce. It was because Amos Burke was a millionaire. He just did police work because, well, it's what he did best.

Captain Burke, who handled homicides out of the L.A.P.D.'s Metropolitan Division, was as handsome, suave, witty, and clever as was say, Bat Masterson. And the reason is elementary—Both Bat Masterson and Amos Burke were played by Gene Barry though television's original Amos Burke was played by Dick Powell.

In "Who Killed Julie Greer?" the first episode of *The Dick Powell Show,* the NBC dramatic anthology series, the actor, director, producer, and founder of Four Star Television, Dick Powell starred as the loaded lawman in what would be the pilot for the Gene Barry series.

Powell began his film career as Harmon in the 1932 film adaptation of the stage play *Blessed Event.* He followed this with a number of other musical roles as crooner before shaking his more boyish image to take on tough guy roles such as tough private dick, Philip Marlowe in the 1944 entry FAREWELL MY LOVELY.

When *Burke's Law* went to series, audiences were already familiar with its star Gene Barry who had played Gene Talbot, the good-looking phys-ed teacher on the 1950s sitcom, *Our Miss Brooks* (See Entry).

Assisting Amos Burke in police procedures were Detective Tim Tilson and Sergeant Les Hart. Tilson was played by Gary Conway who later starred as Captain Steve Burton on the science fiction series, *Land of the Giants,* which aired on ABC from September 22, 1968 to September 6, 1970. Les Hart was played by Regis Toomey who appeared in more than 150 motion pictures. His film roles include Sanders in the 1940 Cary Grant/Rosalind Russell comedy, HIS GIRL FRIDAY, Mr. Miller in the 1947 fantasy, THE BISHOP'S WIFE and John Young in the 1949 science fiction adventure MIGHTY JOE YOUNG. On television he played police contact Lt. McGough in the detective drama *Richard Diamond, Private Detective* (See Entry) and Doctor Barton Stuart on the CBS rural sitcom, *Petticoat Junction* (See Entry).

Beginning in 1964, Eileen O'Neill was added to the cast as policewoman, Sergeant Ames.

Still, with all of this police support, perhaps Amos Burke's strongest relationship was with Henry (Leon Lontoc), who not only served as his houseboy and chauffeur, but as his confidant as well.

When the series was revamped in 1965 to cash in on the James Bond/*The Man from U.N.C.L.E.* craze, the supporting cast was dropped and the series renamed *Amos Burke—Secret Agent.*

Twenty-eight years later, Gene Barry, whose voice was thicker and his now gray hair a little thinner, rolled his limousine onto the prime time schedule with a new limited-run series, again titled *Burke's Law.*

As Leon Lontoc had died on January 22, 1974, Henry was played by Danny Kamekona. The police precinct officer was forensic specialist, Detective Lily Morgan. She was played by Bever-Leigh Danfield who appeared as Christine, a student under Dracula's control in the "Curse of Dracula" segment of the NBC serial *Cliffhangers.*

As for the police detectives, well they were replaced by a handsome young man named Burke, Peter Burke—that's right, Amos' son. He was a brilliant homicide detective who had a Radar O'Reilly quality about him—no matter what requests the senior Burke made, he had already taken care of it.

The junior detective was played by Peter Barton who had made a name for himself on the CBS daytime serial, *The Young and the Restless.*

Whether or not this revival series would catch on with an audience in the 90s was best said in an exchange between Amos and Peter Burke in the series pilot, "Lullaby and Goodnight."

PETER: It's never easy.

AMOS: Burke's Law

C

C.P.O. SHARKEY

December 1, 1976–July 28, 1978.   NBC

Character:	Captain Quinlin
Played by:	Elizabeth Allen
Date(s):	December 1, 1976–August 30, 1977

Replaced by:	Captain "Buck" Buckner
Played by:	Richard X. Slattery
Date(s):	October 21, 1977–July 28, 1978

Actor and comedian Don Rickles played C.P.O. Sharkey, a twenty-four-year Navy veteran in charge of new recruits at the Navy Training Center in San Diego, California.

The original base commander, Captain Quinlin, was played by Elizabeth Allen, a former high fashion model who had played Laura Deane on *Bracken's World.*

This short-lived situation comedy had a sporadic air schedule and was off and on the air a half dozen times before it was finally canceled in 1988.

C.P.O. Sharkey was in one of its hiatuses during the short run of *The Sanford Arms.* When *The Sanford Arms* was canceled on October 14, 1977, after just four episodes, a slightly revamped version of *C.P.O. Sharkey* returned the following Friday.

The change was that Sharkey's female base commander had been replaced by a man, Captain "Buck" Buckner, played by Richard X. Slattery. Slattery had previously played Lieutenant Modeer from 1976 to 1977 on the CBS detective drama, *Switch.*

CACTUS JIM

October 31, 1949–October 26, 1951.   NBC

Character:	Cactus Jim
Played by:	Clarence Hartzell
Date(s):	1949–1951

Replaced by:	Cactus Jim
Played by:	Bill Bailey
Date(s):	1951–October 26, 1951

One of the West's (supposedly) original old timers was Cactus Jim, a grizzly Gabby Hayes type complete with beard, Western vest and chaps with fringes, a neckerchief and beat-up old felt hat. Cactus Jim, originally played by Clarence Hartzell, told his

young audience tales of the Old West and introduced vintage cowboy films that were produced before 1948.

On radio's *Vic and Sade,* Hartzell achieved national recognition as the absent-minded Uncle Fletcher, a role he played for ten years beginning in 1934. Clarence Hartzell left *Cactus Jim* in the summer of 1951 to play the eccentric Uncle Duff on the situation comedy *Those Endearing Young Charms,* which aired on NBC from March 30 to June 17, 1952.

Hartzell was replaced by Bill Bailey who later hosted *The Old American Barn Dance,* which aired on the DuMont network from July 5 to August 9, 1953.

CAGNEY & LACEY

March 25, 1982–August 25, 1988.   CBS

Character:	Detective Christine "Chris" Cagney
Played by:	Meg Foster
Date(s):	March 25, 1982–August 9, 1982

Replaced by:	Detective Christine "Chris" Cagney
Played by:	Sharon Gless
Date(s):	October 25, 1982–August 25, 1988

Character:	Alice Lacey
Played by:	Dana Bardolph
Date(s):	1985–1987

Replaced by:	Alice Lacey
Played by:	Paige Bardolph
Date(s):	1985–1987

Replaced by:	Alice Lacey
Played by:	Michelle Sepe
Date(s):	1987–unknown

Character:	Claudia Petrie
Played by:	Suzanne Stone
Date(s):	March 25, 1982

Replaced by:	Claudia Petrie
Played by:	Jonelle Allen
Date(s):	March 26, 1984

Tyne Daly as Detective Mary Beth Lacey (right) stands behind Meg Foster (left), the second of three actresses to play her partner, Detective Christine ''Chris'' Cagney on the CBS police series, *Cagney & Lacey.*

Character: Detective Marcus Petrie
Played by: Carl Lumbly
Date(s):   March 25, 1982–September 1987

Replaced by: Verna Dee Jordan
Played by: Merry Clayton
Date(s):   September 1987–1988

It began as a television movie, survived three major cast changes, cancellation by the network—twice—and rose to become a critically acclaimed landmark program.

Executive Producer Barney Rosenzweig started it all in 1974 when he commissioned feminist Barbara Corday and her partner, Barbara Avedon, to write a movie script. What Rosenzweig wanted was a female cop show. But, more important, he wanted a show in which the two police women were compadres

similar in nature to the characters of Starsky and Hutch—something that had not been done before.

Rosenzweig pitched the movie around Hollywood, but found no takers. He next approached the networks with the concept as a series, but was turned down twice at every one. Undaunted, he returned to the networks with the project as a television movie, which CBS agreed to produce with the stipulation that they cast Loretta Swit as Chris Cagney opposite Tyne Daly as Detective Mary Beth Lacey.

''They called me up and said, 'What do you think of Loretta Swit as Cagney?' I said, 'Gentlemen, she's perfect. But, you're blowing me out of the water, man—the gal's not available to do a series.' And they said, 'We have a pay-or-play commitment with Loretta Swit. That's who we want. Unless you can come up with a name that's more acceptable to us, that's who you'd better cast.' ''[1]

Rosenzweig wanted Sharon Gless, but was unable to get her because she was under contract to Universal and Loretta Swit got the part.

The movie aired on Thursday, October 8, 1981, and drew a remarkable forty-two share in the ratings, which prompted the executives at CBS to order a series. When Rosenzweig told CBS programming chief Harvey Shephard that he couldn't use Loretta Swit because she was tied up with *M*A*S*H*, Shephard said, ''That's okay—just recast.''[2]

When the casting search began, Rosenzweig recalls being inundated by some of Hollywood's top actresses. The list was finally narrowed down to six or seven. His favorite was Meg Foster, who had played Nora in the NBC series, *Sunshine,* a short-lived situation comedy that aired from March 6 to June 19, 1975. Shephard favored a better-known actress, but when the casting people were brought in, they too liked Ms. Foster and she was hired for the series.

The series, however, did poorly in the ratings and was in danger of being dropped. In an effort to save *Cagney & Lacey,* Harvey Shephard asked Rosenzweig if he would recast Cagney. Shephard's concern was sincere; he believed that the two actresses were too similar. He pointed out that in the pilot with Loretta Swit, at least one was a blonde and the other was a brunette. Rosenzweig defended Ms. Foster and even suggested dying her hair blonde, but the problem was more deep-rooted than that. Both women were too streetwise and Shephard wanted to have more contrast than just physical differences. An unnamed CBS executive was quoted in *TV Guide* as saying that both women were ''too tough, too hard and not feminine.'' He even went so far as to say, ''We perceived them as dykes.''

Sharon Gless, Rosenzweig's first choice, had just completed work as Jane Jeffries on the canceled CBS situation comedy, *House Calls* (See Entry). Rosenzweig knew that Universal had canceled her contract in exchange for replacing Lynn Redgrave in the series and that she was now a free agent.

When Ms. Gless was approached by Rosenzweig, she did not jump at the role because ''She did not want to be known as the

1. Turner, Richard. ''The Curious Case of the Lady Cops and the Shots that Blew Them Away'' *TV Guide,* Vol. 31, No. 41, Issue #1593, October 8, 1983, pp. 52–53.
2. *Ibid.,* p. 53.

actress who went around town replacing other actresses.''[3] Understanding her reservations, Rosenzweig tried to explain to Ms. Gless that she was not replacing another actress, she was finally accepting the role she had been offered two years earlier.

Ms. Gless agreed to do the series after meeting her future co-star, who came to her house bearing a bottle of champagne. When they found that they really liked each other, the deal was clinched and *Cagney & Lacey* resumed production.

Tyne Daly won an Emmy for the 1983, 1984 and 1985 seasons of *Cagney & Lacey* for Outstanding Lead Actress in a Drama Series, beating out her co-star, Sharon Gless, who was nominated in 1983 and 1984. Ms. Gless turned the tables in 1986 by winning the Emmy in the same category.

''The first major cast change in several years in *Cagney & Lacey*, the CBS police series, will take place early in the season when Detective Marcus Petrie (Carl Lumbly) is promoted out of the precinct. Merry Clayton has been added to the cast in the role of Verna Dee Jordan, the replacement for Petrie, which pairs her with the precinct's resident chauvinist, Isbecki (Martin Kove). Sharon Gless replaced Meg Foster as one of the two leads after the first season but the only other previous major change in the original precinct squad (the series is starting its sixth season) was after the death of Sidney Clute (Detective Paul LaGuardia), several seasons back. He was never really replaced by a single individual.''[4]

CAMP RUNAMUCK

September 17, 1965–September 2, 1966.   NBC

Character:	Doc Joslyn
Played by:	Frank DeVol
Date(s):	September 17, 1965

Replaced by:	Doc Joslyn
Played by:	Leonard Stone
Date(s):	September 1965–September 2, 1966

The first episode of this pre-MEATBALLS situation comedy about summer camp featured bandleader/actor Frank DeVol as Doc Joslyn, who gave up his role because of health problems. DeVol may not have appeared on camera for more than one episode, but his theme song, *Camp Runamuck*, was heard weekly. He was also the composer of that classic theme song, *The Brady Bunch*.

The horseshoe-balding actor with the long puss had previously appeared as the building contractor, Myron Bannister, on *I'm Dickens—He's Fenster*. He is also well remembered as the poor man's Doc Severinsen, Happy Kyne, on all 125 episodes of the satirical talk-show spoof, *Fernwood 2–Night*, which ran in syndication from 1977 to 1978.

DeVol was replaced by Leonard Stone, who has similar features but a lot more hair. Stone later played Morton, Patricia

Marshall's (Jean Arthur) rather silent chauffeur on the situation comedy, *The Jean Arthur Show,* which ran on CBS from September 12 to December 5, 1966.

CAPTAIN GALLANT OF THE FOREIGN LEGION

February 13, 1955–September 21, 1963.   NBC-ABC-NBC

Character:	The Colonel
Played by:	Roger Trevielle
Date(s):	February 13, 1955

Replaced by:	The Colonel
Played by:	Daniel Lecourtois
Date(s):	unknown

The title really says it all. Captain Gallant was an officer in the Foreign Legion, headquartered in North Africa. Michael Gallant was played by former Saturday matinee idol Buster Crabbe, who had played Flash Gordon and Buck Rogers. Gallant's young ward, Cuffy, the orphan of a fallen officer, was played by Crabbe's real-life son, Cullen.

It is unclear why the role of the Colonel was played by two actors. It may have something to do with the fact that only the first production season of *Captain Gallant of the Foreign Legion* was filmed in the Sahara Desert, Morocco, Paris and Athens, using real French Foreign Legion officers in supporting roles. When production moved to Libya and Tripoli for the second year of production, some members of the cast and crew may not have been able to follow, or may not have wanted to. It is also possible that Trevielle was actually a member of the Foreign Legion, and remained behind with the other members of his post.

The series was later syndicated under the title, *Foreign Legionnaire.*

CAPTAIN VIDEO AND HIS VIDEO RANGERS

June 27, 1949–August 16, 1957.   DuMont

Character:	Captain Video
Played by:	Richard Coogan
Date(s):	June 27, 1949–December 11, 1950

Replaced by:	Captain Video
Played by:	Al Hodge
Date(s):	December 1950–April 1, 1955

Character:	Dr. Pauli
Played by:	Bram Nossen
Date(s):	June 27, 1949–June 1950

3. Turner, p. 54.
4. *TV Pro-Log: Television Programs and Production News.* TI-Volume 40, No. 2. Television Index Information Services, L.I., New York. Jerry Leichter, Editor and Publisher, September 7, 1987.

Replaced by:	Dr. Pauli
Played by:	Hal Conklin
Date(s):	June 1950–1954

Replaced by:	Dr. Pauli
Played by:	Stephen Elliot
Date(s)	December 16, 1954–March 11, 1955

Character:	Commissioner Bell
Played by:	Jack Orsen
Date(s):	1949–1950

Replaced by:	Commissioner Carey
Played by:	Ben Lackland
Date(s):	1950–1955

Captain James T. Kirk may never have had the chance to command the Starship Enterprise had it not been for his predecessor, Captain Video, who paved the way for future voyages into outer space in the first science fiction space program to air on television.

It was Richard Coogan who piloted the original Galaxy rocket ship for four and later five evenings a week. His schedule was a rather hectic one because after finishing the *Captain Video* broadcast, Coogan dashed from the DuMont Studios, located in Manhattan's Wanamaker's Department Store, to Broadway, where he was starring in *Diamond Lil* with Mae West. Coogan kept up this pace for about a year before leaving *Captain Video* to devote his full energies to the play. It has also been reported that DuMont replaced Coogan because he had asked for a percentage of the merchandising rights for *Captain Video* helmets and games and had been refused.

He was replaced by a thirty-seven-year-old square-jawed actor with sandy hair named Al Hodge. Hodge, who was born in Ravenna, Ohio on April 18, 1913, had previously played the Green Hornet on radio and really had the face and the voice to bring the self-proclaimed "Guardian of the Safety of the Universe" to life. With Hodge at the controls the program gained enormous popularity and continued for nearly five more years, ending in 1955, shortly before the plug was pulled on the DuMont Network.

But not everyone could keep up with Captain Video. Bram Nossen, for instance, who played the evil Dr. Pauli, the President of the Asteroidal Society and a scientific genius in his own right, was suffering from exhaustion and had to leave the show.

When Nossen was replaced by Hal Conklin it was explained in the program that the Captain's arch nemesis had "undergone plastic surgery to hide his identity and trick the Captain."[5]

A third actor, Stephen Elliot, played Dr. Pauli in "The Return of Tobor," which began on December 13, 1954. Stephen Elliot made his first appearance as Dr. Pauli on the December 16, 1954 episode in which he removes his disguise as the dimwitted Sukey and evades capture by Captain Video, escaping in the *Comet* with his accomplice, Forbes.

Starting on January 17, 1955, Stephen Elliot returned in "Dr. Pauli's Planet," a man-made metallic planet built by Dr. Pauli as a base of operations for conquering the universe. This very same synthetic planet idea showed up in the November 8, 1968 episode of *Star Trek,* "For the World Is Hollow and I Have Touched the Sky." An even closer approximation to Dr. Pauli's Planet was the Death Star, a leviathan space station controlled by Grand Moff Tarkin (Peter Cushing) in the 1977 blockbuster, science fiction, STAR WARS.

Dr. Pauli's Planet was last seen in the March 11, 1955 installment of "Dr. Pauli's Planet," appropriately titled "The End of Dr. Pauli's Planet." In the previous installment, wearing space suits, Dr. Pauli and Captain Video, on the hull of the *Comet 2,* were battling when the recoil from Pauli's ray gun sent him hurtling into space. Now, having landed on a desolate piece of space junk, Dr. Pauli vows to get his revenge on the Captain.

It seemed that Richard Coogan left the role of *Captain Video* in time to continue his acting career. He went on to play the starring role of Sheriff Matthew Wayne on the NBC Western, *The Californians.* The series began on September 24, 1957 and Coogan's character was introduced in the middle of the first season. He continued with the series until it ended on August 27, 1959.

Al Hodge wasn't as fortunate and became so identified with his character that he was unable to land regular work in the business. He did play a few bit parts in network dramatic series and hosted several cartoon shows in the New York market.

His last regular appearance was as host of a children's program that featured cartoons and space news. The program, *Space Explorer,* aired on WOR-TV, New York from September 18 to December 29, 1961. Hodge later took odd jobs, including a bank guard and a store clerk.

Sadly, at the age of sixty-six, television's first defender of the universe died of severe emphysema and acute bronchitis on Monday, March 19, 1979, in a nine-dollar-a-day room in Manhattan's George Washington Hotel.

"Official space helmet off, Captain Video, wherever you are."[6]

CAPTAIN Z-RO

1952–1955.   Syndicated

Character:	Jet
Played by:	Bobby Trumbull
Date(s):	1952

Replaced by:	Jet
Played by:	Jeff Silvers
Date(s):	1953

5. Woolery, George W. *Children's Television: The First Thirty-Five Years, 1946–1981. Part II: Live, Film, and Tape Series.* Scarecrow Press, Metuchen, New Jersey, p. 109.
6. Marx, Marvin and Stone, Walter. "TV or Not TV," episode of *The Honeymooners,* October 1, 1955.

Replaced by: Jet
Played by: Bruce Haynes
Date(s):   1954–1955

Society has long been fascinated by the prospect of traveling through time; the topic has been explored in books, motion pictures and on television for decades. There were the 1960 and 1978 science fiction films, THE TIME MACHINE, and the 1979 entry, TIME AFTER TIME—all based on *The Time Machine* by H.G. Wells, published in 1895.

The 1981 comedy, TIME BANDITS, was written by Monty Python graduates Terry Gilliam and Michael Palin. In the 1978 blockbuster, SUPERMAN, the entire population of the planet earth got to go back in time. Two years later Christopher Reeve, as playwright Richard Collier, went back in time in the 1981 romance SOMEWHERE IN TIME. Lest we not forget, there were also the 1985, 1989 and 1990 science fiction films BACK TO THE FUTURE, BACK TO THE FUTURE PART II, and BACK TO THE FUTURE PART III.

On television, Clark Kent, Perry White, Lois Lane, Jimmy Olsen, Professor Tweedle and a crook named Turk Jackson (Jim Hyland) went back to prehistoric times in ''Through the Time Barrier,'' a 1954 episode of the *Adventures of Superman* (See Entry). Captain James T. Kirk and the crew of the Starship Enterprise journeys back in time include ''Tomorrow Is Yesterday'' (January 26, 1967), ''The City on the Edge of Forever'' (April 6, 1967), ''Assignment Earth'' (March 29, 1968), and ''All Our Yesterdays'' (March 14, 1969).

From September 9, 1966, to September 1, 1967, ABC aired the science fiction series, *The Time Tunnel*. *The Time Tunnel,* however, wasn't television's first series about traveling through time; *Captain Z-Ro* was. The closest parallel to the 1955 educational science fiction adventure, *Captain Z-Ro,* may be NBC's dramatic science fiction series, *Quantum Leap,* which premiered on NBC on March 31, 1989.

Scott Bakula plays Sam Beckett, a young scientist who is not only trapped in time (thirty years within his own lifetime), but enters the bodies of people living in the last three decades in order to help them and the people around them. Interestingly, one of the episodes of *Quantum Leap* placed Sam Beckett in the body of a 1950s television actor playing the title role in ''Future Boy: October 6, 1957.'' The episode, which aired on March 13, 1991, starred Richard Herd as Moe/Captain Galaxy, a Captain Video-type television actor who built what he believed to be a working time machine in his own basement.

In the 1950s series, Captain Z-Ro (Roy Steffens) invented a machine with a Lectric Chamber that he used to send himself to a precise year, day, hour and location in order to help resolve some historical struggle that would later make the person famous. It's almost like the *Rocky and his Friends* segment, ''Peabody's Improbable History,'' but without the humor.

The historical events depicted in the episodes of *Captain Z-Ro* were well researched and based on fact, and the trips into the future were based on scientific projections. The Captain's adventures in the past include saving the life of a pony express rider and preventing the Express relay station at Fort Bridger, Wyoming from being burned; assisting Napoleon with the discovery of the Rosetta Stone; thwarting an attempt by the Sheriff of Nottingham to capture Robin Hood; and aiding Molly ''Pitcher'' Hayes during the Battle of Monmouth in 1778.

Captain Z-Ro's young assistant, Jet, originally played by Bobby Trumbull, was replaced twice. First in 1952 by Jeff Silvers. From 1954 to 1955 it was Bruce Haynes who took control of the Spector Wave Length.

CASABLANCA

September 27, 1955–April 24, 1956.   ABC
April 10, 1983–September 3, 1983   NBC

Character: Rick Jason
Played by: Charles McGraw
Date(s):   September 27, 1955–April 24, 1956

Replaced by: Rick Blaine
Played by: David Soul
Date(s):   April 10, 1983–September 3, 1983

Character: Capt. Renaud
Played by: Marcel Dalio
Date(s):   September 27, 1955–April 24, 1956

Replaced by: Capt. Louis Renault
Played by: Hector Elizondo
Date(s):   April 10, 1983–September 3, 1983

Character: Ferrari
Played by: Dan Seymour
Date(s):   September 27, 1955–April 24, 1956

Replaced by: Ferrari
Played by: Reuven Bar-Yotam
Date(s):   April 10, 1983–September 3, 1983

Character: Sasha
Played by: Michael Fox
Date(s):   September 27, 1955–April 24, 1956

Replaced by: Sacha
Played by: Ray Liotta
Date(s):   April 10, 1983–September 3, 1983

Character: Sam
Played by: Clarence Muse
Date(s):   September 27, 1955–April 24, 1956

Replaced by: Sam
Played by: Scatman Crothers
Date(s):   April 10, 1983–September 3, 1983

Sometimes a hit motion picture just doesn't translate well to television, as was proven by two ill-fated attempts to bring the

1942 Humphrey Bogart/Ingrid Bergman classic, CASA-BLANCA, to the small screen. Warner Bros. produced what was essentially a series of pilots for three programs, which aired on a rotating basis under the banner of *Warner Brothers Presents.* This concept was much like the later NBC *Wednesday Mystery Movie,* that featured *Madigan, Cool Million* and *Banacek.*

The three programs being tested by Warner Brothers were *Kings Row, Cheyenne* and *Casablanca.* The first incarnation of the Bogart film ran for a total of ten episodes, the last for only six. Since the series was based on the film, the premise and the characters were pretty much the same except for the inexplicable changes in spellings and the completely different last name of Rick, the owner of Rick's Cafe Americain in the first version.

Two actors from the film appeared in the 1955–1956 series, though not in the same roles as in the motion picture. Marcel Dalio, who was the croupier Emil in the film, instead played Captain Renaud in the series. Dan Seymour, who played Abdul in the motion picture was very well cast as Ferrari, the role which will forever be associated with Sydney Greenstreet. Usually seen in films and on television playing heavies, Dan Seymour may be remembered as Rocko in the 1951 season episode of the *Adventures of Superman,* "The Runaway Robot."

By the time the series was revived, twenty-seven years later, the spellings of the characters' names had been restored to match those used in the film and Rick's last name once again became Blaine. Even the sets had been reconstructed from the blueprints used for the film.

This time around, David Soul, who had gained fame as "Hutch" in the ABC police drama, *Starsky and Hutch,* took over the Bogart role, but not before having second thoughts.

"David Soul, who has Bogey's role in the long-postponed Warner Bros. TV series *Casablanca,* wanted to get out so he could star in *Scarecrow and Mrs. King,* a CBS pilot with Kate Jackson. But Warners wouldn't let him go, so Kate found another leading man: Bruce Boxleitner (*Bring 'Em Back Alive*). Here's not looking at you, David."[7]

Sam was played by Scatman Crothers. Crothers began his career in the 1920s as a jazz musician and singer, but didn't achieve national recognition until nearly fifty years later when he played the garbage man, Louie, on *Chico and the Man.* Following *Chico,* which ran from September 13, 1974, to July 21, 1978, Crothers turned in an outstanding performance as Halloran, the cook, in the 1980 horror film, THE SHINING.

CHARLES IN CHARGE

October 3, 1984–July 24, 1985.   CBS
January 1987–November 1990   Syndicated

Character:	Stan Pembroke
Played by:	James Widdoes
Date(s):	October 3, 1984–July 24, 1985

Replaced by:	Walter Powell
Played by:	James Callahan
Date(s):	January 1987–November 1990

Character:	Jill Pembroke
Played by:	Julie Cobb
Date(s):	October 3, 1984–July 24, 1985

Replaced by:	Ellen Powell
Played by:	Sandra Kerns
Date(s):	January 1987–November 1990

Character:	Lila Pembroke
Played by:	April Lerman
Date(s):	October 3, 1984–July 24, 1985

Replaced by:	Jamie Powell
Played by:	Nicole Eggert
Date(s):	January 1987–November 1990

Character:	Douglas Pembroke
Played by:	Jonathan Ward
Date(s):	October 3, 1984–July 24, 1985

Replaced by:	Sarah Powell
Played by:	Josie Davis
Date(s):	January 1987–November 1990

Character:	Jason Pembroke
Played by:	Michael Pearlman
Date(s):	October 3, 1984–July 24, 1985

Replaced by:	Adam Powell
Played by:	Alexander Polinsky
Date(s):	January 1987–November 1990

Character:	Gwendolyn Pierce
Played by:	Jennifer Runyon
Date(s):	October 3, 1984–July 24, 1985

Replaced by:	Lillian
Played by:	Ellen Travolta
Date(s):	January 1987–November 1990

The business of television has changed greatly since the early days, when viewers were offered a few programs on a few channels for a few hours a day. Today, with twenty-four-hour-a-day broadcasting on VHF, UHF and cable, the television audience has been given an almost inexhaustible menu of programs to choose from. Moreover, the three major networks, ABC, CBS and NBC no longer hold an exclusive on original

7. *TV Guide.* "Insider," Vol. 31, No. 16, April 16, 1983, Issue #1568, p. 25.

programming. Today, Fox Broadcasting has created a strong presence as a fourth network offering viewers original programming.

With the growth of production companies, many high-quality programs, produced exclusively for cable and syndication, never air on the networks, such as the Family Channel's *Zorro* (See Entry).

The first-run syndication market sometimes offers marginally successful series a chance at a second life, which is what happened with *Too Close for Comfort* (See Entry). In that series Ted Knight played a cartoonist, Henry Rush, who has two very attractive daughters, in their twenties, living in the downstairs apartment of his San Francisco duplex. Although the series was canceled by ABC, it was brought back the following season by Metromedia Producers Corporation, which aired the show in syndication on sixty-eight stations.

This shows that cancellation by a network no longer means the death of series. *Charles in Charge* is just one more example of a canceled series finding life, and an audience, after cancellation. The quality of the production was maintained and the series fared quite well on its own.

Charles, a young man played by Scott Baio, took a job as a domestic to help put himself through Copeland College. The couple who employed him, Jill and Stan Pembroke, gave Charles room and board and a pittance in exchange for his services.

The series rose from the network grave in January of 1987, with a new lease on life and practically a completely new cast.

In the revised storyline, Charles and Buddy return from a two-week vacation to the Pembroke House. Charles learns that the Pembrokes have moved to Seattle and sublet their house to the Powell family. Since Ellen's (Sandra Kerns) husband is a Naval commander stationed in the South Seas, Charles gets the job as their live-in helper. This made the Powells Charles' new employers. Charles' pal, Buddy, stuck by his best friend; the rest of the cast was changed.

Some cast members of note include Sandra Kerns who had played Beth MacDonald on the NBC drama, *Flamingo Road*, which aired from January 6, 1981 to July 13, 1982; Jonathan Ward went on to play Kevin Kennedy in the ABC police series, *Heart of the City,* which aired from September 20, 1986 to July 2, 1987; and Nicole Eggert replaced Erika Eleniak on *Baywatch* (See Entry).

The most notable member of the updated cast was Ellen Travolta, who played Charles' mother, Lillian. The older sister of former superstar, John Travolta, she made two appearances during 1977 and one during 1978 as Arnold Horshack's mother on the ABC situation comedy, *Welcome Back Kotter.* She also played a waitress in John's 1978 hit motion picture, GREASE.

CHARLIE WILD, PRIVATE DETECTIVE

December 21, 1950–June 19, 1952.   CBS-ABC-DuMont

Character:	Charlie Wild
Played by:	Kevin O'Morrison
Date(s):	1950–May 1951

Replaced by:	Charlie Wild
Played by:	John McQuade
Date(s):	May 1951–June 19, 1952

Transplanted from the CBS radio program, *Charlie Wild, Private Detective* was another of New York city's tough private eyes, closely following the format established by Ralph Bellamy in *Man Against Crime* (See Entry).

Criminals originally slugged it out with Kevin O'Morrison and later with John McQuade as Charlie Wild.

Wild's loyal secretary, Effie Perrine, was played by Cloris Leachman, who was the second mom on *Lassie* (See Entry), while future kiddie-show icon, Sandy Becker, did the announcing.

CHARLIE'S ANGELS

September 22, 1976–August 19, 1981.   ABC

Character:	Jill Munroe
Played by:	Farrah Fawcett-Majors
Date(s):	September 22, 1976–May 4, 1977
	September 20, 1978
	November 15, 1978
	February 14, 1979
	October 24, 1979
	November 14, 1979
	February 27, 1980

Replaced by:	Kris Munroe
Played by:	Cheryl Ladd
Date(s):	September 14, 1977–February 28, 1981

Character:	Sabrina Duncan
Played by:	Kate Jackson
Date(s):	September 22, 1976–May 16, 1979

Replaced by:	Tiffany Wells
Played by:	Shelley Hack
Date(s):	September 12, 1979–May 7, 1980

Replaced by:	Julie Rogers
Played by:	Tanya Roberts
Date(s):	November 30, 1980–August 19, 1981

To help avoid confusion, let's begin by noting the three original *Angels.* Sabrina Duncan, played by Kate Jackson, was the composed leader and the brains of the team and had the short dark brown hair. The athlete of the group was Jill Munroe, played by Farrah Fawcett-Majors. She was the blonde with the huge smile and the original "Farrah" hair cut. Kelly Garrett, played by Jaclyn Smith, had fluffy brown hair.

These three detectives, all former cops with police training, now worked for the Townsend Investigations Agency headed by Charlie Townsend. Townsend, whom viewers never saw, was voiced by John Forsythe. The male lead we did see was the Angels' contact man, John Bosley, played by David Doyle.

It has been rumored that the producers originally wanted

Heaven sent, were *Charlie's Angels* (clockwise from top left) Kelly Garrett (Jaclyn Smith), Jill Munroe (Farrah Fawcett-Majors) and Sabrina Duncan (Kate Jackson).

Charlie's kimono-clad angels are (clockwise from top) Kelly Garrett (Jaclyn Smith) Kris Munroe (Cheryl Ladd) and Tiffany Wells (Shelley Hack).

Tom Bosley (Howard Cunningham of *Happy Days*) for the role, but were unable to secure him. So, they hired an actor who bore a striking resemblance to Bosley, and then named their character after him as a sort of inside joke. The joke, however, didn't go unnoticed. On the original *Saturday Night Live,* Bill Murray threatened John Belushi, who was playing the Doyle role in an *Angels* skit, that if he gave the producers any trouble he would be replaced by Tom Bosley.

As it turned out, David Doyle was one of only two members of the on-camera cast who did remain with the series through its entire run. Jaclyn Smith was the other.

The series was an instant hit and even though Kate Jackson had been hired as the program's lead, Farrah Fawcett-Majors became the star, initiating what *TV Guide* called ''The Farrah Phenomenon.'' The series also created what has since been referred to as ''Jiggle TV.''

As is so often the result in such cases, Ms. Fawcett-Majors, who was the last *Angel* to be cast, was the first to leave. Her game plan was to capitalize on her newly-found fame to develop a career in the movies. Before production for the second season began, Ms. Fawcett-Majors summarily announced that she would not return for the second season.

This created animosity between her and the other members of the cast and spawned a lawsuit with the production company. She settled out of court by agreeing to appear on *Charlie's Angels* as a guest star in three episodes a season for the remainder of her original three-year contract.

It was explained in the series that Jill had left for Europe to pursue her racing career.

The producers of *Charlie's Angels,* Aaron Spelling and Leonard Goldberg, wanted Cheryl Ladd as Farrah's replacement, largely because they had worked with her in the made-for-television movie, *Satan's School for Girls.* In that film, Ms. Ladd (still using her real last name, Stoppelmoor) played Jody Keller. The ninety-minute TV movie, which aired on ABC on September 19, 1973, also starred future *Angel* Kate Jackson as Roberta Lockhart.

Strange as it may seem, Ms. Ladd didn't want the role, which made Spelling and Goldberg want her that much more. She was finally signed for the series without having to go through the formality of a screen test. When the second season began, Cheryl Ladd was introduced as Kris Munroe, Jill's younger sister who had also come from a police background.

Charlie's Angels was a major disappointment, both person-

Tanya Roberts (left) replaced Shelley Hack as Charlie's newest ''Angel'', Julie Rogers and went on to star as Sheena in the 1984 motion picture of the same name. Pictured with Ms. Hack are Cheryl Ladd (right) as Kris Munroe and Jaclyn Smith (center) as Kelly Garrett, the only ''Angel'' to endure the entire run of the series.

ally and professionally, to the series' star, Kate Jackson. Almost from the beginning, Ms. Jackson had asked for better scripts, but they never materialized. Then, in 1979, she lost the role of Joanna Kramer in KRAMER VS. KRAMER, to Meryl Streep because the producers of *Charlie's Angels* would not allow her to work on the picture. This, coupled with being overshadowed by Farrah's huge success, contributed to her decision to leave the series after fulfilling her three-year contract. She was written out as having a desire to get married and raise a family.

Charlie's newest *Angel* was the ''Charlie Girl,'' Shelley Hack, the television spokesperson for Revlon's perfume, ''Charlie.'' It was publicized that Ms. Hack was selected from more than 150 *Angel* hopefuls who auditioned for the role.

Shelley Hack played Tiffany Wells, the daughter of a friend of the Boston chief of police. But the new *Angel* didn't prove to be very popular, and was written out of the series as having returned to New York to pursue a career in modeling.

The fifth and final season began on November 30, 1980 with a three-hour two-part episode called ''Angel in Hiding'' (also known as ''Street Models'' and ''Hawaiian Angels''), introducing Tanya Roberts as Julie Rogers, the sixth and last of *Charlie's Angels*. Ms. Rogers, a former L.A.P.D. cop, joined the Townsend Agency after the death of her partner, Harry Stearns (Vic Morrow). The concluding episode aired on November 23, 1980.

Tanya Roberts later played the title character in the lavishly produced 1984 adventure film, SHEENA.

THE CHARMINGS

March 20, 1987–February 11, 1988.   ABC

Character:	Snow White Charming
Played by:	Caitlin O'Heaney
Date(s):	March 20, 1987–April 1987
Replaced by:	Snow White Charming
Played by:	Carol Huston
Date(s):	August 1987–February 11, 1988

The Charmings, a spoof of the classic fairy tale by the Brothers Grimm, is set in Van Oaks, California in the present—the result of a spell cast by Queen Lillian White (Judy Parfitt) that put just about everybody from the fairy tale, except the dwarfs, into a sleep that lasted until 1987.

It began as a test series during the spring of 1987 with Caitlin O'Heaney as Snow White Charming, Christopher Rich as Prince Eric Charming, and a particularly nasty Paul Winfield as The Mirror.

Caitlin O'Heaney had previously played another Ms. White, Sarah Stickney White, on the ABC adventure series, *Tales of the Gold Monkey,* from 1982 to 1983.

A slightly revamped version of the show returned in August with a change in cast. ''Carol Huston has replaced Caitlin O'Heaney in the role of Snow Charming (the latter-day Snow White) in ABC's *The Charmings* in the fall episodes. The series had a spring tryout with six episodes.''[8]

CHEERS

September 30, 1982–May 20, 1993.   NBC

Character:	Diane Chambers
Played by:	Shelley Long
Date(s):	September 30, 1982–September 17, 1987
	May 20, 1993
Replaced by:	Rebecca Howe
Played by:	Kirstie Alley
Date(s):	September 24, 1987–May 20, 1993
Character:	Ernie ''Coach'' Pantusso
Played by:	Nicholas Colasanto
Date(s):	September 30, 1982–May 9, 1985
Replaced by:	Woodrow ''Woody'' Tiberius Boyd
Played by:	Woody Harrelson
Date(s):	September 26, 1985–May 20, 1993

The setting—unusual in an anti-drug and alcohol abuse-aware America—was a Boston bar known as Cheers. The establishment is run by handsome ex-Boston Red Sox pitcher, Sam Malone (Ted Danson). Working behind the bar with him is former coach Ernie Pantusso—''Coach'' to everyone—while their abrasive waitress, Carla Tortelli (Rhea Perlman) waits on the customers who aren't seated around the bar. The two most visible stool sitters are Norm Peterson (George Wendt), an overweight and often out-of-work accountant, and his best friend, Cliff ''Cliffy'' Clavin (John Ratzenberger), a dedicated postal worker and pseudo-intellectual with a penchant for sharing bits of trivia that no one cares about.

Without a question, the second most important character of the series was the bar's second waitress, Diane Chambers (Shelley Long), a true intellectual. She was prim and proper and spoke English that seemed stilted in its preciseness. Though her bent toward the arts and her goal to become an author gave her a snooty air, she was also neurotic, compulsive, and even a little ditsy, which made her hard to take seriously.

The producers auditioned more than one thousand actors to fill the four main roles, Sam Malone, Diane Chambers, Coach Ernie Pantusso and Carla Tortelli. This was because they didn't want to use established ''stars''; they preferred relative unknowns who they hoped would become stars as a result of the series. ''You can't compensate for wrong casting with writing.

8. *TV Pro-Log: Television Programs and Production News.* TI-Volume 39, No. 47. Television Index Information Services, L.I., New York. Jerry Leichter, Editor and Publisher, July 20, 1987.

The people responsible for making it possible to go to a place where everybody knows your name are: *Cheers* owner, Sam Malone (Ted Danson, top) and (left to right), bartender Ernie "Coach" Pantusso (Nicholas Colasanto) and waitresses Carla Tortelli LeBec (Rhea Perlman) and Diane Chambers (Shelley Long).

It's a killer to try. That's why we spent so much time on casting,"[9] said Les Charles, the co-producer of *Cheers*.

Somewhere between fifty and seventy-five actors were auditioned for the role of Coach, who was supposed to be a combination of Yogi Berra, Sparky Anderson and Casey Stengel. Among those tested for the part was Sid Caesar, but "Nick was our first choice from the very first time we saw him."[10]

Anyone who has ever seen *Cheers* would agree that Nicholas Colasanto was the perfect choice for the role of Coach, but it was only by a fluke that he even auditioned for the part. Colasanto began his career as an actor on Broadway, appearing with long-time friend Ben Gazzara, but had turned to directing when he joined Gazzara in California and had virtually given up acting. Colasanto's directing credits include episodes of *Columbo, Hec Ramsey, Here Come the Brides, Logan's Run,* *Bonanza* and *The Streets of San Francisco*. It was only at his agent's suggestion that he read for the part of Coach. "I read for them and connected."[11]

At the end of the third season, Colasanto, who had a history of heart trouble, had to be written out of five episodes because he had been hospitalized for two weeks and was home recovering. Viewers were told that "Coach" was on vacation, which explained his absence simply enough, but he never returned to the series.

The cast and crew were stunned to learn that Nicholas Colasanto passed away in his home on the morning of Tuesday, February 12, 1985, because he had stopped by the studio the previous week to announce his return.

Tuesday just happened to be the day *Cheers* was filmed and as a result of the sad news, that evening's filming was canceled. Two days later, NBC aired a special episode of *Cheers* in his memory. The episode selected was "Coach's Daughter."

The program opened with a photograph of Nicholas Colasanto. Ted Danson recorded the voice-over: "This encore presentation of *Cheers* is dedicated with love and appreciation to the memory of Nick Colasanto."

"Cheerio, Cheers," the last episode in which Colasanto appeared as Coach, aired on April 11, 1985. The story has Diane going to Bologna, Italy with Frasier Crane (Kelsey Grammer) and leaving Cheers, presumably for good. In a tearful scene, which is now particularly poignant due to Colasanto's passing, Diane and Coach say their final good-byes as they hug each other tightly.

DIANE: Oh, Coach, I'm going to miss you.

COACH: Oh, I'm going to miss you too, honey.

It is an undisputed fact that one of the most difficult tasks in series television is having to replace an established and loved character like Coach.

The producers decided that they would not recast the role of Coach with another actor. Instead, they wanted to go with a new character, but one who maintained the same childlike innocence and honesty that had endeared the character of Coach to the cast, the crew and, most importantly, the audience.

As a result, the Woody character developed into what some have referred to as a younger version of Coach. This was perfect because that is what replacement characters should be—helping a series continue smoothly without interfering too much with the balance between the established characters. It can, however, be a difficult adjustment for the new cast member.

The first episode of the fourth season was titled "Birth, Death, Love and Rice." It aired on September 26, 1985 and introduced the character of Woody Boyd and addressed the issue of Colasanto's (Coach) death through Woody's initial dialog with Sam Malone.

WOODY: Excuse me, I'm Woody Boyd.

9. Andrews, Bart. *Cheers, The Official Scrapbook.* New American Library, New York, 1987, p. 13.
10. *Ibid.* p. 77.
11. *Ibid.* p. 79.

SAM: Woody, hi, I'm Sam Malone.

WOODY: Howdy. I'm a friend of Coach's. Is he still
            around?

SAM: I'm sorry, Woody, I guess you hadn't heard.
            No. Uh, Coach passed away a couple of
            months ago. But yeah, I'd like to believe he's
            still around.

It is further explained that Woody, a farm boy from Indiana,
had become pen pals with Coach as a result of writing letters for
a bartending job in "the big city." Their friendship began
because Coach was the only one to write back!

Speaking about Woody's character, Ted Danson said, "One
day it just dawned on me that it was like having Coach's son on
the set. Woody just kind of fell into it."[12]

"I'm certainly not trying to do Nicholas Colasanto's character.
I know that a lot of lines written for me are 'Coach' lines, but I
don't know how Coach would have done them."[13] This was
because Harrelson had previously worked in the theater at night
and had never had an opportunity to catch *Cheers* on television.

Woody Harrelson related a story about a girl who managed to
sum up the entire problem of replacing an established character
in a hit series with a back-handed compliment: "I dearly loved
Coach. I never thought he could be replaced in any way, and I
was ready to resent anybody who tried. But 'you,' you're just
strange enough to bring it off."[14]

The audience accepted Woody as Coach's replacement
partly because he exhibited some of Coach's qualities. Woody
also shared something with another popular television character. His middle name is Tiberius, which is what the "T" stands
for in Captain James T. Kirk of *Star Trek*.

With acceptance of Woody, the series continued to gain
popularity and the cast of *Cheers* remained stable for nearly two
years. That's when the announcement was made that one of the
show's co-stars, Shelley Long, had decided to leave the series at
the end of the 1986/1987 season.

"When Shelley came in to read for the part of Diane, Glen
Charles noticed immediately that she didn't have to 'reach' as
other actresses did."[15] "She tested with many different actors,
while Ted Danson tested with different actresses. The day Ted
and Shelley tested together, something magical happened, and
the producers knew they had their Sam and Diane."[16]

The first episode of the series begins with the entrance of Dr.
Sumner Sloane, played by Michael McGuire. Sumner Sloane is
introduced as the professor of world literature at Boston University. He is both Diane Chambers' teacher and her fiancé. Sloane
and Diane stop off at Cheers before heading to the airport to catch
their flight to Barbados, where they are to be married. Sumner
leaves Diane at the pub while he dashes off to retrieve his
grandmother's antique gold wedding ring from his ex-wife.

He returns an hour later, without the ring, at which time he
receives a phone call from his ex-wife. Sumner tells Diane that
he loves her and dashes off a second time to fetch the ring, but
this time he doesn't return. Sam offers Diane a job as a waitress
and the series is under way.

At the end of the fifth season the producers were faced with
an even more difficult casting job than finding a Diane for their
Sam. Now they had to find a replacement for their Diane.

But before Diane's replacement was cast, the producers had
an opportunity to produce one last episode with Shelley Long
that would tie up all of the loose ends between Sam and Diane.

Michael McGuire, who played Dr. Sumner Sloane in the
opening episode, returns to Cheers to tell Diane that he had
submitted her unfinished novel to an editor at Houghton Mifflin
who loved it. The catch was that the novel wasn't completed
and Diane had not written in five years.

Back at Diane's house, Diane tells Sam about the novel and
he is more than willing to postpone their wedding so that she
can finish her manuscript. Sam sits down for a moment while
Diane leaves to get some tea. When Diane returns she is an old
woman. Sam is, of course, day-dreaming about what his life
would be like if he and Diane had married. The daydream
demonstrates that he would have a wonderful life with Diane,
and when he awakens he agrees to marry her.

The ceremony is held at Cheers (where else?) and just as it is
about to conclude, Woody takes a phone call from the editor at
Houghton Mifflin who says that he is going to publish Diane's
book. Sam calls off the wedding to give Diane the opportunity
to finish her novel, which she says will only take her six
months. Diane tells Sam that she *will* return and will see him in
six months. They give each other a friendly kiss and Diane
leaves. Sam stares for a moment at the closed door and says,
"Have a good life."

The episode concludes with another of Sam's daydreams. He
and Diane are both old and gray and are slowly and silently
dancing cheek-to-cheek to a piano rendition of Irving Berlin's
What'll I Do? The scene then fades to black.

James Burrows, the executive producer and director of
Cheers, had made it clear that they were not going to look for
another Diane, but were looking instead for a stronger actress to
play Sam's boss. In the revised storyline, Sam sells Cheers to a
large corporation which places Rebecca Howe (Kirstie Alley)
in charge of the bar.

Meanwhile, Sam is supposed to be off sailing around the
world, as we learn from Woody, who tells Carla's (Rhea
Perlman) old boyfriend, Eddie Le Bec (Jay Thomas) when he
comes into Cheers looking for Sam in the sixth season opener.

EDDIE: Sam around?

12. *Ibid.* p. 121.
13. *Ibid.* p. 122.
14. *Ibid.* p. 124.
15. *Ibid.* p. 35.
16. *Ibid.* p. 39.

WOODY: Oh, didn't you hear? Sam sold the bar to some big corporation, bought a boat—he's sailing around the world with it.

Sam returns to Cheers for a job because his boat had sunk somewhere in the Caribbean. He is broke and doesn't have enough money to buy back Cheers. He even jokes that he doesn't have enough money to buy an ice cube.

He approaches Rebecca Howe and tries to charm her, but gets more than a cold shoulder. She tells him, "You know, Mr. Malone, we've known each other only seconds and I'm already tired of you."

Like the other members of the cast, Kirstie Alley was also virtually unknown to television audiences when she made her first appearance on *Cheers*. Ms. Alley's previous television roles were Casey Collins in the series *Masquerade,* which aired on ABC from December 15, 1983 to April 27, 1984, and Virgilia Hazard in the 1985 miniseries, *North and South.* In 1982 she donned a pair of pointed ears to play Lieutenant Saavik, the half-Vulcan aboard the U.S.S. Enterprise in Paramount Pictures science fiction film, STAR TREK II: THE WRATH OF KAHN. When STAR TREK III: THE SEARCH FOR SPOCK was released two years later, Ms. Alley had been replaced by Robin Curtis.

In a 1987 *TV Guide* interview, Kirstie Alley admitted the difficulty of replacing an established character, saying, "I am stepping into big shoes. I'm an alien and they will just have to learn to accept me." In that same article, Ted Danson said that "She is stepping into a meat grinder . . . Shelley was a little bit bigger than life. Kirstie comes across as more vulnerable. And more relaxed. There was nothing relaxed about Shelley."

An unnamed member of the *Cheers* staff expanded on Danson's comments: "I wouldn't want to walk in here and try to take over for Shelley Long. You can tell it's taking its toll on her."

Rhea Perlman, who played Carla Tortelli on *Cheers,* said, "There are no pretenses about Kirstie. You immediately like her."

Yet with all of the difficulties involved in the delicate process, James Burrows summed up everyone's feelings, saying, "We're thrilled. We wanted to do it a different way, and we did."[17]

The "Cheers 'N' Jeers" section of *TV Guide* echoed Burrows' sentiments. Under the "Cheers" heading, *TV Guide* wrote, "To Kirstie Alley on NBC's Cheers for making us forget what's-her-name. . . . It's only been one season, but already it seems as if Alley has always been part of the gang at our favorite bar."[18]

The National Enquirer ran a story in 1989 that began with the headline "Shelley Long Back on 'Cheers'—And Kirstie Alley's Furious." The subhead read, "She'll Do Three Episodes This Season — Then Return Full-Time."[19] The story was disputed by Maggie Begley, a spokeswoman for Paramount Television "Contrary to the supermarket tabloids, Shelley Long is not coming back to the show."[20] And she didn't.

There is one final note regarding a minor reoccurring character on *Cheers* that bears mentioning. Rebecca Howe's boss was originally Walter Gaines, played by Richard Doyle. Woody, with the blessings of Rebecca Howe, first dated Mr. Gaines' daughter Kelly (Jackie Swanson), whom he later married.

Walter Gaines was later replaced by a new boss, Evan Drake, played by Tom Skerritt who was, for a time, Rebecca's love interest. In a later episode Rebecca explains to Sam that she will not date him because she only dates men who can help her career, such as Evan Drake.

She is made to eat those words when she meets her new boss, Martin Teal, played by Alex Nevil. Teal replaced Mr. Stone (whom we never saw) as the new executive vice president of the corporation that owns Cheers. The joke was that Teal was one of that new breed of executives who appear young enough to have just gotten out of college.

CHEYENNE

September 20, 1955–September 13, 1963.   ABC

Character:	Cheyenne Bodie
Played by:	Clint Walker
Date(s):	September 20, 1955–June 5, 1956
	September 11, 1956–June 17, 1958
	September 21, 1959–June 20, 1960
	September 26, 1960–May 15, 1961
	September 25, 1961–April 30, 1962
	September 24, 1962–September 13, 1963
Replaced by:	Bronco Layne
Played by:	Ty Hardin
Date(s):	September 16, 1958–June 16, 1959

It began as one of three rotating series on *Warner Bros. Presents* in 1955. At that time, it alternated with *King's Row* and *Casablanca.* By the beginning of the 1956–1957 series, the other two programs had been cancelled and *Cheyenne* then alternated with *Conflict.* The following season a new series, *Sugarfoot,* was introduced into the mix.

The series centered around its main character, Cheyenne Bodie, a tough, simple cowboy. His father was a white man, but he was raised by the Indians. Cheyenne was what some might call "a man of few words." He had a straightforward approach to justice and traveled across the American West righting wrongs.

One of the many wrongs *Cheyenne's* star, Clint Walker, was involved with was a dispute with Warner Bros. that had him walk out on his contract because of "difficulties with the studio."[21] Another source put it a little stronger, saying that the

17. Murphy, Mary. "New Face on Cheers. Kirstie Alley *Will* Shock You." *TV Guide,* November 14, 1987, p. 11.
18. "Insider Cheers 'n' Jeers." *TV Guide,* April 9, 1988, p. 31.
19. *The National Enquirer.* February 21, 1989, p. 5.
20. The Associated Press, March 28, 1989.
21. Wooley, Lynn and Malsbary, Robert W. and Strange, Robert G., Jr., *Warner Bros. Television.* McFarland & Company, Inc. Jefferson, North Carolina, 1985, p. 12.

studio refused to bow to Walker's complaints and demands and let him go.

There were several major issues at stake here. First, Clint Walker explained that he originally signed the long-term contract with Warner Bros. because he wanted to do feature films. He did not believe the series would last, so it was actually the success of *Cheyenne* that sparked the dispute.

Furthermore, Walker wanted to be paid $500 for the reruns instead of the $45 he was presently making. He did not want to split his personal appearance fees 50/50 with the studio, and to make his point he turned down $40,000 worth of personal appearances. Walker also wanted permission to record for labels other than Warner Bros., and he wanted more time off. Specifically, he wanted to shoot thirteen episodes a season instead of twenty.

Whether he walked out or was let go is inconsequential. What does matter is that Warner Bros. had a hit series on its hands and no star! The solution was to continue the series under the same title and replace Clint Walker with a new but similar character. The new character was Bronco Layne, an ex-Confederate Army Captain, played by Ty Hardin, who at the time was an unknown.

Walker felt no ill will toward Hardin and was even said to have felt sorry for his replacement because he understood the difficulties of an unknown trying to take over the role of an established character (and star). Being a true gentleman, Walker even offered to appear in the first couple of episodes to help introduce the Bronco Layne character to the *Cheyenne* audience in exchange for Warners releasing him from his contract.

This offer was not accepted by Warner Bros., largely because they felt that if they gave in to Walker's demands, they would be besieged by other walkouts; so the studio stood its ground. Additionally, they were legally able to prevent Walker from performing during the duration of the walkout.

Walker came to terms with the studio early in 1959 and reluctantly returned to *Cheyenne*. Warner Bros. spun off his replacement in a series of his own, *Bronco*.

By this time, Walker had not only lost interest in the series but was becoming typecast, which is why he didn't renew his contract when it ran out in the eighth year. Nevertheless, *Cheyenne* did complete 108 episodes, while *Bronco* was canceled after only sixty-eight.

CHICO AND THE MAN

September 13, 1974–July 21, 1978.   NBC

Character:	Chico Rodriguez
Played by:	Freddie Prinze
Date(s):	September 13, 1974–January 27, 1978

Replaced by:	Raul Garcia
Played by:	Gabriel Melgar
Date(s):	1978–July 21, 1978

This is one of those unfortunate Hollywood stories that began with enormous overnight success and ended in tragedy. It began because television producer James Komack just happened to be

Raul Garcia (Gabriel Melgar, right) as the new "Chico" hugs "The Man" (Jack Albertson, left), who looks heavenward, perhaps in reverence to his former co-star, Freddie Prinz, who committed suicide in 1977.

in the *Tonight Show* audience in December 1973 when a nineteen-year-old and as yet unknown Puerto Rican comic was making his first appearance.

The comic was Freddie Prinze, who was quick to point out that he couldn't really call himself a Puerto Rican because his father was from Hungary. So he would joke that he was a "Hungarican."

Komack, whose other successes include *Get Smart, Mr. Roberts* and *Welcome Back Kotter,* was looking for an ethnic comic to co-star with Jack Albertson in a new situation comedy, *Chico and the Man.* Perhaps that is why he was in the audience.

"The Man" was Ed Brown (Jack Albertson), a cranky old codger from middle America. "Chico" is Chico Rodriguez, a bright young go-getter and a Mexican-American, whom Ed takes into his garage business as his new partner.

The young comedian from New York was tested for the role of Chico, along with several others, and won.

According to Nielsen statistics, the NBC series was the third highest-rated show for the 1974/1975 season, which made Freddie Prinze a household name. He worked to packed houses in Las Vegas, appeared on TV specials and played ex-con Muff Kovak in the made-for-television movie, *The Million Dollar Rip-Off,* which aired on NBC on September 22, 1976.

The success was great. It was also overwhelming and Prinze

began taking pills in an effort to cope with the pressure. His wife, Kathy, a young Las Vegas travel agent whom he had married in 1975, filed for divorce. What was perhaps even more devastating was that she left with their infant son. By this time Prinze had become dependent on Quaaludes and developed a morbid fascination with guns. It was not at all uncommon for Prinze to put a gun to his head and pretend to shoot himself.

Then, on January 27, 1977, he phoned his mother and several friends, telling them that he was going to put an end to his pain. That is when, in the presence of his manager who stayed with him all night, Prinze pulled out a gun he had hidden in the sofa cushions, placed the barrel on the temple of his head and pulled the trigger. Thirty-three hours later, Freddie Prinze was dead.

With the 1977 season drawing to a close, the producers were faced with a difficult decision: cancel the show or replace Freddie Prinze. They decided to replace Prinze, not with another Hispanic comedian, but with a twelve-year-old boy.

The new character was Raul Garcia, played by Gabriel Melgar. He was introduced in the first episode of the 1977–1978 season when he was found hiding in the trunk of Ed's car. It seems that before Ed and Louie (Scatman Crothers) started their return journey from a fishing trip in Tijuana, young Raul Garcia had hitched a ride in the trunk of Ed's car. Since Chico had already left the garage to go into business with his father, there was room in Ed's garage and heart for this young illegal alien.

At the end of the episode, Ed says, "Good night, Chico." When the young boy corrects him, Ed answers, "You're all Chicos to me."

CHiPs

September 15, 1977–July 17, 1983.   NBC

Character:	Officer Frank "Ponch" Poncherello	
Played by:	Erik Estrada	
Date(s):	September 15, 1977–July 17, 1983	

Replaced by:	Officer Steve McLeish
Played by:	Bruce Jenner
Date(s):	1981

Character:	Officer Jon Baker
Played by:	Larry Wilcox
Date(s):	1977–1982

Replaced by:	Bobby Nelson
Played by:	Tom Reilly
Date(s):	1982–1983

Character:	Cadet Bruce Nelson
Played by:	Bruce Penhall
Date(s):	March 20, 1983–1983

Replaced by:	Officer Sindy Cahill
Played by:	Brianne Leary
Date(s):	September 16, 1978–September 15, 1979

Replaced by:	Officer Bonnie Clark
Played by:	Randi Oakes
Date(s):	September 22, 1979–July 18, 1983

CHiPs stands for "California Highway Patrol." The other letters are just thrown in so the acronym could be pronounced. This cops-and-robbers show differed from Broderick Crawford's *Highway Patrol* in that these law enforcement officers rode on motorcycles instead of in cars and they rarely if ever said, "Ten four." The two beefy stars of the show were Erik Estrada as Officer Frank Poncherello and Larry Wilcox as Officer Jon Baker, most often referred to as Ponch and Jon.

When television hunk Erik Estrada temporarily left *CHiPs* because of a contract dispute, it only took a good-looking Olympic gold medalist to replace him. That Olympic star was Bruce Jenner, who won the gold medal for the decathlon in the 1976 Olympics.

Jenner was brought on as a temporary replacement for Estrada and only played Officer Steve McLeish in a few episodes. This was a tough break for Jenner, because Estrada's original co-star, Larry Wilcox, left the series in the fall of 1982 because of his deteriorating relationship with Estrada.

At the time, his plans were to devote 1983 and 1984 to becoming an expert racer of Bilstein Rabbits (Super Vees) and to continue producing. He began his producing career with the 1981 NBC television movie, *Death of a Centerfold: The Story of Dorothy Stratten,* which starred Jamie Lee Curtis.

It may have taken one Olympic athlete to replace Estrada, but it took two actors (one a former champion cyclist) to replace Wilcox. Trainee and later Officer Bobby Nelson was played by Tom Reilly. Nelson's younger brother, Bruce, was played by Bruce Penhall, a former international speedway champion. He had won the World Speedway Championship in both 1981 and 1982 and held eleven international titles.

In March of 1983, Penhall was "promoted to 'main title' billing, taking Tom Reilly's place as Erik Estrada's partner."[22] The full-page promo ad in *TV Guide* hyped: "A Spectacular Night for *CHiPs!* Tonight Bruce Penhall, Motorcycle Speedway Champ of the World, becomes Ponch's new partner!"

Officer Sindy Cahill, played by Brianne Leary, was *CHiPs'* first female officer. A year later, she was replaced by Officer Bonnie Clark, who was played by Randi Oakes; Clark in turn, was replaced by Officer Kathy Linahan, played by Tina Gayle. Ms. Oakes had previously appeared on the opposite side of the

22. Durslag, Melvin. "Life in the Slow Lane. The Macho Biker Gets His Big Break," *TV Guide,* March 19, 1983, p. 36.

law as a car thief named Kim in the December 16, 1968 episode of *ChiPs*.

THE CHISHOLMS

March 29, 1979–March 15, 1980.   CBS

Character: Gideon Chisholm
Played by: Brian Kerwin
Date(s):   March 29, 1979–April 19, 1979

Replaced by: Gideon Chisholm
Played by: Brett Cullen
Date(s):   January 19, 1980–March 15, 1980

Character: Bonnie Sue Chisholm
Played by: Stacey Nelkin
Date(s):   March 29, 1979–April 19, 1979

Replaced by: Bonnie Sue Chisholm
Played by: Delta Burke
Date(s):   January 19, 1980–March 15, 1980

Character: Lester Hackett
Played by: Charles Frank
Date(s):   March 29, 1979–April 19, 1979

Replaced by: Lester Hackett
Played by: Reid Smith
Date(s):   January 19, 1980–March 15, 1980

This rugged Western drama began as a four-part, 12-hour miniseries in which the Chisholm family journeys via wagon train from Virginia to the Ohio territory to build a new life. CBS felt that the ratings were strong enough to warrant a weekly series, and nine months later the Chisholms (with some changes in cast) continued their journey from Wyoming to California. Their ratings, however, were not as high as those for the miniseries and CBS ended their cross-country trek after the ninth episode.

Brian Kerwin, who played Gideon Chisholm, went on to play Deputy Birdwell ''Birdie'' Hawkins on the NBC situation comedy, *Lobo*, which aired from September 18, 1979 to August 25, 1981. He was replaced on *The Chisholms* by Brett Cullen, who later played Bob Cleary on *The Thorn Birds*, a four-part miniseries that aired on ABC from March 27 to March 30, 1983.

The Chisholms' daughter, Bonnie Sue, was played by Stacey Nelkin in the miniseries. She was replaced in the series by Delta Burke, who went on to star as Suzanne Sugarbaker in the hit CBS situation comedy, *Designing Women* (See Entry), which premiered on September 29, 1986. She was later written out and replaced by Julia Duffy, who had earlier replaced Jennifer Holmes on *Newhart* (See Entry).

When Charles Frank accepted the role of Ben Maverick in the CBS Western, *Young Maverick,* he was replaced by Reid Smith, who had played Officer Norm Hamilton in the NBC police drama, *Chase.*

COLT .45

October 18, 1957–June 21, 1960.   ABC

Character: Christopher Colt
Played by: Wayde Preston
Date(s):   October 18, 1957–November 22, 1959
               December 13, 1959
               March 27, 1960–May 3, 1960

Replaced by: Sam Colt, Jr.
Played by: Donald May
Date(s):   December 6, 1959
               January 10, 1960–March 13, 1960
               May 10, 1960–June 21, 1960

Warner Bros. had produced a motion picture, COLT .45, in 1950, starring Randolph Scott as Steve Farrell. A representative of the Colt Firearms Company, Farrell is sent out West on a promotional tour for its new .45–caliber gun. A pair of guns is stolen and the usual good guy vs. bad guy encounter ensues.

When the producers at Warner Bros. Television were told by ABC that they had a sponsor who wanted to buy a new show, they remembered the COLT .45 movie and began developing it for television. The character they created for the series was Christopher ''Chris'' Colt, the son of the inventor of the Colt revolver. Like his theatrical predecessor, Chris Colt was also supposed to be selling guns out West. The plot twist was that Colt was actually an undercover agent working for the United States government. The actor chosen for the lead was six-foot-four Wayde Preston, a handsome young man with curly, sandy-colored hair.

Everything was going well. Warner had just completed shooting the first twenty-six episodes and Wayde Preston had just returned from a twelve-day, cross-country promotional tour that took him from St. Louis to New York. Upon his return to Warner Bros., Preston learned that both ABC and the show's sponsor had dropped the series. This infuriated Preston and he blamed Warner Bros. and the network for not spending enough money to promote the series.

As it turned out, *Colt .45* was going to return to the air in the fall of 1958 with a new sponsor, but not without problems.

Preston, who was becoming more difficult to work with, was himself the cause of his departure from the series. The story that is told deals with the filming of what is referred to as a process shot. The word process refers to a special transparent rear projection screen in front of which actors must perform while filmed action or scenes are taking place behind them.

In this instance, the process shot required Wayde Preston to get on top of a stagecoach while shooting at some outlaws. The coach, of course, was stationary and the filmed footage that was to be projected on the process screen would create the illusion that the coach was moving. Preston refused to do the scene, which he contended was dangerous and would require a stunt double. The only problem was that the scene was *his* close-up.

Christopher Colt (Wayde Preston) ready for a showdown on *Colt 45.*

Producer Cedric Francis was sent to the set to straighten things out and he told Preston, " 'You know, Wayde, maybe you're not right for this business.' Wayde said, 'You may be right,' then got in his car, left the lot and never came back. That was the end of Wayde Preston."[23]

One has to wonder if Warner's earlier problems with *Cheyenne's* Clint Walker in some way precipitated the events that caused Wayde Preston to leave *Colt .45.*

Faced with the pressure to find an immediate replacement for Preston, the producers brought in Donald May. May was the perfect choice for two reasons. One, he was a contract player for Warner Bros. and, two, he had already guest starred on an earlier episode of *Colt .45* as Sam Colt, Jr., Chris's cousin. The plan was simple. Write and produce new episodes with May as the Colt character he had previously played on the series.

While the new episodes were being filmed, ABC aired reruns of the *Colt .45* episodes starring Wayde Preston.

When the new episodes aired no mention was made in the storyline of any explanation either for Chris's absence, or for his cousin Sam's taking over for him as the government's undercover agent. This was a conscious decision by the produc-

ers and may have been one of the factors that contributed to the decline in viewership.

The series was renewed for a third season, but only three new episodes were filmed; reruns were aired to fill the remaining ten weeks.

Donald May was rewarded by Warner Bros. by being given the leading role of reporter Pat Garrison in the 1960s newspaper drama, *The Roaring 20's.*

COLUMBO

September 15, 1971–September 4, 1977.   NBC
February 6, 1989   ABC

Character:	Lieutenant Columbo
Played by:	Bert Freed
Date(s):	July 31, 1960

Replaced by:	Lieutenant Columbo
Played by:	Peter Falk
Date(s):	September 15, 1971–September 4, 1977
	February 6, 1989–

Back in the days of television when Dinah Shore would throw a big kiss to her audience—that's when Lieutenant Columbo was born. To be more precise, television writers and producers Richard Levinson and William Link created the character of Lieutenant Columbo for *The Chevy Mystery Show,* which was the summer replacement for *The Dinah Shore Chevy Show* during the 1960/1961 season.

Their teleplay, ''Enough Rope,'' was the first *Columbo* vehicle and starred Bert Freed as the overly polite and somewhat distracted crime solver. Freed later played Rufe Ryker on the ABC Western, *Shane,* which aired from September 6 to December 31, 1966. His most recognizable role may very well be Posner in the 1971 film, BILLY JACK.

The television production led *Columbo's* creators to the stage, where the title was changed to *Prescription: Murder.* The play, which toured for six months but never made it to Broadway, starred Thomas Mitchell as Lieutenant Columbo. Some years earlier, Mitchell played Gerald O'Hara, Scarlett O'Hara's father in the 1939 David O. Selznick masterpiece, GONE WITH THE WIND. Lieutenant Columbo was Mitchell's last role. The other cast members included Joseph Cotten as the psychiatrist, Agnes Moorehead as his wife and Patricia Medina as his mistress.

When the *Movie of the Week* was created, the network was looking for scripts to produce and approached the Columbo team, who quickly dusted off their *Prescription: Murder* script and adapted it for television. The television cast starred Gene Barry as the psychiatrist, Nina Foch as his wife and Katherine Justice as his mistress. That left the role of the cop to filled.

Levinson and Link said that they originally wanted Bing

---

23. Wooley, Lynn and Malsbary, Robert W. and Strange, Robert G., Jr., *Warner Bros. Television.* McFarland & Company, Inc. Jefferson, North Carolina, 1985, p. 209.

Crosby as Columbo. Crosby, who was semi-retired, said, ''I like the screenplay, but I really just want to play golf.''[24] Their second choice was Lee J. Cobb, but it is not known whether the studio ever offered him the role.

That's when they received a call from their old friend, Peter Falk, who somehow knew that the part was written for him. ''Listen. I'd kill to play this cop. I've got to play this guy Columbo.'' After he auditioned, Levinson and Link agreed with Falk—he had to play this guy Columbo.

The TV movie was a success and when the character returned, to rotate with *McMillan and Wife* and *McCloud,* Peter Falk became a star and his salary rose to a reported $250 thousand per episode, which made him the highest-paid actor on television at the time.

Columbo solved what he thought would be his last case, ''Try and Catch Me,'' on May 23, 1978. Then, more than ten years later, he returned to television as a part of ABC's *Mystery Movie* to solve ''Columbo Goes to the Guillotine,'' which aired on February 6, 1989.

The only other regular on the series was Dog, Columbo's pet. The original basset hound was reported by Falk to have been 103 years old when it was introduced in the first episode of the second season. That dog died about three years later and was replaced by a younger basset hound that had to have white make-up applied to its face to make it look as old as its predecessor.

By the time the new *Columbo* series went into production in 1988, the second dog had also died and was replaced by a third canine actor.

COMBAT!

October 2, 1962–August 29, 1967.   ABC

Character:	Doc Walton
Played by:	Steven Rogers
Date(s):	October 2, 1962–May 14, 1963

Replaced by:	Doc
Played by:	Conlan Carter
Date(s):	September 17, 1963–August 29, 1967

Like *M*A*S*H,* this video reenactment of war lasted longer than the conflict it was depicting. In this instance the war was World War II and the setting was Europe. The stories soft pedal the horrors of war and focus instead on the lives of the men of the Second Platoon of the United States Army Infantry, known as ''K'' Company.

Among these brave soldiers are comedian Shecky Greene as Braddock, Rick Jason as Lieutenant Gil Hanley, and Vic Morrow as Sergeant Chip Saunders, the role that shot him to national fame.

The unit's sawbones, who patched up his fellow solders for the first season, was Steven Rogers as Doc Walton. For the

remainder of the the series, the medical officer, referred to only as ''Doc,'' was played by Conlan Carter, who played C.E. Carruthers on *The Law and Mr. Jones,* which aired on ABC from October 7, 1960 to October 4, 1962.

COMMANDO CODY: SKY MARSHAL OF THE UNIVERSE

July 16, 1955–October 8, 1955.   NBC

Character:	Ted Richards
Played by:	William Schallert
Date(s):	July 16, 1955–July 30, 1955

Replaced by:	Dick Preston
Played by:	Richard Crane
Date(s):	August 6, 1955–October 8, 1955

Character:	Dr. Varney
Played by:	Peter Brocco
Date(s):	July 16, 1955–July 30, 1955

Replaced by:	Baylor
Played by:	Lyle Talbot
Date(s):	August 6, 1955–October 8, 1955

In 1949, theater audiences were treated to the thrilling heroics of a brand-new aerial hero—Rocketman, in a twelve-chapter Republic serial, KING OF THE ROCKETMEN.

Not a superhero, Rocketman was really Jeff King (Tristram ''Tris'' Coffin), a rocket propulsion expert at Science Associates. After a series of unexplained disasters took the lives of a number of top scientists working for Science Associates, King was named Director of Security.

Holed up in a secret cave that had been converted to a full-blown laboratory was Professor Millard, who had been saved from a laboratory explosion by Jeff King. Working with Millard, the inventor of an atomic-powered flying suit (actually a jacket with a pair of jets on the back and an attached helmet), Jeff King took on the secret identity of the Rocketman.

Interestingly, the identity of the Sky Marshal of the Universe is known neither to his assistants Joan and Ted, nor to his superior, Mr. Henderson (Craig Kelly). The ''good guys'' refer to him as Commando Cody while the ''bad guys'' simply refer to him as ''Cody.''

Rocketeering hero Tris Coffin later starred as Captain Tom Rynning, in the syndicated Western, *26 Men,* which ran from October 1957 to 1959.

In an attempt to lure audiences away from the exciting new space adventures on television and back into the theaters, the second serial in the series, RADAR MEN FROM THE MOON, began with a superimposed title over the opening shot: ''Introducing a new character, Commando Cody.'' Essentially the same character as Rocketman, Commando Cody donned the same rocket jacket, which he wore over his gray business

---

24. Meyers, Ric. *Murder on the Air, Television's Great Mystery Series.* The Mysterious Press, New York, 1989, p. 266.

suit—he just removed his hat before putting on the bullet-shaped helmet. Republic also edited in the same stock takeoffs and flying sequences used in the previous films.

For this outing George Wallace donned the rocket suit as he did battle against Retik (Roy Barcroft), the evil ruler of the moon who is hellbent on conquering the earth. Graber, one of the thugs back on earth who is aiding Retik, was played by that daring and resourceful masked rider of the plains, The Lone Ranger—actually actor Clayton Moore who played *The Lone Ranger* (See Entry) on television.

Pitted against invaders from Mars, Commando Cody returned later that year in ZOMBIES OF THE STRATO-SPHERE, which starred Judd Holdren as Larry Martin (a last-minute name change). His lovely assistant, Joan Albright, was played by Aline Towne.

Aiding the Martian leader, Marek (Lane Bradford) was Leonard Nimoy as the Martian henchman, Narab. Nimoy, who would later play Mr. Spock, an alien from the planet Vulcan, on *Star Trek* (See Entry), betrayed Marek and for the first of many times in his screen career helped to save the earth from destruction.

The series then moved to television with Judd Holdren and Aline Towne continuing in their roles while William Schallert, best known for his role as Patty's father, Martin Lane, on *The Patty Duke Show,* joined the cast as Cody's other colleague, Ted Richards.

While the rocket suit worn by Commando Cody remained unchanged, Cody also wore a black domino mask, nearly identical to the one worn by Clayton Moore as The Lone Ranger. In fact, Holdren's facial features so closely resembled Moore's, that one is apt to wonder if the producers were somehow hoping audiences would make a subliminal connection between Commando Cody and the last of the Texas Rangers. It has also been suggested that the producers may have wanted to protect themselves against the possibility of a replacement, figuring viewers wouldn't notice a new actor under a black mask.

It wasn't a bad plan, but they should have had Ted wear a mask as well, because beginning with the fourth episode, "Nightmare Typhoon," he was replaced by Richard Crane as Dick Preston. The scene that explained the replacement takes place in the lab with Cody simply saying to Joan, "Ted was transferred." Not much, but it at least acknowledged the change.

The Lone Ranger wasn't the only other hero connection found in *Commando Cody, Sky Marshal of the Universe*—there is also a strong link to television's Superman.

Even though Rocketman/Commando Cody didn't possess any super powers, which is why he carried a revolver, there was a strong link to one of television's most enduring superhero programs, the *Adventures of Superman.* For one thing, the camera direction and photography of Cody's takeoffs, landings and flying sequences were nearly identical to those used on the *Adventures of Superman.* Even more interesting is the number of supporting players who appeared in episodes of the *Superman* series.

These include Tris Coffin, the first actor to strap on the rocket suit, who may be best remembered for his roles as heavies on the *Adventures of Superman.* In 1951 he was E. J. Davis in "The Case of the Talkative Dummy" and Paul Martin in

"The Mystery of the Broken Statues." Two years later he appeared as Stoddard in the series' sixtieth episode, "Clark Kent, Outlaw." Martian leader Marek (Lane Bradford) guest-starred as Perry White's nephew, Chris White, in the 1951 episode, "Jet Ace." And even Aline Towne, who played Cody's assistant, Joan Albright, had played Kal-El's (Superman) mother, Lara, in the very first episode, "Superman on Earth."

The other replacement in the short-lived *Commando Cody* series was Dr. Varney (Peter Brocco), the aide of The Ruler (Gregory Gray), who only appeared with William Schallert in the first three episodes. Beginning with episode four "Nightmare Typhoon," Lyle Talbot took over as Baylor, but in this case no explanation was given for the character replacement.

THE CORNER BAR

June 21, 1972–September 7, 1973.   ABC

Character:	Harry Grant
Played by:	Gabriel Dell
Date(s):	June 21, 1972–August 23, 1972

Replaced by:	Mae
Played by:	Anne Meara
Date(s):	August 3, 1973–September 7, 1973

Replaced by:	Frank Flynn
Played by:	Eugene Roche
Date(s):	August 3, 1973–September 7, 1973

A distant relative of *Cheers* this ABC situation comedy was produced by Alan King with Howard Morris. The series was given two chances and both failed.

In the first version the corner bar was Grant's Toomb, named after its owner, Harry Grant. Grant was played by Gabriel Dell, who had played the level-headed friend with a job, Gabe Moreno, in seventeen of the original BOWERY BOYS films.

The following summer, a new version of the series aired. Harry was gone and the name of the bar was changed to "The Corner Bar." Its new owners were Frank Flynn and Mae. Mae was played by Anne Meara and her partner, Frank, by Eugene Roche.

Ms. Meara was, of course, the Irish half of the husband and wife comedy team, Stiller and Meara. She later got a job at another television bar, playing the cook, Veronica Rooney, on *Archie Bunker's Place,* the revised edition of *All in the Family,* which occasionally featured Billy Halop, one of Gabe Dell's old BOWERY BOYS co-stars, as Bert Munson.

From 1984 to 1986, Eugene Roche played Bill Parker on the ABC situation comedy, *Webster.*

THE COURTSHIP OF EDDIE'S FATHER

September 17, 1969–June 14, 1972.   ABC

Character:	Etta
Played by:	Karen Wolfe
Date(s):	September 17, 1969–unknown

Replaced by: Tina Rickles
Played by: Kristina Holland
Date(s):   unknown–June 14, 1972

In between *My Favorite Martian* and *The Incredible Hulk,* Bill Bixby starred in this warm situation comedy as widower Tom Corbett, the editor and publisher of *Tomorrow* magazine. His son, Eddie, was played by Brandon Cruz, and their housekeeper, Mrs. Livingston, was played by Miyoshi Umeki.

Every good publisher should have a secretary and Tom's was Etta, played by Karen Wolfe. Etta was later replaced by Tina Rickles, who was played by Kristina Holland. After *The Courtship of Eddie's Father,* Ms. Holland went on to provide the voice of Alice Boyle on the animated cartoon series, *Wait Till Your Father Gets Home.*

COVER UP

September 22, 1984–July 6, 1985.   CBS

Character: Mac Harper
Played by: Jon-Erik Hexum
Date(s):   September 22, 1984–November 3, 1984

Replaced by: Jack Striker
Played by: Antony Hamilton
Date(s):   November 10, 1984–July 6, 1985

Character: Rachel
Played by: Rosemarie Thomas
Date(s):   unknown

Replaced by: Rachel
Played by: Sheree Wilson
Date(s):   unknown

In the style set by *I Spy,* whose undercover agents posed as professional tennis players on a world-wide tour, these agents posed as professional photographer and male model. The photographer, Danielle "Dani" Reynolds, was played by the beautiful Jennifer O'Neill who, in 1971, starred as Dorothy in the definitive coming-of-age film, THE SUMMER OF '42. Her partner, Mac Harper, was played by Jon-Erik Hexum, who had played Phineas Bogg on *Voyagers!,* the NBC science fiction that aired from October 3, 1982 to July 31, 1983.

Hexum was replaced on *Cover Up* after accidentally shooting himself in the head with a prop gun while on the set of the series. Though there were no bullets in the gun, the force of the explosion of the blank at such close range was still enough to kill him.

" 'I got the part about 18 hours before I reported to the set,' says Antony Hamilton, recalling how he was tapped to replace Jon-Erik Hexum on *Cover Up* following Hexum's tragic death. 'I had no time to think about it.' Nor did the Australian actor

seek the part. Having known Hexum, Hamilton didn't think it was 'ethical.' The producers came to him. Despite the sad circumstances, Hamilton, a former model, says that playing Jack Striker—a spy who masquerades as a model—has its rewards: 'It's a wonderful opportunity to vent any frustrations I had as a model in real life.' "[25]

The other famous Australian male model is George Lazenby, who played James Bond in HER MAJESTY'S SECRET SERVICE. The villain in that film was played by Telly Savalas, TV's *Kojak* (See Entry).

And speaking of models, Rosemarie Thomas, who played Rachel, one of Dani's models, was later replaced by Sheree Wilson in the same role.

COVINGTON CROSS

August 25, 1992–October 31, 1992.   ABC

Character: William Gray
Played by: Ben Porter
Date(s):   August 25, 1992–September 4, 1992

Replaced by: Armus Gray
Played by: Tim Killick
Date(s):   September 19, 1992–October 31, 1992

It has by now become standard practice for successful motion pictures to serve as the inspiration for television series. The enormously popular James Bond films of the 1960s, for instance, were translated to television as *The Man from U.N.C.L.E.* The 1978 syndicated science fiction *Battlestar Galactica* was unquestionably a lift of the 1977 film, STAR WARS. The following year, NATIONAL LAMPOON'S ANIMAL HOUSE turned up on ABC as *Delta House,* on NBC as *Brothers and Sisters,* and on CBS as *Co-Ed Fever.* In 1981, PRIVATE BENJAMIN became *Private Benjamin* and the 1989 comedy LOOK WHO'S TALKING begot 1991's *Baby Talk.*

Less often, a film's theme spawns a series that is not so much a direct copy of the film, but one that adopts its spirit and mood. A case in point is Kevin Costner's 1991 big-budget adventure film ROBIN HOOD: PRINCE OF THIEVES, which may very well have been the inspiration for ABC's *Covington Cross,* an action adventure series with a smattering of humor set in 14th-century England.

Covington Cross focused on the lives of the Grays, a wealthy medieval family of powerful land owners with contemporary values and sensibilities. The full-page ad in the September 19–25 issue of *TV Guide* read: "14th Century adventure. 14th Century romance. 20th Century attitude." Television columnist Kay Gardella wrote in the September 6th issue of the *Daily News:* "*Covington Cross* is the one historically flavored series of the new season, sort of an English-style *Bonanza.*" And *Entertainment Weekly*'s satirist Jim Mullens wrote in the September 4, 1992 issue: "*Covington Cross*—*Dallas* set in the Middle Ages. They're working on an episode called 'Who Lanced J.R.?' "

25. *TV Guide.* "Insider," February 16, 1985. Vol 33. No. 7. Issue #1664, pp. 18–19.

Gil Grant, the writer and executive producer of the series, does not dispute these observations because they were precisely what he had in mind. "*Covington Cross* is not intended as a history lesson. It's a 1990s take on family life in the 1350s, presented by a guy who grew up in the 1950s. The stories will often have modern themes, but the action and romance will be straight from the days when knights were knights and chivalry reigned," he explained.[26]

The preview episode of *Covington Cross,* which was also the show's pilot, starred Briton Nigel Terry as Sir Thomas Gray, the lord of Covington Cross Castle and a widower. Cherie Lunghi, who coincidentally had played Guinevere to Nigel Terry's King Arthur in the 1981 action adventure/fantasy film, EXCALIBUR, here played Lady Elizabeth, a neighbor and Sir Thomas' love interest. His beautiful and quite liberated daughter, Eleanor, was played by Ione Skye, the daughter of one of the 1960s most popular folk/rock recording artists, Donovan. Though not yet a household name, she had already appeared on television as Napoleon Bonaparte's little sister in the 1987 miniseries, *Napoleon and Josephine: A Love Story.* Her film roles include Clarissa in the 1986 drama, RIVER'S EDGE; Diane Court in the 1989 dramatic comedy, SAY ANYTHING; and Elyse in the 1992 comedy, WAYNE'S WORLD.

Cedric, Sir Thomas' youngest and gentlest son, was played by Glenn Quinn, who as a recurring regular was simultaneously appearing as Becky's (Lecy Goranson) former boyfriend and now newlywed husband, Mark, on ABC's hit situation comedy, *Roseanne.* The two more rambunctious sons, Knight Richard and Knight William, were played by Jonathan Firth and Ben Porter. The show's heavy, Sir John Mullens, a dark and contemptible character with a greedy eye on the Grays' land, was played by James Faulkner.

And just as Robin Hood had his Friar Tuck, so too did Sir Thomas have his own man of the cloth. In fact the Friar (Paul Brooke), a full-time member of his castle's staff, even suffered from the same male pattern "monk's baldness" as Friar Tuck.

Each of these actors looked to be ideally suited for his role, but there appears to have been a small casting gaffe. Jonathan Firth, the actor who played Richard, and Ben Porter, the actor who played William, looked so much alike in the photography of the show that you couldn't tell which was Cedric and which was William.

Glenn Quinn spoke candidly about the *Covington Cross* casting catastrophe in *Entertainment Weekly:* "I think they're canning one of my brothers. One of them is going off to the Crusades sadly enough. [Test] audiences couldn't distinguish between them—they were like 'Richard, William—who the f—-is who?' I had the same problem."[27]

According to Gil Grant, who spoke to the press via satellite from London on July 13, 1992, when they cast Jonathan Firth and Ben Porter to play the older sons, they looked quite different, even though they were both rail thin and six feet tall. But once they were put in the makeup and the period clothes—

their knight outfits, which all tend to look alike—they seemed indistinguishable. "They were a blur—and they totally blended together. People couldn't tell the difference between either brother," said Grant.[28] So they made a choice to send one off and bring another in.

They very cleverly set it up by reshooting just half-a-scene for the pilot in which it was explained that there was another brother, Armus, who's off fighting in the war.

CEDRIC: Why can't I become a knight?

SIR THOMAS: Because you're going to be a cleric.

CEDRIC: I wasn't meant for the church.

SIR THOMAS: When Armus left, I swore an oath to your mother, Cedric. Though she was losing her eldest son to the Crusades, at least her youngest would be spared the horrors of war. A cleric's blood is not spilled on the battlefield. We have enough knights. Now leave it!

Then, in the first episode after the pilot, "Armus Returns," it was mentioned that William had gone off to war and Tim Killick, this big, hulking guy who looked like no one else in the cast, was introduced as Sir Thomas's eldest son, Armus.

At the opening of this episode, Sir Thomas is preparing for a journey to Sussex for a gathering at the castle of the Duke of Arondale which was being held solely for the purpose of collecting the yearly taxes. Before riding off, Sir Thomas asks his live-in friar to say a prayer for them.

SIR THOMAS: A traveling prayer would be in order. You know, the usual thing—good weather, safe journey—whatever else you can think of.

FRIAR: Of course.

SIR THOMAS: And Friar, perhaps you could say another as well for my sons Armus and our William off to war . . . I worry for them . . . I miss them.

FRIAR: I'll pray the best prayer I can pray for them, Sir Thomas.

The Friar's prayers were answered as Sir Thomas and the viewer learned of Armus' return from a letter delivered to Eleanor. Yet when she approached her father with the sealed document, he feared the worst.

26. Grant, Gil. From a July 1992 press release issued by The Lippin Group.
27. Harris, Mark and Alan Carter. "Covington Cross," *Entertainment Weekly,* New York. September 11, 1992, No. 135, p. 56.
28. Grant, Gil. From the ABC 1992 Summer Press Tour held at the Plaza Room of The Century Plaza Hotel in Los Angeles, California, via Satellite from London on July 13, 1992.

SIR THOMAS: What is it? What's wrong?

ELEANOR: This just came from the king's guard. He said it was about Armus.

SIR THOMAS: Armus? (Takes a long pause while he reads the letter.) He's coming home. (Visibly moved to tears.) He's coming home.

Armus did, of course, come home, but he was not the brave knight that his father and brothers had expected. He had indeed trained long and hard to become a knight, but after killing an opposing soldier, "a boy like himself," in his first encounter, Armus realized that this was not the path his life should take, as he explained to his brother Richard:

ARMUS: The kill came so easily. I'll never forget the incredible feeling of power it gave me. A feeling I had no wish to acquire a taste for.

Being a mountain of a man, not unlike Sir Robin's Little John, what Armus had acquired a taste for was food. So, instead of fighting, he served king and country as the cook for a regiment of some 400 knights engaged in the Crusades. The more important war, however, was the ratings war that *Covington Cross* waged each week, and which was ultimately lost.

CRIME PHOTOGRAPHER

September 26, 1945–December 28, 1945.   CBS
April 19, 1951–June 5, 1952   CBS

Character:	Casey
Played by:	Oliver Thorndike
Date(s):	1945

Replaced by:	Casey
Played by:	Richard Carlyle
Date(s):	April 19, 1951–June 1951

Replaced by:	Casey
Played by:	Darren McGavin
Date(s):	May 3, 1951–June 5, 1952

Character:	Ethelbert
Played by:	John Gibson
Date(s):	April 19, 1951–June 1951

Replaced by:	Ethelbert
Played by:	Cliff Hall
Date(s):	May 3, 1951–June 5, 1952

Crime Photographer, which is also known as *Casey, Crime Photographer* and *Casey, Press Photographer,* is another of the early television series to have its origins in radio.

In "Diary of Death," a 1945 television adaptation of the CBS radio program that premiered in 1943, Oliver Thorndike starred as Casey, the ace crime photographer for the New York daily newspaper, *The Morning Express.* Also appearing in the series were Ruth Ford and John Gibson as Ann and Ethelbert.

The series resurfaced six years later with Darren McGavin as Casey—his first television role. Since his introduction to television, McGavin has appeared in six series and has had guest starring roles on more than 150 programs.

From 1957 to 1959, Darren McGavin was television's first Mike Hammer in *Mickey Spillane's Mike Hammer* (See Entry). He spent the next three years on the Mississippi and Ohio rivers as Captain Grey Holden on the NBC adventure series, *Riverboat* (See Entry). McGavin later played Carl Kolchak on ABC's supernatural series, *Kolchak: The Night Stalker,* which aired from September 13, 1974 to August 30, 1975.

When McGavin took over the role of Casey on *Crime Photographer,* he was joined by Cliff Hall, who replaced John Gibson as Ethelbert, the bartender of the Blue Note Cafe. After leaving *Crime Photographer,* Gibson landed a role on the prime time version of *A Date with Judy* (See Entry), replacing Judson Rees as Judy's father, Melvyn Foster in the ABC comedy series.

D

DANIEL BOONE

December 4, 1960–March 19, 1961.   ABC
September 24, 1964–August 27, 1970   NBC
September 12, 1977–October 4, 1977   CBS

Character: Daniel Boone
Played by: Dewey Martin
Date(s):   December 4, 1960–March 19, 1961

Replaced by: Daniel Boone
Played by: Fess Parker
Date(s):   September 24, 1964–August 27, 1970

Replaced by: Daniel Boone
Played by: Rick Moses
Date(s):   September 12, 1977–October 4, 1977

Character: Rebecca Boone
Played by: Mala Powers
Date(s):   December 4, 1960–March 19, 1961

Replaced by: Rebecca Boone
Played by: Patricia Blair
Date(s):   September 24, 1964–August 27, 1970

Following in the television footsteps of Davy Crockett was Daniel Boone. This legendary American frontiersman and scout was, one, not a fictional character and, two, not always played by Fess Parker. The real Daniel Boone was born in 1734 in a township near Reading Pennsylvania that is now known as Exeter, but was then named Oley.

He was played by George O'Brien in the 1936 motion picture, DANIEL BOONE, and by Bruce Bennett in the 1957 adventure film, DANIEL BOONE, TRAIL BLAZER.

Walt Disney brought Daniel Boone to television at the end of 1960 in what would now be considered a four-part miniseries. With leading man Dewey Martin in the title role, *Daniel Boone* aired as part of *Walt Disney Presents*. The first two installments, entitled, ''The Warrior's Path,'' ran on December 4 and 11 in 1960. The third and fourth installments, ''The Wilderness Road,'' aired on March 12 and 19, 1961.

Since 1955, Martin has appeared in episodes of nearly three dozen series, including *Climax, The Twilight Zone, Mission: Impossible* and *Petrocelli*. He may be better remembered for his co-starring role in the 1952 Kirk Douglas adventure, THE BIG SKY. Coincidentally, the name of the character Martin played in the film just happened to be named Boone.

Daniel's wife, Rebecca Boone, was played by Mala Powers, who played Mona Williams in the later CBS episodes of *Hazel*.

In much the same way that Buster Crabbe was asked to portray Buck Rogers after his successful stint as Flash Gordon, Fess Parker was cast as Daniel Boone after having played a very similar character, Davy Crockett.

The co-producers of this successful *Daniel Boone* series were Aaron Rosenberg and Aaron Spelling, not Walt Disney. It aired on CBS for nearly six years, building an impressive inventory of 165 episodes. Daniel Boone's wife, Rebecca, was played by Patricia Blair, who only one year earlier had played the hotel keeper, Lou Mallory, on the Chuck Connors Western, *The Rifleman*.

Seven years after *Daniel Boone* left the air, CBS tried to bring the character back in a prequel entitled, *Young Dan'l Boone*. They hired twenty-five-year-old Rick Moses to portray the young Kentucky frontiersman and Devon Erickson to play his girlfriend, Rebecca Bryan. Bryan was indeed Rebecca Boone's maiden name and it was refreshing to see the writers stick to the history. Unfortunately, the viewers didn't stick to their sets and the series ended after only four episodes.

A few years later, Ms. Erickson joined the cast of another CBS Western, *The Chisholms*, as Betsy O'Neal.

THE DANNY THOMAS SHOW see MAKE ROOM FOR DADDY

DARK JUSTICE

April 5, 1991–August 27, 1993.   CBS

Character: Judge Nicholas ''Nick'' Marshall
Played by: Ramy Zada
Date(s):   April 5, 1991–April 10, 1992

Replaced by: Judge Nicholas ''Nick'' Marshall
Played by: Bruce Abbott
Date(s):   April 17, 1992–August 27, 1993

Character: Catalana ''Cat'' Duran
Played by: Begona Plaza
Date(s):   April 5, 1991–March 6, 1992

Replaced by: Maria
Played by: Viviane Vives
Date(s):   September 20, 1991–

In an effort to broadcast original programming during the 11:30 p.m. to 12:30 a.m. time slot, usually reserved for talk shows and sitcom reruns, CBS introduced one mystery series and six dramas to rotate under the umbrella title of *Crime Time After Prime Time.* These were *Scene of the Crime, Sweating Bullets, The Exile, Fly by Night, Silk Stalkings, Urban Angel* and *Dark Justice.*

Airing on Fridays was *Dark Justice,* a drama originally starring Ramy Zada as Judge Nicholas Marshall. By day, Judge Marshall metes out justice according to the letter of the law. By night, he adopts a secret identity to bring criminals—who had gotten off on technicalities—to justice.

Assisting the judge in these *Mission: Impossible*-like cases, are Catalana "Cat" Duran (Begona Plaza); former forger and counterfeiter, Arnold "Moon" Willis (Dick O'Neill); and special effects expert, Jericho "Gibs" Gibson (Clayton Prince).

Beginning with "Once Upon a Krestridge," the episode that aired on September 20, 1991, Viviane Vives replaced Bergona Plaza as the judge's assistant, Maria. Cat was killed—shot in the back twice—while saving Nick's life.

"Bump in the Night," the episode of April 17, 1992, featured a major change in cast as Bruce Abbott took over the series' starring role as the vigilante judge, Nicholas Marshall.

A DATE WITH JUDY

June 2, 1951–September 30, 1953.   ABC

Character: Judy Foster
Played by: Patricia Crowley
Date(s):   June 2, 1951–February 23, 1952

Replaced by: Judy Foster
Played by: Mary Linn Beller
Date(s):   July 10, 1952–September 30, 1953

Character: Melvyn Foster
Played by: Judson Rees
Date(s):   June 2, 1951–September 15, 1951

Replaced by: Melvyn Foster
Played by: Frank Albertson
Date(s):   September 22, 1951–February 23, 1952

Replaced by: Melvyn Foster
Played by: John Gibson
Date(s):   July 10, 1952–September 30, 1953

Character: Dora Foster
Played by: Anna Lee
Date(s):   June 2, 1951–February 23, 1952

Replaced by: Dora Foster
Played by: Flora Campbell
Date(s):   July 10, 1952–September 30, 1953

Character: Randolph Foster
Played by: Gene O'Donnell
Date(s):   June 2, 1951–February 23, 1952

Replaced by: Randolph Foster
Played by: Peter Avramo
Date(s):   July 10, 1952–September 30, 1953

This situation comedy was based on a 1941 radio show of the same name and was set in sunny California. The town was never mentioned in the series, though a reviewer once wrote that the family lived in Santa Barbara. It made the leap to televison ten years later and landed on ABC's Saturday daytime schedule.

Starring in the title role was a young Patricia Crowley. She would later become one of television's more frazzled moms, Joan Nash, on the NBC situation comedy, *Please Don't Eat the Daisies,* which aired from September 14, 1965 to September 2, 1967.

When the situation comedy moved to Thursday nights, nearly the entire cast was changed and Ms. Crowley was replaced by Mary Linn Beller. Also in the prime time version, Judy's dad, Melvyn Foster, was played by John Gibson who was the first Ethelbert on the CBS newspaper drama, *Crime Photographer* (See Entry).

The role of Judy's boyfriend, Oogie Pringle, was originated by Richard Crenna on radio and played by Jimmy Sommers in both television versions.

DAVIS RULES

January 27, 1991–April 9, 1991.   ABC
July 9, 1991–September 11, 1991   ABC
December 30, 1991–July 1, 1992   CBS

Character: Robbie Davis
Played by: Trevor Bullock
Date(s):   January 27, 1991–April 9, 1991

Replaced by: Skinner
Played by: Vonni Ribisi
Date(s):   December 30, 1991–July 1, 1992

Comedian Jonathan Winters, whose last regular role on television was Mearth, the son of an Orkian alien, on the ABC situation comedy *Mork & Mindy,* was the star of this domestic sitcom from the Carsey-Werner Company.

Winters, famous for his unique brand of improvisational humor that inspired new talents like Robin Williams, was here playing Gunny Davis, a retired Marine Corps sergeant living with his son, Dwight, (Randy Quaid—who looks like a young Jonathan Winters) and his three young sons, Robbie (Trevor Bullock), Charlie (Luke Edwards) and Ben (Nathan Watt).

The last new first-run episode aired on ABC on April 9,

1991. The series returned for reruns from July 9 to September 11, 1991, and then changed networks, moving over to CBS.

The move left behind Dwight's son, Robbie, with no explanation given. It was as if he never even existed. CBS replaced Robbie with a new kid named Skinner. Skinner (Vonni Ribisi), the fifteen-year-old son of a friend, moved in with the Davis family when his archeologist parents went off on a dig to study primitive tribes in South America.

DAVY CROCKETT

December 15, 1954–December 14, 1955.   ABC

Character:	Davy Crockett
Played by:	Fess Parker
Date(s):	December 15, 1954–December 14, 1955

Replaced by:	Davy Crockett
Played by:	Johnny Cash
Date(s):	November 20, 1988

Replaced by:	Davy Crockett
Played by:	Tim Dunnigan
Date(s):	November 20, 1988
	December 18, 1988

Character:	Andrew Jackson
Played by:	Basil Ruysdael
Date(s):	1954

Replaced by:	Andy Jackson
Played by:	David Hemmings
Date(s):	November 20, 1988–1989

Replaced by:	General Andrew Jackson
Played by:	Matt Salinger
Date(s):	November 20, 1988–1989

This five-part adventure was one of the first of what would today be referred to as a miniseries. It also paved the way for Walt Disney's four-part *Daniel Boone* series.

To keep our frontier heroes straight, Davy Crockett was born in Limestone, Tennessee in 1786, 52 years after Daniel Boone was born in Pennsylvania. Crockett served under General Andrew Jackson in the war of 1812 and was killed while defending the Alamo. Oh, and by the way, both Daniel Boone and Davy Crockett wore coonskin caps.

"Baby boomers, get your coonskin caps out of mothballs: Davy Crockett's coming back. The mid-'50s Disney serial, a cultural phenomenon that made star Fess Parker a fixture on watches and lunch boxes, will be revived next season when Disney launches its new TV show on NBC."[1]

The new *Davy Crockett* was one of four recurring series airing on *The Magical World of Disney,* which was hosted by Walt Disney Company Chairman Michael Eisner, a la Walt Disney. Originally negotiations were under way to have Fess Parker introduce the *Davy Crockett* segments, but that idea was scrapped.

NBC kicked off the new season of *The Magical World of Disney* with a one-hour star-studded special set in Disneyland. During the program clips shown to introduce the new series included *The Absent-Minded Professor* and *Davy Crockett.* The special aired on Sunday, October 9, 1988, but the first *Davy Crockett* episode, "Davy Crockett: Rainbow in the Thunder," didn't run until November 20.

It began with Johnny Cash, as Crockett in his later years, reminiscing with his friend, Andy Jackson, played by David Hemmings.

The young Davy Crockett was played by Tim Dunnigan, who had played Templeton "Face" Peck in *The A-Team* pilot. The younger Andrew Jackson was played by Matt Salinger.

Davy Crockett "was a simple man, full of good humor, hateful of violence and loving of peace. He still makes a fine hero for our time."[2]

THE DEFENDERS

September 16, 1961–September 9, 1965.   CBS

Character:	Walter Pearson
Played by:	Ralph Bellamy
Date(s):	February 25, 1957
	March 4, 1957

Replaced by:	Lawrence Preston
Played by:	E.G. Marshall
Date(s):	September 16, 1961–September 9, 1965

Character:	Kenneth Pearson
Played by:	William Shatner
Date(s):	February 25, 1957
	March 4, 1957

Replaced by:	Kenneth Preston
Played by:	Robert Reed
Date(s):	September 16, 1961–September 9, 1965

For an hour, beginning at ten o'clock on two consecutive Monday evenings in 1957, CBS broadcast *The Defenders* as a two-part teleplay on its *Studio One* program.

The innovative courtroom drama starred Ralph Bellamy and William Shatner as father and son attorneys, Walter and Kenneth Pearson.

"I was still looking around for something on Broadway and

---

1. Francis, Paul. "Fess Up, Fess." *TV Guide,* Vol. 36, No. 11, Issue #1824, March 12, 1988, p. A-3.
2. Hutton, Paul Andrew. "Davey Crockett—He Was Hardly King of the Wild Frontier." *TV Guide,* Vol. 37, No. 5, Issue #1871, February 4, 1989, p. 25.

visited various producers and Herb Brodkin became a good friend of mine—and still is and I've worked for him since. He was the one who put it together and that was how I got the role of Walter Pearson on the *Studio One* production of *The Defenders,*"[3] said Ralph Bellamy.

Appearing with Bellamy in the *Studio One* production was a young Steve McQueen as Joseph Gordon. "Steve McQueen was fresh from the country. He used to appear at rehearsals in Levi's and a rough kind of a jacket and he rode in on a motorcycle. At lunchtime he'd say, 'I'm a meat and potatoes man. I've gotta have some food.' He loved mashed potatoes and gravy—anything that was bulky, and I'd take him to Lupowitz and Moskowitz, a Jewish deli on lower Broadway, where he could get loaded with good food. I liked this fella, Steve, and we became good friends. And although he was just getting started in the business, he was very serious about what he was doing,"[4] Bellamy observed.

The law firm of Pearson & Pearson didn't take on any new clients for four and one-half years. When they did reopen, however, the firm's name had changed to Preston & Preston to reflect the change in the characters' last name, and Walter Preston became Lawrence.

The cast had changed as well. "They wanted me to do the series. Herb Brodkin and Reggie [Reginald] Rose, the show's writer, came out to California to see if they could talk me into doing the series. I didn't want to do it. I turned it down, which may or may not have been the right thing to do. But one does what one thinks is right at the time,"[5] chuckled Bellamy.

Ralph Bellamy, already a leading man in B pictures, had previously starred as the first Mike Barnett in the detective drama, *Man Against Crime* (See Entry). His motion picture roles include Dr. Ladd in the 1932 drama, REBECCA OF SUNNYBROOK FARM. Seven years later, Bellamy played the psychologist, Dr. Shelby, in the much imitated crime drama, BLIND ALLEY. One of his more memorable performances was his self-mocking role as Bruce Baldwin in the 1940 Cary Grant comedy, HIS GIRL FRIDAY. That year he starred in the title role of ELLERY QUEEN, MASTER DETECTIVE, which led to three other entries in the popular Ellery Queen series. He later replaced Wendell Corey on the medical drama, *The Eleventh Hour* (See Entry).

Bellamy was replaced in *The Defenders* by E.G. Marshall, a well-known character actor with nearly twenty films to his credit. Marshall had played such diverse roles as Rayska in the 1948 James Stewart crime drama, CALL NORTHSIDE 777; Lieutenant Commander Challee in Humphrey Bogart's 1954 drama, THE CAINE MUTINY; and the fourth juror in Henry Fonda's 1957 courtroom drama, 12 ANGRY MEN. Four years after *The Defenders,* E.G. Marshall played Dr. David Craig on *The New Doctors* (See Entry).

E.G. Marshall was reunited with his former co-star Robert Reed on the October 9, 1970 episode of Reed's now cult series, *The Brady Bunch.* In that episode, Marcia Brady's (Maureen McCormick) slumber party was in danger of being canceled because her principal, played by E.G. Marshall, had accused her of misbehaving in school.

William Shatner, who went on to become famous as Captain James T. Kirk in the *Star Trek* (See Entry) television series and subsequent films, was replaced by a young Robert Reed, who matured to become one of the favorite sitcom fathers of the '60s and '70s as Mike Brady on *The Brady Bunch.*

Most sources agree that Joan Miller, Kenneth Preston's girlfriend, was played throughout the series by Joan Hackett. One author, however, lists Rosemary Forsyth as having also played the role.

In *The Defenders* pilot Barbara Bolton played Helen Davidson, the role played by Polly Rowles in the series.

On September 30, 1961, an edited version of this pilot aired as the third episode of the series, "Death Across the Counter" (also known as "Death Across the Street"). Ms. Bolton's scenes were cut out of this version and replaced with new footage of Meg Mundy as Lawrence's wife, Frances.

There was also an unaired pilot in which Joan Miller was played by Rosemary Forsyth.

THE DENNIS DAY SHOW

February 8, 1952–August 2, 1954.   NBC

Character:	Kathy
Played by:	Kathy Phillips
Date(s):	1952

Replaced by:	Lois Sterling
Played by:	Lois Butler
Date(s):	1952–1953

Replaced by:	Peggy
Played by:	Barbara Ruick
Date(s):	1953

Replaced by:	Marion
Played by:	Carol Richards
Date(s):	1954

There is a great deal of confusion surrounding this little program which grew out of an alternating segment of *The RCA Victor Show.* Its star, of course, was the bright young singer who replaced tenor Kenny Baker on *The Jack Benny Show.*

The premise was simple enough. Day essentially played himself as a struggling young actor living beyond his means in a luxurious Hollywood hotel in order to bolster his professional image.

Since he was a good-looking eligible bachelor, there had to be a girl in his life and that bill was originally filled by Kathy

---

3. From an exclusive telephone interview with Ralph Bellamy on December 20, 1990.
4. *Ibid.*
5. *Ibid.*

Phillips as Kathy. She was later replaced as Lois, by Lois Butler who was herself replaced by Barbara Ruick as the beautiful blonde, Peggy. And last, but certainly not least, Peggy was replaced by Carol Richards as Marion.

There is conflicting information, however, which states that it was Peggy who replaced Lois Sterling in 1953 and that Marion, who was said to have replaced Peggy in 1954, was played by a second actress, Lois Butler.

The actress who played Peggy was Barbara Ruick, the daughter of Lurene Tuttle and Melville Ruick. During the 1950s, Ms. Ruick was a regular on several popular variety programs including *The Jerry Colonna Show,* which aired from May 28 to November 17, 1951, and *The Johnny Carson Show,* which aired from June 30, 1955 to March 29, 1956. She has also appeared in episodes of *Public Defender, Climax, The Lineup* and *The Millionaire.*

DENNIS THE MENACE

October 4, 1959–September 22, 1963.   CBS
September 26, 1987   Syndicated

Character:	Dennis Mitchell
Played by:	Jay North
Date(s):	October 4, 1959–September 22, 1963

Replaced by:	Dennis Patrick Mitchell
Played by:	Victor DiMattia
Date(s):	September 26, 1987

Character:	Henry Mitchell
Played by:	Herbert Anderson
Date(s):	October 4, 1959–September 22, 1963

Replaced by:	Henry Mitchell
Played by:	Jim Jansen
Date(s):	September 26, 1987

Character:	Alice Mitchell
Played by:	Gloria Henry
Date(s):	October 4, 1959–September 22, 1963

Replaced by:	Alice Mitchell
Played by:	Patricia Estrin
Date(s):	September 26, 1987

Character:	Mr. George Wilson
Played by:	Joseph Kearns
Date(s):	October 4, 1959–1962

Replaced by:	Mr. John Wilson
Played by:	Gale Gordon
Date(s):	May 1962–September 22, 1963

Replaced by:	Mr. George Wilson
Played by:	William Windom
Date(s):	September 26, 1987

Replaced by:	Mrs. Martha Wilson
Played by:	Sylvia Field
Date(s):	October 4, 1959–1962

Replaced by:	Mrs. Eloise Wilson
Played by:	Sara Seeger
Date(s):	Fall 1962–September 22, 1963

Replaced by:	Mrs. Martha Wilson
Played by:	Patsy Garrett
Date(s):	September 26, 1987

Character:	Margaret Wade
Played by:	Jeannie Russell
Date(s):	October 4, 1959–September 22, 1963

Replaced by:	Margaret Wade
Played by:	Kirsten Price
Date(s):	September 26, 1987

Character:	Mr. James Trask
Played by:	Henry Norell
Date(s):	(early episodes)

Character:	Mr. Hall
Played by:	J. Edward McKinley
Date(s):	(later episodes)

As anyone who has ever read Hank Ketcham's comic strip knows, Dennis Mitchell was an adorable blond-haired lad with an unruly cowlick and personality. He wasn't a bad kid and didn't mean to get into trouble—he just did.

When the popular character came to television, Jay North was cast in the title role, with Herbert Anderson as his long-suffering dad, Henry, and Gloria Henry as his mother, Alice.

Living next to the Mitchells were an older couple, the Wilsons, and there should be no arguments—even though there were two, there was really only one "Good ol' Mr. Wilson," as lovingly played by Joseph Kearns. His wife, Martha, could also be played by only one actress, and she was Sylvia Field.

Joseph Kearns died unexpectedly on February 17, 1962, before filming for the season was completed, and was written out of the series. Beginning in May, Lucille Ball's favorite foil, Gale Gordon, was hired to replace Joseph Kearns as Mr. Wilson's brother, John. He was first introduced as a house guest of Mrs. Wilson's while George was away, but eventually Martha left and was replaced by John Wilson's wife, Eloise.

Interestingly, both Mr. Wilsons appeared together on the Eve Arden situation comedy, *Our Miss Brooks.* Gale Gordon played

Good Ol' Mr. Wilson (Joseph Kearns, left) agrees to go camping with Dennis Mitchell (Jay North, right) in a 1959 episode of *Dennis the Menace.*

Good Ol' Mr. Wilson's brother, John (Gale Gordon, left) takes charge of Dennis Mitchell (Jay North, right) in this posed publicity still from *Dennis the Menace.*

the school's principal, Osgood Conklin. Joseph Kearns joined the cast from 1953 to 1955 as Superintendent Stone.

And had he not been working on *Our Miss Brooks,* Lucille Ball might have been able to coax Gale Gordon to co-star with her as Fred Mertz on *I Love Lucy* (See Entry). What would Ethel have said?

The characters all returned to the small tube some twenty-four years later in a one hundred-minute syndicated TV movie *Dennis the Menace* starring newcomer Victor DiMattia in the title role and William Windom, who later appeared on *Murder She Wrote* (See Entry), as Mr. Wilson.

Jim Jansen, a dead ringer for Herbert Anderson, took over as Dennis' dad Henry while Patricia Estrin slipped into the role and Gloria Henry's high heels as Henry's wife, Alice.

Mr. Wilson's bride of forty years, Martha, was played by Patsy Garrett, who had appeared as Mrs. Florence Fowler on the Juliet Mills/Richard Long situation comedy, *Nanny and the Professor,* which aired on ABC from January 21, 1970 to December 27, 1971.

The plot of the one-shot telefilm produced by Dic Entertainment, had Dennis and his friends dig up the Mitchell's front yard in a plan to save Henry the $300 it would cost him to have the trenches cut for an underground lawn sprinkler system. In the process Dennis digs up a real dinosaur bone that turns the Mitchell's home, and the neighborhood upside down when Henry invites his college fraternity brother Dr. Barclay "Bones" Schuyler III (Barton Tinapp), to qualify the find.

Just six years later, Hank Ketcham's characters were brought to the big screen in DENNIS THE MENACE, a major motion picture produced by John Hughes. The film starred Walter Matthau as George Wilson and introduced Mason Gamble as Dennis. The Mitchells were played by Robert Stanton and Lea Thompson and Mrs. Wilson by Joan Plowright.

Bespectacled Margaret Wade, the little girl smitten with Dennis Mitchell, was played here by Amy Satz.

DESIGNING WOMEN

September 29, 1986–May 27, 1993.   CBS

Character:	Suzanne Sugarbaker
Played by:	Delta Burke
Date(s):	September 29, 1986–September 9, 1991

Replaced by:	Allison Sugarbaker
Played by:	Julia Duffy
Date(s):	September 16, 1991–September 7, 1992

Replaced by:	Bonnie Jean "B.J." Poteet
Played by:	Judith Ivey
Date(s):	September 25, 1992–May 27, 1993

Character:	Charlene Frazier Stillfield
Played by:	Jean Smart
Date(s):	September 29, 1986–September 16, 1991

Replaced by:	Carlene Frazier
Played by:	Jan Hooks
Date(s):	September 16, 1991–May 27, 1993

Character:	Vanessa Chamberlain
Played by:	Olivia Brown
Date(s):	1991–1992

Replaced by:	Vanessa Chamberlain
Played by:	Jackee
Date(s):	May 4, 1992

Replaced by:	Etienne Toussant Bouvier
Played by:	Sheryl Lee Ralph
Date(s):	November 6, 1992–May 27, 1993

Given the theme song *Georgia on My Mind,* and a title that is a double-entendre, viewers at first may have been confused as to what to expect from this CBS sitcom. It turned out to be about ''Sugarbakers,'' an interior decorating business in Atlanta that was run by Suzanne and Julia Sugarbaker (Delta Burke and Dixie Carter) along with Charlene Frazier Stillfield (Jean Smart) and Mary Jo Shively (Annie Potts). Meshach Taylor played delivery man Anthony Bouvier, a black ex-con with a winning personality and intellectual bent who later became a full partner in the firm.

After the cancellation of *Designing Women,* Annie Potts went on to replace Susan Dey in the CBS sitcom *Love & War* (See Entry).

However, it wasn't long before audiences knew what to expect—good television, that is until the network programmers began playing time-slot roulette with the series, which in 1987 almost ended with cancellation—twice!

The series did return to become a fixture on the network's Monday night schedule and all seemed well. But then a feud developed between the producers and one of the series' co-stars, Delta Burke. The highly publicized controversy centered on the fact that the executive producers, husband and wife team Harry Thomason and Linda Bloodworth-Thomason, felt that Ms. Burke, who had emerged as *Designing Women*'s central character, was putting on too much weight; she was reported at one point to be nearly 210 pounds. They were afraid that if Delta Burke didn't begin to lose weight, the show might lose its audience.

Delta Burke went public with the story during an interview on *The Barbara Walters Special* that aired on Wednesday, November 14, 1990.

| BURKE: | In the beginning, when I started to put on the weight after the first season, they [the Thomasons] weren't happy about that. And I was trying to do all these extreme diets to keep the weight down. But I was told that CBS would replace me. |

| WALTERS: | If you kept getting fatter. |

| BURKE: | Right. |

| WALTERS: | So you were in a panic? |

| BURKE: | I was in a panic. The unhappier I got, the bigger I got. |

When pressed by Ms. Walters to explain how there could be such unhappiness on the set among the show's executive producers and her co-stars, Delta Burke made some very strong allegations.

| BURKE: | Harry [Thomason] would yell and scream quite a bit at all of us and it's rather frightening. And he did put us all in a room and yell and scream and say how ungrateful we were and throw things at us. And when I tried to leave, he barred the door. And when I tried to phone for help, he ripped the phone out of my hand. And he didn't let me go until he was ready to let me go. And I locked myself in my room because I was afraid he would come . . . and he did. That's not what I'm hired for. I'm not hired to be terrorized and manipulated. |

The Thomasons defended their position, issuing a statement to the media that was read by *Barbara Walters:* ''We are all mentally exhausted from the daily trials and tribulations of Delta Burke.''

Ms. Burke said she wasn't on any sort of a ''star trip,'' because by appearing on *The Barbara Walters Special* she was, in fact, jeopardizing her name, her career and her paycheck, and she hoped that things could be worked out. They weren't.

Matters were further complicated when another of the show's ensemble cast indicated a desire to leave the series. In the May 1991 issue of *Ross Reports Television,* Publisher and Editor Timothy Hunter reported, ''. . . Most people thought that Delta Burke would be the first to leave the cast of CBS-TV's *Designing Women* (Mondays, 9:30–10 p.m. NYT). Her feuds with the producers and other cast members have been fodder for many an article. However, it seems that Jean Smart may be the first to depart. It is rumored that Ms. Smart has informed the show that she will not renew her contract. It is also rumored that Meshach Taylor feels he has been underpaid in comparison to the rest of the cast.''[6] For Ms. Smart, the departure from her successful role had nothing to do with internal pressures or contract demands. She wanted to play a more personal role, that of wife to her husband, Richard Gilliland, and mother to their twenty-one-month-old son, Connor Douglas, and to be able to perform in other projects.

Regardless of who was right, who was wrong and who was caught in the crossfire, the sixth season began on September 16,

---

6. *Ross Reports Television: Casting, Scripts, Production.* Television Index, Inc. Long Island, New York. May 1991, p. 2. Editor Timothy Hunter.

1991 without Burke and with Jean Smart receiving a guest-starring credit for her appearance in this transitional episode.

"The Desk" was more than just the season opener. In fact it was twice the length of the regular episodes. It may be that the writers and producers felt they needed a full hour because the storyline had to explain the departure of Suzanne Sugarbaker and introduce her cousin, Allison. It also had to introduce Jan Hooks as Charlene's younger sister, Carlene Frazier.

Mary Jo's (Annie Potts) line explained how Suzanne sold her share of the business to another, albeit unknown, investor.

MARY JO: You know, businesswise, Suzanne sellin' out was just the best thing that could have happened. You know the cash flow's just totally revitalized everything.

The dialogue between Carlene and Julia (Dixie Carter) addressed the absence of Suzanne.

CARLENE: Why'd she move to Japan anyway?

JULIA: Well, Suzanne was very attracted to the Japanese economy. They have a very large elderly population there and she had dated most of the men in this country.

A more detailed explanation of the revamped series appeared on the pages of the industry publication, *TV Pro-Log:*

"Now that Delta Burke is out, you may wonder what will happen to the character of Suzanne Sugarbaker. Well, the executive producers have decided to send her to Japan to live with her mother, Perky. Perky has been over there since the series started. Jean Smart, who plays Charlene, announced a while ago that she would be leaving *Designing Women* to devote more time to her son Connor. So next season, Charlene's husband, Bill (Doug Barr), will be reassigned to an Air Force base in England and Charlene will go along. Unlike Delta Burke, however, Jean Smart will make the occasional guest appearance. Julia Duffy, who has quit ABC's *Baby Talk,* will join the *Designing Women* cast as a Sugarbaker cousin who buys into the design firm and moves into Suzanne's house. According to Linda Bloodworth-Thomason, '. . . she'll supply the vain, selfish voice we've had on the show for five years.' Jean Smart will be replaced by Jan Hooks, formerly of *Saturday Night Live,* who will play Charlene's kid sister. She'll show up to help with Charlene's baby and then take over as the firm's bookkeeper."[7]

Of the two new cast members, Julia Duffy had the bigger hairdo to fill. Ms. Duffy, who had left *Baby Talk* (See Entry) because she was unhappy playing what she felt to be a shallow and undeveloped character, not to mention being the straight-woman to a baby, tried to fill the vacancy left by Delta Burke's Suzanne Sugarbaker. "But Duffy resists any notion that she is portraying essentially the same spoiled-brat character she plays as Stephanie on *Newhart* [See Entry]. 'There's an arrogance in both characters,' she allows. 'And they're both obnoxious. But [the role of Allison] feels very different inside. She is striving, and wants to be successful, but feels very much like an outsider who would like to be an insider. That's an entirely different feeling from someone like Stephanie, who is languid and assumes that she is adored and has never felt like an outsider.'"[8]

Maybe so, but Allison Sugarbaker was certainly played with the same obnoxious, vain, pretentious and self-centered qualities possessed by Stephanie Vanderkellen, and these were precisely the qualities the producers were looking for. " 'I was very familiar with Julia's [Duffy] work, and I thought she had the kind of character persona that could fill the void that would be left by the departure of Suzanne Sugarbaker,' Bloodworth-Thomason says. 'There are only a handful of actresses who can pull off being whiny and petulant and self-centered, and still be liked by the audience, and Julia Duffy has that quality.' "[9]

" 'I didn't do anything innovative or original,' " says Bloodworth-Thomason bluntly. 'Jan and Julia bring their own personalities to these voices, but they're essentially the same voices.' "[10]

". . . Allison and Carlene, have essentially the same kinds of personalities as the two they replace. 'The shadings may be somewhat different,' says Harry Thomason, 'but it will be the same four distinctive voices we had last year.' "[11]

However, the writers of the Fox sketch-comedy series, *The Edge,* saw it differently—and they called it the way they saw it in the series debut on September 19, 1992.

MARY JO: Where's our friends Delta and Jean Smart?

JULIA: Well, don't you remember, dear? They're gone. We have new friends now.

MARY JO: Oh yeah, but they are not as good.

After Jan Hooks' character is introduced as a "not so smart but likeable" character, Mary Jo does the set up for the arrival of Allison Sugarbaker.

MARY JO: Where's Stephanie from the *Newhart* show?

ALLISON: (Entering from the front door) I'm not Stephanie. I'm (BEAT) . . . Well, I forget what my new name is, but it's certainly nothing like Stephanie. Stephanie was snotty, vain, stuck-

7. *TV Pro-Log: Television Programs and Production News.* TI-Volume 43, No. 43, Television Index Information Services, L.I., New York. Timothy Hunter, Editor and Publisher, June 24–30, 1991

8. Warren, Elaine. "Shake-up at the Sugarbakers': It's Now Re-Designing Women" *TV Guide,* Vol. 39, No. 38. September 21, 1991, Issue # 2008, pp 15–16. Reprinted with permission from *TV Guide Magazine.* Copyright 1991 by New America Publications, Inc.

9. *Ibid.,* p. 15.

10. Harris, Mark. "Designing Women," *Entertainment Weekly,* New York, October 4, 1991, No. 86, p. 27.

11. Warren, pp. 12–13.

up and disliked by all the other characters. And now I'm . . .

JULIA: (Interrupting) Exactly the same.

ALLISON: Well, so what if I am. Delta was just like Stephanie and Stephanie came first, so this is only fair.

Most will agree that Julia Duffy was indeed the ideal choice for the role. But for unexplained reasons, which may have more to do with that unknown quantity known as "chemistry" than with talent, Ms. Duffy's character just never caught on, forcing yet another change in cast for the show's seventh season.

Judith Ivey starred from April 12, 1990 to August 10, 1991 as Kate McCrorey in *Down Home,* the appealing NBC situation comedy that was co-produced by Barton Dean, Ted Danson and Dan Fauci. She accepted the challenge to "join the ailing-without-Delta Burke show [which came] 'out of the blue' from series executive producer Linda Bloodworth-Thomason."[12]

Unlike Julia Duffy's character, which was written very close to Delta Burke's, great care was taken to assure that Judith Ivey's character would not be a clone of her predecessors, while still contributing the same "feel" to the cast mix. "Series creator Linda Bloodworth-Thomason calls Ivey's character 'a cross between [outspoken Texas journalist] Molly Ivins and [outspoken Texas governor] Ann Richards.' "[13]

Before a new character is introduced, it is always a good idea to first explain what happened to the character who was written out.

MARY JO: You know, I tell you, I could just wring Allison's neck for pullin' out her money the way she did. I know that she is a cousin of yours, Julia, but still she could have given us a little notice.

CARLENE: Oh, I don't know, you know those Victoria Secret franchises are real hard to get.

But just when it looks as though the remaining partners are going to have to close the doors to Sugarbakers forever, the phone rings—it's a call from a new customer who, upon being questioned about the money budgeted for the job, said, "The sky's the limit." The new client is Bonnie Jean "B.J." Poteet, the wealthy widow of James Poteet, a millionaire building contractor from Houston who had relocated in Atlanta. Bonnie, who was a court reporter, met her husband in the courtroom, where he was one of the litigants. They fell in love and married, but because of his bad heart, James died on the Conga line during their wedding reception as the band played *Proud Mary.*

Since it is Julia's birthday, everyone comes with her to Ms. Poteet's home so they can leave for a birthday drink after her appointment. Bonnie, who is later called B.J., invites them all to stay and celebrate at her home, which they do. Julia winds up

drinking a little too much and loses the business to B.J. in a game of five-card stud, a game she later admits to knowing nothing about.

B.J., however, who is a recovering alcoholic, didn't drink during the party and feels a little guilty about winning Sugarbakers in the card game. The following morning she offers a sober Julia a chance to win back Sugarbakers in a sudden death game of high card. Julia cuts the deck and draws a picture card. B.J. pulls a card and immediately turns it face down, saying that she should have quit while she was ahead. Julia had won back the business!

B.J. then leaves the room and Julia turns over the face-down card, to find that B.J. had actually drawn an ace. Realizing what B.J. has done, Julia decides to pop the question.

JULIA: Say, B.J., I just had a great idea. Since our business has been revitalized now, you know, I was thinking we could use another partner.

B.J.:   Well, I'm kind of of a personality person, not a trained decorator. What are you looking for?

What they were looking for was, of course, a new partner with money to put into the business, and they found it in B.J. The show ends with everyone standing in a circle, putting their hands on top of each other's in an all-for-one and one-for-all chant.

And as if this were not enough, *Designing Women,* which has already proven itself to be a troubled series with staying power, was forced to endure still another change in cast. This was handled in the sixth and seventh episodes of the seventh season. Part I, "Viva Las Vegas," which aired on November 6, 1992, opened with a discussion about Anthony's rich fiancée, Vanessa Chamberlain, and her unconventional suggestions for their wedding, one of which included getting married in Bermuda with the wedding party dressed in shorts. With the wedding only two weeks away, Anthony receives a shattering telephone call from Vanessa.

CARLENE: Anthony, did she postpone the wedding?

ANTHONY: No, (BEAT) she called it off.

In an effort to cheer Anthony up, B.J. offers to fly everyone to Las Vegas for a good time. They all agree and in a short while find themselves at the Tropicana Resort & Casino. The women try their luck in the casino, while Anthony catches the ten o'clock performance of the Folies Bergère. Headlining the elaborate showgirl song-and-dance number is Etienne Toussant, and during a refrain in the song, *Get My Boogie Down,* she looks over at Anthony and says, "Hello handsome." At the conclusion of the number, just before the cadence, she again singles out Anthony: "Oh, I hope I see you later."

And see him she did, because when the designing women

12. Carter, Alan, "Faces to Watch: Judith Ivey" *Entertainment Weekly,* New York, September 11, 1992, No. 135, p. 54.
13. Tucker, Ken "DESIGNING WOMEN." *Entertainment Weekly,* New York, September 11, 1992, No. 135, p. 54.

returned to Anthony's hotel room they found him in bed with Etienne. It seems they had polished off more than a couple of bottles of champagne and were married at the Isle of Capri Wedding Chapel. Anthony doesn't remember a thing.

The following week, in Part II, "Fools Rush In," Julia is wrestling with the disbelief that Anthony could actually have gotten drunk and married a woman he didn't even know.

JULIA: Are things like this really possible? I mean, do these kinds of things actually happen to people?

CARLENE: They happen to Doris Day and Rock Hudson all the time.

This was an accurate allusion, since that is precisely what happened in the 1961 Rock Hudson/Doris Day comedy, LOVER COME BACK. Anthony even went so far as having annulment papers drawn up. In the end, the newlyweds decided to live up to their wedding vows and make a go of it.

Now although this made for some very good television, it might never have happened had Jackee decided to remain with the series after playing Anthony's fiancée in *Designing Women*'s sixth season finale episode, "Shades of Vanessa." Prior to Jackee's series involvement, Olivia Brown, who played Detective Trudy Joplin on the NBC police drama, *Miami Vice* from September 16, 1984, to July 26, 1989, had made occasional appearances as the sexy but dimwitted Vanessa during the series' 1991/1992 season, though she was talked about more than seen.

Unfazed by all of the changes in cast is Meshach Taylor, who philosophized: "Inevitably, people are replaced in a show. That doesn't mean the show goes down the tubes. Jean and Delta weren't born here; they had lives before, and they have lives now. Meanwhile, it's exciting to work with new people."[14]

DETECTIVE SCHOOL

July 31, 1979–November 24, 1979.   ABC

Character:	Teresa Cleary
Played by:	Jo Ann Harris
Date(s):	July 31, 1979–August 1979

Replaced by:	Maggie Ferguson
Played by:	Melinda Naud
Date(s):	September 1979–November 24, 1979

There were six students enrolled in Nick Hannigan's Detective School which began in the summer of 1979. Hannigan was played by James Gregory, whose Inspector Luger character was already a regular on the successful ABC sitcom, *Barney Miller*, which aired on ABC from January 23, 1975 to September 9, 1982. One of his earlier roles was as President Ulysses S. Grant in *The Wild, Wild West* (See Entry).

One of Hannigan's students was Teresa Cleary, played by Jo Ann Harris, who had appeared as Gloria Bartley in the 1976 miniseries, *Rich Man Poor Man—Book I.*

When *Detective School—One Flight Up* resumed as a regular fall series, "One Flight Up" was removed from the title and the Teresa Cleary character was removed from the cast. She was replaced by Maggie Ferguson, played by the beautiful Melinda Naud, who, just before joining the cast of *Detective School*, played Lieutenant Dolores Crandell on *Operation Petticoat* (See Entry). She holds the distinction of being one of the few characters on that series *not* to be replaced. Her other claim to fame was that she was seen in several episodes of ABC's *Happy Days* as Fonzi's girlfriend, Paula Petralunga.

THE DETECTIVES, STARRING ROBERT TAYLOR

October 16, 1959–September 21, 1962.   ABC-NBC

Character:	Lieutenant James Conway
Played by:	Lee Farr
Date(s):	October 16, 1959–May 27, 1960

Replaced by:	Sergeant Chris Ballard
Played by:	Mark Goddard
Date(s):	September 16, 1960–September 21, 1962

Character:	Lieutenant Otto Lindstrom
Played by:	Russell Thorson
Date(s):	September 16, 1960–May 19, 1961

Replaced by:	Sergeant Steve Nelson
Played by:	Adam West
Date(s):	September 29, 1961–September 21, 1962

Each week, three of the four detectives in the series were assigned to cover a case. The star of the series was motion picture actor Robert Taylor, as Captain Matt Holbrook. His assistant throughout the series was ladies' man Lieutenant John Russo, played by Tige Andrews, who would later star as Captain Adam Greer on *The Mod Squad*.

The other detectives who came and went were not part-for-part replacements; they were there just to keep enough detectives on hand to maintain the case load.

Lee Farr's replacement, Mark Goddard, played Cully on the CBS Western, *Johnny Ringo,* and Elinor Donahue's husband, Bob Randall, on the situation comedy, *Many Happy Returns.* He is, however, best known for his role as the handsome young pilot of the Jupiter II, Major Donald "Don" West, on *Lost In Space.* The weekly science fiction adventure series aired on CBS from September 15, 1965 to September 11, 1968.

And unless you just landed on earth in the Jupiter II, Adam

---

14. Harris, Mark. "Designing Women." *Entertainment Weekly,* New York, October 4, 1991, No. 86, p. 23.

West traded up his squad car for the Batmobile, and became television's caped crusader, Batman.

THE DICK VAN DYKE SHOW

October 3, 1961–September 7, 1966.   CBS

Character: Feona ''Pickles'' Sorrell
Played by: Barbara Perry
Date(s): December 19, 1961
March 14, 1962

Replaced by: Feona ''Pickles'' Sorrell
Played by: Joan Shawlee
Date(s): February 13, 1963
March 6, 1963
April 10, 1963

Character: Freddy Helper
Played by: Peter Oliphant
Date(s): November 21, 1962
February 3, 1964
November 3, 1965

Replaced by: Freddy Helper
Played by: David Fresco
Date(s): November 3, 1965

Character: Edward Petrie
Played by: Will Wright
Date(s): December 12, 1961

Replaced by: Sam Petrie
Played by: J. Pat O'Malley
Date(s): November 7, 1962
March 18, 1964

Replaced by: Sam Petrie
Played by: Tom Tully
Date(s): November 25, 1964
Februry 2, 1966

Character: Clara Petrie
Played by: Isabel Randolph
Date(s): February 21, 1962
November 7, 1962
March 18, 1964
November 25, 1964
February 2, 1966

Replaced by: Clara Petrie
Played by: Carol Veasie (Veazie)
Date(s): December 12, 1961

Character: Sol Pomeroy
Played by: Marty Ingels
Date(s): October 31, 1961
April 11, 1962

Replaced by: Sam Pomeroy
Played by: Allan Melvin
Date(s): March 4, 1964
February 16, 1966

Character: Sam Pomerantz
Played by: Henry Calvin
Date(s): March 6, 1963

Replaced by: Sam Pomerantz
Played by: Allan Melvin
Date(s): October 13, 1965
November 24, 1965[15]
February 16, 1966[16]

Character: Delivery Boy
Played by: Jamie Farr
Date(s): October 17, 1961
October 24, 1961
November 14, 1961
December 19, 1961

Replaced by: Delivery Man
Played by: Frank Adamo
Date(s): January 10, 1962
March 24, 1965

Replaced by: Delivery Man
Played by: Jerry Hausner
Date(s): October 30, 1963

Replaced by: Delivery Man
Played by: Johnny Silver
Date(s): February 5, 1964

Replaced by: Delivery Man
Played by: Henry (Herkie) Styles
Date(s): April 14, 1965

Television, really great television, rarely happens overnight and almost certainly never happens without a great deal of hard work. A case in point is *The Dick Van Dyke Show,* which began as *Head of the Family* and starred Carl Reiner as Robert Petrie.

---

15. In this episode, the name of Rob's Army buddy was changed to a combination of both names—Sol Pomerantz.
16. Ibid.

Who would cast veteran television comedy writer and performer Carl Reiner as Robert Petrie? Why, Carl Reiner, of course. That is because what became the now classic *Dick Van Dyke Show* began as a failed pilot titled, *Head of the Family*, which was written by Reiner during a summer vaction on Fire Island, in 1959.

Between 1950 and 1954, Reiner had been working as a regular cast member on *Your Show of Shows*, which starred Sid Caesar and Imogene Coca. For four months following the cancellation of *Your Show of Shows*, Reiner was a panelist on the NBC quiz program, *Droodles*. He rejoined Sid Caesar on September 27, 1954 in *Caesar's Hour*. On this successful NBC comedy variety show, Reiner played George Hansen in a recurring sketch, "The Commuters."

Caesar's Hour ended on May 25, 1957 and Carl Reiner stayed with Caesar as they moved over to ABC in Caesar's next venture, *Sid Caesar Invites You,* which also featured their former co-star, Imogene Coca. That particular comedy outing began on January 26, 1958 and only lasted for four months, ending on May 25.

Carl Reiner returned to TV game shows for a year, from September 1958 to September 1959, to replace Monty Hall as the host of *Keep Talking,* which also featured a standup comic named Morey Amsterdam as one of the regular panelists. It was in the summer of that year that *The Dick Van Dyke Show* was conceived as a starring vehicle for himself because his wife, Estelle, had told Reiner that he could write better scripts than the ones which had recently been submitted for his consideration. During the next 52 days, Reiner wrote not one, but 13 original episodes of his new situation comedy, *Head of the Family,* one every four days. He submitted the finished scripts to his agent, Harry Kalcheim, who passed them on to actor and producer Peter Lawford for financial backing. At the time, Lawford was married to Patricia Kennedy, which meant that final approval had to come from her father, Joseph P. Kennedy, because it concerned "family money."

With the backing secured, the pilot was filmed with Reiner in the lead as Robert Petrie. Film actress Barbara Britton, who played Sister Clothilde in the 1944 Ray Milland war film, TILL WE MEET AGAIN, co-starred as his wife, Laura Petrie. Their son, Richie, was played by Gary Morgan. The two other key members of the cast were Buddy Sorrell and Sally Rogers. They were played by standup comic Morty Gunty and Sylvia Miles, respectively. The role of Alan Sturdy (who would later become Alan Brady) was played by Jack Wakefield.

Much to Reiner's disappointment, the series wasn't picked up and the unsold pilot aired in 1960 as a segment of the CBS summer series, *The Comedy Spot.* Reiner's agent, however, would not let the idea die and approached producer Sheldon Leonard with the scripts. Leonard was impressed with what he saw and believed that he could sell the series if some changes were made. Those changes included re-casting the part of Robert Petrie.

The actors whom Leonard and his business partner, Danny Thomas, had in mind were Johnny Carson and Dick Van Dyke. Thomas had auditioned the latter for a role on *The Danny Thomas Show* as the young nightclub performer, who was named Pat Hannigan after Pat Harrington, Jr. won the role.

Leonard had seen Dick Van Dyke in the 1958 Broadway review *The Boys Against the Girls.* Van Dyke later won a Tony award for his portrayal of Albert Peterson in the Broadway musical, *Bye Bye Birdie,* a role he later recreated for the 1963 film. At the urging of Leonard, Carl Reiner flew to New York to see Van Dyke in *Bye Bye Birdie* and was so impressed with his performance that he offered him the role of Robert Petrie that evening. But it took a little cajoling on the part of Reiner to get Van Dyke to take the week off from the play that was necessary for him to film the pilot.

They experienced a little more difficulty filling the role of his wife, Laura, and auditioned dozens of actresses for the part. They nearly signed Eileen Brennan but decided that she was too strong to play against Van Dyke. She, of course, gained fame as Capt. Doreen Lewis in both the 1980 motion picture and the 1981 to 1983 television series, PRIVATE BENJAMIN.

With time running out, Danny Thomas remembered auditioning a young actress to replace Sherry Jackson as his daughter, Terry Williams, on *Make Room for Daddy.* The twenty-year-old actress had impressed Thomas but was turned down because, as he told her, "Nobody could believe that a daughter like mine could have a nose like yours![17] The only problem was that he could not now remember her name, although he did recall that she used three names professionally. When one of Thomas' casting people asked him if he could remember any *more* actresses, the three names that had eluded him clicked into place—Mary Tyler Moore.

For a year in 1957, Ms. Moore had one of the most famous pair of legs in show business as she played Sam, secretary to *Richard Diamond, Private Detective* (See Entry), in which only her legs were shown on camera.

When she auditioned for Carl Reiner, one of her lines was "Hello, Rob." And it was her ability to deliver the line naturally that won her the role of Laura Petrie. The supporting members of *The Dick Van Dyke Show* had already been cast.

In a remarkable demonstration of the old "It's not what you know, but who you know" adage, Rose Marie was cast as comedy writer, Sally Rogers. She had played various roles on *Love That Bob,* Bertha on the CBS situation comedy, *My Sister Eileen,* and was a long-time friend of Sheldon Leonard's. She had often asked for a part in one of his projects and easily won the role of Sally. She then recommended Morey Amsterdam for the role of her writing partner, Buddy Sorrell.

Another old friend of Leonard's was Jerry Paris, who was cast as the next-door neighbor, Dr. Jerry Helper. Legend has it that he was hired when Sheldon Leonard saw him eating a hot dog at a Los Angeles Dodgers ball game. He in turn recommended Ann Morgan Guilbert to play his wife Millie Helper. How did Paris know of Ms. Guilbert? Well, she just so happened to be the wife of one of his friends.

Juvenile actor, Larry Matthews, who was born Larry Mazzeo, replaced Gary Morgan, who had turned in a fine performance in the pilot.

The most often talked about, sometimes heard and infre-

17. Smith, Ronald L. *Sweethearts of '60s TV.* St. Martin's Press, New York, 1989, p. 45.

quently seen character on *The Dick Van Dyke Show* was Alan Brady (Alan Sturdy in the pilot), the loud and overbearing boss of the three comedy writers. This fictitious egomaniacal television personality was the star of his own weekly series, *The Alan Brady Show,* and was played by none other than *The Dick Van Dyke Show's* real-life writer and producer, Carl Reiner.

There was, however, another character who was often spoken about and seldom seen, Buddy Sorrell's wife, Pickles. Actually her real name was Feona, as she explained to Sally's boyfriend, Ted Harris (Paul Tripp) in the December 19, 1961 episode, "Sally Is a Girl."[18]

PICKLES: Well, you can call me Pickles, okay?

TED: Pickles, that's an odd name. I never heard anybody called Pickles before.

PICKLES: Yes, it is a strange name, but you see my real name is Feona. And in my neighborhood, everyone named Feona was called Pickles.

TED: Were there many Feonas in your neighborhood?

PICKLES: Just me.

The Pickles character is also a perfect example of a character that is better left unseen, because there is no way for an actor or actress reciting dialogue to live up to their own legend. But the producers apparently didn't see that when they wrote Pickles into five episodes and had her played by two different actresses. The first Pickles Sorrell was played by Barbara Perry, who played Thelma Brockwood on Peggy Cass' simian sitcom, *The Hathaways,* which aired on ABC from October 6, 1961 to August 31, 1962. She was replaced by Joan Shawlee, who played various roles on *The Abbott and Costello Show* during 1951 and 1952, and Lorna from 1959 to 1960 on *The Betty Hutton Show.*

There were also five actors who played Rob's parents—three different fathers and two mothers. His father, Sam (also named Edward), was played by Will Wright, J. Pat O'Malley and Tom Tully. Rob's mother, Clara, was played by both Isabel Randolph and Carol Veasie.

Will Wright only appeared in one episode, "Empress Carlotta's Necklace," while O'Malley and Tully each appeared in two. O'Malley had many television roles including Mr. Harry Burns on *My Favorite Martian,* but is most easily remembered as Bert Beasley, the elderly gent who married the Findlay's second maid, Mrs. Naugatuck on *Maude* (See Entry). The actor who replaced J. Pat O'Malley was Tom Tully. He was seen as Tom Starett in the 1966 Western, *Shane.*

Isabel Randolph, the first Mrs. Clara Petrie, had the opportunity to play Sam's wife opposite both J. Pat O'Malley and Tom Tully. She is known to television audiences as Mrs. Nestor from the Eve Arden situation comedy, *Our Miss Brooks.* Her replacement, Carol Veasie, had played Mrs. Maude Endless, the president of the Pearl River First National Bank in the 1955 NBC situation comedy, *Norby.*

There were many episodes in which the audience was treated to a glimpse of Rob's army days at Camp Crowder in Joplin, Missouri. The first of these was the flashback episode, "Oh, How We Met the Night That We Danced," which aired on October 31, 1961. Rob Petrie's Army buddy, Sol Pomeroy, was played by Marty Ingels. The very next episode, "Harrison B. Harding of Camp Crowder, Mo.," introduced Allan Melvin in the title role. Marty Ingels returned to the role of Sol Pomeroy in the 1962 episode, "Sol and the Sponsor." When he landed the role of Arch Fenster in the ABC situation comedy, *I'm Dickens—He's Fenster,* the role of Rob's Army pal was given to Allan Melvin and the character's name alternated between Sol and Sam.

For the March 6, 1963 episode, "The Sam Pomerantz Scandals," Rob's old Army buddy was Sam Pomerantz, played by the rotund comic actor, Henry Calvin. Although his name may not be familiar to television audiences, the image of Calvin, as Sergeant Garcia, having a "Z" slashed in his clothing at the opening of the Walt Disney version of *Zorro* (See Entry) has been indelibly etched in viewers' minds. The Pomerantz character returned four more times with Allan Melvin replacing Henry Calvin, and once again the character's name bounced between Sam and Sol.

The last reoccurring character of *The Dick Van Dyke Show* ensemble was the delivery boy (sometimes the delivery man). The character appeared in nine episodes throughout the series and was played by five different actors.

The original delivery boy was played by Jamie Farr, who went on to co-star in *M*A*S*H* (See Entry) as Corporal Max Klinger. The Klinger character later replaced Radar O'Reilly as the unit's company clerk when actor Gary Burghoff left the series in the fall of 1979.

After four appearances on *The Dick Van Dyke Show* Jamie Farr was replaced by Van Dyke's long-time friend, Frank Adamo who also served as Van Dyke's personal secretary and stand-in. In addition to his two appearances as the delivery man, Adamo also appeared as a waiter, a beatnik, a veterinarian's assistant, a witness, a guy named Frank, and Dr. Adamo, among others.

The next delivery man was played by Jerry Hausner, who later starred as O.D. Dunstall on the 1964/1965 ABC situation comedy, *Valentine's Day.* He was replaced by Johnny Silver who, in turn, was replaced by Herkie Styles.

Several sources indicate that there were actually two actors, Peter Oliphant and David Fresco, who played Freddie Helper, Richie Petrie's next-door neighbor and best friend. Careful research turned up only one episode in which David Fresco appeared: that was "Odd But True," and Fresco was listed as having played the Potato Man. Peter Oliphant appeared in that same episode as Freddie Helper.

---

18. Ted Harris was played by the well-mannered and soft-spoken children's show host, Paul Tripp. From May 29, 1949 to April 13, 1952, Trip was known to youngsters across America as the host of *Mr. I Magination* and later the host of *Birthday House.* Paul Tripp is also the author of the children's classic *Tubby the Tuba.*

When the book, *The Dick Van Dyke Show: Anatomy of a Classic,* was released in 1983, the former cast members of the series were approached with the possibility of making a reunion movie. Everyone seemed to be for it, including Mary Tyler Moore, but there has been no further movement on the project to date.

If the movie is ever made, the role of Jerry Helper will have to be recast, because Jerry Paris died on March 31 in 1986.

A DIFFERENT WORLD

September 24, 1987–May 8, 1993.   NBC

Character:	Stevie Rallen
Played by:	Loretta Devine
Date(s):	September 24, 1987–1988

Replaced by:	Lettie Bostic
Played by:	Mary Alice
Date(s):	1988

Replaced by:	Carla Meyers
Played by:	Vernee Watson
Date(s):	July 7, 1988

Replaced by:	Jaleesa Vinson
Played by:	Dawnn Lewis
Date(s):	Fall 1988–May 1992

Replaced by:	Kim Reese
Played by:	Charnelle Brown
Date(s):	September 24, 1992–May 8, 1993

Replaced by:	Freddie Brooks
Played by:	Cree Summer
Date(s):	September 24, 1992–May 8, 1993

The first of what potentially could have been several successful spinoff series from NBC's hit *The Cosby Show* starred Lisa Bonet (still Cliff's daughter, Denise Huxtable), now off on her own at Hillman College.

However, unlike *The Cosby Show,* which had a stable cast throughout its eight-season run, *A Different World* suffered cast changes almost immediately. There were several different professors and six Gilbert Hall dormitory directors.

Stevie Rallen was the original director of the dorm, but when Loretta Divine left the show to get married, she was replaced by Mary Alice as Lettie Bostic, a former Hillman student who had returned to complete her education after a leave of absence "to experience life."

When Lettie left, Vernee Watson was hired to play Carla Meyers, but was dropped without explanation after only one episode. "My Dinner With Theo," the episode that introduced Carla Meyers, was quietly presented on July 7, 1988, during the height of the summer reruns to avoid drawing attention to the cast change.

Stepping in for Vernee Watson was Dawnn Lewis as Jaleesa Vinson, and she stayed with the series until May of 1992, when she left to play the teacher, Robin Dumars, on the ABC situation comedy, *Hangin' with Mr. Cooper,* which debuted on September 22, 1992. So while Dawnn Lewis was hangin' with Mr. Cooper, premed student Kim Reese (Charnelle Brown) and archeology major Freddie Brooks (Cree Summer) shared the duties of dorm directors. Kim ran Gilbert Hall while Freddie was responsible for Height Hall.

During the summer of 1992, Jaleesa was married to Colonel Bradford Taylor (Glynn Turman), though the wedding took place off screen. Dawnn Lewis left *A Different World* in May of 1992, but a new actress was not brought in to play Colonel Bradford's wife. Instead, a new student, Charmaine Brown (Karen Maline White) was introduced as a freshman working in the campus eatery, The Pit, which was owned and run by Vernon Gaines (Lou Meyers).

DIFF'RENT STROKES

November 3, 1978–March 21, 1986.   NBC-ABC

Character:	Mrs. Edna Garrett
Played by:	Charlotte Rae
Date(s):	November 3, 1978–September 21, 1979

Replaced by:	Adelaide Brubaker
Played by:	Nedra Volz
Date(s):	1980–1982

Replaced by:	Pearl Gallagher
Played by:	Mary Jo Catlett
Date(s):	1982–1986

Character:	Maggie McKinney
Played by:	Dixie Carter
Date(s):	January 21, 1984–August 31, 1985

Replaced by:	Maggie McKinney
Played by:	Mary Ann Mobley
Date(s):	September 27, 1985–March 21, 1986

New York millionaire Phillip Drummond (Conrad Bain) was an honest, likeable and mild-mannered man. He was the adoptive father to two black brothers, Arnold and Willis, and seemed to have more trouble holding on to his housekeepers than he did in raising his daughter, Kimberly, and her adopted brothers.

Drummond's first housekeeper, Mrs. Jackson, was actually the mother of Arnold and Willis, who were played by Gary Coleman and Todd Bridges. When she died Drummond honored her last request to take care of her boys and later adopted them.

Mrs. Jackson's first replacement was Mrs. Edna Garrett, who was played by Charlotte Rae. Her familiar face has been around television for more than thirty years and is remembered by sitcom fans as Officer Schnauser's wife, Sylvia, on *Car 54, Where Are You?* She left *Diff'rent Strokes* in the summer of 1979 to star in her own spinoff series, *The Facts of Life.* The tie-in between the two series was that Mrs. Garrett accepted the position as a housemother at the exclusive Eastland School for

Girls, which just happened to be the school Kimberly was attending.

In the transitional episode, Drummond is asked to run for city council, but cannot make up his mind. That's when Adelaide Brubaker shows up at the door. She was short, wore her white hair in a bun and was a little feisty.

DRUMMOND: You're probably here about the housekeeping position.

ADELAIDE: Well, I'm not the Avon lady.

Drummond invites Adelaide in so that he may interview her and innocently asks her age. Adelaide becomes incensed and starts for the door, while the kids continue to hound their father to accept the political nomination because he cares about important issues such as low-cost housing for the elderly.

ADELAIDE: Here's your first test, Mr. Politician. I'm seventy-one years old.

DRUMMOND: You don't look a day over thirty.

ADELAIDE: You just got yourself a new housekeeper.

In addition to taking care of the Drummonds for two years, Nedra Volz was appearing simultaneously on *The Dukes of Hazzard* as Miz Emma Tisdale. She eventually left *Diff'rent Strokes* in 1982 and continued for one more year with *The Dukes of Hazzard*. In 1985 she replaced Markie Post on *The Fall Guy* (See Entry).

Once again left without domestic help, Phil Drummond hires Pearl Gallagher (Mary Jo Catlett), who was more like Edna Garrett than Adelaide Brubaker.

The series changed direction slightly when Philip Drummond fell in love with and married a television exercise show hostess, Maggie McKinney, in February 1984. She was originally played by Dixie Carter, but when the series moved to ABC in September 1985, Mary Ann Mobley replaced her as Drummond's wife. Ms. Carter went on to co-star as Julia Sugarbaker in the CBS situation comedy, *Designing Women* (See Entry), which premiered on September 29, 1986.

DOBIE GILLIS *see* THE MANY LOVES OF DOBIE GILLIS

DOC

August 16, 1975–October 30, 1976.   CBS

Character:	Miss Beatrice Tully
Played by:	Mary Wickes
Date(s):	August 16, 1975–September 25, 1976

Replaced by:	Janet Scott, R.N.
Played by:	Audra Lindley
Date(s):	September 25, 1976–October 30, 1976

Doc was one of those likeable situation comedies that regrettably never caught on. When the series began, Joe Bogert, "Doc," was an elderly physician with old-fashioned morals who still cared for his patients as people. Doc was played by Barnard Hughes, and his nurse, Ms. Tully, was played by character actress Mary Wickes. He also had a wife, two daughters, a son-in-law and a grandson. But after twenty-five episodes the series was completely revamped.

Dr. Bogert was now a widower who left his general practice to become the medical director of a free community clinic in New York. The entire original cast was replaced, although Mary Wickes did appear in the first episode of the revised series. Doc's new nurse, Janet Scott, was played by Audra Lindley.

A familiar face in motion pictures since 1932, Mary Wickes played Emma in the 1954 holiday classic, WHITE CHRISTMAS, and Mrs. Squires in the 1962 musical, THE MUSIC MAN. Television audiences may have trouble recalling her as Zelda Marshall on the Saturday morning series, *Sigmund and the Sea Monsters* (See Entry), but should have no trouble remembering her as the less than likeable Miss Esther Cathcart on *Dennis the Menace*.

Her replacement, Audra Lindley, is more readily associated with her role as Helen Roper, the lovingly tolerant, sex-starved wife of Stanley Roper on the ABC situation comedy, *Three's Company* than for this short-lived role.

DR. KILDARE

September 28, 1961–August 30, 1966.   NBC
1972   Syndicated

Character:	Dr. James Kildare
Played by:	Richard Chamberlain
Date(s):	September 28, 1961–August 30, 1966

Replaced by:	Dr. James Kildare
Played by:	Mark Jenkins
Date(s):	1972

Character:	Dr. Leonard Gillespie
Played by:	Raymond Massey
Date(s):	September 28, 1961–August 30, 1966

Replaced by:	Dr. Leonard Gillespie
Played by:	Gary Merrill
Date(s):	September 14, 1972 (syndicated)

It's hard to visualize a urologist named George Winthrop Fish as an engaging lead character for a weekly television series. In reality, Dr. Fish was the inspiration for a series of short stories written by the well-known Western writer, Max Brand. Of course, Brand embellished the stories a bit and didn't make his doctor a urologist. He also changed his name to James Kildare.

The character first appeared on film in the 1937 motion picture, INTERNS CAN'T TAKE MONEY, in which Jimmie Kildare was played by Joel McCrea. McCrea, who appeared in dozens of Westerns, later starred as Marshal Mike Dunbar from 1959 to 1960 in the NBC Western, *Wichita Town.*

Dr. Kildare came to television twenty-four years later in the guise of a young, handsome and relatively unknown actor, Richard Chamberlain, who would play opposite Hollywood legend Raymond Massey as his mentor, Dr. Gillespie. Massey, of course, played Abraham Lincoln in the 1940 drama, ABE LINCOLN IN ILLINOIS, and the role Boris Karloff created on stage, Jonathan Brewster, in the 1944 Cary Grant black comedy, ARSENIC AND OLD LACE.

Chamberlain managed to hold his own and became a star. The series ran for just under five years, at which time he turned to meatier roles in films and on stage. In 1970 he played Peter Tchaikovsky in the biographical musical, THE MUSIC LOVERS, and Aramis in the 1974 film, THE THREE MUSKETEERS.

He returned to television in 1974 in the made-for-television movie, *The Last of the Belles.* He went on to earn critical acclaim as John Blackthorn in the five-part NBC miniseries, *Shogun,* which aired from September 15 through 19, 1980. Three years later, Richard Chamberlain starred as Father Ralph deBricassart in ABC's four-part miniseries, *The Thorn Birds.*

Twenty-three years after *Dr. Kildare* left the air, the actor whom *TV Guide* once called "King of the miniseries" picked up his stethoscope once again to star as Dr. Daniel Kulani in a new CBS medical series, *Island Son.* This hour-long medical drama premiered at 10:00 p.m. on Tuesday, September 19, 1989.

A syndicated version of the "Kildare" series was produced in 1972 by Bristol-Myers/MGM and was based on the same characters. The series was named *Young Dr. Kildare,* after the first of the fifteen black-and-white DR. KILDARE films produced by MGM between 1938 and 1947.

Like its television predecessor, *Young Dr. Kildare* cast an unknown in the title role opposite a well-known actor as Dr. Gillespie. In this version the craggy-faced father figure is played by Gary Merrill, who played Bill Sampson opposite his new bride, Bette Davis, in the 1950 drama, ALL ABOUT EVE. The young intern was played by the then still relatively unknown Mark Jenkins, who later appeared in episodes of *Hawaii Five-O, Barnaby Jones* and *Joe Forrester.*

DR. SIMON LOCKE

Fall 1971–1974.   Syndicated

Character: Chief/Detective Lieutenant Dan Palmer
Played by: Len Birman
Date(s):   1971–1973

Replaced by: Lieutenant Jack Gordon
Played by: Larry D. Mann
Date(s):   1973–1974

Dr. Simon Locke was sort of a poor second cousin to the original *Dr. Kildare* television series. It was produced by *Kildare's* sponsor, Colgate-Palmolive Co., as an inexpensive syndicated answer to fill air time on local stations due to a 1971 ruling by the Federal Communications Commission that sta-

tions must fill the 7:30 p.m. to 8:00 p.m. time slot with local programming.

Its cast included the young and handsome Dr. Simon Locke, played by Sam Groom, and the crusty old Dr. Andrew Sellers (a la Gillespie) was played by Jack Albertson, who had replaced Larry Keating on *Mr. Ed* (See Entry).

With the beginning of the second season, the locale of the show moved from the small town to the big city, with Dr. Locke assigned to the police emergency unit headed by Chief Palmer of Dixon Hills, Canada. Palmer was played by Len Birman.

The series was overhauled by the producers for the last season and an attempt was made to upgrade the quality of the show. Dr. Locke again relocated, this time to Toronto, Canada where he was a surgeon with the Emergency Medical Unit of the Metropolitan Police Department. His new police department superior was Lieutenant Jack Gordon, played by Larry D. Mann. The Canadian-born actor, had previously played Jerry Van Dyke's lawyer friend, Marty Warren, on the situation comedy, *Accidental Family.* The series aired on NBC from September 15, 1967 to January 5, 1968.

THE DON RICKLES SHOW

January 14, 1972–May 26, 1972.   ABC

Character: Arthur Kingston
Played by: Edward Andrews
Date(s):   January 14, 1972
                   February 11, 1972
                   April 14, 1972
                   April 21, 1972

Replaced by: Arthur Kingston
Played by: M. Emmet Walsh
Date(s):   unknown

Today, most television viewers know Don Rickles as king of insult comedy, but early on in his career he had serious acting roles. One fine example was his portrayal of Ruby in the 1958 war drama, RUN SILENT, RUN DEEP, directed by Robert Wise, who later directed STAR TREK: THE MOTION PICTURE. By the late 1960s, however, Rickles' work was anything but serious. This short-lived series was Rickles' second attempt at weekly television and the first at situation comedy. The first *Don Rickles Show* was a comedy/variety program.

The premise of this sitcom was that Rickles was an advertising executive at a New York agency, Kingston, Cohen and Vanderpool, Inc.

Somewhere during the five-month run of the series, Rickles' boss, Arthur Kingston, who was originally played by the wonderful character actor, Edward Andrews, was replaced by M. Emmet Walsh.

Anyone who has ever enjoyed a Doris Day or Tony Randall movie will remember the white-haired actor with the thick-framed glasses. Edward Andrews played Arlene Francis' husband, Gardner Fraleigh, in the 1963 Doris Day/James Garner comedy, THE THRILL OF IT ALL. In 1964 he played Professor Kenton, Barbara Eden's dad in the Tony Randall comedy, THE BRASS BOTTLE, and Burke in the somewhat lengthy Jack Lemmon vehicle, GOOD NEIGHBOR SAM.

A few months after *The Don Rickles Show* left the air, M. Emmet Walsh, the second actor to play Arthur Kingston, played Alex Lembeck on another short-lived situation comedy, *The Sandy Duncan Show,* which aired on CBS from September 17 to December 31, 1972.

THE DONNA REED SHOW

September 24, 1958–September 3, 1966.   ABC

Character:	Mary Stone
Played by:	Shelley Fabares
Date(s):	September 24, 1958–1963

Replaced by:	Trisha Stone
Played by:	Patty Petersen
Date(s):	1963–September 3, 1966

Along with *The Adventures of Ozzie & Harriet, Father Knows Best* and *Leave It to Beaver, The Donna Reed Show* is one of the icons of the television families.

The original Stone household comprised Donna Stone, (Donna Reed), Dr. Alex Stone (Carl Betz), Mary Stone (Shelley Fabares), their teenage daughter, and Jeff Stone (Paul Petersen), Mary's younger brother. In a remarkable bit of casting, Shelley Fabares looked enough like Donna Reed to be her biological daughter, which she wasn't.

This stable, tight-knit group was altered slightly after being on the air for nearly five years. The storyline had Mary Stone leave for college in 1962 and she made only an occasional appearance for the next year. She left the series in 1963 and was replaced by an eight-year-old orphan, Trisha, who was adopted by the Stones.

While still working on *The Donna Reed Show,* Shelley Fabares recorded a hit single, "Johnny Angel," that went to the top of the record charts, earning her a gold record.

The niece of Nanette Fabray (who changed the spelling of her name from Fabares), Shelley appeared in five motion pictures after leaving *The Donna Reed Show.* Her first role was Brie Matthews in the 1964 Fabian outing, RIDE THE WILD WAVES. She then co-starred with Elvis Presley in three pictures: as Valerie in the 1965 beach musical, GIRL HAPPY, Cynthia Foxhugh in the 1966 musical, SPINOUT; and Dianne Carter in the 1967 Presley film, CLAMBAKE.

She later returned to television as Dr. Anne Jamison in *The Brian Keith Show,* which was followed by a number of other sitcoms. But she really came into her own on the CBS situation comedy, *One Day at a Time*, in which she appeared regularly as Francine Webster between 1981 and 1984, along with her famous aunt who played Bonnie Franklin's mother, Katheryn Romano.

A more mature Shelley Fabares, as Christine Armstrong, co-starred as Coach Hayden Fox's (Craig T. Nelson) steady on the ABC filmed situation comedy, *Coach,* which premiered on February 28, 1989.

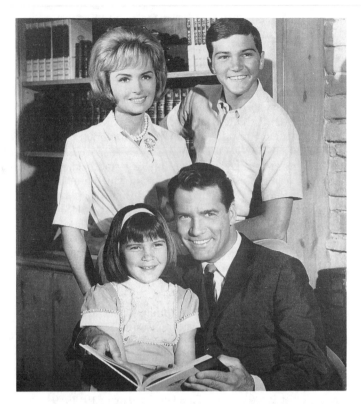

Dr. Alex Stone (bottom right) with (clockwise) his daughter, Trisha, wife Donna and son Jeff in *The Donna Reed Show,* which originally starred Shelley Fabares as the Stone's eldest daughter, Mary, who is not in this picture because she was supposed to be away at college.

When Patty Petersen joined the cast she became the Stones' daughter, replacing Shelley Fabares even though she was so much younger. It was natural for her to play Jeff's younger sister, because in real life—she was. Patty Petersen stayed with the series through the end, but her career didn't blossom the way Shelley Fabares' had and she left acting.

DOORWAY TO DANGER

July 6, 1951–October 1, 1953.   NBC-ABC

Character:	Chief John Randolph
Played by:	Melville Ruick
Date(s):	July 6, 1951–August 1951

Replaced by:	Chief John Randolph
Played by:	Roland Winters
Date(s):	1952

Replaced by:	Chief John Randolph
Played by:	Raymond Bramley
Date(s):	1953

Character: Agent Doug Carter
Played by: Grant Richards
Date(s):   1951

Replaced by: Agent Doug Carter
Played by: Stacy Harris
Date(s):   1953

This weekly half hour of international intrigue began as *Door With No Name,* a summer replacement for *The Big Story.* The head of the government's top-secret agency was Chief John Randolph, originally played by Melville Ruick. Randolph's top agent, Doug Carter, was first played by Grant Richards.

The first season ended in August 1951. When the second began the following July, the name of the series had been changed from *Door With No Name* to *Doorway to Danger.* There was also a new cast. Ruick went on to play Dr. Barton Crane in the CBS medical drama, *City Hospital.*

There was no Agent Carter during this season, but Chief John Randolph was still in charge of the government agency. He was now being played by Roland Winters, who played the first J.R. Boone on the CBS situation comedy, *Meet Millie* (See Entry). From 1965 to 1966, Roland Winters played Leonard J. Costello, the publisher of Pandora Publications and Dick Smothers' boss on *The Smothers Brothers Show.* Roland Winters is better known as the fourth and final Charlie Chan, starring in six films between 1947 and 1949.

Doorway to Danger moved to ABC for the third and final season with yet a new cast. Randolph was now played by Raymond Bramley. Agent Doug Carter was played by Stacy Harris, who went on to become Mayor Clum from 1960 to 1961 in the ABC Western, *The Life and Legend of Wyatt Earp.*

THE DORIS DAY SHOW

September 24, 1968–September 10, 1973.   CBS

Character: Angie Thompson
Played by: Fran Ryan
Date(s):   September 24, 1968–November 1968

Replaced by: Juanita
Played by: Naomi Stevens
Date(s):   December 1968–September 16, 1969

Character: Michael Nicholson
Played by: McLean Stevenson
Date(s):   September 22, 1969–September 6, 1971

Replaced by: Cyril "Cy" Bennett
Played by: John Dehner
Date(s):   September 13, 1971–September 10, 1973

Character: Myrna Gibbons
Played by: Rose Marie
Date(s):   September 22, 1969–September 6, 1971

Replaced by: Jackie Parker
Played by: Jackie Joseph
Date(s):   September 13, 1971–September 10, 1973

The perennially lovely Doris Day graced the small screen in her own situation comedy, *The Doris Day Show,* from 1968 to 1973. Ms. Day played a widow, Doris Martin, who, like *Green Acres'* Lisa Douglass, said "good-bye city life" in favor of a rural one. In this case it was the Martin family ranch.

The adjustment to ranch living, however, proved to be more difficult for the writers and producers than for the Martin family, because they just couldn't seem to settle on the right formula, or cast.

The new series had been on the air for less than three months when Doris Martin's (Day's name in the series) housekeeper was replaced. Aggie Thompson, the first housekeeper, was played by Fran Ryan, who turned up the following season as the second Mrs. Doris Ziffel on *Green Acres* (See Entry). Her domestic replacement, Juanita, was played by Naomi Stevens who, ten years later, played Sergeant Bella Archer on the ABC detective drama, *VEGA$.*

By the end of the first season, Doris again longed for the big city and took a secretarial job at San Francisco's *Today's World* magazine. The publication's editor, Michael Nicholson, was played by McLean Stevenson, who later reached the high point of his television career as Lieutenant Colonel Henry Blake on the critically acclaimed series, *M*A*S*H* (See Entry). His secretary, Myrna Gibbons, was played by Rose Marie, who played comedy writer Sally Rogers on *The Dick Van Dyke Show* in the early 1960s.

The format changed again at the beginning of the third season when Doris, along with her two sons and their dog, moved to San Francisco.

With the start of the fourth season the program's elements were altered drastically. Doris Martin still worked for *Today's World* magazine, now as a staff writer, à la the *Mary Tyler Moore Show.* In this, the next to the last season, the entire cast was dropped, including her boys and their dog. The new editor of the magazine was Cyril Bennett, who was played by John Dehner. A veteran radio actor, John Dehner appeared as a regular in eleven television series. His television roles include Jim "Duke" Williams on the ABC newspaper drama, *The Roaring 20's* (See Entry), which aired from October 15, 1960 to September 21, 1962. His more than 40 film roles include Henry Wheelock in the 1978 picture, THE BOYS FROM BRAZIL.

The new boss, of course, had to have a new secretary. She was Jackie Parker, played by comedienne Jackie Joseph, who was a regular on Bob Newhart's comedy variety show, *The Bob Newhart Show,* which aired on NBC from October 10, 1961 to June 13, 1962.

What all this proves, of course, is that even after landing a regular role on a weekly television series, one is not guaranteed stardom, or even steady work. But in television, "Que Sera Sera."

DOWN THE SHORE

June 21, 1992–August 5, 1993.   Fox

Character:	Miranda Halpern
Played by:	Pamela Segall
Date(s):	June 21, 1992–September 20, 1992

Replaced by:	Sammy
Played by:	Nancy Sorel
Date(s):	December 3, 1992–August 5, 1993

Sixty miles south of New York City, on the New Jersey coast, lies the Monmouth County town of Belmar, a quiet community surrounded by water on three sides: to the west, the Belmar Marine Basin; to the north, the Shark River Inlet; and to the east, the Atlantic Ocean. It is the lure of this water and the clean beaches that draws tourists during the summer months to swell the year-round population of 6,000 to more than 60,000. It also caught creator Alan Kirschenbaum's attention as the ideal setting for his Fox sitcom, appropriately titled, *Down the Shore*.

One of the advantages of vacationing in Belmar is that there are nearly 1,000 rental units available for from a week to the entire summer—ranging from one-room bungalows to seventy-five-year-old ten-bedroom estates. It is one of these Victorian homes that serves as the setting for the Fox sitcom about six friends—three guys and three gals—sharing the $8,000 rent and their lives on weekends during the summer months.

The guys, who have been friends since they were kids, are Zack (Lew Schneider), an inner city junior high school teacher; Aldo (Louis Mandylor), a clothing salesman for Cleanwear Fabrics in New York City's garment district; and Eddie Cheever (Tom McGowan), a computer program writer. Actor McGowan also added a bit of authenticity to the cast: he was actually born in Belmar.

The gals, who worked together in the same unnamed New York advertising agency, were Arden (Anna Gunn), a socialite; Donna Shipko (Cathryn de Prume), an ambitious receptionist; and Miranda (Pamela Segall), an artist.

Since Belmar is a real setting, not a fictional one, scenes of the town and the beach were used in the show's opening, the most recognizable of which is a strip of stores, arcades and eateries known as Belmar Playland, located on Ocean Avenue between 14th and 15th Avenues, and featuring as its main attraction the relaxing diversion of "Rooftop Golf." But because the proper permissions could not be obtained in time for shooting, the house used in the opening and exteriors of transitional scenes is actually located at 215 Lincoln Avenue in the next town over—Avon-by-the-Sea. The number of the house shown on the series, which is shot at Warner Hollywood Studios in California, is 738.

"I Don't Wanna Go Home," the show's theme song, comes from the title track of a 1976 album by the same name. If it seems to have a decidedly down home flavor, it may be because it was written and produced by Jersey Shore native Steven Van Zandt, and performed by *Southside Johnny & the Asbury Jukes*.

Van Zandt, (formerly known as "Miami Steve" when he played lead guitar with Bruce Springsteen's *E Street Band* for nine years) is also the older brother of writer/actor/producer Billy Van Zandt (see: *Anything But Love, I Love Lucy, Newhart, The Odd Couple*).

The first episode of *Down the Shore* is set on the Fourth of July, although the six roommates had been coming down to the shore for about six weeks. As is the case with most pilot episodes, the thrust of the storyline of "Independence Day" was essentially the vehicle used to set up the premise and introduce the characters.

Down the Shore's creator, Alan Kirschenbaum, did an outstanding job with the script for the pilot, directed by John Sgueglia, which played more like a Lanford Wilson stage play than a Fox sitcom.

Introduced as a limited series, *Down the Shore* aired a total of thirteen original episodes before going on hiatus after the September 20, 1992 episode. It should have returned in the summer of 1993, which would have made sense since Belmar is located on the East coast. But this is television and, ignoring the cold winter weather, the original cast went back down the shore, without Pamela Segall's Miranda, on a chilly December 3, 1992, eight days before a powerful Nor'easter hit the area. The hurricane-like squall, which was labeled as one of the worst storms of the century, ripped up Belmar's boardwalk between 17th and 22nd Avenues, devastated homes and businesses, knocked out power, washed out roads and bridges, and forced the suspension of most mass transit.

According to the Fox Broadcasting publicity department, the reason that Pamela Segall did not return to *Down the Shore* was that the writers and producers felt Miranda was a dead-end character. Initially they had felt she had a lot of potential, but she seemed to hit a wall and leave them nowhere to go, with no other avenues to explore in the storylines. So she was written out and replaced by Sammy—a new female character who was totally different.

At the age of 15, Pamela Segall, the daughter of television writer Don Segall (*Fish/The Four Seasons*), appeared in Goldie Hawn's variety special, *Goldie and Kids: Listen to Me,* which aired on ABC on May 8, 1982. From January 18 to April 19, 1986, Ms. Segall played Toni Rutledge on the ABC situation comedy, *The Redd Foxx Show,* and during the 1983/1984 television season played Kelly Affinado on *The Facts of Life.* Her motion picture roles include Delores Rebchuck in the 1982 musical comedy, GREASE 2, and Rebecca in the 1989 dramatic comedy, SAY ANYTHING, which co-starred Ione Skye of *Covington Cross* (See Entry) as Diane Court.

Sammy was played by Nancy Sorel, who portrayed Monique McCallum-Craig from March 27, 1989 to January 25, 1991 on the NBC daytime soap opera, *Generations.* She has also had guest starring roles on *Jake and the Fatman, Doogie Howser, M.D., The Commish* and *Matlock.*

Nancy Sorel made her first appearance as Sammy in "No Hard Feelings," the premiere episode of *Down the Shore*'s second season.

DONNA:	(Entering the house) Hey guys, we need a new roommate.

EDDIE: What are ya talkin' about?

ARDEN: Miranda told us at work that she can't come down anymore.

DONNA: She got a big gallery opening and she wants to stay in the city and paint every weekend.

EDDIE: Well, why can't she paint here?

DONNA: There's too many distractions.

ALDO: Distractions? Like what? (At that moment, Zack tosses a pile of dirty bed linens over the balcony, which land on Eddie's head.)

The solution, of course, was to invite Sammy to move in. After all, she has known Arden since the fourth grade, even though they hadn't seen each other since their high school graduation. Today, Sammy designs expensive jewelry that is exclusive to Bloomingdale's and the Guggenheim Museum.

The childhood friends bump into each other on the beach in Belmar. Sammy is actually on her way to a meeting in Philadelphia but says that she got off the train when she saw the beach. She would have had to have very good eyes to see the beach, because the ocean is seven blocks from the Belmar train station. But since the train from New York to Philadelphia runs on a line that doesn't even pass through Belmar, Sammy would have to have had telescopic vision to see the beach.

Nevertheless, Sammy manages to get off the train, buy a bathing suit and find her way to the beach, where she meets her old school chum. The three women return to the house, where Donna makes the announcement.

DONNA: Hey guys, this is Sammy. She might want to move in.

This is fine with Zack and Eddie, but Aldo has a problem with it because of a one-night tryst with Sammy that broke his unblemished record of 638 conquests. The problem was that on this occasion, Aldo failed to perform, as Sammy explains in purely clinical terms. When the naive Donna fails to get the drift, Sammy puts it in simpler words "His pee pee didn't work."

But since it was Aldo's male ego that was bruised, he lies to his friends about his reasons for not wanting Sammy to move in—he tells the guys that she was a thief.

Of course, by the show's end, Aldo and Sammy work out their differences.

EDDIE: So, she's movin' in?

ALDO: Yeah, yeah, yeah, you know. We talked 'bout it, you know, and she's gonna try to get over me. But she understands it's her problem. I'm cool with it. I don't have any hard feelings.

EDDIE: (Out loud, but almost in an aside) That's funny.

DRAGNET

January 3, 1952–September 10, 1970.   NBC
September 29, 1990–September 1991   Syndicated

Character:	Sergeant Joe Friday
Played by:	Jack Webb
Date(s):	January 3, 1952–September 10, 1970
Replaced by:	Detective Vic Daniels
Played by:	Jeff Osterhage
Date(s):	September 29, 1990–September 1991
Character:	Sergeant Ben Romero
Played by:	Barton Yarborough
Date(s):	December 1951
Replaced by:	Sergeant Ed Jacobs
Played by:	Barney Phillips
Date(s):	Spring 1952
Replaced by:	Officer Frank Smith
Played by:	Herb Ellis
Date(s):	Fall 1952
Replaced by:	Officer Frank Smith
Played by:	Ben Alexander
Date(s):	1953–1959
Replaced by:	Officer Bill Gannon
Played by:	Harry Morgan
Date(s):	January 1967–September 10, 1970
Replaced by:	Detective Carl Molina
Played by:	Bernard White
Date(s):	September 29, 1990–September 1991
Character:	Captain Brown
Played by:	Art Ballinger
Date(s):	unknown
Replaced by:	Captain Nelson
Played by:	Clark Howat
Date(s):	unknown
Replaced by:	Captain Nelson
Played by:	Len Wayland
Date(s):	unknown
Replaced by:	Captain Nelson
Played by:	Byron Morrow
Date(s):	unknown
Character:	Captain Al Trembly
Played by:	Clark Howat
Date(s):	unknown

Replaced by: Captain Lussen
Played by: Don Stroud
Date(s):   September 29, 1990–September 1991

The story you are about to read is true; only the names of the characters and actors have been changed to protect the series.

Jack Webb created *Dragnet* for radio and cast himself in the lead as Sergeant Joe Friday. His partner, Sergeant Ben Romero, was played by Barton Yarborough.

When the opportunity arrived for Webb and *Dragnet*'s producers to move the radio drama to television, the NBC network is said to have recommended casting Lloyd Nolan as Friday, because they did not feel that Jack Webb had the needed "star quality" to carry the series on television.

The pilot episode aired at 7 p.m. on Sunday, December 16, 1951 on *Chesterfield Soundoff Time*, with Webb and Yarborough recreating their radio roles. Then, three days after the program aired, as if it were a *Dragnet* plot element to be followed up by those famous four-notes, "Dum-de-dum-dum," Jack Webb's fifty-year-old co-star, Barton Yarborough, died in Burbank, California of a heart attack.

The sudden and unexpected loss of his friend and co-star broke the creative momentum that Webb had been building up. The episode following the three that had already been filmed with Yarborough was, like the rest of the series, taken from real life. In that episode, as well as on the radio version which was running concurrently, the Ben Romero character died of a sudden heart attack. It was also one of the few times during the series' long run that Sergeant Joe Friday displayed some emotion. "There followed an awkward search for a replacement, one of the few times the first season *Dragnet* stumbled. Part of its success was its frills-less approach. Introducing and reintroducing new partners distracted from the strong stories' linear lines."[19]

Friday's second partner was Sergeant Ed Jacobs. Jacobs was played by Barney Phillips, who looked a lot like Jack Webb. In fact, they looked so much like each other in close-ups that it was actually confusing to watch, so Sergeant Jacobs was quickly replaced by Officer Frank Smith.

The first of the two actors to portray Smith was Herb Ellis. But "Ellis' Smith was a nonentity who did not compare favorably with the seemingly calm Friday."[20] Ellis completed work on the first season and was replaced by Ben Alexander at the start of the second season's programs. Webb released very little information about the cast change to the press because he did not want to draw attention to the replacement and felt that the show should be the star.

Ben Alexander differed from his predecessors in that he somehow seemed to be more "human." He was slightly heavy-set and a little older than Friday. He was also more likeable than Friday. "Alexander looked like everyone's favorite uncle or friendly neighbor. He looked like someone you could trust."[21] And trust him we did, for the next six years.

The *Dragnet* radio program ended in 1955, but the television series continued for four more years.

Nearly eleven years later, Universal television brought Jack Webb back to produce a made-for-television *Dragnet* movie. He would again play the tough, emotionless Joe Friday and planned to reactivate Ben Alexander's commission to play Officer Frank Smith. There was just one glitch. Ben Alexander had just accepted the role of Desk Sergeant Dan Briggs on a new police drama, *Felony Squad,* which aired on ABC from September 12, 1966 to January 31, 1969. During the show's 1967/1968 season, Barney Phillips appeared alongside Alexander as Captain Franks.

Webb found his new partner in Harry Morgan, who would become Officer Bill Gannon. He may have been somewhat shorter and thinner than Ben Alexander, but possessed the same everyman likeable characteristics that had made Alexander's character play so well against Webb's Joe Friday.

Morgan did, however, break the mold of Webb's preference for hiring "unknown" actors for the series. Morgan co-starred as Art Croft in the 1943 Western drama, THE OX-BOW INCIDENT and was Bill Womack in the 1948 crime drama, THE BIG CLOCK. He was also the astute southern judge in the Fredric March/Spencer Tracy drama, INHERIT THE WIND. To television audiences, Harry Morgan was Pete Porter from the CBS sitcom *December Bride* and its spinoff series, *Pete and Gladys,* which kept him in viewers' living rooms from September 19, 1960 to September 10, 1962. He went on to star as one of televison's stronger father figures, Colonel Sherman Potter, in *M*A*S*H* (See Entry) and *After M*A*S*H.*

The later versions of *Dragnet*—that is, *Dragnet 67, Dragnet 68, Dragnet 69* and *Dragnet 70*—suffered from numerous changes in the supporting roles.

Captain Brown, played by Art Ballinger, was replaced by Captain Nelson, who was played by Clark Howat, Len Wayland and Byron Morrow. Clark Howat was then brought back to play Captain Al Trembly, who replaced Captain Nelson. Howat continued with the series, although his name was changed from Trembly to Brooks, and William Boyett played both Sergeant Bill Pailing and Sergeant Sam Hunter.

Dragnet was much more than a television show; it was an institution, and not only was it copied, it was often parodied. The best-known sendup of the no-nonsense, quick-talking Joe Friday was the parody Jack Webb himself performed with Johnny Carson on *The Tonight Show Starring Johnny Carson.*

Another parody, this one a big-budget motion picture version, was released seventeen years later with Dan Aykroyd as Sergeant Joe Friday (the supposed nephew of Jack Webb's Joe Friday) and Tom Hanks as his partner, Pep Streebek. Harry Morgan, Webb's long-time partner, appeared as his Bill Gannon character, who had been promoted to Captain.

The more important revival was a new syndicated *Dragnet* series that varied very little in style and format from the original

19. Meyers, Ric. *Murder On the Air, Television's Great Mystery Series.* The Mysterious Press, New York, 1989, p. 53.
20. *Ibid.*
21. *Ibid.*

series that was canceled some twenty years earlier. There was even a disclaimer flashed on the screen during the closing credits that read: "The characters and events depicted in this photoplay are based on facts; however, the names have been changed to protect the privacy of the individuals."

The new cast members were nice-looking young men in their thirties, but they couldn't be classified as hunks. And although both Jeff Osterhage as Vic Daniels and Bernard White as Carl Molina ran the risk of parodying the Joe Friday and Bill Gannon roles they were taking over, they did an admirable job of portraying solid police work with a lot of fancy fights and gunplay.

Backing them up at headquarters was Captain Lussen, played by Don Stroud, who had played Captain Pat Chambers on *Mickey Spillane's Mike Hammer* (See Entry) and Sergeant Mick Varrick on the Kate Mulgrew detective series, *Kate Loves a Mystery,* which aired on NBC from February 26 to December 6, 1979. Stroud's film credits include Jesse in the 1978 musical biography, THE BUDDY HOLLY STORY, and Friar Bolen in the 1979 shocker, THE AMITYVILLE HORROR.

The original *Dragnet* announcer was Hal Gibney. He was later replaced by George Fenneman, who had served as the on-camera host and announcer of the enormously popular Groucho Marx quiz program, *You Bet Your Life,* which aired on NBC from October 5, 1950 to September 21, 1961, and where the secret "woid" was "longevity."

DREXELL'S CLASS

September 19, 1991–July 9, 1992.   Fox

Character:	Principal Francine Itkin
Played by:	Randy Graff
Date(s):	September 19, 1991–November 7, 1991

Replaced by:	Principal Marilyn Ridge
Played by:	Edie McClurg
Date(s):	November 14, 1991–July 9, 1992

By September 1991, Fox had become a viable network entity premiering new series right along with the big three. *Drexell's Class* was one of Fox's contributions to the twenty-eight new series introduced in the fall of that year.

Instead of creating a star out of an unknown, Fox opted to feature an established actor in the title role. Starring as Otis Drexell in this half-hour sitcom was Dabney Coleman,who began his career as an unspectacular dramatic actor playing supporting roles such as Charlie in the Sidney Poitier/Anne Bancroft 1965 drama, THE SLENDER THREAD, and the salesman in the Natalie Wood/Robert Redford 1966 vehicle, THIS PROPERTY IS CONDEMNED.

Dabney Coleman had turned in a strong performance as McKittrick in the 1983 hit motion picture, WARGAMES, but it was his work in comedies that really made him a star. His successful comedic film roles include Franklin Hart, Jr. in Dolly Parton's 1980 comedy, 9 TO 5, and Ron in Dustin Hoffman's 1982 farce, TOOTSIE.

One of Coleman's earliest comedic television parts was the recurring role of Merle Jeeters, the corrupt mayor of Fernwood in Norman Lear's syndicated comedies *Mary Hartman, Mary Hartman, Fernwood 2–Night,* and *America 2–Night.* He later gained critical acclaim as TV talk show host, "Buffalo" Bill Bittinger in the NBC sitcom, *Buffalo Bill* (May 31, 1983–April 5, 1984).

Coleman drew upon these roles for his characterization of the ornery but likeable Otis Drexell, who was forced into accepting the position of fifth-grade teacher to pay off an enormous IRS debt.

In *Shut Up Kids,* the unaired pilot for the series that became *Drexell's Class,* Suzie Plakson played Principal Francine Itkin. But it was Randy Graff who started as Principal Itkin with the series first episode, "Otis' Last Day." Two months later, Ms. Graff was replaced by Edie McClurg as Marilyn Ridge.

Ms. McClurg has been a familiar face around television since the mid-1970s. She was a regular during the 1976 season of the CBS musical variety show, *Tony Orlando and Dawn,* and the short-lived variety program, *The Big Show,* which aired on NBC from March 4 to June 3, 1980.

In the NBC sitcom miniseries, *The Kallikaks* (August 3–31, 1977), Edie McClurg co-starred as Venus Kallikak. She was also Willamae Jones during the 1981 season of Barbara Eden's NBC situation comedy, *Harper Valley P.T.A.* (January 16, 1981–August 14, 1982). Edie McClurg's most memorable television role to date has been Mrs. Poole, the next-door neighbor on *The Hogan Family,* which began its life as *Valerie* (See Entry).

THE DUKES OF HAZZARD

January 26, 1979–August 16, 1985.   CBS

Character:	Luke Duke
Played by:	Tom Wopat
Date(s):	January 26, 1979–April 2, 1982
	February 25, 1983–August 16, 1985

Replaced by:	Coy Duke
Played by:	Byron Cherry
Date(s):	September 24, 1982–February 25, 1983

Character:	Bo Duke
Played by:	John Schneider
Date(s):	January 26, 1979–April 2, 1982
	February 25 1983–August 16, 1985

Replaced by:	Vance Duke
Played by:	Christopher Mayer
Date(s):	September 24, 1982–February 25, 1983

Character:	Deputy Enos Strate
Played by:	Sonny Shroyer
Date(s):	January 26, 1979–November 5, 1980
	October 22, 1982–August 16, 1985

Replaced by: Reserve Deputy Cletus
Played by: Rick Hurst
Date(s):   1980–1983

Character: Roscoe P. Coltrane
Played by: James Best
Date(s):   January 26, 1979–January 25, 1980
                March 21, 1980–August 16, 1985

Replaced by: Sheriff Grady Byrd
Played by: Dick Sargent
Date(s):   February 1, 1980–March 14, 1980

Character: Mabel
Played by: Ginny Parker
Date(s):   unknown

Replaced by: Mabel
Played by: Lindsay Bloom
Date(s):   October 24, 1978–November 21, 1981

The good guys in this light adventure series were two cousins, Luke and Coy Duke, who did their best to right the wrongs of the corrupt politician, Jefferson Davis, known as "Boss Hogg." The main catalyst for the action of the series seemed to be their car, the "General Lee," which was in reality a souped up 1969 Dodge Charger.

The series and its colorful characters caught on with the public in record time and on November 5, 1980, Sonny Shroyer, who played Deputy Enos Strate, starred in a special two-hour episode "Enos—Strate to the Top," that was the pilot for his own series, *Enos*. In that spinoff episode, Enos accidentally captures two wanted criminals, which impresses the Los Angeles Police Department, and the LAPD subsequently offers Enos a job with the newly formed Division 8 branch of its Metro Squad.

When Enos Strate left *The Dukes of Hazzard,* he was replaced by Reserve Deputy Cletus, played by Rick Hurst, who stayed with the series until 1983 even though Sonny Shroyer returned to *The Dukes of Hazzard* in 1982 when *Enos* was canceled after only 16 episodes, the last of which aired on September 19, 1981.

The Dukes of Hazzard experienced considerable success and became one of CBS's biggest hits, spawning merchandise tie-ins from toy companies to T-shirt manufacturers, including Knickerbocker Toy Company, a division of Warner Communications.

Then, in the spring of 1982, both Tom Wopat and John Schneider decided to put their popularity to the ultimate test, betting that it was them and not the car that viewers were tuning in for each week. They walked out on the series in a bitter

contract dispute, which included a $25,000,000 lawsuit against Warner Bros. Television and a $90,000,000 counter lawsuit by the studio, denying that they had cheated the actors out of their profits from the merchandising rights.

The discrepancy in the royalties came when John Schneider read that Warner Communications had earned $190,000,000 from the sale of *Dukes* merchandise in 1981. "Tom and I said, 'Hey, wait a minute. We're supposed to be getting five percent of that and we each have received only $16,000.' It just didn't add up."[22]

The actors were also suing for increased salaries and for more script control.

Forced to find two suitable replacements, Warner Bros. embarked on a nationwide talent hunt and were reported to have auditioned 2,230 actors before settling on two non-professionals, Byron Cherry and Christopher Mayer. John Schneider spoke candidly about the hiring of Byron Cherry for the role of Coy Duke in a 1982 interview with *TV Guide*. "Byron's one of my best friends from Atlanta," he says. "I coached him for the part and he stayed at my house in Los Angeles while they were testing him."[23]

The revised storyline of the fifth season opener, "The New Dukes," introduced Cherry and Mayer as Luke and Bo's cousins, Coy and Vance, who had returned to Hazzard County to help their uncle Jesse (Denver Pyle) run the farm while Luke and Bo pursued a racing career on the NASCAR circuit.

In a statement issued by Warner Bros. on Wednesday, December 22, 1982, *Dukes* original stars Tom Wopat and John Schneider said, "We are especially happy to be returning to our family on the show, whom we have missed very much. We have good feelings about our return and welcome the opportunity to put the past misunderstandings behind us."

Their return to the program, eighteen episodes later, was heralded in the title, "Welcome Back Bo and Luke." The *TV Guide* listing read "Bo and Luke (John Schneider, Tom Wopat) roar into Hazzard from a triumphant tour on the NASCAR circuit, and not a moment too soon. . . ."[24] This episode also marked the exit of their cousins, Coy and Vance, even though Paul Picard, the producer of the *Dukes of Hazzard,* said, "I'll take Schneider and Wopat back in a minute if they decide to return. I'd also keep Byron Cherry and Chris Mayer. That'd just mean we'd have seven people riding in the General Lee instead of five."[25]

The following season, Christopher Mayer turned up as *Glitter Magazine*'s reporter, Pete Bozak, on the ABC drama, *Glitter,* which aired from September 13, 1984 to December 27, 1985.

Dick Sargent, the mortal who was the second Darrin Stephens on *Bewitched* (See Entry), replaced James Best as Boss Hogg's corrupt sheriff for six weeks. Best had walked off the show because of poor scripts, not because of an argument about dressing rooms—a story that had been circulated.

Hazzard County's telephone operator, Mabel, was originally

22. Davidson, Bill. "Crackup in Hazzard County! Here's the Casualty Report" *TV Guide,* December 25, 1985, p. 14.
23. *Ibid.*
24. *TV Guide* (listing) Vol. 31, No. 8, February 19, 1983, Issue #1560, p. A-106
25. Davidson, Bill. "Crackup in Hazzard County! Here's the Casualty Report." *TV Guide,* December 25, 1985, p. 14.

The Dukes of Hazzard are (clockwise) John Schneider and Tom Wopat as Bo and Luke, with Catherine Bach as their cousin Daisy.

played by Ginny Parker. She was later replaced by Lindsay Bloom, Miss U.S.A., 1973. Miss Bloom, who began her television career on *The Dean Martin Show* as one of the "Ding-a-Ling Sisters," later played Velda on *Mickey Spillane's Mike Hammer* (See Entry).

Luke and Coy and Bo and Vance, however, weren't the only look-alikes in the series to be replaced. In addition to the cast changes, nearly 300 look-alike Dodge Chargers were used during the series. The cars had to be replaced on a regular basis as a result of the two to three cars which were wrecked each week during the five or more jumps filmed during production.

EIGHT IS ENOUGH

March 15, 1977–August 29, 1981.   ABC

Character:	Joan Bradford
Played by:	Diana Hyland
Date(s):	March 15, 1977–April 19, 1977

Replaced by:	Sandra Sue Abbott ''Abby'' Bradford
Played by:	Betty Buckley
Date(s):	November 9, 1977–August 29, 1981

Replaced by:	Sandra Sue Abbott ''Abby'' Bradford
Played by:	Mary Frann
Date(s):	October 18, 1987 (reunion movie)

Character:	Nancy Bradford
Played by:	Kimberly Beck
Date(s):	March 15, 1977

Replaced by:	Nancy Bradford
Played by:	Dianne Kay
Date(s):	March 22, 1977–August 29, 1981

Character:	David Bradford
Played by:	Mark Hamill
Date(s):	March 15, 1977–March 22, 1977

Replaced by:	David Bradford
Played by:	Grant Goodeve
Date(s):	March 22, 1977–August 29, 1981

Character:	Tommy Bradford
Played by:	Chris English
Date(s):	March 15, 1977

Replaced by:	Tommy Bradford
Played by:	Willie Aames
Date(s):	March 22, 1977–August 29, 1981

Character:	Donna
Played by:	Lucy Soroyan
Date(s):	March 15, 1977

Replaced by:	Donna
Played by:	Jennifer Darling
Date(s):	March 29, 1977–April 4, 1981

In a throwback to the 1950s, the Bradford kids—all eight of them—were blessed with a TV family that had both a mother and a father who loved them all very much. The big difference between this family and its video cousins was that these kids were all quite independent.

Dick Van Patten played their intelligent and very even-tempered father, Tom Bradford, a columnist for the *Register,* a newspaper in Sacramento, California. His wife, Joan, was played by Diana Hyland, who had played Susan Winter on *Peyton Place* from 1968 to 1969. Perhaps her most important television credit was the 1977 Emmy award she won for her performance as Mickey Lubitch, Tod Lubitch's (John Travolta) mother in the touching made-for-television movie, *The Boy in the Plastic Bubble.* It also won her the love of her co-star, Travolta.

A great many changes occurred during the first weeks of the series and among the actors who were replaced was Mark Hamill. Hamill, who had played David Bradford in the first two episodes, was replaced by Grant Goodeve. The change in cast worked out for both actors, because that same year Mark Hamill starred as Luke Skywalker in STAR WARS, the science fiction adventure film that paved the way for two sequels as well as other space fantasies such as CLOSE ENCOUNTERS OF THE THIRD KIND and STAR TREK THE MOTION PICTURE and its sequels.

Unlike Hamill, Goodeve didn't become a major star, although the series did provide him with steady work and constant exposure for four years, which opened the doors to guest appearances on many other series including a pair of *Fantasy Island* and *The Love Boat* episodes, a *T.J. Hooker* and a *Murder, She Wrote.* He also appeared as Chris Deegan, from April 20 to November 9, 1983 on the ABC evening soap opera, *Dynasty.*

Classified as a dramatic comedy, *Eight Is Enough,* which was presented as a reflection of real life, hovered in twelfth place for most of its run and climbed to eleventh place during the 1978/1979 season.

With the series underway and the cast in place, there were no plans to make any additional changes until Diana Hyland died of cancer on March 27, 1977. There were only five episodes in the can and this being a reality-based program, the producers were faced with a situation for which they could not have planned. They decided to mimic real life and had Tom Bradford's wife, Joan, die and Tom become a widower for a short while until they could regroup and, as it turned out, recast.

Betty Buckley joined the cast of *Eight Is Enough* that fall as Sandra Sue Abbott, a widow whom Tom Bradford hired as a tutor. She and Tom were married on the November 9, 1977, episode which restored the family unit. It also evoked the emotions of love and resentment that are often exhibited by family members who have a parent replaced. She wasn't their real TV mom and they showed it by calling her Abby, instead of "Mom," even as they grew to love her over the course of the series.

There were only two changes made for the 1987 TV movie *Eight Is Enough: A Family Reunion.* The first was that it aired on NBC instead of ABC, the second a slight change in cast. All of the original actors and actresses who were the Bradford children and Dick Van Patten, who played their dad, overcame their conflicting schedules to appear in this reunion show. Only their mom, actually their stepmother, who was played by Betty Buckley, had to be replaced. This time, however, no mention was made of the change in cast and Mary Frann, who was playing Bob Newhart's wife over on CBS's *Newhart,* was quietly slipped in as Abby Bradford.

The second Mrs. Bradford was unable to shoot the telefilm due to what *TV Guide* called "A compelling assignment in a new Roman Polanski film."[1] That film, released in 1988, was FRANTIC and starred Harrison Ford as Dr. Richard Walker and Betty Buckley as his wife Sondra. A year earlier, Ms. Buckley appeared as the bag lady, Leah, in WILD THING.

THE ELEVENTH HOUR

October 3, 1962–September 9, 1964.   NBC

Character:	Dr. Theodore Bassett
Played by:	Wendell Corey
Date(s):	October 3, 1962–May 22, 1963

Replaced by:	Dr. L. Richard Starke
Played by:	Ralph Bellamy
Date(s):	October 2, 1963–September 9, 1964

Created to capitalize on the success of *Dr. Kildare, The Eleventh Hour* dealt with psychological problems rather than physical ones. During the first season, Wendell Corey starred as Dr. Theodore Bassett. Corey had previously starred as Steve Peck in the CBS situation comedy, *Peck's Bad Girl,* which ran from May 5, 1959 to September 29, 1960. He also starred as Captain Ralph Baxter in the police drama, *Harbor Command,* which was syndicated during 1957 and 1958. His film roles include the role of the prison warden, Captain H. T. Peoples, in the 1952 James Stewart film, CARBINE WILLIAMS.

At the end of the first season, Wendell Corey left *The Eleventh Hour.* There are no hard facts explaining why he left

and all that his replacement, Ralph Bellamy, could recall was: "I think there was some disagreement between him and the management. I don't know what."[2]

Bellamy does recall that he did not feel predisposed to follow Wendell Corey's lead. "I just played the part as I saw it. I never gave it a thought,"[3] he said.

A very well-known film and television actor, Ralph Bellamy had nearly one hundred motion pictures to his credit. His roles in Universal's horror films include Captain Paul Montford in the THE WOLF MAN, 1941, and Erik in THE GHOST OF FRANKENSTEIN, 1942. He also made a cameo in the 1943 musical, STAGE DOOR CANTEEN and played James Morse, the owner of the business that Edward Lewis (Richard Gere) was trying to buy in the 1990 love story, PRETTY WOMAN.

The television roles of Ralph Bellamy include the first Mike Barnett in the early detective drama, *Man Against Crime* (See Entry). His later television work included President Franklin D. Roosevelt in the ABC seven-part miniseries, *The Winds of War,* which aired from February 6 to 13, 1983.

ELLERY QUEEN *see:* THE ADVENTURES OF ELLERY QUEEN

EMPTY NEST

October 8, 1988–.   NBC

Character:	Barbara Weston
Played by:	Kristy McNichol
Date(s):	October 8, 1988–October 24, 1992

Replaced by:	Emily Weston
Played by:	Lisa Rieffel
Date(s):	January 2, 1993–September 18, 1993

Television is good for the environment because it is one hundred percent recyclable. That includes premises for shows, episode plotlines, characters and, of course, the actors themselves. Though this is not an absolute, very often a producer will recycle cast members from their previous series.

A case in point is producer Susan Harris, who produced *Soap* and its spinoff, *Benson* (See Entry), and cast Robert Guillaume as Benson DuBois, the same role he played on *Soap.* Harris then recycled a number of other cast members, putting them in different roles. Caroline McWilliams, who played Sally on *Soap,* was Marcie Hill on *Benson;* and Kene Holliday, who played Eddie Dawson on *Soap,* became Earl DuBois on *Benson.*

One of *Soap*'s outstanding characters was Burt Campbell, brilliantly portrayed by Richard Mulligan who had to wait seven years before appearing in a new Susan Harris series, but it was well worth the wait. He was perfectly cast as a pediatrician,

1. Rense, Rip. "*Eight Is Enough:* A Family Reunion. Hello Again Bradfords: *Now* You Can Say Goodbye." *TV Guide,* October 17, 1987, p. 27.
2. From an exclusive telephone with Ralph Bellamy on December 20, 1990.
3. *Ibid.*

Dr. Harry Weston, a widower raising two grown daughters, in the long-running NBC sitcom, *Empty Nest.*

Empty Nest itself was a spinoff from one of Harris's other major successes, *The Golden Girls,* which premiered on NBC on September 14, 1985. Co-starring as Richard Mulligan's daughters were Kristy McNichol and Dinah Manoff as Barbara and Carol. Barbara was an undercover policewoman, her sister an insecure divorcee.

The small supporting cast included Park Overall as Dr. Weston's nurse, LaVerne Todd, and David Leisure, who achieved national recognition as TV commercial automobile pitch man, Joe Isuzu, as the Weston's annoying and womanizing next-door neighbor, Charlie Dietz. Charlie was a recycled version of Jack Tripper's (John Ritter) best friend, Larry Dallas (Richard Kline), from the ABC sitcom, *Three's Company.*

In keeping with the idea of producers recycling actors, it should come as no surprise that Dinah Manoff played Elaine Lefkowitz during the 1978/1979 season of *Soap.* Prior to her co-starring role on *Empty Nest,* Dinah Manoff appeared on a number of hit series including ''Bomb,'' the March 26, 1979 episode of *Lou Grant,* and ''The Nun,'' the second season premiere episode of the NBC sitcom, *Night Court,* which aired on September 27, 1984. She had, coincidentally, worked with her *Empty Nest* co-star, Kristy McNichol, in ''Sleeping Gypsy,'' the May 9, 1978 episode of *Family.*

But it was Kristy McNichol who came to *Empty Nest* with the strongest resumé. At the age of six, she began her career appearing in television commercials. On November 19, 1973, approximately three years later, Kristy McNichol appeared in the ''Love and the Unsteady Love'' segment of ABC's *Love American Style.* The following year, the busy actress took over the role of Patricia Apple, from Franny Michel, on the CBS drama, *Apple's Way* (See Entry).

Her real break came in 1976 when she was cast as Letitia ''Buddy'' Lawrence in the ABC drama, *Family,* which won her two Emmy awards for Best Supporting Actress in a Drama Series, in 1977 and again in 1979. But things were moving too fast for the young actress and this began to take its toll on her personal life. Still, she put herself together and continued working, appearing on dozens of series including *The Bionic Woman, The Love Boat, Starsky and Hutch* and *Murder, She Wrote.*

No longer the ''cute kid,'' Ms. McNichol, who had matured into an attractive young woman, was cast as Dr. Weston's middle daughter, Barbara. The series was a hit and her success was virtually assured. But midway through the series' fifth season the pressure of the work became too great, forcing Ms. McNichol to leave the series for what was at the time reported as ''health reasons.''

In a December 21, 1992 report on Paramount's *Entertainment Tonight,* guest host Leeza Gibbons reported: ''Actress Kristy McNichol flew the coop from her hit TV series *Empty Nest* earlier this year, saying it was a temporary break because she was suffering from a manic depressive mental disorder. Now the lowdown, according to Kristy's agent, is she has officially retired and has no plans to return to acting.''

Her being an undercover cop made it easy to write her out by having her away on an assignment. One week she was said to be on assignment in Hawaii. And in ''Thanksgiving at the Westons,'' which aired on November 21, 1992, Harry laments to his mixed breed dog Dreyfuss (Bear) about his favorite holiday.

HARRY:	I just wish everybody else was here, all together. I mean Barbara's off working—where I don't know. Emily's off traveling—where I don't know. The only steady reliable one is Carol.

Emily, incidentally, was Harry's youngest daughter, who was supposed to be attending Mount Holyoke College in South Hadley, Massachusetts, though at one point she was said to be away at college in New York. She's often spoken of and even phones home from time to time, but she has never been heard or seen—until now.

It was one terribly fortunate piece of scripting, having an unseen daughter away at college, because it allowed the writers the luxury of bringing in an already ''established,'' albeit unseen, character to replace the one who has left. A similar character switch with brothers William and Cedric was made on ABC's *Covington Cross* (See Entry). The only difference was that instead of being away at college, Armus was off fighting in the Crusades. Whatever works!

Cast in the role of Emily was Lisa Rieffel, who at the age of sixteen played Kim Ginty in the CBS law drama, *The Trials of Rosie O'Neill,* which starred Sharon Gless as Fiona Rose ''Rosie'' O'Neill. She was introduced in the January 2, 1993 episode, ''Emily,'' after being out of touch with her father for more than two months. Inside the Weston household, Dr. Harry Weston and his extremely insecure daughter, Carol, are sitting together on the sofa.

CAROL:	Daddy?
HARRY:	Hmmm?
CAROL:	With Barbara and Emily away, does it remind you of the time I was your only child? Just your one hopeless little mewling baby girl to care for day and night?
HARRY:	Does have its similarities, dear.
CAROL:	Well, pardon me for being a daddy hog, but having you to myself is the one thing that makes me truly happy (hugs a less-than-receptive Harry).

This precious moment is almost immediately interrupted when the front door bursts open.

EMILY:	Hey you guys, I'm home!

Emily is Harry's youngest daughter and is by far more worldly and even more free-spirited than Barbara. Before arriving back home, Emily left college to work in a Vietnamese clinic, rode an old moped over the Himalayas—until it caught fire—and flew to Italy to work as a hand model for two weeks. There she met millionaire ship builder, Gianni (Gian-Carlo Scandiuzzi), who subsequently fell in love with her. She met an opera singer appearing in *Don Juan in Hell,* and he, like her moped, briefly caught fire himself. She was a waitress in Kyoto, Japan and speaks both Japanese and Italian.

In an effort to "share" with her big sister, Emily asks Carol what she has been doing, but the only thing Carol could think of was that she had learned to crack an egg with one hand. When Emily says that she's planning on staying home for a week or so because of boyfriend problems (Gianni), Carol jumps in and offers to help, having herself had thirty-seven "serious" relationships.

Not long after, Charlie strolls into the Westons' kitchen and immediately begins hitting on Emily.

EMILY: I didn't know guys like you still exist. You're like a sketch from *Love, American Style.*

To tie things up neatly Harry asks Emily to consider staying home.

EMILY: (Gingerly) Carol stays?

HARRY: She kind of has squatter's rights.

So guess what? Right, Emily decides to stay (and take Barbara's place), though clips of Kristy McNichol and her superimposed credit did appear in the show's opening along with three new clips featuring Lisa Rieffel and her own close-up and superimposed credit.

EMILY: (To Dreyfuss) Help me Dryf—I'm home.

EVENING SHADE

September 21, 1990–.   CBS

Character:	Molly Newton
Played by:	Melissa Martin
Date(s):	September 21, 1990–May 1991

Replaced by:	Molly Newton
Played by:	Candy Hutson
Date(s):	September 1991

After four successful television series that began with his role as Ben Frazer on *Riverboat* (See Entry), and more than forty motion pictures, Burt Reynolds returned to television on February 13, 1989 as B.L. Stryker, an ex-cop from New Orleans who has seen one too many murders of young women and has retired to his former home in West Palm Beach, Florida. But, he doesn't stay retired for very long before he's drawn back in the thick of things by a rash of serial-type murders of young socialites.

This was an important series for Burt Reynolds. "And he knows that, for him, *Stryker* is not just another TV series. It may be his last chance to save his sinking career."[4]

The series was rather short-lived but it did prove that Burt Reynolds hadn't lost it. As a result, shortly after the demise of *B.L. Stryker,* Reynolds resurfaced as Wood Newton on the CBS sitcom, *Evening Shade.* In the small southern town of Evening Shade, Arkansas, Wood Newton faces life as the coach of a losing high school football team. He's also husband to Ava Evans Newton (Marilu Henner) and father of three children, Taylor (Jay R. Ferguson), Molly (Melissa Martin) and Will (Jacob Parker), ages fifteen, seven and four, respectively.

For unexplained reasons, Candy Hutson replaced Melissa Martin as Wood Newton's daughter Molly beginning in September 1991.

EXECUTIVE SUITE

September 20, 1976–February 11, 1977.   CBS

Character:	Elly Gibson
Played by:	Pauline Myers
Date(s):	September 20, 1976–unknown

Replaced by:	Elly Gibson
Played by:	Kim Hamilton
Date(s):	unknown–Febrary 11, 1977

One of the supporting characters in this short-lived series about the fictitious California conglomerate, the Cardway Corporation, was the wife of Malcolm Gibson (Percy Rodrigues), one of Cardway's board members.

The role was originally played by Pauline Myers who had played Gloria Byrd on the law drama, *Storefront Lawyers,* which ran on CBS from September 16, 1970 to September 1, 1971. Ms. Myers was replaced on *Executive Suite* by Kim Hamilton.

---

4. Jordan, Pat. "Burt Reynolds on the Skids. . . Will B.L. Stryker Be His Deliverance?" *TV Guide,* Vol. 37, No. 9, March 4, 1989, Issue #1875, p.27.

F

THE FACTS OF LIFE

August 24, 1979–September 10, 1988.   NBC

Character:	Edna Garrett
Played by:	Charlotte Rae
Date(s):	August 24, 1979–September 20, 1986

Replaced by:	Beverly Ann Stickle
Played by:	Cloris Leachman
Date(s):	September 27, 1986–September 10, 1988

Character:	Harold J. Crocker
Played by:	Jack Riley
Date(s):	1979

Replaced by:	Steven Bradley
Played by:	John Lawlor
Date(s):	1979–1980

Replaced by:	Mr. Harris
Played by:	Kenneth Mars
Date(s):	1980

Replaced by:	Charles Parker
Played by:	Roger Perry
Date(s):	December 2, 1981–September 21, 1983

Character:	Monica Warner
Played by:	Pam Huntington
Date(s):	unknown

Replaced by:	Monica Warner
Played by:	Marj Dusay
Date(s):	November 18, 1981–December 5, 1987

Character:	Jason Ramsey
Played by:	Duane La Page
Date(s):	unknown

Replaced by:	Jason Ramsey
Played by:	Robert Hooks
Date(s):	unknown

The setting for this spinoff from the NBC sitcom, *Diff'rent Strokes,* was the Eastland School for Girls in Peekskill, New York, though when the school was spoken about on *Diff'rent Strokes* it was referred to as the Eastlake School.

Mrs. Garrett, who was the Drummonds' housekeeper on *Diff'rent Strokes,* accepted the position of Housemother at Eastland. This gave Charlotte Rae her own series and NBC another hit.

In addition to the cast of regular Eastland students, who stayed with the series through its entire nine-season run, there were a number of recurring regulars who moved in and out of the show, none of whom could be classified as direct replacements for others. One of these transient students, Molly Parker, was played by Molly Ringwald who went on to become a motion picture star and charter member of "The Brat Pack" appearing in such films as the 1985 teenage drama, THE BREAKFAST CLUB, in which she played the spoiled little rich girl, Claire Standish.

The first headmaster of Eastland was Harold J. Crocker, played by Jack Riley, the character actor who has made a career out of playing neurotics ever since his role as Mr. Elliot Carlin on *The Bob Newhart Show,* from September 16, 1972 to August 26, 1978. Subsequent headmasters, seen on an infrequent basis, were Steven Bradley, Mr. Harris and Charles Parker.

Monica Warner, the mother of Eastland's attractive young yuppie, Blair Warner (Lisa Whelchel), was played by both Pam Huntington and Marj Dusay. On separate occasions "Tootie" Ramsey played opposite Duane La Page and Robert Hooks, both of whom were playing her dad, Jason Ramsey.

The most important change in the program's cast came in July of 1986 when, after seven successful seasons, Charlotte Rae exited the still popular series. In the storyline, Mrs. Garrett remarries and moves away. Her place is taken by Cloris Leachman, who joins the cast as Mrs. Garrett's sister, Beverly Ann Stickle. The new episodes place added emphasis on her relationship with the four series regulars, Blair, Natalie, Jo and Tootie—played by Lisa Whelchel, Mindy Cohn, Nancy McKeon and Kim Fields respectively.

A familiar face to motion picture and television audiences, Cloris Leachman was Mary Richards' annoying friend, Phyllis Lindstrom, from 1970 to 1975 in the *Mary Tyler Moore Show,* and was later the star of her own spinoff series, *Phyllis,* which aired on CBS from September 8, 1975 to August 30, 1977. She was Frau Blucher in Mel Brooks' 1974 horror film satire, YOUNG FRANKENSTEIN, which also featured Kenneth Mars as Inspector Kemp. Ms. Leachman was also Ruth Martin, the second mom on *Lassie* (See Entry).

Roger Perry, played Charles Parker, Eastland's second head-master, replacing Kenneth Mars as Mr. Harris. Mars later replaced Edward Platt as the Chief of CONTROL on *Get Smart* (See Entry).

THE FALL GUY

November 4, 1981–May 2, 1986.   ABC

Character:	Samantha "Big Jack" Jack
Played by:	Jo Ann Pflug
Date(s):	October 28, 1981–May 5, 1982
Replaced by:	Terri Shannon (Michaels)
Played by:	Markie Post
Date(s):	October 27, 1982–May 2, 1984
Replaced by:	Pearl Sperling
Played by:	Nedra Volz
Date(s):	1985–1986
Replaced by:	Edmond Trent
Played by:	Robert Donner
Date(s):	1986

Lee Majors followed his successful *Six Million Dollar Man* series with *The Fall Guy.* He starred as Colt Seavers, a Hollywood stuntman for the Fall Guy Stunt Association, and uses his unique skills to earn extra money as a bounty hunter for the Los Angeles Criminal Courts System.

During the first two years of the series, Colt received his assignments from a sexy bail bondswoman known as "Big Jack," played by Jo Ann Pflug. In 1982, "Big Jack" was replaced by Terri Shannon, played by Markie Post. The following year, Terri's last name was inexplicably changed to Michaels.

Moviegoers may remember Ms. Pflug as Lieutenant Dish from the 1970 motion picture, M*A*S*H. Her replacement, Markie Post, is best known for her portrayal of Christine Sullivan on NBC's judicial situation comedy, *Night Court* (See Entry).

In a bit of creative casting, the beautiful young Markie Post was replaced by the considerably older Nedra Volz, as the spirited Pearl Sperling. A few years earlier Ms. Volz was busy looking after Gary Coleman as the second of three housekeepers on the NBC situation comedy, *Diff'rent Strokes* (See Entry).

At the end of *The Fall Guy*'s run, Robert Donner, as Edmond Trent, took over for the departed Pearl Sperling. It is possible that you'll remember him as Yancy Tucker, the role he played on *The Waltons* from 1972 to 1979, or as Boss Shorty from the 1967 Paul Newman film, COOL HAND LUKE. But Robert Donner is more readily associated with the role of the eccentric Exidor, that whacked-out holy man from the Robin Williams/Pam Dawber sitcom, *Mork and Mindy.*

FAMILY AFFAIR

September 12, 1966–September 9, 1971.   CBS

Character:	Mr. Giles French
Played by:	Sebastian Cabot
Date(s):	September 12, 1966–September 9, 1971
Replaced by:	Mr. Nigel French
Played by:	John Williams
Date(s):	November 1966–April 1967

Unlike the real world, there is no shortage of good domestic help in Teeveeland—one of the finest being Mr. Giles French, the epitome of a gentleman's gentleman.

His employer, Bill Davis (Brian Keith), was the guardian of three children left orphaned by his brother and sister-in-law, who died in an automobile accident back in Terre Haute, Indiana. There were the six-year-old fraternal twins, Buffy and Jody, and fifteen-year-old Catherine "Cissy" Davis, played, respectively, by Anissa Jones, Johnnie Whitaker and Kathy Garver.

Mr. French was impeccably portrayed throughout the series by the bearded, portly, somewhat stuffy and teddy bear-lovable Sebastian "Sabby" Cabot, "Who naturally loathes children, and who has all the funny lines."[1]

When producer Don Fedderson asked Cabot to take on the role of Mr. French, "Sabby really didn't want it. 'I fought for three years to lose the image of Dr. Hyatt,' he says."[2]

The Dr. Hyatt Cabot was referring to was Dr. Carl Hyatt, a special consultant to the San Francisco based detective agency, Checkmate Incorporated, the role he had played on the series, *Checkmate,* which ran on CBS from September 17, 1960, to September 19, 1962.

His new series, *Family Affair,* had barely gotten off the ground when near disaster struck in November of the first season. "He collapsed at home and was packed off to the hospital with bleeding ulcers. . . . After six weeks [and nine shows in which actor John Williams sat in for him] he recovered, but there was still a lingering doubt about whether or not the condition was malignant."[3]

Cabot's absence and the appearance of John Williams as his brother Nigel were dealt with in the program's scripts with the explanation that the Queen of England had called Giles away on special service. So as not to shirk his responsibilities to the

---

1. Hano, Arnold. "Keith and Kin." *TV Guide,* Vol. 14, No. 40, Issue #705, October 1, 1966, p. 16.
2. Whitney, Dwight. "The Great Faffler." *TV Guide,* Vol. 15, No. 16, Issue #734, April 22, 1967. p. 18.
3. *Ibid.*

Brian Keith (seated, center) starred as Bill Davis, *Family Affair*'s wealthy globe-trotting engineer. He was assisted in raising his orphaned nephew Jody (Johnnie Whitaker, bottom right) and nieces Cissy (Kathy Garver, far left) and Buffy (Anissa Jones, front) by Mr. Giles French (Sebastian Cabot, back right). That's Buffy's favorite doll, Mrs. Beasley, down in front.

FAMILY TIES

September 22, 1982–May 14, 1989.   NBC

Character:	Ellen Reed
Played by:	Tracy Pollan
Date(s):	September 26, 1985–February 13, 1986
Replaced by:	Lauren Miller
Played by:	Courteney Cox
Date(s):	September 13, 1987–May 14, 1989
Replaced by:	Marty Brodie
Played by:	Jane Adams
Date(s):	April 2, 1989–April 9, 1989

The Keatons were a very different television sitcom family. The parents, Steven and Elyse Keaton (Michael Gross and Meredith Baxter-Birney), were products of the sixties and still held on to the values of that era. Their son, Alex P. Keaton (Michael J. Fox), on the other hand, was a child of the eighties. He was outstanding scholastically, always wore a tie and held the "Almighty Dollar" as his talisman. His fifteen-year-old sister, Mallory (Justine Bateman), was a lot more relaxed and spent most of her time shopping and thinking about boys, and not necessarily in that order. Their nine-year-old sister, Jennifer (Tina Yothers), was a good student who tried her best to just be a kid, and was generally ignored by the rest of the family, who were preoccupied with more "adult" concerns. One of these was dating—no, not their own, their kids'.

Consequently, like so many sitcom parents before them, the Keatons played host to a steady stream of boyfriends and girlfriends of their pubescent offspring. But, unlike other sitcom kids, where the weekly crush was hardly worth mentioning, Alex Keaton's girlfriends played a more integral part in the series and should be mentioned.

The first major love interest to enter Alex Keaton's life was Ellen Reed (Tracy Pollan), whom he met in the first part of a two-part episode appropriately titled "The Real Thing."

One of Alex's qualities is his ability to reduce everything to a formula—even love. At the end of his first day as a sophomore at Leland College (although the logo on his sweatshirt read Leland University), Alex enters the Keaton kitchen, where so much of the series took place, and tells his parents that he has narrowed down his choices of the girl he intends to fall in love with to "seven lucky finalists," whom he has selected from photographs in the Leland College Freshman Directory.

Alex goes to the dormitory where his "dream girl," Tricia Armstrong, lives. She is, of course, the beautiful blonde homecoming queen type. He is greeted at the door by Ellen Reed, Tricia's rather plain-looking (by comparison) roommate who comes complete with pony tail and glasses. He invites himself in to wait for Miss Armstrong and manages immediately to get on Ellen's nerves, and they end up in a shouting match.

When Alex gets back home he complains to his mother that

Davis family, his brother Nigel stepped in to cover for him temporarily.

Cabot was able to complete work on the episodes for the second season, but when shooting wrapped up in March he went in to the hospital for an operation which allayed his worst fears and restored the 260–pound actor to full health.

The other Mr. French was played by John Williams, who was Chief Inspector Hubbard in the 1954 Ray Milland/Grace Kelly 3–D mystery, DIAL M FOR MURDER. But in spite of his fine performance in this and dozens of other films, John Williams will perhaps always be remembered not for his film work but as the rather distinguished television huckster for a set of classical music albums in which he so eloquently explained that the familiar theme *A Stranger in Paradise* is actually taken from the Polovtsian Dance Number Two by Borodin.

In 1973 Sebastian Cabot did an admirable job in the classic Edmund Gwenn role of Kris Kringle in the television remake of MIRACLE ON 34TH STREET.

he can't seem to get Ellen off his mind. When he returns to the dorm to pick Tricia up for a date he learns that Ellen is engaged to be married. Back at home, Alex now confides in his dad that he cannot get Ellen out of his mind.

At the big school dance, Alex gets a chance to slow dance with Ellen when Tricia is out of the room, and winds up kissing her. After the dance, Alex offers to drive Ellen to the train station so that she can meet her fiancé in Pennsylvania where they will be married.

Later that evening, back at the Keaton kitchen, Alex admits to his mom that he is in love with Ellen, and he then drives 350 miles to the train station in Lancaster, Pennsylvania to tell her so.

ALEX: (To Ellen) I cannot figure out for the life of me why I love you . . . I'm crazy about you. I'd give anything to be with you. I can't live without you. Okay? Gotta go, see ya.

Ellen admits to Alex that she loves him and will call off her wedding. Then, for the next year, they are ''a thing'' on the series.

Michael J. Fox and Tracy Pollan also became ''a thing'' in real life. When they were married on July 17, 1988, she exited the series.

There followed an entire episode devoted to the fact that Ellen had dumped the great womanizer, Alex P. Keaton, to accept a dance scholarship in Paris. In her attempt to cheer up Alex, who is uncharacteristically depressed by this breakup, Elyse tells her son, ''She's gone to Paris. Great. Now is the time for Alex P. Keaton to get on with his life.''

On the rebound from his broken relationship, Alex begins dating a girl named Sharon (Haviland Morris), only to find that she cannot take Ellen's place—even after he persuades her to let her hair down and tries to get her to put on a pair of glasses so that she'll look like Ellen.

The episode closes with Alex writing one last letter to Ellen. ''Dear Ellen . . . I want you to know that I loved you as much as I could love anyone. . . . I'm moving on, Ellen, but I know I've come out of our relationship richer for the experience. . . . I wish you well. Don't eat too many croissants. I hope you become the greatest dancer in the world. Your pal, no. Your son, no! Love, Alex.''

Soon afterward, Alex meets Lauren Miller when he agrees to participate in a psychology study of over-achievers. They argue and Alex comes home furious to speak with his mother.

ALEX: Nobody's irritated me this much, this fast, since the first time I met Ellen. Oh come on, I know what you're thinking—that I'm falling for this girl? There's no way, it's not true.

Following another one of those helpful mother and son talks, Alex returns to Lauren's dormitory room and tells her ''I want to be with you. I want to hold you. I want to open . . . a joint bank account with you.''

A special two-part episode, which aired in April 1989, dealt with the breakup with Lauren. At the beginning of the episode, Lauren is on her way to a two-week psychology conference being held in Detroit. Meanwhile, Alex gets involved with one of the students in the economics course he is student-teaching. This latest girlfriend, Marty Brodie, hires Alex as an economics tutor and they wind up spending a lot of time together.

The two-parter closes at Leland graduation day when Alex winds up ending both relationships.

Seeing Marty in the graduation hall practicing the piano for the ceremony, we hear Alex's voice as he thinks of the words he is going to use to break up with her.

ALEX: (Voice-over) So even though I know this is going to hurt you, we've got to stop kidding ourselves. We've got to bring this thing to an end.

Meanwhile, Marty has finished playing the piano and Alex sits down next to her on the piano bench to discuss their relationship, but it is Marty who does the talking.

MARTY: Even though I know this is going to hurt you, I think we've got to stop kidding ourselves and we've got to end this.

Their last words to each other are ''Good-bye Mr. Keaton'' and ''Good-bye Ms. Brodie.''

Alex then spots Lauren across the room and realizes that it is now time to tie up the loose ends with her. We again listen in on him thinking through his speech.

ALEX: (Voice-over) I just have to be honest with her and just tell her she's a wonderful, decent, intelligent, unique individual and that we're not in love anymore.

Unfortunately for poor Alex P. Keaton, Lauren gets the upper hand by speaking first.

LAUREN: Alex, you're a wonderful intelligent, decent, honest, unique individual, but we're not in love anymore.

ALEX: Nobody lets me get a word in edgewise.

There is then a moving speech by Lauren explaining why she cannot be Marty and that she will not try to replace Marty. That's when Alex tells her that he isn't seeing Marty anymore either. She then wishes Alex good luck and they hug.

Marty is never seen again, but Lauren turns up for a brief appearance in the series' final episode to wish Alex all the best in New York.

There were no other major character changes during the run of the series except for the episode in which Steven Keaton reminisces about his childhood and we see his parents at middle age and as seniors. His mother, May Keaton, was played by both Maryedith Burrell and Anne Seymour; his dad, Robert Keaton, by both Mark Marias and Norman Parker. The young Steven Keaton was played by Adam Carl.

FANTASY ISLAND

January 28, 1978–August 18, 1984.   ABC

Character:	Tattoo
Played by:	Herve Villechaize
Date(s):	January 28, 1978–May 14, 1983

Replaced by:	Lawrence
Played by:	Christopher Hewett
Date(s):	October 8, 1983–August 18, 1984

The now clichéd opening to ABC's *Fantasy Island* shows a seaplane making its final approach over a lush tropical paradise. The aircraft is spotted by the three-foot-ten-inch Tattoo, played by Herve Villechaize, who makes a beeline for the island's bell tower. Making it just in time, he rings the bell and alerts the staff to the arriving guests by shouting in his hoarse, lisping French-English accent, "The plane, the plane."

Villechaize began his association with the popular television series with the *Fantasy Island* pilot which aired on January 14, 1977. The pint-sized actor first caught the public's imagination playing another character with a two-syllable name and a double meaning, Nick Nack, the henchman to Christopher Lee's Scaramanga in Roger Moore's 1974 James Bond Film, THE MAN WITH THE GOLDEN GUN.

Tattoo's role on *Fantasy Island* was basically to stand next to Mr. Roarke (Ricardo Montalban) who, in his matching white suit, would make comments about about each of the guests as they stepped off the seaplane. Tattoo would ask, "What's her fantasy, boss?" which was the plot device used to set up the various storylines for each week's program, of which there were usually three.

He also stood next to Roarke at the closing of each episode to help wrap the stories up. These really were his key functions in the series and he was given very little else to do. There was, however, at least one episode, "Remember . . . When?" which aired on May 7, 1983, that was devoted to Tattoo.

At the beginning of the episode, Mr. Roarke presents his loyal associate with a miniature car, which Tattoo smashes up after tooling around the island. The accident puts Tattoo in a coma, which is the device used to set up the audience for an episode filled with flashbacks.

It seems that although Villechaize was helping to fulfill nearly everyone's fantasies, including ABC's—which now had another hit on its schedule—he had not been able to fulfill his own.

In a published interview with Ricardo Montalban that appeared in September 1983, Dan Lewis said that there would be major revisions to the series the following season. "Herve Villechaize, the diminutive Tattoo, has departed in a rift over 'dollars and cents,' reported Montalban. 'Herve had been threatening to quit for the last two years,' Montalban says. 'It

José Ferrer (far left) guest-starred as a dying shipping tycoon who enlists the help of Mr. Roarke (Ricardo Montalban, far right) and Lawrence (Christopher Hewett, center) to help him dispose anonymously of his huge fortune in "Random Choices," the December 3, 1983 episode of *Fantasy Island.*

was becoming very difficult. He demanded too much. Maybe he decided to ask for an offer they couldn't meet.' "[4]

In Jeff Rovin's book, *TV Babylon,* Villechaize's reasons for departure were said to be more than just money. It seems that when Wendy Schaal was introduced in 1981 as Mr. Roarke's goddaughter, Julie, Villechaize found his role getting smaller. " 'Suddenly I found myself doing, "Eh, boss, what's this fantasy?" and "Good-bye" and that's it. I was a glorified extra.' He took out his indignation on Schaal, ignoring her on the set and refusing to take publicity shots with her."[5]

The April 23, 1983 edition of *TV Guide* reported: "Despite the strong lead-in provided by *The Love Boat, Fantasy Island* has been slipping in the ratings; most weeks it's not in the top 30. That's one of the reasons that Villechaize's demand for a big salary increase reportedly led the producers to decide the

4. Lewis, Dan. "Problems easily solved on ABC's 'Fantasy Island'." *Asbury Park Press TV Week,* Asbury Park, New Jersey. September 7, 1983, p. 35.

5. Rovin, Jeff. *TV Babylon.* Signet, New York, April 1987, p. 224.

series could survive without him. The new character will be much like the one played by John Gielgud in ARTHUR and the producers are seeking an English actor to play him.' 'We had considerable thoughts about replacing Herve with another small person,' Montalban says. 'But we thought that would be too obvious.' ''[6]

The English actor they hired to portray Mr. Roarke's gentleman's gentleman was the six-foot-two-inch Christopher Hewett, who later played the role of the English housekeeper in ABC's 1985 situation comedy, *Mr. Belvedere*. Hewett said of his predecessor, ''I don't really remember seeing him on the show much. He was always up in a turret, or something.''[7]

Christopher Hewett made his first appearance as Lawrence on *Fantasy Island* in the seventh season opener, ''Forbidden Love.'' In that episode he shows up with a note from Tattoo which says that he is quitting his job and recommends Lawrence as his replacement.

When *Fantasy Island* was cancelled in 1984, David Bianculli wrote a newspaper article that panned the entire series: ''There has been no tearful finale, no star-studded farewell, no conciliatory return of Tattoo. Sometime this summer, ABC's *Fantasy Island* will simply and quietly disappear, sinking into oblivion, like a TV version of Atlantis.''[8]

Bianculli went on to explore the possible reasons for *Fantasy Island's* cancellation and drew this tongue-in-cheek conclusion: ''The key to the success and eventual failure of *Fantasy Island*, has to be Tattoo. When Villechaize was replaced by Christopher Hewett, *Fantasy Island* began to sink. It's Tattoo bad he didn't leave a few years earlier.''[9]

THE FARMER'S DAUGHTER

September 20, 1963–September 2, 1966.   ABC

Character:	Margaret
Played by:	Nancy Rennick
Date(s):	Unknown

Replaced by:	Margaret
Played by:	Barbara Bostock
Date(s):	Unknown

Although the title of this series sounds like a bad traveling salesman joke, it was nothing of the sort. True, Katrin ''Katy'' Holstrum was the daughter of a Swedish farmer from Minnesota, but the series was set miles away from the farm in Washington, D.C.—307 Marshall, Washington, D.C. to be exact.

Katy (Inger Stevens) came to the nation's capital to enlist the aid of her congressman, Glen Morley (William Windom), in securing a government job teaching underprivileged kids in the Belgian Congo. The job never materialized, and Katy wound up taking a job as Congressman Morley's governess to help raise his two children, Danny (Rory O'Brien) and Steve (Mickey Sholdar). It was sort of a Mary Poppins done with a Swedish accent and no magic.

Adjusting to life in the big city was difficult for Katy, but it was made just a little bit easier by her friend Margaret, initially played by Nancy Rennick, who had played Patty Johnson on the 1958 syndicated adventure series, *Rescue 8*. She later played Edith Thorncroft on the NBC dramatic comedy, *Kentucky Jones*, which aired from September 19, 1964 to September 11, 1965.

Even though good friends may last forever, good actresses can come and go. Ms. Rennick was replaced by Barbara Bostock, who went on to play Carol Parker, Rich Little's wife on the ABC situation comedy, *Love on a Rooftop*, which aired from September 6, 1966 to September 8, 1971. The series starred Peter Deuel and Judy Carne as Dave and Julie Willis, the young married couple living in a top-floor apartment. Ms. Carne is most famous as the ''Sock-it-to-me'' girl from *Rowan & Martin's Laugh-In*; Peter Deuel later starred as the first Hannibal Heyes on the ABC Western, *Alias Smith and Jones* (See Entry).

The Farmer's Daughter was based on the 1947 comedy of the same name that starred Loretta Young and Joseph Cotten. The role of Katrin had been offered to Ingrid Bergman, but she turned it down and then saw Loretta Young win the Academy Award that could have been hers.

William Windom, who played Congressman Morley on the series, went on to portray the James Thurber character, John Monroe, in *My World and Welcome to It,* a situation comedy that ran from September 15, 1969 to September 7, 1972. It began on NBC and later moved to CBS. Windom is also known to science fiction fans as Commodore Matt Decker from ''The Doomsday Machine'' episode of *Star Trek* and is supposed to be the father of Commander Will Decker (Stephen Collins) in the 1980 film, STAR TREK: THE MOTION PICTURE.

FELONY SQUAD

September 12, 1966–January 31, 1969.   ABC

Character:	Captain Nye
Played by:	Frank Maxwell
Date(s):	September 12, 1966–April 10, 1967
	September 27, 1968–January 31, 1969

Replaced by:	Captain Franks
Played by:	Barney Phillips
Date(s):	September 11, 1967–March 18, 1968

The commanding officer for the first and last seasons of this Los Angeles-based police drama was Captain Nye, played by

Frank Maxwell. He was replaced temporarily during the 1967/1968 season by Barney Phillips, who was Sargent Joe Friday's second partner on *Dragnet* (See Entry).

While Barney Phillips was taking over the desk duties as Captain Franks, actor Frank Maxwell was playing Colonel Garroway in the ABC situation comedy, *The Second Hundred Years,* which starred Monte Markham as both Luke and Ken Carpenter, and Karen Black as Marcia Garroway. The series aired from September 6, 1967 to September 19, 1968.

FILTHY RICH

August 9, 1982–June 15, 1983.   CBS

Character:	Big Guy Beck
Played by:	Slim Pickens
Date(s):	August 9, 1982–August 23, 1982

Replaced by:	Big Guy Beck
Played by:	Forrest Tucker
Date(s):	October 13, 1982–June 15, 1983

There is no disputing the fact that *Filthy Rich* was meant to be a spoof of the prime-time soap operas *Dynasty, Falcon Crest* and especially *Dallas.*

This rich and powerful family was headed by a deceased Tennessee land baron, Big Guy Beck, who maintained his grip on the family fortune through his videotaped last will and testament, a section of which was played for the family each week.

The original Big Guy Beck seen on the videotape was Western actor Slim Pickens. He was replaced after only a few episodes had been shot. At least one source has indicated that Pickens was replaced because he had died. This cannot be true since he died on December 8, 1983––nearly six months after the last episode of *Filthy Rich* aired on CBS, though it is conceivable that he left for health reasons. Previously, Pickens was seen as Slim on the NBC Western, *The Outlaws.* He later appeared in one episode of *The Mary Tyler Moore Show* as WJM-TV station owner Wild Jack Monroe. That episode, "The 45–Year-Old Man," aired on March 6, 1971.

When *Filthy Rich,* a limited series, returned, Forrest Tucker was seen on the videotapes as Big Guy Beck. Sitcom audiences fondly remember Forrest Tucker as Sergeant Morgan O'Rourke on the ABC series, *F Troop,* which aired from September 14, 1965 to August 31, 1967.

Big Guy's attorney was George Wilhoit, played by David Healy in the pilot and Vernon Weddle during the regular run of the series. Weddle had played Mr. Ames in the three-part miniseries, *East of Eden,* which aired on ABC from February 8 to 11, 1981.

THE FLASH

January 18, 1979.   NBC
September 20, 1990–July 19, 1991   CBS

Character:	The Flash
Played by:	Rod Hasse
Date(s):	January 18, 1979

Replaced by:	Barry Allen/The Flash
Played by:	John Wesley Shipp
Date(s):	September 20, 1990–July 19, 1991

Curiously, DC Comics' super fast superhero, The Flash, didn't make it to the screen until some twenty years after his creation by Gardner Fox. And it is likely that the transition took so long, not for lack of colorful crime-fighting heroes with unusual powers, but because of the special effects technology necessary to make the character believable on film.

But it wasn't until after the box-office success of the 1989 BATMAN, motion picture, that the scarlet speedster was developed for a series of his own.

As it turns out, BATMAN served as much more than an inspiration. The $25,000 Flash costume (of which eight were used each season) was designed by Bob Ringwood, the designer of the muscular Batman costume worn by Michael Keaton. Similarly, the pounding music score was provided by BATMAN composer, Danny Elfman.

The premise of the CBS series, which was produced by Warner Bros., had Barry Allen as a police chemist, who gained the power of super speed when lightning struck his police lab and threw him crashing into a storage rack containing an array of chemicals including aluminum sulfate, glycerin, potassium nitrate, magnesium hydroxide, hydrochloric acid, sulfur, tannic acid and phosphorous. And it was the random mixture of these and other chemicals, combined with the jolt of electricity from the lightning, that altered Barry Allen's metabolism enabling him to move at super speeds.

He was assisted in the police lab by Julio Mendez (Alex Desert). Helping Barry control his amazing abilities was Star Lab's top research scientist, Christina "Tina" McGee, (Amanda Pays), who is the one responsible for designing the costume for Barry's alter ego. Tina explained that the skin-tight suit was based on a Soviet prototype deep sea suit that was able to withstand the pressure of high velocity as well as regulating the wearer's body temperature. It also explains its red color.

There seemed to be some confusion as to the period in which the series was set, because of the mixture of some very 1950s stylized sets that included vintage automobiles, juxtaposed against the 1990's computer technology used by Barry and Julio at Central City's police lab and Tina McGee at Star Labs.

Disappointing was the fact that some of the Flash's other powers, which helped to advance the storylines in the comics, were never explored on the series. One power in particular was The Flash's ability to vibrate his molecules so quickly that he was able to pass through walls and bullets would pass through him.

Another convention altered for television was the storage of the crimson uniform. In the comics, Barry Allen wore a special ring that confined the bright red costume inside a secret compartment.

In the origin story it was explained that a chemical solution swelled the costume to life-size. In later stories the costume of the fastest man alive was released by activating a spring that opened the ring and caused the costume to expand upon contact with the air. By pressing another part of the ring, the uniform shrunk as it was drawn back in by a small, but powerful suction device.

On the television series, Barry had to lug the full-size outfit around in the trunk of his car.

The producers of *The Flash*, who realized that they owed some of their success to Superman, paid homage to The Flash's more famous cousin by casting Robert Shayne as Reggie, the blind newspaper vendor who provided Barry Allen with important leads.

Robert Shayne who, of course, had played Clark Kent's best friend and police contact, Inspector William J. ''Bill'' Henderson on the *Adventures of Superman* (See Entry), appeared in two episodes of *The Flash*, ''Sins of the Father,'' broadcast on November 8, 1990, and ''Sight Unseen,'' which first aired on January 10, 1991.

''The interesting thing about my role on *The Flash* is that after being out of the business for about twenty years—not having made anything—I was called up by the Disabled Actors Committee of the Screen Actors Guild. They had my name on file as a disabled actor because of my blindness and asked, 'Would you play a blind man, Bob?' And I said, 'Of course I'd play a blind man, I am blind!' '' Shayne chuckled.

''A day or so later, I received an invitation to meet the producers and I went over to the Warner Bros. lot where I met the casting director, April Webster.

''They gave me my lines and I read it cold. They said, 'That's fine, Bob, that's fine. You're hired.' I never looked for that job, they looked for me,'' said Shayne happily.[10]

Shayne was also very proud of the fact that he was only one of the two people in the show who knew the identity of The Flash, something neither he, nor any of the other characters had known about Superman on the *Adventures of Superman*.

The Flash actually made his first television appearance in *The Challenge of the Superheroes*, a one-hour special that aired on NBC in 1979 and also featured Adam West and Burt Ward as Batman and Robin and Garrett Craig as television's third Captain Marvel (see SHAZAM!).

Though the stories were engaging enough and the special effects quite outstanding, *The Flash*'s loyal audience was not large enough to warrant the $1.6 million per episode budget and was cancelled after twenty-three episodes—making it just another flash in the pan for Warner Bros. Television.

THE FLYING NUN

September 7, 1967–September 18, 1970.   ABC

Character:	Sister Teresa
Played by:	Naomi Stevens
Date(s):	September 7, 1967–unknown

Replaced by:	Sister Teresa
Played by:	Cynthia Hull
Date(s):	unknown–September 18, 1970

If you are in the habit of checking out the nuns hidden under the huge coronets in the series, you may have witnessed a divine bit of casting. One week Sister Teresa was played by Naomi Stevens and the next by Cynthia Hull. Ms. Stevens can be seen more easily as Juanita, Doris Day's second housekeeper, or as Sergeant Bella Archer on the ABC detective drama, *VEGA$*.

This series, of course, starred Sally Field as Elsie Ethrington, who joined the Convent San Tanco in San Juan, Puerto Rico, where she was ordained as Sister Bertrille. The name of the series refers to the remarkable ability of the ninety-pound nun to fly, which is possible because of her light weight and the unusual aerodynamic design of the coronet worn by the nuns of this order.

She went on from this cute but silly situation comedy, which followed her short stint on *Gidget* (See Entry), to more demanding roles like Sybil Dorsett in NBC's 1976 made-for-television movie, *Sybil*, about a schizophrenic woman with sixteen personalities; it won Sally Field the Emmy Award for Best Actress. Three years later she won the Academy Award for the title role of the 1979 drama, NORMA RAE.

FLYING TIGERS *see* MAJOR DELL CONWAY OF THE FLYING TIGERS

FOREIGN INTRIGUE

1951–1955.   Syndicated

Character:	Robert Cannon
Played by:	Jerome Thor
Date(s):	1951–1953

Replaced by:	Michael Powers
Played by:	James Daly
Date(s):	1953–1954

Replaced by:	Christopher Storm
Played by:	Gerald Mohr
Date(s):	1954–1955

Character:	Helen Davis
Played by:	Synda Scott
Date(s):	1951–1953

Replaced by:	Patricia Bennett
Played by:	Ann Preville
Date(s):	1953–1954

Orginally broadcast as *Foreign Intrigue: Dateline Europe,* this syndicated mystery/adventure series spawned two spinoffs, *Foreign Intrigue: Overseas Adventures* and *Foreign Intrigue: Cross Current.*

In the original series, Jerome Thor starred as Robert Cannon, a foreign correspondent for the Amalgamated News Service.

---

10. From an exclusive telephone interview with Robert Shayne on May 13, 1991.

His Lois Lane-type rival, Helen Davis, was played by Synda Scott.

After two seasons, the series became *Foreign Intrigue: Overseas Adventures* and starred James Daly as a pipe-smoking correspondent for Associated News. Ann Preville played Patricia Bennett who worked for the rival news service, Consolidated Press.

The final thirty-nine episodes of the series featured Gerald Mohr, who played Christopher Storm, an American hotel owner in Vienna who did his part to stamp out the evil doings of the international underworld.

Of the five actors involved with the series over the years, only one managed to achieve a degree of fame: James Daly. Working steadily until his death on July 3, 1978, James Daly appeared in more than one hundred roles in anthology and episodic television series including *Studio One, Omnibus, Dr. Kildare, Gunsmoke* and *Mission Impossible*

He also guest starred as Flint in the *Star Trek* episode,

Taking a break from their chores on the Broken Wheel Ranch are (left to right) Fury (Gypsy), Jim Newton (Peter Graves), Pee Wee Jenkins (Jimmy Baird), Pete, who said he cut his teeth on a branding iron, (William Fawcett), and Joey Newton (Bobby Diamond).

''Requiem for Methuselah,'' which aired on February 14, 1969. Beginning on September 24, 1969, Daly starred for nearly seven years as Dr. Paul Lochner, the chief of staff on the CBS drama, *Medical Center*.

FURY

October 15, 1955–September 3, 1966.   NBC

Character:	Pee Wee Jenkins
Played by:	Jimmy Baird
Date(s):	October 15, 1955–April 5, 1958
Replaced by:	Packey Lambert
Played by:	Roger Mobley
Date(s):	October 11, 1958–September 3, 1966

If they could do it with a boy and his dog, why not a boy and his horse? They did, and *Fury* was the result.

Unquestionably, the star of the show was the horse, Fury, whose real name was Beauty. The stories revolved around widower, Jim Newton, owner of the Broken Wheel Ranch, and his adopted son Joey. Newton was played by Peter Graves, who later starred as Jim Phelps on *Mission Impossible* (See Entry).

Joey was played throughout the series by Bobby Diamond, who was eleven years old when the show first aired. His best friend for the first three seasons was pint-sized (by comparison to Joey) Pee Wee Jenkins, played by Jimmy Baird.

At the start of the fourth season, Baird was replaced by another diminutive young actor, Roger Mobley, who played Joey's friend, Packey Lambert. Baird later played Gustav in the 1964 Disney film, *EMIL AND THE DETECTIVES*.

G

GALACTICA 1980 *see* BATTLESTAR GALACTICA

THE GEORGE BURNS AND GRACIE ALLEN SHOW

October 12, 1950–September 22, 1958.   CBS

Character:	Harry Morton	
Played by:	Hal March	
Date(s):	1950–1951	
Replaced by:	Harry Morton	
Played by:	John Brown	
Date(s):	1951	
Replaced by:	Harry Morton	
Played by:	Fred Clark	
Date(s):	1951–1953	
Replaced by:	Harry Morton	
Played by:	Larry Keating	
Date(s):	1953–1958	
Character:	Bill Goodwin	
Played by:	Bill Goodwin	
Date(s):	1950–1951	
Replaced by:	Harry Von Zell	
Played by:	Harry Von Zell	
Date(s):	1951–1958	

Before George Burns told his wife to "Say goodnight, Gracie" for the two hundred and thirty-ninth time, their popular television series had been on CBS for nearly eight years and the Burnses had gone through four next-door neighbors and two announcers.

Like so many situation comedies to follow, *The George Burns and Gracie Allen Show* relied on playing off their next-door neighbors. The Burnses' neighbors were the Mortons, Blanche and Harry. Blanche was played by Bea Benaderet, who would later appear on *The Beverly Hillbillies* (See Entry), star on *Petticoat Junction* (See Entry) and become the voice of Betty Rubble on *The Flintstones*. Her husband, Harry, was played by four different actors during the run of the series.

The first Harry Morton was played by comic actor Hal March, who went on to play Irma Peterson's second boyfriend on the CBS situation comedy, *My Friend Irma* (See Entry). He later played Winston Burr in the 1964 Rock Hudson/Doris Day romantic comedy, SEND ME NO FLOWERS. He was replaced for a short time by John Brown who had previously played undertaker Digby "Digger" O'Dell from 1949 to 1950 on *The Life of Riley*. Brown was removed from the series after only six months because he was blacklisted for allegedly being a communist.

Brown's replacement was Fred Clark, who later played Gerald B. Hannahan in the 1966 situation comedy, *The Double Life of Henry Phyfe.*

There are several reasons for Clark's departure from *The George Burns and Gracie Allen Show*. In addition to accepting a role in a Broadway show, he had also requested that his salary be increased to $1,500 an episode. The problem was that his asking price was $350 more than George Burns was getting. Clark was dismissed and replaced by Larry Keating, who was paid the more reasonable fee of $750 an episode.

This was also one of those rare moments in television when the audience was let in on the switch.

"On Fred Clark's last show, Blanche was waiting by the door to hit him over the head with a vase because she didn't like the iron deer he had bought for the front door. When Clark entered, Burns walked into the scene and said, 'Hold it!' and then explained to the audience about Clark leaving the show. George introduced Larry Keating—the new Harry—to the audience, then to Bea Benaderet. They bowed, and George said, 'Now let's get back to the story.' Keating exited and then re-entered—and Blanche hit him over the head with the vase."[1]

Keating was a major supporting player in more than forty feature films, which included an outstanding performance as Dr. Cole Hendron in the 1951 science fiction classic, WHEN WORLDS COLLIDE. The following year, he played Mr. G.J. Culverly in the Cary Grant/Ginger Rogers comedy, MONKEY BUSINESS. He also was Wilbur Post's first next-door neighbor on the CBS sitcom, *Mr. Ed* (See Entry).

One source indicates that Harry Morton was also played by Bob Sweeney, a balding actor who played Mr. Oliver Munsey

---

1. Mitz, Rick. *The Great TV Sitcom Book,* Richard Marek Publishers, New York, 1980, p. 36.

from 1955 to 1956 on the Eve Arden situation comedy, *Our Miss Brooks,* and the title role on *Fibber McGee and Molly,* which aired on NBC from September 15, 1959 to January 19, 1960. He went on to direct *The Andy Griffith Show.*

The announcer on the show within a show was first played by Bill Goodwin, who is said to have left *The George Burns and Gracie Allen Show* to host his own program. This is interesting because the quiz program, *Penny to a Million,* that Goodwin did emcee did not go on the air until 1955.

Goodwin later appeared as the narrator of *The Gerald McBoing Boing Show,* which was actually a combination of live action with the Gerald McBoing Boing cartoons. The program aired on CBS from May 30 to October 3, 1958. Since the early episodes of the *The George Burns and Gracie Allen Show* in which Goodwin appeared are not in the syndication package, most television viewers are only familiar with his replacement, Burns' likeable, well-meaning and all-too-often scapegoat, Harry Von Zell.

THE GEORGE GOBEL SHOW

October 2, 1954–June 5, 1960.   NBC-CBS

Character:	Alice
Played by:	Jeff Donnell
Date(s):	October 2, 1954–1958

Replaced by:	Alice
Played by:	Phyllis Avery
Date(s):	1958–March 1959

Just as the *Jackie Gleason Show* was a comedy variety show that featured ''The Honeymooners'' as a regular weekly sketch, George Gobel's program featured a domestic sketch about George and his wife, Alice (which just happened to be the name of Gobel's real-life spouse).

The first of the Mrs. Gobel impersonators was Jeff Donnell who appeared as Anne Carstairs in the 1942 Loretta Young film, A NIGHT TO REMEMBER. One of her later film roles was Dorothy Lawrence in the 1961 beach comedy, *GIDGET GOES HAWAIIAN.* Her television work includes Ethel, the answering-service operator in ABC's short-lived detective series, *Matt Helm,* and May Parker in the *Spider-Man* pilot which aired on CBS on September 14, 1977.

Ms. Donnell was replaced by Phyllis Avery who stayed with the program until it moved from NBC to CBS, at which time the George and Alice sketches were dropped. One of her more visible television roles was Ruth Wilkinson on the NBC high school drama, *Mr. Novak,* on which she appeared from 1964 to 1965.

GET CHRISTIE LOVE!

September 11, 1974–July 18, 1975.   ABC

Character:	Lieutenant Matt Reardon
Played by:	Charles Cioffi
Date(s):	September 11, 1974–unknown

Replaced by:	Captain Arthur P. Ryan
Played by:	Jack Kelly
Date(s):	1975

In this short-lived action-based police drama, *Laugh-In's* Teresa Graves starred in the title role. Her first no-nonsense superior was Lieutenant Reardon, played by Charles Cioffi. Reardon was soon replaced by Captain Ryan, played by Jack Kelly. Shortly thereafter, the entire series was cancelled.

Charles Cioffi had previously played Major Caldwell on *Assignment Vienna,* which aired on ABC from September 28, 1972 to June 9, 1973. His replacement, Jack Kelly, had played James Garner's brother, Bart, on the popular Western, *Maverick,* which aired on ABC from September 22, 1957 to July 8, 1962.

GET SMART!

September 18, 1965–September 11, 1970.   NBC-ABC

Character:	The Chief of CONTROL
Played by:	Edward Platt
Date(s):	September 18, 1965–September 11, 1970

Replaced by:	Commander Drury
Played by:	Kenneth Mars
Date(s):	February 26, 1989

Character:	Agent 44
Played by:	Victor French
Date(s):	December 11, 1965–January 29, 1966

Replaced by:	Agent 13
Played by:	Dave Ketchum
Date(s):	December 3, 1966–December 7, 1967

Replaced by:	Agent 44
Played by:	Al Molinaro
Date(s):	December 3, 1969–December 19, 1969

Maxwell Smart (Don Adams), Agent 86, was Mel Brooks' and Buck Henry's answer to James Bond, Simon Templar, John Steed, Napoleon Solo and every other secret agent worth his silencer. The main difference was that Maxwell Smart was a buffoon who managed to solve his cases in spite of himself, with a lot of luck and a little help from his beautiful female assistant, Agent 99, played by Barbara Feldon.

And just as 007 received his orders from M, and Napoleon Solo and Ilya Kuryakin got their assignments from Mr. Waverly, Agent 86 got his marching orders from the Chief of CONTROL, a secret branch of the United States Intelligence Agency set up during the 1960s to deal specifically with KAOS, the international criminal organization of evil that was formed circa 1957 to dominate the world.

Edward Platt, as the Chief (his real first name was Thaddeus though he sometimes used the cover name of Howard Clark), was the series father figure and Smart's foil for all 138 hilarious episodes.

Ten years after *Get Smart!* left the air, Universal Pictures released a feature-length motion picture, THE NUDE BOMB, which was based on the original series and starred Don Adams as Maxwell Smart. The film was later released on television as *The Return of Maxwell Smart.* Sadly, Edward Platt died on March 20, 1974, and had to be replaced in the film. The producers chose Dana Elcar, who has had guest roles on more than 150 television series including everything from *Naked City, Gunsmoke* and *Bonanza* to *The Incredible Hulk* and *The A-Team.* He starred as Detective Tony Baretta's first boss, Inspector Shiller, on *Baretta* (See Entry), and Colonel Lard, U.S.M.C. on *Baa Baa Black Sheep.*

On November 7 and 14, 1969, Dana Elcar appeared as the KAOS doctor in the two-part *Get Smart* episode, "And Baby Makes Four." But Dana Elcar will most certainly be remembered for his portrayal of Peter Thornton on the long-running adventure series, *MacGyver,* which aired on ABC from September 29, 1985, to April 25, 1992.

Even though Dana Elcar was referred to as "The Chief," he no longer worked for CONTROL, but for PITS, the Provisional Intelligence Tactical Service. It is interesting that the writers felt compelled to create the acronym PITS, since neither CONTROL nor KAOS stood for anything, in the way that U.N.C.L.E. and T.H.R.U.S.H did.

Barbara Feldon did not appear in the motion picture as Agent 99. She was replaced by three female agents who were given numbers which corresponded to women's measurements—they were simply introduced out of order. Agent 34 was played by Sylvia Krystel, Agent 36 by Pamela Hensley, and Agent 22 by Andrea Howard.

Panned by the critics, the movie still earned enough money at the box office to warrant making a television movie. It was originally scheduled to air in the fall of 1988, but was delayed until February of 1989 because of a writers' strike that began before the script had been completed.

The made-for-television movie, *Get Smart, Again!,* finally made it to the air on February 26, 1989, and reunited much of the original cast, including Barbara Feldon as Agent 99. This time around, however, headquarters was neither CONTROL or PITS, but the USIA (United States Intelligence Agency), and its head was referred to as a Commander instead of a Chief—specifically, Commander Drury. This made Kenneth Mars the third actor to play Maxwell Smart's superior, a role which had changed drastically from the father figure played by Edward Platt in the original television series. The producers expressed their love and sense of loss by including a special screen credit which read "Dedicated to Ed Platt, 'The Chief'."

Kenneth Mars is a comedian and actor who has appeared in episodes of many serious detective shows including *McMillan and Wife, Barnaby Jones, Ironside* and *Columbo.* His work in situation comedies includes *Car 54, Where Are You?, That Girl* and *Alice.* He was a regular of *The Don Knotts Show* from 1970 to 1971 and *The Carol Burnett Show* in 1979. Mars even put in an appearance as Tom Orlando in Part III of the *Get Smart!* episode, "A Man Called Smart," which aired on April 22, 1967.

Among his recurring roles on television were Harry Zarakardoson in the CBS situation comedy, *He & She,* which aired from September 6, 1967, to September 11, 1970. Mars also turned up as Mr. Harris, the third of four headmasters on *The Facts of Life* (See Entry).

One of the silliest, but perhaps best-remembered recurring roles played by Kenneth Mars was that of one of Barth Gimble's more frequent guests, William W.D. "Bud" Prize, the man who was under the care of a chinodontist to correct his underbite. Barth Gimble (Martin Mull) was host of *Fernwood 2-Night,* the *Mary Hartman, Mary Hartman* spinoff which aired in syndication between 1977 and 1978.

Aiding Max and 99 in more than a dozen of their weekly missions against KAOS were a number of other agents, the most popular of whom was Agent 13, who provided CONTROL agents with "inside" information. Inside, because 13 was always found hiding in unlikely and uncomfortable locations, including a mailbox, a wall safe and a washing machine. This bitter but likeable agent was always played by Dave Ketchum, who played Mel Warshaw on the ABC situation comedy, *I'm Dickens—He's Fenster.*

But before (and after) Agent 13 was Agent 44. The first Agent 44, assigned to hide inside a clock, a cello case and a medicine cabinet, was Victor French, who earned his place in television history as Michael Landon's sidekick. In *Little House on the Prairie,* Victor French played Mr. Isaiah Edwards, and on NBC's *Highway to Heaven* (September 19, 1984–August 4, 1989) he co-starred as Mark Gordon.

CONTROL Agent 44 returned after Dave Ketchum packed it in, only this time it was eagle-nosed Al Molinaro hiding inside a working pot-bellied stove. Molinaro is better known to aficionados of the television sitcom as Murray the cop from *The Odd Couple* and for replacing Arnold on *Happy Days* (See Entry).

With the continued popularity of television reunion movies and series, there are sure to be another dozen or so *Get Smart!* television movies in the future. . . would you believe six? How about. . . ? Well, in any event we are sure to be watching reruns of *Get Smart!* for years to come. . . and loving it!

GIDGET

September 15, 1965–September 1, 1966.   ABC-Syndicated

Character:	Francine "Gidget" Lawrence[2]
Played by:	Sally Field
Date(s):	September 15, 1965–September 1, 1966

Replaced by:	Francine "Gidget" Lawrence Griffin[3]
Played by:	Caryn Richman
Date(s):	June 1985 (pilot)
	September 1986–June 1988

2–3. Gidget's first name was also given as Frances.

Character:	Professor Russ Lawrence
Played by:	Don Porter
Date(s):	September 15, 1965–September 1, 1966

Replaced by:	Russ Lawrence
Played by:	William Schallert
Date(s):	June 1985 (pilot)
	September 1986–June 1988

Character:	Jeff "Moondoggie" Matthews
Played by:	Steven Mines
Date(s):	September 15, 1965–September 1, 1966

Replaced by:	Jeff "Moondoggie" Griffin
Played by:	Dean Butler
Date(s):	June 1985 (*Gidget's Summer Reunion*)
	September 1986–June 1988

Character:	Larue
Played by:	Lynette Winter
Date(s):	September 15, 1965–September 1, 1966

Replaced by:	Larue Wilson
Played by:	Jill Jacobson
Date(s):	September 1986–June 1987

Professor Russ Lawrence, a happy father (Don Porter) hugs his loving daughter Francine (Sally Field) in the wholesome fun-in-the-sun TV show that took its title from his daughter's nickname, *Gidget.*

Whenever television trivia buffs hear the word fidget, they think of *The Little Rascals.* When they hear the word midget, they think of Zero Zero Zero, Minus One; and when they hear the name Gidget, they immediately think of Sally Field.

The television character was obviously based on the motion pictures which in turn were taken from a novel Frederick Kohner wrote about his daughter that made the best-seller list in 1957. Before splashing around in the surf on the small screen, Gidget was first brought to life by Sandra Dee in the 1959 movie GIDGET. The character returned in a number of sequels and was subsequently played by Deborah Walley and Cindy Carol.

TV's Gidget was played by an eighteen-year-old actress who, although unknown at the time to television audiences, was most likely known around Hollywood because she was the daughter of screen actress Margaret Field and the step-daughter of Jock Mahoney. Formerly a Hollywood stuntman, Mahoney made the successful transition to acting as The Range Rider in all seventy-eight episodes of the 1952 syndicated series of the same name. He was also the screen's thirteenth Tarzan.

In another of those remarkable Hollywood stories of being in the right place at the right time, Sally Field had enrolled in an actors' workshop at Columbia Pictures after her graduation from high school, and this resulted in her winning the role of Gidget.

Only thirty-two episodes of *Gidget* were produced during its one-season run, but that was enough to establish Ms. Field as a valuable television commodity, and with the introduction of the 1967 fall season she flew into Americans' hearts as Sister Bertrille in *The Flying Nun* (See Entry). When *The Flying Nun* left the air in 1970, Sally Field turned up as Clementine Hale in the ABC Western, *Alias Smith and Jones.* That series ran until

January 1973 and by September 14, Sally Field was on NBC in the situation comedy, *The Girl with Something Extra,* which ran until May 24, 1974. Five years later she won an Academy Award for her portrayal of the title character in the motion picture NORMA RAE.

Gidget's dad, Professor Russ Lawrence, was played by Don Porter, who played James Devery, the second manager of the Bartley House Hotel on the *Ann Sothern Show* (See Entry).

As in the motion pictures, the apple of Gidget's eye was Jeff "Moondoggie" Matthews. But unlike the films, where Jeff figured prominently in the stories, in the series he was said to be away at college and appeared infrequently. When he was in town, he was played by Steven Mines, who is perhaps more familiar for his soap opera work. He was the first of four actors to play Paul Stewart, the son of Dr. David Stewart on the CBS daytime soap opera, *As the World Turns.* In 1966, Mines was the first of two actors to play David Martin on NBC's daytime soap, *Days of Our Lives.* He was also Fred Morgan on the especially short-lived (by soap opera standards) NBC afternoon soap opera, *Paradise Bay,* which ran from September 27, 1965 to July 1, 1966.

Larue was the one friend of Gidget's who was seen more frequently than Gidget's beau, "Moondoggie." She was played by Lynette Winter. After completing work on *Gidget* she went on to play the second Henrietta Plout on the rural sitcom, *Petticoat Junction* (See Entry).

The first of three attempts to return *Gidget* to weekly television was the ninety-minute pilot, *Gidget Grows Up*, which aired on ABC more than thirteen years after the original series left the air. In this made-for-television movie, Gidget was played by Karen Valentine, another cute, perky actress who made a name for herself playing Alice Johnson in the ABC drama, *Room 222*. It was also the role which earned her an Emmy in 1970 for Best Supporting Actress in a Comedy Series. *Room 222* ran from September 17, 1969 to January 11, 1974. Ms. Valentine once said that she hated the word "cute," but like it or not, she is indeed cute and it is undoubtedly one of the factors that helped her win the Gidget role.

Gidget's understanding father was played by an actor who made a career out of being a womanizer in his own situation comedy, *The Bob Cummings Show*, which aired from January 2, 1955 to September 15, 1959 (See Entry).

The "Moondoggie" character, Jeff Matthews, was changed to Jeff Griffin and was played by Paul Petersen, who had played Donna Reed's lovable son, Jeff, on *The Donna Reed Show*. Gidget's friend, Larue, didn't turn up in this first pilot at all.

The second of the *Gidget* pilots, *Gidget Gets Married*, aired on ABC three years later and subjected *Gidget* fans to a bit of culture shock. Because now, not only had the Gidget character grown up, but she was of all things (gulp) a housewife! Her hubby was, of course, "Moondoggie," whose last name was now Stevens.

Our little Gidge was now brought to life by Monie Ellis, while her now domesticated beach bum, Jeff, was played by Michael Burns, who as a child actor appeared in episodes of *Alfred Hitchcock Presents, Lassie* and *The Lone Ranger*. By 1963 Burns had joined the cast of *Wagon Train* as Barnaby West, a thirteen-year-old orphan.

Hollywood leading man Macdonald Carey took on the responsibilty of becoming Gidget's father, Russell Lawrence, in this second ill-fated attempt to return the *Gidget* series to the air. Among Carey's film roles were Cesare Borgia in the 1949 Paulette Goddard drama, BRIDE OF VENGEANCE, and his starring role as newsman Larry Wilder in the 1950 drama, THE LAWLESS. He starred on television as Dr. Tom Horton on the daytime soap opera, the *Days of Our Lives,* a role which lasted for more than twenty years. But, perhaps more memorable than his on-screen role is his famous voice-over narration, "Like the sands through the hourglass, so are the days of our lives," which was heard at the beginning of each day's program.

They say that "the third time's a charm" and that old axiom proved to be true with *Gidget's Summer Reunion,* which managed to finally pave the way for *The New Gidget* series. The lucky actress was Caryn Richman, who had a few years earlier played Elena Dekker on *Texas,* the soap opera spinoff from *Another World* that ran on NBC from August 4, 1980 to December 31, 1982. Her faithful husband, now Jeff Griffin, was played by Dean Butler, who had played Almanzo Wilder from 1979 to 1983 on Michael Landon's *Little House on the Prarie.*

Even with Jeff married to Gidget, the true father figure on the series (though seen infrequently) was played by William Schallert, a man who made a career out of playing likeable and understanding dads and dad types. His best known "dad" role

was that of Martin Lane, Patty Lane's dad on *The Patty Duke Show,* which ran on ABC from September 18, 1963 to August 31, 1966.

For an actor who was not a leading man, William Schallert may have appeared in more television series than any other actor—more than 200 to date! He was Dobie's English teacher, Mr. Leander Pomfritt, on more than twenty episodes of *The Many Loves of Dobie Gillis* (See Entry). The particular episodes in which Schallert appeared aired between October 6, 1959 and April 17, 1962.

Science fiction fans will remember Schallert as the Federation's dedicated but somewhat misguided Undersecretary for Agriculture, Nilz Baris, in the *Star Trek* episode, "The Trouble with Tribbles," which aired on December 29, 1967.

Not surprisingly, William Schallert has also appeared in a number of motion pictures. He played Professor Elliot in the very well done 1951 science fiction film, THE MAN FROM PLANET X. On a sillier note, Schallert played the hotel clerk in the 1959 Rock Hudson/Doris Day comedy, PILLOW TALK.

This *Gidget* entry also reintroduced the character of Gidget's best friend, Larue. In the pilot, Larue Powell was played by Anne Lockhart, the daughter of Lassie's "mom," June Lockhart. For a short time during 1979, Ms. Lockhart played Sheba on the small screen version of STAR WARS, *Battlestar Galactica.* She was also the only cast member in the pilot who did not appear in *The New Gidget.* Larue was instead played by Jill Jacobson, who during 1986 played Erin Jones on the CBS evening soap opera, *Falcon Crest.*

There was even an animated version of *Gidget* produced in 1973, *Gidget Makes the Wrong Connection,* which featured the voice talent of Kathi Gori as Gidget. Ms. Gori also provided voices for other animated cartoon characters including Sara on *Bailey's Comets* and Rosemarie on *Hong Kong Phooey.*

Still, even after television audiences have had the opportunity to see four actresses (five if you count the animated special) in the title role, Sally Field will always be able to say, "That Gidget is mine."

GILLIGAN'S ISLAND

September 26, 1964–September 4, 1967.   CBS

Character:	Ginger Grant
Played by:	Tina Louise
Date(s):	September 26, 1964–September 4, 1967
Replaced by:	Ginger Grant
Played by:	Judith Baldwin
Date(s):	October 14, 1978 (*Rescue from Gilligan's Island.* NBC movie, part I)
	October 21, 1978 (part II)
	May 3, 1979 (*The Castaways on Gilligan's Island.* NBC movie)
Replaced by:	Ginger Grant
Played by:	Constance Forslund
Date(s):	May 15, 1981 (*The Harlem Globetrotters on Gilligan's Island.* NBC movie)

Television's most famous castaways wave ''Aloha'' to their island guests in this, the first of three reunion movies, *Rescue from Gilligan's Island.* Pictured (left to right) are: Roy Hinkley, ''The Professor'' (Russell Johnson); Thurston Howell, III (Jim Backus); Mrs. Lovey Howell (Natalie Schafer); Skipper Jonas Grumby (Alan Hale, Jr.); Gilligan (Bob Denver); Ginger Grant (Judith Baldwin); and Mary Ann Summers (Dawn Wells).

Character:	Thurston Howell III
Played by:	Jim Backus
Date(s):	September 26, 1964–September 4, 1967

Replaced by:	Thurston Howell IV
Played by:	David Ruprecht
Date(s):	May 15, 1981 (*The Harlem Globetrotters on Gilligan's Island.* NBC movie)

Once a television series gets on the air and stays on for as long as *Gilligan's Island* did, we come to know the actors as the characters they portray, and find it hard to imagine anyone else in those roles.

As the creator and producer of *Gilligan's Island,* [Sherwood] ''Schwartz's first choice for the role of Gilligan was Jerry Van Dyke, who, represented by Schwartz's original agent, was advised to take a different pilot.''[4] ''The only other person I have ever talked to was Bob Denver,'' remembers Schwartz. ''William Morris got in touch with me and said they had a perfect guy.''[5] Denver, of course, won the role.

The part of ''The Skipper'' was played from the beginning by Alan Hale, Jr. Among the actors who were tested for the role and turned down was Carroll O'Connor. Can you imagine *Gilligan's Island* with Carroll O'Connor and Jerry Van Dyke?

''The movie star'' mentioned in ''The Ballad of Gilligan's Isle,'' is Ginger Grant who, during the entire three-season run of

4. Green, Joey. *The Unofficial Gilligan's Island Handbook,* Warner Books, Inc., New York. 1988. p. 4.
5. *Ibid.*

Gilligan's Island, was played by Tina Louise. But Ms. Louise was not always Ginger, not before and not after. In the unaired pilot for the series Kit Smythe starred as the glamorous actress.

The original pilot for *Gilligan's Island* also starred two other actors who never made it to the actual series. The Professor was played by John Gabriel, and Mary Ann by Nancy McCarthy.

For ninety-eight weeks, *Gilligan's Island* was served up piping hot to the viewing public like a seven-course gourmet meal without a dessert. The dessert being a finale episode in which the seven stranded castaways are rescued.

In an interview on the February 18, 1989 edition of *Entertainment This Week,* Sherwood Schwartz, speaking about *Rescue from Gilligan's Island,* said that "Every week somebody would write in and say 'Whatever happened to those people on *Gilligan's Island?*' It was the audience that asked for that show and I was, at least, aware enough to pick that up." A stand-up comic picked up on this and asked his audience, "Remember the episode of *Gilligan's Island* when they almost got rescued?"

A rescue episode was never produced at the conclusion of the series' run because Schwartz believed that *Gilligan's Island* was going to be renewed for a fourth season, which it was not. But Schwartz always felt that it would be very satisfying to the public to produce such an episode. All of the members of the original cast agreed to recreate their roles in *Rescue from Gilligan's Island,* a two-hour made-for-television movie that was shown in two parts on NBC—not CBS, the series' original network.

The original Ginger, Tina Louise, was asked to join her fellow co-stars in the reunion movie even though producer Schwartz had anticipated difficulties signing her. In his book, *Inside Gilligan's Island,* Sherwood Schwartz said, "Tina was even more of a problem than I anticipated. That's because she *wasn't* as adamant as I thought she would be. First, she said she might do it after all. Then she changed her mind again. And again. And again."

"Finally, she said she would agree to do Ginger if I made her an offer that she couldn't refuse. The Godfather sum she mentioned was one-tenth of the budget of the entire show. It was far more than any of the other performers were being paid."

"It was out of the question. I would have to renegotiate all the other deals if I gave Tina what she asked for. I would have been left with seven Castaways and no money to do the show."[6]

"As much as I wanted to get together with everybody for old time's sake—I thought, well, that'll be fun—I was afraid of confusing the casting agents," explains Louise. "I thought if they paid me something worthwhile, then I'll say, 'Okay, well, I'm doing this for money—I do have a child[7] to support—and I'll overcome my emotional hesitations.' "[8]

Ms. Louise never had to deal with her emotional hesitations

because her replacement was cast with only five working days to spare before shooting was to begin. Schwartz explained: "Millie Gussie, our casting director, found Judy Baldwin, a beautiful, tall, redhead who had ample proportions where Tina Louise had ample proportions. Judy became Ginger for *Rescue from Gilligan's Island,* and our Castaways were now complete."[9]

Rescue aired on two consecutive Saturdays and did phenomenally well in the ratings. It earned a 30.2 with a fifty-two share making it the fifth highest-rated show of 1978 and one of the highest-rated television movies in history. It also paved the way for other reunion movies based on series such as *The Andy Griffith Show, The Beverly Hillbillies, Get Smart!, Perry Mason, The Brady Bunch* and *Gunsmoke.*

The high ratings *Rescue* received naturally prompted the network to ask for more. What they asked for was a new one-hour weekly series. What Schwartz wanted was to do one two-hour movie special each year. They settled on a new two-hour movie, *The Castaways on Gilligan's Island.* If the movie did well, NBC would then discuss the production of seven hour-long episodes based on the new premise, which had the Castaways operating a ritzy resort, "The Castaways," on the island. This second television movie featured the same cast as the first film. This time, the ratings were not as impressive, but they were still strong enough to warrant another outing, which turned out to be the last.

The six original stalwarts all signed on while the Ginger role was recast one last time for *The Harlem Globetrotters on Gilligan's Island.* The third and final Ginger Grant was played by Constance Forslund.

However, before shooting commenced, Jim Backus, who had been with *Gilligan's Island* from the beginning, became very ill. "After a while it became obvious that Jim would be unable to do his traditional role of Thurston Howell III in the film. I refused to recast the role with anyone else. Nobody could play Thurston Howell III like Jim. . . . Instead, we rewrote the script to bring in an heir to the Howell fortunes, Thurston Howell IV. The part was played by David Ruprecht. David did a wonderful interpretation of Jim's Howell characterization, without trying to do an imitation of Thurston Howell III."[10]

Toward the end of the shooting schedule, Backus phoned Schwartz and told him that he felt well enough to come in to film a scene if Thurston Howell III could be worked back into the script?

". . . I quickly added Jim to an existing scene at the end of the film, with the excuse that Thurston Howell III had just returned from a trip visiting one of his many enterprises."[11]

A podium is quickly put into place by hotel employees and Thurston Howell III steps up to congratulate his son and the Harlem Globetrotters on their victory against the robotic ball club.

---

6. Schwartz, Sherwood. *Inside Gilligan's Island. From Creation to Syndication.* McFarland & Company, Inc., Jefferson, North Carolina, 1988, pp. 222–223.

7. Tina Louise has a daughter named Caprice.

8. Green, Joey. *The Unofficial Gilligan's Island Handbook.* Warner Books, Inc., New York, 1988, p. 14.

9. Schwartz, *op. cit.,* p. 223

10. Schwartz, *op. cit.,* p. 150

11. *Ibid.*

HOWELL: Ladies and gentleman, your attention please. I would like to thank the Globetrotters on behalf of all of us for saving our island. (The crowd cheers wildly and Howell tries to calm them down.) A miniture hubbub, a minature hubbub. And to show our gratitude, you're invited to stay here free—off-season, of course.

If you want to be a real stickler, Dawn Wells (Mary Ann Summers) actually played Ginger on two separate occasions. In the ninety-second episode, "The Second Ginger Grant," Ms. Wells, as Mary Ann, assumes Ginger's personality traits after she takes a fall and bumps her head.

There were also two animated versions of *Gilligan's Island,* and the second one, *Gilligan's Planet,* featured the voice of Dawn Wells as the voluptuous movie star. *Gilligan's Planet* aired on CBS from September 18, 1982 to September 10, 1983.

The New Adventures of Gilligan, which aired on ABC from September 7, 1974 to September 4, 1977, featured the voice of Jane Webb as Ginger Grant.

And that's the way it was each week my friends where you were sure to get a smile, from seven stranded castaways, there on Gilligan's Isle.

THE GIRLS

January 1, 1950–March 25, 1950.   CBS

Character: Cornelia Otis Skinner
Played by: Bethel Leslie
Date(s):   January 1, 1950–February 1950

Replaced by: Cornelia Otis Skinner
Played by: Gloria Stroock
Date(s):   February 1950–March 25, 1950

This live CBS situation comedy, also known as *Young and Gay,* originally starred Bethel Leslie as Cornelia Otis Skinner, one of two Bryn Mawr graduates living in New York's Greenwich Village during the "Roaring '20s."

Ms. Leslie, who from 1965 to 1968 was the second of three Dr. Maggie Powers on the NBC daytime soap opera, *The Doctors,* left *The Girls* to work in a play, which during the 1950s was considered to be more acceptable work for an actress.

The actress who did not have the good fortune to be working on Broadway was Gloria Stroock, who took over the role until the series left the air a few weeks later. By coincidence, Ms. Stroock, also played a character named Maggie. In her case it was Maggie, the housekeeper, on *The NBC Sunday Mystery Movie, McMillan and Wife* (See Entry), which ran from September 29, 1971 to August 21, 1977.

THE GOLDBERGS

January 10, 1949–October 19, 1954.   CBS-NBC-DuMont

Character: Jake Goldberg
Played by: Philip Loeb
Date(s):   January 10, 1949–June 1951

Replaced by: Jake Goldberg
Played by: Harold J. Stone
Date(s):   February 1952–July 4, 1952

Replaced by: Jake Goldberg
Played by: Robert H. Harris
Date(s):   July 1953 October 19, 1954

Character: Sammy Goldberg
Played by: Larry Robinson
Date(s):   January 10, 1949–July 1952

Replaced by: Sammy Goldberg
Played by: Tom Taylor
Date(s):   April 1954–October 1954

In 1949, after nearly twenty years as a popular radio program, *The Goldbergs,* a domestic comedy about a middle-class Jewish family living in the Bronx, New York, became one of television's first situation comedies—but not before first becoming a Broadway play, *Molly and Me.*

Gertrude Berg, the creator, writer and producer of *The Goldbergs,* also starred as Molly, the central figure in the series. Her husband, Jake, who had been played by James R. Waters on radio, was replaced by Philip Loeb, who had played Timothy Hogarth in the 1938 Marx Brothers comedy, ROOM SERVICE. Waters did not appear in the play because he had died on November 20, 1945.

The stage production began its pre-Broadway run in the fall of 1947 and ended in 1949, at which time the cast moved into the new medium—television.

The television series went along without any changes in cast until 1951 when the red scare struck the series' co-star, Philip Loeb, who was listed in Senator McCarthy's publication, *Red Channels,* as being a Communist sympathizer. Presumably he had been singled out because of his work as one of the founders of the Actors Equity union, created to protect the interests of stage actors.

Some light was shed on this dark subject by Hasha Mintz, the widow of Eli Mintz, the actor who played Molly's Uncle David Romaine on *The Goldbergs:*

"Philip Loeb was originally called before the Senate hearings when Senator McCarthy was in his heyday. It was based on his actor's union activity and the fact that he had innocently signed certain petitions. This man was not a Communist, because we knew him and he was not the type of person to be involved with revolutionary movements. His only concern was to represent the interests of the working class of actors. And in no way could these activities have been construed as threatening to overthrow the government.

"They put this man through the worst kind of torture. You know, when you have to get up and defend yourself when you're innocent and really have nothing to hide, how do you present a case for yourself? What can you really use for evidence when you didn't do anything?" she asked rhetorically. "The man was going through hell. This man was an actor. Theater was his life. And what was done to him was totally unjust,"[12] she said furiously.

The way the story was previously reported was that General Foods, which sponsored *The Goldbergs* with its Sanka Coffee product, offered Loeb $85,000 to leave the show, but Loeb refused the offer and the sponsor dropped the series. Gertrude Berg stood by her co-star and was quoted in the *New York Times* as saying, "I believe him. There is no dispute between Philip Loeb and myself." But the outside pressure of losing the series and putting twenty people out of work was too great and so, reluctantly, Mrs. Berg paid Loeb $85,000 and the series returned to the air with a new actor, Harold J. Stone, in the co-starring role of Jake Goldberg.

"I can't attest to that [the $85,000 payoff], but what I know is that Philip Loeb had a seven-year ironclad contract with Gertrude Berg that guaranteed that he would be with the program as long as it remained on the air. It also stipulated that he would receive yearly increases in salary,"[13] said Mrs. Mintz.

Meanwhile, Loeb, like so many other victims of blacklisting, testified under oath that he was not a member of the Communist Party, but it did no good and his career and his life began to fall apart. On September 1, 1955, at the age of sixty-one, embittered, despondent and alone, the actor committed suicide in his New York City hotel room, taking an overdose of sleeping pills. The *New York Times* wrote, "Philip Loeb died of a sickness commonly called 'The Black List.'"

The second of three actors to play Jake Goldberg was Harold J. Stone, who told how he became Molly's second husband.

"Philip Loeb had already left the series when I got a call from Gertie Berg to replace him, but I no more wanted to play the part than the man in the moon! I met Gertrude at her apartment on Park Avenue in New York and suggested George Tobias, a great friend of Gertie's, for the part. And that's all we talked about in that meeting—George Tobias. I was doing *Stalag 17* on Broadway, playing Stosh ["Animal"], a role I had taken over from from Bob [Robert] Strauss when he left for Hollywood to do the film version.

"A few days later, I got a call from Gertie's secretary, Fanny Merrill, that Gertrude wanted to see me up at the NBC studios on the ninth floor. After finishing a matinee performance of *Stalag 17,* my agent, Mildred Weber and I went to meet her at NBC. When we got up there I heard Fanny ask Gertie, 'What about George?' and Gertrude answered 'Don't worry about that.' I was a young man then and I didn't want to play the part—that's why I suggested she ask George Tobias to come in from California.

"Anyway, this was a Wednesday after I had just finished a matinee. We were up on the ninth floor of NBC where they had a camera standing by. They sort of grayed my hair a little bit and put glasses on me. Then Gertrude and I ad-libbed together in front of the camera.

"The next day was Thursday, and after that evening's

performance of *Stalag 17* who should come in to my dressing room but George Tobias. He was complaining. 'Jesus Christ, I came into town because I had a three o'clock appointment with Gertrude and she didn't show up until seven o'clock!' he shouted. She asked George to read the part and at first he used a little accent and she said 'No accent.' She then told him that they were going into rehearsal for the Monday night's live performance on Friday.

"So George said, 'Look, you've got to give me three days,' and she said, 'That's the end of it.'

"Now, on Friday I was doing *The Ed Sullivan Show* with Bea [Beatrice] Lillie and Reggie [Reginald] Gardner. I was rehearsing a show for the Lamb's Club with Bobby Clark and Brandon Peters—and then, of course, I was doing *Stalag 17* at night. At eleven o'clock in the morning on Friday, when I was rehearsing, the phone rang. On the other end was Mildred and she said, 'Hello Jake,' and that was it.

"So here was Jake, a guy who was surrounded by all of these Jewish people and was supposed to be working in New York's garment center and Gertrude wanted me to speak like an Oxonian—without any accent. We rehearsed for about five hours that Sunday and on Monday night, at seven o'clock, I went on live—with Gertrude Berg holding me by the hand.

"I did *The Goldbergs* until the end of the season, which was in July, when the show went on hiatus. And since my contract for *Stalag 17* was up in May and *The Goldbergs* wasn't scheduled to go back into production until October, my wife and I went on a two-week vacation to Hyannis and the Cape. Incidentally, when I was doing *The Goldbergs,* George Tobias was hired to play Stosh in the road production of *Stalag 17.*

"When I got back from vacation, there was some sort of contract problems with Gertrude and the network and then they canceled the show. So I went to London to do *Stalag 17* and just kept on working. When I came back from England, I found out that the show was back on the air and Bob [Robert H.] Harris was doing the part and that was that,"[14] said Stone, very matter-of-factly.

"A couple of months later I got a call from Fanny Merrill who said, 'Gertrude wants to talk with you but she was embarrassed to call,' and I asked, 'Why?' 'Well, she would like you to replace George Tobias on her radio program, *The House of Glass.* It was like a kick in the ass, but I was working so much, what the Hell did I care? I didn't want to play Jake in the first place. So I asked her, 'Is she going to pay me?' and Fanny answered, 'Yes,' so I said, 'Sure, I'll do it,'"[15] chuckled Stone.

There was never any resentment between Harold J. Stone and Robert H. Harris, and to prove it, they worked together in an episode of CBS's 1950's police anthology series, *Crime Syndicated.* "I played a stevedore, Jim [James] Gregory played a detective, Bob played a mobster and Bob's wife, Viola, played my wife,"[16] laughed Stone.

Stone was also teamed up with Robert H. Harris in "The

---

12. From an exclusive telephone interview with Eli Mintz's widow, Hasha Mintz, on February 9, 1991.
13. From an exclusive telephone interview with Eli Mintz's widow, Hasha Mintz, on February 9, 1991.
14. From an exclusive telephone interview with Harold J. Stone on February 9, 1991.
15. *Ibid.*
16. *Ibid.*

Greatest Monster of them All,'' the February 14, 1961 episode of *Alfred Hitchcock Presents*. He worked for Hitchcock again in the 1956 crime film, THE WRONG MAN, in which he played Lieutenant Bowery. In 1960 he played David in the wide-screen spectacular SPARTACUS, but Stone said that his favorite role was Nick Barbella in SOMEBODY UP THERE LIKES ME, which was released the same year as THE WRONG MAN. In 1963, Harold J. Stone played Doctor Sam Brant in the Roger Corman science fiction film, X—THE MAN WITH THE X-RAY EYES.

In addition to his earlier television work, Harold J. Stone played publisher Hamilton Greeley on William Windom's situation comedy, *My World and Welcome To It*, which aired from September 15, 1969 to September 7, 1972. Probably his best remembered television role since *The Goldbergs* was Sam Steinberg, on *Bridget Loves Bernie*, which aired on CBS from September 16, 1972 to September 8, 1973.

The third and final actor to serve as Molly's Jake was Robert H. Harris, who played Raymond Schindler on *The Court of Last Resort*, the crime series that aired on both NBC and ABC between October 4, 1957 and February 17, 1960.

''I don't think Robert Harris was even remotely disturbed by the fact that Jake had been played before by any one else. I'm not even sure if he had seen Phil Loeb do the role on television or heard him on radio,''[17] said Robert H. Harris's widow, Viola Harris.

''I know only that he had been approached by Mrs. Berg to do this role after the difficulties with Phil and after the show went back on the air. And at that time Robert Harris was extremely busy in television, doing as many as three and four shows at the same time. I know today that may sound incredible, but in those early days of live television when they had *Studio One* and *Danger* and *Suspense*, that's exactly what he did. He was extremely active and successful at that time, doing a variety of roles on these programs. And as a character actor, his interest really lay in playing these varied roles instead of tying himself up in a series, which was then not considered so impressive a credit as it is today. Today, one dies to get into a series, but he did not. He preferred to play different roles as a character actor. And so it was at that point that Harold Stone assumed the role in *The Goldbergs* for a very brief period. Mrs. Berg came back to Bob after Harold Stone had been in the role for five months, and asked him to do it.

''He agreed, but only with the proviso that it would not be an exclusive contract and that he would be free to do other roles whenever possible. She agreed and he did just that.

''Yet in the years to come it was this one role as Jake Goldberg that everybody remembers and not all those other brilliant roles he had played. He did not imitate Phil Loeb. He did not think in terms of playing this role as anybody else did.

He moved in to play this role as he moved in to play any role which is *as he saw it to be played*,''[18] said Mrs. Harris.

Robert H. Harris wasn't really a stranger to *The Goldbergs*; he had appeared in some of the very early episodes as Mr. Mendell, Jake's younger partner in the dress business. In the 1950 theatrical release MOLLY, Erno Verebes played Mr. Mendell.

''When Bob [Harris] went on *The Goldbergs* to play Jake, I went in to play Mrs. Mendell. It was a steady role, in that I always played it, but it didn't come up that often, perhaps once in every three months,''[19] concluded Mrs. Harris.

Certainly one of the program's most beloved characters was the slight-framed, nasal-voiced old man known affectionately as Uncle David. But the actor who played this ''everyone's favorite uncle'' for the entire run of the series was neither nasal-voiced nor old when he played the part, as explained by his widow, Hasha Mintz:

''When plans got underway for the TV production, she [Gertrude Berg] had a special script written for audition purposes only. Eli had been in the Broadway show prior to that and she used to playfully needle him by saying things like, 'Do you want to be on TV with me? One of these days we may be on TV, darling?' and always acting as though she was going to protect him to see that he gets on television also.

''In that initial audition, Larry Robinson and Arlene McQuade played the Goldbergs' children, Sammy[20] and Rosalie; Mrs. Berg played Molly; Philip Loeb played Jake; and Menasha Skulnik played Uncle David for this one-time audition for the TV cameras,''[21] recalled Mrs. Mintz.

''Menasha Skulnik was cast in the pilot because he had played Uncle David on the radio version of *The Goldbergs*. According to Gertrude Berg's autobiography, *Molly and Me: The Memoirs of Gertrude Berg*, she had seen Skulnik performing in the Yiddish theater on New York's Second Avenue and was taken by his personality and his brand of comedy, and created the role of Uncle David *for him* to play for what turned out to be the show's last season on radio.

''She wanted to use him for the Broadway production, but he probably didn't want to do it because he was making more money than she could have paid him. There was very little money in television in those days and he was making more starring in his own Second Avenue theater productions,''[22] she speculated.

''Menasha was the one who recommended Eli for the part of Uncle David, because he could do an imitation of Menasha's voice.

''When Eli came for the formal screen test, there were at least forty other actors there trying out for the same part, while Mrs. Berg had promised him all along that he was going to get the part. And he did not know that Menasha had already auditioned with the entire cast in the pilot.

---

17. From an exclusive telephone interview with Robert H. Harris's widow, Viola Harris, on February 9, 1991.
18. From an exclusive telephone interview with Robert H. Harris's widow, Viola Harris, on February 9, 1991.
19. *Ibid.*
20. Sammy was played by Tom Taylor.
21. From an exclusive telephone interview with Eli Mintz's widow, Hasha Mintz, on February 9, 1991.
22. From an exclusive telephone interview with Eli Mintz's widow, Hasha Mintz, on February 9, 1991.

"Among the actors auditioning for the part of Uncle David was Irving Jacobson, who was a top level performer in the Yiddish theater—he would have been suitable. Later, he played Sancho Panza in the Broadway production of *Man of La Mancha* and when he left the play, Eli was auditioned to become his replacement.

"A more unlikely candidate was Zvee Scooler. He was very well known on Yiddish radio, but didn't fit the part at all,"[23] said Mrs. Mintz.

"But up until the time of the Broadway play, there was very little consideration given to the way Uncle David should look, because it wasn't necessary for radio.

"Eli was in his forties at the time he got the role of Uncle David for the Broadway play and there was no way he could pass for this old character. So Eli took it upon himself to try out different makeups. He worked with crepe hair to create mustaches and tried on different wigs until he finally came up with the way we know Uncle David's appearance. He created that at home—in front of mirrors. He showed Gertrude Berg and the director of the play what he had in mind and they thought it was great and let him do it the way he conceived it. He even supplied his own clothes that he bought on the Bowery instead of using what the costumer was supplying. This was because he had a better feel for what was correct for this character than they did. Eli felt that at sixty-five, which was presumably the age of Uncle David, he would dress the same way he had always dressed. People don't put on old people's clothing just because they get older. The ones who look dowdy, looked dowdy when they were thirty. So that was the way Uncle David came to be known visually.

"When they were preparing for Eli's screen test for the TV series, he went up to the producer, Worthington Minor, before he had put on the Uncle David makeup and Mr. Minor did not recognize him. He didn't know that the guy playing Uncle David was a young man.

"Now, this was the early days of television, before the role of the emerging unions were very well defined, so Eli asked Mr. Minor, 'Who will do my makeup for the Monday performance?' and Mr. Minor answered, 'Well, who did your makeup for the camera test?' Eli responded, 'I did.' So Mr. Minor said, 'So you do it, because no one is going to do it better.' And Eli continued to do it until the union decided who did what. At first, the union makeup artist would allow Eli to do basic makeup and would just do some finishing touches like adding a little whitening to his eyebrows. Eli was still doing his own makeup for quite a while before the union makeup artists took over completely,"[24] concluded Mrs. Mintz.

GOMER PYLE, U.S.M.C.

September 25, 1964–September 9, 1970.   CBS

Character:	Corporal Johnson
Played by:	Jerry Dexter
Date(s):	September 25, 1964–episode #7

Replaced by:	Corporal McCabe
Played by:	Richard Sinatra
Date(s):	(episode #10)

Replaced by:	Corporal Nick Cuccinelli
Played by:	Tommy Leonetti
Date(s):	September 1964–September 10, 1965

Replaced by:	Tommy
Played by:	Jack Larson
Date(s):	September 17, 1965

Replaced by:	Corporal Boyle
Played by:	Richard Sinatra
Date(s):	(episode #35)

Replaced by:	Corporal Chuck Boyle
Played by:	Roy Stuart
Date(s):	1965–April 5, 1968

Replaced by:	Corporal Duke Slater
Played by:	Ronnie Schell
Date(s):	October 4, 1968–September 9, 1970

In addition to the "few good men" stationed at Camp Henderson in Los Angeles there is one Gomer Pyle, a former resident of Mayberry, North Carolina. Actor Jim Nabors developed this dim-witted, naive and honest-as-the-day-is-long southerner on *The Andy Griffith Show* (See Entry). It didn't take long for the producers, Aaron Ruben in particular, to recognize the enormous potential of this character. So, at the end of the 1963/1964 season, CBS gave Nabors his very own series, *Gomer Pyle, U.S.M.C.*

The transition, from fillin' station attendant to Marine Private, occurred on the May 19, 1964 episode of *The Andy Griffith Show,* which was appropriately titled, "Gomer Pyle, U.S.M.C."

According to Napoleon Bonaparte, "An army marches on its stomach," but as we have learned from programs such as *M*A*S*H,* it is often the aides to the officers who are the backbone of the military. Camp Henderson was no different and in the case of series co-star Frank Sutton, who played B Company's platoon sergeant, Vince Carter, he too required a good officer to do the paperwork and generally run the office.

As we all know, good help is hard to find and Sergeant Carter went through five corporals during his enlistment, one of whom was played by two different actors.

Episodes one through seven of *Gomer Pyle, U.S.M.C.* were set in boot camp, where Corporal Johnson served as Sergeant Carter's aide. Johnson was played by Jerry Dexter, who for twenty years (from the late 1960s through the 1980s) lent his voice to dozens of Saturday morning cartoon characters. Some of his more popular character voices include the superhero Aqualad on the CBS series *Aquaman,* which aired from September 9, 1967 to September 7, 1969; Gulliver on *The Adven-*

23. *Ibid.*
24. From an exclusive telephone interview with Eli Mintz's widow, Hasha Mintz, on February 9, 1991.

Flirting with Lou Ann Poovie (Elizabeth MacRae) outside soundstage 9, during a break in filming *Gomer Pyle, U.S.M.C.,* are Corporal Duke Slater (Ronnie Schell, left) and Sergeant Vince Carter (Frank Sutton).

tures of Gulliver, which aired on ABC from September 14, 1968 to September 5, 1970; and Alan on *Josie and the Pussycats,* which aired on CBS from September 12, 1970 to September 9, 1972.

The first corporal to sit behind the khaki desk at Camp Henderson was Corporal McCabe, played by Richard Sinatra who later returned for one episode as Corporal Boyle. Replacing McCabe was Nick Cuccinelli, played by singer Tommy Leonetti, a member of The Hit Paraders chorus from 1957 to 1958 on *Your Hit Parade.* Leonetti as Cuccinelli, sat in the hot seat for one year before the series. His first replacement lasted for only one episode, but that is not how it was planned.

It is an episode especially worth watching, if only for its value as television nostalgia. This is because Cuccinelli's replacement, Tommy, was played by Jack Larson, Superman's pal, Jimmy Olsen, the young whippersnapper who was balled out each week by the editor-in-chief of the Metropolis *Daily Planet* on the *Adventures of Superman.* It was a rare appearance by Larson, who was last seen in an uncharacteristically funny performance as Kenneth Dexter, a young nightclub performer with very little talent, on the ''Big Max Calvada'' episode of *The Dick Van Dyke Show,* which aired on November 20, 1963.

Jack Larson explained that it was nothing short of a miracle that he appeared on *Gomer Pyle, U.S.M.C.* at all because he had no intention of doing any more acting after the *Adventures of Superman:*

''I had quit acting, I had felt very typed with Jimmy Olsen and when George Reeves died in 1959 I just decided that I was going to quit acting. Since I write and had other things to do, I did quit.

''In 1964 a friend of mine, actor John Kerr, who had starred as Tom Robinson Lee in the 1956 drama, TEA AND SYMPA-THY, and Lieutenant Cable in the 1958 musical, SOUTH PACIFIC, had also quit acting. He had already directed an L.A. production of *Who's Afraid of Virginia Woolf?* and his current project was a Los Angeles stage production of *Androcles and the Lion* for ANTA (American National Theater Academy), a very distinguished production company.

''At the time I was writing for a Jerome Robbins project called American Laboratory Theater and I certainly didn't want to think about acting. John Kerr, however wanted me to do *Androcles* for him. Jack [Kerr] and I were old, old, old friends and he wouldn't take 'no' for an answer. And Kate Drain Lawson, a great lady of the theater who had worked with Virgil

Thomson and John Houseman on the original 1933 production of *4 Saints in 3 Acts,* also wanted me to do *Androcles,* which she was producing for ANTA.

"I got brow-beaten into it. Jack would be on my doorstep and say, 'Are you just going to quit acting without doing something that would challenge you? It's George Bernard Shaw and it's going to be a good production.'

"Finally, very unwillingly, I agreed to do it and we had a success with it. Suddenly there was a lot of good press and I got offered 'a' *Gomer Pyle* and I thought, 'Why not?' I had only seen *Gomer Pyle* once and thought Jim Nabors was terrific. I thought, well, as long as I'm on the stage doing *Androcles* I may as well pick up some money during the day and do this—but there was a misunderstanding.

"I don't remember the ins and outs of it, but they were under the impression that I would do a running character. And they paid me quite a good amount of money to do this thing and so I did it. I was still performing at night on the stage and I went to do this for two or three days. I really had no intention of doing a running character whatsoever, and I didn't know I was replacing anybody.

"They were all very, very nice, but the producers were surprised that I hadn't been told by my agent, Harold Gefsky, that they were thinking of having me on *Gomer Pyle* as a running character. When this became apparent, I sidestepped the issue with them, but told my agent that it was out of the question.

"Well, they were very cranky that I wasn't going to do this. There was a real nice man who may have been the one who had negotiated this whole thing, and when he learned that I wasn't going to do the series, he was very dismayed.

"I was doing *Androcles* under very distinguished circumstances and I was very glad I did *Androcles,* but it didn't make me want to act again at that time. Just because it was so difficult being typed.

"When I originally did Jimmy in *Superman* there was a lot of live television. You couldn't at that time, at all, cross over into film. If it were today, somebody would have starred me in a film because I was very popular, like Michael J. Fox. But you were considered 'the enemy' if you were on television. The film studios stood against that. We're talking about the early fifties to the mid-fifties. It just was a very disheartening experience.

"As a kid, I was under contract with Warner Bros. They were very nice to me and they always gave me a run on something. FIGHTER SQUADRON was the first thing I ever did; it was for Raoul Walsh. The last film I did was an independent, released through Warner Bros., JOHNNY TROUBLE. But other than that I was just typed. I would go to an audition and they'd say, 'We'd love to have you, but we don't want Jimmy Olsen in our movie.' It's a depressing experience being typed and I thought, I have other things to do than to go up against this.

"I would like to act again, but only if it were the right thing. But I would never do another television series. I mean doing one in my lifetime was enough. I'm proud and delighted I did *Superman,* but I'd never do that grind again,"[25] said Larson.

Since leaving the *Adventures of Superman* Jack Larson has collaborated with Virgil Thomson on the opera, *Lord Byron.* The work was commissioned by the Metropolitan Opera and was broadcast live from Lincoln Center in a program hosted by John Houseman.

"I wrote the libretto," said Larson, "and Virgil Thomson, who was America's greatest composer of opera, wrote the music. His music, my libretto. Libretto is like a play and you set it to music. That is certainly the most famous work I've done. I have two works that the Joffrey Ballet do. One is called *The Relativity of Icarus,* which I did with another composer, Gerhard Samuel. And, I continue to work with composers."[26]

At this writing Larson was completing *Parson Weems' Life of Washington,* an unfinished work he began with Virgil Thomson. "It's a music-theater work that I'm finishing up with a protégé of Virgil Thomson,"[27] concluded Larson.

In addition to his work as a librettist, Larson was the associate producer of the 1988 drama, BRIGHT LIGHTS, BIG CITY, which starred Michael J. Fox as Jamie Conway.

The next corporal assigned to Sergeant Carter was Corporal Boyle, who was actually played by two actors. The first was Richard Sinatra, who like Larson only appeared in one episode, but he proved to be far less memorable than Jack Larson. Richard Sinatra lasted a bit longer in the Navy when he played Seaman D'Angelo in the NBC adventure comedy, *Mr. Roberts,* which remained afloat from September 17, 1965 to September 2, 1966.

The Corporal Chuck Boyle that everyone does remember was the one played for nearly four years by the very likable, hazy-voiced actor, Roy Stuart. Coming from a background in musical theater in New York, Roy Stuart said he worked "In any number of flops including *Cafe Crown,* which opened at the Martin Beck Theater in New York on a Friday and closed on a Saturday."[28]

Stuart said that when he came out to California to perform in summer stock theater, he had no intention of staying or doing episodic television. The play he came to California to work in was *The Bells Are Ringing.* It ran at the Valley Music Theater in the San Fernando Valley and starred Gordon and Sheila MacRae.

He began his work in television because, "Alan Young saw me in that [*The Bells Are Ringing*]. *Mr. Ed* was the first thing I ever did—I played the optometrist on *Mr. Ed.* He [Young] got me on that show. . . and I was frightened of that damned horse,"[29] said Stuart.

One of his next roles was an episode of *Please Don't Eat the Daisies,* which was directed by Peter Baldwin. "I was a young

---

25. From an exclusive telephone interview with Jack Larson on September 8, 1990.
26. *Ibid.*
27. *Ibid.*
28. From an exclusive telephone interview with Roy Stuart on August 30, 1990.
29. *Ibid.*

New York actor and I just loved the theater and loved what I was doing and I had no intention of staying out here—at all. And I got lucky and did a lot of episodic stuff,"[30] he said.

By coincidence, Peter Baldwin was also directing *Gomer Pyle, U.S.M.C.* When Roy Stuart went to work on *Please Don't Eat the Daisies* he and the director developed what he referred to as "an instant rapport."[31] As a result, after Stuart finished that show he was told by his agent that he had been booked on *Gomer Pyle, U.S.M.C.* without having to go through an audition. This was because he had been requested by Peter Baldwin.

Stuart was actually only booked for one episode of *Gomer Pyle, U.S.M.C.*, and as he tells it, "Frank Sutton and I just ignited. I guess he saw in me a kindred spirit from the theater. When I got on the show I want you to know that I had no idea that they were looking for a Corporal Boyle. I had no idea that Frank [Sutton] was the final say so in that particular situation because it was someone he wanted to work with. I didn't know any of that background. If I knew it, maybe I would have felt differently,"[32] said Stuart.

Roy Stuart never fell into the trap of wanting to do an impression or copy of the character he was replacing because he had never seen the series. "I was protected in my ignorance," he said. "I didn't know, I didn't care. It was a joke to me. . . it was all a dream to me. I didn't know that I had replaced someone or that I had to act a certain way. If I had known it, maybe I would have felt differently, but I had nothing to lose."[33]

By comparison, Stuart, who when working in summer stock rehearsed one show and did another at the same time seven days a week, felt that going into a studio and doing one take, which took about sixty seconds, was like a vacation.

Working on a year-to-year contract, Stuart ended his hitch on *Gomer Pyle, U.S.M.C.* at the end of his fourth year, not to take a vacation from his vacation, but because he had accepted a five-picture deal at Universal. "Aaron Ruben graciously let me out [of my contract],"[34] he said. Stuart might have stayed on for another season, but "I really just didn't understand that I was doing as well as I did. But it wasn't as hard as working in a play."[35]

The producer who had lured Roy Stuart away from television was Aaron Ruben's cousin, Nat Hiken, who was the producer and director of *Car 54, Where Are You?* The first of Hiken's five pictures was the Don Knotts/Anne Francis comedy, THE LOVE GOD. The film was written and directed by Nat Hiken and featured Roy Stuart as Joe Merkel. It was released in 1969, but the 54–year-old Hiken never saw it because he had died in Brentwood, California on December 7, 1968. Consequently, Stuart never completed his five-picture deal because, as he reflected, "When Nat passed away, the other four pictures passed away with him."[36]

Roy Stuart's resumé includes appearances on dozens of television programs and more than 400 commercials. One of his most famous commercials was the classic "smelly feet" spot in which the dog faints. The dog in that commercial was Benji and Stuart jokes, "My feet made that dog a star!"[37]

His more recent television work includes playing the dry cleaner who was Blanche's (Rue McClanahan) boyfriend on *Golden Girls* and an episode of *The New Munsters*. His latest film appearance was as the businessman in the 1991 Mel Brooks comedy, LIFE STINKS. Yet with all of his credits Stuart admits, "I am amazed that people still recognize me from that show [*Gomer Pyle*]. Not from anything else I've done." When asked if that bothers him he confessed, "I love it, I love it,"[38] concluded Stuart.

Instead of hiring a new actor to portray Boyle or introduce a new character, the producers took the same route that the producers of *M*A*S*H* took later, using an already established member of the cast in a new position. On *M*A*S*H* (See Entry) Corporal Max Klinger (Jamie Farr) was promoted to the 4077th's company clerk—the spot left vacant by the departed Walter "Radar" O'Reilly (Gary Burghoff). *Gomer Pyle*'s producers moved Ronnie Schell's Duke Slater character into the Sergeant's office to finish out the run of the series.

Originally a stand-up comedian, Ronnie Schell, first snuck onto television as a contestant on the Groucho Marx quiz program, *You Bet Your Life*. In addition to his role on *Gomer Pyle, U.S.M.C.*, Ronnie Schell appeared concurrently on two other situation comedies. He was Harvey Peck, one of Ann Marie's (Marlo Thomas) agents on the ABC situation comedy, *That Girl* (See Entry), during 1966 and 1967, and starred as morning disc jockey Larry Clarke on the CBS sitcom, *Good Morning World*. That series ran from September 5, 1967 to September 17, 1968. From 1969 to 1971, Schell was a regular on *The Jim Nabors Hour,* surprise, surprise, surprise.

Sergeant Carter's last Corporal got to work alongside his first on the ABC Saturday morning cartoon, *Goober and the Ghost Chasers,* which aired from September 8, 1973 to August 31, 1975. Ronnie Schell provided the voice of Gilly while Jerry Dexter did the voice of Ted.

Gomer Pyle, U.S.M.C. received its honorable discharge from CBS on September 9, 1979, after an incredible total of 230 roll calls.

---

30. From an exclusive telephone interview with Roy Stuart on August 30, 1990.

31. *Ibid.*

32. *Ibid.*

33. *Ibid.*

34. From an exclusive telephone interview with Roy Stuart on August 30, 1990.

35. *Ibid.*

36. *Ibid.*

37. *Ibid.*

38. *Ibid.*

GOOD ADVICE

April 2, 1993–May 7, 1993.   CBS

Character:	Ronnie Cohen
Played by:	Estelle Harris
Date(s):	April 2, 1993
Replaced by:	Lynn Casey
Played by:	Kiersten Warren
Date(s):	April 9, 1993–May 7, 1993

Shelley Long, who was no longer drunk with the success of her role as Diane Chambers on the hit series *Cheers* (See Entry), returned to television six years later as Susan DeRuzza, Ph.D., a prominent marriage counselor and best-selling advice author, in the short-lived CBS series, *Good Advice.*

Sharing the suite of offices with Doctor DeRuzza were Jack Harold (Treat Williams), an unattached divorce attorney, and Artie Cohen (George Wyner), a chiropractor and owner of the office building.

Susan separated from her philandering husband, Joey (Christopher McDonald), when she returned home early from a promotional tour for her latest book and found a woman hiding in her closet.

The DeRuzza's son, Michael, was played by Ross Malinger.

Borrowing from a page out of television sitcom history, Artie's mother Ronnie (Estelle Harris) served as the office receptionist for all three practices, just as Carol Kester (Marcia Wallace) served as receptionist for both psychologist Bob Hartley (Bob Newhart) and dentist, Jerry Robinson (Peter Bonerz) on *The Bob Newhart Show,* which aired on CBS from September 16, 1972, to August 26, 1978.

Mrs. Cohen, a nosey and totally obnoxious old biddy, was replaced in the second episode by Lynn Casey (Kiersten Warren), a pretty young receptionist.

All three practices were closed four weeks later when the show was cancelled after its sixth episode, "Turning Thirteen," had aired.

In hindsight, Ms. Long should have taken some good advice in 1987 and stayed with *Cheers.*

GOOD MORNING MISS BLISS *see:* SAVED BY THE BELL

GOOD SPORTS

January 10, 1991–July 13, 1991.   CBS

Character:	Stu Ramsey
Played by:	Arthur Burghardt
Date(s):	January 10, 1991
Replaced by:	"Downtown" Bobby Tannen
Played by:	Ryan O'Neal
Date(s):	January 10, 1991–July 13, 1991

The full-page promotional ad in *TV Guide* read "Join us right after CHEERS—on another network!" Those who did were treated to a very promising situation comedy about former lovers who are now the co-anchors of cable sports programs, *Sports Central* and *Sports Chat.* And, oh yes, they don't get along.

The setting is the Rappaport Broadcasting System, owned and operated by Mr. R.J. Rappaport (Lane Smith), who is a caricature of cable television mogul Ted Turner. The network operates the *RSCBC,* a religious channel, *RAP"HA"PORT,* a twenty-four-hour comedy channel and, of course, *RSCN,* the Rappaport All Sports Cable Network.

The co-anchors of *Sports Central* are Gayle Roberts (Farrah Fawcett) and Stu Ramsey (Arthur Burghardt). The premiere episode, "Pros And Ex-Cons," opens with a Sunday broadcast that features the weekly segment, "Stump Stu," to which viewers submit sports trivia questions in an attempt to stump Stu. Gayle prefaces each week's question by saying that as long as she has worked on the show, she has never known Stu to have been stumped.

The question that was sent in by Alan Ross of Waco, Texas, read , "Only one player in the history of the major leagues has ever hit five consecutive switch-hit home runs." The question baffles Stu and quickly drives him crazy. He then stands up and turns to the video wall of nine television monitors behind the anchor desk, becomes disoriented and asks, "Will someone please get this hat off my head?" He then begins turning monitors off until all that remains are the letters spelling his name "STU." He then repeats his name four times and collapses on the anchor desk, face down, right in front of Gayle. Gayle covers with a joke and quickly goes to a commercial. Stu had, of course, died—on camera.

The lucky actor who knew he was going to be written out the moment he read the script was Arthur Burghardt. Daytime soap opera fans may remember him as Dr. Jack Scott on ABC's *One Life to Live,* while sitcom addicts may know him from his occasional appearances on *Diff'rent Strokes* as Alex DuPrey, the father of Willis Jackson's (Todd Bridges) girlfriend, Charlene (Janet Jackson).

At the gathering following Stu Ramsey's funeral, Mr. Rappaport tells Gayle that he will give her total approval on Stu's replacement.

Enter Ryan O'Neal as "Downtown" Bobby Tannen, a washed-up ex-football star who had played with the Jets, L.A. Rams and Oakland Raiders. Rappaport tries to sell the nostalgia of having Tannen join the RSCN family to his staff of "yes men," and calls to mind Woodstock, the New York Jets winning the Super Bowl, the New York Mets winning the pennant and films like LOVE STORY. This is doubly funny because Ryan O'Neal, the co-star of the series, starred as Oliver Barrett IV in that sentimental 1970 drama.

But, when Mr. Rappaport introduces Bobby Tannen to Gayle Roberts, she gives him more than just a cold shoulder, and Rappaport remarks, "That was downright ugly." The reason for Gayle's immediate dislike of Tannen is that she had been jilted by him some years earlier—worse yet, he didn't even remember her. Gayle tries to refresh his memory and relates the details of their two-day tryst.

It seems that while the New York Jets were in Maine to play the Detroit Lions, Bobby Tannen crashed a party at Gayle's sorority house. She was introduced to him by her unseen friend Robin Blankman. Tannen took her dancing at the Shangri-la and later went back to her apartment in Ann Arbor, where they indulged in a love-making session that went on for forty-eight hours. He missed his plane back to New York and was fined for missing two days of football practice.

It is hard to imagine that anyone could forget an affair with someone who looked like one of *Charlie's Angels,* (See Entry), but maybe he didn't recognize her because she had changed her name (which was probably done for professional reasons).

You see, when Gayle first met Bobby Tannen, her last name was not Roberts, but Gordon—Gayle Gordon! Bobby is still baffled—that is until his mom (Lois Smith) comes in to confirm Gayle's story.

> MRS. TANNEN: I remember being worried sick that you slept with the guy that played Mr. Mooney on the *Here's Lucy* show.

Bobby's first on-air experience was on *Sports Chat* and their first guest was professional basketball player and actor Kareem Abdul-Jabbar.

> KAREEM: I want to say how sorry I was about Stu.
>
> GAYLE: Me too.
>
> KAREEM: He was a great man.
>
> GAYLE: He's the reason I'm here today.
>
> BOBBY: Me too.

Unfortunately for Bobby, the job he had wanted so badly only lasted for three months; *Good Sports* was pulled from the CBS schedule after the seventh episode. The reason—low ratings.

In the April 13, 1991 issue of *TV Guide,* executive producer Brad Grey said that the show might return to the schedule later in the year, but not until after some reworking, including an all-new writing staff. The first assignment for the new writers would be to make the show more of a romantic comedy, because surveys had shown that audiences didn't enjoy seeing the bickering between the series' co-stars, who are actually lovers in real life. The real problem was that the audience wasn't a lover of the series; it was canceled by both Rappaport and CBS after just fifteen episodes.

GOOD TIMES

February 1, 1974–August 1, 1979.   CBS

Character:	Florida Evans
Played by:	Esther Rolle
Date(s):	February 1, 1974–1977
	1978–August 1, 1979

Replaced by:	Willona Woods
Played by:	Ja'net DuBois
Date(s):	September 21, 1977–August 1, 1979

Character:	James Evans
Played by:	John Amos
Date(s):	February 1, 1974–March 2, 1976

Replaced by:	Carl Dixon
Played by:	Moses Gunn
Date(s):	February 9, 1977
	February 23, 1977
	March 2, 1977

If you watched *Good Times* during the seventies you may have associated with and even admired the characters' struggle to get ahead in this, the first television series which attempted to accurately depict black life in America.

It began as a successful spinoff from Beatrice Arthur's CBS sitcom *Maude* (See Entry), on which Esther Rolle played Florida Evans, the Findlay's maid (the first of three). In that

Enjoying the *Good Times* are John Amos, as James Evans, and Esther Rolle, as his wife and Maude Findlay's former housekeeper, Florida.

spinoff episode, it was explained that Florida's husband Henry didn't want his wife working as a maid anymore.

During the course of her employment, the two women had built a close relationship that transcended employer and employee and in a tearful scene the two friends say good-bye to each other.

MAUDE: Oh, we'll visit.

FLORIDA: Mrs. Findlay, you know we'll never visit each other.

MAUDE: I know.

John Amos had always played Florida's husband on *Maude,* but somewhere between Tuckahoe, New York and the South Side of Chicago his name was changed from Henry to James.

The series started out in seventeenth place during its first season and jumped to number six during the 1974/1975 season, but dropped out of the top twenty for the remainder of its run.

The trouble started at the beginning of the 1975/1976 season when John Amos got into a contract dispute with the producers. Their differences, which were reported to have centered primarily on money, were settled but the tension between the actor and the producers was heightened when an article, "Bad Times on *Good Times*" ran in *Ebony* magazine. In that article, both John Amos and Esther Rolle complained about the show, the producers and the writers. As a result, Amos was released from his contract in September of 1976.

It was explained in a two-part episode, which aired on September 22 and 29, 1976, that James got a job in rural Mississippi working at a garage. But before the excited Evans family had a chance to move to Mississippi to begin their new lives, they received word that James had been killed in an automobile accident. And regardless of the explanations given by the producers for this twist, it was obviously designed to prevent Amos from returning to the series, like Archie Bunker on *All in the Family* (See Entry) and Colonel Henry Blake on *M*A*S*H* (See Entry).

Prior to leaving the series John Amos was quoted as saying, "The only regrets I would have leaving *Good Times* is that it might mean that the show would revert to the matriarchal thing—the fatherless black family."[39] Amos was apparently right, because that is exactly the way the Washington-based National Black Media Coalition saw it. They were also more vocal than Amos and demanded that Norman Lear, the show's executive producer, make casting changes so that *Good Times* would not present blacks in this stereotypical manner.

The situation was rectified by introducing Carl Dixon, the owner of a small appliance shop. Dixon, who was played by Moses Gunn, married Florida in an unseen wedding in the summer of 1977 restoring the family unit—almost. Almost, becsuse Esther Rolle left the series before the 1977/1978 season began. Her reasons for walking out related primarily to the

portrayal of Jimmie Walker's character, J.J. Her feelings are best explained in her quote in *Ebony:* "I resent the imagery that says to black kids that you can make it by standing on the corner saying 'Dyn-O-Mite!' He's 18, and he doesn't work. He can't read or write. He doesn't think."

Jimmie Walker's rebuttal explained that the character of Fonzi on *Happy Days* and all of the students known as "sweathogs" on *Welcome Back Kotter* could not be thought of as true representations of white teenagers.

In this case, the producers took a more relaxed stance and did not have Florida killed off, as they hoped Ms. Rolle would return to the series. They first explained that she was away on her honeymoon. Later it was explained that she had been ill and moved to Arizona with Carl for her health.

In her absence, Willona Woods (Ja'net DuBois), the sexy next-door neighbor, took care of the Evans family.

Noble as it was, Walker's explanation was overruled and Esther Rolle returned to the series, partly as a result of her being unemployed for a year. "I must admit," she said, "there was a bit of practicality behind my decision to come back. Having been off regular salary for a year, my funds were getting depleted."[40] In addition to replacing the producers and having the stories center more on her, Ms. Rolle also won the authority to consult on the scipts. Furthermore, she was reassured that the J.J. character would be toned down a bit and they promised that they would attempt to make him more intelligent.

Ms. Rolle concluded by saying that she hoped that these improvements were not being made too late to save the show, but it was indeed too late.

GREEN ACRES

September 15, 1965–September 7, 1971.   CBS

Character:	Doris Ziffel
Played by:	Barbara Pepper
Date(s):	September 15, 1965–1969

Replaced by:	Doris Ziffel
Played by:	Fran Ryan
Date(s):	1969–1970

This long-running rural comedy was about a New York lawyer and his wife who bought the farm—literally. The lawyer was Oliver Wendell Douglas (Eddie Albert), who believed that farm living was the life for him. His wife Lisa (Eva Gabor), on the other hand, would rather have stayed in New York.

The rundown farm they purchased was in Hooterville, just a few miles from neighboring sitcom *Petticoat Junction*. Hooterville must have been a pretty nice place to live, because there was only one minor change in cast throughout all 170 episodes.

The character was Doris Ziffel, the wife of the farmer, Fred Ziffel, who was played throughout the series by Hank Paterson. For most of the series, Mrs. Ziffel was played by Barbara

39. Mitz, Rick. *The Great TV Sitcom Book.* Richard Marek Publishers, New York, 1980, p. 318.
40. *Ibid.,* p. 320.

Pepper. When Ms. Pepper died at the age of fifty-six on July 18, 1969, she was replaced by Fran Ryan, who had played numerous roles on television. Among her more memorable portrayals are Aggie Thompson on *The Doris Day Show* (See Entry) and Miss Hannah on *Gunsmoke* from 1974 to 1975. She was also Gertrude Gouch, the Stuart's second housekeeper on Sid and Marty Krofft's Saturday morning live-action fantasy, *Sigmund and the Sea Monsters* (See Entry).

Oh yes, there was one more character replaced—several times in fact. That character was Arnold Ziffel, the son of Fred and Doris. Actually, only *they* considered Arnold to be their son, for you see, Arnold was a pig. Lots of them, to be more exact. And not all of them males or "boar pigs," which is the proper term to use when referring to immature males.

The very first Arnold was indeed a "boar," while many of the subsequent Arnolds, Arnold doubles and Arnold stand-ins were females or "gilts." How many Arnold Ziffels were there? Without reviewing signed contracts or matching hoof prints, it is difficult to tell. One can safely assume, though, that anywhere from 12 to 24 Arnolds were used over the course of the series. These calculations are based on the fact that there were two to four different pigs used each season.

Why were so many different swine used to portray the television-watching Ziffel? The simple truth of the matter is that as pigs go, they are only "cute" for so long. "The rapid turnover in Arnolds is due to the fact that upon attaining a weight of about 200 pounds, pigs cease being 'cute.' 'Sounders,' 'suckling pigs,' 'weanling pigs,' 'shoats,' 'boar pigs,' 'gilts,' and young 'stags' and 'barrows'—all immature pigs, in fact—are cute enough for TV, but mature hogs (whether sows or boars) are not."[41]

Arnold (which ones are not clear) even managed to hog two PATSY Awards, for Best Animal Actor of the Year, a feat that WKRP newsman Les Nessman would be proud to report.

THE GROWING PAYNES

October 20, 1948–August 3, 1949.   DuMont

Character:	Mr. Payne
Played by:	John Harvey[42]
Date(s):	October 20, 1948–1949

Replaced by:	Mr. Payne
Played by:	Ed Holmes
Date(s):	1949

Character:	Mrs. Payne
Played by:	Judy Parrish
Date(s):	October 20, 1948–1949

Replaced by:	Mrs. Payne
Played by:	Elaine Stritch
Date(s):	1949

John Harvey and Judy Parrish were the stars of this very early live situation comedy about an insurance salesman and his family that aired locally in New York during 1948. While actor John Harvey was also known as John Henry, Judy Parrish, who was always known as Judy Parrish, had previously starred as Gene O'Donnell in NBC's television mystery series, *Barney Blake, Police Reporter.*

When *The Growing Paynes* moved to the DuMont network, the roles were taken over by Ed Holmes and Elaine Stritch. Among her many other roles, Ms. Stritch has the distinction of being the first Trixie Norton in *The Honeymooners* (See Entry). She was also a regular panelist on *Pantomime Quiz* from 1953 to 1955 and again in 1958. From October 5, 1960 to April 12, 1961, Ms. Stritch starred as Ruth Sherwood in the CBS situation comedy, *My Sister Eileen.*

Using the name "Eddie," Holmes became a regular on DuMont's musical variety program, *Starlit Time,* which ran from April 9 to November 26, 1950.

GUN SHY

March 15, 1983–April 19, 1983.   CBS

Character:	Clovis
Played by:	Keith Mitchell
Date(s):	March 15, 1983–April 12, 1983

Replaced by:	Clovis
Played by:	Adam Rich
Date(s):	(never aired)

In this Western comedy, based on the 1975 Walt Disney film THE APPLE DUMPLING GANG, Keith Mitchell appeared as Clovis, the role played by Brad Savage in the film.

Juvenile actor, Adam Rich, who made a name for himself at the age of eight playing Nicholas Bradford on the heartwarming dramatic comedy *Eight Is Enough,* actually played Clovis in the first two episodes filmed. He was then replaced by Jackie Coogan's grandson, Keith Mitchell, who interestingly enough had played Clovis in *Tales of the Apple Dumpling Gang,* the pilot for the series, which aired in October 1983. Young Mitchell had previously been seen during 1979 and 1980 as Jeffrey Burton on the CBS drama, *The Waltons.*

When CBS aired *Gun Shy,* they began with the four episodes featuring Mitchell. Due to poor ratings, the series was canceled before the episodes starring Adam Rich ever aired.

---

41. Hobson, Dick. "A Pig for All Seasons." *TV Guide,* Vol. 18, No. 14, Issue #888, April 42, 1970, p. 26.
42. Some sources list John Harvey as John Henry.

GUNSMOKE

September 10, 1955–September 1, 1975.   CBS

Character:	Chester Goode
Played by:	Dennis Weaver
Date(s):	September 10, 1955–April 11, 1964
Replaced by:	Festis Haggen
Played by:	Ken Curtis
Date(s):	January 18, 1964–September 1, 1975
Character:	Sam
Played by:	Glen Strange
Date(s):	September 13, 1971–1974
Replaced by:	Sam
Played by:	Robert Brubaker
Date(s):	February 11, 1974–September 1, 1975

In much the same way that radio's Lone Ranger (See Entry) Brace Beemer, lost the television role to Clayton Moore because of his stocky build, William Conrad, radio's Marshal Matt Dillon, lost out to James Arness. But unlike Clayton Moore, who was replaced for a short time by another actor, James Arness was always Marshal Dillon on television, although the producers' first choice was John Wayne. Wayne was the one who recommended Arness for the part.

When it came to sidekicks, however, the Lone Ranger only had one—Tonto, and he was always played by Jay Silverheels. Marshal Dillon had two. Then again, *The Lone Ranger* only aired for eight years, while *Gunsmoke* ran for twenty! And it is that longevity which was the main reason why Marshal Matt Dillon's trusted deputy, Chester Goode, rode out of Dodge City.

For nine years, Dennis Weaver limped alongside the six-foot, seven-inch lead before he decided, with the encouragement of his wife, Geraldine Stowell, that it was time to stand firmly on both of his good legs. "I wanted to grow as an actor, to create, to expand," he says, "and quitting *Gunsmoke* was the biggest decision I had to make in my life. In addition, I just couldn't see fit to make only one solitary character my entire life's work as an actor. Oh, from the standpoint of money, it couldn't be beat. Chester's remuneration grew beyond my expectations, in fact is still coming in every month from residuals. But money is a drag if you allow it to become an end instead of a means. So I discussed how I felt with Gerry [Stowell], and we decided I'd have to make a clean break with Chester and *Gunsmoke* if I was ever going to fully accomplish what I wanted as an actor."[43]

Dennis Weaver began by starring in his own series, *Kentucky Jones,* which aired on NBC from September 19, 1964 to September 11, 1965. Weaver played Kenneth "Kentucky" Yarborough Jones in the uneven dramatic comedy that combined a little of the West, a little comedy, a little drama and a little Chinese orphan. It also had little ratings and was canceled after twenty-six episodes.

Undaunted, Dennis Weaver reappeared two years later as an Everglades wildlife officer, Tom Wedloe, in what turned out to be his second hit series, *Gentle Ben.* This CBS weekly adventure series aired from September 10, 1967 to August 31, 1969. His third and biggest success came riding into New York City as Sam McCloud, the deputy marshal from Taos, New Mexico. *McCloud* aired as a regular feature of NBC's *Four-in-One* and, later, *The NBC Mystery Movie* which aired from September 16, 1970 to August 28, 1977.

Just as Chester Goode limped out of *Gunsmoke,* Festis Haggen strolled in. Festis was played by Ken Curtis, who had a few years earlier starred as one Jim Buckley on *Ripcord* (See Entry).

Anyone living in Dodge City, Kansas was sure to hanker for a drink every so often. That's when they'd stop by the Long Branch Saloon and ask the bartender, Sam, to pour them a drink. If he poured you enough drinks you might have been too stiff to notice that in 1974 Sam changed from Glen Strange to Robert Brubaker.

Strange had been around Hollywood for years and often played heavies such as the Frankenstein monster in the 1948 Abbott and Costello horror classic, *ABBOTT AND COSTELLO MEET FRANKENSTEIN.* He later terrorized the Lone Ranger as outlaw Butch Cavendish in the first three introductory episodes of *The Lone Ranger* (See Entry). The other Sam was played by Robert Brubaker, who played Deputy Blake, the second of three deputies in *U.S. Marshal,* the spinoff series of *The Sheriff of Cochise* (See Entry).

---

43. Miller, Leo O. *The Great Cowboy Stars of Movies and Television.* Arlington House Publishers, New York, 1979, p. 160.

H

THE HALLS OF IVY

October 19, 1954–September 29, 1955.   CBS

Character:	Dr. Merriweather
Played by:	Ray Collins
Date(s):	October 19, 1954–unknown

Replaced by:	Dr. Merriweather
Played by:	James Todd
Date(s):	Unknown–September 29, 1955

British motion picture star Ronald Colman and his wife, Benita Hume, starred in this early television adaptation of their radio series by the same name. Colman played Dr. William Todhunter Hall, the president of Ivy College, and Ms. Hume played his wife, Vicky.

One of Dr. Hall's associates was Dr. Merriweather, who was also referred to as Professor Merriweather. When this radio series made the move to the new medium, Merriweather was played by the radio and motion picture actor Ray Collins, who appeared in more than seventy-five motion pictures including the 1941 Orson Welles classic, CITIZEN KANE, in which he played Boss Jim Geddes. He will be best remembered, however, for his television role as Lieutenant Arthur Tragg on the original *Perry Mason* (See Entry). He was later replaced by James Todd.

HANGING IN

August 8, 1979–August 29, 1979.   CBS

Character:	Maude Findley
Played by:	Beatrice Arthur
Date(s):	unknown

Replaced by:	Louis Harper
Played by:	Bill Macy
Date(s):	August 8, 1979–August 29, 1979

This deceptively simple series could actually be described as four series in one. The first was *Hanging In*—itself a non sequitur since very few members of the cast were actually able to "hang in."

Hanging In started as a spinoff from the long popular CBS series, *Maude* (See Entry), which was losing steam after five very successful seasons. To counteract the loss in audience, major changes in cast and plot were planned. The next-door neighbors, the Harmons, and Maude's daughter, Carol, were to be written out of the series by having them move out of town. Maude's husband, Walter (Bill Macy), would retire while Maude started a new career in Washington as a congresswoman.

The exact set-up was that Maude and Walter would move to Washington, D.C. because she had accepted an appointment to complete the term of office of a congressman who had died. After completing just two episodes, Beatrice Arthur decided that she had taken her character as far as she could. "One can only live with the same character for so long, and it is time for both of us to take a rest."[1] Naturally, *Maude* folded.

The producers, still having faith in the concept, reworked the format slightly, leaving most of the original script and cast intact. In the place of Maude Findley was a retired pro football star played by John Amos. The altered series was titled, *Mr. Dooley*. Not long afterward, in a scenario reminiscent of his departure from *Maude* (See Entry), John Amos left the series among reports of "creative differences."

Exit John Amos, enter Cleavon Little as Mr. Dugan, while everything else remained the same. The new pilot was shot and previewed to a group of black politicians who felt that the series was in poor taste. Consequently the show never aired, even though on-air promos had already run on CBS and the program listing appeared in the March 11, 1979 edition of *TV Guide*: "A new Congressman (Cleavon Little) has inherited more than a Capitol Hill office from his late predecessor. . . ."

The producers went back to the drawing boards and revised the show one more time. The title was changed to *Hanging In,* the setting moved from Washington D.C. to the fictitious Braddock University, and Bill Macy, now as Louis Harper, replaced Cleavon Little.

Little had previously made a name for himself playing Bart, the black sheriff in the 1974 Mel Brooks' Western spoof, BLAZING SADDLES. The same year that *Hanging In* failed, Bill Macy succeeded as Stan Fox, the man who helped Navin Johnson (Steve Martin) market the "Opti-Grab" glasses in his motion picture, THE JERK. Twelve years later, it was creative differences with Frankie Faison that won Cleavon Little the lead in the Fox sitcom, *True Colors* (See Entry).

---

1. Mitz, Rick. *The Great TV Sitcom Book.* Richard Marek Publishers, New York, 1980, p. 311.

Hanging In finally hit the air on August 8, 1979, but was canceled four weeks later, even after all the work that had gone into saving a series that the producers had believed in so strongly.

HAPPY

June 8, 1960–September 8, 1961.   NBC

Character:	Happy Day
Played by:	David Born
Date(s):	June 8, 1960–September 8, 1961

Replaced by:	Happy Day
Played by:	Steven Born
Date(s):	June 8, 1960–September 8, 1961

No, this is not just another one of those instances where twin babies were used to allow for more time on camera, as with Joey on *All in the Family* (See Entry). This one is important to mention because Happy Day, played by the Born twins, was more than just another baby on a TV series; Happy was the star of the series. The gimmicks that made him a star were his ability to use facial expressions and a voice-over to speak his mind. Back in 1960, television audiences might have compared this to Cleo, the blabby basset hound provided by Mary Jane Croft on Jackie Cooper's situation comedy, *The People's Choice*, which aired on NBC from October 6, 1955 to September 25, 1958.

Today's audiences would undoubtedly compare this series to the 1989 comedy, LOOK WHO'S TALKING and its television spinoff, *Baby Talk* (See Entry), that featured the Bruce Willis-like voice of Tony Danza as the baby Mickey Campbell (Ryan and Paul Jessup).

HAPPY DAYS

January 15, 1974–July 12, 1984.   ABC

Character:	Chuck Cunningham
Played by:	Gavan O'Herlihy
Date(s):	January 15, 1974–1974

Replaced by:	Chuck Cunningham
Played by:	Randolph Roberts
Date(s):	September 10, 1974–December 1974

Character:	Arnold (Matsuo Takahashi)
Played by:	Pat Morita
Date(s):	1974–1976
	1982–1983

Replaced by:	Alfred Delvecchio
Played by:	Al Molinaro
Date(s):	1976–1982

Character:	Harry Malph
Played by:	Mike Monahan
Date(s):	April 2, 1974

Replaced by:	Mickey Malph
Played by:	Alan Oppenheimer
Date(s):	unknown

Replaced by:	Mickey Malph
Played by:	Jack Dodson
Date(s):	unknown

Character:	Eugene Belvin
Played by:	Dennis Mandel
Date(s):	October 1980–September 1982

Replaced by:	Melvin Belvin
Played by:	Scott Bernstein
Date(s):	September 1982–September 1983

Character:	Raymond ("Spike")
Played by:	Danny Butch
Date(s):	1974–1977

Replaced by:	Charles "Chachi" Arcola
Played by:	Scott Baio
Date(s):	September 12, 1978–March 16, 1983
	October 12, 1982
	November 16, 1982
	November 23, 1982
	January 25, 1983
	March 1, 1983
	September 27, 1983–July 19, 1984

Character:	Bag Zombroski
Played by:	Neil J. Schwartz
Date(s):	1974–1975

Replaced by:	Bill "Sticks" Downey, Jr.
Played by:	John Anthony Bailey
Date(s):	1975–1977

Replaced by:	Daphnie
Played by:	Hillary Horan
Date(s):	1976–1977

Replaced by:	Charles "Chachi" Arcola
Played by:	Scott Baio
Date(s):	September 12, 1978–July 19, 1984
	(see above)

Somehow, when the 1970s arrived, nostalgia for the 1950s came in with them. On Broadway, the musical *Grease* was a hit, as was the 1973 motion picture, AMERICAN GRAFFITI. Television's contribution to this seemingly simpler time in our history was *Happy Days,* which, originally titled *New Family in Town,* was a show about young people in the 1970s that avoided the issues of alcohol, drugs and sex; this is what the network wanted, but the show was a little tame and the idea was shelved.

Producer Garry Marshall got a second chance after George Lucas' 1950s nostalgic comedy, AMERICAN GRAFFITI, became a box-office hit in 1973. Marshall not only set his show in the 1950s, but hired AMERICAN GRAFFITI's clean-cut star, Ron Howard, to star in his series as Richard "Richie" Cunningham.

Like *The Honeymooners, Happy Days* began as a skit on another program. Specifically, it was a segment on the popular anthology series, *Love, American Style,* which aired on February 25, 1972. In that pilot, "Love and the Happy Days,"[2] all the elements and most of the regulars of what would become a popular television series, were present. Those not present were Tom Bosley, Erin Moran and Gavan O'Herlihy.

Tom Bosley's role as Howard, the head of the Cunningham household, was played by Harold Gould, who is remembered as Rhoda Morgenstern's father, Martin, on Valerie Harper's sitcom, *Rhoda. The Mary Tyler Moore Show* spinoff aired on CBS from September 9, 1974 to December 9, 1978. Howard's wife, Marion, was played by Marion Ross, who later starred as Sophie Berger in the CBS dramatic comedy, *Brooklyn Bridge,* which premiered on September 20, 1991. Richie Cunningham's sister Joanie was played by Susan Neher, and their brother, Chuck, by Ric Carrott.

The pilot was produced by Garry Marshall, but didn't sell as a series right away. By the time ABC asked Marshall to go ahead with his project, Harold Gould was no longer available, so Tom Bosley was cast—which is why David Doyle and not Tom Bosley became John Bosley on *Charlie's Angels* (See Entry).

It is not really clear why Chuck's character was recast, but then nothing about Chuck was very clear. The second actor to play the big brother—the first on the series—, was Gavan O'Herlihy, the son of veteran television actor Dan O'Herlihy. Gavan later appeared as Airk Thaughbaer in WILLOW, the 1988 fantasy directed by Ron Howard. O'Herlihy appeared as Chuck Cunningham in about half a dozen episodes; his replacement, Randolph Roberts, appeared in only two.

Very little character development was given to Chuck. All we know is that he played basketball and went away to college. Perhaps he went with Mike Douglas on *My Three Sons* (See Entry).

Randolph Roberts returned to make one final appearance as Chuck in the classic Christmas episode. The miracle of this 34th episode of the series is that it's the first time the audience gets to see Fonzie's (Henry Winkler) apartment, a depressingly small and cluttered room with his motorcycle parked in the middle. When the Cunninghams find that Fonzie has no place to spend Christmas, he is invited to share the holiday with them.

The next episode, "The Cunningham Caper," finds Richie at home, sick in bed. He hears noises downstairs, which he figures are being made by his friends Potsie (Anson Williams) and Ralph (Donny Most). It turns out to be a burglar (Herb Edelman), and Richie tells him that he, Joanie and Chuck bought the present the burglar is taking for their parents. It was the last time that Chuck was even mentioned. In fact, the final episode of the series, when Howard toasts the marriage of Joanie and Chachi, he excludes Chuck completely.

HOWARD: What can I say? *Both* of my children are married now and they're starting out to build lives on their own. . . .

This obvious and probably intentional omission was addressed nearly fourteen years later during the closing sequence of *The Happy Days Reunion Special,* which aired on ABC on Tuesday, March 3, 1992.

The entire cast is assembled, family portrait style, for one grand farewell, which took a number of takes to get right. Five bloopers are shown, one of which included some playful banter among Henry Winkler, Ron Howard, Tom Bosley and the rest of the cast.

HENRY: Good night, everybody, and thank you for being a part of our family.

RON: Here's to *Happy Days.*

TOM: Chuck? Is that you Chuck? Marion . . . which Chuck?

CAST: (Jokingly turning to each other and repeating Tom Bosley's question) Which Chuck?

In a fitting bit of Hollywood justice, Randolph Roberts appeared as Ron in "The Battle of Bel Air," the January 10, 1984 episode of *The A-Team,* the series that is credited with pulling the plug of the *Happy Days* jukebox.

Images like the jukebox were almost as important to the series as the actors. The largest of these images was the place where the jukebox was kept, "Arnold's Drive-In," the familiar 1950s burger and malt shop with the bright red neon sign that was often the central location for the series action. This haven, located somewhere between home and school, or school and home, depending on which way you were traveling, was run by a very likable Japanese American who was more American than Japanese.

Everyone on *Happy Days* seemed to like Arnold, who was portrayed by comedian and actor Pat Morita. But producer James Komack, who had produced the successful Gabe Kaplan sitcom, *Welcome Back Kotter,* liked him even more. Naturally, Morita left the supporting role in *Happy Days* to star in his own situation comedy, *Mr. T and Tina.* Morita played the Japanese inventor Taro Takahashi (Mr. T for short) opposite Susan Blanchard as his children's governess, Tina Kelly. Sometimes, however, a starring role isn't all it is cracked up to be and the ABC situation comedy ran for only five episodes between

---

2. Before airing as a segment of *Love American Style,* the *Happy Days* pilot was titled *New Family in Town.*

September 25 and October 30, 1976. In retrospect, perhaps Arnold shouldn't have sold the restaurant.

From the standpoint of the series, continuity never presented a problem as Arnold's was sold to Al Delvecchio, who didn't even change the name of the place. Al was big, had a huge nose and was Italian—nothing at all like Arnold, except that not only was he as likable, he was quite lovable.

The actor who played Al was already a familiar nose—er face—on the small screen, having played officer Murray Greshner from 1970 to 1975 on *The Odd Couple* (See Entry), the role created by Herb Edelman in the 1968 motion picture. Al Molinaro also got a chance at a starring role in a series. In his case it was a *Happy Days* spinoff, *Joanie Loves Chachi.* This made the transition a little easier for Molinaro than for Morita, because he was simply continuing the character he had already developed. The tie-ins, however, were not enough to keep the series afloat and in a short time the series was canceled. Fortunately for the cast, most of them had a series to go home to: they returned to the security of *Happy Days,* where Pat Morita was already making occasional guest appearances as Arnold.

Richie's two best friends were Warren "Potsie" Webber (Anson Williams) and Ralph Malph (Donny Most). Harry Malph, Ralph's sometimes seen father, was played by three actors during the eleven-year run of the series. The first was Mike Monahan, who appeared as Harry Malph in the tenth episode of the series, "Because She's There."

The next time Mr. Malph appeared on *Happy Days* he was not only played by a different actor (Alan Oppenheimer), but his name had been changed to Mickey. Fans of the ABC science fiction adventure series, *The Six Million Dollar Man* (See Entry), will remember Alan Oppenheimer as the first actor to play scientist Dr. Rudy Wells. The second Mickey Malph and third actor to be featured as Ralph's father was Jack Dodson, who for five years played Mayberry's most eligible bachelor, Howard Sprague, on both *The Andy Griffith Show* and its spinoff series, *Mayberry R.F.D.*

Without a doubt, the most colorful and the most popular character was Milwaukee's most likable hood, the Fonz, or Fonzie as his friends called him (short for Arthur Fonzarelli). Henry Winkler, the Yale Drama school graduate, who accepted the part of Fonzie, written originally as a small role for a recurring regular, eventually became the star of the show.

In a logical piece of character development, Fonzie, a high school dropout, later went back to school to earn his degree and then became Jefferson High's auto shop instructor. One of his students was a nerd named Eugene Belvin (Dennis Mandel), who was ga-ga over Joanie's friend, Jenny Piccalo. Jenny was played by Cathy Silvers, the daughter of comedian and actor Phil Silvers.

At the end of the 1981/1982 season, Eugene decided to go to college and left the show. Perhaps he enrolled in the same college that kept Chuck away from home. The following season, Eugene was replaced by his brother Melvin (Scott Bernstein), who was more interested in Howard Cunningham's niece, K.C. (Crystal Bernard), than in Jenny.

Fonzie also had a couple of cousins added to the cast of the show. The first was a tough adolescent, played by Danny Butch to be a younger version of Fonzie. His name was Raymond, but he preferred to be called "Spike." He wore sunglasses and a leather jacket that was identical to his cousin Fonzie's and did everything his cousin did, or at least tried to. The character lasted three years before being replaced by an older cousin, Charles Arcola (Scott Baio), "Chachi" to everyone.

Baio was handsome and had enough charisma to become the heartthrob of every teenage girl in America, including Joanie Cunningham, who ran away with him in 1982 to co-star in their own series, *Joanie Loves Chachi.* But if Joanie loved him, the public didn't love the show, so both characters returned to the security of the *Happy Days* series and were married in the show's final episode, as previously mentioned.

Nearly everyone was invited to the wedding, with the exception of Richie's band, which was formed in the eleventh episode of the 1974 season in an episode titled "Give the Band a Hand." The four-piece combo had Richie on the keyboard, Ralph on the sax, Bag (Neil J. Schwartz) on the drums, and Potsie providing the vocals on the only song they knew, Elvis Presley's *All Shook Up.* Richie kept insisting that they come up with a name for the group, and through the years they had several. Originally, their combo was referred to as "The Happy Days Band."

Over the course of *Happy Days*' eleven-season run, the band featured three other drummers, Bill "Sticks" Downey, Jr. (John Anthony Bailey), Daphnie (Hillary Horan), and finally Charles "Chachi" Arcola, himself. It was at this point that the band's name was changed to the Velvet Clouds. And even though he wasn't responsible for the music at the wedding, Charles was later put in charge of his own hit series, *Charles in Charge* (See Entry).

After putting down his drumsticks, Neil J. Schwartz reprised his role as one of the song-and-dance men in limbo, for the Showtime cable network's series, *Steambath,* which aired on August 16, 1984. The cable series was based on the PBS *Hollywood Television Theater* production of the off-Broadway play, which aired on April 30, 1973 and starred Jose Perez, Bill Bixby, Herb Edelman and Valerie Perrine.

The Band's second drummer, John Anthony Bailey, later appeared as C.C. in the "Wonderbug" segment of *The Krofft Supershow,* which aired on Saturday mornings from September 11, 1976 to September 2, 1978.

And if you're a Hillary "Hildy" Horan fan, you can catch a glimpse of her as the "Girl in Car" in *The Munsters* (See Entry) reunion movie, *The Munsters Revenge.*

HARDCASTLE & MCCORMICK

September 18, 1983–July 23, 1986.   ABC

Character:	Lieutenant Michael Delaney
Played by:	John Hancock
Date(s):	1984–1985

Replaced by:	Lieutenant Frank Harper
Played by:	Joe Santos
Date(s):	1985–July 23, 1986

Buffy and Jody's reserved and even-tempered Uncle Bill (Brian Keith), from CBS's *Family Affair,* starred as Milton C. Hardcastle, a tough, no-bull, retired judge who was fed up with criminals who managed to slip through the court system and get off scot-free because of a legal loophole, lack of evidence, or technicalities.

To even up the score and set the record straight, the athletic sixty-five-year-old Hardcastle, who had recently stepped down from the bench, sets out to bring these slippery characters to justice, a premise later adapted by CBS's *Dark Justice* (See Entry). But it is too big a job to go it alone, so he teams up with Mark ''Skid'' McCormick (Daniel Hugh-Kelly). McCormick is a twice-convicted felon and almost legendary racing car driver, who faces a stiff prison sentence for auto theft.

Rather than convict and sentence him, Judge Hardcastle, who presides over this final case of his judicial career, opts to have Mark released in his custody. Running down criminals isn't exactly community service, but it sure beats the alternative.

Judge Hardcastle called in markers from both sides of the track and John Hancock appeared during the series' 1984/1985 season as his police contact, Lieutenant Michael Delaney. The following season, Joe Santos took over the beat as Lieutenant Frank Harper.

The versatile Hancock appeared as Wilcox in the March 24, 1978 ABC musical special, *Cindy,* which Donald Bogle, author of *Blacks in American Films and Television,* called ''The Cinderella tale done in sepiatone.'' He later had a recurring role as Judge Richard Armand on NBC's law drama, *L.A. Law.* His motion picture credits include the roles of Sergeant Washington in the 1984 drama, A SOLDIER'S STORY, and Reverend Bacon in the 1990 Tom Hanks/Bruce Willis comedy, BONFIRE OF THE VANITIES. But the television role of *Love & War*'s (See Entry) irascible Ike Johnson, which might have made John Hancock a household name, was cut short when the actor died of a sudden heart attack on October 12, 1992.

Joe Santos, who played *Hardcastle & McCormick*'s second police contact, came to the series after having played Detective Dennis Becker on *The Rockford Files.* He later appeared in two very short-lived situation comedies. From March 22 to September 12, 1980, Santos starred as Norman Davis on NBC's *Me and Maxx,* and from March 6 to April 7, 1984 he was Domingo Rivera on ABC's *a.k.a. Pablo.*

THE HARDY BOYS MYSTERIES

January 30, 1977–August 26, 1979.   ABC

Character:	Nancy Drew
Played by:	Pamela Sue Martin
Date(s):	January 30, 1977–January 29, 1978

Replaced by:	Nancy Drew
Played by:	Janet Louise Johnson
Date(s):	February 12, 1978–April 22, 1978

Character:	George Fayne
Played by:	Jean Rasey
Date(s):	1977

Replaced by:	George Fayne
Played by:	Susan Buckner
Date(s):	1977–1978

The Hardy Boys Mysteries and *The Nancy Drew Mysteries* are based on the characters that appeared in the children's novel series created by Edward Stratemeyer and his daughter Harriet Adams during the early 1900s. Originally, Pamela Sue Martin played Nancy Drew in her own series, *The Nancy Drew Mysteries* (See Entry), which alternated on Sunday nights with *The Hardy Boys Mysteries.*

Then, much to her displeasure, she appeared during the fall of 1977 as Nancy Drew, with the Hardy Boys, Joe (Shaun Cassidy) and Frank (Parker Stevenson). It was obvious that the producers had more in mind than just crossover episodes. ''Martin had balked at the idea of merging the two shows and was replaced when the decision to merge was final.''[3] Ms. Martin later starred as the first Fallon Carrington Colby on the ABC evening soap opera, *Dynasty,* a role which lasted from January 12, 1981 to May 9, 1984. She was replaced on November 20, 1985 by Emma Samms.

The second Nancy Drew was played by eighteen-year-old actress Janet Louise Johnson, who was introduced as the new Nancy Drew in the two-part episode, ''Voodoo Doll,'' which aired on February 12 and 19, 1978. The following week, February 26, 1978, Ms. Johnson appeared in ''Mystery on the Avalanche Express.'' The next week's episode was a *Hardy Boys* mystery only.

The last episode in which Nancy Drew appeared was the next to the last episode of the season. ''Arson and Old Lace'' aired on April 1, 1978 and marked the end, on television, of the character created by Carolyn Keene. Carolyn Keene was actually the pseudonym used by Harriet Adams for the *Nancy Drew* series.

Always at her best friend's side was George Fayne, who was first played by Jean Rasey. She was replaced by Susan Buckner, a former Miss Washington and Miss America finalist who went on to play construction worker Lucy Davis on the situation comedy, *When the Whistle Blows,* which aired on ABC from March 14 to July 27, 1980.

HARRY AND THE HENDERSONS

January 12, 1991–September 3, 1993.   Syndicated

Character:	Harry
Played by:	Kevin Peter Hall
Date(s):	January 12, 1991–June 1991

3. McNeil, Alex. *Total Television.* Penguin Books, New York, 1984, p. 279.

The mystery girl in the center is Janet Louise Johnson, who took over the role of Nancy Drew from Pamela Sue Martin. She is flanked on the left by Shaun Cassidy as Joe Hardy and on the right by Parker Stevenson as Frank Hardy.

Replaced by: Harry
Played by: Dawan Scott
Date(s):   June 1991–November 13, 1992

Replaced by: Harry
Played by: Brian Steele
Date(s):   November 20, 1992–September 3, 1993

Character: Samantha Glick
Played by: Gigi Rice
Date(s):   January 12, 1991–September 1991

Character: Tiffany ''Tiffy'' Glick
Played by: Cassie Cole
Date(s):   January 12, 1991–September 1991

Replaced by: Brett Douglas
Played by: Noah Blake
Date(s):   September 1991–September 3, 1993

Replaced by: Darcy Farg
Played by: Courtney Peldon
Date(s):   January 10, 1992–November 13, 1992

Replaced by: Hilton Woods, Jr.
Played by: Marc Dakota Robinson
Date(s):   November 20, 1992–September 3, 1993

Character: Uma Farg
Played by: Julie McCullough
Date(s):   January 10, 1992
                April 10, 1992

Replaced by:	Ema Farg
Played by:	Angela Vesser
Date(s):	January 17, 1992–April 4, 1992

Character:	Walter Potter
Played by:	David Coburn
Date(s):	January 12, 1991–June 1991

Replaced by:	Dr. Arenson
Played by:	Nan Martin
Date(s):	1992

What was to have been a thirty-minute TV comedy wended its way through the jungle of Hollywood production offices until it landed squarely on Steven Spielberg's desk, and his Amblin Entertainment studio produced HARRY AND THE HENDERSONS for theatrical release in 1987. Four years later, it made its way back through the quagmire to find a new home in the syndicated television market.

The story, about your typical American family, the Hendersons, who run into a Bigfoot—literally—and make him part of their family was the idea of six-foot-nine-inch comedian Brad Garrett, who wanted to play the missing link in his script. But when Spielberg took on the project, the loveable Sasquatch, named Harry, wound up being played by the even taller Kevin Peter Hall, a Washington University basketball star. White bread husband and wife George and Nancy Henderson were played by John Lithgow and Melinda Dillon. The adorable Henderson kids, Sarah and Ernie, were played by Margaret Langrick and Joshua Rudoy.

As the scene fades at the end of the 110–minute film, Harry is seen walking back into the forest where he is joined by his fellow creatures. Four years after walking out of theaters, the seven-foot-two-inch Kevin Peter Hall, as the eight-foot Sasquatch, was squeezed into the small screen in a syndicated series based on the motion picture.

In the opener, the Hendersons are returning from their vacation in the Pacific Northwest and traveling on Interstate 5 in Seattle. Suddenly, and without warning, a huge hairy creature (presumably the legendary Bigfoot) steps onto the road and is struck by the Henderson's 4x4 van. Believing that they have killed the creature, they decide to tie it to the roof of their van and bring it home.

The creature, however, is not dead—only stunned. Upon awakening, he ingratiates himself with the Hendersons and they allow him to become part of their family. And like ALF, who at first lived in a laundry basket next to the washing machine and later moved to the Tanner's attic, so he wouldn't be discovered by the authorities, the Sasquatch was allowed to live in the Henderson's loft.

The only member of the film's cast who made the transition to television was Kevin Peter Hall as Harry. George was played by Bruce Davison and his wife, Nancy, by Molly Cheek. Their kids, Sarah and Ernie, were played by Carol-Ann Plante and Zachary Bostrom.

The supporting cast originally consisted of a young biologist, Walter Potter (David Coburn), who was concerned for Harry's well-being and whom George would call if Harry were ill or acting strangely. Dr. Arenson (Nan Martin) later took over these veterinary responsibilites on a semi-regular basis, with no explanation given as to what happened to Walter.

The Henderson's next-door neighbor was Samantha Glick (Gigi Rice), a TV reporter for *The News at 5* on Channel 10. Her daughter, Tiffany (Cassie Cole), was the first outsider to see the missing link and called him "Hairy Guy," which the Hendersons changed to Harry. Both of these characters later learned of the secret, which they took with them to television limbo when they were written out in the fall of 1991.

They were replaced by Nancy's brother, Brett Douglas, who moved in with his sister and brother-in-law to help out with George's new magazine, *A Better Life*. He was also meant to be a pal to young Ernie (Tiffy was too young—about five or six). When this formula didn't work, Courtney Peldon was brought on as the new neighbor, Darcy Farg.

Now Darcy, who comes from rich but never-seen parents, is looked after by her cousin Uma Farg, who was played by Julie McCullough in only two episodes. The first was "The Love Mask," which aired on January 10, 1992. The second was "Sarah's First Job," which aired on April 10, 1992. In between, Angela Vesser played her cousin/nanny Ema Farg.

Darcy was fine when she first moved in—although Ernie didn't really like her. She was an "icky girl," and he had no interest in girls, icky or otherwise, even though they were on the same Pee Wee softball team. It looked as if the writers wanted to keep Ernie a kid and Darcy was just too rich, feminine and spoiled to be a tomboy, so they replaced her with a new guy neighbor for Ernie—Hilton Woods, Jr., the son of the town's chief of police.

HARRY-O

September 12, 1974–August 12, 1976.   ABC

Character:	Detective Lieutenant Manuel "Manny" Quinlan
Played by:	Henry Darrow
Date(s):	September 12, 1974–December 26, 1974 February 27, 1975

Replaced by:	Lieutenant K.C. Trench
Played by:	Anthony Zerbe
Date(s):	March 13, 1975–April 29, 1976

Nearly all of the critics seem to agree that Harry Orwell was perhaps the best television adaptation of the Philip Marlowe-type character. The original concept called for a television adaptation of the popular DIRTY HARRY films of the 1970s, which starred tough guy Clint Eastwood. *Harry-O*'s creator, Howard Rodman, resisted the studio's suggestion and built a series with plenty of action but without "obligatory" violence and car chases.

Had things gone as originally planned by the producers at Warner Bros., *Harry-O* would have been *Nick-O* played by Telly Savalas. As it turned out, Savalas was pursuing a career in feature films in Europe and turned the role down because he was not interested in doing television at the time. He obviously had a change of heart, because in 1973 he accepted the lead in *Kojak*.

When David Janssen was cast, the character's name was changed from Nick to Harry and the series became *Harry-O*. "See? It's that simple to create a television show. Just add *Kojak* to DIRTY HARRY and you get *Harry-O*."[4]

Television's "fugitive," David Janssen took on the role in two pilots for the series. The *Harry-O* telefilm, which aired on March 11, 1973, was actually a second attempt. The first pilot, *Such Stuff as Dreams Are Made Of,* starred David Janssen but was originally written for Telly Savalas and never aired. The second pilot produced, *Smile Jenny, You're Dead,* was written specifically for David Janssen and aired on ABC on February 3, 1974. Neither of these pilots featured Harry-O's adversarial ally, Lieutenant Manny Quinlan, although the first pilot did feature Mel Stewart as Lieutenant Arvin Grainger. Stewart is best-remembered as George Jefferson's brother, Henry, on *All in the Family* (See Entry).

During the first season of the series, Harry Orwell's ex-partner and police contact was played by Henry Darrow, who some years later played Don Diego de la Vega, on the 1983 situation comedy, *Zorro and Son* (See Entry). He was also the second actor to play Zorro's father, Don Alejandro de la Vega, in the Family Channel's updated *Zorro* (See Entry). But Henry Darrow was not the first, but the second actor to play Lieutenant Quinlan. The first actor quit. Harvey Frand, the executive in charge of production was on location with the *Harry-O* crew the first day of shooting.

" 'The day we started the actor playing Harry's police contact quit.' Frand thought it best to mention no names. 'He was an actor who was unhappy,' he related. 'There was some friction between him and the producer. He was later replaced by Henry Darrow (as Lieutenant Manuel Quinlan).' "[5]

"I didn't read for the part of Manny Quinlan," said Darrow, "they cast me in it. I had just lost out to Earl Holliman for the part of Lieutenant Crowley on *Police Woman,* so I felt pretty down about that, and then very shortly thereafter I was told by my agent that I was playing this character on *Harry-O*. I had been given six scripts and the character was called Milt Bosworth. That's when I learned that Clu Gulager had been signed for the role of Lieutenant Bosworth. But he turned it down. He didn't want to go down to San Diego and live there for those five or six months. He didn't want to do it and it was just one of those many things that happen in this business. Initially, I didn't want to do *Zorro* (See Entry) and Efrem Zimbalist, Jr. did it. Clu didn't want to do *Harry-O* and *bam,* I walked right into it. They changed the character's name to Manny Quinlan and I just packed up and went down to San Diego and that was it."[6]

After the twelfth episode of the series was completed Henry Darrow was written out. "I didn't decide to leave. They moved the location of the show from San Diego to Malibu and didn't take me with them. I think the only thing that was really upsetting was that David [Janssen], the crew and other people knew that I was not coming to Malibu with the company. I could tell that something was wrong, but I didn't know what it was.

"David had finished shooting in the morning and I had another scene after lunch. After I finished the scene David said, 'I'd like to talk to you,' and then he told me. He said, 'Hank, we're moving the show up to Malibu and I'm going alone.' I asked him what happened and he said, 'It had nothing to do with you. I fought for you but they said, "It's either you, alone, or nothing."

"I later had a talk with Abby Greschler who was David's agent at the time and he said 'Henry, I just wanted you to know that David really wanted you to come with him, but the network said "We're just taking David." ' "

"You have to remember that there was a company of anywhere from seventy-five to one hundred people with per diems, hotel rooms and all transportation. It was an expensive show to shoot because we were in San Diego. The first thing you save immediately by bringing the show up here is rooms for seventy-five to one hundred people; then there are per diems multiplied by seventy-five to one hundred people. And all the perks. And all the drivers that are necessary to get the cast and crew back and forth from the location. There never was a studio, we always shot on location and that was one of the reasons it was such an expansive production,"[7] Darrow explained.

To explain the departure of Lieutenant Quinlan, the episode "Elegy for a Cop" was produced. In that story, while Lieutenant Quinlan is bringing his drug-addicted niece home to Los Angeles he is murdered by guest star Sal Mineo, who had played Walter Scheerer in the *Harry-O* pilot. In their book, *Crime & Detective TV,* the authors point out that this poignant episode was "one of the few times on TV that a regular character has been killed off rather than simply written out—or ignored."[8]

The listing in *TV Guide* read: "Former series regular Henry Darrow returns in the role [Manny Quinlan]."

"As it turned out, they had some extra footage, which included chase sequences: left over from the *Harry-O* pilot. And when you see the episode in which I was shot, they used all those motorcycle sequences from the old footage of David Janssen chasing Sal Mineo. I only worked one day on that episode and they saved themselves about three or four days of shooting. They also saved themselves some money and footage. That's the way things happen in marvelous Hollywood,"[9] chuckled Darrow.

Since networks feel comfortable following formulas that have worked in the past, they insisted on replacing Lieutenant

4. Meyers, Ric. *Murder On the Air, Television's Great Mystery Series.* The Mysterious Press, New York, 1989, p. 192.
5. Meyers, Ric. *Murder On the Air, Television's Great Mystery Series.* The Mysterious Press, New York, 1989, pp. 197–198.
6. From an exclusive telephone interview with Henry Darrow on January 19, 1991.
7. From an exclusive telephone interview with Henry Darrow on January 19, 1991.
8. Collins, Max Allan and Javna, John. *The Best of Crime and Detective TV.* Harmony Books, New York, 1988, p. 18.
9. From an exclusive telephone interview with Henry Darrow on January 19, 1991.

Quinlan with another police contact, which went against Rodman's instincts. Like it or not, the new character who would be the thorn in Harry Orwell's side was added to the cast for the last episode of the first season, ''Street Games.'' His name was Lieutenant K.C. Trench and Anthony Zerbe was cast to play him.

The same critics who had lauded *Harry-O* during its first season felt that the second and final season did not equal the quality of the earlier episodes. In spite of the critics' disappointment, Anthony Zerbe won an Emmy in the 1975/1976 season for Outstanding Continuing Performance by a Supporting Actor in a Drama Series. Among the many series Zerbe appeared in are *Mission Impossible, Gunsmoke, Mannix, Little House: A New Beginning* and *The Man from U.N.C.L.E.: The 15 Years Later Affair.*

HAVE GUN-WILL TRAVEL

September 14, 1957–September 21, 1963.   CBS

Character:	Hey Boy
Played by:	Kam Tong
Date(s):	April 12, 1958–June 18, 1960
	November 26, 1960–September 21, 1963

Replaced by:	Hey Girl
Played by:	Lisa Lu
Date(s):	October 1, 1960–November 19, 1960

Before the electronic age when ''assignments'' could be delivered on a hidden tape recorder carrying a prerecorded message that self-destructed in five seconds, earlier ''guns for hire'' had to have their assignments delivered by hand and Paladin was the Old West's answer to the A-Team. A West Point graduate and former U.S. Army weapons officer, Paladin moved West where the posh San Francisco Hotel Carleton served as his base of operations. His business cards carried the inscription, ''Have Gun Will Travel,'' followed by ''Wire Paladin, San Francisco.''

Those wired calls for help were personally delivered by the hotel's Oriental houseboy. This hotel messenger was referred to throughout the series as Hey Boy and was always played by Kam Tong. Tong left *Have Gun-Will Travel* to co-star as Kam Chang, Frank Garlund's foster brother, in the CBS dramatic adventure, *Mr. Garlund,*[10] which aired from October 7, 1960 to January 13, 1961.

Back at the hotel, Hey Boy was replaced by Hey Girl, played by Lisa Lu, but only for one season because *The Garlund Touch* didn't seem to have the Midas touch. It was canceled after thirteen episodes and Kam Tong returned to his role on *Have Gun-Will Travel,* supplanting Ms. Lu. Lisa Lu's next regular series was *Anna and the King,* in which she played Anna Owens opposite Yul Brynner's King of Siam. This short-lived adaptation of Margaret Landon's novel and subsequent stage play ran on CBS from September 17 to December 31, 1972.

HAWAII FIVE-O

September 26, 1968–April 26, 1980.   CBS

Character:	May
Played by:	Maggie Parker
Date(s):	September 26, 1968–February 19, 1969

Replaced by:	Jenny Sherman
Played by:	Peggy Ryan
Date(s):	October 8, 1969–1976

Replaced by:	Luana
Played by:	Laura Sode
Date(s):	1978–1980

Character:	Detective Danny ''Danno'' Williams
Played by:	James MacArthur
Date(s):	September 26, 1968–April 5, 1979

Replaced by:	James ''Kimo'' Carew
Played by:	William Smith
Date(s):	October 4, 1979–April 26, 1980

Character:	Detective Kono Kalakauna
Played by:	Zulu
Date(s):	September 26, 1968–March 7, 1972

Replaced by:	Detective Ben Kokua
Played by:	Al Harrington
Date(s):	September 12, 1972–February 26, 1974

After James MacArthur left *Hawaii Five-O,* Steve McGarrett (Jack Lord) could no longer shout ''Book 'em Danno,'' demonstrating again that old adage that nothing lasts forever, even on televsion.

In a *TV Guide* interview MacArthur said, ''After eleven years I decided it was enough. I wanted to do other things. I didn't quit for any one thing in particular. I haven't spoken to Jack [Lord]. I was out of the country and I told my agent to call the producers with my decision. I didn't think it was necessary to tell Jack. I suppose it will be hard to imagine *Hawaii Five-O* without Danny . . . but that's the way it goes.''[11]

The new character was ''Kimo'' Carew, played by stuntman William Smith, who was quite different from the actor he was hired to replace. MacArthur had a rounder, more boyish face; Smith's face was hard and worn and his physical build was much bigger than McArthur's.

His first major television role was gunfighter Joe Riley on the

---

10. This series was originally titled *The Garlund Touch;* it was changed on November 11, 1960.
11. *TV Guide, n.d.*

NBC Western, *Laredo,* which aired from September 16, 1965 to September 1, 1967. Smith once said that he had won that role, not because of his acting ability, but more than likely because he was able to ride tall in the saddle and squint real well. Movie buffs may recognize William Smith as the vampire in the 1973[12] horror film, GRAVE OF THE VAMPIRE.

But James MacArthur was not the first person replaced on this, television's longest continually running police/detective show.

Gilbert Kauhi used Zulu as his professional name, and was a popular character actor, disc jockey and stand-up comedian in Hawaii who had minor roles in the 1959 motion picture, GIDGET and the 1966 historical drama, HAWAII.

It is true that Zulu had become dissatisfied with his role because he felt his abilities were not being fully utilized, but this is not why he left *Hawaii Five-O.* It has been suggested that Zulu was fired over an incident in which Jack Lord forbade him to accept an honorary membership in the United States Coast Guard, an honor which Lord reportedly felt should have been reserved for himself. The change in cast had little affect on the series, which revolved around the Steve McGarrett character.

The other minor character that was replaced was McGarrett's secretary. The second actress to assume the role was Peggy Ryan, who as a teenager danced with Donald O'Connor. In 1943 she played Jan Warren in TOP MAN. The following year she played Patsy Monahan in THE MERRY MONAHANS.

The pilot film for *Hawaii Five-0* aired on September 20, 1968, and had a few different faces. McGarrett's assistant, Danny Williams, was played by Tim O'Kelly, but it was felt that he was a little too hard-looking, so he was replaced by James MacArthur. Yet when MacArthur left the series, he was replaced by an actor who was perhaps more similar to O'Kelly than to himself. The original Governor of Hawaii was played by veteran actor Lew Ayres who had played in the 1930 ALL QUIET ON THE WESTERN FRONT and had starred as Dr. James Kildare in nine films beginning with the 1938 medical drama, YOUNG DR. KILDARE. This film series later inspired the successful *Dr. Kildare* television version starring Richard Chamberlain. When the series was sold, Ayres did not wish to move to Hawaii and was replaced by Richard Denning. He had starred in the title role of the *Michael Shayne* detective series.

HAWAIIAN EYE

October 7, 1959–September 10, 1963.   ABC

Character:	Chryseis "Cricket" Blake
Played by:	Connie Stevens
Date(s):	October 7, 1959–January 1, 1963
	February 26, 1963–September 10, 1963
Replaced by:	Sunny Day
Played by:	Tina Cole
Date(s):	January 8, 1963–March 5, 1963

It must always be kept in mind that the "business" in "show business" is at least as important as the "show," if not more so. And *Hawaiian Eye* was created by Warner Bros. to satisfy advertisers' cravings for another program along the lines of *77 Sunset Strip.* In fact, except for its locale, it is more of a carbon copy of *77 Sunset Strip* than one might imagine. First, both shows had three male leads. Second, there was also an Hawaiian Suzanne, an Hawaiian Kookie, an Hawaiian Roscoe (Kim), and an Hawaiian Lieutenant (Quon).

When *The Roaring 20's* came around, you had a combination of elements from both of these shows, with Dorothy Provine becoming the Connie Stevens of the 1920s. *Bourbon Street Beat* has the two male leads, the female secretary (like Suzanne) and the junior detective (like Kookie or Roscoe). It seems that all Warner Bros. did to create a new series was change the locale and maybe the time period.

As it was originally conceived by Executive Producer William T. Orr, *Hawaiian Eye* was going to be *The Islander* and was to be set in the Caribbean. When the decision was made to move the locale to Hawaii, the working title was *Diamond Head.* Shortly before production began, the series became *Hawaiian Eye.*

The macho male leads of this detective series were Robert Conrad as Tom Lopaka and Anthony Eisley as Tracy Steele. At the start of the third season, Grant Williams, who had made several guest appearances during the second season, joined the cast as Greg MacKenzie, which brought the total number of private dicks to three—until Anthony Eisley left the cast at the end of the season. Shortly thereafter, Troy Donahue, who had starred as Sandy Winfield, II on *Surfside Six* (See Entry), joined the cast of *Hawaiian Eye* as Phil Barton, the director of special events at the Hawaiian Village Hotel.

In his book *Murder on the Air,* author Ric Meyers said that the actors, Connie Stevens in particular, were severely overworked, which resulted in her physical collapse in 1962.

At the beginning of 1963, Connie Stevens was suspended by the studio. Her last appearance on *Hawaiian Eye* was in the episode broadcast January 1, 1963, "Go Steady with Danger." The producers replaced her with Tina Cole, whom they knew as a singer from the *King Cousins.* The old King's Cole became Sunny Day, the new employee of Hawaiian Village Hotel.

She was introduced in the "Kupikio Kid" episode, which aired on January 8, 1963. In that episode Tom Lopaka and Phil Barton must suppress their interest in Sunny Day in order to rescue a kidnapped college student, Peter Kirk (Evan McCord).

Seven episodes later, in "Two Million Too Much," Connie Stevens returned to *Hawaiian Eye.* She and Tina Cole appeared together in the "Blow Low, Blow Blue" episode which aired on March 5, 1963.

In 1967 Tina Cole became Mrs. Robbie Douglas on *My Three Sons,* while Connie Stevens became the second Thalia Menninger in *Bring Me the Head of Dobie Gillis,* the 1988 reunion movie based on *The Many Loves of Dobie Gillis* (See Entry)

---

12. Some sources give 1972 as the release date of GRAVE OF THE VAMPIRE.

HAZEL

September 28, 1961–September 5, 1966.   NBC-CBS

Character:	George Baxter	
Played by:	Don DeFore	
Date(s):	September 28, 1961–September 6, 1965	
Replaced by:	Steve Baxter	
Played by:	Ray Fulmer	
Date(s):	September 10, 1965–September 5, 1966	
Character:	Dorothy Baxter	
Played by:	Whitney Blake	
Date(s):	September 28, 1961–September 6, 1965	
Replaced by:	Barbara Baxter	
Played by:	Lynn Borden	
Date(s):	September 10, 1965–September 5, 1966	

Iron-willed maid Hazel (Shirley Booth) shows her hungry boss, "Mr. B." (Don DeFore), just how small a piece of cake he's allowed to eat.

Of all the live action series based on comic strip characters, *Hazel* was one of the most successful. It was based on the characters cartoonist Ted Key created for the *Saturday Evening Post* in 1943.

Hazel, the housekeeper for the Baxter family, was brought to life by Shirley Booth, the stage actress who won a Tony award in 1950 for her portrayal of Lola in William Inge's play, *Come Back, Little Sheba.* Her television role won her two Emmy awards in successive seasons, 1961/1962 and 1962/1963, and both in the same category, Outstanding Continuing Performance by an Actress in a Series (Lead).

George Baxter was an attorney with Butterworth, Hatch and Noell and was played by Don DeFore, who had played Ozzie Nelson's first neighbor on *The Adventures of Ozzie & Harriet* (See Entry). George's wife, Dorothy Baxter, was played by Whitney Blake, who was a regular on the syndicated comedy/variety program, *The David Frost Revue,* which aired between 1971 and 1973.

Don DeFore got his role as "Mr. B." on *Hazel* from Mitchell Gertz, the same agent who got him the job in BATTLE HYMN, which he filmed in 1956 while *The Adventures of Ozzie & Harriet* (See Entry) was on hiatus.

"Agent Mitchell Gertz said, 'Don, I'm pleased you said you'd like for me to represent you. You've been handled very badly in this business and I want to get you your own TV show!' That's something I've been hoping for,"[13] said DeFore.

"One Sunday, Mitch [Gertz] and his girlfriend and Marion and I drove out to Ojai [California] and during the trip he said, 'Don, there was a pilot made for a new series and the production company doesn't like it; as a matter of fact they're unhappy with the performer they hired as the husband. I saw the pilot and it was lousy, and I know they're going to try to get you for it. But my advice is to turn it down because whatever female star

they get—Thelma Ritter or Shirley Booth—she's going to demand a big salary and huge percentage and there will be very little offered to you!' So I said, 'Okay, Mitch, I want you to handle it!'

"I finally went ahead and did the first three years with *Hazel,* but because the production company's attitude toward me had incorporated one Jack Warner's treatment of actors—'keep 'em back on their heels,' that office and I were constantly at odds. However, Shirley Booth and I got along just great. I thoroughly enjoyed every minute with her. She was marvelous in the series and it was a great show for me,"[14] said DeFore.

"At the end of the first year of *Hazel,* Ted Key, the creator of the long-running *Saturday Evening Post* panel, sent me an original cartoon as a Christmas present. It was Hazel standing there holding a scroll-list of things that rolled clear to the floor. Mr. B. is standing in front of her and she is saying, 'All right, Mr. B. You want me to tell you what Don DeFore has that you haven't got?' "[15] DeFore laughed with pride.

Hazel Burke was about as loyal as employees get and she never left her employers or the series. Her employers, however, did skip town, or rather the country, on her.

When the series began, Hazel was employed by George and

---

13. Don DeFore in a letter to the author dated March 6, 1991.
14. Don DeFore in a letter to the author dated March 6, 1991.
15. *Ibid.*

Dorothy Baxter, who lived at 123 Marshall Road in an unspecified city that has appeared in some printed sources as Hydsberg, New York. Living with them was their son, Harold, who was played by Bobby Buntrock. In the very first episode of the series, co-star Don DeFore managed to get his ten-year-old son, Ron, a bit part as one of Harold's neighborhood friends.

"My cousin Pat DeFore and a friend, Dick Severy, also appeared in that episode with me as friends of Harold Baxter,"[16] explained Ron DeFore. "In that episode we were playing football in a park with Harold. Each of us had some shouting lines, but no long speaking parts. It was the first time I was involved in a television production as opposed to just watching, which I did get to do a lot of,"[17] said the younger DeFore.

"I can recall watching them shoot a scene with a balloon vendor and remember wondering why it took so long to film something that would only wind up on the screen for twenty or thirty seconds,"[18] he said.

With Hazel Burke in charge of the Baxter's household, everything went along fine for more than three seasons until the series changed networks and Hazel changed families.

"It was before the close of our third year, during our hiatus, when I was writing my first book. It was about our eldest daughter, Penny, who, after graduating from high school at the age of seventeen, went to Korea to work in an orphanage as a volunteer. I took her letters, as well as a trip to Korea, and wrote *With All My Love,* which was published by Prentice Hall,"[19] explained DeFore.

"After Penny returned home, she attended the San Jose Nursing College, while I continued work on the book. I'd finished over half of the manuscript and decided that I needed some on-the-spot verification. I called my wife from the set of *Hazel* on our last day of shooting before hiatus time and said, 'Mar, we're going to Korea and I hope Penny has a semester break so that she can go with us. Fortunately she did, and we all headed for 'the Land of the morning calm.'

"Then, in Korea," chuckles DeFore, "I get a wire from the producer of *Hazel* that said, 'You'd better get back here because we're going to start shooting right away.' Before leaving for Korea I'd gone to an attorney, who'd bettered my contract. The amended contract was accepted and I returned to work, and that was it,"[20] explained DeFore.

In addition to writing, one of Don DeFore's other hobbies was woodworking, making antique tables and antique shelves. DeFore's son, Ron, recalled the time his dad nearly cut off a finger on his left hand while working with his radial saw. "My dad's whole hand was bandaged. He does a lot of woodworking at home and he had put on a nine-inch blade where he normally worked with a six-inch one. For six weeks he had this huge

bandage on his left hand; fortunately the finger was saved. There are several episodes of *Hazel* in which my father is seen with this bandage,"[21] recalled Ron DeFore.

At first the producers tried to shoot around DeFore's hand so that it wasn't visible on the screen. But that began to cause more trouble than it was worth so DeFore asked that his bandage be written into the show. The first idea was to say that Mr. B. had been bitten by the neighbor's dog. According to Don DeFore, that excuse was never used. He then recounted the dialogue that was used to explain his injury.

"BOSS: George, what happened to you?

GEORGE: Well, I was out playing baseball.

BOSS: How could you hurt your hand like that playing baseball?

GEORGE: Hazel was up to bat."[22]

DeFore also laughed about the fact that since reruns of *Hazel* were rarely shown in consecutive order, George Baxter's bandaged arm turned up at various times during the reruns and he would get letters from fans asking him if he had hurt his hand again.

Hazel then moved from NBC to CBS. "The attorney representing me and the studio phoned to tell me that the studio was not going to pick up my option for the fifth year! I said, 'Well, that's fine. I'm just leaving for New York to do other things!' "[23] said DeFore.

Don DeFore did leave for New York and the fifth season began without him or Whitney Blake. Consequently, Hazel was forced to change families. The storyline explained that George had been transferred to Saudi Arabia and that his wife, Dorothy, was traveling to the Middle East with him. It was further explained that the Baxters felt it best to leave their son, Harold, with his younger brother's family so that the youngest Baxter could complete his schooling in Hydsburg, uninterrupted. Naturally, Hazel went along with the deal and both Shirley Booth and Bobby Buntrock moved in with Steve and Barbara Baxter, who were played by Ray Fulmer and Lynn Borden.

Before his death at age eighty on December 22, 1993, Don DeFore devoted his time to writing. Projects in the works included *Hollywood—DeFore 'N After, Ragged Strangers,* a murder mystery that involved a major city's crooked D.A., and his Hollywood comedy-drama, *Flesh Peddler.*

---

16. Ron DeFore in a letter to the author dated March 3, 1991.
17. *Ibid.*
18. *Ibid.*
19. Don DeFore in a letter to the author dated March 6, 1991.
20. *Ibid.*
21. Ron Defore in a letter to the author dated March 3, 1991.
22. From an exclusive telephone interview with Don DeFore on August 17, 1990.
23. *Ibid.*

HEAD OF THE CLASS

September 17, 1986–June 25, 1991.　ABC

Character:　　　Charles "Charlie" Moore
Played by:　　　Howard Hesseman
Date(s):　　　　September 17, 1986–April 25, 1990

Replaced by:　　Billy MacGregor
Played by:　　　Billy Connolly
Date(s):　　　　September 11, 1990–June 25, 1991

Character:　　　Jawaharlal Choudhury
Played by:　　　Jory Husain
Date(s):　　　　September 17, 1986–May 1989

Replaced by:　　Alex Torres
Played by:　　　Michael DeLorenzo
Date(s):　　　　September 27, 1989–June 25, 1991

Character:　　　Maria Borges
Played by:　　　Leslie Bega
Date(s):　　　　September 17, 1986–May 1989

Replaced by:　　Viki Amory
Played by:　　　Lara Piper
Date(s):　　　　September 27, 1989–June 25, 1991

Character:　　　Janice Lazarotto
Played by:　　　Tannis Vallely
Date(s):　　　　September 17, 1986–May 1989
　　　　　　　　June 25, 1991

Replaced by:　　Aristotle McKenzie
Played by:　　　De'Voreaux White
Date(s):　　　　September 27, 1989–June 25, 1991

Charlie Moore's (Howard Hesseman) I.H.P. (Individualized Honors Program) on *Head of the Class* was by all measures the complete antithesis of Gabe Kotter's (Gabriel Kaplan) S.G.R.A. (Special Guidance Remedial Academics) on ABC's *Welcome Back Kotter,* which aired from September 9, 1975 to August 10, 1979. Mr. Kotter taught the "sweathogs"; Mr. Moore taught the "nerds."

For Mr. Charlie Moore, what began as a two-day substitute teaching assignment at New York's Fillmore High School turned into a full-time teaching assignment that lasted for four seasons. Class began on a Thursday morning at 8:05, when Mr. Moore bumped into Assistant Principal Bernadette Meara (Jeannetta Arnette) and asked for directions to room 19. Ms. Meara gave him directions—and a warning.

MS. MEARA:　Oh, Mr. Moore. I'd better warn you about your
　　　　　　　first period class . . .

MR. MOORE:　. . . Warn me? I've taught in the toughest high
　　　　　　　schools in New York City.

What Mr. Moore didn't understand was that this was not a class of problem students—this was a class of whiz kids.

During the run of the series, three of the ten kids who were enrolled in the I.H.P. program, Jawaharlal, Maria and Janice, were written out and replaced by new students, introduced in the premiere episode of the fourth season, "Back to School."

Mr. Moore first broke the news to his class that Jawaharlal would not be returning. "Jawaharlal's family has moved to California . . . business opportunities." He was replaced by Alex Torres, who corrected Mr. Moore after being introduced as Al.

ALEX:　　My name is Alex Torres. My friends call me
　　　　　Alex. Nobody calls me Al. Okay?

Maria left when she was accepted into the High School for the Performing Arts. "Maria decided that she was born to sing," said Mr. Moore. Her replacement was Viki, an attractive blonde whose father had been transferred to New York from Florida.

Janice, an adolescent and a certified genius, left Fillmore for Harvard because, as Mr. Moore related, "Janice and her parents decided that she's accomplished enough here so she'll move on to college." She did, however, return as a special guest star for the second part of the series' graduation episode.

Aristotle McKenzie, the student replacing Janice, has a story that is just the opposite of Maria's. He transferred out of the Performing Arts High School, where he studied filmmaking, writing, acting and painting, not because he couldn't cut it, but because "My mom said, 'Get a life.' She said, 'Do something real like a doctor or lawyer or something.' So, I gotta do this and I gotta do college to make her happy."

Head of the Class, which may have aspired to be the *Star Trek* of the twentieth century by having one representative from each of the world's racial groups, was left with an imbalance when Jory Husain left the series. To right this inequity, Jonathan Ke Quan was added to the cast as Jasper Quan. Moviegoers may remember Jonathan Ke Quan (who went by the name of Ke Huy Quan) as Indiana Jones' young sidekick, Short Round, in the 1984 blockbuster, INDIANA JONES AND THE TEMPLE OF DOOM.

Eventually, Howard Hesseman, who had achieved television fame as Dr. Johnny Fever on *WKRP in Cincinnati* (See Entry), felt it was time for Mr. Moore to move on, and he was replaced by Scottish comedian Billy Connolly. "Where's Class," the first episode with Connolly, has his character, Billy MacGregor, entering the I.H.P. classroom carrying a bicycle without any wheels—they'd been stolen.

BILLY:　　Is this room 19, I.H.P.? I'm Billy MacGregor.
　　　　　(PAUSE) Your new teacher.

The difference between the two teachers was immediately perceptible. Foremost was the obvious fact that Billy MacGregor spoke with a thick Scottish accent that was melodious and quite pleasing to the ear. Of greater importance was his more open relationship with the students, as can be seen by comparing his first moments in class with Mr. Moore's.

On Charlie Moore's first day he wrote "Mr. Moore" on the blackboard and told the class that they could call him by his first name then he underlined the word "Mr." Mr. MacGregor, on the other hand, also told the class to address him by his first name. "Billy. Call me Billy," he said, and they did until the series ended with a sentimental two-part finale, "It Couldn't Last Forever," which aired on June 18 and 25, 1991.

It was naturally Billy who broke the news to the I.H.P. class:

BILLY:	Morning, geniuses. . . . Oh, before we have any lessons at all, I'm afraid I've got some rather sad news for ya.
CLASS:	(VARIOUS VOICES) Like what?
BILLY:	A couple of weeks after graduation, the entire school is going to be demolished.

Toward the end of the episode, just before the graduation ceremony, Billy gives the class his last good-bye, telling them to "Go forth, the world awaits!"

The final scene has Billy returning to the now empty classroom one last time. He writes "Billy Was Here!" on the blackboard, tells Bernadette to follow her dream to travel and see the world, then pauses, turns off the room light, and says, "So long, geniuses."

Though this may be the last time the students at Fillmore High get to see Billy MacGregor, it is not the last time audiences do. Billy Connolly returned on January 31, 1992, in his own spinoff series, appropriately titled *Billy*. The continuing plot has Billy moving to Berkeley, California to teach poetry at Community College, which would be just great except for the fact that Billy's work permit, which was issued on September 29, 1989, had expired on September 30, 1991.

In order to legally stay in the country (and the series) Billy convinces one of his night school poetry students, Mary Springer (Marie Marshall), to marry him—which she does. Billy then moves into a basement apartment Mary built specifically for him. Naturally, Mary is a divorced mother (her husband left and moved to Australia) with three adorable TV kids: six-year-old Annie (Clara Bryant), ten-year-old Laura (Natanya Ross) and fourteen-year-old David (Johnny Galecki).

HELLO LARRY

January 26, 1979–April 30, 1980.   NBC

Character:	Diane Alder
Played by:	Donna Wilkes
Date(s):	January 26, 1979–August 10, 1979
Replaced by:	Diane Alder
Played by:	Krista Errickson
Date(s):	October 12, 1979–April 30, 1980

After deciding to leave his plum role as Lieutenant Colonel Henry Blake on *M*A*S*H* (See Entry), McLean Stevenson has become a man in search of a series. One such ill-fated attempt was the short-lived sitcom, *Hello Larry,* in which he played Larry Alder, the host of a radio phone-in program on Portland, Oregon's KLOW-Radio.

He is also divorced and has won custody of his two daughters, Ruthie and Diane, ages thirteen and sixteen. Larry actually had three daughters, if you count the fact that Diane was played by two actresses. Ruthie was played by Kim Richards, while Diane was played by both Donna Wilkes and Krista Errickson.

The Alder family wasn't always the Alder family. They actually began the series as the Adlers, which was changed to Alder soon after *Hello Larry*'s premiere.

The series aired on a very erratic schedule, but somehow managed to rack up forty-four episodes, after which the names of the entire cast were changed to unemployed.

HERE'S LUCY *see:* THE LUCY SHOW

THE HIGH CHAPARRAL

September 10, 1967–September 10, 1971.   NBC

Character:	Anna Lee
Played by:	Joan Caulfield
Date(s):	September 10, 1967
Replaced by:	Victoria de Montoya Cannon
Played by:	Linda Cristal
Date(s):	September 10, 1967–September 10, 1971

Even though *The High Chaparral* was created and produced by David Dortort, who had begun producing *Bonanza* some eight years earlier, the series was only moderately successful, running for just four years.

The locale was the High Chaparral Ranch in Tucson, Arizona during the 1870s. The ranch took its name from the chaparral bush that was indigenous to that area of Arizona. The series had an added aura of realism because most of the filming was done on location in Arizona, not on a back lot in California.

"All of the beautiful location stuff was shot in Arizona at the Old Tucson Movie Studio, that served as a backdrop to many great Western movies, including THE MARK OF ZORRO, GUNFIGHT AT THE O.K. CORRAL, HOMBRE and RIO LOBO. Episodes of *Bonanza, The Wild, Wild West* and *Little House on the Prairie* were also shot there. Today, the *High Chaparral* set is serving as a fort in *The Young Riders*. Interior shots were divided between a sound stage on Paramount's lot and a little sound stage in Old Tucson,"[24] recalled Henry Darrow, who played Manolito Montoya in the series.

Using the *Bonanza* formula, stories centered on the struggles of the Cannon family to make a success of their cattle ranch.

Heading up the cast was Leif Erickson as "Big" John

24. From an exclusive telephone interview with Henry Darrow on December 13, 1991.

On location at the Old Tucson Movie Studio in Arizona are the cast of *The High Chaparral*. Seated at the bottom is Mark Slade as Billy Blue Cannon, and, clockwise, from top left, Cameron Mitchell as Buck Cannon, Leif Erickson as Big John Cannon, Henry Darrow as Manolito Montoya, and Linda Cristal as Victoria Cannon.

Cannon, owner of the High Chaparral; Cameron Mitchell as John's brother, Buck; and Mark Slade as John's son, Billy Blue Cannon.

Joan Caulfield, who had played the first Liz Cooper in the 1950s situation comedy, *My Favorite Husband* (See Entry), starred as John Cannon's first wife, Anna Lee. She was killed by the arrow of an Apache Indian in the Western's two-hour pilot, "The High Chaparral." John's second marriage, to Victoria Montoya (Linda Cristal), was said to have been an act of appeasement to his professional rival, Don Sebastian Montoya (Frank Silvera).

Henry Darrow, who played Don Sebastian's son, Manolito, a ranch hand on the High Chaparral, shared his recollections of working on that first episode:

"Joan Caulfield, who died at the end of the first hour of the two-hour pilot, knew her character was going to be killed and that she was not going to be a regular on the show. During the second hour, the characters of Victoria and Manolito were introduced. During that introduction, I save Big John's life and when he says, 'Thanks,' I say, 'You're welcome. Put your hands up, I'm taking your horse.' So I steal his horse and his gun. He later returned the favor by saving me from the Federales. I did, however, find it interesting that Big John Cannon continued to visit Anna Lee's grave site for seven or eight more episodes." [25]

A few years after *The High Chaparral,* Henry Darrow played Detective Lieutenant Manny Quinlan on the David Janssen detective drama, *Harry-O* (See Entry). He later began a long-running association with *Zorro* (See Entry) and even guest-starred in the syndicated science fiction series, *Star Trek: The Next Generation.* In the episode "Conspiracy," Henry Darrow played Savar, a Starfleet admiral whose body was taken over by an insect-like alien.

Though Linda Cristal has appeared in guest-starring roles in a number of series including *Rawhide, Voyage to the Bottom of the Sea, Bonanza, Police Story* and *Barnaby Jones,* she may be best known to soap opera fans from her recurring role on ABC's *General Hospital.*

HILL STREET BLUES

January 15, 1981–May 19, 1987.   NBC

Character:	Sergeant Phil Esterhaus
Played by:	Michael Conrad
Date(s):	January 15, 1981–1984

Replaced by:	Captain Frank "Francis" Furillo
Played by:	Daniel J. Travanti
Date(s):	February 2, 1984

Replaced by:	Officer/Sergeant Lucille "Lucy" Bates
Played by:	Betty Thomas
Date(s):	February 9, 1984

Replaced by:	Sergeant Stanislaus "Stan" Jablonski
Played by:	Robert Prosky
Date(s):	September 27, 1984–May 19, 1987

Mention the show *Hill Street Blues* and two very strong images are immediately called to mind. One is the theme music written by Mike Post; the other, the voice of Sergeant Esterhaus warning his police officers, "And, hey—let's be careful out there." The music continued with the series to the end, the voice did not.

Hill Street Blues was one of those unique programs that should have been an immediate success, but it wasn't until later on. It did, however, win a great deal of critical acclaim during its first season. To put the phrase "critical acclaim" into the proper perspective, *Hill Street Blues* as a series was nominated for an amazing total of twenty-one Emmy Awards, and in six categories they were competing against themselves, so they could only have won fifteen. By the time the curtain had come done, *Hill Street Blues* had won eleven Emmys. Here is how it went down.

Executive Producers Steven Bochco and Michael Kozoll and producer Gregory Hoblit won for Outstanding Drama Series.

Daniel J. Travanti won for Outstanding Lead Actor in a Drama Series, and Barbara Babcock won for her role as Grace Gardner in the March 25 episode, "Fecund Hand Rose." She beat out fellow *Blues* co-star Veronica Hamel, who was also nominated.

Michael Conrad won in the category of Outstanding Supporting Actor in a Drama Series. His competition included two of his co-stars, Charles Haid and Bruce Weitz, who played Officer Andy Renko and Detective Mick Belker.

Both Barbara Bosson and Betty Thomas were nominated for Outstanding Supporting Actress in a Drama Series, but lost out to Nancy Marchand, who played Mrs. Margaret Pynchon on *Lou Grant.*

The award for Outstanding Directing in a Drama Series went to Robert Butler for his premiere episode, "Hill Street Station." He beat out *Blues* directors Georg Stanford Brown, who was nominated for the February 21 episode, "Up In Arms," and Corey Allen for his March 26 episode, "Jungle Madness."

In the writing category, Michael Kozoll and Steven Bochco won for their teleplay, "Hill Street Station." They beat out themselves for the script they did for "Jungle Madness."

William H. Cronjager took home the award for Outstanding Cinematography for "Hill Street Station," while Jeffrey L. Goldstein, the art director, and Joseph A. Armetta, the set director, were nominated for Outstanding Art Direction, but didn't win.

Mike Post's music was nominated for Outstanding Achievement in Music Composition for a Series or Dramatic Underscore and lost to *Buck Rogers in the 25th Century* composer Bruce Broughton for his March 12 score, "The Satyr." However, Samuel Horta did win for Outstanding Achievement in Film Sound Editing for the premiere episode. And four film editors, Bernard Balmuth, Ray Daniels, A. David Marshall and Thomas H. Stevens, Jr. were nominated, but did not win.

25. From an exclusive telephone interview with Henry Darrow on December 13, 1991.

Why then was the series almost canceled? Simple, it was doing lousy in the ratings. Of course, after the attention garnered from these awards, people began tuning in—week after week, for the next six years.

There is no doubt, that one of the most beloved members of the crew at Hill Street Station was Sergeant Esterhaus, played by Michael Conrad, who most assuredly would have remained with the series were it not for his death. Even though he appeared in episodes through 1984, some of these were actually filmed before his death in 1983.

With more than eighty television credits, which included episodes of *Naked City, Wagon Train, I Spy* and *The Dick Van Dyke Show,* he is also well remembered for his role as Mike Stivic's uncle, "Cas" (Casimir) Stivic, in the two-part flashback episode of *All in the Family,* "Mike and Gloria's Wedding," which aired on November 11 and 18, 1972.

When Michael Conrad died of cancer on November 22, 1983, he left a gaping hole in the large ensemble cast, and like a sore that will not heal, it took some time to replace him. The episode of February 2, 1984 dealt with the loss of the character.

In *The Best of Crime & Detective TV,* Max Allan Collins and John Javna wrote that the character of Grace Gardner (Barbara Babcock), the middle-aged widow of another officer in the precinct, was hastily written back into the series. "Grace was written abruptly, briefly back in to announce Phil had died during typically exquisite sex with her."[26]

Phil's superior, Captain Frank Furillo, played by the series' star, Daniel J. Travanti, handled the famous roll call scene in that episode and announced that Sergeant Esterhaus had died of a heart attack.

In the following week's episode, Officer Lucy Bates is promoted to Sergeant to take over the vacancy left by the passing of Esterhaus, but she didn't last in this role and eventually a replacement was hired—but not before more than 200 actors were auditioned. " 'Sometimes I think I've considered every middle-aged actor in town,' moaned NBC's vice president of talent in 1984. '[But] you always come back to thinking of Michael.' "[27]

The actor they finally settled upon was Robert Prosky, who was quite different in demeanor and style from his predecessor. Although he had been in the business for more than twenty years, this was his only regular role in a television series. His other television work includes the "Home Town" episode of *Lou Grant* that aired on November 23, 1981, and an NBC miniseries, the two-part telefilm, *World War III,* aired on January 31, 1981 and February 1, 1982. In it, Prosky played Colonel General Aleksei Rudenski.

On *Hill Street Blues,* his character, Sergeant Stan Jablonski, was a brusque heavyset Pole who was more of a do-it-by-the-book kind of cop.

The writers gave Jablonski, who was introduced in the "Mayo, Hold the Pickle" episode, a catch phrase of his own to use at the end of roll call. But when he bellowed "Let's do it to them before they do it to us," it didn't touch the same emotional nerve as Sergeant Esterhaus' loving axiom. Which only goes to prove that even writers have to be careful out there.

HOGAN'S HEROES

September 17, 1965–July 4, 1971.   CBS

Character:	Sergeant James Kinchloe
Played by:	Ivan Dixon
Date(s):	September 17, 1965–1969[28]

Replaced by:	Sergeant Richard Baker
Played by:	Kenneth Washington
Date(s):	September 20, 1970–July 4, 1971

Character:	Helga
Played by:	Cynthia Lynn
Date(s):	September 17, 1965–1966

Replaced by:	Hilda
Played by:	Sigrid Valdis
Date(s):	1966–1970

Stalag 13 was a German prisoner-of-war camp and probably television's most unlikely setting for a situation comedy, yet somehow it seemed to work—most likely because there was practically no violence. What violence there was, was only superficial, as the Germans were all played as bone heads.

The premise for this hit series was that a band of prisoners, each an expert in a specific discipline, worked together to sabotage the Nazis' war effort from their base of operations inside a P.O.W. camp in Germany. The series lost a plagiarism suit to the producers of the the Broadway play, *Stalag 17,* which was written by Donald Bevan and Edmund Trzcinski. In the play, Harold J. Stone, who starred as Stosh, appeared as a German officer on several episodes of *Hogan's Heroes.* He was also the second of three actors to play Jake on *The Goldbergs* (See Entry).

The play was later turned into a successful motion picture starring William Holden as Sefton and Otto Preminger as Oberst Von Scherbach. Stone's role was played by Robert Strauss.

The truth of the matter is that the series also resembled the 1963 Steve McQueen film, THE GREAT ESCAPE. As in the motion picture, each of the allied prisoners featured on *Hogan's Heroes* was an expert in a particular discipline. Colonel Robert E. Hogan (Bob Crane) was the senior P.O.W. and the brains of the outfit, just as Richard Attenborough was in THE GREAT ESCAPE. Corporal Peter Newkirk (Richard Dawson) was an excellent mimic, as well as able to sew uniforms and forge papers, like the Donald Pleasence character, Colin. Louis LeBeau (Robert Clary) was a Frenchman and the unit's chef—

26. Collins, Max Allan and John Javna. *The Best of Crime and Detective TV.* Harmony Books, New York, 1988, p. 51.
27. *Ibid.,* p. 59
28. Some sources give 1970 as the date Ivan Dixon left *Hogan's Heroes.*

okay, so there was no French chef in THE GREAT ESCAPE, but you get the idea.

Rounding out Hogan's band of merry men were Sergeant Andrew Carter (Larry Hovis), an explosives expert, and Sergeant James Kinchloe, the electronics and communications expert.

Kinchloe, "Kinch" as he was affectionately called by his fellow inmates, was played by Ivan Dixon, who got his start in motion pictures by working as a stunt double for Sidney Poitier in the 1958 film, THE DEFIANT ONES. He then appeared as Asagai in Poitier's 1961 film, A RAISIN IN THE SUN, and played Lonnie in the 1976 comedy, CAR WASH. Perhaps his most famous film portrayal was Duff Anderson in the 1964 film, NOTHING BUT A MAN.

While still working on *Hogan's Heroes,* Ivan Dixon embarked on a new career—directing. After directing several episodes of the series, Dixon left *Hogan's Heroes* to direct motion pictures. His first was the 1972 blacksploitation film, TROUBLE MAN, which starred Mr. "T" as Robert Hooks and Paul Winfield as Chalky Price. The following year he both produced and directed his next film in the genre, THE SPOOK WHO SAT BY THE DOOR.

Dixon returned to television to direct episodes of dozens of series including *Airwolf, Bret Maverick, Delvecchio, The Nancy Drew Mysteries, Wonder Woman, The Righteous Apples* and *The A-Team.* Ivan Dixon was nominated for an Emmy during the 1966/1967 season for Outstanding Single Performance by an Actor in a Leading Role in a Drama for the *CBS Playhouse* production of *The Final War of Olly Winter.*

Meanwhile, back at Stalag 13, Colonel Hogan was unable to operate without his electronics expert and so Sergeant Richard Baker was drafted to take Kinch's place. Kenneth Washington was cast as Baker, a role virtually identical to the one played by Dixon.

There were very few women on *Hogan's Heroes,* only three turning up with any regularity. Most of the others were either Nazi spies, or contacts from the underground. There was, however, one beautiful and brilliant female rocket scientist thrown in for good measure.

The most frequently seen actress in a recurring role was Colonel Klink's (Werner Klemperer) secretary. The second was the beautiful Russian spy, Marya (Nita Talbot), and the third was General Alfred Burkhalter's (Leon Askin) sister, Gertrude Linkmeir. Frau Linkmeir was played by Kathleen Freeman, who had played Katie the maid on *Topper* (See Entry).

The Kommandant's first secretary, Helga, was played by Cynthia Lynn during the first season. After leaving the series, Ms. Lynn was not immediately replaced and there were a number of episodes shot without a secretary. The position was eventually filled by Sigrid Valdis, as Fraulein Hilda. The new actress, a beautiful blonde who looked very much like Helga, just happened to be married to the star of the series, Robert Crane.

To introduce viewers to Klink's new secretary, the writers had General Burkhalter introduce his sister to Colonel Klink, in the hope that they would hit it off and get married. Actually, she was already married to a soldier named Otto. He had been reported missing in Russia, though Frau Linkmeir refused to believe that he wasn't coming back. General Burkhalter felt otherwise.

BURKHALTER:	I said you'd have a secretary the first thing this morning.
KLINK:	Yes sir, you did. What time will she be here.
BURKHALTER:	She's here, right now.
KLINK:	You don't mean your sister?
GERTRUDE:	What is wrong with that?
KLINK:	Oh, no, no, nothing. Its a wonderful idea, but you see it's very complicated work.
GERTRUDE:	What is so complicated about it? I can make twice the mess I see here.
KLINK:	Well, you see, work has been piling up since Fraulein Hilda left . . .
HOGAN:	Believe me, we were mighty happy when Hilda took a leave of absence. She and the Colonel were quite a pair.

As it turned out, Hilda and Hogan were also quite a pair, as was reported in the December 5, 1970 issue of *TV Guide:* "Bob Crane is learning that a TV series can turn into a family thing: he recently married Sigrid Valdis, who decorates *Hogan's Heroes'* drab prison-camp setting as the Kommandant's eye-popping secretary."[29]

Werner Klemperer performed as narrator in the "Mostly Mozart Festival" which aired live from Lincoln Center on July 11, 1990. During intermission, Klemperer was interviewed by host Hugh Downs, who asked him about his portrayal of Colonel Klink. "When I decided to say yes and do it, I did make one qualification that was important to me," said Klemperer. "And that is, if there were ever to be a segment in which Klink came out the winner, I would not want to be with the show anymore. So he was always a loser, which is the way it ought to have been."

That simple philosophy, along with his precise timing and delivery, which Klemperer has attributed to his sense of music, may have made Colonel Klink a loser, but it made actor Werner Klemperer a winner. For the 1967/1968 season Klemperer won an Emmy Award for Outstanding Performance by an Actor in a

Supporting Role in a Comedy. For his work during the 1968/1969 season of *Hogan's Heroes* he took home his second Emmy. That one was for Outstanding Performance by an Actor in a Supporting Role in a Series for which he beat out Greg Morris from *Mission Impossible* and Leonard Nimoy from *Star Trek*.

HOLLYWOOD JUNIOR CIRCUS

March 25, 1951–January 19, 1952[30].   NBC-ABC

Character:	Ringmaster
Played by:	Art Jacobson
Date(s):	March 25, 1951–July 1, 1951 (NBC)

Replaced by:	Ringmaster
Played by:	Paul Barnes
Date(s):	September 8, 1951–January 19, 1952 (ABC)

Character:	Clown
Played by:	Carl Marx
Date(s):	March 25, 1951–July 1, 1951 (NBC)

Replaced by:	Buffo the Clown
Played by:	unknown
Date(s):	September 8, 1951–January 19, 1952 (ABC)

One of many circus-oriented shows in television's early days was *Hollywood Junior Circus*. The gimmick was that instead of taking place inside the Big Top, *Hollywood Junior Circus* was set behind the tent, where the performers rehearsed their acts.

The program was originally slated to air on the CBS television network beginning on January 27, 1951. When the network failed to run the program, the sponsor, Hollywood Candy Company, sued CBS for one million dollars. Eventually, the program aired Sunday evenings from 5:30 to 6:00 on NBC. The ringmaster was Art Jacobson and the clown was played by Carl Marx.

When the show moved to Saturday mornings on ABC the ringmaster was replaced by Paul Barnes and the new circus clown was Buffo. Buffo the Clown appeared as himself in "The Audition," the sixth episode of *I Love Lucy*, which originally aired on November 19, 1951. The script was actually a reworking of the unaired pilot for the series and featured Pepito the Clown in the role.

HOME IMPROVEMENT

September 17, 1991–.   ABC

Character:	Lisa
Played by:	Pamela Denise Anderson
Date(s):	September 17, 1991–September 15, 1993

Replaced by:	Heidi
Played by:	Debbe Dunning
Date(s):	September 15, 1993–

From the first time Ralph Bellamy appeared on screen as Mike Barnett on *Man Against Crime* (See Entry) television has offered male viewers characters who were the unattainable role models for a guy who was truly a man's man—until now. That is, Tim Allen's Tim Taylor character is not only attainable—it's surpassable.

Tim Taylor is the host of *Tool Time*, a big budget cable "do-it-yourselfer" television show produced in Detroit.

The highly rated show, which has made Tim a local celebrity, features Tim and his low key, but highly competent assistant Al Borland (Richard Karn), sharing advice and humor (often at Al's expense) on home repair and construction projects to the delight of a fairly large studio audience for a cable operation.

But the reason that Tim "The Tool Man" Taylor is a fully attainable role model is that regardless of how macho he thinks he is, he's really quite incompetent in the use of tools, which are supplied by his sponsor, Binford. Assisting Tim and Al is Lisa, the curvaceous coveralled "Tool Girl," cast from the same mold as those real-life models that grace the Makita Power Tools calendar.

Tool Time is an obvious takeoff on the popular PBS series, *This Old House,* whose popular host Bob Vila has made a couple of guest appearances on *Home Improvement* as a guest on Tim's show.

Keeping Tim humble at home is his wife Jill, who is played so well by Patricia Richardson, that it's hard to believe she's really a TV sitcom wife and mother of three young sons: Brad (Zachery Ty Bryan), Randy (Jonathan Taylor Thomas) and Mark (Taran Smith).

The series, which is based on the standup comedy of Tim Allen caught on quickly and eventually knocked *Roseanne* out of the number one spot in the ratings, earning Allen and Richardson several *TV Guide* covers—the true yardstick of success in the business.

Audiences keep coming back to *Home Improvement*. In fact, the only one not coming back to *Home Improvement* is former *Playboy* Playmate, Pamela Denise Anderson, who left her small, but highly visible recurring role on the ABC sitcom for a meatier role on an equally high rated syndicated dramatic adventure series, *Baywatch,* where she was simultaneously playing lifeguard C.J. Parker.

Debbe Dunning, who replaced Pamela Denise Anderson as *Tool Time*'s "Tool Girl," had made an earlier appearance as Kiki, a guest on *Tool Time*. First, she caught Tim's eye—then Tim caught it from Jill.

Tim Taylor introduced the new Binford "Tool Girl" to his audience on the September 15, 1993 episode, "Maybe Baby."

TIM:	Of course you all know our new "Tool Girl." I want you to say "Howdy" to Heidi.
AUDIENCE:	(In Unison) Howdy Heidi.

---

30. Some sources give March 1, 1952 as the last date the series aired.

TIM: Of course, our old ''Tool Girl'' moved on to bigger and better things.

AL: Oh, did she accept that offer from Bob Vila?

TIM: She went on to college. We both know that.

There is no question that Tim's construction capabilities are questionable. What is uncontestable is that the producers and cast of *Home Improvement* did know how to build a hit sitcom.

THE HONEYMOONERS

October 1, 1955–May 9, 1971.   DuMont-CBS-ABC

Character:	Alice Kramden
Played by:	Pert Kelton
Date(s):	June 4, 1949–September 26, 1952 (*Calvalcade of Stars*. DuMont)

Replaced by:	Alice Kramden
Played by:	Audrey Meadows
Date(s):	September 20, 1952–June 18, 1955
	October 1, 1955–September 22, 1956
	September 29, 1956–June 22, 1957
	October 3, 1958–January 2, 1961
	February 2, 1976 (*The Second Honeymoon*. ABC)
	November 28, 1977 (*The Honeymooners Christmas*. ABC)
	February 13, 1978 (*The Honeymooners Valentine Special*. ABC)
	December 10, 1978 (*The Honeymooners Christmas Special*. ABC)

Replaced by:	Alice Kramden
Played by:	Sue Ane Langdon
Date(s):	September 29, 1962–October 27, 1962 (*Jackie Gleason and his American Scene Magazine*. CBS)

Replaced by:	Alice Kramden
Played by:	Sheila MacRae
Date(s):	September 17, 1966–September 12, 1970 (*The Jackie Gleason Show*. CBS)
	December 12, 1970 (*The Jackie Gleason Special*. CBS)
	November 11, 1973 (*The Jackie Gleason Special*. CBS)

Character:	Trixie Norton
Played by:	Elaine Stritch
Date(s):	1950–September 26, 1952 (*Calvalcade of Stars*. DuMont)

Replaced by:	Trixie Norton
Played by:	Joyce Randolph
Date(s):	September 20, 1952–June 18, 1955
	October 1, 1955–September 22, 1956
	September 29, 1956–June 22, 1957
	October 3, 1958–January 2, 1961

Replaced by:	Trixie Norton
Played by:	Patricia Wilson
Date(s):	September 29, 1962–June 4, 1966 (*Jackie Gleason and his American Scene Magazine*. CBS)

Replaced by:	Trixie Norton
Played by:	Jane Kean
Date(s):	September 17, 1966–September 12, 1970 (*The Jackie Gleason Show*. CBS)
	December 12, 1970 (*The Jackie Gleason Special*. CBS)
	November 11, 1973 (*The Jackie Gleason Special*. CBS)
	February 2, 1976 (*The Second Honeymoon*. ABC)
	November 28, 1977 (*The Honeymooners Christmas*. ABC)
	February 13, 1978 (*The Honeymooners Valentine Special*. ABC)
	December 10, 1978 (*The Honeymooners Christmas Special*. ABC)

Character:	Mrs. Gibson (Alice's mother)
Played by:	Ethel Owen
Date(s):	October 1, 1955–September 22, 1956

Replaced by:	Mrs. Gibson (Alice's mother)
Played by:	Pert Kelton
Date(s):	March 4, 1967 (*The Jackie Gleason Show*. CBS)

Replaced by:	Mrs. Gibson (Alice's mother)
Played by:	Templeton Fox
Date(s):	February 2, 1976 (*The Second Honeymoon*. ABC)

Twenty-six years before *Saturday Night Live,* the Saturday evening staple was *Calvalcade of Stars.* It was a low-budget variety show hosted by an up-and-coming comedian and was broadcast live in front of a studio audience.

The program's first host was Jack Carter, who left *Cavalcade* in February 1950 to host NBC's new variety series, *Saturday Night Revue.* He was replaced by Jerry Lester, another former vaudevillian, who only lasted until July of that year. He went on to become television's first late-night talk show host, on NBC's *Broadway Open House.*

The producers wanted the suave English-born quiz show panelist Peter Donald to take over the show. He turned it down, but not before recommending Jackie Gleason, who played television's first Chester A. Riley on the NBC situation comedy, *The Life of Riley* (See Entry).

Just as *Saturday Night Live* featured comedy sketches and a musical guest, *Cavalcade* offered show girls and musical extravaganza numbers in addition to comedy sketches. The recurring sketch on *Cavalcade of Stars* was titled "The Honeymooners" and starred Jackie Gleason and Pert Kelton as Ralph and Alice Kramden, a married couple living in a sparsely-furnished cold-water apartment in Brooklyn, New York. The original sketch, which lasted only twelve minutes, caught on and became a regular feature on the program, just as "The Coneheads" were visited regularly on *Saturday Night Live.*

Gleason and his ensemble cast took *The Honeymooners* on a whirlwind U.S. tour in July 1952, during which they gave four live performances each day. It was a hectic schedule for anyone, but it took its toll on Pert Kelton. "One day she went on in her Alice role, left the stage to get sick, and reappeared to pick up her squawk with Ralph."[31] The audience, cast and crew all thought the piece of business was part of the show. It was not. Pert Kelton was suffering from a coronary thrombosis and collapsed at the end of the day.

The cast returned to New York when the *Honeymooners* road tour ended in August. Gleason's contract with DuMont had also ended. This gave him the opportunity to move to CBS, where his program would be aired on more affiliate stations. He also had more control and more money.

In addition to her heart ailment, Ms. Kelton was also suffering from a disease known as blacklisting, as her name appeared in *Red Channels* as a Communist sympathizer and Gleason was left with no choice but to replace her. "She had to be taken off the show because the sponsors wouldn't renew it,"[32] said Hasha Mintz, the widow of Eli Mintz, who played Uncle David on *The Goldbergs* (See Entry).

Ms. Kelton's parents were vaudevillians and she herself entered show business at the age of three. She made her debut on Broadway in the 1925 musical, *Sunny.* Her most famous motion picture role was Mrs. Paroo, in the 1962 musical comedy, THE MUSIC MAN.

Finding a new actress to play Alice Kramden was not an easy task because each actress was being compared to the Alice Kramden that Pert Kelton had created. One actress who auditioned, was initially turned down because Gleason felt she was too young and too pretty. She was Audrey Meadows, who had played Linda Lovely on *The Bob and Ray Show* (See Entry). "I told him that he was out of his mind. So I hired a photographer to visit my apartment at 5:30 A.M., wake me up and take pictures without makeup. Gleason looked at them and said: 'Jeez, she really is a dowdy broad!' "[33] The very unflattering stills did the trick and Audrey Meadows became *The Honeymooners* second, and now definitive, Alice Kramden.

Long unhappy with the weather in New York, Gleason moved to Miami Beach, Florida in 1962, where he produced *Jackie Gleason and his American Scene Magazine,* with Sue Ane Langdon as Alice Kramden and Patricia Wilson as Trixie

Norton. There was no Ed Norton in the earlier episodes because Art Carney had left the ensemble to pursue other acting opportunities including two episodes of *Batman.* Carney played Batman's Robin Hood-type merry nemesis, Archer, in "Shoot a Crooked Arrow" and "Walk the Straight and Narrow," which aired on September 7 and 8, 1966.

Unlike her predecessors, Sue Ane Langdon was good looking—but times had changed. Her television credits include Kitty Marsh, Bentley Gregg's fourth secretary on the John Forsythe situation comedy, *Bachelor Father* (See Entry).

It was reported that when Art Carney returned to make several guest appearances as Ed Norton, he encountered personality conflicts with Ms. Langdon, and ultimately she quit. This didn't faze Gleason; he is quoted as saying, "Who needs her?"

Apparently he didn't need her, because Audrey Meadows returned to play Alice Kramden in "The Adoption," the last of the Miami Beach episodes to be filmed in black and white. It is a particularly touching episode in which the Kramdens attempt to adopt a baby.

In the fall of 1966 *Jackie Gleason and his American Scene Magazine* was gone, but Jackie Gleason wasn't. In its place was a new *Jackie Gleason Show.* This version, a more sophisticated and much slicker version of Gleason's earlier *Cavalcade of Stars,* was a musical variety show featuring sketches, one of which was "The Honeymooners."

Gleason's loyal sidekick, Art Carney, was back in the role of Ed Norton, but both he and Ralph had new wives—that is, new actresses playing their ever-lovin' spouses, Alice and Trixie. This was because both Audrey Meadows and Joyce Randolph, who had played their wives in the black and white DuMont series, were not interested in moving to Miami; they were enjoying their marriages without the daily grind of working on a television series.

The fourth and final actress to play Alice Kramden was Sheila MacRae, the singer, actress/impressionist wife of actor Gordon MacRae, who among other hardships had to face the fact that she had to dye her hair an orangey-red.

"I just couldn't *get* Alice Kramden at first. Does she have nothing to do all day but yell at Ralph?" said Sheila MacRae in a *TV Guide* interview which ran on September 23, 1967. In comparing her interpretation of the Alice Kramden character with Audrey Meadows' portrayal, Ms. MacRae said, "*My* Alice is sweeter. *My* Alice cries." This kinder, gentler Alice worried some friends and critics and they advised her to stand up to Ralph more, but Gleason said, "The very fact that I've rehired her means that I like her very much. She can continue to play Alice as long as she wants to."

She wanted to for a total of forty all-singing, all-dancing episodes that even included a trip to Europe with Ralph and the Nortons. These were followed up by two Jackie Gleason specials.

On February 2, 1976 the now familiar Miami Beach opening, which began with a sweeping shot from the water heading

31. McCrohan, Donna. *The Honeymooners' Companion. The Kramdens and the Nortons Revisited.* Workman Publishing, New York, 1978, p. 14.
32. From an exclusive telephone interview with Eli Mintz's widow, Hasha Mintz, on February 9, 1991.
33. Barber, Rowland. *TV Guide*: Vol. 24, No. 30, Issue #1217, July 24, 1976, p. 13.

toward the mainland, featured a slight change in Johnny Olsen's introduction because Audrey Meadows, the quintessential Alice, had returned for four *Honeymooners* specials, beginning with *The Second Honeymoon*: "From beautiful Gussman Hall in Miami, the sun and fun capital of the world, Jackie Gleason presents *The Honeymooners,* starring Jackie Gleason and Art Carney, Audrey Meadows and Jane Kean. And away we go!"

It should now come as no surprise that there were also four different actresses to portray Mrs. Norton. The first Trixie Norton, a former burlesque queen, was played by Elaine Stritch, but only once. Ms. Stritch went on to play the second Mrs. Payne on *The Growing Paynes* (See Entry).

The next actress to play Alice's best friend was Joyce Randolph, who had appeared with Gleason on *Cavalcade of Stars* in a serious sketch in which they were former sweethearts who had been reunited. When Jackie Gleason needed a new Trixie on short notice he remembered Ms. Randolph's performance and said, "Get me that serious actress." And just as Audrey Meadows became Alice, Joyce Randolph became Trixie, a role she stayed with until Jackie Gleason relocated his productions in Miami in 1962.

That's when Patricia Wilson stepped in to play opposite Sue Ane Langdon's Alice on *Jackie Gleason and his American Scene Magazine.* Ms. Wilson came to television from a Broadway career that had won her a Critic's Circle nomination for Best Actress of the Season for her portrayal of Marie LaGuardia in *Fiorello!.* Her co-star was Tom Bosley, who would go on to play Howard Cunningham on *Happy Days* (See Entry). Patricia Wilson later rejoined her former co-star in an episode of *Happy Days.* Some of her other television roles include appearances on *Starsky and Hutch, The Mary Tyler Moore Show* and *Ellery Queen.*

The last actress to play Mrs. Edward L. Norton was Jane Kean, who had appeared with Jackie Gleason in the Broadway production of *Along Fifth Avenue.* She had also appeared on *Cavalcade of Stars.* She was hired by Gleason without an audition—he controlled the casting along with everything else.

Like Sheila MacRae, Ms. Kean also found it difficult to step into a role that had been so ingrained in the minds of the audience. "I found my own Trixie," she says. "I didn't want to copy Joyce Randolph. Otherwise it would be impersonation, not acting."[34]

From time to time, Alice's mother would show up and create the now classic "mother-in-law" arguments between Ralph and Alice. During the black and white DuMont days, Mrs. Gibson was played by Ethel Owen.

By the time *The Honeymooners* moved to Miami, Gleason had begun to delegate some of the work. One of the jobs he had relinquished was casting. The new casting director completely surprised Gleason with what some might view as an inspired bit of casting; others might find it crude and insensitive.

The casting brouhaha was caused by the hiring of Pert Kelton, the first actress to play Alice Kramden, to now play Alice's mother, Mrs. Gibson. It was, of course, no surprise to Ms. Kelton, who reveled in the role, which included the jazz

waltz, "That's What Comes of Marrying for Love," written especially for her by Lyn Duddy and Jerry Bresler. And true to form, she criticizes Ralph at every turn.

On October 30, 1968, a little more than a year later, Pert Kelton died at the age of sixty-one. "Baby, you're the greatest."

HONG KONG

September 28, 1960–September 20, 1961.   ABC

Character: Fong
Played by: Harold Fong
Date(s):   September 28, 1960–unknown

Replaced by: Ling
Played by: Gerald Jann
Date(s):   1960–September 20, 1961

Australian-born actor Rod Taylor, who starred as Mitch Brenner in Alfred Hitchcock's 1963 thriller, THE BIRDS, played Glenn Evans, an American foreign correspondent who lived and worked in Hong Kong.

When the series premiered, Evans' houseboy, Fong, was played by Harold Fong. A few week's later Gerald Jann took over as Evans' new houseboy, Ling. It is as simple as that.

HOOPERMAN

September 23, 1987–March 29, 1989.   ABC

Character: Susan Smith
Played by: Debrah Farentino
Date(s):   September 23, 1987–December 7, 1988

Replaced by: Dr. Platt
Played by: Pamela Bowen
Date(s):   December 14, 1988–unknown

The somewhat wacky John Ritter, formerly the star of *Three's Company,* settled down a bit in his next regular series, *Hooperman*—as a cop with a lighter side.

Detective Harry Hooperman lived in a building in which the handyman was neither George Utley nor Ralph Kramden, but an attractive woman, Susan Smith, with whom Hooperman was romantically involved. But just when things were getting juicy (Susan was pregnant with Hooperman's child), the producers decided to put an end to their relationship. Susan suffered a miscarriage in what was Debrah Farentino's last appearance on the series.

The reason Susan Smith left San Francisco was not so much to help her start a new life, but to allow Harry Hooperman to have one. Executive producer Robert Myman said in a *TV Guide* interview, "The show is going to be a lot more of

34. McCrohan, Donna. *The Honeymooners' Companion. The Kramdens and the Nortons Revisited.* Workman Publishing, New York, 1978, p. 48.

Hooperman as a single guy. There won't be one, but several women in and out of his life.''[35]

The following week, the first of those women, Dr. Platt, came into Hooperman's life. In that episode Hooperman suffers a hernia while trying to lift an overweight crook. He, of course, mistrusts hospitals and surgeons—that is, until he meets his anesthesiologist, Dr. Platt, played by Pamela Bowen.

HOPALONG CASSIDY

August 7, 1948–1950.   Syndicated
June 24, 1949–December 23, 1951   NBC

Character:	Uncle Ben; Spike; Windy; Shanghai
Played by:	George ''Gabby'' Hayes
Date(s):	1935–1939[36]
Replaced by:	California
Played by:	Andy Clyde
Date(s):	1940–1948[36a]
Replaced by:	Red Connors
Played by:	Edgar Buchanan
Date(s):	June 24, 1949–December 23, 1951

William Boyd starred in sixty-six HOPALONG CASSIDY features between 1935 and 1948. He was offered the starring role of Buck Peters, the handsome ranch foreman, but preferred to play Hopalong Cassidy, who was written as a much more interesting character.

Producer Harry ''Pop'' Sherman had planned to cast character actor James Gleason in the Cassidy role. Among Gleason's most memorable roles is that of Joe Pendleton's (Robert Montgomery) boxing manager, Max Corkle, in the 1941 fantasy, HERE COMES MR. JORDAN.

The part of the ranch foreman, Buck Peters, was ultimately given to Charles Middleton, who is perhaps best known as Ming the Merciless from the three FLASH GORDON serials produced in 1936, 1938 and 1940.

There is a great deal of confusion as to how many television shows were actually produced. One source says there were thirty-nine films shot for syndication, another says there were fifty-two. A third source says there were fifty-four and a fourth reports ninety-nine. A fifth source quotes 106 and a sixth researcher puts the total number of *Hopalong Cassidy* episodes at 118. The official television industry source book, *The B.I.B.* (*Broadcast Information Bureau Source Book*) is among those listing ninety-nine episodes.

Fortunately, some sense can be made from this widely conflicting data.

The bulk of the HOPALONG CASSIDY films were produced between 1935 and 1946, and it was William Boyd who purchased the television rights to these *fifty-four* pictures, which were the first to air on the small screen. Between 1946 and 1948 another twelve HOPALONG CASSIDY features were produced, which brings the total number to sixty-six.

Additional confusion arises from the fact that one source indicates that only the last dozen HOPALONG CASSIDY films were shown on television. This contradicts the information on the original contract, which clearly stated that these last HOPPY entries could not be aired on television until 1953, which was the year *Hopalong Cassidy* left the air.

William Boyd signed a contract with NBC in May 1952 to produce *fifty-two* new *Hopalong Cassidy* programs exclusively for television.

Now get out your calculators and follow along. If it is true that only the first fifty-four features were allowed to air on television before 1953, we can add those fifty-four to the fifty-two made-for-television films and arrive at a figure of 106. If all sixty-six features did indeed air on television, then sixty-six plus the fifty-two-episode television series equals 118. This explains all but the researchers who arrived at the sums of thirty-nine and ninety-nine films. To them I suggest that they recheck their sources, load fresh batteries into their calculators and recheck their ''cypherin'.''

Using this information we must now determine the number of Hoppy's ''sidekicks'' that television audiences actually saw.

There is no question that the first HOPALONG CASSIDY films television viewers saw were from the first fifty-four features. To bring the Western adventures of Hopalong Cassidy to the small screen, William Boyd added narration and at times even shot new footage, which was intercut with the original films. This was done to hide the fact that these were not all original programs.

That many of the motion pictures were shot some fifteen years earlier, is really quite amazing, since the handsome cowboy actor was fifty-four[37] years old when the program first aired on NBC.

If we assume that television audiences were treated to all sixty-six HOPALONG CASSIDY feature films, they were able to enjoy both Gabby Hayes and Andy Clyde as Hoppy's faithful sidekick.

During 1935, George Hayes played three different characters. In the original HOP-ALONG CASSIDY Western, Gabby Hayes played Uncle Ben. In the next installment, THE EAGLE'S BROOD, he turned up as Spike. In the third film of that year, BAR 20 RIDES AGAIN, his character was named Windy.

The first film produced the following year, CALL OF THE

---

35. *TV Guide.* Vol. 36, No. 45, Issue #1858, November 5, 1988, p. A2.

36. These are the dates the original HOPALONG CASSIDY films were produced. It is not possible to determine the actual dates each of these films were aired on television.

36a. *Ibid.*

37. Actor William Boyd may actually have been only fifty-one years old. There are two conflicting dates of birth: 1895 and 1898.

PRAIRIE, cast George Hayes as Shanghai. Thereafter, Gabby Hayes played Hopalong Cassidy's whiskered companion, Windy Halliday, in eighteen of the next twenty-two installments.

The Windy character was replaced in 1940 by California, played in all but one of the remaining forty pictures by Andy Clyde. If it is true that the last twelve HOPALONG CASSIDY films never made it to television, then the home audience would never have seen Andy Clyde as California.

The one certainty is that Edgar Buchanan did indeed play Red Connors in all fifty-two television episodes. The character of Red Conners, played by Frank McGlynn, Jr. only appeared in the initial film, after which he was dropped.

The gravel-voiced Buchanan went on to play the title role in the syndicated Western, *Judge Roy Bean,* which was produced by Screencraft and first aired in December 1955. Had the show gotten off of the ground with Tele-Voz a few years earlier, Chill Wills would have been the judge.

Most of America remembers Edgar Buchanan fondly as Uncle Joe, who was movin' kinda slow at the junction, *Petticoat Junction* (See Entry).

HOTEL

September 21, 1983–May 5, 1988.   ABC

Character: Laura Trent
Played by: Bette Davis
Date(s):   September 21, 1983

Replaced by: Mrs. Victoria Cabot
Played by: Anne Baxter
Date(s):   September 28, 1983–1986

The 1983 Fall Preview Issue of *TV Guide* hyped ABC's new Wednesday night entry, explaining that as with *The Love Boat,* each hour-long episode of *Hotel* would comprise several ministories woven together. The article went on to introduce the series' regular characters and the actors who would be playing them. "All of them will be watched by those famous Bette Davis eyes. She plays Laura Trent, the hotel's aristocratic owner."[38]

The *TV Guide* listing for the two-hour premiere also promoted the fact that "Bette Davis has a recurring role in this series (based on Arthur Hailey's novel) as Laura Trent, owner of San Francisco's prestigious St. Gregory Hotel, where she gives manager Peter McDermott (James Brolin) a free hand, with an occasional raised eyebrow."[39]

"Davis started work on *Hotel* in April. But after filming only two episodes she visited her doctor, Vincent Carroll, complaining of a breast lump and a circulatory dysfunction. . . . The breast lump was found to be malignant and a mastectomy was performed. Davis remained in the hospital [Cornell Medical Center] for testing on the circulatory disorder. Shortly after she suffered three strokes in a row."[40]

When Ms. Davis recovered from her medical ordeal "she abruptly informed Aaron Spelling that she would not be returning to *Hotel* and that as far as she was concerned, that episode in her life was over. . . . Her reasons for walking out on her lucrative *Hotel* commitment were, as usual, complex and dichotomous. She claimed she hated the scripts, thought them 'garbage.' She felt also that James Brolin and Connie Sellecca were the real stars because they were 'young and cute' and that she, with all her hard won expertise, was being 'cameoized' and 'downgraded' and 'pushed aside'."[41]

Inasmuch as this all took place before the two-hour movie aired, there was enough time to replace Ms. Davis. In fact, the following week's listing in *TV Guide* read: "Laura Trent's sister-in-law, the hotel overseer (Anne Baxter), is visited by an old flame (Stewart Granger)."[42] It was explained in the storyline that Ms. Trent was away on an "extended trip" and that her sister-in-law, Victoria Cabot, would be in charge of the St. Gregory hotel in her absence.

On December 4, 1985, Anne Baxter suffered a stroke while hailing a cab on the streets of New York City. She lingered for eight days, then died on December 12. But thanks to the magic of film, she didn't check out of the series until 1986; her character was written out as having died. At the time of her death, stories were circulated in the media that Ms. Baxter was not replaced because the producers felt that she was irreplaceable.

The coincidences surrounding these two great women of Hollywood are quite interesting. Film historians have pointed out that Ms. Baxter often appeared to be following in the footsteps of Bette Davis.

Anne Baxter played the young aspiring actress, Eve Harrington, in the 1950 dramatic comedy, ALL ABOUT EVE, which starred Bette Davis as Margo. Twenty years later, the Academy Award-winning film came to the Broadway stage as the musical *Applause* with Lauren Bacall cast in the Bette Davis role. When Ms. Bacall left the play in 1971, she was replaced by Anne Baxter.

Newspaper columnist Jack O'Brian wrote in his June 18, 1984 syndicated column: "When Bette Davis got sick and had to drop out of TV's hit-series, *Hotel,* cynics supposed her replacement, Anne Baxter, simply had life imitate art—à la Baxter's buttering Bette in ALL ABOUT EVE to steal the role in the play-within-a-film; no, Bette had okayed Anne without telling her in advance; real pal."

38. *TV Guide.* Fall Preview issue. Vol. 31, No. 37, September 10, 1983, Issue #1589. p. 59.
39. *TV Guide.* Vol. 31, No. 38, Issue #1590, September 17, 1983, p. A-156.
40. Quirk, Lawrence J. *Fasten Your Seat Belts.* William Morrow, New York, 1990, pg. 434.
41. *Ibid.,* pp. 435–436.
42. *TV Guide.* Vol. 31, No. 39, Issue #1591, September 24, 1983, p. A-159.

HOUSE CALLS

December 17, 1979–September 13, 1982.   CBS

Character: Ann Anderson
Played by: Lynn Redgrave
Date(s):   December 17, 1979–December 21, 1981

Replaced by: Jane Jeffries
Played by: Sharon Gless
Date(s):   January 4, 1982–September 13, 1982

In 1979, CBS took the moderately successul motion picture HOUSE CALLS and turned it into a moderately successful television series. The 1978 motion picture ran for ninety-eight minutes. The 1979–1982 sitcom ran for just thirty-four episodes.

In the motion picture, Walter Matthau plays Dr. Charley Nichols opposite Glenda Jackson as Ann Atkinson. The TV series cast former *M*A*S*H* (See Entry) surgeon, Wayne Rogers, as Dr. Charley Michaels and Lynn Redgrave as Dr. Ann Anderson.

With eight episodes already in the can, Ms. Redgrave entered into a contract dispute with the show's producers. The primary issue was over (what else?) money, but Ms. Redgrave, who had recently given birth, also wanted the right to breastfeed her baby on the *House Calls* set. With no agreement reached, Ms. Redgrave was released from her contract and written out of the series.

There is, however, still some confusion over the actual number of episodes Ms. Redgrave appeared in before leaving the series. Most sources indicate that she left *House Calls* after the eighth episode, which aired on February 18, 1980. But she did appear in three more episodes before the series went on hiatus on March 17, 1980.

When the series returned on November 2, 1981, *TV Guide* still listed Ms. Redgrave as Ann in eight more episodes, with the last one airing on December 21, 1981.

When production, which had been interrupted by a writers' strike, resumed, it was explained that Ann Anderson had gone back to her former husband in England. Her replacement, Jane Jeffries, just happened to have once had a "thing" with Dr. Michaels, which allowed the storyline to continue virtually unchanged for the remainder of the series.

Jane Jeffries was played by Sharon Gless, who shortly after leaving *House Calls* became the third Chris Cagney in the rocky but successful police series, *Cagney & Lacey* (See Entry).

Lynn Redgrave went on to star in two other failed sitcoms. The first was *Teacher's Only,* in which she starred as English teacher Diana Swanson. The series aired on NBC from April 14, 1982 to May 21, 1983. The 1989 television season hailed the ABC sitcom *Chicken Soup,* as a Stiller and Meara-type romance between the Jewish Jackie Fisher (Jackie Mason) and the Catholic Maddie (Lynn Redgrave). But the series never had a chance to heat up before it was poured down the drain. It ran from September 12, 1989 to November 7, 1989.

HOW TO MARRY A MILLIONAIRE

October 1958–1960.   Syndicated

Character: Greta Hanson
Played by: Lori Nelson
Date(s):   1958–1959

Replaced by: Gwen Kirby
Played by: Lisa Gaye
Date(s):   1959–1960

Character: Mr.Tobey
Played by: Joseph Kearns
Date(s):   1958–unknown

Replaced by: Mr. Blandish
Played by: Dabbs Greer
Date(s):   1958–1960

The inspiration for this syndicated sitcom was the 1953 Cinema-Scope comedy, HOW TO MARRY A MILLIONAIRE, which starred Betty Grable, Marilyn Monroe and Lauren Bacall. Although it is obvious that the series is based on the motion picture, the closing credits read, "Based on Screenplay by Nunnally Johnson and a play by Dale Eunson and Katherine Albert."

The story is a simple one. Three extremely sexy and attractive young women pool their resources to rent a posh New York penthouse apartment, to lend credibility to their ultimate goal, which is expressed quite clearly in the title of the series.

The three scheming sweeties are Loco Jones (Barbara Eden), "Mike" McCall (Merry Anders) and Greta Hanson (Lori Nelson).

Unhappy with the size of her role, Lori Nelson up and quit after the first season. She said that she was interested in landing more substantial roles, but she never did. Her most famous screen credit is that of Helen Dobson, the beautiful scientist in the 1955 3–D science fiction film, REVENGE OF THE CREATURE.

Greta's absence is discussed by Mike and Loco in the first episode of the second season, "Cherchez La Roommate." In this episode, Greta's former roommates, Mike and Loco, are upset by her leaving. Loco is particularly disturbed by the fact that Greta has married a gas station owner and moved to California. She is consoled by Mike who suggests that it must have been "true love."

The two remaining golddiggers place an ad in the newspaper for a new roommate, which is how they meet Gwen Kirby.

Gwen, like all good replacement characters, is almost a carbon-copy of her predecessor (she borrows Mike and Loco's nylons and uses Loco's bubble bath—just like Greta; her first name even begins with the same letter).

For reasons which cannot be explained, or determined by either *TV Guide* or *Variety,* the apartment house manager was at times Mr. Blandish and other times Mr. Tobey. Both characters appeared in various first season episodes; Mr. Blandish is more prominent in second season stories.

Even though there are two managers (sometimes called the

landlord by the girls), there is no reference by anyone to what happened to Mr. Blandish when Mr. Tobey shows up for the rent, and vice versa.

Mr. Blandish was played by Dabbs Greer, who appeared three times on the *Adventures of Superman* and later played Reverend Robert Alden on Michael Landon's family series, *Little House on the Prairie* (See Entry). Mr. Tobey was played by Joseph Kearns, who possibly left the series in 1959 so that he could play the first "Good Ol' Mr. Wilson" on *Dennis the Menace* (See Entry).

HOWDY DOODY

December 27, 1947–September 24, 1960.   NBC-Syndicated

Character:	Buffalo Bob Smith
Played by:	Bob Smith
Date(s):	December 27, 1947–September 3, 1954
	January 17, 1955–September 24, 1960
	September 1976 (*The New Howdy Doody Show*)

Replaced by:	Cornelius J. "Corny" Cobb
Played by:	Bobby "Nick" Nicholson
Date(s):	September 6, 1954–(various)
	September 1976 (*The New Howdy Doody Show*)

Replaced by:	Ed Herlihy
Played by:	Ed Herlihy
Date(s):	September 1954 (rotating)

Replaced by:	George "Gabby" Hayes
Played by:	George "Gabby" Hayes
Date(s):	September 1954 (rotating)

Replaced by:	Ben Grauer
Played by:	Ben Grauer
Date(s):	September 1954 (rotating)

Replaced by:	Gene Rayburn
Played by:	Gene Rayburn
Date(s):	September 1954 (rotating)

Replaced by:	Wright King
Played by:	Wright King
Date(s):	September 1954 (rotating)

Replaced by:	Bison Bill
Played by:	Ted Brown
Date(s):	October 1954–September 1955

Character:	Clarabell Hornblow
Played by:	Bobby "Bob" Keeshan
Date(s):	1948–June 1950
	June 23, 1950–December 23, 1952

"Buffalo" Bob Smith never turned in a wooden performance when providing the voice for his alter-ego, and the show's title character, Howdy Doody.

Replaced by:	Clarabell Hornblow
Played by:	Gil Lamb
Date(s):	June 1950–June 22, 1950

Replaced by:	Clarabell Hornblow
Played by:	Bernie Morshen
Date(s):	December 1952

Replaced by:	Clarabell Hornblow
Played by:	Henry McLaughlin
Date(s):	unknown

Replaced by:	Clarabell Hornblow
Played by:	Bobby "Nick" Nicholson
Date(s):	unknown

Replaced by:	Clarabell Hornblow
Played by:	Lew Anderson
Date(s):	September 1976 (*The New Howdy Doody Show*)

Character:	Howdy Doody
Played by:	Bob Smith (voice)
Date(s):	December 27, 1947–1954
	May 1956–September 24, 1960

Replaced by:	Howdy Doody
Played by:	Allen Swift (voice)
Date(s):	1954–May 1956

Character:	Princess Summerfall Winterspring
Played by:	Judy Tyler
Date(s):	1951–November 1953

Replaced by:	Papoose Gina Runningwater
Played by:	Gina Ginardi
Date(s):	January 26, 1954–September 1955

Replaced by:	Story Princess
Played by:	Alene Dalton
Date(s):	September 1955–December 1956

Replaced by:	Happy Harmony
Played by:	Marilyn Patch
Date(s):	September 1976 (*The New Howdy Doody Show*)

Character:	Zippy the Chimp
Played by:	Zippy (a chimpanzee)
Date(s):	–1957

Replaced by:	Kokomo Junior
Played by:	Kokomo Junior (a chimpanzee)
Date(s):	1957–September 24, 1960

It was two days after Christmas and the city of New York was buried in twenty-five inches of clean, wet and sparkling white snow. Because of the storm, the Duke Ellington Orchestra had canceled its performance for the evening. John Wayne's TYCOON and Gregory Peck's GENTLEMAN'S AGREEMENT didn't play that night because the movie houses didn't open. Walt Disney's BAMBI didn't brave the storm either, because Radio City Music Hall was closed. Even Broadway was dark.

Then, at five o'clock on this snowy Saturday, December 27, 1947, something magical happened. Nearly all of the 15,000 television sets able to receive the signal broadcast by NBC television in New York were tuned to a new children's program, *Puppet Playhouse.*

It was different, it was entertaining and it kept the kids spellbound for an entire hour. It was only meant to air three times, but that single Saturday night broadcast changed the course of television history. The program aired 2,342 more times over the next thirteen years before it faded to black on September 24, 1960. What was so significant about this little program, which featured the Frank Paris marionettes? It was, you see, the beginning of what would eventually become *The Howdy Doody Show.*

On this initial broadcast there was no ''Peanut Gallery,'' no Clarabell the Clown and no Howdy Doody. While the first two

had not yet evolved, there was a Howdy in the making. And puppeteer Frank Paris was still building him.

To cover for the missing ingredient, Bob Smith explained that Howdy Doody was hiding in the drawer of his desk. The gimmick was for Smith to speak to the shy and reclusive puppet and then have the camera cut to a close-up of the drawer while Smith, who was by no means a ventriloquist, answered in the familiar hayseed voice he had created on radio as Elmer.

The actual marionette was completed in January 1948 and was introduced by using the same scenario as before. The only difference was that this time the desk drawer wasn't empty; when the camera cut to the close-up of the drawer, out popped Howdy.

The kids erupted with joy and so did the staff, though this Howdy, the first of three puppets, looked more like Edgar Bergen's Mortimer Snerd than the Howdy Doody we all remember. This first design was painstakingly based on Smith's ignorant-voiced Elmer character and looked every bit as stupid. He had thick strands of yellow mop-like hair that stuck straight up, ears that stuck out, and a chin that a pelican would have been proud of.

As the series continued, it gained enormous popularity. It became so popular, in fact, that a top toy buyer at Gimbel's called the show's producer, Martin Stone, to discuss merchandising rights to a Howdy Doody doll. Before a deal could be struck, however, ownership rights to the character needed to be assessed. What Stone determined was that NBC owned the rights to the Howdy Doody marionette, while Bob Smith owned the program.

Meanwhile, Gimbel's rival, Macy's, approached the puppet-master directly in what must have been reminiscent of a scene from the 1947 film, MIRACLE ON 34TH STREET. Macy's later broached the subject with Bob Smith and Martin Stone who subsquently told Paris that he held no rights to the puppet. Paris did, however, hold the puppet itself in a cloth bag, and left the meeting with it after telling Smith and Stone, ''*Well. If you think you own him, you just see how you're going to do your show tonight!*''[43] The ''tonight'' Paris alluded to was 5:00 p.m., just four hours away.

The solution was so staggeringly simple, it was inspired. It was an election year. In Washington, President Harry S Truman was running against Thomas E. Dewey. In the *Howdy Doody* storyline, Howdy was running against the mysterious Mr. X for President of the kids and this is where the inspiration came in. The election storyline had already been introduced with the original Howdy marionette, and no one had any intention of altering Howdy's physiognomy. . . until now.

That afternoon, *Howdy Doody* opened with a shot of a United States map while Bob Smith announced that Howdy was at that very moment flying to Portland, Oregon to participate in the presidential primaries. Howdy was, of course, in radio contact with Mr. Smith.

These two-way radio conversations were handled in much the same manner as the ''empty desk drawer'' programs had been. Whenever Howdy spoke, the camera cut to a shot of the

---

43. Davis, Stephen. *Say Kids! What Time Is It? Notes from the Peanut Gallery.* Little Brown and Company, Boston, 1987, p. 49.

map. This kept the kids at bay, but the sponsors began to get antsy after a couple of weeks because there was no puppet for Buffalo Bob to do the commercials with. This dilemma was soon remedied by using a ploy that would later turn up in countless television series, including *Captain Video and his Video Rangers* (See Entry).

The writers already knew that a completely new Howdy had been designed by two artists working for Walt Disney studios, Norman Blackburn and Mel Shaw, and was at that moment being built in Los Angeles by Thelma Dawson, who had also submitted sketches to NBC. The show's writer then created what is now known as "the old plastic surgery excuse."

The Peanuts were told on previous broadcasts how handsome Howdy's opponent, Mr. X, was so it was okay for Bob to buffalo the kids. . . just a little. Smith told the youngsters that no women would vote for Howdy because he was just too ugly, and that he was going to have plastic surgery done to make him look better. Howdy soon radioed Buffalo Bob to tell him that the operation was a complete success and that he was on his way back home. Oh, just one more thing, the doctor had conveniently ordered Howdy to keep the bandages on his face for a few more weeks.

At the end of that day's program, Howdy Doody, who had parachuted out of his plane, was seen hanging on to his parachute, which was dangling from the ceiling of the NBC studio. His head was, of course, bandaged. This was not yet the new marionette being built in California, but an interim one made by a local puppet maker, Dorothy Zuconic, and it was this second Howdy Doody who did the commercials with Buffalo Bob that the sponsors had so desperately desired.

"On the next show, Mr. Smith asked the Peanut Gallery, 'Do you know what plastic surgery is, kids?'

" 'Nooooo!'

" 'Well, if people think their nose is too big, they get the doctor to take a little off. It really doesn't hurt a bit! Remember, it won't hurt Howdy, but it'll help him beat Mr. X, the handsomest man in the world!' "[44]

The new marionette that Velma Dawson constructed was unveiled on the June 8, 1948 broadcast. The switch was accomplished by wrapping the new puppet's head in bandages, to match the one that had been on the air for the past month. Then, at the end of that day's show, Buffalo Bob Smith, with the assistance of Clarabell the Clown, carefully and dramatically unwrapped the bandages to reveal the now adorable red-haired, freckle-faced little puppet that today we recognize as Howdy Doody.

Anyone who has ever seen *Howdy Doody* surely remembers the rather inept clown, Clarabell. In the earlier shows there was no clown at all. Clarabell was another one of those instances where a character grew out of necessity.

If you were lucky enough to have been a member of one of those first live studio audiences you might remember a young man in a sports jacket showing you to your seat, handing out prizes and telling you to keep quiet. That 20–year-old former page was Bobby Keeshan, and when NBC executive Warren Wade saw Keeshan on camera he ordered *Howdy Doody*'s producer, Roger Muir, to "get that guy into some kind of circus outfit."[45]

The circus outfits that NBC had on hand were two clown costumes; one had polka dots and the other had zebra stripes. They chose the latter, although Clarabell was occasionally seen wearing the other one. After a few days it was decided that this guy in the clown suit should have a clown's face to match, so NBC makeup artists, Dick Smith created one and Clarabell was born.

In October 1952, Bob Smith hired Bob Nicholson, a young radio musician from Boston. This was done because Smith, who was also a musician, wanted to add more music to the program. He had tried desperately to do this with Bobby Keeshan, and at one point arranged for him to take music lessons, but it was to no avail. Keeshan displayed an immediate resentment toward Nicholson because he feared that Nicholson had been hired to replace him as Clarabell, and he wasn't far off the mark. Keeshan also wanted more money and a piece of the million-dollar merchandising pie, and began to organize a cast strike.

The other members of the *Howdy Doody* staff who sided with Keeshan were Dayton Allen, who provided the voices for Mr. Bluster, the Inspector and Flubadub; Bill Lecornec, who played Chief Thunderthud and was the voice of Dilly Dally; and Rhoda Mann, the only puppeteer who could handle the unwieldy Howdy Doody marionette.

The group hired an agent to negotiate for them and retained the services of a puppetmaker to create a new set of marionettes so that in the event that they were fired, they would be prepared to produce their own show.

On the evening of December 23, 1952 the four disgruntled employees did a benefit at the Brooklyn Navy Yard at the request of Bob Smith, who was never directly involved in their negotiations. When they returned to the studio to rehearse that evening's show, the entire cast and crew was assembled by Roger Muir, who made the announcement: "We've had a dispute with Bobby, Dayton, Rhoda and Bill. We've decided that since they're not going to discharge their agent, we're going to discharge them. You're all excused. You can go."[46]

Keeshan had been replaced earlier, in June 1950, for two weeks by Gil Lamb. The reason given for Keeshan's firing then was that Bob Smith, Roger Muir and Eddie Kean were fed up with having to write special business for Clarabell because Keeshan couldn't read lines or play a musical instrument. His replacement, Gil Lamb, was described as a dancer and a mime who had been theatrically trained. He was also about six-foot-three and everyone noticed the switch. NBC affiliate stations were barraged with phone calls from outraged viewers and Bobby Keeshan was (reluctantly) rehired.

This time, regardless of the public's sentiments, Keeshan, along with the others, would have to be replaced.

Bobby Keeshan, would later become Captain Kangaroo, the

44. Davis, Stephen. *Say Kids! What Time Is It? Notes from the Peanut Gallery.* Little Brown and Company, Boston, 1987, p. 50.
45. Davis, p. 43.
46. Davis, p. 137.

gentle, lovable, intelligent and thoughtful children's show host whose program became a staple on CBS for more than 25 years after its initial broadcast on October 3, 1955.

Luckily, Bob Smith was the voice of Howdy, so all the producers had to do was pull a few strings and hire another puppeteer to replace Rhoda Mann. It was Rufus Rose who filled that slot on the puppet bridge temporarily; he was later replaced by Lee Carney while he became the show's puppetmaster, responsible for building new puppets while maintaining the old ones. They covered for the missing Clarabell by simply saying that he was hiding. But Clarabell couldn't hide forever, so Bernie Morshen, the show's property master, donned the familiar costume. He only lasted for about a week before someone suggested Bobby Nicholson. Nicholson refused at first, but when NBC offered him a better contract he sat down in the makeup chair. The costume and makeup looked great on Nicholson, but there was still some concern that the change would be noticed by the show's toughest critics, the kids.

To make the transition, writer Eddie Kean developed a storyline that had the missing Clarabell found at the bottom of Doodyville Harbor confined in an old-fashioned diving suit, the one that had the heavy spherical helmets with the grilled windows all around (like the one worn by Diver Dan). The clown was rescued after a full week with the diving helmet "stuck" on his head. When it was finally removed, no one noticed that Clarabell was no longer being played by the same actor. Better still, this new Clarabell showed a lot more enthusiasm and was also able to play the piano, the trombone and even the xylophone, in addition to the "Yes" and "No" bicycle horns worn on the front of his costume.

Voice man Dayton Allen was replaced by "The Man of a Thousand Voices," Allen Swift. A former stand-up comic, Swift was just breaking into television. Among his accomplishments was the fact that he ad-libbed 200 silent Max Fleischer *Out of the Inkwell* cartoons for Bray Studios so they could be sold to television. His more famous cartoon voices include Odie Colognie, Itchy Brother and Tooter Turtle from *King Leonardo and his Short Subjects*. The show aired on NBC from October 15, 1960 to September 28, 1963 and was produced by TOTAL Television, Leonardo Productions, Inc. The animation was supervised by Harvey Siegel, who was the production supervisor for *Rocky and His Friends*.

Howdy Doody's producers would have been satisfied with any reasonable voices for the show's stringed players, but Swift told them that he could most likely duplicate the original voices if he had a sample to listen to. He was given some recordings to practice with over the weekend and when he returned on Monday, he could duplicate all but one of the voices perfectly. The final piece to the puppet voice puzzle was Dilly Dally, the one voice even Allen Swift could not pick up.

Since it was generally felt that the mild-mannered Bill Lecornec was coerced into joining Keeshan and the others in their protest, he was approached, and eventually rehired.

There were no "major" casting problems for nearly two years. Then the unthinkable happened. On Sunday, September 5, 1954, at five o'clock in the morning, Bob Smith suffered a massive heart attack and was not expected to live. The diagnosis of his condition was coronary thrombosis, posterior, severe.

Thankfully, Smith was as strong as a buffalo and did not die, although he did spend the next nine weeks in the hospital.

That Monday, September 6th, Bobby Nicholson hosted *Howdy Doody;* his character was renamed Cornelius Cobb. The audience was told that Buffalo Bob was away on a secret mission. This solved one problem, but created another. Since Nicholson was hosting *Howdy Doody* as Corny Cobb, he couldn't portray Clarabell. The situation was further compounded by the fact that without Bob Smith, there was no voice for Howdy!

During the period of time that the auditions were being held for Bob Smith's replacement, Buffalo Bob was replaced by several different actors, who hosted the program on a rotating basis. These included Bobby Nicholson, Gabby Hayes and Ed Herlihy. But there was still no voice for the freckle-faced marionette. The solution to this dilemma is perhaps more easily seen by television historians than it was by those involved at the time. Why didn't they just ask "The Man of a Thousand Voices" if he could duplicate Howdy's voice? After all, when the original cast was fired, Allen Swift took over the voices of most of the other characters.

In Stephen Davis's book, *Say Kids! What Time Is It?*, Swift says he was asked by Bob Smith if he could do Howdy's voice and told Smith he couldn't so as not to bruise Smith's ego. In reality, although Swift had never actually attempted the voice, he felt confident that he could do it.

Howdy Doody producer Roger Muir gave Swift his second weekend homework asignment. This time his charge was to practice Howdy Doody's voice. Swift took his assignment seriously and worked diligently all weekend on perfecting the voice. When he felt he had mastered it, he tried it out on a friend's son who was blind and only knew Howdy by the sound of his voice. When Swift did his impression for the youngster, the child believed that Howdy Doody was right there with him in the room. Swift knew he had the voice down.

Everyone associated with the program, including Bob Smith, liked Allen Swift's Howdy so much that even after Buffalo Bob returned, Swift continued to provide the voice for Smith's alter ego. This freed Bob Smith from prerecording Howdy's voice on a cumbersome acetate recording system. When Allen Swift was fired in May 1956, Bobby Nicholson took over the voices of Mr. Bluster, the Inspector and Flubadub. Allen's swift departure was one result of cutbacks created by a drop in the ratings, caused by a new kids' program on ABC—*The Mickey Mouse Club*. Swift's contract was up for renewal and NBC just didn't pick up his option. The talented voice-man went on to host *The Popeye Show with Captain Allen Swift* on WPIX-TV, New York.

In the meantime, the auditions for Buffalo Bob's replacement continued. One performer who didn't make the grade was a twenty-nine-year-old singer, Merv Griffin, who had a hit single with the Freddy Martin novelty tune, "I've Got a Lovely Bunch of Coconuts," in 1949.

One of the better-known hosts at the time was Ben Grauer. A veteran newscaster, Grauer covered the opening of the 1939 World's Fair, was the first to broadcast from an airplane in 1949 and, for twenty years, helped Americans ring in the new year as he hosted the festivities from New York's Times Square.

Some of the other temporary hosts during September 1954 were Ed Herlihy, Wright King and Gene ''The Match Game'' Rayburn.

Eventually, the perfect full-time replacement for Bob Smith was found. He was New York radio disc jockey, Ted Brown, who assumed the Buffalo's duties as Bison Bill. Brown heard about the auditions from one of the Colgate Girls dancers he was working with on an NBC TV game show. While taking their bows after a show, one of the girls whispered to him, out of the corner of her mouth, that Bob Smith had suffered a heart attack and that NBC was looking for a replacement. Brown passed the audition and on one October evening, rode onto the set atop a white horse. He was wearing an old-style cowboy blouse and a white Stetson hat.

Two months later Smith's doctor offered him a Christmas present. He could go back to work, but only if he did not travel to New York. Since everyone wanted Buffalo Bob back, the radio studio that had been built in the basement of his New Rochelle, New York home for Smith's drive-time radio show was converted into a one-camera television studio featuring a ceiling-to-floor-length drape on the back wall, which served as the backdrop. Smith sat behind a dark wooden desk which was placed directly to the right of a seven-foot grand piano. It was a little cramped, but it did enable Buffalo Bob to get back on the air beginning with the January 17, 1955 broadcast.

Things were just getting back to normal when Bobby Nicholson became disenchanted with the Clarabell role.

''After two years I begged Roger Muir: 'Get me out of the goddamned clown suit.' I just couldn't stand it anymore. I was a serious musician who practiced for hours every day, and I was spending my life in makeup and telling children to shut up.''[47]

The director of the morning *Bob Smith Show,* Howard Lawrence Davis, was very taken by a talented member of The Honeydreamers, Lew Anderson. Anderson was a musician and singer who also happened to be a natural comic and a good ad-libber. Perhaps more important, he had already made an occasional appearance from Buffalo Bob's basement studio, as the Northwoodsman, Trapper John.

The Clarabell costume fit Anderson like a glove, and with his makeup on, no one could tell the difference. There was not as much concern over the Clarabell replacement as there had been when Nicholson took over, so no special introductory scripts were written. The only adjustment made was that Clarabell was written out of a couple of episodes so that Anderson could observe the show, which he had never seen. A few days later, Anderson stepped in as the sixth and final Clarabell and no one was the wiser.

Bison Bill made his last appearance on *Howdy Doody* in September 1955. A white horse, taller than the original steed that brought him to Doodyville, was used to help him make his exit. After a small ceremony Bison Bill said ''Well, kids, I guess it's time to say goody-by.'' It was at that moment that Ted Brown, who had done the best he could to fill Buffalo

Bob's boots, heard the horse relieving himself right on the set—everyone's a critic!

The regular female citizen of Doodyville was Princess Summerfall Winterspring. Originally she was a marionette, but she didn't have the appeal among young girls that the producers had hoped for. Consequently, there was very little demand for Princess Summerfall Winterspring products. The decision was made to replace the puppet, voiced by Rhoda Mann, with a live actress.

The actress who got the part was a beautiful eighteen-year-old charmer, who was said to have been able to sing like Judy Garland and Ethel Merman. Judy Tyler had won the audition by lying about her age (she was really 17) and by wearing a tight-fitting bra to help make her look younger.

The transition was again handled ''on camera'' as Chief Featherman (a marionette) escorted the Princess marionette back to the Tinka Tonka tribe to care for her aging parents. He then returned to Doodyville with a ''new'' princess. Following a rather elaborate Indian ceremony, a curtain parted and out stepped Judy Tyler, who stayed with *Howdy Doody* until she was nineteen. She appeared in various roles on the comedy-variety show, *Caesar Presents,* which aired on NBC from July 4 to September 12, 1955.

Judy Tyler's second and last film was the 1957 Elvis Presley dramatic musical, JAILHOUSE ROCK. In it, Ms. Tyler played Elvis' love interest, Peggy Van Alden. In the final scene of the film you could almost see, by the way Elvis held Ms. Tyler and lovingly nudged his head against hers, that there may have been more genuine attraction than acting taking place.

On July 4, 1957, three days after completing work on the film, Ms. Tyler and her new husband, Greg Lafayette, were involved in a horrible traffic accident on U.S. Highway 30. They survived the crash, but Lafayette died two hours later and Ms. Tyler the following morning.

In January 1954, the producers began looking for a replacement for Judy Tyler, largely because sales of Princess paraphernalia had dropped off.

The new Indian princess was Papoose Gina Runningwater. Sixteen-year-old ''Gina Ginardi was hired to replace Judy Tyler as the Princess, but she was ineffectual and was eventually let go. 'She didn't last too long,' one cast member recalls. 'Why? Because you don't replace Bob Hope with Morty Putz.'''[48]

The third Indian princess was not a young ''papoose,'' but a more mature mother figure in the person of the Story Princess as played by Alene Dalton beginning in September 1955. But she too was short-lived and left the show just prior to the ninth-anniversary telecast at the end of December 1956. Perhaps her serene story-telling just didn't fit in with the fast-paced antics of the other Doodyvillians.

The last female replacement on the original *Howdy Doody* show was Marty Barris, who played Peppy Mint, a character that was even shorter-lived than the Story Princess.

Zippy, the last regular member of the *Howdy Doody* cast to

47. Davis, Stephen. *Say Kids! What Time Is It? Notes from the Peanut Gallery.* Little Brown and Company, Boston, 1987. pp. 175–176.
48. Davis, Stephen. *Say Kids! What Time Is It? Notes from the Peanut Gallery.* Little Brown and Company, Boston, 1987, p. 163.

be replaced, was neither man nor wood. Zippy was a chimpanzee. And when he made the mistake of biting Buffalo Bob, he was replaced by the much tamer Kokomo Junior. A similar simian sacking occurred on *The Abbott and Costello Show* when Bingo the chimp bit Lou Costello. Bingo, however, was not replaced.

Howdy Doody left the air on September 24, 1960, only to return in a syndicated version that was shot in Florida in 1976. This slicker *Howdy Doody* show featured all of the regulars with the exception of "The Princess" character, who was now Happy Harmony, the Doodyville school teacher played by Marilyn Patch.

HUNTER

September 18, 1984–August 30, 1991.   NBC

Character:	Captain Lester Cain
Played by:	Michael Cavanaugh
Date(s):	September 18, 1984
Replaced by:	Captain Lester Cain
Played by:	Arthur Rosenberg
Date(s):	September 28, 1984–October 5, 1984
Replaced by:	Captain Dolan
Played by:	John Amos
Date(s):	November 2, 1984
	November 9, 1984
	March 23, 1985
	April 13, 1985
Replaced by:	Captain Wyler
Played by:	Bruce Davison
Date(s):	September 21, 1985–May 13, 1986
Replaced by:	Captain Charlie Devane
Played by:	Charles Hallahan
Date(s):	September 27, 1986–August 30, 1991
Character:	Detective Sergeant Dee Dee McCall
Played by:	Stepfanie Kramer
Date(s):	September 18, 1984–September 12, 1990
Replaced by:	Officer Joann Molinski
Played by:	Darlanne Fluegel
Date(s):	September 19, 1990–January 9, 1991
Replaced by:	Sergeant Chris Novak
Played by:	Lauren Lane
Date(s):	September 9, 1991–August 30, 1991

It is no surprise that the action formula created by Clint Eastwood as Harry Callahan in the first DIRTY HARRY film

in 1971 would eventually carry over to the small screen. What is surprising, however, is that it took thirteen years and five Dirty Harry films before it did. What is not surprising is that it was Stephen J. Cannell's action factory that did it.

Stephen J. Cannell Productions had scored a hit a few years earlier with *The A-Team*. The major difference between the two Cannell productions was that on *The A-Team* (See Entry), very rarely was anyone ever struck by a bullet, let alone killed. On *Hunter* the bullets regularly hit their mark, to the smirking pleasure of Detective Sergeant Rick Hunter (Fred Dryer).

That *Hunter* was violent is a given, but more importantly, the violence was not gratuitous. At crucial moments following chase scenes, when most television cops restrain themselves and read the baddies their Miranda rights, Hunter pulls the trigger. As cold-blooded as it may sound, there is definitely an emotional satisfaction in seeing murderers get theirs.

The actor cast as Hunter, television's answer to Dirty Harry, was Fred Dryer, who played defensive end for the New York Giants from 1969 to 1971 and was later traded to the Los Angeles Rams. His character, Rick Hunter, is an honest cop with an interesting skeleton in his closet—he's the son of a mobster. *TV Guide* said that you had to like Dryer because "He looks like Richard Widmark and talks like Clint Eastwood."[49]

Hunter's partner, Dee Dee McCall, also known as "The Brass Cupcake," is the widow of a cop named Steve who was shot and killed in the line of duty. Dee Dee, played by Stepfanie Kramer, had previously played Claudia in the situation comedy, *We Got It Made,* which aired on NBC from September 8, 1983 to March 30, 1984.

It's tough enough putting your butt on the line every day, and tougher when you're taking orders from a superior with whom you don't see eye-to-eye. It's even tougher when you don't even know who your superior is going to be from week to week, which is exactly what happened to *Hunter.*

In the series' debut on September 18, 1984, Hunter's boss, Captain Lester Cain, was played by Michael Cavanaugh, but by the October 5th episode Cain was already being played by another actor, Arthur Rosenberg.

A few weeks later, the precinct had a new leader, Captain Dolan, played by *Good Times* (See Entry) star, John Amos. He lasted for nearly six months but was ultimately replaced by Bruce Davison as Captain Wyler. Davison had previously played alien John Langley in the prime time science fiction, *V: The Series,* which aired on NBC from October 26, 1984 to March 22, 1985. He played George Henderson on TV's *Harry and the Hendersons.*

A few months later, Captain Wyler was replaced by Captain Charlie Devane. Devane, played by Charles Hallahan, may be best remembered as Ernie in the critically-acclaimed CBS series, *The Paper Chase,* which aired from September 9, 1978 to July 17, 1979.

Still, none of these changes was very disruptive to the continuity of the series, which did manage to maintain its leads until September of 1990, when Stepfanie Kramer was written out in the special two-part episode, "Street Wise."

The method for writing out Hunter's partner was to introduce

---

49. *TV Guide* Vol. 32, September 8, 1984, Issue # 1641, p. 70.

her old flame, Dr. Alexander "Alex" Turner, (Robert Connor Newman), who had proposed marriage to her. Dee Dee's decision is made more difficult by the fact that Alex wants to accept a research grant offered to him by Oxford University. Saying "yes" would mean that Dee Dee would have to leave the force and move to England with her new husband. Alex is offered a similar position at U.C.L.A. and says to Dee Dee, "Now all I need is a reason to stay. I believe you owe me the answer to a very important question." The answer to the question, popped in Part I, was "Yes, Alex. Yes."

The seasoned detective is naturally torn between her love of Alex and her job, but it is the shooting death of a fellow officer and the subsequent killing of his murderer by Hunter that helps her put her life into perspective. She has a heart to heart with Hunter.

HUNTER: He loves you very much. Do you love him?

DEE DEE: Yeah. I never thought that I could feel like this again after Steven died. But I do.

Following the beautiful wedding ceremony, Hunter and Captain Devane pause for a moment on the steps of the church.

DEVANE: Well, looks like the end of an era.

HUNTER: Oh, I don't know, Charlie. I think it could be the beginning of a new one.

The new era began with the seventh season opener on September 19, 1990, in which Darlanne Fluegel joined the cast as Officer Joann Molinski in the first of a two-part episode entitled, "Deadly Encounters."

Darlanne Fluegel came to the staff of the L.A.P.D. after a stint as Julie Torello, the estranged wife of Lieutenant Mike Torello on the NBC police drama, *Crime Story,* during 1978 and 1987.

In the January 9, 1991 episode, "Fatal Obsession," Joann is killed off—shot three times by a psychopathic woman, Loreen Arness (Ellen Wheeler). She is replaced by Sergeant Chris Novak, played by Lauren Lane.

In the article, "TV's Top Cop Flops with His Women Costars," that appeared in the March 9, 1991 issue of *TV Guide,* Darlanne Fluegel's publicist spoke about Fluegel's departure from the series, saying that it "was a mutual decision" and that she wanted to pursue other projects. Series star Fred Dryer, however, was a little blunter: "The chemistry wasn't there between Darlanne and me to have a love affair on screen. And Hunter needed to have a relationship with some female cop he's working with. So we had to bring in another woman."

THE HUNTER

July 3, 1952–December 26, 1954.   CBS-NBC

Character:	Bart Adams
Played by:	Barry Nelson
Date(s):	July 3, 1952–1954

Replaced by:	Bart Adams
Played by:	Keith Larsen
Date(s):	1954

International intrigue was big business in the early days of television. This entry in the genre was a CBS summer replacement series. It originally starred Barry Nelson as the wealthy American businessman, Bart Adams, who, among other things, was a master of disguise, not unlike the Rolland Hand character on *Mission Impossible* (See Entry).

When the series moved to the NBC network on September 26, 1954, some new episodes were produced with Keith Larsen in the lead.

While episodes of *The Hunter* were still airing in 1953, Barry Nelson turned from espionage to comedy in his role as George Cooper on the CBS sitcom, *My Favorite Husband.*

No longer disguised as Barry Nelson, Keith Larsen starred as the title character in the television Western, *Brave Eagle,* which aired on CBS from September 28, 1955 to June 6, 1956. He later played Drake Andrews on the CBS adventure series, *The Aquanauts* (See Entry). His film roles include Colonel Paul Tibbets, Jr. in the 1947 drama about the development of the atomic bomb, THE BEGINNING OF THE END, and Lieutenant Anson Harris in the 1970 disaster film, AIRPORT.

Barbara Eden as Jeannie gave viewers plenty of navel observatory time in *I Dream of Jeannie: 15 Years Later,* the 1985 pilot for a new series that co-starred Wayne Rogers in the Larry Hagman role of Captain Anthony ''Tony'' Nelson.

I

I DREAM OF JEANNIE

September 18, 1965–September 1, 1970.   NBC

Character: Captain/Major Anthony ''Tony'' Nelson
Played by: Larry Hagman
Date(s):   September 18, 1965–September 1, 1970

Replaced by: Major Anthony ''Tony'' Nelson
Played by: Wayne Rogers
Date(s):   October 20, 1985 (*I Dream of Jeannie . . . 15 Years Later*. NBC)

Replaced by: Mr. Bob Simpson
Played by: Ken Kercheval
Date(s):   October 20, 1991 (*I Still Dream of Jeannie.* NBC)

Character: Anthony Nelson, Jr. (as a baby)
Played by: unknown
Date(s):   October 20, 1985 (*I Dream of Jeannie . . . 15 Years Later*. NBC)

Replaced by: Anthony Nelson, Jr. (age 7)
Played by: Brandon Call
Date(s):   October 20, 1985 (*I Dream of Jeannie . . . 15 Years Later*. NBC)

Replaced by: Anthony ''Tony/J.R.'' Nelson, Jr. (age 12)
Played by: MacKenzie Astin
Date(s):   October 20, 1985 (*I Dream of Jeannie . . . 15 Years Later*. NBC)

Replaced by: Anthony ''Tony'' Nelson, Jr.
Played by: Christopher Bolton
Date(s):   October 20, 1991 (*I Still Dream of Jeannie.* NBC)

Character: General Wingard Stone
Played by: Philip Ober
Date(s):   September 18, 1965
               October 9, 1965

Replaced by: General Martin Peterson
Played by: Barton MacLane
Date(s):   1965–1969

Character: General Winfield Schaeffer
Played by: Vinton Hayworth
Date(s):   1969–1970

Replaced by: General Hatten
Played by: Michael Fairman
Date(s):   October 20, 1985 (*I Dream of Jeannie . . . 15 Years Later*. NBC)

Replaced by: General Wescott
Played by: Al Waxman
Date(s):   October 20, 1991 (*I Still Dream of Jeannie.* NBC)

Character: Jeannie's mother
Played by: Florence Sundstrom
Date(s):   unknown

Replaced by: Jeannie's mother
Played by: Lurene Tuttle
Date(s):   unknown

Replaced by: Jeannie's mother
Played by: Barbara Eden
Date(s):   unknown

Character: Captain/Major Anthony Nelson's mother
Played by: Spring Byington
Date(s):   November 14, 1967

Replaced by: Captain/Major Anthony Nelson's mother
Played by: June Jocelyn
Date(s):   unknown

In 1965, the U.S. space program was in full swing and was capturing the headlines and the imagination of the American public. On March 23, Grissom and Young's Gemini 3 piloted the first manned spacecraft to alter its orbital path. On June 3, Edward H. White II became the first American astronaut to

197

walk in space. And on September 18, 1965, Captain Anthony "Tony" Nelson of the United States Air Force was launched into orbit aboard the Stardust One spacecraft. What distinguished this flight from the others was that it launched the careers of Larry Hagman and Barbara Eden, the stars of this first situation comedy based "loosely" on the lives of these brave Americans. To be fair, their careers had already been launched; what this series did was put them into orbit.

In that first episode, the final stage of Captain Nelson's spacecraft misfired shortly after launch. When "control" (it was not referred to as mission control) realized that the Stardust One would not be able to maintain orbit, it was decided to abort the mission and bring Tony back home. The seventh fleet was notified to make the recovery, but Nelson's capsule had crashlanded, off course, stranding him on what looked like a tiny tropical island (referred to by Dr. Bellows [Hayden Roarke] as a desert island), presumably in the Pacific, although it was never mentioned where the island was located until the extension episode *I Dream of Jeannie . . . 15 Years Later.*

While on the beach, Captain Nelson finds a bottle, and when he opens it, out pops a genie—a beautiful genie at that. At first she speaks only in an ancient tongue. Nelson realizes the ramifications of releasing a genie from a lamp or bottle, as the case may be, and asking for a wish or three. But because of the language barrier, when Tony asks Jeannie to produce a rescue plane, she "blinks" a falcon. He then asks her for a boat, and when Jeannie conjures up a slave ship he responds by saying, "You're older than you look." He finally wishes the genie could speak English and then, in mid-sentence, Jeannie says, "Somehow I must find a way to please thee, master." She follows this up with, "Thou may ask anything of thy slave, master."

Captain Nelson then describes a helicopter to Jeannie and she produces one. He is afraid to take her home with him because he is afraid her presence could damage his career, so he sets her free. But Jeannie blinks herself back into her bottle and rolls it into Nelson's survival kit, which he, of course, takes home with him. Their relationship blossoms and their lives are never the same again.

Jeannie was played throughout the series by Barbara Eden who was Loco Jones in the 1950s situation comedy, *How to Marry a Millionnaire* (See Entry). In an interesting switch, the year before *I Dream of Jeannie,* Ms. Eden played Sylvia Kenton in the Universal comedy, THE BRASS BOTTLE. In this film, Sylvia is engaged to Harold Ventimore (Tony Randall), who purchases a three-foot-tall Kum Kum at an auction as a gift for his fiancée's father, Professor Anthony Kenton (Edward Andrews), a professor of Egyptology. When Harold opens the bottle, Burl Ives appears in a cloud of dark green smoke as the genie, Fakrash Alamash. Randall spends the rest of the film trying to keep the good-intentioned genie a secret from Barbara Eden.

Before any series can get on the air, there are always a few problems to be addressed. With *I Dream of Jeannie,* it was Barbara Eden's garb that needed attention—specifically, her harem pants.

Harem pants are traditionally cut to reveal the belly and navel. It is, after all, pretty difficult to perform a belly dance without exposing one's belly. The harem pants of Ms. Eden's costume, which is otherwise relatively authentic, were purposely designed to "hide" her navel. Navels were a taboo on television during the sixties.

"In that pre-Cher era, NBC censors required Eden to wear the only waist-high harem pants in existence.[1] 'With all the world's problems,' she [Barbara Eden] shrugs, 'I could care less whether my navel showed.' "[2]

Barbara Eden's ex-husband, Michael Ansara, who earlier starred as Cochise in *Broken Arrow,* remembers the "navel" incident a little differently. "It was a publicity man's idea—just public relations to build publicity on the show and build it up. They made a big issue out of NBC wanting to censor the idea of showing a navel on television. Things have changed a lot since then, of course, but that was a 'no-no' in those days. In one scene, her costume was cut a little low and it showed the navel, and they made a big, big issue out of that and kept it going on and on and on for a long time. Even to the point when she [Barbara Eden] did the *I Dream of Jeannie* reunion movie, they were still talking about her navel. So much was made out of that. It was really nothing to begin with. It was good publicity,"[3] said Ansara with a smile in his voice.

He was also able to dispel another ugly rumor—that Ms. Eden's navel was in some way deformed. "She had a perfectly normal navel. She had a very good midriff and a good-looking stomach,"[4] he concluded.

"During the sixties, network censors and executives were beginning gingerly to relax their mandates, but still Jeannie concealed the navel that men dreamed of. The pretty, homespun Kansas farm girl, Mary Ann, on *Gilligan's Island* was forced to hike her hip-huggers to hide her belly button."[5]

The producers of *Laugh-In* thought that perhaps they could debut Ms. Eden's navel, but they couldn't get the NBC censors to permit it either.

The harem costume seen throughout most of the 1985 reunion movie appears almost identical to the pink one used on the series. But for those patient viewers there is a prize in store at the very end of the movie, when Jeannie, at Tony's request, "blinks" herself into a beautiful white harem outfit which reveals Ms. Eden's navel in all its glory.

During the production of *Gilligan's Island* (See Entry), Dawn Wells, who played the innocent Mary Ann Summers, faced exactly the same problem. CBS has a similar ruling, which *Gilligan's Island* executive producer Sherwood Schwartz referred to as the " 'Intermittent Navel' rule." The network

---

1. The waist-high harem outfit wasn't exactly an original idea. In the 1964 comedy, THE BRASS BOTTLE, genie Tezra (Kamala Devi) wore a costume strikingly similar to the one designed for Ms. Eden.
2. Breu, Giovanna. *People,* July 10, 1978, pg. 75.
3. From an exclusive telephone interview with Michael Ansara on January 15, 1991.
4. *Ibid.*
5. Cox, Stephen. *The Addams Chronicles.* Harper Collins, New York, 1991. p. 52.

doctrine stated that "it was okay if a female navel appeared and disappeared. Permanent view of a female navel was *verboten*."[6] Schwartz satisfied the CBS censors by having Ms. Wells pull her hip huggers up an inch. Then when she walked, sometimes you saw her navel, sometimes you didn't, thereby creating what Schwartz called the peek-a-boo navel. Seventeen years later, Schwartz gave the CBS logo an eyeful when he costumed Mary Ann and Ginger for the 1981 reunion movie, *The Harlem Globetrotters on Gilligan's Island:* both Mary Ann's and Ginger Grant's navels made special appearances in their cheerleaders' low-cut grass skirt outfits.

Jeannie's loving "master" was played by Larry Hagman for the entire run of the series. Fifteen years later, when the reunion movie was being produced, Hagman had become a major television star as the rich and not so honest J.R. Ewing on the CBS evening soap, *Dallas.*

A caption underneath a photo of Barbara Eden dressed in her updated "Jeannie" costume read, "A light check on the *Jeannie* set reveals Eden in fine form, but even her genie powers couldn't persuade her original co-star Larry (J.R.) Hagman to return to the sequel."[7] In the article that followed, co-star Bill Daly was quoted as saying, "This is crazy—nothing's changed since 1965!"[8] "Needless to say, some things have changed. Wayne Rogers will play astronaut Tony Nelson, the part originally played by Larry Hagman (the *Dallas* star reportedly was willing to return for a cameo, but not the whole show)."[9]

It's a good thing that television genies don't hold grudges, because five years after the *Jeannie* reunion movie, Barbara Eden signed on to appear in several episodes of the thirteenth season of *Dallas.* Ms. Eden played a woman interested in buying Ewing Oil. It was the first time that she and Larry Hagman had appeared together since 1970.

The first words spoken by Wayne Rogers as Major Tony Nelson are: "Jeannie? Honey, I'm home." This was the perfect setup for Jeannie to say something silly like "Oh, Tony, you colored your hair." But as with Dick Sargent's first appearance on *Bewitched* (See Entry), no reference was made that might draw attention to the replacement actor—as if we didn't notice.

A detail that the audience may have noticed, if they looked closely enough, was that the space shuttle "Liberty Seven" being flown by Major Nelson was in reality the "Columbia," which is visible for just a moment during the triumphant touch-down sequence (courtesy of stock NASA footage).

Wayne Rogers is best known as Hawkeye's first swampmate, Trapper John McIntyre, in the highly-acclaimed CBS dramatic situation comedy, *M*A*S*H* (See Entry).

To bring up to date any viewers who may not have seen any of the original 139 episodes which have been running endlessly since 1965, in the reunion movie Jeannie blinks herself and her twelve-year-old son, Tony Jr. (MacKenzie Astin), to "the island in the Pacific" where she met his father. Then, via a short

refilmed sequence with Wayne Rogers that condenses slightly and alters the storyline of the first episode, Jeannie tells her son how she and Captain, now Major, Nelson first met and fell in love.

Other flashback scenes depict Tony Jr. as an infant and very briefly as a seven-year-old. The infant or infants used were uncredited, while Brandon Call's name appeared in the closing credits as "Tony Jr. at 7." The juvenile actor who played Tony Jr. for the remainder of the made-for-television movie was MacKenzie Astin, the son of Patty Duke of *The Patty Duke Show* (See Entry) and John Astin of *The Addams Family* (See Entry). In an obvious allusion to Larry Hagman's famous role, Tony Jr. is also referred to as "J.R." It was also during the 1985 season that MacKenzie Astin joined the cast of *The Facts of Life* as Andy Moffet.

Even though *I Dream of Jeannie* didn't go on the air until 1965, the writers for *The Tonight Show Starring Johnny Carson's* 29th and final anniversary show (October 3, 1991; NBC) took some liberty with the conflicting air dates to make a point about the advances in television by addressing Jeannie's undressed belly in Johnny Carson's opening monologue: "People often ask what has been the biggest changes in television?—there's too many to even enumerate. But back then in 1962, you could not show Barbara Eden's navel on *I Dream of Jeannie,* and today, kids named Doogie are losing their virginity in prime time."

Seventeen days later—exactly six years after *I Dream of Jeannie . . . 15 Years Later* aired—NBC blinked the now 4,233–year-old Jeannie back for a second made-for-television movie, *I Still Dream of Jeannie,* against competition that included the first of ABC's two-part *Dynasty, The Reunion* and the CBS broadcast of the 88th World Series.

Ms. Eden's costume has gone through a second redesign, with the harem pants now cut low enough to fully reveal Jeannie's navel. *TV Guide* ran an article in its October 19–25, 1991 issue that featured a color still of Barbara Eden in one of her two updated costumes, but the audience's interest should have been further piqued by the fact that the photo did not give a peek at Ms. Eden's navel, which had been airbrushed out. And even though—according to official *I Dream of Jeannie* navel observatory time—Ms. Eden's navel was clearly visible for more than seven minutes of the two-hour special, the TV movie did miserably in the ratings.

I Still Dream of Jeannie only pulled a 12.3 in the ratings with a 19 share, which put it in 39th place for the week. The poor ratings may have had something to do with the fact that Colonel Nelson (neither Larry Hagman nor Wayne Rogers) was not in the revival movie. Not surprisingly, no one seemed to wonder why Wayne Rogers did not return to reprise the role he had taken over in *I Dream of Jeannie . . . 15 Years Later,* but everyone wanted to know why Larry Hagman wasn't back.

On the October 18, 1991 episode of the popular internation-

6. Schwartz, Sherwood. *Inside Gilligan's Island. From Creation to Syndication.* McFarland & Company, Inc., Jefferson, North Carolina, 1988, pp. 155–156.
7. *People,* October 21, 1985. p. 61.
8. *Ibid.*
9. *Ibid.*

ally syndicated talk show *Geraldo*, a member of the studio audience asked guest Barbara Eden why Hagman had not been recruited to return to the role he had created twenty-six years ago.

QUESTION: Why is Larry Hagman not in the special now this weekend? I thought he was the master?

EDEN: We asked him. We wanted him to be. He finished thirteen years, you know, of *Dallas* and he was very tired. And what he told me was that he went to Europe for a vacation—I believe him.

GERALDO: Were you disappointed?

EDEN: I was.

Tony's absence was explained at the top of the movie, which began with beautiful NASA footage of a space-shuttle launch. The technique used was to over-dub scripted dialogue supposedly being spoken by mission control flight controllers.

VOICE 1:   Good luck on the mission, Colonel Nelson. Don't do anything we wouldn't do.

VOICE 2:   Oh Tony, your wife called. She wants you to pick up a loaf of bread on the way home.

The problem with this dialogue is that NASA would never engage in such light chatter during the launch, which is one of the most critical stages of a shuttle mission. Then again, this is only television, and the setup is important.

With Colonel Nelson out of the picture Tony Jr. (Christopher Bolton) asks his mother to save her magic for "the big things," which include making sure his father would be back in time to hear his speech on "What America Means to Me," which he will be presenting at the state finals in Austin, Texas. There is just one hitch—Jeannie must know where Tony is in order for her to transport him back. Problem is, Colonel Nelson is on a secret mission and his whereabouts are classified. This sets Jeannie off on her own mission—to locate her husband.

Complicating matters is "Jeannie": Jeannie's not so nice twin sister (played by Barbara Eden wearing a dark wig) wants her sister to return to Mesopotamia so that she may go to the plane of reality. She pleads her case with the wise sage Sham-Ir (Peter Breck), who must abide by the laws of the sacred scrolls which say, "A genie without an earthly master must return to Mesopotamia within three moons." And because Tony is in space, he no longer qualifies as an "earthly" master. But instead of enforcing the law, he grants Jeannie a fortnight to find a temporary master until her real master returns. Roger Healey (Bill Daly), who already knows Jeannie's secret, is disqualified because he is not single.

In a plot twist, Tony Jr. is kidnapped by some slapstick crooks and it is Ken Kercheval as "J.R." 's school guidance counselor, Mr. Bob Simpson, who helps Jeannie rescue him.

Back at the Nelson residence, just two minutes to midnight, Jeannie, who has not found a new master, says her goodbyes to Tony Jr. Just then, Mr. Simpson returns for his missing car keys and Jeannie does some fast talking to get him to say he'll be her new master; she promises not only to make him new keys, but to provide two new cars. Jeannie then asks Simpson if it's money he wants, and blinks a barrage of bills which begin to rain down on the befuddled educator. Simpson says, "All right—I'll be your new master." Jeannie and Tony Jr. jubilantly hug and dance, but Mr. Simpson interrupts: "Excuse me. Somebody please tell me what's going on?" Tony Jr. and Jeanie simultaneously plant kisses on Simpson's cheeks—FREEZE FRAME. Jeannie then unfreezes, looks at the camera and blinks on the closing credits.

Over the course of the series, Tony Nelson answered to a number of different generals, which is no earth-shattering news and had no effect on the series whatsoever, since the general was such a minor character. Even had this been a reality-based series, it is general practice for military men to transfer or be transferred on a regular basis.

Here are their dossiers. General Wingard Stone, who appeared in the first episode of the series, was played by Philip Ober who played Mr. William Beevor in the THE BRASS BOTTLE with Barbara Eden. He was also, at one time, married to Vivian Vance, the actress who played Lucy Ricardo's best friend on *I Love Lucy*. In the *I Love Lucy* episode, "Don Juan Is Shelved," Phil Ober was hired at the last minute to play Dore Schary, the head of the MGM studios, because the real Dore Schary decided, at the last minute, not to appear in the episode as himself.

General Stone and his daughter Melissa (Karen Sharpe) were written out of *I Dream of Jeannie* after the fourth episode. Stone was said to have accepted a position as a foreign ambassador; Melissa married an old boyfriend.

General Martin Peterson was portrayed by Barton MacLane, the same actor who starred as United States Marshal Frank Caine on the NBC Western, *The Outlaws*, (See Entry).

General Peterson's replacement, General Winfield Schaeffer, was played by Vinton Hayworth, who was the magistrate Galindo on the Walt Disney *Zorro* series. In *I Dream of Jeannie . . . 15 Years Later* Tony Nelson's commanding officer was General Hatten. General Hatten was played by Michael Fairman who had, a year earlier, taken on the role of Inspector Knelman on the CBS police drama, *Cagney & Lacey*.

In the most recent of the *I Dream of Jeannie* reunion movies a General Norman Schwarzkopf look-alike, Al Waxman, played General Wescott of the Lyndon B. Johnson Space Center. Viewers may have recognized Waxman because of his role as Lieutenant Albert Samuels in the CBS police drama, *Cagney & Lacey*.

Jeannie's mom was played by Florence Sundstrom, Lurene Tuttle, Barbara Eden and Spring Byington.

Ms. Sundstrom may be more familiar to television audiences as Belle Dudley, the role she played from 1955 to 1956 on the William Bendix version of *The Life of Riley*. As Vinnie Day, Ms. Tuttle was one of the only members of the cast who wasn't replaced on the CBS situation comedy, *Life with Father* (See Entry). She played Doris Dunston on yet another CBS situation comedy, *Father of the Bride*, which aired from September 29,

1961 to September 14, 1962. She later played Hannah Yarby, the head nurse on *Julia.*

The first actress to play Anthony Nelson's mom was Spring Byington, who is fondly remembered as Lilly Ruskin in that entertaining CBS situation comedy, *December Bride,* which aired from October 4, 1954 to April 20, 1961, and featured a young Harry Morgan as Pete Porter before he starred in his own spinoff series, *Pete and Gladys.*

In addition to her work in television, Ms. Byington appeared in more than thirty motion pictures. She played Marmee in the 1933 drama, LITTLE WOMEN; Miss Ettie Coombes in the original 1935 horror film, THE WEREWOLF OF LONDON; Mrs. Mitchell in the 1941 Gary Cooper holiday classic, MEET JOHN DOE; and Mrs. Suzi Robinson in the light comedy, PLEASE DON'T EAT THE DAISIES.

I LOVE LUCY

October 15, 1951–June 24, 1957.   CBS

Character:	Alvin Littlefield
Played by:	Gale Gordon
Date(s):	May 26, 1952
	June 9, 1952

Replaced by:	Mr. Chambers
Played by:	Arthur Q. Bryan
Date(s):	December 1, 1952

Character:	Charlie Appleby
Played by:	Hy Averback
Date(s):	November 2, 1953

Replaced by:	Charlie Appleby
Played by:	George O'Hanlon
Date(s):	January 14, 1957

Character:	Little Ricky Ricardo
Played by:	James John Gauzer
Date(s):	January 19, 1953

Replaced by:	Little Ricky Ricardo
Played by:	Richard Lee Simmons (twin)
Date(s):	unknown

Replaced by:	Little Ricky Ricardo
Played by:	Ronald Lee Simmons (twin)
Date(s):	unknown

Replaced by:	Little Ricky Ricardo
Played by:	Joseph David Mayer (twin)
Date(s):	October 4, 1954–May 30, 1955

Replaced by:	Little Ricky Ricardo
Played by:	Michael Lee Mayer (twin)
Date(s):	October 4, 1954–May 30, 1955

Replaced by:	Little Ricky Ricardo
Played by:	Richard Keith (Keith Thibodeaux)
Date(s):	October 8, 1956–September 25, 1960

Quite simply, *I Love Lucy* was, is, and probably always will be television's most popular situation comedy. And whether it was because of its popularity or the way television was run in the early days, there was very little tampering with the cast.

The idea for the series grew out of an offer to Lucille Ball to recreate on television the Liz Cooper role she was then playing on the radio version of *My Favorite Husband* (See Entry), opposite Richard Denning as her husband George. Ms. Ball instead suggested a new concept to star herself and her real-life husband, Cuban bandleader Desi Arnaz, but was turned down because William Paley at CBS didn't feel that Desi would be acceptable to the public as her husband because he was Cuban.

To prove him wrong, the Arnazes decided to strike out on their own. They produced a television pilot which they paid for with a $5,000 loan they had obtained. The show was sold to the Philip Morris Tobacco Company. And now with a sponsor in hand, CBS changed its mind about the "salability" of Lucille Ball and Desi Arnaz.

The new show was to be produced by Jess Oppenheimer and written by Oppenheimer, Madelyn Pugh (later Madelyn Davis) and Bob Carroll, Jr., the latter two both graduates of the *My Favorite Husband* radio show. Because the radio show was performed in front of a live audience the gags were played for laughs, so Lucille Ball knew Madelyn's and Bob's ability to write visually, which is why they were asked to write the script for the pilot.

Published sources have indicated that Lucy and Desi played Lucy and Larry Lopez in that unaired pilot. This is incorrect and was clarified by writer Bob Carroll, Jr. in an interview which aired on April 30, 1990 as part of *I Love Lucy: The First Show.*

This hour-long special, written and produced by Billy Van Zandt and Jane Milmore, featured the original pilot along with film clips, taped interviews with Lucy and Desi, Bob Carroll, Jr. and Madelyn (Pugh) Davis, and new taped wraparounds featuring Lucy and Desi's daughter, Lucie Arnaz.

Coproducer Billy Van Zandt explained that previously published stories of how the lost pilot was located under a bed were not completely accurate. "Executive Producer Bud Grant was a close friend of Joanne Perez, the widow of Pepito the Clown. The stories about the episode being lost and found under her bed are untrue. I made that up for P.R. reasons. Joanne knew what she had in her possession, she just didn't know it was the pilot,"[10] said Van Zandt.

---

10. From an exclusive telephone interview with Billy Van Zandt on January 7, 1991.

"And she didn't know people were looking for it. She just assumed that everyone connected with the show had a copy," [11] interjected co-producer Jane Milmore.

"She would show it during parties at her home," continued Van Zandt. "Finally, around the time CBS had aired the lost *I Love Lucy* Christmas show, Joanne [Perez] heard on the radio that people were looking for the pilot and wondered if it was the film she had been showing all of these years. Joanne called Bud [Grant] and asked if her print was the film they were looking for and he said, 'Yes, it is.' The next day, Bud went to CBS and made a deal with the stipulation that they could have the footage as long as GTP Productions could produce the special.

"Now this is four years since I had guest starred on *Life With Lucy* as a delivery man for a florist, and here we were interviewing Bob Carroll, Jr. and Madelyn (Pugh) Davis for our show. It was pretty wild. They are incredibly sharp and it was great meeting them," [12] said Van Zandt excitedly.

"They worked very similarly to the way Billy and I work," added Ms. Milmore. "They came in and looked at our office and my desk was neat and Billy's was a mess. They were amazed because that is exactly the way their office looked when they were writing *I Love Lucy*," [13] she said.

"In terms of who does the structuring, who does the dialogue, who does the storyline, it was identical to the way Jane and I work," [14] added Van Zandt.

When Van Zandt and Ms. Milmore were asked who handled what duties for their own work, Jane Milmore laughed, "Same as them." [15] Van Zandt glibly added, "The men did the same thing and the women did the same thing. The only difference is, everything we've learned about writing sitcoms we learned from them, and everything they've learned about writing sitcoms they learned from themselves." [16] Speaking about the naming of what became *I Love Lucy* (and the characters), Bob Carroll, Jr. said, "We were going to call it *The Lucy and Larry Lopez Show* but at that time there was a famous band leader, Vincent Lopez, and we thought that might be a little confusing for the audience, so we made it the Ricardos." [17]

The writers also used the same basic structure that had worked for them on Ms. Ball's radio program, with the husband and wife as the central characters and an older couple as their neighbors and chief foils. "We'd always planned to have neighbors on the show. In those days all the shows had neighbors. The people had to have somebody to talk to. But in the pilot there just wasn't room, there was too much else, and besides . . . we hadn't cast them yet," [18] explained *I Love Lucy* co-writer Madelyn (Pugh) Davis.

Producer Oppenheimer and the Arnazes wanted to hire Gale Gordon and Bea Benaderet to play Fred and Ethel Mertz, which were ostensibly the same sort of roles they had played on *My Favorite Husband,* but both were unavailable. Gale Gordon already had made a commitment to play Osgood P. Conklin, the principal of Madison High on the CBS radio program, *Our Miss Brooks.* He did, however, find time to join Lucille Ball in two episodes of *I Love Lucy* and later became her regular nemesis on *The Lucy Show* (See Entry), *Here's Lucy,* four *Lucy* comedy specials and her final series, *Life with Lucy,* which aired on ABC from September 20 to November 15, 1966.

Over at CBS television, Bea Benaderet was already playing Blanche Morton opposite the first of four Harry Mortons on *The George Burns and Gracie Allen Show* (See Entry).

The role of Fred Mertz had been offered to James Gleason (Max Corkle in the 1941 fantasy, HERE COMES MR. JORDAN) but he turned it down because "he didn't do television."

How then did William Frawley become Fred Mertz? As the story is told, Lucy didn't find William Frawley, the sixty-four-year-old Frawley found her. He was a well-known character actor who had appeared in many motion pictures including his highly visible role as Charlie Halloran, Judge Harper's confidant and political adviser in the 1947 Christmas classic, MIRACLE ON 34TH STREET.

He had worked with Lucille Ball before, when he played Martin in the 1945 MGM musical extravaganza, ZIEGFELD FOLLIES, but now had a reputation as being unstable and an alcoholic. Desi read Frawley the riot act, telling him that "if he ever showed up late to the set or couldn't perform, except because of illness, more than once, he'd be bounced out of the show." [19]

Fred Mertz' wife, Ethel Mae, was played by Vivian Vance, who was chosen by the program's director, Marc Daniels. He brought Lucy and Desi to a theater in La Jolla, California to see Ms. Vance performing in a summer theater production, *The Voice of the Turtle.* She, of course, got the part.

Auditions being part and parcel of show business, Ricky Ricardo had to pass an audition to get his job at "the club," the Tropicana. Though it was understood that there was a club owner, he was only seen three times. What is interesting is that the first time Ricky's boss is seen on camera, it is in "Lucy's Schedule": Gale Gordon appears as Mr. Littlefield, the "new" boss of the Tropicana. Mr. Littlefield is an extremely fastidious gent and after the Ricardos arrive an hour late for a dinner at the Littlefields (because Lucy set the clock back an hour to give herself more time to get ready) Ricky puts her on a strict time schedule. Two weeks later Gale Godon was back as Mr. Littlefield in "Ricky Asks for a Raise," but Mr. Littlefield and

11. From an exclusive telephone interview with Jane Milmore on January 7, 1991.
12. From an exclusive telephone interview with Billy Van Zandt on January 7, 1991.
13. From an exclusive telephone interview with Jane Milmore on January 7, 1991.
14. From an exclusive telephone interview with Billy Van Zandt on January 7, 1991.
15. From an exclusive telephone interview with Jane Milmore on January 7, 1991.
16. From an exclusive telephone interview with Billy Van Zandt on January 7, 1991.
17. *I Love Lucy: The First Show.* April 30, 1990. CBS.
18. *Ibid.*
19. Mitz, Rick. *The Great TV Sitcom Book.* Richard Marek Publishers, New York, 1980, p. 43.

his wife Phoebe (Edith Meiser) were never seen or heard from again. When "Ricky Loses His Voice" in the December 1, 1952 episode, it was Arthur Q. Bryan as Mr. Chambers who had trouble hearing him. Ricky's voice eventually returns—Mr. Chambers does not.

After the first 166 episodes were completed in the Ricardos' New York apartment, they moved to Connecticut for a taste of rural life. They did meet new neighbors in Connecticut, Ralph and Betty Ramsey, but these were not replacements for good old Fred and Ethel, who soon moved to Connecticut to join their closest friends.

Ralph Ramsey was played by Frank Nelson, who may have already been a familiar face to *Lucy* viewers, as he had appeared in eight *I Love Lucy* episodes. His most memorable character was that of quizmaster Freddie Fillmore, a part he played twice. His first appearance was in "The Quiz Show," the fifth episode of the series, on November 12, 1951. His second appearance as the radio show host was in the more memorable "Lucy Gets Ricky on the Radio" episode, in which Lucy gives Ricky the answers she stole—the only problem was that those answers were for a different set of questions! This episode originally aired on May 19, 1952.

Lucy's Connecticut neighbor, Betty Ramsey, was played by Mary Jane Croft, who was also no stranger to the *I Love Lucy* audience, as she had appeared in five earlier *Lucy* episodes before landing her recurring role. We met Mary Jane Croft as Cynthia Harcourt in the "Lucy Is Envious" episode, in which Lucy must portray a woman from Mars, from the Empire State Building, to promote the opening of a science fiction movie. If the promoter who hired Lucy looks familiar, that's because he's Herb Vigran, who turned up regularly as different crooks on the *Adventures of Superman*. Ms. Croft turned up regularly on *The Lucy Show* (See Entry), replacing Vivian "Viv" Bagley as Lucy's best friend. Her earlier work included *The Adventures of Ozzie & Harriet* (See Entry).

Back at the Ricardos' New York apartment there were only two regular characters who were played by more than one actor.

The first was Lucy and Ricky's on-screen son, Little Ricky, who was played by one infant, two sets of twins and an adorable five-year old who could speak a little Spanish, play the drums and looked enough like his television parents to have actually been their real son.

The infants and younger Little Rickys were played by twins because of the California child labor laws, which stipulated that children appearing on television and in motion pictures could "work" for only two hours each day. The infant Lucy gave birth to on the January 19, 1953 episode was played by James John Gauzer. He was replaced by the Simmons twins, who were replaced in turn by the four-year-old Mayer twins. It was reported that after working for a short time on *I Love Lucy,* Mrs. Mayer began to have second thoughts about having her boys in show business, and the three of them left the series and the industry.

The replacement for the Mayer twins was Keith Thibodeaux, a talented youngster who was billed as "The World's Tiniest Professional Drummer." This publicity intrigued Desi Arnaz, who, after seeing the youngster perform, signed him to a seven-year contract. He was given the stage name Ricky Keith. Ricky Keith became the envy of thousands of the nation's

youngsters not because he was appearing on television's most popular situation comedy but because he got to have Superman—the real Superman, George Reeves—land an appearance at his fifth birthday party.

But before the party was booked, Lucy and Ricky had to entertain their boring and competitive friends, Charlie and Caroline Appleby. The Applebys had come to visit in an earlier episode entitled "Baby Pictures," which starred Hy Averback as the overly proud father of Little Stevie, a boy the same age as the Ricardos' son. The name Hy Averback has appeared on television credits more often as a director than an actor. His most memorable television role was as Benny's father, Mr. Romero, on the Eve Arden situation comedy, *Our Miss Brooks.* Averback's directing credits include *The Real McCoys, F Troop* and *M*A*S*H.*

In the "Lucy and Superman" story, Ricky practices whipping out his snapshots from his inside breast pocket, so that he will be able to beat Charlie Appleby to the draw.

It's too bad he didn't have a snapshot of Charlie, because he would have noticed that Charlie was now being played by a different actor, George O'Hanlon. He had a pleasant enough face, but his most redeeming trait was his voice. It's a little difficult to pick up while watching him, but if you close your eyes when he says "Of course, every once in a while, Stevie does somthin' so cute I just can't resist telling about it," what you will hear is the voice of *Hanna-Barbera*'s futuristic family man. Meet George Jetson, the role O'Hanlon played in two versions of the half-hour series and a feature film, *JETSONS: THE MOVIE,* which was released in 1990 shortly after O'Hanlon's death.

George Reeves, who appears as Superman, probably has the most appropriate and prophetic line in the entire series.

In the story, when Lucy was afraid that Superman wouldn't be able to put in an appearance at Little Ricky's birthday party as she had promised, she dresses in a homemade Superman costume and winds up getting her cape caught on a drainpipe as she tries to make her entrance via the window.

Superman, who didn't want to disappoint Little Ricky, does show up at the party and is called upon to rescue Lucy, who is stuck on a narrow ledge outside the Ricardos' apartment. Superman effortlessly moves the piano away from the window and leaps out onto the building's ledge to save her.

Ricky is furious and begins yelling at Lucy.

RICKY: Of all the crazy things that you've done in the fifteen years that we've been married, this is really . . .

SUPERMAN: Wait a minute Mr. Ricardo, you mean to say that you've been married to her for fifteen years?

RICKY: Yeah, fifteen years.

SUPERMAN: And they call me Superman!

I MARRIED JOAN

October 15, 1952–October 6, 1955.   NBC

Character:	Minerva Parker
Played by:	Hope Emerson
Date(s):	October 15, 1952–1953
Replaced by:	Beverly
Played by:	Beverly Wills
Date(s):	1953–October 6, 1955

I Married Joan was in many respects very similar to *I Love Lucy.* There was an attractive, somewhat ditsy wife whose husband was more level-headed and had a very distinctive voice. On *I Love Lucy,* Ricky spoke with a funny Cuban accent. But if you thought that Ricky had a funny voice, you should have heard Judge Bradley Stevens. He sounded just like Mr. Magoo! But that was okay, because he was Mr. Magoo— actually, Jim Backus, who, at the time, was the voice of the U.P.A. cartoon, *Mr. Magoo,* and later became Thurston Howell III on *Gilligan's Island* (See Entry).

Just like Lucy Ricardo, Joan Stevens (Joan Davis) had a next-door neighbor with whom she was often in cahoots. Her name was Minerva Parker and she was portrayed by Hope Emerson, who had played Olympia La Pere in the 1949 Spencer Tracy/Katharine Hepburn comedy, ADAM'S RIB. Five years after leaving *I Married Joan,* Ms. Emerson played "Mother" on *Peter Gunn* (See Entry).

Minerva's replacement was a young college student, Beverly, who was Joan Stevens' sister on the series and Joan Davis's daughter in real life. Even though you couldn't tell that Beverly was Joan Davis's daughter by the credits, because her name was Beverly Wills, you could certainly tell she was her daughter by the way she spoke, which was exactly like her mother. What a girl, what a whirl, what a life.

I REMEMBER MAMA *see:* MAMA

IN THE HEAT OF THE NIGHT

March 6, 1988–May 3, 1988.   NBC
July 26, 1988–

Character:	Chief Bill Gillespie
Played by:	Carroll O'Connor
Date(s):	March 6, 1988–April 4, 1989
	May 16, 1989–
Replaced by:	Captain Thomas Dugan
Played by:	Joe Don Baker
Date(s):	April 25, 1989–May 16, 1989

Contrary to popular belief, it is possible for an actor to overcome typecasting and become a star in a very different type of role. Larry Hagman managed to leave Major Nelson behind when he left *I Dream of Jeannie* (See Entry) and became J.R.

Ewing on *Dallas.* Buddy Ebsen did it when he left *The Beverly Hillbillies* and became Barnaby Jones. And much to everyone's surprise, audiences no longer laugh when they catch sight of Carroll O'Connor, who now plays the tough Sparta, Mississippi police chief Bill Gillespie on the NBC police drama, *In the Heat of the Night,* which began as a made-for-television movie and a six-episode limited-run series. Gone is Archie Bunker, now replaced by no-nonsense Gillespie.

The portrayal of the somewhat gruff police chief is not so much a departure for O'Connor as it is a return to the sort of roles he has been playing in motion pictures and on television for more than thirty years. Carroll O'Connor has played serious roles in such motion pictures as LONELY ARE THE BRAVE, the 1962 Western in which he plays a truck driver named Hinton, who kills Jack Burns, played by Kirk Douglas, as he tries to cross a busy superhighway on horseback. He was Major General Hunter in the war drama, THE DEVIL'S BRIGADE, and General Colt in the 1970 picture, KELLY'S HEROES. Back in 1963, O'Connor appeared as Casca in the Elizabeth Taylor/Richard Burton film, CLEOPATRA.

His work on television prior to his starring role in the landmark Norman Lear situation comedy, *All in the Family,* includes appearances in episodes of *The Untouchables, Naked City, Dr. Kildare, Ben Casey, I Spy* and *Mission Impossible.*

The good news about *In the Heat of the Night* was that the limited-run series, which was to have its last installment air on May 3, 1988, turned into a regular weekly series. The bad news was that at the end of the 1989 season, Carroll O'Connor had to go into the hospital for coronary bypass surgery.

O'Connor's replacement was Joe Don Baker, who made his first appearance on the April 25, 1989 episode, "Forever Fifteen," but isn't named Chief Gillespie's replacement until the May 2, 1989 episode, "Ladybug, Ladybug."

There is no change in the series opening credits, which still include "starring Carroll O'Connor." The credits for this and the next few episodes include "Special guest appearance by Joe Don Baker."

The transition, which began the previous week is handled very neatly. The Chief is attending a month-long symposium on domestic terrorism, in Washington D.C., as the representative from Mississippi.

As the camera dissolves to the interior of the Sparta police headquarters, Detective Virgil Tibbs (Howard Rollins) is reading a letter from Chief Gillespie to his staff: "I am amazed at how sophisticated law enforcement is becoming, but Virgil, I guess that's no surprise to you. Before I sign off: Jamison, stay away from that piano, and Parker, be ready to answer the telephone. Best, Chief Bill Gillespie."

After Tibbs finishes reading, he is giving a few orders to his men when he is interrupted by Councilwoman Lorraine White (Pamela Garmon).

WHITE:	Gentleman, may I introduce your new acting chief of police, Thomas Dugan.
DUGAN:	Ain't my idea, guys. I'd just as soon be farmin'

or fishin' or playin' golf. Miss[20] White twisted my arm.

Mrs. White explains to Detective Tibbs that Captain Dugan is a temporary replacement for Chief Gillespie because the City Council did not want the police department "to be rudderless for a month."

The scene is also meant to create some tension and distrust between Tibbs and his men and the new acting chief, but that plot element doesn't last very long. Dugan assures Mrs. White that not only doesn't he anticipate any problems, he expects everyone to get along just fine. The tension isn't very strong between the two men and by the end of the episode Tibbs is calling Dugan, Tom, as they shake hands in an attempt to make the best of the temporary situation. In the episodes that follow, Dugan soon proves himself to be a good cop and an all-right guy.

Chief Gillespie is reintroduced in the May 16, 1989 episode, "The Pig Woman of Sparta," in which the men, bearing a cake and fixings for a welcome-home party, discover his home ransacked, Joann (Lois Nettleton) unconscious, and the Chief nowhere in sight.

The full-page promotional ad which ran in many editions of the October 21, 1989 *TV Guide* to hype the third-season opener read, "Emmy-winner Carroll O'Connor returns!" Didn't he already return on May 16th?

And yes, this series and lead characters are taken from the 1967 Academy Award-winning drama, IN THE HEAT OF THE NIGHT. Virgil Tibbs was played by Sidney Poitier and O'Connor's role was played by Rod Steiger who, from certain angles, looks remarkably like O'Connor.

THE INVISIBLE MAN

November 4, 1958–September 22, 1960.   Syndicated
September 8, 1975–January 19, 1976   NBC

Character:	Dr. Peter Brady
Played by:	Unknown
Date(s):	November 4, 1958–September 22, 1960
Replaced by:	Dr. Daniel Westin
Played by:	David McCallum
Date(s):	September 8, 1975–January 19, 1976
Character:	Sir Charles
Played by:	Ernest Clark
Date(s):	November 4, 1958–unknown
Replaced by:	Sir Charles
Played by:	Ewen MacDuff
Date(s):	unknown

Being seen on a weekly television series is not always a requirement for notoriety. Charlie Townsend was never seen on *Charlie's Angels,* Gladys Porter was never seen on *December Bride* nor was Orson on *Mork & Mindy.*[21] Still, they were all quite real and very popular characters.

The possibility of not being seen has often troubled actors, which is one of the reasons why Bela Lugosi turned down the original offer to portray the Frankenstein monster. The role was also devoid of dialogue, which further troubled Lugosi. After some rather unimpressive screen tests, it was perhaps the idea that he would be totally unrecognizable under the monster's make-up that scared him away. The actor who wasn't afraid of the Frankenstein monster was Boris Karloff. And it was that unseen role which made him a star. Yet, Karloff turned down the lead in THE INVISIBLE MAN for much the same reason Lugosi turned down the role of the monster. And that is also the role which catapulted Claude Rains to stardom.

A quarter of a century later, producer Ralph Smart decided to resurrect H.G. Wells' tale of the invisible one by adapting it for the small screen in a twenty-six episode syndicated series which he produced in England. Only this time the scientist, Dr. Peter Brady, chose to use his unique appearance, or lack thereof, to do good working as an agent with British Intelligence.

In this very interesting series, produced in England, Smart chose to keep the actor's face and name anonymous, to heighten believability. Audiences either saw an actor completely wrapped in bandages or simply heard his voice (when he was invisible). That is actually more than the production crew heard, as the voice of Dr. Peter Brady, who spoke with an American accent, was looped in during post production.

The identity of the actor, or actors, along with the secret of invisibility, is yet to be uncovered. There is some speculation that it may have been writer, producer and director, Ralph Smart behind those Foster Grants, but this is unconfirmed. British authors Leslie Halliwell and Philip Purser wrote in 1980 that the actor underneath the bandages was Tim Turner, but this too is only hearsay. What can be confirmed is that Tim Turner did appear as "Nick" in the tenth episode of the series, "Man in Disguise."

Authors Tim Brooks and Earle Marsh wrote in the fifth edition of *The Complete Directory to Prime Time Network TV Shows: 1946–Present* that Dr. Peter Brady/The Invisible Man was played by "an obscure actor named Jim Turner."

In 1957, Ralph Smart used the idea of an unknown actor for his little-known syndicated series, *The Iron Mask,* which is based on the Alexandre Dumas story. *The Man in the Iron Mask* was produced again with Richard Chamberlain in the dual role of King Louis XIV and his twin brother Philippe, in an NBC made-for-television movie that aired on January 17, 1977.

The Cabinet Minister, Sir Charles, in *The Invisible Man* series was initially played by Ernest Clark. After Clark vanished from the series, Ewen MacDuff materialized to carry on as Sir Charles.

---

20. In the same scene, Virgil Tibbs refers to her as Mrs. White, which is how she is listed in the credits.
21. Audiences never even heard Gladys Porter's voice, but the voice of Charles Townsend was provided by John Forsythe and the voice of Orson was Ralph James.

The next scientist to meddle in things men should leave alone came along fifteen years later. His name was Dr. Daniel Westin (incorrectly referred to as Mike Weston in a *TV Guide* article, "How to Make an Invisible Man) and he was played by former U.N.C.L.E. agent, David McCallum.

His misfortune grew out of his experiments in "teleportation." Teleportation, as everyone knows, is the system that went awry in the 1958 science fiction classic, THE FLY and all subsequent sequels, remakes and sequels of remakes.

In the pilot film, Dr. Westin explained to his boss, Walter Carlson (Jackie Cooper),[22] how his system worked.

> DR. WESTIN: We're working on a process whereby we transport matter from one point to another at the speed of light. In order to do that we first have to transform that matter, right?

There are several distinct differences among this series, the motion picture, the British television version. In the motion picture, Dr. Jack Griffin (Claude Rains) injected himself with monocaine, a drug made from a flower that grows in India. He also had to be buck naked to be invisible. In this series, Dr. Westin's clothes are also invisible, which allows him and the NBC censors to maintain their modesty. There is one small glitch. Although the clothing worn by him turns invisible, when the effects of the process begin to wear off, clothes remain invisible longer than the person. This is made clear in one scene when Dr. Westin, who is still invisible, begins to get dressed. "Modesty compels me to put this on since my clothes will be appearing after the rest of me."

In the film, eating presents a particular problem, as Griffin explains. "I must always remain in hiding for an hour after meals. The food is visible inside me until it is digested."

Dr. Westin faced no such problem. He explained, "Everything I take into my body—drugs, food, whatever—becomes invisible."

In the first television series, Dr. Brady works for the government, while Dr. Westin vehemently opposes warfare. When he is presented with the possibility that his discovery could fall into the wrong hands he declares, "As far as I'm concerned, the U.S. military is the wrong hands."

And unlike the motion picture and the 1958 series, in which both invisible men had to don bandages, gloves and eyewear (goggles in the first, sunglasses in the latter) to be seen, Dr. Westin relied on another advance in modern technology.

Dan's good friend was Dr. Nick Maggio, the world's leading plastic surgeon and the inventor of Dermapleque, a process designed to replace patients' missing skin tissue. Nick modifies his process, which he then calls "Dermaplex," to literally paint on Daniel's face and hands. Dermaplex is a latex-like material from which a skintight mask and gloves were made, à la *Mission Impossible*. This not only eliminated the need for messy bandages, safety pins and adhesive tape, but allowed actor David McCallum to do something no previous actor has been able to achieve in the part—to be seen throughout most of the series, which itself became invisible after only thirteen episodes.

Nick Maggio was played by Henry Darrow, who explained why he didn't continue in the role when the project went to series: "I had an offer, but it was not a good offer, which was to do six out of thirteen episodes, and I didn't want to sign up for that. I originally asked for thirteen out of thirteen and they turned that down, so I asked for eleven out of thirteen and they said, 'No.' I guess they figured that with the rest of the cast and the weekly bad guys they wouldn't have enough time to use my character in every episode, so I said that's it and turned down the series."[23]

Henry Darrow had played Lieutenant Quinlan on *Harry-O* (See Entry). He later played Zorro on *Zorro and Son* and most recently replaced Efrem Zimbalist, Jr. as Zorro's father, Don Alejandro de la Vega on the new *Zorro* (See Entry).

A few months later *The Gemini Man* appeared on the NBC schedule. Sam Casey, played by Ben Murphy, a government agent for INTERSECT who became invisible after being exposed to radiation in an underwater explosion while he was attempting to retrieve a space capsule. This series vanished after only five episodes.

There were also thirteen episodes of a rarely seen syndicated series, *The Invisible Man,* produced in Japan in 1966. A three-part miniseries, starring Pip Donaghy in a more faithful adaptation of the original story by H.G. Wells, aired on the Arts & Entertainment Cable network in September of 1985. And finally, those wacky guys who gave us *Gilligan's Island,* Sherwood and Lloyd J. Schwartz, produced a pilot for a proposed situation comedy entitled *The Invisible Woman* which starred Alexa Hamilton as Sandy Martinson and their favorite castaway, Bob Denver, as biochemist Dudley Plunkett. The pilot aired on NBC on February 13, 1983, but the series never materialized.

IRONSIDE

September 14, 1967–January 16, 1975.   NBC
May 4, 1993   NBC

Character:	Sergeant Eve Whitfield
Played by:	Barbara Anderson
Date(s):	September 14, 1967–April 15, 1971
	May 4, 1993

Replaced by:	Officer Fran Belding
Played by:	Elizabeth Baur
Date(s):	October 5, 1971–January 16, 1975
	May 4, 1993

Raymond Burr starred as the wheelchair-bound Chief Robert T. Ironside for so long that it appeared as though a miracle had occurred when he walked back into the courtroom as Perry Mason (See Entry) in 1985.

The reason for the wheelchair is that Chief Ironside of the San Francisco Police Department was crippled by an assassin's bullet that shattered his spinal column. He continued his work for the force along with a team of special agents.

22. In the series, Craig Stevens took over the Jackie Cooper role of Walter Carlson. Stevens is best known for his role as Peter Gunn (See Entry).
23. From an exclusive telephone interview with Henry Darrow on January 19, 1991.

During the long and successful run of *Ironside,* which lasted for 120 episodes, there was only one change in supporting cast.

Sergeant Eve Whitfield was played for the first four of eight seasons by Barbara Anderson. The role won her an Emmy in 1968 for Outstanding Performance by an Actress in a Supporting Role in a Drama. She was nominated twice more for Emmys, but lost both times. In 1969 she lost to Susan Saint James in the category of Outstanding Continued Performance by an Actress in a Supporting Role in a Series, and in 1970 to Gail Fisher of *Mannix* in the same category she had won in 1968.

The 1970/1971 season was her last, and she left in a contract dispute. *TV Guide* wrote, "The pretty new face is Elizabeth Baur, who joins the series as Off. Fran Belding."[24]

Ms. Baur had just completed work as Teresa O'Brien, on the CBS Western, *Lancer,* which aired from September 24, 1968 to September 9, 1971. Ms. Baur, the daughter of 20th Century Fox casting director Jack Baur, had a bit part as the fourth policewoman in the "Nora Clavicle and the Ladies's Crime Club" episode of *Batman,* which aired on January 18, 1968.

"Twenty-five years ago the story began. Now Raymond Burr is back as Ironside. He came back to save a young woman accused of murder. A twenty-fifth Anniversary event. Retiring was easy. Coming back could be deadly." So spoke the thick-voiced announcer in the teaser promo before the showing of *The Return of Ironside* began on May 4, 1993. The two-hour made-for-television movie reunited all of the members of the original cast including both Barbara Anderson and Elizabeth Baur. Back was Don Galloway as Detective Sergeant Ed Brown and Don Mitchell as Mark Sanger, now a judge.

Also appearing was Dana Wynter as Mrs. Katherine "Kate" Ironside. This was not a replacement as Ms. Wynter had appeared in two episodes of the series as Ironside's girlfriend and "long lost love." The only change was her name. In the December 11, 1969 episode, "Beyond a Shadow," Dana Wynter appeared as Tracy Oliver, while in the September 27, 1973 episode, "In the Forests of the Night," her name was changed to Alexandra. Would the real Mrs. Ironside, please stand up.

ISIS

September 6, 1975–September 2, 1978.   CBS

Character: Cindy Lee
Played by: Joanna Pang
Date(s):   September 6, 1975–September 3, 1977

Replaced by: Renee Carroll
Played by: Ronalda Douglas
Date(s):   September 17, 1977–September 2, 1978

For forty-four episodes girls . . . and boys (of all ages) tuned in to CBS every Saturday morning to watch the live action adventures of *Isis,* television's newest superhero.

The great appeal of this show was twofold . . . and centerfold. There were superhero adventures for the younger viewers and the lovely actress and model JoAnna Cameron (who, as Marilyn Michele, appeared topless in the 1971 comedy, B.S. I LOVE YOU) for those viewers who were past puberty . . . way past according to the demographics of viewer mail.

Isis was the second live adventure series to be offered by CBS from the Filmation Studios, which later produced *Jason of Star Command* and *Land of the Lost.* The first was *Shazam!* (See Entry). *Isis* (*The Secrets of Isis*), with the start of the 1977/1978 season, focused on a Larkspur, California, high school science teacher, Andrea Thomas. The thing that set this show apart from other superhero adventures was that this superhero was a woman, and a very beautiful one at that.

The legend for this character did not come out of the pages of dusty old comic strips and comic books like Superman, Tarzan, Wonder Woman and Sheena. *Isis* sprang from the mind of Marc Richards at Filmation Studios. His creation was billboarded as the "Dedicated foe of evil, defender of the weak, and champion of truth and justice." (Superman already had the "American Way" covered.)

Andrea gets her powers from an Egyptian amulet she finds while on a scientific expedition in Egypt. The talisman originally belonged to an Egyptian queen who had received it from the Royal Sorcerer, Thuhaupee.

Miss Thomas tapped into the powers of Isis, the Egyptian goddess of fertility (of all things),[25] by holding the pendant, which she wore as a necklace, and calling out, "O mighty Isis." That's all it took to lose her glasses, lengthen her hair and outfit her in an adorable little white tunic with a short skirt. Other accouterments included a headband and necklace with magic stones in matching settings. But Isis couldn't just leap into the air like Superman and Captain Marvel. She had to summon the power of flight by reciting a little iambic pentameter: "O Zephyr winds which blow on high, lift me now so that I may fly."

Like Filmation's *Shazam!,* each episode of *Isis* was dripping with valuable social lessons such as honesty, friendship and trust.

In a Superman-like role reversal, the superhero with the double identity in this series also has a co-worker who is just a little too thick to make the connection. Andrea's Lois Lane-type is a fellow science teacher at Larkspur High School, Rick Mason, played by Brian Cutler. Dr. Barnes, who was head of the science department, was played by Albert Reed, who had played Inspector Frank Dawson on the NBC police series, *Chase,* which ran from September 11, 1973 to August 28, 1974.

The high school student/teaching assistant most often seen kissing up to Miss Thomas for the first two years was Cindy Lee, played by Joanna Pang.

In 1977 the program grew from a segment of *The Shazam! Isis Hour* to its own time slot, where it appeared as *The Secrets of Isis.* Cindy Lee was gone and a new student, Renee Carroll, played by Ronalda Douglas, took her place.

24. *TV Guide.* Vol. 19, No. 40, Issue #966, October 2, 1971, p. A39.
25. Some sources incorrectly refer to Isis as the goddess of nature.

IT TAKES A THIEF

January 9, 1968–September 14, 1970.   ABC

Character:	Chief Noah Bain
Played by:	Malachi Throne
Date(s):	January 9, 1968–April 22, 1969
Replaced by:	Wallie Powers
Played by:	Edward Binns
Date(s):	September 25, 1969–September 14, 1970

Since *It Takes a Thief* was essentially about a former bad guy, why not have his superior played by a former bad guy.

Robert Wagner starred as Alexander Mundy, a professional cat burglar now working for the S.I.A. branch of the United States Government in exchange for his eventual release from the San Jobel Prison.

His superior officer, Chief Noah Bain, was played by Malachi Throne, himself a former Bat villain, False Face, on *Batman* (See Entry).

After the first two seasons, Noah Bain's role was stolen by Edward Binns, who appeared for the remainder of the series as Mundy's superior, Wallie Powers. Binns had previously starred as Detective Lieutenant Roy Brenner in the CBS police drama, *Brenner*. The initial run of the series aired from June 6, 1959 to September 1962. Ten new episodes were shot in 1964 and added to the fifteen episodes that were already airing as reruns. *Brenner* left the air on September 13, 1964.

J

JASON OF STAR COMMAND

September 9, 1978–September 5, 1981.   CBS

Character:	Commander Canarvin
Played by:	James Doohan
Date(s):	September 9, 1978–September 1, 1979

Replaced by:	Commander Stone
Played by:	John Russell
Date(s):	September 15, 1979–September 5, 1981

Having already gone where no man had gone before, James Doohan, who had played Chief Engineer Montgomery Scott, "Scotty" to his friends, on the NBC science fiction, *Star Trek,* was given a command of his own in 1978. Each Saturday morning Doohan (sans his familiar Scottish accent) appeared as Commander Canarvin, the head of Star Command, the secret section of Space Academy, which was located on a man-made planetoid.

"Obviously I'm typecast. Not only as a Scotsman, which I didn't play on *Jason of Star Command,* but I'm also typecast as a spacemen. They were looking for someone who obviously knows how to handle himself in space. That is so ridiculous. An actor should be able to play any kind of character, but they put these little tags behind actors' names such as 'Has done space.' In other words, you don't get the part in ALIEN unless you've done space before,"[1] explained Doohan.

Under the guidance of Commander Canarvin, Jason, played by Craig Littler, sets off on dangerous and exciting adventures in his Starfire spacecraft—usually to thwart the evil Dragos' attempts to enslave planets for his empire.

Dragos was played by character villain Sid Haig, who has probably been beaten up on television more times than any other actor. He was caught repeatedly on *Mission Impossible,* was an outlaw on the pilot for *Alias Smith and Jones,* and was beaten up by the A-Team. Even Agent 86 got the drop on him in "The Greatest Spy on Earth" episode of *Get Smart,* which aired on NBC on November 5, 1966.

"I stayed with *Jason of Star Command* for one year before quitting because they just didn't give me enough to do,"[2] said Doohan. "I was the commander, but while Craig [Littler] was off doing all the stuff I was back at Star Command and I only had a couple of words to say in every episode. You know, it's fun going to the bank, but that's not enough to keep an actor interested. It certainly wasn't enough to keep me interested anyway,"[3] Doohan concluded.

The initial run of fifteen- and later twenty-minute serialized installments of *Jason of Star Command* aired as a regular segment on *Tarzan and the Super 7* program and ended on September 1, 1979.

A week later, *Jason of Star Command* appeared as its own half-hour live-action show with one major difference. Commander Canarvin was replaced by the somewhat taller Commander Stone, who was played by John Russell. Like Doohan, John Russell also had a past of standing up for law and order. The major difference was that Russell meted out justice in the Old West instead of in outer space. His most famous role was that of Marshall Dan Troop in the ABC Western series, *The Lawman,* which aired from October 5, 1958 to October 2, 1962.

THE JEFFERSONS

January 18, 1975–July 23, 1985.   CBS

Character:	Lionel Jefferson
Played by:	Mike Evans
Date(s):	January 18, 1975–August 2, 1975
	September 23, 1979–July 23, 1985

Replaced by:	Lionel Jefferson
Played by:	Damon Evans
Date(s):	September 13, 1975–September 16, 1979

When the Jeffersons moved on up and out of Queens to their swanky East Side apartment, George (Sherman Hemsley) and Louise's (Isabel Sanford) son, Lionel, was still being played by Mike Evans, who had played Lionel all along on *All in the Family* (See Entry).

Apparently, the good life didn't agree with Lionel, because within nine months of movin' on up, he moved out. "There was

---

1. From an exclusive telephone interview with James Doohan on September 13, 1990.
2. *Ibid.*
3. *Ibid.*

Just one big happy family—hardly. This is an obvious posed shot of *The Jeffersons* cast who were never this chummy on the series. Forcing smiles are (clockwise, from the top left): in-laws Tom Willis (Franklin Cover), Helen Willis (Roxie Roker), and Jenny Willis Jefferson (Berlinda Tolbert); Lionel Jefferson (Damon Evans), Olivia ''Mother'' Jefferson (Zara Cully), George Jefferson (Sherman Hemsley), Louise ''Wheezie'' Jefferson (Isabel Sanford) and annoying neighbor Mr. Harry Bentley (Paul Benedict).

no question of money. He was unhappy and, speaking for myself, he was not alone. It was by mutual agreement,''[4] said Producer Norman Lear.

This was the wording used in the CBS press release issued on

July 18, 1975: ''Damon Evans replaces Mike Evans, no relation, who by mutual agreement left *The Jeffersons* following completion of the first season. Evans is a singer as well as an actor and had appeared in the off-Broadway musical *Hair*

---

4. Mitz, Rick. *The Great TV Sitcom Book*. Richard Marek Publishers, New York, 1980, p. 346.

and came to television by way of a twenty-week recurring role on the CBS soap opera, *Love of Life*.''

Lionel's character was rewritten to explain that he had decided to move out of his parents' apartment, but would return occasionally for visits. When he did return, it was Damon Evans who did the visiting.

The real Lionel, Mike Evans, went over to Danny Thomas' situation comedy, *The Practice,* to play Lenny. In less than a year (January 30, 1976--January 26, 1977) *The Practice* folded, leaving Evans without series work.

Meanwhile, replacement Damon Evans left *The Jeffersons* at the end of the 1978/1979 season. That is when Lionel became one of those *Twilight Zone* characters that are spoken about but never seen. Finally in September 1979, Mike Evans, the original Lionel Jefferson, returned to his old TV family after being away for four years.

Lionel was the only member of the cast to have come and gone and come again. Everyone else remained intact. There were, however, three changes in cast from the introduction of these characters on *All in the Family.*

In the episode ''Lionel's Engagement,'' which aired on February 9, 1974, Lionel's fiancée, Jenny, was played by Lynne Moody. Her parents, the Willises, were played by Charles Aidman and Kim Hamilton.

Lynne Moody later played the first Tracy Curtis Taylor on *That's My Mama* (See Entry) and Polly Dawson on *Soap* from 1979 to 1981.

Charles Aidman has made more than one hundred appearances on episodic television including several episodes of *The Californians, Gunsmoke* and *Mannix.* He was the astronaut in the *Twilight Zone* episode, ''And When the Sky Was Opened,'' and later became the narrator of the updated *Twilight Zone* series, which aired on CBS from September 27, 1985 to December 12, 1986. He also was seen briefly in 1968 as James West's assistant, Jeremy Pike, in four episodes of *The Wild Wild West* (See Entry).

On *The Jeffersons* Tom Willis was played by Franklin Cover; his wife, Helen, by Roxie Roker; and their daughter, Jenny Willis (later Jenny Willis Jefferson), by Berlinda Tolbert.

JEFF'S COLLIE *see:* LASSIE

JIMMY HUGHES, ROOKIE COP

May 8, 1953–July 3, 1953.   DuMont

Character:	Officer Jimmy Hughes
Played by:	William ''Billy'' Redfield
Date(s):	unknown

Replaced by:	Officer Jimmy Hughes
Played by:	Conrad Janis
Date(s):	unknown

One of television's earliest rookie cops was Jimmy Hughes who had just returned to New York after serving a military hitch in Korea. He joined the force in order to avenge the death of a cop who had been killed in the line of duty while he was overseas. That cop was Jimmy's father.

The earlier episodes of this short-lived series starred Billy Redfield in the title role. Redfield later was part of television history on *The Marriage,* the NBC sitcom which only ran from July 8 to August 19, 1954. It made history because it was the first network series to be telecast in color.

The second actor to play Jimmy Hughes was Conrad Janis, who is best know to television sitcom audiences as Frederick McConnell, Mindy's dad on *Mork & Mindy,* which aired on ABC from September 14, 1978 to June 10, 1982. Mindy was played by Pam Dawber, her alien roommate by Robin Williams.

JOE & VALERIE

April 24, 1978–January 19, 1979.   NBC

Character:	Frank Berganski
Played by:	Bill Beyers
Date(s):	April 24, 1978–May 10, 1978

Replaced by:	Frank Berganski
Played by:	Lloyd Alann
Date(s):	January 5, 1979–January 19, 1979

Character:	Stella Sweetzer
Played by:	Pat Benson
Date(s):	April 24, 1978–May 10, 1978

Replaced by:	Stella Sweetzer
Played by:	Arlene Golonka
Date(s):	January 5, 1979–January 19, 1979

Joe Pizo and Valerie Sweetzer had one of those storybook teenage romances. During the day they both held down fairly ordinary jobs, she at a cosmetics counter in a department store and he in his dad's plumbing store. But when the sun set their lives were magically transformed on the lighted dance floor of the discotheque where they first fell in love.

''When I was cast for *Joe & Valerie* they told me that we want the series to start with the very last frame of SATURDAY NIGHT FEVER. There is no question that John Travolta opened the door to the industry that made the New York street kid 'hot,' ''[5] explained series star Paul Regina.

Just like real teenagers, their initial courtship lasted just four weeks.

When the series returned from hiatus on January 5, 1979, Joe's roommate, Frank, was being played by Lloyd Alann and Valerie's mom, Stella, was being played by Arlene Golonka,

---

5. From an exclusive telephone interview with Paul Regina on January 30, 1993.

who more than ten years earlier had played Millie Swanson on the *Andy Griffith Show* (See Entry) spinoff, *Mayberry R.F.D..* A year before that she played Mrs. Margie Myers on the Marlo Thomas sitcom, *That Girl* (See Entry).

"There were two sets of four episodes and that's where the cast changes were made. Also, our set was changed from a disco to a bar, not to mention my marital status from single to married. [Joe and Valerie's whirlwind romance led to their marriage on the January 12, 1979, broadcast]. After the first four episodes we were [Fred] Silvermanized. We went from very streetwise single people in a disco to the more acceptable married couple in a corner bar. We played pool more than we drank—which made us more acceptable to middle America. And I think that it was these changes that torpedoed the show—it took the heart out of it," said Regina.

"Although I never heard any reasons for the cast changes, one can surmise that after the shows began airing there was another quality they wanted out of the Frank Berganski character. So rather than medium height, blond and very coiffured they went to darker hair, taller look—I think they were trying to sell more posters.

"The change from Pat Benson to Arlene Golonka may have had something to do with Pat's characterization of Valerie's divorced mother. Pat's Stella was very quirky and you never knew where she was going to go next. By comparison, Arlene Golonka was more of a stable mother figure,"[6] concluded Regina.

Joe & Valerie's honeymoon ended one week later when the series was canceled after a total of eight episodes. Ah, young love.

THE JOE PALOOKA STORY

1953.   Syndicated

Character: Knobby Walsh
Played by: Luis Van Rooten
Date(s):   1953

Replaced by: Knobby Walsh
Played by: Sid Tomack
Date(s):   1953

Heavyweight boxer Joe Palooka began in 1928 as a comic strip drawn by Ham Fisher, and came to television by way of motion pictures. The first bell sounded in 1934. That Reliance/United Artists film, PALOOKA (also known as JOE PALOOKA), starred Stuart Erwin as the prize fighter and Jimmy Durante as his manager, Knobby Walsh. Erwin later starred in his own situation comedy, *The Stu Erwin Show* (See Entry).

Unrelated to this JOE PALOOKA comedy was a series of B pictures produced by Monogram between 1946 and 1951. These films starred Joe Kirkwood, Jr. in the title role. His manager was played at various times by Leon Errol, James Gleason and William Frawley.

As the good-natured protagonist, Joe Palooka rarely smelled blood, but Joe Kirkwood, Jr. did smell money. Kirkwood purchased the television rights to the character and produced thirty-nine episodes of *The Joe Palooka Story* for syndication, with himself cast as Palooka.

Television's Knobby Walsh was first played by Luis Van Rooten who had played Dr. Thompson from 1949 to 1950 on the NBC soap opera, *One Man's Family*. Van Rooten was also the first Caribou Jones in the DuMont adventure series, *Major Dell Conway of the Flying Tigers* (See Entry).

The second Knobby was played by Sid Tomack, the same actor who played Jim Gillis to Jackie Gleason's Chester Riley in *The Life of Riley* (See Entry) and Irma's first boyfriend, Al, on the CBS situation comedy, *My Friend Irma* (See Entry).

THE JOEY BISHOP SHOW

September 15, 1962–September 20, 1964.   NBC
September 27, 1964–September 7, 1965.   CBS

Character: Freddy
Played by: Guy Marks
Date(s):   1962

Replaced by: Larry Corbett
Played by: Corbett Monica
Date(s):   1963–September 7, 1965

Nice guy comedian Joey Bishop originated the character of Joey Barnes, an assistant press agent in the Los Angeles firm, Wellington, Willoughby and Jones. The series, which first aired on September 20, 1961, featured a large cast, and just never seemed to work. Hence a revised *Joey Bishop Show* was born on September 15, 1962.

The only holdover from the first cast was Joey Bishop as Joey Barnes. Everything else had changed. His job, his cast, and eventually his network.

Bishop, who was referred to as a comedian by everyone, played a Johnny Carson-type talk show host. Like all good talk show hosts, Joey Barnes had an agent. His original agent was Freddy, who was played by Guy Marks. Five years later Marks co-starred on Tim Conway's Western situation comedy, *Rango*, which aired on ABC from January 13 to September 1, 1967.

Joey's new agent was his former writer, Larry Corbett, who was played by comedian Corbett Monica, said to have won "The 1963 TV Writer of the Year Award" in the episode "Joey vs. Larry the Writer." In a conversation with Joey, Larry says, "I write 'em—you tell 'em." But before Corbett Monica played Larry, he played Johnny Edwards, a comedian at the Purple Pussycat Night Club in a 1963 episode, "Joey's Replacement."

Interestingly enough, Monica's first television appearance was on a 1961 segment of the *The Jack Paar Show*, which was in fact the predecessor to the real *The Tonight Show Starring Johnny Carson*.

---

6. From an exclusive telephone interview with Paul Regina on January 30, 1993.

JOHNNY JUPITER

March 21, 1953–June 13, 1953   DuMont
September 5, 1953–June 12, 1954   ABC/Syndicated

Character: Ernest P. Duckweather
Played by: Vaughn Taylor
Date(s):   March 21, 1953–June 13, 1953

Replaced by: Ernest P. Duckweather
Played by: Wright King
Date(s):   September 5, 1953—May 29, 1954

Johnny Jupiter was a puppet with a social conscience, and the program, which was named after this inquisitive little inhabitant of the planet Jupiter, may have also raised the social consciousness of the American viewing public.

The *Johnny Jupiter* program was produced by Martin Stone, who owned Kagran, the merchandising division of *Howdy Doody,* and later produced the Jackie Gleason classic, *The Honeymooners.* The program, officially classified as a children's program, was, according to its principal writer, Jerry Coopersmith, really aimed at the entire family. In a *New York Times* article Coopersmith said, "We know that both children and adults watch the show, but I don't write for either group."

The little Jupiterian with the peanut-shaped head commented on American society while conversing with Ernest P. Duckweather, a janitor at the television studio who just couldn't keep his hands off of the broadcast equipment. His fiddling accidentally put him in contact with two emissaries of the planet Jupiter, Johnny and B-12, and Johnny's robot friends, Major Domo, the head robot,[7] and Reject, the factory-rejected robot. When Ernest speaks to Johnny, Major Domo and Reject on his TV screen, they are hand puppets, but when Reject comes to earth he appears as a human-size robot played by an actor inside of a costume.

Gilbert Mack was the talent responsible for providing the voices for all of the puppets, but no screen credit is given to the actor playing the life-sized Reject.

Duckweather was originally played by Vaughn Taylor, who played Joseph Peterson in the 1964 crime drama, FBI CODE 98, originally produced in 1962 as a pilot for a potential series, which never aired. He also appeared as the dog in the NBC science fiction special based on Charles Darwin's theory of evolution. The forty-five-minute special aired on November 10, 1946.

The series left the DuMont network in September 1953. At that time several changes were made in the series. Duckweather was no longer a lowly janitor but a clerk in the Frisby General Store. Electronics was now his hobby and was the means to achieving the same end—communicating with his pals on Jupiter. Mr. Horatio Frisby was played by Cliff Hall and Ernest P. Duckweather was now played by Wright King, who in 1960 co-starred as Steve McQueen's young sidekick, Jason Nichols, on the CBS Western, *Wanted: Dead or Alive.*

JULIA

September 17, 1968–May 25, 1971.   NBC

Character: Paul Cameron
Played by: Paul Winfield
Date(s):   March 11, 1969–January 27, 1970

Replaced by: Steve Bruce
Played by: Fred Williamson
Date(s):   September 15, 1970–May 25, 1971

Joining the ranks of television programs with single parents—such as *The Andy Griffith Show, The Courtship of Eddie's Father, Nanny and the Professor, My Three Sons, Family Affair* and *The Lucy Show*—was *Julia.* Not such a big deal on the surface. But what made *Julia* so unusual was not that she was a single mother like Doris Day's Doris Martin on *The Doris Day Show,* but that she was a black female—the first to star in her own network television series. In a *TV Guide* article, January 1968, Art Peters wrote, in language which now dates itself, "Diahann Carroll may be the first Negro woman star of a weekly television drama series, if present plans jell and a pilot film she recently made is picked up by NBC."

The plans did jell, with only one minor change: the series became a situation comedy instead of a drama. What was perhaps more significant was that Ms. Carroll's character, Julia Baker, was a professional woman—a nurse, not a domestic.

In the storyline, Julia was a single parent because her husband was killed in Vietnam. This, of course, left her open for dating. Her first relationship was with Paul Cameron, played by the outstanding dramatic actor, Paul Winfield. Schooled at UCLA, Paul Winfield has appeared in more than three dozen episodes of series, including *Perry Mason, Mission: Impossible, Room 222* and *Ironside.* He received an Emmy nomination for his portrayal of Dr. Martin Luther King in the NBC miniseries which aired from February 12 to 14, 1978. Winfield's motion picture credits include Clark Tyrell, the captain of the U.S.S. Reliant, who selflessly gave his life by turning a phasor on himself to protect his friend and comrade, Admiral James T. Kirk (William Shatner) in STAR TREK II: THE WRATH OF KHAN.

At the start of *Julia*'s third season handsome ex-football pro Fred Williamson picked up the ball dropped by Winfield.

Williamson, a surprisingly talented actor for a former sports figure, has appeared in more than a dozen motion pictures. His roles include Spearchucker in the 1970 war comedy, M*A*S*H, and Ben in the 1975 Richard Pryor comedy, ADIOS AMIGO, which he also wrote, produced and directed.

---

7. A major-domo is defined in *Webster's II New Riverside University Dictionary* as "1. The chief steward or butler in the household of a sovereign or noble."

JUSTICE

April 8, 1954–March 25, 1956.   NBC

Character:	Jason Tyler
Played by:	Gary Merrill
Date(s):	April 8, 1954–June 23, 1955

Character:	Richard Adam
Played by:	Dane Clark
Date(s):	1954–June 1955

Replaced by:	Richard Adam
Played by:	William Prince
Date(s):	October 2, 1955–March 25, 1956

Taking his lead from Jack Webb's successful police drama, *Dragnet,* which was based on real stories taken from the files of the Los Angeles police department, producer David Susskind used the files of the National Legal Aid Association as the basis for his live series, *Justice.* The program was actually the brainchild of John Rust, an executive of the U.S. Steel Corporation, who originally produced the show in the summer of 1953 on ABC's experimental program, *Album.*

The first regular character to appear in this series was Legal Aid attorney Jason Tyler. Tyler was played by Gary Merrill who was so convincing in the role that the February 12, 1955 issue of *TV Guide* reported, "One woman, for instance, insisted that actor Merrill be assigned to handle her Legal Aid case." Merrill turned down the case, but did accept other roles on television such as Dr. Leonard Gillespie on the syndicated series, *Young Dr. Kildare* (See Entry). He has also appeared as Walter Guilfoyle in the ABC crime show, *The Mask,* which ran from January 10 to May 16, 1954.

Gary Merrill's last regular series role was as Lou Sheldon, city editor of *The Globe,* on all fifteen episodes of the CBS newspaper drama, *The Reporter,* which aired from September 25 to December 18, 1964. He has, however, made dozens of appearances in episodes of *Alfred Hitchcock Presents, Rawhide, The Twilight Zone, Ben Casey, Medical Center* and *Movin' On.*

Merrill was replaced by attorney Richard Adam, who was played by both Dane Clark and William Prince. Clark, who appeared in episodes of many early television series including *Wagon Train* and *The Untouchables,* later played Lieutenant Arthur Tragg on the reunion episode of *Perry Mason* (See Entry). Perhaps not so coincidentally, Clark's replacement, William Prince, had previously co-starred with Gary Merrill as Peter Guilfoyle on *The Mask.* In addition to appearing in at least as many series as Gary Merrill, William Prince starred in the title role of the NBC soap opera, *Young Dr. Malone,* from 1958 to 1963. Some of his episodic television appearances were on *Studio One, Inner Sanctum, Kojak, Quincy, M.E.* and *Little House: A New Beginning.*

One other actor, Dennis O'Keefe, was listed in *TV Guide* as "the Legal Aid man" in "The Deadly Silence" episode which aired on September 16, 1954. In 1957 Dennis O'Keefe was hired to host the NBC suspense program, *Suspicion,* but left after two weeks. He was not replaced until the summer of 1959, when Walter Abel hosted several reruns of the programs that were produced after O'Keefe's departure.

K

KAREN

January 30, 1975–June 19, 1975.   ABC

Character:	Dale Busch
Played by:	Denver Pyle
Date(s):	January 30, 1975

Replaced by:	Dale Busch
Played by:	Charles Lane
Date(s):	February 6, 1975–June 19, 1975

After school let out for the cast of *Room 222,* Karen Valentine, who had played Alice Johnson, emerged as a bona fide television star. The successful series aired on ABC from September 17, 1969 to January 11, 1974 and earned Ms. Valentine an Emmy in 1970 for Outstanding Performance by an Actress in a Supporting Role in a Comedy.

When she was not teaching English at Walt Whitman High, Karen Valentine was teaching the rest of the country about *Love American Style,* in many of the blackout sketches which appeared on that ABC series. She then graduated to her own situation comedy, *Karen,* in which she played Karen Angelo, the single, spunky and quite cute staff member working for the Capitol Hill citizens' committee, Open America.

Karen Valentine once complained that she hated the word "cute," which was so often used to describe her. But, she is cute. And it is clearly okay to be cute in Hollywood, because that is one of the reasons she was given the opportunity to work for Open America on her very own sitcom.

The founder of Open America, Dale Busch, was played on the first episode only by that handsome hillbilly, Denver Pyle. Pyle's television credits include Briscoe Darling on *The Andy Griffith Show,* Buck Webb on *The Doris Day Show* and Uncle Jesse Duke on *The Dukes of Hazzard.*

For the remaining twelve episodes of *Karen,* Charles Lane took over the role and responsibilities of Dale Busch. For those who don't recognize his name, Charles Lane is unquestionably the industry's nastiest man. In fact, he has made a fine career as the quintessential curmudgeon since the early 1930s. Frankly, on film he has never, ever been a nice guy. He was the all too inquisitive reporter in Frank Capra's black comedy, ARSENIC AND OLD LACE. Quite simply, Charles Lane is the epitome of someone you just love to hate.

Mayberry's Sheriff, Andy Taylor, said it best: "You know somethin', Barney, when that man's time comes he ain't gonna go like everybody else, he's just gonna nasty away!"

Sheriff Taylor was actually speaking to Deputy Fife about Ben Weaver (Tol Weaver), who was evicting a struggling young family from their home in "Andy Forecloses," an episode of *The Andy Griffith Show.* But maybe he was really speaking about all of the Charles Lane types of the world.

If you still can't place Charles Lane, here are a few more clues. Among his many guest roles on *I Love Lucy,* Charles Lane played Ricky's accountant, who does his penny-pinching best to keep Lucy Ricardo on a budget in "The Business Manager" episode which aired on October 4, 1954. He rejoined Lucy for a short time as Mr. Barnsdahl on *The Lucy Show* (See Entry). He co-starred as

Karen Valentine, however, was not television's first Karen. Debbie Watson (right) starred as the title character in *Karen* opposite Mary LaRoche (left) as Barbara Scott, in a segment of NBC's *90 Bristol Court* sitcom which aired from October 5, 1964 to January 4, 1965.

Ned Cooper with Dobie Gillis' mom, Florida Friebus as Jenny Ludlow, on his own short-lived sitcom, *Love Nest,* which was syndicated during the 1974/1975 season.

Charles Lane reached the zenith of his crotchetiness, in what is perhaps his best-remembered role, Homer Bedloe. Mr. Bedloe was the vice-president of the C.F. & W. Railroad on *Petticoat Junction* (See Entry), where for five years, from 1963 to 1968, he did everything within his authority to close down the Hooterville station and take the Cannonball out of service.

Wherever Charles Lane is today, he is without a doubt being a major pain in the ass!

KNIGHT RIDER

September 26, 1982–August 8, 1986.   NBC
May 19, 1991   NBC

Character:	Bonnie Barstow
Played by:	Patricia McPherson
Date(s):	September 26, 1982–May 6, 1983
	September 30, 1984–August 8, 1986
Replaced by:	April Curtis
Played by:	Rebecca Holden
Date(s):	October 2, 1983–September 30, 1984
Replaced by:	Shawn McCormick
Played by:	Susan Norman
Date(s):	May 19, 1991

Not unlike *The Dukes of Hazzard* (See Entry), the true star of this action series was an automobile. In this case it was a sleek, black Pontiac Trans-Am named KITT, which was short for Knight Industries Two Thousand. What set this vehicle apart from others in its class, such as James Bond's Aston Martin and Batman's Batmobile, was not just its 300 m.p.h. speed, its flamethrowers or smoke bombs. KITT had something only one automobile had before—KITT could speak. But this car was not former undercover cop Michael Knight's (David Hassel-hoff) mother. The car and the money to finance his crime-fighting efforts were bequeathed to Michael Young by a dying millionaire, Wilton Knight, who saved his life and gave him a new face, a new name and a new car.

The haughty voice of the car was provided by William Daniels, who was Benjamin Braddock's father in the 1967 comedy, THE GRADUATE. While providing the voice for KITT, William Daniels was also saving lives as Dr. Mark Craig on the NBC medical drama, *St. Elsewhere.*

Keeping the car's onboard computer in top running order was the beautiful computer whiz, Bonnie Barstow, played by Patricia McPherson in the first, third and fourth seasons. During her one-season absence, the computer programming and maintenance were handled by April Curtis, played by Rebecca Holden.

Ms. Holden's career seemed to be cruising along at an accelerated clip, as she had indicated in a 1984 *TV Guide* interview in which she said that she expected her relatively small role on *Knight Rider* to be expanded to include some comedy and perhaps even an occasional song and dance number. It was at about that time that the announcement was made that Ms. Holden would not be returning for the third season because Patricia McPherson was coming back to reprise her role as April Curtis.

Knight Rider 2000 was a two-hour made-for-television movie that aired Sunday, May 19, 1991—more than five years after the cancellation of the original series. It was set in the near future (February 19, 2000) and was geared to sell as a new series, but hasn't appeared to date.

Returning were David Hasselhoff as Michael Knight, Edward Mulhare as Devon, the head of the Knight Foundation, and William Daniels as the erudite voice of KITT. Missing were most of the original KITT and Bonnie Barstow.

The person responsible for dismantling KITT was foundation scientist and engineer Russ Maddock (Carmen Argenziano), who sold off most of the electronic components to research firms in order to keep the Knight Foundation solvent. KITT's body was recycled.

Naturally, Devon was able to persuade Michael, who left the foundation in 1990 to operate an unprofitable bass charter boat, to return. And it was Michael who insisted that Maddock buy back the computer components that made KITT, KITT.

Maddock was able to get most of the electronics back, except for one memory chip that was sold for medical research and was used to save the life of a cop who had been shot in the head at point blank range.

That cop, Shawn McCormick, played by Susan Norman, quit the force after her accident and joined Knight Industries where her computer-aided memory could be of enormous help tracking down the gun runners and crooked cops. This made Michael's new partner much more than KITT's computer whiz—it made her a part of KITT.

The familiar black Trans Am was replaced by a sleek red and more futuristic-looking Knight 4000 that was based on the Dodge Stealth.

KOJAK

October 24, 1973–April 15, 1978.   CBS
November 4, 1989–April 7, 1990   ABC

Character:	Detective Robert ''Bobby'' Crocker
Played by:	Kevin Dobson
Date(s):	October 24, 1973–April 15, 1978
Dates(s):	December 3, 1990 (*The ABC Saturday Mystery,* ''It's Always Something.'' ABC)
Replaced by:	Detective Winston Blake
Played by:	Andre Braugher
Date(s):	November 4, 1989 (*The ABC Saturday Mystery,* ABC).
	December 2, 1989 (*The ABC Saturday Mystery,* ABC).
	January 6, 1990 (*The ABC Saturday Mystery,* ABC)
	February 3, 1990 (*The ABC Saturday Mystery* ABC).
	April 7, 1990 (*The ABC Saturday Mystery,* ABC).

In this unusual scenario, the made-for-television-movie *The Marcus-Nelson Murders* was *not* planned as a pilot. But after writer Abby Mann and director Joseph Sargent won Emmy awards, producer Matthew Rapf began the work of developing the series which would become *Kojak*.

The series was named *Kojak* after the lead character in the *Marcus-Nelson Murders*. Choosing Telly Savalas to play the hero is a prime example of casting against type. Except for his role as Big Joe in the 1970 war film, KELLY'S HEROES, this bald-headed actor with the crooked nose and the mole on his left cheek had most often played heavies such as Ernst Stavro Blofeld in the 1969 James Bond film ON HER MAJESTY'S SECRET SERVICE. Savalas made a wonderful Bond villain; it is just too bad that James Bond wasn't in the film.[1]

During the early 1970s Telly Savalas bounced around the industry and did some regrettable work in foreign films for audiences in France, Spain, Italy and Mexico. This experience, coupled with his earlier decision to turn down the lead in *Harry-O*, moved him to accept the role of Lieutenant Theo Kojak. The decision was the right one because it led to a steady paycheck, public recognition and adulation, an Emmy and a Golden Globe award, and that all-too-elusive intangible—stardom.

As in many police dramas, Savalas worked with an ensemble cast who played the other members of his team at Manhattan South's 13th Precinct. Among the most visible were Captain Frank McNeil, (Dan Frazer), Lieutenant Robert Crocker (Kevin Dobson), Detective Saperstein (Mark Russell), and Detective Stavros, who was listed in the opening credits during the first and second seasons as Demosthenes. Demosthenes was the bushy-haired rotund actor who played Stavros. This, however, was only his middle name. His first and last names were George Savalas; he was Telly's brother. And it is likely that this bit of nepotism was intentionally kept from the public until the character caught on, which he did. From the third season on George Savalas' name appeared in the credits.

The *Kojak* series ended in 1978, only to return seven years later in a two-hour made-for-television movie, *Kojak: The Belarus File*, which aired on CBS on Saturday, February 16, 1985.

In this film, all of the members of the original cast returned to recreate their roles, except for Kevin Dobson. It was reported in *TV Guide* that Dobson "sent his regrets from *Knots Landing*,"[2] where he was starring as attorney Mack MacKenzie—Michelle Lee's new husband in the series. On *Kojak*, his character was not replaced, just written out of the storyline as Lieutenant Kojak was working on the case with Dana Sutton, a State Department official played by Suzanne Pleshette.

With the success of *Kojak: The Belarus File,* Kojak was promoted to a police inspector when he returned on February 2, 1987 in *Kojak: The Price of Justice.* The story, like that of *The Belarus File,* was based on a novel. This one was adapted from *The Investigation* by Dorothy Uhnak. *Kojak: The Belarus File* was taken from *The Belarus Secret* by John Loftus. The major difference in this *Kojak* installment was that none of the regular

cast members appeared, nor were there any character-for-character replacements.

The next time Telly Savalas turned up as Theo Kojak was as one of the regulars of the *ABC Saturday Mystery,* which also featured Peter Falk as Columbo, Jaclyn Smith as Christine Cromwell and Burt Reynolds as B.L. Stryker.

First up was "Ariana," in which Inspector Kojak is maneuvered into a case involving the kidnapping of an adorable little Greek girl whose name is (what else?) Ariana.

Assisting the former Lieutenant is Detective Winston Blake, played by Andre Braugher. Blake actually worked for Captain Rastelli (Joe Grifas), but at the inspector's request, was transferred to assist Kojak as his legman, in very much the same capacity as Crocker had.

The second *Kojak* movie, "It's Always Something," reunited Lieutenant Theo Kojak and Bobby Crocker, who was now a big shot with the D.A.'s office. Two hours later, the case solved, Crocker returned to Knots Landing where he assumed his second television identity as Mack, and Detective Blake picked up where he left off with his new boss before he was so nostalgically interrupted.

There was one other change made in the series beginning with *Kojak: The Belarus File*—Kojak's lollipops. The previous suckers of choice, orange-flavored Tootsie Roll Pops, were replaced by a less caloric and more dentally hygienic brand of sugar-free pops, which came wrapped in clear cellophane.

KUNG FU

October 14, 1972–June 28, 1975.   ABC
January 27, 1993   Syndicated

Character:	Kwai Chang Caine
Played by:	David Carradine
Date(s):	October 14, 1972–June 28, 1975
	February 1, 1986 (*Kung Fu: The Movie.* CBS)

Replaced by:	Kwai Chang "Grasshopper" Caine (age 6)
Played by:	Stephen Manley
Date(s):	October 14, 1972–June 28, 1975

Replaced by:	Kwai Chang "Grasshopper" Caine (older)
Played by:	Radames Pera
Date(s):	October 14, 1972–June 28, 1975

Replaced by:	Kwai Chang Caine
Played by:	David Carradine
Date(s):	January 27, 1993–

Character:	Master Po
Played by:	Keye Luke
Date(s):	October 14, 1972–June 28, 1975

1. In all fairness, Australian male model George Lazenby was hired to replace Sean Connery in this lavishly produced picture.
2. Rosenthal, Sharon. *TV Guide,* Vol. 33, No. 7, Issue #1664, February 16, 1985, p. 34.

Replaced by:	Ping Hai "The Ancient"
Played by:	Kim Chan
Date(s):	January 27, 1993–

Character:	Peter Caine
Played by:	Chris Potter
Date(s):	January 27, 1993–

Replaced by:	Peter Caine (as a boy)
Played by:	Nathaniel Moreau
Date(s):	January 27, 1993–

This offbeat Western probably did more to revitalize interest in the martial arts than Olympic gold medalist Mark Spitz did for swimming.

Born to Chinese and American parents, Caine fled to the American West after he was forced to kill a royal nephew in an uprising which left his beloved teacher, Master Po, dead.

The adult Caine was always played by David Carradine. David's father was horror film legend John Carradine, one of whose earliest film appearances was the bit role of the lost huntsman in the 1935 Universal horror classic, THE BRIDE OF FRANKENSTEIN. In that short but memorable scene, Carradine's deep, resonant tones are unmistakable as he spots Frankenstein's monster in the blind hermit's shack. The hermit (O.P. Heggie) says, "This is my friend." Carradine responds in utter dismay, "Friend? This is the fiend that's been murdering half the countryside; good heavens man, can't you see?" He, of course, could not see, but Hollywood did see Carradine's potential, which led to his appearing in nearly one hundred and seventy films. His television appearances include the second episode of *Kung Fu*, "Dark Angel," which aired on November 11, 1972 and also featured his other son, Robert.

One of the devices *Kung Fu* employed to develop the storyline was the incorporation of regular flashback sequences in which we would see Caine as a boy being taught by Master Po (Keye Luke) and Master Kan (Philip Ahn), who lovingly called him "Grasshopper."

In the pilot for *Kung Fu*, which aired on ABC on February 22, 1972, Keith Carradine, David's younger brother, played Middle Caine—a younger Kwai Chang Caine.

David Carradine had previously starred as Shane in the television series based on the classic 1953 Western of the same name. *Shane* aired on ABC from September 10 to December 31, 1966.

Almost twenty years after *Kung Fu* left the air, it returned in an all new and updated version for the syndication market, *Kung Fu: The Legend Continues*. It is set in the present and David Carradine is playing another Kung Fu master, the grandson and namesake of Kwai Chang Caine; in effect he is playing his own grandson.

Supporting him with traditional Chinese wisdom and philosophy, supplied in the original series by Master Po (Keye Luke), is Chinatown's apothecary, Ping Hai, also known as "The Ancient." He is the voice of reason for the community, its doctor, father confessor—and, like Caine, a priest. A spokesman for Warner Television explained that Ping Hai was developed as a character to relate the wisdom and metaphysical elements of Kung Fu that only an ancient can convey, but was not intended to be a teacher to Kwai Chang Caine, who was himself a teacher to his long-lost son Peter, played by Chris Potter.

Peter Caine is something of a maverick police detective with a "Dirty Harry" bent, who, although he does remember his Kung Fu training and the sacred philosophy taught to him by his father fifteen years earlier (shown in flashback sequences featuring Nathaniel Moreau as Peter), has become much more cynical living in the brutal world of crime that he has vowed to put an end to.

He is kept in check by his superior, Captain Paul Blaisdell, played by Robert Lansing.

L

L.A. LAW

October 3, 1986–.   NBC

Character:	Michael Kuzak
Played by:	Harry Hamlin
Date(s):	September 15, 1986–April 18, 1991

Character:	Victor Sifuentes
Played by:	Jimmy Smits
Date(s):	September 15, 1986–May 16, 1991

Character:	Grace Van Owen
Played by:	Susan Dey
Date(s):	October 3, 1986–May 21, 1992

Character:	Tommy Mullaney
Played by:	John Spencer
Date(s):	December 6, 1990–

Character:	Zoey Clemmons
Played by:	Cecil Hoffmann
Date(s):	February 7, 1991–November 5, 1992

Character:	Abby Perkins
Played by:	Michele Greene
Date(s):	September 15, 1986–May 16, 1991

Character:	Cara Jean ''C.J.'' Lamb
Played by:	Amanda Donohoe
Date(s):	November 8, 1990–May 21, 1992

Character:	Gwen Taylor
Played by:	Sheila Kelley
Date(s):	May 10, 1990–May 19, 1994

Character:	Rosalind Shays
Played by:	Diana Muldaur
Date(s):	November 30, 1989–March 21, 1991

Character:	Daniel Morales
Played by:	A Martinez
Date(s):	October 22, 1992–May 19, 1994

Character:	Susan Bloom
Played by:	Conchata Ferrell
Date(s):	October 10, 1991–May 21, 1992

From the creative team of Steven Bochco, who created the Emmy Award-winning *Hill Street Blues* (See Entry), and Terry Louise Fisher, the former producer of *Cagney and Lacey* (See Entry), sprang *L.A. Law,* an involving series about the high-profile Los Angeles law firm of McKenzie, Brackman, Chaney and Kuzak. During the long and successful run of the series, it won fifteen Emmy Awards, four of which were for Best Drama.

Using the multiple-story format that became popular with *The Love Boat* (See Entry) and *Fantasy Island* (See Entry), the rather large ensemble cast of nine attorneys of *L.A. Law* dealt with a number of different and intriguing cases each week—many on the cutting edge of current controversial issues such as sex discrimination, animal rights, abortion and AIDS.

Featured in some of the on-air promotional ads for the series was a blonde, attractive and all-grown-up Susan Dey as Deputy District Attorney Grace Van Owen. At fifteen, Ms. Dey represented the epitome of femininity to millions of pubescent teenage boys as Laurie, Keith's sister on the ABC sitcom, *The Partridge Family.*

As the show caught on and the other characters were given a chance to develop, promos began to feature less and less of Ms. Dey and reflected a more even balance among cast members. These included Richard Dysart as the firm's senior partner, Leland McKenzie; Alan Rachins as Douglas Brackman, Jr.; Harry Hamlin as Michael Kuzak; Jill Eikenberry as Ann Kelsey; Corbin Bernsen as Arnie Becker; Michael Tucker as tax attorney Stuart Markowitz; Jimmy Smits as Victor Sifuentes; and Michele Greene as Abby Perkins.

Two very important characters who were not attorneys were Arnie's legal secretary Roxanne Melman, played by Susan Ruttan, and the retarded clerk, Benny Stulwicz, played with great aplomb and love by Larry Drake.

Off the tube, Larry Drake, who remained with the series, has made a number of big screen appearances. He played Robert G. Durant in the 1990 science fiction, DARKMAN, and the title role in the 1992 thriller, DR. GIGGLES.

Other *L.A. Law* recurring regulars included Cynthia Harris as

Iris Hubbard; Joyce Hyser as Alison Gottlieb; and Dann Florek as David Meyer.

Due to the realistic nature of *L.A. Law,* new characters were introduced when actors in established roles left the series. This was by no means a new practice. While series such as *M*A*S*H* (See Entry) endeavored to fill cast vacancies with new characters serving the same basic function within the structure of the series, the new attorneys introduced on *L.A. Law* were not so easily interchangeable. No direct comparisons can, or should be drawn, therefore, between the original cast members and their replacements. All that can be said is that new characters were introduced as older ones departed.

Diana Muldaur, who joined the *L.A. Law* cast as Rosalind Shays, in the November 30, 1989 episode, "One Rat—One Ranger," was written out during the show's fifth season.

Initially, her appearance was a welcome one as it was hoped that as a new partner she could infuse the struggling agency with the more lucrative cases she was known to attract, which were very much needed.

Even though her less than congenial personality often put her at odds with the other members of the firm, it did make for more interesting television viewing. This is precisely why her recurring character became even more prominent during *L.A. Law*'s fifth season, which began on October 18, 1990 with an episode title that said it all, "The Bitch Is Back." In that season's opener, Rosalind Shays returns to sue her former partners for allegedly forcing her out of the law firm, which causes tempers to flare between the other partners.

Diana Muldaur was literally dropped from the series when her character, Rosalind Shays, plunged to her death after accidentally stepping into an empty elevator shaft, in an episode titled "Good to the Last Drop," which aired on March 21, 1991.

A familiar face on television for more than thirty years, Diana Muldaur has appeared in episodes of nearly 200 shows, from *Dr. Kildare* to *Murder, She Wrote.* Her series roles include Belle in the ABC drama *The Survivors,* which aired from September 29, 1969 to September 17, 1970, and Sam's girlfriend, Chris Coughlin, on the successful police drama, *McCloud,* which ran on NBC from September 16, 1970, to August 29, 1978.

To science fiction fans, Diana Muldaur is fondly remembered as Dr. Ann Mulhall/Thaalassa in "Return to Tomorrow" and Dr. Miranda Jones in "Is There in Truth No Beauty?"— two episodes of *Star Trek* which aired on February 9 and October 18, 1968, respectively. Nearly a century later, Diana Muldaur took over the medical duties on the Starship Enterprise as Doctor Katherine "Kate" Pulaski, replacing Gates McFadden as Doctor Beverly Crusher on *Star Trek: The Next Generation* (See Entry).

Harry Hamlin's character, Michael Kuzak, left the firm during the 1991 season to establish his own firm. It was highly publicized that Susan Dey was leaving the series before the beginning of the 1991/1992 season, but she didn't.

She did eventually leave *L.A. Law* at the end of the 1991/1992 season to co-star in the CBS sitcom, *Love and War,* which debuted on September 21, 1992. In her new role, Ms. Dey played Wallis "Wally" Porter, an uptown girl, who is newly divorced from a self-centered actor, named Kip (Michael Nouri). The series co-starred Jay Thomas as Jack Stein, a no-nonsense newspaper columnist who likes to hang out at the Blue Shamrock bar, which was recently purchased, on an impulse, by Wally. John Hancock played bartender Ike Johnson and had to be written out of *Love and War* (See Entry) when he died on October 12, 1992. Ms. Dey also had to be written out when she left the series due to creative differences.

Michael Cumpsty, whose Frank Kittridge character was brought into the firm by Susan Bloom (Conchata Ferrell), found a new identity as Mr. Terhorst on Bob Newhart's third CBS situation comedy, *Bob,* which premiered on September 18, 1992.

Abby Perkins (Michele Greene), who left McKenzie, Brackman, Chaney and Kuzak in May of 1991 to open her own law firm and then returned, left for good on October 10, 1991. She turned up in "Everything Old Is New Again," the second episode of the ABC series, *Jack's Place,* which aired on June 9, 1992. Ms. Greene was featured in that episode as Jack Evans' (Hal Linden) daughter, whom he hadn't seen for twenty-eight years. In fact, when she sat down to have dinner, at the cabaret restaurant, she was treated royally, because her father mistook her for a food critic.

Other new *L.A. Law* cast members who were introduced included John Spencer, as Tommy Mullaney; Cecil Hoffmann (Mullaney's ex-wife) as Assistant District Attorney Zoey Clemmons; and Amanda Donohoe as Cara Jean "C.J." Lamb.

In an article that appeared in the May 8, 1992 issue of *Entertainment Weekly,* Executive Producer Rick Wallace admitted that the sixteen-member ensemble cast had become unwieldy. " 'We're going to have to talk about changes,' says Wallace. 'The cast is too large to service our characters as well as we'd like. We can't afford to lose track of Arnie Becker for three weeks.' Though he won't name names, Wallace says the cast will shrink considerably."

Not only did they adhere to this mandate, they actually had characters Douglas Brackman and Leland McKenzie discuss it in the seventh season premiere episode, "L.A. Lawless," as they look at the glass door to the firm's offices that is being relettered by a sign painter.

DOUGLAS:	Always good to start with a clean slate, Leland.
LELAND:	Yeah, if you say so.
DOUGLAS:	Leaner and meaner law machine. A clear reflection of the times.
LELAND:	All well and good, but perhaps we've been short-sighted. I can't help feeling we must be doing something wrong with all the comings and goings this past year . . . we should install a revolving door.

Metaphorically, this is what they did, as a number of major cast changes, long hinted at, were made in "L.A. Lawless," the premiere episode of the series' seventh season, which aired on October 22, 1992. In addition to Grace Van Owen, who was said to have moved to New York, C.J. Lamb was written out as having joined the professional golf tour. Featured more prominently was Sheila Kelley as secretary and intern law student Gwen Taylor. Joining the cast was A Martinez as the firm's new partner, Daniel Morales.

Martinez, now playing a single father who left his private practice in Santa Barbara to take up criminal law at the Los Angeles partnership, was one of those unusual bits of casting as he had played the convicted murderer Hector Rodriguez in the May 17, 1990 *L.A. Law* season finale, "The Last Gasp."

In a coincidental parallel (or deliberate inside joke), Daniel Morales left his practice in Santa Barbara to join McKenzie, Brackman, Chaney & Becker; while actor A Martinez left the NBC soap opera *Santa Barbara,* where he had played Cruz Castillo since 1984, to join the cast of *L.A. Law.* His previous legal experience comes from his role as Attorney Roberto Alvarez, who worked for Neighborhood Legal Services in Los Angeles' Century City, on the CBS crime/law drama, *Storefront Lawyers,* which aired from September 16, 1970 to September 1, 1971.

LAND OF THE LOST

September 7, 1974–September 2, 1978.   NBC
September 7, 1991–September 3, 1994   NBC

Character:	Rick Marshall
Played by:	Spencer Milligan
Date(s):	September 7, 1974–November 1976

Replaced by:	Jack Marshall
Played by:	Ron Harper
Date(s):	November 1976–September 2, 1978

Replaced by:	Tom Porter
Played by:	Timothy Bottoms
Date(s):	September 7, 1991–September 3, 1994

Character:	Holly Marshall
Played by:	Kathy Coleman
Date(s):	September 7, 1974–September 2, 1978

Replaced by:	Annie Mary Porter
Played by:	Jennifer Drugan
Date(s):	September 7, 1991–September 3, 1994

Character:	Will Marshall
Played by:	Wesley Eure
Date(s):	September 7, 1974–September 2, 1978

Replaced by:	Kevin Porter
Played by:	Robert Gavin
Date(s):	September 7, 1991–September 3, 1994

Character:	Chaka
Played by:	Philip Paley
Date(s):	September 7, 1974–September 2, 1978

Replaced by:	Stink
Played by:	Bobby Porter
Date(s):	September 14, 1991–September 3, 1994

Character:	Sleestak Leader
Played by:	Jon Locke
Date(s):	September 7, 1974–unknown

Replaced by:	Enik
Played by:	Walker Edmiston
Date(s):	unknown–September 3, 1977

Replaced by:	Shung
Played by:	Tom Allard
Date(s):	September 21, 1991–September 3, 1994

Character:	Nim
Played by:	R.C. Tass
Date(s):	September 7, 1991–September 5, 1992

Replaced by:	Nim
Played by:	Ross Kramer
Date(s):	October 3, 1992–September 3, 1994

Character:	Keeg
Played by:	Brian Williams
Date(s):	September 7, 1991–September 5, 1992

Replaced by:	Keeg
Played by:	Bret Davidson
Date(s):	October 3, 1992–September 3, 1994

Due to continually rising production costs and the diminishing returns of live action versus cartoon animation, Saturday morning television was a veritable wasteland until 1969. Then Sid and Marty Krofft introduced series that featured actors wearing life-sized costumes in shows like *H.R. Puffnstuf, The Bugaloos, Lidsville* and *Sigmund and the Sea Monsters* (See Entry).

But 1974 marked the return of the live-action science fiction adventure series to children's television. These intrepid explorers who dared to go where no man had gone . . . in a very long time, were no doubt the incentive for Norm Prescott and Lou Scheimer, co-owners of Filmation Studios, to bring out some of their own live action series, including *Shazam!* (See Entry), *Isis* (See Entry), *Ark II, Space Academy* and *Jason of Star Command* (See Entry).

But it was Krofft Productions, run by Sid and Marty Krofft, whose contribution to live action science fiction began with *Land of the Lost,* a series that featured live actors, special effects and excellent stop-motion model animation.

The adventure began when forest ranger Rick Marshall (Spencer Milligan) took his children Will and Holly (Wesley Eure and Kathy Coleman) on a rafting expedition down the Colorado River. Then something extraordinary happened. As their raft was tossed over the falls, the threesome was caught in a time vortex and transported to the Land of the Lost, a world inhabited by dinosaurs and other strange creatures.

The Land of the Lost was built by a race of reptilian/humanoid creatures known as the Sleestak (played by the members of a Los Angeles high school basketball team, with Jon Locke as their first leader) who also posed a threat to the Marshall family. Though they were a highly intelligent race, they hunted with bows and arrows.

The world is controlled by a series of triangle-like devices called Pylons. Inside each Pylon is a series of colored crystals that are very dangerous to disturb because they maintain the delicate balance of this closed universe. They also hold the key to the time doorway that is the only way out of this world. Furthermore, if one person leaves, another must take his or her place to keep the universe in balance.

During Rick Marshall's time in this lost world, the main creatures encountered, besides dinosaurs, were the Palcus, simian-like missing link-type creatures. The Palcus had sharp fangs, were covered in fur and stood no more than three and one-half feet tall. They were intelligent, spoke their own language and, apart from a gamy odor, were generally friendly and very likable. The leader of this group was Ta (Scott Fullerton). In the first episode of the series, Chaka (Philip Paley) was befriended by the Marshalls. The other Palcus are not as friendly as Chaka.

Spencer Milligan escaped from his Purgatory at the opening of the 1976/1977 season. It happened when Rick began experimenting with the crystals in one of the Pylons and found the time doorway by moving one of the crystals. He was swept away before he could go back to get Will and Holly; he did not intentionally leave them.

To maintain harmony in the closed universe, Will and Holly's dad was replaced by their uncle Jack Marshall. Jack was an engineer who was, of course, searching for his lost relatives at the time the earthquake occurred, and it was he who watched over the kids during the remaining two seasons. Notice that the writers chose the name ''Jack,'' a one-syllable first name with the same number of letters as their dad's. It also ended in a ''k'' to give it a familiar ring.

To advance the story line a new Sleestak, Enik (Walker Edmiston), was introduced to the series. The Sleestaks were green lizard-like humanoids, not unlike the Gorn from *Star Trek*'s ''Arena'' episode. This may be more than an interesting comparison, as two prominent *Star Trek* writers, David Gerrold and D.C. Fontana, wrote some of the very fine scripts for *Land of the Lost*. A third contributor was actor Walter Koenig, who played Mr. Chekov in the *Star Trek* (See Entry) television series and all seven feature films.

The character Koenig was responsible for creating was Enik, a Sleestak who fell through a Time Doorway and is now in his future, where his race has reverted to a primitive state, which is the reason why only Enik can speak. His mission is to find the Time Doorway and to return to his present to prevent his race from becoming savages in the future. Although the savage Sleestak in the Land of the Lost respect Enik, they also consider him an enemy for befriending the Marshall family.

Enik, was not the original name intended, as Walter Koenig, its creator, explained: ''I wanted Eneg, because that is 'Gene' spelled backwards—a little inside joke.[1] The Gene that Koenig was referring to was Roddenberry, the creator and producer of *Star Trek*—It was Koenig's way of tipping his hat and saying ''Thanks.'' Another possible spelling for the Sleestak's name was Enig, which happens to be the last four letters of Walter's last name.

Some years later, George Peppard, as John ''Hannibal'' Smith, donned a Sleestak costume in the ''Double Heat'' episode of *The A-Team,* which aired on October 23, 1984.

Depending on one's perspective, being catapulted to the Land of the Lost may have been an unsettling experience for most actors. But in the case of Ron Harper, *Land of the Lost* may very well have been looked upon as an improvement upon his previous encounter with time travel as astronaut Alan Virdon, who crashed into *The Planet of the Apes* on September 13, 1974.

Exactly seventeen years after *Land of the Lost* premiered on NBC, it returned to the same network in a brand-new, revamped and completely updated version. It used the same logo title carved into the side of a volcano, and the premise was only altered slightly as this new family, the Porters, entered the Land of the Lost through a fissure in the earth that swallowed up their camper, whereas the Marshalls had entered the time vortex on a raft. It was explained visually during the opening credits, which was supported by a descriptive theme song. ''Our vacation began mapping out a plan, the map never showed danger down the road. We felt our camper shaking as the earth was quaking. There's nowhere to hide, it's the ride of our lives. Now we've crossed the line, fallen through time—living in the Land of the Lost. What a world we found deep underground—living in the Land of the Lost. . . .''

While the juvenile actors portraying the Porter kids have yet to make a name for themselves in the business, the actor playing their father already has. Cast as Tom Porter is Timothy Bottoms, the eldest brother of Joseph and Sam, who had starred as Adam Trask in the three-part, eight-hour miniseries, *John Steinbeck's ''East of Eden,''* that aired on ABC on February 8, 9 and 11, 1981. Certainly his most famous movie role was Sonny Crawford in the 1971 drama, THE LAST PICTURE SHOW.

Some of the other revisions to the story include the fact that the Porters have built themselves a treehouse to live in, and they refer to the immediate area surrounding the dwelling as, ''The Compound.'' Similarly, the Marshalls found a safe haven in a cave they called High Bluff. Both series featured a threatening tyrannosaurus rex and a cute pet dinosaur. The Marshalls nicknamed their thunder lizards after the creatures' personalities (Grumpy and Dopey respectively), which happened to be the names of two of Walt Disney's seven dwarfs.

The Porters referred to the tyrannosaurus rex that harassed them as Scarface, because of the huge gash along the right side of its head. Annie named their baby parasaurolophus Natasha (Tasha for short)—after her mother. Though it didn't come from Disney, it did come from another popular cartoon—

---

1. From an exclusive telephone interview with Walter Koenig on January 25, 1991.

Natasha was the name of the femme fatale on *Rocky and His Friends.*

The second episode of the new *Land of the Lost,* "Something's Watching," introduced the Pakuni and a beautiful dark-haired Sheena-like jungle girl named Christa (Shannon Day), who tools around the jungle aboard a triceratops named Princess.

In the teaser, Kevin went out to shoot some videotape (they were well equipped for their camping trip) and was chased up a tree by some wolves that he initially referred to as "prehistoric pitbulls." In climbing the tree Kevin dropped the camcorder, which happened to record a pair of eyes watching the attack on him, from behind some hedges.

But just when it looks as though Kevin is going to be caught by the predators, a primeval cry ("Aaaaa-Oooooo") [that was right up there with Tarzan's famous jungle yell (See Entry)] caused the carnivorous canines to break off their attack.

Back at the treehouse, Kevin reviews the footage he shot earlier in the day and notices the outlines of two humanoid creatures moving behind the bushes. This prompts a decision to return to the spot where the video was shot, in the hope that he may find intelligent beings who may be able to show the Porters the way back to their own time.

As they continue their search, the trio notices a simian-like creature drinking at the water's edge. Annie gets closer in an attempt to befriend it, while Tom is bitten by a presumably poisonous iguana that had crawled into his binocular bag.

All of these events are being watched by the beautiful jungle woman who approaches the Porters after Tom is bitten. The kids ask her (in English) to help their father. She seems to get their drift and Kevin uses the van to take her to a distant location where there are plants that will serve as an antidote to the lizard's venom. This is quite similar to the plot used by Wolf Larsen in the 1991 version of *Tarzan* (See Entry).

Annie uses the time to introduce herself and her reptilian friend to the monkey-boy.

ANNIE: This is Tasha. I am Annie—Annie Porter.

STINK: I Stink!

ANNIE: Your name is Stink?

The scene dissolves to the van where Kevin is playing a similar "Jane, Tarzan, Jane, Tarzanesque" game with his traveling companion, who is directing him to the location of the medicinal plants.

KEVIN: What's your name? Your name, you know? My name's Kevin.

CHRISTA: (Repeating his words) Kevin, Kevin.

KEVIN: Well, not exactly.

CHRISTA: (Pointing to herself) Christa.

The Sleestak are introduced in "Shung the Terrible," the third episode of the revised series.

While the Porters should be conserving fuel, because the dinosaurs chasing them won't be turning into gasoline for another sixty-five million years or so, they drive about the Land of the Lost as if there's a Sinclair station just down the road. This time, however, they leave the sleeping Tasha in the back of the van while they go off to have a picnic lunch.

Two slapstick Sleestak, Nim (R.C. Tass) and Keeg (Brian Willams) stumble upon the four-wheel drive, get in, and during their fumbling release the emergency brake, causing the vehicle to roll down a hill and stop at the entrance to a cave.

Inside the cave is Shung, the leader of these three Sleestak criminals who were banished to the Land of the Lost to die. He wants to have the van as his chariot and Tasha as his dinner—but he gets neither.

It is Annie who learns from Christa that these creatures are the Sleestak—and that they are up to no good.

CHRISTA: Long ago they catch many Pakuni. Stink's mama and papa. Make work very hard. Pakuni get sick and die.

Stink was played by the diminutive Bobby Porter, who also served as the show's stunt coordinator. Shung was played by the six-foot-nine-inch-tall character actor, Tom Allard, who doubled as the amphibious humanoid, Namaki, who was introduced in the October 10, 1992 episode, "Life's a Beach."

Serving under Shung were two fumbling Sleestak flunkies, Nim (R.C. Tass) and Keeg (Brian Williams), both of whom were replaced at the start of the second season; Tass by Ross Kramer and Williams by Bret Davidson.

Do the Porters ever get out of the Land of the Lost? Only time will tell.

LARAMIE

September 15, 1959–September 17, 1963.   NBC

Character: Andy Sherman
Played by: Bobby Crawford, Jr.
Date(s):   September 15, 1959–June 13, 1961

Replaced by: Mike Williams
Played by: Dennis Holmes
Date(s):   September 26, 1961–September 17, 1963

Set in Laramie, Wyoming, this Western series revolved around two brothers, Slim and Andy Sherman (John Smith and Bobby Crawford, Jr.), who, after the death of their father, were left with the responsibility of keeping the Sherman family cattle ranch afloat. The youngest and least often seen member of the Sherman clan was Andy.

The Sherman boys were said to have been raised by their dad, with the help of his close friend, Jonesey. Jonesey was played by singer and songwriter Hoagy Carmichael, whose hit tunes include *Star Dust* and *Georgia on My Mind.* The producers apparently had something else on their minds because at the beginning of the second season Jonesey was gone.

The character who joined the cast was not a new ranch hand but a peace officer, Sheriff Mort Corey, who cannot really be considered a replacement character for Jonesy. Laramie's sheriff was played by Stuart Randall, who had just dismounted from his role as Art Sampson on another NBC Western, *Cimarron City*. *Cimarron City*, which is not to be confused with the CBS Western *Cimarron Strip*, ran from October 11, 1958 to September 16, 1960, and featured *Laramie* star John Smith as Lane Temple.

Juvenile actor, Bobby Crawford, Jr., who had played Andy Sherman, was gradually written out of the series from the very beginning because he did not have as strong an audience appeal as Robert Fuller's character, Jess Harper. Fuller appeared in the first episode as a drifter, but it was young Crawford who drifted out of the series. His replacement was Dennis Holmes, who played Mike Williams, a boy who had been orphaned when his parents were killed in an Indian attack.

Neither of these young actors continued their television series work after leaving *Laramie*. Bobby Crawford's younger brother, Johnny, fared much better. He was one of the original Mouseketeers on *The Mickey Mouse Club*, Mark McCain on *The Rifleman* series and even hitched a ride on the Starship Enterprise as High Commissioner Ferris in "The Galileo Seven" episode of *Star Trek*, which aired on January 5, 1967.

LASSIE

September 12, 1954–September 12, 1971.   CBS
September 29, 1989–September 8, 1991   Syndicated

Character:	Jeff Miller
Played by:	Tommy Rettig
Date(s):	September 12, 1954–December 1, 1957
Replaced by:	Timmy Martin
Played by:	Jonathan "Jon" Provost
Date(s):	September 8, 1957–August 30, 1964
Replaced by:	Cully Wilson
Played by:	Andy Clyde
Date(s):	1958–1964
Replaced by:	Corey Stuart
Played by:	Robert Bray
Date(s):	September 6, 1964–April 13, 1969
Replaced by:	Bob Erickson
Played by:	Jack De Mave
Date(s):	October 13, 1968–March 8, 1970
Replaced by:	Scott Turner
Played by:	Jed Allan
Date(s):	October 20, 1968–March 8, 1970
Replaced by:	Will McCulloch
Played by:	Will Nipper
Date(s):	September 29, 1989–September 8, 1991

Character:	Ellen Miller
Played by:	Jan Clayton
Date(s):	September 12, 1954–December 1, 1957
Replaced by:	Ruth Martin
Played by:	Cloris Leachman
Date(s):	December 1, 1957–May 25, 1958 (episode #141)
Replaced by:	Ruth Martin
Played by:	June Lockhart
Date(s):	September 7, 1958–August 30, 1964
Replaced by:	Dee McCulloch
Played by:	Dee Wallace Stone
Date(s):	September 29, 1989–September 8, 1991
Replaced by:	Paul Martin
Played by:	Jon Shepodd
Date(s):	December 1, 1957–May 25, 1958 (episode #141)
Replaced by:	Paul Martin
Played by:	Hugh Reilly
Date(s):	September 7, 1958–August 30, 1964
Replaced by:	Chris McCulloch
Played by:	Chris Stone
Date(s):	September 29, 1989–September 8, 1991
Character:	George "Gramps" Miller
Played by:	George Cleveland
Date(s):	September 12, 1954–December 1956
Replaced by:	Uncle Petrie Martin
Played by:	George Chandler
Date(s):	December 8, 1957–1959
Character:	Sylvester "Porky" Brockway
Played by:	Donald Keeler
Date(s):	September 12, 1954–June 8, 1958
Replaced by:	Boomer Bates
Played by:	Todd Ferrell
Date(s):	September 7, 1958–May 31, 1959
Character:	Doc Peter Wilson
Played by:	Frank Ferguson
Date(s):	October 31, 1954
Replaced by:	Dr. Frank Weaver
Played by:	Arthur Space
Date(s):	October 30, 1955–1964
Character:	Sheriff Clay Horton
Played by:	Richard Garland
Date(s):	October 30, 1954

Lassie starred as *Jeff's Collie* while Tommy Rettig co-starred as Jeff.

Lassie and her second owner, Timmy (Jon Provost), look as though they may be daydreaming about whom they are going to help next.

Replaced by:	Sheriff Jim Billings
Played by:	House Peters, Jr.
Date(s):	unknown

Lassie was the heartwarming story of a boy and his dog, an old man and his dog, a forest ranger and his dog and . . . you get the picture. The star of the show was not the humans but the highly intelligent collie named Lassie.

Lassie—all six of her, were trained by Rudd Weatherwax, the same animal trainer who worked with the chimpanzees for a series that Jack Larson turned down in favor of continuing with the *Adventures of Superman* (See Entry). Just as there were many Rintys in *The Adventures of Rin Tin Tin* (See Entry), there too were many Lassies—which should come as no great surprise. There is, however, one big surprise and that is, whenever someone called "Here Lassie, here girl," the dog that came running was really a laddie. Now that's what I call acting.

The very first Lassie raced across the pages of *Lassie Come Home,* a 1940 novel by Eric Knight. Three years later this novel was turned into a surprisingly successful film of the same name, starring fifteen-year-old Roddy McDowall as Joe Carraclough and eleven-year-old Elizabeth Taylor as Priscilla. Also starring in the film was Alan Napier, who became Bruce Wayne's loyal butler, Alfred, on the *Batman* television series.

Napier had a chance to work with the young man again some twenty-three years later when Roddy McDowall appeared as that literary louse, Bookworm, in the April 20 and 21, 1966 *Batman* episodes, "The Bookworm Turns" and "While Gotham City Burns."

The original collie dog used in LASSIE COME HOME was

a bitch—and so was her excessive shedding! That is why Weatherwax replaced her with Pal, a male collie and Lassie's stunt double that he had bought for $10. Ever since, all of the Lassies have been males.

Jon Provost, the second boy to own the cuddly collie, actually worked with five different Lassies during his tenure—three main dogs, a stand-in and a stunt double for long shots and fight scenes. The first dog Provost worked with had been with the series for a few years and was affectionately referred to as "the old man." Having already worked for a number of years on the series he was retired after the first season with Jon Provost. The second dog was replaced, not because of age, but because of an accident on the set. During an interview on the July 7, 1989 edition of the short-lived CBS late-night desk and chair talk program, *The Pat Sajak Show,* Jon Provost related the story of how an out-of-control camera dolly accidentally knocked over some studio lights on the set where Lassie was standing next to June Lockhart. No one was injured in the mishap, but the dog associated the accident with Ms. Lockhart and became upset every time he had to work in scenes with her.

LASSIE COME HOME was followed by six more feature films and a radio program before becoming a long-running television series. On TV, the first lucky owner of the prodigious pup was Jeff Miller, who inherited the collie from a neighbor. Jeff lived on the family farm in Calverton with his widowed mother, Ellen (Jan Clayton), and her father-in-law, George Miller (George Cleveland), whom he called Gramps.

Ellen's husband, Johnny, was Gramps's son. In episode 9, from the 1956 season, Gramps tells Jeff that he got Johnny a rifle when he was twelve years old and put that "gun away ten years ago when we heard about your father.'' Ten years ago would place it in 1944, during World War II. Nothing more is said until episode 81, when it is mentioned that Johnny lost his life attempting to save twenty men in his squadron.

Casting for Jeff began in 1953 and dozens of kids were tested. When the field was narrowed to three finalists, each boy was asked to spend a week at the dog's house. The role would then be awarded to the kid who got along the best with the dog. That kid turned out to be Tommy Rettig, who said that he had never seen any of the LASSIE movies.

Rettig was by no means a ''discovery''; the young actor was already one of the industry's biggest juvenile stars. His first film role was as Tommy Reed in the 1950 drama, PANIC IN THE STREETS. Three years later he starred as Bart Collins, a boy who has a nightmare about a piano school where 500 boys are held captive and forced to play on an enormous bilevel piano. The 1953 film, THE 5,000 FINGERS OF DR. T., a rather bizarre comic adventure, was co-written by Ted Geisel, who is better known as Dr. Seuss.

Jeff's mom was played by Jan Clayton, who had been a regular panelist during 1953 and 1954 on the popular game show, *Pantomime Quiz*. Her father-in-law, George, was played by George Cleveland who very often played the crusty old prospector in Westerns. He was Mr. Plummer in the 1945 John Wayne picture, DAKOTA and played Judge Benbow in the 1947 Abbott and Costello Western comedy, THE WISTFUL WIDOW OF WAGON GAP. Seen occasionally was Donald Keeler as Jeff's friend, ''Porky.''

By 1957 it was decided that Tommy Rettig, who would celebrate his sixteenth birthday on December 10, had outgrown Jeff. Rettig himself has also been quoted as saying that he had tired of the role that had limited his social time to Saturday nights.

Provost also told, on the previously mentioned *The Pat Sajak Show*, how he was hired to become Lassie's new master after being recommended for the part by the wife of a producer he was doing a show for in Japan: ''I met the producer and the directors and everybody said, 'Okay, you're great, you look fine for the part, but you gotta get Lassie's approval.' I went and lived with Rudd Weatherwax and Lassie for a week. Lassie and I got along great, so they figured if we got along great in that kind of setting, that we could work together . . . and we did.''

It's true that the two did get along well together, but no matter how much Lassie liked the lad, trainer Weatherwax still had to intervene to encourage the canine to lick the little boy's face a second time after getting a tongue full of makeup. Jon Provost elaborated: ''So Rudd [Weatherwax] had some tricks and one of them was a little bit of tuna fish oil or a little bit of butter behind the ear, you know.''[2]

Unbeknownst to the audience, when Lassie discovered a runaway orphan on the September 8, 1957 episode, the boy would eventually become her new owner. The adorable blond-haired little boy, Timmy, played by Jon Provost, had run away from an orphanage and was found by Lassie and brought to the farm, where he temporarily found asylum with the Millers.

That's when the changes really started happening. First, Gramps died. In reality, actor George Cleveland, who was in his seventies, died on July 15, 1957, just as production was starting for the new season. Producer Robert Maxwell, who co-produced the episodes of the *Adventures of Superman* shot in 1951, wanted to incorporate Cleveland's heart attack into the storyline and was even said to have consulted a child psychologist with his idea. Needless to say, the show's sponsor, Campbell's Soups, was unhappy with the plot scenario. Maxwell compromised by deleting specific references to ''death'' and using euphemisms such as ''Gramps's gone'' and ''Everybody loved him.'' The sponsors did, however, permit Maxwell to include a scene in which Timmy kneels and asks God to ''take care of Gramps in heaven.''

Without a husband, a fifteen-year-old boy and an old man to help her run the farm, Ellen Miller packs it in and sells the property to Paul and Ruth Martin, a lovely young couple who just happen to be childless. Since Jeff, who was going off to high school, would be unable to care for Lassie in the city, he gave her to Timmy.

The reason Ellen Miller didn't adopt Timmy, which was one of the options open to the producers, was that Jan Clayton had resigned from the series. Ms. Clayton said that she had tired of wearing Ellen Miller's ratty old dress week-after-week.

Her leaving opened the door to Timmy's adoption by Paul and Ruth Miller (Jon Shepodd and Cloris Leachman). Today, Ms. Leachman is better known for her broad comic skills in such television roles as Mary Richards' friend, Phyllis, on *The Mary Tyler More Show* and her own spinoff, *Phyllis* (See Entry).

These parents lasted for only one year before they were replaced by Hugh Reilly and June Lockhart. While Hugh Reilly was seen only rarely on television, June Lockhart has an ongoing list of film and television credits to her name. Reilly's most visible performance prior to *Lassie* was as the first host of the *TV Reader's Digest* anthology series during 1955.

One of Ms. Lockhart's earlier parts was as Priscilla in the 1945 drama, THE SON OF LASSIE. This was, of course, the role originated by Elizabeth Taylor in LASSIE COME HOME. Her second most famous TV role was Maureen Robinson, the mother of Judy, Penny and Will Robinson on *Lost In Space*, which aired on CBS from September 15, 1965 to September 11, 1968. This outer space series eventually landed her just outside Hooterville, where as Dr. Janet Craig she replaced Kate Bradley at the junction in *Petticoat Junction* (See Entry).

Timmy's sometimes-seen friend, Boomer Bates, was played by Todd Ferrell. His Uncle Petrie, the ''Gramps'' replacement character, was played by George Chandler, who had appeared in dozens of B pictures. One of his more prominent roles was as Amos Hart in the 1942 Ginger Rogers film, ROXIE HART. He later appeared as a weasely hood in a couple of episodes of the *Adventures of Superman*. He was Scratchy in ''The Face and the Voice'' and Bates in ''Blackmail.'' He also appeared as the manager of the Crumbly Hotel in ''Flight to the North,'' which starred Chuck Connors as Sylvester J. Superman.

---

2. From an interview with Jon Provost on the July 3, 1989 edition of *The Pat Sajak Show*. CBS.

Lassie's veterinarian, Doc Peter Wilson, was played in episode eight by Frank Ferguson, who appeared as Gus Broeberg from February 10, 1956 to May 18, 1958 on the NBC equine adventure series, *My Friend Flicka.* In 1955, Ferguson was replaced in episode 34, "The Witch" by Arthur Space as Dr. Frank Weaver.

Interestingly enough, five years after joining *Lassie,* Arthur Space was cast in another adventure series about a horse. While still appearing on *Lassie,* Arthur Space played Velvet Brown's (Lori Martin) father, Herbert, on *National Velvet,* which aired on NBC from September 18, 1960 to September 10, 1962.

Arthur Space also turned up in "The Seven Souvenirs," the episode of the *Adventures of Superman* that followed "Flight to the North," which guest-starred George Chandler. Space played Mr. Jasper, owner of Jasper and Company, Chemical Engineers, the inventor of a metal alloy that turned into pure radium, after he tricked Superman into exposing the metal (fashioned into souvenir knives) to his X-ray vision.

Law and order was maintained from episode 4 by Richard Garland as Sheriff Clay Horton. Sheriff Horton, who left law enforcement to run a garage, was replaced in episode 73 by House Peters, Jr. as Sheriff Jim Billings. Peters, the son of the handsome hero of the silent screen, House Peters, generally played heavies in Westerns, including several segments of *The Lone Ranger.* These episodes included "Jim Tyler's Past," February 16, 1950, and "Man Without a Gun," June 15, 1950.

By the time 1964 rolled around, the producers felt that at the age of fourteen, one of their stars was getting a little long in the tooth. That star turned out not to be Lassie, but Jon. Their parting was a mutually agreeable one, for as Provost explained during his interview on *The Pat Sajak Show,* "I was tired of being Timmy."

This time, instead of introducing a new family, they had the Martins move to, of all places, Australia! The plotline explained that there was a need for American farmers overseas, which prompted the good-natured Martins to sell the farm and move to the land down under. Unfortunately, due to the strict quarantine laws, Timmy had to leave Lassie behind. So he decided to give his cute canine to an elderly friend, Cully Wilson, who promised to take good care of the pooch. Andy Clyde, who played Cully, played similar roles to George Cleveland in dozens of two-reeler Westerns. His grizzly features and toothless grin made him one of the more familiar comic sidekicks. Clyde is also remembered as Amos McCoy's (Walter Brennan) irascible friend and neighbor, George MacMichael, on *The Real McCoys,* which aired from October 3, 1957 to September 22, 1963, first on ABC and later on CBS.

Cully didn't maintain ownership of Lassie very long because he soon had a heart attack—just like Gramps. Maybe they were allergic to Lassie's fur. Anyway, being the resourceful dog that she was, Lassie ran for help and was befriended by Corey Stuart, a firefighting forest ranger.

It was obvious that in Cully's condition, he could no longer take proper care of the pup and so he gave her to the forest ranger. Together they enjoyed four years of companionship and adventure before Ranger Stuart met with a terrible accident in the October 13, 1968 episode, "The Holocaust," as explained in the *TV Guide* listing: "To help check a raging forest fire, Corey parachutes into the inferno, where he's trapped by

flames." Jack De Mave is introduced as forest ranger Bob Erickson in this episode.

In the following Sunday night's episode, the second of this exciting two-part story, Lassie seems instinctively to sense that her master is critically ill and begins a desperate search to locate the hospitalized forest ranger. This episode introduces Jed Allan as Ranger Scott Turner. And it is with these two new forest rangers that Lassie spends the next two years.

Seemingly frustrated with human companionship, Lassie goes off on her own from 1970 until the series is finally cancelled in 1971 after more than 500 adventures.

But there was more. In 1972 a syndicated series placed Lassie in the care of California rancher Keith Holden (Larry Pennell). Keith's assistant was played by Larry Wilcox, who later co-starred as Officer Jon Baker on the police drama, *CHiPS* (See Entry).

Also appearing in the series were Skip Burton and Joshua Albee as Keith's sons, Ron and Mike. The Holdens' neighbor, Lucy Baker, was played by Pamelyn Ferdin, and the veterinarian, Sue Lambert, by Sherry Boucher.

The following year, Lassie appeared in her first animated series, *Lassie's Rescue Rangers,* which starred the voice of Ted Knight as Ben Turner, the head of a family-run Rocky Mountain rescue team. Ben's wife, Laura, was provided vocally by Jane Webb. Their son and daughter, Jackie and Susan, featured the voice talents of Lane Scheimer and Erica Scheimer. The forty-eight half-hour episodes were produced by Filmation and aired on ABC from September 8, 1973 to August 30, 1975.

A two-part pilot, *Lassie: The New Beginning,* aired on ABC on September 17 and 24, 1978, and starred Shane Sinutko and Sally Boyden as Lassie's new masters, Chip and Samantha Stratton. Their uncle Stuart was played by John Reilly.

A second syndicated series, *The New Lassie,* barked its way onto television on September 29, 1989. In "Roots," the November 4, 1989 episode, the updating of the story actually begins twenty-five years earlier.

Timmy Martin (Jon Provost) is taken away from his adoptive parents, Ruth and Paul Martin. Now Timmy, who begins using his middle name, Steve, is adopted by the McCulloch family. In 1986, Chris McCulloch (the father), rescues a young collie puppy from a car wreck—a puppy they keep as Lassie.

Three years later, Ruth Chadwick (June Lockhart)—formerly Ruth Martin and since renamed—manages to trace her puppy to the McCullochs. She and Timmy (now Steve) are reunited. She, of course, wanted to take her dog back, but when she sees how much young Will McCulloch and the dog love each other, she allows them to keep Lassie.

An interesting side note is that in addition to introducing Jon Provost as Chris McCulloch's brother, Steve, the dog used in the series was a seventh-generation descendant of the original Lassie, trained by Rudd Weatherwax's son, Bob.

In November 1990, the producers of the syndicated series threw another bone to fans of television nostalgia. That treat was an episode written by and starring Lassie's first master, Tom Rettig. At age forty-eight, Rettig played a college computer science professor who helps train Lassie to operate a computer by pushing a mouse (the hand-held device used to control computer functions that takes the place of a keyboard) around with his nose. Good girl, Lassie.

LAVERNE & SHIRLEY

January 27, 1976–May 10, 1983.   ABC

Character:	Mrs. Havenhurst
Played by:	Helen Page Camp
Date(s):	May 18, 1976–October 1976

Replaced by:	Mrs. Edna Babish De Fazio
Played by:	Betty Garrett
Date(s):	October 19, 1976–1981

This was the first of two shows with names joined by an ampersand to be spun off from *Happy Days.* The other was *Mork & Mindy.*

The main characters of the show, Laverne De Fazio (Penny Marshall) and Shirley Feeney (Cindy Williams), had only made a couple of small guest appearances on *Happy Days,* but that was enough to get them started. These were single girls, one a man-crazy realist, the other a naive romanticist. They worked in the bottle-capping division of the Shotz Brewery in Milwaukee, Wisconsin, and lived together for six seasons in an apartment building near Pfister Park. The year was 1959.

Their first landlady was Mrs. Havenhurst, played for only a few episodes by Helen Page Camp. She later moved into a middle-class garden apartment in Queens, New York on *13 Queens Boulevard.* She played Eileen Brennan's neighbor, Mildred Capestro. The series was evicted from the ABC schedule after only eight episodes, which aired from March 20 to July 24, 1979.

Laverne and Shirley's new landlady was Mrs. Edna Babish, who was played by Archie Bunker's old next-door neighbor on *All in the Family* (See Entry). Mrs. Babish, a widow, didn't stay with the series to the end, but she did stay long enough to marry Frank De Fazio, Laverne's widowed dad who was played throughout the series by Phil Foster.

The show itself was a huge hit and started out in the number three spot in the ratings during the 1975/1976 season. The following season it moved to the number two spot and then stayed at number one for the next two seasons.

Yet, with all of the apparent success, the series took a beating from many critics who saw it as being simplistic and inane slapstick with no substance. One comment in particular dealt with the fact that the cast often appeared to be yelling their lines. *TV Guide* wrote, "Perhaps their shouting is due to playing before a live audience—the idea may be to drown out their groans, or possibly to wake them up."

Dr. Isaac Asimov, the author of 467 books, on subjects ranging from physics and chemistry to science fiction and the Bible, had another opinion of the show. This great man of letters admitted in his October 22, 1983 *TV Guide* article, "Three Cheers for This Battle of the Sexes . . . and for Loni, Too," that *Laverne & Shirley* was one of his favorite shows on television. Why? "It is an old, old literary custom to deify male friendship as the noblest of emotions: Damon and Pythias,

David and Jonathan, the Cisco Kid and Pancho, Hawkeye and B.J.—one for all and all for one.

"Not so with women. Women have no loyalty and can't be trusted—at least as they are portrayed. Cats and back-biters, all of them. Show me two women 'friends' and introduce a man—any man—and it is knife-in-the-back time at once. But not Laverne and Shirley. They have their spats and arguments, sure. We all do. Bring on the showdown, however, and there they are shoulder to shoulder. They are totally different. Laverne is a man-crazy fighter and Shirley is a prim and proper maiden who doesn't like to sweat, but each places friendship first."[3]

So, regardless of what the critics say, if *Laverne & Shirley* is good enough for Dr. Isaac Asimov, it is certainly good enough for me. And as their good friend Fonzie would say, "End of convo."

LAW & ORDER

September 13, 1990–.   NBC

Character:	Detective Sergeant Max Greevey
Played by:	George Dzundza
Date(s):	September 13, 1990–September 17, 1991

Replaced by:	Detective Phil Cerreta
Played by:	Paul Sorvino
Date(s):	September 17, 1991–November 18, 1992

Replaced by:	Detective Lennie Briscoe
Played by:	Jerry Orbach
Date(s):	November 25, 1992–

Dragnet followed the investigation and apprehension of the criminals for twenty-five minutes, then, just before the final commercial break, the announcer would intone, "In a moment, the results of that trial." *Law & Order* was different; it spent an equal amount of time following the police investigation and the trial, dividing the hour-long format into two distinct thirty-minute segments.

Though innovative, this was not a new concept in police dramas. It had been explored some twenty-seven years earlier with *Arrest and Trial,* a ninety-minute crime drama that aired on ABC. The thirty-episode series, which aired September 15, 1963 to September 13, 1964, starred Ben Gazzara as Detective Sergeant Nick Anderson and Chuck Connors as Deputy District Attorney John Kerr.

Leading the weekly investigations on *Law & Order* were Detective Sergeant Max Greevey and his younger partner, Detective Mike Logan. Greevey was portrayed by George Dzundza, who previously starred as Gordon Feester in *Open All Night,* an ABC sitcom that aired from November 28, 1981 to March 5, 1982. Logan was played by Christopher Noth.

In the courtroom were Michael Moriarty and Richard Brooks as Assistant District Attorneys Ben Stone and Paul Robinette.

---

3. Asimov, Isaac. "Three Cheers for This Battle of the Sexes. . . and for Loni, Too." *TV Guide,* October 22, 1983. Reprinted with permission from *TV Guide Magazine,* copyright 1983 by News America Publications, Inc.

Because George Dzundza was said to be unhappy with the amount of screen time he was given on the series, the second season opener, ''Confession,'' began with the murder of Max Greevey and the introduction of Stone's new partner, Detective Phil Cerreta, played by Paul Sorvino.

The Brooklyn-born Sorvino, who starred as George Platt in the short-lived CBS sitcom, *We'll Get By* (March 14–May 30, 1975) and as Sergeant Bert D'Angelo in the Quinn Martin police drama, *Bert D'Angelo/Superstar* (February 21–July 10, 1976), also co-starred as Paul Cicero in the Academy Award-nominated 1990 crime drama, GOODFELLAS.

Shortly into *Law & Order*'s third season, which began on September 23, 1992, Stone was faced with a new crisis: the long-planned departure of his second partner. Actor Paul Sorvino had asked to leave the series in order to devote more time to his opera singing.

The episode, ''Prince of Darkness,'' begins with a gangland-style hit on a young Colombian family enjoying a birthday celebration at a local restaurant. Mrs. Natalie Ortega (Carrell Myers), the twenty-seven-year-old guest of honor, is killed at the scene. Her twenty-eight-year-old husband, Manuel (Gary Perez) later dies in the hospital. Their little girl, Felice (Catherine Gardner), survives.

The thrust of the story is to convict Gaitan (Carlos Sanz), the professional Colombian drug cartel hit man also known as El Diablo/The Prince of Darkness, by tying him to the purchase of an Austrian-built Sterol Commando 223 high-velocity automatic weapon with an adjustable ejector. Cerreta and Logan manage to locate George Lobrano (Mark Margolis), the gun dealer who sold Gaitan the murder weapon. But during the police setup to buy an identical piece for $3,500, the edgy and neurotic Lobrano pumps two slugs into Detective Cerreta's gut at close range. Cerreta remains conscious long enough to hold onto his assailant until his partner can get to him. He then slowly slides down the wall. ''Thirty years . . . a charmed life. I never even fired . . . I can't breathe . . . I can't breathe.'' In the hospital, Cerreta tells Logan that although the bullet passed near his spine, he isn't going to be paralyzed.

The storyline is continued in the following week's episode, ''Point of View,'' which also introduced Jerry Orbach, who starred as Harry McGraw in the CBS detective series, *The Law and Harry McGraw* (September 27, 1987–Februay 10, 1988), as Mike Logan's new partner, Lieutenant Lennie Briscoe. Orbach's motion picture credits include Gus Levy in the 1981 crime drama, PRINCE OF THE CITY, Dr. Jake Houseman (''Baby's'' dad) in the 1987 Jennifer Grey/Patrick Swayze film, DIRTY DANCING; and the voice of the French candlestick, Lumière, in the 1991 Disney animated feature, BEAUTY AND THE BEAST.

The November 25, 1992 *Law & Order* teaser began with a patrol car on night duty cruising the streets. The cops see a man and a woman come out of a bar; the slovenly cop, Livick, discounts it as nothing, though his more astute female partner, Officer Jenna Adams (Samaria Graham), is not so sure. The two officers go on break and park their car at the intersection of Broadway and Murray. He's stuffing his face with a doughnut and she's sipping a cup of coffee, when a call comes in over the police radio—a 1024, ''man down, shots fired.''

The scene, which by this time is buzzing with police activity, is on the street outside the bar they had passed earlier, and the man, one Thomas ''Tommy'' Xavier Duff, has been shot and killed.

Lieutenant Lennie Briscoe (Jerry Orbach), a tired-looking plain-clothes cop walks into the investigation, which in his opinion, is being handled sloppily by detective Carillo (Rick Ramirez), and then comes on like gangbusters.

BRISCOE: Put it back (PAUSE) . . . exactly where you found it.

CARILLO: Your beeper not workin'?

BRISCOE: What I was doin', I don't wear a beeper. Usual treatment of a crime scene, Carillo—you stirrin' it with a stick? Hey, hey! Before you stomp all the evidence into the paper, could I see the diagram?

CARILLO: (To Logan) Hey, Briscoe's your new partner?

LOGAN: It's temporary.

CARILLO: You hope.

Of course, if Christopher Noth had stuck around for a few more minutes, he would have seen that Jerry Orbach received starring credit, which meant that he would indeed be around for a while. He would also have read that Paul Sorvino was making a special guest-starring appearance.

When the show returned after the first commercial, credits are fading in and out as Briscoe and Logan are walking down the street trading some expository small talk.

BRISCOE: You know, Logan, I don't have any problems with your jinx.

LOGAN: That so?

BRISCOE: Hey, two partners shot. A lotta guys'd say you're a black cat. The fact is my ex-wives are both thrilled I got this. They're under the mistaken impression that I'm heavily insured.

LOGAN: Hey, Briscoe, don't forget, it's a temp job. The minute my partner's off his back, your ex-wives get very disappointed.

BRISCOE: Fine. I like short matches. Just don't ever ask me to be the first one through the door. The days when I took chances are history.

Unhappy with his new partner, Logan goes to the hospital to visit Cerreta, whom he lovingly calls ''Big Daddy,'' to find out when he's coming back. Logan's disappointed when Cerreta explains that although he isn't paralyzed, he is experiencing some weakness in his legs because one of the bullets caused some minor damage to a couple of nerves in his spine.

CERRETA: (Painfully) Mike, I'm not gonna be on the street with you anymore. What I'm saying is, that even with the physical therapy and everything . . . as your partner, I wouldn't be a hundred percent.

LOGAN: Hey now, wait a minute, Phil. Any percent you give is enough.

CERRETA: Not for me. The chief of detectives has offered me the administrative desk at the one-ten.

LOGAN: Hey, what can I say? I meant, that's a big bump in your salary—that's good.

Resigned to the fact that Phil isn't coming back and that Lennie Briscoe is going to be his new partner; and mellowed by Briscoe's dedication to the job, Mike Logan, who initially resented Briscoe temporarily using *one* of Phil's desk drawers, softens, after tripping over Briscoe's archive box of belongings.

LOGAN: How many times do I gotta trip over this thing? (Lifting it on to Briscoe's desk.) Why don't you put this junk away, like maybe in your drawers?

LEAVE IT TO BEAVER

October 4, 1957–September 26, 1958.   CBS
October 3, 1958–September 12, 1963   ABC
September 1986–September 1989   TBS

Character: George Haskell
Played by: Karl Swenson
Date(s):   unknown

Replaced by: George Haskell
Played by: George O. Petrie
Date(s):   unknown

Character: Agnes Haskell
Played by: Ann Doran
Date(s):   unknown

Replaced by: Agnes Haskell
Played by: Ann Barton
Date(s):   unknown

Character: Benjy's mother
Played by: Sara Anderson
Date(s):   unknown

Replaced by: Benjy's mother
Played by: Ann Doran
Date(s):   unknown

Character: Gwen Rutherford
Played by: Helen Parrish
Date(s):   January 24, 1958

Replaced by: Gwen Rutherford
Played by: Majel Barrett
Date(s):   unknown

Replaced by: Gwen Rutherford
Played by: Margaret Stewart
Date(s):   unknown

Character: Violet Rutherford
Played by: Wendy Winkleman
Date(s):   unknown

Replaced by: Violet Rutherford
Played by: Veronica Cartwright
Date(s):   unknown

Character: Julie's father
Played by: Ross Elliott
Date(s):   unknown

Replaced by: Julie's father
Played by: Bill Baldwin
Date(s):   unknown

Character: Mary Ellen Rogers
Played by: Pamela Beaird
Date(s):   unknown

Replaced by: Mary Ellen Rogers
Played by: Janice Kent
Date(s):   September 1986–September 1989

Character: John Bates
Played by: Carleton G. Young
Date(s):   unknown

Replaced by: John Bates
Played by: Allan Ray
Date(s):   unknown

Character: Judy Hessler
Played by: Jeri Weil
Date(s):   unknown

Replaced by: Penny Woods
Played by: Karen Sue Trent
Date(s): (last season)

Character: Mr. Haller
Played by: Howard Wendell
Date(s): unknown

Replaced by: Mr. Farmer
Played by: Frank Wilcox
Date(s): unknown

The Adventures of Ozzie & Harriet, Father Knows Best, Leave It to Beaver and *The Donna Reed Show* are four of the most popular family sitcoms that made their debuts during the 1950s. *Leave It to Beaver* stands above the rest for its more accurate depiction of middle America family life in a small town during the 1950s. The characters behave more realistically; they are not larger than life. Moreover, their weekly problems, for the most part, were plausible dilemmas that could be solved by common sense and a quiet talk.

The show's title character, "Beaver" or "The Beave," as he was often called, was played by a talented nine-year-old who had previously played Arnie Rogers in Alfred Hitchcock's 1955 comedy, THE TROUBLE WITH HARRY.

Beaver, which was actually a nickname for Theodore, has absolutely nothing to do with oversized incisors. The unusual moniker was coined by his older brother, Wally. It seems that as a youngster, Wally had trouble pronouncing "Theodore" and called his brother "Tweeder." The boys' parents, Ward and June, intervened and suggested "Beaver" instead. And from the pilot to this day, so it has always been—Jerry Mathers as the Beaver.

Beaver's older brother Wallace, whose name was not part of the show's title, and whose nickname, "Wally," was a little more traditional, was played by Tony Dow. However, in the 1957 pilot, *It's a Small World,* Wally was played by Paul Sullivan and Ward by Max Showalter, who was at the time using the stage name Casey Adams. Max Showalter appeared in such notable films as the 1960 Academy Award-winning drama, ELMER GANTRY, and the 1971 Sean Connery crime adventure, THE ANDERSON TAPES. On television, he played Gus Clyde in the short-lived CBS situation comedy, *The Stockard Channing Show,* which aired from March 24 to June 28, 1980.

Not only did audiences accept these characters as real, but when viewers were given the opportunity to choose a favorite TV mom and dad, Ward and June Cleaver always made the top of the list.

Ward, an intelligent, even-tempered and patient man, was played with great ease by Hugh Beaumont. Playing ex-con Dan Grayson, Hugh Beaumont was named Man of the Year by the Metropolis Daily Planet in "The Big Squeeze," a 1953 episode of the *Adventures of Superman.*

Beaumont's strong all-American handsome features and pleasingly resonant speaking voice, that had a Fred MacMurray quality to them, made him a fairly popular second lead in war dramas in roles such as John McGinnis in 1942's FLIGHT

LIEUTENANT and Captain Hennessey in the 1945 Errol Flynn film, OBJECTIVE BURMA. Working during Hollywood's B-movie heyday, Hugh Beaumont, as Dr. Jud Bellamin, helped Dr. Roger Bentley (John Agar) save the earth from THE MOLE PEOPLE in 1956.

At the Cleaver household, Ward would never hit or spank his sons, although he was not above punishing them. But before he meted out his very fair brand of discipline, Ward would take his boys into his study to discuss the matter with them. He usually sat on the edge of his bank officer-like desk, while Beaver and/or Wally sat in the chairs that faced it. And, as so many parents do, when the Cleaver lads were being reprimanded they were often called by their legal names at least once. At times, Mr. Cleaver even asked Wally and the Beave what they thought their punishment should be. How enlightened.

Mrs. Cleaver, June (Barbara Billingsley), had a similar easy-going temperament, and few will argue that she wasn't the perfect mother role model. Jim Henson also felt so, which is why he cast Barbara Billingsley as Nanny for his delightfully imaginative CBS Saturday morning animated series, *Jim Henson's Muppet Babies,* which debuted on September 14, 1985. All that is ever seen of Nanny is her red-and-white stockinged feet, but Ms. Billingsley's voice is unmistakable.

Writers/directors Jim Abrahams, David Zucker and Jerry Zucker also knew that if anyone could bring the races together, it was Mrs. Cleaver, which is why they cast Barbara Billingsley as "Jive Lady" in their 1980 disaster movie spoof, AIRPLANE!

This may all sound blasé since it now reflects traditional parenting for the nineties, but it may very well have something to do with the fact that today's parents were raised, at least in part, by the Cleavers. Even TV sitcom parents of twin boys, like Jesse and Rebecca Katsopolis (John Stamos and Lori Loughlin) from ABC's *Full House,* have, on occasion, referred jokingly to each other as Ward and June.

Leave It to Beaver was also one of the handful of shows that didn't revolve around a broken family. Better still, none of the main characters was ever written out. What may *not* be recalled is that there were at least nine recurring characters who wound up being played by different actors.

Certainly the show's most famous recurring regular was Wally's best friend, a rather slimy character named Eddie Haskell. He was a cutup, a wiseass, a prankster, and general troublemaker. He spoke to parents and those in authority with a syrupy insincerity peppered with false compliments that was blatantly obvious to everyone—everyone but Eddie.

In the original pilot, the Eddie Haskell character was a young man named Frankie. He was played by the future *Saturday Night Live* regular, Harry Shearer. Once in a while, Eddie's mother and father, Agnes and George, would turn up. At first they were played by Karl Swenson and Ann Doran. Swenson, a popular radio actor during the 1930s and 1940s, may best be remembered by television audiences as Lars Hanson, which he played from 1974 to 1978 on *Little House on the Prairie.* His wife, Agnes, was played by Ann Doran, who had appeared as Clara Randolph in the 1952 motion picture, HERE COME THE NELSONS, which was adapted from *The Adventures of Ozzie & Harriet* radio series.

The second Mrs. Haskell was played by Ann Barton, and her

husband by George O. Petrie, who is known as Harve Smith-field to fans of the CBS evening soap opera *Dallas* which aired from April 2, 1978, to May 3, 1991. Ms. Doran later appeared on *Leave It to Beaver* as one of two actresses to play Benjy's mother. Sara Anderson was the other.

Another prominent resident of Mayfield was Wally's dense and overweight friend, Clarence Rutherford, whom everyone called "Lumpy." Lumpy was always played by Frank Bank and his father by Richard Deacon, but his mother Gwen, initially referred to as Geraldine, was played by three different actresses: Helen Parrish, Majel Barrett and Margaret Stewart. "Lumpy Rutherford" was the episode that featured Helen Parrish as the first Mrs. Rutherford. Her other television credits include "Bill of Sale," an episode of the CBS police series, *Racket Squad,* that aired on November 29, 1951.

The other two actresses who played Lumpy's mom are best remembered for their association with television science fictions that aired on NBC. Margaret Stewart played Thirza in the undersea adventure, *Operation Neptune,* which aired from June 28 to August 16, 1953. Majel Barrett, who later married Gene Roddenberry, is known to millions of Trekkers as Nurse Christine Chapel in the live action series, as well as lending her voice to her character and the computer in the animated *Star Trek* television series. By the time the first theatrical feature, STAR TREK: THE MOTION PICTURE, was released in 1980, Majel Barrett's character had been elevated to that of doctor. Majel Barrett also provided the voice for the Enterprise computer in all seven feature films and the syndicated series, *Star Trek: The Next Generation.*

Two different actresses appeared as Lumpy's sister, Violet. Wendy Winkleman first played the role. Veronica Cartwright, who from 1964 to 1966 played Jemima Boone on *Daniel Boone,* later became Violet Rutherford.

Wally's first girlfriend was Julie Foster (Cheryl Holdridge), a former Mouseketeer on *The Mickey Mouse Club* during the 1950s. Her dad was played by Ross Elliott and Bill Baldwin. From 1967 to 1970, Ross Elliott played Sheriff Abbott on the NBC Western, *The Virginian.* The second actor to play Julie's dad was Bill Baldwin, who played the second campaign manager on the 1952 NBC variety show, *Mayor of Hollywood* (See Entry).

But the real love of Wally's life was Mary Ellen Rogers, who was played by Pamela Beaird. This was also the character chosen by the writers of the revival series, *The New Leave It to Beaver,* to become Mrs. Wallace Cleaver. The actress chosen to play the role was Janice Kent, who had played Cheryl on the short-lived CBS sitcom, *The Ted Knight Show,* which aired on CBS from April 8 to May 13, 1978.

Wally, of course, did not hold the franchise on friendships. Beaver too had a number of good friends. There was Gilbert Bates (Stephen Talbot); Richard Rockover (Richard Correll); a younger Lumpy Rutherford type, Larry Mondello (Rusty Stevens); and Hubert "Whitey" Witney (Stanley Fafara). Fafara's character was later changed to Harrison "Tuey" Brown.

While Larry's mother was always played by the same actress, Madge Blake, who endeared herself to a generation as Bruce Wayne's Aunt Harriet on *Batman,* Gilbert had two dads: Carleton G. Young and Allan Ray. Young had played Harry

Steeger on the crime drama, *The Court of the Last Resort,* which premiered on NBC on October 4, 1957 and moved in August of 1959 to ABC, where its last broadcast aired on February 17, 1960.

Though she cannot really be classified as a friend, Judy Hessler (Jeri Weil) was one of Beaver's classmates. Judy was an obnoxious little girl who kissed up to teachers and got under the skin of Beaver and his friends. She was replaced by Karen Sue Trent as Penny Woods, who was basically the same character.

Cornelia Raeburn, the principal at the Grant Avenue School, was played by Doris Packer, but over at Mayfield High, to which Wally, Eddie and Lumpy had graduated, there were two different principals: Mr. Haller, played by Howard Wendell, and Mr. Farmer, played by Frank Wilcox. From 1962 to 1966, Frank Wilcox appeared on *The Beverly Hillbillies* as John Brewster, the president of the O.K. Oil Company.

Sure, *Leave It to Beaver* was just a television situation comedy. Still, I'd like to believe that right now, somewhere in America, there is a mom standing on the front step with a cold pitcher of just-made lemonade, a father who only lectures his kids, and a little boy who appears to be limping home from school because he's walking in the street and up and down every time he steps on the curb with his right foot.

THE LIEUTENANT

September 14, 1963–September 5, 1964.   NBC

Character:	Lieutenant Samwell "Sanpan" Panosian
Played by:	Steve Franken
Date(s):	September 14, 1963–October 12, 1963
Replaced by:	Lieutenant Harris
Played by:	Don Penny
Date(s):	October 19, 1963–September 5, 1964

The stories for this peacetime military drama centered around the personal and professional lives of three U.S. Marine officers stationed at the Camp Pendleton Marine Base in Oceanside, California: Captain Raymond Rambridge (Robert Vaughn), Second Lieutenant William Rice (Gary Lockwood) and Lieutenant Samwell Panosian (Steve Franken).

The first episode of the series to feature Steve Franken aired four days before his last appearance on *The Many Loves of Dobie Gillis* (See Entry). Four weeks later, Franken was gone; because he had left the series after filming only five episodes.

His replacement, Lieutenant Harris, was played by Don Penny who later played Seymour Schwimmer from 1967 to 1968 on *That Girl.*

While Robert Vaughn kept his feet on the ground as Napoleon Solo on *The Man from U.N.C.L.E.* and General Stockwell in *The A-Team* (See Entry), Gary Lockwood gained fame as Frank Poole, one of the Discovery astronauts in Stanley Kubrick's 1968 science fiction, 2001: A SPACE ODYSSEY.

THE LIFE AND LEGEND OF WYATT EARP

September 6, 1955–September 26, 1961.   ABC

Character:	Bat Masterson
Played by:	Mason Alan Dinehart III
Date(s):	September 6, 1955–1957

Replaced by:	Ed Masterson
Played by:	unknown
Date(s):	unknown

Replaced by:	Deputy Hal Norton
Played by:	William Tannen
Date(s):	January 22, 1957–April 1, 1958

Character:	Mayor Hoover
Played by:	Selmer Jackson
Date(s):	September 4, 1956–1957

Replaced by:	Jim ''Dog'' Kelly
Played by:	Paul Brinegar
Date(s):	September 4, 1956–June 10, 1958

Replaced by:	Jim ''Dog'' Kelly
Played by:	Ralph Sanford
Date(s):	October 28, 1958–1959

Character:	John H. ''Doc'' Holliday
Played by:	Douglas V. Fowley
Date(s):	April 23, 1957–December 3, 1957 September 15, 1959–September 26, 1961

Replaced by:	John H. ''Doc'' Holliday
Played by:	Myron Healy
Date(s):	April 22, 1958–September 8, 1959

Character:	Deputy Virgil Earp
Played by:	John Anderson
Date(s):	March 25, 1958

Replaced by:	Deputy Virgil Earp
Played by:	Ross Elliot
Date(s):	May 26, 1959–September 8, 1959

Character:	Sheriff Johnny Behan
Played by:	Lash La Rue
Date(s):	October 27, 1959–May 31, 1960

Replaced by:	Sheriff Johnny Behan
Played by:	Steve Brodie
Date(s):	October 25, 1960–June 20, 1961

Supposedly based on the real-life lawman Wyatt Earp, it is safe to say that most of these stories had much more basis in the ''legend'' than in the ''life'' of this frontier lawman. He also never had a great-nephew, Clarence, which Sheriff Andy Taylor later proved on *The Andy Griffth Show* episode, ''Wyatt Earp Rides Again,'' which aired on January 31, 1966.

Marshal Earp's first duty was to find himself a deputy. His first choice was Bat Masterson, played by Mason Alan Dinehart III. Four years later Bat Masterson would return to television in his own series starring Gene Barry.

When Bat became a county sherriff, Wyatt Earp gave the job to Bat's brother Ed, but he didn't last long. The Marshal's third and final sidekick was Hal Norton, played by William Tannen.

The first mayor of Dodge City was Mayor Hoover. He was played by Selmer Jackson, who joined the series the same day that Wyatt Earp's friend, Jim ''Dog'' Kelly, arrived. Kelly, who was first played by Paul Brinegar, was later elected as the new mayor of Dodge City.

The character lasted with the series for two years although Brinegar was replaced by Ralph Sanford. He may have left Dodge City, but actor Paul Brinegar didn't leave the Old West. His next regular job was the role of Wishbone on the CBS Western, *Rawhide* and from 1969 to 1970 he played Jelly Hoskins on *Lancer*.

The infamous ''Doc'' Holliday should have looked familiar to Wyatt Earp, and to regular viewers as he was originally played by Douglas Fowley. This was the same actor who had played Doc Fabrique in the earlier episodes of *The Life and Legend of Wyatt Earp,* which took place back in Ellsworth, Kansas. When Fowley took a holiday from the series in 1958, he was replaced temporarily by the handsome character actor, Myron Healy. One of Healy's more notable roles on television was as Major Peter Horry in all six hour-long episodes of the Revolutionary War drama, *Swamp Fox,* which aired on *Walt Disney Presents* from October 23, 1959 to January 22, 1960. He is also remembered for his role as Gunner Flinch, the lily-livered gunslinger who never really shot anyone, on ''The Bully of Dry Gulch'' episode of the *Adventures of Superman.*

Although no direct, or even indirect, correlation can be found, it is still interesting to note that the name of the Marshal in the first episode of *The Life and Legend of Wyatt Earp* was Whitney Ellsworth. Coincidentally, Whitney Ellsworth was the name of the producer of the *Adventures of Superman* from 1953 to 1957.

Douglas V. Fowley turned to comedy after leaving *The Life and Legend of Wyatt Earp.* His next series role was Grandpa in the Western situation comedy, *Pistols 'n' Petticoats,* which aired on CBS from September 17, 1966 to August 19, 1967. Two years later he turned up as Robert Redford on *Detective School.*

Nepotism prevailed even in the Old West when Wyatt Earp replaced Deputy Hal Norton with his brother Virgil. During the short life of the character, he was played by two different actors. The first was John Anderson, who has appeared in episodes of more than 500 television programs including *Gunsmoke, Have Gun—Will Travel, Steve Canyon, Perry Mason, Dr. Kildare, Car 54, Where Are You?, Mission: Impossible* and *M*A*S*H.* From September 21, 1976 to March 8, 1977, he played Scotty in the ABC miniseries, *Rich Man, Poor Man—Book II*. During January and February, 1979, John Anderson played President Franklin D. Roosevelt in the miniseries, *Backstairs at the White House*. His nearly three dozen film roles include the car salesman, California Charlie, in the 1960 horror film, PSYCHO.

Anderson's replacement was Ross Elliot, who after his short stint as Deputy Virgil Earp played Sheriff Abbott on *The Virginian*, another Western series with innumerable cast changes.

The last regular character to be played by more than one actor was Sheriff Johnny Behan. The producers initially pinned the tin star on Alfred La Rue, who was dubbed ''Lash'' when a publicity man came up with the gimmick of giving him a whip. Like Zorro and later, Indiana Jones, La Rue lived up to his moniker and became proficient with the prop. He starred in twenty-three Westerns including RETURN OF THE LASH, 1947; DEAD MAN'S GOLD, 1948; MARK OF THE LASH, 1949; and KING OF THE BULLWHIP in 1950. His last feature was FRONTIER PHANTOM, released in 1952.

Hugh O'Brian proved that old axiom, ''Cowboys Never Die,'' when he turned up twenty-eight years later as Wyatt Earp in a special two-hour episode of *Paradise*, which aired on CBS on Sunday, September 10, 1989. He was joined by Gene Barry, who recreated his role as Bat Masterson.

LIFE GOES ON

September 12, 1989–May 23, 1993.   ABC

Character:	Paige Thatcher
Played by:	Monique Lanier
Date(s):	September 12, 1989–April 1990

Replaced by:	Paige Thatcher
Played by:	Tracey Needham
Date(s):	October 1990–May 23, 1993

Life Goes On boasts two television firsts. It was the first series to employ a Beatles song for its theme and the first to co-star an actor with Down's syndrome.

The song was *Ob-La-Di,Ob-La-Da* by John Lennon and Paul McCartney. The actor was twenty-three-year-old Chris Burke. Burke played Charles ''Corky'' Thatcher, an eighteen-year-old with Down's syndrome who, in the premiere episode, was being ''mainstreamed''—for the second time. He had previously attended a special school named Fowler. Corky's parents, Drew and Libby, were played by Bill Smitrovich and Patti LuPone.

One of the conflicts explored in the pilot dealt with Corky's enrollment in the same freshman class at Marshall High School as his younger sister, Rebecca—''Becca'' (Kellie Martin). Becca's concern was that her brother would embarrass her.

The other conflict was that Becca's older sister, Paige, has come back home to live with the family, after breaking up with her live-in boyfriend, Glen. But Monique Lanier, the actress who created the role of Paige, only lived with the series until April 1990, when she was replaced by Tracey Needham, proving that television series, like life—goes on.

THE LIFE OF RILEY

October 4, 1949–August 22, 1958.   NBC-DuMont

Character:	Chester A. Riley
Played by:	Jackie Gleason
Date(s):	October 4, 1949–March 28, 1950

Replaced by:	Chester A. Riley
Played by:	William Bendix
Date(s):	January 2, 1953–August 22, 1958

Character:	Peg Riley
Played by:	Rosemary DeCamp
Date(s):	October 4, 1949–March 28, 1950

Replaced by:	Peg Riley
Played by:	Marjorie Reynolds
Date(s):	January 2, 1953–August 22, 1958

Character:	Chester ''Junior'' Riley, Jr.
Played by:	Lanny Rees
Date(s):	October 4, 1949–March 1950

Replaced by:	Chester ''Junior'' Riley, Jr.
Played by:	Wesley Morgan
Date(s):	January 2, 1953–August 22, 1958

Character:	Babs Riley
Played by:	Gloria Winters
Date(s):	October 4, 1949–March 28, 1950

Replaced by:	Babs Riley
Played by:	Lugene Sanders
Date(s):	January 2, 1953–August 22, 1958

Character:	Jim Gillis
Played by:	Sid Tomack
Date(s):	October 4, 1949–March 28, 1950

Replaced by:	Jim Gillis
Played by:	Tom D'Andrea
Date(s):	January 2, 1953–1955
	1956–August 22, 1958

Replaced by:	Calvin Dudley
Played by:	George O'Hanlon
Date(s):	1957–1958

Character: Olive ''Honeybee'' Gillis
Played by: Veda Ann Borg
Date(s):   January 2, 1953–1955

Replaced by: Olive ''Honeybee'' Gillis
Played by: Marie Brown
Date(s):   unknown

Replaced by: Olive ''Honeybee'' Gillis
Played by: Gloria Blondell
Date(s):   January 2, 1953–1955

Replaced by: Belle Dudley
Played by: Florence Sundstrom
Date(s):   1955–1956

Character: Pa Riley
Played by: James Gleason[4]
Date(s):   unknown

Replaced by: Pa Riley
Played by: James Gavin
Date(s):   unknown

Character: Carl Stevenson
Played by: Bill Green
Date(s):   unknown

Replaced by: Carl Stevenson
Played by: Emory Parnell
Date(s):   unknown

Replaced by: Mr. Cunningham
Played by: Douglas Dumbrille
Date(s):   January 2, 1953–August 22, 1958

Character: Constance Ganaway
Played by: Pamela Britton
Date(s):   unknown

Replaced by: Constance Ganaway
Played by: Sheila Bromley
Date(s):   unknown

If you are living the life of Riley, you are most likely able to enjoy the finer things in life without having to work. But the expression does not come from the television series or even the radio series. It came from a song written in 1883 by Pat Rooney, *Is That Mr. Reilly?*[5] The comic lyrics tell what Mr. Reilly would do if he became wealthy. The expression ''Living the life of Riley'' didn't enter popular usage until around 1910, and

didn't enter the airwaves until 1943, with William Bendix in the role of Chester A. Riley.

The program did make the move to television, but without William Bendix. He was unable to accept the part because he had previous movie commitments. These included a motion picture version of THE LIFE OF RILEY in which he repeats the role he created on radio. Some of the other films Bendix worked on during that period include the 1948 comedic drama, THE TIME OF YOUR LIFE, in which he played the bartender, Nick. The film was based on the 1939 play by William Saroyan, in which Bendix had made his Broadway debut as an Irish cop.

Also released in 1948 was THE BABE RUTH STORY, starring William Bendix as baseball's greatest left-handed batter. This may be Bendix's most memorable film role as he portrayed Ruth with such accuracy that one has trouble catching the cuts between Bendix and newsreel footage of Ruth. There is also an interesting bit of trivia attached to William Bendix's involvement in the picture. Before becoming an actor, William Bendix had played minor league baseball and as a youngster was actually a bat boy for the real ''Bambino.''

During 1949, William Bendix co-starred as Sir Sagamore in the Bing Crosby musical comedy, A CONNECTICUT YANKEE IN KING ARTHUR'S COURT, and played Blake in the Robert Mitchum crime film, THE BIG STEAL.

Auditions were held and two pilots were shot with different actors as Riley. The first pilot, which never aired, starred, of all people, Lon Chaney, Jr., who had become famous in horror films during the 1940s, playing troubled men who usually wind up as monsters. His most famous role was Lawrence Talbot in THE WOLF MAN.

When Chaney didn't work out, they tried character actor Herb Vigran, who later appeared on the *Adventures of Superman* as any of half a dozen different crooks, including Legs Leemy, Mugsy Maples, Georgie Gleap and Si Horton. He also appeared in an episode of *I Love Lucy* (See Entry). This pilot did air on April 13, 1948 and also starred Alice Drake as Peg Riley, Lou Krugman as Jim Gillis, and Jo Gilbert as his wife, Olive.

The actor who finally brought Chester A. Riley to the small screen on a weekly basis was a newcomer to television named Jackie Gleason. Gleason appeared in twenty-six episodes which aired between 1949 and 1950 on NBC and DuMont. His wife, Peg, was played by Rosemary DeCamp, who had played the same role on radio and in the motion picture with William Bendix. Their son, Junior, was played by Lanny Rees, who appeared as the newsboy in THE TIME OF YOUR LIFE, which also featured William Bendix. The Riley's daughter, Babs, was played by Gloria Winters, who after appearing in an episode of *The Lone Ranger* on June 9, 1950, flew off into the Western blue as Skylar King's niece, Penny, in the television Western, *Sky King,* which aired on ABC from September 21, 1953 to September 12, 1954. Her replacement in the William Bendix version of *The Life of Riley* was Lugene Sanders, who had starred as television's first Corliss Archer in *Meet Corliss Archer* (See Entry).

---

4. One source indicates that James Gleason appeared as the postman on *The Life of Riley* series from 1954 to 1957.
5. Some sources give ''Are You the O'Reilly?'' as the title of Pat Rooney's song.

Riley's best friend and next-door neighbor, Jim Gillis, was played by Sid Tomack, who had played the second Knobby Walsh in *The Joe Palooka Story* (See Entry). But Gleason's portrayal of Riley failed to garner an audience and the series was canceled after the first season.

The concept was still a good one and three years later the program returned with a new cast, headed up by William Bendix as Riley and Marjorie Reynolds as Peg. This time the chemistry worked and the series remained on the air for five years, during which time a total of 217 episodes were produced.

Other members of this second cast included Pa Riley, who was first played by James Gleason, who had played the part of Gillis in THE LIFE OF RILEY motion picture. Gleason, a well-known character actor with a distinct Brooklyn, New York accent that is reminiscent of Mel Blanc's characterization of Bugs Bunny, played boxing manager Max Corkle in the 1941 fantasy, HERE COMES MR. JORDAN.

Because two separate series were produced, there were understandably some minor changes in the storyline, which also affected the cast. In the Herb Vigran pilot, Chester Riley was a riveter for the Cunningham Aircraft Company in Los Angeles, but his boss never appeared.

The Jackie Gleason version also had Chester Riley employed as a riveter, but at Stevenson Aircraft and Associates. His boss, Carl Stevenson, was played by both Bill Green and Emory Parnell.

Three years later Riley, now William Bendix, was back at Cunningham Aircraft. This time there was a Mr. Cunningham and he was played by Douglas Dumbrille.

Riley's best friend, "Gillis," was played throughout the series by Tom D'Andrea. His wife, "Honeybee," however, was played by Veda Ann Borg, Marie Brown and Gloria Blondell (Joan Blondell's sister).

For a time the Gillises left town and were replaced by Calvin and Belle Dudley. Mrs. Dudley was played by Florence Sundstrom, and her husband, Calvin, by George O'Hanlon, who had played the second Charlie Appleby on *I Love Lucy* (See Entry).

LIFE WITH FATHER

November 22, 1953–July 5, 1955.   CBS

Character:	Clarence Day, Jr.
Played by:	Ralph Reed
Date(s):	1953–1954

Replaced by:	Clarence Day, Jr.
Played by:	Steven Terrell
Date(s):	1954–1955

Character:	Whitney Day
Played by:	Ronald Keith
Date(s):	1953–1954

Replaced by:	Whitney Day
Played by:	B. G. Norman
Date(s):	1954–1955

Replaced by:	Whitney Day
Played by:	Freddy Ridgeway
Date(s):	1955

Character:	John Day
Played by:	Freddie Leiston
Date(s):	1953–1954

Replaced by:	John Day
Played by:	Malcolm Cassell
Date(s):	1954–1955

This early fifties situation comedy centered on the Day household on West 48th Street in New York. The focal point of the stories was the somewhat eccentric Wall Street banker, Clarence Day, Sr. He was a gourmet and an equestrian, and truly a man of the '90s—the *1890s*, that is. That is why he was also opposed to progress and dead set against such advances as the telephone.

The television program was based on a series of autobiographical articles written by Clarence Day, Jr. for *The New Yorker* magazine during the 1920s. In 1935, Day wrote a best-selling novel, *Life with Father,* which subsequently led to a hit play written by Howard Lindsay. The success of the play, which ran on Broadway for more than 3,000 performances, led to a 1947 motion picture starring William Powell as Clarence Day.

Thirty years after Clarence Day, Jr. penned his first article, the series was brought to television with Leon Ames as Clarence Day, Sr. and Lurene Tuttle as his wife, Vinnie. Ames later replaced Larry Keating as Wilber Post's next-door neighbor on *Mr. Ed* (See Entry). From 1968 to 1970, Lurene Tuttle played Hannah Yarby, the head nurse on the *Julia* series.

Both the patriarch and the matriarch of this Victorian family stuck it out for all twenty-six episodes, which is more than could be said for their red-headed children. We know that the Days' children were redheads because *Life with Father* was the first live network series to be broadcast in color from Hollywood.

LIFE WITH LUIGI

September 22, 1952–June 4, 1953.   CBS

Character:	Luigi Basco
Played by:	J. Carrol Naish
Date(s):	September 22, 1952–December 22, 1952

Replaced by:	Luigi Basco
Played by:	Vito Scotti
Date(s):	April 9, 1953–June 4, 1953

Character:	Pasquale
Played by:	Alan Reed
Date(s):	September 22, 1952–December 22, 1952

Replaced by:	Pasquale
Played by:	Thomas Gomez
Date(s):	April 9, 1953–June 4, 1953

Character:	Rosa
Played by:	Jody Gilbert
Date(s):	September 22, 1952–December 22, 1952

Replaced by:	Rosa
Played by:	Muriel Landers
Date(s):	April 9, 1953–June 4, 1953

Among the mainstays of radio were the ethnically-oriented family sitcoms. Slowly, as television came into its own, one-by-one these programs made the transition to the visual medium.

Joining the ranks of *Mama,* which was about a Scandinavian family, and *The Goldbergs,* about a Jewish family, was *Life with Luigi,* a show about an Italian immigrant.

But unlike Molly Goldberg, who was played by the Jewish writer and actress, Gertrude Berg, Luigi Basco was played by an Irish-American actor, J. Carrol Naish, who had created the role on radio in 1948.

Naish's characterization of the Italian immigrant Luigi Basco was so convincing that he actually became typecast. He eventually broke out of his typecast image and played the famous oriental detective, Charlie Chan, in all thirty-nine episodes of *The New Adventures of Charlie Chan,* which were produced in England during 1956 and 1957.

Prior to his work on television, J. Carrol Naish made a name for himself as a versatile character actor in the motion picture industry, beginning in 1930 with GOOD INTENTIONS, SCOTLAND YARD. He was the Grand Vizier in the 1935 epic adventure, LIVES OF A BENGAL LANCER, and Rasinoff in the 1939 adventure, BEAU GESTE. A few years later, he played Daniel, Boris Karloff's hunchbacked assistant, in the 1944 Universal horror film, HOUSE OF FRANKENSTEIN, a role to which Naish brought much tenderness and pathos. He played Chief Sitting Bull twice: first in the 1950 comedy, ANNIE GET YOUR GUN, and again in the 1954 Western, SITTING BULL.

Luigi's friend Pasquale, the owner of Pasquale's Spaghetti Palace, was played by Alan Reed, the same actor who played him on the radio version. He was seen on camera in later situation comedies such as *Mr. Adams and Eve,* in which he played the studio boss, J. B. Hafter, and *Peter Loves Mary,* where he played Happy Richman. *Mr. Adams and Eve* aired on CBS from January 4, 1957 to September 23, 1958. *Peter Loves Mary* ran on NBC from October 12, 1960 to May 31, 1961. He turned up as different characters on different episodes of *The Beverly Hillbillies,* his most memorable being the eccentric artist, Sheldon Epps, in "Clampett A-Go-Go."

Alan Reed, Jr. is definitely more recognizable off-camera as the voice of that Ralph Kramden of the Stone Age, Fred Flintstone.

Even though few changes were made in the television version of *Life with Luigi,* the series was not as popular as it had

been on radio. It was temporarily taken off the air in December of 1952.

It returned in the spring of 1953 with a brand new cast. In the lead was Vito Scotti, a comic genius who built his career playing humorous Italian characters in dozens of films and television programs. He has appeared in episodes of *The Addams Family, Batman, Zorro and Son,* the comedy takeoff of *Zorro* (See Entry), and most recently turned up in the September 8, 1990 premiere episode of the NBC situation comedy, *The Fanelli Boys,* which in many ways picks up where *Life with Luigi* left off.

THE LINEUP

October 1, 1954–January 20, 1960.   CBS

Character:	Inspector Matt Grebb
Played by:	Tom Tully
Date(s):	October 1, 1954–1959

Replaced by:	Inspector Dan Delaney
Played by:	William Leslie
Date(s):	September 30, 1959–January 29, 1960

Character:	Inspector Fred Asher
Played by:	Marshall Reed
Date(s):	October 1, 1954–1959

Replaced by:	Inspector Charlie Summers
Played by:	Tod Barton
Date(s):	September 30, 1959–January 20, 1960

Long before Karl Malden set out to clean up *The Streets of San Francisco,* Inspectors Matt Grebb and Fred Asher were hard at work tracking down suspects and putting them in *The Lineup* for their victims to identify.

For this series the producers raided the files of the San Francisco Police Department (the producers of *Dragnet* and *Justice* had already gotten their hands on those of the Los Angeles Police Department and the National Legal Aid Society).

For the first six years, *The Lineup* aired as a weekly half-hour series on Friday nights. It was moved to Wednesday nights in the fall of 1959 and expanded to sixty minutes. At that time Grebb and Asher were replaced by Inspectors Delaney and Summers, although Inspector Matt Grebb, who was played by Tom Tully, did return for the November 4, 1959 episode, "Run for the City," which starred Robert Vaughn and Susan Oliver.

The actors who played the first set of police inspectors not only had more police experience, but more acting experience than their successors. Tom Tully, who played Inspector Matt Grebb, appeared in more than one dozen feature films including the 1944 Cary Grant war drama, DESTINATION TOKYO. His other regular television role was Tom Starett in *Shane,* the short-lived Western which starred *Kung Fu* (See Entry) lead David Carradine.

Grebb's partner, Fred Asher, played by Marshall Reed,

turned up twice as a replacement for Robert Shayne, who played one of television's most well-known police inspectors, Bill Henderson, on the *Adventures of Superman* (See Entry).

LITTLE HOUSE ON THE PRAIRIE

September 11, 1974–March 22, 1983.   NBC

Character:	Charles Ingalls
Played by:	Michael Landon
Date(s):	September 11, 1974–September 21, 1982
	February 7, 1983
	December 12, 1983
	February 6, 1984
Replaced by:	John Carter
Played by:	Stan Ivar
Date(s):	September 27, 1982–March 21, 1983

Character:	Caroline Ingalls
Played by:	Karen Grassle
Date(s):	September 11, 1974–September 21, 1982
	February 6, 1984
Replaced by:	Sarah Carter
Played by:	Pamela Roylance
Date(s):	September 27, 1982–March 21, 1983

Character:	Carrie Ingalls
Played by:	Lindsay Green Bush
Date(s):	September 11, 1974–September 21, 1982
Replaced by:	Carrie Ingalls
Played by:	Sidney Green Bush
Date(s):	September 11, 1974–September 21, 1982

Character:	Grace Ingalls
Played by:	Wendi Turnbeaugh
Date(s):	1978–1982
Replaced by:	Grace Ingalls
Played by:	Brenda Turnbeaugh
Date(s):	1978–1982

Character:	Mr. Isaiah Edwards
Played by:	Victor French
Date(s):	October 2, 1974–March 5, 1975
	November 5, 1979
	September 27, 1982–March 21, 1983
	December 12, 1983
	February 6, 1984
	December 17, 1984

Replaced by:	Jonathan Garvey
Played by:	Merlin Olsen
Date(s):	September 12, 1977–May 11, 1981

Character:	Grace Edwards
Played by:	Bonnie Bartlett
Date(s):	October 2, 1974
	September 10, 1975–May 12, 1980
Replaced by:	Alice Garvey
Played by:	Hersha Parady
Date(s):	September 12, 1977–February 4, 1980
Replaced by:	Grace Edwards
Played by:	Corinne Michaels
Date(s):	March 1, 1982–unknown

Character:	Eva Beadle
Played by:	Charlotte Stewart
Date(s):	September 18, 1974–1978
Replaced by:	Eliza Jane Wilder
Played by:	Lucy Lee Flippen
Date(s):	September 17, 1979–1982

Replaced by:	Laura Ingalls
Played by:	Melissa Gilbert
Date(s):	September 11, 1974–September 21, 1982
	September 27, 1982–March 21, 1983
	December 12, 1983
	February 6, 1984
	December 17, 1984
Replaced by:	Hannibal Applewood
Played by:	Richard Basehart
Date(s):	February 25, 1976
Replaced by:	Etta Plum
Played by:	Leslie Landon
Date(s):	September 27, 1982–March 21, 1983

Character:	Nellie Oleson
Played by:	Alison Arngrim
Date(s):	September 11, 1974–May 11, 1981
	November 15, 1982
	December 17, 1984
Replaced by:	Nancy Oleson
Played by:	Allison Balson
Date(s):	October 5, 1981–1983

A little girl, Laura Ingalls, was born in 1867 in a small log cabin built on the edge of Wisconsin's Big Woods. As she grew older she traveled across America with her family in a covered wagon built by her father, Charles, whom she called ''Pa.'' Their journey across Kansas and Minnesota eventually led them to the Dakota Territory, where Laura married Almanzo Wilder. In 1935, at the age of sixty-eight, Laura Ingalls Wilder published *Little House in the Big Woods,* the first of more than a dozen such books about her childhood that have been enjoyed by three generations of youngsters.

One of those readers was a man by the name of Michael Landon, who used the title of the second book, *Little House on the Prairie,* for his warm and loving television series which was set near Walnut Grove, Plumb Creek, Minnesota. Michael Landon starred as Charles Ingalls. Laura was played by Melissa Gilbert.

Pa's best friend was Isaiah Edwards. Victor French played Mr. Edwards beginning with the two-hour made-for-television movie which aired on March 30, 1974. He then made five guest appearances on the series, the first being "Mr. Edwards' Homecoming," which aired on October 2, 1974, and the last episode, "To See the World," which aired on March 5, 1975.

Victor French didn't pay another visit to the *Little House on the Prairie* until after the cancellation of his own situation comedy, *Carter Country,* which aired on ABC from September 15, 1977 to August 23, 1979. When he did come back on November 5, 1979, it was in an episode that centered on his character, "The Return of Mr. Edwards."

In his absence, Merlin Olsen, as Jonathan Garvey, a new neighbor and friend of Charles Ingalls, joined the cast at the start of the fourth season in an episode titled, "Castoffs." Jonathan's wife Alice was the replacement for Isaiah's wife, Grace. Later in the series, Alice died in a fire that destroyed the Sleepy Eye school for the blind in the two-hour episode of February 4, 1980, "May We Make Them Proud."

This was only the second professional acting job for Merlin Olsen who came to television by way of football. For fifteen years, from 1962 to 1977, Olsen played defensive tackle for the Los Angeles Rams. What is interesting is that his screen persona is the complete opposite of his NFL days when he was a member of the Rams' "Fearsome Foursome."

His first role was as Perlee Skowrin in the "Nine Lives" episode of *Kung Fu,* which aired on February 15, 1973. He went on to star as John Michael Murphy on the *Little House on the Prairie*-like NBC drama, *Father Murphy.* The series, which was created and produced by Michael Landon, aired from November 3, 1981 to June 17, 1984. Merlin Olsen later starred in two short-lived series. He was Buddy Landau in the situation comedy, *Fathers and Sons* (NBC, April 6 to May 4, 1986) and Aaron Miller on the NBC drama, *Aaron's Way,* which aired from March 9 to May 25, 1988. He is also very well known as the spokesman for a long-running series of commercials for FTD Florists.

Mr. Edwards, who had already come and gone several times during the run of the series, returned again in the March 1, 1982 episode, "A Promise to Keep." This time he was returning to Walnut Grove after he and his wife had been separated due to his drinking. He may, however, have thought that he was still suffering from the effects of alcohol when he found a completely different wife waiting for him. But even though he couldn't let on that she looks different, the explanation is a simple one. Mrs. Grace Edwards was now being played by Corinne Michaels, who starred as Stephanie Marshall in the syndicated drama special, *Princess,* which aired in April 1980.

For the ninth and last season, the popular series went through several major revisions. The most dramatic was the absence of series star Michael Landon, who had made the decision to leave the series in 1982.

First, the title was changed to *Little House: A New Beginning.* Second, Charles, who had fallen on hard times, was forced to sell his home and property to John and Sarah Carter (Stan Ivar and Pamela Roylance). He then moved his family to Burr Oak, Iowa where there was a job waiting for him. To help with continuity, Victor French returned as a series regular. And there was a new school teacher, the fifth.

The first school teacher, Miss Beadle, a sweet and kind woman, left the series in 1978 after marrying and having a baby. During Miss Beadle's tenure, she was replaced in one episode, "The Troublemaker," by Richard Basehart, who was formerly the captain of the Seaview in *Voyage to the Bottom of the Sea.*

In the storyline, some of the older kids in the class were "troublemakers." They would intentionally drop books when Miss Beadle turned around to write on the board and were generally disrespectful to her. The school board felt that because she was unable to control her class they would replace her with a tougher teacher, although Charles Ingalls was against it.

They hired Hannibal Applewood (Basehart) as Miss Beadle's replacement. He was an absolute tyrant and not above disciplining the students by rapping the backs of their hands with a ruler. Charles became suspicious of his abusive actions and showed up at the school just as Applewood was about to lower his ruler on Laura's hand. Charles grabbed the ruler out of his hands and cracked it in two over his knee.

When the program returned from the last commercial break Miss Beadle had been reinstated as the schoolmarm. Back in the classroom, Ms. Beadle has her back turned to the students as she's writing on the chalkboard. One of the students purposely drops a book to the floor but instead of his classmates smirking, they turn and give him dirty looks—they don't want to take a chance of losing her as their teacher again.

Walnut Grove's second schoolmarm was Eliza Jane Wilder, the sister of Laura Ingalls' future husband, Almanzo. She taught her first class in "Back to School," the two-part episode that opened the sixth season. In 1982, Eliza Jane fell in love with Harve Miller and felt humiliated when he failed to return her affections and married someone else. Now that Laura and Almanzo (Dean Butler) were married, she no longer felt needed and left Walnut Grove. Eliza Jane did turn up in several later episodes, but never resumed teaching in Walnut Grove.

The actress who played Eliza Jane in this dramatic series, Lucy Lee Flippen, is also known for her much lighter role as Flo Castleberry's sister, Fran, from the CBS situation comedy, *Flo.*

Harve Miller was played by James Cromwell, who had played Archie Bunker's co-worker and friend, Stretch Cunningham, on *All in the Family* during the 1974 season.

The kids who attended Walnut Grove's one-room schoolhouse were next instructed by Laura Ingalls, who at the time only had a couple of years on the school's older students.

In the ninth-season episode, "Times Are Changing," which took place during the spring of 1887, Almanzo's brother,

Royal, dies of a heart attack. Laura gives up teaching so that she can devote her time to raising her brother-in-law's daughter, Jenny (Shannen Doherty) and her own daughter, Rose. Michael Landon's daughter, Leslie, stepped in to take over the teaching chores as Etta Plum in the "Times Are Changing" episode.

Walnut Grove's wealthy owners of the town's general store were Nels and Harriet Oleson (Richard Bull and Katherine MacGregor). Prior to his serving as the proprietor of the general store, Richard Bull had served under Richard Basehart's command as the first of three ship's doctors on *Voyage to the Bottom of the Sea* (See Entry).

The Oleson's obnoxious daughter, Nellie, had been with the series since the beginning. In the two-part episode "He Loves Me, He Loves Me Not," which aired on May 5 and 12, 1980, Nellie married Percival Dalton (Steve Tracy). At the end of the seventh season, Percival returned to New York with Nellie and their children to help Percival's mother after his father's death.

The eighth season began on October 5, 1981 with a two-part episode, "The Reincarnation of Nellie."

Mrs. Oleson was so lonely without her "dear" Nellie that she went into a state of deep depression. Her spirits were lifted when she came face to face with an orphan named Nancy—a Nellie look-alike who was twice as obnoxious. The Olesons immediately adopted the girl, who filled the void left by their daughter.

For the first few seasons, Laura had a dog named Jack. In one episode her mother had to prod her to attend to her pet, who needed to be fed and played with. On this particular day, Laura just didn't feel like doing it, even though it was her responsibility. Begrudgingly, she went outside to bring Jack his food and found him lying there dead.

This traumatized Laura and she vowed never to own another dog as long as she lived. That's when a stray dog began following her everywhere she went, including to and from school. Laura did everything she could to keep the dog away from her and even went so far as to pitch some stones at him, but she could not get the stray to leave her alone. Needless to say, the dog began to grow on her and that's how this new pooch, whom she named Bandit, came to take the place of Jack.

Two other members of the Ingalls family should be mentioned. Laura's younger sister, Carrie, who was with the series from the beginning, and her baby sister, Grace, who was born in 1978.

Because of what is now standard practice in the television industry, each of these younger characters was actually portrayed by a set of twins: Carrie by Lindsay and Sidney Green Bush, and Grace by Wendi and Brenda Turnbeaugh.

LOBO

September 18, 1979–August 25, 1981.   NBC

Character:	The Governor
Played by:	William Schallert
Date(s):	December 30, 1980

Replaced by:	The Governor
Played by:	Mark Roberts
Date(s):	unknown

Lobo, the spinoff of a spinoff, was a crime drama starring Claude Akins as Elroy P. Lobo, a sheriff of questionable integrity meting out his idea of justice in Atlanta, Georgia.

The basis for the series was *B.J. and the Bear* (See Entry), an adventure series about a trucker who had formerly flown a helicopter during the Vietnam War and traveled with Bear, his pet chimpanzee.

Co-starring in the series was Claude Akins as the corrupt Orly County, Georgia sheriff, Elroy P. Lobo, who had it in for B.J.

Then on September 18, 1979, just a few months after *B.J. and the Bear* had completed its run, Claude Akins's popular Lobo character was spun off in *The Misadventures of Sheriff Lobo* which aired on the same network. Accompanying Lobo in the move was Deputy Perkins, played by Miles Watson. Introduced were Deputy Birdwell "Birdie" Hawkins (Brian Kerwin), and his father, Mayor Hawkins, played by William Schallert. The series lasted for twenty-two episodes ending its run on September 2, 1980, but not before spinning off a second time.

The locale shifted from Orly, to Atlanta, Georgia where the Governor hired Sheriff Lobo and his deputies, Birdie and Perkins, to restore law and order to a city whose crime is spiraling out of control.

Without noticeably showing any signs of an identity crisis, character actor William Schallert, who had previously played Mayor Hawkins, was here the Governor of Georgia.

Later in the series, Schallert, who is best remembered as Martin Lane from *The Patty Duke Show* (See Entry) and later Border Hodges on *The Torkelsons* (See Entry), was replaced by Mark Roberts as the Governor.

THE LONE RANGER

September 15, 1949–September 12, 1957.   ABC

Character:	The Lone Ranger
Played by:	Clayton Moore
Year(s):	September 15, 1949–March 8, 1951
	September 9, 1954–September 12, 1957

Replaced by:	The Lone Ranger (as a boy)
Played by:	unknown
Year(s):	September 15, 1949

Replaced by:	The Lone Ranger
Played by:	John Hart
Year(s):	September 11, 1952–September 3, 1953

Character:	Tonto
Played by:	Jay Silverheels
Year(s):	September 15, 1949–September 12, 1957

Replaced by:	Tonto (as a boy)
Played by:	unknown
Year(s):	September 15, 1949

The Lone Ranger ranks sixty-ninth among the top one hundred longest-running television programs of all time, with a full eight seasons under its double-holstered gun belt. During the 1950–1951 season, *The Lone Ranger* strode into the number seven spot with a Nielsen rating of 41.2 percent of the audience.

Clayton Moore, who will be eternally linked with the role of the Lone Ranger, was not the first, nor will he be the last actor to play the unknown Texas Ranger. Before he donned the black mask, there had already been several actors portraying the character created by George W. Trendle in 1933.

The first to play the Lone Ranger on radio was George Seaton, who left broadcasting to become one of America's leading film writers and directors. His first foray in the field was as the writer/director of the 1937 Marx Brothers comedy, A DAY AT THE RACES. Ten years later, he won an Academy Award for writing and directing the holiday season classic, MIRACLE ON 34TH STREET, and in 1969, at the age of fifty-eight, Seaton wrote and directed AIRPORT.

The actor who replaced George Seaton as the Lone Ranger was Earle W. Graser. He died tragically in an automobile accident at the age of thirty-two on April 8, 1941; his funeral was attended by hundreds of adoring fans.

Brace Bell Beemer, the man who had been the announcer on *The Lone Ranger* radio program, next assumed the duties as the voice of the daring and resourceful masked rider of the plains. There was one problem, however: Beemer's voice, a deep resonant bass, was easily distinguished from Graser's. Even though the public knew of Graser's death, the producers of *The Lone Ranger* still felt it was necessary to get the audience to accept the new voice. The changeover was handled by having the Lone Ranger injured in the storyline. The injury was said to have caused him to lose his voice, and only his breathing was heard. As the story continued over the next few episodes, the Lone Ranger gradually healed and when he was fully recovered his new voice was heard—only slightly altered from his injury. And, for the next thirteen years, Brace Bell Beemer was the voice of the man in the mask.

There had also been two motion picture serials produced by Republic Pictures, which were very loosely based on the character. The first serial, THE LONE RANGER, was produced in 1938 and starred Lee Powell as Allen King/The Lone Ranger.

In 1939, a second serial, THE LONE RANGER RIDES AGAIN, starred Robert Livingston as Gill Andrews/The Lone Ranger. Both serials starred Chief Thunder-Cloud as Tonto. The voice of the Lone Ranger was, in both films, provided by the diminutive actor, Billy Bletcher, who later appeared in several episodes of *The Lone Ranger* television series.

At the end of the 1940s, Trendle began casting for a forthcoming television series, *The Lone Ranger*. The logical choice for the role might appear to have been Brace Beemer, for two reasons. The first was that even before Beemer became the Lone Ranger on radio he had been called upon to make personal appearances as the masked man for WXYZ-Radio in Detroit, because it was felt that he fit the description of the character. Secondly, he was an accomplished equestrian.

Some sources indicate that Beemer, who wanted the television role, even went so far as to go on a diet to take off some weight, but he was still turned down. Certainly this was not because of his voice, but more likely because of his stocky build and lack of film experience.

Word soon got around that Beemer had been rejected and literally hundreds of actors were tested for the part, including Robert Livingston, who played the Lone Ranger in the 1939 serial.

One of the actors who auditioned for the role was Clayton Moore, who was born in Chicago, Illinois, on September 14, 1908, 1914 or 1915, depending on the source. Clayton Moore's agent sent George W. Trendle and Jack Chertok, the show's producers, prints of several Westerns which featured Moore in either starring or co-starring roles.

These films may have included the 1940 United Artists Western, KIT CARSON, in which Moore appears as Paul Terry; the 1947 Republic Pictures film, ALONG THE OREGON TRAIL, which featured Moore as Gregg Thurston; the 1948 Republic Pictures serial, ADVENTURES OF FRANK AND JESSE JAMES; and the 1949 Republic Pictures twelve-chapter serial, THE GHOST OF ZORRO, in which Clayton Moore starred as Ken Mason/Zorro.

Whether it was Moore's acting ability, his distinctive voice, or his impeccable diction, he became, then and forever after, the Lone Ranger.

Then in 1950, at the end of the second season, it is rumored that Clayton Moore, who received an estimated $500 an episode, asked Trendle for a substantial raise, which resulted in a salary dispute. When Trendle refused to pay the increase, Moore said *adios* to Chertok and rode off into the sunset.

There are also stories of Clayton Moore receiving poor treatment on the set of the series, such as having to sit on boulders during breaks in location shooting instead of having a chair available for him.

Whether it was the salary, his treatment, or other demands which Moore may have made, George W. Trendle hired John Hart to replace him as the Lone Ranger for the fourth and fifth seasons, which consisted of a total of fifty-two episodes (twenty-six per season). John Hart was born in Los Angeles, California circa 1921. Hart said:

"The guy who was producing it [*The Lone Ranger*] in those days was Jack Chertok and he was probably one of the cheapest guys who ever worked in Hollywood. Clayton Moore had done quite a few *Lone Ranger*s and I'm sure they had some dispute with him. Probably he wanted to get paid. In those days they thought you could wear a mask and you couldn't identify any particular actor. Several other guys had played the Lone Ranger on radio and in serials. . . . I kind of looked like the comic strip more than Clayton did, and the comic strip was a big deal then. I don't know how many other actors they looked at, but I got the part.

"I had worked on *The Lone Ranger* as bad guys when Clayton was the Lone Ranger, so they knew me and they knew I could do a lot of dialogue and make it believable."[6]

The first episode of *The Lone Ranger* TV series in which

6. Hise, James Van. *Who Was That Masked Man? The Story of The Lone Ranger.* Pioneer Books, Las Vegas, Nevada, 1990, p. 128.

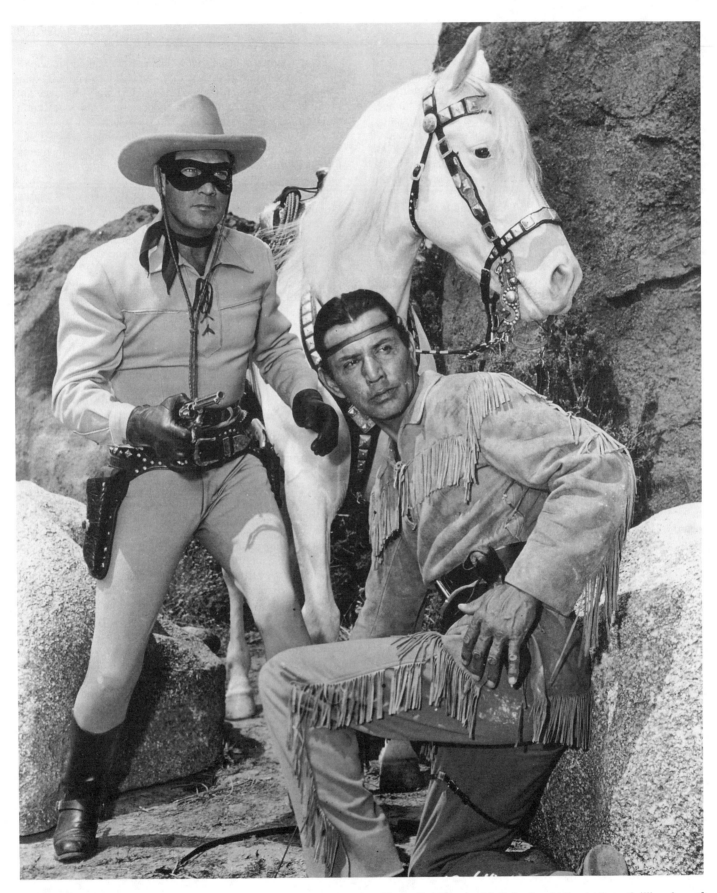

The Lone Ranger (Clayton Moore, left) and his faithful Indian companion, Tonto (Jay Silverheels), defending justice in those thrilling days of yesteryear.

For a short while, John Hart (pictured) played the daring and resourceful masked rider of the plains, but it wasn't long before Clayton Moore returned to the role he will always own.

John Hart appeared was "Rifles and Renegades," which aired on May 4, 1950. In that episode, John Hart played a guard at Fort Maddox who is only referred to as "Sergeant." Although it is unlikely that either actor knew then what strange turn of events lay ahead for him, it is understandably very interesting to watch them together.

In the familiar closing scene of this episode, which dealt with a crooked Army major who was selling guns to the Indians, it is John Hart who inquires about the identity of the masked stranger:

SERGEANT: Say, Lieutenant, what is that masked man's name? I've never seen the likes of him before.

LT. "SKIP" HAINES: I just found out who he is, Sergeant. The Indian, Tonto, told me (PAUSE) he's The Lone Ranger.

Even though the black mask covered John Hart's face (and his entire nose, due to a change in the mask's design), his voice and mannerisms were enough to tip off viewers that there had been a change in cast, long before the closing credits rolled.

By the 1952/1953 season, *The Lone Ranger* had slipped below number fifteen in the ratings, which may have been what prompted Jack Chertok to run an audition to replace John Hart. After reviewing the finalists in California, George Trendle decided to rehire Clayton Moore for the 1954 season. The only other option he had was to try out a third actor as the Lone Ranger, which presented him with the same risk as when he hired Hart.

In 1961, after completing 221 thirty-minute episodes (thirty-nine of which were shot in color) and two LONE RANGER feature films with Jay Silverheels as Tonto, Clayton Moore retired to Minneapolis, Minnesota. He moved later to Calabasas, California.

In 1947, John Hart played Jack Armstrong in the 1947 Columbia serial and in 1957 was Hawkeye in all thirty-nine episodes of the syndicated adventure, *Hawkeye and the Last of the Mohicans*. In that series, Lon Chaney, Jr. played the last member of the Mohican Indians, Chingachgook, Hawkeye's blood brother.

Hart reprised the role of the Lone Ranger one last time during the 1976/1977 season of *Happy Days*. The episode centered around getting a special birthday present for "The Fonz" (Henry Winkler).

When the Cunninghams heard that the Lone Ranger was appearing at the county fair, Chachi (Fonzie's young cousin played by Scott Baio) explained that the Lone Ranger had been Fonzie's idol ever since he was a kid and that meeting him would be the perfect birthday gift.

In the program's last scene, Fonzie is in Arnold's restaurant, slow dancing with his girlfriend to *Misty*, which is playing on the jukebox.

Howard Cunningham, played by Tom Bosley, sneaks into Arnold's behind the couple, drops a coin in the jukebox and pushes a button which replaces *Misty* with Rossini's overture to the opera *William Tell*. A moment later the rest of the cast enters Arnold's and shouts "Surprise," as John Hart enters in full regalia as the Lone Ranger.

RANGER: Are you the one they call "The Fonz?"

FONZIE: (NODS HIS HEAD IN STUNNED AGREEMENT)

RANGER: I understand you've been wanting to meet me for a number of years.

FONZIE: (NODS AGAIN)

RANGER: I'd like to say it gives me great pleasure to meet a man who has patterned his life after mine.

FONZIE: Wow (AS HE SHAKES LONE RANGER'S HAND AND WON'T RELEASE GRIP).

RANGER: Well, with all of these loyal friends, you must be a good-hearted man.

FONZIE: (A SQUELCHED AND BREATHY) Wow.

RANGER: I'd like to leave you with something that can stand as a symbol to our meeting and our friendship. (THE LONE RANGER HANDS FONZIE A SILVER BULLET)

FONZIE: (CLOSE UP OF FONZIE AS RANGER EXITS UNNOTICED) (FONZIE MOUTHS THE WORDS "A silver bullet" AND THEN KISSES IT. HE THEN REGAINS HIS VOICE) Mr. Lone Ranger . . . Where is that masked man?

MARION: Oh Arthur, I'm afraid he's left.

FONZIE: But I didn't get a chance to thank him.

HART: (HEARD FROM OUTSIDE) Hi-yo Silver, Away!

In the 1981 motion picture, THE LEGEND OF THE LONE RANGER, John Hart played Lucas Striker, the editor of the *Del Rio Dispatch*. In a scene involving John Reid, Lucas and Amy Striker, John Hart has the opportunity to thank Reid (The Lone Ranger) for saving his niece's life:

LUCAS: Oh, Mr. Reid, I'm Lucas Striker.

AMY:	My uncle.
REID:	It's a pleasure to meet you, sir.
LUCAS:	Amy told me what you did. I just can't thank you enough. If anything happened to her . . . (HE BEGINS TO WALK)
REID:	Well, uh, you know your niece, uh, was very courageous, sir. She never compromised an inch.
AMY:	Perhaps you might join us for supper tonight.
REID:	Thank you. I'd like to, but I can't. Have to be at the Ranger post before dark.
LUCAS:	Joining the Rangers?
REID:	No sir, my brother.
LUCAS:	I see.

An even more interesting fact about this motion picture is that the Lone Ranger was played by three different actors: juvenile actor Marc Gilpin portrayed John Reid as a boy, and Klinton Spilsbury played the Lone Ranger as an adult. The third actor, James Keach, who wasn't seen on-camera at all, was responsible for dubbing all of Klinton Spilsbury's dialogue in the film. When James Keach was asked how he landed the role, he said that he had to audition for the part and beat out 300 competitors.

Dubbing the voice for another actor and making it sound authentic is no small accomplishment. When James Keach was asked about the difficulties of dubbing the Lone Ranger's voice for Klinton Spilsbury, he said that the three most difficult factors were trying to achieve the proper "Rhythm, tone and nuance."[7] Keach's performance was so skillful that even under close scrutiny it is virtually impossible to detect that the voice of the Lone Ranger is not Spilsbury's.

James Keach is a man of many talents. He was born James Peckaham Keach on December 7, 1947 in Flushing, New York, the son of Mary and Stacy Keach, Sr. Stacy Keach, Sr., an actor and a drama coach, is perhaps best remembered as the ingenious Professor Carlson on *Get Smart,* from 1966 to 1967.

In 1971, after leaving Yale University, James Keach made his film debut in the TV movie, *Orville and Wilbur,* in which he and his brother, Stacy, co-starred as the brothers Wright.

Keach has also appeared in the 1978 films, COMES A HORSEMAN and "FM." In 1980, James Keach worked as writer and producer as well as acting in THE LONG RIDERS,

the story of the notorious James Brothers. An interesting note about this film is that it starred four sets of brothers: James and Stacy Keach, Keith and Robert Carradine, Randy and Dennis Quaid, and Nicholas and Christopher Guest. James Keach later appeared as Yuri, the Latvian pilot, in THE EXPERTS, the 1989 comedy which he produced for Paramount. The film starred John Travolta as Travis and was directed by *Second City* TV star, Dave Thomas.

Patrick Montoya played Tonto as a boy in THE LEGEND OF THE LONE RANGER and Michael Horse portrayed the Lone Ranger's faithful Indian companion as an adult.

An article on THE LEGEND OF THE LONE RANGER, which appeared in the December 24, 1987 issue of *TV Guide,* incorrectly stated that the voices of both the Lone Ranger and Tonto had to be dubbed. A concerned reader set the record straight in a letter to *TV Guide,* which ran in the January 23, 1988 issue:

"Although I can agree with most of your criticism of the movie 'THE LEGEND OF THE LONE RANGER' in your Dec. 24 'Previews' page . . . you made a serious error. I played Tonto in the film—and I did not have my voice dubbed." The letter was signed, "Michael Horse, North Hollywood, Cal."

The young actors who portrayed the Lone Ranger and Tonto as boys in the flashback sequence in the first episode of *The Lone Ranger* television series, "Enter The Lone Ranger," were not listed in the closing credits.

Portly actor William Conrad, who is today familiar to television audiences as "Cannon," "Nero Wolfe" and J.L. (Fatman) McCabe, lent his deep rich voice to the mysterious masked rider of the plains in the 1976 animated version of "The Lone Ranger."

Conrad's voice, however, may be even more familiar to television audiences as the narrator of the Jay Ward-Bill Scott cartoon, *Rocky and His Friends,* which was produced in Mexico City under the supervision of Harvey Siegel. Conrad also provided the opening narration for the 1979 science fiction series *Buck Rogers in the 25th Century,* before the format was revised in 1981.

The Lone Ranger's faithful Indian companion, Tonto, was played for the entire television series by Jay Silverheels, a mixed-breed Mohawk Indian. Tonto said that he was a Potawatomie Indian from up North in the same episode which starred John Hart as the guard from Fort Maddox.

Due to conflicting records, Jay Silverheels' date of birth is difficult to pinpoint, but it seems reasonably certain that he was born between 1918 and 1920, the son of a Mohawk chief on the Six Nations Indian Reservation in Ontario, Canada.

His first film role was the Mexican-Indian, Coatl, in the 1947 film, CAPTAIN FROM CASTILE. Three other films Jay Silverheels appeared in prior to landing the role of Tonto were THE PRAIRIE, 1947, and KEY LARGO, YELLOW SKY and FURY AT FURNACE CREEK, all released in 1948.

Jay Silverheels also appeared in a number of films produced at the same time as *The Lone Ranger* was in production, which may explain his occasional absence from the series. These films include the 1950 Western, BROKEN ARROW, in which he

---

7. James Keach in a letter to the author dated May 31, 1988.

played Geronimo. In 1951 Silverheels appeared as Little Crow in the Alan Ladd Western, RED MOUNTAIN. In 1952 he co-starred as Chingachgook in THE PATHFINDER. Silverheels again played Geronimo in the 1952 Western, BATTLE AT APACHE PASS, and was the lead Indian warrior in YANKEE BUCCANEER.

In 1954, Jay Silverheels appeared as Taos in DRUMS ACROSS THE RIVER. Two years later, Jay Silverheels played Geronimo for a third time in the Audie Murphy Western, WALK THE PROUD LAND. Also in 1956, Jay Silverheels played Tonto opposite Clayton Moore's Lone Ranger in a film of the same name. Two years later both actors reprised their roles in THE LONE RANGER AND THE LOST CITY OF GOLD.

In 1968 Clayton Moore and Jay Silverheels appeared together in a now classic television commercial created by Stan Freberg for Jeno's pizza rolls.

Although Clayton Moore retired from films three years after THE LONE RANGER AND THE LOST CITY OF GOLD, Jay Silverheels continued acting and appeared briefly in the 1961 Western adventure series, *Frontier Circus*, which aired Thursday evenings on CBS for a total run of twenty-six episodes. He also appeared in episodes of *Pistols and Petticoats, Gentle Ben* and *The Partridge Family*. Then in 1970 he made a cameo appearance as Tonto in the 1970 comedy, THE PHYNX.

During the 1960s, Jay Silverheels founded the Indian Actors Workshop in Hollywood, California. In August of 1979, Jay Silverheels became the first American Indian to have his star set in Hollywood's Walk of Fame. On Wednesday, March 5, 1980 at the age of sixty-two, Jay Silverheels died of complications from pneumonia at the Television and Motion Picture Country House in Woodland Hills, California.

The following year Clayton Moore appeared as the Lone Ranger in two black and white commercials that introduced Amoco Silver gasoline.

Shepard Menkin, who provided the voice for Tonto in the Filmation animated version of *The Lone Ranger*, which aired from 1966 to 1969 on CBS, had previously lent his voice to Clyde Crashcup on *The Alvin Show*, which aired on CBS from October 4, 1961 to September 5, 1962.

Silver, The Lone Ranger's silver white stallion, was actually portrayed by more than one horse—six to be exact. There were, however, only four "Silvers" at any given time during the production of *The Lone Ranger*.

Since the horses were all albinos, they were very sensitive to the heat and the bright sunlight, which is why backup horses had to be kept nearby, and in the shade, at all times. "Hi-Yo *Silver*, Away!"

THE LONG HOT SUMMER

September 16, 1965–July 13, 1966.   ABC

Character:	"Boss" Will Varner
Played by:	Edmond O'Brien
Date(s):	September 16, 1965–December 30, 1965

Replaced by:	"Boss" Will Varner
Played by:	Dan O'Herlihy
Date(s):	January 6, 1966–July 13, 1966

Character:	Jody Varner
Played by:	Paul Geary
Date(s):	September 16, 1965–March 2, 1966

Replaced by:	Jody Varner
Played by:	Tom Lowell
Date(s):	March 9, 1966–July 13, 1966

The characters, title and basic storyline for this dramatic series came from the 1958 motion picture of the same name. The film, written by Irving Ravetch and Harriet Frank, Jr., was itself based on three works by William Faulkner: his 1940 novel, *The Hamlet,* and two short stories, "Barn Burning" and "The Spotted Horse."

The series is set in Frenchman's Bend, Mississippi, a town controlled by Will Varner, much as Mr. Potter ran Bedford Falls in the Frank Capra classic, IT'S A WONDERFUL LIFE.

The first of the "Boss" Varners is played by Edmond O'Brien, who brought many memorable characters to the screen including Gringoire in the 1939 film, THE HUNCHBACK OF NOTRE DAME, and Tom Gaddis in the 1962 prison picture, THE BIRDMAN OF ALCATRAZ. In 1962, O'Brien earned an Academy Award for his portrayal of Oscar Muldoon in THE BAREFOOT CONTESSA.

In all likelihood, Edmond O'Brien left the series after the fourteenth episode because of his failing health, which in later years developed into Alzheimer's disease. His replacement was Dan O'Herlihy, the real-life father of Gavan O'Herlihy, who played the first Chuck Cunningham on *Happy Days* (See Entry).

Varner's ineffectual son, Jody, was played for the first twenty-three episodes of the series by Paul Geary, who had played Johnny Ramos on the CBS political drama, *Slattery's People,* from September 21, 1964 to November 26, 1965.

The last three episodes featured Tom Lowell as Jody Varner. Lowell was seen as Private Billy Nelson during the 1963/1964 season of the ABC war drama, *Combat!*

As it turned out, *The Long Hot Summer* was neither hot nor long; it was canceled after the twenty-sixth episode.

LOU GRANT

September 20, 1977–September 13, 1982.   CBS

Character:	Carla Mardigian
Played by:	Rebecca Balding
Date(s):	1977

Replaced by:	Billie Newman	
Played by:	Linda Kelsey	
Date(s):	October 18, 1977–September 13, 1982	

Character:	National Editor	
Played by:	Sidney Clute	
Date(s):	September 20, 1977–1979	

Replaced by:	National Editor	
Played by:	Emilio Delgado	
Date(s):	November 26, 1979–September 13, 1982	

Spinoffs are by no means unusual or out of the ordinary. What usually happens is that situation comedies such as *All in the Family* spin off other situation comedies such as *Maude* and *Good Times.* Television dramas such as *Dynasty* spin off other dramas such as *The Colbys.* What is unique about *Lou Grant* is that it was the first drama to be spun off from a situation comedy—*The Mary Tyler Moore Show.*

The transition occurred when the staff of WJM television on *The Mary Tyler Moore Show* were fired in that program's last episode. After being canned, the news producer, Lou Grant, played by Edward Asner, got serious and moved from Minneapolis to Los Angeles, where he landed a job as the city editor for the *Los Angeles Tribune, "The Trib"* for short.

Among the talented reporters on his staff was Carla Mardigian, a young investigative reporter played by Rebecca Balding, who had played Carol David from September 14, 1978 to 1979 on the ABC situation comedy, *Soap.* Her next regular series role after *Lou Grant* was Corky Crandall in *Makin' It,* the second ABC adaptation of the hit motion picture, SATURDAY NIGHT FEVER, which aired from February 1 to March 23, 1979. The first was *Joe & Valerie* (See Entry).

While one source indicated that Ms. Balding appeared only in a few episodes of *Lou Grant,* others indicate that she remained with the series for the entire first season, which ended on March 6, 1978. This would seem unusual since her replacement, Linda Kelsey, made her first appearance on October 18, 1977, which was only the fifth episode of the series. In either case, there is no argument that Ms. Balding left and was replaced by Ms. Kelsey as Billie Newman.

One of Linda Kelsey's most recognizable roles prior to *Lou Grant* was in the *M*A*S*H* episode, "The Nurses," which aired on October 19, 1976. Her most recognizable role following *Lou Grant* was as Kate Harper in the NBC situation comedy, *Day By Day,* which aired from February 29, 1988, to June 25, 1989. This intelligent young woman portrayed by Ms. Kelsey became an integral part of the series and was the focus of many episodes. She eventually married on the fifth season opener, which aired on November 2, 1981. In that episode, aptly titled, "Wedding" Billie Newman marries a baseball scout, Ted McCovey, played by Cliff Potts.

The *Trib*'s first National Editor was played by Sidney Clute, who is better known as Detective Paul La Guardia from the CBS police drama, *Cagney & Lacey.* The actor who replaced Clute, Emilio Delgado is known to children all over the world as Luis from *Sesame Street.* Other than that, the cast stayed intact until the series was finally put to bed on September 13, 1982, after 114 episodes.

LOVE & WAR

September 21, 1992–.   CBS

Character:	Wallis "Wally" Porter	
Played by:	Susan Dey	
Date(s):	September 21, 1992–Summer 1993	

Replaced by:	Dana Palladino	
Played by:	Annie Potts	
Date(s):	September 20, 1993–	

Character:	Ike Johnson	
Played by:	John Hancock	
Date(s):	September 21, 1992–November 9, 1992	

Replaced by:	Abe Johnson	
Played by:	Charlie Robinson	
Date(s):	December 7, 1992–	

Susan Dey, who first graced the airwaves as Laurie Partridge on *The Partridge Family,* returned to her situation comedy roots as Wallis "Wally" Porter in CBS's *Love & War.* This came after nearly six years of playing Deputy District Attorney Grace Van Owen on NBC's successful law drama, *L.A. Law* (See Entry). The public side of Wally Porter was as a successful restaurateur at "Chez Wally," located on East 72nd Street, a chic eatery where the elite meet to eat and where Woody Allen had his own table. The private Wally Porter was just coming off a sloppy divorce from a five-and-one-half-year marriage to Kip Zakaris, a struggling actor for whom she fell when she saw him play Jet Number 2 in an off, off, off-Broadway production of *West Side Story*—seems she just loved the way he snapped his fingers.

Opposite Exit 3, which leads to South Street and the Manhattan Bridge, and just across from the Family Court of the City of New York, in a neighborhood whose chief industry is selling hubcaps, lies a little bar and grill named The Blue Shamrock.

Its owner, Ike Johnson (John Hancock), was a scowling black man in his early fifties. He laid down the law to Wally when she came into the bar after concluding her divorce proceedings twenty minutes earlier. She was not only forced to sell her restaurant, but had to pay alimony to her ex-husband.

IKE:	Before I serve you, let's get one thing straight. I don't break anything bigger than a twenty. I don't make blender drinks. If you've got a sob story, you're looking for somebody to tell it to, you came to the wrong place. I am not your average comforting bartender with a soft shoulder. That is an ugly stereotype. I don't like people—I never will.

That said, Wally orders a double 100–proof vodka, straight up, with two onions.

Other Blue Shamrock regulars were sanitation worker Ray Litvak (Joel Murray) and two newspaper writers for the *Daily Register;* columnist Mary Margaret "Meg" Tynan (Suzie Plakson) and Jack Stein (Jay Thomas), who writes "The Stein Way," the paper's opinion column—eight-and-one-half-inches, he brags.

Almost immediately, Jack hits on Wally and sparks fly (both love and hate). It is this relationship around which the show revolves. Before their first date, which takes place in the second half of the hour-long premiere episode, a somewhat inebriated Wally boasts, "I have the magic touch. I can turn any dump into someplace great. Even a dump like this." She then proceeds to play a negotiating game to buy the bar from Ike, who insists he's not selling the Blue Shamrock. That is until she offers him $70,000--twice its worth. Ike agrees to stay on and run things for a percentage of the profits, which the two say they will negotiate in good faith at a later date.

In "Step 2," the following week's episode, a sixth regular is introduced to the cast. Joanna Gleason plays Nadine Berkus, a suburban housewife and mother, whose husband is serving time in prison for stock fraud. She is hired by Wally to work as a waitress at the Blue Shamrock.

That the series had trouble finding an audience at first may be because its title, *Love & War,* initially *Love Is Hell,* was very similar in wording and sound to several other programs that were on the air at the time, or had been recently canceled. These included the ABC law drama, *Civil Wars;* the situation comedy, *Anything But Love; Law & Order,* and *P.S. I LUV U.*

In spite of the possible audience confusion, the series, which has its main characters talk directly into the camera for audience asides, as George Burns did in *The George Burns and Gracie Allen Show,* was just beginning to hold its own. Tragedy struck after only nine episodes, when John Hancock died of a massive heart attack in his home on October 12, 1992.

The loss of a fellow actor is always difficult for the cast and crew, but the death of John Hancock must have been especially difficult for Susan Dey, who had worked with him during her tenure on *L.A. Law.* Most significant was the May 16, 1991 episode, "Since I Fell for You," in which John Hancock, as Judge Richard Armand, presided over the wedding ceremony between Grace Van Owen (Susan Dey) and Victor Sifuentes (Jimmy Smits).

Standing out among Hancock's many television credits was his role as Lieutenant Michael Delaney during the 1984/1985 season of the ABC detective series, *Hardcastle & McCormick* (See Entry). He also played Gold Tooth in the NBC serial, *Stop Susan Williams,* which aired from February 27 to May 1, 1979, and Lieutenant Tony Bakersmith in the six-part CBS miniseries, *Scruples,* which aired on February 25, 26, and 28, 1980.

One of John Hancock's most recognizable film roles was as the psychiatrist, Dr. Croce, in the 1979 Blake Edwards comedy, *10.* In the film, Dr. Croce tried to get to the bottom of George Webber's (Dudley Moore) fixation on Jennifer "Jenny" Miles (Bo Derek) by asking him to rate Jenny "On a scale from one to ten?" To which George answered, "Eleven."

In an October 20, 1992 *New York Times* article by Bernard Weinraub, series co-creator Diane English said, "'There are no rules for this sort of thing. It completely blindsides and devastates you. . . .

" '. . . When John died,' said Ms. English, 'we shut the show down for a week. We gathered together on the stage and sat in a circle. We did a lot of crying. I asked everyone to talk about what the episode [explaining Ike's death] might be. Each cast member was able to provide some wonderful little piece of business and some way the character would approach this great bartender that they all loved. By the end of a couple of hours, I had a yellow pad with a lot of great ideas. We all felt better. It was very cathartic for us. I wrote the episode in three days.' "

"For John," the tribute episode written by Ms. English, aired on November 16, 1992, and began with a voice-over by Jack Stein.

JACK:	He was the kind of guy you'd expect to find in a place like the Blue Shamrock. On a night like tonight, you could always go rest your elbows on his bar, and lose yourself in the feeling that time is standing still. Somehow you felt connected to something. Maybe some old tradition of New York City bars. But mostly, it was about the bartender. He was the real reason why you were there. And now he's gone. Ike Johnson died yesterday, and with him went a little piece of this great old town.

Because Ike had died in a chair while watching television, the regular Blue Shamrock barflies half jokingly blamed Kip for Ike's death, because it was possible that he was watching *Surf and Turf,* a really lousy television pilot that featured Kip as an undercover meat inspector who drove a Ferrari.

Ignoring the pleadings of Ike's longtime friends not to publicly recognize Ike's death, Wally decides to go ahead with a memorial party at the bar, complete with Ike's favorite foods made from recipes she found in a drawer. These delicacies included chili, chicken fried steak, little hot dogs wrapped in American cheese, and Rice Krispy squares.

The biggest surprise was the number of people who turned out for the party to pay their respects as Wally observed: "For a guy who said he didn't like people, people sure liked him."

It was because Ike was liked so much that the producers were presented such a huge casting problem. Right from the start Diane English felt that Ike's replacement should be a close relative, such as a brother, son, or even a sister.

The producers interviewed a number of black actors and actresses before settling on Charlie Robinson, who would be introduced as Ike's brother, an unemployed auto worker from Detroit. Robinson joined the series with an already high acceptance rating; he was already known to television audiences as Mac Robinson, the longest-tenured of the three court clerks on NBC's *Night Court* (See Entry).

To ease the new character into the series, Charlie Robinson only appeared briefly in the December 7, 1992 episode "Not Tonight, Honey."

ABE:	I'm looking for some guy named Wally Porter.

WALLY:	I'm Wally Porter.
ABE:	I'm Abe Johnson (BEAT), Ike Johnson's brother.
CAST:	(Together) Ike Johnson's brother?
ABE:	Yeah, he left me a stake in this place—twenty percent. Got a copy of the will right here.

With the same audacity as his brother, Abe insists Wally write him a check, but after she explains that the bar would first have to show a profit . . .

ABE:	As part owner, I've got to protect my investment. There's only one thing to do . . . offer myself a job . . . I accept.

At the end of the 1992/1993 season, in what was reported by the media as "creative differences," Susan Dey relinquished her role on *Love & War*. And thanks to the fact that she left on her own accord and in good health, it was possible for the producers to take a much lighter approach with the introduction of her replacement—*Designing Women*'s (See Entry) Annie Potts.

The episode, "Just in Time," opens with Nadine in a tizzy—none of the customers seem to be happy because they have either gotten the wrong food, or the food they did get was lousy.

ABE:	Oh, I can't believe she's deserted us.

The "she" Abe is referring to was Wally Porter. Why she deserted them is set up by Ray Litvak (Joel Murray), a New York City sanitation worker and Blue Shamrock regular.

RAY:	I still can't believe Wally would just leave town like this. Ever since I heard, I kept thinking about Jack. He must be a complete wreck.

In a futile attempt and trying to appear unaffected, Jack casually enters the Blue Shamrock. He's calm, collected, and even a bit reserved. But he can't keep the act up for very long and quickly falls apart, ranting about "The Year of the Woman" as he quotes something Wally wrote to him in a "Dear Jack" letter.

JACK:	"Oh, I'm sorry Jack, I can't marry you. But I suddenly feel empowered to go find myself in Paris. . . ." Oh, I can't believe she left me. Why would she do something like that?
MEG:	Maybe she had mileage that was about to expire.
JACK:	You know what she did? She left me a letter.

I've read it a million times: "Dear Jack, I don't know where to start, so I'll just start by saying I love you very, very much—which is why I have to leave you . . . I met you on the day of my divorce and now you've asked me to marry you. As much as my heart wants to say 'yes,' it would be wrong to make that kind of commitment when I don't know who I am yet.

Now that the audience has learned what happened to Wally, the next question that comes to mind is the ownership of the restaurant, which was answered in a letter Wally wrote to Abe: "Dear Abe, The Blue Shamrock is now yours. I bought it from your brother, so giving it to you seems like the right way to close the circle. P.S. Sorry about all the debt."

With these explanations given, it was time to introduce Wally's replacement, which comes after a short conversation between new soulmates, Jack and Kip, when Jack accidentally bumps into a woman coming into the restaurant. The woman is Dana Palladino (Annie Potts), who after trading barbs with Jack, makes her way to the bar, reaches out and shakes Abe's hand: "We can negotiate my salary later. Where's the kitchen? I'm ready to start. . . ."

ABE:	Whoa. How do I know you're really a chef?
DANA:	My God, we really are starting from scratch here, aren't we? All right. Palladino. Daughter of the famous modern artist, Dante Palladino. Trained in the great kitchens of Europe. Personal chef to Mick Jagger during his "Steel Wheels" tour. A year and a half cooking on the Alaska pipeline just to learn about salmon. Rising star in one of New York's most important restaurants. I'm the luckiest thing that's happened to you in a long time. So come on, let's go, it's time to cook.

THE LOVE BOAT

September 24, 1977–September 5, 1986.   ABC

Character:	Cruise Director Julie McCoy
Played by:	Lauren Tewes
Date(s):	September 24, 1977–September 8, 1984
	November 30, 1985
	November 21, 1986
	December 25, 1986
	February 27, 1987
Replaced by:	Cruise Director
Played by:	Diane Ladd
Date(s):	September 22, 1984
Replaced by:	Cruise Director Judy McCoy
Played by:	Patricia "Pat" Klous
Date(s):	September 22, 1984–February 27, 1987

Replaced by:	Kelly Donaldson
Played by:	Kim Johnston Ulrich
Date(s):	February 12, 1990

Character:	Yeoman-Purser Burl "Gopher" Smith
Played by:	Fred Grandy
Date(s):	September 24, 1977–September 5, 1986

Replaced by:	Chief Purser Isaac Washington
Played by:	Ted Lange
Date(s):	February 12, 1990

With a formula that had already proven itself in police and medical dramas, each episode of *The Love Boat* tells more than one story (usually three). These individual stories about adult relationships, each scripted by a different writer, are interwoven into a single one-hour program. But unlike their dramatic cousins, which often deal with life and death struggles, these stories deal with romance.

The Love Boat differs from *Love American Style,* which featured similar type vignettes, because its tales of love have a more structured framework, thanks to a regular cast of characters that operate the cruise ship and interact with the passengers who are played by some of Hollywood's biggest stars.

Having big-name guest stars is definitely a coup for a weekly television series, but it is by no means a first. In the 1950s and early 1960s, programs like *Wagon Train* (See Entry) were able to attract big-name guest stars because of good scripts, good pay and good treatment. In the 1970s and 1980s, *Love Boat* was the series that attracted them, but it wasn't just the money and "star treatment" that brought them out. It was the lure of the open seas and the opportunity to take a working vacation aboard a luxurious cruise ship.

And as the seasons passed, the ports of call of this luxury liner of love became even more exotic: the Love Boat cruised through the Panama Canal and made port in China, Greece and Alaska.

The crew of *The Love Boat* included Captain Merrill Stubing (Gavin MacLeod); Adam Bricker, the ship's doctor (Bernie Kopell); Yeoman-Purser Burl "Gopher" Smith (Fred Grandy); Isaac Washington, the ship's bartender (Ted Lange); and Cruise Director Julie McCoy (Lauren Tewes).

The casting was perfect, but as with so many other programs, it didn't happen overnight, or by magic. It was the result of trial and error and three pilot films.

The first of these pilots, *The Love Boat I,* aired on ABC on September 17, 1976, and starred Ted Hamilton as Captain Thomas Allenford, II; Dick Van Patten as Dr. Adam O'Neal; Sandy Helberg as "Gopher"; Theodore Wilson as Isaac; and Teri O'Mara as the cruise director, Jeri Landers.

By the time the *The Love Boat II* set sail on January 21, 1977, the captain, Tom Madison, and the cruise director, Sandy Summers, were being played by Quinn Redeker and Diane Stilwell, while the other regulars were already being played by the actors who would eventually appear in the series. With the voyage of *The Love Boat III,* on May 5, 1977, the captain and

The Love Boat set sail for more than nine seasons under the command of Captain Merrill Stubing (Gavin MacLeod, center) and his crew, (clockwise from bottom right): Cruise Director Julie McCoy (Lauren Tewes), Yeoman-Purser Burl "Gopher" Smith (Fred Grandy), Bartender Isaac Washington (Ted Lange), Ship's Doctor Adam Bricker (Bernie Kopell), and Captain Stubing's daughter Vicki (Jill Whelan).

cruise director had become Merrill Stubing and Julie McCoy, played by Gavin MacLeod and Lauren Tewes.

MacLeod was already known to viewers for his seven-year stint as Murray Slaughter, WJM-TV's head newswriter on *The Mary Tyler Moore Show.* Ms. Tewes had considerably less exposure, having only made guest appearances on episodes of *Charlie's Angels* and *Starsky and Hutch.*

The actor who played bartender Isaac Washington had earlier played Junior on the ABC situation comedy, *That's My Mama,* which co-starred Theodore Wilson as Earl Chambers. Wilson, you will recall, is the actor who played Isaac in the initial *Love Boat* pilot.

And if "Doc's" face and voice didn't seem familiar, it is not becuse he hadn't worked on television before. On the contrary, Bernie Kopell has worked steadily in television since 1961. The reason he may not be immediately recognizable is that he most often plays roles under heavy makeup and uses fake accents. Among his eight appearances on *Bewitched,* Kopell turned up as a century-old apothecary, a Viennese psychiatrist and a

German U-Boat captain. On *The Doris Day Show* he played Italian restaurant owner Louie Palucci, and on *The Odd Couple* he played an expert in ESP research. But his most famous recurring character role is Siegfried, the diabolical and twisted KAOS agent, on *Get Smart*.

It was smooth sailing on *The Love Boat* for six seasons until one of the crew members fell overboard—figuratively speaking, of course.

Lauren Tewes, the perky twenty-four-year-old ingenue who had beaten out more than one hundred other actresses for the plum role of Julie, had developed a serious drug problem and almost killed herself with an overdose of cocaine. "'I didn't shoot it,' she says. 'I didn't speedball [inject a mixture of heroin and cocaine, the combination that killed John Belushi]. But I almost OD'd. I had so much money, I didn't know what money could buy. I certainly didn't think it could buy your own death.'"[8]

Miraculously, Ms. Tewes' addiction to cocaine didn't kill her, but it did kill her career. Executive producer Douglas S. Cramer failed to pick up her option for another year.

In a satellite interview with WABC-TV New York's Jill Rappaport, Lauren Tewes said "I didn't take that job thinking 'Well, now I'm going to be a star.' And the side effects are that you become a star. And another side effect of my unhappy life at the time was that I became a drug addict."

The seventh season of the series began on September 22, 1984 with a cruise to Alaska and a new cruise director, as described in the *TV Guide* listing for the episode titled "The Crew's Cruise Director." "... The new cruise director (Diane Ladd), a cynical, unfriendly woman, alienates everyone on board except Julie's sister Judy (new regular Patricia Klous) ..."

Not quite the newcomer her predecessor was, Patricia Klous gained high visibility as the star of her own series, *Flying High*, in which she played Marcy Bowers. The short-lived CBS sitcom took to the air on September 29, 1978 and was grounded on January 23, 1979 after only eighteen flights.

Pat Klous also appeared as Fran Linhart, the social director at a resort hotel in *Aloha Paradise*, a *Love Boat* clone starring Debbie Reynolds as Sydney Chase. Produced by Aaron Spelling Productions, the ABC sitcom faded into the sunset after just eight episodes, which aired from February 25 to April 29, 1981.

Ms. Klous, however, continued working for Aaron Spelling Productions and even took two cruises on *The Love Boat* as a passenger before she was asked to become one of its crew members, as explained by Douglas S. Cramer. "We put her under contract in 1983, just to sit on our bench until the proper spot for her came along. As it turned out, she very well could have ended up as a lead in two of our new shows this season, *Finder of Lost Loves* or *Glitter*. Instead, the Lauren Tewes situation came to a head and we immediately thought of Pat as a replacement for Lauren in *The Love Boat*. Pat was right there, sitting on our bench, and we felt she was perfect for the role."[9]

In what must have been an uncomfortable situation for Pat

Klous, Lauren Tewes returned to the series on November 30, 1985 in a guest role recreating her Julie McCoy character. In the episode "Trouble in Paradise," Julie is reintroduced as Judy's sister who left to get married and was now having marital problems.

This guest shot was followed by three more Tewes appearances in *The Love Boat* specials, "The Shipshore Cruise," November 21, 1986; "The Christmas Cruise," December 25, 1986; and "Who Killed Maxwell Thorne?" which aired on February 27, 1987.

The Love Boat: A Valentine Voyage, a two-hour made-for-television movie that aired on February 12, 1990, reunited most of the original cast. Left on shore were both Patricia Klous and Lauren Tewes, who were replaced by a new cruise director, and Fred Grandy, who was replaced by his old shipmate, Isaac.

Kelly Donaldson (Kim Johnston Ulrich) was said to have been in that position for more than one year, while the ship's former bartender had been promoted to Chief Purser. This change in status was necessary because Fred Grandy, who had been the purser since the second pilot film, did what many actors seem to be doing—he gave up acting and went into politics.

Grandy began his political career in 1986 when the people in his home state of Iowa elected him as one of their six congressmen to serve in the United States House of Representatives.

Isaac Washington's promotion from bartender to Purser was dealt with at the beginning of the Valentine's Day special.

CAPTAIN:	Isaac?
ISAAC:	I'm sorry I'm late, Captain. I was polishing my new stripes.

A few minutes later, Isaac bumps into an old friend, police lieutenant Logan (Tom Bosley), and we learn what the stripes are for as the two old friends greet each other.

ISAAC:	Lieutenant Logan.
LOGAN:	Isaac! Hey, you got your stripes!
ISAAC:	Chief Purser. Finally! An officer and a gentleman.

For most of the series, two different vessels served as "The Love Boat," the Pacific Princess and the Island Princess. Then, in May 1985, after eight years of faithful service, these ships were replaced. "Look for another cast replacement on ABC's

8. Murphy, Mary. "Stardom and Cocaine: Why Lauren Tewes Couldn't Handle Them." *TV Guide*, Vol. 33, No. 11, March 16, 1985, Issue # 1668, p. 7.
9. Davidson, Bill. "Patricia Klous of The Love Boat." *TV Guide*, Vol. 32, No. 49, December 8, 1984, Issue # 1664, p. 20.

The Love Boat. No, Capt. Merrill Stubing (Gavin MacLeod, below) isn't about to ship out—but the ship itself is. Executive producer Aaron Spelling is said to be so hopeful that the series will stay afloat in the ratings for another two seasons that he's decided to trade up. The Pacific Princess, the cruise ship currently seen in exterior shots, will be replaced by the Royal Princess, a more elegant vessel said to be in the same class as the QEII.''[10]

LOVES ME, LOVES ME NOT

March 20, 1977–April 27, 1977.   CBS

Character:	Sue
Played by:	Udana Power
Date(s):	March 20, 1977–unknown

Replaced by:	Sue
Played by:	Phyllis Glick
Date(s):	unknown–April 27, 1977

In between her series work in *The Partridge Family* and *L.A. Law,* Susan Dey appeared in a little known and short-lived situation comedy, *Loves Me, Loves Me Not,* that named the show's characters after the characters in the reading primer, Dick and Jane.

Behind the scenes were successful sitcom producer Susan Harris and co-executive producers Paul Junger Witt and Tony Thomas, who might call this one ''the hit series that got away,'' as it only lasted for six episodes.

Susan Dey played Jane Benson, a beautiful grammar school teacher who was dating Dick Phillips, a bungling newspaper reporter played by Kenneth Gilman.

Art Metrano played Tom, the editor of the newspaper and Dick's best friend, while Jane's best friend, Sue, was at first played by Udana Power, then by Phyllis Glick.

The problem with Dick and Jane's courtship was that viewers quickly fell out of love with the series. See Dick. See Jane. See Dick run after Jane. See viewers tune out. See network cancel series.

THE LUCY SHOW

October 1, 1962–September 2, 1974.   CBS

Character:	Vivian Bagley
Played by:	Vivian Vance
Date(s):	October 1, 1962–June 1965

Replaced by:	Mary Jane Lewis
Played by:	Mary Jane Croft
Date(s):	September 1965–September 2, 1974

Character:	Mr. Barnsdahl
Played by:	Charles Lane
Date(s):	October 1, 1962–1963

Replaced by:	Theodore J. Mooney/Harrison Otis Carter
Played by:	Gale Gordon
Date(s):	October 1, 1962–September 16, 1968
	September 23, 1968–September 2, 1974

Character:	Chris Carmichael
Played by:	Candy Moore
Date(s):	October 1, 1962–June 6, 1965

Replaced by:	Kim Carter
Played by:	Lucie Arnaz
Date(s):	September 23, 1968–September 2, 1974

Character:	Jerry Carmichael
Played by:	Jimmy Garrett
Date(s):	October 1, 1962–1966

Replaced by:	Craig Carter
Played by:	Desi Arnaz, Jr.
Date(s):	September 23, 1968–September 1971

Connecticut life must have agreed with Lucy, even if her marriage to Desi Arnaz didn't, because that is where she decided to set up housekeeping for her next situation comedy, *The Lucy Show,* which for the first month was titled, *The Lucille Ball Show.*

Lucy moved from Westport to Danfield, Connecticut and set up housekeeping at 132 Post Road. Her new alias was Lucy Carmichael and her new husband . . . well, there was no new husband—Lucy Carmichael was a widow, which was the basis for the storyline of many an episode.

Finding a new husband was important not only for Lucy, but for her two teenaged kids. Lucy's daughter, Chris, was played by Candy Moore, who played Jeff Stone's girlfriend, Bibi Barnes on *The Donna Reed Show* from 1963 to 1965. Her brother, Jerry Carmichael, was played by Jimmy Garrett who was a relative unknown both before and after he did the series.

And when it came to friendship, Lucy could always count on her friend Vivian Bagley, played by Vivian Vance, very well known to audiences as Ethel Mertz from the original *I Love Lucy* series (See Entry).

Money, or rather the lack of it and schemes to get more of it, was the basis for the second most popular storylines. Not too long afterward, the need to pay the bills drove Mrs. Carmichael back into the work force at the Danfield First National Bank. The president of the bank was Mr. Barnsdahl, played by that well-known tightwad, Charles Lane, who had played Dale Busch on *Karen* (See Entry). But to long-time fans of the program, money became synonymous with Mooney, who became the new president of the bank. His full name was

10. ''Insider.'' *TV Guide,* February 16, 1985, Vol. 33, No. 7, Issue #1664, p. 19.

Theodore J. Mooney, but Lucy never called him anything but Mr. Mooney, and he always referred to her as Mrs. Carmichael, as only Gale Gordon could enunciate it. In fact, Gale Gordon's ''Mrs. Carmichael!'' echoes in our ears almost as well as Ricky Ricardo's enunciation of ''Lucy!''

This was a sitcom marriage made in heaven and planned for more than ten years, because Lucille Ball had always wanted to work with Gale Gordon on a television series. In fact, she had really wanted him to play Fred Mertz on *I Love Lucy* (See Entry). Now he was finally available and here to stay.

However, they didn't stay in Connecticut. Lucy moved to 708 Gower Street, San Francisco, possibly to get away from that tyrannical boss of hers. But when she accepted her new position as secretary to the vice president of the Westland Bank, just who do you think her boss was? That's right, Mr. Mooney. There was no explanation given as to why he gave up the presidency of Danfield for a vice presidency at Westland, but knowing Mr. Mooney, Westland must have offered him more money, or he never would have left Connecticut. Of course, he could have decided to leave Danfield First National to get away from Mrs. Carmichael, but no such luck, she was there waiting for him.

There were also cast changes in the making. Lucy's daughter, Chris, was no longer in the series and her housemate, Vivian, was relegated to a few guest appearances. Her new co-conspirator was Mary Jane Lewis, played by Mary Jane Croft, last seen back in Connecticut as the Ricardo's next-door neighbor, Betty Ramsey, during the 1957 season of *I Love Lucy* (See Entry).

When the series returned on September 23, 1968, it had been completely revamped. First, the series had a new name, *Here's Lucy.* Lucy had a new name, Lucy Carter. She had two new kids, who were in real life her two old kids: Lucie Arnaz as Kim Carter and Desi Arnaz, Jr. as Craig Carter. One of the episodes of the series, ''Kim Finally Cuts You Know Who's Apron Strings,'' was actually a pilot for Lucie Arnaz's own series.

She did get her own series, *The Lucie Arnaz Show,* but it wasn't until ten years later. In that series, a sitcom, Lucie played psychologist Jane Lucas. Ms. Arnaz's CBS sitcom didn't quite have the staying power of her mother's: it lasted only two months, running from April 2 to June 11, 1985. She was, however, given the honor of hosting *I Love Lucy: The First Show,* a special presentation of the lost pilot to her parents' *I Love Lucy* (See Entry) series.

With her real kids in tow, the title of Ms. Ball's series might have been changed to *Family Affair,* but that name had already been taken by the series which aired on CBS an hour after *Here's Lucy.*

Lucy no longer worked for a bank but for The Unique Employment Agency, which advertised ''Unusual Jobs for Unusual People.'' The agency was run by her brother-in-law, Harrison Otis Carter, who was not played by a member of the family but by—you guessed it—Gale Gordon, who was just as stuffy and irascible as ever.

Confident in his abilities as an actor and knowing full well that this time that kid on television really was Lucy's son, Desi Arnaz, Jr. left the series in 1971 to pursue other opportunities which included episodes of *Night Gallery, The Mod Sqaud* and *The Streets of San Francisco.* He made appearances on *The Love Boat* and *Fantasy Island* and even did a pilot, *Wacked Out,* which co-starred *The A-Team*'s Amy Allen, Melinda Culea. The pilot aired on NBC on September 26, 1981, but was never produced as a series.

Arnaz did manage to land his own series in 1983, playing Walter Nebicher, the computer nerd who was the head of the Los Angeles Police Department's computer section. Nebicher created a computer character with the combined abilities of the world's finest sleuths, from Sherlock Holmes to James Bond, which accidentally turns into a handsome holographic super-hero who steps out of his computer to fight crime in the real world. The science fiction police show was titled *Automan,* and it materialized on ABC from December 15, 1983. The plug was pulled on April 2, 1984, after twelve fairly entertaining episodes.

M

M*A*S*H

September 17, 1972–September 19, 1983.   CBS

Character:	Lieutenant Colonel Henry Blake
Played by:	McLean Stevenson
Date(s):	September 17, 1972–March 18, 1975

Replaced by:	Colonel Sherman Potter
Played by:	Harry Morgan
Date(s):	September 19, 1975–September 19, 1983

Character:	Captain John F. X. ''Trapper John'' McIntyre
Played by:	Wayne Rogers
Date(s):	September 17, 1972–March 18, 1975

Replaced by:	Captain B.J. Hunnicut
Played by:	Mike Farrell
Date(s):	September 12, 1975–September 19, 1983

Character:	Major Frank Burns
Played by:	Larry Linville
Date(s):	September 17, 1972–March 15, 1977

Replaced by:	Major Charles Emerson Winchester, III
Played by:	David Ogden Stiers
Date(s):	September 20, 1977–September 19, 1983

Character:	Corporal Walter Eugene ''Radar'' O'Reilly
Played by:	Gary Burghoff
Date(s):	September 17, 1972–March 24, 1980

Replaced by:	Corporal Maxwell Q. Klinger
Played by:	Jamie Farr
Date(s):	October 8, 1972–September 19, 1983

Character:	Lieutenant Father Francis Mulcahy
Played by:	George Morgan
Date(s):	September 17, 1972

Replaced by:	Father Francis Mulcahy
Played by:	William Christopher
Date(s):	September 24, 1972–September 19, 1983

Character:	Igor Straminsky
Played by:	Joseph Perry
Date(s):	February 18, 1973

Replaced by:	Igor Straminsky
Played by:	Jeff Maxwell
Date(s):	February 9, 1974–February 21, 1983

Character:	Major Donald Penobscott
Played by:	Beeson Carroll
Date(s):	March 15, 1977

Replaced by:	Lieutenant Colonel Donald Penobscott
Played by:	Mike Henry
Date(s):	November 22, 1977

Character:	Nurse Baker
Played by:	Jean Powell
Date(s):	unknown

Replaced by:	Nurse Baker
Played by:	Linda Kelsey
Date(s):	October 19, 1976

The acronym ''M*A*S*H,'' which stands for Mobile Army Surgical Hospital, became a part of the nation's vocabulary when the 1968 novel by Dr. H. Richard Hornberger, using the pseudonym, Richard Hooker, was turned into the Academy Award-winning motion picture, M*A*S*H in 1970.

The film, which starred Donald Sutherland as Hawkeye Pierce and Elliott Gould as ''Trapper John'' McIntyre, succeeded in poking fun at war—the Korean War to be exact—while at the same time showing graphic operating-room scenes.

This juxtaposition of comedy and carnage appealed to Twentieth Century-Fox, which hired Gene Reynolds to produce the project for television. Reynolds, in turn, hired screenwriter Larry Gelbart to work on the pilot script and it is Gelbart who received the screen credit, ''developed for television by.''

The series, which was also a social anti-war statement on the

Vietnam war, starred Alan Alda and Wayne Rogers in the Captain Benjamin Franklin "Hawkeye" Pierce and "Trapper" John McIntyre roles, with Loretta Swit replacing Sally Kellerman as Major Margaret "Hot Lips" Houlihan. The other characters in this ensemble cast, Colonel Henry Blake, Major Frank Burns and Corporal "Radar" O'Reilly were played by McLean Stevenson, Larry Linville and Gary Burghoff. Burghoff was the only holdover from the motion picture in which Blake and Burns were played by Roger Bowen and Robert Duvall.

In the film, the role of the company chaplain was a small one, so the character of Father Mulcahy was introduced and expanded—perhaps to add some morality to the madness of war. In the pilot episode, which aired as the series' first episode, the military man of the cloth was played by George Morgan. William Christopher played him for the remainder of the series.

In a January 1983 story for the Associated Press, Jerry Buck quoted executive producer Burt Metcalfe: "It was agreed that the show could survive the comings and goings of the actors. Except for Alan Alda." Even though Metcalfe was never faced with the problem of having to replace Alan Alda, his theory was put into practice when he had to replace four of the show's main characters.

M*A*S*H premiered in 1972 with McLean Stevenson as commanding officer Lieutenant Colonel Henry Blake. The 4077th remained under his command for three full seasons but his reign ended when NBC signed actor McLean Stevenson to a long-term contract. His two most popular situation comedy series for NBC were The McLean Stevenson Show, which aired from December 1, 1976 to March 3, 1977, and Hello Larry, which aired from January 26, 1979 to April 30, 1980. He also appeared in two lesser-known and less successful series for the other two networks. In the Beginning aired on CBS from September 20 to October 18, 1978, and Condo aired on ABC from February 10 to June 16, 1983, and featured James Victor who later co-starred as Sergeant Mendoza on the new Zorro (See Entry).

"The producers [of M*A*S*H] dealt with another contract dispute in a more ingenious fashion, when McLean Stevenson grew restless to break out on his own during the second and third years. 'I'm tired of being one of six,' he complained. 'I want to be one of one.'

"When Stevenson made it clear he wouldn't be returning for a fourth year, the producers planned Colonel Blake's final appearance in absolute secrecy. When the actor got his copy of the complete script, he was shocked to discover that Colonel Blake was to be shot down over the Sea of Japan after his final appearance. 'I felt it was vindictive,' he told David Reiss, author of M*A*S*H: The Exclusive, Inside Story of Television's Most Popular Show, 'that the real motive was to prevent me from doing a show where I might want to continue being Henry Blake, M.D.' But after his anger softened, he was forced to admit, 'It did make one hell of a show.' "[1]

Television critic Phil Kloer of the Atlanta Constitution shed a little more light on the subject of Colonel Blake's untimely demise: "That show [M*A*S*H] really came of age, I think, when they killed Henry Blake. The reason for it, I've been told, was that McLean Stevenson was such a pain to work with that the writers wanted to make sure there would never, ever be pressure put on them to write him back into the script, for any reason."[2] And Rick Mitz reported in The Great TV Sitcom Book that Colonel Blake's fate was kept a secret from the rest of the cast so that their reactions would be genuine when Radar delivered the news. To keep the news of Colonel Blake's death a secret, Gary Burghoff wasn't given his lines until the scene was ready to be filmed.

In one of those rare instances when the listing in TV Guide didn't give away the surprise ending, the episode "Abyssinia, Henry" was described this way: "It's a red-letter day for the 4077th after Henry (McLean Stevenson) learns that he has been discharged. Sentimental moments mix with bon-voyage hoopla as the C.O. prepares to take leave and Frank (Larry Linville) prepares to take command."

But it was Radar who dropped the bomb on the members of the 4077th—and the viewing public—when he staggered into the operating room looking as though he was suffering from shell shock.

TRAPPER: Radar, put a mask on!

HAWKEYE: If that's my discharge give it to me straight, I can take it.

RADAR: (Noticeably upset and holding back tears) I have a message: Lieutenant Colonel Henry Blake's plane was shot down over the sea of Japan. It spun in. There were no survivors.

Unbeknownst to the viewers was that this episode would also be the last time they saw Hawkeye's practical-joking bunkmate, "Trapper." His departure would be the basis for the first half of the hour-long episode, "Welcome to Korea," which also introduced Colonel Blake's replacement.

It was not the writers, but the actor himself who asked to be written out. It started when Alan Alda began to emerge as the central character, which is what was promised Rogers when he made his commitment to the series. It continued with a contract dispute that lasted for months and placed Rogers at the receiving end of a $2.9 million breach-of-contract suit. He beat it with his business savvy and the keen negotiating skills of an investment counselor that has earned William Wayne McMillan Rogers, III the nickname, "The Wizard."

Rogers continues to act and starred as Jake Axminster from February 3 to August 10, 1976 in Stephen J. Cannell's short-lived detective series, City of Angels, which aired on NBC. He also replaced Larry Hagman as Tony Nelson in I Dream of Jeannie: 15 Years Later, the extension episode of I Dream of Jeannie (See Entry).

"Wayne Rogers' departure, for instance, made more sense to

_____

1. Waldron, Vince. Classic Sitcoms. A Celebration of the Best of Prime-Time Comedy. MacMillan Publishing Company, New York, 1987, p. 250.
2. Javna, John. The Best of TV Sitcoms. Harmony Books. New York, 1988, p. 87.

the survivors than did McLean Stevenson's. As William Christopher put it, 'Wayne was a leading-man type. It didn't seem unreasonable for him to go off on his own.' "[3]

The episode "Welcome to Korea," was another of *M*A*S*H*'s one-hour episodes. It began with Frank Burns throwing around his weight as the acting C.O. and Hawkeye returning from "R&R" in Tokyo.

The writers again called upon Corporal O'Reilly to be the bearer of bad news. He finds Hawkeye, who is suffering from what he called "The Mount Rushmore of hangovers," taking a shower with his clothes on.

RADAR: I just want you to know that we couldn't reach you. And we really tried.

HAWKEYE: What'd you need me for. You had Frank Burns and trusty Trapper John, Champion of the Oppressed and Molester of registered nurses.

RADAR: He's gone, Hawkeye. He got his orders, he's been shipped stateside.

Radar tells Hawkeye that Trapper left for the Military Air Transport Service at Kimpo only a couple of hours earlier. When Hawkeye hears Radar ask Frank Burns for permission to pick up Trapper's replacement at Kimpo, Hawkeye forces Radar to let him drive the jeep to Kimpo so that he can say good-bye to his best friend.

Meanwhile, in eager anticipation of breaking in a new man, Major Margaret Houlihan (Loretta Swit), who is assisting Frank with the administration of the camp, drools over the credentials of the incoming surgeon, who graduated from Stanford Medical School in the top ten of his class.

At Kimpo, Hawkeye and Radar arrive too late to catch Trapper and Hawkeye laments to Radar, after looking at the flight manifest,

HAWKEYE: I missed Trapper by ten minutes. Ten lousy minutes!

Captain Hunnicut (Mike Farrell) is located by Radar and introduced to an uninterested Hawkeye who is still miffed about missing Trapper. On their way back to the jeep they discover there *is* no jeep—it's been stolen. But instead of reporting it, they go to the base officers' club for a drink. Captain Hunnicut, who previously told Captain Pierce to call him B.J., asks the meaning of his drinking buddy's nickname.

B.J.:   Hawkeye, why Hawkeye?

HAWKEYE: That's from *The Last of the Mohicans*. My father was crazy about that book. He was crazy about Indians.

The three comrades in arms steal a General's jeep that is parked outside the officers' club. En route to the 4077th, they meet up with a unit of soldiers and are attacked by snipers and missile fire, which gives B.J. his first taste of war—a taste that makes him sick to his stomach.

Before returning to camp, Hawkeye takes his new-found friend to Rosie's Bar, the local watering hole. When Radar (who only drinks Grape Nehi) pulls into camp with the two officers, they are falling-down drunk. Margaret's high expectations of the new medical officer are quickly dashed when he addresses Frank as "Ferret Face."

This new surgeon joined the 4077th with a long list of credits which include appearances on episodes of *McHale's Navy, Marcus Welby, M.D., Banacek* and *Harry-O.* The casting of Mike Farrell as Wayne Rogers' replacement was not a sudden decision but something the producers had considered once before: ". . . my agent had gotten a phone call saying that there were some contract difficulties with Wayne and would I be available to replace him if the need arose. So when I read that he was definitely leaving, I wondered if I would hear from the show again.

"It was a long, slow process with Wayne, so it was months later when I finally did hear from the show and they asked me to come in and talk to them about it. I made it very clear right then that I was not interested in replacing Wayne as Trapper. It had to clearly be a new character. I had no wish to do Trapper at all. Wayne had done it well and was well accepted by the public in that role. The *M*A*S*H* people said right off that it would be a new role, B.J. Hunnicut, and that he would be different from Hawkeye the womanizer."[4]

Captain Hunnicut's disrespect for the acting C.O. in the "Welcome to Korea" episode didn't really matter since Major Burns' command officially ended on September 19, 1952, at exactly 1600 hours (military time for 4:00 p.m.). And if you haven't already guessed it, Radar was the one who delivered the crushing news to Frank. He took it quite well while in the mess tent, but threw a tantrum back in his quarters.

This wasn't the first time that Frank was called upon to command the 4077th. In "Henry, Please Come Home," which aired on November 19, 1972, he was put in charge when Colonel Blake was transferred to Tokyo. This command didn't last very long either; Henry returned at the end of the episode.

In "Welcome to Korea," Burns' replacement drove his own jeep into camp and honked his horn at a sunbathing Radar. Radar, with his eyes still closed, told the unknown driver with uncharacteristic feistiness, "Stick that horn in your ear." The voice that brought the young Corporal back to reality was that of his new commanding officer—"On your feet soldier. I'm Colonel Potter."

Potter was not silly or irreverent like his predecessor who always wore a fishing cap and would have been completely lost without Radar. Colonel Potter was referred to as "Regular Army." Much older than anyone in the camp, he was a career man. He came on a little gruff at first, but softened up after his first session in the operating room, after which he joined Pierce

3. Prelutsky, Burt. "The Troops Scatter—but the Memories Linger." *TV Guide,* Vol. 31, No. 7, February 12, 1983, Issue # 1559, p. 21.
4. Kalter, Suzy. *The Complete Book of M*A*S*H.* Harry N. Abrams, Inc. Publishers, New York, 1984, p. 101.

and Hunnicut for a drink in "The Swamp," the nickname for their home away from home.

Even though everyone acted as though they had never met this man before, they had—it is just that he was a different person. Before Harry Morgan took over the command of M*A*S*H 4077, he appeared in the first episode of the 1974/1975 season, "The General Flipped at Dawn," which aired on September 10, 1974." He played General Bartford Hamilton Steele, a West Point graduate, spit-and-polish military man who was strictly G.I. on the outside, and certifiably nuts on the inside. He insisted on protocol and detested waste. Some of the suggestions he made were for Frank to clip the hair in his nose, Father Mulcahy to polish up his cross, and Colonel Blake to clean and re-use their wooden tongue depressors.

The order that broke the camel's back came after a conversation with Ward Officer Martin "Marty" Williams (Theodore Wilson), one of the unit's chopper pilots. General Steele asked him how far it was to the front and how much fuel was consumed to get there. His answer was twenty minutes to the front with fuel consumption at twenty gallons an hour. The general found this wasteful and mandated a very unpopular solution:

STEELE: We're going to have to move your unit closer to the front, Colonel.

BLAKE: You mean where the guys are fighting, sir?

STEELE: You do your best business on Main Street (aside) General Cornwallis.

TRAPPER: It's not all that pleasant being on the fifty-yard line, General.

BLAKE: It's very dangerous, sir.

STEELE: Danger is our business. Get your second in command and we'll find a new location. M*A*S*H means MOBILE, Army, Surgical, Hospital. And mobile you shall be.

The 4077th, of course, didn't make the suggested move, but the next season Harry Morgan moved in as the new commanding officer. Of his eleven television series Harry Morgan is best remembered for his first, second and fifth. His first role was as Peter Porter, Lily Ruskin's (Spring Byington) next-door neighbor on *December Bride,* which aired on CBS from October 4, 1954, to September 24, 1959. His second series, *Pete and Gladys,* was a spinoff of *December Bride* that aired on CBS from September 19, 1960 to September 10, 1962. The fifth series which Morgan put his indelible mark on was *Dragnet* (See Entry), in which he played Officer Bill Gannon, Joe Friday's fifth partner.

When *TV Guide* asked Harry Morgan how he felt about replacing McLean Stevenson, he said, "I was afraid. Mac was enormously popular. My fear lasted only until about noon of that first day, though. You just couldn't ask for a better role than Sherman Potter. Potter has made me a better person. He's such a decent human being that, after eight years, some of that is bound to rub off."[5]

One of the subplots of "Welcome to Korea" was the disappearance of Major Burns, who had trouble dealing with the fact that he had not been made Colonel Blake's replacement. He turned up at the end of the episode and continued to be the butt of Hawkeye's, and now B.J.'s, humor and practical jokes. Early in 1977, Burns disappeared again—this time for good.

The episode, "Fade Out, Fade In," began with Radar's concern over the fact that Major Burns was overdue from his "R&R."

COL. POTTER: It's not like Burns. He's a lousy surgeon, a pain in the butt; however, he's always on time.

RADAR: I know, that's why I'm worried.

Margaret has returned early from her honeymoon with Donald Penobscott (who does not appear in this episode) and it is believed that Frank may have gone to Tokyo in an attempt to have a last tryst with Margaret, or, worse yet, to sabotage her wedding and/or her honeymoon. With Frank AWOL, the 4077th is down one surgeon. To fill the spot, Colonel Potter asks Radar to call Colonel Baldwin (Robert Symonds) at Tokyo General Hospital to get a surgeon to fill in for forty-eight hours until Frank is located. The surgeon Colonel Baldwin assigns is Charles Emerson Winchester, III (David Ogden Stiers), a pompous Bostoner who has just won $672.17 from him in a game of cribbage.

En route to the 4077th, Winchester's jeep comes under attack by mortar fire. The driver (James Lough) leaves the jeep and takes cover moments before it is blown up. Without a vehicle, the driver leaves Winchester to find his own way to the M*A*S*H unit. Winchester arrives unceremoniously riding on the back of one of the local's ox carts.

Colonel Potter is kept apprised of Frank's whereabouts and antics by Sergeant Williamson of the Military Police. From the sound of things, it would seem that Frank has gone off the deep end. Williamson's first report told of an inebriated Burns who accosted a blonde WAC in Seoul (he pretended to be shampooing her hair and then begged her to let him clip her toenails). The second report found Burns on a bus trying to bite the buttons off the uniform of a Red Cross worker while yelling, "Margaret, Margaret."

The final report on Major Burns comes from Frank himself, in a one-sided phone conversation with Colonel Potter (Larry Linville did not appear in this episode). As related by Potter to O'Reilly, Pierce and Hunnicut, the intoxicated major spotted a couple on the street whom he mistook for Margaret and her new

5. Prelutsky, Burt. "The Troops Scatter—but the Memories Linger." *TV Guide,* Vol. 31, No. 7, February 12, 1983, Issue # 1559, p. 20.

husband, Donald Penobscott. He followed them into a public bath and, in full uniform, joined them in the tub. He grabbed the woman and began crying. Naturally these people, Brigadier General Kester and his wife, weren't who Frank thought they were. After being held for psychiatric observation, Frank was transferred. Colonel Potter orders the group to offer a toast to their former colleague. B.J. suggests something tender, their C.O. insists on something sentimental. They raise their glasses and Hawkeye says, "Good-bye ferret face."

Hawkeye's initial joy about Frank's transfer later turns to rage after a phone conversation with his former Swampmate.

> HAWKEYE: The Army, in its infinite wisdom, has not only cleared Frank of the charges—they have assigned him to a veteran's hospital in Indiana and promoted him to Lieutenant Colonel.

Infuriated with the news, Hawkeye tosses the phone out the door.

Frank's transfer also puts the pressure on Colonel Potter to find a replacement. He looks no further than Major Winchester, who, although a boorish snob, is an outstanding surgeon. Needless to say, Winchester is greatly displeased at his reassignment.

> WINCHESTER: And if I refuse?

> COL. POTTER: You'll be making gravel at Leavenworth!

The reasons given for Larry Linville's departure weren't as harsh as those given for the departure of McLean Stevenson and Wayne Rogers. He explained: "My contract was up at the end of Year Five and I had the option to negotiate or take a walk. I felt I had done everything possible with the character, so I told them I was leaving. I'm not sorry I left. I went on to do television, movies-of-the-week, and theater. I was saturated with playing only Frank."[6]

One of the television roles Larry Linville went on to play was the dopey Air Force General, Major General Kevin Kelley, in *Grandpa Goes to Washington,* which starred Jack Albertson as Senator Joe Kelley. The short-lived sitcom aired on NBC from September 7, 1978 to January 16, 1979.

A number of minor supporting characters were replaced over the course of the series. One was Igor, the company's culinary character, regularly seen dishing out the swill known as "mess." In "The Long-john Flap" he was played by Joseph Perry and thereafter by Jeff Maxwell, who made his premiere in "Crisis," in which the camp was forced to deal with a shortage of fuel for both their bodies and the equipment.

Major "Hot Lips" Houlihan conducted a long-distance romance with a Major Donald Penobscott which was consummated with their joining in "Margaret's Marriage." The officer who took the sacred vow was Beeson Carroll, who later played W.D. Hall on the CBS drama, *Palmerstown, U.S.A.,* which aired from March 20, 1980 to June 9, 1981.

The only other on-camera appearance of the often-mentioned Donald was in "The M*A*S*H Olympics." By this appearance he'd been promoted to Lieutenant Colonel and was now played by Mike Henry, who was supposed to be television's first Tarzan (See Entry).

A number of actresses worked regularly on the series, but appeared as different nurses. One in particular, Nurse Baker, was played by both Jean Powell and Linda Kelsey, the latter of whom co-starred as reporter Billie Newman on *The Mary Tyler Moore Show* spinoff, *Lou Grant* (See Entry).

The last major character to be discharged from the 4077th was Corporal Walter "Radar" O'Reilly. Gary Burghoff *is* Radar, and not just because he was the only actor to play the character on the series; he also holds the distinction of being the only actor from the 1970 motion picture to recreate his role for the series. It was perfect casting; there was no one else who could have brought the lovable innocence to this character as well as the diminutive Burghoff.

One of the reasons given for Burghoff's departure after seven seasons and 169 episodes was, according to John Javna, that "he was suffering severe burnout and didn't like being recognized on the street."[7]

" 'I was angry and rebellious,' Gary says, 'because I thought that if I allowed myself to be Radar and talk to people about him, I wouldn't be able to be myself.' "[8]

It was pretty much the consensus of the cast and crew that Burghoff was quite taken with himself, possibly because he had worked on the motion picture. "Loved Radar, hated Burghoff" was the sentiment expressed by his former co-workers, who felt that Burghoff's personality problems may have been the reason he was so rude to them. Explosive incidents with the actor range from his being reprimanded by Alan Alda for continually showing up late, to the time Wayne Rogers threw a chair at him.

Still, the Radar character was so beloved that he was given a two-part farewell, "Good-bye, Radar, Part 1 and Part 2," which aired on October 8 and 15, 1979. His final appearance on the series was actually the March 12, 1979 episode, "The Party," but he was wooed back for this special two-parter that would be Radar's last hurrah, though his character was the catalyst for two later episodes.

The two-part tear-jerker began innocently enough with the camp's electrical generator crapping out during a session in the O.R. "Damn, I'll be glad when Radar gets back," barks Colonel Potter. This is because Radar was the only one in camp with the ability to finagle a new generator.

Filling in for Radar during his absence (he is supposed to be on his way back from R&R in Tokyo) is Klinger who, after coming up empty-handed, is scolded by Colonel Potter for not being able to produce a generator. He admits, "Nobody wants Radar back more than me, sir."

6. Kalter, Suzy. *The Complete Book of M*A*S*H.* Harry N. Abrams, Inc., Publishers, New York, 1984, p. 101.
7. Javna, John. *The Best of TV Sitcoms.* Harmony Books, New York, 1988, p. 87.
8. Rovin, Jeff. *TV Babylon,* Signet, New York, April 1987, p. 229.

Upon Radar's return to camp, Colonel Potter declares, "Welcome back, son, I think I missed you even more than I miss Mildred [Mrs. Potter]."

Radar's efforts to locate a generator are interrupted by the news that his Uncle Ed has died.

B.J.: How 'bout you, Radar? You all right?

RADAR: Huh? Yeah, I'm okay. I don't want to be, but I guess I have to be, I'm the man of the family now.

COL. POTTER: That's right, son, and you're going home. Go get yourself a DA-7 Hardship Discharge and type your name on it.

The company clerk not only prepares to leave, but actually does his darnedest to divest himself of his duties, once screaming at his replacement Corporal Klinger, "I'm not the clerk anymore. You're the clerk!"

Clerk or no clerk, Radar's loyalty to his country and his duties drives him to assist Klinger in one last-ditch attempt to secure a new generator—but he doesn't succeed. This places the medical staff in an awful predicament when wounded are flown in just before dark.

Then, in what Colonel Potter called "a brainstorm," Radar managed to pull them through the crisis (with the assistance of some clever writing) by ordering a nearby camp to send every available jeep and truck to the 4077th. There, under Radar's guidance, the doctors prepare to operate al fresco, ringed by U.S. Army vehicles with their headlights trained on the operating tables.

Being the one responsible for saving all those lives gives Radar second thoughts about his discharge and he tells the Colonel that he has decided to stay. It is only after several speeches and some loving yelling by his friends, particularly Hawkeye and Colonel Potter, that he changes his mind and agrees to accept the Colonel's offer and go home.

A bon voyage party is planned to say good-bye to this, the most gentle of soldiers in this man's army. This "shove off soirée," as the Colonel called it, however, has to be put off when a new complement of wounded is brought into camp, and Radar and Hawkeye, his idol, never get a chance to say a good-bye. Radar, who will be leaving in a couple of hours, tells Hawkeye that he'll find him before he has to go. Where he finds him is in the operation room. Hawkeye looks up from his patient and catches a glimpse of Radar, in his dress uniform, looking through the dirty plastic window. Not knowing what to do, Hawkeye pauses for a moment, stands up straight and with his bloodied surgical glove, salutes his friend. Stepping back from the window, the corporal returns the Captain's salute. He quietly walks to the waiting jeep and gets in.

DRIVER: Where ya headed?

RADAR: Ottumwa, Iowa.

DRIVER: Never heard of it. Guess anywhere you live is home.

Then Radar delivers his final words: "I'm ready. Let's go."

And the jeep, carrying Radar, drives off into the sunset. The show could easily have ended there, but there was still one more commercial break, and for the epilogue the writers tried to pull one more tear out of the audience by having Colonel Potter discover Radar's teddy bear in Hawkeye's bed. It was almost as if Radar was saying, "Now that I've grown up, I won't be needing this anymore, but wanted you to have it to remember me by."

He, of course, left something much larger to remember him by: Corporal Max Klinger, an interesting choice as his replacement. Actually, Klinger was another of those one-minute superstars to emerge from a one-shot appearance—just as Christopher Lloyd was on *Taxi* (See Entry). And like Lloyd, the casting was perfect—too perfect to dismiss the actor after one episode. As with Kip and Henry (Tom Hanks and Peter Scolari) in the ABC situation comedy, *Bosom Buddies,* and Tony Curtis and Jack Lemmon as Joe and Jerry in the 1959 motion picture SOME LIKE IT HOT, there was never any question about Klinger's masculinity—not an easy feat to pull off. There was never any doubt that this hairy Lebanese with the shark-fin nose was anything more than a desperate soldier bucking for a Section Eight psychiatric discharge.

After his appearance in "Chief Surgeon Who?" Jamie Farr, who really was from Toledo, Ohio, became a regular member of the 4077th. As his character became more popular his role grew in size, until he seemed the logical choice to replace his buddy Corporal O'Reilly—and he was. Keen-eyed viewers may recall seeing Jamie Farr in dozens of roles on episodic television. His appearances include *Hazel, My Favorite Martian, I Dream of Jeannie, The Andy Griffith Show* and four episodes of *The Dick Van Dyke Show* (See Entry). During his period of enlistment he was a regular panelist on Chuck Barris' wacky program, *The Gong Show.*

After his honorable discharge from the Army he appeared in the spinoff series, *AfterM*A*S*H* (See Entry).

In addition to the transition episode that bids au revoir to Radar and acclimates Klinger to his new duties as the company clerk, there were a couple of other episodes that focused on this changing of the guard. In fact, the good-bye to Radar can actually be thought of as a four-parter: the first two parts featuring Gary Burghoff as the lovable Corporal. The third episode was, "Period of Adjustment." Airing on October 22, 1979, one week after Part 2 of "Good-bye, Radar," the story was set two weeks after Radar's departure. Continuing the storyline in which B.J. had made arrangements for his wife Peg to meet Radar when his plane stopped over in San Francisco, B.J. eagerly reads a letter from home, which sets the tone for the episode.

B.J.: Hey guys, listen to this. Peg says the meeting with Radar went just as we planned. "Erin and I went to the airport and we spent two or three hours with him. He sure is a cute little guy and so nice. Sweetheart, it was really funny when Erin first saw Radar in his uniform. She ran up to him and said, 'Hi, daddy.' "

The greater part of the episode has the members of the 4077th praising Radar and berating Klinger, who hasn't quite gotten the hang of the job yet. But as mad as Klinger is, it is nothing compared to that of B.J.'s anger; he is deeply hurt that he was not there to have his toddler call *him* daddy. He's so angry that he lashes out and smashes the still in the Swamp and slugs Hawkeye.

He then goes on a drinking binge with Klinger that ends in Colonel Potter's office. Colonel Potter apologizes to Klinger and tells him of his own difficulties when replacing the camp's beloved colonel. "Nobody was jumping for joy over me. I was no Henry Blake—never tried to be." He then orders Klinger to make the job his own, and concludes by saying, "As of right now, Radar's office is closed and Klinger's is open."

In the back room B.J. apologizes to Hawkeye for hitting the best friend he ever had and begins to cry uncontrollably. He lets out all of his pent-up anger while Hawkeye tries to console him by holding his friend close to him.

The fourth Radar-related episode, "The Foresight Saga," aired on April 13, 1989, near the end of the ninth season, and was more upbeat than the third episode.

The senior officers of the M*A*S*H 4077th are assembled in Colonel Potter's office; purpose, to hear the colonel read a letter from Radar. Gary Burghoff doesn't appear, but the words and tone of the letter ring true. He says that he is making the farm a success and that it will be their best year ever. The letter is signed, "Sincerely yours, in long-distance affection, Walter O'Reilly, Gentleman Farmer." They all say how much they loved and miss Radar, except Winchester, who says, "Actually, you know, I never thought I'd miss old Radar—I was right of course."

Hawkeye then comes up with the brilliant idea to phone Radar and say hello, but they fail to reach Radar. Colonel Potter does speak with Edna O'Reilly, Radar's mom, whose voice at first he mistakes for her son's. What the colonel learns in this conversation is that Radar had stretched the truth a bit in his letter because he was too embarrassed to tell his friends that things are very tough. They couldn't afford to hire any help to run the farm and Radar had to take an evening job in the general store so they'd have enough money to pay the mortgage.

Enter Park Sung (Rummel Mor), a Korean boy whose refugee family the M*A*S*H doctors once helped when their village was bombed out. Just days before he has repaid the favor of their saving his grandmother from pneumonia by bringing cabbage and other fresh vegetables to Igor (Jeff Maxwell) for the camp's mess.

Realizing that Park Sung is a farming whiz, B.J., Hawkeye, Colonel Potter and Father Mulcahy simultaneously come up with the same idea. Get Radar to sponsor Park Sung. Radar and his mom will get the help they need around the farm and Park Sung will have an opportunity to live and go to school in the United States.

The entire cast returned to the United States after the two-and-one-half-hour special, "Good-bye, Farewell and Amen," which aired on February 28, 1983 and was seen by an audience of 125 million.

MAJOR DAD

September 17, 1989–April 9, 1993.   CBS

Character:	Merilee Gunderson
Played by:	Whitney Kershaw
Date(s):	September 17, 1989–April 9, 1993
Replaced by:	Gunnery Sergeant Alma Lou "Gunny" Bricker
Played by:	Beverly Archer
Date(s):	September 17, 1990–April 9, 1993

After allowing nearly twenty years to pass since *Gomer Pyle, U.S.M.C.* (See Entry) marched off the CBS prime time lineup, the network gave United States Marines another crack at sitcom stardom.

This time, however, instead of being a gentle buffoon, the show's leading character, Major John D. "Mac" MacGillis, U.S.M.C., was a smart, do-it-by-the-book Marine, adjusting to life at a stateside base during peacetime. Wearing the uniform of "The Few, The Proud" was Gerald McRaney, who at first was in some ways reminiscent of the Mr. Banks character played by David Tomlinson in the fanciful 1964 musical, MARY POPPINS.

But instead of being worn down by a magical nanny, Mac falls head-over-spit-polished-heels for Polly Cooper (Shanna Reed), a liberal reporter for the *Oceanside Chronicle* who had tarred and feathered him in an article she wrote. Nevertheless, Mac falls for the attractive widow and her three daughters, Elizabeth (Marisa Ryan), Robin (Nicole Dubuc), and Casey (Chelsea Hertford).

In the first season, Whitney Kershaw, who appeared as Mary Kathrun during the 1984 season of the CBS evening soap opera, *Knots Landing*, played Mac's secretary, Merilee Gunderson. Beginning with the second season she was replaced by Beverly Archer as Gunnery Sergeant Alma Lou "Gunny" Bricker. Among Ms. Archer's earlier television credits are Lorraine from the short-lived NBC situation comedy, *The Nancy Walker Show* (September 30–December 23, 1976), and Iola Boylen during the 1986 season of *The Carol Burnett Show*'s first-run syndicated spinoff, *Mama's Family*.

MAJOR DELL CONWAY OF THE FLYING TIGERS

April 7, 1951–May 26, 1951.   DuMont-Syndicated

Character:	Major Dell Conway
Played by:	Eric Fleming
Date(s):	April 14, 1951–May 26, 1951
Replaced by:	Major Dell Conway
Played by:	Ed Peck
Date(s):	July 29, 1951–March 2, 1952

Replaced by:	Major Dell Conway	
Played by:	Arthur ''Art'' Fleming	
Date(s):	1953	

Character:	Caribou Jones	
Played by:	Luis Van Rooten	
Date(s):	April 14, 1951–May 26, 1951	

Replaced by:	Caribou Jones	
Played by:	Bern Hoffman[9]	
Date(s):	July 29, 1951–March 2, 1952	

This low-budget adventure series, also known as *Flying Tigers,* aired live over the DuMont television network during the 1950s.

The flying hero, Major Dell Conway was first played by Eric Fleming, who achieved television fame from 1959 to 1965 as Gil Favor, the trail boss in charge of the cattle drive on the CBS Western series, *Rawhide* (See Entry).

In an unaired pilot, *Ding Howe of the Flying Tigers,* based on the real Flying Tigers of World War II, Richard Denning starred as Ding Howe, which was very much the same type of character as Major Dell.

On *Major Dell Conway of the Flying Tigers,* Conway's assistant, Caribou Jones, was played by Luis Van Rooten. Born Luis d'Antin Van Rooten in Mexico City on November 29, 1906, this small balding actor often played heavies during his motion picture career. He was educated at the University of Pennsylvania as an architect, but decided to turn to acting. His first role was as the German Nazi leader, Heinrich Himmler, in the 1944 film, THE HITLER GANG. He was Edwin Orlin in the 1948 Ray Milland drama, THE BIG CLOCK, and Hoenig in the 1951 Bob Hope comedy, MY FAVORITE SPY. In an unusual coincidence, Van Rooten again played Himmler in his last film, EICHMAN, which was released in 1961.

Following *Major Dell Conway of the Flying Tigers,* Luis Van Rooten appeared as boxing manager Knobby Walsh in the syndicated series, *The Joe Palooka Story* (See Entry). Character actor Luis Van Rooten, who was also a recognized horticulturist, died in Chatham, Massachusetts on June 17, 1973 at the age of 66.

Major Dell Conway of the Flying Tigers soon moved from its Saturday evening time slot to Sunday afternoon. The program also left the DuMont network. With its return as the syndicated series *Flying Tigers,* and with the change in day and time, came a change in cast. The new Major Dell Conway was Ed Peck, the tough gravel-voiced actor who turned up occasionally as the no-nonsense Officer Kirk on ABC's nostalgic '50s situation comedy, *Happy Days.* The new Caribou Jones was played by Bern Hoffman.

In the syndicated series, Ed Peck was replaced with Arthur ''Art'' Fleming as the leader of a brave group of fly boys whose lives were always in jeopardy. These later episodes were set during World War II and detailed the adventures of the Flying Tigers—the American volunteers who fought to free the Chinese from the Japanese by shooting down Zeros.

As a matter of fact the series lead's career remained in *Jeopardy,* as the host of that intelligent NBC game show for more than ten years. He even appeared in a cameo role as the host of *Jeopardy* aboard the very punny 1982 comedy, AIRPLANE II: THE SEQUEL

Fleming's earlier acting roles include Jeremy Pitt from the 1958/1959 season of the NBC Western, *The Californians,* and Ken Franklin in the 1959 syndicated crime drama, *International Detective.*

MAKE ROOM FOR DADDY

September 29, 1953–September 14, 1964.   ABC CBS
September 23, 1970–September 2, 1971   ABC

Character:	Margaret Williams	
Played by:	Jean Hagen	
Date(s):	September 29, 1953–1956	

Replaced by:	Kathy ''Clancey'' Williams	
Played by:	Marjorie Lord	
Date(s):	October 7, 1957–September 14, 1964	
	September 23, 1970–October 2, 1971	

Character:	Teresa ''Terry'' Williams	
Played by:	Sherry Jackson	
Date(s):	September 29, 1953–September 28, 1958	
	September 23, 1970–September 2, 1971	

Replaced by:	Teresa ''Terry'' Williams	
Played by:	Penny Parker	
Date(s):	1959–1960	

Replaced by:	Patty Williams	
Played by:	Lelani Sorenson	
Date(s):	unknown	

Replaced by:	Linda Williams	
Played by:	Angela Cartwright	
Date(s):	October 7, 1957–September 14, 1964	
	November 6, 1967	
	September 14, 1968	
	September 23, 1970–September 2, 1971	

Replaced by:	Jesse Leeds	
Played by:	Jesse White	
Date(s):	1955–1957	

---

9. Some sources say that Bern Hoffman played Major Dell Conway's sidekick, Caribou Jones, in *both* versions.

Replaced by:	Phil Arnold
Played by:	Horace McMahon
Date(s):	September 29, 1953–1954
Replaced by:	Phil Brokaw
Played by:	Sheldon Leonard
Date(s):	May 3, 1967
Character:	Louise
Played by:	Louise Beavers
Date(s):	unknown
Replaced by:	Louise
Played by:	Amanda Randolph
Date(s):	unknown
Character:	Pat Hannegan
Played by:	Pat Harrington, Jr.
Date(s):	1960
Replaced by:	Bill Johnson
Played by:	unknown
Date(s):	September 23, 1970–September 2, 1971

In much the same manner that Carl Reiner would later develop (with the help of Sheldon Leonard) the concept for his hit situation comedy, *The Dick Van Dyke Show* (See Entry), so too did Danny Thomas use his real life as the basis for *Make Room for Daddy*. The only difference was he didn't know he had come up with the idea. It happened by accident at the end of his meeting with Louis "Lou" F. Edelman and Melville "Mel" Shavelson, the producer and the writer for Thomas' 1951 musical, I'LL SEE YOU IN MY DREAMS. Thomas had just been given the go-ahead by ABC to develop his own show and his two friends had come over to hash over some ideas. Thomas was hot on the idea of a situation comedy, because it would enable him to get off the nightclub circuit and spend more time with his family, but nothing seemed to work.

"That's when Mel Shavelson got up to leave, and I began my long pleading to come up with *something* that would allow me to stay in Los Angeles with my kids. That I was away on the road so much that they hardly knew me, that they called me 'Uncle Daddy,'[10] that I didn't know my girls' dress sizes, that I wanted my son to know me as something more than a telephone pal. And that's when Mel leaped to his feet and yelled, 'That's the concept. I can write it overnight.' "[11]

The title for the show, *Make Room for Daddy*, was suggested by Danny's wife, Rose Marie (not the actress who starred as Sally Rogers on *The Dick Van Dyke Show*), as an outgrowth of their unusual lifestyle. It seems that when her husband was away on the road, their two daughters, Marlo and Terre, slept in the master bedroom with her. Consequently, the girls took over their father's dresser drawers, filling them with their own clothing. When their father returned they had to clear out of his room and "make room for daddy."

Thomas named his character Danny Williams, after his brother whose name was William. In true Ozzie Nelson tradition, the actor who played Danny's son (Rusty Hamer) used his own first name, while the Williams' daughter Terry (Sherry Jackson), had a more traditional spelling of his youngest daughter's name. To top off the cast of characters, Thomas used his eldest daughter's name, Margaret (today known as Marlo), for the name of his TV spouse, a role originally played by Jean Hagen, who had earned an Oscar nomination for her portrayal of Lina Lamont in the 1952 Gene Kelly musical, SINGIN' IN THE RAIN.

The show was a qualified success. It won the Sylvania Award 1953 for the best new show of the year. The following year *Make Room for Daddy* won the Emmy award for Best Situation Comedy Series, while Danny Thomas won the 1954 Emmy award for Best Actor Starring in a Regular Series.

At the 1955 season Emmy awards, Jean Hagen was nominated in the categories of Best Actress (Continuing Performance) and Best Actress in a Supporting Role, but lost to Lucille Ball and Nanette Fabray. But as Danny Thomas explained, "Things were not so fine. Jean Hagen, in the all-important role of my wife, was aloof in her dealings with the rest of us, sometimes even snobbish. I guess it had to do with her stage training, and the fact that she had played fairly significant roles both in the theater and in films. Her professional and personal habits tended to annoy me as well. On stage, she began by being just as cool in her part as she was in real life."[12] In addition to her attitude, Thomas spoke of Ms. Hagen's husband, who expressed a great deal of displeasure with the the show's new director, former screen toughie Sheldon Leonard, who had taken over from William Asher. "I don't want my wife to be directed by that gangster actor."[13] It has also been reported that Ms. Hagen, who owned seven percent of the series, quit after three seasons because she felt that she was doing a thankless job on the series, which regularly featured Thomas and the children more prominently than her. Thomas recalled that "She said she wanted to get to more serious work in the theater and the cinema."[14]

The 1955 season ended with Danny tearfully explaining Margaret's absence to the kids: "Mommy has gone to heaven."

The storyline picked up the following season with Danny Williams as a widower trying to raise Rusty and Terry by himself while he began dating a bevy of beautiful women, each of whom would try to win the kids over in the hopes of becoming their new stepmother. But none, including Marilyn Maxwell, was able to take their mother's place. "It was fun working with new beautiful women every week or two. The

10. "Uncle Daddy" was chosen as the title for the show's first episode.
11. Thomas, Danny. *Make Room for Danny*. Danny Thomas with Bill Davidson. G.P. Putnam's Sons, New York, 1991, p. 186.
12. Thomas, Danny. *Make Room for Danny*. Danny Thomas with Bill Davidson. G.P. Putnam's Sons, New York, 1991, p. 186.
13. *Ibid.*, p. 192.
14. *Ibid.*, p. 194.

only problem was that none of them really fit the bill as a permanent replacement for Jean Hagen.''[15]

One evening, as a diversion from the grueling work of a hit series, Thomas and his wife decided to take in a play, *Anniversary Waltz,* that was being done at a small theater on Wilshire Boulevard. Whether or not they enjoyed the play is immaterial; what is more significant is that they were both quite taken with the performance of the female lead, Majorie Lord.

After the curtain came down the Thomases went backstage to meet the young actress and Danny invited her to the studio to discuss the possibility of her playing one of Danny Williams' ''weekly dates.''

The storyline Sheldon Leonard and the show's writers came up with had Marjorie Lord playing a widowed nurse, Kathleen ''Kathy'' O'Hara, hired to care for Rusty, who had come down with the measles. The interaction between Ms. Lord and the cast was so good that she was written into a second episode in which she catches the measles from Rusty and is quarantined in the Williams' house. Being cooped up with Danny Williams may not have seemed like a picnic, but a budding romance developed and culminated in a marriage proposal by Kathy after Danny had botched his. This was the last episode of the season and of the series on ABC.

In the fall the series, renamed *The Danny Thomas Show,* premiered in *I Love Lucy*'s recently vacated prime time spot on the CBS schedule. A couple of minor changes were made to the series at this point. Kathy, whose maiden name was changed to Daly, was joined by her daughter Patty (Lelani Sorenson). A short time later, she was replaced by Angela Cartwright as Kathy's daughter Linda. It should also be noted that Kathy's maiden name was never Clancey. This was only a nickname given to her by Danny.

While movie-goers will remember Angela Cartwright as Brigitta Von Trapp in the 1965 Julie Andrews film, THE SOUND OF MUSIC, television audiences know her better as Penny Robinson from the CBS science fiction *Lost in Space* (September 15, 1965–September 11, 1968).

Sherry Jackson was written out of the series as Danny's daughter Terry because she had outgrown the part; it was explained that she had gone off to college—but she wasn't written out for good.

During the interim period, former Mousketeer Annette Funicello was brought in temporarily as Gina Minelli, a foreign exchange student from Italy.

Terry returned to the Williams' residence at the start of the 1959 season with a new actress (Penny Parker) taking Sherry Jackson's place. One of more than a dozen actresses who auditioned for the role was Mary Tyler Moore (whom Danny Thomas later cast in *The Dick Van Dyke Show*).

The now maturing young woman became romantically involved with Pat Hannegan, a nightclub performer played by comedian Pat Harrington, Jr., who had been a regular member of the ensemble cast on *The Steve Allen Show* from 1958 to 1961. He later co-starred as the macho handyman Dwayne Schneider on *One Day at a Time.*

The man responsible for Danny Williams' career was his agent, played during the course of the series by three different actors. The first, Jesse Leeds, was played by Jesse White, who appeared on two of Ann Sothern's sitcoms. From February 1, 1953 to September 10, 1957, Jesse White played Cagney Calhoun on *Private Secretary.* Following *The Danny Thomas Show* he went back to work for Ms. Sothern as Oscar Pudney for the 1960/1961 season of *The Ann Sothern Show.* His highly lauded film roles include the hospital aid, Wilson, in the 1950 James Stewart comedy, HARVEY, and J. Sinister Hulk, in the 1971 Boris Karloff beach comedy horror film, THE GHOST IN THE INVISIBLE BIKINI. White was also the long-running commercial spokesman, ''the lonely repairman'' for Maytag, before being replaced by *WKRP in Cincinnati*'s Gordon Jump at the end of 1989.

Danny's second agent, Phil Arnold, was played by Horace McMahon, who had played Lieutenant Monahan in the 1951 Kirk Douglas/Eleanor Parker police drama, DETECTIVE STORY, which was not unlike the Captain Willis role he played on television's *Martin Kane, Private Eye* (See Entry).

Even *The Danny Thomas Show* director/producer Sheldon Leonard went before the cameras once as Danny's agent, Phil Brokaw, in the episode titled ''The Road to Lebanon.''

To help keep the house in order, the Williamses employed a housekeeper named Louise. The first actress to take on this role, Louise Beavers, had plenty of practice, having played the third of four of TV's *Beulah*'s (See Entry).

The popular show went out of production in 1964. Danny Thomas decided to call it quits, but the series was revived six years later as *Make Room for Granddaddy,* which updated the characters in much the same manner as *Ozzie's Girls* updated *The Adventures of Ozzie & Harriet* (See Entry) and *The New Leave It to Beaver* updated *Leave It to Beaver* (See Entry).

Danny Thomas, Marjorie Lord, Rusty Hamer and Angela Cartwright all returned to reprise their roles. In an interesting switch, Penny Parker, who was the last actress to play Terry Williams, was replaced by Sherry Jackson, who had originated the role on *The Danny Thomas Show.* She was now married to someone by the name of Bill Johnson, since Pat Harrington, Jr. did not return to the role of Pat Hannegan. But Bill Johnson was one of those TV characters who was mentioned but never seen. He was supposed to be stationed overseas and it was because of Terry's plans to join him that she had to leave her son with Danny.

MAMA

July 1, 1949–March 17, 1957.   CBS

Character:	Dagmar Hanson
Played by:	Iris Mann
Date(s):	July 1, 1949–1949
Replaced by:	Dagmar Hanson
Played by:	Robin Morgan
Date(s):	1950–July 27, 1956

15. Thomas, *op. cit.,* p. 195.

Replaced by:	Dagmar Hanson
Played by:	Toni Campbell
Date(s):	December 1956–March 17, 1957

Character:	Uncle Chris
Played by:	Malcolm Keen
Date(s):	July 1, 1949–1951

Replaced by:	Uncle Chris
Played by:	Roland Winters
Date(s):	1951–1952

This is another of those instances where there is confusion surrounding the actual title of a show, which may or may not have been changed or replaced. The title of the play and the motion picture, on which this series is based, is *I Remember Mama,* and all versions are based on the best-selling book, *Mama's Bank Account,* by Kathryn Forbes.

Many highly regarded published sources list this show simply as *Mama,* but an equal number of similarly respected sources list the program's title as *I Remember Mama.* But which is correct?

One of the published sources listing the program as *Mama* is *TV Guide,* the undisputed bible of television viewing and history. One finds, however, that programs with particularly lengthy titles, such as *The Life and Legend of Wyatt Earp* (See Entry), were listed in *TV Guide* as *Wyatt Earp.* This practice was instituted to save space and prevails today, with *Superman* being cited for the *Adventures of Superman* (See Entry) and *Dobie Gillis* for *The Many Loves of Dobie Gillis* (See Entry). This in no way diminishes the usefulness of *TV Guide* because there is no confusion about the program being aired, but it does show how the correct names of series can become confused or lost over time.

The final authority, of course, lies in the programs themselves, and this, in many instances forces us to rely mostly on memory, as many of the early series were broadcast live. But the proof is in the viewing: one kinescope from 1949 which has survived confirms the title as *Mama.*

As the show's opening theme plays, Katrin narrates, "This old album brings back so many memories of San Francisco, of growing up, of all the happy, artless days that seemed so long ago. Here is our house on Steiner Street, where I was born. And these are the neighbors and friends I recall so well. And my aunts and their children. And I remember my family as we were then: my little sister Dagmar, my big brother Nels, and of course, Papa. But most of all when I think back to those happy days, most of all I remember Mama." And as the last three words are spoken, the title *Mama* appears on the screen.

This beloved family program about the lives of a Norwegian family did experience several changes in cast during its weekly prime time run. Peggy Wood played Marta "Mama" Hanson and Judson Laire was Lars "Papa" Hanson. Their daughter, Dagmar, was initially played by Iris Mann during 1949. Her replacement, Robin Morgan, remained with the series until it ended its prime time run after which she became a regular panelist on the radio and television quiz program, *Juvenile Jury* and starred as Corliss Archer in the 1956 special, *Meet Corliss*

Archer (See Entry). Her first motion picture role was Mother Cabrini as a child in the 1947 religious drama, CITIZEN SAINT. In the 1980 edition of *The Great TV Sitcom Book,* author Rick Mitz says that Ms. Morgan later became a poet and a well-known feminist.

Uncle Chris, who was played by Malcolm Keen for the first three years of the series, was replaced by Roland Winters, who was the second of three actors to portray John Randolph on *Doorway to Danger* (See Entry).

More than seven years after *Mama* began, CBS felt that the program had run its course and canceled it on July 27, 1956. The viewing public didn't take kindly to this decision and mobilized to save *Mama,* as if it were their own mothers who had been turned out by the cold cruel CBS. The network received thousands of letters, wires, petitions, and telephone calls demanding the program to be returned to the air. There were even newspaper editorials supporting the public's outrage.

Right or wrong, CBS bent to the pressure and returned the program, with all but one member of the original cast, to the air on Sunday afternoons beginning in December 1956.

Toni Campbell became the third juvenile actress to play Dagmar.

The revival just didn't work and thirteen weeks later, on St. Patrick's Day, March 17, 1956, *Mama* became a memory. Perhaps they might have had better luck if the Hansons had been Irish?

MAN AGAINST CRIME

October 7, 1949–August 19, 1956.   CBS-DuMont-NBC

Character:	Mike Barnett
Played by:	Ralph Bellamy
Date(s):	October 7, 1949–April 4, 1954

Replaced by:	Pat Barnett
Played by:	Robert Preston
Date(s):	June 29, 1951–August 1951

Replaced by:	Mike Barnett
Played by:	Frank Lovejoy
Date(s):	July 1, 1956–August 26, 1956

This no-nonsense, tough-as-nails private detective wasn't afraid to use his fists, which was a good thing, since he didn't use a gun. He was first played by well-known B actor Ralph Bellamy, who appeared in one hundred and seven feature films and more than twenty made-for-television movies since he began acting in 1930. His regular series include *The Eleventh Hour* (See Entry) and *The Defenders* (See Entry).

"*Man Against Crime* was one of the first, if not *the* first private detective series on the air at the very beginning of television. It was kind of a formula. A case was introduced at the beginning of the program and then it went into the story. It was a very popular show. It was on three networks at one time—there wasn't much on the air in those early, early days.

"The radio studios weren't equipped for TV, so we actually shot *Man Against Crime* live on the second or third floor above

Grand Central Station, where they were doing some experimenting with television. We did our show there and they also did *Ford Theater* and *Mama* there.

"This was, of course, before any national, cross-country hookups and we did *Man Against Crime* on kinescope and mailed it to other cities,"[16] said series star Ralph Bellamy.

Bellamy went on to explain that he was cast as detective Mike Barnett because he was starring as Jim McLeod, a similar character, in the Broadway production of *Detective Story.* In 1951, the play was made into a motion picture with Kirk Douglas as McLeod. Bellamy didn't appear in the film because he was still doing the role on the New York stage, but he did contribute to the production of the film.

"In my own preparation for the part on stage, I had become well-acquainted with the police department and the various police headquarters. When Willie [William] Wyler, the producer and director of the DETECTIVE STORY film, came to New York I helped him with the making of the picture by taking him around to give him the background he needed," said Bellamy.

Ralph Bellamy also cleared up the confusion that has long existed as to the period of time he stayed with the series. Some sources indicate that he was gone for nearly two years, while other sources report that he was only away for six weeks.

"I did leave *Man Against Crime* for a summer vacation for six weeks during the summer of 1951. I had asked for the time off after a solid year of work," Bellamy said.

While on vaction in England, Ralph Bellamy decided to go shopping for a piece of wardrobe that, as he recalls, began a trend that continues to this day—the detective's trenchcoat. "While I was in England I went to Aquascutum, one of the world's biggest men's shops, to buy a trenchcoat. I said, 'I want a trenchcoat with a belt, a wide collar and everything you can put on it—I want everything on it.' The salesman said to me, in his proper English accent, 'Oh do you mean one like Danny Kaye's?' He was being serious, because Danny Kaye wore a trenchcoat like that on the street, but I found it amusing and laughed. After that every private detective who came along wore a trenchcoat—but I think I was the first," chuckled Bellamy.

Ralph Bellamy's caseload on *Man Against Crime* was temporarily taken over by that most famous of music men, Robert Preston, whose name starts with "P," which rhymes with "T" and that spells talented.

"The producers told me that they had signed Bob [Robert Preston] as my replacement. I knew Bob and thought that was great," Bellamy said. Since this was only going to be a temporary replacement, and there were no extenuating circumstances, Ralph Bellamy was happy to appear in a transition episode introducing Robert Preston as his brother, Pat Barnett, who was supposed to have just arrived from Ireland.

"We started the first rehearsal, which included both of us with Pat just arriving from Ireland. And whatever he [Preston] had to say, he had the goddamnedest Irish brogue you ever heard in your life! I asked the director, 'What's going on here?'

and he said, 'I think he's doing fine, don't you?' and I said, 'No! What about that Irish accent?' It was so thick that you couldn't understand him. It was a joke—and it was on me!'' chuckled Bellamy.

When Ralph Bellamy returned from his vacation in England, Robert Preston traded his trenchcoat for a lab coat and became a doctor on the ABC documentary series, *Anywhere U.S.A.* He appeared in episodes of dozens of other television series and made-for-television movies for the next 30 years, including a regular role as Hadley Chisholm in *The Chisholms.* The CBS miniseries began as a four-part program which aired from March 29 to April 19, 1979. It later ran as a nine-episode series from January 19 to March 15, 1980. Preston's forty film roles include Digby Geste in the 1939 Gary Cooper/Ray Milland version of BEAU GESTE. Preston received an Academy Award nomination for his portrayal of Toddy in the 1982 Blake Edwards comedy, VICTOR/VICTORIA. His most famous role was when he turned River City upside down as Professor Harold Hill in the 1962 musical, THE MUSIC MAN.

Man Against Crime left the air for two years and then returned during the summer of 1956 on a new network (NBC) with a new actor (Frank Lovejoy) in the lead. Whether he was afraid of his adversaries or a drop in the ratings, Frank Lovejoy took no chances and carried a gun. It didn't help and his series was shot down after just one month.

The following summer Frank Lovejoy turned in his gun and turned on his tough guy act for a new detective drama, *Meet McGraw,* which premiered on NBC on July 2, 1957. In November 1958 the series moved to ABC, where it remained until October 8, 1959.

Lovejoy was already experienced at crime dramas, having starred as Howard Taylor in THE SOUND OF FURY in 1950. His other film roles include Lieutenant Tom Brennan in the 1953 3–D Vincent Price horror film, HOUSE OF WAX, and General Ennis C. Hawkes in the 1955 James Stewart war drama, STRATEGIC AIR COMMAND.

"Sometimes you can stay with a thing too long. As a matter of fact, I think I had somewhat of that feeling in *Man Against Crime,* and even in pictures. You can be cast for a certain kind of part in different pictures that has a resemblance to the same kind of character, which is not good for you. As a matter of fact, one time, out here in California, I was visiting Mark Hellinger, a friend of mine from New York. Mark, a very popular columnist who had written the first Broadway theater column, had come to California because he was trying to become a producer. He had an office on the Warner Bros. lot and later produced HIGH SIERRA with Humphrey Bogart and THE ROARING TWENTIES with Bogart and Cagney.

"It was just a social call and we were sitting in his office at Warner Bros. He was sitting at his desk when the phone rang. He excused himself and took the call. Lying on his desk was a script that was pointed toward me so that I was able to read the title—which I did. After the title it gave a list of characters. And after each character's name was a short description. Halfway down the list, next to the name of a character, it said, 'A naive, but charming fellow from the midwest or southwest. A typical Ralph Bellamy part'," laughed Bellamy.

"In pictures like THE AWFUL TRUTH and HIS GIRL FRIDAY, I played the kind of parts that had a resemblance to each other. And this is dangerous for an actor. If this happens— you're stuck. So I went back to New York and stayed there for about ten years doing one play right after the other," he said.

When asked about his favorite film role he answered, "I suppose I'd have to say F.D.R., because I admired the man as well as knowing him," Bellamy concluded.

During Universal's horror heyday, Ralph Bellamy played Captain Paul Montford in the 1941 Lon Chaney, Jr. classic, THE WOLF MAN. One of Bellamy's most recent motion picture roles was as James Morse in the 1990 film, PRETTY WOMAN.

THE MAN FROM U.N.C.L.E.

September 2, 1964–January 15, 1968.   NBC

Character:	Mr. Alexander Waverly
Played by:	Leo G. Carroll
Date(s):	September 2, 1964–January 15, 1968
Replaced by:	Sir John Raleigh
Played by:	Patrick Macnee
Date(s):	April 5, 1983 (*The Man From U.N.C.L.E.: The 15 Years Later Affair*. CBS)

This show, which was sort of a James Bond times two, appeared at the height of the popularity of the James Bond films precipitated by the success of FROM RUSSIA WITH LOVE, which was released in 1963.

The cast remained constant throughout the series and the first change wasn't until a revival episode was filmed nearly ten years after *The Man from U.N.C.L.E.* first aired. The head of U.N.C.L.E.'s New York office, Mr. Waverly, had to be recast because the actor who played him, Leo G. Carroll, had died on October 16, 1972.

Leo G. Carroll, a likeable British actor who wasn't "too British" for American tastes, had starred in two comedy series before taking on the responsibilities of maintaining peace in the free world. The later of the two was the ABC situation comedy, *Going My Way,* in which he played Father Fitzgibbon. But it was his earlier situation comedy, *Topper,* that made him a household name. Carroll also played Mr. Waverly on *The Girl from U.N.C.L.E.,* the short-lived spinoff of *The Man from U.N.C.L.E.,* that starred Stefanie Powers as April Dancer. This series ran concurrently with *The Man from U.N.C.L.E.,* beginning on September 13, 1966. It ended on August 29, 1967--five months before *The Man from U.N.C.L.E.* took a slug in the back of its ratings. Carroll's extensive film credits include Joseph in the 1939 Academy Award-winner, WUTHERING HEIGHTS and the professor in the riveting 1959 Alfred Hitchcock spy adventure, NORTH BY NORTHWEST. A few years earlier, Leo G. Carroll played a different kind of scientist. As Professor Gerald Deemer, his experiments with artificial food created a

The men from U.N.C.L.E. are (clockwise from center) agents Napoleon Solo (Robert Vaughn) and Ilya Kuryakin (David McCallum), with Leo G. Carroll as Mr. Alexander Waverly, the head of U.N.C.L.E.

one-hundred-foot-tall Theraphosidae in the 1955 science fiction, TARANTULA.

Replacing Leo G. Carroll's Mr. Waverly as the new head of the United Network Command for Law Enforcement was Sir John Raleigh, played by Patrick Macnee. Macnee had previously starred as John Steed in *The Avengers* (See Entry). The made-for-television movie was more than just a reunion, it was actually a pilot for a new *The Man from U.N.C.L.E.* series which was never produced.

The early part of the movie brings the audiences up to date on what former U.N.C.L.E. agents, Napoleon Solo (Robert Vaughn) and Ilya Kuryakin (David McCallum) are doing. We are also introduced to their new superior, Sir John Raleigh.

It was good fun to see Solo and Kuryakin together again, risking life and limb for the betterment of mankind. It was also fun to see George Lazenby as James Bond lending his fellow agents a hand.

Though the series was never made, the two super-spies were reunited on October 31, 1983 in an episode of *The A-Team* (See Entry) nostalgically titled, "The Say Uncle Affair."

Patrick Macnee later spoofed himself and his fellow secret

agents in a series of car commercials for the Sterling. The beautifully photographed commercials feature the Monty Norman James Bond theme music as the sleek Sterling automobile winds its way around scenic mountain roads. When the car stops, Macnee steps out and alludes to the fact that we might have been expecting someone else to step out of the new car—James Bond, of course.

MANHUNT

September 1959–1961.   Syndicated

Character:	Detective George Peters
Played by:	Charles Bateman
Date(s):	1959–1960 (episodes 1–13)

Replaced by:	Detective Bruce Hanna
Played by:	Rian Garrick
Date(s):	1959–1960 (episodes 14–23)

Replaced by:	Detective Dan Kramer
Played by:	Chuck Henderson
Date(s):	1959–1960 (episodes 24–39)

Replaced by:	Detective Paul Kirk
Played by:	Michael Steffany
Date(s):	1960–1961 (episodes 40–52)

Replaced by:	Detective Phil Burns
Played by:	Robert Crawford
Date(s):	1960–1961 (episodes 53–65)

Replaced by:	Detective Carl Spencer
Played by:	Todd Armstrong
Date(s):	1960–1961 (episodes 66–78)

This syndicated police drama may have the distinction of being the only show in the history of television to have intentionally planned to write characters out. The idea was to use two established actors to anchor the series and to use the series as a proving ground for new talent.

The series stars were Victor Jory as Detective Lieutenant Howard Finucane of the San Diego Police Department and Patrick McVey as police reporter Ben Andrews. Assisting Finucane as police department detectives were six different actors.

The pilot for *Manhunt* was produced in 1954 with Broderick Crawford. The pilot didn't sell and Crawford didn't get to say "10–4!, 10–4!" for another year, when he starred as Captain Dan Matthews in his own syndicated series, *Highway Patrol*.

Once again actual police files were used as the basis for stories. This time it was the San Diego, California police department that opened its files to the television scriptwriters. Certainly every production company wanted another *Dragnet*, but to Screen Gems this series also presented a cost-effective way of testing their new male contract players.

Series star Victor Jory was fairly good-natured about the revolving door Screen Gems had installed for his assistant because he enjoyed being the one to show the ropes to up-and-coming actors. And of the six actors who got their start on *Manhunt*, two went on to achieve a modest amount of success.

Charles Bateman went on to star as twin brothers Marshal Rick January and Dr. Ben January in the 1960 syndicated Western, *Two Faces West*. The series was produced by Matthew Rapf, who went on to produce *Kojak* (See Entry).

The only member of the group to make a name for himself in motion pictures was Todd Armstrong. In his first film, Armstrong played Lieutenant Omar Stroud in the 1962 drama, WALK ON THE WILD SIDE. But it was the 1963 science fiction adventure, JASON AND THE ARGONAUTS, that earned him his, albeit short-lived, "leading man" status as Jason. It also stands as one of Ray Harryhausen's finest works in special effects and stop-motion animation. Armstrong's later films, including the two Westerns, KING RAT and A TIME FOR KILLING, never brought him the kind of success he had achieved with his second film.

THE MANY LOVES OF DOBIE GILLIS

September 29, 1959–September 18, 1963.   CBS

Character:	Maynard G. Krebs
Played by:	Bob Denver
Date(s):	September 29, 1959–October 27, 1959
	November 17, 1959–September 18, 1963

Replaced by:	Jerome Krebs
Played by:	Michael J. Pollard
Date(s):	October 27, 1959
	November 10, 1959

Character:	Milton Armitage
Played by:	Warren Beatty
Date(s):	October 6, 1959–January 19, 1960

Replaced by:	Chatsworth Osborne, Jr.
Played by:	Steve Franken
Date(s):	1960–September 18, 1963

Character:	Clarice Armitage
Played by:	Doris Packer
Date(s):	1959–1960

Replaced by:	Mrs. Chatsworth Osborne, Sr.
Played by:	Doris Packer
Date(s):	1960–September 18, 1963

Character:	Leander Pomfritt
Played by:	Herbert Anderson
Date(s):	September 29, 1959

Replaced by:	Leander Pomfritt
Played by:	William Schallert
Date(s):	October 6, 1959–April 17, 1962

Character:	Mr. Millfloss
Played by:	Lee Goodman
Date(s):	unknown

Replaced by:	Mr. Millfloss
Played by:	Marvin Kaplan
Date(s):	March 7, 1961

Character:	Charlie Wong
Played by:	James Yagi
Date(s):	September 29, 1959

Replaced by:	Charlie Wong
Played by:	Guy Lee
Date(s):	October 6, 1959–September 18, 1963

Character:	Dean Hollister
Played by:	Addison Richards
Date(s):	unknown

Replaced by:	Dean Hollister
Played by:	Paul Tripp
Date(s):	unknown

Character:	Zelda's sister
Played by:	Sherry Alberoni
Date(s):	unknown

Replaced by:	Zelda's sister
Played by:	Jeri Lou James
Date(s):	unknown

Replaced by:	Zelda's sister
Played by:	Larrain Gillespie
Date(s):	unknown

Replaced by:	Zelda's sister
Played by:	Glenda Padgett
Date(s):	unknown

Replaced by:	Zelda's sister
Played by:	Judy Harriett
Date(s):	unknown

Replaced by:	Zelda's sister
Played by:	Marlene Willis
Date(s):	unknown

Replaced by:	Zelda's sister
Played by:	Anna Maria Nanasi
Date(s):	unknown

Character:	Thalia Menninger
Played by:	Tuesday Weld
Date(s):	September 29, 1959–September 20, 1960

Replaced by:	Linda Sue Faversham
Played by:	Yvonne Craig
Date(s):	May 2, 1961–November 21, 1962

Character:	Imogene Burkhart
Played by:	Jody Warner
Date(s):	March 8, 1960

Replaced by:	Dr. Imogene Burkhart
Played by:	Jean Byron
Date(s):	1960–1961

Perhaps it would be more appropriate if the producers had named this program *The Many Versions of Dobie Gillis.* There were actually three distinct storylines, each resulting in cast changes designed to retain as much as possible from the previous format. This often included recasting the same actors in new, but similar roles.

On *M*A*S*H* (See Entry) they brought in a new colonel with a new actor playing him. On *The Many Loves of Dobie Gillis* they brought in a new school teacher, played by the same actress who played the old school teacher. Why bother getting a new actress?

Maybe it would be easier if we went down to the park, sat down on the white marble bench in front of the Rodin statue, put our fist under our chin and crouched down a little to think this thing through.

Dobie Gillis, played by Dwayne Hickman, was an all-American boy. He was clean cut, didn't smoke or drink, and had blonde hair . . . some of the time. Even his neighborhood was all-American where nary a crime was committed for the four years we knew him. Maybe the reason that there was no crime was because Dobie Gillis lived in Central City, which also happens to be the hometown of police scientist Barry Allen, who is known in superhero circles as The Flash.

Basically, Dobie Gillis was a girl chaser. He wasn't a womanizer like Chuck MacDonald, the character played by Bob Cummings on *The Bob Cummings Show* from 1955 to 1959. He was simply looking for that one special girl. As it turned out, he looked for her for four years and she was right there under his nose the whole time. She was the less-than-beautiful Zelda Gilroy, who was always played by Sheila James. This scenario was very much like the one for *The Bob Cummings Show,* which had its handsome star chasing after beautiful models when the one girl who really loved him was his less-than-beautiful assistant, Schultzy, played by Ann B. Davis. The difference was that in the 1977 reunion pilot, *Whatever Happened to Dobie Gillis?,* Zelda finally gets her man and becomes Mrs. Zelda Gillis. Schultzy never did get her MRS degree, but she did get the housekeeper's job on *The Brady Bunch.*

Without a doubt, though, the character on the program who loved Dobie the most wasn't a girl at all. It was Maynard G. Krebs (Bob Denver), Dobie's closest friend, who often seemed to care more about Dobie than Dobie. This lovable beatnik, who viewed life with a child-like innocence, said it all when he called Dobie "good buddy." The actor who played this most loyal of friends, Bob Denver, a few years later, was himself referred to as "little buddy," by the Skipper of the S.S. Minnow on the CBS situation comedy, *Gilligan's Island.* Denver, as everyone knows, starred in the title role of that series—Gilligan . . . not Island.

The Many Loves of Dobie Gillis was barely underway when Uncle Sam decided that he needed Bob Denver more than Dobie did. As it turned out, he didn't. Not wanting to pass up a good storyline, the writers decided to have Maynard drafted on the series and wrote a special transition episode, "Maynard's Farewell to the Troops," in which everyone from his best friend Dobie Gillis to Riff Ryan, the owner of the record shop, to Charlie Wong at the ice cream parlor, to his own father, tells Maynard how much they really "dig" him, but that he should get lost for a while. That's when Maynard misreads a draft classification letter and tells everyone he has been drafted.

Dobie feels lousy and everyone shows up at a going-away party at Charlie Wong's, which was complete with a painted banner that read "Like Farewell, Maynard."

Later, down at the induction center, when Maynard learns that he hadn't been drafted, he insists on enlisting because, as he told the captain at the induction center, "They don't especially love me when I'm around, only when I'm like leaving."

His friends even chipped in for two going-away gifts, a lightweight, weather-resistant two-suit bag and a shockproof, waterproof, solid steel watch with a sweep second hand. With the consent of Maynard's parents, the Army reluctantly takes him.

Our fears about Maynard's well-being in the service are dispelled when Dobie goes to visit him following his basic training. What Dobie finds, to his disbelief, is that Maynard has become one of the finest new recruits in the service and that his commanding officer, Major Walter L. Bradbury, has made him an acting corporal.

Dobie, returning to Maynard's parents' house to relay the good news about their son's progress in the Army, hears the sound of a bongo drum coming from Maynard's room. He rushes in to see what is going on and finds another beatnik-type sitting on Maynard's bed wearing headphones and playing a single bongo drum. He introduces himself and Dobie learns that this Krebs house guest is Maynard's cousin Jerome from New Orleans.

Michael J. Pollard appeared again as Jerome Krebs in the following week's episode, "The Sweet Singer of Central High." It was also his last appearance, because it didn't take the Army long to find out about Bob Denver's neck injury and to classify him 4–F. When Denver returned to the series it was explained that Maynard was discharged as a hardship case.

Impish Michael J. Pollard made a name for himself as C.W. Moss in the 1967 Warren Beatty crime film, BONNIE AND CLYDE. Some of his most memorable television roles include Barney Fife's klutzy cousin Virgil on the April 30, 1962 episode of *The Andy Griffith Show.* He was Jahn on the *Star Trek* episode "Miri," which aired on October 27, 1966. In 1990, at the age of fifty-one and not looking much older than he

did on *The Many Loves of Dobie Gillis,* Michael J. Pollard appeared on the syndicated adventure series, *Superboy,* as that prankster from the fourth dimension, Mr. Mxyzptlk.

On *The Many Loves of Dobie Gillis,* Warren Beatty played Dobie's sophisticated rival, Milton Armitage, but quit because he thought his role was unrealistic. His replacement, Steve Franken, played an even broader fool. His name was Chatsworth Osborne, Jr., the son of the terribly wealthy Chatsworth Osborne, Sr., and he spoke with an affected English accent. Obviously Franken didn't find the role too demeaning as he stuck with it for the remainder of the series.

Of the actors who played Dobie's rivals, Warren Beatty fared far better than Steve Franken, who achieved some later successes, but never on the scale of Beatty's. For a short while he played Lieutenant "Sanpan" Panosian on *The Lieutenant* (See Entry). He also appeared in two pilots which aired, but never went to series: in the first he had a guest role as Henry Maitland in the science fiction pilot, *The Stranger,* which aired on NBC on February 26, 1973; in the other, he was Jay on the ABC situation comedy, *Three for Tahiti,* which starred Robert Hogan as Kelly and Bob Einstein as Muk. Einstein later gained somewhat dubious fame as the ill-fated stuntman, Super Dave Osborne. As Dr. Dick Moran, Steve Franken co-starred in all thirteen episodes of the NBC situation comedy, *Tom, Dick and Mary,* which ran from October 5, 1964 to January 4, 1965.

Warren Beatty, on the other hand, went on to achieve superstardom as an actor, producer and director. His first film role after *Dobie Gillis* was Bud Stamper in the 1961 drama, SPLENDOR IN THE GRASS, which won an Academy Award for writer William Inge. Seven films later he starred as Clyde Barrow in BONNIE AND CLYDE, a film he also produced. The real turning point in his career came with the release of his 1975 comedy, SHAMPOO, which he produced and cowrote. His most recent success was with the 1990 crime film, DICK TRACY, which he produced, directed and starred in.

Milton Armitage's mom was always played by Doris Packer, and come to think of it, so was Chatsworth's "Mumsie." It was one of those unusual casting decisions: the talent was so right for the part that even after leaving the series for a year in 1960 to play Clara Mason on the NBC sitcom, *Happy,* Packer returned to play another, but remarkably similar character. Gale Gordon did the same thing on *The Lucy Show* (See Entry), although he never left the series.

Right from the first episode the one beautiful, gorgeous, soft, round and creamy girl of Dobie's dreams was Thalia Menninger, played by Tuesday Weld. Dobie met Thalia in the series' first episode when they went to Jackpot night at the Bijou Theatre. In all fairness, it was Thalia who approached Dobie. She was looking for a "jackpot partner" to increase her chances of winning the $100 prize, which she promised to split. This sort of teasing went on for the first year of the series and then she split.

With a couple of films already under her belt, Tuesday Weld had very little trouble returning to the big screen. She played Selena Cross in the 1961 dramatic sequel, RETURN TO PEYTON PLACE, Christian in the 1965 drama, THE CINCINNATI KID, and Barbara Ann Greene in the 1966 comedy, LORD LOVE A DUCK.

Poor Dobie, what was he to do without his Thalia? No

problem in sitcomland. Just cast a new actress to replace her. It took nearly a year to find the right spark, who turned out to be Yvonne Craig. She played Linda Sue Faversham who like Thalia, only wanted the finer things in life. She must have also hated crime, because on September 14, 1967 she became Gotham City's one and only Batgirl on the hit television series, *Batman.* Dobie sure knew how to pick 'em, didn't he?

In the first episode of the series, Dobie's teacher was Mr. Pomfritt, who taught Social Studies I. He was played for this episode only by Herbert Anderson, who in his short tenure wasn't able to teach Dobie a thing. He did, however, manage to teach his son, Dennis, a few things over the next four year. That is because just days after Dobie's social studies class ended, Anderson became Henry Mitchell on the long-running series, *Dennis the Menace.*

Another Central High teacher was Mr. Millfloss, first played by Lee Goodman and later by Marvin Kaplan, the round-faced little actor who was later heard as the whiny voice of Choo-Choo on the animated series *Top Cat,* which aired on ABC from September 27, 1961 to March 30, 1962. His most highly visible role on television was as Henry, a regular patron from 1977 to 1985 at Mel's Diner on *Alice.*

When school let out the kids liked to stop by the Charles Wong Ice Cream Parlor, which served thirty-one flavors of ice cream and strawberry wonton sundaes, Thalia's favorite. The owner, Charlie Wong, was played by James Yagi in the first episode and thereafter by Guy Lee.

The last of the series' three formats (the second being Dobie, Maynard and Chatsworth in the Army) had the boys enrolled in St. Peter Pryor Junior College, which was headed by Dean Hollister.

Their matriculation began on September 26, 1961, and continued for the remainder of the series run. Addison Richards, the first actor to play Hollister, was previously seen as the Colonel in the CBS dramatic anthology series, *Pentagon U.S.A.,* which aired from August 6 to September 24, 1953. He also played Doc Gamble on the NBC sitcom, *Fibber McGee and Molly,* which ran from September 15, 1959 to January 19, 1960. Richards was replaced by the gentle actor Paul Tripp, who wrote the 1940s children's classic *Tubby the Tuba,* and is most fondly remembered for playing host to children's programs *Mr. I Magination* and *It's Magic.* The first of these aired on CBS from May 29, 1949 to April 13, 1952, the other on CBS from July 31 to September 4, 1955. For youngsters fortunate enough to have grown up in the east, Paul Tripp is also remembered as the friendly host of *Birthday House,* which was broadcast on WNBC-TV, New York. Tripp did do some adult roles, including an appearance on *The Dick Van Dyke Show* (See Entry).

Perhaps the strangest change in cast was the role of Imogene Burkhart, who started out as a friend of Dobie Gillis and turned into a middle-aged teacher with the same name.

Here is how it happened. In the show's first format, Jean Byron played math teacher, Ruth Adams. Then on the March 8, 1960 episode, "The Chicken from Outer Space," Jody Warner played Central High student Imogene Burkhart. The writers must have liked the character's name, because they used it later as the name of another teacher played by Jean Byron, who had played the math teacher not long before.

If you think the students began to see double when Jean Byron emerged as Imogene Burkhart, she herself was later faced with an even more confusing predicament as Natalie Lane, the mother of Patty and the aunt of Cathy, who were cousins . . . identical cousins, on *The Patty Duke Show.*

It also appears that Ms. Burkhart might have been engaged in a little teacher's tryst with Mr. Pomfritt, because it was William Schallert who wound up as her level-headed husband, Martin, on *The Patty Duke Show.*

On January 18, 1968, Ms. Byron was reunited with Yvonne Craig on the "Nora Clavicle and the Ladies' Crime Club" episode of *Batman.* Ms. Byron played Mrs. Millie Linseed and Ms. Craig was, of course, Batgirl.

As for Zelda's sister . . . well, let's just say her parents were strong supporters of the Foster Child program and leave it at that.

In another of the popular "fifteen years later" reunion movies, Dwayne Hickman, Bob Denver, Sheila James, William Schallert and Steve Franken returned to recreate their roles in *Bring Me the Head of Dobie Gillis,* which aired on CBS on Sunday, February 21, 1988.

Following the opening credits and some teaser dialogue by the townspeople to set up the premise for the show, we find Dobie Gillis just where we left him in 1963, sitting on the stone bench mimicking the pose of the statue of the Thinker which lies just a few feet behind him. Dobie lifts his head off his clenched fist, turns and speaks directly into the camera:

> DOBIE: Since we've seen each other,[17] I've graduated from pharmacy school, got married, bought a little house, settled down. And let's go back to "got married." I'm sure you'll recall I always wanted a girl who was tall and blonde and dreamy. Well, the girl I married isn't exactly tall or blonde or . . .

The girl Dobie married was Zelda Gilroy. The girl he wanted to marry was Thalia Menninger, now played by the grown up Connie Stevens who is blonde and dreamy every day of the week.

MARK SABER

October 5, 1951–May 15, 1960.   ABC-NBC

Character:	Mark Saber
Played by:	Tom Conway
Date(s):	October 5, 1951–June 30, 1954

Replaced by:	Mark Saber
Played by:	Donald Gray
Date(s):	October 13, 1957–May 15, 1960

---

17. It should be noted that the last time Dobie Gillis actually saw us was in the updated pilot, *Whatever Happened to Dobie Gillis?* which aired on CBS on May 10, 1977.

Character: Sergeant Tim Maloney
Played by: James Burke
Date(s):   October 5, 1951–June 30, 1954

Replaced by: Barney O'Keefe
Played by: Michael Balfour
Date(s):   December 23, 1955–October 12, 1956

Replaced by: Judy
Played by: Teresa Thorne
Date(s):   1956

Replaced by: Stephanie Ames
Played by: Diana Decker
Date(s):   1956–1957

Replaced by: Pete Paulson
Played by: Neil McCallum
Date(s):   1957–1958

Replaced by: Pete Paulson
Played by: Gordon Tanner
Date(s):   1958

Replaced by: Bob Page
Played by: Robert Arden
Date(s):   1958–1960

Here is another of those series that began well enough, left the air, and returned completely revamped. This fine crime drama began with the British plainclothes detective Mark Saber working for the Homicide Division of the New York Police Department. As with Lieutenant Kojak, plainclothes meant tailored pinstriped suits. Saber was played by the British actor Tom Conway, who not only was the brother of George Sanders but took over his brother's role as the Falcon in nine RKO motion pictures made between 1943 and 1946. He was first introduced as Tom in this motion picture series, THE FALCON'S BROTHER, released in 1942. His last recorded television appearance was in the *Perry Mason* episode, "The Case of the Simple Simon," which aired on April 2, 1964.

The sophisticated detective's assistant, Sergeant Tim Maloney, was more of a regulation cop. He was played by James Burke when the series began but was replaced when the series returned as *The Vise* on October 12, 1956. Burke's film roles include Detective Reardon in the original 1934 version of Damon Runyon's LITTLE MISS MARKER and Luke in the 1941 Humphrey Bogart classic, THE MALTESE FALCON.

The setting had also changed from New York to more exotic ones in London, Paris and the French Riviera. This was what the *Man Against Crime* (See Entry) had attempted to do with backdrops, but *Mark Saber* was actually filmed in England, which helped.

The revised storyline made Mark Saber a one-armed P.I. who was formerly a private detective for Scotland Yard. Unusual concept, but how do you cast the part? Simple, just hire one-armed British leading man, Donald Gray. Gray, who lost his arm during the second world war, began his career on radio as an actor and announcer before turning to film. He starred as

scientist James Martin in the 1937 crime film, STRANGE EXPERIMENT. In the 1953 romance, ISLAND OF DESIRE, Gray plays RAF pilot William Peck, who is seriously injured after making a crash-landing on a remote island. Fortunately there is a nurse, played by Linda Darnell, stranded on the same island and she manages to save Peck's life by—what else?—amputating his arm.

In addition to the plot change and several changes in titles—*Saber of London* was another—Saber went through an inordinane number of assistants, much like Detective Lieutenant Finucate on *Manhunt* (See Entry), and if *Mark Saber*'s producers weren't intentionally using the series to test new actors, as was the case with *Manhunt,* they should have considered it.

Although none of these replacements went on in regular series work in the United States, they did work in films. Michael Balfour appearead as Machiavelli's Prince in Ray Bradbury's 1966 science fiction, FAHRENHEIT 451. Diana Decker played Jean Farlow in the 1962 dramatic comedy, LOLITA. Neil McCallum played Sully in the 1962 Steve McQueen picture, THE WAR LOVER, and Robert Arden co-starred as Guy Van Stratten in Orson Welles' 1962 drama, MR. ARKADIN.

MARRIED . . . WITH CHILDREN

April 5, 1987–. Fox

Character: Steve Rhoades
Played by: David Garrison
Date(s):   April 5, 1987–1990
                  February 28, 1993

Replaced by: Jefferson D'Arcy
Played by: Ted McGinley
Date(s):   January 6, 1991–

At first glance, *Married . . . with Children* seems like dozens of other sitcoms set in the Chicago suburbs. There's the typical sitcom husband and wife, with the typical sitcom beautiful blonde daughter, the typical sitcom bright son and the typical sitcom family dog. Living next door are the typical sitcom wacky next-door neighbors. But that's only at first glance. Peggy and Al Bundy are just a little bit too "typical." Al (Ed O'Neill) is a shoe salesman who barely earns enough money to support his family and displays some disgusting personal habits that are best left unmentioned. His typical sitcom wife, Peggy (Katey Sagal), spends her days just lounging around the house watching television and eating chocolates. She rarely goes to the supermarket and refers to the kitchen stove as "that big hot thing."

The Bundy's beautiful teenage daughter, Kelly (Christina Applegate), is an air-headed tramp with a great figure, which is great for the ratings. Kelly's younger brother, Bud (David Faustino), is a con artist who fancies himself a lady killer, but isn't.

Living next door is a perky and bright young couple, Steve and Marcy Rhoades (David Garrison and Amanda Bearse),—

young bankers in love. And Buck—well, Buck's just a dog. But even bankers can't stay in love forever and the Rhoadeses officially split up on February 11, 1990.

In reality, actor David Garrison, who had co-starred as Norman Lamb on the NBC situation comedy, *It's Your Move* (September 26, 1984 to August 10, 1985), left *Married . . . with Children* to star as Charlie in a revival of the Stephen Sondheim musical, *Merrily We Roll Along,* a part that earned him the Helen Hayes Award. ''The opportunity to work with Steve Sondheim comes along very rarely in life,''[18] said Garrison.

This was not really a departure for the talented actor/singer/ dancer/musician who had starred on Broadway as Groucho Marx in *A Day In Hollywood/A Night in the Ukraine,* which ran from 1980 to 1981, and as Charlie Brown's pooch in *Snoopy,* which ran from 1982 to 1983. *Merrily We Roll Along* was scheduled to open on Broadway, but closed after ten weeks in Washington.

Garrison said that he and the creators and executive producers of *Married . . . With Children* had been friends since his days on *It's Your Move* and had an amicable parting. From watching the series it seemed as though Steve was expected to return because he was not written out for quite some time. Garrison himself admitted that ''In fact we sort of left it open so he [Steve Rhoades] could come back as a guest and wreak havoc.''[19]

He did just that as the pirate feared for his singing in the dream episode of *Married . . . with Children,* ''Peggy and the Pirates,'' which aired on February 28, 1993. This came nearly three years after his stint as Stan, David Stuart's (Stephen Collins) best friend on the short-lived sitcom, *Working It Out,* which aired on NBC from August 22 to December 26, 1990.

To explain Steve's departure from *Married . . . with Children,* and to help his jilted wife put her life back together, a special two-part episode was written and produced. The first of these aired on Sunday, February 11, 1990, and opens up with Peg telling Al that she needs a vacation. Marcy then walks in, declares her hatred of men and asks Peg to read a Dear John (or a Dear Joan in this case) letter she found on her pillow when she came home from work.

PEG: Dear Marcy . . .

MARCY: Dear Marcy my sweet patutie! The geek is leaving me!

PEG: Oh, Steve doesn't mean that. He loves you.

MARCY: I guess you're right. He probably meant to say that when he wrote this: ''Frankly I'm sick of you. You disgust me. I had a full head of hair when I met you and I'm sure my nose grew during our marriage.'' He says he's going to Yosemite to be a park ranger. He's rejected

materialism and all the evils brought about by the quest for money . . . oh, and he's suing me for alimony.

Peg then sells Al's 19–inch remote-control color television and pushes Marcy into selling Steve's stereo so they'll have enough money to fly to Las Vegas, Nevada for a vacation. The remainder of the episode, including the second part which aired the following Sunday (February 18), revolves around their winning and losing money, with Al and the kids coming to their rescue.

It soon became obvious to the producers and writers that a single Marcy was just not working out. So, on January 6, 1991, Marcy remarries.

The episode starts right off with Marcy bringing her latest problem into the Bundy's living room. She's just returned from what she described as a ''wild'' bankers' convention at which she awoke one morning with a strange man in her bed, a wedding ring on her finger and a T-shirt that read, ''I WENT TO CLYDE'S NO BLOOD TEST REQUIRED CHAPEL AND ALL I GOT WAS THIS LOUSY T-SHIRT.''

While a befuddled Marcy tries to reconstruct her actions, Ted McGinley, walks in to the whoops, hoots and hollers of the audience.

The audience may have been reacting to the handsome blonde actor because they recognized him from his roles on *Happy Days* as Roger Phillips and on *The Love Boat* as ship's photographer Ashley ''Ace'' Covington Evans. They might even have remembered him from the December 17, 1989 episode of *Married . . . with Children,* in which he played Norman, Peggy's fantasy husband in the Bundy's send-up of the Frank Capra Christmas classic, IT'S A WONDERFUL LIFE.

MARCY: It's hard to believe that I'm now Mrs . . . Darling, what's your last name?

JEFFERSON: D'Arcy.

MARCY: Marcy D'Arcy? Marcy D'Arcy? What have I done?

What she has done is managed to marry a very good looking guy. But since she doesn't remember the wedding, they decide to pool their $2,040 in savings (Marcy's $2,000, Jefferson's $40) to throw a wedding they will remember.

Al and Peg see dollar signs and offer to handle the wedding and reception for the D'Arcys. What they do, of course, is cut everything to the bone. They eliminate nearly everyone on the D'Arcy's guest list, order two pounds of twelve-cent-a-pound cold cuts for sixty guests, including friends of Kelly and Bud. A Hostess Twinkie becomes the wedding cake, and Buck the maid of honor.

Al even found a way to save money on the preacher by

18. David Garrison during an interview on *Regis & Kathie Lee.* August 22, 1990. ABC.
19. *Ibid.*

having the ceremony officiated via short wave radio by Captain Hank, the captain of a garbage scow, whom he paid off with a bottle of Red Eye and a *Playboy* magazine.

But the pièce de résistance was Al's gift to Marcy—the information that Jefferson is an ex-con. What Al didn't learn until after the wedding was that Jefferson was sent to prison for committing a white collar crime—selling plots of land around Lake Chicamocomico, a toxic waste pond, the very same retirement property into which Al had just sunk his D'Arcy wedding profits. Tough break, Al.

THE MARSHAL OF GUNSIGHT PASS

March 12, 1950–September 30, 1950.   ABC

Character:	Marshal
Played by:	Russell ''Lucky'' Hayden
Date(s):	March 1950

Replaced by:	Marshal Eddie Dean
Played by:	Eddie Dean
Date(s):	March 1950–September 30, 1950

It is true that some of the scenes in *The Lone Ranger* were shot on a soundstage dressed with dirt, trees and shrubs, but they did go outside when they had to film chases. This was not the case with *The Marshal of Gunsight Pass*, where everything was done live in the confines of a studio with unrealistic backdrops.

The first Marshal of this short-lived Western, which was based on the radio series of the same name, was played by Russell Hayden. Hayden is better known to audiences as Lucky Jenkins, from more than two dozen HOPALONG CASSIDY Westerns made between 1937 and 1941. He lived up to his nickname ''Lucky'' when he was smart enough to dismount from this series before it ran itself into the ground.

The new Marshal, Eddie Dean, was played by Eddie Dean, himself a popular singing cowboy. The only problem was, the show didn't have a song.

MARTIN KANE, PRIVATE EYE

September 1, 1949–June 17, 1954.   NBC

Character:	Martin Kane
Played by:	William Gargan
Date(s):	September 1, 1949–1951
	1957 (syndicated version)

Replaced by:	Martin Kane
Played by:	Lloyd Nolan
Date(s):	1951–1952

Replaced by:	Martin Kane
Played by:	Lee Tracy
Date(s):	1952–1953

Replaced by:	Martin Kane
Played by:	Mark Stevens
Date(s):	1953–1954

Character:	Happy McMahon
Played by:	Walter Kinsella
Date(s):	September 1, 1949–August 1953

Replaced by:	Don Morrow
Played by:	Don Morrow
Date(s):	January 1954–June 17, 1954

Character:	Lieutenant Bender
Played by:	Fred Hillebrand
Date(s):	1949–1950

Replaced by:	Captain Willis
Played by:	Horace McMahon
Date(s):	1950–1951

Replaced by:	Sergeant Ross
Played by:	Nicholas Saunders
Date(s):	1950–1952

Replaced by:	Captain Leonard
Played by:	Walter Greaza
Date(s):	1951

Replaced by:	Captain Burke
Played by:	Frank Thomas
Date(s):	1951–1952

Replaced by:	Lieutenant Grey
Played by:	King Calder
Date(s):	1952–1954

The first incarnation of this live detective series starred William Gargan, who had originated the role on radio and was the fourth and final actor to play Ellery Queen in the long-running motion picture series. Taking over the role from Ralph Bellamy, Gargan appeared in the last three Ellery Queen pictures, CLOSE CALL FOR ELLERY QUEEN, DESPERATE CHANCE FOR ELLERY QUEEN and ENEMY AGENTS MEET ELLERY QUEEN. All were released in 1942. In 1940 William Gargan was nominated for an Academy Award for his portrayal of Joe in the 1940 Carole Lombard/Charles Laughton drama, THEY KNEW WHAT THEY WANTED.

Gargan left *Martin Kane, Private Eye* after the second season to become a producer, but didn't achieve any great success. The *Martin Kane, Private Eye* series continued until 1954, with three other actors in the role he had created. The first of these was Lloyd Nolan, who had also been a successful actor in B movies. A couple of Nolan's more memorable performances were as McShane in A TREE GROWS IN BROOKLYN, and as the federal investigator, Inspector George A. Briggs, in THE HOUSE ON 92ND STREET. Both films were released in 1945. His acting career was still going strong in the 1960s and he turned in a fine performance as Admiral Garvey in the 1968 war drama, ICE STATION ZEBRA. Television audiences may remember Lloyd Nolan as Dr. Morton Chegley, on *Julia*.

The third to play this New York wisecracking detective was Lee Tracy, who most often played reporters in films during the 1930s. He played a reporter named Lee in the 1932 horror film, DR. X, a studio press agent named Space in the 1933 Jean Harlow comedy, BOMBSHELL, and Brad McKay, an investigative newspaper reporter in the 1943 mystery, THE PAYOFF. A few years after leaving *Martin Kane,* Lee Tracy played Lee Cochran, a tough newspaper reporter-columnist in the syndicated crime drama, *New York Confidential*.

The last, or at least, what was thought to be the last Martin Kane was played by Mark Stevens, who went on to star as the second Steve Wilson in the newspaper crime drama, *Big Town* (See Entry).

As far as the network run of *Martin Kane, Private Eye* was concerned, Stevens *was* the last actor to portray Kane. However, three years later the character was revived in a syndicated series that moved the locale from New York to London and Paris. There was even an episode that was secretly filmed in Denmark's famed Elsinore castle.

These thirty-nine episodes, which were now titled *The New Adventures of Martin Kane,* and were syndicated under the title *Assignment Danger,* starred, interestingly enough, the first Martin Kane, William Gargan, who was trying to revive his acting career.

Back in the early days of television it was common practice to work the sponsor into the program and J. Walter Thompson used Happy McMahon's Tobacco Shop for this purpose. The shop served as Kane's hangout until the end of the 1953 season. Happy McMahon was played by Walter Kinsella. When the shop was no longer incorporated into the storylines, Happy left his shop to Don Morrow, who pitched Old Briar pipe tobacco and Encore cigarettes under his own name.

Ironically, it was smoking that put an end to William Gargan's acting career in 1960 when he had his larynx removed because of throat cancer. Only able to speak with the assistance of a mechanical voice box, William Gargan devoted the last nineteen years of his life to the fight against cancer, which was highlighted by his 1969 autobiography, *Why Me?*

Among the many actors to play Martin Kane's police contact over the series' seven-year run, was Frank Thomas who, with his wife, Mona, played Mr. and Mrs. Eggleston on the situation comedy, *Wesley.* In real life the Thomases were the parents of Frankie Thomas, who is known to children of the fifties as Tom Corbett, Space Cadet.

Another Thomas, Danny, later hired Captain Willis (Horace McMahon) to play one of his agents on *Make Room for Daddy* (See Entry).

THE MARY TYLER MOORE COMEDY HOUR

March 4, 1979–June 6, 1979.   CBS

Character:	Crystal
Played by:	Doris Roberts
Date(s):	March 4, 1979

Replaced by:	Ruby Bell
Played by:	Dody Goodman
Date(s):	March 11, 1976–May 6, 1979

Although classifed as a variety series, *The Mary Tyler Moore Comedy Hour* used the show-within-a-show format to give guest stars an opportunity to perform. That internal show was *The Mary McKinnon Show* and Mary Tyler Moore played Mary McKinnon. The other regular characters included her producer, her secretary, the show's head writer and a writer-director.

At home, Mary had a housekeeper, Crystal, who was played by Doris Roberts in the first episode. Thereafter, Mary McKinnon's housekeeper was Ruby Bell, played by Dody Goodman, who could also be seen as Blanche, helping out Eve Arden in the principal's office in the 1978 musical comedy, GREASE.

Both actresses later appeared in Norman Lear's syndicated soap opera spoof, *Mary Hartman, Mary Hartman,* which aired between 1976 and 1978. Dody Goodman, who played Mary Hartman's (Louise Lasser) mother, Martha Schumway, was heard at the opening of the episode calling, "Mary Hartman, Mary Hartman."

Ms. Roberts, who played evangelist Dorelda Doremus on the series, is fondly remembered by television trivia buffs as "Angie's mom," Theresa Falco, on the ABC situation comedy, *Angie.* That short-lived series aired from February 8, 1979 to October 2, 1980. Unquestionably, the role that Doris Roberts is most associated with is Mildred Krebs, the second secretary/receptionist on *Remington Steele* (See Entry).

THE MARY TYLER MOORE SHOW

September 19, 1970–September 3, 1977.   CBS

Character:	Bonnie Slaughter
Played by:	Sherry Hursey
Date(s):	unknown

Replaced by:	Marie Slaughter
Played by:	Tammi Bula
Date(s):	unknown

Character:	Chuckles the Clown
Played by:	Mark Gordon
Date(s):	unknown

Replaced by:	Chuckles the Clown
Played by:	Richard Schaal
Date(s):	unknown

Who was replaced on the *Mary Tyler Moore Show?* Well, if you were watching it every week and don't remember seeing any replacements, you may not have been watching closely enough, because there were a couple. Minor characters, mind you, but legitimate replacements nonetheless. And no, they didn't include John Amos, who enjoyed good times throughout the series run as Gordy the weatherman.

Juvenile actress Sherry Hursey appeared as newswriter Murray Slaughter's daughter, Bonnie. On the next occasion we had to see her, not only was she being played by a different actress (Tammi Bula) but her name had been changed to Marie. This might have had something to do with the fact that Murray's wife, played by Joyce Bulifant, was also named Marie.

Murray, of course, was always played by Gavin MacLeod, who went on to pilot *The Love Boat* (See Entry) as Captain Merrill Stubing.

There were also two different bartenders on the series, but since each one worked in a different establishment, it is difficult to say whether this should be considered a replacement. Tony, (Chuck Bergansky) worked at the Ballantine Bar, where Lou Grant's girlfriend, Charlene McGuire (Sheree North), sings. But when Lou just wanted to hang out, he went over to the Happy Hour Bar where he was served by Peter Hobbs.

MATLOCK

September 20, 1986–August 21, 1992.   NBC
November 5, 1992–August 18, 1994   ABC

Character:	Charlene Matlock
Played by:	Linda Purl
Date(s):	September 20, 1986–May 1987
Replaced by:	Lee Ann McIntyre
Played by:	Brynn Thayer
Date(s):	May 8, 1992 (NBC)
	September 1992–August 18, 1994 (ABC)
Character:	Tyler Hudson
Played by:	Kene Holliday
Date(s):	September 20, 1986–September 12, 1989
Replaced by:	Conrad MacMasters
Played by:	Clarence Gilyard, Jr.
Date(s):	September 19, 1989–May 8, 1992 (NBC)
	September 1992–August 18, 1994 (ABC)

Andy Griffith must have figured that if it worked for Buddy Ebsen, it would work for him—and he was right. Ebsen, of course, left his established *Beverly Hillbillies* (See Entry) character of Jed Clampett behind and returned to weekly television not in another rural comedy, but as a private investigator in *Barnaby Jones* (See Entry).

Similarly, Andy Griffith hung up the Sheriff Andy Taylor uniform he wore on *The Andy Griffith Show* and put on a light-colored suit to become Benjamin "Ben" Matlock, Atlanta's leading defense attorney.

Aiding in Matlock's quest for justice were his daughter Charlene (Linda Purl) and Tyler Hudson (Kene Holliday). Charlene, like her dad, was an attorney, while Hudson was a brilliant stock market investor who was called upon to do much of the legwork, just as Paul Drake had done for Perry Mason (See Entry). In fact, *Matlock* was very much the *Perry Mason* of

the South. Holliday, who had played Sergeant Curtis Baker on the ABC situation comedy, *Carter Country,* from September 15, 1977 to August 23, 1979, left Matlock's employ at the end of the third season.

The series' fourth season began with a special two-hour episode titled "The Hunting Party," which introduced Clarence Gilyard, Jr. as Conrad MacMasters, a police deputy who winds up replacing Tyler Hudson as Ben's new investigator.

The firm was originally named "Matlock and Matlock," but was changed to "Ben Matlock, Attorney at Law," when Charlene left in 1987 to set up her own law practice in Philadelphia.

If Charlene looked familiar to viewers, it may have been because she appeared regularly on *Happy Days* as Richie Cunningham's girlfriend, Gloria, from 1974 to 1975 and was reincarnated for the 1982/1983 season as Fonzie's romantic interest, Ashley Pfister. During her absence from the nostalgic sitcom, Linda Purl played Betsy Bullock on the CBS drama, *Beacon Hill,* which aired from August 25 to November 4, 1975.

The *Matlock* pilot, *Diary of a Perfect Murder,* which aired on March 3, 1986, featured Lori Lethin as Charlene.

In the last first-run episode on NBC, a two-hour movie, *The Assassination,* Brynn Thayer appeared as Ben's estranged daughter, Lee Ann McIntyre—not Charlene. She is divorced and working as a prosecutor in Philadelphia, but pitches in to help her father's investigation to clear a judge who has been framed for the mayor's assassination.

Lee Ann's character (played by Brynn Thayer) continued with the series when it made its network move to ABC.

MAUDE

September 12, 1972–April 29, 1978.   CBS

Character:	Phillip
Played by:	Brian Morrison
Date(s):	1972–1977
Replaced by:	Phillip
Played by:	Kraig Metzinger
Date(s):	1977–1978
Character:	Florida Evans
Played by:	Esther Rolle
Date(s):	September 12, 1972–February 5, 1974
Replaced by:	Mrs. Nell Naugatuck
Played by:	Hermione Baddeley
Date(s):	September 30, 1974–September 5, 1977
Replaced by:	Victoria Butterfield
Played by:	Marlene Warfield
Date(s):	September 12, 1977–April 29, 1978

If there was one thing that *All in the Family* could do better than teach us about our foibles and prejudices, it was the ability to create spinoff sitcom. *Maude* was the first of three—four if you count *Archie Bunker's Place* as a separate series.

The Maude Findlay character was introduced on the twenty-fifth episode of *All in the Family,* "Cousin Maude's Visit," which aired on December 11, 1971. In the storyline Maude Findlay (Beatrice Arthur) made the trek from Tuckahoe to Queens, New York to care for her Cousin Edith who, along with the rest of the family, was stricken with a nasty case of the flu. The character received such a favorable reaction from the audience that a spinoff series was planned. In "Maude," the pilot that aired as an episode of *All in the Family,* Archie is forced to attend the wedding of Maude's daughter, Carol. This pilot aired on March 11, 1972, and featured Marcia Rodd as Carol. This may have confused Mike Stivic (Rob Reiner) a bit because the last time he saw Marcia Rodd she was playing his old girlfriend, Marilyn Sanders, in "Mike's Mysterious Son," the January 22 episode of *All in the Family,* in which she turned up on the Bunkers' doorstep with "Rob's" four-year-old son—which he wasn't. Then again, it might have been a relief to him.

Six months later, when the series premiered, Carol Traynor was played by Adrienne Barbeau. A succession of guest appearances on series and made-for-television movies followed her role on *Maude.* These included the role of Margo Dean, on the two-hour telefilm, *Return to Fantasy Island,* which aired on ABC on January 20, 1978. She also appeared in the "Teacher's Aide" episode of *The Twilight Zone,* which aired on CBS on November 8, 1985.

Adrienne Barbeau's motion picture credits include Stevie Wayne in the 1980 horror film, THE FOG, and Maggie in the 1981 action thriller, ESCAPE FROM NEW YORK, both directed by her ex-husband John Carpenter. The following year Ms. Barbeau played Alice Cable in Wes Craven's comic book character horror film, SWAMP THING and currently provides the voice for Catwoman in Fox's stylish *Batman* animated series. Television viewers were treated to a rare guest appearance, when Adrienne Barbeau appeared as a mobster's (Alex Rocco) girlfriend in "You Bet Your Life," the October 3, 1993 episode of *Daddy Dearest.* The Fox sitcom, which stars Richard Lewis and Don Rickles, is produced by Billy Van Zandt and Jane Milmore, who worked with Lewis when they were the executive story editors on *Anything But Love* (See Entry). Billy Van Zandt and Adrienne Barbeau were married at her home in Los Angeles on New Year's Eve in 1992.

A previous marriage (on *Maude*) had left Carol with a nine-year-old son, Phillip, who for most of the series was played by Brian Morrison. However, before the start of the last season, Morrison left and Kraig Metzinger was brought in to finish out the series.

Maude was, without a doubt, in complete control of the household, but she did have some help with the domestic chores. The first of her live-in housekeepers was Florida Evans, played by Esther Rolle. Ms. Rolle explained how producer Norman Lear convinced her to accept the part she had initially turned down by emphasizing that they were not looking for the Louise Beavers or Hattie MacDaniel type. " 'No! I don't want to be no Hollywood maid,' she said. 'They don't want a *black* woman, they want something they cooked up in their heads.' "[20] But it was this kind of fire that she displayed at her audition that sold her to Lear.

Lear made certain that Maude echoed his sentiments by explaining to Florida that she would not be treated like a maid, but more like a member of the family, which included using the front door, dining and drinking with the family. This may have been a very magnanimous gesture on the part of Mrs. Findlay, but it wasn't acceptable to Florida, who preferred using the kitchen door, because it saved her steps when bringing in the groceries. Furthermore, since Florida didn't drink in the afternoon, she had no desire to spend "happy hour" with Maude and her husband, Walter (Bill Macy), who was not quite as thoroughly cowed as Maude might have liked. But in spite of their differences, these two women became close friends and a strong bond developed between them. Esther Rolle had also developed a strong bond with the television audience. So strong, in fact, that she was forced to end her relationship with Maude so that she could star in her own series, *Good Times* (See Entry).

Where other producers might take the safe route and cast another round black actress to take over the chores of the Findlay household, Norman Lear showed his boldness by completely rewriting the role of the maid so that she'd have an almost opposite appearance and personality. First of all, she was white. Secondly, she loved to suck back a few, and third, she wasn't even from the United States—she was English. Not upper-crust English, mind you, but a working class Englishwoman. Her name was Mrs. Naugatuck and she was played by the British stage actress, Hermione Baddeley. Depending on whom you talk to, Mrs. Naugatuck was better liked, as liked, or less liked than her predecessor. She obviously did not garner enough popularity to get her own series, but the Naugatuck character was probably least liked by the actress playing her. She was quoted in Rick Mitz's *The Great Sitcom Book* as having had trouble adjusting to delivering her lines in an Americanized English "so she switched to an accent that was half-American, half-Cockney. In time, Baddeley became disgruntled with the show—in any accent. 'My parts were getting smaller and smaller,' she said. 'I didn't want it to get to the 'Yes, mum, no, mum thing.' "[21] It never came to that, but she did eventually leave the series. The writers had already developed a storyline in which Mrs. Naugatuck is courted by Bert Beasley (J. Pat O'Malley.)

The writers picked up on this angle and used the old "gets married and moves away" story. In this case, Mrs. Naugatuck marries Bert and the newlyweds are said to be returning to their childhood home across the great pond. Audiences may also recall O'Malley as the second of three actors to play Rob Petrie's father on *The Dick Van Dyke Show* (See Entry).

Still, as liberated and as capable as Maude was, she was still

20. Riley, John. *TV Guide,* Vol. 22, No. 26, Issue #1104, June 29, 1974, p. 17.
21. Mitz, Rick. *The Great TV Sitcom Book.* Richard Marek Publishers, New York, 1980, p. 310.

unable to run the damn house without any help. The producers fished the final ethnic domestic out of the Caribbean. Her name was Victoria Butterfield and she was played by Marlene Warfield. The new equation just never resulted in any degree of success, proving that Warfield plus Butterfield equals canceled.

MAVERICK

September 22, 1957–July 8, 1962.   ABC

Character:	Bret Maverick
Played by:	James Garner
Date(s):	September 22, 1957–March 13, 1960

Replaced by:	Cousin Beauregard "Beau" Maverick
Played by:	Roger Moore
Date(s):	September 18, 1960–May 6, 1962

Replaced by:	Brent Maverick
Played by:	Robert Colbert
Date(s):	March 26, 1961–July 8, 1962

The thrill of it all was that if it were not for his role as Bret Maverick, James Garner might never have been given the opportunity to kiss Doris Day.

This TV Western was a little off the beaten path. Its hero, Bret Maverick, lived by Shakespeare's line from *Henry IV*, "The better part of valor is discretion," and it was not uncommon for him to steal out of town to avoid becoming involved in any gunplay.

Making his first television appearance in the September 20, 1955 episode of *Cheyenne*, a show he would appear on three more times, it was his portrayal of the witty card-playing peacekeeper that allowed Jim to garner his success.

Bret's brother, Bart, was introduced in "Hostage," the series' eighth episode, which aired on November 10, 1957. The intention in adding the character was twofold. First was the concern that a more straightlaced presence was needed to keep the series from becoming a sitcom. Second, the new actor, Jack Kelly, could help relieve some of the burden of production by appearing solo in several episodes each season in order to allow Garner some time off—but it wasn't enough.

The Merriam-Webster dictionary defines *Maverick* as "an independent individual who refuses to conform with his group." And James Garner lived up to the definition when he left the series at the end of the third season after Warner Bros. refused to meet his new contract demands. It was a scenario nearly identical to the one involving Clint Walker and the same studio during the production of *Cheyenne* (See Entry).

The problem was compounded by a writers' strike at the end of 1959, which prompted Warner Bros. to temporarily suspend Garner until new scripts were available. Garner sued the studio and when the court ruled in his favor, he was amicably released from his contract in December 1960.

This separation between James Garner and Warner Bros. had nothing whatsoever to do with any jealousy toward his co-star, Jack Kelly, whom Garner liked very much.

His departure from television gave Garner the additional free time he wanted and the freedom to work in motion pictures, which were less grueling and more financially rewarding. Audiences were rewarded by being able to enjoy his work in more than thirty films. He palled around with Tony Randall in the 1962 comedy, BOYS' NIGHT OUT. In 1963 he played Doris Day's husband, Dr. Gerald Boyer, in THE THRILL OF IT ALL. That same year he joined Steve McQueen, Richard Attenborough, Charles Bronson, James Coburn, Donald Pleasence and David McCallum in the highly successful prisoner-of-war drama, THE GREAT ESCAPE.

James Garner returned to television as a modern-day Maverick-type, Jim Rockford, in his hit detective series, *The Rockford Files,* which aired on NBC from September 13, 1974 to July 25, 1980.

Of greater significance is that James Garner returned to reprise his *Maverick* role three times. The first was in *The New Maverick,* the pilot for *Young Maverick,* wherein Charles Frank starred as Beau's son, Ben. The pilot aired on CBS on September 3, 1978. A total of thirteen episodes of *Young Maverick* were produced but only eight aired. The first episode, "Clancy," which aired on November 28, 1979, once again featured James Garner as Bret Maverick. The series played out its hand on January 16, 1980.

The following year, James Garner returned again, this time in a pilot for his own *Maverick* revival series, *Bret Maverick,* which placed *Maverick* on NBC, the last of the three networks to air one of the incarnations. Even though this series was not a major success it did air a total of eighteen episodes, which is more than twice the number recorded by its predecessor.

The first episode, "Welcome to Sweetwater," picks up after the pilot in which Maverick won $100,000, the Lazy Ace ranch and "The Red Ox" saloon in a high stakes poker game. The first scene shows Maverick standing on the steps of his newly-acquired home watching the wagons bringing in crates of his belongings. The ranch foreman, Cy Whitaker (Richard Hamilton), questions Maverick on the activity:

WHITAKER: What's all this stuff, anyway?

MAVERICK: Twenty years of leave behinds. Things I was movin' too fast to take with me. Souvenirs, books, tools of the trade.

WHITAKER: And just what trade is that?

Maverick never dignified that question with an answer.

What was needed now was another actor qualified to replace the departed Garner. As a result of the Clint Walker incident, Warner Bros. had already established a position of not giving in to actors' demands, so there was never any thought given to bringing Garner back.

In 1960 Roger Moore appears as Beau Maverick. He is introduced in the fourth season's first episode, "Bundle from Britain," and we learn that Cousin Beau has been in England since the end of the Civil War, which is supposed to explain his polished appearance and impeccable English accent.

It is also most likely that the casting of Moore dictated the writing of the part as the Englishman, rather than the other way around. Roger Moore was not a newcomer to the series, but had actually appeared during its first season. In that episode, "The Rivals," which aired on January 25, 1959, Roger Moore played Jack Vandergelt, a handsome millionaire who trades places with Bret—but only temporarily. Now, as Beau, he trades places with him for good.

Accepting the role as Beau Maverick was a gamble for Moore that paid off in a big way. He went on to play the first Simon Templar in *The Saint* (See Entry) and to take over Sean Connery's duties as 007 in seven JAMES BOND films.

Robert Colbert joined the series in 1961 as the fourth and youngest Maverick, Brent. He made his first appearance in the town of Sunburst in "The Forbidden City" episode, and had overlapping appearances with both Bart and Beau. But he did not add enough Maverick to *Maverick* and after twenty-nine more episodes, twelve of which were repeats of earlier episodes starring the one and only Maverick, James Garner, the producers realized that they no longer held a winning hand and the series folded. This did not prevent Robert Colbert from transporting his career via his co-starring role as Dr. Doug Phillips on the science fiction series, *The Time Tunnel,* which aired on ABC from September 9, 1966 to September 1, 1967. He later found happiness on the ABC soap opera, *The Young and the Restless,* as Stuart Brooks, a role he played from 1973 to 1983.

James Garner returned to television as Jim Doyle, a sort of modern day Maverick-like politician, in the NBC situation comedy, *Man of the People,* which premiered on September 15, 1991.

MAYBERRY R.F.D. *see* THE ANDY GRIFFITH SHOW

MAYOR OF HOLLYWOOD

July 29, 1952–September 18, 1952.   NBC

Character:	Secretary
Played by:	Jeanne Dyer
Date(s):	July 29, 1952–August 7, 1952

Replaced by:	Secretary
Played by:	Lina Romay
Date(s):	August 14, 1952–September 18, 1952

Character:	Campaign Manager
Played by:	Lou Crosby
Date(s):	July 29, 1952–July 31, 1952

Replaced by:	Campaign Manager
Played by:	Bill Baldwin
Date(s):	August 7, 1952–September 18, 1952

Walter O'Keefe, as himself, mounted a fictitious political campaign to become the mayor of Hollywood. Although this half-hour summer series, which was broadcast live, was classified as a variety program, it did feature two regulars as

O'Keefe's political aides—his campaign manager and his secretary.

About halfway through his two-month campaign, both actors were replaced, Ms. Dyer by Latin singer, Lina Romay, and Crosby by Bill Baldwin.

In 1968, as part of *The Summer Smothers Brothers Show,* which aired sixteen summers after *The Mayor of Hollywood,* the Smothers' deadpan editorial comedian Pat Paulsen mounted a similar campaign for the U.S. presidency, using the slogan "If nominated I will not run, and if elected I will not serve." He flew to several cities and, standing at the base of the portable stairs after deplaning, gave exactly the same speech, the only change being the name of the city. Not wanting to get involved in the "equal time" law, CBS ended his campaign before the election in which Paulsen earned a surprising number of write-in votes.

McMILLAN AND WIFE

September 29, 1971–August 21, 1977.   NBC

Character:	Mildred
Played by:	Nancy Walker
Date(s):	September 29, 1971–February 16, 1975

Replaced by:	Agatha
Played by:	Martha Raye
Date(s):	December 5, 1976–August 21, 1977

If "Mac" and Sally McMillan reminded you of Nick and Nora Charles, there's good reason—Nick and Nora were the models for this updated version of *The Thin Man.* The leads were Rock Hudson as San Francisco Police Commissioner Stewart "Mac" McMillan and Susan Saint James as his beautiful wife, Sally. Their rather outspoken maid, Mildred, was played superbly by Nancy Walker.

This four-foot-eleven-inch tall red-headed fireball has played the owner of Rosie's Diner, the quicker pickerupper expert on the Bounty paper towel commercials for more than twenty years. She spent the first thirty years of her professional career as a New York stage actress and didn't make it to series television until she was nearly fifty.

Her first duty was as a part-time housekeeper, Emily Turner, for Bill Davis in *Family Affair.* Her introductory episode of *Family Affair* was "Meet Emily," which aired on October 8, 1970. She stayed with the series until March 1, 1971.

Her reason for leaving the employ of the McMillans was to star as Sophie in a new CBS situation comedy, *Keep the Faith.* The pilot, which starred Bert Convy as Rabbi Miller, aired on April 14, 1972, but it never went to series.

Walker's most famous role on television, by far, was Ida Morganstern, Rhoda's mother. The part began as a guest shot on *The Mary Tyler Moore Show*'s episode "Support Your Local Mother," which aired on October 24, 1970. Two years later she appeared again in "Enter Rhoda's Parents," which aired on October 7, 1972. Her last appearance on *The Mary Tyler Moore Show* was in "Rhoda's Sister Gets Married," which aired on September 29, 1973.

Her return to series work came when Valerie Harper left *The Mary Tyler Moore Show* for her own successful spinoff, *Rhoda,* which aired on CBS from September 9, 1974 to December 9, 1978. Nancy Walker continued in her role as Rhoda's mother from the first episode to September 20, 1976. She walked out on her TV daughters (Rhoda also had a sister, Brenda [Julie Kavner]) to star in her own series. *The Nancy Walker Show* premiered on ABC on September 30, 1976 with Ms. Walker as Nancy Kitteridge, a Hollywood theatrical agent. But ABC closed her agency after only thirteen episodes, the last show airing on July 11, 1977.

As it turned out, Nancy Walker was not the only one to leave *McMillan and Wife* at the end of the fifth season—Susan Saint James also left in a contract dispute. This casting upset was dealt with by having Mrs. McMillan killed in a plane crash, and the series title was shortened to *McMillan.* Mildred's sister, Agatha, was Mac's new domestic. The December 5, 1976 listing in *TV Guide* brought viewers up to date: "Commissioner McMillan (Rock Hudson) begins a sixth season a fully adjusted widower, vacationing in Las Vegas where, as luck would have it, his new girlfriend is robbed of a fortune in diamonds. Martha Raye replaces Nancy Walker as Mac's doting new house-keeper."

Coming from a background similar to Nancy Walker's and having much the same acting style, Martha Raye was the perfect choice for her replacement, even without red hair! Like Ms. Walker, her parents were in vaudeville, she worked on radio and on Broadway. She starred in her own comedy variety show, *The Martha Raye Show,* which aired on NBC from September 20, 1955 to May 29, 1956. After picking up after Mac for the last season of *McMillan,* Martha Raye found happiness from 1982 to 1984 as Mel Sharples' loud-mouthed mom, Carrie, on the CBS sitcom, *Alice.*

MEET CORLISS ARCHER

July 12, 1951–August 5, 1956.   CBS-Syndicated-NBC

Character:	Corliss Archer
Played by:	Lugene Sanders
Date(s):	July 12, 1951–August 10, 1951
	January 26, 1952–March 29, 1952

Replaced by:	Corliss Archer
Played by:	Ann Baker
Date(s):	1954 (syndicated series)

Replaced by:	Corliss Archer
Played by:	Robin Morgan
Date(s):	August 5, 1956 (special)

Character:	Harry Archer
Played by:	Fred Shields
Date(s):	July 12, 1951–August 10, 1951
	January 26, 1952–March 29, 1952

Replaced by:	Harry Archer
Played by:	John Eldridge
Date(s):	1954 syndicated series

Replaced by:	Harry Archer
Played by:	Jerome Cowan
Date(s):	August 5, 1956 (special)

Character:	Janet Archer
Played by:	Frieda Inescort
Date(s):	July 12, 1951–August 10, 1951

Replaced by:	Janet Archer
Played by:	Irene Tedrow
Date(s):	January 26, 1952–March 29, 1952

Replaced by:	Janet Archer
Played by:	Mary Bain
Date(s):	1954 (syndicated series)

Replaced by:	Janet Archer
Played by:	Polly Rowles
Date(s):	August 5, 1956 (special)

Character:	Dexter Franklin
Played by:	Bobby Ellis
Date(s):	July 12, 1951–August 10, 1951
	January 26, 1952–March 29, 1952
	1954 (syndicated series)

Replaced by:	Dexter Franklin
Played by:	Warren Berlinger
Date(s):	August 5, 1956 (special)

The 1943 radio program about a pretty but unpredictable teenaged girl, *Meet Corliss Archer* (which was almost a carbon copy of *A Date with Judy*), was turned into a live television program of the same name in 1951. With the radio series still on the CBS network, the actors who were playing Mr. and Mrs. Archer, Fred Shields and Frieda Inescort, added the television series to their weekly schedule.

The first teenager to appear on television in the title role was Lugene Sanders, who later became the second Babs on *The Life of Riley* (See Entry). Her boyfriend, Dexter, was played by Bobby Ellis, who was the fifth Aldrich on *The Aldrich Family* (See Entry).

The series went on hiatus in August 1951 and when it returned the following January, Irene Tedrow had replaced Frieda Inescort as Mrs. Archer. Unlike her predecessor, Ms. Tedrow continued to work in series television. She played Mrs. Lucy Elkins, the woman who owned the cat, on *Dennis the Menace* from 1959 to 1963 and Mrs. Ring during the 1965 season of *Mr. Novak.*

Meet Corliss Archer turned up two years later as a filmed syndicated series with an entirely new cast except for Bobby Ellis as Dexter.

The only actor of note from this version is handsome John

Eldridge, whose film credits include Barry Jones in the 1934 Edward G. Robinson mystery, THE MAN WITH TWO FACES, and the first executive in the 1950 Ronald Colman comedy, CHAMPAGNE FOR CAESAR. John Eldridge's television roles include several appearances on *The Lone Ranger,* though his most visible parts may be the heavies he played on the *Adventures of Superman.* These include the man with the tulips, Burt Burnside, in "Shot in the Dark," and the notorious "Mr. X" in "Superman's Wife," in which he manages to imprison Superman, Lois, Jimmy and Perry White in a submerged diving bell.

A third cast for *Meet Corliss Archer* was assembled in 1956 for a comedy special that was broadcast in color. It starred juvenile actress Robin Morgan, who played the third Dagmar on *Mama* (See Entry). Harry Archer was played by Jerome Cowan, already known to television audiences as the second Collins in the newspaper drama, *Not for Publication* (See Entry). He later co-starred as Herbert Wilson on the Walter Brennan situation comedy, *The Tycoon,* which aired on ABC from September 15, 1964 to September 7, 1965.

MEET MILLIE

October 25, 1952–March 6, 1956.   CBS

Character:	J.R. Boone, Sr.
Played by:	Earl Ross
Date(s):	October 25, 1952–June 1953

Replaced by:	J.R. Boone, Sr.
Played by:	Roland Winters
Date(s):	June 1953–March 6, 1956

Meet Millie Bronson, an attractive secretary working in Manhattan. She is secretly in love with Johnny Boone, Jr. The fly in the ointment is that John, Sr. is her boss!

The title character was played throughout this series by Elena Verdugo, who later played Consuelo Lopez on *Marcus Welby, M.D.,* which aired on ABC from September 23, 1969, to May 11, 1976.

Although she did not originate the Millie character on radio, she did eventually replace radio's Millie, Audrey Totter, while still playing the character on the television series. Ms. Bronson's boss on radio was played by Earl Ross and he carried over the role to the television series for the first year. His replacement was Roland Winters, who was the second of three John Randolphs on *Doorway to Danger* (See Entry).

MELROSE PLACE

July 8, 1992– .   Fox

Character:	Sandy Louise Harling
Played by:	Amy Locane
Date(s):	July 8, 1992–October 28, 1992

Replaced by:	Jo Reynolds
Played by:	Daphne Zuniga
Date(s):	November 11, 1992–

While the 1980s closed out as the domain of a generation of baby boomers who were thirty something, the nineties began as the decade for the next generation who were twenty something. There were a number of series which targeted young adults, such as *Ferris Bueller* and *Parker Lewis Can't Lose* (See Entry), but it was Fox Broadcasting that set the standards for the new wave of television programs aimed at this new upscale audience.

The flagship series that spoke to teens (and preteens for that matter) was *Beverly Hills, 90210*—probably because it didn't revolve around a sitcom family with sitcom problems. The good-looking cast was headed by Shannen Doherty and Jason Priestley as fraternal twins Brenda and Brandon Walsh. The program, set in a posh neighborhood in sunny Beverly Hills, California, was at one point during the 1991 season the number one show watched by teens.

Two years later, the series spun off *Melrose Place,* another ensemble drama focusing on the lives of eight "twentysomething" adults who were all living in an apartment building in one of L.A.'s trendiest neighborhoods.

After auditioning literally hundreds of unknown actors for each of the plum roles, the engaging eight were Josie Bissett as aspiring designer Jane Mancini; Thomas Calabro as medical intern Michael Mancini, Jane's new husband and manager of the apartment building they all live in; Amy Locane as actress Sandy Louise Harling; Doug Savant as social worker Matt Fielding; Grant Show as construction worker Jake Hanson; Andrew Shue as struggling writer Billy Campbell; Courtney Thorne-Smith as college graduate Alison Parker; and Vanessa Williams as aerobics instructor Rhonda Blair.

Andrew Shue was the only first-season cast member who was not one of the producer's first choices. He took over the role of Billy from Stephen Fanning, who was dropped several days after filming began.

The beautiful Amy Locane, who at the age of twelve played Andrea Winger on NBC's *Spencer* (later titled *Under One Roof*), became the first to leave the cast after being with the series for just thirteen episodes.

The change came on November 11, 1992, when Sandy Louise Harling (Amy Locane) moved to New York to star in a soap opera and Jo Reynolds (Daphne Zuniga) moved into apartment #6, and into Jake's life as his new love interest.

Ms. Locane's other television work includes the "Love and the Teenager" episode of ABC's *The New Love American Style,* which aired on January 7, 1986. Her film credits include the part of Cheryl Anderson in the 1989 Donald Sutherland drama, LOST ANGELS, and Allison in CRY-BABY, a 1990 musical comedy starring Johnny Depp.

As Allison Bradbury in the 1985 dramatic comedy, THE SURE THING, Daphne Zuniga played a prudish all-American girl, while on Fox's *Melrose Place* she played a tough-talking photographer from New York, who moved to the West Coast to revive her career and escape her past.

THE MEN FROM SHILOH *see* THE VIRGINIAN

MICHAEL SHAYNE, PRIVATE DETECTIVE

September 30, 1960–September 22, 1961.   NBC

Character:	Lucy Hamilton
Played by:	Patricia Donahue
Date(s):	September 30, 1960–1961

Replaced by:	Lucy Hamilton
Played by:	Margie Regan
Date(s):	1961

Well before Crockett and Tubbs hit the Miami vice scene, Michael Shayne, played by Richard Denning, dressed a lot more conservatively than Don Johnson, and used his fists to fight crime in Miami Beach, Florida.

Lucy Hamilton conveniently served as Shayne's secretary and romantic interest. The first of the actresses to play Lucy was Patricia Donahue, who got her detective training as Nora Charles's friend, Hazel, on *The Thin Man.*

The pilot for this series, *Michael Shayne, Detective,* starred Mark Stevens and Merry Anders and aired on NBC on September 28, 1958.

MICKEY SPILLANE'S MIKE HAMMER

January 1958–1959.   Syndicated-NBC
January 26, 1984–September 9, 1987

Character:	Mike Hammer
Played by:	Darren McGavin
Date(s):	January 1958–1959

Replaced by:	Mike Hammer
Played by:	Stacy Keach
Date(s):	January 26, 1984–September 9, 1987

Character:	Captain Pat Chambers
Played by:	Bart Burns
Date(s):	January 1958–1959

Replaced by:	Captain Pat Chambers
Played by:	Don Stroud
Date(s):	January 26, 1984–September 9, 1987

If you like your police dramas packed with violence and sex, you'll love Mike Hammer, based on the stories of novelist Mickey Spillane. No other cop show could boast more blood than Mike Hammer.

The pilot for the original series starred Brian Keith, who later became famous as Buffy and Jody's Uncle Bill on *Family Affair.*

Stacy Keach slugged his way through the streets of New York as *Mickey Spillane's Mike Hammer,* in this violent 1980s series.

Realizing that Keith had been miscast, *Crime Photographer*'s (See Entry) second Casey, Darren McGavin, was brought in to replace him in the cold-blooded syndicated series which chalked up seventy-eight highly successful episodes. The series was so hot that it took more than twenty years to cool down enough for the networks to give the series a try. When they did, very little was changed except the cast.

The Mike Hammer of the eighties was played by Stacy Keach, of whom John Huston once said, ''The audience will go to see whatever character he projects. Each character is a star in itself. He, Stacy, is a constellation.'' Huston was right, because the series earned him a Golden Globe nomination in 1985. Not surprisingly, the character of Mike Hammer was a particular favorite of Keach's.

More accurately, Stacy Keach is really Stacy Keach, Jr., the son of Stacy Keach, Sr., who played Professor Carlson on *Get Smart!* His brother, James, who is an actor and producer, once lent his voice to the man in the mask in *The Lone Ranger* (See Entry).

Keach, who has nearly two dozen feature films to his credit, began with the role of Blount in the 1968 drama, THE HEART IS A LONELY HUNTER. In 1972 he starred as Roy Fehler in the police drama, THE NEW CENTURIONS, and appeared in the Western, JUDGE ROY BEAN. In addition to playing serious cops and cowboys, Keach also did a number of comedies—two for Cheech and Chong. In their 1978 outing, UP IN SMOKE, he played Sergeant Stedenko. Three years later he turned up as Sarge in CHEECH AND CHONG'S NICE DREAMS.

His numerous television roles include the heroic, rugged, self-effacing Union Cavalry officer, Jonas Steele, in the CBS miniseries, *The Blue and the Gray,* which aired from November 14 to November 17, 1982.

One of his most satisfying accomplishments was learning how to walk a tightrope for his title role in the Broadway play, *Barnum.* The rope was thirty-five-feet long, a half-inch in diameter and was suspended six feet above the stage.

"It took me four months to learn how to do that, and when I finally got it down pat, audiences started taking it for granted that my character was an accomplished wire-walker and there was thus no suspense in my getting up there and taking the thirty-five-foot walk. So I inserted a fake fall, saving myself by grabbing the wire with my hands, and that kept the suspense alive. Thing is, when in my life will I ever use that skill again?" said Keach.

Mike Hammer's secretary on the Keach series was Velda, played in the pilot by *Charlie's Angels* (See Entry) beauty, Tanya Roberts. But Ms. Roberts "was unable to reprise the role because of other commitments with Columbia features." A nationwide talent search ensued. Jay Bernstein, executive producer of *Mickey Spillane's Mike Hammer,* said, "Historically, Velda has been a brunette who can handle the gift of gab as well as a gun. What we're looking for is a well-endowed actress who is as agile as she is attractive and can handle one-liners like Claudette Colbert."[22] They found her in Lindsay Bloom, who fit nicely into the role and Ms. Roberts' wardrobe. Ms. Bloom, who remained throughout the entire run of the series, had been Hazzard's second telephone operator on *The Dukes of Hazzard* (See Entry).

Among Mike's friends, Captain Pat Chambers of the New York Police Department, was played by Don Stroud, who later appeared in the syndicated revival of *Dragnet.*

Incidentally, in 1984 Columbia Pictures released SHEENA, which starred a blonde Tanya Roberts in the title role. It seems logical to assume that this is what occupied her time during 1983.

MISSION: IMPOSSIBLE

September 17, 1966–September 8, 1973.   CBS
October 23, 1988–February 24, 1990   ABC

Character:	Daniel "Dan" Briggs
Played by:	Steven Hill
Date(s):	September 17, 1966–April 22, 1967

Replaced by:	Jim Phelps
Played by:	Peter Graves
Date(s):	September 10, 1967–September 8, 1973
	October 23, 1988–February 24, 1990

Character:	Rollin Hand
Played by:	Martin Landau
Date(s):	September 17, 1966–April 20, 1969

Replaced by:	Paris
Played by:	Leonard Nimoy
Date(s):	September 28, 1969–March 17, 1971

Replaced by:	Nicholas Black
Played by:	Thaao Penghlis
Date(s):	October 23, 1988–April 20, 1989

Character:	Cinnamon Carter
Played by:	Barbara Bain
Date(s):	September 17, 1966–April 20, 1969

Replaced by:	Lynn
Played by:	Alexandra Hay
Date(s):	September 28, 1969

Replaced by:	Meredyth
Played by:	Dina Merrill
Date(s):	October 12, 1969–October 19, 1969

Replaced by:	Tracey
Played by:	Lee Meriwether
Date(s):	October 5, 1969–January 18, 1970

Replaced by:	Beth
Played by:	Sally Ann Howes
Date(s):	October 26, 1969

Replaced by:	Gillian Colbee
Played by:	Anne Francis
Date(s):	December 7, 1969

Replaced by:	Lisa
Played by:	Michele Carey
Date(s):	December 14, 1969

Replaced by:	Wai Lee
Played by:	Barbara Luna
Date(s):	December 21, 1969

Replaced by:	Monique
Played by:	Julie Gregg
Date(s):	December 28, 1969

No matter how many times IMF leader Jim Phelps (Peter Graves, bottom right) reviewed the dossiers of potential agents, he always seemed to choose the same four: (clockwise, from top) Cinnamon Carter (Barbara Bain), Rollin Hand (Martin Landau), Barney Collier (Greg Morris) and Willie Armitage (Peter Lupus).

Replaced by:	Nora
Played by:	Antoinette Bower
Date(s):	February 8, 1970

Replaced by:	Valerie
Played by:	Jessica Walter
Date(s):	March 1, 1970

Replaced by:	Roxy
Played by:	Lynn Kellog
Date(s):	March 29, 1971

Replaced by:	Dana Lambert
Played by:	Lesley Warren
Date(s):	September 19, 1970–March 17, 1971

Replaced by:	Casey
Played by:	Lynda Day George
Date(s):	September 18, 1971–March 30, 1973

Replaced by:	Mimi Davis
Played by:	Barbara Anderson
Date(s):	September 16, 1972–November 18, 1972

Replaced by:	Sandy
Played by:	Marlyn Mason
Date(s):	December 9, 1972

Replaced by:	Andrea
Played by:	Elizabeth Ashley
Date(s):	January 19, 1973

Replaced by:	Casey Randall
Played by:	Terry Markwell
Date(s):	October 23, 1988–February 18, 1989

Replaced by:	Shannon Reed
Played by:	Jane Badler
Date(s):	February 18, 1989–February 24, 1990

Character:	Barnard "Barney" Collier
Played by:	Greg Morris
Date(s):	September 17, 1966–September 8, 1973

Replaced by:	Grant Collier
Played by:	Phil Morris
Date(s):	October 23, 1988–February 24, 1990

Character:	Willie Armitage
Played by:	Peter Lupus
Date(s):	September 17, 1966–September 8, 1973

Replaced by:	Max Harte
Played by:	Tony Hamilton
Date(s):	October 23, 1988–February 24, 1990

Your mission, should you decide to accept it, is to remain on the air with consistently high ratings through nine seasons and two incarnations. As always, should you, or any of your IM force be caught in contract negotiations, or a poor "TVQ" survey, the secretary will disavow all knowledge of your actions. This series will self-destruct in twenty-four years. Good luck Dan . . . er, Jim.

That's basically how the series began each week, with the head of the Impossible Missions Force (IMF) listening to a recorded briefing of the proposed assignment while perusing still pictures supplied to him in an accompanying envelope.

When *Mission: Impossible* went on the air, the team leader was Dan Briggs, played by Steven Hill. Hill was replaced at the start of the second season by Peter Graves as Jim Phelps. The other original members of the team were Rollin Hand (Martin Landau), a master of disguise, Cinnamon Carter (Barbara Bain), the female operative, Barney Collier (Greg Morris), the electronics expert and Peter Lupus as strongman Willie Armitage.

Together, they worked undercover for a top secret government agency to plan and execute intricate assignments often involving the assassination of dictators and despotic leaders of fictitiously named foreign countries. The results of all this somehow protected and preserved the free world without directly involving or implicating the United States government.

The star of the series was supposed to be Steven Hill, who played John Tower in the 1958 drama, THE GODDESS, and Ted Widdicombe in the 1963 Burt Lancaster/Judy Garland drama, A CHILD IS WAITING. But Hill didn't become the star. "His role in *Mission: Impossible* might have been the one to bring him the sort of recognition he has missed, but it has been overshadowed by the flashier part and more flamboyant acting style of Martin Landau, who was originally to have been only an occasional guest star but who has been in almost every episode of the series."[23]

Of concern to the producers was that Hill's commitment to follow his Orthodox Jewish tradition had, at times, hindered production. Hill had a clause in his contract that allowed him to be released from the set every Friday so that he would have sufficient time to drive home before sundown. Furthermore, Steven Hill did not work on Jewish holidays, which resulted in three episodes being shot almost exclusively with Landau.

Patrick J. White, the author of *The Complete Mission: Impossible Dossier,* added that "In addition to Steven Hill's orthodox requirements, he was difficult at times and was even suspended for one episode for refusing to run up a studio staircase, as per the script."[24]

Whatever the reason, the second season of *Mission: Impossible* began with Peter Graves taking Hill's role as the leader of the IMF team. Saving the world was nothing new for Peter

23. Radditz, Leslie. *TV Guide,* Vol. 15, No. 6, February 11, 1967, Issue #724, p. 22.
24. White, Patrick J., from a letter to the author dated March 27, 1992.

Graves; he had done so many times before as the star of several popular B science fiction films. In the 1956 film, IT CONQUERED THE WORLD, Peter Graves starred as Paul Nelson, who saved earth from a Venusian invasion. A year later, Graves was back defending the world against giant grasshoppers in BEGINNING OF THE END.

Before *Mission: Impossible,* Peter Graves starred as Jim Newton in *Fury* (See Entry) and Christopher Cobb in the 1960/1961 syndicated Western, *Whiplash.*

The *Mission: Impossible* pilot, filmed in 1965, featured Martin Landau as Rollin Hand in what was written as a one-shot guest-starring role. So impressed was the CBS network with the character and Landau's performance that they urged him to sign on as a regular. Landau declined the offer. He had already turned down the producers of *Star Trek* when they had offered him the role of the half-human half-Vulcan, Mr. Spock. Landau was at that time not interested in committing to a weekly television series; he wanted to continue his work in motion pictures.

His previous film roles include Leonard in Alfred Hitchcock's 1959 drama, NORTH BY NORTHWEST, and the Duke in the Glenn Ford/Debbie Reynolds comedy, THE GAZEBO, released that same year. In 1966 he played Jesse Coe in the Steve McQueen Western, NEVADA SMITH.

Like Lucille Ball, who signed yearly contracts, Martin Landau worked without a standard five-year contract and still managed to appear in twenty-six of the first twenty-eight episodes. Even more surprising is that he continued with the series and by the third season had won a salary increase to $6,500 per episode, up $1,500 from his first-season salary.

Landau's wife, Barbara Bain, who was appearing in the series as Cinnamon Carter, had signed a five-year contract which gave her a modest $1,000 per episode. That part with the small salary, however, earned Mrs. Landau two big Emmy awards. In both the 1966/1967 and 1967/1968 seasons, Barbara Bain won for Outstanding Continued Performance by an Actress in a Leading Role in a Dramatic Series, beating out Diana Rigg in *The Avengers* and Barbara Stanwyck in *The Big Valley* on both occasions. Barbara Bain had become a star and demanded a salary more commensurate with her new Hollywood status. This being a reasonable request and one quite common in the industry, Ms. Bain's per episode salary was upped to $2,500.

By the end of the third season, *Mission: Impossible* was an unqualified success and had become a part of the national consciousness.

It was at this point that Martin Landau asked, through his attorney, E. Gregory Hookstratten, for an increase in salary to $11,000 per episode for the upcoming fourth season, and a guarantee of $12,500 for the fifth. Paramount agreed to an increase to $7,000 per episode, but would budge no further, as that was the salary being paid to the top-billed star of the series, Peter Graves.

At this point " 'That dollar differential in terms of Marty was

only one small part of the veritable floodgate that it would have opened,' [Douglas S.] Cramer maintained, rejecting this alternative."[25]

Compounding the problem was the questionable return of Barbara Bain to the series. In a situation that seems to have gotten blown out of proportion, Ms. Bain was called by the associate producer of *Mission: Impossible* on a Friday afternoon, seven days prior to the scheduled start of shooting, and asked to report to Paramount on that coming Monday to discuss makeup and wardrobe. Ms. Bain said she explained that due to previous commitments, which included the filming of promotional messages for the Heart Association, she could not be at the studio until Wednesday.

" 'When it first appeared that Barbara was not going to show up for the first show," Cramer explained, 'and we didn't know whether that was temporary or permanent, it was everybody's decision that we should go after the biggest promotable name [to replace her].' "[26] That name was Dina Merrill.

Things got even uglier, with suits and counter suits between Paramount and Barbara Bain, the end result being that Alexandra Hay replaced Ms. Bain in the September 28, 1969 episode, with Dina Merrill appearing on October 12. To keep the record straight, Ms. Merrill's episode was actually shot first, even though it aired after Ms. Hay's.

These actresses were followed by one of *Batman*'s (See Entry) three Catwomen, Lee Meriwether, and ten other "guest spies" throughout the fourth season.

In an awkward moment at the 1969/1970 Emmy Awards ceremony, Barbara Bain and Lesley Warren accidentally bumped into each other. Both actresses retained their composure and exchanged pleasantries. Ms. Bain wished Ms. Warren well, while Ms. Warren told the three-time Emmy winner that she had always enjoyed her performances. The reason this tête-a-tête was so uncomfortable was that Ms. Warren had recently been signed as *Mission: Impossible*'s new female agent, Dana.

In a bold departure from the established and well-liked character of the perfectly coifed and more aloof Cinnamon played by Barbara Bain, Lesley Warren's younger Dana character had long brown hair and girlish freckles. But the casting of Ms. Warren was no accident. It was more of an edict from CBS-TV president Robert D. Wood, who was making aggressive moves at the network to attract a younger audience, and Lesley Warren fit the bill. One of her best-remembered performances prior to *Mission: Impossible* was in Rodgers and Hammerstein's February 22, 1965 special, *Cinderella,* in which she starred in the title role—her first.

But even before Lesley Warren even had a chance to settle in to her character, she was supplanted by Lynda Day George, whose Casey character was somewhere in between Dana and Cinnamon.

Among the nine other actresses to appear as the female member of the IMF team in guest-starring roles—their names were never included in the main title credits—was Jessica

---

25. Lewis, Richard Warren. "Is This Mission Possible?" *TV Guide,* Vol. 17, No. 42, Issue #864, October 18, 1969. p. 36
26. *Ibid.*

Walter, who achieved film stardom as Evelyn Draper in Clint Eastwood's chilling 1971 drama, PLAY MISTY FOR ME. Television audiences will also recognize Ms. Walter as the voice of Fran Sinclair on the ABC situation comedy, *Dinosaurs,* which premiered on April 26, 1991.

Meanwhile, over on the very next sound stage, Paramount's premiere science fiction series, *Star Trek,* was just about to be canceled after completing its third season. One of the show's co-stars, Leonard Nimoy, still had two years remaining on his five-year contract. And without the bangs and pointed ears, Leonard Nimoy's facial characteristics were strikingly similar to Martin Landau's.

"At the end of the third season, Martin Landau and Barbara Bain were involved in some very difficult negotiations with Paramount. Landau had been working on a season-to-season contract, and was free to negotiate for whatever he thought were his best interests for the season to come. By the time it became clear that *Star Trek* was to be canceled, it was also evident that Landau and his wife, Barbara Bain, were not going to successfully complete their negotiations for a fourth season on *Mission: Impossible.* Having reached an impasse, and having decided to move off in another direction, the studio contacted my agent about the possibility of my moving into the *Mission: Impossible* show,"[27] said Nimoy.

The July 12, 1969, *TV Guide* announced "Leonard Nimoy has become a *Mission: Impossible* regular, replacing Martin Landau, who left the series because of a salary dispute."[28]

"For the next year and a half I settled into the business of being a man of a thousand faces. It was fun for a while.... My character was called 'Paris.' I often wondered if perhaps that name was chosen for me because of my success in a one-name character called Spock.... All of this was fun for a while but eventually I realized that I had done it. I had played the South American dictator, I had played the Greek shipping magnate, I had played the European revolutionaries. Having done that, and without the sustenance of personal involvement in the material, the fun began to wear thin. In the middle of the second season I told my agent that I would like to ask for a release from the series."[29]

Nimoy beamed out of *Mission: Impossible* on good terms and says that he has never regretted his decision.

Leonard Nimoy, however, wasn't the only one from *Star Trek* to appear on the series. For three months during the 1972 season the IMF was joined by Barbara Anderson as Mimi. Ms. Anderson had worked with Leonard Nimoy in the "Conscience of the King" episode of *Star Trek,* in which she played Lenore Karidian. Because *Mission: Impossible* was produced at Paramount, right next door to the *Star Trek* sound stage, *Star Trek* fans will have a field day looking for the veritable gold mine of *Star Trek* regulars and guest stars. These include Mark Lenard, George Takei, David Opatoshu, Ricardo Montalban, William Windom, William Schallert, Lee Meriwether, Joan Collins, William Shatner and Gary Lockwood.

On February 6, 1971, Cincinnati Reds' catcher Johnny Bench appeared in what *TV Guide*'s "TV Teletype: Hollywood" reported as "one of those minor roles that Hollywood reserves for front-running athletes." Another athlete, tennis star Arthur Ashe, was said to have been interviewed as a possible replacement for Greg Morris, but nothing came of the rumor after Morris was given a token $500–per episode salary increase and a new dressing room.

One of the team's standby agents, Dr. Doug Robert, who often used the alias "Lang," was played by Sam Elliott, who replaced Peter Lupus in a number of episodes from October 17, 1970 to March 30, 1973, when a doctor was needed instead of a strongman.

"Sam Elliott was hired for the series in an attempt to freshen up the show, and because the series' producer thought that Peter Lupus was expendable. Lupus' absence, however, resulted in a negative response from series viewers,"[30] said author Patrick J. White.

Mission: Impossible ended on September 8, 1973, after successfully completing 172 impossible missions.

This, however, was not the end of *Mission: Impossible:* the series was given a second life in 1988, when ABC found a way to circumvent a strike by the Writer's Guild of America. "The network has also ordered at least 13 episodes of *Mission: Impossible,* being produced in Australia by Paramount with a new cast, but with old scripts culled from the successful series."[31]

The new series had a lot going for it. A proven formula, tested scripts, and the original star of the series, Peter Graves, recreating his role as the leader of the IM force.

Still, the casting of Graves may have been just as big a gamble as recasting the role—and not because of the fifteen years that had passed. Even at sixty-three years old, Graves was just as handsome as ever. The problem was that one of Graves' most recent roles was not the usual straight dramatic part he had played throughout his career. The white-haired Graves had very recently appeared as Captain Oveur in the 1980 and 1982 satirical spoofs, AIRPLANE! and AIRPLANE II: THE SEQUEL. This presented the possibility that audiences would no longer accept Graves in the role of the hero, and might laugh at his portrayal of Mr. Phelps. Fortunately, audiences didn't laugh, but even so, the series only enjoyed a modicum of success.

Except for Graves, who was still playing Jim Phelps, the rest of the cast featured new actors playing different characters, although each was pretty much a clone of his or her predecessor. One unseen actor who returned to *Mission: Impossible* was Bob Johnson, the same actor who provided the voice on the recorded message for the original series.

Nicholas Black (Thaao Penghlis) was the master of disguise, Max Harte (Tony Hamilton), the muscle; Casey Randall (Terry Markwell), the beautiful female operative.

The characters were all introduced in the first episode of the

27. Nimoy, Leonard. *I Am Not Spock.* Del Rey, New York, 1977, pp. 124–125.
28. "Joseph Finnigan Reports." TV Teletype: Hollywood. *TV Guide,* Vol. 17, No. 28, July 12, 1969, Issue #850.
29. Nimoy, Leonard. *op cit.,* pp. 126–128.
30. White, Patrick, J., from a letter to the author dated March 27, 1992.
31. *Ross Reports Television: Casting, Scripts, Production.* Television Index, Inc. Long Island, New York, August 1988, p. 1. Editor Jerry Leichter.

A close variation of the cast shot shown at the close of ''The Fortune,'' the February 18, 1989, episode in which team member, Casey Randall (Terry Markwell, left) is murdered. Pictured (left to right) behind the departed Casey are Tony Hamilton as Max Harte, Phil Morris as Grant Collier, Thaao Penghlis as Nicholas Black and Peter Graves as the inimitable Mr. Phelps.

series, which also reintroduced Peter Graves as Jim Phelps, first seen observing a funeral from a vantage point elsewhere in the cemetery. The funeral was for Thomas D. Copperfield (Vince Martin), a handsome young agent killed in the episode's teaser. Jim Phelps had a personal interest in the young man because he was a team leader for the IMF. More importantly, he was Phelps' protégé and like a son to him.

The audience is reintroduced to the series through some familiar images and sounds. Phelps stops a fisherman (Reg Gilliam) on a pier and trades an obviously contrived bit of coded dialogue with him. The fisherman walks away and leaves Phelps with his fishing gear. Opening up the tackle box, Jim Phelps removes a small rectangular box and places his thumb on a white button. A red beam is seen moving up and down, obviously scanning his fingerprint. The box unlocks and re-

veals a combination LCD screen/laser disc player, with no way to insert the disc. That is when Phelps punches in the code ''3–5-9'' on the calculator keypad, which opens up the laser disc player. Phelps drops the mini-disc in the slot and a familiar voice is heard.

RECORDED VOICE: Welcome back, Jim, though I wish it weren't under these circumstances. This is the man we believe was responsible for the death of your friend, Tom Copperfield. . . .

As the message continues, still images appear on the LCD screen, thus eliminating the need for a separate package of photographs. At the end of the message Phelps is given the sobering reminder that if he or any of his IM force are caught or killed, the secretary will disavow any knowledge of their actions. And just like the old tapes, these discs also self-destruct in five seconds, with the same type of smoke that was previously seen engulfing the reel-to-reel tape recorder.

The credits begin to appear and the scene changes to Phelps' apartment. When he hits a button on a TV-type remote control, the coffee table opens up to reveal a built-in computer keyboard and video disc player.

PHELPS: Time does march on.

Other new technology includes a projection screen that unfolds from one of the room's support columns. Phelps punches one of the keyboard's function keys and an image appears on the screen as the same familiar voice introduces him to each of his new team members.

Jim Phelps is told that Nicholas Black is an expert in languages and disguises and teaches drama at an unnamed eastern university when not working for the IMF. Casey Randall is a top designer whose fiancé was killed in a tourist bombing in Rome. Ms. Randall aided the IMF in apprehending her fiance's killers and has presumably stayed within the employ of the IMF. Max Harte's background includes organizing his own mission to locate his brother, a Vietnam P.O.W.

The next team member evokes a bit of nostalgia for both Phelps and the audience.

RECORDED VOICE: Grant Collier. That's right, Jim, Barney Collier's son. (Image of Grant on the screen moves to the right as a still of Greg Morris as Barney pushes in from the left to form a split screen showing both father and son on the screen.) And where Barney left off, his son picked up. Grant graduated from MIT at sixteen where one of his professors called him one of the greatest inventive minds to come out of MIT in twenty years.

Each of these selections is made by depressing a two-key combination which displays the word ''ACCEPTED'' on the screen, which is a whole lot neater than throwing them into separate piles on the floor.

One more button is depressed on the keyboard and the photographs of all four operatives are displayed on the screen together. Superimposed across the center of the screen are the words ''MISSION TEAM.''

An hour later, with the murderer of Copperfield brought to justice, the entire team stops by the cemetery to pay its respects. Then Nicholas asks Phelps a question that will be the setup for the rest of the series.

NICHOLAS: What do you do now, Jim?

PHELPS: Well, I think I'll have to stay. It would be a shame to break up a nice team like this, wouldn't it? (Sneak in Lalo Schifrin theme and display credits.)

Tom Copperfield, however, was not the only member of the IMF team to be killed in the line of duty. The promotional ad in the February 18, 1989 issue of *TV Guide* said, ''In twenty years, we've never lost a member of our team. But we can't beat the odds forever. . . .''

The lost team member was Casey Randall (Terry Markwell), who got hers at the very beginning of ''The Fortune,'' the twelfth episode produced for the new series. She was replaced by Jane Badler as Shannon Reed.

The episode is set in the Florida Keys where Casey is seen trying to escape from the grounds of a deposed dictator, Luis Berezan (Michael Pate), and his wife Emelia (Barbara Luna), an Imelda Marcos-type character who has stolen millions from her country's national treasury, leaving her people in a state of virtual poverty. During the assignment briefing, Phelps explains that Shannon Reed, who has a degree in broadcast journalism and has been working for the Secret Service for the last five years, is being brought in to assist with this mission. He goes on to explain that the Secretary has sent Casey on a special assignment and that they are scheduled to rejoin her.

What Jim doesn't know is that in the teaser, Casey was caught by the Berezans' security force and given a lethal injection by Mrs. Berezan herself. While the team is busy making preparations for the upcoming mission, a story on a newscast catches Jim's attention.

NEWSCASTER: Turning now to the local news here in Florida. Fort Lauderdale police are seeking help in identifying the body of a young woman. A woman whose body was washed up on a Florida beach earlier today who carried no identification . . .

Phelps recognizes Casey from the picture shown on the screen, but does not share the shocking news with his team. It is only after he goes to the police and identifies the body that he informs Casey's co-workers, who are understandably upset by the news.

PHELPS: I know how you all feel. She was like a daughter to me. We *will* nail whoever did this. That's a promise.

At the end of the episode, all of the Berezans' stolen money is returned and in an uncharacteristic display of violent emotion, Jim Phelps grabs Mrs. Berezan and says, ''It's all over, Emelia. You're going to jail for the rest of your life . . . and that's too good for you.''

This episode also reveals to the viewer something that has often been talked about, but never shown—the disavowing of an IMF team member. We are shown a closeup of a computer screen with the names of the IMF team members. Casey Randall's name has been highlighted and her photograph shows up at the bottom right portion of the screen. Her file is c2386625. Her status was active. Her age, 28. Her profession was listed as ''Designer,'' and her fiancé (incorrectly referred to as her husband), J. Randall, is listed as deceased. The cursor highlights the ''Change Status'' selections and selects ''deceased.'' The other two choices are ''inactive'' and ''retired.'' Large type in a rectangular red band appears on the screen—''DISAVOWED.''

The scene fades to a still of the team (really the cast shot) which shows Casey with the other IMF team members. The credits come up cold, without the familiar Lalo Schifrin theme. All of which is an obvious attempt to evoke a tear or two from the viewer. It doesn't, the reason being that Casey was only on the IMF for a short time and there was never enough character development to make audiences love her or miss her.

The new female member of the cast, Jane Badler, who was famous for her role as Diana in the NBC science fiction, *V*, was given a starring credit at the beginning of this transition episode and the following week her name appeared as part of the regular opening credits, which showed scenes of her on the show.

Grant Collier, the electronics genius, was supposed to be Barney Collier's son and in fact he really was. He was played by Greg Morris's son, Phil Morris. Father and son were reunited in the fifth episode of the first season, ''The Condemned,'' in which ''Greg Morris reprises his original series role as Grant's father Barney, who's awaiting execution in a Turkish prison, framed for a murder involving a corrupt police official.''[32]

The senior Morris returned for the second season's two-part premiere, ''The Golden Serpent.'' In this two-parter, which aired on September 21 and 28, 1989, Barney works with the Impossible Missions Force to bust an international drug ring.

''MISSION may be the only non-anthology series in the history of television whose popularity was based not upon stars or characters, but upon story,'' says Patrick J. White. ''It lost its original leading man and the star duo of Landau and Bain, yet ultimately ran longer without them than with; actors like Lesley Ann Warren and Sam Elliott failed as regulars, while Lynda Day George and Peter Lupus succeeded. The true stars were the plots themselves, and as long as the scripts were clever and imaginative, the show was a success, regardless of who was written into or out of *Mission: Impossible*.''[33]

ABC disavowed all knowledge of the new *Mission: Impossible* as a first-run series after the thirty-fifth episode.

MR. ED

October 1, 1961–September 8, 1965.   CBS

Character:	Kay Addison
Played by:	Edna Skinner
Date(s):	October 1, 1961–1963

Replaced by:	Winnie Kirkwood
Played by:	Florence MacMichael
Date(s):	December 1963–1965

Character:	Roger Addison
Played by:	Larry Keating
Date(s):	October 1, 1961–1963

Replaced by:	Paul Fenton
Played by:	Jack Albertson
Date(s):	1963

Replaced by:	Gordon Kirkwood
Played by:	Leon Ames
Date(s):	1963–1965

It is possible that the reason *Mr. Ed* doesn't get the same bad rap from television critics as *My Mother the Car*, a sitcom about a 1928 Porter that talks, is because there were never any motion pictures about a talking car. *Mr. Ed*, on the other hand, stands firmly in the hoof prints left by Donald O'Connor's joking jackass. And perhaps having a motion picture relative somehow legitimized Wilbur Post's pontificating palomino.

Mr. Ed is a horse, of course, of course. And as everyone knows, ''no one can talk to a horse, of course. That is, of course, unless the horse is the famous Mr. Ed''—who, incidentally, will never speak unless he has something to say.

The jackass was Francis the talking mule, the star of six films co-starring Donald O'Connor and one co-starring Mickey Rooney. The first film in the series, FRANCIS, was released in 1949; the last, FRANCIS IN THE HAUNTED HOUSE, in 1956. The six Donald O'Connor films were directed by Arthur Lubin and featured Chill Wills as the voice of Francis. The Mickey Rooney picture tapped the voice talent of Paul Frees, who among other things was the voice of Rocky and Bullwinkle's nemesis, Boris Badenov.

All of the FRANCIS films were based on a novel by David Stern. Silly as they may sound, the FRANCIS pictures earned Universal a good deal more money than expected and made FRANCIS a valuable commodity. Director Arthur Lubin thought so as well, and tried to buy the rights from the studio; they wouldn't sell even though they were no longer producing films in the FRANCIS series.

In retrospect this was a poor decision on Universal's part, because they haven't done anything with the FRANCIS character since 1956; all Arthur Lubin had to do was locate another source, which he did when he found a series of stories about a talking horse in *Liberty* magazine.

Lubin's concept was to have an average young couple, an architect and his wife, Wilbur and Carol Post, purchase a new home at 17230 Valley Spring Road in Southern California that came complete with a horse, as Roger Addison (Larry Keating), the house's owner and the Posts' neighbor, explained to Wilbur in the first episode of the series.

ROGER: You see, the people who rented this house before you bought it owned this horse. Well,

---

32. *TV Guide*. Vol. 36, No. 47, November 19, 1988, Issue #1860, p. A-67.
33. White, Patrick, J., from a letter to the author dated May 21, 1992.

Mister Ed horsing around with next-door neighbor Kay Addison (Edna Skinner) in this CBS publicity photo.

they had to leave in a hurry and said you can keep 'im, you can sell 'im—do anything you want with him.

WILBUR: We'll keep him!

Naturally, Carol had a different opinion. She wanted to sell him, but Wilbur managed to get his way.

Later in the episode, while brushing the horse down, Wilbur learns that he can speak.

WILBUR: I never thought owning a horse could mean so much to me. I guess that's because when I was a little boy, I wanted a pony. Of course, it's been a long time since I was a little boy.

MR. ED: It's been a long time since I was a pony.

Arthur Lubin, who had been trying to bring the talking animal show to television since 1954, had also been dead set on hiring Alan Young to play the horse's owner, Wilbur Post. But at the time, Alan Young, who wanted no part of the silly series, had left for England after CBS suspended him for his insistence that they film his live series, *The Alan Young Show*. Three years later a disappointed, but not defeated Lubin cast Scott McKay and Sandra White as Wilbur and Carlotta Pope in the pilot for the series, which was to be called *The Wonderful World of Wilbur Pope*. In that pilot, Ray Walker and Peggy Coverse played the Post's next-door neighbors, John and Florence Reese. The role of Mr. Ed went—literally—to a dark horse candidate. Still, even with the financial support of both the star and producer of *The Burns and Allen Show,* George Burns and Al Simon, the networks weren't interested in the program.

In 1960 Arthur Lubin's luck changed. He was still betting on his horse to win a series commitment, but he somehow knew all along that the missing ingredient was Alan Young. Young, who hadn't worked in the United States for several years, had lost his clout as a top commodity and reluctantly agreed to do Lubin's horse opera. But even with Young in the saddle, the networks still weren't willing to add *Mr. Ed* to their programming stable.

Fortunately, before *Mr. Ed* was put to sleep, the automobile manufacturer Studebaker-Lark had the horse-sense to sponsor the series in syndication. Thirty-nine weeks later, after seeing a favorable audience reaction to the series, CBS made the riskless decision to fill the open Sunday 6:30 p.m. slot with *Mr. Ed.* Any trepidations they might have had about airing the series were quickly allayed when *Mr. Ed* finished with a Nielsen rating of 20.

The main cast, as in so many television sitcoms of the day, was a foursome: Wilbur and Carol Post (Alan Young and Connie Hines) and their next-door neighbors, Roger and Kay Addison (Larry Keating and Edna Skinner).

The choice of character names is very interesting. Two of them were used in Arthur Lubin's FRANCIS films. In FRANCIS, Mickey McCardle played Captain "Addison" and

in FRANCIS GOES TO WEST POINT (1952), William Reynolds played a character named Wilbur.

The actor cast as Roger, who was most often referred to by his last name, had already worked with Lubin in FRANCIS GOES TO THE RACES. In this third talking mule entry released in 1951, Larry Keating was cast as the head steward. He had also worked for George Burns and Al Simon as the fourth actor to play Harry Morton on *The George Burns and Gracie Allen Show* (See Entry).

Actress Edna Skinner, who in 1954 replaced Kathleen Freeman on *Topper* (See Entry), explained how she was lassoed into playing Mrs. Addison and then fired after four years. "A very close friend of mine, Constance Moore, was going to play Kay Addison. But when they put Connie together with Connie [Hines] they looked like the Bobbsey Twins, so they quickly had to do something to get somebody else.

"I had just come out of retirement to fill in for a friend of mine who was doing a production of *Dinner at Eight* in La Jolla. My agent heard they were looking for the fourth character in *Mr. Ed* and they had to film the second pilot right away. Arthur Lubin was in Europe directing THE THIEF OF BAGHDAD with Steve Reeves, so I went down to the Filmways studio and was directed in my screen test by George Burns, who did everything for me on the set. Larry [Keating] played the test with me and said, 'That's my Kay—no question about it. She'll be just fine.' The ironic thing that happened was that Connie [Moore]'s sister wound up being my stand-in,"[34] said Ms. Skinner.

But working on *Mr. Ed* wasn't as easy as pitching horseshoes, as Edna Skinner related.

"Everybody had to fight for every line. And I was told by Larry, 'Don't read your lines well in the read-throughs,' because while I'd be giving my all Larry would say to me, 'If you do that Edna, we're not going to have a scene here,' because if we did too good a job, Alan [Young] would have the scene cut! It was Larry who taught me to read 'dead' and he and Connie and I all fought very hard to make it a foursome, because working with Alan was one of the most difficult things I did in my life. Nobody was to be anybody with Alan. But thanks to the technical staff and to the marvelous direction and the marvelous writing, the show was a smash—but at no time was it an easy show to do because Alan had his nose in the air with it. That is nothing against Alan as a person. I had nothing against Alan as a person. We were never friends, none of us ever were. It was purely a professional thing.

"Ed and I got along just beautifully and as a matter of fact I had to be told to keep away from the horse, because Kay wasn't supposed to know anything about Mr. Ed's gift of gab.

"Everybody in the world talks to their pets, but they don't want anybody to really know that, so *Mr. Ed* helped everyone feel better knowing that they weren't insane talking to their animals," she said.

Then, on August 26, 1963 the unexpected happened—Larry Keating, who had long suffered with leukemia, died.

"There has always been a show business superstition sur-

---

34. This and subsequent quotations from Edna Skinner in this *Mr. Ed* entry are from an exclusive telephone interview with Ms. Skinner on September 17, 1989.

rounding the death of someone while working on a series. That's why they didn't sign someone else to play Roger. They had marvelous chances to sign Jerome Courtland, or Sebastian Cabot, but at that time Alan wanted more and more scenes with the horse.

"It was one of the most horrible, horrible things that could happen to somebody, because I was six months away from my twentieth year in films. The Screen Actors Guild came in because they had to pay me off and I said, 'I don't want to be paid for what I'm not going to do.' So they used me in seven shows with Jack Albertson as my brother, Paul Fenton," said Ms. Skinner.

In a somewhat contrived scene from the introductory episode with Jack Albertson, Kay has just given Wilbur a new set of golf clubs for his birthday.

KAY:	Happy birthday, neighbor.
WILBUR:	Oh, Kay, for me? You shouldn't have. I mean they're so expensive.
PAUL:	Yeah, a hundred seventy-four dollars and . . .
KAY:	Brother dear. Why don't you go back in the house and play with your blocks.

"Then that weekend they had my agent and me up to the Nasser brothers'[35] private estate in the redwood forest. Being a lover of nature, I went for a ride among the redwoods with Ira Stewart, Arthur's assistant director. And during that ride Ira said, 'Edna, you know there's no sense of just pulling wings off flies—you're out!' I had no inkling whatsoever! Then he said, 'I don't want you to meet with the *San Francisco Chronicle* until nine o'clock in the morning, and Edna, handle it with dignity.'

"I told Arthur [Lubin] that we will always remain friends, but the truth of the matter is that I was, for the first time, dumped as a successful actress.

"They had this successful foursome—the two sophisticates, Larry and me, playing against Connie and Alan. But instead of having Kay remarry, they got Florence MacMichael and Leon Ames as the new neighbors. They could pay two people less than what they were paying me because I had been working on the series for four years," said Ms. Skinner.

In the all-important episode that introduces the Posts' new neighbors, the names of the old neighbors, the Posts' best friends, are never mentioned. No explanation is given as to where the Addisons went, or that they were the ones who sold the Posts their home. It is also conceivable, but not likely in '60s sitcomdom, that the Addisons didn't actually move away, but just had a major falling out with the Posts and just stopped speaking to them.

The new characters, Colonel Gordon Kirkwood (Leon Ames) and his wife, Winnie (Florence MacMichael), are intro-duced in a scene that has Colonel Kirkwood phoning Wilbur Post from a phone booth.

WILBUR:	(Answering the phone) Hello.
COLONEL:	Wilbur Post?
WILBUR:	Yes.
COLONEL:	Gordon Kirkwood here.
WILBUR:	Kirkwood?
COLONEL:	Your C.O., 361st Airborne, remember?
WILBUR:	Yes! Colonel Kirkwood, sir, how are you?
COLONEL:	Mrs. Kirkwood and I just arrived in town and I thought I'd give you a ring.
WILBUR:	I'm very glad you did, sir.

During the phone conversation, Wilbur invites the Kirk-woods to dinner. The Colonel accepts the invitation and practically forces them to move in to the Addisons' old place.

WILBUR:	You and Mrs. Kirkwood plan to stay in town long, Colonel?
COLONEL:	Well, in fact, we've decided to settle down here in Southern California.
CAROL:	Oh wonderful. Oh Wilbur, you know there's a house right on our block that's just been put up for sale. Maybe you'd like to take a look at it.
WILBUR:	That's a beautiful place and the price is right. And what's more, you'll be our neighbors.

"One of the men working on the series—I will not mention a name—said, 'You're just a piece of meat, you might as well be just as dead as Larry,' which was a wonderful way to say good-bye. So for me, the last memories of *Ed* are very unhappy. The truth of the matter is that Alan Young could have backed the staying of anyone in the cast because he and Mr. Lubin and Mr. Simon all had a piece of the show. Mr. Alan Young is a very self-centered man—has been for a long, long time and has done that with many, many performers that he has worked with.

---

35. James and Edward Nasser, or Nassour, were at the time the owners of Filmways Studios.

That's just a part of him. There's no hatred anywhere here, but it damn near killed me!'', Ms. Skinner confessed.

"The last night I left *Mr. Ed* I remember putting things in bags. I remember packing my dressing room. I remember saying good-bye to my crew, who gave me a lovely farewell, and I remember going backstage and kissing the horse good-bye.

"Nobody else was around. No executives. No leading man, no leading woman—nobody. I think that has to be one of the heartbreaks of my life. And Alan has never, to this day, said, 'Hello, how are you?' or whatever. And when they did that I remembered what that gentleman over at Filmways said: 'You're just a piece of meat, you might as well be just as dead as Larry.' Then I suddenly realized that it was true about the entertainment business. And after you've done everything, and given everything—including being part of a legend—then that's why I got out of it and went into another career,'' she said.

The other career Edna Skinner went into was writing about game fishing. She turned out nearly 500 feature magazine articles and a book, *The Hotspots*. Her sister, Ann, did the photography and Ms. Skinner, a champion fisherman, did the writing.

Today Ms. Skinner's love of nature and dedication to preserving the environment is evident in her expenditure of time and money on the Dolphin Research Center located in the Florida Keys.

"After Larry passed on and the cast changed, the scenes with Ed and Alan go on forever. I mean forever! So it has nothing to do with Edna Skinner being out of the show. As long as Larry Keating was alive, then he had scenes with Alan, and then Connie and I had scenes, and then Larry and I had scenes, and Alan and Connie had scenes, but the horse was the star! And anybody who said that the horse wasn't the star was a dirty liar. And anybody who resented that was an ass! Alan Young, to his dying day, will never have a part like that again. The horse made Alan a star and he could never accept that,'' said Ms. Skinner.

She also spoke about plans for a MR. ED feature that was written and scheduled to be shot in Japan, but, as she recalled, the deal fell through because the producers had not purchased the movie rights from the widow of the author who wrote "The Talking Horse" stories for *Liberty* magazine.

"Arthur has since sold his rights to *Mr. Ed* to CBS and for a long time CBS had planned on doing an updated *Mr. Ed* like the new *Leave It to Beaver*. They were going to revamp the whole show and make *Mr. Ed* something awful. To tell you God's truth, I'm glad it didn't come out. I hope it stays gone because the original is such a legend. I hope that it doesn't sound like sour grapes, but my feeling is that I hope the legend stays as it was because I don't want to see it maligned. I just don't want to see something that beautiful go down the bloody tubes because of some modern moron's idea of what *Mr. Ed* should be during the 1990s,'' concluded Ms. Skinner.

Mr. Ed was, for the entire series, played by the equine thespian, Bamboo Harvester, although another horse was used in the pilot.

Saturday Night Live alumnus Eddie Murphy returned to television, after a triumphant foray into the movies, with a clever and innovative pilot for CBS that never made it to series status. In that pilot, *What's Alan Watching?*, which aired on February 27, 1989, Shelley Berman appears in a satirical documentary about *Mr. Ed*. Since Bamboo Harvester had died at the age of 33 on February 28, 1979, the role of Ed was played by an up-and-coming horse named Tizz. The actor who provided the voice was uncredited.

The Gary Shandling Show: 25th Anniversary Special was a mock anniversary show à la Johnny Carson that featured old clips (shot in black and white specifically for this one-time special). The first clip, supposedly from 1960, was an interview with Mr. Ed which was full of "bleeps" because of foul language used by Ed.

GARY: How does a horse like yourself get interested in acting?

ED: When I was growing up, I went to the movies and I saw Francis the Talking Mule. And something just clicked. I figured if that a . . . "BLEEP" could do it. . . .

This clever tribute was only flawed by the fact that the date 1960 was superimposed at the start of the clip. *Mr. Ed* didn't air until October of the following year. Still, it was nice to see that America still has a soft spot for one of the most popular hoofers in show business.

MR. PEEPERS

July 3, 1952–June 12, 1955.   NBC

Character:	Royala Dean
Played by:	Norma Crane
Date(s):	1952

Replaced by:	Nancy Remington
Played by:	Patricia Benoit
Date(s):	1952–June 12, 1955

By day, Robinson J. Peepers was a timid, soft-spoken and mild-mannered biology instructor at Jefferson Junior High School in Jefferson City. But by night, Robinson J. Peepers became . . . a timid, soft spoken and mild-mannered biology instructor at Jefferson Junior High School in Jefferson City. And that was the whole point of this situation comedy that didn't have to yell at its audience to get laughs.

And please, by no means should Mr. Peepers be confused with Philip Boynton, the shy biology teacher who taught at Madison High on *Our Miss Brooks* (See Entry). They were nothing alike.

The star of the series was a young comedian named Wally Cox, who wasn't so much playing a character as he was playing himself. He continued to play that character for the rest of his acting career.

Mr. Peepers was originally produced as a summer replacement series and was only scheduled for an eight-week run. During that time the principal of Jefferson High was played by Joseph Foley, who had played the second Mr. Bradley on *The Aldrich Family* (See Entry).

Surprisingly, Robinson Peepers did have a girlfriend and during the initial eight-week run she was played by Norma Crane.

As scheduled, *Mr. Peepers* was dismissed from the air to make way for NBC's new fall schedule, which put *Doc Corkle* in their time slot. Much to the network's chagrin, *Doc Corkle* was immediately diagnosed as a terminal case by both the television critics and the viewing public. In response, NBC quickly buried the good doctor and brought Mr. Peepers back to teach biology.

It was from this point on that Jefferson High did without a visible principal. Superintendent Bascomb (Gage Clark), however, was highly visible. Gage Clark was later visible as Dr. Gordon on the Betty White sitcom, *Date with the Angels,* which aired on ABC from May 10, 1957 to January 29, 1958.

Wally Cox, by the way, did eventually get to play a superhero, of sorts. From October 3, 1964 to September 1, 1973 meek little Wally Cox lent his voice to Shoeshine Boy, who was that champion of the oppressed, lifting the spirits of those in trouble when they heard him cry out that awe-inspiring rhyme as he flew to their rescue: "Plane nor jet, nor even frog . . . it's just little old me, Underdog."

THE MONKEES

September 12, 1966–August 19, 1968.   ABC-Syndicated
September 1987–1987

Character: Davy
Played by: David Jones
Date(s):   September 12, 1966–August 19, 1968

Replaced by: Larry
Played by: Larry Saltis
Date(s):   September 1987–1987

Character: Peter
Played by: Peter Tork
Date(s):   September 1987–1987

Replaced by: Dino
Played by: Dino Kovas
Dates: September 1987–1987

Character: Micky
Played by: Micky Dolenz
Date(s):   September 12, 1966–August 19, 1968

Replaced by: Jared
Played by: Jared Chandler
Date(s):   September 1987–1987

Character: Mike
Played by: Mike Nesmith
Date(s):   September 12, 1966–August 19, 1968

Replaced by: Marty
Played by: Marty Ross
Date(s):   September 1987–1987

Television managed to tap into the enormous success of The Beatles, their 1964 A HARD DAY'S NIGHT feature film in particular, by creating their own fab four, which was named after a popular mammal instead of an insect. Both spellings were, of course, altered to avoid confusion.

The studio did not find a struggling garage band to catapult to stardom, but chose to start from scratch and wound up auditioning 437 hopeful actors and musicians before making their final decisions. What they decided upon was a mix of two actors and two musicians. Peter Tork and Mike Nesmith both played the guitar. Micky Dolenz and David Jones were the actors. Jones brought with him three years of experience on the BBC. He had a successful run on Broadway as the Artful Dodger in *Oliver,* a role that won him a Tony award nomination. He had also made some appearances on episodic television in the United States.

The most familiar face in the group is Micky Dolenz. Perhaps not immediately recognizable, but if you know that he starred as Corky, the homeless orphan in *Circus Boy,* his childhood features begin to come into focus. His name, however, may not be remembered, because when he took the acting job in 1956, he also took a stage name, Braddock, and used the more traditional spelling of Mickey for his first name. *Circus Boy* aired on NBC from September 23, 1956 to September 8, 1957, and on ABC from September 19, 1957 to September 11, 1958.

Together this talented foursome became The Monkees, and their songs, which included *Last Train to Clarksville* and *I'm a Believer,* sold more than eight million albums. When the series left the air, the group disbanded, although the two actors, Dolenz and Jones, did get together for several reunion concerts.

A 3/4 *Monkees* reunion was launched in 1985. The MTV cable network aired a *Monkees* marathon of their original series during the summer of 1986. Missing was Mike Nesmith, who had become a very successful music video producer and could not fit the concert tour into his full schedule. It is also clear that money was not a problem for Nesmith, who inherited quite a large sum of the green stuff from his mother, who was the inventor of some white stuff—Liquid Paper Correction Fluid— which is now manufactured by the Gillette Company.

With the original Monkees on tour, Columbia Pictures smelled revival, but instead of asking Davy, Peter, Micky and Mike to reprise their roles in a reunion movie or series, they opted to find four new Monkees.

While three of our Monkees were on tour in England, Columbia Pictures instituted a lawsuit that "requests that a British court in the Chancery Division grant an injunction that restrains Jones, Dolenz and Tork from making concert or personal appearances using the name [*Monkees*], advertising or promoting the name or printing or selling merchandise using the name."[36]

Meanwhile, back in the States, a nationwide talent hunt was mounted to locate the four actor/musicians who were to become *The New Monkees.* The media hype connected with the search helped keep the project in the news.

---

36. *The Hollywood Reporter.* Hollywood, California. Thursday, May 4, 1989, p. 34.

Only *The Monkees* could be happy about being stuck in cement in this scene from the ''Your Friendly Neighborhood Kidnappers'' episode. Kneeling (left to right) are: Mike (Mike Nesmith), Davy (David ''Davy'' Jones), Micky (Micky Dolenz) and Peter (Peter Tork).

Once assembled, *The New Monkees* went into production. The show was set in a huge gothic mansion which came complete with a butler, Manfred, played by Gordon Oad-Heim. In addition to the usual *Monkees* antics, in each episode there were two very elaborately-produced music videos to help promote their new albums. But the entire misguided project ended after the first season. America already had The Monkees and as for these new guys, ''Hey, Hey, they weren't the Monkees.''

THE MOTHERS-IN-LAW

September 10, 1967–September 7, 1969.   NBC

Character: Roger Buell
Played by: Roger C. Carmel
Date(s):   September 10, 1967–1968

Replaced: Roger Buell
Played by: Richard Deacon
Date(s):   September 15, 1968–September 7, 1969

If you liked *The Mothers-in-Law* it may have something to do with the fact that you loved Lucy, as this late 1960s sitcom had the same executive producer as *I Love Lucy*—Desi Arnaz. He even went so far as to appear on the series as Raphael del Gado, a Mexican bullfighter who was a friend of the mothers-in-law, Eve Hubbard (Eve Arden) and Kaye Buell (Kay Ballard).

The Hubbards and the Buells took friendship to the extreme in this very entertaining situation comedy. They were next-door neighbors for fifteen years and when their kids (Jerry Buell and Susie Hubbard), played by Jerry Fogel and Deborah Walley, graduated from high school, they married and set up residence in the Hubbards' garage, which they converted into an apartment. But even with all this love there was a fair amount of bickering between the two families. Worse yet was the bickering between Kaye's husband Roger and the producers. Roger was played by Roger C. Carmel during the first season only; he left in a contract dispute.

A wonderfully funny character actor, Roger C. Carmel was known for his wildly broad characterizations such as Andreyev in the 1966 Dean Martin comedy, THE SILENCERS, Batvillain Colonel Gumm on *Batman,* and the inimitable Harry Mudd in two of the lighter episodes of *Star Trek.* The Batman episodes, ''A Piece of the Action'' and ''Batman's Satisfaction,'' aired on March 1 and March 2, 1967. Carmel's appearances on *Star Trek* were in the October 13, 1966 episode, ''Mudd's Women'' and ''I, Mudd,'' which aired on November 3, 1967.

Since Jerry looked more like his mother, it didn't matter that Carmel was replaced by Richard Deacon, who had played producer Mel Cooley on the *Dick Van Dyke Show.* This was an interesting choice since Roger Buell was supposed to be a television writer on this series.

Deacon joined the cast of *The Mothers-in-Law* in the second-season opener, which deals with parental plans to hold a formal wedding for their children, who were actually married the previous year. Jeanette Nolan played Kay's grandmother, who has traveled all the way from Italy to attend the ceremony.

Richard Deacon's long list of credits include Lumpy's dad, Fred Rutherford, on *Leave It to Beaver,* which aired from October 4, 1957 to September 12, 1963. He played several roles on *Mr. Ed* including the voice of ''Moko the Mischievous Martian.'' And speaking of aliens, Deacon played the skeptical Dr. Harvey Bassett in the classic 1956 fiction film, INVASION OF THE BODY SNATCHERS.

THE MUNSTERS

September 24, 1964–September 1, 1966.   CBS-NBC-Syndicated

Character:	Herman Munster
Played by:	Fred Gwynne
Date(s):	September 24, 1964–September 1, 1966
	February 27, 1981 (*The Munsters' Revenge*)

Replaced by:	Herman Munster
Played by:	John Schuck
Date(s):	October 8, 1988–September 1991

Character:	Count Dracula ''Grandpa''
Played by:	Al Lewis
Date(s):	September 24, 1964–September 1, 1966
	February 27, 1981 (*The Munsters' Revenge*)
	September 4, 1988 (*Best of The Munsters.* TBS)

Replaced by:	Count Dracula ''Grandpa''
Played by:	Howard Morton
Date(s):	October 8, 1988–September 1991

Character:	Lily Munster
Played by:	Yvonne DeCarlo
Date(s):	September 24, 1964–September 1, 1966
	February 27, 1981 (*The Munsters' Revenge*)

Replaced by:	Lily Munster
Played by:	Lee Meriwether
Date(s):	October 8, 1988–September 1991

Character:	Marilyn Munster
Played by:	Beverley Owen
Date(s):	September 27, 1964–December 17, 1964

Replaced by:	Marilyn Munster
Played by:	Pat Priest
Date(s):	December 24, 1964–September 1, 1966
	September 4, 1988 (*Best of The Munsters.* TBS)

Replaced by:	Marilyn Munster
Played by:	Jo McDonnell
Date(s):	February 27, 1981 (*The Munsters' Revenge*)

Replaced by:	Marilyn Munster
Played by:	Hilary Van Dyke
Date(s):	October 8, 1988–September 1991

Character:	Edward ''Eddie'' Wolfgang Munster
Played by:	Butch Patrick
Date(s):	September 24, 1964–September 1, 1966
	September 4, 1988 (*Best of The Munsters.* TBS)

Replaced by:	Edward ''Eddie'' Wolfgang Munster
Played by:	K.C. Martel
Date(s):	February 27, 1981 (*The Munsters' Revenge*)

Replaced by:	Edward ''Eddie'' Wolfgang Munster
Played by:	Jason Marsdan
Date(s):	October 8, 1988–September 1991

Character:	Doctor Edward Dudley
Played by:	Paul Lynde
Date(s):	October 29, 1964
	November 1964
	January 28, 1965

Replaced by:	Doctor Edward Dudley
Played by:	Dom DeLuise
Date(s):	January 13, 1966

The typical American Family (at least that's how *The Munsters* saw themselves) are (clockwise, from top left): Herman Munster (Fred Gwynne), Count "Grandpa" Dracula (Al Lewis), Marilyn Munster (Pat Priest), Eddie Munster (Butch Patrick), and Lily Munster (Yvonne DeCarlo).

"When you are walking the street at night and behind you there's no one in view, but you hear mysterious feet at night, then the Munsters are following you." These words are hardly as memorable as "They're creepy and they're kooky. Mysterious and spooky. They're altogether ooky. The Addams Family." Nonetheless they are the words to the theme song from television's first family of fright—actually the second—*The Munsters.*

The first horror family of television was *The Addams Family* (See Entry) who made their ABC network debut at 8:30 p.m. on Friday, September 18, 1964. Just six days later, and an hour earlier, *The Munsters* burst onto CBS's Thursday night schedule.

The reason the words to *The Munsters'* theme song may not sound familiar is that on the series the theme song was only an instrumental. The lyrics, written by Bob Mosher, the coproducer of the series, were only sung on a children's record, *At the Munsters;* they were never used for the TV series.

Although it may be tempting, or even fun, to compare the two programs, it is really not fair, since they are two very separate and unique entities, each with its own humble beginnings.

The Addams Family is based on the series of ghoulish cartoons by Charles Addams that appeared in *The New Yorker,* while *The Munsters* have their roots planted in the classic Universal horror films from the 1930s and 1940s.

What is so much fun about *The Munsters* is that even though their outward appearance is that of Universal's monsters, they see themselves as, and act like, the typical American family. In fact, in the December 17, 1964 episode, "Family Portrait," *Event* magazine's computer randomly selects the Munsters as just that.

Herman Munster is the dad. He stands seven-feet three-inches tall and is a direct knock-off of Karloff's Frankenstein monster. His wife, Lily, is a more motherly version of Vampira. Their son, Eddie, is a werewolf, and Herman's father, whom everyone in the household refers to as "Grandpa," is supposed to be Count Dracula.

We know he's the Prince of Darkness because that is how he is addressed by Herman's boss, Mr. Gateman (John Carradine), in this scene set around the dinner table in "The Musician," which aired on March 3, 1966.

GATEMAN: Count Dracula. . . .

GRANDPA: (Preoccupied and to himself) There was something from some garden chicken soup from Liberace. . . ..

LILY: Grandpa, our guest is speaking to you.

GRANDPA: Eh, yes, young man.

GATEMAN: (Taken back at being called a young man) You've been quiet as a customer all evening.

GRANDPA: I'm basically shy.

Living with the Munsters is their blonde niece, Marilyn. She's beautiful to us, but to them, she looks abnormal and is referred to as "the black sheep of the family."

The Munsters first appeared on film in four separate pilots. Two fifteen-minute pilots (one color, one black and white) with Joan Marshall as Lily; one, a fifteen-minute pilot with Yvonne DeCarlo as Lily; and the other, a thirty-minute pilot with Yvonne DeCarlo as Lily (both in black and white).

The differences among these pilots seem to be the makeup on the characters. The pilots show hideous creations. They were greatly humanized for the series. These were all but unseen as CBS used clips of the Joan Marshall pilot for their 1964 Fall Preview show.

Ex-cops Muldoon and Schnauser (Fred Gwynne and Al Lewis) from *Car 54, Where Are You?*'s 53rd precinct, were signed as Herman and Grandpa. Al Lewis recreated the phone call that got him the role on *The Munsters:* " 'Hi, this is Jerry Henshaw here at the new creative department at Universal Studios and we're interested in you. We're doing a new series and we'd love to have you for the pilot.' I asked them to send me a couple of scripts, which they did. A few days later, Sunday, Jerry phoned to make the arrangements for me to fly out [from New York to California] and said, 'Oh, and by the way, you're flying out with Fred Gwynne.' I said, 'Oh that's nice.' And that's it," said Lewis.

Al Lewis went on to explain that he had never had any discussions with Gwynne about the possibility of their working together on a new series. It seems likely that Universal liked the way Lewis and Gwynne worked together on *Car 54, Where Are You?* but Lewis said that was never discussed with him.

In *The Munsters,* author Stephen Cox wrote that the role of Grandpa Munster was offered to Bert Lahr, who was at that time already in his late sixties. Lahr, of course, is best remembered for his role as the timid king of the forest in the 1939 MGM classic, THE WIZARD OF OZ.

"I didn't know that they had considered Bert for the role of Grandpa, but he would have been very funny. I do know that after about four or five episodes we took a hiatus and they screen-tested a number of people to replace me because Hunt Stromberg, Jr., the head of CBS television in California, did not like me. He didn't know me personally, but he didn't like the way I was doing the role and gave instructions to test other actors, so I do know that they screen-tested four, five or six other people during that hiatus period. That I do know because it was told to me by my dear friend Perc Westmore, who made me up and in turn had to make up those others for their screen tests,"[37] said Al Lewis.

Mrs. Munster, who in the first two presentation films was named Phoebe, was played by Joan Marshall, who did a lot of television work during the 1950s. Her most famous television character prior to this role was Sailor Duval in the 1959 syndicated series, *Bold Venture.* This was a particularly difficult role to step into because it had already been done on radio by Lauren Bacall who played opposite her husband, Humphrey

---

37. From an exclusive telephone interview with Al Lewis on October 19, 1990.

Bogart, as Slate Shannon. In the TV series Sailor Duval and Slate Shannon were played by Joan Marshall and Dane Clark.

Little Eddie Munster was played by Happy Derman, and Marilyn by Beverley Owen, who went on to work in the series. Her earlier work was on two of the most popular daytime soap operas. On *All My Children* she was the second of three actresses to play Ann Tyler Martin, and on *Another World* Ms. Owen played Dr. Paula McCrea.

The Munsters project interested the network, and another test in black and white was ordered with two changes in cast. Mrs. Munster, renamed Lily, was played by Yvonne DeCarlo and Eddie by Butch Patrick.

Yvonne DeCarlo was a well-known leading lady of the 1940s. Her first starring role was as the Viennese dancer, Salome, in the 1945 drama, SALOME, WHERE SHE DANCED. In 1949 Yvonne DeCarlo played Anna opposite Burt Lancaster's Steve Thompson in the 1949 crime film, CRISS CROSS. Seven years later she co-starred as Sephora in Cecil B. DeMille's 1956 epic, THE TEN COMMANDMENTS.

Interestingly enough, the series' stars, Fred Gwynne and Al Lewis were opposed to the casting of Yvonne DeCarlo because they thought she was wrong for the role. But she quickly proved them wrong. The young man hired to play Eddie Munster was Butch Patrick, a juvenile actor who had already starred as Billy Davis in the delightful 1961 fantasy, THE TWO LITTLE BEARS. The following year he appeared in flashback sequences of PRESSURE POINT. In the film, Barry Gordon played Bobby Darin as a boy and Butch Patrick was his playmate.

Patrick's television appearances include a CLIO-winning commercial for Kellogg's Corn Flakes and a six-month stint as Johnny on the ABC daytime soap opera, *General Hospital*. He later had a recurring role as Greg Howard during the 1963 season of *The Real McCoys*. He also did a number of guest shots as Ernie Douglas's friend, Gordon, during the 1968/1969 season of *My Three Sons*. The following season, Butch Patrick returned to *My Three Sons* and although he looked the same, his name had been changed to "Yo Ho."

For a time Butch Patrick's stand-in was Felix Silla, the midget actor who played Cousin Itt on the competing series, *The Addams Family.*

Landing the role of Eddie Munster was not so much luck as it was all in a day's work, as Butch Patrick explained: "I was flown out from Illinois, where I was vacationing with my grandmother, and taken to the studio for a one-shot interview with two other children, who were apparently the best of the 500 or so kids they had interviewed. I auditioned with Joan Marshall, who played Lily before Yvonne DeCarlo. Although Billy Mumy wasn't there, I think he had been offered the part, but I had heard rumors that his mom turned it down because she didn't want him hidden under all that makeup."[38]

It is fairly obvious that none of the members of *The*

Munsters's cast or crew suffered from triskaidekaphobia (the fear of the number thirteen) because the number always played in their favor. The Munsters lived at 1313 Mockingbird Lane and Butch Patrick was thirteen years old when he worked on the feature film, MUNSTER, GO HOME! Stephen Cox wrote (on page 13 of his book *The Munsters*), "The first Munster episode reportedly received a rating of 13, which, ironically, the cast felt was their lucky number."[39]

Depending on one's perspective, the number thirteen was simultaneously lucky and unlucky when the series completed its thirteenth episode, "Family Portrait." This is because the thirteenth episode was the last appearance of Beverley Owen as Marilyn Munster.

Ms. Owen, a Universal contract player, was unhappy during the entire first season of production. "She cried on the set every day because she wanted to leave the show and they wouldn't let her. Eventually we just screamed bloody murder, Fred [Gwynne] and I, because it was terrible for the show, so they replaced her,"[40] recalled Al Lewis.

It is never easy when a member of an established ensemble cast leaves a series, and in some instances it can be quite traumatic. Beverley Owen's departure from *The Munsters* was especially difficult for the youngest member of the cast. "I had a crush on Beverley—a kid's crush, like you might have on a school teacher. Beverley was my first date. When MARY POPPINS was released, Beverley drove all the way down to our house, picked me up and took me out to Grauman's Chinese Theatre to see the film,"[41] recalled Patrick fondly.

After she was released from her seven-year contract, Beverley Owen returned to her home in New York and got married, which earned her the coveted role of Mrs. Jon Stone. Stone, incidentally, was the original co-executive producer of *Sesame Street.*

Beverley Owen was no stranger to the phenomenon of being written out, as she came to *The Munsters* after replacing Diana De Vegh as Ann Tyler Martin in the ABC daytime soap opera, *All My Children.* She was then replaced by Judith Barcroft. On another network, NBC, and another soap, *Another World,* she played Doctor Paula McCrea. There were also guest appearances on network Westerns such as "The Invaders," the January 1, 1964 episode of *The Virginian.*

The second actress to play Marilyn Munster was Pat Priest. She explained how the casting search led the producers to select her as The Munsters' "unfortunate" niece: "I hadn't seen the show and had no idea what it was like. I'd never seen the girl I was replacing. I didn't know what she looked like at all.

"The day I tested, there were four other girls, Linda Foster[42] being one of them. We went to Universal for the test and they put us in one of Marilyn's dresses. The makeup man did the makeup and hair and, as I recall, the test, which was just a monologue, was done on the set of *The Munsters.*

"This was on a Monday that I tested, and they notified me on

---

38. From an exclusive telephone interview with Butch Patrick on November 15, 1991.
39. Cox, Stephen. *The Munsters.* Contemporary Books, 1989, p. 13.
40. From an exclusive telephone interview with Al Lewis on October 19, 1990.
41. From an exclusive telephone interview with Butch Patrick on November 15, 1991.
42. Linda Foster starred as Doris Royal on *Hank,* an NBC situation comedy that aired from October 17, 1965 to September 2, 1966.

Tuesday that I had gotten the part. I signed the contracts on Wednesday and started work on Thursday,"[43] recalled Ms. Priest.

" 'Ten girls tested for the part of Marilyn,' says executive producer Bob Mosher. 'We chose Pat because she had a matter-of-fact, utterly composed manner that we needed for Marilyn, who, after all, has to remain unmoved by her weird surroundings.' "[44]

Show business has been a part of Pat Priest's life ever since she was about fourteen years old. She got her start in a road show she did for the Bountiful First Ward Church. Bountiful is a suburb located about ten miles north of Salt Lake City, Utah. In that show, directed by Pat's mother Ivy Baker Priest, she lip-synched the Beatrice Kay novelty record, *Hooray, Hooray, I'm Going Away with the Man in the Little White Coat.* This led to requests for appearances at the Lion's Club and the Rotary Club and eventually even some local television programs in Salt Lake City.

"In 1952, when my mother was appointed treasurer of the United States, we went to Washington D.C. While I was in my senior year of high school there was a television program, *The Art Lamb Show* on WTTG, that featured record pantomimes. They were looking for a girl to replace one who was leaving and some friends of mine talked me into auditioning, and so I went down and did one of my record pantomimes and got the job. I went on to do local television commercials in Washington and then I married in Washington D.C. My husband, Pierce A. Jensen, Jr., was a Naval officer, so whenever he was transferred I'd go to the local television station and do commercials.

"When I came to Southern California in 1962 [Jensen was transferred to Point Mungu and the couple moved to Thousand Oaks, California] I got an agent and actively started pursuing a career in television and started doing television commercials. In the first commercial I ever did, I played the mom in the Kellogg's Rice Krispies commercial in which I baked those little, marshmallow squares.

"I went on to do commercials for all the major brands like Clairol, Ford, Parkay Margarine, Little Friskies and Pillsbury. I also did all the interviewing for the Coffeemate commercials featuring the blindfold tests to see if they could tell the difference between Coffeemate and real cream.

"Then I started working small parts in a lot of television shows. I played Bill Bixby's girlfriend in an episode of *My Favorite Martian* and the girlfriend of a young man who was turned into a little boy on *Bewitched.* I also auditioned for the role of Mary Ann on *Gilligan's Island,* along with Raquel Welch and Dawn Wells.

"The very first thing I did was a semi-regular part of Nurse Hollis on *Dr. Kildare.* Linda Evans and I started together and when we were off camera we would sit together and chit-chat. She went on to do *Big Valley* and I went on to do *The Munsters,*"[45] said Priest.

Yet with all of the hard work in casting, writing, makeup and production, *The Munsters* ended its first season in eighteenth place. When they didn't even make the top twenty the following season, the network executioner chopped *Munsters* from the schedule in the fall of 1966. But as everyone knows, you can't kill a monster (or Munster, as the case may be) and the cast rose from the dead of television cancellation to appear in a full-color feature film, MUNSTER, GO HOME! The ninety-six-minute feature, which has been said to have originally been filmed for television, starred the members of the television cast, except for one—Pat Priest.

"They [the producers] had a young contract player named Debbie Watson and apparently everybody had been signed for the movie—but me. I did not know that they wanted to use her. One of the assistant executive producers came on the set of *The Munsters,* took me aside and told me that I would not be doing the movie. When I asked, 'Why' he said, 'Because they (Connolly, Mosher and Universal) felt you were too old.' I started to cry, I was so upset, and Al [Lewis], who was like a sweet father to me, was the one that talked to me and calmed me down. They [the cast] all felt that it wasn't right, but they couldn't do anything about it," [46] concluded Ms. Priest.

"They had Debbie Watson, whom they were trying to groom as the new Sandra Dee, under contract and had already given her a shot in her own series [see *Karen*]. I also believe that they thought that Pat [Priest] was too old for the role because several lines in the script referred to Marilyn as a teenager,"[47] added Butch Patrick.

But even though she was no longer a teenager, Pat Priest did continue to act after *The Munsters.* "I tested with Abby Dalton and Michael Learned for the role of Olivia on *The Waltons* and Michael Learned got the role." One of the more notable roles she did land was Lila Nivens, Sue Ann Nivens' sister in the classic episode of *The Mary Tyler Moore Show,* "Sue Ann's Sister," in which the audience finally gets to see Sue Ann's (Betty White) bedroom. The episode aired on October 9, 1976.

Three members of the original cast (Fred Gwynne, Al Lewis and Yvonne DeCarlo) were reunited for a 1981 TV movie titled *The Munsters' Revenge,* for which they recreated their original roles. The Munsters' youngsters, Eddie and Marilyn, were played by K.C. Martel and Jo McDonnell. A few years later, K.C. Martel appeared as Dale Troutman in the short-lived NBC drama, *The Best Times,* which aired from April 19 to June 7, 1985. The year before *The Munsters' Revenge,* Jo McDonnell made a guest appearance as Susan Webster in *Once Upon a Spy,* a pilot for ABC that starred Eleanor Parker and Ted Danson. The two-hour made-for-television movie aired on September 19, 1980.

For Fred Gwynne and Yvonne DeCarlo this would be the last time they would play the characters with which they will always be associated.

Gwynne had returned to his first love—art. He had written

---

43. From an exclusive telephone interview with Pat Priest on October 19, 1990.
44. *TV Guide,* March 27, 1965, p. 35
45. From an exclusive telephone interview with Pat Priest on October 19, 1990.
46. From an exclusive telephone interview with Pat Priest on October 19, 1990.
47. From an exclusive telephone interview with Butch Patrick on November 15, 1991.

and illustrated a number of popular children's books, including *The King Who Rained, The Story of Ick, A Chocolate Moose for Dinner* and *The Sixteen Hand Horse.* He also appeared as Frenchy Demange in the 1984 film, THE COTTON CLUB, and was Arthur in the 1984 romantic thriller, FATAL ATTRACTION. He had also become one of the busiest voice-over talents in the advertising industry as the commercial spokesman for dozens of national brand products, including Maytag, Hyundai and U.S. Air.

Al Lewis, on the other hand, continues to appear as "Grandpa" and shows no signs of ever giving up his most famous role. He appeared in character in a series of nostalgic television commercials for McDonald's that also featured Buddy Ebsen as Jed Clampett and Don Adams as Maxwell Smart. Late in the 1980s he hosted the Saturday afternoon monster flicks on the TBS cable network's *Super Scary Saturday,* and for a time even had his own 900 number for the Grandpa Munster Fan Club.

Al Lewis has taken his character one step further and opened Grandpa's, an Italian Restaurant at 252 Bleecker Street in New York's Greenwich Village, and two Grandpa's comedy clubs— one on Central Avenue in Yonkers and the other on New Dorp and Ross on Staten Island.

In 1988, TBS brought Al Lewis back to tape some wraparounds for a retrospective of *The Munsters* that reunited him with Butch Patrick and Pat Priest. The listing in *TV Guide* for the two-hour special titled *The Best of The Munsters* read, "A behind-the-scenes look at life at 1313 Mockingbird Lane and the cast members' favorite episodes."

"Since we were older, I was now the head of a blood bank and Eddie was owner of a mortuary and Grandpa—was still Grandpa,"[48] reminisced Pat Priest.

This two-hour special preceded an updated syndicated series titled *The Munsters Today,* which premiered on October 8 that year.

The explanation for the new series was summed up quite succinctly in the *TV Guide* listing. "One of Grandpa's bungled experiments causes the Munsters to sleep for more than 20 years, but when they wake up in the 1980s, it's business as usual for the unusual clan."

This explains how they got into the 1980s, but it doesn't explain why they all looked and sounded so differently. Except for Lee Meriwether as Lily, who looked and sounded very much like Yvonne DeCarlo, the other members of the cast were far from being clones. Batfans will, of course, remember Ms. Meriwether as Catwoman in the 1966 motion picture based on the series, *Batman* (See Entry).

Herman was played by comedian and actor John Schuck, who had appeared as Frankenstein's monster in the ABC Halloween special *The Halloween That Almost Wasn't,* which aired on October 30, 1979.

Schuck, who is three inches shorter than Fred Gwynne, spoke in *TV Guide* about the reduced amount of makeup he wore for the part. "I wanted makeup that wouldn't constrict me . . . Fred did a lot of mouth work because that was about the only thing on him that still moved. I'm a lot more user-friendly."[49]

Of his most popular television roles, which include Sergeant Charles Enright on *McMillan and Wife* and Murray the cop on *The New Odd Couple* (see *The Odd Couple* entry), John Schuck is perhaps best remembered as Gregory "Yoyo" Yoyonovich on the ABC situation comedy, *Holmes and Yoyo,* which aired from September 25 to December 11, 1976. He also appeared under heavy makeup as a Klingon ambassador in the 1986 science fiction film, STAR TREK IV: THE VOYAGE HOME.

There is one more actor who also deserves some credit for appearing as Herman Munster—Bill Foster, Fred Gwynne's stunt double. Foster, who also goes by the stage name "Jefferson County," also appeared as the frightened statue of Daniel Boone in the episode, "Herman Munster, Shutter Bug," which aired on October 7, 1965.

Howard Morton, who played Grandpa in *The Munsters Today,* had played Officer Ralph Simpson on the Nell Carter situation comedy, *Gimme a Break,* which aired on NBC from October 29, 1981, to May 12, 1987.

Never afraid to say what is on his mind, Al Lewis spoke candidly about *The Munsters Today.*

"Let's face it—Butch Patrick can't do it, he's thirty-seven years old. Yvonne DeCarlo is too old and too heavy to do it and Pat Priest is a grandmother. The only possible ones who could physically do it are Fred [Gwynne] and myself. Fred will have absolutely nothing to do with *The Munsters.* Not only will Fred not do the role but, my God, he won't even talk about *The Munsters.*

"I did not know they were doing the show. I had heard from a lady who had been an agent of mine many many years ago. She called me one day in New York and asked, 'Did you happen to read the *Hollywood Reporter?*' I said, 'No. I haven't read a trade paper in my life,' and she said to me, 'There was an item in there that said, *Does anyone know the whereabout of Al Lewis who created the role of Grandpa on The Munsters?*' And she said that she called them and said, 'Yeah, I talk to Al occasionally.' And the secretary who answered the call said that they didn't need the information because they had already heard from a number of agents who had told them that Al Lewis has since passed away and they all had clients who could do it much better anyway. So that was the end of that conversation. The head of casting asked if there was any film on me and word was sent back asking if I would consider screen testing for the role I created?

"I told them that I don't know if the lady who is the head of casting had ever been to New York, but R.H. Macy and Company on 34th Street has an immense window in front of which approximately 22,000 people pass every hour. And you can tell her that Al Lewis will hire New York's finest window cleaner to make sure that that window is absolutely spotless and in that window she can kiss my ass!"[50] said Lewis.

---

48. From an exclusive telephone interview with Pat Priest on October 19, 1990.

49. *TV Guide.* Vol. 36, No. 35. August 27, 1988. Issue # 1848. p. A-2

50. This and the following quotations of Al Lewis in this entry on *The Munsters* are from an exclusive telephone interview with Mr. Lewis on October 19, 1990.

Lewis, who was born on April 30, 1910, in Walcott, New York, said, "Eventually, I heard third-hand that I was too old—too old to play a 378–year-old man?

"I will tell you why they're doing the show. I was doing a show for Ted Turner called *Super Scary Saturday* down in Atlanta, Georgia. The president of entertainment for Turner, Bob Levy, came by one day while we were filming and told me that they were doing a new Munsters. He then asked if I would like to see the pilot and I told him I had no interest in it. I then asked him how he happened to have it, and he explained, because they are trying to sell it, and when I asked what he thought of it he said, 'Dreadful, terrible.' "

Lewis has no ill will toward the new cast. He said, "Good luck to them. I hope they run twenty years. I had nothing to do with it. What should I do, wish them all death? That's crazy! Life goes on. If they think they can do it better by not hiring Fred and me, that's great, that's their decision, that's their judgment. The only problem with that is that *The Munsters* has been running for twenty-six years and you're tampering with twenty-six years of memories—that is tough to overcome," concluded Lewis.

The Munsters' second, and certainly the television audience's favorite Marilyn, Pat Priest, also had a few things to say about *The Munsters Today:*

"When I found out about *The Munsters Today,* I was in Atlanta filming a two-hour special, *Best of the Munsters* for TBS. One of the TBS people asked us, 'Have you seen the *New Munsters?*' and we all said, 'No, we haven't.' And they said, 'Well, they sent a copy to us to see if we wanted to buy it. Would you like to see it?' So we went up to one of the offices there and they played it for us.

"I think it's very difficult to try and copy anything that is still on the air. *The Munsters* is still on the air—been on the air for nearly twenty-seven years now—and while a show is still on the air people can compare the new show to the original. Our show was very high-budget at that time. Our sets were very elaborate—more so than the new production. I just find it so hard to compare them. I don't think you can.

"Maybe if they made that show when *The Munsters* had been off the air for a number of years and people couldn't look and see, then you could form a better opinion. But, of course, I'm so prejudiced to our show that I just don't think you can compare the people. They're different people, they're different characters. I don't think there can ever be a duplicate of Fred Gwynne and Al Lewis—I just think they're unique. I wish they hadn't done it,"[51] concluded Ms. Priest.

Butch Patrick, the original Eddie Munster, offered his observations on *The Munsters Today:*

"I've seen *The Munsters Today* and think it's not very good. It's pretty sad—I don't like the show. But, then again, it's a reflection of modern day technology with videotape and color. It's just a whole different ballgame. Our series was like little mini-movies shot in black and white.

"They've updated the series and made Eddie a modern day kid and Jason Marsdan seems to be doing all right with the role—he's making the best of it,"[52] Patrick said.

On *Almost Home* the revamped version of NBC's *The Torkelsons,* (See Entry) Jason Marsdan played Gregory Morgan, a replacment for Aaron Metchik, who played Steven Floyd.

In addition to the live series, the motion picture and reunion episode, there was also a one hour-long animated special produced entitled *The Mini-Munsters.* All of the characters were included except Marilyn, who was replaced by a character called Lucretia. The caricatures of Grandpa, Lily and Eddie were quite good, but for some reason they decided to make Fred Gwynne's character look more like Milton the Monster than Herman Munster.

According to Stephen Cox, *The Mini-Munsters* did not feature the voices of the original cast. Al Lewis is not certain this is completely true because, as he recalled, "I'm a little confused on that because I did do the voice of Grandpa for Hanna-Barbera. I don't know if I did one or two or three episodes—it's vague in my mind—but I know I was at Hanna-Barbera studios on Ventura Boulevard, so I know I did something!"[53] chuckled Lewis.

Before closing the lid on the Munsters' coffin there are a couple of other replacements that should be discussed. The recurring character of Doctor Dudley was played in all but one episode by Paul Lynde, whose claim to fame runs from Kim McAfee's dad, Harry, in the 1963 musical comedy, BYE BYE BIRDIE, to the center square on the long-running NBC game show, *Hollywood Squares.* He was replaced by Dom DeLuise in only one episode, "Just Another Pretty Face," because Lynde was working on *Bewitched* as Samantha's Uncle Arthur.

The voice of The Munster's pet raven was provided in most episodes by Mel Blanc, certainly the world's most famous cartoon voice actor, who brought to life dozens of Warner Bros. cartoons including Bugs Bunny, Daffy Duck and Porky Pig.

There were, however, occasions when Blanc wasn't available and it was Bob Hastings who filled in as the voice of the Munsters' feathered friend. Hastings, who played Lieutenant Elroy Carpenter on *McHale's Navy* from October 11, 1962 to August 30, 1966, and was the second of three Tommy Kelseys on *All in the Family (See Entry),* also appeared in *The Munsters' Revenge* as the Phantom of the Opera.

The final character to be replaced on *The Munsters* wasn't even an actor—it was a prop. The prop was Eddie Munster's Woof-Woof doll, which in the original series had a detailed face that bore a striking resemblance to Lon Chaney Jr.'s portrayal of THE WOLF MAN. The Wolf Man doll used in the pilot was bigger, and had huge fangs and pointed ears near the top of its head (like a real wolf), while the Woof-Woof held by Jason Marsden in *The Munsters Today* looked more like an ALF doll.

---

51. From an exclusive telephone interview with Pat Priest on October 19, 1990.
52. From an exclusive telephone interview with Butch Patrick on November 15, 1991.
53. From an exclusive telephone interview with Al Lewis on October 19, 1990.

MURDER, SHE WROTE

September 30, 1984–.   CBS

Character: Ethan Cragg
Played by: Claude Akins
Date(s):   October 7, 1984–December 16, 1984

Replaced by: Doctor Seth Hazlitt
Played by: William Windom
Date(s):   April 21, 1985–

Character: Sheriff Amos Tupper
Played by: Tom Bosley
Date(s):   October 7, 1984–March 13, 1988

Replaced by: Sheriff Mort Metzger
Played by: Ron Masak
Date(s):   1989–

In her first television series, London-born actress, Angela Lansbury starred as Jessica Beatrice Fletcher, a retired substitute school teacher who became a successful author of Agatha Christie-like murder mysteries when unbeknownst to her, her nephew Grady, (Michael Horton) submitted a novel she wrote to Covington Publishers in New York. The book became a bestseller and Jessica, who lived in Cabot Cove, Maine, became a celebrity.

More importantly, when a murder was committed in Cabot Cove, or for that matter anywhere Jessica happened to be traveling, the police would inevitably enlist her aid. It stands to reason; who better to unravel a murder mystery than someone who creates them for a living?

The "law" in Cabot cove was embodied in one Sheriff Amos Tupper, played by *Happy Days* dad Tom Bosley as a recurring regular.

Claude Akins, who had starred as Sheriff Elroy P. Lobo in *B.J. and the Bear* (See Entry), was introduced in *Murder, She Wrote*'s first season as Ethan Cragg, a Cabot Cove fisherman. As Executive Producer Peter S. Fisher explained, " 'We needed a male presence in the town besides Tom Bosley (who played Sheriff Amos Tupper). His purpose on the show was to be a rough and tough buddy, but I don't think Claude liked the idea of being an occasional second banana. He made it clear he was unhappy. We took him at his word and wrote him out of the show.

'That's when we brought along William Windom as Dr. Seth Hazlitt. We could do more with him, because he was more Jessica's age and temperament. He was also the town doctor, which made it easy to get him into the show. When you're finding bodies, you need both a sheriff and a doctor.' "[54]

Fans of the author and cartoonist James Thurber may remember William Windom as John Monroe, the Thurberesque character in the situation comedy, *My World and Welcome to It*. The series premiered on NBC on September 15, 1969, and then moved to CBS in June of 1972 and ended its network run on September 7th of that year.

Among Windom's many guest roles, one of his best remembered was his portrayal of Commodore Matthew "Matt" Decker in "The Doomsday Machine," the October 20, 1967, episode of *Star Trek*.

And though never made clear in the 1979 film STAR TREK: THE MOTION PICTURE, the Stephen Collins character Willard "Will" Decker, was supposed to be Matt's son.

In 1967, William Windom starred as Mr. George Wilson in the one-shot syndicated telefilm, *Dennis the Menace* (See Entry).

Tom Bosley left *Murder, She Wrote* to solve some murders of his own as Father Frank Dowling in *The Father Dowling Mysteries* which premiered on NBC on January 20, 1989, and moved to ABC the following January where it remained until its cancellation on September 5, 1991. The unusual detective series co-starred Tracy Nelson as Sister Stephanie (often called "Steve" by Bosley) and proverbial nun, Mary Wickes, who played Mary Lazarus in the 1992 Whoopie Goldberg comedy, SISTER ACT.

Replacing Bosley was Ron Masak as Sheriff Mort Metzger, a tough New York cop who was transplanted to Maine.

Before becoming a recurring regular Ron Masak actually made his first appearance on *Murder, She Wrote* in "Footnote to Murder," which aired on March 10, 1985. He appeared two years later in "No Accounting for Murder," which aired on March 22, 1987.

Of his more than six dozen guest roles on episodic television, Ron Masak appeared in "Just a Kid Again," the February 26, 1970, episode of *Bewitched* in which he played department store salesman Irving Bates whom Tabitha (Erin/Diane Murphy) turned into a nine-year-old when she overheard him wishing to be a kid again. His grown-up girlfriend was played by Pat Priest, just one of the five actresses to have played Marilyn on *The Munsters* (See Entry).

MY FAVORITE HUSBAND

September 12, 1953–September 8, 1957.   CBS

Character: Liz Cooper
Played by: Joan Caulfield
Date(s):   September 12, 1953–June 1955

Replaced by: Liz Cooper
Played by: Vanessa Brown
Date(s):   October 11, 1955–December 1955

Character: Gillmore Cobb
Played by: Bob Sweeney
Date(s):   September 12, 1953–June 1955

Replaced by: Oliver Shepard
Played by: Dan Tobin
Date(s):   October 1955–December 1955

Character: Myra Cobb
Played by: Alix Talton
Date(s):   September 12, 1953–June 1955

54. Meyers, Ric. *Murder On the Air, Television's Great Mystery Series.* The Mysterious Press, New York, 1989, p. 280.

Replaced by:	Myra Shepard
Played by:	Alix Talton
Date(s):	October 1955–September 8, 1957

If things had gone the way producers Edmund Hartmann and Norman Tokar had planned it, the opening credits for this series might have read, "Starring Lucille Ball." If it had, we might never have had *I Love Lucy* (See Entry). Lucille Ball had starred in the 1948 radio version of *My Favorite Husband* and CBS naturally wanted her to continue to portray her popular character on television.

Ms. Ball was quite willing to accept the offer providing CBS agreed to one small change in the cast. She wanted her real-life husband, Desi Arnaz, to replace Richard Denning as her sitcom husband, George Cooper. Her reason was purely a selfish one. She wanted to spend more time with her husband, who was away touring the country with his band much of the time. Selfish? Yes. Understandable? Undeniably. Still, as persuasive as she was, Ms. Ball was unable to convince the producers that the audience would believe she was married to a Cuban bandleader . . . which, of course, she was.

Compounding the producer's dilemma was the fact that Ms. Ball's co-stars, Bea Benaderet and Gale Gordon, were not even available to reprise their roles on television.

But even with all of these setbacks, the producers were not dissuaded from pursuing what they believed still to be a good idea and they proved it by recasting the entire show. This is what led to Barry Nelson being cast as Liz Cooper's favorite husband and Joan Caulfield being cast as his wife. Nelson, the year before, had starred as the first Bart Adams on *The Hunter* (See Entry).

The Coopers' Fred and Ethel next-door-neighbor prototypes, Gillmore and Myra Cobb, were played by Bob Sweeney and Alix Talton. A short, balding actor, Sweeney also appeared between 1955 and 1956 as Mr. Munsey on the Eve Arden sitcom, *Our Miss Brooks* (See Entry). If you enjoy whistling along with the closing credits of *The Andy Griffith Show,* Bob Sweeney's name may be familiar to you, as it often appeared under the "Directed by" credit.

This newly-assembled television cast remained stable for the program's first two seasons, but changed at the beginning of the third, when production of the program changed from live to film, as described by Vanessa Brown:

"I never heard the original Lucy shows, but that's where it started. I didn't know about it [the television version of *My Favorite Husband*] until they were replacing Joan Caulfield. As a matter of fact, I didn't even know they were replacing Joan Caulfield. I had just returned to California after playing 'The Girl' in *The Seven Year Itch* in New York. I had just gotten a divorce from Dr. Robert Allen Franklin and was in between jobs and in between husbands. It was a Saturday night and a friend of mine, Alan Reisner, who had directed me in a couple of episodes of *Climax,* said to me, 'Would you like to go over to Bill [William] Dozier's house?' and I said, 'Yeah.'

"Apparently Dozier (the head of CBS' West Coast office) had asked my agent, Lillian Small [Dore Schary's sister], if I would be available to play Liz Cooper in *My Favorite Husband* and had made me a wonderful offer, as far as money was concerned.

"I had no idea about the property and no idea what their problems had been with Joan Caulfield. From what I understand, and this is hearsay that came out afterwards, Joan was getting difficult and wanted too much money to do the filmed show. The negotiations with Joan had broken down. Joan had gotten swelled-headed by her success, they said. She was being difficult and she was asking for too much money.

"It was happening all over the place with a lot of the people who had gotten the early television successes and then became difficult. I think they became difficult for many reasons.

"After I finished that show I said to myself that I'm never going to star in a television show again because you don't have any time off. We were shooting five days and on the weekends we were doing wardrobe. In other words, Joan could have just gotten exhausted as well as cranky.

"I had not had a chance to see the show and I didn't know they were looking for anyone. I didn't even know much about Joan Caulfield except that I had seen her in a couple of movies like BLUE SKIES.

"That was why Alan [Reisner] took me over to see Dozier because he figured 'Maybe Bill [Dozier] will have something for her.' Alan probably knew more than he told me, but didn't want to give me false hopes—friends are like that, they help each other. I think that deal was settled over the weekend. Dozier called Lillian Small on Monday and she called me back with the money offer. I said, 'That sounds fine,' and that was it.

"They all thought very highly of the show out here in California, and Bill Dozier loved the show. CBS in New York, however, expected the show, with me now in the Liz Cooper role, to have the same kind of success they had with Joan Caulfield. What they didn't realize was that even though the show was still *My Favorite Husband,* it had a different texture and a different feel. It was, in effect, a different show and in thirteen weeks it was very difficult to gain a new audience. It takes the public a while to accept a new concept and new people. Had they had the patience to run with it a little longer, we certainly had the writing, producing, directing and acting talent to make the show a success.

"Later on I did something for Norman Lear called *All that Glitters.* There were five us. There was Lois Nettleton, Barbara Baxley, Anita Gillette, myself and Linda Gray, with each of us carrying one story every week, so the work burden was not impossible. Frankly, I don't know how Angela Lansbury does it, because it is so hard on the performer if you want to have any kind of a private life. As a matter of fact I just finished taping a cameo in a new series, *True Colors,* in which I play a crabby, tired, old waitress. And it is only because I am now divorced and I have no children that I can do any kind of work like that, because you have to have total abandonment of everything and just do what you're supposed to do. They rehearse two days and tape with a live audience on the evening of the third day and that's not a hard schedule. The demands of television are voracious. I mean only somebody like Milton Berle can survive.

"We had a very cute dog on *My Favorite Husband.* He was one of those low slung dachshunds and he was very temperamental. When the lights got too hot for him he'd walk off the set. Everybody else was dying, but nobody would dare walk off the set, except the dog. The dog had sense."[55]

The new next-door neighbors to come along were the Shepards. He was Oliver and she was Myra, which was quite a coincidence. Even more astonishing was that even though Myra was supposed to be a different person, it may have looked as though she left Gillmore for Oliver, since she was still being played by Alix Talton.

Dan Tobin was already known to television viewers as Kerwin Tobin from the last season of *I Married Joan,* but one has to wonder if Ms. Talton knew something that no one else knew about her favorite husband, or favorite producer, that allowed him to stay for the entire run of the series.

MY FRIEND FLICKA

February 10, 1956–September 26, 1964.   CBS-ABC-CBS

Character:	Sheriff Walt Downey
Played by:	Hugh Sanders
Date(s):	unknown

Replaced by:	Sheriff Walt Downey
Played by:	Sydney Mason
Date(s):	unknown

It may very well have been the success of *Fury* (See Entry) that spurred CBS on to enter the arena with its own series about "a boy and his horse." In some ways the two series were quite similar, but they were still different enough to make direct comparisons impossible. Both shows revolved around a boy and a wild stallion, but the similarities ended there.

Fury was set in the present and took place on the Broken Wheel Ranch, which was just outside Capitol City. *My Friend Flicka* was set in the early 1900s and took place on the Goose Bar Ranch in Coulee Springs, Wyoming.

On *Fury,* Joey (Bobby Diamond) was given a recently captured black stallion by Jim Newton (Peter Graves) in an effort to gain the orphaned boy's affections. On *My Friend Flicka,* Ken McLaughlin (Johnny Washbrook) was given a brown colt to teach him responsibility.

Both shows had a ranch hand. Pete (William Fawcett), who said he cut his teeth on a branding iron, worked the Broken Wheel while Gus Broeberg (Frank Ferguson) pitched in at the Goose Bar. And both shows had sheriffs: Davis on *Fury,* Walt Downey on *My Friend Flicka.* Sheriff Davis was always played by James Seay, while two actors wore Sheriff Downey's uniform.

Hmmm. Maybe the two shows were similar after all.

It may not be fair to beat a dead horse, but as with so many animal actors, it often took more than one to create the star. To begin with, the main horse used to portray Flicka on the series was a six-year-old Arabian sorrel named Wahama. Her double, a quarter horse gelding named Goldie, was used in most scenes requiring action. There was, however, one problem. Goldie, a former lead horse at the Caliente Race Track in Tijuana, Mexico, was a much harder animal to handle, which necessitated a stunt double for Johnny Washbrook.

Washbrook, who was taught riding specifically for his role on the series, could adequately handle Wahama in the tamer riding scenes. But it took a ten-year-old girl, Steffi Epper, the daughter of a stunt man, to help the boy appear to be making his rite of passage during action sequences.

MY FRIEND IRMA

January 8, 1952–June 25, 1954.   CBS

Character:	Jane Stacy
Played by:	Cathy Lewis
Date(s):	January 8, 1952–June 1953

Replaced by:	Kay Foster
Played by:	Mary Shipp
Date(s):	October 1953–June 25, 1954

Character:	Al
Played by:	Sid Tomack
Date(s):	April 1952–June 1953

Replaced by:	Joe Vance
Played by:	Hal March
Date(s):	November 6, 1953–June 25, 1954

Character:	Professor Kropotkin
Played by:	Sig Arno
Date(s):	April 1952–June 1953

Replaced by:	Mr. Corday
Played by:	John Carradine
Date(s):	October 1953–June 25, 1954

The early days of television were just brimming with beautiful, dumb, scatterbrained secretaries, and Irma Peterson may have been the quintessential one. The show started on radio in 1947 with Marie Wilson as Irma; Cathy Lewis as her roommate, Jane Stacy and Gloria Gordon as their landlady, Mrs. O'Reilly. When CBS introduced a live television version in 1952, all three actresses continued their roles on the new medium.

---

55. From an exclusive telephone interview with Vanessa Brown on February 16, 1991.

One of the unique carryovers from radio was that the show's co-star, Cathy Lewis, also served as the program's narrator and spoke directly to the audience to establish the scenes before the opening curtain.

Stories most often revolved around the two friends' romantic endeavors. Irma's boyfriend is an unemployed con artist named Al, who only uses Irma as a means to his own end; Jane is chasing after her multimillionaire boss, Richard Rhinelander III. Jane's boyfriend was played throughout the series by Brooks West, who, offscreen, was married to *Our Miss Brooks,* Eve Arden.

Al, Irma's good-for-nothing heartthrob, was at first played by Sid Tomack, who had played the first Jim Gillis on *The Life of Riley* (See Entry) and later played the second Knobby Walsh on *The Joe Palooka Story* (See Entry).

The girls' wacky neighbor, Professor Kropotkin, was played by the comic German actor, Sig Arno who had appeared in Charlie Chaplin's first talkie, THE GREAT DICTATOR, which was released in 1940. He later played the dancing instructor in the 1951 Doris Day comedy, ON MOONLIGHT BAY. The good professor was not a man of science, but of music and his instrument was the violin.

One year after the program hit the air, a number of changes in cast had occurred. The audience learned of the most important of these in an opening narration given by the show's star, Marie Wilson. The introduction, which Ms. Wilson gave in character, explained that Jane Stacy had been transferred to Panama. Irma's new roommate was Kay Foster, a newspaperwoman who answered the classified ad Irma had placed in the newspaper. The actress who played Kay Foster was already known to television audiences as Miss Spalding from the CBS situation comedy, *Life with Luigi.*

Irma also had a new boyfriend and a new neighbor. Her boyfriend was played by veteran actor Hal March, who, among many other roles on television, had been the original Harry Morton on *The George Burns and Gracie Allen Show* (See Entry). Her new neighbor was Mr. Corday, who was also in show business. But instead of being a musician, he was an actor—and a rather bizarre actor at that. He was played by that deep-throated master of the macabre, John Carradine. Playing Mr. Corday was Carradine's only continuing role on a television series except for the syndicated series, *Trapped,* which he hosted beginning on July 15, 1951. His more than one hundred other television appearances were roles on episodic television which ran the gamut from mysteries such as *Lights Out,* to Westerns such as *Bonanza,* to science fiction such as *The Twilight Zone,* to sitcoms like *The Munsters.*

Carradine's highly visible motion picture roles include Hatfield in the 1939 Western, STAGECOACH; Casey in the 1940 drama, THE GRAPES OF WRATH; and Aaron in the 1956 biblical epic, THE TEN COMMANDMENTS. One of his least visible roles, though especially fun to watch for, is his part as one of the lost woodsmen who stop by the blind hermit's cottage for directions in the 1935 Universal horror film, THE BRIDE OF FRANKENSTEIN.

Perhaps John Carradine's most notable contribution to television was his son, David, who was the star of *Kung Fu* (See Entry).

MY LIVING DOLL

September 27, 1964–September 8, 1965.   CBS

Character:	Dr. Robert McDonald
Played by:	Robert Cummings
Date(s):	September 27, 1964–1965
Replaced by:	Dr. Peter Robinson
Played by:	Jack Mullaney
Date(s):	1965–September 8, 1965

He was television's most eligible bachelor for more than half a decade. The wholesome, good-looking actor, Bob Cummings, played Bob Collins, a professional photographer with an eye for the ladies both during and after studio hours. The show was *The Bob Cummings Show* (also know as *Love That Bob*) and it aired, at various times on NBC and CBS, from January 2, 1955 to September 15, 1959. Network repeats aired from October 12, 1959 to December 1, 1961.

The second Cummings comedy was *The Bob Cummings*

Ladies' man Bob Cummings, as Dr. Robert McDonald who was entrusted with the responsibility of caring for Dr. Carl Miller's invention, the AF 709, with Julie Newmar who played *Batman*'s first Catwoman and co-starred in *My Living Doll* as the statuesque robot nicknamed "Rhoda."

Show, a short-lived sitcom about Bob Carson (Cummings), a charter pilot. Coincidentally, Bob Cummings occasionally flew a plane on his previous series. This one landed on CBS's Thursday night schedule on October 5, 1961, and crashed five months later on March 1, 1962.

Two years later, Cummings, still as handsome as ever, took on the most difficult role of his career. He played psychologist Dr. Bob McDonald who, instead of chasing women, had one beautiful statuesque redhead placed in his charge. And although she was highly desirable, there could never be a romantic relationship between them because Rhoda Miller (Julie Newmar), a name Dr. McDonald gave to her, was no more than a well-stacked pile of nuts and bolts.

Rhoda, you see, was a robot built by Dr. Carl Miller (Henry Beckman) for United States Space Project AF 709, a program designed to send robots into outer space. Being the dedicated scientist, Dr. Miller calls Rhoda "It," "709," or "The Robot." He doesn't see her as a beautiful woman.

To avoid arousing suspicion, "The Robot" posed as Rhoda Miller, Carl's niece, and she worked as Bob's secretary.

Bob was assigned to care for Rhoda and develop her character. This interesting story element showed up again four years later in an episode of *Star Trek.* That episode, "Requiem for Methuselah," dealt with an android, Rayna Kapec (Louise Sorel), who was encouraged to interact with Captain Kirk (William Shatner) to hasten the development of her emotions.

McDonald displayed great restraint, but the strain must just have been too much for Cummings. He left the series after the twenty-first episode.

Based on available printed information, the explanation given for Bob's hasty departure (which can be attributed to the co-stars' inability to work together) was that he had been sent to Pakistan. Peter Robinson, a bachelor friend of Bob's, played by Jack Mullaney, had fallen in love with the robot and she became his ward for the remaining five episodes.

One may wonder if the examples set by Dr. McDonald and Peter Robinson were good ones, as Rhoda (Julie Newmar) later turned to a life of crime as Catwoman in the BATMAN (See Entry) movie.

It would surely be fun to go back and take another look at *My Living Doll,* but it has been reported that most of the episodes were destroyed by Producer Jack Chertok (*The Lone Ranger*) when the series failed to generate syndication sales in the 1960s.

Film historians and collectors, including Julie Newmar, are seeking prints of the episodes.

MY THREE SONS

September 29, 1960–August 24, 1972.   ABC-CBS

Character:	William Francis Michael Aloysius "Bub" O'Casey
Played by:	William Frawley
Date(s):	September 29, 1960–September 9, 1965

Replaced by:	Uncle Charley O'Casey
Played by:	William Demarest
Date(s):	September 16, 1965–August 24, 1972

Character:	Herbert Blakeley "Sudsy" Pfeiffer
Played by:	Ricky Allen
Date(s):	1961–1963

Replaced by:	Ernie Thompson
Played by:	Barry Livingston
Date(s):	1963–August 24, 1972

Character:	Mike Douglas
Played by:	Tim Considine
Date(s):	September 29, 1960–1965

Replaced by:	Ernie Thompson Douglas
Played by:	Barry Livingston
Date(s):	September 16, 1965–August 24, 1972

Character:	Bob Walters
Played by:	Russ Conway
Date(s):	unknown

Replaced by:	Bob Walters
Played by:	John Gallaudet
Date(s):	unknown

Character:	Jean Pearson
Played by:	Cynthia Pepper
Date(s):	November 17, 1960–November 12, 1964

Replaced by:	Sally Ann Morrison Douglas
Played by:	Meredith MacRae
Date(s):	October 24, 1963–September 16, 1965

"Between 1960 and 1972 millions of American television viewers enjoyed the antics of the Douglas family on *My Three Sons.* Fred MacMurray played Steve Douglas, a widower and the apparently devoted father of three boys. But over the years, it now seems clear, the specter of death continued to stalk the star-crossed Douglas clan—with no acknowledgment ever made by the preternaturally composed dad. Recent films such as VELVET BLUE have exposed the maggots hiding beneath the rock of America's TV suburbia. In that context, those old *My Three Sons* episodes take on a disturbing aspect. Everywhere there are hints of foul goings-on just outside the eye of the camera, just beyond that invisible fourth wall.

"Fred MacMurray rose to fame on the strength of motion pictures such as DOUBLE INDEMNITY—*films noirs* that explored the rictus behind the neighborly smile, the skull beneath the middle-class skin. Perhaps when MacMurray's

Chip Douglas (Stanley Livingston, center) makes a birthday wish while his brother Robbie (Don Grady, far right) helps him blow out the candles on his cake. Standing behind Chip are (clockwise): his brother Mike (Tim Considine), his father, Steve (Fred MacMurray), and grandfather, "Bub" (William Frawley).

advisers were choosing a TV vehicle for the fading movie star in the late 1950s, they deliberately picked a scenario with an underlying tension, a hint of muffled screams beneath the laugh track. Through its twelve seasons *My Three Sons* told the story of a suburban family whose members disappeared with alarming regularity. Steve Douglas's stated alibis for his vanishing family made little sense, should certainly have piqued the interest of local police, and may help explain why the Douglas family abruptly quit 'Bryant Park' for North Hollywood at the start of the 1966–1967 season.

"An examination of the evidence suggests that Steve Douglas was a murderer who eliminated members of his family as they became conscious of his misdeeds. By the time the series left the air, only Chip, the youngest and stupidest of the original three sons, was left witness to Dad's death spree.

"(1) **MRS. STEVE DOUGLAS.** When we first meet the family, in 1960, Steve Douglas is a putative widower raising sons Mike [Tim Considine], Robbie [Don Grady] and Chip [Stanley Livingston] with the help of an old man named Bub [William Frawley], allegedly the boys' maternal grandfather. Although Chip is hardly more than a toddler, no mention is ever made of the late Mrs. Douglas, beyond the fact that her untimely death leaves her husband free to date. [Chip actually

did learn a little about his mom in an episode that required him to write a paper about his mother. What he found out by asking his family members questions was that she was pretty and loved them all very much.]

"(2) **BUB.** In 1964 the jolly grandfather, perhaps beginning to suspect that his daughter's death several years earlier was no accident, suddenly disappears. Dad tells the boys that Bub has gone to 'visit his mother in Ireland' and will be back soon. It seems dubious that Bub, a man in his seventies, could have a living mother, but the trusting sons fall for it. [Actually, Bub didn't go to Ireland to visit his mother. He went to Ireland to help his Aunt Kate celebrate her 104th birthday.]

"As the transition episode opens, the Douglas men are in a tizzy over Mrs. Fedocia Barnett (Reta Shaw), the housekeeper Steve hired on temporarily to help out around the house until Bub returned from Ireland. Fedocia is even tougher and crustier than Bub. Robbie said that she was a grouch, which was an understatement. She seemed to hate socks because she never washed any and when she burned the boys' shirts, she blamed it on 'that cheap iron you gave me to use.' Reta Shaw was a whole lot nicer earlier on in the series when she played Mrs. Bradshaw, the mother of the year. But in the transition episode she was intolerable and totally unreasonable. [Reta Shaw had also played Mrs. Macauley on *The Ann Sothern Show* (See Entry).]

"In the same episode a mysterious seaman arrives at the Douglas home. Dad convinces the boys this rough character is their 'Uncle Charley,' who will stick around to help out until Bub comes home."

[Uncle Charley (William Demarest) was not in the Navy, but the Merchant Marines (the same outfit Popeye the Sailor belongs to). He stops by the house and asks, 'Does Bill O'Casey live in these parts?' The reference to Bill throws Chip because they all know him as Bub—only his brother Charley calls him Bill. It's sort of like Captain James T. Kirk's brother, George Samuel Kirk—only his brother Jim calls him Sam.

Steve invites Charley to stay with them for the three days he'll be laid over before he has to catch his plane to San Francisco in order to meet his ship which is bound for the Caribbean.

The boys all think it's a neat idea, but Fedocia refuses to cook for another "male mouth" and gives Steve her notice. This works out just fine since he was going to fire her anyway, but couldn't get up the nerve.

Charley accepts the invitation and agrees to look after the boys while Steve is away on business. He really makes points with Chip when he shows up unexpectedly at Chip's school's open house in place of Steve, who is stuck out of town on business. They both get all mushy and William Demarest, whose name had already replaced William Frawley's on the opening credits, stays for the rest of the series.]

"Eight years later, Bub has not returned."

"(3) **MIKE.** Eventually the eldest son reaches an age at which he might begin to question his father. Thus, a year after Bub vanishes, Mike disappears. First Dad tells Robbie and Chip that Mike has gone on a honeymoon—and then he announces that Mike has 'moved east.' [In the storyline, it is explained that Mike moved east to accept a job as a psychology professor.] Mike never returns."

[In the earlier episodes, Mike dated Jean Pearson. Jean was

played by Cynthia Pepper in her first televison role. Cute as she was, though, she was no match for Meredith MacRae, who went on to star as Billie Jo Bradley on *Petticoat Junction* (See Entry). Ms. Pepper also landed another series following *My Three Sons*. But playing the title character in *Margie,* which ran on ABC from October 12, 1961 to August 31, 1962, didn't bring her very much recognition.

Cynthia Pepper actually appeared in six episodes of *My Three Sons* before Meredith MacRae was introduced as Sally Ann Morrison. Her last appearance was in ''The Sunday Drive,'' which aired on June 1, 1961. Then, on November 12, 1964, Cynthia Pepper returns in a painfully realistic story, ''Goodbye Again,'' in which Mike confesses to being engaged to Sally Ann Morrison.]

''(4&5) **ERNIE'S PARENTS.** [Since Mike married Sally Ann Morrison on the September 16, 1965 episode, 'The First Marriage,' the Douglas household was going to come up one son short.]

''Down one son, Steve Douglas begins to take a special interest in Chip's little pal Ernie, who has been hanging around the Douglas home for a couple of seasons.

[Chip's original friend on the series was a cute little fellow with dark hair and glasses. His full name was Herbert Blakeley Pfeiffer, but Chip, whose first name was really Richard, just called him ''Sudsy.'' After appearing in a number of episodes including the one in which Chip asks about his mom, ''Sudsy'' disappears and is replaced by another cute young fellow with dark hair and glasses, who looks remarkably like ''Sudsy.'' His name is Ernie Thompson but he had more of a family resemblance to Chip than he did to ''Sudsy'' and for a very good reason. He was played by Barry Livingston, Stanley's younger brother. A very young Barry Livingston, as Barry Martin, had once been seen hanging around the Nelson's home in an episode of *The Adventures of Ozzie and Harriet* while his dad, Fred, took his mom, Carol, to the hospital to have a baby. It was a girl.]

''When Ernie is orphaned [Steve knew Ernie's mother and even asked Chip over the phone if she could fill in for him at the school's open house in the Bub/Uncle Charley transition episode], Steve generously offers to adopt the little boy,'' [but only in so many words. In the episode when Ernie moves in with the Douglases, Chip and Ernie walk into the house through the front door and catch it from Uncle Charley who tells Chip that the front door is only for guests and Ernie isn't a guest, but ''our star boarder.''

Ernestine Colter, from the King's County Children's Welfare Unit, shows up at the Douglases looking for Ernie. Ernie, you see, is on the lam from the County Home and spending the night with his best friend, Chip Douglas.

After Steve Douglas finishes speaking wth Miss Colter, he goes upstairs to check on the boys. Chip thanks his father for not ratting on Ernie who, of course, doesn't want to return to the home because, among other things, they wouldn't let him keep his dog, Wilson.

Chip chimes in, 'Yeah, dad . . . kids with dogs gotta wait longer to get a frosted home. I mean foster home.'

Later . . . Steve goes to Chip's room to say good-night and discovers that Ernie is crying, although he is trying to hide the fact from Chip. Steve decides to have one of his fatherly talks with the lad.

He tells Ernie that when he returns to the Home, his friends aren't going to disappear. He'll still have Uncle Charley, Robbie, Chip, Tramp (the Douglas' dog) and Wilson.

STEVE: And don't forget, Ernie, when things get rough you've always got a friend you can pray to.

ERNIE: Oh, I already did that.

STEVE: Oh, you did?

ERNIE: I prayed for you to come in here.

STEVE: Well, you know Ernie, that's the nicest compliment I've ever had. Why don't you lie down and go to sleep. Good night, Ernie.

Ernie then asks Mr. Douglas if it would ''be baby'' if he asked him to stay in the room until he fell asleep. Steve assures him that ''it wouldn't be baby at all, Ernie.''

ERNIE: Good night, Mr. Douglas.

STEVE: Good night, Ernie.]

''No mention is ever made of how Ernie's parents met their premature death, but it is not long after this that the Douglas clan flees their midwestern home in California. (An even more bizarre note: though it had been established that Chip and Ernie were in the same grammar school class, once Ernie becomes the new third son, Dad claims Ernie is younger than Chip [which he is] and forces Ernie to go back several grades at his new school.''

[Ernie's dog, Wilson, also disappears and is never seen again.]

''(6) **ROBBIE.** In California, Robbie marries a college friend and promptly seeds her with triplets. Robbie, still a teenager, cannot afford to provide for his spawn. Dad invites Robbie, Katie [Tina Cole] and the triplets to live under his roof. [As rare as twins are, triplets are even scarcer. Finding infant triplet boys with fair complexions, light hair and blue eyes was, for all intents and purposes, impossible. And because of the California labor laws allow infants to be photographed for only thirty seconds. The law also stipulates that babies can only be on the set for two hours each day. During that two-hour period, they are allowed to be before the camera for only twenty minutes at a clip; it is during that twenty-minute period that the thirty-second exposure is made. Certainly having two sets of triplets would double the total amount of time that 'baby shots' could be made. This being nearly impossible, the producers opted for two sets of twin boys who not only met the aforementioned criteria, but looked enough like each other so that they could be divided into groups of three for filming, with one to spare.] Dad invites Robbie, Katie and the triplets to live under his roof. Two years later, Robbie is gone—though the pretty Katie continues to live with her missing husband's father.

Visitors are told that Robbie is 'away on a business trip'—though when the series leaves the air, Robbie is still gone.''

[There were several occasions on which Fred MacMurray didn't actually play Steve Douglas. In one episode Josephine Kringle (Pat McNulty), Steve's girlfriend of 30 years earlier, stopped by to visit and Mike drove her to the malt shop. Steve tried to catch up with her, but never did. Maybe it was best, since she had married Steve's high school rival, Larry Peckinpaugh (Dennis Whitcomb) and was now Mrs. Peckinpaugh. In a flashback sequence, George Spicer portrayed Steve Douglas as a boy.

Another time, Steve Douglas took Bub and the boys to Scotland where he was to inherit "The Castle." While there the Douglases of America meet the Douglases of Scotland, including the Laird (Lord) of Douglas, head of the Douglas clan. Fred MacMurray played both parts, just as Patty Duke had played Patty Lane and her cousin Cathy Lane on *The Patty Duke Show* (See Entry), but instead of doing a Scottish accent, his voice was dubbed by Alan Caillou, who had played "The Head" in the science fiction sitcom, *Quark,* which aired on NBC from February 24 to April 14, 1978.

The Castle, by the way, turned out to be the name of a Scottish inn. Steve, being the gentleman he is, turns down the inheritance and returns to the states where he works for Bob Walters, who was played by both Russ Conway and John Gallaudet.]

"We can only wonder how long it was after the series ended its run that lunkhead Chip or ditz Ernie finally asked Dad one question too many and joined Mom, Bub, Mike and Robbie on the long vacation 'to visit Bub's mother' 'on business' 'back east.' ''[56]

MY TWO DADS

September 20, 1987–June 16, 1990.   NBC

Character:	Ed Klawicki
Played by:	Dick Butkus
Date(s):	September 20, 1987–September 1989

Replaced by:	Judge Wilbur
Played by:	Florence Stanley
Date(s):	September 20, 1987–January 10, 1990

Sure, it's another one of those mixed-up television broken families in which a mom had to die to give birth to a show, but if you got past that and gave it a chance, this show might have grown on you, primarily because the show's leads, Michael Taylor, played by comedian Paul Reiser, and Joey Harris (Greg Evigan) were fun to watch together.

The reason we watched them was to see how they were raising ''their'' twelve-year-old daughter, Nicole Bradford (Staci Keanan).

The story given to explain why this young lady had two dads was that they both had had an affair with her mom. When she (try not to cry) died, Nicole was left in the joint custody of not one, but two fathers, neither of whom knows which one really is her dad, probably because her mother didn't know either. But it doesn't matter, because they both love her very much, as all good TV dads should.

Rounding out the cast is ex-Chicago Bears football player Dick Butkus as Ed Klawicki, the owner of the diner, and Florence Stanley as Judge Wilbur, who lives in the same building and serves as a surrogate aunt. Perhaps she felt somewhat responsible, because it was she who placed Nicole in their custody.

In September of 1989, when Dick Butkus left the series, it was covered by having Judge Wilbur buy the diner from him. This kept the cast stable and avoided the need to find another ex-football player who could act. Shortly thereafter, the series was pulled from NBC's schedule.

Butkus, by the way, is actually quite a competent actor and had previously appeared as Richard ''Ski'' Butowski in the short-lived police series, *Blue Thunder,* which aired on ABC from January 6 to September 7, 1984.

Actress Florence Stanley also came from a police series—*Barney Miller.* She carried over her Bernice Fish character in the Abe Vigoda spinoff *Fish. Barney Miller* aired on ABC from January 23, 1975 to September 9, 1982, while *Fish* overlapped from February 5, 1977 to June 8, 1978.

To make family matters worse, Staci Keanan left her two dads to play Lindsay Bowen in a new ABC situation comedy, *Going Places,* which made its network debut on Friday, September 21, 1990. It ended its short run on July 5, 1991.

---

56. The framework for this entry is the complete and unedited article, ''The Disappeared of My Three Sons'' by Bill Flanagan, published in the October 1987 issue of *SPY* magazine. It is reprinted here with permission. All of the information contained within brackets has been added by Steven Lance.

N

NAKED CITY

September 30, 1958–September 11, 1963.   ABC

Character:	Detective Lieutenant Dan Muldoon
Played by:	John McIntire
Date(s):	September 30, 1958–March 10, 1959

Replaced by:	Lieutenant Mike Parker
Played by:	Horace McMahon
Date(s):	March 17, 1959–September 11, 1963

Character:	Detective Jim Halloran
Played by:	James Franciscus
Date(s):	September 30, 1958–September 29, 1959

Replaced by:	Detective Adam Flint
Played by:	Paul Burke
Date(s):	October 12, 1960–September 11, 1963

Out of the eight million stories in the naked city, this well-written and well-produced crime drama managed to tell 137 of them. The first thirty-nine were half-hour episodes. The remaining ninety-eight were hour-long dramas. All of them were filmed in black and white, which added to the realism of this series, shot on location in New York instead of in studios with painted backdrops.

What is unique about this series is that it had two lives. The first ran from September 30, 1958 to September 29, 1959.

The plainclothes detectives, who worked out of Manhattan's 65th precinct, were Muldoon and Halloran. For the entire run of the half-hour series, Halloran was played by a handsome blonde actor, James Franciscus. He eventually gave up police work, but used his experience on the force as a private insurance investigator, Russ Andrews, in *The Investigators,* a short-lived series which aired thirteen episodes on CBS from September 21 to December 28, 1961.

Disillusioned with being a shamus, Franciscus again changed careers and became an English teacher at Jefferson High School in Los Angeles, California as the star of *Mr. Novak,* which aired on NBC from September 24, 1963 to August 31, 1965.

But being a gumshoe was in his blood and when James Franciscus left the teaching profession he returned to the field of insurance investigations as Mike Longstreet, an insurance investigator blinded by an explosion which took the life of his wife, Ingrid. The series, *Longstreet,* produced nearly twice as many episodes as *The Investigators*—twenty-four in all. The hour-long series aired on ABC from September 16, 1971 to August 10, 1972.

His motion picture roles include Major Hoffmann in the 1963 Walt Disney drama, MIRACLE OF THE WHITE STALLIONS. The following year, James Franciscus starred in the title role of YOUNGBLOOD HAWKE, a very interesting picture which featured a host of familiar faces from television, including Suzanne Pleshette, Eva Gabor, Lee Bowman, Hayden Roarke and Werner Klemperer.

Science fiction fans will recall James Franciscus as Tuck Kirby, the self-confident circus promoter who lassoed more than he could handle in the 1969 Western fantasy, THE VALLEY OF GWANGI. This underrated film featured some of stop-motion animator Ray Harryhausen's best work which was supported by an outstanding music score by Jerome Moross. A year later, Franciscus recreated his role as Brent in BENEATH THE PLANET OF THE APES, the second of five films in the series.

On *Naked City,* James Franciscus's partner was a cop named Muldoon. This Muldoon is not to be confused with the comic character on *Car 54, Where Are You?* portrayed by future star of *The Munsters* (See Entry), Fred Gwynne. This Muldoon was played by John McIntire, who also should not be confused with Hawkeye Pierce's swampmate in *M*A*SH* (See Entry).

McIntire chaperoned the young detective for the first twenty-four episodes before he was blown up in a high-speed chase that ended with his car careening into a gasoline truck in ''Ten Cent Dreams,'' which aired on March 10, 1959. McIntire moved West, both figuratively and literally, when he took over the role of wagonmaster on *Wagon Train* (See Entry).

Halloran's new mentor was Lieutenant Mike Parker, played by Irish actor Horace McMahon, who was introduced in ''The Bumper,'' which aired on March 17, 1959. McMahon had previously appeared as Captain Willis on *Martin Kane, Private Eye* (See Entry) and as one of Danny Thomas's agents on *Make Room for Daddy* (See Entry). One of his better film roles was as Monahan, the lieutenant in charge of the New York police precinct in the 1951 drama, DETECTIVE STORY. The irony is that except for McMahon, just about everyone else in the cast was nominated for an Academy Award.

After a hiatus of nearly one year, *Naked City* returned in a revised and expanded version on October 12, 1960. Still with the series from the previous version was Horace McMahon as Lieutenant Mike Parker. His new partner was Detective Adam Flint, played by Paul Burke.

Burke had one of those familiar faces, but it is difficult to say whether it worked for him or against him, because he never really made it big. He did, however, work steadily in television. Aside from his work on *Naked City* his most famous role was as Colonel Joe Gallagher on *Twelve O'Clock High* (See Entry).

His more than one hundred appearances on episodic television include two episodes of the *Adventures of Superman.* His first was as one of the gangsters in the 1953 season episode, "My Friend Superman." During the 1954 season he appeared as the sidekick of Si Horton (Herb Vigran), Matthew Tips, in "Superman Week."

NAME OF THE GAME

September 20, 1968–September 10, 1971.   NBC

Character:	Jeff Dillon
Played by:	Anthony Franciosa
Date(s):	September 20, 1968–September 10, 1971
Replaced by:	Paul Tyler
Played by:	Robert Culp
Date(s):	October 2, 1970
	November 6, 1970

You might say that *Fame Is the Name of the Game,* because it just happened to be the title of the series' pilot which aired on November 26, 1966. That "fame" came in the form of stories published in Howard Publications' *Crime Magazine.*

The magazine's publisher, Glenn Howard, was played by George Macready in the pilot, but by Gene Barry throughout the series.

In an uninspired bit of typecasting, Robert Stack, who had played F.B.I. agent Eliot Ness in *The Untouchables,* was cast as senior editor Dan Farrell, a former F.B.I. agent (no kidding).

Rounding out the main cast was Anthony Franciosa as Jeff Dillon, an investigative reporter and the editor of the People section of *Crime Magazine.*

In place of an ensemble cast, each of these actors appeared in separate episodes on a rotating basis; they were never seen together. This gave them a lighter-than-usual production schedule of three weeks of shooting and one week off. Compared to the seventeen-hour day Robert Stack put in during the production of *The Untouchables,* this was like a vacation.

Although this should have made it easy for the producers to cover for a missing star for a week or two, by having one of the two remaining actors featured in an additional episode, it didn't work out. When Tony Franciosa was suspended by Universal in a script dispute at the start of the second season, he was replaced by Robert Culp as reporter Paul Tyler. The episode, "Cynthia Is Alive and Living in Avalon," aired on October 2, 1970. Cynthia, by the way, was played by Barbara Feldon, who just two weeks earlier appeared for the last time in *Get Smart!* (See Entry) as Agent 99.

Five episodes later, Robert Culp returned to the *Name of the Game* as Tyler in "Little Bear Died Running." The episode, shot on location in New Mexico, dealt with the murder of a senator's son and his Indian friend, who had been the chief suspect.

In television, the name of the game is "change," and since no series lasts forever, when *The Name of the Game* left the air in 1971, Tony Franciosa went on to star as Nick Bianco in the NBC adventure series, *Search,* which aired from September 13, 1972 to August 29, 1973. Two years later he picked up where Dean Martin left off in the movies and starred as television's Matt Helm in the series of the same name, which aired on ABC from September 20, 1975 to January 3, 1976.

Robert Culp had, of course, already made a name for himself as Kelly Robinson in the poplular adventure series, *I Spy,* which aired on NBC from September 15, 1965 to September 2, 1968.

THE NANCY DREW MYSTERIES *see:* THE HARDY BOYS MYSTERIES

THE NEW DOCTORS

September 14, 1969–June 23, 1973.   NBC

Character:	Dr. Ted Stuart
Played by:	John Saxon
Date(s):	September 4, 1969–March 5, 1972
Replaced by:	Dr. Martin Cohen
Played by:	Robert Walden
Date(s):	October 10, 1972–June 23, 1973

The New Doctors, also known as *The Doctors,* was actually only one spoke of a series of rotating dramas on NBC known as *The Bold Ones.* This was very much like *Columbo, McMillan and Wife* and *McCloud,* which were rotating elements of *The NBC Sunday Mystery Movie.*

These hour-long dramas unfolded at the Benjamin Craig Institute in Los Angeles. The founder of this medical research institute was Dr. Benjamin Craig himself. Dr. Craig was played by E.G. Marshall, who had played Lawrence Preston on *The Defenders* (See Entry). In addition to his on-camera work in thirty motion pictures he narrated many of television's *National Geographic* specials. One of his most attention-getting screen roles in recent years was that of the president of the United States in the 1980 adventure film, SUPERMAN II.

Working under Dr. Craig was a gifted heart transplant specialist, Dr. Ted Stuart, played by John Saxon who had played Dirk Fredericks, the head of the Agency which employed Scarecrow and Mrs. King on a series of the same name. That series aired on CBS from October 3, 1983 to September 10, 1987. One of his better film roles was Benny Rampell in Otto Preminger's 1963 epic drama, THE CARDINAL. His more than one hundred appearances on episodic television include two episodes of *The A-Team.* In his first appearance, Saxon turned in a particularly good performance as a crazed Reverend Jim Jones-type cult leader in "The Children of Jamestown," which aired on January 30, 1983.

Long before he became famous as the dedicated newspaper columnist Joe Rossi on *Lou Grant,* Robert Walden joined the cast of *The New Doctors* as Dr. Martin Cohen, Dr. Stuart's replacement. A few years after *Lou Grant* left network television, so did Robert Walden, who co-starred as Joe in Showtime cable network's comedy series, *Brothers,* which first aired in 1984. His co-star, Brandon Maggart, who played Lou on *Brothers,* had appeared as Buddy in the ''Buddy and Jim'' segments of *Sesame Street* during the first few seasons.

A NEW KIND OF FAMILY

September 16, 1979–January 5, 1980.   ABC

Character:	Abby Stone
Played by:	Gwynne Gilford
Date(s):	September 16, 1979–October 21, 1979

Replaced by:	Jessie Ashton
Played by:	Telma Hopkins
Date(s):	December 15, 1979–January 5, 1980

Character:	Jill Stone
Played by:	Connie Ann Hearn
Date(s):	September 16, 1979–October 21, 1979

Replaced by:	Jojo Ashton
Played by:	Janet Jackson
Date(s):	December 15, 1979–January 5, 1980

Contrary to what many people think about overnight stardom, most ''stars'' had to endure some failures before they finally made it. For Eileen Brennan, who went on to star as Captain Doreen Lewis in both the motion picture and television versions of *Private Benjamin* (See Entry), *A New Kind of Family* was one of hers.

Actually, the title doesn't accurately describe the premise. A better title would be *Kit Flanagan and Abby Stone Move Their Families into the Same Apartment Because They Can't Afford to Pay the Rent Individually.* But you know how *TV Guide* would feel about that, so they went with the shorter one.

The reason these women, who didn't know each other before the apartment lease mixup occurred, couldn't afford the rent was, primarily, that they had both lost their breadwinners. Specifically, Kit Flanagan was a widow and Abby Stone a divorcee.

Kit had three kids, Andy, Hillary and Tony, played by David Hollander, Lauri Hendler and Rob Lowe, respectively. Abby had a daughter, Jill, who was played by Gwynne Gilford.

Only four episodes had aired when the network pulled the series. They apparently felt that some recasting might add some spark to the show, so they replaced Abby and Jill Stone with Jessie Ashton and her daughter JoJo.

Mrs. Ashton was played by Telma Hopkins, originally a member of Tony Orlando's backup group, known collectively as ''Dawn.'' She later appeared as Isabelle on the Tom Hanks/Peter Scolari sitcom, *Bosom Buddies,* which aired from November 27, 1980 to September 15, 1984. JoJo was played by Janet Jackson.

But even these changes couldn't save the series; it folded after four more episodes. Some good, however, did come out of the series. Rob Lowe became a major box office attraction in film roles such as Billy in the 1985 drama, ST. ELMO'S FIRE.

Janet Jackson, Michael's sister, had been seen as Penny Gordon Woods on *Good Times* from September 21, 1977 to August 1, 1979, and had the recurring role of Charlene DuPrey on *Diff'rent Strokes* from October 29, 1981 to November 13, 1982. She then played Cleo Hewitt from 1984 to 1985 on the series, *Fame,* before turning back to music and becoming a star in her own right.

THE NEW PEOPLE

September 22, 1969–January 12, 1970.   ABC

Character:	Stanley Gabriel
Played by:	Dennis Olivieri
Date(s):	September 22, 1969–unknown

Replaced by:	Stanley Gabriel
Played by:	Kevin O'Neal
Date(s):	unknown–January 12, 1970

In an unusual series, strangely reminiscent of the feature films based on William Golding's book, *The Lord of the Flies,* a group of forty college exchange students survive a plane crash and struggle to start a better society on Buamo, a remote island in the Pacific.

Dennis Olivieri, the actor who originally played Stanley Gabriel, was rescued from this series by Kevin O'Neal, who replaced him as Stanley Gabriel before ABC deserted the series after only seventeen episodes.

THE NEW PHIL SILVERS SHOW

September 28, 1963–June 27, 1964.   CBS

Character:	Scarpitta
Played by:	Norman Grabowski
Date(s):	unknown

Replaced by:	Scarpitta
Played by:	Henry Scott
Date(s):	unknown

Phil Silvers' civilian character, Harry Grafton, in *The New Phil Silvers Show* wasn't very much different from his wonderful characterization of Sergeant Ernie Bilko.

Instead of running a platoon, he was now a maintenance superintendent. Instead of having a group of soldiers under him, he supervised a group of men. One of these men, Waluska, was played by Herbie Faye, who had played Private Sam Fender on *The Phil Silvers Show,* which aired on CBS from September 20, 1955 to September 11, 1959.

Conflicting information indicates that the character of Scarpitta was played by both Norman Grabowski and Henry Scott; other sources indicate that the character played by Norman Grabowski was named Grabowski on the series, and that he was never played by anyone else.

THE NEW WKRP IN CINCINNATI *see:* WKRP IN CINCINNATI

THE NEW ZOO REVUE

January 24, 1972–September 1975.   Syndicated

Character:	Henrietta Hippo
Played by:	Thomas Carri
Date(s):	1972–1973

Replaced by:	Henrietta Hippo
Played by:	Larri Thomas
Date(s):	1974–1975

This scaled-down takeoff of *Sesame Street* was created by Barbara Atlas, who had built several of the unusual props for *Sesame Street,* and musician-singer-composer, Doug Momary.

The animal characters in this educational series were played by actors wearing full-sized costumes built by Sid and Marty Krofft. Some of the Kroffts' other work include *H.R. Pufnstuf, Sigmund and the Sea Monsters, Lidsville,* and the adult puppet satire, *D.C. Follies,* which was syndicated in 1987. The only human member of the cast was Fred Willard, who played the bartender of the Washington, D.C. pub.

The original actor inside Henrietta Hippo was Thomas Carri. Later on the costume was worn by Larri Thomas.

The transition was naturally seamless, as Henrietta Hippo looked the same in every episode. She also sounded the same in every episode because her voice was not provided by the costumed actor, but by Hazel Shermit.

NEWHART

October 25, 1982–May 21, 1990.   CBS

Character:	Leslie Vanderkellen
Played by:	Jennifer Holmes
Date(s):	October 25, 1982–October 10, 1983

Replaced by:	Stephanie Vanderkellen
Played by:	Julia Duffy
Date(s):	October 17, 1983–May 21, 1990

Character:	Carl
Played by:	Murray Matheson
Date(s):	October 31, 1983

Replaced by:	Michael Harris
Played by:	Peter Scolari
Date(s):	October 15, 1984–May 21, 1990

Character:	Arthur Vanderkellen
Played by:	Richard Roat
Date(s):	October 24, 1983

Replaced by:	Arthur Vanderkellen
Played by:	Jose Ferrer
Date(s):	February 25, 1985–November 16, 1988

Dick Loudon (Bob Newhart) is an author of "How to" books. His titles include *How to Build Plywood Furniture Anyone Would Be Proud Of* and *101 Uses for Garden Hoses.* His most popular work is *Two Can Carve.* His other passion is history. And in his pursuit of the perfect lifestyle, Dick buys the ultimate fixer-upper, the 200–year-old Stratford Inn, located in River City, Vermont.

He and his beautiful wife, Joanna (Mary Frann), move from New York to Vermont to make a go of the inn. Initially, Dick's beautiful wife was going to be played by Dee Wallace, but she became unavailable.

Assisting with the operation are a rather thick handyman named George Utley (Tom Poston) and a very attractive maid, Leslie Vanderkellen. Poston, who had been a regular on *The Steve Allen Show* from 1956 to 1959, appeared as "the Peeper" in several episodes of *The Bob Newhart Show* during 1975, 1976 and 1977.

Juvenile actor Jason Marin played young George Utley in a flashback triggered by the visit of George's lovable Aunt Bess (Ann Morgan Guilbert) in a *Newhart* episode that aired on May 8, 1989. Ms. Guilbert is best remembered from *The Dick Van Dyke Show* as Laura Petrie's dizzy friend and next-door neighbor, Millie Helper. More than twenty years later, she returned to weekly television as Theresa Fanelli in the short-lived situation comedy, *The Fanelli Boys,* which debuted on NBC from September 8, 1990. It was canceled on February 16, 1991, after only nineteen episodes.

Leslie Vanderkellen, a wealthy but level-headed young lady, was attending nearby Dartmouth College and took a part-time job as the Loudon's maid to see how the other half lived—but only for the first season. She was replaced from the second season on by Julia Duffy, as her wealthy, conceited and self-centered cousin, Stephanie.

The writing and producing team of Billy Van Zandt and Jane Milmore, who produced the special on the lost pilot of *I Love Lucy* (See Entry), worked as story editors on *Newhart* during the show's seventh season (1988/1989). They also wrote several episodes, including "Goonstruck," in which Julia Duffy falls in love with a burly stone mason—Ms. Duffy's personal favorite.

Jane Milmore explained how the decision was made to replace Jennifer Holmes with Julia Duffy: "The story we heard was that it wasn't Jennifer's fault. The character just wasn't structured right,"[1] said Ms. Milmore.

Billy Van Zandt added: "Mary Frann and Jennifer Holmes basically served the same purpose on the show. They were straightmen to set up other people and you could have had one person play both of those roles. Julia guest-starred on the series

---

1. From an exclusive telephone interview with Jane Milmore on January 7, 1991.

and knocked everybody's socks off, and that was purely a fluke. It was just supposed to be another guest-star role. But when she came in, the dynamics were just so great that they wanted to bring her back and make her a permanent part of the show. That's why they wrote out Jennifer. I'm sure it wasn't a very pleasant decision to make."[2]

"It wouldn't really have anything to do with talent," added Ms. Milmore. "It was just the way the character was structured and you can't just all of a sudden make a character become a different person the next day. It just doesn't look good. It wasn't her fault. She was playing a nice sensible girl and it wasn't working."[3]

"One of the problems with doing television is that you don't have a road company to go out on tour and work the kinks out before you get in front of the cameras. The fear with a lot of shows is, yes, you have a hit show and yes, everything is working—except that one element. Now, as the producer, you either sit back and let that weak link become a permanent part of your show, or you fix it? Smart producers fix it,"[4] said Van Zandt.

"Sometimes you can fix it by keeping the character and just doing some work on it. Sometimes you can't,"[5] added Ms. Milmore.

Julia Duffy was introduced in a two-part episode that revolved around Dick being hired to write the kiss-and-tell book of steamy movie star Erica Chase (guest star Stella Stevens).

While Dick and his agent, Elliot (Lee Wilkof), are off in New York meeting with Erica Chase and her agent, John Carson, Stephanie has shown up unexpectedly at the Stratford Inn.

From Stephanie's conversation with Joanna we learn that Leslie has gone to Oxford University, in England, to complete her education, and that Stephanie's recent marriage to Carl didn't work out. Stephanie told Joanna that she knew by the time of the reception that the marriage was over, but she stayed with Carl for the weekend because she didn't want to appear flighty. She admitted that her two-day marriage seemed more like a week.

Her personal troubles were compounded by the fact that her rich parents had thrown her out of their posh home, insisting that she grow up, get a job and learn to face reality, which she tried not to think about.

STEPHANIE: I don't know who's going to hire me? I can't do anything. I don't have any experience. I don't have an education. Sometimes I think the only thing I'm good for is looking at (LONG PAUSE) . . . though that's important.

JOANNA: Well, I admit finding a job won't be easy, but . . .

STEPHANIE: It's going to be impossible . . .

JOANNA: No, it isn't. If worst comes to worst, you can always . . .

STEPHANIE: Can always what?

JOANNA: Well, I was going to say, you could always work here . . . oh, what the heck . . . you've got the job.

STEPHANIE: Really? Doing what?

JOANNA: Well, you could do what Leslie used to do. You could be a maid.

STEPHANIE: (Sarcastically) A maid! Oh boy.

Meanwhile, Stephanie's parents have a change of heart and, in a last-ditch effort to bring their daughter back home, Arthur Vanderkellen (Richard Roat) arrives at the Stratford in his private helicopter. Stephanie stands her ground and declines the invitation to return. They hug as he exits, and he tells his daughter that the gates are always open for her.

The next appearance of Mr. Vanderkellen is on February 25, 1985; from this time on he is played by Jose Ferrer, who made four additional appearances on the series.

We get a look at Stephanie's ex-husband, Carl (Murray Matheson), a silver-haired gentleman, when he turns up in the October 31, 1983 episode to find out why Stephanie left him after only two days.

With the opening of *Newhart*'s third season, which was just about one year later, Peter Scolari joined the cast as Michael Harris, a TV producer at WPIV Channel 8. He had just completed work as Henry "Hildegarde" Desmond on the situation comedy, *Bosom Buddies,* which aired on ABC from November 27, 1980 to August 5, 1982.

Newhart really began to click with the introduction of Scolari, whose chemistry with Julia Duffy was casting made in sitcom heaven. Their long courtship did have its rocky periods and eventually led to a split-up.

Then, in the last episode of the seventh season, Michael, with clipboard in hand, went to the local mall to screen women for a date. His perfect woman was a Stephanie Vanderkellen-clone, Jennifer Allen, played to perfection by Jane Milmore.

And it is because of Michael's date with Jennifer that he was finally moved to propose to Stephanie.

Landing the role as Jennifer was no easy task for Ms. Milmore who had been working on the series all season. In fact, not only did she edit scripts and write episodes she was, from time to time, called upon to fill in for Julia Duffy during script reading sessions when Ms. Duffy was unable to attend.

---

2. From an exclusive telephone interview with Billy Van Zandt on January 7, 1991.
3. From an exclusive telephone interview with Jane Milmore on January 7, 1991.
4. From an exclusive telephone interview with Billy Van Zandt on January 7, 1991.
5. From an exclusive telephone interview with Jane Milmore on January 7, 1991.

Ms. Milmore said that after a while she thought that she was able to do a fair impression of Ms. Duffy's Stephanie characterization, though she was not automatically awarded the role.

In fact, she actually had to pass, not one, but three separate auditions. "There were no special favors and it was very hard to audition for people you already worked with. It was extremely painful,"[6] said Jane Milmore.

Inga Swenson gave Stephanie a run for her money, when she appeared on the February 6, 1989 episode as a former maid of the Stratford Inn.

Before the Stratford was closed for good, the producers managed to create one of the best "final" episodes ever produced. It was nostalgic, and as funny as it was absurd.

In that episode, a Japanese investor, Gedde Watanabe, bought up all the land in town. His plans are to turn the area into a giant golf course. Dick Loudon is the only holdout, but he cannot prevent progress and the golf course goes up anyway—built around the Stratford. Then comes the classic moment: Dick steps out of the front door of the inn and is struck in the head by a golf ball. No, he doesn't die. Better—he wakes up in bed after this nightmare and finds sleeping next to him not Joanna, but a surprise guest star, Suzanne Pleshette, as Emily Hartley, the role she played on the original *The Bob Newhart Show,* which aired on CBS from September 16, 1972 to August 26, 1978.

BOB:	Honey. Honey, wake up. You won't believe the dream I just had. Don't you want to hear about it?
EMILY:	All right Bob, what is it?
BOB:	I was an innkeeper in this crazy little town in Vermont.
EMILY:	I'm happy for you. Good night.

Before turning in, Bob looks over at Emily and, as an afterthought, suggests in his inimitable halting delivery that she should consider wearing more sweaters.

NICK & HILLARY *see:* TATTINGERS

NIGHT COURT

January 4, 1984–May 13, 1992.   NBC

Character:	Court Clerk Lana Wagner
Played by:	Karen Austin
Date(s):	January 4, 1984–September 13, 1984

Replaced by:	Court Clerk Charli Tracy
Played by:	D.D. Howard
Date(s):	March 28, 1984

Replaced by:	Court Clerk Mac Robinson
Played by:	Charles "Charlie" Robinson
Date(s):	September 27, 1984–May 13, 1992

Character:	Liz Williams
Played by:	Paula Kelly
Date(s):	January 4, 1984–July 1984

Replaced by:	Billie Young
Played by:	Ellen Foley
Date(s):	January 4, 1984–unknown

Replaced by:	Mary
Played by:	Deborah Harmon
Date(s):	December 13, 1984

Replaced by:	Christine Sullivan
Played by:	Markie Post
Date(s):	September 26, 1985–May 13, 1992

Character:	Selma Hacker
Played by:	Selma Diamond
Date(s):	January 4, 1984–1985

Replaced by:	Florence Kleiner
Played by:	Florence Halop
Date(s):	September 26, 1985–July 1986

Replaced by:	Roz Russell
Played by:	Marsha Warfield
Date(s):	1986–May 13, 1992

Some series find the perfect mix of characters from the very first episode. On others, it may take a bit of tweaking, and on some, replacements may become necessary due to extenuating circumstances. *Night Court* could be convicted of being guilty on all three accounts.

The original cast of this courtroom situation comedy seemed to work just fine. Then, after some minor changes, it might have been called perfect, but it was forced to replace one of the members of its main ensemble cast not once, but twice, due to death.

The first cast member sentenced to TV's "Phantom Zone" was Karen Austin, who played Lana Wagner; she left the series on September 27, 1984. She was replaced by D.D. Howard as Charli Tracy. The position was finally filled by Charlie Robinson as Mac Robinson. Charlie Robinson came to *Night Court* after playing makeup man Newdell Spriggs on Dabney Coleman's situation comedy, *Buffalo Bill,* which aired on NBC from May 31, 1983 to April 5, 1984. By coincidence, one of Robinson's earlier television roles was in *The Buffalo Soldiers,* a sixty-minute pilot for an NBC Western series in which he played Private Wright. It aired on May 26, 1979. He returned to television as a series regular on November 16, 1992, replacing

6. From an exclusive telephone interview with Jane Milmore on January 7, 1991.

Florence Halop fit perfectly into the tiny court matron's uniform left by Selma Diamond in ''Hello, Goodbye,'' the premiere episode of *Night Court*'s second season, which aired on NBC on Thursday, September 26, 1985.

John Hancock on *Love & War* (See Entry) as Ike Johnson's brother, Abe.

The July 8, 1985 issue of TV Pro-Log reported that "Ellen Foley, a regular on NBC's *Night Court* last season, has left to pursue her recording and singing career after changes were suggested in her series character. Markie Post, who left *The Fall Guy* (See Entry) series (she had been playing the bail bonds-woman), was first announced as a regular in the role of a new defense attorney in *Night Court*, but then that announcement was corrected to announce her as a guest star, with no note as to how many guest appearances she will be making. (It should be noted that performers no longer like the description, 'recurring regulars,' and prefer to be termed 'guest stars,' as what they are doing is playing recurring roles. Everything is a matter of status)."[7]

Surprisingly though, Markie Post was not the second, but the sixth actress to fill, or at least try and fill, the position. In the pilot, Gail Strickland was cast as Sheila Gardner, the public defender. She was replaced by Paula Kelly as Liz Williams. Shelley Hack, of *Charlie's Angels* (See Entry) fame, was said to have filmed some test sequences, but she lasted only three days and her segments never aired.

The producers auditioned twelve actresses for the role of Billie Young and awarded it to Ellen Foley, who most recently had appeared with Debbie Allen and Mimi Kennedy in three episodes of an NBC variety show, *Three Girls Three*, which aired on March 30, June 15 and June 29, 1977. Ms. Foley also had a burgeoning musical career, having appeared with Meat Loaf on his hit single, "Paradise by the Dashboard Light."

Deborah Harmon appeared as the public defender, Mary, in the December 13, 1984 episode, in which the patients from a Willowbrook-like mental institution go to court in order to prove that they have been mistreated. Although she has appeared as various nurses in several episodes of *M*A*S*H* and played Prudence opposite Duncan Regehr, television's future Zorro (See Entry), in the made-for-television movie, *My Wicked, Wicked Ways . . . The Legend of Errol Flynn*, she may be best remembered for her role as Joy in *The Ted Knight Show*, which aired on CBS from April 8 to May 13, 1978.

Markie Post's first appearance on *Night Court* was in the October 4, 1984 episode, "Daddy for the Defense." In it she enters the courtroom and introduces herself to the towering Bull Shannon (Richard Moll):

CHRISTINE: You see, the assigned attorney got sick and they called and told me to fill in. I've worked in Legal Aid for three years and this is the first chance I've gotten to try my own cases. I'm ready.

Christine was noticeably nervous because not only was this her first day in court, but her meddling father (Eugene Roche) has come to watch her. Judge Harry T. Stone (Harry Anderson) tries to help her relax. He tells her that he had a terrible first day in court and then innocently compliments her blouse. This doesn't help and Christine demands, "I don't want to be treated any differently just because I have breasts."

Also in that story, Christine's father insults Judge Stone and is thrown in jail on contempt charges. He is later released when Christine makes him apologize, and she and the judge have a final moment together.

HARRY: You know, I'm sorry that you will not be with us permanently. You are a good attorney.

CHRISTINE: I wish I could stay too. I feel like I could learn here.

Well, a year later she got her wish because that's when Markie Post became a regular member of the *Night Court* cast. The episode opens with Harry interviewing Miss Corlin, a beautiful bailiff (and former actress) who is applying for the job as bailiff, which became vacant about six months earlier due to the death of Selma Hacker. Christine enters the courtroom and reintroduces herself to Dan Fielding (John Larroquette), the assistant district attorney, and asks if he remembers her.

DAN: Of course I do. Mardi Gras, New Orleans, '76, French Quarter. Snake Dance.

CHRISTINE: Christine Sullivan. Legal Aid, Manhattan. I was here a year ago.

DAN: That was my second choice. Well I swear I'll never forget you again as long as I live.

CHRISTINE: You probably won't. I've been assigned here permanently.

Christine, however, is only one of the show's new regulars. The other is the replacement for actress/comedian Selma Diamond, who died on May 14, 1985. Selma Hacker, the caustic court matron, was one of the show's most endearing characters, partly because of the interaction between her and the towering bald-headed bailiff, Bull, played by Richard Moll.

Like Markie Post on her first appearance, Florence Halop was listed as Special Guest Star in the closing credits of the September 26, 1985 episode of *Night Court*. Industry sources reported that she would be making an unspecified number of guest-starring appearances on the program during the 1985/1986 season.

The death of actress Selma Diamond was written into the teleplay, with Selma Hacker passing away instead of just moving away. This gave the characters an opportunity to deal

---

7. *TV Pro-Log: Television Programs and Production News.* TI-Volume 37, No. 46. Television Index Information Services, L.I., New York. Jerry Leichter, Editor and Publisher, July 8, 1985. p. 1.

openly with the loss of one of their family and made for a bittersweet episode.

Bull, who spent the greater part of his day with Selma, lumbers into the courtroom stinking drunk. Harry asks him why he's been drinking and he explains that he was out toasting his best friend, Selma, who was going to be replaced that day by another bailiff. The inebriated Bull then recites a painfully honest poem: "Out with the old, in with the new. Get sick and die and we'll replace you too."

Near the conclusion of the story, when Bull sobers up, Harry tells him, "I don't know why we live and I don't know why we die, but I do know that as long as we're here, we'd better hold on to each other real tight."

The two friends hug warmly, only to be interrupted by a short woman in a bailiff's uniform who looks and sounds an awful lot like Bull's departed friend.

FLORENCE: In case you're interested, the music has stopped.

Harry asks the woman if he can help her and she tells him that she has come for the bailiff's job. Harry explains that there are procedures that must be followed and asks her if she has any references. She says she has none. He then makes the mistake of asking her how long she has been working as a bailiff. Without missing a beat the crackly-voiced woman answers, "One hundred-and-six years."

Looking up at Bull's bald pate, Florence asks, "What's with the hair?" Thinking she's talking about Harry's funny new haircut—which was joked about earlier in the episode—he tells her that he knows what she means but that she shouldn't say anything that might hurt Judge Stone's feelings to which she responds, "You—are a very weird man."

Bull smiles and asks, "Can I keep her, Harry?" Being the sensitive and perceptive person he is, Harry realizes the striking similarities between Florence and Selma, and tells Florence that she's hired.

In the episode's final scene, Bull is seated quietly on the table in the courtroom. Florence comes in and asks him what's wrong. He tells her that he is suffering from a terrible hangover, and she shouts that it serves him right for abusing alcohol.

Bull smiles and tells his new co-worker that Selma used to care enough to yell at him too.

FLORENCE: Tell me, what was this Selma like?

BULL: Well, she was kind of abrasive. She was short and she had a funny voice. [all of qualities possessed by Florence.]

FLORENCE: How pathetic.

Though this is very touching, what was more pathetic was that on July 15, 1986, Florence Halop died. The producers were understandably gun-shy about casting a third actress of the same age to fill this role. They opted for a brash, outspoken, black comedienne and actress, Marsha Warfield, who had been a regular on *The Richard Pryor Show* during 1977.

There was one other semi-regular character replaced on *Night Court,* but it didn't attract very much interest, because the character herself never spoke or was spoken to for the show's first two seasons. The character was the court stenographer, originally played by an older, more matronly woman. Her replacement was Lisette Hocheiser, a pretty, curly-haired blond who was just a little bit off.

Lisette (Joleen Lutz) brought this somewhat dizzy and ditsy stenographer to Judge Harry Stone's courtroom with a host of idiosyncrasies, including a pet goldfish named Orca, a stuffed giraffe named Too Tall, and a lamp named Sparky.

NOT FOR PUBLICATION

May 1, 1951–May 27, 1952.   DuMont

Character:	Collins
Played by:	William Adler
Date(s):	May 1, 1951–August 27, 1951

Replaced by:	Collins
Played by:	Jerome Cowan
Date(s):	December 21, 1951–May 27, 1952

Collins was a big-hearted reporter on the *New York Ledger,* and it is from his point of view that these dramas were written. This fifteen-minute series, which was also known as *Reporter Collins,* first starred William Adler as the reporter.

In December 1951, the program was expanded to a half hour and Adler was replaced by Jerome Cowan, a very prolific actor. Cowan appeared in more than one hundred films during his career, which started in 1936 and spanned more than thirty-five years. It began with his portrayal of O'Roarke in the 1936 Merle Oberon drama, BELOVED ENEMY and continued through the 1960 Jerry Lewis comedy, VISIT TO A SMALL PLANET, in which he played George Abercrombie.

One of the roles for which Jerome Cowan is well-remembered is Miles Archer, Humphrey Bogart's partner in the 1941 classic crime drama, THE MALTESE FALCON. In one of the film's most graphically disturbing scenes, Archer is killed, at the end of Bush Street, by a gunshot that delivers such force that he is literally thrown backward over a barrier.

One of Cowan's lighter roles was as Herbert Wilson on the Walter Brennan situation comedy, *The Tycoon,* which aired on ABC from September 14, 1964 to September 7, 1965.

NURSES

September 14, 1991–June 18, 1994.   NBC

Character:	Greg Vincent
Played by:	Jeff Altman
Date(s):	September 14, 1991–September 12, 1992

Replaced by:	Luke Fitzgerald
Played by:	Markus Flanagan
Date(s):	September 19, 1992–June 18, 1994

Character: Jack Trenton
Played by: David Rasche
Date(s):   September 19, 1992–June 18, 1994

The original diagnosis given to *Nurses* by *TV Guide* in its 1991 "Fall Preview" issue was grim. "If *Nurses* isn't Feverishly Funny, they'll be calling it FLATLINERS II." Still, it had a lot going for it: a good cast headed by comic Jeff Altman (formerly of the 1980 NBC comedy variety show, *Pink Lady*), a good time slot (between *Empty Nest* and *Sisters*), and a producer, Susan Harris, who created *Soap, The Golden Girls* and *Empty Nest*. It also had a very talented pair of supervising producers in the persons of Billy Van Zandt and Jane Milmore. The team had previously worked on *Newhart* (See Entry) and *Anything But Love* (See Entry), and went on to become the executive producers of the outrageous Fox situation comedy, *Martin*.

The premise was simple. Five nurses—four women: Sandy Miller (Stephanie Hodge), Annie Roland (Arnetia Walker), Julie Milbury (Mary Jo Keenen), and Gina Cuevas (Ada Maris), and one man, Greg Vincent (Jeff Altman)—working on the West wing of the third floor of Community Medical Center, in Miami—the same facility Doctor Harry Weston (Richard Mulligan) worked out of on *Empty Nest*. These dedicated professionals were overworked, underpaid and, all too often, unappreciated. But it was their lighthearted camaraderie that got them through the day, as well as the show's first season.

And, as is so often the case, the patient outlived the diagnosis, though it was forced to go through a castectomy at the opening of the second season. The operation, which took place in the second season premiere episode, "Slime and Punishment," was practically painless.

Male nurse, Greg Vincent, was replaced by two new characters. Markus Flanagan as paramedic and loner, Luke Fitzgerald, and David Rasche as Jack Trenton.

The exposition for Markus Flanagan's character took place at the show's opening. Luke Fitzgerald barges into the nurse's lounge where a meeting (he is supposed to be attending) is taking place.

SANDY:	Annie, why doesn't the new guy have to be here for shift report?
LUKE:	(Interrupting the meeting) Hi, you guys done yet?
ANNIE:	I'm tryin' to start.
LUKE:	Wow, timing sucks. Call me when you're done.
ANNIE:	Luke, what makes you think you can just waltz in here whenever you feel like it?
LUKE:	Hey, I said I was going to be late.
ANNIE:	You didn't call this mornin'.
LUKE:	No, the day I started I told you I was just generally goin' to be late.

But Luke is not a slacker, he was actually in the hospital doing rounds two hours before his regular shift was due to start. The slacker was Jack Trenton, the slick venture capitalist convicted of insider trading, bribery and fraud, and sentenced to 8,000 hours of community service.

Actor David Rasche is best known to television viewers as Detective Inspector Sledge Hammer from the offbeat detective sitcom, *Sledge Hammer,* which aired on ABC from September 23, 1986 to June 30, 1988.

O

THE ODD COUPLE

September 24, 1970–July 4, 1975.   ABC
October 29, 1982–June 9, 1983

Character:	Felix Unger
Played by:	Tony Randall
Date(s):	September 24, 1970–July 4, 1975

Replaced by:	Felix Unger
Played by:	Ron Glass
Date(s):	October 29, 1982–June 9, 1983

Character:	Oscar Madison
Played by:	Jack Klugman
Date(s):	September 24, 1970–July 4, 1975

Replaced by:	Oscar Madison
Played by:	Demond Wilson
Date(s):	October 29, 1982–June 9, 1983

Character:	Officer Murray Greshner
Played by:	Al Molinaro
Date(s):	September 24, 1970–July 4, 1975

Replaced by:	Officer Murray Greshner
Played by:	John Schuck
Date(s):	October 29, 1982–June 9, 1983

Replaced by:	Officer Murray Greshner
Played by:	Jerry Adler
Date(s):	September 24, 1993 (*The Odd Couple: Together Again. CBS*)

Character:	Myrna Turner
Played by:	Penny Marshall
Date(s):	September 22, 1972–July 4, 1975
	September 24, 1993 (*The Odd Couple: Together Again. CBS*)

Replaced by:	Maria
Played by:	Liz Torres
Date(s):	October 29, 1982–June 9, 1983

Character:	Gloria Unger
Played by:	Janis Hansen
Date(s):	1971–July 4, 1975

Replaced by:	Frances Unger
Played by:	Telma Hopkins
Date(s):	October 29, 1982–June 9, 1983

Replaced by:	Gloria Unger
Played by:	Barbara Barrie
Date(s):	September 24, 1993 (*The Odd Couple: Together Again. CBS*)

Character:	Leonard Unger
Played by:	Leif Garrett
Date(s):	September 26, 1974

Replaced by:	Leonard Unger
Played by:	Willie Aames
Date(s):	Fall 1971

Character:	Edna Unger
Played by:	Pamelyn Ferdin
Date(s):	December 17, 1971

Replaced by:	Edna Unger
Played by:	Doney Oatman
Date(s):	unknown–July 4, 1975

Replaced by:	Edna Francis Unger
Played by:	Toni Kalem
Date(s)	September 24, 1993 (*The Odd Couple: Together Again. CBS*)

Character:	Dr. Melnitz
Played by:	Bill Quinn
Date(s):	October 29, 1970–unknown

Replaced by:	Dr. Nancy Cunningham
Played by:	Joan Hotchkis
Date(s):	1970–1972

Character: Speed
Played by: Gary Walberg
Date(s):   September 24, 1970–July 4, 1975

Replaced by: Speed
Played by: Christopher Joy
Date(s):   October 29, 1982–June 9, 1983

Character: Roy
Played by: Ryan McDonald
Date(s):   1970–1971

Replaced by: Roy
Played by: Bart Braverman
Date(s):   October 29, 1982–June 9, 1983

Replaced by: Roy
Played by: Dick Van Patten
Date(s)   September 24, 1993 (*The Odd Couple: Together Again.* CBS)

Character: Vinnie
Played by: Larry Gelman
Date(s):   September 24, 1970–July 4, 1975

Replaced by: Vinnie
Played by: Marvin Braverman
Date(s):   October 29, 1982–June 9, 1983

Character: Cecily Pigeon
Played by: Monica Evans
Date(s):   September 24, 1970–July 4, 1975

Replaced by: Cecily Pigeon
Played by: Sheila Anderson
Date(s):   October 29, 1982–June 9, 1983

Character: Gwendolyn Pigeon
Played by: Carole Shelley
Date(s):   September 24, 1970–July 4, 1975

Replaced by: Gwendolyn Pigeon
Played by: Ronalda Douglas
Date(s):   October 29, 1982–June 9, 1983

Character: Oscar's mother
Played by: Elvia Allman
Date(s):   unknown

Replaced by: Oscar's mother
Played by: Fran Ryan
Date(s):   unknown

Character: Mimi Greshner
Played by: Jane Dulo
Date(s):   unknown

Replaced by: Mimi Greshner
Played by: Alice Ghostley
Date(s):   November 1970

Sometimes a good thing on Broadway becomes a good thing in motion pictures, then becomes a good thing on television. This time it was Neil Simon's 1965 Broadway play, which asks the question: "Can two divorced men share an apartment without driving each other crazy?"

The Broadway run of *The Odd Couple* starred Walter Matthau as *New York Herald* sportswriter Oscar Madison and Art Carney as his fastidious television news-writer roommate. When Carney took time off, Paul Dooley filled in for him. Ultimately, Jack Klugman replaced Walter Matthau after Matthau left the play in 1966. He also spent a year in London, where his portrayal of Oscar Madison won him several British acting awards. Back in Las Vegas, Nevada, Mickey Rooney said, "Hey kids, let's put on a play," and Tony Randall took him up on it. Rooney played the sportswriter and Randall became Felix Unger.

By 1968, Doc Simon was ready to take his play to the large screen. He cast his Broadway star Walter Matthau as Oscar and Jack Lemmon as Felix, and the film won him an Academy Award nomination for best screenplay.

The next logical stop for this property was television. With at least six different actors and nine different combinations to choose from, it was Jack Klugman and Tony Randall who became television's odd couple. There are, of course, many factors that went into this casting decision. It may even have had something to do with the fact that as costumed actors they had appeared together as opponents pitted against Captain Video and his Video Rangers. One never knows. What one does know is that these two men accepted the roles and stayed with the series for all 114 episodes. Their supporting players were headed up by Al Molinaro, cast as Murray the cop. There was apparently no attempt to match the look of Murray in the film, as played by the tall and balding Herb Edelman. TV's Murray was overweight and had a big nose. In fact, it was his nose that was responsible for one of the series' funniest moments, and it happened by accident.

" 'During rehearsals I was waiting to make my entrance,' Molinaro recounts, 'and Tony and Jack were having problems with the scene and I was behind the door saying, "For God's sake, Tony, let's go." I'm yelling through the peephole and I'm sticking my nose through there, popping that little door open. Garry Marshall [the producer] is standing there watching, and he says, "Wait a minute! We've got to rewrite the scene. Al doesn't come in at all. He just sticks his nose through the door".' "[1]

That scene ran in the episode in which Felix had Oscar sequestered in their apartment so that he could concentrate on writing his book. When there was a knock at the door Oscar

1. Pollock, Bruce. "The Minute that Makes a Career." *TV Guide,* July 25, 1981, pp. 12–15.

asked Felix who it was. Then, without a word being spoken, Molinaro poked his protruding proboscis into the apartment's peephole door. The door popped open and the audience split their sides laughing at the sight of it.

Luck was with Molinaro and he was out of work for only a very short time after *The Odd Couple* went out of production. On Garry Marshall's other hit series, *Happy Days* (See Entry), Pat Morita, who had played the owner of Arnold's, had just left. Marshall acted quickly and wrote Molinaro in as Alfred Delvecchio, the new owner of Arnold's.

Officer Greshner's often talked about but infrequently-seen wife, Mimi, was played by both Jane Dulo and Alice Ghostley. The latter had played Esmerelda on *Bewitched* (See Entry) and replaced Aunt Bee on *The Andy Griffith Show* (See Entry).

There were several other infrequently seen characters on *The Odd Couple* who were played by more than one actor.

While Oscar's marriage was childless, Felix and Gloria Unger had a boy, Leonard, and a girl, Edna. Leonard was initially played by juvenile actor Leif Garrett, who starred as Endy Karras in the CBS drama, *Three for the Road*. The short-lived series, which starred Alex Rocco as his widowed father Pete, aired from September 14 to November 30, 1975. Garrett, who was a contemporary of Shaun Cassidy's, entered the recording arena for a short time, but his potential as a teenage idol was never fully realized.

The second young man to play the younger Unger was Willie Aames, who had a more successful career. His biggest score came when he played Tommy Bradford on the ABC family-oriented dramatic comedy, *Eight Is Enough*. He also played Buddy Lembeck, the only other member of the situation comedy *Charles in Charge* to remain with the series, when it moved from the CBS network to first-run syndication.

Leonard's sister, Edna, was played by two young actresses. The first, Pamelyn Ferdin, was the voice of Lucy Van Pelt in the CBS animated specials, *It Was a Short Summer, Charlie Brown* and *Play it Again, Charlie Brown*. Both aired on CBS, the first on September 27, 1969 and the second on March 28, 1971. Six years later she enlisted in the CBS Saturday morning live-action series, *Space Academy,* where she appeared as Cadet Laura Gentry from September 10, 1977, to September 8, 1979.

Her replacement on *The Odd Couple* was seen in several unsuccessful pilots. Ms. Oatman played Julie McCain in the ABC drama, *Delta County U.S.A.* She also appeared in a pilot for an NBC series called *Full House,* in which she played Susan Campbell. The pilot aired on August 2, 1976 and was in no way connected to the successful sitcom of the same name that premiered on ABC on September 22, 1987.

Being the neurotic hypochondriac that Felix is, the most important member of his extended family was his doctor. His name was Dr. Melnitz, a crusty practitioner who, somewhat begrudgingly, still made house calls. Felix first rang the doctor on October 29, 1970, to help Oscar with his severe stomach pains, which Melnitz diagnosed as the beginnings of an ulcer. As Felix showed the doctor out of the apartment, Melnitz stopped and said, "Oh, and one other thing. I won't make another house call unless he cleans his room."

The episode concludes with Dr. Melnitz offering Felix and Oscar one more piece of advice: "I want you to both promise me . . . that if this trouble ever occurs again . . . you won't waste

a minute . . . that you'll pick up the phone . . . and call another doctor." True to character, Felix ignored the doctor's advice and called him on several other occasions.

For six years prior to his work as Dr. Melnitz on *The Odd Couple,* Bill Quinn poured the drinks as Sweeney the bartender on *The Rifleman.* He spent six more years, from 1978 to 1983, sitting on the other side of the bar for his recurring role as the blind curmudgeon, Mr. Van Ranseleer, one of the regulars at Kelsey's Bar on *All in the Family.*

The doctor who covered for Dr. Melnitz was an attractive physician by the name of Nancy Cunningham. It goes without saying that Felix wanted only Dr. Melnitz, but when Dr. Cunningham arrived, Oscar wanted only her. Dr. Cunningham, Nancy to Oscar, became their new physician, although Dr. Melnitz was often referred to.

When you're a writer for a newspaper, there has to be an editor over you. On the *Daily Planet,* Clark Kent had Perry White and on *The New York Herald,* Oscar Madison had William Donnoley. Bill Donnoley was played by *Get Smart*'s (See Entry) Chief of CONTROL, Edward Platt.

Felix loses Oscar's job for him by forcing him to quit after his request for a raise is denied. Oscar then goes to work for a sophisticated *Playboy*-type magazine named *Harem.* John Astin turned in a memorable performance with his wonderful characterization of Oscar's Hugh "Heff" Hefner-type boss, Beau "Buffy" Buffington. Astin, who is best remembered as Gomez Addams from *The Addams Family,* later navigated the ill-fated series *Operation Petticoat* (See Entry) for one season.

Every boy has to have a mother and in *The Odd Couple,* Oscar had two of them. Elvia Allman, the first actress to play Mrs. Madison, had years before played the first of three Cora Dithers on the situation comedy, *Blondie* (See Entry). The other actress to admit to being Oscar Madison's mom was Fran Ryan, who had played the second Doris Ziffel on the rural sitcom, *Green Acres* (See Entry).

Still, *The Odd Couple* did prove that not every actor is expendable. This was accomplished by the hiring of Monica Evans and Carole Shelley, the British actresses who had played the Pigeon sisters on Broadway and in the 1968 motion picture.

In 1975, DePatie-Freleng, that wonderful animation studio that brought us *The Pink Panther,* adapted Neil Simon's characters for a Saturday morning cartoon, *The Oddball Couple.*

Oscar became a slob of a pooch named Fleabag and Felix a fastidious feline named Spiffy, both of whom were magazine writers. Their secretary, the Myrna Turner of the pet set, was Goldie Hound. A total of sixteen half-hour programs was produced featuring the voices of Paul Winchell as Fleabag, Frank Nelson as Spiffy, and Joan Gerber as Goldie. The series aired on ABC from September 6, 1975 to September 3, 1977, before it was scratched from the schedule.

The real significance of *The Odd Couple* lies not in the minor changes in cast that have already been discussed, but in the reasons why the producers, Garry Marshall in particular, felt compelled to take a series that was well-cast, well-acted, well-written and generally well-directed and well-produced, and try to do it again using many of the original scripts, but with a completely new cast. Please understand, the second cast, many of whom were black actors and actresses, did their best to pull off something that they knew was going to be compared yell-for-yell and honk-for-honk with its predecessor, which was and is still running successfully in syndication around the country.

The part of Felix was given to Ron Glass, who was so good as the literate and well-spoken Detective Ron Harris on the police precinct sitcom *Barney Miller,* which aired on ABC from January 23, 1975 to September 9, 1982. Oscar Madison was played by Demond Wilson, who robbed the Bunkers with Cleavon Little on the October 9, 1971 episode of *All in the Family,* "Edith Writes a Song." Wilson later stole America's funny bone as the hard-working son of the junk tycoon of Watts, Fred G. Sanford, on the runaway hit situation comedy, *Sanford and Son* (See Entry).

Other members of the cast included Liz Torres as Oscar's secretary, Maria, replacing Penny Marshall, Laverne of *Laverne and Shirley,* who had played opposite Jack Klugman as his secretary, Myrna Turner. Ms. Torres was another graduate from *All in the Family,* where she played Teresa Betancourt from 1976 to 1977. She also replaced Barbara Colby as Julie Erskine on Cloris Leachman's situation comedy, *Phyllis* (See Entry).

Felix's wife, who had been Gloria during the seventies, was now named Frances and was played by Telma Hopkins, who had played Jessie Ashton on *A New Kind of Family* (See Entry).

One of the few white actors in the series was John Schuck, who replaced Fred Gwynne as Herman Munster on *The Munsters* (See Entry), and now replaced Al Molinaro as Officer Murray Greshner. Another was Billy Van Zandt. "On *The New Odd Couple* I was Felix's photography lab assistant. It was supposed to be a recurring role, but I don't remember 'recurring.' I think I only 'curred.' I appeared in one episode of the show before it got killed. I played a jerky Jerry Lewis-type character. This, however, was not replacing a role seen on the original series. I believe the character's name was John—named after John Tracy, the director of that episode.

"I remember that it aired on New Year's Eve [December 31, 1982], so that no one could watch it because they'd be out of the house. That's how bad it was," said Van Zandt.

"At one point during the rehearsal Ron Glass and Demond Wilson, with scripts in front of them, accidentally juxtaposed who was reading whose role and they kept doing the scene. And at one point, Demond Wilson just stopped and said to the writers, 'Excuse me. I think we have a little trouble here. If we can't tell the difference between our two characters, how is the audience supposed to? I don't think you've done enough work.' "[2]

In his book, *Blacks in American Films and Television,* author Donald Bogle, one of today's foremost experts on blacks in American popular culture, wrote, "Although Glass gave the show some professional spit-and-polish, the material itself was never adapted to a black milieu with a new black point of view that might have made the series—and its characters—fresh and appealing. One never senses a black community from which these men have come or in which they now live. Consequently, the old criticism of so many black sitcoms applied: it does strike one as a white show done in blackface. Still it wasn't *that* bad of a series."[3]

"*The Odd Couple* will be back, starring Jack Klugman and Tony Randall. Howard Koch is the executive producer for Paramount Television. Karl Kleinschmidt and Garry Marshall are the writers." That entry was published in the June 1989 issue of *Ross Reports Television,* but the project was put on hold when Klugman underwent throat cancer surgery that resulted in the removal of one of his vocal cords.

Marilyn Beck and Stacy Jenel Smith, in the October 30, 1990 edition of *The Star-Ledger,* wrote: "Producer Howard W. Koch, who had to scrap plans for a *The Odd Couple* TV reunion movie with Klugman and Tony Randall because of Jack's physical condition, reveals the project is back on. 'He's coming along just great—and we expect to see the project come to fruition in early '91.' "

Well, it did happen, but not until late '93. The project *The Odd Couple: Together Again* reunited the cast of the hit series for the wedding of Felix's daughter—sorta. Back in the lead roles were Tony Randall and Jack Klugman as Felix Unger and Oscar Madison. Penny Marshall returned as Oscar's secretary, Myrna and Gary Walberg as their poker playing buddy, Speed—but everyone else had been recast! Dick Van Patten, who is best loved for his role as TV dad, Tom Bradford from the ABC dramatic comedy, *Eight is Enough,* showed up at the poker game as Roy. Gloria Unger was played by Barbara Barrie, whose past television roles include Elizabeth Miller on *Barney Miller* and Aunt Margo on *Double Trouble,* which aired on NBC from April 4, 1984 to August 21, 1985. The adult Edna Unger was played by Toni Kalem.

Most disappointing, however, was the absence of Al Molinaro as Murray the cop. For this reunion movie the producers cast Jerry Adler as Officer Greshner.

The made-for-television movie opened with the same clips and narration that has become ingrained on the minds of television audiences: "On November thirteenth, Felix Unger was asked to remove himself from his place of residence . . . that request, came from his wife." To bring the story and viewers up to date, the narration was extended: ". . . Can two divorced men live in the same apartment without driving each other crazy? Yes, and no. For five wonderful turbulent years they lived together. It was many things, but never dull. But this too came to an end. Felix did return to his ex-wife Gloria. They remarried—a day Oscar Madison declared to be the 'happiest of his life.' How ironic that the wedding of Felix's daughter was destined to bring them together again."

ONE DAY AT A TIME

December 16, 1975–September 2, 1984.   CBS

Character:	David Kane
Played by:	Richard Masur
Date(s):	December 16, 1975–1976

2. From an exclusive telephone interview with Billy Van Zandt on January 7, 1991.
3. Bogle, Donald. *Blacks in American Film and Television, an Illustrated Encyclopedia.* Garland Publishing, Inc. New York, 1988, p. 294.

Replaced by: Nick Hendris
Played by: Ron Rifkin
Date(s): November 23, 1980–1981

Character: Annie Horvath
Played by: J.C. Dilley
Date(s): 1983–1984

Replaced by: Annie Horvath
Played by: R.C. Dilley
Date(s): 1983–1984

Replaced by: Annie Horvath
Played by: Paige Maloney
Date(s): 1983–1984

Replaced by: Annie Horvath
Played by: Lauren Maloney
Date(s): 1983–1984

This is yet another situation comedy cranked out by the successful producer of such ground-breaking series as *All in the Family, The Jeffersons* and *Sanford and Son*. And after the others, this story of a thirty-four-year-old divorcee raising two children hardly raised an eyebrow. But, like its cousins, it did manage to raise a few consciences about divorce and women's rights during its successful nine-year run.

The vulnerable woman around whom the series was based was Ann Romano, played by Bonnie Franklin. Her two daughters, Barbara and Julie Cooper (who kept their father's last name), were played by MacKenzie Phillips and Valerie Bertinelli. MacKenzie's papa, John Phillips, was the Papa of the popular rock group, the Mamas and the Papas. MacKenzie has been around show business all of her life.

Valerie was the daughter of an executive at General Motors, and her most visible television role prior to her work on the series was as the cute kid in the Nestlé's hot cocoa commercials. That cute kid, eventually grew into a beautiful young woman who went on to star in a great many television movies. Then, on March 21, 1990, Ms. Bertinelli, emerged as private eye, Sydney Kells, in her very own CBS comedy series, *Sydney,* which ended its short run on August 6, that same year. Valerie Bertinelli returned three years later in her third television series, *Café Americain,* which premiered on NBC on September 18, 1993.

Ms. Phillips didn't have it so easy; she was fired from the series during its 1978/1979 season, largely because drugs and alcohol had taken over her life. Her dismissal from the series was explained by having Julie and her new husband, Max Horvath (Michael Lembeck), move to Houston, where Max had been offered a new job with the airline that had recently laid him off.

Yes, MacKenzie Phillips was written out of *One Day at a Time,* but she was not forgotten—or replaced. With her drug problem in check, she and Michael Lembeck returned to the series on November 8, 1981, and the following fall, Julie gave birth to a daughter, Annie, who was played by two sets of twins.

At the start of the series, Ann Romano was dating David Kane (Richard Masur), who had just completed work as

Clifford Ainsley, the manager on Norman Lear's short-lived sitcom, *Hot l Baltimore,* which aired on ABC from January 24 to June 6, 1975.

The relationship between Ann and David heated up to the point where it looked as though they would be married, which was almost the case. In a two-part episode that aired during the fall of 1976, Ann called off their wedding and David moved out of her life and the series. This was really no surprise; it was just too early in the series to alter the formula by having Ann get remarried.

In fact, Ann didn't get romantically involved again for four years until Nick Hendris, played by Ron Rifkin, was introduced as her new advertising partner. The business relationship soon turned into a full-blown romance, but Nick was tragically killed off in an automobile accident in 1983. The series died the following year, but is still going strong in syndication. For two years following his untimely death, Ron Rifkin appeared as Dr. Lantry on the CBS evening opera, *Falcon Crest.*

OPERATION PETTICOAT

September 17, 1977–August 10, 1979.   ABC

Character: Lieutenant Commander Matthew Sherman
Played by: John Astin
Date(s): September 17, 1977–August 25, 1978

Replaced by: Lieutenant Commander Sam Haller
Played by: Robert Hogan
Date(s): September 25, 1978–August 3, 1979

Character: Lieutenant Nick Holden
Played by: Richard Gilliland
Date(s): September 17, 1977–August 25, 1978

Replaced by: Lieutenant Michael "Mike" Bender
Played by: Randolph Mantooth
Date(s): September 25, 1978–August 3, 1979

The inspiration for this unsuccessful television series was an extremely successful motion picture of the same name, which earned an Academy Award nomination for its screenplay and earned Cary Grant a boatload of money. OPERATION PETTICOAT, was released in 1959 and starred Cary Grant as Admiral Matt Sherman and Tony Curtis as Lieutenant Nick Holden.

Translated to the small screen, the pink submarine, the U.S. Sea Tiger, was piloted by John Astin who had once played the Riddler on *Batman* (See Entry), but was most famous as the lovable lunatic, Gomez Addams, on the popular series based on the cartoons of Charles Addams, *The Addams Family.*

Prior to that he co-starred with Marty Ingels in the situation comedy, *I'm Dickens . . . He's Fenster.* He was Harry Dickens, Ingels was Arch Fenster. The series aired on ABC from September 28, 1962 to September 13, 1963. Astin, who was at one time married to actress Patty Duke, appeared in dozens of roles—usually as an eccentric—on episodic television, including once on *The Odd Couple* (See Entry).

The Captain's second in command, Lieutenant Nick Holden, was played by Richard Gilliland, who had played Sergeant Steve DiMaggio on *McMillan and Wife* from 1976 to 1977.

When the series failed to commandeer a respectable audience, it was taken off the air after only twenty-two episodes, recast and put back on the air one month later with Robert Hogan as the Sea Tiger's new commanding officer, Lieutenant Commander Haller. Hogan had been Sergeant Ted Coopersmith on the NBC detective series, *Richie Brockelman, Private Eye*, which aired from March 17 to August 24, 1978.

Haller's exec/nuisance was Lieutenant Mike Bender, played by Randolph Mantooth, who also happened to be a graduate of *Detective School*, where he played Eddie Dawkins. Mantooth is also remembered for his long-running role of Paramedic John Cage, on Jack Webb's dramatic series, *Emergency*, which aired on NBC from January 22, 1972 to September 3, 1977.

The only two members of the original crew who were not reassigned were Lieutenant Dolores Crandall and Seaman Broom. Broom (Melinda Naud) went on to play Maggie Ferguson on *Detective School* when she was discharged from this series in 1979. Rubber-faced comic actor Jim Varney who had appeared as Virgil Sims on the syndicated talk show parody, *Fernwood 2–Night*, gained national recognition in a series of commercials that turned his fictitious friend, Vern, into a household name. Many people still think Varney *is* Vern, but that's about as dumb as his character Ernest P. Worrell, who noses right up to the wide-angle lens and shouts, ''Hey, Vern!''

As unbelievable as it might seem, Varney went on to star as Ernest in several motion pictures including ERNEST GOES TO CAMP, released in 1987, and ERNEST SAVES CHRISTMAS, released in 1988. That same year Varney brought his character to Saturday morning TV in a Pee-wee Herman-type children's program, appropriately titled, *Hey, Vern, It's Ernest!*, which premiered on CBS at eleven a.m. on Saturday, September 24th. In 1993, Jim Varney stepped into a new character, Jed Clampett, in the big screen version of *The Beverly Hillbillies*.

There is no fair way to compare the Sea Tiger's first crew with its second. Therefore, what follows are the names of the crews/cast members—unsung heroes all—who gave their acting careers to make this series a success:

Serving under Lieutenant Commander Matthew Sherman were Major Edna Hayward, Yvonne Wilder; Lieutenant Ruth Colfax, Dorrie Thompson; Lieutenant Claire Reid, Bond Gideon; Yeoman Alvin Hunkle, Richard Brestoff; Ensign Stovall, Christopher J. Brown; Seaman Dooley, Kraig Cassity; Chief Herbert Molumphrey, Wayne Long; Seaman Gossett, Michael Mazes; Chief Tostin, Jack Murdock; Seaman Horwich, Peter Schuck; Lieutenant Watson, Raymond Singer; Seaman Williams, Richard Marion; Seaman Ramone Gallardo, Jesse Dizon; and Corporal Maurice Milgrim, James Ray.

Captain Haller's crew included Lieutenant Katherine O'Hara, Jo Ann Pflug; Lieutenant Betty Wheeler, Hilary Thompson; Chief Stanley Dobritch, Warren Berlinger; Yeoman Alvin Hunkle, Richard Brestoff; Lieutenant Travis Kern, Sam Chew, Jr.; Seaman Horner, Don Sparks; Seaman Doplos, Fred Kareman; Chief Manhiannini, Martin Azarow; and Seaman Kostos, Peter Mamakos.

The change in crew did the show no good and the series continued to sink in the ratings. With only nine new episodes aired, ABC put *The New Operation Petticoat* in permanent dry dock.

OUR MISS BROOKS

October 3, 1952–September 21, 1956.   CBS

Character:	Mr. Philip Boynton
Played by:	Robert Rockwell
Date(s):	October 3, 1952–September 30, 1955
Replaced by:	Gene Talbot
Played by:	Gene Barry
Date(s):	December 20, 1955–September 21, 1956
Character:	Mrs. Nestor
Played by:	Nana Bryant
Date(s):	1955
Replaced by:	Mrs. Nestor
Played by:	Isabel Randolph
Date(s):	1955–1956
Character:	Martha Conklin
Played by:	Virginia Gordon
Date(s):	1952–1953
Replaced by:	Martha Conklin
Played by:	Paula Winslow
Date(s):	1953–1956

If there was ever any doubt in anyone's mind as to who the quintessential school teacher is, it is Eve Arden, who began her role as Miss Constance ''Connie'' Brooks on radio in 1948, continued through a long-running television series and followed with a 1956 motion picture. But her tenure didn't end there. In the 1978 Robert Stigwood/Alan Carr musical, GREASE, Eve Arden is promoted to the role of Rydell High's Principal McGee.

The principal back at Madison High, Osgood Conklin, was played by Gale Gordon, and this was the role which prevented him from becoming Fred Mertz on *I Love Lucy* (See Entry). Incidentally, the first actress to play Mrs. Conklin on *Our Miss Brooks* was Gale Gordon's real-life wife, Virginia Gordon.

Our Miss Brooks, however, was interested in much more than being Madison's English teacher. What she aspired to was to become Madison's biology teacher's wife.

The part of the shy and perhaps thick-headed man of science was played by Jeff Chandler on radio. It was rumored that when the role was being cast for television, Chandler was advised by the producers to pursue a movie career, basically because they didn't feel he had the right ''look'' for television. Fortunately, he did have the right look for motion pictures and starred in more than forty films between 1947 and 1961.

The actor selected to portray Mr. Boynton on the small

screen was Robert Rockwell, who was not only handsome, but also had a beautifully resonant speaking voice.

Rockwell's early work in B films gained him very little recognition and he turned to television in the early 1950s. His first four recorded roles on the small screen were in episodes of *The Lone Ranger*.

In 1951 Robert Rockwell earned his place in television's hall of fame by playing Superman's Krytonian father, Jor-El, in the "Superman on Earth" episode of the *Adventures of Superman*. Trivia buffs will be interested to learn that Rockwell played this role outfitted in Buster Crabbe's old costume from the FLASH GORDON serials.

Soap opera fans will recognize Robert Rockwell as Dr. Greg Hartford, a role he played on *Search for Tomorrow* from 1977 to 1978.

Even though Miss Brooks never lost interest in Mr. Boynton, viewers began to lose interest in the series. To spruce things up some major changes were introduced at the beginning of the 1955/1956 season. First, Madison High School was demolished to make way for a new superhighway. Second, Mr. Conklin and Miss Brooks joined the staff of Mrs. Nestor's Private Elementary School, as principal and dramatics teacher, respectively.

The school was always run by a Mrs. Nestor, the first one being played by Nana Bryant. The second Mrs. Nestor, Isabel Randolph was introduced as the first Mrs. Nestor's sister-in-law.

Mr. Boynton was left in the lurch and was replaced by not one, but three suitors. They differed from Boynton in that they were the aggressors in the little game of romance.

The first, a confirmed bachelor by the name of Mr. Munsey, was played by Bob Sweeney, the same actor who had played Liz Cooper's first next-door neighbor, Gillman Cobb, on the CBS situation comedy, *My Favorite Husband* (See Entry). Mr. Munsey was replaced by the school's athletic director, Clint Albright, played by William Ching. Albright's romantic overtures were displaced by those of the Maharajah of Boongadddy, who was played by actor/director producer Hy Averback, the narrator and the producer of the syndicated version of *Meet Corliss Archer*. Finally, there was the rather handsome gym teacher with the good physique, Gene Talbot. Talbot was played by the debonair Gene Barry, who had made a name for himself as Dr. Clayton Forrester in the superb 1953 adaptation of H.G. Wells' science fiction masterpiece, THE WAR OF THE WORLDS, which also featured Robert Rockwell in a minor role as the Ranger.

On television, Gene Barry gained fame as the man who wore a cane and derby hat, "they called him Bat, Bat Masterson." The popular Western aired a total of 108 episodes on NBC between October 8, 1958 and September 21, 1961. Two years later, Gene Barry exchanged his derby and cane for a chauffeured limousine when he took on the role of Amos Burke, the multimillionaire police captain on *Burke's Law* (See Entry), which employed Hy Averback as one of its directors. *Burke's Law* ran on ABC from September 20, 1963 to August 31, 1965.

Still, none of these suitors suited Miss Brooks. They didn't suit the television audience either. So Robert Rockwell's Mr. Boynton character was reintroduced at midseason. Romantically, not much happened between the two, however, and the

series went out of production and into reruns, while a feature film opened in the theaters.

All of the regulars recreated their roles for what could be considered the final episode of *Our Miss Brooks*, in which Brooks and Boynton consummated their relationship by finally tying the knot.

Our Miss Arden later starred as Eve Hubbard in the NBC situation comedy, *The Mothers-in-Law*, and recreated her role as Principal McGee in GREASE 2, which was released in 1982.

Robert Rockwell continues to appear in commercials and on episodic television. During 1990 he was cast as a handsome, white-haired granddad in a series of long-running television commercials for Werther's Original candies. He still looked and sounded great, but that didn't make it any easier to think of Jor-El as someone's grandfather.

Isabel Randolph, the second of the two actresses to portray Mrs. Nestor, had played Mrs. Boone to both Mr. Boones on the CBS situation comedy, *Meet Millie*.

OUT OF THIS WORLD

September 1987–1991.   NBC-Syndicated

Character:	Beano Froelich
Played by:	Joe Alasky
Date(s):	September 1987–September 1990

Replaced by:	Mick
Played by:	Tom Nolan
Date(s):	September 1990–June 1991

"Would You Like to Swing on a Star?" was the song used as the theme of this first-run syndicated sitcom that began its life on NBC during the pre-prime-time half-hour. It was one of five different shows that aired from 7:30 p.m. to 8:00 p.m. over each of the five NBC-owned stations to win back some of the audience lost to the highly successful game show, *Wheel of Fortune*. The other four shows were *Marblehead Manor, She's the Sheriff, You Can't Take It With You* and *We Got It Made*.

It seems apparent that *Out of This World* borrowed its concept from the ABC science fiction series, *Starman* (September 19, 1986– September 4, 1987), in which an alien, played by Robert Hays, returns to earth fourteen years later to help raise the son he had fathered.

In *Out of This World*, the half-human/half-alien child was Evie Garland (Maureen Flannagan), a thirteen-year-old girl who had developed the extraterrestrial ability to "freeze" time. In a departure from the ABC series, Evie's dad (a native of the planet Antares) never assumed human form; he was only seen as a flashing light and heard as a disembodied voice emanating from a crystalline cube that Evie kept on her night table.

Evie's mom, Donna, was played by Donna Pescow, who had played Angie Falco Benson from February 8, 1979 to October 2, 1980 in the ABC situation comedy, *Angie*.

Joe Alasky appeared on the series in the recurring role of Donna's brother, Beano, the owner of a diet clinic. When Beano was said to be away on business, he was replaced by Tom Nolan as Donna's other brother, Mick, a musician. One of Tom

Nolan's earlier television credits was the role of Officer Hubbell in the short-lived Lindsay Wagner police drama, *Jessie*, which ran on ABC from September 18 to November 13, 1984.

Also appearing as a recurring regular on *Out of This World* was Doug McClure, who had gained fame as Trampas in the NBC Western, *The Virginian*, and may be known to science fiction fans for his role as David Innes in the 1976 film, AT THE EARTH'S CORE.

THE OUTLAWS

September 29, 1960–September 13, 1962.   NBC

Character:	U.S. Marshal Frank Caine
Played by:	Barton MacLane
Date(s):	September 29, 1960–June 22, 1961

Replaced by:	Marshal Will Forman
Played by:	Don Collier
Date(s):	October 5, 1961–September 13, 1962

Character:	Deputy Marshal Will Forman
Played by:	Don Collier
Date(s):	September 29, 1960–June 22, 1961

Replaced by:	Deputy Marshal Chalk Breeson
Played by:	Bruce Yarnell
Date(s):	October 5, 1961–September 13, 1962

The first season of this Western, which was set in the town of Stillwater, Oklahoma during the 1890s, allowed viewers to experience the Old West from the outlaw's point of view.

On the side of justice was United States Marshal Frank Caine and his Deputy, Will Forman. The marshal was played by Barton MacLane, who later joined the United States Air Force for his role as General Martin Peterson on *I Dream of Jeannie* (See Entry). His deputy, Will Forman, was played by Don Collier, who later played Sam Butler on *The High Chaparral*, which aired on NBC from September 10, 1967 to September 10, 1971.

The scenario for this series did a complete flip-flop at the beginning of the second season, and now presented the stories from the lawman's perspective.

To maintain continuity and avoid having to cast a new Marshal to replace Caine, the writers juggled their existing cast and promoted his former deputy, Will Forman, to full marshal. This change in status made Don Collier Barton MacLane's replacement as the new marshal, and he took on his own deputy, Chalk Breeson, played by Bruce Yarnell.

OWEN MARSHALL, COUNSELOR AT LAW

September 16, 1971–August 24, 1974.   ABC

Character:	Jess Brandon
Played by:	Lee Majors
Date(s):	September 16, 1971–January 26, 1974

Replaced by:	Ted Warrick
Played by:	David Soul
Date(s):	February 2, 1974–April 6, 1974

Replaced by:	Danny Paterno
Played by:	Reni Santoni
Date(s):	October 3, 1973–April 6, 1974

Canadian-born actor Arthur Hill starred in the title role of the Santa Barbara, California defense attorney who differed from typical television lawyers not only in that he was older than most, but also because he showed more compassion than many of his contemporaries.

Like many established attorneys, Marshall didn't go it alone; he always had a young law partner at his side. The difficulty is in trying to figure out which one at what time.

While one source says that Danny (Reni Santoni) became Owen Marshall's assistant during the last season, another states that it was David Soul who appeared on the series during its third season.

This much is known: Lee Majors, the actor who played Marshall's first young law partner, Jess Brandon, went on to star as Colonel Steve Austin in the ABC science fiction adventure series, *The Six Million Dollar Man*. Since this new series premiered on January 18, 1974, there were several weeks during which Majors was working on both series simultaneously. The end result was that the last two *Owen Marshall, Counselor at Law* episodes Majors filmed, were aired during the same weeks as the first two episodes of his new series, *The Six Million Dollar Man*.

The attorney-turned-cyborg spoke about his displeasure with his role on *Owen Marshall, Counselor at Law* in an article by Bill Davidson that appeared in the May 18, 1974 issue of *TV Guide*.

"One of the things that bothered me about that show is that I'm a country boy from Kentucky and never really learned to tie a necktie. Also, I like action, staying in shape, and all the exercise I ever got was walking from the counsel table to the judge's bench in the courtroom on Sound Stage 27."

David Soul's first appearance as Ted Warrick on *Owen Marshall, Counselor at Law* was highlighted in the February 2, 1974 issue of *TV Guide*. "The battle over defining obscenity is waged in 'A Foreigner Among Us,' starring Rick Nelson as a bookstore owner [Vic] and Darren McGavin as the small-town mayor [McClain] who wants to censor his inventory. David Soul joins the cast as Owen's colleague, Ted Warrick."

Even though it is certain that David Soul joined the cast as a regular at this time, he had made an earlier guest appearance, as a character named Doug in the November 9, 1972 episode, "Love Child," which starred Patty Duke as Lois.

Among David Soul's early roles on television was Makora, one of the innocent inhabitants of Gamma Trianguli VI on the *Star Trek* episode, "The Apple," which aired on October 13, 1967. David Soul went on to greater fame one year after *Owen Marshall, Counselor at Law* when he became Detective Ken "Hutch" Hutchinson on ABC's hit police series, *Starsky and Hutch*, which aired from September 3, 1975 to August 21, 1979.

Because sources differ, it cannot be positively determined whether or not David Soul was replaced by Reni Santoni, as Danny Paterno, but it appears that Danny was around to help out.

P

PARKER LEWIS CAN'T LOSE

September 2, 1990–September 27, 1992.   FOX

Character:	Judy Lewis (Parker's mom)
Played by:	Annie Bloom
Date(s):	September 2, 1990–August 4, 1991

Replaced by:	Judy Lewis (Parker's mom)
Played by:	Mary Ellen Trainor
Date(s):	August 11, 1991–September 27, 1992

With his portrayal of Ferris Bueller in John Hughes' 1986 comedy, Matthew Broderick began a trend that would spawn two television series and last into the 1990s.

The 1986 motion picture, FERRIS BUELLER'S DAY OFF, starred Broderick as a well-off teenager living in one of Chicago's upper-crust suburbs, whose popularity, charm and good looks allowed him to get away with murder—figuratively, of course. He talks directly to the camera and tells the audience that what he really needs is a day off from school. So, for the balance of the film's 103 minutes, Bueller (whose first name is reminiscent of an amusement park ride) takes his best friend Cameron Frye (Alan Ruck) and his girlfriend, Sloane Peterson (Mia Sara), on a pleasure cruise in Cameron's dad's prize possession, a classic 1961 red Ferrari 250 GT convertible.

NBC, which secured the rights to the film's characters, premiered *Ferris Bueller* with Charlie Schlatter in the driver's seat on Monday, September 17, 1990. In the show's opening scene Schlatter, talking to the camera, says (as he pulls a life-size cardboard cutout of Matthew Broderick out of his closet), "Come on, Matthew Broderick as me? No way. he's too white bread. Two dimensional. Too, too, tootsie good-bye." Schlatter then proceeds to saw off Broderick's head with a chain saw, after which he delivers what may very well be the most important line ever spoken on the magic box: "This is television—this is real."

Real or not, *Ferris Bueller* didn't last very long on television, ending its run on December 23, 1990. *Parker Lewis,* on the other hand, has.

Who's Parker Lewis? Just the title character of Fox net-work's shameless knock-off of *Ferris Bueller,* described in *TV Guide*'s 1990 Fall Preview issue: "If you had to go through high school again—what a thought—you'd want to be Parker Lewis. Well, actually, you might want to be Ferris Bueller, but he's playing on another network. Let's start again. If you had to go through high school as a Ferris Bueller clone, you'd want to be Parker Lewis (Corin Nemec)."[1]

Two very minor supporting roles in this fast-paced sitcom were Parker's parents. Parker's dad, Martin Lewis, which sounds like the name of an old comedy team, has from the very start been played by Timothy Stack. His wife, Judy, originally played by Annie Bloom, lost her job during the second season and was replaced by Mary Ellen Trainor—categorically proving that only Parker Lewis can't lose.

THE PARTRIDGE FAMILY

September 25, 1970–August 31, 1974.   ABC

Character:	Christopher "Chris" Partridge
Played by:	Jeremy Gelbwaks
Date(s):	September 25, 1970–1971

Replaced by:	Christopher "Chris" Partridge
Played by:	Brian Forster
Date(s):	September 17, 1971–August 31, 1974

Character:	Walter Renfrew
Played by:	Ray Bolger
Date(s):	October 9, 1970–Fall 1972

Replaced by:	Walter Renfrew
Played by:	Jackie Coogan
Date(s):	December 8, 1973

Character:	Snake
Played by:	Rob Reiner
Date(s):	January 6, 1971

---

1. *TV Guide.* "Fall Preview," Vol. 38, No. 37, September 15, 1990, Issue #1955, p. 27.

Replaced by: Snake
Played by: Stuart Margolin
Date(s):   October 13, 1972

The undisputed king of the teen idols of the early 1970s was David Cassidy, whose face graced the covers of more teen magazines and posters, and whose voice played from more radios than just about any other teenage idol up to that time.

He inherited his boyish good looks from his strikingly handsome father, Jack Cassidy, and his mother Evelyn Ward, both talented actors and singers.

The role that made David famous was Keith Partridge, the oldest kid in the family singing sensation, *The Partridge Family* that included his mom Shirley, his sister Laurie, his brother Danny, his younger sister Tracy, and his youngest brother Chris. The Partridges were said to have been based on The Cowsills, the singing family from the sixties who hit it big with their cover of the title song from the enormously successful Broadway musical, *Hair*.

Keith Partridge's television mother, Shirley, was, in fact, his real-life stepmother, Shirley Jones, an accomplished performer with many credits to her name, including the role of Marion Paroo in the 1962 musical, THE MUSIC MAN.

Keith's sister, Laurie, was played by Susan Dey, who enjoyed a renewed popularity as the strikingly beautiful Deputy District Attorney, Grace Van Owen, on *L.A. Law* (See Entry).

Danny Bonaduce, who played their younger brother Danny, later became a popular disc jockey in the Philadelphia market, and Suzanne Crough, who played Tracy Partridge, appeared as Stevie Friedman in the 1977 dramatic comedy, *Mulligan's Stew,* which aired on NBC from October 25 to December 13.

The youngest of the Partridge Family boys was Christopher, who was played by two juvenile actors. The first, Jeremy Gelbwaks, dropped out of sight after he dropped out of the series. The second actor to play young Chris, Brian Forster, joined the cast at the beginning of the second season and lent his voice to two animated series that also featured the other Partridge kids doing their own voices. These were *Goober and the Ghost Chasers,* which aired on ABC from September 8, 1973 to August 31, 1975, and *Partridge Family: 2200 A.D.,* which aired on CBS from September 7, 1974 to March 9, 1975.

Although Keith Partridge did not appear in the ABC series, he was present in the CBS version. The only difference was that his voice sounded more like Chuck McLennan and his mom's sounded like Sherry Alberoni. But, that is probably because those are the actors who did them.

On the original series, Shirley's father, Walter Renfrew, was played by two of Hollywood's great character actors, Ray Bolger and Jackie Coogan. Bolger has already achieved immortality as the Scarecrow in the 1939 classic, THE WIZARD OF OZ, while his replacement, Jackie Coogan, who starred in the title role of Charlie Chaplin's 1921 feature, THE KID, will forever be remembered by television audiences as Uncle Fester from *The Addams Family*. Ray Bolger appeared as Shirley's father in three episodes of *The Partridge Family;* while Jackie Coogan only played Renfrew once. He did, however, appear as an agent on the December 8, 1973 episode in which Danny wanted to become a comedian.

In *The Partridge Family* episode, "A Man Called Snake,"

Rob Reiner was introduced as the local motorcycle-riding hoodlum, Snake—who else? A few years later, Rob Reiner became a household name when he assumed the role of Archie Bunker's "meatheaded" son-in-law, Mike Stivic, on Norman Lear's landmark situation comedy, *All in the Family*.

As a result of Reiner's commitment to *All in the Family* he was unable to repeat the role of Snake. The second actor to pull up on the motorcycle was Stuart Margolin, who had appeared as an inmate in the November 27, 1970 episode, "Go Directly to Jail." In that episode Margolin arranged for the Partridges to perform at the prison.

Even though Margolin continued to get steady work in television, he never achieved the degree of fame or instant recognition that Reiner did. In 1976 Stuart Margolin starred as Rabbi David Small in the pilot film for NBC's *Lannigan's Rabbi,* but lost out to Bruce Solomon for the series role. TV viewers who do recognize Margolin most often refer to him as the guy who was in all of those blackout segments on *Love American Style,* which aired on ABC from September 29, 1969 to January 11, 1974.

THE PATTY DUKE SHOW

September 18, 1963–August 31, 1966.   ABC

Character: Sue Ellen Turner
Played by: Kitty Sullivan
Date(s):   1963–1965

Replaced by: Gloria
Played by: Kelly Wood
Date(s):   1964–1965

Character: J.R. Castle
Played by: John McGiver
Date(s):   1963–1964

Replaced by: William Smithers
Played by: Ralph Bell
Date(s):   later episodes

Character: T.J. Blodgett
Played by: Alan Bruce
Date(s):   unknown

Replaced by: T.J. Blodgett
Played by: Robert Carson
Date(s):   unknown

Character: Monica Robinson
Played by: Laura Barton
Date(s):   unknown

Replaced by: Monica Robinson
Played by: Kathy Garver
Date(s):   unknown

"Only in the last year have I begun to look at it with any fondness." These were the words of Patty Duke that *Entertainment Weekly* columnist Mark Harris quoted in his November 2, 1990 article, "Patty Dukes It Out."

It is reassuring to learn that Anna Duke is now able to join so many of us who have always looked upon her work on *The Patty Duke Show* with great fondness.

That you know who Patty Duke is goes without saying. You might, however, like to know who Rita McLaughlin is. If you can't place her face, it is probably because you never got to see it. As a matter of fact, all you ever saw was the back of her head whenever Patty spoke to Cathy and Cathy spoke to Patty, because she was the actress who helped to make us believe that Patty and Cathy were cousins—identical cousins.

In her 1987 best-selling autobiography, *Call Me Anna*, written with Kenneth Turan, Patty Duke wrote, "Although the directors may have changed frequently, the cast remained steady." She was, of course, referring to the main cast, which included her father, Martin "Poppo" Lane (William Schallert); her mother, Natalie (Jean Byron); her brother Ross (Paul O'Keefe); and her long-suffering boyfriend, Richard Harrison, who was always played by Eddie Applegate.

There were, however, four members of the supporting cast who did change, yet very few of them went on to any great success in television, although there were a few gemstones hidden among the quartz.

Martin Lane's first employer, J.R. Castle, was played by John McGiver, who appeared in three series following *The Patty Duke Show*. The most famous of these was the superhero spoof, *Mr. Terrific,* in which McGiver played Barton J. Reed, the subchief for the Bureau of Special Projects—in short, the man responsible for Mr. Terrific.

The good-looking young waiter at Leslie's Ice Cream Parlor, Louie, was played by Bobby Diamond, who as a youngster starred as Joey Newton on *Fury.*

The second actress to play Patty's friend, Monica Robinson, is best remembered as Buffy and Jody's older sister, Cissy, on *Family Affair.*

And if you watch *The Patty Duke Show* very closely for Mr. Castle's secretary, Miss Gordon, you ought to recognize Phyllis Coates, the very first of television's Lois Lanes in the *Adventures of Superman* (See Entry).

Executive producer Sheldon Pinchuk, with Patty Duke-Pearce as co-producer, brought Ms. Duke's life to network television on November 11, 1990, in a blatantly honest adaptation of her autobiography, *Call Me Anna.*

In that two-hour made-for-television movie, Jenny Robinson portrayed Ms. Duke-Pearce during the period she was involved with *The Patty Duke Show.* As a youth, she was played by Ari Meyers; as an adult, she played herself.

PEE-WEE'S PLAYHOUSE

September 13, 1986–August 3, 1991.   CBS

Character:	King Cartoon
Played by:	Gilbert Lewis
Date(s):	September 13, 1986–unknown
Replaced by:	King of Cartoons
Played by:	William Marshall
Date(s):	unknown

Pee Wee Jenkins was Joey's best friend on *Fury* (See Entry). Pee Wee Russell, was a Jazz musician born in 1906 who played clarinet with Eddie Condon. Pee Wee King wrote *The Tennessee Waltz,* and in the 1934 Laurel and Hardy classic, MARCH OF THE WOODEN SOLDIERS, Stannie Dum (Stan Laurel) loses one of his Pee Wees. But the character to which that childish moniker will forever belong is Pee-wee Herman, the concoction of Paul Rubenfeld, the talented comedian and writer from Peekskill, New York who now goes by the professional name of Paul Reubens.

Reubens first introduced his child-like character during a stint with a West Coast improvisational group, the Groundlings, and gained national recognition with a sixty-minute cable special, *The Pee-wee Herman Show,* which aired on HBO on September 11, 1981. Set in Pee-wee's Playhouse, this bitingly funny satire that was meant to spoof 1950s children's programs turned out to be the basis for his later Saturday morning series.

In 1985, before taking over Saturday mornings, Reubens brought his character to the big screen in an improbable motion picture, PEE-WEE'S BIG ADVENTURE. The big surprise in Pee-wee's big adventure was that it made big bucks—thirty-five million to be exact. Not bad for a film that cost around six million to make.

The following fall, Pee-wee Herman opened his Playhouse on CBS and demonstrated his leadership role in innovating programming, including an eclectic mixture of live action, puppetry, stop-motion animation, claymation, great music and a smidgen of special effects thrown in to complement simple creative scripts.

The thing that makes *Pee-wee's Playhouse* such a fun place to visit is all of the interesting characters: Miss Yvonne, the girl with the biggest hair; Conky 2000, the robot; Jambi the genie; Chairry, the chair; Globey, the globe; Floory, the floor; Clockey, the clock; Pterri, the Pterodactyl and . . . well, you get the picture.

One of the highpoints in each of these thirty minutes of madness and mayhem is a visit by the King of Cartoons, who brought with him a 1930s vintage Merrie Melodies animated short which he shows after introducing it in a grand manner: "Ladies and gentleman, boys and girls . . . let the cartoon begin."

These wonderful examples of animation, whose original running times were from nine to twelve minutes, were edited to run about two minutes. Thankfully, with the introduction of the series' fifth season in 1990, the time allotted for these glimpses of celluloid gold was often expanded to allow the cartoon to run at nearly its full length.

The first actor to play King Cartoon was Gilbert Lewis, who had played Spanish Harry in the violent 1973 crime film, GORDON'S WAR. *New York Times* columnist Howard Thompson wrote, "This is a worthy film, whose format and substance—a black theme dramatized for practical, constructive purposes—remain exceeded by its goal."

The second actor to wear the crown of Cartoons was William

Marshall, a polished actor with a booming baritone voice, who had played another king, King Dick, in the 1952 Dale Robinson/Anne Francis film, LYDIA BAILEY.

To many, he is the perfect Othello, the role he played in the *Omnibus* series during the 1950s. Because of his dignified presence, wonderful control of the English language and deep rich voice, William Marshall fared admirably in the the title role in the 1972 blaxploitation horror film, BLACKULA.

William Marshall has appeared on episodes of *Rawhide, Bonanza* and *Tarzan.* He also played Judge Marcus T. Block in all six episodes of the crime series, *Rosetti and Ryan,* which aired on NBC between September 22 and November 10, 1977.

In addition to these credits, William Marshall may be best remembered for his role as Dr. Richard Daystrom, the designer of the multitronic computer unit, M-5, which he tested aboard the Starship Enterprise on the March 8, 1968 episode, "The Ultimate Computer." Interestingly enough, this episode happens to be one of the favorite episodes of actor James "Scotty" Doohan.

It should also be noted that with the introduction of William Marshall as the King, the screen credit was changed from "King Cartoon" to "King of Cartoons."

PERRY MASON

September 21, 1957–May 22, 1966.   CBS
September 16, 1973–January 20, 1974   CBS
December 1, 1985–November 29, 1993   NBC

Character:	Perry Mason
Played by:	Raymond Burr
Date(s):	September 21, 1957–May 22, 1966
	December 1, 1985–November 29, 1993
Replaced by:	Perry Mason
Played by:	Monte Markham
Date(s):	September 16, 1973–January 20, 1974
Character:	Della Street
Played by:	Barbara Hale
Date(s):	September 21, 1957–May 22, 1966
	December 1, 1985–November 29, 1993
Replaced by:	Della Street
Played by:	Sharon Acker
Date(s):	September 16, 1973–January 20, 1974
Character:	Paul Drake
Played by:	William Hopper
Date(s):	September 16, 1973–May 22, 1966
Replaced by:	Paul Drake
Played by:	Albert Stratton
Date(s):	September 16, 1973–January 20, 1974

Character:	Paul Drake, Jr.
Played by:	William Katt
Date(s):	December 1, 1985–May 15, 1988
Replaced by:	Ken Malansky
Played by:	William R. Moses
Date(s):	February 12, 1989–November 29, 1993
	December 1, 1985–November 29, 1993
Character:	Gertie Lade
Played by:	Connie Cezon
Date(s):	September 21, 1957–May 22, 1966
Replaced by:	Gertrude "Gertie" Lade
Played by:	Brett Somers
Date(s):	September 16, 1973
Character:	Hamilton Burger
Played by:	William Talman
Date(s):	September 16, 1973–May 22, 1966
Replaced by:	Hamilton Burger
Played by:	Harry Guardino
Date(s):	September 16, 1973–January 20, 1974
Character:	Lieutenant Arthur Tragg
Played by:	Ray Collins
Date(s):	September 21, 1957–May 13, 1965
Replaced by:	Lieutenant Steve Drumm
Played by:	Richard Anderson
Date(s):	September 12, 1965–May 22, 1966
Replaced by:	Lieutenant Arthur Tragg
Played by:	Dane Clark
Date(s):	September 16, 1973–January 20, 1974

Ladies and gentlemen of the jury, picture if you will, Fred MacMurray as Perry Mason. "Impossible," you say? Then you concur with *Perry Mason*'s creator, Erle Stanley Gardner, who couldn't picture MacMurray as Mason either and passed him up in favor of Raymond Burr. Just imagine if Fred MacMurray had gotten the role as Mason, what Burr would have been like as Steve Douglas on *My Three Sons!*

Two other recognizable actors who were also auditioned for the role were Richard Carlson and Efrem Zimbalist, Jr. William Hopper also read for the role of Perry Mason, but instead of being sent away with the others, he was hired as Perry's leg man, Paul Drake. One source even says that Hopper, who was the son of actress and gossip columnist Hedda Hopper, had already been signed for the role of Mason, but traded parts with Raymond Burr shortly before production was to begin.

The character of Perry Mason was not a new one; he had in fact been around for quite some time. He was created by Erle Stanley Gardner, an attorney turned novelist, who published his first Perry Mason novel, *The Case of the Velvet Claws* in 1933. Most of the ingredients were present save Perry Mason's trademark courtroom scene; this didn't appear until the following year in *The Case of the Sulky Girl.*

But Gardner and the producers had more to go on than just characters on paper—Perry Mason had already appeared on radio and in six motion pictures.

Moviegoers became familiar with Warren William as Perry Mason in four features: THE CASE OF THE HOWLING DOG, 1934; THE CASE OF THE CURIOUS BRIDE, 1935; THE CASE OF THE LUCKY LEGS, 1935; and THE CASE OF THE VELVET CLAWS, 1936. Ricardo Cortez took over as Mason in the 1937 entry, THE CASE OF THE BLACK CAT. It was Donald Woods who played Perry Mason in the 1937 feature, THE CASE OF THE STUTTERING BISHOP, which turned out to be the last in the series.

For twelve years, from the late 1930s and early 1940s, radio listeners got to know John Larkin as the brilliant defense attorney.

The actor finally selected for the part on television was Raymond Burr, who went to read for the part of District Attorney Hamilton Burger. This was because Burr had more often played heavies than heroes in films. He played the greedy ivory hunter Vargo in the 1953 jungle adventure, TARZAN AND THE SHE-DEVIL, and Lars Thorwald in Alfred Hitchcock's suspenseful 1954 thriller, REAR WINDOW.

In 1956, Raymond Burr, starred as American newspaperman Steve Martin in scenes that were inserted in the American version of Japan's GODZILLA, KING OF THE MONSTERS. Burr reprised his role for the sequel, GODZILLA 1985.

Raymond Burr did, however, have one outstanding legal credit to his name: he had played Marlow, the prosecuting attorney in the 1951 Academy Award-winning drama, A PLACE IN THE SUN.

Even with the fine ensemble cast of players, audiences tuned in each week to see Perry Mason defend those who had been wrongly accused; but there were at least five occasions on which Raymond Burr did not even appear on the series.

The first three occasions were in 1963 when Burr was unable to work during his convalescence from minor surgery. Another actor was not brought in to play Mason, but there were guest stars who appeared in the role of the attorney in these episodes.

Bette Davis starred in the January 31, 1963 episode, "The Case of the Constant Doyle." "The Case of the Two-Faced Turnabout," which aired on February 14, 1963, featured Hugh O'Brian. The third actor to fill in for Raymond Burr was Walter Pidgeon, who appeared in the February 28, 1963 episode, "The Case of the Surplus Suitor."

More than a year and a half later, Michael Connors, who as Mike Connors became television detective Joe Mannix, played counselor Joe Kelly in "The Case of the Bullied Bowler," which aired on November 5, 1964.

The last guest star to substitute for the missing Mason was Barry Sullivan in "The Case of the Thermal Thief," which aired on January 14, 1965. "I remember I fought it, I didn't want to do it. Because I didn't think anybody else *should* do it. Because I loved Raymond [Burr] in that role," said Sullivan.

He went on to say why Raymond Burr wasn't available. "I

think he had some dental work done that was giving him a problem, that's my recollection," Sullivan recalled.

"I was living down at Malibu, it was the summertime, and I didn't want to drive into town. I had rented a house down there for the summer and I just hated the whole goddamn business and decided to take a little time off because I had been working my ass off. It was a hot summer and I just wanted to go down to the beach. I said to the producers 'Nobody should do it but Raymond Burr. Why don't you shut down for a week or two until he's ready to go?'" explained Sullivan.

The producers, however, didn't take Sullivan's advice and coaxed him into doing the episode, which "Was one of those scripts they rewrote in a hurry,"[2] he concluded.

Perry's loyal secretary, Della Street, was always played by Barbara Hale on the long-running television series. Earlier in her career she had played Miss Brand in the 1949 anti-war drama, THE BOY WITH THE GREEN HAIR. That same year she co-starred as Ellen Clark, the nurse Jolson (Larry Parks) falls in love with in JOLSON SINGS AGAIN. Barbara Hale worked with another of the screen's famous detectives when she played dancing star Peggy Callahan in THE FALCON IN HOLLYWOOD. This film, released in 1944, was the eighth in a series of sixteen FALCON features.

In the courtroom, "the enemy" was Hamilton Burger, the District Attorney played by William Talman; following his work on *Perry Mason,* he appeared in episodes of *Have Gun—Will Travel, Gunsmoke* and *The Wild Wild West.*

He may have starred as Boss J.W. "Big Jim" Gettys in Orson Welles' crowning achievement, the 1941 biographical drama, CITIZEN KANE, but Ray Collins is no doubt best remembered for his portrayal of Lieutenant Tragg on *Perry Mason.* Collins died on July 11, 1965, and was replaced at the beginning of the eighth season by Richard Anderson as Lieutenant Steve Drumm.

Richard Anderson is well-known to television audiences as Oscar Goldman from the science fiction adventure series, *The Six Million Dollar Man* (January 18, 1974–March 6, 1978; ABC) and *The Bionic Woman* (January 14, 1976–September 2, 1978; ABC/NBC). He later appeared as Braddock in the first Perry Mason telefilm, *Perry Mason Returns.*

He had dealt with futuristic topics and technologies some eighteen years earlier in the landmark science fiction film, FORBIDDEN PLANET. In that film Anderson played Chief Quinn, the Scotty-like engineer who was murdered by the invisible Id. Though Quinn's body was graphically described as having been plastered all over the communications room of the C57–D, the audiences of 1956 were spared a visual depiction of the carnage.

Sometimes a character in a television series is ever-present but infrequently seen. In *Perry Mason* it was Mason's receptionist and switchboard operator, Gertie Lade. But when she was seen, she was played by Connie Cezon.

In 1965 Raymond Burr was interviewed by Dwight Whitney for an article that appeared in the April 28 issue of *TV Guide.* In that article Burr spoke about his determination to stick with *Perry Mason* for a ninth season because he wanted the series to

2. From an exclusive telephone interview with Barry Sullivan on February 15, 1991.

end on a high note. This philosophy was permeated by his dissatisfaction with the convoluted scripts produced during the show's eighth season. Reflecting on Burr's commitment to the role of Perry Mason, Whitney prophetically wrote, "I could visualize Burr waiting for that 'great year' to go out on until Perry Mason was defending cases from a wheelchair—which at his current rate may not be too far away." The journalist wasn't far off; less than two years later, that is precisely what Raymond Burr was doing on *Ironside* (See Entry).

The last case Raymond Burr handled as Perry Mason on CBS was "The Case of the Final Fade-Out," which fittingly featured Erle Stanley Gardner in a guest-starring role as the judge.

An attempt was made in 1973 to revive the series as *The New Adventures of Perry Mason,* with a completely new cast headed by Monte Markham in the title role. He was backed-up by Sharon Acker as Della Street, Albert Stratton as Paul Drake, Dane Clark as Lieutenant Arthur Tragg, and Harry Guardino as Hamilton Burger.

Dane Clark was one of two actors to play Legal Aid attorney, Richard Adams on *Justice* (See Entry).

The producers even expanded the role of Mason's receptionist, Gertrude. She was played by Jack Klugman's wife, Brett Somers, who had a recurring role as Blanche Madison on *The Odd Couple* (See Entry).

But even with this high-caliber cast, the series never caught on. This can be attributed to the lack of chemistry among the players and the indelible memory left by the original cast.

The idea of new *Perry Mason* episodes was still very appealing, but it wasn't until 1985 that the right formula was put together. In fact, it might have been called *Classic Perry Mason* because it starred the only two actors who could make it work—Raymond Burr and Barbara Hale.

The man responsible for putting it together was Fred Silverman, as was explained by his business partner, Dean Hargrove: "He had already talked to Raymond [Burr] and had discussed the idea with NBC. He then asked me if I would write the two-hour movie, which I did, and that's how it began," said Hargrove.

There was, however, one small glitch. William Hopper, the actor who had played Paul Drake, the third member of the Perry Mason team, had died on March 6, 1970.

Dean Hargrove explained how he handled the situation. "Since there were only two members of the original cast who could return, I devised the character of Paul Drake, Jr. We cast Bill [William] Katt in the role, because I wanted to give the movie some suspense and some action, which is what Bill brought to it." Hargrove went on to deny that nepotism played any part in Katt's receiving the role.

"That was completely coincidental. I'd always been a fan of Bill's and as I sat down to devise the character, I thought this would be perfect for Bill Katt. I didn't even know at that time that Barbara [Hale] was his mother," Hargrove explained.[3]

The listing in *TV Guide* trumpeted the first of these made-for-television movies.

" 'Perry Mason Returns'—and so does Raymond Burr, as Erle Stanley Gardner's redoubtable criminal lawyer, a role he played on TV from 1957 to 1966. In this 1985 TV-movie, Mason gives up a judgeship to defend his former secretary Della Street (Barbara Hale, who played Della in the series), who's facing a murder charge. Hale's son William Katt plays private eye Paul Drake Jr. Additional Cast—Paula Gordon: Holland Taylor; Braddock: Richard Anderson; Kathryn Gordon: Kerrie Keane; David Gordon: David McIlwraith; Bobby Lynch: James Kidnie; Prosecutor: Cassie Yates."[4]

William Katt was introduced as private investigator Paul Drake Jr. in a scene that takes place in a local jazz club. Drake is playing the saxophone on stage. Perry Mason is seated in the audience.

After the number, Drake spots Mason and leaves the stage to join his friend at his table, but winds up getting cross-examined by the prominent attorney.

MASON: Hello Paul.

DRAKE: How are ya?

MASON: Good. Yourself?

DRAKE: Good. Good. I talked to Della, she seems to be doing okay. I already talked to a contact of mine downtown and I think I can get into the property and sneak a look at the evidence. Might take a little finagling, but I think I can do it.

MASON: You play here often?

DRAKE: I sit in with these guys now and then and, uh, let off a little steam. Make 'em sound good. Do we have a date for the preliminary hearing yet?

MASON: Not yet. How's the Drake Detective Agency these days?

DRAKE: A little bit more my style than my father's but, uh, I'm doin' fine.

MASON: How many operatives do you have?

DRAKE: One.

MASON: One besides yourself?

DRAKE: No, just one . . . me.

---

3. From an exclusive telephone interview with Dean Hargrove on March 25, 1991.
4. *TV Guide.* November 30, 1985, Vol. 33, No. 48, Issue #1705.

MASON: What happened to the others?

DRAKE: I decided to reduce the overhead.

MASON: Last time I saw you, you were working on a novel. How's it coming?

DRAKE: I'm about half way through—give or take a chapter.

MASON: That's what you said last time I saw you.

DRAKE: Why am I getting the third degree here?

MASON: Because we're talking about Della's life. I need an experienced investigator. (To the waitress) Check, please.

DRAKE: I'll get it. I am an experienced investigator.

MASON: Paul, I worked with your father many years. I've known you all your life. I know you're smart and I'm sure you're good. But I don't know if you're ready for this one. Sorry to be blunt, it's the way I feel.

Mason gets up and leaves. Drake hurriedly pays the check and dashes outside to catch Mason.

DRAKE: (Shouting to stop him) Perry! Hey, come on, I like to play the sax now and then—Sherlock Holmes had a violin. I liked to write, so did Dashiell Hammett. All I'm saying is, I run my life and my business to suit me. But I am quite capable. And my lifestyle might not click with you, but Della means too much to me. I'm not taking no for an answer. I'm working this case.

MASON: Meet me tomorrow. Eleven a.m., your office. Be on time. (Mason drives away.)

In Drake's office Paul tells Mason that he doesn't need to be filled in on the case because he went downtown that morning, made copies of the police report and an itemized copy of the physical evidence being held in "Property."

Mason asks Drake to run down some leads and when he leaves the room, Mason remarks to Della.

MASON: Hope I'm doing the right thing with him.

STREET: I'm the one who should be concerned, and I'm

not. You'll see.

Later, following another meeting between Mason, Drake and Street, Della compliments Drake on his investigation.

STREET: Nice work, Paul.

DRAKE: Thank you, Della. (Drake leaves)

STREET: (To Mason) You didn't think so?

MASON: Think what?

STREET: That it was nice work.

MASON: Oh, yes.

STREET: You didn't mention it.

MASON: He's still on the case, isn't he?

Of course, at the end of the program Mason acknowledges Drake's work and makes friends with him as the three principals get into Drake's jeep.

MASON: (To Drake) Ah, before I forget—nice work.

DRAKE: (To Mason) You too.

Drake laughs and the three of them drive off to the haunting strains of the theme music by Richard Shores and Fred Steiner, paving the way for twenty more *Perry Mason* television movies.

William Katt appeared as Paul Drake, Jr. in a total of nine *Perry Mason* movies-of-the-week before calling it quits, as Dean Hargrove explained.

"Bill had other things that he wanted to do for his own career. One of the things he left to do was *Top of the Hill,* a series he did for Steven J. Cannell and that took him out of the *Perry Mason* series. So we were required to devise another character to replace him.

"We had cast Billy [William R.] Moses in *Perry Mason: The Case of the Lethal Lesson* and established his character, Ken Malanski, as a law student, with an eye toward his becoming a replacement for Paul Drake." [5]

Perry Mason: The Case of the Lethal Lesson aired on February 12, 1989, and featured William R. Moses as a law student accused of killing one of his classmates—which he didn't.

William R. Moses went on to appear as Ken Malansky in

_____

5. From an exclusive telephone interview with Dean Hargrove on March 25, 1991.

seventeen of the twenty-six *Perry Mason* telefilms since Perry proved his innocence.

Starting on December 4, 1981 and ending in 1986, Moses played Cole Gioberti on the CBS evening soap opera, *Falcon Crest.*

Incidentally, William Katt has been upholding justice ever since he played Ralph Hinkley on the superhero spoof, *The Greatest American Hero,* which aired on ABC from March 18, 1981 to February 3, 1983.

On the evening of Monday, November 29, 1993, beginning precisely at nine p.m., Raymond Burr tried his last case as Perry Mason on the NBC network as touted in the show's teaser: "For thirty-five years, he's thrilled you with the greatest mysteries. Tonight daytime's biggest stars join Raymond Burr in his final performance as Perry Mason . . . The Master of mystery in his unforgettable final case . . . And now, Perry Mason's last case."

"The Case of the Killer Kiss" revolved around the cast and crew of *Mile High,* a fictitious daytime serial taped at B and B studios where series heartthrob, Mark Stratton (Sean Kanan) died of anaphylactic shock leading to total cardiac arrest from an allergic reaction set off by a walnut oil-based lipstick worn by his leading lady Charlotte Grant (Krista Tesreau).

Also appearing in this final outing were *General Hospital*'s Genie Francis as Kris Buckner and Stuart Damon as Alex Straub; *Another World*'s Linda Dano as Sandra Drake; *Days of Our Lives*' Arleen Sorkin as Peg Ferman and *The Young and the Restless*' Michael Tylo as producer Evan King. Two years earlier Michael Tylo was co-starring as Luis Ramon, the first of two Alcaldes in the Family Channel's *Zorro* (See Entry).

Mr. Burr, who had lost his battle with kidney cancer, on September 12, 1993, did, however, receive a favorable review from *TV Guide* for this, his final performce: "*Perry Mason: The Case of the Killer Kiss* is formulaic, Raymond Burr's last film turns out to be one of the better entries in the Mason series." Eighteen days later, NBC aired *A Perry Mason Mystery: The Case of the Wicked Wives,* starring Paul Sorvino as Anthony Caruso, a lawyer defending the widow of a murdered fashion photographer. In this, the first of the post-Raymond Burr *Perry Mason* series Barbara Hale and William R. Moses continued thier characterizations of Della Street and Ken Malansky.

Co-Executive Producer Dean Hargrove said, "There will be no attempt to recast the role of Perry Mason in any of the movies or projects we have planned. The character will continue because it's owned by the Erle Stanley Gardner estate. There will probably be some additional *Perry Mason Mysteries* which will use the *Perry Mason* format, but will feature guest attorneys,"[6] concluded Hargrove.

Case closed.

PETER GUNN

September 22, 1958–September 25, 1961.   NBC
April 23, 1989   ABC

Character:	Peter Gunn
Played by:	Craig Stevens
Date(s):	September 22, 1958–September 25, 1961
Replaced by:	Peter Gunn
Played by:	Peter Strauss
Date(s):	April 23, 1989
Character:	Mother
Played by:	Hope Emerson
Date(s):	September 22, 1958–1958
Replaced by:	Mother
Played by:	Minerva Urecal
Date(s):	September 21, 1959–September 25, 1961
Replaced by:	Mother
Played by:	Pearl Bailey
Date(s):	April 23, 1989
Character:	Edie Hart
Played by:	Lola Albright
Date(s):	September 22, 1958–September 25, 1961
Replaced by:	Edie
Played by:	Barbara Williams
Date(s):	April 23, 1989
Character:	Lieutenant Jacoby
Played by:	Herschel Bernardi
Date(s):	September 22, 1958–September 25, 1961
Replaced by:	Lieutenant Herschel Jacoby
Played by:	Peter Jurasik
Date(s):	April 23, 1989
Character:	Babby
Played by:	Billy Barty
Date(s):	September 22, 1958–September 25, 1961
Replaced by:	Spec
Played by:	David Rappaport
Date(s):	April 23, 1989

When actor, writer, producer and director Blake Edwards created *Peter Gunn* in 1958 it became television's first detective series produced exclusively for the medium. All of its predecessors were taken from characters appearing on radio, or in films and novels.

Oh sure, *Peter Gunn* possessed elements of some of the other television sleuths like Richard Diamond and Mike Hammer. The difference was that Gunn wasn't as rough around the edges as his contemporaries. He was more reserved and well polished.

6. From an exclusive telephone interview with Dean Hargrove on January 3, 1994.

He was cool. He wore his hair short, neat and never out of place—like Dick Van Dyke's Rob Petrie on *The Dick Van Dyke Show*. He was always impeccably dressed and his speech was peppered with glib remarks that made him seem more like Simon Templar and James Bond than any previously seen television detective. Craig Stevens brought him to life.

One of Gunn's favorite hangouts was Mother's, a classy jazz club where his girlfriend, Edie Hart, sang. Mother, a tall woman with a tough side, was initially played by the six-foot-two-inch tall Hope Emerson, who had played Minerva Parker on the NBC situation comedy *I Married Joan* (See Entry).

As of September 22, 1959, Hope Emerson joined the cast of *The Dennis O'Keefe Show,* a situation comedy in which she played Hal Towne's (O'Keefe) housekeeper, Sarge. The series left the air on June 7, 1960, and Ms. Emerson died on April 25 of that year.

Over on the set of *Peter Gunn,* Minerva Urecal had been brought in to replace Hope Emerson as Mother and made her first appearance in the second season's premiere episode, "Protection," but the new actress didn't have the same chemistry with the series' star. According to Craig Stevens, "The character was so identified with Hope that we didn't use Mother as much after that."[7] Somehow, this worked to the show's advantage, because Lola Albright, the actress who was playing Edie Hart, had been asking for a bigger role. She got her wish at the beginning of the series' third season when Mother's was changed to Edie's. Naturally, this change expanded her part.

The importance of the chemistry among cast members was illustrated during *Peter Gunn*'s first season. It was an instance in which Herschel Bernardi, the actor playing Gunn's police contact, Lieutenant Jacoby, fractured his thigh in a car accident and producer Blake Edwards refused to write him out. Instead, the cast and crew set up shop at North Hollywood Emergency Hospital in order to film scenes with Bernardi for use in three episodes. The policeman's injury was described as being the result of an attack.

One of Peter Gunn's more colorful informants was a pint-sized pool hustler named Babby. He was played by the same midget who had played Little Tom on *Circus Boy* from September 23, 1956 to September 11, 1958. He also appeared as Billy Longfellow, in a fantasy-like episode of *My Three Sons*.

Blake Edwards took his characters to the big screen in a 1967 feature film titled GUNN. In this extension of the television series only Craig Stevens recreated his role as the ex-cop turned private investigator. " 'I was terribly upset when they couldn't do it,' Stevens recalled. 'Lola had just had an accident and Blake was afraid she might not be up to it, while Herschel was on Broadway in *Zorba*. Blake talked to Hal [Harold] Prince [*Zorba's* director] I don't know how many times, but they just couldn't work out a suitable schedule.' "[8] Lola Albright's role went to Laura Devon and Herschel Bernardi's to Edward Asner. Mother was played by M.T. Marshall

Twenty-two years later (twenty-eight after the series left the air), *Peter Gunn* returned to television in a two-hour ABC Sunday Night movie on April 23, 1989. However, the time period in which the film is set was 1964. Speaking over exciting titles and clips, just before the teaser, the thick-throated ABC announcer intoned, "Get set for girls . . . guns . . . and goons because Peter Strauss is taking charge as Peter Gunn."

The movie opened with the electrocution-murder of a mob boss who was taking a swim in the pool outside his palatial estate. The scene didn't use any dialogue, just like so many openings of the original series. Cut to the animated opening credits, set to the beat of Henry Mancini's driving theme. Cut to Mother's jazz club, with Pearl Bailey as its owner and Barbara Williams as the singer, Edie.

Included in the elements gleaned from the original series is the diminutive pool-playing tipster, now named Spec and played by David Rappaport, who starred as Simon McKay in his own detective series, *The Wizard,* which premiered on CBS on July 7, 1987.

Gunn's police contact is still Lieutenant Jacoby but as an inside acknowledgment to the original series co-star, Blake Edwards, who wrote, produced and directed this made-for-television movie, gave Lieutenant Jacoby the first name of Herschel.

In this well made telefilm, Peter Gunn tells his new secretary, Maggie Dugan (Jennifer Edwards), that Peter Gunn's Private Detective Agency (Gunn Investigations is engraved on the doorplate) has been in business since July 5, 1957. The date doesn't jibe with the original series premiere, but undoubtedly holds some significance for Blake Edwards—as does this series to many aficionados of the genre.

PETTICOAT JUNCTION

September 24, 1963–September 12, 1970.   CBS

Character:	Kate Bradley
Played by:	Bea Benaderet
Date(s):	September 24, 1963–1968
Replaced by:	Cousin Mae
Played by:	Shirley Mitchell
Date(s):	February 24, 1968
Replaced by:	Aunt Helen
Played by:	Rosemary DeCamp
Date(s):	February 24, 1968–March 30, 1968
Replaced by:	Dr. Janet Craig
Played by:	June Lockhart
Date(s):	November 16, 1968–September 12, 1970
Character:	Billie Jo Bradley
Played by:	Jeannie Riley
Date(s):	September 24, 1963–September 7, 1965

7. Meyers, Ric. *Murder on the Air, Television's Great Mystery Series.* The Mysterious Press, New York, 1989, p. 82.
8. Meyers, *op. cit.,* p. 86.

Posed around the dog centerpiece are (standing, left to right): Owner of the General Store, Sam Drucker (Frank Cady), Billie Jo Bradley (Gunilla Hutton), Betty Jo Bradley (Linda Kaye Henning), and the Cannonball's engineers, Floyd Smoot (Rufe Davis) and Charlie Pratt (Smiley Burnette). Seated (left to right) are: Bobbie Jo Bradley (Lori Saunders), Kate Bradley (Bea Benaderet) and Uncle Joe (Edgar Buchanan), who was movin' kinda slow at the junction—*Petticoat Junction*.

Replaced by:	Billie Jo Bradley
Played by:	Gunilla Hutton
Date(s):	1965–1966

Replaced by:	Billie Jo Bradley
Played by:	Meredith MacRae
Date(s):	September 13, 1966–September 12, 1970

Character:	Bobbie Jo Bradley
Played by:	Pat Woodell
Date(s):	September 24, 1963–1965

Replaced by:	Bobbie Jo Bradley
Played by:	Lori Saunders
Date(s):	1965–September 12, 1970

Character:	Charley Pratt
Played by:	Smiley Burnette
Date(s):	September 24, 1963–1967

Replaced by:	Wendell Gibbs
Played by:	Byron Foulger
Date(s):	1968–1970

Character:	Selma Plout
Played by:	Virginia Sale
Date(s):	1964–1965

Replaced by:	Selma Plout
Played by:	Elvia Allman
Date(s):	1965–1970

Character:	Henrietta Plout
Played by:	Susan Walther
Date(s):	1965–1966

Replaced by:	Henrietta Plout
Played by:	Lynette Winter
Date(s):	1966–1970

The last line of the *Petticoat Junction* theme song is: "And that's Uncle Joe. He's a movin' kinda a slow at the junction." This may be true, but he was the only one. Nearly everybody else moved in and out of the series faster than the Cannonball.

The Cannonball was a steam engine from the 1890s and in spite of the efforts made by Homer Bedloe to close her down, the railroad stayed in service during the entire run of the series. Bedloe, a nasty old so-and-so, was played by Charles Lane, who later co-starred as Dale Busch in the situation comedy, *Karen* (See Entry).

The Cannonball's conductor was always Floyd Smoot (Rufe

Davis), but there were two different engineers during the seven-year run of *Petticoat Junction*. Charlie Pratt, played by Smiley Burnette, was at the throttle for the first four years of the series. Earlier in his career, he appeared in dozens of Western pictures as Gene Autry's sidekick, Frog. Later, as himself, Smiley Burnette saddled up next to Charles Starrett in fifty-six DURANGO KID Westerns.

Burnette was replaced by Byron Foulger as Wendell Gibbs, when he died at the age of fifty-six on February 16, 1967. In *The Great Cowboy Stars* by Leo O. Miller, his former co-star, Charles Starrett, spoke of his friend's passing.

"We worked together for a long time. I found it fun to work with him. He always had a story for me. If I felt a little down, he could pick me up. By the same token, if he felt a little down, I could pick him up. We really got along fine and worked well together. I was both shocked and saddened by his sudden death from a heart attack."[9]

Only a year before firing up the old Cannonball, Byron Foulger appeared as Mr. Nash, the father of sitcom superhero *Captain Nice,* which aired on NBC from January 9 to August 28, 1967.

The star of *Petticoat Junction* was Bea Benaderet as Kate Bradley, the owner of the Shady Rest hotel in the quiet farming community of Hooterville. She was a widow and the mother of three beautiful daughters, Billie Joe, Bobbie Jo and Betty Jo. She was actually the mother of six beautiful daughters, as there were a total of five different actresses who stepped in and out of Billie Jo's and Bobbie Jo's petticoats over the course of the series, but more about them later.

Kate was the matriarch of the Bradleys and the guiding force behind this spinoff from *The Beverly Hillbillies* (See Entry), in which Bea Benaderet had played Granny's Cousin Pearl. She had co-starred as Blanche Morton on *The George Burns and Gracie Allen Show* (See Entry) and was even Lucille Ball's first choice for the role of Ethel Mertz on *I Love Lucy* (See Entry).

For a period during the beginning of 1968, Ms. Benaderet became ill and was temporarily replaced, first by Shirley Mitchell as Cousin Mae, and then, in four episodes, by Rosemary DeCamp as Aunt Helen. The *TV Guide* listing for the episode of February 24, 1968 read, "Cousin Mae takes over the hotel while Kate is away, and manages to rile just about everybody in once-happy Hooterville." In the fifth episode, "Kate's Homecoming," Ms. DeCamp appeared to make a smooth transition back to Bea Benaderet. Ms. DeCamp is well known for her earlier series role as Bob Collins' (Bob Cummings) nagging sister, Margaret, in *Love That Bob.* She had also appeared as Helen Marie, Ann Marie's mom on *That Girl.*

Ms. Benaderet continued in her role as Kate Bradley for eight more months. She died of lung cancer on October 13, 1968, and was replaced by Lassie's mom (really Timmy's mom), June Lockhart. She had initially joined the cast as a replacement for Hooterville's Doctor Barton Stuart, who was played by several different actors, the last being Regis Toomey, who held the role from September 29, 1968 to 1969. During the 1950s he played Lieutenant McGough on *Richard Diamond, Private Detective* (See Entry). Previously, as Detective Sergeant Les Hart, he

---

9. Miller, Lee O. *The Great Cowboy Stars of Movies & Television.* Arlington House Publishers, New York, 1979, p. 76.

worked with Amos Burke in *Burke's Law* from September 20, 1963 to August 31, 1965.

Another resident seen sporadically through the run of the series was Bert Smedley. And just about every time he showed up, he was played by a different actor.

With many of the episodes' storylines revolving around the love lives of one or more of the "Jo" Bradleys, the series needed to have an antagonist. Enter Kate's neighbor, Selma Plout, and her daughter Henrietta, who competed with Betty Jo for the attention and affection of handsome pilot Steve Elliot (Mike Minor), who crash-landed in the series in the fall of 1966.

Selma was initially played by Virginia Sale, who co-starred with her husband, Sam Wren, in *Wren's Nest*, one of television's first situation comedies. It aired on ABC from January 13 to April 30, 1949. Her daughter, Henrietta, on *Petticoat Junction* was played by Susan Walther. Ms. Sale left the series in 1965 while Ms. Walther remained for another year with Elvia Allman as her mother. Ms. Allman had replaced Margaret Hamilton as Morticia's mother, Esther Frump, on *The Addams Family* (See Entry). When Walther left *Petticoat Junction* in 1966 her role was taken over by Lynette Winter, who had just completed work as Larue on *Gidget* (See Entry).

The real confusion, however, centered on the Bradley girls, Billie Jo, Bobbie Jo and Betty Jo. The other Joe living at the junction was Uncle Joe, who referred to himself as the manager of the Shady Rest. He was played throughout the series by Edgar Buchanan, who had been one of several cowboy sidekicks on *Hopalong Cassidy* (See Entry).

To make things simpler, let us begin with Betty Jo who was played by Linda Kaye (Henning). In their *Complete Directory to Prime Time Network TV Shows, 1946–Present,* Tim Brooks and Earle Marsh wrote, "The one regular who was most likely to stay, however, was Linda Kaye Henning. Her father, Paul Henning, was the producer of *Petticoat Junction* as well as *Green Acres*." They called it right, because she did stay and no one else did.

Billie Jo Bradley was played by three different actresses and Bobbie Jo by two. The first actress to appear as Billie Jo was an ambitious brown-eyed blonde from Fresno, California, Jeannie Riley.

In Fresno, during her pre-*Petticoat Junction* show business career, Jeannie Riley was the star of the Hacienda nightclub's underwater ballet. Her first big break in Hollywood came when she was signed to play one of Kate Bradley's daughters. " 'She was pushing all the time,' says someone who knew her then. As a result, she was generally disliked by the rest of the cast, which included such veteran unpretentious types as the late Bea Benaderet, and there were no regrets when Jeannie decided to leave for what she felt would be a bigger and better career in motion pictures."[10]

That bigger and better career included the roles of Bambi Berman in the 1967 Jerry Lewis comedy, THE BIG MOUTH, and Lorraine in Dick Van Dyke's 1969 comedy, THE COMIC. Her motion picture work was followed by a number of guest shots on programs such as *The Virginian, Gomer Pyle, U.S.M.C.* and *The Man from U.N.C.L.E.* On September 5, 1967 she appeared in two unsold pilots for NBC, *Li'l Abner* and *Sheriff Who?*

Then, on June 15, 1969, she found a home as one of the first regular members of the *Hee Haw* gang and stayed with the cornpone *Laugh-In* until September of 1971. Two years later Jeannie Riley played Lulu McQueen in the Bob Denver syndicated Western sitcom, *Dusty's Trail.* Co-starring with her, as Betsy, was Lori Saunders, the second of *Petticoat Junction's* Bobbie Jo Bradleys.

Jeannie Riley's replacement was Gunilla Hutton, who left the junction in 1966. Three years later Ms. Hutton joined Jeannie Riley as a new member of the large *Hee Haw* family. This led to singing engagements at country fairs with Roy Clark.

That left Meredith MacRae, the third and final Billie Jo Bradley—probably the best-known of all the actresses to appear on the series, not only because she was the daughter of famous parents, Gordon and Sheila MacRae, but because she had played Sally Ann Morrison on *My Three Sons* (See Entry). After *Petticoat Junction* left the air, Ms. MacRae became the cohost of a local Los Angeles, California talk show, *Mid-Morning LA.*

For whatever reason, the recasting done for Billie Jo was rather loose; the replacement actresses looked only a little bit like their predecessors.

There was also a fourth actress who was actually the first to play Billie Jo. In the unaired pilot for the series, Sharon Tate played the part, but she was dropped from the series when the producers learned that she had done a nude layout for *Playboy* magazine. Funny though it didn't bother them when they hired her later for the role of Janet on *The Beverly Hillbillies.*

In the case of Bobbie Jo, Lori Saunders could have been Pat Woodell's twin. It had been reported that Ms. Woodell left *Petticoat Junction* to pursue her acting career, but she had actually spent more than six years working with Erhard Seminar Training, the self-realization program more commonly known as EST.

In 1983, from May 2 to 13, Lori Saunders, Linda Kaye Henning, Gunilla Hutton and Meredith MacRae appeared on a special edition of ABC's popular game show, *Family Feud,* subtitled "TV's All-Time Favorites." Their team captain was Frank Cady, who had played Sam Drucker on *Petticoat Junction* and *Green Acres.* When the feud was over, *Petticoat Junction* had won $22,000 for United Cerebral Palsy, beating out the likes of *The Brady Bunch* and *Leave It to Beaver.*

PHYLLIS

September 8, 1975–August 30, 1977.   CBS

Character:	Julie Erskine
Played by:	Barbara Colby
Date(s):	September 22, 1975

Replaced by:	Julie Erskine
Played by:	Liz Torres
Date(s):	September 29, 1975–March 1, 1976

10. Raddatz, Leslie. *TV Guide,* Vol. 17, No. 28, Issue #850, July 12, 1969, p. 15.

Replaced by:	Dan Valenti
Played by:	Carmine Caridi
Date(s):	September 20, 1976–August 30, 1977

By the time *Phyllis* premiered on September 8, 1975, she was already a familiar character to television audiences because we had known her for five years as Mary Richards' landlady and friend on *The Mary Tyler Moore Show* from September 19, 1970 to January 18, 1975.

The casting director for *The Mary Tyler Moore Show* was Ethel Winant, a vice president at CBS. She explained how she cast Ms. Leachman in the role: "Cloris was clearly Phyllis, to me. I could have cast Phyllis immediately. I knew Cloris was Phyllis, I just knew it. One of the hard things was that Jim [Brooks] and Allan [Burns] saw her not as a comedienne. She'd been doing the mother on *Lassie* (See Entry) and all these dramatic roles."[11]

After repeatedly bringing Ms. Leachman in to audition for the role of Phyllis Lindstrom, Ethel Winant finally got the producers to see it her way and Cloris Leachman became Phyllis, the role she carried over into her own spinoff series.

The new setup was that Phyllis' husband, Lars, had died and Phyllis was leaving Minneapolis for a new life in San Francisco, where she landed a job with Erskine's Commercial Photography Studio.

The original actress to play Julie Erskine, the owner of the studio, was Barbara Colby, who made her first television appearance on Lieutenant Columbo's third case, "Murder by the Book." In that episode, which aired on September 15, 1971, Barbara Colby plays Lily La Sanka, the proprietor of a small store who is murdered by Jack Cassidy. Some of her other television work includes episodes of *The F.B.I.* and *McMillan and Wife.*

The ABC special, *A Brand New Life,* starred Cloris Leachman in her Emmy-winning performance as Victoria Douglas and featured Barbara Colby as Jessica Hiller. The ninety-minute drama aired on February 20, 1973.

Barbara Colby guest-starred in the fifth season opener of the *The Mary Tyler Moore Show,* playing Sherry, the prostitute with the heart of gold. This outstanding episode, "Will Mary Richards Go to Jail?" aired on September 14, 1974, and dealt with Mary's conviction for not releasing the identity of a news source. A judge sends Mary to jail for contempt of court and it is there that she meets Sherry.

Ms. Colby made a return appearance as Sherry in "You Try to Be a Nice Guy," which aired on February 8, 1975.

These previous associations with both Cloris Leachman and the *Mary Tyler Moore Show* people clearly had something to do with her being cast in *Phyllis.* She only appeared as the studio's owner, Julie Erskine, in one episode, however, because she was murdered before other episodes were filmed.

The story pieced together on this still unsolved mystery placed Ms. Colby and her roommate, actor James Kiernan, leaving a drama class they taught on Ellis Street in the Palms section of West Los Angeles. It was a little before midnight on Thursday, July 24, 1975, when two black youths emerged from a light-colored van and ordered the couple to put their hands up. The actors complied, but instead of robbing them, the youths each fired their small-caliber hand-guns and fled.

Ms. Colby died instantly when a bullet perforated her lung. Kiernan was rushed to the hospital but died shortly after 1:30 a.m. at Brotman Memorial Hospital in Culver City, from the bullet which struck him in the chest very near to his heart. It has been speculated that Ms. Colby may have been singled out as a target because of the promiscuous roles she played, such as Sherry on *The Mary Tyler Moore Show.*

Phyllis' star, Cloris Leachman, taped an emotional eulogy to her co-worker and friend, which CBS opted not to air.

" 'As some of you may know, shortly after we filmed tonight's episode last July, Barbara Colby, who played the part of Julie, was tragically killed. She was a superb actress and one of the most joyful and giving people I have ever known.' Leachman went on to explain, 'We could have written out the character, but this would not have fooled you, and more important, it would not have fooled us.' However she assured viewers that while another actress would be assuming Colby's role, 'it is impossible to replace her as a person.' "[12]

The actress given the difficult task of replacing Barbara Colby during the first season was Liz Torres.

In an attempt to improve *Phyllis'* weak ratings, and perhaps put the Barbara Colby tragedy behind them, several changes were made in the series with the start of its second season.

Since Phyllis no longer worked for Julie Erskine, Ms. Torres was able to leave the series to accept the role of Teresa Betancourt, Archie Bunker's housekeeper, on *All in the Family.* She followed this up by playing Maria, Oscar Madison's secretary in the updated version of *The Odd Couple* (See Entry).

Phyllis Lindstrom's new employer was the San Francisco Board of Supervisors and her new boss, an executive with the department, was Dan Valenti. The actor who played Valenti was Carmine Caridi who among other things appeared as a detective in the 1971 Sean Connery action film, THE ANDERSON TAPES.

It is unlikely that *Phyllis* will ever be seen again since only forty-eight episodes were completed, which is less than half the total usually needed for syndication.

PLEASE DON'T EAT THE DAISIES

September 14, 1965–September 2, 1967.   NBC

Character:	Herb Thornton
Played by:	Harry Hickox
Date(s):	1965–1966

Replaced by:	Herb Thornton
Played by:	King Donovan
Date(s):	1966–1967

11. Alley, Robert S. and Brown, Irby B. *Love Is All Around, The Making of the Mary Tyler Moore Show.* Delta Book, Dell Publishing, New York, 1989, p. 13.
12. Rovin, Jeff. *TV Babylon,* Signet, New York, April 1987, p. 94.

The roots for *Daisies* were planted in a best-selling novel by Jean Kerr, a play and a 1960 motion picture starring Doris Day and David Niven as Kate and Lawrence MacKay. In the series, their names were Joan and James Nash and they were played by Patricia Crowley and Mark Miller.

The Nash's next-door neighbors were Marge and Herb Thornton. Marge was played in all fifty-eight episodes by Shirley Mitchell. Her husband was initially played by Harry Hickox. Hickox, who had just completed work on the ABC comedy, *No Time for Sergeants,* in which he played Sergeant King, was replaced by a different King, King Donovan. Donovan had played Harvey Helm, from 1956 to 1958, on *The Bob Cummings Show.* Donovan's real-life wife was Imogene Coca, who replaced Irene Ryan's Granny as "Granny's Maw" in the 1981 *Beverly Hillbillies'* (See Entry) reunion show, *The Return of the Beverly Hillbillies.*

THE POWERS OF MATTHEW STAR

September 17, 1982–September 11, 1983.   NBC

Character:	General Frederick Tucker
Played by:	John Crawford
Date(s):	September 17, 1982–November 19, 1982

Replaced by:	Mr. Wymore
Played by:	James Karen
Date(s):	February 11, 1983–September 11, 1983

Ehawk, the Crown Prince of the planet Quandris, lived on earth as Matthew Star, a typical, albeit exceedingly handsome, teenager, attending Crestridge High School.

He lived in Crestridge, California with his guardian Dehay, under the guise of Crestridge High science teacher, Walt Shepherd.

Star was played by Peter Barton, who began his television career as Bill Miller, Shirley Jones's teenage son in the dramatic comedy *Shirley,* which aired on NBC from October 26, 1979, to January 25, 1980.

Shepherd was played by Academy Award winner Louis Gossett Jr., who played The Drac, the androgynous reptilian alien in the 1985 science fiction film, ENEMY MINE.

Ehawk a.k.a. Star, was sent to earth as an infant to develop his powers of telepathy, telekinesis, astral projection and transmutation and would be picked up by a spaceship in his year of 8312 to return to his home planet to fight for freedom.

While hiding out on earth from his Quandrian enemies, Matthew used his extraordinary powers to help solve crimes for the government under the direction of General Frederick Tucker. General Tucker was eventually replaced by Major Wymore.

In the series pilot, which aired on April 15, 1983, Star's first name was David and Gerald S. O'Loughlin appeared as his guardian, Max.

Matthew Star was given his powers by Executive Producer Harve Bennett, who breathed new life into the STAR TREK motion picture series by collaborating on the story of STAR TREK II: THE WRATH OF KHAN and served as both the writer and producer of STAR TREK III: THE SEARCH FOR SPOCK (1984); STAR TREK IV: THE VOYAGE HOME (1986); and producer on STAR TREK V: THE UNDISCOVERED COUNTRY (1989).

Bennett left Paramount to become the creator and executive producer of the Warner Bros. syndicated science fiction, *Time Trax,* which premiered in 1993 and starred Dale Midkiff as Captain Darien Lambert and Henry Darrow as The Chief.

The *Star Trek* (See Entry) connection goes still further as Leonard Nimoy (Mr. Spock) served as one of the directors on *The Powers of Matthew Star,* directing the November 19, 1982, episode while Walter Koenig (Ensign Pavel Chekov) wrote the November 26, 1982, episode. And Henry Darrow, who played Don Alejandro de la Vega on *Zorro* (See Entry) had appeared as Savar, a Vulcan Starfleet admiral in the "Conspiracy" episode of *Star Trek: The Next Generation.*

PRIVATE BENJAMIN

April 6, 1981–September 5, 1983.   CBS

Character:	Captain Doreen Lewis
Played by:	Eileen Brennan
Date(s):	April 6, 1981–September 5, 1983

Replaced by:	Major Amanda Allen
Played by:	Polly Holliday
Date(s):	January 3, 1983–January 10, 1983

Character:	Harriet Benjamin
Played by:	Barbara Barrie
Date(s):	November 30, 1981

Replaced by:	Harriet Benjamin
Played by:	K Callan
Date(s):	January 3, 1983

It was the 1980 motion picture, PRIVATE BENJAMIN, that triggered this military sitcom. The film was produced by Goldie Hawn and won her an Academy Award nomination for her portrayal of the title character. Hawn's co-star, Eileen Brennan was also nominated for an Academy Award for her portrayal of Captain Doreen Lewis.

When the TV series was cast, Brennan was available and Hawn was not, so Brennan was hired to recreate her role as Captain Lewis and an unknown, Lorna Patterson, was cast as Private Judy Benjamin.

The premise was that a JAP (read Jewish American Princess) joins the United States Army in search of a more exciting lifestyle. This was toned down quite a bit from the motion picture, in which Judy Benjamin joined the service after her husband died while making love to her on their wedding night. Other than that minor detail, everything else was pretty much the same.

During the abbreviated run of this marginally popular sitcom, viewers had the pleasure of meeting Private Benjamin's mother on two separate occasions—who was each time played by a different actress.

The first appearance of Mrs. Benjamin was in the episode, "Bye Bye Benjamin," which featured Barbara Barrie, the same actress who had played Harriet Benjamin in the 1980 motion picture.

Her name may sound familiar to television audiences because she has appeared on nearly one hundred series. But as Tim Brooks pointed out in *The Complete Directory to Prime Time TV Stars,* "This fine-featured, understanding woman looks like she was born to play somebody's mother on a TV sitcom. In fact she has had many such roles, but none of them lasted long enough to become closely identified with her." And that includes this one, because when Judy Benjamin's mom showed up in "Captain Lewis, Matchmaker," she was played by a different actress. That actress was K Callan, who had co-starred as Katie Wabash in the NBC situation comedy, *Joe's World,* which aired from December 28, 1979 to July 26, 1980.

Disaster struck *Private Benjamin* in October 1982 when the series co-star, Eileen Brennan, was hit by a car and seriously injured. The producers acted quickly and brought in Polly Holliday as a temporary replacement for Captain Lewis.

Ms. Holliday, who had played Flo on *Alice* (See Entry), was introduced in the appropriately titled January 3, 1983 episode, "The Replacement," and returned the following week in "Judy's Cousin."

Eileen Brennan recovered from her injuries, but the series never recovered from its poor showing in the ratings. This forced CBS to give *Private Benjamin* a dishonorable discharge after only thirty-six episodes.

PROJECT U.F.O.

February 19, 1978–August 30, 1979.   NBC

Character:	Major Jake Gatlin
Played by:	William Jordan
Date(s):	February 19, 1978–September 14, 1978

Replaced by:	Captain Ben Ryan
Played by:	Edward Winter
Date(s):	September 21, 1978–August 39, 1979

Jack Webb, the talented no-nonsense actor and highly successful producer of fact-based series such as *Dragnet, Adam 12* and *Mobile One,* looked to the stars for his next inspiration. Not the stars living in Hollywood, mind you, but the stars of the universe.

This series, which investigated the sightings of U.F.O.s, was based on actual cases documented in the declassified files of the United States Air Force's *Project Blue Book.* Each of the twenty-six episodes opened with the following explanatory narration by Jack Webb:

"Ezekiel saw the wheel. This is the wheel he saw. [Shot of a drawing which resembled a twin wheel-shaped space station.] These are Unidentified Flying Objects that people say they are seeing now. Are they proof that we are being visited by civilizations from other stars? Or, just what are they? The United States Air Force began an investigation of this high strangeness in a search for the truth. What you are about to see is part of that twenty-year search."

Heading up the investigative team during the first season were U.S.A.F. Major Jake Gatlin and his assistant, U.S.A.F. Staff Sergeant Harry Fitz. Fitz was played by Caskey Swaim. The good Major was played by William Jordan, who went on to play Joseph Oppenheimer, a scientist working for the Delos Corporation in *Beyond Westworld.* This was an even shorter-lived series than *Project U.F.O.,* with a total of five episodes produced and only three airing between March 5 and March 19, 1980.

Fitz's superior officer for the last thirteen investigations was Captain Ben Ryan, played by Edward Winter, who may be more familiar to television audiences as Barkley Foods Vice President William "Bud" Coleman, from the television adaptation of the hit motion picture 9 TO 5. The television sitcom aired on ABC from March 25, 1982, to October 27, 1983.

R

RAWHIDE

January 9, 1959–January 4, 1966.   CBS

Character:	Gil Favor
Played by:	Eric Fleming
Date(s):	January 9, 1959–December 7, 1965

Replaced by:	Rowdy Yates
Played by:	Clint Eastwood
Date(s):	January 9, 1959–January 4, 1966

''Roll-in' roll-in' roll-in', tho' the streams are swollen, keep them dog-ies roll-in' Rawhide.''

To interpret the opening line to the show's popular theme song, the cattlemen depicted in this Western series were responsible for cattle drives which took them overland and across flooded rivers and streams from San Antonio, Texas to Sedalia, Kansas.

The trail boss and presumed star of the series was Eric Fleming, who had played Major Dell Conway in *Major Dell Conway of the Flying Tigers* (See Entry). His ramrod, Rowdy Yates, was played by Clint Eastwood, who had not yet caught the public's attention. *Rawhide* changed all that, making him a television star.

Both actors had previous motion picture experience. Fleming had starred as the handsome and heroic astronaut, Captain Neil Patterson, in the 1958 science fiction film that has since become a cult classic, THE QUEEN OF OUTER SPACE. His *Rawhide* co-star, Clint Eastwood, also got his motion picture start in science fiction films. His first was as the lab technician who had a mouse in his pocket in REVENGE OF THE CREATURE. Also appearing in this film was John Bromfield as Joe Hayes, one year prior to his first television series role as Sheriff Frank Morgan in the syndicated police drama, *The Sheriff of Cochise* (See Entry). This 1955 3–D science fiction was the second of three CREATURE films and the first film to be broadcast in 3–D on television.

Fleming, who had a reputation in the business for being difficult, left the series in 1965 to retire in Hawaii, but almost immediately came out of retirement when he landed the role as Edgar Hill in the 1966 Doris Day comedy, THE GLASS BOTTOM BOAT, that was filming on location there.

Back on the plains of *Rawhide* Clint Eastwood took over the duties as trail boss Rowdy Yates. Since Eastwood had already become a star, this change in status was of little importance to his career, which skyrocketed with his roles as The Man with No Name in A FISTFUL OF DOLLARS, 1964; FOR A FEW DOLLARS MORE, 1967; and THE GOOD, THE BAD, AND THE UGLY, 1967.

He became even more popular (if that is possible) in 1971 with his portrayal of Harry Callahan, in the police drama DIRTY HARRY, which spawned five (to date) subsequent sequels.

He was elected mayor of Carmel, California in 1986 and has since added producing and directing to his already impressive list of credits.

Eric Fleming was not as fortunate. He left *Rawhide* at the peak of his and the series' popularity, to star in motion pictures. But his career and life literally went down the river when he drowned on September 28, 1966. ''In the summer of 1966, Fleming got a co-starring role with Anne Heywood in *High Jungle,* a film set to be part of ABC's *Off to See the Wizard* series. He went down to Peru to do location footage on the Huallaga River, a tributary of the Amazon 350 miles northeast of Lima. On September 28, he and actor Nico Minardos were preparing for a shot in a canoe when it capsized in rough water. Minardos made it to shore, but Fleming didn't. Search parties recovered his body four days later.''[1]

The *Rawhide* theme is responsible for saving the lives of Elwood and Jake (Dan Aykroyd and John Belushi) in their 1980 comedy, THE BLUES BROTHERS. In one of the film's most outrageous scenes, the boys are booked into a rowdy Western bar. The only Western song they know is the theme to *Rawhide,* which they play with all their hearts. ''Cut 'em out! Tie 'em in! Ride 'em in! Turn 'em in! Cut 'em out! Ride 'em in . . . Rawhide.''

REASONABLE DOUBTS

September 26, 1991–.   NBC

Character:	Kay Lockman
Played by:	Nancy Everhard
Date(s):	September 26, 1991–September 29, 1992

Replaced by:	Maggie Zombro
Played by:	Kay Lenz
Date(s):	October 13, 1992–

---

1. *Reruns.* Published by Richard Tharp, 1981, p. 10.

The first television series to star a hearing-impaired actress since the introduction of closed captioning in 1980 was the hour-long police drama, *Reasonable Doubts.* Starring as Assistant District Attorney Tess Kaufman was Marlee Matlin, who won an Academy Award for Best Actress for her portrayal of Sarah Norman in the 1986 dramatic love story, CHILDREN OF A LESSER GOD.

In the NBC series, Ms. Matlin, who worked for the Chicago District Attorney's office, was teamed with Richard "Dicky" Cobb (Mark Harmon), a police detective working for the investigative unit out of the felony division. Although there might have been some attraction between the two unlikely partners, Dicky was caught up in a sticky relationship with a jealous and manipulative bartender named Kay Lockman.

The problem with Nancy Everhard's character, as seen by the show's creator, Robert Singer, was her distance from the legal profession, which is why they decided to kill her off and introduce a new attorney, Maggie Zombro. Actually, Kay Lenz made her first appearance as attorney Maggie Zombro in "Aftermath," the eighth episode of the series' first season, which aired on November 15, 1991. She appeared again in "One Woman's Word," which aired on November 29, 1991, and later turned up in "Burning Desire," the first of a three-part episode that aired on March 4, 1992, and "Love Is Strange," the second part, which aired on March 17, 1992. The following week, Ms. Lenz appeared in the March 24, 1992 episode, "Maggie Finds Her Soul." She also guest-starred in "Home to Roost," an unaired episode from the show's first season.

Kay Lockman's death came in "Forever My Love," the premiere episode of the second season, which aired on September 29, 1992. She was killed by a ruthless hood who fatally wounded her during a robbery at the bar.

THE REDD FOXX SHOW

January 18, 1986–April 19, 1986.   ABC

Character:	Jim-Jam
Played by:	Nathaniel Taylor
Date(s):	January 18, 1986–February 15, 1986

Replaced by:	Jim-Jam
Played by:	Theodore Wilson
Date(s):	February 22, 1986–April 19, 1986

Character:	Toni Rutledge
Played by:	Pamela Segall
Date(s):	January 18, 1986–March 1986

Replaced by:	Byron Lightfoot
Played by:	Sinbad
Date(s):	March 1986–April 19, 1986

Redd Foxx returned to television in this warm situation comedy about Al Hughes, a crotchety old man who owns a combination coffee shop and newsstand in Manhattan. In his care is Toni Rutledge, (Pamela Segall), an orphaned white child he was coerced into adopting.

Hughes' friend, Jim-Jam, originally played by Nathaniel Taylor, was replaced after a couple of weeks by Theodore Wilson, who had starred as Phil Wheeler on the *Sanford and Son* (See Entry) spinoff, *The Sanford Arms.*

In an attempt to save the failing series after just three months on the air, several major cast changes were made. These included dropping Toni by having her sent away to a boarding school and introducing Sinbad as Al's new foster son, Byron Lightfoot.

A former *Star Search* winner, Sinbad went on to co-star as the dormitory director, Walter Oakes, in the *Cosby* spinoff, *A Different World.* He later starred in his own series, *The Sinbad Show,* which premiered on the Fox network on Thursday, September 16, 1993.

Redd Foxx returned to network television on Wednesday, September 18, 1991, as Al Royal in the CBS sitcom, *The Royal Family* (See Entry).

REMINGTON STEELE

October 1, 1982–March 9, 1987.   NBC

Character:	Bernice Foxx
Played by:	Janet DeMay
Date(s):	October 1, 1982–April 12, 1983

Replaced by:	Mildred Krebs
Played by:	Doris Roberts
Date(s):	September 20, 1983–March 9, 1987

If you were a beautiful, talented, young detective, but couldn't get any cases because you were a beautiful, talented, young detective, what would you do? Laura Holt (Stephanie Zimbalist), whipped up a fictitious boss with a classy name. His name was Remington Steele and when Laura Holt Investigations was renamed Remington Steele Investigations, the business took off.

As one might imagine, clients did begin to get a bit edgy when they never saw Steele, so Laura hired someone to become him. That someone was a handsome and suave con man (Pierce Brosnan) who was poised to steal a collection of gems that she has been hired to protect. This partnership by mutual agreement was largely the result of the strong romantic attraction between them.

Although a unique entry into the television spy/detective genre, this one has many similarities with other notables in the category. If the series seems to conjure up memories of *Moonlighting*'s Maddie and David, it may have something to do with the fact that *Moonlighting* was developed for ABC by Glen Gordon Caron, who wrote for *Remington Steele* during its first season.

One can also equate *Remington Steele* with *The Avengers.* And if Pierce Brosnan reminds you of James Bond, you are in good company, because the producers of the James Bond films also felt that Pierce Brosnan reminded them of James Bond. So much so that in 1987 when Roger Moore decided to turn in his Walther PPK, Pierce Brosnan was being considered to replace him as the new double-o-seven. He lost out to Timothy Dalton when NBC exercised its option to pick up the series—and Brosnan—for a fifth season.

Assisting with the office chores were Bernice Foxx (Janet DeMay) as the agency's receptionist and secretary, and Murphy Michaels as Laura's original partner. Michaels was played by James Read, who appeared as George Hazard in ABC's pre-Civil War miniseries, *North and South*, which aired in six parts from November 3 to 10, 1985.

The second season of *Remington Steele* got off to a wonderful start with a lavish two-hour episode that almost rivaled a James Bond film, complete with a fine music score by Richard Lewis Warren that borrows heavily in style and content from the familiar themes composed by Monty Norman and John Barry.

Largely filmed on location in Acapulco, "Steele Away with Me" also introduced Mildred, Laura and Steele's new assistant, and explained what happened to Bernice and Murphy. Mildred was played by Doris Roberts, who had played Crystal, Mary McKinnon's first housekeeper on *The Mary Tyler Moore Comedy Hour* (See Entry).

The *Remington Steele* movie opened with a series of diamond robberies in Cairo, London, Amsterdam and San Diego, California. This was followed by a cut to the exterior of Remington Steele's office building.

Inside, the elevator bell rings and out marches a frumpy, yet very determined-looking woman carrying a large briefcase. The music is ominous and punctuated with kettle drums.

This humorless middle-aged woman turns a corner and enters the offices of Remington Steele. The outer office is filled with secretarial applicants waiting to see Laura Holt, who, it turns out, has been detained for her 9:30 a.m. appointment with this representative from the Internal Revenue Service because of a murdered man who mysteriously turned up in her living room.

By this time, the no-nonsense woman has introduced herself to Remington Steele. Her name is Mildred Krebs and she is there because a routine check showed that Remington Steele had not filed an income tax return the previous year. No wonder—he didn't exist!

Steele sneaks out of the office and returns four hours later with Laura in hand. Mildred has a few questions for Ms. Holt.

MILDRED: Now, according to the corporate returns, which you signed Ms. Holt, the company employed a Bernice Foxx as a secretary/receptionist.

LAURA: Unfortunately, Ms. Foxx is no longer with us.

STEELE   Yes. Terrible loss there. She ran off with a saxophone player. No doubt to join some hot licks in New York, eh?

When questioned about Murphy Michaels, who also served as an investigator, Laura explained that he had left Remington Steele Investigations to open his own firm in Denver, Colorado. Steele added that Murphy would be working closely with the coroner's office because he had always had a flair for autopsy reports.

This tense but enlightening meeting breaks up when Steele agrees to allow Mildred Krebs to come by his apartment to check for personal items that might have been purchased with the company's money. Krebs warns Steele that for six years she worked as a member of the fraud squad and that if she finds any improprieties, he could face a prison sentence.

As promised, Krebs shows up the following morning—just in time to catch Steele on his way to the airport to meet Laura in Acapulco, where the mysterious murder had taken her investigation. Believing that Steele is skipping the country to avoid prosecution for income tax evasion, Mildred follows him to Mexico. Steele drags her up to his hotel room against her will, but does permit her to phone her I.R.S. supervisor—almost. Because no sooner does Mildred pick up the phone than Steele says "Miss Krebs, forgive me," then slugs her with a right cross. Together, Laura and Steele use strips of torn sheets to tie and gag the unconscious woman, whom they leave lying on the bed.

Later, as they are untying Mildred as a show of good faith, Laura offers her a job because of the investigative talent and initiative she has shown in tracking down Steele. Mildred reminds Laura that since she is still working for the I.R.S., Laura's offer could be construed as a bribe. Laura denies the offer is a bribe and Steele chimes in with, "I wouldn't have you on a platter."

The wind is knocked out of her sails when gung ho Mildred, who still believes that she is conducting an investigation for the I.R.S., calls her supervisor, only to be told that she will be placed on suspension if she is not back in the office within the hour.

As the episode progresses, Laura and Steele begin to rely on Mildred to help them with their investigation. Bitten by the espionage bug, Mildred confesses to Steele, as she helps him set up his hang-glider, "I can't believe this is happening to me . . . any of this. It's like a dream, like a fantasy. It's like a James Bond movie." She hit it right on the head, because that is exactly what it was like.

The case is wrapped up and the final scene of the episode takes place back in the offices of Remington Steele Investigations where Laura and Steele are interviewing an attractive young woman.

Mildred marches in, announcing that she is on official business from the I.R.S. She surreptitiously thanks the applicant being interviewed and ushers her out of the office.

Mildred then tells Steele that she has figured out how to get him off the hook with the I.R.S. for not filing his last tax return as long as he pays the penalties and interests due Uncle Sam. She concludes by telling them that it was also her last official act for the I.R.S.

MILDRED: I got discharged for dereliction of duty. I stayed too long in Mexico.

LAURA: Oh, I'm terribly sorry, Mildred. It was basically our fault.

MILDRED: You remember that job you offered me? I know you did it so I'd go easy on you.

LAURA: No, no, no, no, no. You were very helpful with the case.

MILDRED: I'm not very good at begging. I could grovel a little.

LAURA: I think it would be wonderful for all concerned.

And it was.

RICHARD DIAMOND, PRIVATE DETECTIVE

July 1, 1957–September 6, 1960.   CBS-NBC

Character:	"Sam"
Played by:	Mary Tyler Moore
Date(s):	July 11, 1957–May 17, 1959
Replaced by:	"Sam"
Played by:	Roxanne Brooks
Date(s):	May 24, 1959–September 6, 1960
Character:	Lieutenant Dennis McGough
Played by:	Regis Toomey
Date(s):	July 1, 1957–September 23, 1957
Replaced by:	Lieutenant Pete Kile
Played by:	Russ Conway
Date(s):	1959–1960

A favorite question of television trivia buffs is: "Whose legs were seen at the beginning of *Richard Diamond, Private Detective?*" The surprise answer is Mary Tyler Moore's. By now, though, the question has been asked so often that the answer is hardly much of a surprise.

A far more stimulating question is: "Who replaced Mary Tyler Moore as 'Sam' on *Richard Diamond, Private Detective?*"

Born on December 29, 1936,[2] in Brooklyn, New York, Mary Tyler Moore first graced the television screen in 1954 as "Happy Hotpoint," the dancing Hotpoint elf. Through the magic of early special effects, the eighteen-year-old actress was reduced in size so that she could pop out of the Hotpoint refrigerator's ice-cube tray during the commercials that aired as part of *The Adventures of Ozzie and Harriet.* Her memorable lines were: "Hi, Harriet. Aren't you glad you own a Hotpoint?" Shakespeare it ain't, but that refrigerator did open the door to her first regular television role, "Sam." Not Darrin's Sam, but the switchboard operator who worked for the answering service used by private investigator Richard Diamond. It was never clearly explained why he used an answering service, but it was certainly cheaper than maintaining an office and paying a secretary to run it. Besides, who needed an office when he owned a car with a built-in telephone—quite impressive for 1957. The series, which is about an ex-New York City cop who becomes a private investigator, was based on the radio series created by Blake Edwards.

The radio program, which aired from 1949 to 1952, starred Dick Powell as Richard Diamond and it was Powell himself who eventually brought the series to television via his production company, Four Star Productions. But instead of casting himself in the role, he chose newcomer David Janssen. Janssen, of course, later went on to star in *Harry-O* (See Entry) and *The Fugitive.*

The most intriguing element about the television series, which turned the glib detective into a more serious character, was that "Sam's" face was never seen on-camera; she was lit and photographed to keep her body in shadow. Audiences only knew her by her shapely legs and velvety-smooth voice that was never raised above a whisper.

"I spoke in a very low sexy voice," says Mary. "I don't do that anymore."[3]

It may not sound like very much of a role, but it was enough to earn her legs a photo layout in the May 30, 1959 issue of *TV Guide*, titled " 'Sam' Models the Latest in Hosiery." And it was in that article that her name (Mary Moore) was finally revealed. It was also said to have been responsible for prompting her departure from the series, but at the end of the article *TV Guide* wrote, "Meanwhile, back at the *Richard Diamond* switchboard, a new 'Sam' has replaced Miss Moore. The new 'Sam' has nice legs too—even though they're only seen in black and white."

In his book *Sweethearts of 60s TV,* Ronald L. Smith wrote, "In thirteen weeks, Mary was a leggy legend. Naturally, Mary asked for a raise. When she didn't get it, she left the show."[4]

In hard numbers, the money Ms. Moore was speaking about was an $80 paycheck for each episode of *Richard Diamond, Private Detective.* But in an article, "Sam's Sad Song," which appeared in the August 15, 1959 issue of *TV Guide,* Mary Tyler Moore said, "I was promised more money after the first 13 episodes, but after we filmed 13, the producer was replaced and I didn't get the money. So I left."

Four Star Films' Dick Powell offered yet another reason for Ms. Moore's dismissal: "She got too much publicity and spoiled the gimmick."

A few months after leaving *Richard Diamond, Private Detective,* Mary Tyler Moore recreated her "Sam" role on the October 9, 1959 episode of *77 Sunset Strip,* "The Kookie Caper." She auditioned for the role of Terry Williams, Danny's daughter on *Make Room for Daddy* (See Entry), but lost out to Sherry Jackson, with whom she appeared in the *77 Sunset Strip* episode.

Determined to succeed, Ms. Moore picked up episodic work on more than a dozen programs, including *Steve Canyon, Hawaiian Eye* and *The Aquanauts.* Three years later, Mary Tyler Moore settled down in New Rochelle, New York as Laura Petrie, the wife of Rob Petrie on *The Dick Van Dyke Show.* She later gained even greater recognition for her work on *The Mary Tyler Moore Show.*

Diamond's New York police contact was Lieutenant McGough, played by Regis Toomey, who appeared as Detective Sergeant Les Hart on *Burke's Law* (See Entry) and Doctor Stuart on *Petticoat Junction* (See Entry). When Diamond moved his

2. Some sources give 1937 as the year Mary Tyler Moore was born.
3. Smith, Ronald L. *Sweethearts of '60s TV.* St. Martin's Press, New York, 1989, p. 45.
4. *Ibid.*

operation to Hollywood, California, his new police department liaison was Detective Kile, played by Russ Conway.

The answer to the question asked at the beginning of this entry is Roxanne Brooks, whose legs appeared in the last five episodes of the eighteen filmed for the 1959 season. Unfortunately, Ms. Brooks' legs never carried her to the success achieved by her predecessor, but that's shoe biz.

THE RIFLEMAN

September 30, 1958–July 1, 1963.   ABC

Character:	Hattie Denton
Played by:	Hope Summers
Date(s):	September 30, 1958–November 8, 1960
Replaced by:	Miss Millie Scott
Played by:	Joan Taylor
Date(s):	November 15, 1960–July 1, 1963
Character:	Eddie Holstead
Played by:	John Harmon
Date(s):	September 30, 1958–unknown
Replaced by:	Lou Mallory
Played by:	Patricia Blair
Date(s):	October 15, 1962–July 1, 1963
Character:	Jay Burrage
Played by:	Edgar Buchanan
Date(s):	January 6, 1959–May 19, 1959
Replaced by:	Jay Burrage
Played by:	Jack Kruschen
Date(s):	unknown
Replaced by:	Jay Burrage
Played by:	Ralph Moody
Date(s):	January 24, 1961–July 1, 1963

From 1949 to 1951 Brooklyn-born Chuck Connors was a professional ball player. He was first baseman with the Brooklyn Dodgers and played the infield with both the Chicago Cubs and the Los Angeles Angels.

Then, in 1954, Connors turned in his mitt and bat to become an actor. He gave a memorable performance in his very first televison role, which was on a 1954 episode of the *Adventures of Superman,* "Flight to the North."

As Sylvester J. Superman, a visitor to Metropolis from his home in Skunk Hollow County, he and his mule, Lillybell, answer a personal ad in the *Daily Planet* that is meant for Superman. The ad was placed by Margie Holloway, who wanted Superman to deliver a lemon meringue pie to her fiancé, Steve, who is stationed in Iceville, Alaska.

Naturally, things get fouled up before the real Superman shows up to save the day. Connors' reaction to seeing Super-

man take off is one of the funniest lines in the entire series: "Waaal, if that don't beat all! He just jumped in the air and kep' on goin'!"

Connors followed up this role with more than two dozen appearances on everything from comedies to dramas. His big break came when he landed the starring role in *The Rifleman,* one of the better television Westerns.

Here's the setup: widower Lucas McCain (Chuck Connors) and his twelve-year-old son, Mark (Johnny Crawford), become homesteaders in North Fork, New Mexico, where Lucas does his best to operate a small ranch. The town of North Fork was your typical Western town complete with a general store and a hotel with a saloon.

The first owner of the general store, Hattie Denton, was played by Hope Summers, who later played Aunt Bee's friend, Clara Edwards, on *The Andy Griffith Show.* She was replaced later on by the younger and considerably more attractive Joan Taylor, who was introduced as McCain's love interest, Miss Millie Scott, in an effort to revive the series' sagging ratings.

The owner of the hotel, the Madera House, was Eddie Holstead, who was played by John Harmon. Three episodes into the last season, a new owner of the hotel was introduced in an episode cleverly titled, "Lou Mallory." Depicted as something of a con artist bent on buying up land in North Fork, the new owner of the hotel, which she renamed Mallory House, wasn't really as bad as she was made out to be.

Every decent Western town has got to have a sawbones and North Fork's was Jay Burrage, played during the course of the series by three different actors.

The first was Edgar Buchanan, who had played one of the West's loyal sidekicks, Red Connors, on *Hopalong Cassidy* (See Entry), and later, Uncle Joe on the CBS situation comedy, *Petticoat Junction.* The second was Jack Kruschen, who turned up occasionally between 1985 to 1986 as "Papa" Papadopolis on the ABC sitcom, *Webster.* Just as the series star had appeared in a 1954 episode of the *Adventures of Superman,* so did Ralph Moody, the third actor to play the town's doc.

In "Test of a Warrior," Moody played Okatee, a devious Indian Medicine Man bent on preventing the wise Great Horse from becoming the tribe's new chieftain. Superman, of course, flew in to see that Okatee was defeated.

RIPCORD

September 1961–1963.   Syndicated

Character:	Chuck Lambert
Played by:	Paul Comi
Date(s):	1961–1962
Replaced by:	Charlie Kern
Played by:	Shug Fisher
Date(s):	1962–1963

Thirty minutes of heart-stopping excitement dropped in on America's homes when television's only school for skydiving, Ripcord, Incorporated,[5] opened for business in 1961.

---

5. Some sources say that the skydiving school was named "Skydivers, Inc."

This syndicated adventure series revolved around two sky-diving instructors, Ted McKeever (Larry Pennell) and Jim Buckley (Ken Curtis), who hit the silk each week to fight crime and effect daring rescues.

And since you can't be a parachutist unless you have an airplane to jump from and a pilot to fly the aircraft, Ripcord, Inc. had Chuck Lambert on the payroll. On camera it was Paul Comi who first buckled into the cockpit, but he bailed out in the middle of the first season. He was replaced by Shug Fisher, who played pilot Charlie Kern.

Before taking to the air, Paul Comi had his feet firmly planted on the ground in the town of Gunnison, where he served as Deputy Sheriff on the 1960 syndicated Western series, *Two Faces West*. Later he made it to deep space aboard the Starship Enterprise, as one of the ship's navigators on *Star Trek* (See Entry).

Naturally, neither actor in *Ripcord* actually piloted the aircraft; in reality it was flown by the very talented stunt pilot, Cliff Winters. Winters was once nearly killed in a mid-air collision while filming an episode in 1962. The footage of that near-disaster later found its way into two episodes of the series.

Oh, and while we're on the subject, it was skydiver Lyle Cameron who made it appear that Ted and Jim were doing the jumps. Larry Pennell and Ken Curtis never set foot out of an airborne plane.

RIPTIDE

January 3, 1984–April 18, 1986.   NBC

Character:	Tammy
Played by:	Marla Heasley
Date(s):	January 3, 1984–1984

Replaced by:	Tammy
Played by:	Robin Evans
Date(s):	1984–1986

Character:	Lieutenant Ted Quinlan
Played by:	Jack Ging
Date(s):	January 3, 1984–December 10, 1985

Replaced by:	Lieutenant Joanna Parisi
Played by:	June Chadwick
Date(s):	1985–April 18, 1986

The producers of the enormously successful adventure, *The A-Team,* turned out this entry in the private detective genre which used a cabin cruiser, docked at Slip 7 on Pier 56 in sunny Southern California, as the base of operations.

The ship, the Pier 56 Detective Agency (later called the Riptide Detective Agency), and the series was piloted by three Army buddies. The two hunks, Cody Allen and Nick Ryder were played by Perry King and Joe Penny. Their computer nerd electonics expert, Murray ''Boz'' Bozinsky, was played by Thom Bray.

The series seemed to have all the right elements of a Stephen

J. Cannell production: good scripts, excellent cinematography, a great music track, a likeable cast, car chases, a helicopter and lots of beautiful women in bikinis. But apparently the mix wasn't quite right, becuase the series was canceled after only 56 episodes were shot.

If more hands were needed on a particular case, the boys sometimes recruited Mama Jo (played by Anne Francis in the first episode) and her all-girl crew of the Contessa, the charter boat docked next to theirs.

One of the members of Mama Jo's crew, Tammy, was originally played by Marla Heasley, but she left the crew of the Contessa to replace the departed Melinda Culea as the new female member of *The A-Team* (See Entry).

Ms. Heasley's replacement on *Riptide* was Robin Evans, who had played Terri Collins in *The Eyes of Texas II*, the second of two pilots for an NBC series which was never picked up. This one aired on July 5, 1980. She also had a small role, billed as ''girl,'' in the nostalgic comedy pilot, *High School, U.S.A.*. This was the first of two pilots to feature two generations of television's favorite kids, from Dwayne Hickman, Tony Dow and Angela Cartwright to Michael J. Fox and Nancy McKeon. It aired on NBC on October 16, 1983.

The recurring role of the police department liaison for the Riptide Detective Agency was played initially by the tough-talking Jack Ging, who had already made several guest appearances on *The A-Team* (See Entry). He left *Riptide* and would go on to play the recurring role of General ''Bull'' Fulbright on that series.

The new police lieutenant on *Riptide* wasn't another tough cop, but an attractive female. It was reported in the September 30, 1985 issue of *TV Prolog* that June Chadwick's character, Joanna Parisi, was designed to be both an antagonist and a love interest.

RIVERBOAT

September 13, 1959–January 16, 1961.   NBC

Character:	Captain Grey Holden
Played by:	Darren McGavin
Date(s):	September 13, 1959–January 16, 1961

Replaced by:	Captain Brad Turner
Played by:	Dan Duryea
Date(s):	February 29, 1960–March 7, 1960

Character:	Ben Frazer
Played by:	Burt Reynolds
Date(s):	September 13, 1959–January 2, 1961

Replaced by:	Bill Blake
Played by:	Noah Beery, Jr.
Date(s):	September 19, 1960–January 16, 1961

The first *Enterprise* to sail across the small screen was not a starship, but a riverboat—a riverboat that had been won in a poker game by Grey Holden, who served as Captain for most of the series. Captain Holden was played by Darren McGavin, who earlier starred as Casey on the CBS drama, *Crime Photographer,* and was television's first Mike Hammer in *Mickey Spillane's Mike Hammer* (See Entry). Dan Duryea took over the wheel in two episodes of *Riverboat:* "The Wichita Arrows" and "Fort Epitaph."

Piloting the stern-wheel riverboat for the first half of the first season was Ben Frazer, who was played by Burt Reynolds, in his first television series role. When his character was dropped, Reynolds landed a recurring role as the halfbreed blacksmith, Quint Asper, on *Gunsmoke.* Burt's tenure with the series ran from September 29, 1962 to June 1, 1963. He went on to star as Lieutenant John Hawk in his own police series, *Hawk,* which aired on ABC, September 8 to December 1966, and then was revived on NBC as reruns from April to August 1976.

He later achieved superstardom in motion pictures, beginning with his role as Lewis in the 1972 backwoods horror film, DELIVERANCE, and followed up in 1977 and 1980 as Bandit in SMOKEY AND THE BANDIT and SMOKEY AND THE BANDIT II.

In 1988 Burt Reynolds returned to weekly television as B.L. Stryker and made a guest appearance as himself in an episode of *Carol and Company* the following year. *B.L. Stryker* didn't last very long, but that didn't keep good ol' boy Burt down, because he returned on September 21, 1990 as Wood Newton in the CBS comedy, *Evening Shade.*

In an interesting casting move, young and handsome Burt Reynolds was replaced on *Riverboat* by the much older Noah Beery, Jr., the son of actor Noah Beery, Sr. and the nephew of Wallace Beery.

Beery's roles on television span from his days as Joey the clown on *Circus Boy* to Joseph "Rocky" Rockford, Jim Rockford's dad on *The Rockford Files,* a role that earned him two Emmy award nominations for Outstanding Continuing Performance by a Supporting Actor in a Drama Series.

Among the more than eight-dozen passengers who took a trip on the hundred-foot-long Mississippi paddlewheeler were two actors who later flew aboard the U.S.S. Enterprise in classic episodes of *Star Trek.*

Ricardo Montalban guest-starred as Khan in the February 16, 1967 episode, "Space Seed," which later spawned the 1982 motion picture sequel STAR TREK II: THE WRATH OF KHAN. The rotund Stanley Adams starred as Cyrano Jones in the December 29, 1967 tale, "The Trouble with Tribbles," and the animated entry, "More Trouble with Tribbles," which aired on October 6, 1973.

THE ROARING 20'S

October 15, 1960–January 20, 1962.   ABC

Character:	Scott Norris
Played by:	Rex Reason
Date(s):	October 15, 1960–June 3, 1961

Replaced by:	Jim "Duke" Williams
Played by:	John Dehner
Date(s):	October 7, 1961–January 20, 1962

In 1920 a flapper was a wild and free young woman. She drank, smoked, danced to jazz music and often threw caution to the winds in her pursuit of a good time. In 1960 the word "flapper" became synonymous with actress Dorothy Provine, who starred as Delaware "Pinky" Pinkham, the owner of New York's Charleston Club in the newspaper crime drama, *The Roaring 20's.*

The show was set during the same period as *The Untouchables,* which had premiered on ABC the previous year and was going like gangbusters. This was not a direct copy of *The Untouchables,* although there were many similarities. The major differences were that this series was set in New York City and followed the exploits of two newspaper reporter/columnists working for the *New York Record.* There was, however, plenty of violence.

Pinky's posh speakeasy was often frequented by shady underworld types—local crime bosses, crooked politicians, bootleggers, mobsters and just your run-of-the-mill hoods.

The newspapermen she helped were Pat Garrison and Scott Norris. Donald May apeared as Garrison in all forty-five episodes, but Rex Reason, who played Scott Norris, disappeared at the beginning of the second season and was replaced by John Dehner as Duke Williams in the new season's second episode, "Kitty Goes West." There was some friction between the two journalists because Duke always tried to beat Garrison to the stories.

Prior to his work on *The New York Record,* Rex Reason starred as newspaper editor Adam MacLean in the 1958 syndicated Western, *Man without a Gun.* Before that he was known for his work in science fiction films. His most famous role was in 1955 as the earth scientist, Dr. Cal Meacham, in THIS ISLAND EARTH.

Reason's counterpart, John Dehner, later appeared as Cy Bennett, Doris Martin's second boss, on *The Doris Day Show* (See Entry).

THE ROOKIES

September 11, 1972–June 29, 1976.   ABC

Character:	Officer Willie Gillis
Played by:	Michael Ontkean
Date(s):	September 11, 1972–March 25, 1974

Replaced by:	Officer Chris Owens
Played by:	Bruce Fairbairn
Date(s):	September 9, 1974–June 29, 1976

The next generation of police officers was showcased in this series about three young rookies assigned to Station Number 7 of the Southern California Police Department.

Officers Terry Webster (Georg Stanford Brown), Willie Gillis (Michael Ontkean), and Mike Danko (Sam Melville) have come to the force from different backgrounds, but all share the single philosophy of nonviolent police work.

This approach to law enforcement is tempered by their superior and mentor, Lieutenant Eddie Ryker, a hardened and more experienced officer, who is also less idealistic. Lieutenant Ryker was played by Gerald S. O'Loughlin for the entire series, although Darren McGavin, the first captain of the Enterprise on *Riverboat* (See Entry), created the role in the series pilot.

Rookie Gillis' last assignment of the second season placed him on juvenile detail, "but the duty proves particularly trying for Willie, who encounters more pain and death than he's emotionally prepared to handle."[6] The duty must have been even worse than described in *TV Guide* because when the third season began, Gillis was gone.

In "An Ugly Way to Die," "The idealistic young cops begin a third season with a search for an arsonist who murders firemen. Bruce Fairbairn joins the cast as an intense new officer assigned to work with an unreceptive Terry Webster (Georg Stanford Brown)"[7]

When the last case was wrapped up in 1976, Fairbairn went behind the scenes of the fictitious soap opera, *Generations,* as Bobby Danzig on the CBS drama, *Behind the Screen,* which aired from October 9, 1981 to January 8, 1982. Two years later he joined the cast of an honest-to-goodness CBS evening soap opera, *Knots Landing,* as Ray Geary.

ROSEANNE

October 18, 1988–.   ABC

Character:	D.J. Conner
Played by:	Sal Barone
Date(s):	October 18, 1988

Replaced by:	D.J. Conner
Played by:	Michael Fishman
Date(s):	November 22, 1988–

Character:	Becky Conner
Played by:	Lecy Goranson
Date(s):	October 18, 1988–October 12, 1993

Replaced by:	Becky Conner
Played by:	Sarah Chalke
Date(s):	November 16, 1993–

In the annals of sitcomdom, Roseanne and Dan Conner were literally two of the biggest sitcom parents to appear on the small screen—which they filled edge-to-edge.

The title character was played by standup comedienne Roseanne Barr who in May of 1989 was reported to have tipped the scales at 212 pounds while her six-foot-three co-star, John Goodman, weighed in at 260 pounds.

As in *The Donna Reed Show, Roseanne*'s central character was the woman of the household, not the husband—but that's where the similarities end. In place of the usual understanding, syrupy-sweet TV mom, Roseanne was out-and-out acerbic, albeit honest. Roseanne Barr had no illusions about not fitting into the mold of the traditional sitcom mom, as she explained in a 1989 *TV Guide* interview:

"I'm not Lucy tryin' to hide 20 bucks from Ricky, or June Cleaver glidin' around a dustproof house in pearls and heels. I'm a woman who works hard and loves her family, but they can drive her *nuts.*"[8] There was never any question that the Conners loved their children, and each other, it was just the unconventional (by sitcom standards) way they showed it as they verbally tormented their three kids and good-naturedly flung caustic barbs at each other. "It's a pleasure to see real family situations approached with humor,"[9] wrote Timothy Hunter in *TV Pro-Log.*

Instead of frittering her days away baking brownies, Roseanne Conner worked an eight-hour shift on the assembly line at Wellman Plastics in Lanford, Illinois. Husband Dan was a small building contractor and did the best he could to stay employed installing drywall. He later opened his own business, Lanford Motorcycles, that went belly-up in the fifth-season opener, "Terms of Estrangement." Roseanne quit her job at Wellman at the beginning of the second season and has subsequently worked at a beauty salon and as a waitress, until she finally opened her own diner "The Lunch Box." So even though Roseanne did work for several different employers over the years, these were not direct replacements.

Another change worth noting is Roseanne's last name. Beginning with the fourth season opener, "A Bitter Pill to Swallow," which aired on September 17, 1991, Roseanne Barr officially began using her new married name, Roseanne Arnold. She married comedian and comedy writer Tom Arnold, her second husband, on January 20, 1990. And in the episode of October 27, 1992, "Halloween IV," Sara Rue played Roseanne as a teenager.

Remarkably, *Roseanne,* which was the second-highest-rated series on television in its first season and toppled *Cosby,* the number-one-rated series, in its second season, has never won an Emmy, though in 1992, Laurie Metcalf, who played Roseanne's sister, Jackie Harris, won an Emmy for Best Supporting Actress in a Comedy Series.

Co-star John Goodman was nominated several times, while Roseanne Arnold received her first nomination for Best Actress in a Comedy Series in 1992. However, at the forty-fourth annual Emmy Awards, held at the Pasadena Civic Auditorium on August 29, 1992, the svelte statuette went to *Murphy Brown*'s star, Candice Bergen.

The Conners were the semi-proud parents of three children. Michael Fishman appeared as their son, D.J. However, the first episode of the series, "Life and Stuff," featured Sal Barone as their six-year-old son. And although some published sources indicate that Sal Barone appeared only in this pilot episode, *TV Guide* listed Barone as the actor playing D.J. in "We're in the

6. *TV Guide.* Vol. 22, No. 12, Issue #1095, March 23, 1974.

7. *TV Guide.* (Fall Preview issue). Vol. 22, No. 36, September 9, 1974, Issue #1119, p. A-59.

8. Hicks, Jack. "TV's Battle of the Sexes: With Roseanne, It's No Holds Barred." *TV Guide,* Vol. 37, No. 4, January 28, 1989, Issue # 1870, p. 4.

9. Hunter, Timothy. *TV Pro-Log: Television Programs and Production News.* Volume 44, Number 4, September 23–29, 1991, p.1.

Money,'' the October 25, 1988 episode. *TV Guide* gives the first appearance of Michael Fishman as D.J. in ''Language Lessons,'' the November 22, 1988 episode of the series.

D.J.'s older sisters were Darlene, played by Sarah Gilbert and Becky, played for the first six seasons by Lecy Goranson. When Ms. Goranson decided to attend college, she was written out of the series by having her character marry her boyfriend, Mark Healey and move away to Minneapolis. Mark was played by Glenn Quinn, who from August through October, 1992 appeared as Cedric Gray on the exciting, but all too short-lived ABC Medieval adventure series, *Covington Cross*.

Becky's character was not immediately replaced becuase there existed an open invitation to Ms. Goranson to return to the series as her schedule permitted. According to an article that appeared in the August 22, 1992 edition of *USA Today* ''Becky will elope with Mark, but the newlyweds will drop in from time to time and drive the household nuts. According to Tom Arnold, Ms. Goranson '. . . has decided to go off to college. She has our blessing. She'll still be on several episodes this year. She's a big part of our show and we wish her all the best.' '' But, by November 1993, it was evident that she would not be returning to the series and because she was a ''big part of their show,'' the producers opted to recast the role and reintroduce the character.

The ''Homecoming'' episode opens with Roseanne on the phone with Darlene telling her that she should come home for her father's twenty-fifth reunion of his high school football team because her sister Becky is also coming home. What Roseanne neglected to tell Darlene is that she may not recognize her sister who would be played by a new actress, Sarah Chalke.

Things are not going well financially for the young couple and Roseanne, against her better judgement, invites the kids to move into the house—just until they can put away enough money to get on their feet. So it looks like it will be all in the family for the foreseeable future.

During the closing credits, the Conners are sitting together watching television. We are looking at the back of the set, but can hear the familiar *Bewitched* theme song playing.

ROSEANNE: I can't believe they replaced that Darrin.

JACKIE: Why? It was a hit show, they knew they could get away with anything.

BECKY: (Sighs) Oh well, I liked the second Darrin much better.

ROUTE 66

October 7, 1960–September 18, 1964.   CBS
June 8, 1993–July 13, 1993   NBC

Character:	Tod Stiles
Played by:	Martin Milner
Date(s):	October 7, 1960–September 18, 1964

Replaced by:	Nick Lewis
Played by:	James Wilder
Date(s):	June 8, 1993–July 13, 1993

Character:	Buzz Murdoch
Played by:	George Maharis
Date(s):	October 7, 1960–June 1, 1962

Replaced by:	Linc Case
Played by:	Glenn Corbett
Date(s):	March 22, 1963–September 18, 1964

Replaced by:	Arthur Clark
Played by:	Dan Cortese
Date(s):	June 8, 1993–July 13, 1993

Named after a highway that traversed the United States from Chicago to Santa Monica, this series was nothing like the 1969 series, *Then Came Bronson,* whose closing theme song spoke of ''Goin' down that long lonesome highway.''

Route 66 was anything but lonesome. In fact, that is what helped to make this series such a success. The stars were two young men, Tod Stiles (Martin Milner), the poor little rich kid whose fortune went belly-up when his father died unexpectedly, and his sidekick, Buzz Murdoch (George Maharis), who grew up in what was known as the Hell's Kitchen section of New York.

Together they traveled across the county in Tod's beautiful Chevrolet Corvette convertible, making new friends, finding romance and helping out a ''neighbor'' or two. They even learned a valuable lesson every once in a while. But most of all, they enjoyed their freedom.

Suffering from a case of hepatitis, series co-star George Maharis was forced to pull off *Route 66* in June of 1962. Since it's just no fun to drive aimlessly across the country alone, Tod picked up Linc Case (Glenn Corbett), a Vietnam war hero from Houston who, like the Jim Bronson character in *Then Came Bronson,* was searching for himself and the meaning of life.

Corbett appeared in dozens of shows including episodes of *Gunsmoke, The Man from U.N.C.L.E., Bonanza* and a couple of *Alias Smith and Jones*. He even turned up as astronaut Zefrem Cochrane in the ''Metamorphosis'' episode of *Star Trek,* which aired on NBC on November 10, 1967. Still, Glenn Corbett did not have another regular series role until the fall of 1976, when he joined the cast of the NBC daytime soap opera, *The Doctors,* as Jason Aldrich. Evening soap opera fans may remember him as Paul Morgan from the CBS entry, *Dallas.*

NBC planned a revival of *Route 66* for 1993 and issued press releases that explained the updated premise. Nick Lewis (James Wilder) is Buzz Murdoch's son but never knew of his father's existence. After Buzz's death, Nick inherits his dad's only worldy possession—the perfectly preserved red-and-white 1962 Corvette.

He takes off on Route 66 and gives a lift to a hitchhiker, Arthur Clark, a good-natured adventurer played by Dan Cortese, who was at the time a hot young comedian who had

Cruising down *Route 66* in their Chevrolet Corvette convertible are Tod Stiles (Martin Milner, left) and Buzz Murdoch (George Maharis, right).

made a name for himself as the hip huckster in a series of MTV-style ads for Burger King in 1992 and 1993. He also hosted sports segments on the MTV cable music network.

Like the Lewis and Clark expedition that began in 1803 to explore the territory of the Louisiana Purchase, this Lewis and Clark team cruised what John Steinbeck called ''the mother road,'' in search of adventure, ducking trouble and discovering America as did Buzz and Tod and Buzz and Linc in the carefree sixties.

If the boys watched their speed, they may have been able to complete the trip on a single tank of gas, as the limited-run series ran out of fuel after just four episodes.

THE ROYAL FAMILY

September 18, 1991–May 13, 1992.   CBS

Character:	Alexander Alphonso ''Al'' Royal
Played by:	Redd Foxx
Date(s):	September 18, 1991–November 27, 1991

Replaced by:	Aunt ''Cocoa'' Ruth
Played by:	Jackee
Date(s):	November 27, 1991–May 13, 1992

The Royal Family marked the triumphant return to television of Redd Foxx, who had not had a regular television series since *The Redd Foxx Show* left the ABC schedule on April 19, 1986.

What made this show work was that no one tried to reinvent Foxx, they gave Al the same irascible character traits that the audience knew and loved when he played Fred Sanford on *Sanford and Son* (See Entry).

The first episode of the series, which is set in Atlanta, Georgia, introduced Al as a postal worker (supposedly one of Atlanta's first black postal carriers) who has just retired and is looking forward to spending time with his wife, Victoria (Della Reese). That is until their daughter, Elizabeth (Mariann Aalda) shows up.

ELIZABETH: Dexter and I are getting a divorce.

AL: (Excitedly) Yes, yes, yes!

VICTORIA: Al, if you don't shut up that's going to be the last "Yes" you hear in this bedroom for a long time. (TO ELIZABETH) Well, if there's anything you need, baby, we're here for you.

ELIZABETH: Well, actually I'm glad that you said that. There seems to be some sort of legal tie-up with the house and I was hoping that until things get straightened out, that the kids and I could stay here.

Elizabeth's three children are a sixteen-year-old daughter, Kim (Sylver Gregory), a fifteen-year-old son, Curtis (Larenz Tate), and an adorable preschooler named Hillary (Naya Rivera). Mariann Aalda plays the Royal's daughter, Elizabeth (who incidentally has the same name as Fred Sanford's deceased wife on *Sanford and Son*).

The show was just beginning to catch on when the sixty-eight-year-old Redd Foxx died of a sudden heart attack shortly after collapsing during a rehearsal.

In a creative move to save the promising but fledgling series, the producers addressed Foxx's/Al's death in the storyline of the November 27, 1991 program. The sentimental and tasteful episode, "New Beginnings," shared warm good-byes from family members and friends, including a guest appearance by Redd Foxx's lifelong friend, Slappy White, as Shag. It also featured a moving rendition of the gospel song, *Take It to the Lord in Prayer,* sung by Della Reese.

The episode also introduced Jackee as Della Reese's estranged half-sister, Ruth, who has come to live with Victoria to help her cope after Al's death. Jackee, who at the time was still using her last name, Harry, had previously starred as Sandra Clark on the NBC situation comedy, *227,* which aired from September 14, 1985 to August 12, 1989.

Then, for some unexplained reason, when *The Royal Family* returned on April 8, 1992, Jackee's character had been redefined as Victoria and Al's long-lost daughter who had run away from home when she was seventeen—to which Redd Foxx might growl, "Mother, father! She's Victoria's half-sister, you big dummy!"

THE RUGGLES

November 3, 1949–June 19, 1952.   ABC

Character: Margaret Ruggles
Played by: Irene Tedrow
Date(s):   November 3, 1949–unknown

Replaced by: Margaret Ruggles
Played by: Erin O'Brien-Moore
Date(s):   1950–June 19, 1952

This early situation comedy starred veteran character actor Charlie Ruggles as an insurance salesman and head of the household. His missus was at first played by Irene Tedrow, who went on to become the second of four Janet Archers in *Meet Corliss Archer* (See Entry).

Charlie Ruggles starred in more than eighty motion pictures including the 1935 comedy, RUGGLES OF RED GAP. This has always caused some confusion because of the actor's last name. To set the record straight, *Ruggles of Red Gap* was a novel written in 1915 by Harry Leon Wilson about an English butler, Marmaduke Ruggles, who moves to the town of Red Gap in the American West.

In the film, the title role was played by Charles Laughton, while Charlie Ruggles plays his friend, an American rancher named Egbert Floud. Charlie Ruggles' more than fifty appearances in episodic television include the November 25, 1965 episode of *The Munsters,* "Herman's Driving Test," in which he played the incompetent license bureau chief.

He lent his distinctively friendly voice to the animated Aesop, who appeared regularly on ABC's intelligent animated series, *Rocky and his Friends,* which aired from September 29, 1959 to September 23, 1961.

RUN, JOE, RUN!

September 7, 1974–September 4, 1976.   NBC

Character: Sergeant William Corey
Played by: Arch Whiting
Date(s):   September 7, 1974–August 1975

Replaced by: Josh McCoy
Played by: Chad States
Date(s):   September 6, 1975–September 4, 1976

In his book *Saturday Morning TV,* author Gary Grossman wrote, "In 1974, NBC gave a show to a German shepherd with a David Janssen complex. *Run, Joe, Run!* attempted to combine Janssen's *The Fugitive* with *The Adventures of Rin Tin Tin.*" This was a fair assessment of this live-action Saturday morning adventure series about Joe, a German shepherd with a price on his head. The price is $200, and it was placed there by the United States Army because it was believed that Joe had attacked his master during his training for the K-9 Corps.

This, of course, was not the case, but the canine knew it was better to high-tail it out of there until he could be proven innocent.

The dog's trainer, Sergeant William Corey (Arch Whiting), the only person who could vindicate the pooch, takes out after his former student, but is called back to active duty before having the opportunity to prove Joe's innocence.

Some ten years earlier, Arch Whiting, as Crewman Sparks, served aboard the Seaview under Admiral Nelson's command on the ABC science fiction *Voyage to the Bottom of the Sea,* which aired from September 14, 1964 to September 15, 1968.

Joe, who was still on the lam when the second season began, met up with and became the traveling companion of a mountain man and backpacker, Josh McCoy (Chad States), who was unaware of the dog's past.

S

THE SAINT

1963–1966   Syndicated
May 21, 1967-September 12, 1969   NBC-CBS

Character: Simon Templar, "The Saint"
Played by: Roger Moore
Date(s):   1963–1966
                       May 21, 1967–September 12, 1969

Replaced by: Simon Templar, "The Saint"
Played by: Ian Ogilvy
Date(s):   December 21, 1979–August 15, 1980

Replaced by: Simon Templar, "The Saint"
Played by: Andrew Clarke
Date(s):   June 12, 1987

Replaced by: Simon Templar, "The Saint"
Played by: Simon Dutton
Date(s):   October 1989–January 1990

Character: Inspector Claude Teal
Played by: Ivor Dean
Date(s):   1964–September 12, 1969

Replaced by: Inspector Claude Teal
Played by: Winsley Pithy
Date(s):   1963 (one episode only)

Replaced by: Inspector Claude Teal
Played by: Norman Pitt
Date(s):   1963 (one episode only)

Replaced by: Inspector John Fernack
Played by: Kevin Tighe
Date(s):   June 12, 1987

Replaced by: Inspector Claude Teal
Played by: David Ryall
Date(s):   October 15, 1989

Certainly The Saint was a hero, but he also had a touch of larceny about him and often worked outside the law to achieve his ends, which were to bring evil doers to justice. He was not a straightforward lawman like Jack Webb's Sergeant Joe Friday or even the Lone Ranger, but was more a combination of Robin Hood, James Bond and Zorro.

Like all three, he was a gentleman. Like Robin Hood and Zorro, he took ill-gotten gains and returned them to their rightful owners. Like James Bond he was sophisticated, and like Zorro, was independently wealthy.

Simon Templar first appeared as The Saint in a novel by Leslie Charteris in the late 1920s. Radio audiences were treated to the voices of Edgar Barrier, Brian Aherne, Tom Conway and even Vincent Price as The Saint. The inspector was played by John Brown.

By 1938 Simon Templar had arrived on the big screen in THE SAINT IN NEW YORK, the first of nine SAINT feature films that would star Louis Hayward, George Sanders and Hugh Sinclair as the debonair sleuth. The last of these features, THE SAINT'S GIRL FRIDAY, was released in 1954. The Saint has even appeared in several French films with Jean Marais in the title role.

Creator Charteris was never completely satisfied with the portrayal of his character on film; he felt it had been watered down. This prompted him to establish his own televison production company for the sole purpose of producing an "authentic" *Saint* series. It was to star David Niven, but never made it much past the development stage.

About ten years later, Sir Lew Grade's Associated Television committed to a video series starring Roger Moore. Sir Lew cast Moore because he was already known to both British and American audiences as Ivanhoe and Maverick and this would, it was hoped, insure the success of the series that reached American viewers in May of 1967.

In 1973, Roger Moore stepped into Sean Connery's tuxedo as James Bond in LIVE AND LET DIE. The following year, when Moore appeared on NBC's *Tonight Show Starring Johnny Carson* to promote his latest feature film, GOLD, Carson introduced him as Maverick, The Saint and James Bond all rolled up into one. Roger Moore is talented, speaks very well and is extremely handsome. Yet one of his most endearing qualities is that he is self-effacing and tries not to take himself too seriously. This is what makes him so good at portraying characters who are just a little bit larger than life.

Moore continued as the Saint for all 114 episodes, with Ivor Dean as Scotland Yard's Inspector Claude Eustace Teal. There were, however, a couple of episodes early on in the series in which the inspector was played by Winsley Pithy and Norman Pitt.

Simon Templar was back in *Return of the Saint,* an updated

albeit short-lived version which first aired on CBS on December 21, 1979. This new Templar was played by Ian Ogilvy, who had appeared as Mike in a 1967 Boris Karloff horror film, THE SORCERERS, which also featured Ivor Dean as Inspector Matalon.

A third attempt to bring back *The Saint* starred Australian-born actor Andrew Clarke in a failed 1987 pilot. Commenting on his non-British accent in the May 16, 1978 issue of *TV Guide,* Clarke said, "I just have to smooth out my g'dy's and talk out of the front of my mouth instead of the middle, the way both Americans and Australians do."

Simon Dutton became television's fourth Simon Templar in "The Brazilian Connection," the first in a series of made-for-television movies which aired under the umbrella title of *Mystery Wheel of Adventure.* Much like *The NBC Sunday Mystery Movie,* which alternated *Columbo, McMillan and Wife* and *McCloud,* the syndicated *Mystery Wheel of Adventure* alternated *The Saint* with *Dick Francis Mysteries* and *Star Trap.*

The first of these new *Saint* adventures, "The Brazilian Connection," featured Kevin Tighe as Inspector John Fernack who worked out of the New Scotland Yard. Tighe had played paramedic Roy DeSoto on the Jack Webb drama *Emergency,* which aired on NBC from January 22, 1972 to September 3, 1977. In a scene between Teal and his superior, Teal summed up his relationship with The Saint: "Templar and I go back rather a long way. . . . We have kind of . . . an understanding."

SANFORD AND SON

January 14, 1972–September 2, 1977.   NBC

Character:	Fred Sanford
Played by:	Redd Foxx
Date(s):	January 14, 1972–September 2, 1977
	March 15, 1980–July 10, 1981

Replaced by:	Grady Wilson
Played by:	Whitman Mayo
Date(s):	September 13, 1974–September 2, 1977

Character:	Lamont Sanford
Played by:	Demond Wilson
Date(s):	January 14, 1972–September 2, 1977

Replaced by:	Cal Pettie
Played by:	Dennis Burkley
Date(s):	March 15, 1980–July 10, 1981

Character:	Officer Swanhauser
Played by:	Noam Pitlik
Date(s):	1972

Replaced by:	Officer "Smitty" Smith
Played by:	Hal Williams
Date(s):	1972–1976

Replaced by:	Officer "Happy" Hopkins
Played by:	Howard Platt
Date(s):	1972–1976

Character:	Donna Harris
Played by:	Lynn Hamilton
Date(s):	January 14, 1972–September 2, 1977

Replaced by:	Evelyn "Eve" Lewis
Played by:	Marguerite Ray
Date(s):	March 15, 1980–July 10, 1981

Fred Sanford was the proprietor of Sanford and Son, a junk shop located at 9114 South Central, in the Watts section of Los Angeles. He was sixty-five years old but didn't feel it or act it, as was evident from this conversation he had with his fiancée, Donna Harris (Lynn Hamilton), a practical nurse.

> DONNA: You know what they say. You're as young as you feel.

> FRED: Yeah, well I'm sixty-five. And people say I look fifty-five. And I feel forty-five. I'd settle for thirty-five. But you make me feel twenty-five.

He was ornery, cantankerous, set in his ways, didn't trust anyone and was one of the most popular characters on television for more than five years. It began when Screen Gems bought the American television rights to a popular British series, *Steptoe and Son.*

The first pilot (produced in 1965 by NBC) starred Lee Tracy, who had been the third of four actors to play Martin Kane in *Martin Kane, Private Eye* (See Entry). Steptoe's son was played by Aldo Ray, who had co-starred as Chet Keefer in the 1952 dramatic comedy, THE MARRYING KIND, with Judy Holliday. When the pilot didn't sell, *All in the Family*'s producer, Norman Lear, purchased the rights from Screen Gems.

Lear's pilot starred Barnard Hughes and Paul Sorvino, but it didn't sell either. He created a hit when he recast with black actors. The characters' names were changed from Steptoe to Sanford because that was really Redd Foxx's last name, and Lamont was the name of one of his closest friends.

Fred Sanford was at his best when arguing with his son, Lamont. He'd threateningly ask him, "How'd you like one across your lips?" And he'd call Lamont "dummy" in much the same manner that Archie Bunker called his son-in-law, Mike, "meathead."

For a short time during the 1974/1975 season, Redd Foxx left the series in a dispute over script control, working conditions and money. Fred's friend, Grady Wilson (Whitman Mayo), already a regular on the series, moved into the Sanford house for a while to look after Lamont. For the first two weeks, Fred's absence was covered by saying that he was attending the funeral of a friend back in St. Louis.

Foxx eventually returned after windows were installed in his dressing room and the *Sanford and Son* rehearsal hall. He also

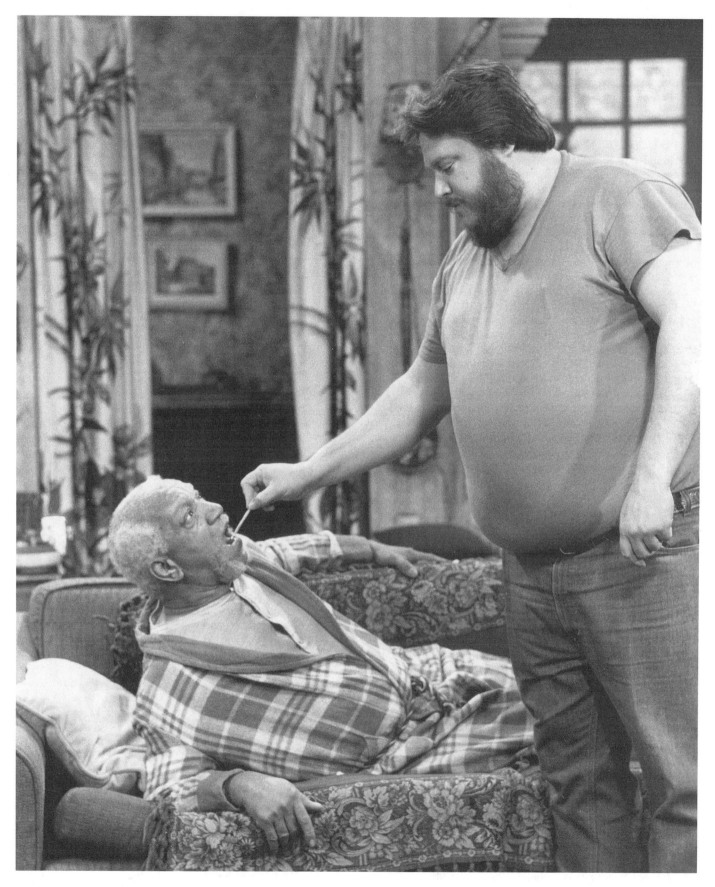

Fred G. Sanford (Redd Foxx, left) is convinced that his partner, Cal Pettie (Dennis Burkley), is trying to kill him in ''Gaslight,'' the June 5, 1981 episode of *Sanford*.

got a golf cart so that he could move more quickly and easily around the long corridors at NBC, an increase in salary and a percentage of the show's profits.

Foxx finally left *Sanford and Son* in 1977 because of a commitment he had made to ABC for his own variety series, *The Redd Foxx Comedy Hour,* which aired from September 15, 1977 to January 26, 1978.

Demond Wilson, who remained with the series, soon found himself locked in a contract dispute over money; he was now *Sanford and Son*'s only star. One source reported that Wilson also wanted a Silver Cloud Rolls-Royce, which at the time was valued at $85,000, in exchange for signing a long-term contract. His demands were rejected and he too left the junkyard.

The network didn't want to lose the audience it had built and revamped the show, which premiered on September 16, 1977 as *The Sanford Arms,* named after the rooming house run by Fred's sister-in-law, Esther Anderson (LaWanda Page), who, like Grady, had been a regular on *Sanford and Son.*

Baby I'm Back was more than just a title for a new sitcom; it also hailed Demond Wilson's return to a weekly series. In the program, Wilson played Raymond Ellis, who has returned after deserting his wife seven years earlier, only to learn that she has just had him declared legally dead. The series didn't live long either and aired on CBS only from January 30 to August 12, 1978. Wilson's next regular series role was as Oscar Madison in the rehashed version of *The Odd Couple* (See Entry).

The Redd Foxx Comedy Hour didn't do very well and was canceled after sixteen programs, but Redd Foxx had no series to return to because *The Sanford Arms* had been canceled after only four episodes had aired.

An attempt was made to revive Foxx's initial hit, *Sanford and Son,* but without co-star Demond Wilson the storyline had to be reworked. What emerged was *Sanford,* set back at the Sanford and Son junkyard, which looked exactly the same but had somehow been mysteriously relocated to 4707 South Central, Los Angeles.

It was explained that Lamont had left Sanford and Son to work on the Alaska pipeline. This gave Fred the opportunity to sell a share of "The Sanford Empire" to Cal Pettie for $2,000. Cal (Dennis Burkley) was an overweight white Southerner who moved in with Fred, whom he politely called "Mr. Sanford." He was sincere, friendly, and did everything he could to make *Sanford and Son* more successful. He was also the butt of Fred's jokes, just as Lamont had been.

Audiences may remember Dennis Burkley as Mac Slattery, a role he played on *Mary Hartman, Mary Hartman* from 1977 to 1978, or for his supporting role as Sam Dickey in the *Maude* spinoff, *Hanging In.*

The new love interest for Fred Sanford was Eve Lewis, a rich widow from Beverly Hills, played by Marguerite Ray.

Only slightly more successful than *The Sanford Arms,* *Sanford* closed its doors for good after twenty-three episodes.

SAVED BY THE BELL

November 30, 1988–December 21, 1988.   DISNEY
August 20, 1989–   NBC

Character:	Zachary "Zack" Ray Morris
Played by:	Mark-Paul Gosselaar
Date(s):	November 30, 1988–September 4, 1993
Replaced by:	Scott Erickson
Played by:	Robert Telfer
Date(s):	September 11, 1993–September 3, 1994
Character:	Karen
Played by:	Carla Gugino
Date(s):	November 30, 1988–December 21, 1988
Replaced by:	Jessica "Jesse" Myrtle Spano
Played by:	Elizabeth Berkley
Date(s):	August 20, 1989–September 4, 1993
Replaced by:	Vicki Needleman
Played by:	Bonnie Russavage
Date(s):	September 11, 1993–September 3, 1994
Character:	Nicole "Nikki" Coleman
Played by:	Heather Hopper
Date(s):	November 30, 1988–December 21, 1988
Replaced by:	Kelly Kapowski
Played by:	Tiffani-Amber Thiessen
Date(s):	August 20, 1989–September 4, 1993
Replaced by:	Lindsay Warner
Played by:	Natalia Cigliati
Date(s):	September 11, 1993–September 3, 1994
Character:	Mickey
Played by:	Max Battimo
Date(s):	November 30, 1988–December 21, 1988
Replaced by:	Albert Clifford "A.C." Slater
Played by:	Mario Lopez
Date(s):	August 20, 1989–September 4, 1993
Replaced by:	Tommy De "Tommy D" Lucca
Played by:	Jonathan Angel
Date(s):	September 11, 1993–
Character:	Lisa Marie Turtle
Played by:	Lark Voorhies
Date(s):	August 20, 1989–September 4, 1993
Replaced by:	Megan Jones
Played by:	Bianca Lawson
Date(s):	September 11, 1993–

Character:	Samuel "Sam" "Screech" Powers
Played by:	Dustin Diamond
Date(s):	November 30, 1988–September 4, 1993

Replaced by:	Barton "Weasel" Wyzell
Played by:	Isaac Lidsky
Date(s):	September 11, 1993–September 3, 1994

Character:	Ox
Played by:	Troy Froman
Date(s):	unknown–September 4, 1993

Replaced by:	"Crunch" Grabowski
Played by:	Ryan Hurst
Date(s):	September 11, 1993–

Character:	Peter Morris
Played by:	Robert Pine
Date(s):	unknown

Replaced by:	Derek Morris
Played by:	John Sanderford
Date(s):	October 13, 1990
	October 10, 1992

Here's a live-action sitcom aimed at teens and preteens that originated on cable and earned a prominent place on a network's Saturday morning lineup as an alternative to the usual animated fare.

This is not as far-fetched as it sounds because it was produced for the Disney Channel by NBC Productions—an industry first. As originally conceived, *Saved by the Bell* was titled *Good Morning, Miss Bliss* and first aired as a pilot on NBC on July 11, 1987. The story was set in an unnamed school in Indianapolis and centered around the warm-hearted and revered grade school teacher, Miss Carrie Bliss. The title role was played by longtime Disney favorite, Hayley Mills, in her first American television series. Ms. Mills, who won a special Academy Award for her portrayal of Pollyanna in the 1960 Disney comedy of the same name, went on to star in a number of other well-known family oriented comedies. One of Hayley's most famous Disney films was 1961's THE PARENT TRAP, in which she played twins Sharon McKendrick and Susan Evers. Four years later, Hayley Mills starred in two more successful Disney features. She played Nikky Ferris in the action/adventure film, THE MOON-SPINNERS, and Patti Randall in the enjoyable comedy, THAT DARN CAT.

Editor and Publisher Timothy Hunter reported in the February 6–12, 1989, edition of *TV Pro-Log* that "*Good Morning, Miss Bliss,* the NBC Productions sitcom recently cancelled by the Disney Channel, will move to NBC's Saturday (noon-1 p.m. NYT) lineup on a date to be announced. Hayley Mills, who played the title character, has left the show; hence the series will shift focus from a junior high school teacher to five or six of her students and be retitled *Saved by the Bell.*"

The location was moved to the fictional Bayside High School in the equally fictional town of Palisades, California, while the focus of the stories shifted from the standpoint of the teacher to that of the teenage students. Although not a direct replacement, Dennis Haskins assumed the authority figure role of Mr. Richard Belding, the school's principal. He actually replaced Oliver Clark, who appeared as Gerald Belding in the original NBC pilot.

When the show moved from the Disney Channel to NBC, the only students saved by the producers were the wealthy Lisa Marie Turtle (Lark Voorhies); the handsome blonde preppy, Zachary Ray "Zack" Morris (Mark-Paul Gosselaar); and the class nerd, Samuel "Screech" Powers (Dustin Diamond). Added to the cast were the tall and lithe Jessica "Jesse" Myrtle Spano, played by Elizabeth Berkley, who appeared as Deborah, the high-priced call girl, in "The Death of Sheila," the October 3, 1992 episode of the CBS action drama *Raven.*

Tiffani-Amber Thiessen, who graduated from the Valerie Bertinelli school of wholesome sitcom good looks, played Kelly Kapowski, Zack's first girlfriend and captain of Bayside's cheerleaders. To emphasize the importance of their relationship, Screech once said that Kelly and Zack were the hottest couple since Betty and Barney Rubble. Kelly watchers may have spotted Ms. Thiessen in "There's a Girl in My Ficus," the January 28, 1990 episode of *Charles in Charge.* She also played Heather McCoy, Bud Bundy's dance date, in "What Goes Around Comes Around," the February 25, 1990 episode of *Married . . . With Children.*

The muscular and deep-dimpled Mario Lopez enrolled as A.C. Slater. Lopez's previous television work includes the role of Tomas Del Gato on the short-lived situation comedy, *a.k.a. Pablo,* which aired on ABC from March 6 to April 17, 1984. He was also the host of NBC's teen reality series, *Name Your Adventure,* which debuted on Saturday, September 12, 1992.

Although Dennis Haskins' Mr. Belding character serves as the adult authority figure, the parents of the Bayside students are seen occasionally—so occasionally that hardly anyone realized that Zack Morris has had two different dads with two different names.

During the *Good Morning, Miss Bliss* years, Zack's dad Peter (Robert Pine) and Carrie Bliss (Hayley Mills) developed a thing for each other when they both fell overboard during a weekend rafting trip. Now, it wasn't made clear why Zack's dad was free to date, but it made things all the more confusing when Mrs. Morris (Melody Rogers) showed up at The Attic dance club in the "Fake I.D.'s" episode of *Saved by the Bell,* which aired on October 19, 1991.

In the October 13, 1990 episode, "Rent-A-Pop," Mr. Belding requests a meeting with Zack's dad to discuss his son's failing grades, "F's" in Science and History, a "D" in English and a "C" in Math.

But Zack ducks the confrontation by hiring James (Mark Blankfield), an actor who worked as a waiter at The Max, Bayside's burger hangout, to impersonate his father. For Zack, this was neither unusual nor the least bit stressful. But the self-assured young man should have been disturbed when his real father showed up later on in the episode, since his name had been changed from Peter to Derek and he looked completely different. That's because he was being played by a different actor, John Sanderford, who appeared again in the October 10, 1992 episode, ''Drinking and Driving.''

Saved by the Bell's fourth season began on September 19, 1992, with an episode titled ''The New Girl.'' It introduced Leanna Creel as a leather-wearing, motorcycle-riding student, Tori Scott, who had a harder edge than Jesse and Kelly, and was reminiscent of Nancy McKeon's Jo Polniaczek character on *The Facts of Life.*

Although a spokesperson for the series denied the fact that Tori was a replacement for either Kelly or Jesse, neither was ever seen in episodes with Tori, though Tiffani-Amber Thiessen did appear in a *Saved By the Bell* promo with Leanna Creel.

The popular cast, who were merchandised on items from books and calendars to Barbie-like dolls, would leave the series at the end of the 1992/1993 television season.

To effect the proper closure, and to make way for the new class of Bayside freshmen, the episode ''Wrestling with the Future,'' which aired on October 10, 1992, was written to explain where each of them would go after graduation.

Zack, who had never studied a day in his life and scammed his way through high school, somehow got accepted to Yale University. Kelly, who couldn't afford to go away to school, planned to take a job while attending Community College. Bayside's ultimate jock, A.C. Slater, won a full wrestling scholarship to the University of Iowa. Jesse was accepted to Columbia University. Lisa would make her mark at the Fashion Institute. And the class geek, Screech Powers, was accepted to no less than five schools of higher learning, including Emerson College, the University of Southern California, Clemson University, Princeton University, and the Barbizon School of Modeling, though he had not made up his mind which offer he was going to accept.

The choice of colleges became moot when NBC decided to spin off the three teen heartthrobs in their own primetime series, *Saved By the Bell: The College Years* as explained in an on air promo that ran just before the pilot aired on May 22, 1993.

ZACK:	Hey, don't even think of touching that remote.
SLATER:	That's right, because over the summer, Zack and I decided to go to college together.
ZACK:	It's gonna be great.
SCREECH:	(Popping up from behind the bed Zack and Slater were seated on) Don't forget me, I'll be there too.
SLATER:	So hang with us—we're going to college right now.

The pilot opened with the Bayside grads getting settled in their dorm suite (number 218) at California University and meeting Kelly, Jesse, and Lisa's replacements, Leslie (Anne Tremko), Alex Tabor (Kiersten Warren), and Danielle Marks (Essence Atkins).

Taking on the awesome duties of authority figure was former L.A. Raiders defensive tackle Bob Golic as former San Francisco 49ers linebacker, Michael ''Mike'' Rogers, the Resident Director of the dorm.

When the 1993 fall season rolled around, Mr. Belding, the only regular character to continue with the series, had a brand new class of freshmen to deal with on Saturday mornings.

The new class was introduced in ''The Date Lottery,'' which premiered on the NBC Saturday morning schedule on September 11, 1993. The cast was, as expected, dollar-for-dollar and pound-for-pound interchangeable with the cast that had just graduated from Bayside. Heading the group was Scott Erickson (Robert Telfer), a shrewd schemer and transfer student from Bayside's rival school, Valley High. His musclebound friend was Tommy De Lucca and the new resident geek was Weasel (Isaac Lidsky).

The new ''most popular girl in the school'' is Lindsay Warner (Natalia Cigliati). Her friends are the socially concious and politically correct Vicki Needleman (Bonnie Russavage) and Megan Jones (Bianca Lawson) who (like Lisa and Screech) is the object of Weasel's affections.

And following in the heavy footsteps of the Bayside Tigers is the new football team lunkhead ''Crunch'' Grabowski (Ryan Hurst).

Meanwhile *Saved by the Bell*'s ''classic cast'' remains in high school for perpetuity in rerun syndication.

SEA HUNT

January 1958–1961.   Syndicated
1987–1988   Syndicated

Character:	Mike Nelson
Played by:	Lloyd Bridges
Date(s):	January 1958–1961

Replaced by:	Mike Nelson
Played by:	Ron Ely
Date(s):	1987–1988

No one else in Hollywood seems to love the water quite as much as Ivan Tors, who has more liquid assets than any other producer. In addition to two versions of *Sea Hunt,* Tors' other aquatic television adventures include *The Aquanauts/Malibu Run,* (1960–1961); *Danny and the Mermaid,* (a 1978 pilot); *Flipper* (1964 to 1967); and *Primus* (1971). His motion pictures include the 1960 feature version of FLIPPER and the 1966 adventure, AROUND THE WORLD UNDER THE SEA, which starred Lloyd Bridges as Dr. Doug Standish.

Sea Hunt is based on the adventures of former Navy frogman Mike Nelson, who works off his boat, the *Argonaut* (as in Jason and the . . .). He now accepts underwater assignments from civilians, law enforcement agencies and even the military.

Most of the 156 black-and-white episodes were filmed in the crystal clear waters of Florida's Silver Springs, which over the years has played host to more than twenty motion pictures—years before Disney and Universal located studios in Florida.

These films include the 1939 jungle picture, TARZAN FINDS A SON and portions of THE YEARLING, SMOKEY AND THE BANDIT, MOONRAKER and NEVER SAY

NEVER AGAIN. Also filmed at Silver Springs were the 1954, 1955 and 1956 horror films, THE CREATURE FROM THE BLACK LAGOON, REVENGE OF THE CREATURE and THE CREATURE WALKS AMONG US, that starred swimming champion Ricou Browning as the Creature in the underwater sequences.

Browning was called back to Silver Springs in 1957 by Ivan Tors, who used him as a stunt man and double for Bridges, or other guest stars, on occasions when filming at greater depths was necessary. Female guest stars were doubled by Miss Zale Perry.

The athletic and rugged series star, Lloyd Bridges, who had already appeared in more than twenty-five motion pictures, continued his motion picture and television career following the cancellation of *Sea Hunt*. Some of his film roles include the co-pilot in the 1941 fantasy, HERE COMES MR. JORDAN; Finch in the 1949 drama, HOME OF THE BRAVE; and astronaut Floyd Oldham in the 1950 science fiction, ROCKETSHIP X-M.

Bridges later returned to television to star in the title role of the police series, *Joe Forrester,* which aired on NBC from September 9, 1975 to August 30, 1976.

In 1980 he played the neurotic flight controller, McCroskey, in the daffy disaster film spoof, AIRPLANE! More than twenty-five years and nearly one dozen series later, Ivan Tors refilled Mike Nelson's air tanks for a brand-new color version of *Sea Hunt*. The updated version, filmed in the Bahamas and British Columbia, starred Ron Ely as Mike Nelson. Ely had gained fame in *Tarzan* (See Entry) and had co-starred as Mike Madison in one of Tors' earlier series, *The Aquanauts* (See Entry).

In this new *Sea Hunt,* Mike Nelson is a widower and is assisted by his daughter, Jennifer (Kimber Sissons), an oceanography student.

Another former Tarzan, Denny Miller, made a guest appearance on "The Big Blowup" episode of the new *Sea Hunt,* which aired on November 7, 1987. Miller, who had appeared in more than 300 television programs, admits that he probably got the part on this one, not because of his acting ability but because of the built-in publicity gimmick of having "two former Tarzans" doing battle in a big fight scene staged on the beach.

Sea Hunt, by the way, was not only the name of the series, it was also the name of Mike's boat.

SEALTEST BIG TOP *see:* SUPER CIRCUS

SEARCH

September 13, 1972–August 29, 1973.   NBC

Character:	Dr. Barnett
Played by:	Ford Rainey
Date(s):	1972

Replaced by:	Dr. Barnett
Played by:	Keith Andes
Date(s):	1973

Search was an unusual high-tech detective adventure series, kind of like a *Six Million Dollar Man From U.N.C.L.E.*.

The Washington, D.C.-based World Securities Corporation was headed up by a Mr. Waverly-type character, B.G. Cameron, played by Burgess Meredith. Working for Cameron were three super-agents, each of whom had a super-miniaturized transmitter/receiver surgically implanted in his ear, a sensing device implanted in his body and a body detector implanted under his skin.

It was these transistorized electronic devices that enabled Cameron to both monitor and direct the activities of his agents from mission control. Agents Hugh Lockwood, Nick Bianco and Christopher R. "C.R." Grover were known to World Securities Corporation as Probe One, Omega Probe and Standby Probe.

In real life they were Hugh O'Brian, Tony Franciosa and Doug McClure, who had served justice, respectively, as Wyatt Earp, Jeff Dillon, and Trampas in *The Life and Legend of Wyatt Earp, The Name of the Game* and *The Virginian.*

The senior research director of the unit was Dr. Barnett, originally played by Ford Rainey, who appeared during the 1976 season of *The Bionic Woman* as Jim Elgin, Colonel Steve Austin's (*The Six Million Dollar Man*) stepfather.

In 1973, the producers were forced to search for another actor to play Dr. Barnett. They came up with Keith Andes, who had played Neil in the 1957 musical comedy, THE GIRL MOST LIKELY.

The show most likely to be canceled in 1983 was *Search,* and after twenty-six episodes[1] its audience was searching for something else to watch.

SECRETS OF ISIS *see:* ISIS

SESAME STREET

November 10, 1969–.   PBS

Character:	Mr. Hooper
Played by:	Will Lee
Date(s):	November 10, 1969–1982

Replaced by:	David
Played by:	Northern J. Calloway
Date(s):	unknown–1989

Replaced by:	Gina
Played by:	Alison Bartlett
Date(s):	1986

Replaced by:	Mike
Played by:	Ward Saxton
Date(s):	January 28, 1991

---

1. Some sources say that there were only twenty-six episodes aired, while other sources put the total at twenty-three.

Character:	Mr. Hanford
Played by:	Leonard Jackson
Date(s):	November 1989–September 1990

Replaced by:	Mr. Hanford
Played by:	David L. Smyrl
Date(s):	November 1990–

Character:	Gordon
Played by:	Matt Robinson
Date(s):	November 10, 1969–1972

Replaced by:	Gordon
Played by:	Hal Miller
Date(s):	1972–1973

Replaced by:	Gordon Robinson
Played by:	Roscoe Orman
Date(s):	November 1974–

Character:	Big Bird
Played by:	Frank Oz
Date(s):	November 10, 1969–unknown

Replaced by:	Big Bird
Played by:	Caroll Spinney
Date(s):	(present)

"Can you tell me how to get, how to get to *Sesame Street?*" The answer to the musical question posed in the theme song might be, "Practice, practice, practice . . . your alphabet."

Puppets have been a part of television from its inception. In fact, in the mid-nineteen twenties, Scottish inventor John Logie Baird used the head of a ventriloquist dummy named Stuckey Bill to test his mechanical television system. At the end of that decade, the television engineers at RCA broadcast images of a Felix the Cat papier-maché doll from New York to Kansas to test the resolution of a sixty-line receiver. And since those initial tests, scores of puppets, marionettes and ventriloquist dummies have graced the small screen. They include Johnny Jupiter, Rootie Kazootie, Kukla and Ollie, Bunny Rabbit and Mr. Moose, Clownie, Froggie, Farfel, King Friday, Jerry Mahoney and, of course, Howdy Doody.

Surprisingly, forty years later the more mature medium plays host to more—not fewer—puppets. The next generation includes puppets by Sid and Marty Krofft, Spittin' Image and Paul Fusco. But the most prominent of the group, and the inspiration for many others, are known collectively as Muppets. A Muppet combines the characteristics and operating techniques of both marionettes and puppets—hence the name. This lovable and ever-growing menagerie of felt and foam rubber was created by Muppeteer Jim Henson, who, along with his partner, Frank Oz, built the Muppet empire known as Henson Associates, or "Ha!"

Henson's creations have been around television since the early sixties and have appeared on programs such as *The Ed Sullivan Show.* But it wasn't until Joan Ganz Cooney, the creator of *Sesame Street,* asked Henson to create a family of Muppets for *Sesame Street* that the word Muppet became a household word.

Together with the humans who live in this New York City-like neighborhood, the inhabitants of *Sesame Street* have taught preschoolers the alphabet, how to count to twenty, math basics and important social skills such as friendship and sharing.

Two of the main human characters on *Sesame Street* are Susan and Gordon. Susan has always been played by Loretta Long, but there have been three different Gordons—two with hair and one without.

Matt Robinson, the first actor to play Gordon, wasn't really an actor at all, but one of *Sesame Street*'s writers. He was asked to play Gordon because he fit the part. Robinson agreed to take it on with the understanding that it would only be a temporary situation and that he would eventually leave and be replaced.

"My understanding is that since no one could have possibly predicted what a tremendous success *Sesame Street* was going to become, Matt took on the assignment without really knowing what he was getting himself into. He assumed it would be kind of fun to try out for a while and ended up doing the first three seasons. By then he realized that he had gotten a little more than he had bargained for, so he moved on and they hired another actor, Hal Miller,"[2] explained Roscoe Orman, the third actor to play Gordon. Robinson's other television credits included writing and producing for the NBC situation comedy, *The Cosby Show.*

But Hal Miller did not seem to have the popularity that Robinson had had and was only with *Sesame Street* for one season before it was decided to recast the part.

It might seem a little easier to have created a new character, rather than keep introducing new actors as Gordon, but there was some method to this madness, as Roscoe Orman explained. "Because Gordon and Susan were a couple, it would have been terribly complicated to get into that whole area of divorce and remarriage; it was better left alone," he said. He went on to explain how he was cast as *Sesame Street*'s third Gordon.

"I first heard about the opportunity through a friend of mine, Stan Lathan, who has directed segments of *Sesame Street* in addition to episodes of *Eight Is Enough, Falcon Crest, Fame, Remington Steele* and *That's My Mama.*

"Stan came to see me in *The Sirens,* a play by Richard Wesley that was performed at The Manhattan Club in New York. I played the role of Duane Carter, a jazz musician who attempts to reunite with his wife and daughter after nearly ten years of separation.

"After the performance, Stan came backstage and mentioned that they were looking for someone to replace one of the actors on *Sesame Street* and asked if I would be interested in trying out.

---

2. This and subsequent quotations from Roscoe Orman in this *Sesame Street* entry are from an exclusive telephone interview with Mr. Orman on April 27, 1991.

"At the time, my wife and I were expecting our first child and the idea of a steady acting job on television sounded very attractive, so I said, 'Sure, why not?' "

As usual, a number of actors were being auditioned for the role. Orman made the final cut when the group was narrowed down to the three finalists who would then have to audition with some children and Muppets. The other two actors were David Downing and Robert Guillaume.

In Roscoe Orman's audition with kids he was asked to improvise the concept of up and down. "The joke was to get them to jump up and then, when they came down, say, 'No, no, no, you're coming down, I don't want down, I want up," said Orman. "Then I did a scene with Oscar the Grouch—my first time ever working with a Muppet. The thing I remember most was that I kept looking at Caroll Spinney, who plays Oscar, down in the trash can. I could not, for the life of me, remember to look at the green rag on this guy's hand—it was so foreign to me, so I suppose it was my scene with the kids that made them feel I was a good bet."

It is never easy to assume a role created by another actor, but working with a cast of preschoolers was particularly difficult as Roscoe Orman explained: "The kids who were on the show that first season would not accept me as Gordon. One day there's Hal as Gordon and the next day there's this new guy who says he's Gordon.

"They knew that this other guy was Gordon, so for me, who looked nothing like him, to all of a sudden be called Gordon, was very confusing to the kids, both on the show and at home, because they just assume that we *are* that person we're playing. So there was no way that I was Gordon to them."

Many times when a role is recast an effort is made to hire an actor who looks like the actor he is replacing, as in the case of Darrin on *Bewitched* (See Entry) and Ellery Queen on *The Adventures of Ellery Queen* (See Entry). In this case, physical characteristics were never a factor, because Roscoe Orman bore no resemblance to Hal Miller. "I actually looked less like Hal than I did like Matt. There are some people who say that there is a similarity between me and Matt, but Hal and I looked nothing alike," chuckled Orman.

The most obvious physical difference between Roscoe Orman and the other two actors who had played Gordon, is that Orman's Gordon is bald. This happened by accident, because at the time of Roscoe Orman's audition he had just completed work on the blaxploitation action adventure, WILLIE DYNAMITE, a story about a garish New York City pimp that starred Orman in the title role. "I decided to shave my head for that role because I thought it was really suitable for that character and I liked the look, and it just kind of stuck. I still had that look, which included a mustache and goatee when I went to see the *Sesame Street* people. And during my first year on *Sesame Street,* I had the goatee as well. Then when I shaved it off between seasons, the producers said 'No, you can't change anything because your looks are supposed to stay the same,' because the kids identified with me as being this person who looked a certain way," said Orman.

During a hiatus in 1976, after his first season of playing squeaky clean Gordon on *Sesame Street,* Roscoe Orman returned to the streets as Tyrone, the infamous pimp on the daytime soap opera, *All My Children.* The role was only supposed to be a one-time guest shot, but wound up becoming a running character. "Once it became clear to the producers of *Sesame Street* that I had this other persona going on simultaneously, they asked me about it and I had to make a choice. I knew that character wasn't going to be around too much longer anyway and my commitment to *Sesame Street* was so much stronger that I know I made the right choice to leave the soap opera and continue with *Sesame Street,*" said Orman.

He later switched to the right side of the law and moved into film roles like Captain Wallenger in the 1986 thriller, F/X. On television, Roscoe Orman played Lieutenant Connors in "The Condemned," the January 11, 1977 episode of *Kojak,* and Captain Ralston in the premiere episode of the CBS science fiction, *Hard Time on Planet Earth,* which aired on March 1, 1989.

One of the unique aspects of Roscoe Orman's character on *Sesame Street* is that Gordon is one of the only humans to have a last name. "As you know, Gordon is a school teacher, and when we recently decided to do some segments in the classroom we couldn't have the students addressing me as 'Gordon,' so I suggested Mr. Robinson, in honor of Matt Robinson, the first Gordon," he concluded.

Among the non-human inhabitants of *Sesame Street* are Ernie and Bert, Cookie Monster, Oscar the Grouch and a yellow canary named Big Bird. The name Big Bird is not only an understatement, it is a contradiction. It is true that he is "big"—seven-feet tall, but he has the personality, charm and innocence of a six-year-old. In some ways, the character is reminiscent of the Harveytoons overgrown duck, Baby Huey.

At first, it was Henson's associate, Frank Oz, inside the Muppet that was similar in design to their commercial success, the La Choy Chinese Dragon. In time, Big Bird was turned over to Caroll Spinney, the same Muppeteer who brings Oscar to life.

The best friend of the bird, who is loved by everyone on *Sesame Street,* was a kindly old human storekeeper, Mr. Hooper, played by Will Lee from the series' inception in 1969.

One of Will Lee's first acting jobs was as Joe Bonaparte in the Clifford Odets play, *Golden Boy*—a part he took over from John Garfield. He played Herman in the 1941 Red Skelton comedy, WHISTLING IN THE DARK, and was the beggar in the 1948 musical drama, CASBAH.

Like a kindly old uncle, or grandfather, Mr. Hooper was always eager to listen to his young friends and help them better understand the world around them. And in a fitting tribute, it was Mr. Hooper who taught one of life's most valuable lessons—death.

When actor Will Lee died of a heart attack on Tuesday, December 7, 1982, after minding the store for more than a dozen years, the writers and producers of this important children's program were faced with a very delicate decision—how to explain Mr. Hooper's absence to thousands of preschoolers. The choices were many. They could have ignored it. They could have cast another Will Lee-type and continued without mentioning it. Or they could have said that Mr. Hooper decided to retire, move away and take life easy in Florida. Instead, the daring and insightful writers and producers decided to meet the crisis head on and made the difficult decision to admit that Mr. Hooper had died.

Executive producer Dulcy Singer was quoted in an Associated Press wire story in August of 1983 as saying "We felt we ought to deal with it head-on. If we left it unsaid, kids would notice. Our instincts told us to be honest and straightforward."

The intelligent and sensitive script, written by Norman Stiles, took a rather direct approach because children do not understand euphemisms such as "passed away." What was avoided was discussion about Mr. Hooper's illness and old age, so as not to frighten youngsters who think their parents are old. The segments aired as part of program number 1839 on November 21, 1983---Thanksgiving day.

The setup was a silly segment with Big Bird bending all the way over and putting his head through his legs. Gordon (Roscoe Orman) comes along and questions Big Bird's silliness.

GORDON: Big Bird, why are you doing that?

BIG BIRD: What?

GORDON: That, with your head between your legs?

BIG BIRD: Oh, because.

GORDON: Because why?

BIG BIRD: Just because.

The next scene takes place in the arbor outside Mr. Hooper's store, where two small square restaurant tables are set up. There are coffee cups set in front of them and the adults are just talking and enjoying each other's company. The main topic of discussion is Mr. and Mrs. Williams' new baby, Leandro. Big Bird asks if he and his friends (children watching at home) can listen. The grownups welcome Big Bird into their group, but he decides to leave when the conversation turns to "boring" politics. Big Bird returns in the next segment with presents for the adults, who are still chatting in the arbor.

BIG BIRD: It's time for your presents. Well, I just drew pictures of all my grown-up friends on *Sesame Street* and I'm going to give 'em to ya. I'm going to be an artist when I grow up.

As Big Bird distributes the caricatures to the assembled residents of *Sesame Street,* they all react with joy at seeing their likenesses translated to paper.

BIG BIRD: And last, but not least . . . Ta da! (revealing a caricature of Mr. Hooper, which everyone compliments him on.) Well, I can't wait till he sees it. Hey where is he? I want to give it to him. I know, he's in the store.

BOB: Big bird, he's not in there.

BIG BIRD: Oh, then where is he?

MARIA: Big Bird, don't you remember we told you? Mr. Hooper died. He's dead.

BIG BIRD: Oh yeah, I remember. Well, I'll give it to him when he comes back.

SUSAN: Big Bird, Mr. Hooper's not coming back.

BIG BIRD: Why not?

SUSAN: Big Bird, when people die they don't come back.

BIG BIRD: Ever?

SUSAN: No, never.

BIG BIRD: Why not?

LUIS: Well, Big Bird, they're dead. They can't come back.

BIG BIRD: (Worried) He's gonna come back. Why, who's goin' to take care of the store? And who's gonna make my birdseed milkshakes and tell me stories?

DAVID: Big Bird, I'm going to take care of the store. Mr. Hooper, he left it to me. I'll make you your milkshakes and we'll all tell you stories and we'll make sure you're okay.

SUSAN: Sure, we'll look after you.

BIG BIRD: Well, it won't be the same.

BOB: You're right, Big Bird. It will never be the same around here without him. But you know something. We can all be very happy that we all had a chance to be with him and to know him. And to love him a lot when he was here.

OLIVIA: And Big Bird, we still have our memories of him.

BIG BIRD: Yeah, memories, right. Memories, that's how I drew this picture [of Mr. Hooper], from memory. And we can remember him and remember him and remember him and remember him as much as we want to. But I don't like it. It makes me sad.

DAVID: We all feel sad, Big Bird.

BIG BIRD: He's never coming back?

DAVID: Never.

BIG BIRD: Well, I don't understand. You know everything was just fine. Why does it have to be this way? Give me one good reason?

GORDON: Big Bird, it has to be this way . . . because.

BIG BIRD: Just Because?

GORDON: Just Because.

BIG BIRD: Oh. You know? I'm goin' to miss you Mr. Looper.

MARIA: That's Hooper, Big Bird. Hooper.

They all get up and surround Big Bird to comfort and reassure him. The camera slowly pulls out and the scene fades to black.

The episode closed with the introduction of Mr. and Mrs. Williams' new baby, and Big Bird philosophizes, ''You know what the nice thing is about new babies? Well, one day they're not here and the next day . . . here they are.''

Roscoe Orman, who had the most important lines in this touching segment, paused for a moment to reflect on the production of this landmark episode. ''It had a very special significance to all of the cast members and we tried to do it in one take because it wasn't so much an acting assignment as a real sharing of our feelings, because Will [Lee] was one of us and very beloved. It was, in a very real way, our tribute to Will,''said Orman.

Things got back to normal with David (Northern J. Calloway) running Hooper's Store, with the assistance of Gina (Alison Bartlett) as the store clerk, until his sudden death, which was reported in *The New York Times* on January 13, 1990: ''The Westchester County Medical Examiner's office said Mr. Calloway had been taken to a psychiatric facility, Stony Lodge Hospital, in Ossining, where he had lost consciousness shortly after his arrival. He was then taken to Phelps Memorial Hospital in North Tarrytown, N.Y., where he was

pronounced dead. The cause of death has not been determined.''

Having already dealt with the death of one character, the writers wisely chose a different more straight-forward approach this time and wrote David out as having purchased his grandmother's farm out West. Gina continued to run Mr. Hooper's Store for the time in between David and the new owner, Mr. Hanford.

Since Mr. Hooper's death the name of the store was changed to *Hooper's Store* and is often simply referred to as *Hooper's*.

Mr. Hanford, who is supposed to be a retired fireman, was played for a short time by Leonard Jackson. In 1973, Jackson starred as Mr. Brooks in the highly rated comedy, FIVE ON THE BLACK HAND SIDE. That same year he also appeared as Archie in the black vampire film, GANJA AND HESS. He later joined the first season cast of the PBS series, *Shining Time Station* (See Entry).

One of the newest residents of *Sesame Street* is a young man named Mike. He's played by Ward Saxton, who helped to explain how Mr. Hanford came in to take over Hooper's Store: ''It was interesting, because they were introducing a new Muppet, Preston Rabbit, and as part of the introduction we all sang this *Hello, My Name Is* song. We would each sing a line and fill in our own names. I sang 'Hello, my name is Mike and I'm glad you're here today.' Mr. Hanford, who was just supposed to be someone else in the neighborhood, sang his part and filled in his name and he assimilated very quickly.

''In the script they just said that Mr. Hanford now owns Hooper's Store. There was an episode devoted to the refurbishing of the store after it was wrecked by a couple of Muppet carpenters, Biff and Sully, while they tried to hang up a framed dollar bill.

''It was my impression that when the renovations were completed it would have been a more modern, or even high-tech store, but when it was completed it was simply a nice updated version of what was there before and wasn't terribly different, which is more in keeping with the usual *Sesame Street* style.

''In the storyline, both Big Bird and Snuffy (the woolly, elephant-like Muppet) wanted to be the first customer in the new store and Snuffy wound up getting stuck in the front door. Because we all ran in through the side door to help Snuffy, no one was singled out as having been Mr. Hanford's 'first' customer. Snuffy, however, was given the honor of being the first one to be stuck in the door,''[3] smiled Saxton.

There was even one episode in the 1991 season in which Mike was given the responsibility of taking over Hooper's Store for a day.

MIKE: (to camera) Oh, hi. Welcome to *Sesame Street*. Gina had to go do some errands, so I offered to take care of the store until she got back.

Saxton went on to tell how he won the role of Mike. ''In 1988 a casting call was put out that they were looking for young people, preferably teenagers. At that time the character of Gina (Alison Bartlett) had already been on for a few seasons and was

---

3. From an exclusive interview with Ward Saxton on March 21, 1991.

very well established and they were looking for more people in her age group to interact with her.

"When I first read for the casting director, Julie Mossberg, I read as I would for any dramatic production and she said, 'No, no, I want you to do it again and I just want you to be yourself.' Which I did. She then brought me in to meet the producer, Lisa Simon, and after that I went in one more time to be put on tape.

"I auditioned with Jim Martin, a Muppeteer who was working the Muppet, Herry, although the script was between Gina and Telly, so instead of Gina, I played Gino and called the Muppet, Telly.

"They then said to me that this Muppeteer may go off the script and to just do my best to go along with him, and I said 'Sure.' We got through most of the script and then he started making things up just to test me and I started throwing things back at him. I remember asking, 'So Telly, what's your last name?' and the Muppeteer answered, 'Oh, I don't have a last name.' 'But everybody has a last name. Come on, think,' I continued. He said, 'Monster, Telly Monster.' Then he turned to me and asked, 'So Gino, what's your last name?' 'I don't have one, there's a writers' strike going on, you know.' Well, that just cracked them up and I was asked to appear in four shows that season as 'Teenager.'

"The following season, I became a contract performer. I think originally my character was going to be called 'Jeff,' but Sonia Manzano, who plays Maria and is also one of the writers, suggested that I looked more like a 'Mike,' so from that moment on, I was 'Mike,' "[4] said Saxton.

Ward Saxton's first professional acting job was as the kid with the pie-eating-grin on the 1982 Celentano's Pizza commercial. His other roles include the *After School Special,* "Oh Boy, Babies!" in which he was allowed to use his real first name, Ward.

77 SUNSET STRIP

October 10, 1958–September 9, 1964.   ABC

Character:	Gerald Lloyd "Kookie" Kookson III
Played by:	Edward "Edd" Byrnes
Date(s):	October 10, 1958–June 14, 1963
Replaced by:	Joey
Played by:	Craig Curtis
Date(s):	April 22, 1960
Replaced by:	J.R. Hale
Played by:	Robert Logan
Date(s):	October 13, 1961–June 14, 1963

Every handsome detective and private eye seen on television since 1958 owes thanks for a bit of his success to Stuart Bailey and Jeff Spencer, who opened up their detective agency at 77 Sunset Strip in Hollywood, California on October 10, 1958.

The head of the agency, Stuart Bailey, was played by the debonair Efrem Zimbalist, Jr., the only cast member to remain with the series from beginning to end. After ABC closed the agency, Efrem Zimbalist, Jr. went to work for *The F.B.I.* as Inspector Lewis Erskine and stayed with the department for nine years. *The F.B.I.* aired on ABC from September 19, 1965 to September 8, 1974. Some years later and with silver-white hair, but still just as handsome, Efrem Zimbalist, Jr. appeared as Don Alejandro de la Vega, the first father of television's third *Zorro* (See Entry).

Bailey's handsome young partner on *77 Sunset Strip* was Jeff Spencer. He was played by Roger Smith, who had played Doyle Hobbs on *Father Knows Best* from 1957 to 1958. Two years after leaving *77 Sunset Strip,* Roger Smith starred in the title role in the maritime misadventures of *Mr. Roberts,* which aired on NBC from September 17, 1965, to September 2, 1966.

Back on Sunset Strip, "Kookie," the hip parking lot attendant at Dino's Lodge, located next door at number 79, was attracting a lot of attention with his jive expressions like "the ginchiest." But it was the incessant combing of his hair that drove teenage girls crazy and made him a recording star. The song he sang was "Kookie, Kookie, Lend Me Your Comb," and when it was recorded with Connie Stevens and released as a single, it went to the top of the charts.

From that time on there was no question that "Kookie" was the star of the show and Edd Byrnes knew it. He asked for more money and for his role to be expanded. When he didn't get it, he walked out on the series, and most of the time he wasn't even mentioned. It was like he was never there, although his name still appeared in the opening theme.

In the April 22, 1960 episode, "Stranger than Fiction," they needed a parking lot attendant to get the cars and Craig Curtis was brought in as Joey. In another episode, it was explained that Kookie wasn't around because he was away at finger-printing school.

The show's executive producer, William T. Orr said, "We had a contract dispute with Edd in which he decided it would be to his advantage not to play 'Kookie' anymore, and we put Bobby Logan in the role."[5]

Byrnes got his expanded role by becoming Mr. Gerald Lloyd Kookson, III, a fully vested partner in Bailey and Spencer's detective firm, while Robert Logan, as J.R. Hale, took over at Dino's, adding his own brand of lingo to pop culture by using initials to represent words and phrases. "B&S," for example, stood for Bailey and Spencer, while "N.T.I." meant nothing to it.

Logan later appeared on Walt Disney's *Daniel Boone* as Jericho Jones during 1965 and 1966. His motion pictures include the starring role as Skip Robinson in a warm series of back-to-nature films, THE ADVENTURES OF THE WILDERNESS FAMILY, 1975; FURTHER ADVENTURES OF

---

4. From an exclusive interview with Ward Saxton on March 21, 1991.
5. Wooley, Lynn, Malsbary, Robert W., and Strange, Robert G., Jr. *Warner Bros. Television.* McFarland & Company, Inc., Jefferson, North Carolina, 1985, p. 101.

THE WILDERNESS FAMILY—PART 2, 1978; and MOUNTAIN FAMILY ROBINSON, 1979.

SHAZAM!

September 7, 1974–September 3, 1977.   CBS
January 18, 1979   NBC

Character: Captain Marvel
Played by: Jackson Bostwick
Date(s):   September 1, 1974–September 1976

Replaced by: Captain Marvel
Played by: John Davey
Date(s):   September 1976–September 3, 1977

Replaced by: Captain Marvel
Played by: Garrett Craig
Date(s):   January 18, 1979

One thing's for sure, you can never have enough superheroes. It was because of Superman's immense popularity that Captain Marvel was born in the number 2 issue of *Whiz Comics* in February 1990. Captain Marvel was conceived by Ralph Daigh and Bill Parker and drawn by Clarence C. Beck. Like Superman's creators, Joe Shuster and Jerry Siegel, they based their character on a real-life personality.

Superman and his alter ego, Clark Kent, are said to have been based on the likeness of Steve Allen; Captain Marvel's looks are reported to have been fashioned after Fred MacMurray. And like Superman, Captain Marvel (who wore a red suit, with a gold cape) had superhuman strength, was impervious to bullets and could fly.

If he sounds a lot like Superman to you, he sounded even more like Superman to National Comics, which later became DC Comics. And even though the characters' histories are very different (Captain Marvel's alter ego was a young boy, Billy Batson), National Comics brought a suit against Fawcett Publications for copyright infringement. Fawcett voluntarily shelved the character after a lengthy litigation that ended in 1953.

In 1941, before the character was dropped by Fawcett, Republic Pictures produced THE ADVENTURES OF CAPTAIN MARVEL, a twelve-chapter serial starring Tom Tyler as Captain Marvel and Junior Coghlan as young Billy Batson.

In an interesting twist, the very company that was responsible for the demise of Captain Marvel purchased the rights in 1972. It reintroduced the character in a new series of comics that caught the attention of Lou Scheimer, a fan of the original *Captain Marvel* comics.

Scheimer was partners with Norm Prescott in Filmation Studios (which produced a series of successful Saturday morning superhero cartoons including *Superman, Batman, The Lone Ranger* and *Tarzan*). Filmation purchased the rights and brought Captain Marvel to Saturday morning TV, not as a cartoon, but in a thirty-minute live-action adventure series. Some major adjustments were made to the property to help a new generation of kids better relate to the character.

In the comics, Billy Batson was a broadcaster for WHIZ-Radio; Shazam was an aged wizard he found living in an abandoned subway tunnel. This ancient sorcerer gave Billy the power to transform himself into the superhero Captain Marvel by shouting his name out loud.

In the Filmation series, Scheimer and Prescott replaced the single wizard with six "elders" (Solomon, Hercules, Atlas, Zeus, Achilles and Mercury) who appeared in animated form to brief Billy (Michael Gray) on his weekly mission. The dark-haired teenager, cast from the David Cassidy school of handsome TV teens, played Ronnie from 1972 to 1973 on *The Brian Keith Show,* which was originally titled *The Little People* during its first season on NBC.

Adult supervision was taken over by a mysterious gray-haired man known only as Mr. Mentor, who chauffeured Billy and himself from adventure to adventure in his twenty-five-foot RV—which sure beats living in an abandoned subway tunnel.

Mentor, who lived up to his name by counseling Billy in the ideas of honesty, cooperation and good citizenship, was played by Les Tremayne, the English-born character actor with the beautiful tenor voice who in 1958 replaced Florenz Ames as Inspector Richard Queen in *The Further Adventures of Ellery Queen* (See Entry).

Under Mentor's guidance, Billy Batson did his best to help those in need. When things got out of hand—usually during the last five minutes of the show—he would shout "SHAZAM!" This magical chant, a combination of the first letters of each of the elders' names, transformed Billy into Captain Marvel (Jackson Bostwick), a tall, dark and handsome actor with classic superhero chiseled features.

As if this transformation wasn't confusing enough to the impressionable viewers at home, in 1976 when Michael Gray shouted "SHAZAM!" he turned into John Davey instead of Jackson Bostwick, who had left the series in what was reported to be a contract dispute.

A third actor, Garrett Craig, played Captain Marvel in an NBC special *The Challenge of the Superheroes.* The 1979 telefilm also featured Adam West and Burt Ward as Batman and Robin and Rod Hasse as The Flash (See Entry).

John Davey, television's second Captain Marvel, appeared in the "Mr. Wrong" episode of *Room 222,* which aired on December 8, 1972, and two episodes of the ABC police drama, *The Rookies.* His first guest shot was in "The Veteran," the February 26, 1973 episode of *The Rookies.* His second, "The Old Neighborhood," aired on November 25, 1974.

Jackson Bostwick, who was a regular cast member on *The Red Skelton Show,* which aired on NBC from September 14, 1970 to August 29, 1971, hasn't been heard from since—SHAZAM!

SHEENA, QUEEN OF THE JUNGLE

1956–1957.   Syndicated

Character: Sheena
Played by: Irish McCalla
Date(s):   1956–1957

Character:	Sheena (stunt double)
Played by:	Raul Gaona
Date(s):	1956

Replaced by:	Sheena (stunt double)
Played by:	unknown
Date(s):	1956–1957

The survivor of a plane crash in Africa as a child, Sheena was raised in the jungle, a friend of the animals, has a pet chimpanzee, and is a strong and valiant fighter all of which sound like a familiar character.

Sheena was born in the minds of cartoonists S.M. Iger and Will Eisner in 1937 as their answer to Edgar Rice Burroughs' popular jungle lord comic strip, *Tarzan.*

The liberated woman of the wild caught on and soon appeared in comic books and a series of pulp novels. Then, in 1955, Sheena accomplished a feat that would take Tarzan another eleven years to achieve. Sheena became a television series. Actually, the color pilot was shot in 1955; the black-and-white episodes didn't go into production until the following year.

Unlike the TARZAN films, which were shot primarily in Florida and California, *Sheena, Queen of the Jungle* was filmed in the jungles (Las Espacas) of Mexico, a location later used for the *Tarzan* television series (See Entry). The *Sheena* cast and crew stayed in a little town south of Cuernavaca.

In 1945, at the age of seventeen, the statuesque beauty Irish McCalla began her professional career as a pinup model. At one point of her career, she graced the covers of seven different magazines in the same month. She also did work with Vargas and a photographer named Kelly, the photographer responsible for creating the poster that gave Marilyn Monroe her start.

Kelly learned about the search for an actress to play Sheena because the producers were testing every actress in town for the role, and he suggested that Irish should give it a try. Primarily a model, Irish McCalla had had some minor television experience, having appeared in bits on *The George Gobel Show* and *The All Star Review* (with Jack Carson) much in the same manner that Carol Wayne appeared on *The Tonight Show Starring Johnny Carson.* "Just when they needed a tall, big-busted blonde to throw jokes at,"[6] explained Ms. McCalla.

There was no need for Irish McCalla to rehearse for the role of Sheena. "I grew up with the comic strip and played Sheena when I was a kid in Nebraska. My brother was Tarzan and I was Sheena. Sheena was just a female Tarzan," she said.

Irish took Kelly's suggestion and arranged for a screen test, which happened to be scheduled on the same day as Anita Ekberg's. "We tested the same day. I tested before her, but at the time she was Miss Sweden and had just gotten out of her contract with Universal," said Ms. McCalla. "She [Anita Ekberg] was very well known. I was very well known in the pinup world, but she was known in the movie world too, as she had already done some bit parts in a couple of pictures and she was chosen for the part.

"But she didn't show up for the pilot shoot, out in California's Arcadia Gardens. So they called me up to see if I would take her contract (which turned out to be lousy) and just go ahead and take over. So that's what I did. I think my mother put it best when she said, 'Now they're paying you for what you used to do for free!' I said to myself, 'My God, they're paying me and I'm still playing.' "

Ms. McCalla explained that she believed the reason Ms. Ekberg turned down the Sheena role was that she had been offered a contract with John Wayne's production company.

In the two or three weeks that passed between the time that Irish McCalla was signed and shooting began, the script was rewritten, a costume was made for her and Irish was sent out to Jungle Land to spend time with her co-star, Chim, who was being played by a short, dark, and hairy chimpanzee named Neil.

The pilot was sold and went into production in 1956 with Irish McCalla in the title role. She also performed her own stunts in the first dozen episodes. Things were swinging along until Irish came down with what she jokingly referred to as "Montezuma's Revenge" and the "Aztec Two-step."

Production on the thirteenth episode of *Sheena* continued even though Ms. McCalla had not fully recovered from her illness. She had lost a lot of weight and was a little weak. Nevertheless, she went ahead with a stunt that required her to swing (on high parallel bars) from one tree to another, where she was supposed to knock a guy out of the second tree into the river. "About halfway between them I started sliding on the rope. I pulled myself up enough so that my knees hit the tree—which resulted in bark and blood all the way from the knee to the ankle, but it saved my face and upper body. In doing that, I tore the ligaments in my left arm and I was sent back to the States for treatment. When I returned, I just didn't do any stunt work from then on," she said.

When Ms. Ekberg failed to show up for the filming of the pilot episode, Irish McCalla filled out Ms. Ekberg's leopardskin very nicely. Now the problem was finding a stunt double who also stood five feet nine and one-half inches tall with the measurements of $39\frac{1}{2}$–$24\frac{1}{2}$–38. The problem was compounded by the fact that "They were really too cheap to send a stunt woman from the coast," said Ms. McCalla. The compromise was to hire a man and dress him up in a wig and padded bra.

The first of the two drag queens of the jungle was a young dark-skinned Mexican stuntman who wasn't nearly as tall as Irish. To cover for his dark complexion, all of his shots were done from the back and at a sizable distance. Ms. McCalla recalls that the name of this Mexican athlete was Raul Gaona, and his replacement was a lighter-skinned Spanish acrobat and trapeze artist, whose name cannot be confirmed. Irish chuckled that these doubles were easy to spot because "They ran more like girls than I did!"

The series wrapped after only twenty-six episodes and when Irish McCalla returned to the United States, "I had hardly gotten off that plane when I did *The Milton Berle Show* with

---

6. This and following quotations from Irish McCalla in this *Sheena, Queen of the Jungle* entry are from an exclusive telephone interview with Ms. McCalla on December 9, 1990.

Pre-dating Lynda Carter's *Wonder Woman* by nearly twenty years was the beautiful and statuesque Irish McCalla as television's first female superhero, *Sheena, Queen of the Jungle.*

Debra Paget and a singer named Elvis Presley, who I hadn't even heard of because I was out in the jungle,'' she recalled.

Her limited work in motion pictures includes a starring role as Jerrie Turner in the 1958 horror film, SHE DEMONS, and Big Pearl in the 1960 Western, FIVE BOLD WOMEN.

A new queen of the jungle was brought to life on the wide screen in SHEENA, a big-budget production released in 1984 and starring former *Charlie's Angels* (See Entry) beauty Tanya Roberts in the title role.

"I did see the film and think that Tanya Roberts is a good actress and a beautiful girl, but I think they needed somebody bigger. She's very athletic, but she just didn't seem very big to me, because according to the legend established in the comics, Sheena's supposed to be a really tall girl," said Ms. McCalla.

"In the beginning, I spoke to the producer of the film and they were going to have me play Sheena's mother in a scene with a plane crash, but then the script was changed and the part never materialized.

"The film was beautifully photographed, but I think one of the reasons that it bombed was that they altered the Sheena legend and tried to change Sheena. The thing I objected to was that stupid thing where they tried to make her appear supernatural by making her look as though she had a headache every time she talked to the animals. That wasn't Tanya's fault, that was just stupidity on the part of the writers and producers.

"I just felt that they didn't do right by her. From what I hear, she worked her tail off and did the stunts and everything else. I just felt that she got short-changed."

Today, Irish McCalla is a successful painter. Some of her most popular works are oil paintings of the Old West, which have been commissioned for a series of collector's plates and limited-edition prints.

In closing, Irish McCalla offered a piece of advice to all actors and actresses who may feel saddled with their continuing roles in a series: "If you have a good deal, stick with it. Because where else are you going to get the fame and money?"

THE SHERIFF OF COCHISE

1956–1960. Syndicated

Character:	Deputy Olson
Played by:	Stan Jones
Date(s):	1956–1958
Replaced by:	Deputy Blake
Played by:	Robert Brubaker
Date(s):	1958
Replaced by:	Deputy Tom Ferguson
Played by:	James Griffith
Date(s):	1959–1960

The title of this popular syndicated series sounds as though the action was taking place in the Old West. In reality, the series was more in line with *Highway Patrol* than with *Gunsmoke*. The time was the present (the present being the years between 1956 and 1960) and the setting was in the real Cochise County in Arizona. There were shoot-outs, but the chases involved cars, not horses.

The Sheriff of Cochise was Frank Morgan, played by John Bromfield, who played "Snakehips" MacKay in the 1952 war film, FLAT TOP, which starred Sterling Hayden and featured TV's first Lois Lane, Phyllis Coates, as Dorothy.

A television series set in a real town, rather than a fictitious one, turned Cochise into a bona fide tourist attraction. To show its appreciation, the city of Cochise honored actor John Bromfield by swearing him in as a deputy sheriff during a special July 4th celebration in 1957 that also included a parade with Bromfield as Grand Marshal.

Sheriff Morgan's first deputy, Olson, was played by Stan Jones, who was the creator of the series. In addition to acting, Jones was a popular songwriter and composed such songs as *Ghost Riders in the Sky*. Jones selected Cochise as the setting for the series because he had been born and raised there.

Producer Mort Briskin managed to keep the series fresh by altering the storyline after the initial seventy-eight episodes were shot.

The new plot began with Sheriff Morgan escorting a deranged murderer (Jack Lord) to a nearby United States marshal. Lord, who was completely off his nut, escaped after killing the marshal. Morgan immediately filled the vacant position and took over tracking down the escaped convict. With that, the title of the series was changed to *U.S. Marshal* and Stan Jones was replaced by Robert Brubaker as Deputy Blake. Brubaker replaced Glenn Strange as Sam, the bartender on *Gunsmoke* (See Entry).

Deputy Blake only lasted for one season and was then replaced in 1959 by Deputy Tom Ferguson. Ferguson was played by James Griffith who had co-starred as Pat Garrett in the 1954 Western, THE LAW VS. BILLY THE KID and appeared as Krenner in the 1960 science fiction film, THE AMAZING TRANSPARENT MAN.

Having a combined total of 156 episodes, more than enough for a hefty syndication package, the program was retitled *Man from Cochise* and reissued in 1960 by NTA.

SHINING TIME STATION

January 29, 1989–. PBS

Character:	Mr. Conductor
Played by:	Ringo Starr
Date(s):	January 29, 1989–May 27, 1989
Replaced by:	Mr. Conductor
Played by:	George Carlin
Date(s):	November 18, 1991–
Character:	Harry Cupper
Played by:	Leonard Jackson
Date(s):	January 29, 1989–May 27, 1989
Replaced by:	Billy Two Feathers
Played by:	Tom Jackson
Date(s):	November 18, 1991–

Character: Matthew "Matt" Jones
Played by: Jason Woliner
Date(s):   January 29, 1989–May 27, 1989

Replaced by: Dan Jones
Played by: Ari Magder
Date(s):   November 18, 1991–

Character: Tanya
Played by: Nicole Leach
Date(s):   January 29, 1989–May 27, 1989

Replaced by: Kara
Played by: Erica Luttrell
Date(s):   November 18, 1991–

Replaced by: Becky
Played by: Danielle Marcot
Date(s):   November 18, 1991–

With the premiere of *Shining Time Station* a new generation of youngsters was introduced to The Beatles' drummer, Ringo Starr, but not as a musician. The ex-Beatle, who had turned to acting in 1968 with his portrayal of the Mexican gardener, Emmanuel, in the sex farce CANDY, was here playing a magical eighteen-inch-high railroad man known only as Mr. Conductor.

Shining Time Station was an old-time train depot located on the Indian Valley Railroad. It had been closed for a number of years until it was purchased by Stacy Jones (Didi Conn). In the show's first episode, "A Place Unlike Any Other," Stacy shared her dreams for Shining Time Station with her nephew Matt:

STACY: This is my plan. I'm gonna make this old station as good as it ever was. There'll be passengers rushing around going to far-away places. Oh, it's going to be a very busy station, just like the days when my granny used to run it. And then lots of trains will want to stop here.

Older viewers might see a connection between Shining Time Station's female stationmaster and the famous railroad engineer from Tennessee, Casey Jones, who was himself the subject of a syndicated series in 1957 starring Alan Hale, Jr., but there is no indication that any relationship exists.

One of the other cast regulars on *Shining Time Station* was locomotive engineer and master mechanic Harry Cupper. Harry was played by Leonard Jackson who, in 1989, became the first of two actors to play Mr. Hanford on *Sesame Street* (See Entry).

Rounding out the cast are Harry's granddaughter, Tanya, and the show's heavy, Schemer (Brian O'Connor), whose name is synonymous with his personality traits.

In addition to making appearances to give Matt advice, Mr. Conductor also narrated the British-produced segments of

Thomas the Tank Engine & Friends, which is based on the railway series by The Rev. W. Awdry.

Except for Didi Conn and Brian O'Connor, when this charming series returned for a second season everyone else in the cast had been replaced: Leonard Jackson by Tom Jackson as Billy Two Feathers and Jason Woliner by Ari Magder as Dan Jones. Nicole Leach, who played Tanya, was replaced by not one, but two new kids, Erica Luttrell and Danielle Marcot, who took over as Kara and Becky. The biggest loss, however, was Liverpudlian Ringo Starr as Mr. Conductor, who was replaced by New Yorker George Carlin.

"This season, the balance is decidedly more American with the departure of Starr, who has been replaced by comedian George Carlin. So far, Carlin seems awkward and self-conscious as Mr. Conductor, rolling his eyes and mugging too much. Where Starr narrated the Thomas tales with a lilting, conversational murmur, Carlin puts a cutesy archness into his delivery that's condescending and annoying."[7]

Nevertheless, as Stacy Jones observed in the first episode "There's just something about this place."

SIGMUND AND THE SEA MONSTERS

September 8, 1973–October 18, 1975.   NBC

Character: Zelda Marshall
Played by: Mary Wickes
Date(s):   September 8, 1973–1974

Replaced by: Gertrude Gouch
Played by: Fran Ryan
Date(s):   1974–October 18, 1975

Continuing with the trend they had begun in 1969, Sid and Marty Krofft introduced *Sigmund and the Sea Monsters,* the third in their line of live-action Saturday morning fantasy series featuring actors in full-size puppet-like costumes and teen heartthrobs as the central characters. The other two series were *H.R. Pufnstuf,* starring Jack Wild as Jimmy, and *Lidsville,* which starred Butch Patrick as Mark. Wild's most famous role prior to *H.R. Pufnstuf* was that of the Artful Dodger in the 1968 motion picture OLIVER. Patrick had gained fame as Eddie, television's wee werewolf on *The Munsters* (See Entry). *H.R. Pufnstuf* premiered on NBC on September 6, 1969, and ended on September 1, 1974. *Lidsville* began on ABC on September 11, 1971, and concluded its seventeen-episode run on NBC on August 31, 1974.

Sigmund and the Sea Monsters also employed a former child star from a 1960s television series. Johnnie Whitaker, who played Johnny Stuart on *Sigmund,* was known to millions as Bill Davis' (Brian Keith) adopted son, Jody, on the popular CBS sitcom, *Family Affair.* Whitaker's co-star, Scott Kolden, who played Johnny's brother Scott, came to *Sigmund and the Sea Monsters* fresh from his role as Scott Reynolds on *Me and the Chimp,* which starred Ted Bessell as his father Mike. The

7. Tucker, Ken "Two Tickets to Ride." *Entertainment Weekly,* January 10, 1992, No. 100, pp. 78–79.

short-lived situation comedy aired on CBS from January 13 to May 18, 1972.

The title character of *Sigmund and the Sea Monsters* was Sigmund Ooz, an adorable six-tentacled sea monster who was disowned by his family because of his inability to scare humans. After leaving his cave, which was located at Dead Man's Point on Cypress Beach, California, Sigmund meets up with and is befriended by the Stuart brothers, who (obeying the first rule of fantasy sitcoms) keep him a secret by allowing him to live in their clubhouse, located behind their home at 1730 Ocean Drive.

Among the people Sigmund is being hidden from is the Stuarts' housekeeper, Zelda Marshall, who was played by Mary Wickes in the first season. The gawky character actress with the hooked nose had been cast as a housekeeper or a nurse with a quick wit and a sharp tongue on stage, in films and on television since the '30s.

Her first film role was as the nurse, Miss Preen, in the 1941 Bette Davis comedy, THE MAN WHO CAME TO DINNER, the part she created in the 1939 Broadway production by Moss Hart and George S. Kaufman. One of her more familiar motion picture roles was the nun, Sister Clarissa, in the 1966 comedy, THE TROUBLE WITH ANGELS, and its more dramatic 1968 sequel, WHERE ANGELS GO . . . TROUBLE FOLLOWS.

Television audiences will no doubt remember Mary Wickes best as Miss Esther Cathcart, one of the Mitchells' more annoying neighbors on *Dennis the Menace*. Her talents still being in demand, Ms. Wickes left *Sigmund and the Sea Monsters* to play Doctor Joe Bogert's nurse, Miss Tully, on the first season of the CBS situation comedy, *Doc* (See Entry).

The actress replacing her as the Stuarts' new housekeeper, Gertrude Gouch, was Fran Ryan, who was the first Doris Ziffel on CBS's rural situation comedy, *Green Acres* (See Entry).

Sigmund, incidentally, was played by dwarf actor Billy Barty, who played Inch in Tim Conway's very short-lived sitcom, *Ace Crawford, Private Eye,* which aired on CBS from March 15 to April 12, 1983.

SISTERS

May 11, 1991–. NBC

Character:	Reed Halsey
Played by:	Kathy Wagner
Date(s):	May 11, 1991–June 22, 1991

Replaced by:	Reed Halsey
Played by:	Ashley Judd
Date(s):	September 21, 1991–

Character:	Alex Reed (as a teenager)
Played by:	Alexondra Lee
Date(s):	May 11, 1991–September 7, 1991

Replaced by:	Alex Reed (as a teenager)
Played by:	Sharon Martin
Date(s):	September 21, 1991–

Character:	Teddy Reed (as a teenager)
Played by:	Jill Novick
Date(s):	May 11, 1991–September 7, 1991

Replaced by:	Teddy Reed (as a teenager)
Played by:	Devon Pierce
Date(s):	September 21, 1991–

Character:	Frankie Reed (as an adolescent)
Played by:	Rhianna Janette
Date(s):	May 11, 1991–September 7, 1991

Replaced by:	Frankie Reed
Played by:	Tasia Schutt
Date(s):	September 21, 1991–

Character:	Thomas Reed
Played by:	John McCann
Date(s):	May 25, 1991

Replaced by:	Thomas Reed
Played by:	Peter White
Date(s):	October 12, 1991
	November 23, 1991

One of the series that raised many eyebrows in recent years was NBC's adult drama, *Sisters*. The controversy surrounded the teaser for the show's pilot, "Moving In, Moving Out, Moving On," which had the four main characters seated in a steam-filled sauna discussing the ins and outs of having multiple orgasms. The scene was edited out by the network before it aired, though it was shown in its entirety on *The Tonight Show Starring Johnny Carson*.

The four sisters (who have boys' names because their father wanted sons) on whom the series centered were each very different. Alexandra "Alex" Reed-Halsey (Swoosie Kurtz) is the wife of a wealthy plastic surgeon, Wade (David Dukes); Georgiana "Georgie" Reed-Whitsig (Patricia Kalember) is a part-time real estate agent and married to John (Garrett M. Brown); Francesca "Frankie" Reed (Julianne Phillips) is a high-powered marketing analyst; and Theodora "Teddy" Reed-Margolis (Sela Ward) is an artist.

In addition to good casting and good scripts, *Sisters* employed the television contrivance of the nineties: another set of actors was cast to explore the minds and emotions of the main characters. Two other shows using this gimmick were Fox's *Herman's Head* (debut September 8, 1991) and *Charlie Hoover* (November 9, 1991–February 2, 1992), which starred the late comedian Sam Kinison as Hugh, Charlie's (Tim Matheson) hedonistic conscience.

Doubling as the sisters during their youth were Alexondra Lee as Georgie, Jill Novick as Teddy, and Rhianna Janette as little Frankie. They were replaced by Sharon Martin as Alex, Devon Pierce as Teddy, and Tasia Schutt as Frankie.

Alex Reed-Halsey's daughter, Reed Halsey, was played during the first season by Kathy Wagner. With the start of the second season, the role was taken over by Ashley Judd.

Thomas Reed, the girls' late father, was first seen in flashback sequences played by John McCann, and later by Peter White.

THE SIX-MILLION-DOLLAR MAN

January 18, 1974–March 6, 1978.   ABC

Character:	Dr. Rudy Wells
Played by:	Alan Oppenheimer
Date(s):	January 18, 1974–April 27, 1975

Replaced by:	Dr. Rudy Wells
Played by:	Martin E. Brooks
Date(s):	September 14, 1975–March 6, 1978

The title for this series is taken from the price tag spent by the Office of Scientific Intelligence (O.S.I.) to save the life of Colonel Steve Austin (Lee Majors), a test pilot and astronaut who was seriously injured in the crash of a moon-landing craft he was testing over a desert.

The operation that saved his life and turned him into a cyborg (part human and part machine) was performed by Dr. Rudy Wells, an expert in cybernetics who is working for OSI, a top secret government agency. Dr. Wells was able to replace Austin's left eye, right arm and both of his legs with nuclear-powered prosthetic devices that give him superhuman abilities.

The Dr. Rudy Wells who performed this advanced surgery on Steve Austin was played by Martin Balsam in the ninety-minute pilot which aired on ABC on March 7, 1973. Among Martin Balsam's more than three dozen film roles are Milton Arbogast, the private detective who gets his with a bread knife in Alfred Hitchcock's 1960 horror classic, PSYCHO. Balsam won an Academy Award for his performance as Arnold Burns in the 1965 comedy, A THOUSAND CLOWNS and was wonderful as the gay interior decorator, Haskins, in Sean Connery's 1971 crime picture, THE ANDERSON TAPES, which also featured Carmine Caridi from *Phyllis* (See Entry).

Of the more than one hundred television appearances Balsam has made over the years, his only regular series role was from September 23, 1979 through 1981, as Archie Bunker's partner, Murray Klein, on the *All in the Family* spinoff, *Archie Bunker's Place*.

By the time *The Six Million Dollar Man* went on the air, in 1974, Balsam had been replaced by Alan Oppenheimer, who in addition to later playing Captain Dinnerty on the police drama, *Eischeid,* from September 21, 1979 to September 2, 1983 provided voices for many Saturday morning cartoons including Mighty Mouse in the 1979 *Mighty Mouse* series and both Dr. Zarkov and Ming the Merciless in *The New Adventures of Flash Gordon,* which aired on NBC from September 8, 1979 to September 20, 1980.

At the start of the second season Martin E. Brooks took over as OSI's brilliant doctor. He continued playing Dr. Rudy Wells in the spinoff series, *The Bionic Woman,* which starred Ford Rainey of *Search* (See Entry) as Jim Elgin.

Brooks returned to his role in two later Bionic Man/Bionic Woman telefilms, *The Return of the Six-Million-Dollar Man*

and the Bionic Woman, which aired on NBC on May 17, 1987, and *The Bionic Showdown: The Six-Million-Dollar Man and The Bionic Woman,* which aired on Sunday, April 30, 1989.

For a year, beginning in 1983, Brooks appeared as Edgar Randolph on the CBS evening soap opera, *Dallas.*

SKY KING

October 14, 1951–September 3, 1966.   NBC-ABC-CBS

Character:	Clipper King
Played by:	Ron Hagerthy
Date(s):	September 16, 1951–1952

Replaced by:	Bob Carey
Played by:	Norman Ollestad
Date(s):	1955–1956

Replaced by:	Mickey
Played by:	Gary Hunley
Date(s):	1955–1956

"Out of the blue of the Western Sky comes Sky King," television's first flying cowboy and hero to a generation of future pilots and lawmen.

The weekly adventures of *Sky King* were originally produced by Jack Chertok, who was also the producer of *The Lone Ranger.* And like Clayton Moore's Lone Ranger, Kirby Grant's Sky King also pitted his wits and his fists against the outlaws in order to bring them to justice.

He did occasionally strap on a holster and did have a rifle stowed aboard the *Songbird,* but these were more precautionary measures. King avoided violence at all costs and used these guns sparingly, and never to kill.

His main weapon was the *Songbird,* a beautiful twin-engine monoplane, a Cessna 310–B (originally a Cessna P-50) with fuel tanks in the wings permitting extended flights of up to one thousand miles before refueling. From the sky, King could easily track down cattle rustlers, or locate a boy lost in the mountains from the sun's reflection on his canteen. For some unexplained reason, in the fifty-sixth episode of the series, "Designing Women," Sky refers to his plane as the Flying Arrow instead of the Songbird.

Living with King on the Flying Crown Ranch in Arizona were his niece, Penny (Gloria Winters), and his nephew, Clipper (Ron Hagerthy), both of whom could and did occasionally pilot the *Songbird.*

It is obvious that a great deal of thought went into choosing just the right name for a hero with the ability to fly a plane. The writers didn't just pick his name out of the clear blue . . . or did they? The name they came up with was Schuyler (pronounced SKY-LER), or Sky for short.

His nephew was Clipper, a name used by Pan American Airways in 1939 for its Boeing four-engine, twenty-two-passenger Dixie Clippers, which were essentially flying boats like the Grumman Goose used in the 1982 adventure series, *Tales of the Gold Monkey.* The name Clipper also calls to mind those three-masted sailing ships built during the first half of the nineteenth century that were designed for speed. One of the most famous American ships of this type was the *Flying Cloud.*

Clipper, a Jimmy Olsen-type character, did his best to help out his "Uncle Sky" for the show's first season on NBC.

The show went out of production in 1952 because of a rift between the advertising agency and the show's sponsors, Peter Pan Peanut Butter.

The cast members went their separate ways, Kirby Grant to Chicago to work as a writer and director for Wilding Pictures, while Ron Hagerthy enlisted in the military to serve his country—for real—during the Korean War.

With a brand new sponsor, *Sky King,* which had been known as *Sky King Theater* during the first season, resumed production. The new sponsor was Nabisco, and the new opening of the show began with the the announcer's line, "Out of the blue of the Western Sky comes Sky King," with the *Songbird* flying toward and over the camera. The next line belonged to the sponsor—"Brought to you by Nabisco"—and was illustrated by the triangle-shaped Nabisco logo which had been animated to appear as though it had flown past the camera as the plane had.

Perky Gloria Winters was back as Sky's niece, Penny, and two young men, Bob Carey and Mickey, were introduced to the cast, presumably as replacements for Clipper, who was still serving overseas.

Sky King, was originally created for ABC radio in 1946 by Robert M. Burtt and Wilford G. Moore and starred, at various times, the voices of Jack Lester, Earl Nightingale, Roy Engel and, according to at least one source, John Reed King, who as far as anyone knows was no relation to Sky King or The Lone Ranger. Penny was played by Beryl Vaughn and Clipper by both Jack Bivens and Johnny Coons.

When the television series was being cast, Kirby Grant, who had played Peter Evans opposite Abbott and Costello in their 1944 comedy, IN SOCIETY, tested with Barbara Whiting as his niece, Penny, while Gloria Winters, who had played the first Babs Riley on *The Life of Riley* (See Entry) with Jackie Gleason, tested with another actor who was vying for the role of Sky King.

Kirby Grant died in Florida on October 30, 1985, the result of a freak automobile accident that occurred while he was on his way to witness a launch of the Space Shuttle.

SPACE: 1999

1975–1977. Syndicated

Character: Professor Victor Bergman
Played by: Barry Morse
Date(s):   1975–1976

Replaced by: First Officer Tony Verdeschi
Played by: Tony Anholt
Date(s):   1976–1977

It was hyped as the most expensive science fiction series ever produced for television, and it was. The only problem was that the money went into special effects, pyrotechnics and models instead of scripts.

Space: 1999 was little more than *Fireball XL-5* without the marionettes. At times it was hard to tell the difference when watching the emotionless, wooden perfomances turned in by the cast, which was headed up by former *Mission Impossible* (See Entry) stars, Martin Landau and Barbara Bain. It was supposed to star Robert Culp and Katherine Ross, but both actors turned down the opportunity.

Following in the ion trail left by *Star Trek,* Landau's character, Commander John Koenig, interestingly enough, was given the last name of the actor who played Ensign Pavel Chekov on *Star Trek* (See Entry)—Walter Koenig.

If in *Space: 1999,* the spacecraft flight sequences seemed reminiscent of shows such as *Supercar, Fireball XL-5, Stingray, Captain Scarlet and the Mysterons* and *The Thunderbirds,* it is because it was produced by Gerry and Sylvia Anderson, who had brought all of the aforementioned programs to life. They even created the alien creature "Sylvia" for the *Star Trek* episode, "Catspaw," which aired on October 27, 1967. A close eye on the television screen at the end of the episode will spot the wires on the marionette used in that death sequence.

One of the main differences between *Space: 1999* and *Star Trek* was the approach to alien lifeforms. *Star Trek* wore its "Prime Directive" of noninterference like a medal of honor. Furthermore, the crew of the U.S.S. Enterprise was instructed time and time again to fire only when absolutely necessary and then to have their phasors set on stun. Conversely, *Space: 1999*'s credo seemed to be shoot first and ask questions later.

Co-star Barry Morse was known to American television audiences as the relentless Indiana Police Lieutenant, Philip Gerard, who stayed on the trail of Dr. Richard Kimble (David Janssen) for four years in *The Fugitive,* which aired on ABC from September 17, 1963 to August 29, 1967. And his presence as Professor Victor Bergman, the swaggering scientific genius and chief officer of Moonbase Alpha was highly touted.

Not surprisingly, Morse's past popularity didn't carry over, primarily because the typical *Space: 1999* viewer had probably never seen *The Fugitive.* Perceiving that Morse had not caught on with the audience, the writers had Bergman killed off and replaced by a younger officer, Tony Verdeschi, who was listed as both the First Officer and the Security Officer.

Tony Anholt, the actor who was hired to play Verdeschi, had previously appeared as the French agent, Paul Buchet, in the 1972 syndicated adventure series, *The Protectors.* The American agent in that series, Harry Rule, was played by ex-*Man from U.N.C.L.E.* star, Robert Vaughn.

Another unusual aspect of *Space: 1999* lies not in its production, but in its distribution. Unusual because this expensive hour of programming was not produced for a network, like NBC's *Star Trek,* but was designed for first-run syndication. This gave network competitors a run for their money and was reportedly, but never admittedly, responsible for the network cancellations of CBS's *The Invisible Man, Fay, The Montefuscos* and *Three for the Road.* Over on ABC, the casualty was *The Barbary Coast,* which starred *Star Trek*'s former starship captain, William Shatner, as Jeff Cable.

To television programmers space isn't the final frontier, syndication is. And while *Space: 1999* never even made it into the 1980s, *Star Trek* gives every indication of the television schedule through 1999 and beyond.

SPACE PATROL

March 9, 1950–June 1, 1952.   KECA-TV ABC

Character: Commander Kitt Corey
Played by: Glen Denning
Date(s):   March 9, 1950–unknown

Replaced by: Commander Buzz Corey
Played by: Ed Kemmer
Date(s):   September 11, 1950–Febrary 26, 1955

"Space Patrol! High adventure in the wild, vast regions of space! Missions of daring in the name of interplanetary justice! Travel into the future with Buzz Corey, Commander-in-Chief of the Space Patrol!"

First there was Captain Video, then there was Buck Rogers and now there was Commander Buzz Corey to defend the galaxy.

The space serial was created by Mike Moser, a veteran of the United States Navy Air Force during World War II. It has been reported that Moser worked in the Navy Fleet Air Electronics Unit and was also responsible for training hurricane-hunter squadrons.

The first Commander Corey to blast off aboard the X-R-Z was Glen Denning, as Kitt. His exciting galactic adventures, set in the thirtieth century, began on Los Angeles television station KECA-TV, as a local program.

Because of conflicting information, it is difficult to say for sure, but it appears likely that *Space Patrol* first aired on KECA-TV on Thursday, March 9, 1950, and not March 13 as some sources indicate, as the program was shown on Tuesdays and Thursdays during that period.

Information is also sketchy as to how long Glen Denning played Kitt Corey on *Space Patrol* before being replaced by Ed Kemmer.

Kemmer was quoted in Gary H. Grossman's *Saturday Morning TV* as saying, "I missed the first twenty-five or thirty daily shows," which put Denning's last appearance in September of 1950 if Kemmer was referring to the Tuesday/Thursday schedule. This makes sense since this science fiction serial made the transition from a program of local origination to the ABC network on September 11, 1950, when the schedule was expanded from two shows to four or five times a week, depending on which source you read. Some sources indicate that *Space Patrol* aired on three weeknights and one Saturday morning edition; other sources say the space opera aired on a Monday-through-Friday schedule.

If these were the "daily shows" Ed Kemmer was referring to, then Glen Denning played Kitt Corey until October 13 or October 20, 1950.

The second Commander Corey was Buzz, introduced as Kitt's brother. He was played by Ed Kemmer, a military pilot who was shot down over Germany on his forty-eighth mission, an experience he no doubt brought to his role as the intrepid

commander of the spaceship *Terra*. And just as the *U.S.S. Enterprise* on *Star Trek* (See Entry) went through several redesigns, Commander Corey piloted the *Terra*s *I* through *V*.

The organization Commander Buzz Corey was working for was the United Planets, an alliance comprised of earth, Mars, Venus, Jupiter and Mercury. An interesting comparison can be made with Captain James T. Kirk, of the Starship Enterprise, whose loyalties were to the United Federation of Planets, which was made up of planets outside of our solar system, including Altair VI, Rigel IV, Orion, Vega IX and, of course, Vulcan.

Space hero Ed Kemmer later starred as Roy Selby on the CBS daytime soap opera, *The Clear Horizon,* which aired from July 11, 1960 to June 11, 1962. Selby was an Army Signal Corps officer, supposedly stationed in Alaska before being reassigned to Cape Canaveral, Florida. Joining Ed Kemmer was Richard Coogan as astronaut, Mitchell Corbin. Coogan, you may recall, had starred as the first Captain Video on television's first space opera, *Captain Video and his Video Rangers* (See Entry).

One of Commander Corey's adversaries was that master of disguise, Mr. Proteus, played by Marvin Miller, who in 1956 narrated the syndicated adventure series, *Stories of the Century* (See Entry). That same year he also provided the voice for Robby the Robot in the ground-breaking science fiction film, FORBIDDEN PLANET.

SPENCER

December 1, 1984–July 5, 1985.   NBC

Character: Spencer Winger
Played by: Chad Lowe
Date(s):   December 1, 1984–December 29, 1984

Replaced by: Spencer Winger
Played by: Ross Harris
Date(s):   March 23, 1985–July 5, 1985

Character: George Winger
Played by: Ronny Cox
Date(s):   December 1, 1984–December 29, 1984

Replaced by: Ben Sprague
Played by: Harold Gould
Date(s):   March 23, 1985–July 5, 1985

Character: Millie Sprague
Played by: Frances Sternhagen
Date(s):   March 23, 1985–July 5, 1985

On December 1, 1984, NBC placed a full-page ad in *TV Guide* promoting its new series, *Spencer*. The ad read: "He's honest—to a fault. He's wry—with a twist. He's funny—without a doubt. He knows the meaning of life. And he's not impressed."

Three months later, another full-page ad ran in *TV Guide*. This one read "When you get three generations under one roof—especially these three generations—the roof is really gonna blow! Here's the next great new family comedy!''

It may sound like two different shows, but it was really the same one—after a major overhaul. Why? Because series star Chad Lowe, the boyishly handsome younger brother of the equally handsome teen matinee idol, Rob Lowe, apparently had second thoughts about his worth to the network and left the series following a contract dispute.

The changes were explained to viewers in the March 23, 1985, *TV Guide* listing for the debut of the revamped series, *Under One Roof.* '' 'Spencer' has a new title, a new actor (Ross Harris) and new characters: Harold Gould and Frances Sternhagen play Spencer's grandparents who, in the opener, fill a void left by Spencer's father, who has left Doris (Mimi Kennedy) for a twenty-three-year-old.'' The identity of the twenty-three-year-old was never revealed. What is known is that Ross Harris had played Dylan Chaplin on the NBC sitcom, *United States,* which aired from March 11 to April 29, 1980.

When *Spencer* began, the slightly off center, girl-obsessed sixteen-year-old had a mom, Doris, played by Mimi Kennedy, and a dad, George, played by Ronny Cox. Ms. Kennedy had previously played Nan Gallagher on the situation comedy, *The Two of Us,* which aired on CBS from April 6, 1981 to August 10, 1982. Cox, who played George Winger on *Spencer,* had ten years earlier, played another George—Apple, in the CBS drama, *Apple's Way.*

Spencer's grandfather, Ben Sprague, was played by busy character actor Harold Gould, who is perhaps best remembered as Rhoda Morgenstern's father, Martin, from Valerie Harper's CBS situation comedy, *Rhoda,* which aired from September 9, 1974 to December 9, 1978.

Spencer also had a younger sister, Andrea (Amy Locane), and two pals, Herbie Bailey and Wayne. While Wayne was played throughout the short run of the series by Grant Heslov, Herbie was played by David Greenlee in the pilot and thereafter by Dean Cameron. Cameron later starred as Jeff Spicoli in the CBS situation comedy, *Fast Times,* which, if all the episodes of the series, which ran from March 5 to April 23, 1986, were spliced together, would have run just slighty longer than the 92–minute 1982 motion picture on which it was based—FAST TIMES AT RIDGEMONT HIGH.

STAND BY FOR CRIME

January 11, 1949–August 27, 1949.   ABC

Character:	Inspector Webb
Played by:	Boris Aplon
Date(s):	January 11, 1949–April 1949
Replaced by:	Lieutenant Anthony Kidd
Played by:	Myron Wallace
Date(s):	May 1949–August 27, 1949

The fact that *Stand By for Crime* was broadcast live provided the producers with a unique opportunity to involve viewers in the program. Each week Inspector Webb, chief of the Homicide Squad, presented a murder mystery complete with enough clues to solve the case, but that's where the program stopped. At that point viewers were invited to phone in and try to solve the case along with a guest celebrity detective who would also offer a suggestion as to who the guilty party was. After the calls, which were broadcast during the program, the guilty party was revealed.

Nearly thirty years later, from April 12 to March 17, 1979, a similar concept was tried by NBC. The name of the program was *Whodunnit?* and it was hosted by the thirty-year announcer of *The Tonight Show Starring Johnny Carson,* Ed McMahon. This half-hour program had three contestants competing for cash prizes for solving a murder that was staged on the program. A panel of experts included ''celebrity'' attorneys F. Lee Bailey and Melvin Belli, the latter of whom played Gorgan on the October 11, 1968 *Star Trek* episode, ''And the Children Shall Lead.''

The show's host, Ed McMahon explained how *Whodunnit?,* a British television series, was brought to the United States:

''Fred Silverman was over in England having dinner with Sir Lew Grade. At dinner he [Silverman] said, 'I saw a show last night that I'm interested in called *Whodunnit?* Do you know who owns it? Lew Grade excused himself and got up from the table. When he returned, fifteen minutes later, he said, 'I now own it. Do you want it?' And Fred [Silverman] said, 'Yes.'

''I won the audition to be the host and we put it on. The problem was that it was a very expensive show to produce because each week we had to have a different set. These included an airport, an old mansion and a luxury liner. When we didn't get the numbers [ratings] that they wanted, *Whodunnit?* was cancelled after only six weeks,''[8] said McMahon.

Nine years later, the producers of *Matlock* devised an episode in which two endings were filmed and then asked viewers to call a 900 phone number (at a cost of fifty cents per call) to vote for the ending they wanted to see. During the final commercial break, the results were tabulated and the ending preferred by the viewers was aired. This gimmick was also used for episodes of *The A-Team* and *Married: With Children.*

Inspector Webb (Boris Aplon) only stood by for crime for four months, at which time he was replaced by Lieutenant Anthony Kidd, who was played by a thirty-one-year-old actor named Myron Wallace in his first network television role. Prior to this, his first acting job on television, Wallace served as narrator for radio programs such as *The Lone Ranger* and *The Green Hornet.*

Myron Wallace's later television work still confined him to the role of emcee or moderator on such programs as *Majority Rules, Guess Again* and *Who's the Boss?* His big break came on September 24, 1968, more than ten years after he had given up acting for broadcast journalism and changed his first name from Myron to Mike. For it was as Mike Wallace that he became famous as the head correspondent for the highly rated CBS newsmagazine program, *60 Minutes.*

---

8. From an exclusive telephone interview with Ed McMahon on December 12, 1990.

STAR TREK

September 8, 1966–September 2, 1969.   NBC

Character:	Navigator
Played by:	Don Eitner
Date(s):	September 15, 1966
Replaced by:	Lieutenant Commander Gary Mitchell
Played by:	Gary Lockwood
Date(s):	September 22, 1966
Replaced by:	Lieutenant Alden
Played by:	Lloyd Haynes
Date(s):	September 22, 1966
Replaced by:	Lieutenant Kevin Riley
Played by:	Bruce Hyde
Date(s):	September 29, 1966
Replaced by:	Lieutenant John Farrell
Played by:	Jim Goodwin
Date(s):	October 6, 1966
	October 13, 1966
	October 27, 1966
Replaced by:	Lieutenant Dave Bailey
Played by:	Anthony Hall
Date(s):	November 10, 1966
Replaced by:	Lieutenant Andrew Stiles
Played by:	Paul Comi
Date(s):	December 15, 1966
Replaced by:	Lieutenant Vincent DeSalle
Played by:	Michael Barrier
Date(s):	January 12, 1967
	March 2, 1967
Replaced by:	Lieutenant Spinelli
Played by:	Blaisdell Makee
Date(s):	February 16, 1967
Replaced by:	Lieutenant DePaul
Played by:	Sean Kenney
Date(s):	January 19, 1967
	February 23, 1967
Replaced by:	Ensign Pavel Chekov
Played by:	Walter Koenig
Date(s):	September 15, 1967
Replaced by:	Ensign Jana Haines
Played by:	Victoria George
Date(s):	January 5, 1968

"Space—the final frontier. These are the voyages of the Starship Enterprise. Her five-year mission to explore strange new worlds, seek out new life and new civilizations, to boldly go where no man has gone before."

These now immortal words were spoken by William Shatner at the opening of each episode of *Star Trek,* just before the opening theme and credits kicked in at warp speed.

To say that *Star Trek* was the most important series ever to air on televison may be a slight overstatement. But that its contribution has forever altered the course of television and popular culture is undisputable. And to think of television without *Star Trek* is unimaginable.

Perhaps even more important is the way *Star Trek* has changed the way we think about ourselves, our planet and the universe. From the very inception, creator Gene Roddenberry bucked then current "safe" trends in television programming, making the designation U.S.S. Enterprise (named the Yorktown in the first draft) stand for United Space Ship instead of the less controversial United States Spaceship. Roddenberry believed that this unified world concept was paramount to his vision of the future. This same idea was carried over to the crew members, who were representative of many nations, cultures and even other worlds.

James T. Kirk (William Shatner), the ship's Captain, was an American from the nation's Midwest (Riverside, Iowa to be exact). The doctor was from the south, the chief engineer was Scottish, and the helmsman was predominantly Japanese. The communications officer was a black woman from the United States of Africa on Terra whose name, Uhura, means "freedom" in Swahili, and the ship's first officer was an alien—half human, half Vulcan.

The person hired by Gene Roddenberry to handle general research assignments was Kellam De Forest, who ran an independent research company located on the Paramount Studios' lot. In a letter dated May 18, 1965, Gene Roddenberry asked De Forest to check out any clearance problems with the names being considered for the Captain of the starship. These names were Flagg, Drake, Christopher, Thorpe, Richard, Patrick, Raintree, Boone, Hudson, Timber, Hamilton, Hannibal, Neville, Kirk and North.

Through most of the development stages, the name of the Captain was Robert April. It was changed twice shortly before production was to begin on the pilot, first, to Winter and then to Christopher Pike.

The actor cast in the role was Jeffrey Hunter. The 1964 pilot, titled *The Cage,* didn't sell, and when the second attempt was made Hunter was working on a motion picture and was unavailable. The actor hired to replace him as the captain of the Enterprise was William Shatner.

There were also a number of other cast changes made from the pilots to the series.

J.M. Colt, the Captain's lovely yeoman, played by Laurel Goodwin, was not retained for the series, though she was seen in pilot footage cut into the two-part episode, "The Menagerie" which aired on November 17 and 24, 1966. Ms. Goodwin's replacement was Grace Lee Whitney, who appeared as Yeoman Janice Rand during the show's first season, from September 8, 1966, to April 13, 1967. Ms. Whitney later appeared briefly in the first three STAR TREK motion pictures.

In the first *Star Trek* pilot, the executive officer of the Enterprise was an efficient, emotionless woman with dark hair,

Star Trek's 23rd-century crew of the Starship Enterprise are (clockwise, from center) Captain James T. Kirk (William Shatner), Dr. Leonard "Bones" McCoy (DeForest Kelley), Engineer Montgomery "Scotty" Scott (James Doohan), Ensign Pavel Chekov (Walter Koenig), Nurse Christine Chapel (Majel Barrett), Communications Officer Uhura (Nichelle Nichols), Helmsman Sulu (George Takei), and Mr. Spock (Leonard Nimoy).

referred to as "Number One," and billed as M. Leigh Hudec in the credits of both the pilot and, later, "The Menagerie." Changing her hair to blonde and her name to Majel Barrett, she became Nurse Christine Chapel in the *Star Trek* series. On August 6, 1969 she also became Mrs. Gene Roddenberry.

In the second pilot, with Number One gone, the alien Mr. Spock (Leonard Nimoy) was moved into her more prominent position as the ship's second in command. Many of Number One's role characteristics were given to Mr. Spock, which helped to make his character more fascinating.

A long-standing supporting role in science fiction films and television series was the ship's doctor, and *Star Trek* was no exception.

Originally conceived as a worldly gentleman in his sixties, the ship's Doctor, Phillip Boyce, was played by John Hoyt, who appeared in the two-part episode, "The Menagerie," which aired on November 17 and 24, 1966.

Susan Sackett, who was the assistant to Gene Roddenberry on the STAR TREK motion pictures, said, "All along, Gene [Roddenberry] had wanted DeForest Kelley, but he was working on other projects, a couple of which were for Gene, so he wasn't available to play the doctor.

"When Gene did the second pilot, *Where No Man Has Gone Before,* John Hoyt wasn't available, so they cast Paul Fix. Finally De Forest Kelley became available."[9] And he was given the role he was meant to play all along.

Thanks to the second pilot, *Star Trek* was launched as a regular weekly series on September 8, 1966, with a core of principal players who would, for the most part, not only remain as loyal crew members for seventy-nine assignments during its five-year mission that really only lasted for three seasons, but would go on to make six big-budget motion pictures.

There was, however, one post aboard the bridge crew of the Enterprise that wasn't filled by a principal player during the first season of the series: the role of the ship's navigator. The plum position in the chair next to Mr. Sulu (George Takei) was filled throughout the first season by a number of different actors, each playing a different character, not every one of whom was even identified.

Where No Man Has Gone Before, Star Trek's second pilot, aired on September 22, 1966 and used the navigator's position for the episode's guest star, Gary Lockwood, who played Chief Navigator Lieutenant Commander Gary Mitchell. Lloyd Haynes appeared as Lieutenant Alden, Mitchell's relief. Lockwood was no stranger to space or science fiction, having co-starred as astronaut Frank Poole in Stanley Kubrick's 1968 groundbreaking science fiction film, 2001: A SPACE ODYSSEY.

The first significant navigator to have any real visibility was in the September 15, 1966 episode, "Charlie X." He was played by Don Eitner and his character didn't even have a name. He was simply listed in the closing credits as "Navigator."

Bruce Hyde starred as Lieutenant Kevin Riley in "The Naked Time," which aired on September 29, 1966. When he left the bridge, communications officer Lieutenant Uhura (Nichelle Nichols) temporarily assumed his duties. She was then replaced by Frank da Vinci as Lieutenant Brent. Bruce

Hyde returned as Kevin Riley in the December 8, 1966 episode, "The Conscience of the King," which co-starred Arnold Moss as Anton Karidian/Kodos the Executioner.

For three episodes during the first season, "The Enemy Within," "Mudd's Women" and "Miri," Jim Goodwin occupied the navigator's station. These episodes originally aired in 1966 on October 6, 13 and 27.

The next actor to have a guest-starring role as a navigator was Anthony Hall, who played Lieutenant Dave Bailey in "The Corbomite Maneuver." Unlike most of the other navigators whose subsequent whereabouts are virtually unknown, Lieutenant Bailey's disappearance was not only explained, but was a key element in the episode. The reason that Dave Bailey was never seen again was because he chose to stay aboard Balok's (Clint Howard) ship, the Fesarius, as a representative of the United Federation of Planets.

Even though Peter Duryea was seen in the next episode as Chief Navigator Jose Tyler, he cannot be considered a replacement. This is because he actually predates all Enterprise navigators, as he was featured in the flashback scenes taken from the 1964 pilot, *The Cage,* that were integrated into the two-part episode, "The Menagerie," which aired on November 17 and 24, 1966.

In this episode, Spock has taken control of the Enterprise in order to return Christopher Pike, his former captain, now an aged and grotesquely deformed quadriplegic, to Talos IV, where he can be given the illusion of youth and health. The wheelchair-bound Captain was played by Sean Kenney, who later became Lieutenant DePaul, one of the starship's many navigators.

There were, of course, a number of episodes during *Star Trek*'s first season when the on-screen navigator spoke few, if any, lines of dialogue and was generally not even included in the closing credits. In "The Balance of Terror," Paul Comi had a fairly substantial role as Lieutenant Andrew Stiles. At first he mistrusted Mr. Spock because he looked similar to the Federation's foes, the Romulans. Mr. Stiles has a change of heart, though, when Spock is the one who saves his life. Before beaming aboard the Enterprise, Paul Comi flew in earth's atmosphere as Chuck Lambert, the first of two pilots featured on *Ripcord* (See Entry).

The relief navigator in "The Squire of Gothos" and "This Side of Paradise" was Lieutenant Vincent DeSalle, who was played by Michael Barrier. Mr. DeSalle was later promoted to assistant chief engineer in the "Catspaw" episode, which aired on October 27, 1967.

A slight slipup in story continuity caused Khan Noonian Singh (Ricardo Montalban), the genetically engineered criminal with the superior intellect, to make a flagrant faux pas.

In the 1982 motion picture, STAR TREK II: THE WRATH OF KHAN, Clark Terrell (Paul Winfield) and Pavel Chekov (Walter Koenig), the captain and first officer of the U.S.S. Reliant, beam down to the surface of what they believe to be Ceti Alpha VI. They are there to insure that the planet is devoid of all life before the Genesis device can be tested.

The inventor of Genesis, Doctor Carol Marcus (Bibi Besch),

---

9. From an exclusive telephone interview with Susan Sackett. December 10, 1990.

STAR TREK   380

warns the landing party that "There can't be so much as a microbe, or the show's off." The show is the test of the Genesis device that was designed to turn a lifeless planet or asteroid into a living planet covered with a rich vegetation that should never have grown there.

On the planet's surface Terrell and Chekov find Khan, who, after looking the captain over, says, "I don't know you." He then walks over to the other starship officer. "But you . . . I never forget a face. Mr. (he pauses as he tries to remember) Chekov, isn't it? I never thought to see your face again."

He must have mistaken Chekov for Lieutenant Spinelli (Blaisdell Makee), who was the navigator aboard the Enterprise when Kahn was there fifteen years earlier in the *Star Trek* television episode, "Space Seed," which aired on February 16, 1967. Kahn's confusion is somewhat understandable, if not forgivable as Blaisdell Makee appeared as Mr. Singh in the September 29, 1967 episode "The Changeling." Perhaps he was a distant relative of Khan's.

With the first season winding down, Sean Kenney, who doubled as the injured Captain Pike in *The Menagerie*, appeared as the ship's navigator, Lieutenant DePaul, in the February 23, 1967 episode, "A Taste of Armageddon." He also played DePaul, the helmsman of the Enterprise in "Arena," which aired on January 19 that same year.

On September 15, 1967, *Star Trek* began a new season, its second, with a new navigator—its eleventh. The first episode, "Amok Time," featured Walter Koenig as Chief Navigator Ensign Pavel Chekov. There are a couple of conflicting explanations as to why the navigator's post was filled by a young Russian.

"According to NBC, a staff reporter for *Pravda*, the Russian newspaper, had reviewed a *Star Trek* episode he had seen televised in Germany. The critic was understandably upset at seeing an internationally (and interplanetarily) staffed spaceship without a Russian prominently in view. The *Pravda* reporter mentioned that since *Star Trek* is a show about space and space exploration, there should *certainly* be a Russian aboard since Russia was the first nation to begin man's ventures into outer space. The news report had far-reaching effects, and when Gene Roddenberry saw it, he could not help but agree."[10]

Susan Sackett, who is the co-author with Gene Roddenberry of *Star Trek: The First Twenty-Five Years,* shared her recollections of Koenig's hiring: "It was not as if they were looking for a permanent ensign and then found Walter [Koenig]. It's just that they needed to have a Russian character. The producers also decided at that time that they needed a young permanent crew member who would help bring in the younger audience. They got lucky because Walter Koenig filled both bills by being Chekov, a young Russian!"[11]

Walter Koenig, the actor who played Mr. Chekov, remembers the circumstances surrounding his hiring a little differently:

"I played the part of a Russian on an episode of *Mr. Novak,* 'A Boy Without a Country,'[12] and Joe [Joseph] D'Agosta, who was casting director on the *Novak* show, was by 1967 the casting director on *Star Trek* and he had brought my name up.

"I had also worked for Gene Roddenberry in a leading role in the 'Mother Enemy' episode of *The Lieutenant*[13]. I played a guy who was trying to get into Officer's Candidate School and was being prevented because my mother, played by Neva Patterson, was a communist.

"Joe [Joseph] Pevney, one of *Star Trek*'s two alternating directors, was in the room when I came to read. He had used me in a leading guest role in 'Memo from Purgatory,' an episode of *The Alfred Hitchcock Hour*[14] written by Harlan Ellison. [Ellison's book was titled *Memos from Purgatory.*]

"So three of the four people involved in the decision of who was going to be cast in this part already knew my work. Only Gene Roddenberry's co-producer, Gene Coon, didn't know me and he brought in another actor, Anthony Benson, to read.[15]

"After the audition I didn't even go home because they asked me to hang around. I waited around for about forty-five minutes when *Star Trek*'s costume designer, Bill [William Ware] Theiss, came into the room and asked me to follow him.

"I followed Bill over to the wardrobe building where he took out one of those cloth tape measures and began measuring me from my crotch to my cuff, and I asked 'What are you doing?' and he answered, 'I'm measuring you for the costume.' That's how I learned that I was in *Star Trek*."[16]

Unlike James Doohan, who did a number of different accents for the producers and casting people before the Scottish one was chosen, Walter Koenig was only called upon to provide his Russian accent because by the time he and Benson were brought in for the final audition, it had already been decided that Chekov was going to be a Russian character.

Koenig's recollection of his being cast in *Star Trek* differs slightly from previously published sources, in that he does not subscribe to the stories circulated about the article in *Pravda*.

"My understanding is that it was pure studio hype. They just decided that it was logical that they had a Russian since the cosmonauts were the first people in space. Originally they were going to have an English kid patterned after Davey Jones of the *Monkees* [See Entry]."

Koenig went on to explain that he had never actually seen an entire episode of *Star Trek* prior to his being cast and was not aware of the fact that there had already been other actors filling the navigator's role. "I did tune it in once, but when I saw those styrofoam rocks I said to myself, 'Boy this looks really phony,' and I never sat through it," said Koenig.

10. Asherman, Alan. *The Star Trek Compendium.* New York: Pocket Books 1986, pg. 69.
11. From an exclusive telephone interview with Susan Sackett. December 10, 1990.
12. The "A Boy Without A Country" episode of *Mr. Novak* aired on December 10, 1963.
13. The "Mother Enemy" episode of *The Lieutenant* aired on April 4, 1964.
14. The "Memo from Purgatory" episode of *The Alfred Hitchcock Hour* aired on October 24, 1964, during the program's third season.
15. Anthony Benson appeared with Walter Koenig in the December 15, 1966 episode of *Jericho*.
16. This and the following recollections by Walter Koenig in this *Star Trek* entry are from an exclusive interview with Mr. Koenig on January 25, 1991.

In retrospect, Walter Koenig explained, "Occasionally they would have a guest actor play that part. Sometimes they simply had a stand-in just sit there at the navigator's console. I wasn't told it was going to be a running role. I was told that if they liked what they saw, there was a chance that it would recur. It was also predicated on the audience reaction. I didn't have a contract that first season. I literally didn't know from week-to-week whether I'd be coming back, and would try to sneak a look at the next week's script to see if my character was in it. And until the show went on the air, I don't beleive they felt totally comfortable with the Chekov character. But when the episodes began airing, they got a very positive reaction from the audience. A lot of fan magazine coverage and a lot of mail. At the peak, I was getting six- to seven-hundred letters a week and I was put under contract beginning with the third season.

"What happened was very fortunate. It is my understanding that during the hiatus between the first and second season, George Takei was working on THE GREEN BERETS and the shooting schedule went overtime and he couldn't get back in time to start. So in a way, I was sort of forced into that position because he wasn't there to take up the slack. Possibly because the producers didn't want to have two rotating actors—I became the person," Koenig said.

Yet even when Chekov was the ship's permanent navigator, there was at least one occasion when he needed to be replaced on the bridge. Not because Koenig wasn't appearing in the episode, but because Chekov was being held captive on the planet below. In "The Gamesters of Triskelion," Ensign Jana Haines (Victoria George) covered for Mr. Chekov, who had his hands full with a butch drill thrall named Kloog while Captain Kirk was being trained for combat by Shahna, played by the curvaceous green-eyed actress, Angelique Pettyjohn. Rank doth have its little privileges.

Star Trek ended its network run in 1969, but on September 15, 1973 it was brought back as a half-hour animated series produced by Filmation Studios, which later produced *Land of the Lost* (See Entry) and *Jason of Star Command* (See Entry). The Saturday morning *Star Trek* cartoon featured the voices of all—well, nearly all—of the original cast as their astro alter egos. Missing was Walter Koenig as Mr. Chekov. According to Walter Koenig, this was by no means an oversight but a conscious decision by the producers to cut expenses: "I wasn't invited. Filmation was trying to save money. In fact they wanted to eliminate George [Takei] and Nichelle [(Lieutenant Uhura) Nichols] from the cast as well. They wanted Jimmy [Doohan] and Majel [Barrett] to do the voices for their characters. And Leonard [Nimoy], to his credit, said that he wouldn't do it unless they were included because they were part of the original series and important to its success. They had to cut it somewhere and since I had the least seniority and had already written an episode, I guess that they felt that I had somehow been paid for my involvement and that that would be the easiest way to go. They cut my character completely and put an alien navigator in Chekov's place."

The episode written by Koenig was "The Infinite Vulcan." It aired on October 20, 1973, and featured the Retlaw plant that

has the unique characteristic of mobility. The inside joke is that Koenig named the plant after himself by spelling his first name backwards.

The new navigator of the Enterprise was an orangey alien named Lieutenant Arex whose voice was provided by James Doohan.

"They [the producers] asked, 'Can you do this voice?' and I answered, 'Well, let's test and see what kind of a voice you like,' " said Doohan.

In addition to providing the high-pitched mechanical-sounding voice for Mr. Arex, James Doohan was usually the voice of each episode's "guest alien" and of more than twenty other characters during the twenty-two-episode run, which ended on October 12, 1974.

"I didn't even use any accent on doing the voice of that [Mr. Arex], but used changes of tone. My main objective was to do more than three voices, because then they had to double my pay,"[17] Doohan explained.

What James Doohan was referring to was the fact that the union rules at that time allowed the producers to ask voice talent to provide up to three voices for their salary. If a fourth voice was required, the actor would receive a second paycheck and would then be obligated to provide two additional voices.

James Doohan continues to recreate his role as Chief Engineer Mongomery Scott and has done so in all six STAR TREK motion pictures. He also said that he does as many as thirty-five to forty *Star Trek* and related conventions every year, as does his fellow co-star, Walter Koenig.

Some of Walter Koenig's other credits include the starring role of Colonel Jason Grant in the 1989 science fiction adventure, MOONTRAP, in which he not only commands his own ship, but also gets the girl. He landed the role because of a comment he made in a *Star Trek* cover story that appeared in *Time* magazine. "The writer of MOONTRAP read my quote that I would be interested in doing other projects if they were offered to me. And strictly on the basis of that quote they contacted me and asked if I would be interested in getting involved,"[18] said Koenig.

In the film there are several subtle allusions to Koenig's continuing affiliation to *Star Trek*. His opening voice-over begins with the words, "The final frontier." He says, "Nice move, bringing up the Russians," and is seen wearing a black T-shirt with a graphic of two humpback whales and the moon. The whales are an obvious reference to the 1986 STAR TREK "save the whales" entry, STAR TREK IV: THE VOYAGE HOME.

Along with his work as an actor, Walter Koenig is also the author of two books, *Chekov's Enterprise: A Personal Journal of the Making of Star Trek: The Motion Picture,* published in 1980 by Pocket Books, and a satirical fantasy, *Buck Alice and the Actor-Robot,* which was published in August 1988.

Koenig has also had a number of his scripts produced for television series other than *Star Trek.* These include episodes of *Family, The Powers of Matthew Star* and Filmation's *Land of the Lost* (See Entry).

Ahead warp factor one.

17. From an exclusive telephone interview with James Doohan on September 13, 1990.
18. From an exclusive telephone interview with Walter Koenig. January 25, 1991.

STAR TREK: THE NEXT GENERATION

October 3, 1987–May 23 1994.   Syndicated

Character: Dr. Beverly Crusher
Played by: Gates McFadden
Date(s):   October 3, 1987–unknown
                September 28, 1989–May 23, 1994

Replaced by: Dr. Katherine "Kate" Pulaski
Played by: Diana Muldaur
Date(s):   November 26, 1988–July 22, 1989

Character: Alexander
Played by: Jon Steuer
Date(s):   unknown

Replaced by: Alexander
Played by: Brian Bonsall
Date(s):   unknown

"Space—the final frontier. These are the voyages of the Starship Enterprise. Its continuing mission to explore strange new worlds. To seek out new life and new civilizations. To boldly go where no one has gone before."

The subtle changes made in this familiar opening voice-over, now spoken by Patrick Stewart, help to let the viewer know that they are no longer in the twenty-third century, but in the twenty-fourth, and that this is not *Star Trek,* but *Star Trek: The Next Generation,* which is set seventy-eight years after the first series.

There is no question that this well-written and well-produced science fiction took a little more getting used to than most new television series. That is primarily due to the nearly twenty-year familiarity with the original crew of the Starship Enterprise, who were concurrently appearing in a continuing series of highly successful big-budget motion pictures.

Star Trek: The Next Generation's production associate, Susan Sackett, warns viewers against the temptation to compare *The Next Generation* to the original *Star Trek* series. "They're really not comparable except for the Enterprise. Other than that they have a captain, but the characters were created totally from scratch," she said.

Even Paramount's submission guidelines for speculative script submissions clearly stated that no stories should be submitted for consideration that involve any of the original characters or their descendants.[19] Still, one may feel compelled to compare the two series.

On a very basic level one might try to draw the conclusion that the writers and producers were just taking scripts from the original *Star Trek* and dividing up the parts. Steve Simels made this observation about the series' first season in his article "Re-'Generation'," which appeared in the September 25, 1992 issue of *Entertainment Weekly:* "Individual episodes stand out

as exceptions, of course—most notably 'The Big Goodbye,' in which the crew inhabits a stylish holodeck re-creation of the world of [Dixon Hill] a fictional Sam Spade-type '40s detective. But most of them are essentially retreads of the original *Star Trek* series (like 'The Naked Now,' a virtual rewrite of 'The Naked Time')."

"Let's see, we'll take this line from Captain Kirk and give half to Captain Jean-Luc Picard (Patrick Stewart) and half to Commander Riker (Jonathan Frakes)."

While Patrick Stewart, as Captain Jean-Luc Picard, possesses the strong-willed, dedicated and resourceful side of Kirk, Jonathan Frakes, as first officer Commander William Riker, takes the brash, impulsive and more passionate side of Kirk. Number One's name even evokes a feeling of Kirk. It would appear to be more than mere coincidence that the first three letters of "Riker" are the reverse of the first three letters of "Kirk" and Commander Riker's first name is the same as Shatner's.

It is also very easy to assume that Mr. Spock's role was also divided between two new characters, Data and Troi. Lieutenant Commander Data (Brent Spiner) is a sentient android—a humanoid-type robot with a clockwork ticker for a brain and superhuman strength, easily comparable to Mr. Spock's intelligence, impeccable logic and superior physical abilities.

These similarities were not ignored but met head on by writers and producers, and they broke their own rule about referring to the original cast in the program's two-hour pilot, "Encounter at Farpoint." In a scene between Commander Data and a visiting Starfleet Admiral, we learn that the more things change, the more they stay the same. This high-level officer is never mentioned by name, but in a discussion between Commander Riker and Lieutenant Worf (a Klingon Starfleet officer played by Michael Dorn) we learn that this visitor came aboard in a shuttlecraft instead of being transported, and any *Star Trek* fan worth his Dilithium crystals could figure out that this visiting dignitary was Dr. Leonard McCoy, the chief medical officer who flew aboard the original Enterprise in *Star Trek* (See Entry). He was played by De Forest Kelley, wearing even more aging makeup than he did in "The Deadly Years" episode of the original series.

The scene cuts to find McCoy arguing with Data about his age:

MCCOY: What about my age?

DATA: Sorry, sir. If that subject troubles you.

MCCOY: Troubles me? What's so damn troublesome about not havin' died? How old do you think I am anyway?

DATA: One hundred thirty-seven years, Admiral. According to Starfleet records.

---

19. In addition to DeForest Kelley's guest appearance as an elderly Dr. McCoy in the first episode, later episoses featured Mark Lenard as Ambassador Sarek and Leonard Nimoy as Mr. Spock.

Star Trek: The Next Generation's 24th-century crew of the Starship Enterprise are (left to right): Wesley ''Wes'' Crusher (Wil Wheaton), Lieutenant ''J.G.'' Geordi La Forge (Levar Burton), Counselor Deanna Troi (Marina Sirtis), Commander William ''Will'' Riker (Jonathan Frakes), Captain Jean-Luc Picard (Patrick Stewart), Chief Medical Officer Dr. Beverly Crusher (Gates McFadden), Lieutenant Worf (Michael Dorn), Security Chief Tasha Yar (Denise Crosby), and Brent Spiner as the android, Lieutenant Commander Data.

MCCOY:	Explain how you remember that so exactly.

DATA:	I remember every fact I'm exposed to, sir.

MCCOY:	(after looking carefully at both sides of DATA's head) I don't see no points on your ears, boy, but you sound like a Vulcan.

DATA:	No sir, I'm an android.

MCCOY:	Hmpf, almost as bad.

In "Angel One," Commander Data displays another of his Spock-like characteristics.

RIKER:	To travel the distance we did in two days, at warp one, would have taken the Oden escape pod five months.

DATA:	Five months, six days, eleven hours, two minutes . . .

RIKER:	Thank you, Data.

DATA:	. . . and fifty-seven seconds.

Lieutenant Commander Deanna Troi (Marina Sirtis), on the other hand, is a half-human, half-Betazoid who, as an empath, has a remarkable gift of being able to "sense" feelings and emotions of other beings, which is not unlike Mr. Spock's ability to perform a Vulcan mind meld.

Incidentally, a second holdover from the original *Star Trek* series was Majel Barrett, who did not turn up as either Number One or Nurse Christine Chapel, but as Deanna Troi's mother in the "Haven" episode. She also continued to provide the voice of the Enterprise computer, as she had done in both the original and the animated series.

The trick, of course, to accepting this alien cast is to somehow get beyond the comparisons and enjoy *Star Trek: The Next Generation* for its own merits, which are many.

The focal point of this series is a fifth-generation Enterprise, which requires many similar crew positions needed to man her. There is a transporter chief, a ship's doctor, a chief engineer and a security chief.

Following in Doctor McCoy's footsteps is Doctor Beverly Crusher (Gates McFadden), whose time is divided between her duties as the ship's chief medical officer and her sixteen-year-old prodigy, Wesley. This brilliant young man soon earns the rank of ensign and works in that capacity aboard the Enterprise while studying for his entrance exam to Starfleet Academy. Surprisingly, Wesley fails the first test and returns to the Enterprise as his mother decides to leave.

Susan Sackett explained that the reason why Gates McFadden left *Star Trek: The Next Generation* was that the producers "Wanted to try a different direction for the role of the doctor, because they weren't sure it was working between Picard and Doctor Crusher. They decided at the end of the season to try a different spin on it,"[20] said Ms. Sackett.

Doctor Crusher was replaced by Diana Muldaur, who appeared as a very different sort of doctor on the original *Star Trek* series. In the second-season episode, "Return to Tomorrow," which aired on February 9, 1968, Diana Muldaur guest-starred as Doctor Ann Mulhall. Eight months later during *Star Trek*'s third season, Ms. Muldaur appeared as Doctor Miranda Jones in the October 18, 1968 episode, "Is There in Truth No Beauty?"

Her first appearance as Doctor Pulaski on *Star Trek: The Next Generation* was in an episode titled "The Child."

On the bridge of the Enterprise, Captain Picard asks Data if the new doctor has reported in yet, but has to be reminded of her name by the android. Picard enters the turbolift so that he may meet up with his new officer, who is in the ship's lounge on the forward section of deck ten. He is joined in the turbolift by Wesley Crusher who is wrestling with the decision of whether to stay aboard the Enterprise or join his mother at Starfleet Medical.

WESLEY:	Hello, Captain.

PICARD:	Ensign. I'm sorry this mission will delay your reunion with your mother.

WESLEY:	That's alright. It will give me the time to finish some projects I have to do. (After a long pause, Wesley continues) It's going to be hard leaving the Enterprise.

PICARD:	Mixed feelings for all of us. It's always hard leaving any ship. Just as it was for your mother when she left to become head of Starfleet Medical. But moving from one assignment to another is part of the life that you're choosing.

Wesley chose to stay aboard the starship and after securing the captain's permission, is instructed to contact his mother.

PICARD:	Mr. Crusher, communicate with your mother at Starfleet headquarters. Give her my regards and tell her that you have my permission to remain on the Enterprise, but I will abide by her wishes.

"Sometime during the second season it became apparent that 'no we shouldn't have done it after all and it was a mistake,' and they went back and corrected it," explained Ms. Sackett.

She also wanted to emphasize that the return of Gates McFadden to the role of the ship's doctor was not influenced by

---

20. All the quotations from Susan Sackett in this *Star Trek* entry are from an exclusive telephone interviw with Ms. Sackett on December 10, 1990.

outside sources such as fan pressure or a letter-writing campaign, and didn't have anything to do with the actress herself.

"It was just that this particular chemistry wasn't what they [the producers] were hoping it would be and they decided that the other chemistry was more effective and went back to it.

"People kept reading a lot more into it than there was and it just wasn't that way at all. It was simply a matter of testing the waters, like a shakedown run of a new ship, and you try new things when you try a new show. This was suggested by one of the producers and they tried it. Diana [Muldaur] was great, but the chemistry wasn't right, so they went back with Gates [McFadden]," said Ms. Sackett.

Ms. McFadden returned to the series in the episode titled "Evolution," in which she laments having missed two inches of Wesley's growth during her year away at Starfleet Medical.

The reintroduction of her character continues in a scene in the captain's quarters.

PICARD:	I know how difficult it was for you, being away.
CRUSHER:	Tell me about him.
PICARD:	Well, he's becoming a very fine officer. He works as hard as any member of the crew. Riker says his studies are on line . . .
CRUSHER:	No. Tell me about *him*.
PICARD:	He's his father's son. Honest, trusting, strong.

On *Star Trek: The Next Generation,* the role of the chief engineer has been deemphasized, while the role of the security officer, Lieutenant Tasha Yar (Denise Crosby), has been added to the regular bridge crew. She was also the first of the new cast members to leave the series—killed on Vegra II by a creature named Armus in the May 7, 1988 episode, "Skin of Evil." This hellacious alien—a black oil slick-like creature that could take on humanoid form—was referred to by Captain Picard as "Pure evil."

Leaving the series was actually Ms. Crosby's idea "If I only got to say, 'Hailing frequencies open,' I would slowly go mad," says Crosby. "I would never have taken the role if I'd known it would be reduced to that of a glorified extra."[21]

Paramount has no intention of replacing Tasha. "They have just amplified and expanded Worf's role . . . a little double duty there," said Susan Sackett.

Lieutenant Worf's role was further expanded with the arrival of his son. Worf first learns that he is a father in the "Reunion" episode, when his former Klingon mate, Ambassador K'Ehleyr (Suzie Plakson), is beamed aboard the Enterprise with their son, Alexander (Jon Steuer). K'Ehleyr had not told Worf that she was pregnant and had given birth, nor had she told Alexander that Lieutenant Worf was his father.

Matters were further complicated by the fact that Worf, who still had strong feelings for K'Ehleyr, could not take the Klingon oath of marriage because, in order to preserve the empire, he had accepted discommendation from the high council when his father was accused of treason for collaborating with the Romulans at Khitomer.

In a struggle for control of the Klingon Empire, K'Ehleyr was murdered by a Klingon named Duras, who was then summarily killed by Worf. With Alexander's mother dead it was time for the young Klingon to confirm what he expected.

ALEXANDER:	(To Worf) Are you my father?
WORF:	Yes, I am your father.

The young Klingon, however, does not remain aboard the Enterprise, but is instead sent to earth to live with the human parents who had raised his father.

At the end of the 1990 season, Wil Wheaton, the teenaged actor who played Dr. Beverly Crusher's son, Ensign Wesley Crusher, left the series. And in a scenario strangely reminiscent of the pre-Chekov Enterprise, "Now we have the 'ensign of the week' sitting in his chair," joked Susan Sackett.

In subsequent episodes Lieutenant Worf's son Alexander was reintroduced, perhaps in an effort to help fill some of the void left by the departure of Wesley, who was said to be off attending Starfleet Academy.

Taking over the role of Alexander was child actor Brian Bonsall, who for four seasons played Andrew "Andy" Keaton, clone and little brother of Michael J. Fox's popular television character, Alex P. Keaton, on the highly successful NBC situation comedy, *Family Ties.*

One of the other *Star Trek* guest stars to return to the updated series was Mark Lenard, who recreated his role as Mr. Spock's father in "Sarek." And since the lifespan of a Vulcan is so much longer than that of humans, Ambassador Sarek, now two hundred and two years old, has taken a new wife, Perrin (Joanna Miles). His first wife, Amanda, was played by Jane Wyatt, who is known to a generation as Margaret Anderson, Jim Anderson's wife on *Father Knows Best.*

Engage.

STORIES OF THE CENTURY

1955–1956.   Syndicated

Character:	Frankie Adams
Played by:	Mary Castle
Date(s):	1955–unknown

Replaced by:	Jonsey Jones
Played by:	Kristine Miller
Date(s):	September 10, 1955–1956

21. P.F. *TV Guide.* March 27, 1988, p. A-3. Quote by Denise Crosby.

In 1954, Jim Davis, as Bill Cameron, rode on the *Last Stagecoast West,* the pilot for *Stories of the Century.* As an agent for the Railroad Protection Association, it was Bill Cameron's job to see that the railroad was, in a manner of speaking, kept on track, by protecting it from robbers, Indians and other unsavory types during the 1890s. Assisting him in the pilot was Mary Castle as Louise McCord.

With some minor adjustments, the show went to series the following year and both actors were back. The series, which was at first titled *Outlaws of the Century* and also known as *The Fast Guns,* starred Jim Davis as Matt Clark, a detective for the Southwest Railroad, and Mary Castle as his partner, Frankie Adams.

Shortly thereafter, Kristine Miller replaced Mary Castle as Matt's new partner, Jonsey Jones. She made her first appearance in "Rube Burrows," an episode which first aired in syndication on September 10, 1955.

In comparison to *Death Valley Days,* which first aired in 1952, *Stories of the Century* seemed to have a slicker look. This may have been due to the use of stock footage taken from the library of motion pictures produced by Republic Pictures,which also produced this series.

Thirty-nine episodes later, the show was derailed and Kristine Miller went on to appear in episodes of many other programs including *Science Fiction Theater, The Millionaire, Wagon Train, Father Knows Best* and *The Donna Reed Show.*

The series was narrated by another Miller, Marvin, who had appeared regularly on *Space Patrol* (See Entry) and is certainly best remembered as Michael Anthony, the executive secretary to John Beresford Tipton on *The Millionaire,* which aired on CBS for more than five years beginning on January 19, 1955 and ending on September 28, 1960.

THE STREETS OF SAN FRANCISCO

September 16, 1972–June 23, 1977.   ABC
January 27, 1992   NBC

Character:	Inspector Steve Keller
Played by:	Michael Douglas
Date(s):	September 16, 1972–June 3, 1976
	September 30, 1976, October 7, 1976
Replaced by:	Inspector Dan Robbins
Played by:	Richard Hatch
Date(s):	September 30, 1976–June 16, 1977
Replaced by:	Inspector/Lieutenant David Connor
Played by:	Conor O'Farrel
Date(s):	January 27, 1992
Replaced by:	Inspector Sarah Burns
Played by:	Debrah Farentino
Date(s):	January 27, 1992

Picking up where Inspectors Matt Grebb and Fred Asher left off in *The Lineup* (See Entry), Karl Malden hit the streets of San Francisco in 1972 as Detective Lieutenant Mike Stone, a homicide detective with twenty-three years of experience on the force. Working with Stone on the San Francisco Police Department was Inspector Steve Keller, a smart, young detective who got his education in college instead of on the streets.

Steve was played by "Kirk's son," Michael Douglas, in his fourth outing on the small screen. His first was in "The Experiment," a *CBS Playhouse* presentation which aired on February 25, 1969. This was followed by appearances on *The FBI* and *Medical Center,* and as Craig in the made-for-telvision movie, *When Michael Calls,* which aired on CBS on February 5, 1972.

Douglas strolled off the streets of San Francisco in 1976 and was written out as having quit the force to take up teaching. What he really took up was producing and starring in motion pictures.

In 1978 he played Dr. Mark Bellows in COMA. The following year he played Richard Adams in THE CHINA SYNDROME, a film he also produced. Michael Douglas really hit it big in 1984 as the producer and star of the romantic comedy adventure film, ROMANCING THE STONE, which he followed up with the role of Dan Gallagher in the 1987 psychological romantic thriller, FATAL ATTRACTION.

His replacement on *The Streets of San Francisco* was the boyishly handsome but much less intense actor Richard Hatch, whose most memorable television role was as Captain Apollo, the Luke Skywalker clone in the STAR WARS rip-off, *Battlestar Galactica.* In between *Battlestar Galactica* and *The Streets of San Francisco,* Richard Hatch was seen as Harmon Fairnella on the soap opera spoof, *Mary Hartman, Mary Hartman,* during the 1977 and 1978 seasons.

NBC returned Karl Malden to the streets of San Francisco on January 27, 1992, in a two-hour made-for-television movie, *Back to the Streets of San Francisco.*

In this, the first of two proposed Movies-of-the-Week, which was originally titled *Return to the Streets of San Francisco,* Mike Stone has been elevated to the rank of Captain. But like James T. Kirk, who was promoted to Admiral in the 1980 feature, STAR TREK: THE MOTION PICTURE, but still longed to be a captain, Captain Stone still saw himself as "just a cop."

Reporting to Captain Stone were two sharp young detectives, Sarah Burns (Debrah Farentino) and David Connor (Conor O'Farrell). Both have risen quickly through the ranks of the department and are being considered for a promotion to lieutenant.

It was Stone who had made the recommendation that helped Officer Burns become an inspector; but because he felt she was still "wet behind the ears," Stone was championing Connor's bid for lieutenant—partly because he sincerely believed he was the right person for the job and partly because David reminded him of his former partner, Steve Keller. Detective Connor, who resents being compared to Detective Keller, wants the promotion, but only if he earns it on his own merits.

Steve Keller is now a professor of criminology at a local university, but stays in touch with his old partner and close friend, Mike Stone. In one scene he is supposed to be on the other end of the phone, but we only see Captain Stone arranging the dinner meeting for 7:30 that evening.

Mike goes to the restaurant, the Market Roastery, and waits

around until 9:21, but Steve never shows. Steve's wife Ann is concerned because she hasn't seen or heard from her husband either, but Mike tells her not to worry—even though he is.

Being a cop through and through, Mike initiates an investigation which turns up Steve's car, a 1973 silver Porsche, that was spotted in the San Francisco Bay by a member of the Dolphin Club. When the car is pulled from the water, Steve is not inside. Is Steve dead, or alive? Stone's worst fears are confirmed later that evening.

CONNOR: Mike . . . uh . . .

STONE: If it's about Sarah . . .

CONNOR: No, someone else.

STONE: Go ahead, say it.

CONNOR: It's Steve. They pulled his body from the bay about two hours ago, near Pier 7. It's a positive I.D.

STONE: (Gets up from his desk, turns toward the wall and begins to weep.)

CONNOR: Coroner said he was strangled with a wire garrote around his neck. (PAUSE) I'm sorry.

Later, at the cemetery, Mike stands there stone-faced until the service is over. His daughter Jean (Darleen Carr) then asks:

JEAN: Are you ready to go?

STONE: The last time we met, it was me he was worried about. (Very emotional) I'm gonna miss him.

Back at home, Stone falls asleep in his easy chair while looking through some mementos and begins to dream about Steve, who is shown in flashback clips taken from the original series—the only time Michael Douglas is seen in this TV movie.

It turns out that Steve Keller was strangled by Karl Murchinson, a.k.a. Karl Strauss, a murderer whom Steve and Mike Stone had arrested. Murchinson (Nick Scoggin), who was convicted of first degree murder on April 22, 1971, and sentenced to life at San Quentin on June 18, 1971, had recently been released due to an unknown technicality in his case, and was out to get the men who put him away.

The movie ended with a shootout between Stone and Murchinson on the roof of an old fort in San Francisco. Murchinson runs out of bullets and throws his gun down. Stone, wanting revenge, begs the murderer, who told him that Keller died screaming for mercy, to pick the gun up—which, under police procedurals, would have "legally" allowed Stone to shoot and kill Murchinson in self-defense. But this scenario is never played out as Detective Burns arrives on the scene with

uniformed backup. Stone, who realizes that his emotions have clouded his judgment, hands his gun to Detective Burns, slugs Murchinson twice in the face, takes his gun back and walks away while the young detective takes the murderer into custody and reads him his rights.

Making it safe once again to walk the streets of San Francisco.

THE STU ERWIN SHOW *see:* THE TROUBLE WITH FATHER

SUPER CIRCUS

January 16, 1949–June 3, 1956.   ABC

Character:	Ringmaster
Played by:	Claude Kirchner
Date(s):	January 16, 1949–December 1955
Replaced by:	Ringmaster
Played by:	Jerry Colonna
Date(s):	December 25, 1955–June 3, 1956
Character:	Queen of the Super Circus
Played by:	Mary Hartline
Date(s):	January 16, 1949–December 1955
Replaced by:	Ringmaster's assistant
Played by:	Sandra Wirth
Date(s):	December 25, 1955–June 3, 1956
Character:	Cliffy the Clown
Played by:	Cliff Soubier
Date(s):	January 16, 1949–December 1955
Replaced by:	clown
Played by:	Jerry Bergen
Date(s):	December 25, 1955–June 3, 1956
Character:	Nicky the Clown
Played by:	Nick Francis
Date(s):	January 16, 1949–December 1955
Replaced by:	clown
Played by:	Baron (twin)
Date(s):	December 25, 1955–June 3, 1956
Character:	Scampy the Clown
Played by:	Phillip Bardwell "Bardy" Patton
Date(s):	January 16, 1949–July 1953
Replaced by:	Scampy the Clown
Played by:	Sandy Dobritch
Date(s):	July 1953–December 1955

Replaced by: clown
Played by: Baron (twin)
Date(s):   December 25, 1955–June 3, 1956

The world's greatest showman, P.T. Barnum, once said, "There's a sucker born every minute," and since everyone's a sucker for a pretty face, what better way to garner an audience for a television program than a circus starring a pretty face. The circus was *Super Circus* and its pretty face was Mary Hartline, a beautiful blonde and former model who had captured the fancy of television viewers across America and become something of a phenomenon.

This was perfectly all right with Claude Kirchner, who served as the ringmaster for this weekly variety show featuring honest-to-goodness circus acts ranging from jugglers and acrobats to animal acts with horses, dogs, chimpanzees and elephants.

Strange as it may seem, *Super Circus* was originally conceived as a radio program, as its host, Claude Kirchner, explained: "About 1946 or 1947 we did an audition for a radio show, that was going to be called *Super Circus,* but it didn't sell. When television came into Chicago, the producer, Phil Patton, said, 'What the hell, that ought to make a pretty good television show.' That's how we got on television."[22]

Since a circus wouldn't be a real circus without clowns, *Super Circus* had three of them: Cliffy, Nicky and Scampy. Cliffy, played by Cliff Soubier, a popular radio actor from the 1940s and 1950s, provided the slapstick humor. Nicky was the musician and acrobat, while Scampy was a midget clown who dressed identically to Cliffy.

The truth of the matter was that Scampy wasn't really a midget at all, but "Bardy" Patton, the son of the show's producer, Phil Patton. Bardy literally saved the day by stepping into the oversized shoes when the real midget who had been hired never showed up.

Little boys, unlike midgets, do tend to grow up, and by July of 1953 young Patton was replaced by a younger and smaller lad, Sandy Dobritch, who at the time was just nine years old.

Super Circus was broadcast from Chicago's ABC affiliate, WENR/WBKB Television, until December of 1955 when production was moved to New York.

"It's difficult to explain why the show was moved to New York, but that was television management in those days and they weren't very bright. The New York show only lasted about three months anyway.

"We decided not to go, because we knew it wouldn't work. Once they take the show out of Chicago and start to fool around with it, it would start to lose its character. It just didn't work out and we were glad to get rid of it. Frankly, eight years on the air is long enough," said Kirchner.

The handsome six-foot-five ringmaster with the booming voice moved to New York and became the host of WOR-TV's *Terrytoons Circus.*

"I was the only one who moved to New York," said Kirchner. He explained how *Terrytoons Circus* was developed: "The seven to seven-thirty p.m. half hour became available on channel nine [WOR-TV, New York]. I said, 'Let's program it for children' and they said, 'Don't do it,' recalled Kirchner who went ahead with it anyway.

"We got a-hold of some Terrytoon cartoons and I got a clown puppet, Clownie, which I did the voice for. It worked very, very well and became quite popular.

"Now the original cartoons were Terrytoons—that's how the program got its name. But after the show became popular they put some money into it and we got other cartoons. We continued to call it *Terrytoons Circus* even though we didn't use Terrytoons and since the Terrytoons people didn't care, we just didn't change it. It was *the* children's show in New York and it was on for thirteen years," he recalled.

From September 22, 1962 to March 16, 1963, Claude Kirchner starred as the ringmaster of *Magic Midway,* a direct clone of *Super Circus* that even featured a baton-twirling majorette and three clowns, Bill Bailey as Boom-Boom, Phil Kiley as Coo-Coo, and Douglas Anderson as magician Mr. Pocus.

"*Magic Midway* was a show I sold to Marx Toys. I didn't produce it, but I was the one who got it together, but it wasn't very good," admitted Kirchner.

Mrs. Helen Bailey, Bill Bailey's widow, said that her husband was cast for television's newest circus show because "He had worked for seven and one-half years on *Big Top,* beginning as a warm-up clown."[23] The head clown on *Big Top* was Ed McMahon who told how he got the job.

"A guy by the name of Charlie Vanda, a big radio honcho in Hollywood, was brought in by Don Thornburg to run WCAU. WCAU was the CBS affiliate in Philadelphia that was owned by *The Bulletin* newspaper,"[24] said McMahon.

"Vanda and I had become good friends and when he got the idea for *Big Top* he said to me, 'I want you to be the ringmaster.' I said, 'That sounds wonderful, that sounds great.' You know, I'm six-foot-four and looked good in a red blazer," chuckled McMahon.

"So, I was all set to be the ringmaster when they sold the show to CBS. But CBS had a man under contract in New York named Jack Sterling. Jack Sterling was the number one, red-hot morning radio personality in New York City. He replaced Arthur Godfrey when Godfrey got so big that he couldn't do morning radio anymore. CBS owned him and they said, 'We'll buy the show, but we want Jack Sterling to be the ringmaster.'

"Shortly thereafter, Vanda took me to dinner and said, 'Ed, I'm awfully sorry. You can't be the ringmaster, or I can't sell the show.'

"I could understand CBS's point. They've got Jack Sterling

---

22. This and all remarks by Claude Kirchner in this *Super Circus* entry are from an exclusive telephone interview with Mr. Kirchner on April 11, 1991.

23. From an exclusive telephone interview with Bill Bailey's widow, Mrs. Helen Bailey, on November 23, 1990.

24. This and subsequent remarks by Ed McMahon in this *Super Circus* entry are from an exclusive telephone interview with Mr. McMahon on December 12, 1990.

under contract, they're buying a show out of Philadelphia from an affiliate to put on the network and they want their man in it. But at the time, it was a very crushing blow because it was a tough career move for me to lose. To have been the ringmaster on a network show in the early days of my career would have been quite spectacular for me. That's when Charlie Vanda asked, 'How would you like to be the chief clown?'

"Well, I had never thought about being a clown. I'd already worked in a suit and tie in this business from day one. After I thought about it, it intrigued me. So I became the chief clown, but still used my own name, Ed McMahon. I hired a fellow by the name of Chris Keegan as my right-hand-man clown. Every week I wrote a clown sketch and if I needed extra people, I would use Bill Bailey as an extra man," McMahon recalled.

In July 1952, after doing *Big Top* for a couple of years, Ed McMahon returned to active duty in the Marine Corps. "I spent nearly a year and a half in Korea as a Marine pilot. Now, while I was gone, Bill Bailey replaced me as the head clown. But when I returned in September 1953, I was reinstated as the chief clown and stayed with the show until it went off the air," McMahon said.

In addition to his having been the announcer on *The Tonight Show Starring Johnny Carson* for thirty years, Ed McMahon still hosts and acts as consultant on *Star Search*.

"*Star Search* is like having a baby. It's my baby. Everybody coming out of *Star Search* now is finding success in this business. And it thrills the hell out of me. We had a young lady, Angela Teek, who was the first actress to recreate the role of Kay in *Oh Kay* when it returned to Broadway in 1991.

"Sinbad is, of course, a big success story, as are Tiffany and Sawyer Brown. And Sam Harris, our first winner, just did an off-Broadway play for which he wrote forty-two original songs. Everybody seems to be finding work and that's wonderful," beamed McMahon.

On *Big Top,* which Mrs. Bailey referred to as the *Sealtest Big Top,* Bill Bailey had not yet become Boom-Boom, but was known as Wee Willie. Bailey got his job on *Magic Midway* from a recommendation by Doug Anderson, who was hired to play the masked magician Mr. Pocus on the program.

It wasn't a live program like Kirchner's *Super Circus* and Mrs. Bailey explained how Bill would travel to New York from his home near Camden, New Jersey to tape two shows on a Saturday.

For his final skit on *Magic Midway,* Bailey used his youngest son, William "Willie," whom he dressed in identical costume and makeup. In the skit, Boom-Boom, in a small clown car, drove into one end of a car wash. A few moments later, Willie exited from the other end in an even smaller car. The sign on the car wash read, "No Shrinking."

During the sixties, a pilot, *Clowning Around,* was shot with Bill Bailey as one of three clowns who got involved in a fire company. The unaired pilot was submitted to Walt Disney Studios which responded by saying, "That film is excellent, but television is not ready for it."

In 1990, Bill "Boom-Boom" Bailey passed away. What is ironic is that he died on August 7, the last day of National Clown Week, a program he helped to institute. It was signed into law by President Richard M. Nixon in 1971. For posterity, Helen Bailey donated Bill's "Boom-Boom" costume to the National Clown Museum in Delavan, Wisconsin, where it is on permanent display.

Old "C.K." or "Skinnybones," as his hand puppet Clownie would rib him, later hosted *Super Adventure Theater,* a Saturday morning program featuring science fiction films from the fifties, that was broadcast locally over WOR-TV, New York.

"That was just because we had so many sponsors on the evening show that it just spilled over and we did the same thing on Saturday," Kirchner said. Remembering the films, he laughed. "They were terrible."[25]

For years, Claude Kirchner did the voice-overs for Marx toy commercials like the ones for "The Great Garloo, by Marx!" Today, Kirchner, who likes to take it easy, does occasionally pop into the studio and give his vocal chords a workout. His voice, which is just a little bit thicker than it was during his Marx heyday, still has plenty of punch and can be heard on a number of national television commercials including Final Touch fabric softener.

The heartthrob of *Super Circus,* Mary Hartline, went on to her own program, *The Mary Hartline Show,* but it only lasted for a few months, airing on ABC from February 12 to June 15, 1951.

SUPERBOY *see:* THE ADVENTURES OF SUPERBOY

SUPERMAN *see:* ADVENTURES OF SUPERMAN

SURFSIDE 6

October 3, 1960–September 24, 1962.   ABC

Character:	Lieutenant Snedigar
Played by:	Donald Barry
Date(s):	October 3, 1960–1961

Replaced by:	Lieutenant Gene Plehan
Played by:	Richard Crane
Date(s):	1961–September 24, 1962

Three good-looking private investigators who live and work off their houseboat "with a beautiful girl in a yacht docked next door"—sounds like a great formula doesn't it? Producer Stephen J. Cannell apparently thought so too, which may explain why twenty-two years later many of the series' successful elements turned up in his action adventure series, *Riptide* (See Entry).

SurfSide 6 was by no means a copy of other Warner Bros. series, but it did borrow many elements from Warner's other successful detective series, including one of its stars. These "other series" were *77 Sunset Strip* (See Entry) and *Hawaiian*

25. From an exclusive telephone interview with Claude Kirchner on April 11, 1991.

Eye, both of which were still running when *SurfSide 6* set sail. *Bourbon Street Beat,* however, had been cancelled on September 26 of that year.

Warner Bros. moved Richard Long's character, Rex Randolph, from Bourbon Street to 77 Sunset Strip, and Van Williams' Kenny Madison became Ken Madison on *SurfSide 6.* His two partners, Dave Thorne and Sandy Winfield II, were played by Lee Patterson and Troy Donahue. The girl in the yacht, Daphne Dutton, was played by Diane McBain.

Rounding out the cast was the very well rounded Margarita Sierra as Cha Cha O'Brien, an entertainer in the Boom Boom Room in Miami Beach's lavish Fontainebleu Hotel.

This was the main cast of *SurfSide 6,* and it remained intact all the while the show was anchored on ABC's schedule. The only change in the cast was that of the supporting role of the police lieutenant. For the first year of the series, Donald Barry appeared as Lieutenant Snedigar. He left *SurfSide 6* in 1961 and from 1963 to 1964 appeared as Mr. Gallo on the NBC drama, *Mr. Novak.* The new police contact, Lieutenant Gene Plehan, was played by Richard Crane for the remainder of the series.

Blond heartthrob Troy Donahue, already a motion picture star, became the Hawaiian Village Hotel's new social director, Philip Barton, on *Hawaiian Eye* from October 2, 1962 to September 10, 1963. His co-star, Van Williams became television's *Green Hornet,* which aired on ABC from September 9, 1966 to July 14, 1967.

T

T. AND T.

January 1988–1990.   Syndicated

Character:	Amanda "Amy" Taler	
Played by:	Alex Amini	
Date(s):	1988–1989	

Replaced by:	Terri Taler
Played by:	Kristina Nicoll
Date(s):	1990

Character:	Detective Jones
Played by:	Ken James
Date(s):	1988

Replaced by:	Detective Dick Hargrove
Played by:	David Hemblen
Date(s):	1990

The "Ts" in the title of this syndicated detective drama which starred former *A-Team*er, Mr. T, actually stood for "Turner" and "Taler." T.S. Turner, was played by Mr. T, and Amy Taler by Alex Amini. This should not be confused with the short-lived ABC sitcom, *Mr. T and Tina* that starred Pat Morita as Taro Takahashi "Mr. T." and Susan Blanchard as "Tina" Kelly—not Tina Turner.

In this outing, Mr. T, dressed to the nines in dark pinstripe suits, played a former boxer and ex-con, T.S. Turner. He worked as private investigator for attorney Amanda Taler, who had Turner released from prison after proving his innocence.

Of course, no show featuring Mr. T would be complete unless we saw him bash some bad guys, which he did at least once in each episode, but not before returning to the gym where he worked out to change into his street-fighting leather outfit—in the grand superhero tradition. The first season, T.S. lived with his Aunt, Martha Robinson (Jackie Richardson), and his niece, Renee (Rachael Crawford).

T. and T. was less explosive and less violent during its second season, which featured several important changes. The most important was that, for the most part, Turner gave up dressing like a dandy, was involved in fewer brawls, and set up office at Decker's Gym, owned by his close friend, Danforth "Dick" Decker (David Nerman).

By the third season, T.S. Turner's police contact, Detective Jones (Ken James), had been replaced by Detective Dick Hargrove (David Hemblen).

It would seem that the reason the series was picked up for a third season by The Family Channel, was because it had by that time toned down much of the violence, but it wound up returning to those roots before going out of production in 1990.

TABITHA

September 10, 1977–January 14, 1978.   ABC

Character:	Tabitha Stephens
Played by:	Liberty Williams
Date(s):	April 24, 1976
	(First pilot. ABC)

Replaced by:	Tabitha Stephens
Played by:	Lisa Hartman
Date(s):	May 7, 1977
	(Second pilot. ABC)

Replaced by:	Tabitha Stephens
Played by:	Lisa Hartman
Date(s):	November 12, 1977–August 25, 1978
	(Tabitha spin-off series. ABC)

Character:	Adam Stephens
Played by:	Bruce Kimmel
Date(s):	April 24, 1976
	(First pilot. ABC)

Replaced by:	Adam Stephens
Played by:	David Ankrum
Date(s):	May 7, 1977
	(Second pilot. ABC)

Replaced by:	Adam Stephens
Played by:	David Ankrum
Date(s):	November 12, 1977–August 25, 1978
	(Tabitha spin-off series. ABC)

Character:	Roberta
Played by:	Barbara Cason
Date(s):	April 24, 1976.
	(First pilot. ABC)

Replaced by:	Marvin Decker
Played by:	Mel Stewart
Date(s):	May 7, 1977
	(Second pilot. ABC)

Replaced by:	Marvin Decker
Played by:	Mel Stewart
Date(s):	November 12, 1977–August 25, 1978
	(Tabitha spin-off series. ABC)

Samantha Stephens' daughter, Tabitha, returned to television in a pilot for her own spin-off series five years after *Bewitched* (See Entry) was canceled by ABC.

On *Bewitched*, Tabitha was born on January 13, 1966, which would make her a little over ten years old. But through the magic of television, and perhaps the twitch of a nose or two, Tabitha, played by Liberty Williams, appeared as a twenty-four-year-old editorial assistant at San Francisco's *Trend* Magazine. Her younger brother, Adam, played by Bruce Kimmel, also worked at the publication.

The pilot didn't sell and the show was completely revamped and recast for the second pilot. Tabitha was now played by Lisa Hartman and her brother by David Ankrum.

In the second pilot the setting moved from the San Francisco magazine to the newsroom of California television station KXLA, where Adam worked with his sister, Tabitha, who was a production assistant.

The Stephens' original boss at *Trend* Magazine was the editor, Roberta (Barbara Cason). When the locale shifted to KXLA-TV in the second pilot and subsequent series, the new authority figure was the producer of "The Paul Thurston Show," Marvin Decker, played by Mel Stewart. Stewart had played George Jefferson's brother, Henry, on the early episodes of *All in the Family*.

TARZAN

September 8, 1966–September 10, 1969.   NBC-CBS
September 28, 1991–September 12, 1992   Syndicated

Character:	Tarzan
Played by:	Ron Ely
Date(s):	September 8, 1966–September 10, 1969

Replaced by:	Tarzan
Played by:	Joe Lara
Date(s):	April 15, 1989

Character:	Jane Parker
Played by:	Joanna Barnes
Date(s):	February 23, 1968

Replaced by:	Jane Porter
Played by:	Kim Crosby
Date(s):	April 15, 1989

"AAAAEEYAA—EEYAA—EEOOO!!!" Anyone hearing that unmistakable blood-curdling jungle yell knows that Tarzan cannot be far away. Yet a television version of the classic character created by Edgar Rice Burroughs was a good idea that was a long time in coming. There were, however, no shortage of Tarzans in the movies as explained by Danton Burroughs, the director of Edgar Rice Burroughs, Inc. and the grandson of Tarzan's creator: "There have been forty-seven films starring eighteen different Tarzans, fifty-seven television episodes and thirty-six animated TV shows. Gordon Griffith was the screen's first Tarzan. He played the jungle lord as a boy in the 1918 silent picture, TARZAN OF THE APES, which starred Elmo Lincoln in the title role. If you want to get really technical, the baby used in that movie was really the first Tarzan, but no one's been able to find the name of the infant used."[1]

As it turns out, Ron Ely, who played Tarzan in all fifty-seven episodes of this popular adventure, holds the distinction of being the first actor to play the lord of the jungle on a weekly series.

It has been incorrectly stated in other sources that the first attempt to bring the ape-man to television was in 1959 when a fifty-eight-minute color pilot, *Tarzan the Ape Man,* was shot with Dennis "Denny" Miller, a former basketball player from UCLA, in the title role. These sources went on to say that when the pilot didn't sell to television, it was released theatrically after twenty-two minutes of additional footage was taken from the black-and-white TARZAN films and tinted to match.

Denny Miller cleared up the confusion, stating emphatically that "It was a feature from the start."[2] Miller later went on to replace Robert Horton as the new trail scout on *Wagon Train* (See Entry).

"MGM realized that they had a remake clause for the very first Weissmuller film, TARZAN THE APE MAN. Tarzan was making money—not a lot of money—but enough for MGM to take advantage of the clause and produce TARZAN THE APE MAN with Dennis "Denny" Miller as Tarzan and Joanna Barnes as Jane Parker. In fact, that's exactly how Bo and John Derek were able to produce their 1981 remake,"[3] explained Gabe Essoe, the author of *Tarzan of the Movies.*

The 1981 remake of TARZAN THE APE MAN was produced by Bo Derek and directed and photographed by her husband, John. It starred Miles O'Keefe as the lord of the jungle, opposite Bo Derek as Jane.

The storylines of both remakes are basically the same as that of the 1932 Johnny Weissmuller film which introduces the characters of Tarzan, Jane and Tarzan's pet chimpanzee, Cheetah. It then follows their battle against greedy ivory hunters who are looking for the location of the secret graveyard of the elephants and one million pounds of ivory.

---

1. From an exclusive telephone interview with Danton Burroughs on March 21, 1991 and a correspondence with the author dated April 19, 1991.
2. From an exclusive telephone interview with Denny Miller on April 3, 1991.
3. This and following quotations from Gabe Essoe in this *Tarzan* entry are from an exclusive telephone interview with Mr. Essoe on April 3, 1991.

"It seems to me that they were going to do a pilot with Lex Barker, who played Tarzan from 1949 to 1953. But Lex wanted out of his loincloth because he had a larger career in mind," said Gabe Essoe.

Gordon Scott replaced Lex Barker and was put under contract by Sol Lesser, who found him working as a lifeguard in Las Vegas. Gordon Scott's first Tarzan film was TARZAN'S HIDDEN JUNGLE, 1955. This was followed by TARZAN AND THE LOST SAFARI, 1957; TARZAN'S FIGHT FOR LIFE, 1958; and TARZAN'S GREATEST ADVENTURE, 1959.

The first real attempt to bring Tarzan to television began with the filming of two half-hour pilot episodes starring Gordon Scott and Eve Brent. Scott had already played Tarzan in four motion pictures and Eve Brent had played Jane in the 1958 entry, TARZAN'S FIGHT FOR LIFE, Scott's third jungle outing.

When no sponsor could be found, the episodes were released theatrically, but not before being edited into one film, TARZAN AND THE TRAPPERS, with additional footage added to bring the time up to seventy-four minutes. The black-and-white feature, which pits the ape-man against trappers who are hoping to take treasures from a lost jungle city, eventually found its way to television, airing for the first time on May 5, 1966.

"The pilots were shot directly after TARZAN FIGHTS FOR LIFE was done. They utilized the same locations and cast. The biggest difference was that the pilot was shot in black-and-white while the feature was made in color," said Essoe. He further speculated that the pilot was shot as a half-hour black-and-white series because those were the requirements of the syndication market at that time, even though networks were airing hour-long programs like *Bonanza* and *Maverick*.

"The pilots didn't sell because they were bad—it's that simple. They didn't have enough quality to merit their being bought by one of the syndicators. It is a weak story and lacks production value. If they had a stronger story, they might have sold it. Instead, it came across as kiddie fare and in those days the programmers were looking for something that could compete with the adult Westerns like *Gunsmoke* and *Bonanza*, but it couldn't."

"Sol Lesser was not what you'd call a good movie maker. I don't know if Sol would have been able to recognize a good story if he tripped over one. He was a guy who was able to make pictures cheaply and bring them in under budget. His films always made money because he didn't spend anything on them. In retrospect a lot of his films are somewhat embarrassing," said Essoe.

So, it wasn't until Ron Ely donned his skimpy $30 loincloth, fashioned out of antelope skin in 1966 that the legendary superhero, created in 1912 by Edgar Rice Burroughs, began making regular appearances on network television.

Had it not been for an aggressive chimpanzee, the six-foot-four-inch Ron Ely might never have become Tarzan. It had already been released that Mike Henry, who had played the

Lord of the Jungle in the 1966 feature film, TARZAN AND THE VALLEY OF GOLD, and two other Tarzan pictures released in 1967 and 1968, would be television's first Tarzan. The turn of events came when the chimpanzee playing Cheetah was supposed to kiss Tarzan, but bit Mike Henry on the chin instead. The wound resulted in eighteen stitches, Mike Henry's return to the United States, and two separate lawsuits totaling $875,000.

Even though Henry had thrown in his loincloth two days before filming for the television series was scheduled to start, there was still no need for producer Sy Weintraub to institute a new talent search. That had been done once before and although Mike Henry had won the role, there were several other actors who stood out from the more than 300 others who auditioned for the part. Five were given screen tests and Ron Ely emerged the winner.

By no means a newcomer to the business, Ron Ely landed his first series role in 1961, replacing Keith Larsen on *The Aquanauts* (See Entry). Even more interesting was that Ely had already been cast to play a Tarzan impostor in one of the television episodes.

There was life for Ely after *Tarzan* and he appeared in more then twenty other series including *The Courtship of Eddie's Father*, *The New Adventures of Wonder Woman* and five episodes of *Fantasy Island*. His next regular series role was in an updated version of *Sea Hunt* (See Entry).

Tarzan's young ward, Jai, an orphan, who served as Ely's "Boy," was played by Manuel Padilla, Jr. There was, however, no Jane. In fact, the only regular member of the *Tarzan* cast was Vickie, the chimpanzee who played Cheetah.

This live-action series was followed by several Saturday morning animated adaptations of the character. These included *Tarzan: Lord of the Jungle,* which aired on CBS from September 11, 1976 to September 2, 1978, and *The Tarzan/Lone Ranger/Zorro Adventure Hour,* which aired on CBS from September 12, 1981 to September 11, 1982. In both versions, the voice of Tarzan was provided by Robert Ridgely.

For whatever reason, it took ten years before the jungle legend returned to the small screen. The February 1989 edition of *Ross Reports Television* reported that "Joe Lara, selected as the 18th Tarzan in film and television history, has started work in Hawaii on *Tarzan in Manhattan*." The Ron Ely *Tarzan* series was filmed in Brazil and later in Mexico.

"There's no doubt about it, Lara represented a good image for *Tarzan*. When they went through the selection process, the number of actors interviewed went into the hundreds. They finally selected Joe Lara because all the women at American First Run thought he was 'a killer.'

"As a former model, Lara had not acted before, so he went through some acting classes and got shaped up for the part of Tarzan. It was a good film with a very good cast that included Tony Curtis,"[4] said Burroughs.

Tarzan in Manhattan is in many respects a takeoff of the 1942 Tarzan adventure, TARZAN'S NEW YORK ADVENTURE, which starred the quintessential Tarzan and Jane,

---

4. This and subsequent remarks by Danton Burroughs in this *Tarzan* entry are from an exclusive telephone interview with Mr. Burroughs on March 21, 1991 and a correspondence with the author dated April 19, 1991.

Johnny Weissmuller and Maureen O'Sullivan. It wasn't the lure of Broadway, but the kidnapping of Boy (Johnny Sheffield) that brought the Lord of the Jungle to the Big Apple.

The 1989 telefilm smells more of pilot than it does of the jungle, where only a few opening scenes take place. Instead of Boy, who does not appear at all in this made-for-television movie, Tarzan's faithful chimpanzee, Cheetah, is the one who is captured and taken to New York. He is trapped by employees of the philanthropic Brightmore Foundation for some very unethical and unsavory primate research which involves the feeding of ground-up brains of one chimpanzee to another—all in the name of science, of course.

Tarzan boards a plane at the Kaduna Air Field in Africa and makes one connection (which we do not see) in Atlanta. He arrives in New York aboard Eastern Airlines flight 100, goes through customs, is arrested and thrown in a cell on Riker's Island. Inside the cell, he gets out of his street clothes, pulls the bars off the window and makes a thirty- to fifty-foot dive into the East River while being shot at by prison guards.

In the city, wearing just a loincloth, he hails a cab by letting out his famous jungle yell. This, by the way, is the very same recording used in both the Ron Ely series and the Johnny Weissmuller films. Incidentally, if you were wondering why no one person, not even the multi-talented Carol Burnett, can quite duplicate the range of the yell, it is not for lack of talent, but because it was never done by just one person.

Buster Crabbe, who was the screen's eighth Tarzan, and who is better known to Saturday matinee-goers as Flash Gordon and Buck Rogers, explained that "the yell" used by Weissmuller, himself and most of the other Tarzans was actually created in a recording studio by his father-in-law, a sound engineer.

Danton Burroughs elaborated: "MGM spared no expense on the Tarzan Yell. The unearthly howl, or victory cry of the bull ape, was made up of five sound tracks: 1. The cry of a mother camel robbed of her young; 2. The sound of a hyena howl run backward with volume lowered; 3. Soprano note sung by Lorraine Bridges recorded at reduced speed to give a flutter; 4. The growl of a dog recorded faintly; 5. The sound track of Weissmuller yelling amplified." Burroughs went on to point out that Johnny Weissmuller mastered the yell and was able to emit a perfect imitation.

Getting back to the telefilm, Tarzan is picked up and befriended by an attractive cabby, "Jane" Porter (Kim Crosby).

There are some funny moments in the film. One of the most memorable lines is spoken by Tarzan when a group of local street hoods, lead by Juan Lipshitz (Jimmy Medina Taggart), break into Jane's apartment. "Where's the dude?" asks a smug Juan, and he is answered by an equally smug Tarzan, "The Dude is here." Tarzan then proceeds to beat up the hoods and sends them running.

Luckily Jane's father, Archimedes "Archie" Porter (Tony Curtis), just happens to be a private detective, so he can help Tarzan locate his primary primate, Cheetah.

Another of the better moments is the scene in which Tarzan is stopped by two of New York's finest.

COP: What's your name, buddy?

TARZAN: My name's Tarzan . . . of the Apes. Formerly John Clayton, III, son of Lord and Lady Greystoke.

COP: Yeah, and I'm Han Solo and this is my sidekick Chewbacca.

In an unsatisfying conclusion, following a fairly exciting chase scene on the grounds of the Brightmore estate, Brightmore (Jan-Michael Vincent) really doesn't get thrashed enough by Tarzan for killing chimpanzees. Worse yet, Tarzan who is about to depart for Africa with Cheetah, decides at the last moment to remain in the city with Jane.

American First Run Studios went to Mexico in 1991 to film a new Tarzan series for syndication, starring Wolf Larson as television's third Tarzan. "I did like Joe Lara's portrayal of Tarzan. He was another good representation of Tarzan. However, we have selected a new Tarzan, Wolf Larson. He is going to star in the new Tarzan series that will begin shooting the first twenty-five episodes this spring [1991]—so we'll be looking at Tarzan, number nineteen," explained Burroughs.

This most recent Tarzan premiered in the New York market on WWOR-TV on Saturday, September 28, 1991. In addition to Wolf Larson as Tarzan, the new cast included Lydie Denier as Jane, a research scientist, and Sean Roberge as Roger Taft, a teenager serving in the "Boy" role. The storyline of this debut episode "Tarzan and the Unwelcome Guest," explained that Jane was in the jungle working for the Wildlife Institute, the only environmental charity supported by Roger's wealthy father.

It was Jane who had persuaded Mr. Taft (Chuck Shamata) to fund her program, which was designed to save endangered species, including plants as well as animals.

Mr. Taft, who owns twenty-one hotels in twelve different countries, arrives in the jungle to tell Jane he's cutting her funding and taking his son back to civilization. When Taft neglects to take his Digitalis, a heart medicine, Tarzan concocts an elixir from the local fauna and saves the city slicker's life. This puts everything into better perspective for the profit-oriented Taft and he softens his position and extends the research grant for an additional six months, as well as allowing his son to stay on with Jane and Tarzan.

The producers of the new Tarzan offered viewers a nostalgic treat in the November 2, 1991 episode, "Tarzan the Hunted," by casting Ron Ely as Gordon Shaw, a ruthless trophy hunter who upon his arrival in the jungle exclaimed, "There should be something worth killing here." That something, as it turned out, was the lord of the jungle himself—Tarzan.

In summing up, Danton Burroughs managed to put Tarzan in the proper perspective. "My grandfather wrote Tarzan of the Apes in 1911. The story first appeared in the October issue of All-Story Magazine. It was a huge success that generated twenty-five more stories in the Tarzan series. Every new generation discovers Tarzan on film and in newspapers, books, magazines, merchandising, etc. Tarzan's visual image has changed innumerable times and yet there's still that one Tarzan that I follow faithfully in my grandfather's books who shows no sign of age and will live on forever."

TATTINGER'S

October 26, 1988–April 26, 1989.   NBC

Character: Winnifred Tattinger
Played by: Chay Lentin
Date(s):   October 26, 1988–January 11, 1989

Replaced by: Winnifred Tattinger
Played by: Jessica Prunell
Date(s):   April 20, 1989–April 26, 1989

Tattinger's was one of New York's great bistros, catering to the more refined tastes of its elegant patrons with linen tablecloths and dinner music supplied by a piano player. But running it was too much pressure for its owner, Nick Tattinger (Stephen Collins), and he sold the restaurant and flew off to Paris after being shot by a drug dealer.

In the premiere episode, Nick has returned to New York to escort his daughter, Nina (Patrice Colihan), to her debutante's ball and to visit with Winnifred (Chay Lentin), the youngest of his two teenage daughters.

Whether it was the lure of the restaurant business or the fact that he couldn't stand to see it run into the ground, Nick buys back the restaurant from its incompetent owner—his ex-wife, Hillary (Blythe Danner).

Nick had barely gotten things going when NBC closed the doors to Tattinger's for renovations after just nine episodes.

The hour-long dramatic comedy returned two months later with a new name, a new look, a new length (thirty minutes) and a new daughter, as Jessica Prunell replaced Chay Lentin as Winnifred.

The return episode began with the regular opening of Tattinger's with the '40s New York-style theme which suddenly slowed down as if there was something wrong with the recorder. Then the still image burns away, like the map at the opening of Bonanza, to reveal a new credit, Nick & Hillary, and a new upbeat theme song.

Much like the later restaurant series, Love & War (See Entry), Nick & Hillary began with a voice-over to set up the show. This one was handled by Tattinger's former maitre d', Sid Wilbur (Jerry Stiller), who is now working as its bartender.

SID: Tattinger's, one of New York's premiere restaurants. That is, before business went bust. Critics said our patrons are elegant, elite, stodgy. But our atmosphere was lush, romantic, boring. For as head waiter, I preferred stodgy and boring. To think it all began with a phone call.

The phone call Sid was referring to was from Nick, who phoned to tell Hillary that their accountant, Arnold Wepner, had run away to Brazil with all of their money—and that he was going after him.

With Nick gone, Hillary took it upon herself to revamp the losing restaurant, transforming it into a hot spot for the chic crowd with a dance floor, nouvelle cuisine and an aloof hostess, Marti (Anna Levine), and Spin, a slightly off-center maitre d'

played by Chris Elliott, the slightly off-center son of Bob and Ray's Bob Elliott.

These are the first people Nick meets upon his return from Rio de Janeiro, and he does a double-take when he hears that their names are Spin and Marti. Spin then mistakes Nick for a customer.

SPIN: Rappaport, party of six. Right this way.

NICK: I'm not Rappaport.

This is a particularly prophetic line. A similar series, Jack's Place, debuted on May 26, 1992, and starred Hal Linden who had himself starred in the 1985 Broadway play, I'm Not Rappaport.

Perhaps the cleverest line in the opener was an allusion in the line delivered by Stephen Collins during an argument with Hillary.

NICK: All of a sudden, bailing out of a fiery Grumman Goose over Guatemala seems like a fond memory.

And indeed it was a fond memory, as Stephen Collins flew a Grumman Goose in his first network series, Tales of the Gold Monkey, which aired on ABC from September 22, 1982 to July 6, 1983. He also flew aboard the refitted Starship Enterprise as Wil Decker in STAR TREK: THE MOTION PICTURE, the first of seven feature films, released in 1979.

TAXI

September 12, 1978–July 27, 1983.   ABC-NBC

Character: John Burns
Played by: Randall Carver
Date(s):   September 12, 1978–December 5, 1978

Replaced by: "Reverend" James "Jim" Caldwell Ignatowski
Played by: Christopher Lloyd
Date(s):   September 25, 1979–July 13, 1983

Character: Mr. MacKenzie
Played by: Stephen Elliott
Date(s):   February 12, 1981

Replaced by: Ben Ratledge
Played by: Allen Goorwitz (a.k.a. Allen Garfield)
Date(s):   November 4, 1982

Way back in the 1932 crime film, TAXI!, James Cagney starred as Matt Nolan, a tough independent hack going up against the union. In 1953, Dan Dailey starred as Ed Nielson, a New York cabbie who picks up a pregnant Irish immigrant and spends nearly the entire day driving her around searching for her husband. Twenty-three years later, Robert De Niro starred as

Travis Bickle, a Vietnam vet who turns vigilante to free a young prostitute (Jodie Foster) from the clutches of her pimp in TAXI DRIVER.

There were also the 1929 romantic comedy, TAXI FOR TWO; the 1928 Chester Conklin comedy, TAXI 13; and the 1944 musical, TAXI TO HEAVEN. And the only thing any of these motion pictures has in common with the successful television series is that the word "Taxi" appears in their titles.

Taxi is an original and was created by James Brooks, Stan Daniels, David Davis and Ed. Weinberger, all of whom were writers and producers of the highly successful sitcom, *The Mary Tyler Moore Show.*

The premise is simple elegance. In New York's Sunshine Cab Company a group of cabbies, with nothing in common except their work, are brought together night after night to drive their cabs and wind up sharing each other's lives.

The central figure is Alex Reiger, a level-headed and compassionate middle-aged man who, though no choice of his own, somehow becomes the confidant and mentor of all of the other cabbies, who range from a would-be boxer to a never-will-be actor. Alex is played to perfection by Judd Hirsch, who had starred as Sergeant Dominick Delvecchio on the surprisingly short-lived detective drama, *Delvecchio,* which aired on CBS from September 9, 1976 to July 17, 1977. The producers who wanted Hirsch and ultimately wooed him into accepting the role, were also considering Tony Curtis.

The five-foot-tall dispatcher, Louie De Palma, was played by one of Hollywood's biggest talents, Danny DeVito. Louie was so rotten that he made the Grinch seem like Mother Theresa.

The first owner of the Sunshine Cab Company was Mr. MacKenzie, who appeared in "The Boss' Wife," in which Louie is invited to dinner by Mrs. MacKenzie (Eileen Brennan) in order to make her husband jealous. Allen Goorwitz appeared in "Crime and Punishment" as Ben Ratledge, the second owner of the struggling cab company.

One of the original cab drivers was John Burns, a sensible but introverted young man. To him, driving a cab in Manhattan was his French Foreign Legion. And it helped him forget his troubles, including a broken relationship. Randall Carver played John Burns and appeared in most of the first-season episodes. In one of those unfortunate situations for an actor (as with Jennifer Holmes on *Newhart* [See Entry]) Carver's character was dropped because the producers felt it wasn't working.

"Curiously, he wasn't 'written out' of the show: no mention is made in any episode about why John is no longer around. He simply disappears after the episode 'Memories of Cab 804, Part II.' "

" 'To my understanding, the characters of John Burns and Tony Banta [Tony Danza] were too similar,' says Randall Carver. 'Both Tony and I were playing innocent and naive characters, so you had two actors there playing the same notes. Some of the lines were almost interchangeable. . . . By the sixth or seventh episode, I was already feeling pretty insecure about the longevity of my character. I could see the writing on the wall.' "[5]

The last episode in which Carver appeared as John Burns was "Memories of Cab 804, Part II." In that episode Alex delivers a baby in the back seat of the cab.

Since Carver's character was eliminated because it wasn't working and perhaps too similar to Tony Banta's, there was not a direct replacement for his character. There was, however, another cabbie added to the cast and it came about purely by accident.

In the eighth episode of *Taxi,* "Paper Marriage," Christopher Lloyd appeared in a guest shot as Reverend Jim Ignatowski, a pastor ordained in 1968 by the Church of the Peaceful. Actually, his name was James Caldwell, but he changed it to Ignatowski because he thought it was "Star-Child" spelled backwards.

Reverend Jim was brought in to officiate at a wedding ceremony between Andy Kaufman's wacky Latka Gravas character and a prostitute who agreed to marry the illegal alien to prevent him from being deported.

" 'He wasn't intended to be a permanent character,' recalled writer Glen Charles. 'But,' adds executive producer Ed. Weinberger, 'from the first minute Christopher Lloyd hit the stage, he was destined to stay. That very night, we all agreed we had to get him on the show.' "[6]

The reason that Jim had to be added to the cast was the way Christopher Lloyd created and portrayed him. With the other actors, *Taxi*'s director, Jim Burrows, said, "We had guys reading for us, doing drunks, evangelical preachers. . . ."[7] But the character didn't have any past. Christopher Lloyd gave him that past, depicting him as a burned-out survivor of the '60s who admitted taking just one too many "recreational" drugs. His favorite rock group is The Kinks, his favorite food is Spaghetti O's, and his favorite television program, *The Bob Newhart Show.*

What began as a one-shot appearance grew to become one of the show's most popular characters and earned Christopher Lloyd two Emmy awards. This recognition was given to him for Outstanding Supporting Actor in a Comedy Series for both the 1981/1982 and the 1982/1983 television seasons.

During a break in the production of *Taxi* Christopher Lloyd co-starred as the rotten Butch Cavendish in the 1981 feature, THE LEGEND OF THE LONE RANGER. And if it were not for his distinctive hoarse voice, he would have been completely unrecognizable as the Klingon Kruge in the 1984 science fiction film, STAR TREK III: THE SEARCH FOR SPOCK. In fact when Captain Kirk (William Shatner) says, "Wait. Give me a chance to talk," you almost expect Kruge to answer "Okey-dokey."

One of the oddities about Jim Ignatowski's character on *Taxi* was that underneath it all there was a brilliant man and a philosopher who sometimes managed to make it to the surface.

At the end of "Zen and the Art of Cab Driving," which aired on March 19, 1981, Jim philosophized about the television medium: "What's great about television is that when an important event is happening, no matter what time of day, or where in the world it is happening . . . you can always change the channel."

5. Sorensen, Jeff. *The Taxi Book.* St. Martin's Press, New York, 1987, pp. 39–40.
6. Waldron, Vince. *Classic Sitcoms. A Celebration of the Best of Prime-Time Comedy.* MacMillan Publishing Company, New York, 1987, p. 439.
7. Pollock, Bruce. "The Minute that Makes a Career," *TV Guide,* July 25, 1981, p. 14.

THE TED KNIGHT SHOW *see:* TOO CLOSE FOR COMFORT

THE TEMPERATURE'S RISING

September 12, 1972–August 30, 1974.   ABC

Character: Dr. Vincent Campanelli
Played by: James Whitmore
Date(s):   September 12, 1972–September 4, 1973

Replaced by: Dr. Paul Mercy
Played by: Paul Lynde
Date(s):   September 25, 1973–January 8, 1974
                       July 28, 1974–August 30, 1974

Character: Dr. Jerry Noland
Played by: Cleavon Little
Date(s):   September 12, 1972–September 4, 1973
Date(s):   September 25, 1973–January 8, 1974
                       July 28, 1974–August 30, 1974

Character: Nurse Annie Carlisle
Played by: Joan Van Ark
Date(s):   September 12, 1972–September 4, 1973

Replaced by: Martha Mercy
Played by: Sudie Bond
Date(s):   September 25, 1973–January 8, 1974

Replaced by: Edwina Mofitt
Played by: Alice Ghostley
Date(s):   July 28, 1974–August 30, 1974

Character: Nurse Mildred MacInerney
Played by: Reva Rose
Date(s):   September 12, 1972–September 4, 1973

Replaced by: Miss Tillis
Played by: Barbara Cason
Date(s):   September 25, 1973–August 30, 1974

Replaced by: Nurse Ellen Turner
Played by: Nancy Fox
Date(s):   September 12, 1972–September 4, 1973
                       July 28, 1974–August 30, 1974

Replaced by: Nurse Amanda Kelly
Played by: Barbara Rucker
Date(s):   September 25, 1973–unknown

Replaced by: Nurse Amanda Kelly
Played by: Sharleen Cotright
Date(s):   unknown–August 30, 1974

Character: Miss Llewellen
Played by: Olive Dunbar
Date(s):   September 12, 1972–September 4, 1973

Replaced by: Nurse Reed
Played by: Mary Batten
Date(s):   September 25, 1973–August 30, 1974

Character: Dr. David Amherst
Played by: David Bailey
Date(s):   September 12, 1972–September 4, 1973

Replaced by: Dr. Lloyd Axton
Played by: Jeff Morrow
Date(s):   September 25, 1973–August 30, 1974

Character: Nurse ''Windy'' Winchester
Played by: Jennifer Darling
Date(s):   September 25, 1973–August 30, 1974

Character: Dr. Charles Cleveland Claver
Played by: John Dehner
Date(s):   September 25, 1973–August 30, 1974

This innocuous slice of life in a big city hospital went through more new blood than a real hospital. In the debut episode, a game of bingo is being broadcast in code over the hospital's public-address system. During the next two years the series went through three different casts and never scored ''bingo'' in the ratings.

The series was set in Washington D.C.'s Capitol General Hospital with Doctor Vincent Campanelli as the chief of staff. The network didn't skimp on talent; the role was played by veteran Hollywood character actor, James Whitmore, though the focal point of the series was Doctor Jerry Noland. Doctor Noland, a real cutup with an affinity for gambling, was played by the very likeable Cleavon Little.

Little broke into situation comedy and the Bunkers' house at the same time. Along with Demond Wilson, Cleavon Little was one of the two cat burglars who put Archie's recorded dog to sleep in the October 9, 1971 episode of *All in the Family,* ''Edith Writes a Song.'' By far his most famous role to date is not on television but as Bart, the ever resourceful sheriff in the 1974 Mel Brooks Western comedy, BLAZING SADDLES.

For the second season, the producers cleaned house and replaced the entire hospital staff except Cleavon Little.

The title of the series was also changed at that time to *The New Temperature's Rising Show.*

Taking the place of James Whitmore as the hospital's administrator was comedian Paul Lynde. Lynde, as Doctor Paul Mercy, was a non-practicing doctor looking after his mother's investment in what has now become a private hospital.

This format didn't catch on either, so a third version was tried without Doctor Mercy's meddlesome mother (Sudie Bond) and with a number of other cast changes.

The series was finally put out of its misery on August 30, 1974.

TERRY AND THE PIRATES

1952–1953.   Syndicated

Character:	Burma
Played by:	Mari Blanchard
Date(s):	November 1952 (pilot)

Replaced by:	Burma
Played by:	Gloria Saunders
Date(s):	1952–1953

Character:	Hot Shot Charlie
Played by:	Jack Kruschen
Date(s):	November 1952

Replaced by:	Hot Shot Charlie
Played by:	Walter Tracy
Date(s):	1952–1953

Terry Lee, Burma, Hot Shot Charlie, Chopstick Joe and the evil Dragon Lady were all characters from a popular comic strip created by Milton Caniff in 1934. In 1952 they were brought to television, not in an animated cartoon, but in a syndicated live-action adventure series.

The hero of the strip and the television series was Terry Lee (John Baer), a colonel in the United States Air Force who ventures to the Far East in search of an abandoned gold mine willed to him by his grandfather.

As luck would have it, before Terry is able to find the gold mine, he is captured by Lai Choi San (Gloria Saunders), better known as the "Dragon Lady," who in the comics was an opium dealer. Terry manages to escape her deadly clutches and continues his search for the lost mine, while at the same time doing everything he can to thwart The Dragon Lady.

In the first episode, which was actually the pilot for the series, Hot Shot Charlie was played by Jack Kruschen, who later played Tully in the short-lived adventure series, *Hong Kong,* which aired on ABC from September 28, 1960 to September 20, 1961. Kruschen, who also played Sam Markowitz on the CBS situation comedy, *Busting Loose* (January 17, 1977–November 16, 1977), may be more familiar to today's television audiences from his recurring role as "Papa" Papadopolis in the popular ABC situation comedy, *Webster,* which aired from September 16, 1983 to September 11, 1987. Walter Tracy took over the role of Hot Shot Charlie when the series went into production because Kruschen was busy with other commitments.

In the twenty-six episodes of *Terry and the Pirates* that were filmed, both Mari Blanchard and Gloria Saunders played the role of Terry's sexy girlfriend, Burma, but Mari Blanchard only played Burma in the first episode. After the pilot was shot, Mari was put under contract by Universal and couldn't do the series. Yet neither of these attractive actresses could hold a candle next to their comic strip counterpart. But, then again, not everyone can be a Jessica Rabbit.

THAT GIRL

September 8, 1966–September 10, 1971.   ABC

Character:	Dr. Leon Bessemer
Played by:	Dabney Coleman
Date(s):	September 8, 1966–June 1, 1967

Replaced by:	Jerry Bauman
Played by:	Bernie Kopell
Date(s):	unknown–September 10, 1971

Character:	Judy Bessemer
Played by:	Bonnie Scott
Date(s):	1966–1967

Replaced by:	Margie Bauman
Played by:	Arlene Golonka
Date(s):	1967–October 3, 1968

Replaced by:	Ruth Bauman
Played by:	Carolyn Daniels
Date(s):	January 23, 1969

Replaced by:	Ruth Bauman
Played by:	Alice Borden
Date(s):	November 6, 1969–September 10, 1971

That girl was, of course, Marlo Thomas, as aspiring actress Ann Marie. Her guy was Donald Hollinger (Ted Bessell), a reporter for *Newsview* magazine. That guy, Dr. Leon Bessemer, and his wife Judy, were Ann's neighbors when the series began. Judy was played by Bonnie Scott. Her husband, Dr. Bessemer, was played by Dabney Coleman, who later starred as Bill Bittinger in the situation comedy, *Buffalo Bill,* which aired on NBC from May 31, 1983 to April 5, 1984.

That other guy, Jeremiah "Jerry" Bauman, was one of Donald's co-workers who later became Ann's neighbor after his marriage to Margie.

Jerry was played by Bernie Kopell, a young actor who had already appeared on episodes of *McHale's Navy, The Beverly Hillbillies* and *My Favorite Martian.* But he really came to the attention of the television viewing public as Conrad Siegfried, the vice president of public relations and terror for KAOS, on *Get Smart!* His later success came as Doctor Adam Bricker on *The Love Boat.*

The other girl on *That Girl* was Jerry's wife, the lovely Mrs. Margie Bauman, who was played by Arlene Golonka in three episodes of the series: "Rain, Snow and Ice" (1967), "Old Man's Darling" (April 25, 1968), and "The Hijack and the Mighty" which aired on October 3, 1968.

The attractive blonde actress, who has guested on more than one hundred series, is best known for her continuing role as Millie Swanson, Ken Berry's romantic interest on *The Andy Griffith Show* (See Entry) spinoff, *Mayberry R.F.D..* She later took over the role as the second Stella Sweetzer on the NBC situation comedy, *Joe & Valerie* (See Entry).

What should have been even more disturbing to Ann Marie than losing one of the diamond earrings given to her by her boyfriend, Donald, on the January 23, 1969 episode, was the fact that Jerry's wife had not only changed her name, but turned into two completely different women.

The identity crisis began when Jerry's wife's first name changed from Margie to Ruth. Jerry still looked the same because he was still being played by Bernie Kopell. His new wife, Ruth, on the other hand, looked totally different because she was now being played by Carolyn Daniels. One of Ms. Daniels' only other television credits was as Stella Maguire in the third adaptation of Elmer Harris' 1940 play, *Johnny Belinda.* The two-hour special aired on ABC on October 22, 1967.

To further confuse the already befuddled Ann Marie, a third actress, Alice Borden, turned up as Jerry's wife, Ruth, on the November 6, 1969 episode of *That Girl.* The episode is about the time that Don had to write a television comedy script about the day that he and Ann were snowbound in an airport with her parents.

No explanation was ever given as to why the actresses playing Margie/Ruth were replaced, but one can easily imagine Ann's reaction upon meeting Jerry's third wife: ''Ohhhh Dawwwwnald!''

THAT'S MY MAMA

September 4, 1974–December 24, 1975.   ABC

Character:	Tracy Curtis Taylor
Played by:	Lynne Moody
Date(s):	September 4, 1974–April 16, 1975
Replaced by:	Tracy Curtis Taylor
Played by:	Joan Pringle
Date(s):	September 10, 1975–December 24, 1975
Character:	Earl Chambers
Played by:	Ed Bernard
Date(s):	September 4, 1974–September 11, 1974
Replaced by:	Earl Chambers
Played by:	Theodore ''Theo'' Wilson
Date(s):	September 18, 1974–December 24, 1975

On *The Andy Griffith Show,* Floyd Lawson (Howard McNear) proved to the residents of Mayberry, North Carolina that a little light chit-chat and a friendly game or two of checkers could prove to be even more important than one's tonsorial skills. The barber's shop was also a good setting for character interaction on a weekly sitcom. Perhaps that is where the show's producers, Alan Blye and Chris Bearde, got the notion that it would work in Washington, D.C., the location of Oscar's Barber Shop.

The shop was no longer run by Oscar, who had passed on, but by his twenty-five-year-old son, Clifton Curtis, played by Clifton Davis. Davis began his televison career with Karen Valentine in blackout sketches on ABC's *Love American Style.* He reached the height of his popularity as Reverend Reuben

Gregory, the young handsome minister of a Philadelphia church, opposite Sherman Hemsley as Deacon Ernest Frye in the spirited NBC sitcom, *Amen,* which premiered on September 27, 1986.

Clifton's mama, as in ''That's my. . .,'' was played by Theresa Merrit who, according to Donald Bogle, author of *Blacks in American Films and Television,* ''came across nonetheless as the all-sacrificing, large, dowdy, warmhearted mammy.''

While Curtis led a bachelor's life, his married sister, Tracy, served as a more traditional example. The original Tracy was played by Lynne Moody, who was the original Jenny Willis. Jennie Willis, you'll recall got engaged to Lionel Jefferson (the first one played by Mike Evans) in the *All in the Family* episode, ''Lionel's Engagement,'' which aired on February 9, 1974. When Lionel and his parents moved on up to the East Side of New York in their own spinoff series, *The Jeffersons* (See Entry), Jenny was played by Berlinda Tolbert.

Ms. Moody appeared in episodes of many weekly series including *Lou Grant, Trapper John, M.D.* and *T.J. Hooker.* Her other regular roles include Polly Dawson on the soap opera spoof, *Soap,* and Nurse Julie Williams on Elliott Gould's CBS situation comedy, *E/R.* She appeared on *Soap* from 1979 to 1981 and on *E/R* from September 16, 1984 to July 24, 1985.

A Program Information release issued by ABC Press Relations on July 8, 1975 said, ''Joan Pringle has been signed to play the series role of Tracy, Clifton's married sister, in *That's My Mama,* premiering for its second season on ABC Television Network, Wednesday, Sept. 10 (8:30–9:00 p.m. EDT). She succeeds Lynne Moody, who left the series to pursue a career in feature films.''

A very busy actress, Joan Pringle played Diana Sanger on *Ironside* during the 1974/1975 season and later co-starred as Sybil Buchanan on *The White Shadow.* Her many guest roles include appearances on *Banacek, Toma, Lucas Tanner* and *Sanford and Son.*

In an unusual bit of casting, the postman, Earl Chambers, was played in the first two episodes by Ed Bernard and was then replaced by Theodore Wilson, who had appeared in both of those episodes as another character. This is not unlike the case of Vincent Gardenia who appeared in ''The Bunkers and the Swingers'' episode of *All in the Family* that aired on October 28, 1972, and then joined the cast as the Bunkers' next-door-neighbor, Frank Lorenzo in the September 15, 1973 episode, ''We're Having a Heat Wave.''

From 1978 to 1980, Ed Bernard joined Joan Pringle on *The White Shadow* in his role as Jim Willis. Theodore Wilson later played Phil Wheeler on *The Sanford Arms* during the 1977 season, and Sweet Daddy on *Good Times* from 1978 to 1979.

THE THIN MAN

September 20, 1957–June 26, 1959.   NBC

Character:	Lieutenant Ralph Raines
Played by:	Stafford Repp
Date(s):	September 20, 1957–1958

Character:	Lieutenant Steve King
Played by:	Tol Avery
Date(s):	September 20, 1957–1958

Replaced by:	Lieutenant Harry Evans
Played by:	Jack Albertson
Date(s):	1958–June 26, 1959

Dashiell Hammett, the detective writer who created Sam Spade in the 1930 novel, *The Maltese Falcon*, four years later created the sophisticated husband and wife detective team of Nick and Nora Charles, who were undoubtedly the role models for future husband and wife detective teams such as *McMillan and Wife*.

The title of the series, *The Thin Man*, refers not to Nick Charles, but to Clyde Wynant, Nora's father, who was played in the 1934 theatrical release, THE THIN MAN, by Edward Ellis.

Nick and Nora, who were played in six films by William Powell and Myrna Loy, were brought to the small screen in seventy-two half-hour episodes by Peter Lawford and Phyllis Kirk.

Nick was a retired detective living in New York's Greenwich Village with his beautiful and wealthy wife, Nora, and her wire-haired fox terrier, Asta. Nick's police experience served him well in his second career—as an editor of mystery novels for a New York publishing house. But it is his wife's inability to stay out of trouble that forces him continually to return to his former profession—sleuthing.

As everyone knows, any good private detective must have a police contact and Nick had his. From 1957 to 1958, Lieutenants Raines and King filled the bill. Ralph Raines was played by Stafford Repp, who later became O'Hara, Gotham City's chief of police on *Batman*. Tol Avery, who played Lieutenant Steve King, went on to play Speaker Bert Metcalf in the political drama, *Slattery's People*, which aired on CBS from September 21, 1964 to November 26, 1965.

Both were replaced the following season by Jack Albertson as Lieutenant Harry Evans. Albertson began his long and distinguished television career by playing a Broadway newspaper columnist who served as the two-time host of the 1948 variety series, *Broadway Jamboree*. In 1976, he won an Emmy for his work as Ed Brown on the NBC situation comedy, *Chico and the Man*.

13 EAST

July 29, 1989–August 25, 1990.   NBC

Character:	Nurse Kelly Morrison
Played by:	Barbra Isenberg
Date(s):	July 29, 1989–September 2, 1989

Replaced by:	Nurse A.J. Gilroy
Played by:	Rosemarie Jackson
Date(s):	April 14, 1990–August 25, 1990

Character:	Nurse Janet Tom
Played by:	Ellen Regan
Date(s):	July 29, 1989–September 2, 1989

Replaced by:	Sidney Cooper
Played by:	Eric Glenn
Date(s):	April 14, 1990–August 25, 1990

Character:	Gertrude Boynton
Played by:	Marie Denn
Date(s):	July 29, 1989–September 2, 1989

Replaced by:	Father Frankie
Played by:	Philip Proctor
Date(s):	April 14, 1990–August 25, 1990

13 East is not an address in a New York neighborhood; it is Ward 13 East of a large hospital. The location was never specified, but it may have been Texas, since the sitcom was taped in Irving.

The supervisor of the nursing station of the hectic, not to say chaotic, ward was Head Nurse Maggie Poole (Diana Bellamy).

Working under her were Nurse Monique Roberts (Jan Cobler), Nurse Kelly Morrison (Barbra Isenberg), Nurse Janet Tom (Ellen Regan), and volunteer Gertrude Boynton (Marie Denn).

Wayne Powers played hospital administrator Wayne Frazier, and Timothy Wade made the rounds as Dr. Warren Newman, who was always coming on to the very attractive Nurse Roberts.

Right from the start, *13 East* was listed in *TV Guide* as a limited-run series. Nevertheless the producers still felt compelled to recast three of the roles after just six episodes had aired.

The show returned without Nurses Kelly Morrison and Janet Tom, Doctor Warren Newman and Gertrude Boynton. Their duties were assumed by Nurse A.J. Gilroy (Rosemarie Jackson), Sidney Cooper (Eric Glenn) and Father Frankie (Philip Proctor). Four months and ten episodes later, the entire cast was discharged.

THOSE ENDEARING YOUNG CHARMS

March 30, 1951–June 26, 1952.   NBC

Character:	Abby Charm
Played by:	Fern Parsons
Date(s):	March 30, 1951–December 1951

Replaced by:	Abby Charm
Played by:	Betty Arnold
Date(s):	May 1951–June 26, 1952

Character:	Connie Charm
Played by:	Pat Matthews
Date(s):	March 30, 1951

Replaced by: Connie Charm
Played by: Charon Follett
Date(s):   May 1951–June 26, 1952

Here's an idea that may have been ahead of its time—a fifteen-minute situation comedy broadcast live from Chicago. Unlike the majority of situation comedies where the television family depends on the livelihood of only one member of the family, *Those Endearing Young Charms* managed to get the entire family involved in a mail-order business that specialized in household gadgets for collectors.

The head of the household, Ralph Charm, was played by Maurice Copeland. His son, Clem, and Uncle Duff were played by Gerald Garvey and Clarence Hartzel respectively. His wife, Abby, and daughter, Connie, however, were played by two different sets of actresses, none of whom went on to any role of note. The changes in cast occurred when the series moved from a local program to the NBC network.

It would appear that what the Charms could not sell wasn't kitchen gadgets, but commercials, which is usually the reason a program is taken off the air as this one was.

On November 12, 1955, approximately three years after the Charms closed up shop, Ralph Kramden and Ed Norton purchased two thousand Happy Housewife Helpers that were left unclaimed in a warehouse. These remarkable household gadgets, not unlike some of those sold through catalogs by the Charms, were described so eloquently and so succinctly by Norton as a combination corkscrew and wart remover. But instead of selling them through the mail or door-to-door, Ralph and Ed decided to sell them on television in the "Better Living Through TV" episode of *The Honeymooners*.

Based on the short run of *Those Endearing Young Charms*, one would have to assume that they weren't all that endearing.

THOSE TWO

November 26, 1951–April 24, 1953.   NBC

Character: Vivian
Played by: Vivian Blaine
Date(s):   November 26, 1951–May 19, 1952

Replaced by: Martha
Played by: Martha Stewart
Date(s):   May 26, 1952–April 24, 1953

Long before CNN, when the evening news ran for only fifteen minutes and when actors used their own first names, there aired an interesting little show called *Those Two*. The gimmick employed in this fifteen-minute series was to use a situation comedy structure to combine guest performers, music and dance.

Vivian Blaine starred as Vivian, a nightclub singer. Her accompanist, Pinky, was played by none other than Pinky Lee. Pinky was gaga over Vivian, but she had no interest in him. In fact she had so little interest that Vivian Blaine left the series in 1952 and was replaced by Martha Stewart as the nightclub singer, Martha.

Vivian Blaine is known to moviegoers of the forties and fifties and to film buffs of today for her work as Emily Joyce in the 1945 Rodgers and Hammerstein musical, STATE FAIR, and as Miss Adelaide in the 1955 Marlon Brando musical comedy, GUYS AND DOLLS. More recently, television audiences may remember Ms. Blaine as Betty McCullough, the next-door neighbor on the silly soap opera, *Mary Hartman, Mary Hartman.*

Vaudeville comedian Pincus Leff was known to millions of adults and children from one or another of his adult variety or Saturday morning children's shows on which he sported his trademark black-and-white checkered hat, shirt and matching suit. He played The Stagehand from April 5 to November 9, 1950 on the NBC situation comedy, *The Pinky Lee Show,* and made headlines on September 20, 1955, when his whirlwind six-day-a-week show caused him to collapse on the air—not from a heart-attack, as was rumored, but from what Lee said was poisoning from a nasal drip.

THREE'S COMPANY

March 15, 1977–September 18, 1984.   ABC

Character: Chrissy Snow
Played by: Suzanne Somers
Date(s):   March 15, 1977–September 29, 1980

Replaced by: Cindy Snow
Played by: Jenilee Harrison
Date(s):   December 16, 1980–1982

Replaced by: Terri Alden
Played by: Priscilla Barnes
Date(s):   October 6, 1981–September 18, 1984

Character: Stanley Roper
Played by: Norman Fell
Date(s):   March 15, 1977–March 11, 1979

Character: Helen Roper
Played by: Audra Lindley
Date(s):   March 15, 1977–March 11, 1979

Replaced by: Ralph Furley
Played by: Don Knotts
Date(s):   September 25, 1979–September 18, 1984

Character: Jim
Played by: Paul Ainsley
Date(s):   unknown

Replaced by: Bob
Played by: Brad Maule
Date(s):   unknown

If you think three's a crowd, just ask Jack Tripper, who will tell you that a single guy living with two young attractive women makes *Three's Company*. Pictured are (clockwise, from center): John Ritter as Jack Tripper, Priscilla Barnes as Terri Alden, Richard Kline as Larry Dallas, Don Knotts as Ralph Furley, and Joyce DeWitt as Janet Wood.

Replaced by:	Steve	Replaced by:	Kelly
Played by:	Paul Ainsley	Played by:	Frances Lee McCain
Date(s):	unknown	Date(s):	unknown

Replaced by: Mike
Played by: Brad Blaisdal
Date(s):   unknown

Character: Lily
Played by: Pamela Dunlap
Date(s):   unknown

Here is yet another variation on the popular theme used in the 1959 Marilyn Monroe comedy, SOME LIKE IT HOT. And in this one, the man living with two women doesn't even have to dress up the way Joe and Jerry (Tony Curtis and Jack Lemmon) did in the Monroe film. Still, the setup is not completely perfect. For Jack Tripper has to pretend he's a homosexual when he's around the landlord, Mr. Roper, so as not to be evicted. So maybe he would be better off if he dressed up as a woman. Then again, that was already done in the ABC situation comedy, *Bosom Buddies,* which starred Tom Hanks and Peter Scolari as Kip and Henry, who cross-dress to save money on rent by moving to the Susan B. Anthony Hotel.

Money was one of the driving forces behind this series as well. In the first episode, Janet Wood (Joyce DeWitt) and Chrissy Snow's (Suzanne Somers) roommate, Eleanor Garvey (Marianne Black), got married and moved out. This left Janet and Chrissy in need of a replacement roommate to help them pay the rent on their Los Angeles, California[8] apartment. Finding the perfect roommate can be a laborious and time-consuming task, but all Janet and Chrissy had to do was look in their bathtub. That's where they found Jack Tripper (John Ritter) sleeping after a wild going-away party for Eleanor, the night before.

The landlords of the apartment house were Stanley Roper and his wife Helen. Mrs. Roper, played by Audra Lindley, was like one of our favorite aunts, or one of our mom's friends whom we enjoyed seeing while growing up. She was warm, friendly, considerate and full of life. Her husband, Stanley, had checked out of the human race long ago and was cheap with his money and himself. Helen would have loved to be a mother but Stanley always seemed to have a headache.

They were, however, popular characters. So popular, in fact, that in March 1979 the producers decided to spin them off into their very own series. The Ropers officially became *The Ropers* on March 13, 1979, after a two-part transitional episode appeared on *Three's Company.*

The premise was that the Ropers had sold their apartment house and moved into the Royal Dale Condominium Town House in Santa Monica's posh Cheviot Hills section—presumably to enjoy their retirement.

The snobbish real estate agent, Jeffrey P. Brookes, III was played by Jeffrey Tambor, who occasionally turned up as Judge Alan Wachtel on *Hill Street Blues.* He vehemently denies being a snob, but as his wife Ann (Patricia McCormack) points out in the first episode, his father's name was Al so how could he be J.P.B, III?

The Brookes' adorable "made-for-television sitcom kid," David, was played by Evan Cohen.

In the first part of the two-parter, Brookes, who is president of the Royal Dale Homeowners Association, doesn't want the Ropers as neighbors and Stanley doesn't want to part with the buck to purchase unit #46. Of course, in the end, it all works out.

ANN: Well, it looks like we got our new neighbor.

JEFFREY: I'm afraid it does.

The Ropers, who had moved in to the CBS schedule on March 13, 1979, moved out on May 22, 1980, after only twenty-eight episodes.

Back in the old neighborhood, Jack, Janet and Chrissy, who are holding a garage sale, stop by the Regal Beagle for a glass of Coke. At the neighborhood bar, they meet up with Jack's friend, Larry Dallas (Richard Kline), who lives upstairs in apartment 304, and show him one of the signs from their garage sale. It reads "Garage Sale on Sunday 31st. Junk and all kinds of wonderful things."

JANET: (To Larry) It's the Roper's garage. When they moved, they left a lot of stuff in there and they said we could do anything we want with it.

What they are doing is selling the stuff to raise money for their rent. Just then a stranger (Don Knotts) walks in to the bar and introduces himself to the bartender[9] as Ralph Furley, while Larry looks on.

FURLEY: (To the bartender) I'll be running things over at the old Roper's building.

LARRY: Oh, then you're the new owner?

FURLEY: Well, not exactly. My brother, Bart, bought the building, but I'm going to be the new manager. Landlord in residence so to speak. I'll be in total charge.

It was about this time that one of the series' co-stars, Suzanne Somers, who had become a bona fide media star complete with merchandising featuring her likeness, felt that she was not being fairly compensated for her contribution to the series.

The dispute with NRW Productions, according to an Associated Press story, involved Ms. Somers' $30,000–a-week salary. Her demands included a raise to $150,000 a week and ten percent of the show's profits. "Mickey Ross of NRW contended that Miss Somers on at least two occasions failed to report for taping at the last minute. It was then that her appearances were limited to one minute."[10]

These cameo appearances were usually in the form of a quick telephone call placed to Janet and Jack. She was supposed to be in Fresno looking after her sick mother. There were also episodes in which she did not appear at all and Chrissy was eventually written out.

" 'There were too many problems involved,' said Bernie West, a partner in NRW Productions. 'There was too much unhappiness. She's been passing around T-Shirts saying "Free Suzanne." Well, she's free now.' "[11]

Ms. Somers was left in the show's opening credits while her fate was being decided. What was finally decided was the introduction of a replacement character.

The main cast was easily restored to three by introducing a

---

8. Later on the series it was mentioned that they were living in Santa Monica, California.
9. At various times throughout the series, the bartender at the Regal Beagle has been Jim, Bob, Steve and Mike. Likewise, Lily and Kelly were waitresses seen at the bar.
10. Associated Press. Saturday, April 4, 1981.
11. *Ibid.*

new roommate. In the first scene, Mr. Furley comes in to "the kids' " apartment asking for the overdue rent. Jack tells him that they only have two-thirds of the money because Chrissy is not around. To prove his depressed financial situation, Jack picks up a pile of mail that he believes is all bills and discovers a letter from Chrissy. Hoping it contains a check for her portion of the rent, he rips the envelope open and finds a smaller envelope addressed to Mr. Furley. Jack hands Furley his envelope and puts down the letter from Chrissy.

FURLEY: Dear Mr. Furley. I owe you one month's rent. Chrissy Snow. (Furley pauses) Look, kids, I can give you one more day. After that, it's out of my hands.

JANET: Mr. Furley, where are we going to get the money?

FURLEY: I don't know. Maybe you ought to get your-selves another roommate until Chrissy comes back.

The next scene is typical of the silly mix-ups and slapstick that helped to make *Three's Company* a hit. First, Mr. Furley comes to the empty apartment to show it to Mrs. Medford (Barbara Stuart). While they are off looking at the kitchen, Larry shows up with his girlfriend, Jennifer (Karen Austin), to show her the apartment. They duck into Chrissy's room when Jack shows up with his beautiful blonde girlfriend and potential roomie, Maxine (Shauna Sullivan). They all eventually bump into each other and begin arguing, when Janet comes in with Bill (Jordan Clarke), her ideal roommate. The arguing is interrupted by a pretty young lady wearing a cowboy hat and boots.

JANET: Who are you?

CINDY: Cindy.

JANET: Cindy?

CINDY: Yeah. Chrissy's cousin. Yeah. She said I could stay here while she's gone. Didn't you get her letter?

That was, of course, the letter that Jack put down and never read.

Cindy then, through the old "what's your sign" scam, gets Bill and Maxine together and suggests they take the one-room apartment she had seen for rent down the street. The suggestion sounds like a good one to them and they leave. She then uses the same ploy to sweet-talk Furley into extending the rent deadline for two weeks, which is when she will be getting her first paycheck from her new job.

With the show recast, everything would seem to be fine, but for some reason the producers must have felt that Jenilee Harrison didn't have the right chemistry with Jack and Janet, so she was moved out of the apartment to make room for an emergency-room nurse, Terri Alden, played by Priscilla Barnes.

It must be noted that Ms. Harrison was not written out. It was simply explained that she had moved into a dormitory at nearby UCLA. She stayed with the series for two years before leaving. In the scenes shown during the opening and closing credits, she could be seen in the background walking with Larry, while Priscilla Barnes was featured more prominently up front with Janet and Jack.

When the gimmick had outworn its freshness, Terri moved to Hawaii and Janet announced her engagement to an art dealer, Philip Dawson. Dawson is played by David Ruprecht, who filled in for Jim Backus as Thurston Howell, III in one of the *Gilligan's Island* (See Entry) extension episodes.

This allows Jack to court and eventually live with Vicky Bradford (Mary Cadorette) and move into their own spinoff series, *Three's a Crowd*.

THROB

September 1986–1988.   Syndicated

Character:	Jeremy Beatty
Played by:	Paul W. Walker
Date(s):	1986–1987

Replaced by:	Jeremy Beatty
Played by:	Sean de Veritch
Date(s):	1987–1988

The beautiful dark-haired Diana Canova, who had played Corinne, Jessica (Katherine Helmond) and Chester (Robert Mandan) Tate's sexy daughter on the soppy syndicated sudser, *Soap,* starred in this syndicated sitcom as Sandy Beatty.

The unusual title of this series stood not for pain, but for the name of a record company that specialized in punk rock albums. Then again, if punk rock isn't your brand of music, it just might make your ears and head throb, which is pretty much the way Sandy felt when she moved from Buffalo to New York City to join the staff of Throb Records.

Heading up the small record label's offices, located in a Manhattan loft, was the younger and shorter Zachary Armstrong (Jonathan Prince), whose heart throbbed for the older and considerably taller thirty-three-year-old divorced mother.

In roughly half of the forty-eight episodes, Sandy's son, Jeremy, was played by Paul W. Walker, and in the remainder by Sean de Veritch.

The cast also included Sandy's co-workers, Meredith (Mary-edith Burrell), Prudence Anne "Blue" Bartlett (Jane Leeves), and Phil Gaines (Richard Cummings, Jr.)

TIMMY AND LASSIE see: LASSIE

TOM CORBETT, SPACE CADET

October 2, 1950–June 25, 1955.   CBS-ABC-NBC-DuMont

Character:	Captain Larry Strong
Played by:	Michael Harvey
Date(s):	October 2, 1950

Replaced by:	Captain Larry Strong
Played by:	Edward Bryce
Date(s):	October 4, 1950–June 25, 1955

Character:	Dr. Joan Dale
Played by:	Patricia Ferris
Date(s):	unknown

Replaced by:	Dr. Joan Dale
Played by:	Margaret Garland
Date(s):	unknown

Character:	Cadet Roger Manning
Played by:	Jan Merlin
Date(s):	1950–1952

Replaced by:	Cadet Roger Manning
Played by:	Jack Grimes
Date(s):	1953–June 25, 1955

Joining the ranks of the space-age defenders of the universe during the 1950s, which included Captain Video, Flash Gordon, Rod Rocket and Buzz Corey, was Tom Corbett. Not yet a full-fledged commander, Tom Corbett was still a student or "cadet" at Space Academy U.S.A., an original idea borrowed from *Space Cadet,* the 1948 novel by Robert A. Heinlein. An idea that has survived into the nineties. In 1977 Filmation aired *Space Academy,* which itself spawned *Jason of Star Command* (See Entry). Lest we forget, *Star Trek,* the standard by which all other space science fictions is measured, has always supported its own Starfleet Academy.

The space cadet on the show—titled *Chris Colby, Space Cadet* for the first broadcast—was thereafter Tom Corbett. He was played by a twenty-nine-year-old actor, Frankie Thomas, whose youthful good looks made him believable as a teenager. He won the role by beating out two twenty-five-year-old actors, Dickie Moore, the adorable youth who played "Dickie" in the OUR GANG comedies, and Jack Lemmon, who is famous as the fastidious half of the odd couple from the 1968 film of the same name. Lemmon also directed KOTCH in 1971.

Thomas was no newcomer to the business. He had appeared in four NANCY DREW films as Ted Nickerson, Nancy Drew's boyfriend.

Captain Larry Strong was played in the first episode by Michael Harvey. In an article written by Earl Blair for *The Big Reel,* associate producer Muriel Buckridge explained why Harvey was replaced after appearing in only one episode of *Tom Corbett, Space Cadet:* "They had a Captain Strong who looked wonderful, but experienced an actor's nightmare in the first episode. He froze on a close-up, could not recover on his own and it was impossible (due to the circumstances of the scene) for any of the actors to give him help. The stage manager did his best, but we finally had to fade out. The experience emotionally shattered the actor and we had to get a new Captain Strong."

The new Captain Strong was played by Edward Bryce who was not nearly as handsome as Michael Harvey but did have a rich baritone voice and was a competent television actor. At one point, he began to think he was just a bit too competent and walked off the series in a pay dispute.

The show's producers, Rockhill Productions, refused to pay the requested increase and began looking for a new Captain Strong. The candidates were quickly narrowed down to three finalists, one of whom was a young actor by the name of Lee Marvin. But he lost the role because he was considered a little too strong for Strong. Luckily, Bryce settled with the producers and returned to *Tom Corbett, Space Cadet.*

The ship's arrogant astrogator, Roger Manning, was played by both Jan Merlin and Jack Grimes. Merlin played Lieutenant Kirby on the post-Civil War Western, *The Rough Riders,* which aired on ABC from October 2, 1958 to September 24, 1959. When Merlin left for California, the part of Cadet Manning was taken over by Jack Grimes, the same actor who later appeared as the third Homer Brown in *The Aldrich Family* (See Entry).

TOMA *see:* BARETTA

THE TONY RANDALL SHOW

September 23, 1976–March 25, 1978.   ABC-CBS

Character:	Roberta "Bobby" Franklin
Played by:	Devon Scott
Date(s):	September 23, 1976–March 1977

Replaced by:	Roberta "Bobby" Franklin
Played by:	Penny Peyser
Date(s):	September 24, 1977–March 25, 1978

Being asked to leave your own series may be more traumatic than being asked to leave your home by your wife, but that is exactly what happened to Tony Randall after five successful years as Felix Unger on *The Odd Couple* (See Entry). Randall managed to find a new home the following season in *The Tony Randall Show.* His new home was Philadelphia, his new name was Judge Walter O. Franklin and his new profession was law.

He works as a judge in the Court of Common Pleas in Philadelphia, and the plots of this entertaining situation comedy deal with the judicial and parental dilemmas of Walter Franklin, a middle-aged widower trying to raise two very bright children. His eleven-year-old son, Oliver Wendell, was played by Brad

Savage. This was television's second character to have been named after the famous jurist, Oliver Wendell Holmes. The other Oliver Wendell was Mr. Douglas (Eddie Albert), a lawyer from New York who moved to *Green Acres* in 1965.

Walter's daughter, Bobby, an eighteen-year-old law student, was initially played by Devon Scott who appeared as Andrea Platt in *We'll Get By.* The short-lived situation comedy, which starred Paul Sorvino as George Platt aired on CBS from March 14 to May 30, 1975.

After only one season on ABC, *The Tony Randall Show* moved to CBS and replaced Devon Scott with Penny Peyser. In the first episode Walter gets on Bobby's case when she tries his patience by dropping out of college and moving in with her boyfriend. It is possible that Walter was so angry with his daughter that he didn't even notice that she looked completely different.

Ms. Peyser may have been a little better prepared for the role of a judge's daughter than Ms. Scott, as her real father, Peter Peyser, was a New York congressman. Her next regular series role following *The Tony Randall Show* was as Cindy Fox, the wife of Harrison K. Fox (John Rubinstein) in the lighthearted crime drama, *Crazy Like a Fox,* which aired on CBS from December 30, 1984 to September 4, 1986.

The Tony Randall Show was adjourned by CBS after forty-four episodes.

TOO CLOSE FOR COMFORT

November 11, 1980–September 15, 1983.   ABC
January 1984–September 1985   Syndicated
April 1986–September 1986 (*The Ted Knight Show*)   Syndicated

Character:	Andrew Rush
Played by:	Jason Willis
Date(s):	1982–1983
Replaced by:	Andrew Rush
Played by:	Eric Willis
Date(s):	1982–1983
Replaced by:	Andrew Rush
Played by:	William Thomas Cannon
Date(s):	1983–1984
Replaced by:	Andrew Rush
Played by:	Michael Philip Cannon
Date(s):	1983–1984
Replaced by:	Andrew Rush
Played by:	Joshua Goodwin
Date(s):	1984–1986

The first-run syndication market sometimes offers marginally successful series a chance at a second life, which is what happened with *Too Close for Comfort.*

The ABC sitcom starred Ted Knight as cartoonist Henry Rush, creator of the *Cosmic Cow* comic strip and the overprotective father of two very attractive daughters, in their twenties, who live in the downstairs apartment of his San Francisco duplex.

Jackie (Deborah Van Valkenburgh) was a brunette and worked in a bank. Her more flirtatious sister, Sara (Lydia Cornell), was a student at San Francisco State College.

Nancy Dussault played Henry's independent wife, Muriel, a freelance photographer cut from the same TV mom cloth as Bonnie Franklin's Ann Romano on the CBS sitcom, *One Day at a Time* (December 16, 1975, to September 2, 1984)—she even looked like Ann.

Rounding out the regular cast was Sara's annoyingly hyper, clutzy and somewhat bewildered college friend, Monroe Ficus, who was played by JM J. Bullock.

TV audiences were as stunned as Henry to learn that at the age of forty-two, Muriel was going to have a baby. It's hard to tell what was more shocking, the fact that the mother was over forty or that the child was going to be born into a sitcom family with both of his natural parents.

Andrew Rush arrived in 1982 and was at first played by twins Jason and Eric Willis. They were replaced for the 1983/1984 season by the Cannon twins, Michael and William. But this being Hollywood, Andrew didn't do his own talking. His baby talk was supplied in voice-overs by Sunni Walton, while his thoughts were enunciated by voice talent Frank Welker, who provided the voice of the Footstool in Walt Disney's 1991 animated feature, BEAUTY AND THE BEAST. This concept of hearing a baby's thoughts predated both the 1989 motion picture, LOOK WHO'S TALKING, and the subsequent 1991/1992 TV series, *Baby Talk* (See Entry).

Too Close for Comfort aired on ABC from November 11, 1980 to September 15, 1983, and ran for a total of sixty-three episodes.

Although the series was canceled by the network, it was brought back the following season by Metromedia Producers Corp., which aired the show in syndication on sixty-eight stations. All of the regular cast returned except the twins playing Andrew; they were replaced by Joshua Goodwin. The setting was also changed from San Francisco to Mill Valley, where Henry had purchased a forty-nine percent share of a weekly newspaper, *The Marin Bugler.*

Beginning in April 1986 under its new name, *The Ted Knight Show* continued as a first-run syndicated series until it was forced into cancellation after the death of series star Ted Knight on August 26, 1986.

Earlier in his career, Ted Knight lent his voice to the Daily Planet's editor-in-chief, Perry White, in Filmation's 1966 animated series, *The New Adventures of Superman.* Other animated characters brought to life by Ted Knight include both Professor Oliver Lindenbrook and Count Saccnuson on *Journey to the Center of the Earth,* which aired on CBS from September 9, 1967 to September 6, 1969.

Knight continued to work for Filmation and for ten years, from September 8, 1973 to September 3, 1983, was the narrator of *Superfriends.*

Born Tadewurz Wladzui Konopka on December 7, 1923, in Terryville, Connecticut, Ted Knight appeared in a number of roles on weekly television series including *Lux Video Theater, Big Town, The Lieutenant, The Outer Limits* and *The Wild Wild West.* But it wasn't until after he had played a newsman quite different from the hard-nosed editor he played on *The New Adventures of Superman* that he achieved national recognition.

For seven years, from September 19, 1970 to September 3, 1977, Ted Knight played WJM-TV's anchorman, Ted Baxter, on the hit TV series, *The Mary Tyler Moore Show.* At the 1972/1973 Emmy Awards, Ted Knight beat out co-star Ed Asner and *M*A*S*H*'s Gary Burghoff and McLean Stevenson for Outstanding Performance by an Actor in a Supporting Role in Comedy. And in 1975, Ted Knight was named TV Father of the Year by the National Father's Day Commission.

TOPPER

October 9, 1953–October 14, 1956.   CBS-ABC-NBC

Character:	Katie
Played by:	Kathleen Freeman
Date(s):	October 9, 1953–1954
Replaced by:	Maggie
Played by:	Edna Skinner
Date(s):	1954–1955

''Anne Jeffreys as Marian Kerby, the ghostess with the mostest . . . Robert Sterling as George Kerby, that most sporting spirit . . . and Leo G. Carroll, host to said ghosts as . . . Topper.''

As with any science fiction or fantasy, if it is well written and well cast—and if you accept the premise—the series will work. All of those factors were in play here and not only does *Topper* work, it works beautifully.

Cosmo Topper's troubles begin when he, a transplanted Englishman and bank vice president, purchases a house in New York. The house you see, or don't see, is still occupied by its former owners, George and Marian Kerby, who were killed in an avalanche while on a skiing vacation in Switzerland. Living . . . strike that . . . residing with the Kerbys is Neil, a lush of a Saint Bernard who was trapped in the snow slide along with the very people he was there to rescue. The three of them returned to the Kerby's former home in the United States only to find a new family living in it.

The Kerbys made their presence known to ''Topper, old man'' as they like to call him, but to no one else. It's the first rule of any fantasy program. Only the audience and one or two characters are to be in on the secret. The ghosts, young and sophisticated, really do like Topper, who is somewhat of a fuddy-duddy. And it is mostly their efforts to help Topper loosen up that gets him into trouble. A fast thinker on his feet, Topper can usually explain away the antics of the ghosts. A typical case is the time the Kerbys carry a cake right by Topper's wife, Henrietta (Lee Patrick). Without missing a beat and with great panache, Topper explains that the reason the cake floated by was that it was very light angel food cake. In another episode Henrietta, who witnesses a case of lipstick just float by her, makes a feeble attempt to explain it away just as her husband has done a hundred times before. When she is questioned about the floating box, she says confidently, ''Of course it floated by. It's lipstick.'' Everyone in the scene just stares at her blankly. She tells herself that whenever Cosmo says things like that, everyone seems to think he's so terribly clever. Problem is, Henrietta just doesn't get it.

Rounding out the Topper household is their housekeeper, Katie, who has been witness to more than her share of goings on. Surprisingly, with three ghosts running around unchecked, there was only one cast member who vanished during the run of this series: the Toppers' housekeeper Katie, played by Kathleen Freeman in her first series role. She left the employ of the Toppers in 1954 to handle the chores as Marilly, the housekeeper for Mayor Thomas Russell in the 1954 syndicated situation comedy, *Mayor of the Town.*

More than ten years later, Kathleen Freeman periodically turned up on *Hogan's Heroes* (See Entry) as General Burkhalter's (Leon Askin) sister, Gertrude Linkmier. She was seen with Imogene Coca and Joe E. Ross as Mrs. Boss in *It's About Time.* This CBS sitcom about two astronauts who cracked the time barrier and crash-landed back on earth during the stone age, ran from September 11, 1966 to August 27, 1967. From 1969 to 1971 she was seen as Flo Shafer on another CBS situation comedy, *The Beverly Hillbillies.*

Kathleen Freeman had already established the character of the Toppers' maid. Her replacement, Edna Skinner, who was hired as the Toppers' cook, Maggie, said that she didn't really experience any difficulty in taking over a role established by another actress. ''There's always going to be the comparison and you have to realize that that's going to happen. And so, rather than do an aping of anything, you must bring your own interpretation to the role,''[12] said Ms. Skinner.

Earlier in her career, Edna Skinner found herself in a similar situation when she was cast to replace Celeste Holm as Ado Annie in the 1943 Broadway production of *Oklahoma* at the St. James Theatre in New York. ''When I replaced Celeste in *Oklahoma,* that was a dilly because about ninety percent of the critics said that I was a carbon copy,'' said Ms. Skinner.

''The Theater Guild didn't want that show reviewed. When you replace somebody they don't want anything reviewed, they just want to slip you in unnoticed,'' she said.

Burton Roscoe, a critic for the *World Telegram,* on the other hand, did notice and gave Ms. Skinner an outstanding review.

It seems that it would be difficult for any new cast member to fit into an already established ensemble, but Edna Skinner said, ''Most casts, like the casts of *Topper* and *Oklahoma,* were absolutely wonderful to me when I went in. I mean they were just absolutely wonderful.''

Five years later, Ms. Skinner went from *Topper,* a show inhabited by ghosts, to *Mr. Ed* (See Entry), a show inhabited by a horse that could talk, and ended up being the one replaced.

An attempt to revive *Topper* was made in 1973 by NBC with a pilot entitled *Topper Returns.* In the updated version, it was Roddy McDowall who returned as Cosmo Topper, Jr., the nephew of the late Cosmo Topper, to monkey around with those ghosts. That explained why Topper looked different, but it did not explain why the ghosts with the most also looked

---

12. All the comments by Edna Skinner in this *Topper* entry are from an exclusive telephone interview with Ms. Skinner on September 17, 1990.

different. The new George and Marian Kerby were played by Stefanie Powers and John Fink. Instead of having a maid or a cook, Cosmo, Jr. had a butler played by Reginald Owen. This failed outing aired on March 19, 1973.

Since there's no keeping a good ghost down, the format was tried a third time, with Kate Jackson as Marian Kerby, Andrew Stevens as George Kerby and Jack Warden as Topper. Wilkins was this Topper's butler and he was played by Macon McCalman. The proper Mrs. Topper (Clara) was portrayed by Rue McClanahan. In this two-hour made-for-television-movie George and Marian were killed in an automobile accident and Topper was their lawyer, not a banker.

All of these television incarnations, as well as a series of TOPPER feature films starring Roland Young in the title role, were loosely based on *Topper: A Ribald Adventure,* a 1932 novel by Thorne Smith. The book was released in London, England in 1939 under the title *The Jovial Ghosts: The Misadventures of Topper.*

THE TORKELSONS

September 21, 1991–June 20, 1992.   NBC
February 6, 1993–July 3, 1993   NBC

Character:	Wesley "Boarder" Hodges
Played by:	William Schallert
Date(s):	September 21, 1991–June 20, 1992
Replaced by:	Brian Morgan
Played by:	Perry King
Date(s):	February 6, 1993–July 3, 1993
Character:	Ruth Ann Torkelson
Played by:	Anna Slotky
Date(s):	September 21, 1991–June 20, 1992
Replaced by:	Molly Morgan
Played by:	Brittany Murphy
Date(s):	February 6, 1993–July 3, 1993
Character:	Steven Floyd Torkelson
Played by:	Aaron Metchik
Date(s):	September 21, 1991–June 20, 1992
Replaced by:	Gregory Morgan
Played by:	Jason Marsden
Date(s):	February 6, 1993–July 3, 1993

The Torkelsons returned rural comedy to the network sitcom scene. It had been absent since CBS's cancellations of *Mayberry R.F.D., The Beverly Hillbillies* and *Green Acres* in 1971. The difference between *The Torkelsons* and the CBS sitcoms was that *The Torkelsons* had more heart.

Just outside of Tulsa, Oklahoma is Pyramid Corners, a speck on the map where the Torkelsons live at house number 855. A family of six that is more than struggling, they are virtually broke—largely because Randall "Randy" Torkelson (played in the November 2, 1991 episode, "Men Don't Leave," by Gregg Henry) walked out on his wife, Millicent (Connie Ray), and their five children.

An eternal optimist, Millicent holds the family together through sheer tenacity and the belief that their luck will change tomorrow. She earns what little money she can with her one-woman reupholstery business that is based on one White sewing machine and her own skill. She saves money in the great Scarlett O'Hara tradition by sewing the kids' clothes out of drapes, bedspreads and bolt ends acquired from the Jenette Mills Oven Mitt Company.

The real star of the show is Millicent's fourteen-year-old daughter, Dorothy Jane (Olivia Burnette), who is embarrassed by her family and tries desperately to break away from the stigma of being poor—she is also their staunchest defender.

Her younger brothers and sisters include twelve-year-old Steven Floyd and his ten-year-old sister, Ruth Ann Torkelson, played in the pilot, "Fence Neighbors," by Benj Thall and Elizabeth Poyer, and thereafter by Aaron Metchik and Anna Slotky.

The love of Dorothy Jane's life was the son of their "fence neighbors," a handsome eighteen-year-old named Riley Roberts (Michael Landes). Further complicating matters is the unrequited love of Kirby Scroggins (Paige Gosney), a boy her own age, who is head-over-heels about Dorothy Jane.

The two tiniest Torkelsons are eight-year-old Chuckie Lee (Lee Norris) and six-year-old Mary Sue (Rachel Duncan).

The missing father figure was filled by television's most prolific character actor, William Schallert.

In the pilot episode, presented on September 21, 1991, with the washer and dryer being repossessed and the mortgage payment overdue, Millicent takes an "I'll never be hungry again" stance and is forced to offer one of her rooms for rent. The newspaper ad is answered by Mr. Wesley Hodges (William Schallert). When Dorothy Jane learns that the room being let is her own, she confronts her mother.

DOROTHY JANE: This room was my sanctuary from the storm. It was the only thing in my life that you didn't make from a curtain or you didn't get handed down to me by some relative that was no where near my size. This is my room! And you gave it to a total stranger off the street!

Willing, as always, to make concessions for her struggling family, Millicent offers to move into the basement and give her room to Dorothy Jane. Mr. Hodges (who is later warmly referred to as Boarder Hodges) overhears this conversation and walks into the room faking exhaustion, declaring that the walk up the thirty stairs on his arthritic knees was both difficult and exhausting. He asks if there is another room available. Millicent tells him that there are only eight "little" steps down to the basement, and he opts for that room.

Proving the old adage that where there's a will there's a way, Millicent wangles a new washer and dryer, forcing the local store to honor its newspaper ad that read, "Step up to quality. Trade in your old washer and dryer and get three months payments free. Any and all trade-ins accepted, regardless of age or condition.'' Millicent's washer and dryer trade-ins were a scrub board and a clothesline.

Television trivia buffs were treated to a very special reunion in an episode when Patty Duke guest-starred as Boarder Hodges' estranged daughter-in-law, Catherine Jeffers. The set-up for this reunion began in an earlier episode in which Boarder Hodges got "another" returned letter from a Molly Jeffers. Not knowing who the mystery woman was drove Millicent's sister-in-law Bootsie (Ronnie Claire Edwards) crazy, but Mr. Hodges, being a private gentleman, did not reveal her identity until the reunion episode.

When a package to Molly was returned to Hodges, he gave it to Mary Sue, telling the little girl it was for her. Inside was a Wedding Barbie meant for his granddaughter Molly's birthday. But like the fourteen letters he had written, this gift was also sent back to him unopened, and that's when Wesley broke down and explained the mystery to Millicent and Dorothy Jane. His heart-wrenching story began with his son Michael, who married a young woman named Catherine. Together they had a little girl and named her Molly. But when Michael died, Catherine remarried and her second husband adopted Molly. And it was Hodges' belief that the letters kept coming back because "I believe I represent a part of her life that she wants to put behind her." That is, however, only his theory, and that's when Millicent decided to intervene and locate his daughter-in-law and tell her how much she and Molly meant to Mr. Hodges.

Starting with the address on the returned package, Millicent called information for Darien, Connecticut to get the telephone number of Catherine Jeffers who lived at 37 Martin Lane, in her attempt to reunite this broken family. The inside jokes here are that William Schallert's character's name on *The Patty Duke Show* was Martin Lane, and Patty (Lane) Duke's sophisticated twin cousin was Catherine.

Millicent's overtures to Catherine did indeed persuade her to make a special visit to Oklahoma with her daughter, Molly (Ashley Peldon).

CATHERINE: Hello, dad. It's been a long time.

HODGES: Maybe I don't have any place in your life anymore.

That, of course, wasn't it at all. Catherine and Molly had never seen the letters or the gift, because the mail had been sent back by Catherine's husband.

Catherine did ask her father-in-law to return to Connecticut with them, but when she saw how much the Torkelson kids loved and needed him, she understood his decision to stay.

CATHERINE: You'll take care of him for us, won't you?

MILLICENT: We sure will.

After living on NBC's Saturday night schedule for nine months, *The Torkelsons* was taken off the air—though not permanently. Eight months later, the Torkelson family returned to NBC's Saturday night lineup on February 6, 1993, after having a major revamping and a name change to *Almost Home.*

"New Moon," the season premiere of *Almost Home,* opens with Dorothy Jane sitting on the steps of her home and speaking to the man in the moon, as she did in every episode.

DOROTHY JANE: Man in the moon, somethin' happened. Although she tried as hard as she could and she scrambled and cajoled and sweet-talked and hollered. My heart does truly go out to her. This time, my mother could not make the mortgage and they're foreclosing this house and kickin' the Torkelsons out of Pyramid Corners, Oklahoma, forever—Yeah!

Millicent says a tearful good-bye to her house and they begin their three-and-one-half-day bus trip from Oklahoma to Seattle, Washington, where she has accepted a job as nanny to Brian Morgan's (Perry King) two irrepressible teenagers, Molly (Brittany Murphy) and Gregory (Jason Marsden). Dorothy Jane explains, in a lengthy opening monologue, that her mother has decided to do what she knows how to do best—be a mother.

Mr. Morgan is a widower and former attorney, who dissolved his law practice so that he could try to make a go of *Molly Gregory,* the shaky mail order catalog business established by his wife that specializes in children's clothes and toys.

After having gone through nearly half-a-dozen nannies, including Mrs. Oliver, Mrs. Mortelli, Mrs. Claymore, Mrs. Connelly and Mrs. Westin, Brian hires Mrs. Torkelson, not only for her own skills, but because he feels her family will be a good influence on his own kids.

Brian Morgan, who had already met the Torkelsons when he had flown out to Oklahoma to interview Millicent for the job, introduces them to his kids.

BRIAN: Let's see if I remember. Now, it's Dorothy Jane, uh, Chuckie Lee and Mary Sue. Right?

GREGORY: Wow, with all those names, you think there'd be more of them.

Come to think of it—there were! Two more to be exact.

Sadly, the first cast casualty was William Schallert as Boarder Hodges. He was replaced by handsome Perry King as Brian Morgan, who, like Mike Brady (Robert Reed) of *The Brady Bunch* and Frank Lambert (Patrick Duffy) of *Step by Step,* had a couple of kids of his own.

And, since Counselor Morgan already had two children, Millicent's five would have been too many—even for a sitcom. So she left her two middle children, Ruth Ann and Steven Floyd, home alone with Boarder Hodges, and no explanation given.

While William Schallert is known for his more traditional roles, including everything from Dobie Gillis' teacher, Mr. Leander Pomfritt, on *The Many Loves of Dobie Gillis* (See Entry), to Patty Duke's father on *The Patty Duke Show,* Perry King's roles have been at the opposite end of the spectrum.

Perhaps best known as Cody Allen from the Stephen J. Cannell detective drama, *Riptide,* Perry King also starred as

Dan Underwood in the short-lived ABC adventure, *The Quest,* which aired from October 22 to November 19, 1982. His more important quest, however, is to survive as a sitcom father. Maybe he should have a talk with the man in the moon.

TOUR OF DUTY

September 24, 1987–August 25, 1990.   CBS

Character:	Private Randy ''Doc'' Matsuda
Played by:	Steve Akahoshi
Date(s):	September 24, 1987–1988

Replaced by:	Private Francis ''Doc Hock'' Hockenbury
Played by:	John Dye
Date(s):	1989–August 25, 1990

Glamorizing war has long been big business for Hollywood studios, which ground out dozens of successful films based on World War II, or what Archie Bunker referred to as ''The big one.''

On a smaller scale, ABC television seemed to wage a one-network battle against the enemy with four World War II dramas. Premiering just days apart were *Combat!* (September 2, 1962–August 29, 1967) and *The Gallant Men* (October 5, 1962–September 14, 1963) followed closely by *Twelve O'Clock High* (September 18, 1964–January 13, 1967) and *The Rat Patrol* (September 12, 1966– September 16, 1968).

The Vietnam War, however, was not as popular—in fact, it was the most unpopular war in the history of America which prodded television producers to take a more subversive approach to venting its antiwar message. *M*A*S*H,* for instance, used the backdrop of the Korean War as a substitute for Vietnam, while Gene Roddenberry's *Star Trek* let us look at the senselessness of war from 200 years in the future.

But it wasn't until 1987 that the Vietnam War was faced head on by CBS, which had in 1965 given us the fanciful sitcom, *Hogan's Heroes.* The series, *Tour of Duty,* was 1967 Vietnam seen through the eyes of the soldiers of Company B, or ''Bravo'' Company, led by Sergeant Zeke Anderson (Terence Knox).

A number of changes were made throughout the run of the series, including a change in locale from the jungles of Vietnam to the Tan Son Nhut airbase located just outside Saigon.

Of all the cast changes, the only direct replacement was that of the company medic. At the start of the second season Steve Akahoshi, who had played ''Doc,'' was replaced by John Dye as ''Doc Hock.''

TRAPPER JOHN, M.D.

September 23, 1979–September 4, 1986.   CBS

Character:	Nurse ''Starch'' Clara Willoughly
Played by:	Mary McCarty
Date(s):	September 23, 1979–October 19, 1980

Replaced by:	Nurse Ernestine Shoop
Played by:	Madge Sinclair
Date(s):	November 23, 1980–September 4, 1986

Character:	Nurse Gloria ''Ripples'' Brancusi
Played by:	Christopher Norris
Date(s):	September 23, 1979–1985

Replaced by:	Nurse Libby Kegler
Played by:	Lorna Luft
Date(s):	Fall 1985–September 4, 1986

Character:	Arnold Slocum
Played by:	Simon Scott
Date(s):	September 23, 1979–1985

Replaced by:	Catherine Hackett
Played by:	Janis Paige
Date(s):	1985–September 4, 1986

There were actually two *After M*A*S*H* television series. This, the first of them, was named for one of the key characters of the *M*A*S*H* (See Entry) series, *Trapper John, M.D.*

In television time, the series was set at the San Francisco Memorial Hospital, twenty-eight years after Trapper John's discharge from the 4077th. In real time, this series aired four years after Wayne Rogers left *M*A*S*H* in a contract dispute.

In the interim, Dr. ''Trapper John'' McIntyre had not only lost a large portion of his hair, he had also completely lost his accent. This is because this Trapper John was not being played by Wayne Rogers, but by Pernell Roberts, who was Adam Cartwright on *Bonanza* (See Entry). Meanwhile, Rogers was preparing for his debut as Dr. Charley Michaels on the CBS situation comedy, *House Calls.* This ex-M*A*S*H surgeon later showed up as astronaut Tony Nelson, Larry Hagman's replacement in the *I Dream of Jeannie* (See Entry) extension episode.

Assisting the hospital's skilled and compassionate chief of surgery was Nurse Clara Willoughly, affectionately referred to as ''Starch,'' who was said to have worked with Trapper in Korea, although in reality there was no Nurse Willoughly or Nurse ''Starch'' on *M*A*S*H.*

Nurse Willoughly, Trapper's scrub nurse, was played by Mary McCarty during the first season of *Trapper John, M.D.* Starch was replaced by Nurse Ernestine Shoop (Madge Sinclair) at the start of the second season because actress Mary McCarty had died on April 3, 1980, while the show was on hiatus. Ms. McCarty, who was also a singer, had been a regular during the 1949 season of the NBC musical variety show, *Admiral Presents the Five Star Revue.*

Ms. Sinclair had appeared as Bell in the ABC five-part miniseries, *Roots,* which first aired on January 23, 1977. She followed that up as Madge, Senator Joe Kelley's (Jack Albertson) secretary on the NBC situation comedy, *Grandpa Goes to Washington,* which aired from September 7, 1978 to January 16, 1979.

Two notable cast changes occurred in the fall of 1985. Judy Garland's daughter and Liza Minnelli's sister, Lorna Luft, joined San Francisco Memorial's staff as Nurse Libby Kegler to replace the departed Nurse Gloria Brancusi. Previously Ms. Luft had guested in "Park Avenue Pirated," the September 21, 1975 episode of *McCloud,* and "Broadway Malady," the January 13, 1985 episode of *Murder, She Wrote.*

Replacing Arnold Slocum (Simon Scott) as the new hospital administrator was Janis Paige as Catherine Hackett. A former Broadway star, Janis Paige co-starred as Peggy Dainton in the 1957 musical, *Silk Stockings,* and Deborah Vaughn in the 1960 comedy, *Please Don't Eat the Daisies.* Her television credits include Kate Lanigan in police drama, *Lanigan's Rabbi,* which aired on NBC from January 30 to July 3, 1977, and Nettie McCoy on the CBS situation comedy, *Gun Shy,* which aired from March 15 to April 19, 1983.

THE TRAVELS OF JAIMIE MCPHEETERS

September 15, 1963–March 15, 1964.   ABC

Character: Buck Coulter
Played by: Michael Witney
Date(s):   September 15, 1963–November 10, 1963

Replaced by: Linc Murdock
Played by: Charles Bronson
Date(s):   November 17, 1963–March 15, 1964

Character: Jenny
Played by: Jean Engstrom
Date(s):   unknown

Replaced by: Jenny
Played by: Donna Anderson
Date(s):   unknown

In an attempt to jump aboard the gravy train, *The Travels of Jaimie McPheeters,* which was preceded by *Wagon Train* and *Rawhide,* was television's third attempt at telling stories of the Old West set outside the usual Western town. The storyline was generally faithful to the 1958 novel, *The Travels of Jaimie McPheeters,* on which it was based, with only minor alterations.

For instance, in Robert Lewis Taylor's novel, which won the Pulitzer Prize in 1959, Doctor Sardius McPheeters and his thirteen-year-old son Jaimie had left their creditors behind in Louisville, Kentucky. In the video version, Doc McPheeters (Dan O'Herlihy) and his twelve-year-old son Jaimie had skipped Paducah, Kentucky and joined the Beaver Patrol wagon train bound for California, where there was gold in "them thar hills."

If the little boy who played Jaimie reminds you of Drew Stephens from the 1983 motion picture SILKWOOD, it is because both parts were played by Kurt Russell—the first at age twelve and the second at age thirty-two.

In the driver's seat when the McPheeters' joined the wagon train was Buck Coulter. A few weeks into the series, the actor

In 1963, twelve-year-old Kurt Russell (right) starred in the title role of the ABC Western, *The Travels of Jaimie McPheeters.* His dad, Sardius "Doc" McPheeters, was played by Dan O'Herlihy.

who portrayed Coulter, Michael Witney, made the ultimate sacrifice, allowing his character to get trampled to death while saving the life of the young McPheeters.

Some of Witney's other television work includes two unsold pilots for CBS. In the first, he played the lead as ex-cop Noah Hendrix in *The Catcher,* which aired on June 2, 1972. The second was as Joe in the comedy, *Miss Stewart, Sir,* which aired on March 31, 1972. His favorite role may have been as the husband to sixties' sensation Twiggy (Lawson). Twiggy later made a name for herself as an actress, starring as Georgina "Georgie" De La Rue in the CBS situation comedy, *Princesses,* which debuted on Friday, September 27, 1991.

The wagonmaster who replaced Buck Coulter, Linc Murdoch, was played by Hollywood tough guy Charles Bronson, whose career fared far better than Michael Witney's. He had appeared in episodes of more than fifty television series from *Gunsmoke* to *Hennessey,* and in two previous series. He played on *Man with a Camera* from October 10, 1958 to January 29, 1960, on ABC. The NBC Western, *Empire,* was fortunate to have Paul Moreno played by Charles Bronson; he was a member of the cast from February 26 to September 17, 1963.

In addition to his television work Bronson had been working in motion pictures since the early fifties. One of his earliest film roles was as the mute sculptor, Igor, in the 1953 3–D horror classic, HOUSE OF WAX. Still it took nearly ten years before Bronson really began to catch the public's attention in roles such as O'Riley in the 1960 Western, THE MAGNIFICENT

SEVEN, and Danny Velinski in the 1963 prisoner-of-war drama, THE GREAT ESCAPE, both directed by John Sturges. The big payoff came ten years later, beginning with his role as Paul Kersey in the original 1974 crime drama, DEATH WISH.

The very pretty young lady, Jenny, traveling west with Jaimie and his dad, was initially played by Jean Engstrom and later by Donna Anderson.

Even though this series was based on an original work, it was by no means an original idea on television, which may be one of the reasons it was left in the dust by *Wagon Train* and *Rawhide* after only twenty-six episodes.

TROUBLE WITH FATHER

October 21, 1950–April 13, 1955.   ABC

Character:	Joyce Erwin
Played by:	Ann Todd
Date(s):	October 21, 1950–1954

Replaced by:	Joyce Erwin
Played by:	Merry Anders
Date(s):	1954–April 13, 1955

Stuart "Stu" Erwin was a very likeable character actor who stepped out onto the boards in 1924. Four years later he began a film career that would span nearly forty years and include more than one hundred motion picture roles. One of his earliest film knockouts was in the title role of the 1934 comedy, JOE PALOOKA.

Just two years later, Stu Erwin was nominated for an Academy Award for his portrayal of Amos Dodd in PIGSKIN PARADE. The 1936 musical comedy is also notable for introducing fifteen-year-old actress, Judy Garland, in her first film role, Sairy Dodd. Co-starring in the picture was Jack Haley as Winston "Slug" Winters. Haley would, of course, go on to play the Tin Woodsman opposite Miss Garland's Dorothy in the 1939 classic, THE WIZARD OF OZ.

By 1950, Stu Erwin had become one of television's many father figures, in his own series, *Life with the Erwins*. The title was later changed to *The Trouble with Father, The Stu Erwin Show* and during the last season, *The New Stu Erwin Show*.

But Stu Erwin differed from other TV dads such as Ozzie Nelson, Jim Anderson and Ward Cleaver in that he was a bit more harried. Okay, he was a little denser too, but he was always quite lovable. Not an easy feat for the father of two daughters or for the principal of Hamilton High School.

At home his wife, June, was played by the real Mrs. Erwin, June Collyer. His daughter Jackie was played by Sheila James, who is best known to television addicts as Zelda Gilroy, one of *The Many Loves of Dobie Gillis* (See Entry).

Jackie Erwin's sister, Joyce, was played by two different actresses. The first, Ann Todd, later appeared in segments of *Climax, G.E. Theater, Alfred Hitchcock Presents* and *Playhouse 90*.

Her replacement, Merry Anders, appeared in dozens of roles on episodic television, including four appearances on *77 Sunset Strip*. She also worked in two other series. Her first was as Val Marlowe in *It's Always Jan*, which aired on CBS from September 10, 1955 to June 30, 1956. Ms. Anders last worked as a regular in a series as "Mike" McCall in the situation comedy, *How to Marry a Millionaire*.

TRUE COLORS

September 2, 1990–August 23, 1992.   Fox

Character:	Ron Freeman
Played by:	Frankie Faison
Date(s):	September 2, 1990–December 8, 1991

Replaced by:	Ron Freeman
Played by:	Cleavon Little
Date(s):	December 15, 1991–August 23, 1992

If you were to cross *Family Ties* with *Cosby* you'd get *True Colors,* an authentic sitcom for the nineties.

Ron and Ellen Freeman (Frankie Faison and Stephanie Faracy) are the happy newlyweds (married just two months in the premiere episode), living with their three kids (his two boys and her girl), Lester (Adam Jeffries), Katie (Brigid Conley Walsh) and Terry (Claude Brooks).

Also residing with the Freemans is Ellen's mother Sara, who was played by Nancy Walker in her last television role. Nancy Walker was lovingly remembered as Rhoda's mom, Ida Morgenstern, on *Rhoda,* and as Mildred from *McMillan and Wife* (See Entry).

Just three months into the series Frankie Faison showed his true colors and left over what was reported in the press as "creative differences." The fact that Faison had been replaced was mentioned in the December 15, 1991 *TV Guide* listing that read "Cleavon Little takes over the role of Ron Freeman."

In addition to being remembered as Bart, the black sheriff from Mel Brooks' 1974 Western comedy, BLAZING SADDLES, Cleavon Little replaced John Amos in the unaired pilot for *Mr. Dugan,* a spinoff of *Maude* that eventually developed into *Hanging In* (See Entry). Faison, on the other hand, will be remembered for not hanging in.

TWELVE O'CLOCK HIGH

September 18, 1964–January 13, 1967.   ABC

Character:	Brigadier General Frank Savage
Played by:	Robert Lansing
Date(s):	September 18, 1964–May 7, 1965

Replaced by:	Colonel Joe Gallagher
Played by:	Paul Burke
Date(s):	September 18, 1964–January 13, 1967

Character: Major General Wiley Crowe
Played by: John Larkin
Date(s):   September 1964–1965

Replaced by: Brigadier General Ed Britt
Played by   Andrew Duggan
Date(s):   September 13, 1965–January 12, 1967

That war is hell goes without saying. That war can be glorified and presented as exciting entertainment is exemplified by this action adventure series set near England during World War II.

It is based on a novel and 1949 motion picture written by Sy Bartlett and Beirne Lay, Jr. Gregory Peck starred in the film and earned an Academy Award nomination for his portrayal of General Frank Savage.

Robert Lansing who brought much of the same intense emotional punch to the role as Peck had in the film, left the series after only one season. It has been revealed in published sources that Lansing became upset when he learned that ABC had decided to reduce his role and move the starting time of the hour-long series from nine thirty to ten o'clock, which is why he left.

On the air, Lansing's disappearance was explained by having General Savage killed—his plane shot down during a mission.

Taking his place was Captain Joe Gallagher, played by Paul Burke, who had been with the series since the beginning. Along with his new responsibilities, Joe Gallagher quickly rose through the ranks and eventually became a Colonel.

It was about this time that Savage's superior officer, Major General Wiley Crowe was replaced by Brigadier General Ed Britt, but this was for an entirely different reason. Actor John Larkin, who had played Mark Grainger on the NBC dramas, *Saints and Sinners* from September 17, 1962, to January 28, 1963, died unexpectedly on January 29, 1965, and had to be replaced. That is when Colonel Gallagher's superior officer became Brigadier General Ed Britt. The actor to don the General's uniform was Andrew Duggan, who starred as Cal Calhoun on *Bourbon Street Beat,* the ABC detective series which aired from October 5, 1959 to September 26, 1960. He also starred as George Rose on the short-lived situation comedy *Room for One More,* which aired on ABC from January 27 to September 22, 1962.

Leaving *Twelve O'Clock High* in no way damaged Robert Lansing's successful acting career. He went on to appear in episodes of many programs including sixteen episodes of *The Equalizer.* His later work includes two series for ABC. In the first he was Peter Murphy/Mark Wainwright in the *The Man Who Never Was,* which aired from September 7, 1966, to January 4, 1967. In the other he was Lieutenant Jack Curtis on *Automan,* which aired from December 15, 1983 to April 2, 1984. He also co-starred with Teri Garr in the March 29, 1968 *Star Trek* episode, "Assignment Earth." In that episode, which was actually a pilot for a proposed series, Robert Lansing played Gary Seven, a human who was trained by an unknown alien race and returned to earth ostensibly to save mankind.

Robert Lansing's replacement on *Twelve O'Clock High,* Paul

Burke, had played Detective Adam Flint on *Naked City* (See Entry).

21 JUMP STREET

April 12, 1987–September 17, 1990.   Fox
1990–1991   Syndicated

Character: Captain Richard Jenko
Played by: Frederic Forrest
Date(s):   April 12, 1978–1987

Replaced by: Captain Adam Fuller
Played by: Steven Williams
Date(s):   April 12, 1987–September 17, 1990

Character: Officer Tom "Tommy" Hanson
Played by: Johnny Depp
Date(s):   April 12, 1987–September 1990

Replaced by: Officer Anthony "Mac" McCann
Played by: Michael Bendetti
Date(s):   1990–1991

Character: Officer Harry Truman "H.T." Ioki
Played by: Dustin Nguyen
Date(s):   April 12, 1987–September 1990

Replaced by: Officer Joey Penhall
Played by: Peter DeLuise
Date(s):   1990–1991

Located just twenty-eight years and a new network away from *21 Beacon Street,* the police drama that starred Dennis Morgan as private investigator Dennis Chase (July 2, 1959–September 24, 1959, NBC; December 27, 1959–March 20, 1960, ABC) was *21 Jump Street,* a youth-oriented police drama that was one of the first successes for Fox Broadcasting.

Working out of an abandoned church at 21 Jump Street in Los Angeles was a special police unit made up of four cops who were even hipper than Peter (Michael Cole), Linc (Clarence Williams III), and Julie (Peggy Lipton) were on *The Mod Squad,* which aired on ABC from September 24, 1968 to August 23, 1973.

The requirements needed to become a member of the Jump Street team were good police training and good genetics. That is to say, the officers on the Jump Street unit had to look youthful enough to pose as students in high school (and later college)—to fight drugs, prostitution and even murder by going undercover inside the city's schools.

Leading this innovative group of undercover cops was Officer Tommy Hanson, played by Johnny Depp. He was originally played by Jeff Yagher, who was replaced by Depp after the pilot had been shot.

The other members of the unit included Officer Joey Penhall (Michael DeLuise), Officer Judy Hoffs (Holly Robinson), and Dustin Nguyen as Officer "H.T." Ioki. Their department superior was Captain Richard Jenko (Frederic Forrest), replaced by Captain Adam Fuller (Steven Williams) when Jenko was killed by a hit-and-run drunk driver.

Three years after jumping onto Fox's schedule, the popular series was dropped, though it did stay in production for the first-run syndication market. Also dropped were two of its regular cast members, Dustin Nguyen and Johnny Depp; the latter went on to star in the title roles of the 1990 John Waters musical comedy, CRY-BABY, and the 1990 Tim Burton romantic science fiction fantasy, EDWARD SCIS-SORHANDS.

Their replacements were Michael Bendetti as Officer "Mac" McCann and Peter DeLuise as Officer Joey Penhall, Doug Penhall's younger brother.

TWO GIRLS NAMED SMITH

January 20, 1951–October 13, 1951.   ABC

Character:	Babs Smith
Played by:	Peggy Ann Garner
Date(s):	January 20, 1951–September 22, 1951

Replaced by:	Babs Smith
Played by:	Marcia Henderson
Date(s):	September 29, 1951–October 13, 1951

Make that "three girls named Smith." The two girls mentioned in the program's title were Frances "Fran" Smith and her cousin Babs, two small-town girls who came to Manhattan in an effort to further their careers—Babs as a model, Fran as a singer. The three girls mentioned, refers not to another character; but to the number of actresses who filled those two roles.

Fran was played throughout the short run of the series by one actress, Peggy French. Babs, on the other hand, was played by two different actresses. The first was Peggy Ann Garner, a child star in films during the 1940s. Her first really noteworthy film role was in the 1944 drama, JANE EYRE, which starred Joan Fontaine in the title role and Peggy Ann Garner in the same role as a child. Certainly her most memorable role as a child actress was as Francie Nolan in the 1945 heart-wrenching drama A TREE GROWS IN BROOKLYN. Her performance was so good, in fact, that she was presented with a special Academy Award for "Best Child Actress."

Two Girls Named Smith was Ms. Garner's only series role, although she did work in more than fifty segments of episodic shows, including *Adventures in Paradise, Perry Mason, The Man from U.N.C.L.E.* and *The Patty Duke Show.* One of her last television appearances was on the September 21, 1967 episode of *Batman,* "Ring Around the Riddler," in which she appeared as television host Betsy Boldface.

Ms. Garner's replacement on *Two Girls Named Smith* (Marcia Henderson) followed up her role as Babs with another early

1950s comedy, *Dear Phoebe,* in which she played Mickey Riley, Bill Hastings' (Peter Lawford) romantic interest. The series aired on NBC from September 10, 1954 to September 11, 1956. Her many other appearances on episodic television include three episodes of *The Millionaire,* an episode of *Richard Diamond, Private Detective,* and two episodes of *Bat Masterson.* In 1961 she co-starred as Joyce Nicoll-Chance in an unsold pilot, *I Married a Dog,* which should not be confused with *Dad's a Dog,* or *Doogie Howser, M.D.* The unsold series pilot for *Dad's a Dog* aired on NBC on August 4, 1990, and starred comedian David Steinberg as Charles Dryden, a serious New York stage actor who moves to Malibu, California when he accepts a job to provide the off-camera voice for a dog in a sitcom. In the 1961 series, *I Married a Dog,* the friction is caused by the fact that Joyce's French poodle is standing between her and her new husband, Peter Chance, who was played by Hal March.

Doogie Howser, M.D. is an ABC series about an adolescent doctor (Neil Patrick Harris) who just happens to have a goofy nickname and has nothing whatsoever to do with dogs.

Two Girls Named Smith was seen Saturdays at noon. Back in the early 1950s it was not an unusual practice for a network to schedule a first-run situation comedy in this fashion. Actually, the idea wasn't such a bad one, but it took more than thirty years to catch on with quality syndicated sitcoms such as *Small Wonder* and *The Munsters Today,* which aired in the New York market on Saturday afternoons.

240-ROBERT

August 28, 1979–September 19, 1981.   ABC

Character:	Deputy Morgan Wainwright
Played by:	Joanna Cassidy
Date(s):	August 28, 1979–December 10, 1979

Replaced by:	Deputy Sandy Harper
Played by:	Pamela Hensley
Date(s):	March 7, 1981–September 19, 1981

In Los Angeles E.S.D. stands for Emergency Service Detail, a division of the Los Angeles County Sheriff's department. Its radio code is 240–Robert.

A team of three dedicated search-and-rescue workers is comprised of Deputy Dwayne L. "Thib" Thibideaux (Mark Harmon), Deputy Theodore "Trap" Roosevelt Applegate III (John Bennett Perry), and their good-looking helicopter pilot, Deputy Morgan Wainright, who for some reason didn't have a catchy nickname like the boys. They just called her Morgan— a rather masculine-sounding name. Still, there was nothing masculine about the beautiful and level-headed Morgan who was played by Joanna Cassidy during the first season. She had previously played Selma "Books" Cassidy on the situation comedy, *The Roller Girls,* which skated onto NBC's schedule on April 24, 1978, and got shoved off on May 10th the same year.

Ms. Cassidy gained high visibility as Dabney Coleman's very attractive television director, Jo Jo White, in the situation comedy, *Buffalo Bill,* which aired on NBC from May 31, 1983 to April 5, 1984. The following year, in an *A-Team*-like scenario, Joanna Cassidy starred in her own series as Elizabeth "Foxfire" Towne, a CIA agent who had served four years in prison "for a crime she didn't commit!" The series, *Code Name: Foxfire,* only lasted for a few weeks on NBC, airing from January 27 to March 22.

The *240–Robert* team returned, after summer reruns, on March 7, 1981, with a slightly different crew, as was pointed out in the *TV Guide* listing: "A young thrill seeker creates dangerous situations for Trap (John Bennett Perry) and two newcomers to the rescue team: chopper pilot Sandy Harper (Pamela Hensley) and Trap's partner Brett Cueva (Stephan Burns), whose lack of teamwork jeopardizes his job with the unit."

The new helicopter pilot was just as sexy as her predecessor,

if not more so, but it apparently wasn't enough to keep viewers tuned in for more than six months.

One of Pamela Hensley's most revealing roles (and costumes) was in the science fiction series, *Buck Rogers in the 25th Century,* in which she appeared in a recurring role as the sinister and often scantily-clad Princess Ardala (as in oh what a doll-a). Try as she might, she couldn't turn Colonel Rogers' (Gil Gerard) head, but as Janet Blake, the public relations director of Hope Memorial Hospital on *Marcus Welby, M.D.,* she did get to marry a doctor. Not Dr. Welby (Robert Young), but his handsome assistant, Dr. Steven Kiley, played by the ever-popular James Brolin. The happy couple were married on the October 21, 1975 broadcast. Ms. Hensley, who first appeared on the series on September 9, 1975, departed on May 11, 1976. She was reunited with her television husband when she checked in to the January 18, 1984 episode of *Hotel,* "Passages."

U

U.F.O.

1972[1].   Syndicated

Character:	Miss Eland
Played by:	Norma Roland
Date(s):	1970

Replaced by:	Miss Holland
Played by:	Lois Maxwell
Date(s):	1970

Ever since the acronym for the phenomenon known as Unidentified Flying Objects was coined in 1950, UFO's have become a part of the American psyche and there have been countless programs, fictional and factual, dealing with the subject. Although the term is meant to refer to any unknown flying object it is equated—even regarded as synonymous with sightings of flying saucers and other "supposed" extraterrestrial visitors.

Sometimes even a known spacecraft such as *Star Trek*'s Starship Enterprise might be classified as a U.F.O. In the January 26, 1967 episode, "Tomorrow is Yesterday," the Enterprise is hurled back into the twentieth century by the gravitational force of a black star and is reported by the staff of the Omaha Air Base as a UFO sighting.

The same year that *Star Trek* was canceled by NBC as a first-run series, Gerry and Sylvia Anderson launched *Captain Scarlet and the Mysterons*, the fifth of their futuristic series featuring their Supermarionation techniques. The storyline establishes Spectrum, an international organization as the vehicle for safeguarding the inhabitants of the planet earth from alien invaders, principally the Mysterons from Mars.

It's all pretty exciting, with wonderfully inventive special effects including the addition of a new technique that used real human hands in plastic gloves to double for the marionettes in close-ups, to create an illusion of dexterity not possible with the puppets.

Apparently, Gerry and Sylvia liked the idea enough to rework it for live actors in *U.F.O.*, their first of two live-action series (*Space 1999* [See Entry] was their other).

In the *UFO* storyline, UFOs are seen as a threat to earth and the world leaders unite to form S.H.A.D.O. (the Supreme Headquarters, Alien Defense Organization). And, so as not to alarm the general public, the entire complex is built underground and under London's Harlington-Straker Film Studios.

Ed Bishop, who provided the voice for Captain Blue on *Captain Scarlet and the Mysterons,* strung along with the Andersons for all twenty-six episodes as Ed Straker, the commander of S.H.A.D.O.

Straker's first secretary was Miss Eland (Norma Roland), whose last appearance was in "Conflict," the sixth episode of the series. She was replaced in episode seven, "Court Martial," by a secretary with a similar-sounding name, Miss Holland.

Miss Holland was played by Lois Maxwell, an actress who may very well be the world's most famous secretary, Miss Moneypenny, having worked for M and appeared with three of the screen's five James Bonds as the first of four Moneypennys.

Ms. Maxwell's James Bond portfolio includes DR. NO, 1962; FROM RUSSIA WITH LOVE, 1963; GOLDFINGER, 1964; THUNDERBALL, 1965; YOU ONLY LIVE TWICE, 1967; ON HER MAJESTY'S SECRET SERVICE, 1969; DIAMONDS ARE FOREVER, 1971; LIVE AND LET DIE, 1973; THE MAN WITH THE GOLDEN GUN, 1974; THE SPY WHO LOVED ME, 1977; MOONRAKER, 1979; FOR YOUR EYES ONLY, 1981; OCTOPUSSY, 1983; and A VIEW TO A KILL, 1985.

On May 9th, 1969, Lois Maxwell appeared with Roger Moore (the screen's second James Bond) in "Simon and Delilah," the twenty-seventh episode of *The Saint*.

UNCLE CROC'S BLOCK

September 6, 1975–February 14, 1976.   ABC

Character:	Rabit Ears
Played by:	Johnny Silver
Date(s):	unknown

Replaced by:	Rabit Ears
Played by:	Alfie Wise
Date(s):	unknown

This was an almost sacrilegious attempt at satirizing children's television programs. What was so misguided about the concept was that it was not aimed at adults, who may have gotten the

---

1. UFO was produced in England in 1970, but wasn't released for syndication in the United States until 1972.

satirical inside jokes, but at children—the very audience it was making fun of.

Airing as part of ABC's Saturday morning lineup, *Uncle Croc's Block* was a program-within-a-program. It centered around a kiddie show host, Uncle Croc (Charles Nelson Reilly), outfitted in a crocodile costume, who, off camera, vocalized the fact that he really didn't like kids or his job very much.

This scenario calls to mind a real children's host, Uncle Don, who was said to have uttered one of broadcasting's most famous bloopers: "I guess that'll hold the little bastards." In reality, Uncle Don, Don Carney (Howard Rice), never said anything of the sort. It was actually concocted by a Baltimore newspaper columnist to fill space on a slow news day. Moreover, *Uncle Don* wasn't even heard in Baltimore!

Uncle Croc's Block, which is supposed to spoof all hosted children's programs, takes a particularly strong jab at *Captain Kangaroo* (Bob Keeshan) with its Captain Klagaroo character.

The other adult characters include Mr. Mean Jeans, a take off of the Captain's lovable Mr. Green Jeans (Hugh "Lumpy" Brannum). There was even a guy in a rabbit suit named "Rabit Ears," possibly a knockoff extension of the Captain's adorable Bunny Rabbit puppet.

Among the actors who played these imposters was a fifty-five-year-old Dead End Kid, Huntz Hall, who had played Horace Debussey "Sach" Jones in all forty-eight of the BOWERY BOYS comedies. The two actors who suited up as what might be considered a Pooka, were Johnny Silver and Alfie Wise.

The network knocked off *Uncle Croc's Block* after only sixteen episodes. The National Association of Better Broadcasters called *Uncle Croc's Block* "A monument of junk."

UNDER ONE ROOF *see:* SPENCER

U.S. MARSHAL *see:* SHERIFF OF COCHISE

THE UNTOUCHABLES

October 15, 1959–September 10, 1963.   ABC
January 11, 1993–October 1, 1994   Syndicated

Character:	Agent Cam Allison
Played by:	Anthony George
Date(s):	October 15, 1959–April 28, 1960
Replaced by:	Agent Lee Hobson
Played by:	Paul Picerni
Date(s):	October 13, 1960–May 21, 1963
Character:	Eliot Ness
Played by:	Robert Stack
Date(s):	October 15, 1959–September 10, 1963
	November 11, 1991 (*The Return of Eliot Ness,* NBC)
Replaced by:	Young Eliot Ness
Played by:	Joseph Gonzalez
Date(s):	January 11, 1993
Date(s):	February 22, 1993
Replaced by:	Eliot Ness
Played by:	Tom Amandes
Date(s):	January 11, 1993–October 1, 1994
Character:	Agent Martin Flaherty
Played by:	Jerry Paris
Date(s):	October 15, 1959–September 10, 1963
Replaced by:	Agent Mike Malone
Played by:	John Rhys-Davies
Date(s):	January 11, 1993–October 1, 1994
Character:	Agent William Youngfellow
Played by:	Abel Fernandez
Date(s):	October 15, 1959–September 10, 1963
Replaced by:	Agent George Steelman
Played by:	Michael Horse
Date(s):	January 11, 1993–October 1, 1994
Character:	Agent Jack Rossman
Played by:	Steve London
Date(s):	1960–September 10, 1963
Replaced by:	Paul Robbins
Played by:	David Elliot
Date(s):	January 11, 1993–October 1, 1994
Character:	Alphonse "Al" "Scarface" "Snorky" Capone
Played by:	Neville Brand
Date(s):	October 15, 1959–September 10, 1963
Replaced by:	Alphonse "Al" "Scarface" "Snorky" Capone
Played by:	Vincent Guastaferro
Date(s):	April 17, 1988 (*Frank Nitti: The Enforcer,* ABC)
Replaced by:	Young Capone
Played by:	Ethan Brosowsky
Date(s):	January 11, 1993
Replaced by:	Alphonse "Al" "Scarface" "Snorky" Capone
Played by:	William Forsythe
Date(s):	January 11, 1993–October 1, 1994

Replaced by:	Frank ''The Enforcer'' Nitti	
Played by:	Bruce Gordon	
Date(s):	October 15, 1959–September 10, 1963	

Replaced by:	Frank ''The Enforcer'' Nitti
Played by:	Anthony LaPaglia
Date(s):	April 17, 1988 (*Frank Nitti: The Enforcer*, ABC)

Replaced by:	Young Nitti
Played by:	Angelo Campo
Date(s):	January 11, 1993

Replaced by:	Frank ''The Enforcer'' Nitti
Played by:	Paul Regina
Date(s):	January 11, 1993–

Character:	Young Louis Basille
Played by:	George Carson
Date(s):	January 11, 1993

Replaced by:	Louis Basille
Played by:	Joe Guzaldo
Date(s):	January 11, 1993–January 18, 1993

Gripping, exciting, and violent stories of Eliot Ness and the Untouchables . . . and not altogether accurate. Oh sure, there was an Al Capone, a Ma Barker and a Dutch Schultz, but they weren't all brought to justice by Eliot Ness. Ma Barker, for instance, was picked up by the FBI and not by The Untouchables. No matter, *The Untouchables* was riveting TV.

Eliot Ness and the Untouchables first screeched onto the small screen in a two-part pilot which aired on *Desilu Playhouse* on April 20 and 27, 1959. This pilot was based on *The Untouchables: The Real Story* written by Eliot Ness with Oscar Fraley and published in 1947.

In the book, Ness told how he chose his nine agents from the more than fifty dossiers of Prohibition agents available to him. And although there were many similarities in the backgrounds and abilities of the characters in the book and on the screen, none of the agents' names were the same in any version of *The Untouchables* except Basile, whose first name was Frank and not Louis.

The real ''Untouchables'' chosen by Eliot Ness were Marty Lahart, an Irishman, a Prohibition Bureau special agent and former postal worker; Sam Seager, a former guard in the death house at Sing Sing; and Barney Cloonan, a big man, who in addition to wanting to get out from behind a desk and in on some action, became what Ness called the ''pen and pencil'' detective for the team, responsible for noting every detail of every raid and running down every lead.

Others were Lyle Chapman, a former end on the Colgate University football team and an honor student with a ''gifted mind''; Tom Friel, from Scranton, was a former Pennsylvania State Trooper; and Joe Leeson from the Detroit division whom Ness praised by saying, ''Leeson's ability as a driver was almost legendary. . . .'' Mike King was ''a drawling Virgin-

ian,'' and Paul Robsky, a telephone expert from New Jersey with a razor-sharp mind.

Last was Bill Gardner, a six-foot-three Indian from the Los Angeles division who had played football for the Carlisle Indians. More than just a football player, Gardner was singled out by Knute Rockne in a *Collier's* magazine article as one of his choices for that year's (1929) All American Team.

A tenth, unofficial man on the elite team was Ness's personal driver, an ex-con named Frank Basile.

Television's first version of *The Untouchables* told the story of the war between mobster Al Capone (Neville Brand) and a prohibition agent named Eliot Ness (Robert Stack).

In the storyline, Eliot Ness met with the new United States District Attorney, Beecher Asbury (Frank Wilcox), on June 24, 1929, and it was during that meeting that he came up with the idea of putting together a special squad of agents from all over the country, a team of agents who were not on the take and could not be bought by the mob—making them ''untouchables.''

After pouring over the files of thousands of agents, Eliot Ness decided on seven agents. Lamaar Kane (Peter Leeds) was a law school graduate out of the Richmond bureau, married and the father of two children. Out of the San Francisco bureau came Eric Hansen (Eddie Firestone), who had worked as a prison guard on San Quentin's death row. Former Boston police officer Martin Flaherty (Bill Williams) was chosen because of his outstanding bureau arrest record. As a former telephone company lineman, Jack Rossman of New York (Paul Dubov) became a member of the elite team because of his wiretapping expertise. William Longfellow (Abel Fernandez), a full-blooded Cherokee Indian, was a second-team All-American in 1924, and Tom Kopka (Robert Osterloh), of the Scranton Bureau, was a former Pennsylvania State Trooper and World War I hero.

The last member of the squad, and Eliot's closest friend, was Joe Fuselli (Keenan Wynn)—a very unusual choice. Not because he was a member of the Prohibition Bureau, or that he had ''the finest pair of driving hands in Chicago,'' but because he was an ex-con who had served five years in Joliet for armed robbery.

Ness is infused with passion when Fuselli is killed for getting too close to the location of the largest of the Capone breweries, located in the Chicago stockyards.

The team acquired its nickname because of a headline that ran in the Final Edition of the *Chicago Record:* ''Untouchables Defy Capone.'' The article, which was read aloud, said, ''They have proven to Capone and his mob that they are Untouchable.''

The success of the television series led producer Quinn Martin to cut the 1959 pilot together and release it as a theatrical motion picture under the title THE SCARFACE MOB in 1962.

Six months after the two-part pilot aired on *Desilu Playhouse* (April 20 and 27, 1959), *The Untouchables,* starring Robert Stack, became a weekly series, with some changes in the roles of his Untouchables. Wire-tap expert Jack Rossman, who was played by Paul Dubov in the pilot, was replaced by Steve London. The full-blooded Cherokee, William Longfellow, played by Abel Fernandez had his last name changed to Youngfellow. Agent Martin Flaherty was taken over by Jerry

Paris, who would later become Dick Van Dyke's dentist and next-door neighbor, Jerry Helper, on *The Dick Van Dyke Show.* Added to the cast was Anthony George as Agent Cam Allison. Missing were Lamaar Kane, Eric Hansen and Tom Kopka.

George left *The Untouchables* to star as Don Corey, the owner of the posh detective agency, Checkmate, Inc., on the CBS series, *Checkmate,* which aired from September 17, 1960 to September 19, 1962, and co-starred *Family Affair*'s (See Entry) butler, Mr. French (Sebastian Cabot) as Carl Hyatt. Anthony George later turned to the daytime soap operas and played Dr. Tony Vincente on *Search for Tomorrow* from 1970 to 1975.

To replace George on *The Untouchables,* the producers chose to cast Paul Picerni, the actor who had played Tony Liguri in the pilot, as Agent Lee Hobson.

In 1987, moviegoers were treated to a major motion picture version of THE UNTOUCHABLES starring Kevin Costner as Eliot Ness and Robert De Niro as Al Capone. Ness' right-hand man, James "Jim/Jimmy" Malone, was played by Sean Connery, who won an Academy Award for Best Supporting Actor, which seemed to be more a gift from the Academy for his past work than recognition of his solid performance in this less-than-stellar film.

Like Joe Fuselli in the original pilot, Malone is killed—here for getting too close to Capone's bookkeeper—which served to fuel Ness' passion to put an end to the reign of organized crime kingpin Al Capone.

The picture began with text that was superimposed on a screen that was absent of sound or narration: "Prohibition has transformed Chicago into a City at War. Rival gangs compete for control of the city's billion dollar empire of illegal alcohol, enforcing their will with the hand grenade and the tommy gun. It is the time of the gang lords. It is the time of Al Capone."

Vincent Guastaferro brought Al Capone back to the small screen in *Frank Nitti: The Enforcer,* an ABC made-for-television movie that starred Anthony LaPaglia as Al Capone's lieutenant, Frank Nitti. The two-hour telefilm about the Chicago gangster, born Francesco Raphael Nitto, aired on April 17, 1988.

Five years later, Eliot Ness and The Untouchables returned to television in a two-hour made-for-television movie that was the pilot for an updated syndicated series. Though there was a line in the closing credits that read, "Based on the television series *The Untouchables,* and books by Oscar Fraley with Eliot Ness and Paul Robsky," none of the real agents was a direct match for any of those depicted on film.

One character, in particular, was Ness' new right-hand agent, Mike Malone. A man of great girth who sported a beard, spoke with a Scottish accent that was "RRR" for "RRR" an unmistakable lift of Sean Connery's Jim Malone character in the 1987 feature.

This two-hour pilot took a different tack from the original series and the theatrical release. Like the others, it began with a short narration. This one used both an on-screen superimposition and a narrator, though there was no attempt to mimic the clipped nasal delivery of Walter Winchell, who served as narrator for the Robert Stack series:

"It is the time of Al Capone, king of Chicago's illegal booze industry. Capone has a stranglehold on America's second largest city. He owns its police department. Its politicians. Its legal system. No one has had the courage to challenge Capone's tyrannical rule . . . until now."

The TV movie opened at some fictional point in the series' future, with Ness and the Untouchables raiding an illegal distillery and becoming engaged in a bloody gun fight that left Tony Pagano, Ness' youngest agent, shot in the the chest. He thought it was his heart and seemed to be near death when he was taken away on a stretcher as Eliot picks up a framed picture of Al Capone with a handwritten note attached: "This town is *mine!*"

NESS: Damn him. How in the name of God did the world get visited by a monster like this?

The answer to Ness' question is told through flashbacks (some filmed in black-and-white) beginning in 1910—an interesting approach that had not been used before. Twenty years later the new Eliot Ness is having the same meeting with the U.S. district attorney that Robert Stack had. This time the district attorney's name is Emerson Q. Johnson (Ned Schmidtke), which was almost historically accurate; the name of the man on which the character was based was George Emmerson Q. Johnson. Here he was at a press conference speaking about the creation of a Federal Task Force to put an end to organized crime in Chicago.

The agent chosen to head up this new task force is Eliot Ness who presents his selections to Mr. Johnson in a scene that is strangely reminiscent of *Mission: Impossible.* Ness brings with him a stack of manila folders and proceeds to present each selection for Johnson's approval—almost like Jim Phelps throwing down the files of the agents he has selected. Ness' narrative is supported through the use of film clips of each man.

Tony Pagano (John Haymes Newton) is from the Detroit office, a Harvard graduate with degrees in Engineering and English. In addition to having an exemplary record, Tony drives midget race cars in his spare time. Paul Robbins (David Elliot), from the St. Louis office, is an ex-fighter pilot for the Army and worked as a district attorney before joining the Treasury Department. George Steelman, a full-blooded Cherokee Indian from the Omaha office, is a former Carlyle University football star and expert wire-tapper. Steelman was played by Michael Horse, the Mescalero Apache who brought Tonto back to the big screen in THE LEGEND OF THE LONE RANGER, the 1982 motion picture based on *The Lone Ranger* (See Entry) television series.

From April 8, 1990, to June 10, 1991, Michael Horse played Deputy Tommy "The Hawk" Hill on the ABC dramatic serial, *Twin Peaks.* Most recently he appeared opposite Wesley Snipes in the 1992 theatrical thriller, PASSENGER 57.

Louis Basille (Joe Guzaldo) is a former mob member who has turned against them after his son was killed by crossfire in a violent street fight. He joined Ness's task force to bring Capone down, but wound up being murdered in the premiere episode for going to the other side. Last, but not least, there was ex-cop Mike Malone (John Rhys-Davies). These were the new Untouchables.

The Eliot Ness of the '90s was played by the handsome, soft-spoken Tom Amandes who possesses a quiet strength which, by his own admission, gives him a James Stewart-like quality.

"I'm a theater actor mainly here in Chicago. I never really have traveled out to either coast looking for work, and have been able to pick up little bits of TV and film work here. Some of the stuff I've done that you would know of was a nice part in Dana Carvey's first film, OPPORTUNITY KNOCKS [1990]. I played his next-door neighbor, Larry. I also played a waiter in the 1992 Dolly Parton film, STRAIGHT TALK."[2] said Amandes.

His limited work on television includes a guest villain on the ABC adventure series *Sable,* which was filmed on location in Chicago and aired from November 7, 1987 to January 2, 1988. "I played an Englishman, Jamison, who had a grudge against Jon Sable (Lewis Van Bergen)," he said.

In an ironic piece of casting, the actor chosen to portray the dedicated treasury agent hellbent on closing down Al Capone's illegal breweries, was himself the spokesperson for a domestic beer.

Radio listeners with a sharp ear may be able to pick up Amandes' friendly, homespun voice on the appealing series of spots for Rolling Rock beer. "I'm Joe Garvey . . . Hi, this is Joe Garvey, philosopher, beer drinker . . . ,'' chuckled Amandes.

"When I got the call for *The Untouchables,* they had me audition for the role of Alexander "Alex" Jamie, who was Ness's brother-in-law, mentor, and boss [In the pilot, the role was played by Patrick Clear.]

"Our producer, Tim Iacofano, and Ernest Dickerson, our director on the pilot, were in the room. I read for the part of Alexander Jamie, they said, 'Thank you,' and I walked out. From what Tim tells me, they kind of looked at each other afterwards and said 'That could be our Eliot Ness.'

"Then I got a call from my agent saying, 'They loved you, they loved you. They want you to read for Eliot Ness.' And I said, sarcastically, 'Yeah, right, they're gonna cast some no-name from Chicago. Get out of here.'

"But I said, 'What the heck. We'll give them our best shot.' and I read through the lines, which were actually Malone's lines from the DePalma film.

"I got a call back and they said they wanted to put me on tape for the producer, Christopher Crowe. At the time I was in rehearsals for *Othello* at the University of Chicago's Court Theater, playing the thankless role of Lodovico," chuckled Amandes. He continued.

"They flew me out to L.A. and initially I read for a room full of their Paramount 'suits' and assorted other people. [After I was through, I] went out of the room and they saw a couple of other guys waiting to be auditioned, though they weren't names that I knew. I do know that Paramount was looking mainly in L.A. for the big roles, so I kind of slipped in the back door.

"After that, [casting director] Mike [Fenton] came out and said, 'Okay, Tom, why don't you give my office a call and set up your flight back to Chicago. We're all set.' I said, 'Okay.' Then he came out a few minutes later and said, 'Oops, change of plans. We want to put all three of you on tape on Monday.' I couldn't, because I would have missed the entire preview week of *Othello* and I really didn't want to do that. So I asked, 'Can I do that now?'

"They agreed and rushed me off to some soundstage and did a little makeup on me. There was a studio audience there, which made me feel right at home, having the theater background.

"That was the seventeenth of September '92. Twelve days later, on the 29th, I was backstage at the Court Theater getting ready for a matinee of *Othello* when I got the message to call my agent and I did. When she told me I got the role, I screamed and the cast from *Othello* came out to congratulate me. It was a very joyous little moment. I was replaced in *Othello* by Danny Sullivan and I was out of there the next day," recalled Amandes.

"I was born in 1959, which is the year the [Robert] Stack series started. I remember it, but it was not something I watched as a kid. I remember seeing it in reruns at some off hour on Sunday mornings—maybe opposite *Bullwinkle*—and at that age, *Bullwinkle* won out," said Amandes.

Compared to Robert Stack, Tom Amandes may seem an unlikely choice to play the driven leader of the Untouchables, but his interpretation of the character is actually much closer to the real Ness, and this is the way the character was written in the script.

"I think the approach that they took with this character was that there was this well-meaning guy that happened to find himself caught in a city where the gangs were taking over and felt he had to do something about it.

"In the pilot, Eliot Ness was written as this kind of gawky, young idealist, which is not Robert Stack at all—which is why *I* got the role. But at the beginning, I would get these calls from Chris Crowe saying 'Listen Tom, they want me to ask you to give it just a little more of that jock Robert Stack kind of feel.' I tried to play the writing and that's what I got out of it. You have to bring a lot of yourself to a role.

"Anytime I've done a role on stage that someone else has done in a film, I've avoided watching it. Just because you don't want to be thinking of other people when you're up there. You've got to start with yourself. Now that I have a couple of episodes under my belt, I'm tempted to pull out some of the Robert Stack videos and watch them," said Amandes, who told how he happened to see the 1987 motion picture starring Kevin Costner.

"At the time THE UNTOUCHABLES was on HBO, I was out of work because I had just quit my job as the artistic director of a theater. To make a few bucks, I took a job at a trade show in Las Vegas doing some sort of a 'Dick Clark' thing. It was absolutely bottom of the barrel in terms of work or career.

"At one point, in the depths of depression, I remember going back to my hotel room and flipping on the TV and there was the Costner movie. The film was shot here in Chicago and had a lot of my friends in it—and there I was in Las Vegas doing a trade show. It's actually quite ironic that I wound up getting this role.

"It was a great movie. I've always loved doing period stuff and I think I watched it twice that week," he said.

Although he would have liked to, Tom Amandes didn't have much time to prepare for his role as Eliot Ness.

"I had two days from the the time I was cast to the time I was

---

2. This and other quotations by Tom Amandes in this entry on *The Untouchables* are from an exclusive telephone interview with Mr. Amandes on February 11, 1993.

in front of the camera. Luckily I didn't have to jump into it full force. We started out with the scenes of the younger Eliot Ness. Paramount was just great. They have a research department with people who pulled out one article after another about Eliot Ness, so I was able to read through these old newspaper clippings.

"I think one of the things that made me an attractive choice was that here I am, this guy who's been living in Chicago. My folks are from Chicago. My mom grew up on Clark Street not far from the St. Valentine's Day Massacre. So these are stories that I kind of grew up with," said Amandes.

"In addition to reading *The Untouchables,* which Eliot Ness wrote with Oscar Fraley, I also spent a bit of time with Jerry Singer, who's with the Department of Alcohol, Tobacco and Firearms, which is what the Department of Prohibition became after Prohibition. He's promised to take me on a raid, which the Paramount people are not too crazy about—but we'll make it a 'light' raid," he laughed.

Discussing the differences between the original series and the one currently in production, Tom Amandes said, "Unlike the Robert Stack version, which focused on the action, we're trying to develop a bit more of the relationships between the men and me and between my wife and me, which I think is important," Amandes said.

Amandes also spoke good-naturedly about the critics' reactions to his portrayal of Eliot Ness—specifically, the comparisons they drew not between himself and Robert Stack, but between himself and another well-known actor.

Laughing about the comparisons, Amandes said, "I'll sum it up in two words: 'Jimmy Stewart,' that's pretty much been the reaction. I respect him a heck of a lot as an actor—as I respect Robert Stack. But I think if you could cast anybody at all for the stuff we're writing, you'd cast a young Jimmy Stewart. You have the integrity, the humor, the engaging quality that he always had.

"I kind of have the curse to look a little bit like him, sound a little bit like him—you put a hat on me and I'm him. For years I've gotten that comparison, no matter what show I'm doing. I was doing George Bernard Shaw a couple of years ago and there it was in the review—it didn't even matter that I was doing an English accent. Back in 1984 I did a biographical piece on Carl Sandberg and the Jimmy Stewart comparison appeared in just about every review. So it's one of those things that I've learned to appreciate. If you're going to be compared with somebody in American movies—who better?" asked Amandes rhetorically. He went on to say, "I take that as positive feedback. We tend to do that in this business anyway—compare actors to other actors.

"Will I be Eliot Ness for the rest of my life? Will I be Jimmy Stewart for the rest of my life? Who knows. What the heck, as long as I'm working," concluded Amandes, philosophically.

Untouchable Tony Pagano was played by John Haymes Newton, who leaped onto the small screen in 1988 as the title character in the Alexander and Ilya Salkind production of *The Adventures of Superboy* (See Entry). He was later replaced by Gerard Christopher. In 1992, Newton was featured in the Touchstone film, ALIVE.

After some questionable police work as a cadet in the 1986 comedy, POLICE ACADEMY 3: BACK IN TRAINING, David James Elliott was tapped by *The Untouchables* producer, Christopher Crowe, to take on the mob as Paul Robbins, who is in part based on Paul Robsky.

Stepping into the Mike Malone role (Jim in the motion picture) created by Academy Award winner Sean Connery is John Rhys-Davies, who worked with Connery in the 1984 blockbuster, INDIANA JONES AND THE LAST CRUSADE. In this, the third of the Indiana Jones films, Rhys-Davies played Indy's Egyptian friend, Sallah, the same role he played in the original 1964 film, RAIDERS OF THE LOST ARK. In a somewhat related credit, Rhys-Davies hosts the critically acclaimed Learning Channel series, *Archaeology.*

Their adversary, Al Capone, was played by William Forsythe, who appeared as the comic-book criminal Flattop in Warren Beatty's 1990 Academy Award-winning film, DICK TRACY. That same year, he was also seen as Polozov in the Timothy Hutton/Nastassja Kinski romantic drama, TORRENTS OF SPRING. Unlike Neville Brand, who played the mobster—who was born in Naples, Italy and raised in Brooklyn—with a distinct Italian accent, William Forsythe, like Al Pacino chose to give him a more regional accent and had him speak a New York street dialect.

Backing up Al Capone was his cousin, Frank Nitti, also known as "The Enforcer," played in this version by Paul Regina, who told how he was cast for the role.

"Initially, I had read for the part of John Torrio [Capone's Godfather in the two-hour pilot]. They liked what I did and they asked me if I'd come back and do it with an Italian accent. I agreed and worked on it over the weekend. But the day before I was supposed to go in to do Torrio again, my agent suggested I read for Nitti, which is the part they cast me in,"[3] said Regina.

This was, of course, not the first time Nitti was brought to the screen. Most recently he was played by Anthony LaPaglia in the 1988 ABC made-for-television movie, *Frank Nitti: The Enforcer,* and the previous year by Billy Drago in THE UNTOUCHABLES motion picture. The Frank Nitti that did battle with Robert Stack's Eliot Ness was played by Bruce Gordon.

"As a kid, I must have seen Bruce Gordon when I watched *The Untouchables,* but I don't really have any memory of his playing the role of Frank Nitti. I just remember Robert Stack standing around and saying, 'This smells of Nitti.' That's all I remember, Stack's way of saying 'Nitti.' By the way, I got to work with Robert Stack in a really touching episode of *Brothers,* directed by Jerry Lewis. I played Cliff Waters on the series and in the episode, which aired in 1986, Robert Stack guest starred as Donald's father, Mr. Maltby," recalled Regina.

Even though Paul Regina had done extensive research for the role, he purposely avoided watching the other portrayals of Frank Nitti so that they would not influence his interpretation, and he said he was influenced by omission.

3. This and following quotations by Paul Regina in this entry on *The Untouchables* are from an exclusive telephone interview with Mr. Regina on January 30, 1993.

''During a press conference at Paramount the question was put to Bill [William Forsythe], 'What is it like playing Capone after De Niro, Jason Robards and Rod Steiger?' I interjected that my personal feeling about playing Nitti is that in the year 2050 when they do the third series, somebody will be asking, 'Now Paul Regina played Frank Nitti from 1993 to the year 2000. What are you going to do different?' I really have an opportunty here to create the definitive Nitti because even though he's been played by a number of other actors, there's no image that comes to mind when you say 'Nitti,' '' said Regina.

One of the reasons that Paul Regina's Frank Nitti was so multi-faceted was that the writers and producers have taken some creative license with his character in order to keep the core cast to manageable numbers, in much the same way that *L.A. Law* (See Entry) trimmed its ensemble. More specifically, instead of introducing additional lieutenants, Paul Regina's Nitti has been painted with broader strokes that include shades of some of the other people who were close to Capone, including his brother, Ralph.

When asked if he would ever consider leaving the role, Regina reflected that, contractural obligations aside, ''It would almost have to be 'Nittimania' before I would even consider such a notion.''

Also featured in both of *The Untouchables* pilots was Eliott Ness's girlfriend/wife. Robert Stack's Ness dated Patricia Crowley as Betty Anderson. Ms. Crowley later played Joan Nash on the NBC situation comedy, *Please Don't Eat the Daisies*. In the 1993 series, Nancy Everhard played Eliot Ness' wife, Catherine. A year earlier, Nancy Everhard's character, Kay Lockman, was written out of the NBC police drama, *Reasonable Doubts* (See Entry), and replaced by Kay Lenz as Maggie Zombro.

Ness concludes the very interesting 1993 telefilm, and sets up the series to come with his closing line to Malone: ''Beginning tomorrow, we're going to start doing some good.''

V

VALERIE

March 1, 1986–July 20, 1991. NBC-CBS

Character:	Valerie Angela Hogan
Played by:	Valerie Harper
Date(s):	March 3, 1986–September 14, 1987
Replaced by:	Sandy Hogan
Played by:	Sandy Duncan
Date(s):	September 21, 1987–July 20, 1991

It began as your usual situation comedy: a working mother, a heartthrob teenage son, his two younger fraternal twin brothers, and a seldom-seen international airline pilot for a dad.

The series title was simple: the first name of the series star, Valerie Harper, was also her character's first name. All perfectly simple and straightforward—but not for long, because the star of the series disappeared.

Conflicting stories reported that Valerie Harper either walked off the show or was removed from the program in an ugly dispute with the production company (Miller Boyett Productions, Lorimar Television and NBC).

When the first episode of the 1987/1988 season aired on September 21, 1987, *Valerie* was retitled *Valerie's Family* and a new character was introduced to take over where Ms. Harper had left off.

Here's what happened according to a Sandy Duncan cover story by Helen Newton that appeared in the December 31, 1988 issue of *TV Guide:*

"Just as the show was going into its second season after a reasonably successful run, the producers found themselves having to replace Valerie Harper. It wasn't like *Dallas,* where cast members can come and go and come again without a ripple. Harper played the central character, the mother of three teenage boys, and her absence was likely to confuse and alienate an audience and make it difficult to sell the show in syndication, which is how the producers make money."[1]

At a point when the show's co-executive producers Thomas L. Miller and Bob Boyett had assurances that Valerie Harper was not going to return to the series, they asked Brandon Tartikoff, president of NBC Entertainment, if they could have Sandy Duncan, who had just completed work on *Act II,* an unsold pilot for that network. Tartikoff said "Great" and Sandy Duncan became Sandy Hogan.

"Despite the awkwardness of stepping into an existing show, Duncan thought the opportunity was great too. . . . 'But I made it clear that I did not want to be in the middle,' Sandy recalls. 'I would only accept if it was absolutely sure that Valerie was not coming back. It's not true that the producers had me in the wings waiting while they got rid of Valerie.' "[2]

The transition episode blends the storyline exposition, comedy and even some good old-fashioned tear-jerking. In one of the first bits of dialogue traded between David Hogan (Jason Bateman) and his dad Michael (Josh Taylor), we learn that Valerie died in an automobile accident six months earlier. Sandy, Michael's recently divorced sister and a high school counselor, has moved from Minneapolis in order to care for her brother's family, and she tells Michael, "I just think it's time for everyone to get on with their lives."

Yet, as in real life, Aunt Sandy does have some difficulty winning her oldest nephew over. David, who has been trying to keep the family together since his mother's death, has become what *TV Guide* described as a "supermom." At the end of the episode Sandy and David have it out. Sandy tells him that deciding to move in with her brother's family was a difficult decision for her and one that she gave a great deal of thought to. She tells David that she made her decision to move in because of her feelings for him and his brothers, her brother and her deceased sister-in-law.

SANDY:	For crying out loud, David. I'm your godmother. I was in the hospital when you were born. I held you in my arms while you were being baptized. I love you so much.
DAVID:	I love you too.

1. Newton, Helen. "Does Jason Bateman Listen to Sandy Duncan? 'Of Course Not,' She Says." *TV Guide,* Vol. 36, No. 53, Issue #1866, December 31, 1988, p. 3.
2. *Ibid.,* p. 2.

SANDY:	Then why won't you let me help you?
DAVID:	I don't know. Just . . . I feel that if I don't hold on tight to everything . . . it'll all just . . . I don't know . . . go away.
SANDY:	David, I'm not going anywhere. I want to be part of this family. But you have to let me. Don't shut me out. Just try me a little. Okay?
DAVID:	I'm really glad you're here. (Sandy stands up and hugs David.)

Things were working out so well with Sandy Duncan in the lead that the producers decided to change the name of the program one last time. The change took place on Monday, June 6, 1988, with on-air teasers run during breaks in that evening's episode of *ALF:*

"*Valerie's Family* is changing its name. Will it be *The Hogan Family? The Hogan Family?* or *The Hogan Family?* Tune in next and find out."

The answer came during *ALF*'s closing credits, as the voice-over said, "Next, *Valerie's Family* becomes *The Hogan Family*—just like that."

And just like that Valerie Harper returned to television. "CBS is premiering *City,* Valerie Harper's return to situation comedy, on Monday, January 29 [1990] (8:30–9 p.m. NYT). Ironically, *The Hogan Family* occupies that time slot on NBC."[3]

In an interview on WWOR-TV's special, *Joe Franklin's First Annual 40th Anniversary Show,* Valerie Harper said about her lawsuit against the producers of *Valerie:* "The truth is, vindication is much sweeter than revenge. I don't have any bad feelings. Everything is fine. I really don't harbor any bad feelings." And why should she when the newspaper headlines read, "Jurors Award Valerie Harper $1.4 Million, Cut of Profits."

The Hogan Family completed its run on NBC on June 18, 1990. Then, on Saturday, September 15, 1990, at the beginning of the series' sixth season, the show moved to CBS and the Hogan family moved to California in a two-part episode entitled "California Dreamin'."

VEGA$

September 20, 1978–September 16, 1981.   ABC

Character:	Sergeant Bella Archer
Played by:	Naomi Stevens
Date(s):	September 20, 1978–1979

Replaced by:	Lieutenant David Nelson
Played by:	Greg Morris
Date(s):	September 19, 1979–June 10, 1981

One of television's sexiest private investigators was Dan Tanna (Robert Urich). Everything about him oozed sex symbol, from his glint of a smile to his fitted blue jeans. Even his name had a sexy rhythm to it and felt good in the mouth.[4]

Dan Tanna lived in and worked out of the posh Las Vegas, Nevada Desert Inn hotel/casino, where he was assisted by the beautiful showgirl Beatrice Travis (Phyllis Davis). He tooled around the city that never sleeps in a red Thunderbird convertible and was on retainer with Phillip Roth, the millionaire owner of the Desert Inn (among other properties).

Like all good P.I.'s, Dan Tanna had his very own police contact. In the pilot, which aired on April 25, 1978, his contact was Lieutenant George Nelson. Lieutenant Nelson was played by Greg Morris, who had starred as Barney Collier on *Mission Impossible* (See Entry).

When the series went on the air, Dan Tanna's link to the Las Vegas police department wasn't George Nelson, but a woman, Sergeant Bella Archer. Naomi Stevens, who played Sergeant Archer, may be remembered as Juanita, Doris Day's second housekeeper on *The Doris Day Show* (See Entry).

One year later, almost to the day, Greg Morris returned to *Vega$* as Lieutenant Nelson, with a new first name, David. And as Morris' role expanded, Ms. Stevens' role diminished and was eventually eliminated from the cast.

In one episode of *Vega$,* "Lost Monday," which aired on January 9, 1980, Greg Morris' son Phillip joined him as Tate. Greg returned the favor when he made a guest shot on the new *Mission Impossible* (See Entry) series in which his son had taken over the role he had established in the original series.

VINNIE & BOBBY

May 30, 1992–September 5, 1992.   Fox

Character:	Jim Wotowski
Played by:	Mike Genovese
Date(s):	May 30, 1992

Replaced by:	Fred Slacker
Played by:	Fred Stoller
Date(s):	June 6, 1992–September 5, 1992

---

3. *TV Pro-Log: Television Programs and Production News.* TI-Volume 35, No. 48, Television Index Information Services, L.I., New York, August 1, 1990.

4. There is, in fact, a real Dan Tanna, who may have been the inspiration for the character's name. He's not a private investigator, but a native of Yugoslavia who defected to the United States in 1952. Twelve years later he opened "Dan Tanna's," a restaurant on Santa Monica Boulevard in Los Angeles that is still today one of Hollywood's favorite "watering holes."

Just as with so many other successful network sitcoms that preceded it, like *All in the Family* and *The Mary Tyler Moore Show,* it was only a matter of time (a little over three years) before the Fox network's flagship series, *Married . . . With Children* would give birth to its own spinoff.

The sitcom, *Top of the Heap,* was introduced in a special episode of *Married . . . With Children* that aired at 9:30 p.m. on Sunday, March 24, 1991, following an episode of the series that aired in its regular time slot. *Top of the Heap* starred Joseph Bologna as Charlie Verducci, a lowlife superintendent of an apartment building in Chicago and Al Bundy's (Ed O'Neill) best friend—figures. Living with his divorced dad was Vinnie (Matt LeBlanc), who was also a blue-collar guy on the make looking for an easy way to get rich quick.

They almost found it in the series opener, "The Agony and the Agony," which aired three weeks later on April 14, 1991. In that episode, Vinnie hopes to "marry money" when he lands a job at a country club brimming with beautiful bachelorettes who were just swimming in money. Vinnie never connected and neither did the series, which was canceled exactly three months later.

What separates Fox from the other three networks is that it gives its new shows a better-than-even chance of catching on before canceling them. So, when *Top of the Heap* didn't make it, Fox revamped the series and returned it to the air on May 30, 1992, as *Vinnie & Bobby.* With Joseph Bologna's character eliminated, Matt LeBlanc starred as Vinnie Verducci. The focus shifted from Charlie and Vinnie to Vinnie and Bobby, their job and their friends.

This time around it was LeBlanc's co-star Robert Torti, as Vinnie's best friend and roommate, Bobby Grazzo, who thought he could get by on his good looks alone, while Vinnie was the one who was striving for success as a businessman. In the meantime, they are both working together as construction workers trying to finish a private home.

Vinnie and Bobby's other co-workers and friends were Bill Beli (John Pinette), Stanley Thompson (Ron Taylor) and Jim Wotowski (Mike Genovese), a lazy, hard-to-understand construction worker who was older than the others.

By the time the second episode of the new series aired on June 6, 1992, Jim had been replaced by a younger worker, Fred Slacker, played by Fred Stoller. Fred was skinny, a bit dimwitted (not to be confused with Bobby's dimwittedness), and had a crush on Winnie Weinstein (Sharyn Leavitt), the post office letter carrier.

Winnie, however, only has eyes for Vinnie—as does the ultra sexy Mona Mullins (Joey Adams), Vinnie's underage (seventeen-year-old) downstairs neighbor, who recreated the same role she played in *Top of the Heap.*

Primetime soap opera fans may remember Mike Genovese as Al Hurley from the 1985 season of CBS's *Falcon Crest.* More recently Genovese's replacement, Fred Stoller, was seen as Sheldon Singer on the short-lived situation comedy, *Singer & Sons,* which aired on NBC from June 9 to June 27, 1990.

Fox placed *Vinnie and Bobby* on top of the "canceled" heap on September 5, 1992.

THE VIRGINIAN

September 19, 1962–September 8, 1971.   NBC

Character:	Judge Henry Garth
Played by:	Lee J. Cobb
Date(s):	September 19, 1962–April 20, 1966
Replaced by:	Morgan Starr
Played by:	John Dehner
Date(s):	February 9, 1966–April 20, 1966
Replaced by:	John Grainger
Played by:	Charles Bickford
Date(s):	September 14, 1966–October 25, 1967
Replaced by:	Clay Grainger
Played by:	John McIntire
Date(s):	November 1, 1967–March 18, 1970
Replaced by:	Colonel Alan MacKenzie
Played by:	Stewart Granger
Date(s):	September 16, 1970–September 8, 1971
Character:	Betsy Garth
Played by:	Roberta Shore
Date(s):	September 19, 1962–March 18, 1970
Replaced by:	Jennifer Garth
Played by:	Diane Roter
Date(s):	November 3, 1965–April 20, 1966
Character:	David Sutton
Played by:	David Hartman
Date(s):	September 18, 1968–April 9, 1969
Replaced by:	Roy Tate
Played by:	Lee Majors
Date(s):	October 14, 1970–September 8, 1971
Character:	Jim Horn
Played by:	Tim Matheson
Date(s):	September 17, 1969–March 18, 1970
Replaced by:	Parker
Played by:	John McLiam
Date(s):	October 14, 1970–1971

The Virginian was . . . well, The Virginian. That's all we knew about him. We never even learned his name. We did know that The Virginian (James Drury), the foreman of the Shiloh Ranch, believed in law and order and did everything he could to enforce it among the residents of Medicine Bow, in the Wyoming Territory.

The Virginian had actually been around for nearly sixty years before coming to television.

The Virginian owes its success to the 1902 novel by Owen Wister and four motion pictures, all by the same name. The first, made in 1921, starred Dustin Farnum. Two years later Kenneth Harlan starred as The Virginian. The most famous version was the one made in 1929 starring Gary Cooper. In 1946, the fourth, and to date the last, remake of THE VIRGINIAN starred Joel McCrea in the title role.

The original pilot for the series, aired on July 6, 1958, did star James Drury as The Virginian, but had Robert Burton cast as Judge Henry.

For the most part, the Universal back lot served as the Wyoming Territory although some location work was done at the Angeles National Forest.

Since the central setting for *The Virginian* was the Shiloh Ranch, the owner of the ranch was an important character—and it was one that changed five times over the course of the series.

The first was Judge Henry Garth, played by Lee J. Cobb who, in 1954, co-starred as Johnny Friendly in the Academy Award-winning motion picture, ON THE WATERFRONT. He went on to star as Attorney David Barrett on *The Young Lawyers,* which aired on ABC from September 21, 1970 to May 5, 1971.

John Dehner, as Morgan Starr, took over the Shiloh for a short spell during 1966. Before settling in the Wyoming Territory during the 1880s, John Dehner lived in New York City during *The Roaring 20's* (See Entry), under the name of Jim ''Duke'' Williams. He later appeared as Dr. Charles Cleveland Claver on the ABC situation comedy, *The Temperature's Rising* (See Entry).

Clay Grainger (John McIntire) bought the ranch when actor Charles Bickford ''bought the ranch'' on November 9, 1967 after having played John Grainger for a little more than one year. Charles Bickford joined the cast of *The Virginian* not long after completing work as Christopher Hale, the second wagon-master of *Wagon Train* (See Entry). Before that he starred in *Naked City* (See Entry) as Detective Lieutenant Dan Muldoon.

The final owner of the property was an Englishman, Colonel Alan MacKenzie (Stewart Granger), who purchased the Shiloh at the beginning of the ninth and final season in ''The West vs. Colonel MacKenzie.''

At that time, the name of the series was changed from *The Virginian* to *Shiloh,* and then to *The Men from Shiloh.* It was also moved ahead in time to the 1890s.

There were other changes made at this time. The ranch hands, David Sutton (David Hartman) and Roy Tate (Lee Majors), were replaced by Jim Horn (Tim Matheson) and Parker (John McLiam).

David Hartman went on to star as Dr. Paul Hunter on *The New Doctors,* the NBC medical drama that aired from September 14, 1969 to June 23, 1973. This was followed by a co-starring role in the television remake of the 1947 motion picture classic, *Miracle on 34th Street.* Hartman played Bill Schaffner (the role John Payne played as Fred Gailey) opposite *Family Affair*'s Sebastian Cabot in the Edmund Gwenn role of

Kris Kringle. This heartwarming Christmas tale first aired on CBS on December 14, 1973.

The next regular series to star David Hartman in the title role was *Lucas Tanner,* an NBC school drama that aired from September 11, 1974 to August 20, 1975. On November 3, 1975, David Hartman left acting to become the first host of the popular ABC morning talk show, *Good Morning America.*

Although the next regular role for Lee Majors was Jess Brandon on *Owen Marshall, Counselor at Law,* the ABC law drama that aired from September 16, 1971 to August 24, 1974, he is more strongly associated with the ABC adventure, *The Six-Million-Dollar Man,* on which he starred as Colonel Steve Austin.

Audiences may recognize Tim Matheson from two other NBC Westerns in which he starred. He was Griff King on *Bonanza* from September 12, 1972 to January 16, 1973, and Quentin Beaudine in *The Quest,* which aired from October 22, 1982 to November 19, 1982. And viewers with a keen ear may recognize Tim Matheson's voice as the title character from television's first animated adventure series, *The Adventures of Jonny Quest,* which premiered on ABC on September 18, 1964.

VOYAGE TO THE BOTTOM OF THE SEA

September 14, 1964–September 15, 1968.   ABC

Character:	Chief Petty Officer Curley Jones
Played by:	Henry Kulky
Date(s):	September 14, 1964–April 19, 1965

Replaced by:	Chief Sharkey
Played by:	Terry Becker
Date(s):	September 19, 1965–September 15, 1968

Character:	Doc
Played by:	Richard Bull
Date(s):	September 14, 1964–unknown

Replaced by:	Doc
Played by:	Wright King
Date(s):	unknown

Replaced by:	Doc
Played by:	Wayne Heffley
Date(s):	December 19, 1965–September 15, 1968

Take two mysterious and virtually unexplored settings, the ocean floor and outer space. Introduce a superatomic submarine populated by a dedicated and highly skilled crew, played by some of Hollywood's biggest names. Introduce a threat to the earth like the Van Allen Radiation Belt gone awry and a saboteur aboard ship. Add some elaborate and expensive sets, a dash of special effects and a giant squid for good measure. Mix well and you get VOYAGE TO THE BOTTOM OF THE SEA, a 1961 science fiction produced by Irwin Allen.

And if you're Irwin Allen, you might also be able to get a long-running and successful television series out of it as well, which he did.

The cast of the motion picture was filled with science fiction, horror and fantasy stars. These includeed a mad scientist, a genie, a ghoul and a ghost. The Captain of the Seaview, Admiral Harriman Nelson, was played by Walter Pidgeon, who had played Doctor Morbius in the 1956 science fiction classic, FORBIDDEN PLANET. His secretary, Cathy Connors, was played by Barbara Eden, who would soon star in her own television series, *I Dream of Jeannie* (See Entry). Commodore Lucius Emery was played by horror film great, Peter Lorre, and the handsome Captain Lee Crane was played by Robert Sterling, who was George Kerby, that sporting spirit on *Topper* (See Entry). The saboteur, incidentally, was played by Joan Fontaine.

The series starred Richard Basehart as Commander Nelson and David Hedison as Captain Lee Crane.

The Seaview's chief petty officer, Curley Jones, was originally played by Henry Kulky. When Kulky died on February 12, 1965, at the age of fifty-four, he was replaced for the remainder of the sub's five-year mission by Terry Becker as Chief Sharkey. Kulky, who began his acting career as "Bomber Kulkavich," a professional wrestler, had played Otto Schmidlap on the William Bendix situation comedy, *The Life of Riley*.

Starship or submarine, every ship has got to have a doctor. Aboard the Seaview it was "Doc," played by Richard Bull, Wright King and Wayne Heffley.

The next regular series role for Richard Bull after his discharge from *Voyage to the Bottom of the Sea* was as the likeably henpecked Nels Oleson, who ran the general store on Michael Landon's warm family drama, *Little House on the Prairie*.

Bull's first replacement, Wright King, began his television career as the second Ernest P. Duckweather on the science fiction sitcom, *Johnny Jupiter* (See Entry). For the 1960 season, Wright King served as Josh Randall's sidekick, Jason Nichols, in the Steve McQueen Western, *Wanted: Dead or Alive*.

The medical duties were taken over by Wayne Heffley in the December 19, 1965 episode, in which a Saturn space probe returns to earth with "The Monster from Outer Space."

WKRP IN CINCINNATI

September 18, 1978–September 20, 1982. CBS
September 14, 1991–July 4, 1993   Syndicated

Character: John "Dr. Johnny Fever" Caravella
Played by: Howard Hesseman
Date(s):   September 18, 1978–September 20, 1982

Replaced by: Dana Burns
Played by: Kathleen Garrett
Date(s):   September 14, 1991–September 6, 1992

Replaced by: Jack Allen
Played by: Michael Des Barres
Date(s):   September 14, 1991–September 6, 1992

Replaced by: Razor D
Played by: French Stewart
Date(s):   September 12, 1992–July 4, 1993

Character: Andy Travis
Played by: Gary Sandy
Date(s):   September 18, 1978–September 20, 1982

Replaced by: Donovan Aderhol
Played by: Mykelti Williamson
Date(s):   September 14, 1991–July 4, 1993

Character: Jennifer Marlowe
Played by: Loni Anderson
Date(s):   September 18, 1978–September 20, 1982

Replaced by: Ronnie Lee
Played by: Wendy Davis
Date(s):   September 14, 1991–January 4, 1992

Replaced by: Nancy Brinkwink
Played by: Marla Jeanette Rubinoff
Date(s):   January 11, 1992–July 4, 1993

Character: Gordon "Venus Flytrap" Simms
Played by: Tim Reid
Date(s):   September 18, 1978–September 20, 1982

Replaced by: Mona Loveland
Played by: Tawny Kitaen
Date(s):   September 14, 1991–July 4, 1993

Character: Bailey Quarters
Played by: Jan Smithers
Date(s):   September 18, 1978–September 20, 1982

Replaced by: Claire Hartline
Played by: Hope Alexander-Willis
Date(s):   September 14, 1991–September 6, 1992

Character: Arthur "Little Big Guy" Carlson, Jr.
Played by: Sparky Marcus
Date(s):   September 18, 1978–September 20, 1982

Replaced by: Arthur "Little Big Guy" Carlson, Jr.
Played by: Lightfield Lewis
Date(s):   September 21, 1991–September 6, 1992

The surprising answer to the question posed in the opening theme of the CBS situation comedy, *WKRP in Cincinnati*, "Baby, if you've ever wondered whatever became of me," was that nine years after being canceled, an updated version returned to first-run syndication.

Here is how it began. WKRP (1530 AM) was a fictional 5,000-watt (originally 50,000-watt) AM radio station broadcasting from the ninth floor of the Flimm Building in downtown Cincinnati, Ohio. The station is owned by Arthur's mother, Mrs. Lillian "Mama" Carlson, played in the pilot by Sylvia Sidney and thereafter by Carol Bruce. WKRP was put on the air by Lillian's husband on December 7, 1941.

Mrs. Carlson, an astute businesswoman in her seventies, has placed her inept middle-aged son, Arthur (Gordon Jump), in charge of the day-to-day operation as general manager of the station. His secretary and the station's receptionist was the beautiful blonde Loni Anderson, who was not only good looking, but had more business savvy than anyone else at WKRP. That's why Mr. Carlson, fully aware of his own shortcomings, left standing orders to pass on all business-related matters to her.

He also had the presence of mind to hire a new program director, which is where the first episode begins. Andy Travis (Gary Sandy), WKRP's new "PD," begins his first day on the job by changing the station's format from beautiful music to rock and roll. Morning disc jockey John Caravella takes Andy's charge in stride and makes the seamless segue—scratching the recording on the air by dragging the tone arm across the easy listening record on the turntable, introducing himself as "Dr. Johnny Fever," and popping on one of the new records given to him by Travis.

Johnny Fever, an over-age holdover from the sixties, was played by Howard Hesseman, who went on to teach the I.H.P. (Individualized Honors Program) class at Fillmore High School on the ABC situation comedy, *Head of the Class* (See Entry).

Richard Sanders played the mild-mannered news director, Les Nessman, who, although he gave the outward impression of a crackerjack journalist, actually had his priorities a little mixed up, and he punctuated his newscasts with farming news and agricultural reports while soft-pedaling the hard news of the day.

In true radio station fashion, Andy Travis brought in his former co-worker, Gordon Simms, a smart black disc jockey, who went by the air name of "Venus Flytrap," to run the graveyard shift. And since you can't run a radio station without selling advertising, Herbert R. "Herb" Tarlek, Jr. (Frank Bonner), the "Joe Isuzu" of the eighties, served as WKRP's general sales manager and general pain in the butt.

Getting the commercials on the air is the responsibility of a radio station's traffic department, which at WKRP was in the able hands of Bailey Quarters (Jan Smithers). Bailey was initially portrayed as a "Plain Jane," complete with pulled-back hair and horn-rimmed glasses, but as the series progressed, she took off her glasses, let her hair down (literally), and began to give Loni Anderson a run for her money as the show's "looker," much in the same manner as Mary Ann competed against Ginger Grant on *Gilligan's Island* (See Entry).

Ms. Anderson, however, won out, by not only replacing Farrah Fawcett-Majors as the nation's newest sex symbol, but by earning one of Hollywood's most coveted titles, that of "Mrs. Burt Reynolds," in April of 1988. Her smile, talent and unstoppable good looks won her the title role in the CBS made-for-television movie, *The Jayne Mansfield Story*, which aired on October 29, 1990. Loni later co-starred as Sydney Kovak, opposite dark-haired beauty Lynda Carter's Carole Stanwyck, on the short-lived NBC detective series, *Partners in Crime*, which aired from September 22 to December 29, 1984.

Then, in September of 1991, something quite out of the ordinary happened—*WKRP in Cincinnati* returned to television with brand-new episodes as a first-run syndicated series.

The new production, which used the same staging blueprint, also included three of the series' original cast members, Gordon Jump, Frank Bonner and Richard Sanders. And to get the show off to a good start, both Howard Hesseman and Loni Anderson returned for a guest appearance in the two-part pilot that reintroduced the series along with its old and new characters. Also returning for the pilot episode was Carol Bruce as Mrs. Lillian Carlson.

The two-part episode began with Mr. Carlson telling his staff that "Mama" Carlson had sold WKRP to Barlow and Associates, a respected media conglomerate from Philadelphia ("Foreigners," Les called them), though it would take about three months before the paperwork cleared through federal agencies to make the sale final.

Meanwhile, the business of running a radio station is still the order of the day. And, as are real radio stations, WKRP was a lot like Oz, where "personnel do come and go so quickly." That opened up the door for "new" employees like the lackluster receptionist, Ronnie Lee, played by Wendy Davis, and Claire Hartline (Hope Alexander-Willis), the new traffic manager.

The new employee of the day was Donovan Aderhol (Mykelti Williamson), a program director hired over the phone by Arthur Carlson. It was explained by Les Nessman that the previous station manager/disc jockey (who had supposedly replaced Andy Travis at some point during the past nine years) was fired "for saying on the radio. . . something you can't say on the radio."

Aderhol had strong credentials, but Mr. Carlson was a might taken aback when he was shown into the office.

CARLSON: This is not a black radio station.

DONOVAN: Good, because I'm not a black program director.

Donovan went on to explain that he could program any radio station format and then zinged Carlson by telling him that he had selected the Cincinnati market because he and his wife felt it would be a nice place to raise little black children. The joke fell a little flat because Carlson, as inept as he seemed to be, was never once portrayed as a bigot.

Johnny Fever's old morning air shift was filled by not one, but two characters—the husband-and-wife team of Burns and Allen (no relation to the original radio team). These two on-air lovebirds were Dana Burns and Jack Allen. Off mike, they were divorcees and frightfully insecure.

At the end of the episode, in a fit of desperation, Mr. Carlson places a telephone call to the one person he can trust to "pull his fat out of the fire" and help him save the station—Jennifer Marlowe. Loni Anderson, who is not seen or heard on the other end of the phone in this episode, makes her guest appearance in the second part, in which she and Johnny pull off an elaborate scheme to prevent WKRP from being sold—for a long time.

In addition to Jennifer and Johnny saving WKRP, the second part also introduced two additional regulars. The first is Arthur Carlson, Jr. (Lightfield Lewis), Mr. Carlson's twenty-one-year-old son, who was hired to handle WKRP's sales and promotions. Arthur, Jr. or "Little Big Guy" as Herb likes to call him, was also a recurring character on the original series. He was played by Sparky Marcus, who as a kid played the eight-year-old minister, Jimmy Joe Jetter, on the satirical soap opera, *Mary Hartman, Mary Hartman*.

Rounding out the staff, and adding the sex appeal that Loni Anderson had brought to the original series, was Tawny Kitaen as the new evening disc jockey, Mona Loveland, whose show was referred to as both "Music 'til Midnight" and "Mona 'til Midnight." Tawny, whose name exudes just about as much sex appeal as the actress herself, had previously co-starred as Debbie Thompson in the 1984 Tom Hanks comedy, BACHELOR PARTY.

Gordon Jump, who in both incarnations of the series played the bumbling and inept, though lovable station manager, Mr. Arthur Carlson, went on to replace another of television's institutions, the lonely Maytag repair man, who had been played for years by comic actor Jesse White. White had played J. Sinister Hulk in the 1966 Boris Karloff beach comedy, THE GHOST IN THE INVISIBLE BIKINI.

Halfway through the first season, two additional cast changes were introduced to the series. The first was the addition of the word "New," inserted between "The" and "WKRP" in the opening titles. The second was the hiring of a new receptionist.

CARLSON: Who would have thought that finding a new receptionist could be so much trouble. Why did Ronnie have to leave anyway?

DONOVAN: Well, don't blame her, chief. Getting a master's degree is pretty important stuff.

Among the applicants interviewed for the vacancy left by Ronnie Lee, were Ms. Milner (Nancy Rubin) and Roy Bender (Michael Stanton), a couple of real oddballs.

The person finally hired for the position was Nancy Brinkwink (Marla Rubinoff), who held a B.A. degree in communications from Dennison College and was a former buyer for Studor and James in Cincinnati. She admitted to leaving that career because all of the men she worked with were either married or gay.

To further complicate matters, Nancy was one of Herb's former girlfriends and still lusted after him, while he, very uncharacteristically, ran the other way.

The updated version of *WKRP in Cincinnati* fared well enough in the ratings to warrant a second season, which brought about a couple of very interesting cast changes.

It seems that Jack and Dana had good reason to be insecure about their jobs after all, because in the second season premiere episode Burns and Allen were out and a new personality and former monk, Razor D (French Stewart), billed in the *TV Guide* advertisement as an outrageous "Shock Jock," was in as the new morning jock, using "The Razor Man" as his air name. Perhaps the most shocking thing about him was that he never worked in radio before and faked his entire résumé to get the job, as he explained to Donovan: "So I just invented a few things about myself."

Razor got his nickname, not because he was on the cutting edge of music, but because he was the barber for the Brendisian Order of Our Lady of. . . Forgetfulness. He was a monk for two years and had taken the vow of silence. He confessed, "Boy, did I fall off that wagon!" "Fall" was an understatement, because in Razor D's first hour on the air at WKRP he managed to attack the city government, the state government, the federal government, the president, the Supreme Court and the guy who sells juicers on cable TV—and still had time to give away free condoms to listeners who called in on the request line.

Even more interesting was the fact that in the November 14, 1992 episode, Howard Hesseman returned to *The New WKRP in Cincinnati*. "The spin doctor is in. After a 10–year absence from the deejay booth, Howard Hesseman, a.k.a. Dr. Johnny Fever, returns to liven up the airwaves in five episodes of *The New WKRP in Cincinnati*, starting this week. Although Hesseman made a few appearances on the syndicated hit last season, he never got back into the studio he called home in the original *WKRP*, which aired on CBS in the early '80s. . . . 'I keep saying, you can't go home again, but you can certainly cruise the *hood*.' "[1]

Johnny returned to WKRP to pay his respects to the family and friends of the recently deceased (and never seen) overnight deejay, Moss Steiger, and winds up taking over his midnight to six a.m. air shift.

Moss' voice, which was provided by Chuck Blore, a popular producer and voice-over talent of particularly outlandish radio commercials, was heard over the station's monitor in French Stewart's first episode as Razor D.

Upon his arrival, Johnny sneaks into the air studio and surprises Les who has just completed his on-air eulogy for Moss Steiger, whom he referred to as the "midnight to dawn radio personality on WKRP for the past twenty-three years." This is either an error in math on the part of the writers, or use of dramatic license, because Venus Flytrap worked the graveyard shift until 1982.

In any event, after a short exchange of pleasantries between Johnny and Les, Fever asks the journalist how Moss died.

LES: Well, um, he went up on the roof to smoke a cigarette and he, um, fell off. Well, actually he hit on the marquee of the theater on the Fourth Street side. And then, somehow, an air conditioning unit came lose and fell on him. That knocked him off the marquee and into the street. That's where the bus hit him.

JOHNNY: How he would've wanted to go.

Hesseman made four other guest appearances on the series during that season, and then went behind the scene to direct two others. He joins fellow actor, Frank Bonner, who directed the episode in which Johnny returned to WKRP.

So baby, now you'll never have to wonder, wonder what ever happened to them. They're livin' on the air in syndication, on TV stations across the nation. They're at WKRP in Cincinnati.

WAGON TRAIN

September 18, 1957–September 5, 1965.   NBC-ABC

Character:	Major Seth Adams
Played by:	Ward Bond
Date(s):	September 18, 1957–March 8, 1961
Replaced by:	Christopher Hale
Played by:	John McIntire
Date(s):	March 15, 1961–September 5, 1965

1. Wolf, Jeanne, Mark Schwed and Ed Weiner. "Grapevine," *TV Guide,* Vol 40, No. 46, Issue #2068, November 14, 1992, p. 4.

Striking a pose as they lean against one of *Wagon Train*'s covered wagons are (left to right) Charlie Wooster (Frank McGrath), Christopher Hale (John McIntire), Bill Hawks (Terry Wilson), and Cooper Smith (Robert Fuller).

Character:	Flint McCullough
Played by:	Robert Horton
Date(s):	September 18, 1957–March 20, 1960
	February 15, 1961–June 13, 1962

Replaced by:	Duke Shannon
Played by:	Scott Miller
Date(s):	1961–1964

Replaced by:	Cooper Smith
Played by:	Robert Fuller
Date(s):	September 16, 1963–May 2, 1965

As the granddaddy of all Western trail programs, *Wagon Train*'s unique premise of trekking across the country gave the writers a wealth of people and stories to draw on for each week's episode.

Leading the weekly odyssey to California from St. Joseph, Missouri, was Ward Bond as wagonmaster Major Seth Adams. Bond, a veteran Hollywood actor generally appeared in minor roles in more than 150 feature films and several dozen television shows. Possibly his most famous film role was as Lov

Bensey in the 1941 drama, TOBACCO ROAD. It is, however, without question that the film that led to his role on *Wagon Train* was the 1950 Western, WAGONMASTER, in which he starred as Elder Wiggs, the wagonmaster leading a wagon train of Mormons out of Crystal City to their promised land—*Utah*.

Ward Bond went to the last roundup in Dallas, Texas on November 6, 1960. As his death fell right at the beginning of the shooting schedule for the 1961/1962 television season, a new wagonmaster had to be found immediately. That actor was John McIntire, who the season before had played Detective Lieutenant Dan Muldoon on *Naked City* (See Entry). Now, as Chris Hale, he would lead the wagons across the country for the remainder of the series' eight-year run.

As any frontiersman knows, it is good practice to send a scout ahead to help guide the wagon train through uncharted territory and avoid danger with unfriendly Indians. When the wagons first left Missouri in 1957 their trusty scout was Flint McCullough, played by Robert Horton.

Horton left the series over what some sources reported as his dissatisfaction with Westerns. Apparently, it was only his dissatisfaction with *this* Western because in 1965 he showed up in the title role of his own Western series, *A Man Called Shenandoah*, which aired on ABC from September 13, 1965 to September 5, 1966.

Horton was replaced in 1961 by Scott Miller as Duke Shannon. "Bob Horton told me that the reason he was going to leave was that his five-year contract was up, even though they had offered him somewhere in the neighborhood of a million dollars for the next year. That was a big chunk of money for television in those days—it is now too, for that matter. However, Bob wanted to sing on stage. That was his big love and he was going to spend all of his time and effort trying to get work on Broadway—which, fortunately for him, he did. He wound up doing a musical, *110 in the Shade*. It was about a cowboy so he hadn't quite escaped the typecasting, but I understand that the play was very successful and ended up running for nearly two years. That's the only reason he ever mentioned to me,"[2] said Scott Miller, who is better known as Denny Miller.

Some insiders, like Gabe Essoe, the author of *Tarzan of the Movies*, say that there was more to Horton's departure from the series than a desire to be a song and dance man:

"Robert Horton was a successful character on *Wagon Train*, but he and Ward Bond did not see eye-to-eye in many ways. Industry rumors hinted that Robert Horton was a homosexual, while Ward Bond was extremely macho, coming out of the John Wayne mold of their drinking, boozing, fighting, brawling days. Ward Bond would constantly be on Horton's ass about being a pansy. It got very unsettling to a lot of people, not just Horton. And that set the replacement process in motion,"[3] said Essoe.

"There was a personality clash with Ward, but that's all I know. There were differences, but I don't know what the differences were. I only worked with the two of them on several occasions before Ward [Bond] passed away. But on all the occasions that I was there, there wasn't even so much as a flare-up. I had heard that there had been arguments before, differences of opinion about the way a scene should go, but that happens all the time and that's so usual that you come to expect it. Movies and television are art by committee. It's a collaborative effort and everybody gets together and throws in their two cents—some people just have a little more money in their pocket. However, there was that friction, I won't deny that," said Miller.

Denny Miller didn't just come in and take over for Robert Horton. It was a gradual transition and both actors appeared together for an entire season of episodes. When Denny Miller started with the series he had a relatively small role, but it grew as the seasons passed.

"You know when they ride up to you and you're standing there by yourself on the plains and somebody asks, 'Which way did they go?' In the beginning, I was just allowed to shrug my shoulders—that was my part. I was standing there, but I wasn't allowed to tell them which way they went. The next year I could point, and by the third year I could actually tell them. Sometimes I even got to take them there, that was the progression. I did 110 episodes and I didn't even know where they were most of the time.

"Then Bobby [Robert] Fuller came along and took over for me

as the new trail scout, Cooper Smith. I was a contract player. My contract went from year to year with yearly options—their option, of course. When the series went from sixty to ninety minutes in 1963, they decided to add a couple of new cast members. One was Michael Burns as Barnaby West, as an interest for the kids. The other was Bobby Fuller as Cooper Smith. I was told by the producer, Howard Christie, that Bobby Fuller was very popular in Europe and Japan because he had played Jess Harper on *Laramie*, which was seen in those markets.

"The following season, when the show went back to sixty minutes they had to cut back on the cast. Since he was popular with the viewers in three markets and I was only popular in one, they decided to keep him. It stands to reason that if they were going to cut one of us out, it was to their advantage to cut me, even though I was supposedly getting more mail than anybody on the show at that time.

"That was the explanation I was given when I was let go. *Wagon Train* continued on with Bobby for one more season after that," explained Miller.

"The Family Channel recently aired a one-hour retrospective on *Wagon Train* called *Wagon Train's Thirty and Still Rollin'*. They had asked Bob Horton to host it, but he was unavailable, so I was the one who got to ride in on horseback and introduce clips from the series, which included many big names in guest-starring roles.

"When *Wagon Train* was on the air it was one of the main catalysts responsible for breaking down the Hollywood cast system. Movie stars would condescend to do television if it was on shows like *Wagon Train* and *G.E. Theater* because these shows had quality writing and the guest stars were given good parts, good money, and were treated very well.

"So every week, for a hundred and some weeks, I'd work with stars like Bette Davis, Barbara Stanwyck, Franchot Tone and Ann Blyth. It was just incredible that they could get such big names to appear in a weekly television series.

"The running parts would introduce the character, whoever it was that week, and then kind of fade away while the guest star would have the meat of the hour show to themselves. At the end of the show, the regulars would come back and sit around the fire and talk about the guest stars after they had gone," recalled Miller.

Today, at fifty-seven, with more than 300 television credits, Denny Miller still makes an occasional guest shot as a cowboy. His most recent were two appearances on the Family Channel's Western, *Bordertown*.

THE WALTONS

September 14, 1972–August 20, 1981.   CBS

Character:	John "John Boy" Walton, Jr.
Played by:	Richard Thomas
Date(s):	September 14, 1972–March 17, 1977
	March 16, 1978
	March 23, 1978

---

2. This and following quotations by Denny Miller in this *Wagon Train* entry are from an exclusive telephone interview with Mr. Miller on April 3, 1991.
3. From an exclusive telephone interview with Gabe Essoe on April 3, 1991.

Replaced by:	John "John Boy" Walton, Jr.
Played by:	Robert Wightman
Date(s):	November 22, 1979–August 20, 1981

Character:	Reverend Matthew Fordwick
Played by:	John Ritter
Date(s):	October 26, 1972–December 23, 1976

Replaced by:	Reverend Hank Buchanan
Played by:	Peter Fox
Date(s):	September 15, 1977–August 20, 1981

Character:	John Curtis Willard
Played by:	Marshall Reed (twin)
Date(s):	1978–August 20, 1981

Replaced by:	John Curtis Willard
Played by:	Michael Reed (twin)
Date(s):	1978–August 20, 1981

Character:	Thelma
Played by:	Dorothy Shay
Date(s):	unknown

Replaced by:	Callie Mae Jordan
Played by:	Dorothy Tristan
Date(s):	unknown

Just before saying their "good-nights" Jason Walton (Jon Walmsley) on the guitar leads *The Waltons* in a wholesome sing-along. Leaning on the piano are Mary Ellen Walton Willard (Judy Norton-Taylor) and Ben Walton (Eric Scott). Seated on the piano stool are John Boy Walton (Richard Thomas, left) and Erin Walton (Mary Elizabeth McDonough). Perched on John Boy's knee is Elizabeth (Kami Cotler), and sitting on the floor next to Jason is Jim-Bob Walton (David W. Harper).

Watching *The Waltons* makes viewers wish they too were growing up in Jefferson County, Virginia during the Depression.

The Waltons, like *Little House on the Prairie* and *The Wonder Years*, was presented as a recollection being told by one of the now grown family members. On *Little House* it was Laura Wilder, and on *The Wonder Years* it was Kevin Arnold. The reminiscences of the Waltons were told by John Walton, Jr., who was distinguished from his father by the nickname, "John Boy." Each loving memory was narrated by Earl Hamner, Jr., the show's creator and coproducer.

Except for "John Boy," the extended Walton family, which consisted of a mother and father, seven children and their grandparents, remained constant throughout the series' run. "John-Boy," who was really the central character in the series, was played by Richard Thomas for six of the program's nine years on the air. It has been reported that Richard Thomas tired of his role and wanted new challenges. His leaving the series was handled by having "John-Boy" leave Walton's Mountain to pursue a writing career in New York, where his first novel was accepted by a publisher. Thomas went on to star as Henry Fleming in the NBC adaptation of *The Red Badge of Courage*, which aired on December 3, 1974. He returned briefly to *The Waltons* for two more episodes, "John Boy's Return" and "The Revelation," before calling it quits.

Thomas' later television work was exclusively in made-for-television movies and includes the role of Jim Warner in the fourteen-hour miniseries, *Roots: The Next Generation*, which aired on ABC from February 18 to 25, 1979.

The second actor to portray "John Boy" on *The Waltons* was Robert Wightman, who made his first appearance in "The Waiting," that season's emotional Thanksgiving episode that found "John Boy" in a comatose condition in a Washington, D.C. hospital. The young man eventually recovers and the family is so overjoyed to have him back that they don't even notice that he looks completely different.

Over the long and successful run of the series, there were several other changes in the supporting cast. The young preacher, Reverend Matthew Fordwick, was played for four years by John Ritter, who essentially left to star in his own situation comedy, *Three's Company*, although he did appear in the "Dealer's Choice—Blackmail" episode of *Hawaii Five-O*, which aired on February 3, 1977. In "The Hawk," the first episode of the sixth season, Reverend Fordwick has left

Walton's Mountain to serve in the Navy, while the good reverend's replacement, Hank Buchanan (Peter Fox), has begun to keep company with ''John Boy's'' sister, Erin (Mary Elizabeth McDonough).

Just as John Ritter left to star in *Three's Company*, Peter Fox also left the serenity of *The Waltons* to appear in a sitcom. In his case it was for the role of Eric ''Otter'' Stratton in the ANIMAL HOUSE clone, *Delta House*, which aired on ABC from January 18 to April 28, 1979.

''John Boy's'' sister, Mary Ellen (Judy Norton-Taylor), a nursing student, eventually married a young doctor, Curtis Willard, during the 1976/1977 season. The following season she gave birth to a baby boy, John Curtis, who was (as are most infants and young children on television series) played alternately by twins. These young thespians were Marshall Reed and his brother Michael Reed. Marshall, by the way, was not the same actor who replaced Robert Shayne on the *Adventures of Superman* (See Entry).

The original owner of the Dew Drop Inn, Thelma (Dorothy Shay), later sold it to Callie Mae Jordan (Dorothy Tristan).

In what could also be considered a replacement, ''John Boy's'' mother, Olivia (Michael Learned), was replaced by her cousin, Rose Burton (Peggy Rea). The on-screen explanation was that Olivia left to work as a nurse in an Army hospital, after she had been released from a sanitarium, where she was treated for tuberculosis. Meanwhile, Rose, who had been with the series since 1979, stepped in to help out the family in her cousin's absence.

This change was necessitated by the fact that Michael Learned asked to be written out of the series when her contract expired in 1980. She, like Richard Thomas, wanted to pursue other roles. Those she found included a number of made-for-television movies and two short-lived series, *Nurse* and *Hot House*. In the first, a medical drama that aired on CBS from April 2, 1981 to May 21, 1982, she played Nurse Mary Benjamin. The second series aired on ABC from June 30 to August 25, 1988. She also went on to a very successful career in motion pictures.

Good night, Olivia. Good night Callie Mae. Good night, Thelma. Good night, John Curtis. Good night, John Curtis. Good night, Reverend Buchanan. Good night, Reverend Fordwick. Good night, ''John Boy.''

WEREWOLF

July 11, 1987–August 21, 1988.   Fox

Character:	Janos Skorzeny
Played by:	Chuck Connors
Date(s):	July 11, 1987–February 28, 1988

Replaced by:	Nicholas Remy
Played by:	Brian Thompson
Date(s):	1988–August 21, 1988

The only way to kill a werewolf, according to the lore established in the 1941 Universal horror film classic, THE WOLF MAN, is with a silver bullet fired from a gun by someone who loves the werewolf enough to care. It may sound like a job for the Lone Ranger, but fathers, lovers and best friends work best.

In 1987, the Fox Broadcasting network decided to update this tale with a weekly series titled *Werewolf*. It starred John J. York as Eric Cord, a graduate student who is bitten by his roommate—a werewolf—that he managed to kill with a silver bullet.

Aside from taking a silver slug, the only way to free himself from the ancient curse, and stay alive, was to go to the source. That is, Eric had to locate and kill the one werewolf responsible for perpetuating the bloodline—Captain Janos Skorzeny. Skorzeny was played by Chuck Connors, the former star of *The Rifleman*.

Eric's cross-country search for Captain Skorzeny is reminiscent in many ways of Michael Alden's (Frank Converse) search for his would-be murderers on *Coronet Blue* (May 29, 1967 to September 4, 1967; CBS) and Ben Richards' (Christopher George) search for his brother on *The Immortal* (September 24, 1970 to September 8, 1971; ABC). Though it is perhaps most like Dr. David Bruce Banner's (Bill Bixby) search for a cure on *The Incredible Hulk*. For like Banner, Eric Cord needed a ''cure'' for his affliction. Similarly, he was often placed in the position where his alter ego would emerge (naturally under the full moon) and wreck havoc. And, like his muscle-bound green cousin, Eric's werewolf seemed to prey only on bad guys and other werewolves. One difference was that the Hulk only roughed up the baddies, while Eric usually killed them.

Eventually, Eric found and killed Captain Skorzeny, only to learn that he was not the ''source'' but only one of many werewolf pack leaders. The loup-garou he should have been after was a cunning 2,000–year-old werewolf by the name of Nicholas Remy (Brian Thompson), so Eric's search continued.

WESLEY

May 8, 1949–August 30, 1949.   CBS

Character:	Wesley Eggleston
Played by:	Donald Devlin
Date(s):	May 8, 1949–July 1949

Replaced by:	Wesley Eggleston
Played by:	Johnny Stewart
Date(s):	July 1949–August 30, 1949

This live situation comedy could certainly be considered a forerunner of series such as *James at 15* and *The Wonder Years*. The stories centered on Wesley Eggleston, a boy who, according to the old Wonder Bread commercials, was in his ''Wonder Years'' (ages six through twelve) and about to become a teenager. The first young man to play Wesley was Donald Devlin. He was replaced after only two months in the role by Johnny Stewart, who stayed with the series until it was canceled at the end of the month.

Both of these juvenile stars regularly appeared in vignettes on Paul Tripp's children's series, *Mr. I. Magination*, which aired on CBS from April 24, 1949 to June 28, 1952.

As an adult, John Stewart was credited as the theme performer for the ABC pilot, *Fly Away Home*, which aired on September 18, 1981.

Wesley's parents were played by show business husband and wife team, Frank and Mona (Bruns) Thomas. The Thomas' real son, Frankie, became famous to younger television viewers as *Tom Corbett, Space Cadet* (See Entry).

WHAT A COUNTRY!

September 27, 1986–April 1987.   Syndicated

Character:	Principal Joan Courtney	
Played by:	Gail Strickland	
Date(s):	September 1986–January 1987	
Replaced by:	Principal F. Jerry "Bud" McPherson	
Played by:	Don Knotts	
Date(s):	January 17, 1987–April 1987	

In this syndicated sitcom the aliens weren't from outer space, but from all over the world—our world. That's because these were the type of aliens who had to register at the post office each year.

This diverse cultural group of immigrants was brought together at a Los Angeles night school, where they were preparing for their citizenship tests under the guidance of their teacher, Taylor Brown (Garrett M. Brown).

The star student was Nikolai Rostapovich, played by Russian comedian Yakov Smirnoff. His fellow classmates included Ali Nadeem (Vijay Amritraj), a Pakistani; Laslo Gabov (George Murdock), a Hungarian; Robert Moboto (Harry Waters, Jr.), an African; Hispanics Victor Ortega (Julian Reyes) and Maria Conchita Lopez (Ada Maris); and Yung Hi (Leila Hee Olsen), an Asian.

Joan Courtney, the school's principal at the beginning of the series, was played by Gail Strickland. She went on to appear in "Steal Me a Story," the November 15, 1987 episode of the CBS detective series, *Murder She Wrote*. That same year, she guest-starred in "A Dream of Wild Horses," the December 2, 1987 episode of Michael Landon's inspirational fantasy, *Highway to Heaven*, on NBC.

Principal Courtney's replacement, Bud McPherson, was played by Don Knotts, who carved his name in the history books as Mayberry's Deputy Barney Fife on *The Andy Griffith Show* (See Entry).

THE WHIRLYBIRDS

1956–1959.   Syndicated

Character:	Janet Culver	
Played by:	Sandra Spence	
Date(s):	1956–1957	
Replaced by:	Helen Carter	
Played by:	Nancy Hale	
Date(s):	1957–1959	

If Sky King was the West's first flying cowboy then Chuck Martin and Pete "P.T." Moore were the second and third—third and fourth if you count Clipper.

But instead of flying a fixed-winged aircraft like the Songbird, Chuck (Ken Tobey) and "P.T." (Craig Hill) flew helicopters for their company, Whirlybirds, Incorporated. Their choppers didn't have catchy names like King's Cessna either, but for the record, the serial numbers of their Bell Ranger helicopters were N2838B and N975B.

Operating out of Longwood Field in California, Chuck and "P.T." performed much the same service for their California-based clients as Sky and his niece and nephew did for the residents in and around the fictional Grover City, Arizona.

The Whirlybirds was filmed on the Iverson Ranch in California, the same location used for much of the *Sky King* series.

The offices of Whirlybirds, Incorporated were looked after, for the first season by Janet Culver (Sandra Spence), and thereafter by Helen Carter (Nancy Hale). Sandra Spence was one of the two young ladies who alternated in the part of Burma in *Terry and the Pirates* (See Entry), and Nancy Hale had appeared as Bess Murdock on the syndicated Western, *Annie Oakley*.

The two chopper pilots who actually did all of the flying sequences for Chuck and "P.T." were Earl Gilbreath and Rod Parker.

240–Robert (See Entry), a 1979 adventure series that utilized helicopters in daring rescue and emergency situations, owed much to this distant cousin.

THE WHITE SHADOW

November 27, 1978–August 12, 1981.   CBS

Character:	Jim Willis	
Played by:	Jason Bernard	
Date(s):	November 27, 1978	
Replaced by:	Jim Willis	
Played by:	Ed Bernard	
Date(s):	December 4, 1978–April 1, 1980	
Replaced by:	Sybil Buchanan	
Played by:	Joan Pringle	
Date(s):	November 27, 1978–August 12, 1981	
Character:	James Hayward	
Played by:	Thomas Carter	
Date(s):	November 27, 1978–April 1, 1980	
Replaced by:	Wardell Stone	
Played by:	Larry Flash Jenkins	
Date(s):	October 16, 1980–August 12, 1981	
Character:	Curtis Jackson	
Played by:	Eric Kilpatrick	
Date(s):	November 27, 1978–March 11, 1980	

Replaced by:	Jesse B. Mitchell
Played by:	Stoney Jackson
Date(s):	October 16, 1980–August 12, 1981

Character:	Milton Reese
Played by:	Nathan Cook
Date(s):	November 27, 1978–April 1, 1980

Replaced by:	Teddy Rutherford
Played by:	Wolfe Perry
Date(s):	October 16, 1980–August 12, 1981

Character:	Abner Goldstein
Played by:	Ken Michelman
Date(s):	November 27, 1978–April 1, 1980

Replaced by:	Eddie Franklin
Played by:	Art Holliday
Date(s):	October 16, 1980–August 12, 1981

Character:	Ricky Gomez
Played by:	Ira Angustain
Date(s):	November 27, 1978–April 1, 1980

Replaced by:	Paddy Falahey
Played by:	John Laughlin
Date(s):	October 16, 1980–August 12, 1981

Character:	Bill Donahue
Played by:	Jerry Fogel
Date(s):	November 27, 1978–1979

Replaced by:	Nick Vitaglia
Played by:	John Mengatti
Date(s):	1979–August 12, 1981

Character:	Katie Donahue
Played by:	Robin Rose
Date(s):	November 27, 1978–1979

Character:	Manager Phil Jefferson
Played by:	Russell Phillip Robinson
Date(s):	1979–April 1, 1980

Who knows what raw talent lurks in high school basketball players? The White Shadow knows.

The "White Shadow" was Ken Reeves (Ken Howard), a former forward on the professional basketball team, the Chicago Bulls. Forced into an early retirement by a knee injury, Reeves accepts a job as the basketball coach for Carver High, an inner-city school in Los Angeles.

He got the job through an old friend, Jim Willis, the school's principal, who was played in the first episode by Jason Bernard and thereafter by Ed Bernard.

Willis stayed on as principal until the end of the second season. When he left, the school's guidance counselor, Sybil Buchanan (Joan Pringle), was promoted and became the school's new principal.

Even though it may appear that there was a typographical error in the cast credits, rest assured that Jason Bernard and Ed Bernard are two different actors. Before joining *The White Shadow*, Ed Bernard had played Tony Baylor on the detective drama, *Cool Million*, which aired as one of the spokes of *The NBC Wednesday Mystery Movie*, rotating from September 20, 1972 to August 22, 1973 with George Peppard's *Banacek* and Richard Widmark's *Madigan*. Ed Bernard continued his police work as Detective Joe Styles on Angie Dickinson's hit series, *Police Woman*, which aired on NBC from September 13, 1974 to August 30, 1978.

Following Jason Barnard's tenure as the principal on *The White Shadow*, he played Deputy Inspector Marquette on *Cagney & Lacey* for the 1982/1983 season. This was followed up with the role of Fletch, the technical genius on the short-lived series, *High Performance*, which ran from March 2 to 23, 1983.

Four members of the school's basketball team graduated at the end of the show's second season, just like at a real high school. A fifth player, Curtis Jackson (Eric Kilpatrick), never made it to graduation. In "The Death of Me Yet," Jackson, an innocent bystander, is killed by a stray bullet during a liquor store holdup—a day before the "big game."

The vacancies were filled during the third season with four new cast members. Wardell Stone (Larry "Flash" Jenkins), Jesse B. Mitchell (Stoney Jackson) and Teddy Rutherford (Wolfe Perry) joined the series with previous acting credits. Jenkins had a small role in two 1975 films, the dramatic comedy, COOLEY HIGH, and Diana Ross' MAHOGANY. Jackson played Phones in the 1975 musical drama, ROLLER BOOGIE, and appeared in THE CONCORDE—AIRPORT '79. Perry also appeared on the PBS series, *Up and Coming*.

The fourth new member of the cast, Art Holliday, who played Eddie Franklin, studied at the Lee Strasberg Theater Institute in New York and appeared in the off-Broadway productions *Ceremonies in Dark Old Men* and *Slow Dance on the Killing Ground*.

Upon his graduation from *The White Shadow*, Stoney Jackson went on to co-star with Nicholas Campbell in *The Insiders*. In this all-too-obvious copy of *Miami Vice*, Stoney Jackson played undercover investigative reporter James Mackey. The hour-long drama series aired on ABC from September 25, 1985 to June 23, 1986.

The other characters who joined the series were not direct replacements for characters who had departed.

THE WILD WILD WEST

September 17, 1965–September 7, 1970.   CBS

Character:	General Ulysses S. Grant
Played by:	James Gregory
Date(s):	September 17, 1965

Replaced by:	General Ulysses S. Grant	
Played by:	Roy Engle	
Date(s):	September 24, 1965–September 7, 1970	

Replaced by:	Robert T. "Skinny" Malone
Played by:	Harry Morgan
Date(s):	May 9, 1979
	October 7, 1980
	October 8, 1980

Character:	Dr. Miguelito Loveless
Played by:	Michael Dunn
Date(s):	October 1, 1965–December 13, 1968

Replaced by:	Miguelito Loveless, Jr.
Played by:	Paul Williams
Date(s):	May 9, 1979

The Wild Wild West rode in on the crest of a wave created by the latest James Bond success, GOLDFINGER, and its television counterpart, *The Man from U.N.C.L.E.* (See Entry). The difference was that instead of being set in the present, *The Wild Wild West* took place shortly after the American Civil War.

Just as James Bond had a license to kill, the producers of *The Wild Wild West* took license with the technology employed by its stars and villains—technology that would not have been possible during that period in history. Then again, it was only a television show!

The heroes, James T. West (Robert Conrad) and Artemus Gordon (Ross Martin), were a couple of Secret Service agents employed by the United States government. They took their orders directly from President Ulysses S. Grant, in much the same manner as agent 007 took his orders from "M" and Napoleon Solo and Ilya Kuryakin took theirs from Mr. Waverly—although President Grant did not appear in every episode as "M" and Waverly did.

The series premiere, "The Night of the Inferno," starred James Gregory as the eighteenth president of the United States. His first assignment for West and Gordon was to thwart the efforts of Juan Manolo (Nehemiah Persoff), who was bent on claiming the U.S. Territory for himself. James Gregory is much better known for his comedic role as Inspector Luger on *Barney Miller* and Nick Hannigan on *Detective School* (See Entry).

After the first episode, whenever President Grant made an appearance on the series he was portrayed by Roy Engle.

Two attempts were made to revive the series, with its original stars recreating their roles. The first was *The Wild Wild West Revisited*, in which the agents' superior, President Grant, was replaced by Robert T. Malone, the head of the United States Secret Service. He was played by Harry Morgan, who was at that time still working on *M*A*S*H* (See Entry).

One of the duo's most popular and most persistent adversaries was a little man who went by the name of Dr. Miguelito Loveless, played in ten episodes by Michael Dunn, a true dwarf.

Of his more than two dozen other television appearances he may be remembered as Mr. Big, the KAOS operative in the pilot episode of *Get Smart*, "Mr. Big." Following his stint on *The Wild Wild West*, Michael Dunn appeared as Alexander, the court jester in the *Star Trek* episode, "Plato's Stepchildren," which aired on November 22, 1968. This ground-breaking episode presented television's first-ever interracial kiss when Captain Kirk (William Shatner) is forced into making love to Lieutenant Uhura (Nichelle Nichols) by Parmen (Liam Sullivan), king of the planet Platonius.

The villain in the updated version of *The Wild Wild West* was Miguelito Loveless, Jr., the son of their former adversary. It was necessary to create this new character because Michael Dunn had died shortly after the original series ended production. This new deranged dwarf wasn't a real dwarf at all, but the diminutive singer and actor Paul Williams, who had played Little Enos Burdette in the 1977 Burt Reynolds comedy, SMOKEY AND THE BANDIT.

In the second pilot, *More Wild Wild West*, Harry Morgan again appeared as Robert T. Malone. The new villain, Professor Albert Paradine II, was played by Jonathan Winters, whose many television roles include Mearth, Mork's full-grown son on the ABC situation comedy, *Mork & Mindy*.

At the beginning, Robert Conrad performed most of his own stunts until he was injured in 1968. That is when Charles Aidman was brought in as West's assistant, Jeremy Pike. The idea was to ease the workload on the series' star while he recuperated. The four episodes in which Aidman appeared that season were "The Night of the Camera," November 29, 1968; "The Night of Miguelito's Revenge," December 13, 1968; "The Night of the Pelican," December 27, 1968; and "The Night of the Janus," which aired on February 14, 1969.

The stuntmen who were hired to double for Conrad and Martin were Fred Stromose and Bob Herron.

WILLY

September 18, 1954–July 7, 1955.   CBS

Character:	Mr. "Papa" Dodger
Played by:	Wheaton Chambers
Date(s):	unknown

Replaced by:	Mr. "Papa" Dodger
Played by:	Lloyd Corrigan
Date(s):	unknown

A bright law school graduate, Willy Dodger, returns to Renfrew, New Hampshire to open up a legal practice. The only problem is that the citizens of Renfrew are a mite hesitant to give the young attorney a chance. Not because Willy isn't a good lawyer, but because Willy is really "Willa," a young woman played by June Havoc.

In the show's first format, which ran on CBS from September 18, 1954 to March 31, 1955, both Wheaton Chambers and Lloyd Corrigan were featured as her dad.

The next month, Willy moved from New Hampshire to New York to work in show business as the legal counselor for the Bannister Vaudeville Company. Her boss, Mr. Bannister, was played by Hal Peary, who created the character of Throckmorton P. Gildersleeve on the *Fibber McGee and Molly* radio program during the 1940s. He later appeared as Herb Woodley with the first cast of television's *Blondie*.

Willy's second format, which ran from April 7 to July 7, 1955, co-starred Sterling Holloway as Willy's friend, Harvey Evelyn (a man with a woman's name), the manager of a theatrical repertory company. Holloway later played the first professor on the *Adventures of Superman* (See Entry).

WONDER WOMAN

November 7, 1975–September 11, 1979.   ABC-CBS

Character:	General Philip Blankenship
Played by:	Richard Eastham
Date(s):	November 7, 1975–July 30, 1977
Replaced by:	Joe Atkinson
Played by:	Normann Burton
Date(s):	September 16, 1977–unknown
Character:	Queen Hippolyte, "The Queen Mother"
Played by:	Cloris Leachman
Date(s):	November 7, 1975
Replaced by:	Queen Hippolyte, "The Queen Mother"
Played by:	Carolyn Jones
Date(s):	November 8, 1976
Replaced by:	Queen Hippolyte, "The Queen Mother"
Played by:	Beatrice Straight
Date(s):	September 16, 1977–September 11, 1979

Wonder Woman was television's first female superhero to have her own series since Irish McCalla starred as *Sheena, Queen of the Jungle* (See Entry) in 1956. Back on September 14, 1967, Yvonne Craig joined Gotham City's dynamic duo in the supporting role of Batgirl on ABC's *Batman*.

Diana Prince (Wonder Woman) was conceived in 1941 by a psychologist, William Marston, four years after the first appearance of Sheena. Wonder Woman first came to television as one of the *Super Friends*, an animated Saturday morning superhero adventure series which premiered on September 8, 1973. She was joined by Superman, Batman and Robin, and Aquaman. In 1967 ABC made a four-minute pilot for *Wonder Woman* with Ellie Wood Wallas in the title role.

But it wasn't until ten years later that Warner Bros. was able to bring the immortal crime-fighting Amazon princess to prime time television in a live action series. They tested the waters with a *Wonder Woman* made-for-television pilot in which Cathy Lee Crosby was cast in the title role. Now that's incredible! It aired as the ABC Movie of the Week on March 12, 1974. The storyline did tell of a race of superhuman women living on Paradise Island. Unfortunately, it was set in the present instead of 1942 and its leading lady didn't look anything like the character depicted in the comic books or on the animated series. Not just because her hair color was wrong, but because the authentic *Wonder Woman* costume had also been scrapped.

The upshot was that even though the pilot had tested poorly, the ratings were strong enough to prove to Warner Bros. that a *Wonder Woman* series could be successful if handled properly. The idea was reworked by producers Douglas S. Cramer and Wilfred Lloyd "Bud" Baumes, who understood that Warner Bros. liked the comic book character and decided to make a more faithful translation from comic book to TV screen.

In a 1977 *TV Guide* interview, Douglas S. Cramer related their new thinking: "We'll put it back in 1942, an age of innocence when you could tell the good guys from the bad guys; and we'll get a dark-haired girl who *looks* like the girl in the strip. She should be built like a javelin-thrower, but with the sweet face of a Mary Tyler Moore."[4]

That decision led them to cast Lynda Carter, the 1972 "Miss World U.S.A.," who was now trying to make it as an actress in Hollywood. At that time she had appeared in only one episode of the ABC police drama, *Nakia*, which aired from September 21 to December 28, 1974, and in an unaired pilot titled *Shamus*. But that was enough experience for delivering lines such as "Follow me, Major. I'll teach those dirty Nazi agents a thing or two about democracy."

The actor cast as Major Steve Trevor, a U.S. fighter pilot, was Lyle Waggoner. Trevor was nursed back to health by the beautiful Amazon after his plane crashed on Paradise Island.

The leader of this society of remarkable women was Queen Hippolyte—referred to as "The Queen Mother." In the first pilot, with Cathy Lee Crosby, "The Queen Mother" was played by Charlene Holt.

For the second pilot, Cloris Leachman, the actress who had been the first mother on *Lassie* (See Entry), became the Queen of the Amazons. This second pilot led to a series of *Wonder Woman* specials in which Carolyn Jones, best known on television as Morticia Addams on *The Addams Family*, became the new potentate of Paradise Island. When the series was reworked and updated in September of 1977, Beatrice Straight was seen in the role of Queen Hippolyte.

By the way, upon learning about the Nazi threat, it was "The Queen Mother" who urged Diana to return with Major Trevor and assume the identity of Diana Prince, Yeoman 1st Class.

Steve and Diana's superior officer, from March 31, 1976 to July 30, 1977, was General Philip Blankenship. He was played by Richard Eastham who was seen from October 16, 1957 to October 9, 1959 as Harris Claibourne on the ABC Western, *Tombstone Territory*.

In the updated and revamped version of *Wonder Woman*, Normann Burton took over the responsibility as Joe Atkinson before Major Trevor himself was appointed as Diana's superior officer. Burton was later seen as Burt Dennis, on *The Ted Knight Show*, which aired on CBS from April 8 to May 13, 1978. The tall, talented and handsome Lyle Waggoner is best remembered for his eleven-year tenure on *The Carol Burnett Show*. Waggoner appeared in sketches with Carol Burnett and Harvey Korman from September 11, 1967 to August 9, 1978.

---

4. Davidson, Bill. *TV Guide*. Vol. 25, No. 5, Issue # 1244, January 29, 1977, p. 24.

Y

THE YOUNG INDIANA JONES CHRONICLES

March 4, 1992–July 24, 1993.   ABC

Character:	Henry "Indiana/Indy" Jones, Jr. (age 9)
Played by:	Corey Carrier
Date(s):	March 4, 1992–July 24, 1993
Replaced by:	Henry "Indiana/Indy" Jones, Jr. (age 17)
Played by:	Sean Patrick Flanery
Date(s):	March 4, 1992–July 24, 1993
Replaced by:	Henry "Old Indy" Jones, Jr. (age 93)
Played by:	George Hall
Date(s):	March 4, 1992–July 24, 1993

Among the many talents of writer/producer George Lucas is his ability to create hit motion pictures and then follow them up, not with sequels, but prequels—that is, the stories and events leading up to the films instead of after them—as he did with his STAR WARS trilogy.

George Lucas has now taken his INDIANA JONES trilogy one step further—one step back, to be more precise—with the creation of a television series, *The Young Indiana Jones Chronicles.*

The first Indiana Jones theatrical release, RAIDERS OF THE LOST ARK (1981), starred Harrison Ford (Han Solo from the STAR WARS trilogy) as Professor Henry Jones, Jr. The role was originally offered to Tom Selleck, who was under contract to Universal and had to drop out because CBS wanted him to play Thomas Sullivan Magnum for its new detective drama, *Magnum, P.I.,* which aired from December 11, 1980 to September 12, 1988.

RAIDERS OF THE LOST ARK was an enormously popular fantasy adventure that paid homage to the Saturday afternoon cliffhangers of the 1930s by borrowing some of their production style. As a result the intense level of excitement doesn't let up for one hundred and fifteen minutes—leaving audiences exhausted, yet thoroughly satisfied.

It should also go without saying that this film, which won Academy Awards for both editing and visual effects, is a tough act to follow and perhaps best left alone. But that did not stop Lucas and director Steven Spielberg from turning out two more successful features in the series: a prequel, INDIANA JONES AND THE TEMPLE OF DOOM, 1984; and INDIANA JONES AND THE LAST CRUSADE, 1989.

At this point, any other producer might have decided to call it quits, but not George Lucas. Four years later he created a wide-screen spectacular for the small screen—*The Young Indiana Jones Chronicles,* a weekly adventure series predating the three films by following Young Indy's adventures from the age of nine.

The approach taken by creator and executive producer George Lucas was to set the series in the present and have the stories unfold as flashbacks triggered by the reminiscences of the now ninety-three-year-old Professor Jones. These wraparounds, which were done as prologues and epilogues at the beginning and end of each show, featured George Hall as the Old Indy in character makeup that was closely modeled after the seventy-eight-year-old countenance of four-time Academy Award-winning director, John Ford.

One of George Hall's most recognizable film roles was Grandpa Walker in the 1988 sports comedy, JOHNNY BE GOOD, that starred Anthony Michael Hall and Robert Downey, Jr.

In the two-hour made-for-television movie, "The Young Indiana Jones and the Curse of the Jackal," we learn that Henry Jones, Jr. took his nickname, "Indiana," from his pet dog. The first hour of the telefilm followed Young Indy at age nine; the second hour jumped ahead eight years to Indy at age seventeen.

The nine-year-old Indy was played by eleven-year-old Corey Carrier, who was a member of the Lenox School Band in the 1987 comedic horror film, THE WITCHES OF EASTWICK. His other film appearances include the 1990 comedies, MY BLUE HEAVEN, which starred Steve Martin and CRAZY PEOPLE, which starred Dudley Moore and Daryl Hannah.

The teenaged Indy was brought to life by Sean Patrick Flanery, who said that he literally watched each of the three Indiana Jones movies more than two dozen times so that he could learn to imitate some of Harrison Ford's mannerisms such as walking, turning around, putting on his hat, cracking a whip and even riding a horse.

In the second half of the two-hour pilot, Young Indy learns to use a whip and is befriended by the extremely likable Belgian, Remy Baudouin, a rather rotund gentleman played by the forty-year-old Belgian actor, Ronny Coutteure, whose native tongue is French—which accounts for Remy's accent. It is Remy who gives Jones his first gun before going into battle, and who then shares a most valuable piece of advice with his young friend: "There is only one rule, Indiana—stay alive."

And stay alive he did, bringing large-screen adventure to the small screen each week in stories featuring Indy at either age, nine or seventeen, but not both as had been done in the pilot.

''Still globe-trotting in his second season, Indy isn't as young as he used to be; actor Sean Patrick Flanery (the teenage Indy) will wield the bullwhip alone as the producers phase out the adventures of little Indy, who was played last season by Corey Carrier.''[1]

All in all, counting River Phoenix, who played Young Indy in the 1989 theatrical film, there have actually been five different actors cast in the role that will nevertheless always be associated with Harrison Ford.

YOUNG DR. KILDARE *see:* DR. KILDARE

1. Tucker, Ken. *Entertainment Weekly.* No. 135, From Friday September 11, 1992. Time, Inc. Magazine Co., 1675 Broadway, New York, NY 10019, p. 20.

Z

ZORRO

October 10, 1957–September 24, 1959.   ABC
October 30, 1960   ABC
November 6, 1960   ABC
January 1, 1961   ABC
April 2, 1961   ABC
January 5, 1990–September 11, 1993   Family Channel

Character: Zorro/Don Diego de la Vega
Played by: Guy Williams
Date(s):   October 10, 1957–September 24, 1959

Replaced by: Don Diego de la Vega/Zorro Sr.
Played by: Henry Darrow
Date(s):   April 6, 1983–June 1, 1983

Replaced by: Don Carlos de la Vega/Zorro, Jr.
Played by: Paul Regina
Date(s):   April 6, 1983–June 1, 1983

Replaced by: Don Diego de la Vega/Zorro
Played by: Duncan Regehr
Date(s):   January 5, 1990–September 11, 1993

Character: Don Alejandro
Played by: George J. Lewis
Date(s):   October 10, 1957–September 24, 1959

Replaced by: Don Alejandro
Played by: Efrem Zimbalist, Jr.
Date(s):   January 5, 1990–May 27, 1990

Replaced by: Don Alejandro
Played by: Henry Darrow
Date(s):   September 14, 1990–September 11, 1993

Character: Bernardo
Played by: Gene Sheldon
Date(s):   October 10, 1957–September 24, 1959

Replaced by: Felipe
Played by: Juan Diego Botto
Date(s):   January 5, 1990–September 11, 1993

Character: Captain Enrique Montasario
Played by: Britt Lomond
Date(s):   October 10, 1957–1959

Replaced by: Magistrate Galindo
Played by: Vinton Hayworth
Date(s):   1957–1959

Replaced by: Alcalde Luis Ramon
Played by: Michael Tylo
Date(s):   January 5, 1990–February 24, 1991

Replaced by: Alcalde Ignacio DeSoto
Played by: John Hertzler
Date(s):   September 1, 1991–September 11, 1993

Character: Sergeant Demitrio Lopez Garcia
Played by: Henry Calvin
Date(s):   October 10, 1957–September 24, 1959

Replaced by: Sergeant Jaime Mendoza
Played by: James Victor
Date(s):   January 5, 1990–September 11, 1993

Character: Anna Maria Verdugo
Played by: Jolene Brand
Date(s):   1958–September 24, 1959

Replaced by: Victoria Escalante
Played by: Patrice (Camhi) Martinez
Date(s):   January 5, 1990–September 11, 1993

"Out of the night when the full moon is bright comes the horseman known as Zorro. This bold renegade carves a 'Z' with his blade, a 'Z' that stands for Zorro. Zorro, the fox so cunning and free, Zorro who makes the sign of the 'Z.' Zorro, Zorro, Zorro, Zorro, Zorro!"

The opening theme song from the Walt Disney production of *Zorro* ends with the name "Zorro" repeated five times, but this actually falls quite a few Zorros short, as there have been more than two dozen actors responsible for bringing the legendary swordsman of Old California to life. Four of these were in television versions, the rest in full-length motion pictures and movie serials in the United States and abroad.

Guy Williams in the title role of the classic Disney production of *Zorro*.

Duncan Regehr as Zorro in the Family Channel's lavishly produced 1990's incarnation of the legendary swordsman of Old California.

The black-cloaked crusader made his first appearance in *The Curse of Capistrano,* a series of six short stories by Johnston McCulley that ran in *All Story* magazine beginning with the August 9, 1919 issue. These stories were collected and released in 1924 as the novel, *The Mark of Zorro.*

It was Douglas Fairbanks, Sr. who first brought McCulley's colorful character to the screen in the 1920 silent film, THE MARK OF ZORRO. This was followed by two twelve-chapter serials: ZORRO RIDES AGAIN (1937) and ZORRO'S FIGHTING LEGION (1939). The first starred John Carroll, and Reed Hadley was under the mask in the latter.

In 1938, Warner Bros. released THE ADVENTURES OF ROBIN HOOD starring Errol Flynn in the title role. Two years later, Twentieth Century-Fox released THE MARK OF ZORRO. Jay Robert Nash and Stanley Ralph Ross point out in *The Motion Picture Guide* that ZORRO was "Fox's answer to Warner Bros.' THE ADVENTURES OF ROBIN HOOD." The film even features some of the same supporting cast. Basil Rathbone, who played Sir Guy of Gisbourne was cast as Zorro's adversary, Captain Esteban Pasquale. Eugene Pallette, who was Robin's Friar Tuck, played another man of the cloth, Father Felipe while Montagu Love, who had been the Bishop of Black Canons in THE ADVENTURES OF ROBIN HOOD, became Diego's father, Don Alejandro. The dual-personality role of Don Diego Vega and Zorro was taken on by Tyrone Power and stands as one of his best performances.

One of the most important factors contributing to the success of any superhero character is what is known as the legend or origin; that is, the explanation of how an ordinary person becomes extraordinary. Equally as important as the powers, talents and special skills of such superheroes, are their relationships with others.

In the Tyrone Power version, Don Diego Vega had two living parents, Don Alejandro (Montagu Love) and Senora Isabella Vega (Janet Beecher), neither of whom knew of his double identity. Diego does, however, take Fra Felipe (Eugene Pallette) into his confidence when he hands him two bags of swag.

DIEGO: Quick, hide this plunder.

PADRE: Plunder?

DIEGO: Don't stand there gaping at me like a fish, put it away.

PADRE: What is this?

DIEGO: It's some of the Alcalde's gold. And this (holding up a jeweled necklace) I took from his charming wife. It's pretty, don't you think?

PADRE: You took?

DIEGO: Have you seen this one, Padre? (Holding Zorro's mask up to his face.)

PADRE: Zorro?!

This is the last time the audience sees Zorro's mask for shortly afterward, the tyrannical Alcalde deduces Zorro's secret identity and throws him in prison, eliminating the need for Don Diego to continue the charade. At the end of the picture, Don Diego, with the assistance of the good Padre and the peons (pronounced "pay-owns") defeat the Alcalde's lancers and force the despot into publicly returning the office of Alcalde to his predecessor, Don Alejandro, who now, along with everyone else in Los Angeles, knows that his son is (or, at least was) Zorro.

Throughout the 1930s and 1940s there were also a number of ZORRO serials. The 1949 entry THE GHOST OF ZORRO, for example, starred an actor who later became famous wearing another black mask that stood for justice in the Old West. The actor was Clayton Moore—the first of television's Lone Rangers (See Entry).

"There were some stunt doubles such as Yakima Canutt, who although they were never credited, probably played Zorro more than anyone else before Guy Williams,"[1] said Bill Yenne, author of *The Legend of Zorro.* Canutt also doubled for Lon Chaney, Jr. (Akhoba, chief of the Rock Tribe) in the 1940 science fiction adventure film, ONE MILLION B.C., that starred Victor Mature and Carole Landis.

Eight years later, Walt Disney studios brought Johnston McCulley's characters to television, first in a series of seventy-eight half-hour episodes, and later in four hour-long segments shown during the seventh season of *Walt Disney Presents.* Both versions featured the same cast.

The Zorro legend in these Disney films differs slightly from the Tyrone Power film and from each other. To begin with, the name of the most important family in Southern California has evolved to "de la Vega." Tyrone Power's Don Diego had both a mother and a father, while in the Disney versions he had only a father. Throughout most of the Power film, Don Diego keeps his alter ego a secret from everyone, including his father. This secrecy was maintained through the first fifty-three half-hour Disney *Zorro*s, but in the fifty-fourth episode, "Amnesty for Zorro," which aired on January 1, 1959, Don Diego's secret is revealed to his father, Don Alejandro.

The discovery is made when Alejandro prevents Diego from dueling with Ricardo Delano (Richard Anderson) for the hand of Anna Maria Verdugo (Jolene Brand), so that he can fight on for the liberation of the peasants, with Don Alejandro supporting his son's crusades as Zorro.

The origin story, which was retold in comic book form by Alex Toth, begins in 1820 with Diego aboard a ship returning to Spanish California from Spain, where some three years earlier he was sent to study. In the opening scene, Don Diego is seen on deck dueling with the ship's captain. When they finish their sport, the seaman tells Diego that Los Angeles

---

1. From an exclusive telephone interview with Bill Yenne on July 19, 1991.

is no longer the way he remembers it; a new tyrannical commandante (who is bent on becoming the richest man in Los Angeles) has taken over the Pueblo de Los Angeles and has imposed a harsh military rule over its citizens. Furthermore, Diego is told he should expect to have his baggage searched upon his arrival.

This disturbing news clears up the vagueness of his father's last letter to him, which Diego asks his dumb manservant and closest friend, Bernardo (Gene Sheldon), to fetch for him so that he may reread it. "My dear son, it is with a heavy heart that I ask you to give up your studies and come home. Certain matters have arisen that I cannot face alone." Realizing that no one must suspect that his father has summoned him home, he orders Bernardo to burn the letter and throw his fencing trophies and other mementos overboard.

Diego tells Bernardo that he must find a way to deal with the tyrant who has taken over the pueblo, and Bernardo, miming the use of a sword, suggests a show of force. Diego disagrees with the suggestion as he explains:

DIEGO: No, Bernardo. When dealing with a powerful enemy we must play another game. You know the old proverb: 'When you cannot clothe yourself in the skin of a lion, put on that of a fox.'

Understanding that Diego must present himself in a different light to throw off the authorities, Bernardo suggests that he portray himself as a genteel man of letters who is more interested in literature, science, art and music than politics—the perfect cover for the skillful swordsman who would soon become the champion of the people.

Bernardo then motions to Diego that he too wants to portray a character he is not. Diego instructs him to play the fool. Bernardo suggests that he pretend to be deaf as well as dumb.

It is a dangerous notion that is put to the test when their coach arrives in Los Angeles. The gullible Sergeant Garcia believes the ruse and when questioned by his superior, Commandante Montasario, Garcia proceeds to insult Bernardo to his face, saying that he has the face of a donkey, smells like a goat, and is the son of a baboon. Bernardo's response is a trusting smile. This, however, is not enough to convince Montasario who fires a rifle at the ground while Garcia and Bernardo are unloading Diego's baggage from the top of the coach. Fortunately, Bernardo manages to ignore the sound of the shot, but Garcia is startled and drops a trunk he is attempting to unload. It is this charade that convinces Captain Montasario of Bernardo's handicaps.

Back at the de la Vega hacienda, Don Diego accomplishes the painful task of convincing his father of his lack of interest in politics, which is necessary to protect Don Alejandro from retribution. Retiring to his room Diego tells Bernardo what he has just done.

DIEGO: Remember what I said this morning? If you cannot clothe yourself in the skin of a lion, put on that of a fox? From now on I shall be Zorro, the fox (as he scars a "Z" on a piece of sheet music with his sword).

No explanation, however, is given of the origin of the costume, which is seen for the first time in the episode when Zorro rides into town to free his neighbor, Nacho Torres (Jan Arvan), who was imprisoned by Montasario for speaking out against political injustice.

In another episode, to further protect himself from arousing any suspicion, Diego teaches Bernardo how to play the guitar.

DIEGO: If you are ever going to cover for me when I'm out riding as Zorro, it must sound as if I'm here practicing.

Later in that same episode Don Diego instructs Bernardo to use his musical skill.

DIEGO: Tonight, you must lock yourself in my room and play the guitar as well as you can. (Bernardo makes the sign of the 'Z' in the air with his index finger.) Yes, and I must be back before my father misses me.

In this continuation of the origin story, which retells and expands on some of the legend, Don Diego makes it quite obvious that he realizes how foolish it would be for Zorro to ride Diego's white horse, Phantom. He then tells Bernardo of another horse, Toronado, a black stallion that even his father doesn't know about because he had left the colt with a shepherd to care for while he was away in Spain. Diego explains to Bernardo that the horse will be kept in a secret cave below the hacienda and shows him the secret entrance through the fireplace that he says he found as a boy and believed was built by his grandfather as a means of escaping from possible Indian raids.

Walt Disney cast the handsome thirty-three-year-old Guy Williams as Zorro/Don Diego de la Vega (as he was billed in the credits). This was a real break for Williams, who had failed to break into the business in 1952 and had returned to New York to pursue a career in modeling, which was a little closer to his goals than some of his earlier occupations such as soda jerk and garment worker.

It is reported that one of the main reasons that Guy Williams won the coveted role was that in addition to standing six-foot three-inches tall and sporting Don Diego's characteristic mustache and long sideburns, he was the only actor among those auditioned who knew how to fence. He learned the art from his father, an avid fencer.

To further prepare for the role, Williams took guitar lessons from Vincente Gomez and a refresher course in fencing from Fred Cavens, who was to be the fencing master for the Disney series. Another Cavens, Albert, was the Belgian fencing master who took on the responsibility of preparing both Douglas Fairbanks, Sr. and Tyrone Power for their roles as the champion swordsman and also served as Power's stunt double in his more strenuous scenes.

For his second television series Guy Williams traded in his mask, black costume and cape for a space suit, to become Professor John Robinson. The juvenile CBS science fiction, *Lost in Space* (September 15, 1965–September 11, 1968), co-starred Jonathan Harris as Dr. Zachary Smith. Years earlier,

Harris, as Don Carlos, had crossed swords with Williams' Zorro.

Diego's father, Alejandro, was played by George J. Lewis, who himself had played Zorro in the 1944 serial, ZORRO'S BLACK WHIP. He also appeared as the traitor Collins, who staged the ambush of the Texas Rangers for Butch Cavendish in the first two episodes of the three-part origin story of *The Lone Ranger* television series. In the second episode, "The Lone Ranger Fights On," Collins conveniently falls to his death, thus protecting the Lone Ranger's secret. His other appearances on *The Lone Ranger* include "Pay Dirt" (March 23, 1950), "The Trouble at Black Rock" (February 8, 1951), and "The Return of Don Pedro O'Sullivan" (October 25, 1956), in which the Lone Ranger impersonates the red-haired Mexican revolutionary.

Just as in the motion picture, Don Diego is friends with Father Felipe at the Mission de San Gabriel, but does not take him into his confidence, as Tyrone Power had.

In place of Father Felipe, who was Diego's mentor and later confidant in THE MARK OF ZORRO, Disney introduced Diego's mute manservant, Bernardo. The very likable middle-aged actor, who bore a slight resemblance to comedian Ed Wynn, was Gene Sheldon. His early film roles include Ali, the genie, in the fanciful 1945 musical comedy, WHERE DO WE GO FROM HERE? He was also Sam Jordan in the 1951 Mitzi Gaynor musical, GOLDEN GIRL, and Puffo in the 1954 Martin and Lewis comedy, THREE RING CIRCUS.

It is somewhat surprising that one of the most vivid images of these *Zorro* episodes is not of the dark horseman riding his black stallion, but of Zorro's blade cutting a "Z" in the front of the rotund Sergeant Garcia's pants. The mark was actually cut below the Sergeant's beltline and were it an inch or two lower, the baritone-voiced actor, who sang the lead vocal for the *Zorro* theme song (later released on Buena Vista Records), could very well have become a soprano.

On April 10, 1957, a few months before his debut as Sergeant Garcia, Henry Calvin had an opportunity to showcase his vocal talents as Wilfred Shadbolt in the NBC special adaptation of Gilbert and Sullivan's operetta, *The Yeoman of the Guard*.

Henry Calvin was perfectly cast as the bulbous, bumbling sergeant of the pueblo lancers and Zorro's foil. He also provided most of the comic relief in the series. Garcia once explained how he managed to rise through the ranks, in an answer to a question from the jewel thief, Carlos Murietta (Kent Taylor).

CARLOS:　　How did anyone as stupid as you become sergeant?

GARCIA:　　Wasn't easy. I was a private for a long time. Then one day I saw the Commandante kissing the Magistrato's wife, and the next thing you know I . . . I am a sergeant, senor, because I possess the natural qualities of leadership.

When not playing Sergeant Garcia, Disney tapped in to Henry Calvin's Oliver Hardy impression for several of the studio's films. In the 1960 Disney drama, TOBY TYLER, Henry Calvin as Ben Cotter was teamed with his *Zorro* co-star,

Gene Sheldon, who played Sam Treat. A year later, in the Christmas musical BABES IN TOYLAND, Calvin played Gonzorgo opposite Gene Sheldon's Roderigo; like his Bernardo character on *Zorro*, Gonzorgo was played as a mute. These were essentially the Oliver Dee and Stanley Dum roles played by Oliver Hardy and Stan Laurel in the 1934 version of the film that is also known as MARCH OF THE WOODEN SOLDIERS.

Television viewers were treated to Henry Calvin's Oliver Hardy in "The Sam Pomerantz Scandals," the March 6, 1963 episode of *The Dick Van Dyke Show* (See Entry).

Since the hefty sergeant posed no real threat to Zorro, the true villain of the series was Captain Montasario, the Alcalde or "mayor" of the pueblo de Los Angeles who imposed unfair taxes on the good people and forced the Indians under his rule to work as slave labor. This incarnation of evil was played by Britt Lomond, who went on to play Johnny Ringo in the 1960/1961 season of *The Life and Legend of Wyatt Earp*.

Montasario was eventually killed and replaced by Sergeant Garcia, who served for a while as the garrison's Acting Commandante; but it was Vinton Hayworth, as Magistrate Galindo, who became the people's oppressor and Zorro's adversary. Hayworth later turned to the right side of the law when he took on the role of Captain Anthony Nelson's commanding officer, General Winfield Schaeffer, on the Barbara Eden sitcom, *I Dream of Jeannie* (See Entry).

Though not a new series, Zorro returned to television on October 29, 1974, in *The Mark of Zorro*, an ABC made-for-television movie that was essentially a remake of the 1940 film. Wearing Zorro's black mask and cape in the ninety-minute feature was Frank Langella, who went on to star as another black-caped character in the 1979 remake of DRACULA.

The other members of *The Mark of Zorro* cast included Jorge Cervera, Jr. as Sergeant Gonzales, Tom Lacy as Fray Felipe and Yvonne DeCarlo, who had created the role of Lily on *The Munsters* (See Entry), as Icela Vega.

Diego's father, Don Alejandro, was played by Gilbert Roland, who had guest-starred as the bandit, El Cuchillo, in two of the hour-long Disney *Zorro*'s, "El Bandido" and "Adios El Cuchillo," that aired on October 30 and November 6, 1960. Ricardo Montalban, who played Captain Esteban, had appeared as Ramon Castillo in "Auld Acquaintance," the April 2, 1961 episode of the half-hour Disney *Zorro*. Among his many motion picture and television appearances, Ricardo Montalban is best remembered as Mr. Roarke from *Fantasy Island* and as Kahn Noonian Singh in the 1982 science fiction, STAR TREK II: THE WRATH OF KHAN.

Zorro returned to television on September 12, 1981, in a series of Saturday morning cartoons that aired as one of the segments of the *Tarzan/Lone Ranger/Zorro Adventure Hour*. The series was produced by Norm Prescott and Lou Scheimer's Filmation Studios and aired through September 11, 1982.

Providing the voices for the animated characters were Henry Darrow as Don Diego and Zorro, Carlos Rivas as Don Alejandro, Don Diamond as Sergeant Gonzales, and Christine Avila as Maria. For a short time, Fernando Lamas replaced Henry Darrow as Don Diego and Zorro.

Henry Darrow, who had played Detective Lieutenant Manny Quinlan on *Harry-O* (See Entry) explained how he landed the role of Zorro: "I auditioned for Lou Scheimer while Norm Prescott directed. When Norm took my tape to CBS they told him, 'Henry has to be a little careful, because the show is for young kids and there's too much inflection in his voice—he sounds a little too sexy when he talks with the girl.' I said, 'What?' and Lou said 'Just do what you're doing, just don't give us so much inflection. Make it a little straighter.'

"To be better prepared for the role, I started to watch some of those Saturday morning cartoons and realized that there is a certain sound to the voice—a kind of a brightness. Part of the reason for that 'sound,' that may seem as though you are talking to yourself, is because you *are* talking to yourself. You rarely tape with another actor—you tape separately. I never did a scene with another actor, I just came in and did my stuff and left. Then someone else would come in and do theirs. That's why you couldn't give a scene too much inflection at the end of a sentence or phrase, because the other actor wouldn't be aware of what you did. And when they came in to record their lines it wouldn't sound as though we were really talking to each other,"[2] he said.

Darrow did, however, get to talk to other actors when he took on the role of the more mature Don Diego de la Vega/Zorro Sr. in the Walt Disney satire, *Zorro and Son,* which may have been inspired by George Hamilton's moderately successful 1980 film, ZORRO, THE GAY BLADE. The Disney-produced series aired a total of five episodes on CBS from April 6 to June 1, 1983.

The setting for this short-lived situation comedy is old California around 1845, twenty-five years after Diego first became Zorro. It begins with Diego's faithful servant, Bernardo (Bill Dana), asking Diego's son, Don Carlos (Paul Regina), to return from Spain to help his father, whose sword is losing some of its z-z-zip, stand up to the new commandante, Paco Pico (Gregory Sierra). Sierra, who has appeared on *All in the Family, Barney Miller* and *Soap,* may be best remembered as Fred Sanford's next-door neighbor, Julio Fuentes, on *Sanford and Son.*

The commandante's dimwitted subordinate, Sergeant Sepulveda, was played by Richard Beauchamp who had played Rodriguez on Don Rickles' situation comedy, *C.P.O. Sharkey.* And in what may be more than a stranger-than-truth coincidence, the offices for the Family Channel's *Zorro* production were located on South Sepulveda Boulevard in Los Angeles, California. There was also a Corporal Sepulveda (Tabare Carballo) serving under Sergeant Mendoza in the Family Channel's production of *Zorro.*

Diego does his best to school his son in the Zorro tradition, but the generation gap widens when Don Carlos, a gambling womanizer, introduces guns and other modern weaponry into his repertoire.

Another departure from the original legend is that Bernardo, Digeo's mute servant in the original Disney series, talks a blue streak in this revival, as Bill Dana, famous for his Jose Jimenez character, explained in a 1983 *TV Guide* interview: " 'I'm

playing Bernardo,' says Dana, 'as if he were Jose, back under a different name.' "

One of the funnier gags comes from fast-talker John Moschitta, Jr. as the Commandante's informer, Corporal Cassette, a human tape recorder who can repeat overheard conversations word-for-word—forward, backward and at fast and slow speeds.

"I had my first audition at Disney," said Darrow, "and read for the casting director and the producer, Eric Cohen, and they liked me very much. After a little time went by I was asked to read for the people at CBS, which included producer Kevin Corcoran and director Peter Baldwin. Fernando Allende had already read for the part of Don Carlos and I was scheduled to read with Paul Regina. He and I hit it off well. I remember saying to Paul, 'Paul, I want to pantomime a little fencing as part of the audition.' He knew his dialogue by heart and I knew most of mine and it went quite well. It was a scene where I revealed to him that I was Zorro, and he just breaks up laughing because he didn't believe me. In fact, that was one of the scenes that was cut from the opening segment of *Zorro and Son.*

"Eric Cohen, who was responsible for casting John Travolta in *Welcome Back, Kotter,* had the same kind of a feeling about Paul Regina because there was a similarity between them.

"They liked my style for Don Diego/Zorro and wanted Paul because he was a little more modern and he had sort of a similarity and an attitude like John Travolta's,"[3] Darrow said.

"I was the right age, the right look. I'm half Italian, a quarter Puerto Rican and a quarter Mexican, so I had Hispanic blood in me—which helped to open the door that made me the third actor to play the son of Zorro," said Paul Regina. Douglas Fairbanks, who had played Zorro in the 1920 feature, THE MARK OF ZORRO, took on the dual roles of both father (Don Diego) and son (Don Cesar) de Vega in the 1925 United Artists release, DON Q, THE SON OF ZORRO. Twenty-two years later, George Turner played Zorro Jr. in Republic Picture's thirteen-chapter serial, THE SON OF ZORRO, released in 1947.

"Not only did I grow up watching the original Disney *Zorro,* but I initially read with Guy Williams, who was asked to reprise his character from the earlier series. They were trying to coax him out of retirement, and didn't succeed. I had heard that they had also considered Cesar Romero for the Don Diego/Zorro role. But obviously, when Henry came in the magic happened and that's the way they went,"[4] Regina said.

Henry Darrow, who does bear a resemblance to Douglas Fairbanks, Sr., admitted to "borrowing" Fairbanks' entrance for his own on *Zorro and Son:*

"I stole that from him. I told Peter Baldwin that I wanted to be cocked and seated on the banister, with my back against the wall or wood beam connected to the banister, like Fairbanks. Then when the guy looks up and says, 'Who's that?' all the peasants answer, 'It's Zorro!' It's fun to capture a bit of cinematic history and I figured, 'Why not?' So I just stole it outright," laughed Darrow.

2. From an exclusive telephone interview with Henry Darrow on January 19, 1991.
3. From an exclusive telephone interview with Henry Darrow on January 19, 1991.
4. From an exclusive telephone interview with Paul Regina on January 30, 1993.

"My favorite Zorro was Tyrone Power, that was the version that I recalled. I researched the part by going to bookstores looking for old books and magazine pictures of Zorro,"[5] Darrow said.

Speaking about Henry Darrow, Paul Regina said "Going to work to see Henry Darrow was like going to school. It was an absolute joy. Something clicked in him with his Zorro character. I just saw this man being able to do the silliest, most ridiculous and strangest things. Henry just ate it alive. It was just so much fun to watch him work. You never knew what he was going to do. You never knew what little twist he was going to add—which was everything from physical schtick to that twinkle in his eye. It was just wonderful. When I got off camera, I had the best seat in the house. It wasn't like I was working. I would think to myself 'I can't believe I'm getting to watch this.' I really wish that show had stayed on, just so I could have seen what more could have come out of Henry," said Regina admiringly. It wasn't long before Darrow's enthusiasm for the larger-than-life character began to rub off on Paul Regina, who related the the story of his own metamorphosis: "There was one moment in an episode where I was standing on a wall after having saved the girl. I remember now that when I gave her that salute I was personally very aware of that little moment. I took my sword and flipped it, cocked my head and made sure the key light hit my eye, and thought to myself, 'God, I'm Zorro . . . I'm Zorro!,'"[6] recalled Regina with great enthusiasm.

"We started shooting the series and when the first dailies came back they were a little concerned that Don Carlos was too modern," said Darrow. "I think what starts to happen is there are so many people who have ideas as to how to play a part, it becomes a committee kind of approach to directing—it's intimidation by numbers.

"By the time we were shooting episode three and going into episode four, we had hit a stride and a few people felt a little leery about showing the first episode, which had a different feel than the later episodes, but we had to air it because that was the show that set up the series and introduced all of the characters.

"So after six weeks, we placed seventy-three out of seventy-four shows on the air, and that was the end of it,"[7] Henry Darrow said.

"I think the reason *Zorro and Son* did so poorly in the ratings was that CBS put it on ahead of a program called *Square Pegs*. Now *Square Pegs* was the lowest-rated show on television—second to none—and the other two networks had very high-rated shows airing against it in that time slot, *The Fall Guy* on ABC and *Real People* on NBC," explained John Gertz, president of *Zorro Productions, Inc.* "*Zorro and Son* was well-produced with good production values and was actually pretty funny. It would have been better received had it not, by a fluke of fate, been put back-to-back with such a terrible show. It simply had no lead in,"[8] he added.

Darrow continued "It was a lot of fun to do and I even got to wear Guy Williams' wardrobe, which had to be shortened because he was three inches taller than me. "The working conditions were great and the scripts were marvelous. I remember one scene where Don Carlos asks me why I became Zorro, and I told him, 'There are a lot of advantages, I get to fight for justice, help the poor, save the people and sometimes . . . I just put on the outfit, hit the bars and score like a bandit, son,' "[9] laughed Darrow.

"Zorro would duel for fifteen minutes to subdue three bad guys and then my character, who had recently attended the university in Spain, would walk in and say, 'Dad, twenty minutes to subdue these guys?' Then I'd throw one gas bomb and 'poof'—that was it!"[10] chuckled Regina.

This was not the first time Henry Darrow had been on the Disney lot; we had done a screen test for the part of one of the heavies for the original *Zorro* series. "I screen-tested opposite Shirley Knight (who lost out to Jolene Brand), but I was a little too young. While waiting to audition I watched this one particular actor, Carlos Romero, who was very smooth, quiet and low key. I remember turning to the other young guys standing there and saying, 'This guy's terrible, he's got no guts, no balls.' Then it's my turn and I overact a storm, and continued to do it take-after-take until the director, Bill Whitney, who had seen enough, said, 'Thank you very much, thank you.' Then, as I was walking off the set, I overheard him say to someone, 'We have a Latin Barrymore on our hands.' I didn't get the part, but was very flattered by what I felt to be an enormous compliment. I just wasn't right for the role, I wasn't ready to do a part like that,"[11] confessed Darrow.

There were two more Zorros in the series. Jerry Wills doubled for Darrow in the scenes requiring difficult horsemanship, such as rearing and falls, while a second double, George Ruge, did most of the fencing and fighting scenes. He's easy to spot because he's slimmer and moves much more quickly than Henry Darrow.

This, however, was not the last time Henry Darrow would stand up for the oppressed as a de la Vega in old Los Angeles, but it would not be before the role of Zorro was taken over by another actor.

More than thirty years after Disney's *Zorro* series rode off into the night, the Family Channel introduced a well-written and lavishly produced new *Zorro* series. The first episode of the new *Zorro*, "Dead Men Tell No Tales," premiered on January 5, 1990 and, like the original, opened with an exciting and catchy theme song that even included an identical phrase "out of the night," possibly a tip of the hat to the composers of the original. And while the Disney theme was sung by Henry

5. From an exclusive telephone interview with Henry Darrow on January 19, 1991.
6. From an exclusive telephone interview with Paul Regina on January 30, 1993.
7. From an exclusive telephone interview with Henry Darrow on January 19, 1991.
8. From an exclusive telephone interview with John Gertz on December 11, 1991.
9. From an exclusive telephone interview with Henry Darrow on January 19, 1991.
10. From an exclusive telephone interview with Paul Regina on January 30, 1993.
11. From an exclusive telephone interview with Henry Darrow on January 19, 1991.

Calvin and an all-male chorus, this one was belted out by a woman with equal effect.

"When daggers are pointed at innocent hearts and muskets are ready to fire, where tyrants ride high and govern with fear and the forces of evil conspire, then from out of the night a hero must ride with courage that even a mask won't disguise. They turn to the man called Zorro—Zorro! When he's larger than life and defender of all, he's this man who the people acclaim, he's the one who fights back for the poor and oppressed, a hero—whose name is Zorro; his name is Zorro!"

"This new version of *Zorro* features a masterful casting job: Physically, Duncan Regehr is a perfect new Zorro; he looks like a youthful version of the Zorro from the '50s, Guy Williams, right down to the little mustache that resembles a black French fry. And Regehr plays the part well, capturing this masked swordsman's playfulness and romanticism. At the same time, Regehr is careful to keep his interpretation from slacking off into a winking, campy character."[12]

Henry Darrow, the actor who took over the role of Don Alejandro de la Vega in the second season, expressed some fatherly admiration regarding the casting of Duncan Regehr as his son Don Diego/Zorro: "Duncan's Zorro is probably the most complete in terms of physical talents—top fencer, an excellent horseman—powerful and graceful in fight sequences—the quickest study in regards to fight and fencing sequences I've seen. His Zorro has *dash* and *flash*. After all, the name of the show is *Zorro* and you've got to go for it and he does! His Diego is straighter than my portrayal on *Zorro and Son*, but serves as a better role model for young people by focusing on music, theater and the arts."[13]

The supporting cast for the first season includes Efrem Zimbalist, Jr. as Don Alejandro; Michael Tylo as the corrupt Alcalde, Luis Ramon; James Victor as the less-than-competent sergeant of the guards, Jaime Mendoza; and Patrice (Camhi) Martinez as Victoria Escalante, the owner of the pueblo's gathering place, Victoria's Tavern, and Zorro's love interest. Jolene Brand was introduced as Anna Maria Verdugo, Zorro's love interest, during the 1958/1959 season of the Walt Disney series, but theirs never became the ongoing relationship that existed between Zorro and Victoria. Their relationship was not unlike the eternal triangle that existed between Lois Lane, Clark Kent and Superman.

Patrice Martinez, the only member of the *Zorro* cast to appear in the unaired pilot, co-starred as Carmen in the 1986 Chevy Chase/Steve Martin/Martin Short comedy, THE THREE AMIGOS, and was the chartreuse receptionist in the doctor's office in the 1988 comedy, BEETLEJUICE. She used her married name "Camhi" during *Zorro*'s first and second seasons, but returned to Martinez after her divorce, which was finalized prior to the filming of third season episodes. The pilot starred Patrick James as Don Antonio de la Cruz/Zorro and Val De Vargas as the Alcalde.

As in each of the other versions, there too was a Felipe in this new series, but this time he wasn't the padre of the mission. In this '90s production of Johnston McCulley's eternal hero of Spanish California, Felipe, played by Juan Diego Botto, replaced the Bernardo character as Diego's servant and confidant. And just as Bernardo was mute but not deaf, so too is Felipe.

He helps the de la Vegas around the hacienda, cares for Toronado, and is always ready to offer his assistance to the defender of the people. To purists, this departure from the tradition of Zorro's mature manservant may seem a little jarring, but it may be a better alternative. There always seemed to be something demeaning about Bernardo's having to act ignorant, and it made viewers feel uncomfortable. The young Felipe exhibits a natural innocence that is not only refreshing, but works very well within the framework of the *Zorro* tradition and stays very close to the original legend—one of the keys to its success.

"I did not personally favor casting a child in the role of Felipe," said John Gertz. "I thought that if you're going to keep the character of a mute servant, who is also pretending that he cannot hear, then you need to get a really talented mime. It was, and still is, my feeling that no adolescent either has the talent or could be taught the talent of miming to the extent that I would be satisfied. Regrettably, in my opinion, Felipe does little more than flail his arms around a bit. There is no talented miming there,"[14] said Gertz.

The origin story, "Zorro: The Legend Begins," was presented as a two-hour special on Saturday, February 17, 1990, and differed slightly from the Disney version.

What is interesting is that The Family Channel aired this movie, which explains the origin of Zorro and introduces the main cast of characters, more than a month after the beginning of the weekly series, which, for a short time, left newcomers to the legend in the dark. This was, according to John Gertz, due in part to the fact that the script for the "Legend" episode was not approved as originally written and had to go back for several rewrites before being produced.

A couple of other replacements of interest were not in the cast, but in Zorro's costume. In the origin story, for instance, Zorro's hat did not have the band with the silver conchos that he wears in the half-hour episodes. And his sword was more akin to the thin four-sided blade of a fencing epee. This weapon was later replaced with a wider-bladed saber. But it was this hat without the conchos and the foil-like sword that appeared in all of Duncan Regehr's publicity stills that ran for the entire first season of the series.

Irish McCalla, the actress who played Sheena in the 1950s series, *Sheena Queen of the Jungle* (See Entry), said, "I love the new Zorro. I think he's just marvelous. I loved the other one too, and I'm glad they stayed with the character and didn't try to give him any weird powers."[15]

When Duncan Regehr, who stands two inches taller than Guy Williams, was asked if he had ever seen his predecessor's

12. Tucker, Ken. *Entertainment Weekly*. Issue #1. From Friday 2/16/90. The Time, Inc. Magazine Co., 1675 Broadway, New York, NY 10019. p. 103.
13. From an exclusive telephone interview with Henry Darrow and a letter to the author dated December 5, 1991.
14. From an exclusive telephone interview with John Gertz on December 11, 1991.
15. From an exclusive telephone interview with Irish McCalla on December 9, 1990.

portrayal of Zorro, he explained, "I might have seen it in passing, but I can say quite honestly that I've never seen an episode of the Disney series. When I first got this role somebody gave me some tapes of the Disney series and said, 'You might want to look at these.' I said, 'I'm not looking at these,' and put them on the shelf where they've been ever since. I don't know what they thought I wanted to do with the part, but my only intention was to make it my own—as I do with any role. I don't want to copy what's been done before. That makes it kind of boring, don't you think?"[16]

Regehr went on to explain how he got the role: "I was under contract to ABC for the Disney series, *Earth*Star Voyager* when this thing first came up and I tried to get out of the contract. They said, 'No, we won't let him out to do *Zorro*, we think this show will go.' Then they changed the network (NBC) and time slot for it and they dropped the show. So then I was free, and the *Zorro* people came back to me and asked if I was still interested, and I said, 'Yes.'

"They had already made a pilot by that point and it was said to have been a failure. I heard it was terrible. I believe they recast all of the roles except Victoria, who was and still is being played by Patrice Martinez," Regehr said.

"It's interesting to play a role and to try and please somebody else's vision, but still get your own licks in. For instance, the *Zorro* production people said, 'We really want you to look a lot like the Guy Williams character,' and I said, 'I don't care about Guy Williams. I don't care what he did. My choice for Don Diego was to go for a much more bookish kind of guy, to the point of his wearing a pair of early spectacles, and he forgets things and he's very much the absent-minded professor that the townspeople come to every once in a while to solve difficult scientific problems, rather than the more caballero type of guy that I've developed, which makes the studio very happy. They feel there's more romance involved in that and I say, 'Okay, fine, I'll do it that way if that's what you want.

"I did, however, allow them to dictate the style of my hair and the shape of the mustache. At first they insisted I have this tiny little mustache like the one worn by Guy Williams. You'll notice it's a little thicker in the second season and in the third season you'll see that the mustache is even a little bit thicker, so there are things that I am changing as I go along. They're little things . . . things that I wanted to do originally, but unfortunately, you can't win those battles the first day. You have to wait three years before you can do what you want to and then they'll say, 'Oh yeah, great!' You just have to get them sold on it.

"If we were shooting the pilot tomorrow I would give Don Diego a little mustache and long hair—blonde hair! That's how I'd play him. And when he became Zorro the hair would, of course, disappear underneath that wraparound mask and the hat and all you would have is the man with the mustache. There would be much more contrast between the two characters. There's a certain amount of dramatic license there anyway, since Don Diego happens to be the only six-foot-five caballero in the Los Angeles pueblo—I wonder why they can't figure out

that he's Zorro? But that's true of any of the superheroes, like when Clark Kent takes off his glasses and becomes Superman, but nobody recognizes him," explained Regehr.

Another difference in the way Duncan Regehr portrays the characters of Don Diego and Zorro is the accent and the voice. Douglas Fairbanks, Sr. was silent, so the audience never heard him speak. Tyrone Power essentially used his own voice, while Guy Williams added a slight Spanish intonation. Duncan Regehr's interpretation, like Power's, does not speak with an accent, although he does push his voice into a deeper and throatier register giving the character a thicker sound. "There are differences between Don Diego and Zorro; it's very, very subtle, but there is a little bit of a difference. I tried to work on a voice that I thought would sound right coming out of a mask. In a way, it's almost a disembodied kind of a voice. Because there's really not too much else you can tell a story with. You're whole face is just about gone so you can't really express too much with that, and your eyes are very shadowed most of the time because of the mask . . . and the hat. So you've got to use body language more, which I've tried to do," Regehr said.

The only portion of Regehr's face that is visible is his mouth, and he takes full advantage of his infectious smile. "I call it twinkling. It's actually something I got from Don Taylor who directed me in *My Wicked, Wicked Ways . . . The Legend of Errol Flynn* [January 21, 1985]."

Much of Zorro's body language comes through in the fencing scenes, one of the most important aspects of the character, as Duncan Regehr discussed: "I guess I've been at it about eighteen years. I trained with Patrick Crean, who's a great old fencer and doubled Errol Flynn. Presently I work with Peter Diamond, who is unquestionably the world's greatest film coordinator/fencer.

"I liked books when I was a kid because we didn't have television. I was fascinated with Robin Hood as a child and have read every story that was ever written about him. I was involved in theater at a very young age. I had my first professional job on the stage at the age of sixteen and that's really where I learned to fence. It was a tool, that's all. It came to me very naturally. It's a little like riding a bike, it's something you never forget.

"There are different ways of fencing. If you watch me in *My Wicked, Wicked Ways,* in which I played Errol Flynn, I fenced the way Errol Flynn fenced in his movies. If you flip on *Zorro* you'll see that I have developed a totally different style of fencing to match the character. I fence how I think my character of Zorro would fence. You've got to find the right style for the character," Regehr explained.

One of the factors working against the actors is the temperature. Duncan Regehr elaborated: "The heat is really extraordinary to work in. It was 115 to 120 last year. It's unbelievably hot, especially wearing an all-black costume. One day I took the hat off and was burned on the forehead, right where one of the metal studs was on the band—right through the hat! Now that's hot. When I played Don Diego, they had to pat makeup on it to hide the big red mark it had left.

---

16. This and following remarks by Duncan Regehr in this *Zorro* entry are from an exclusive telephone interview with Mr. Regehr on January 17, 1991.

"And to get the horses to do anything in that heat is a major task, because they just don't want to move. In fact, there were actually three or four horses who served as Toronado. One we call 'the dead horse' because he'll behave and do close-ups and ride into town nicely. We've got another one that does jumping very, very well and we've got another one that does rearing," continued Regehr.

Duncan Regehr was no stranger to heroes and superheroes, as can be seen from his earlier television credits, which include a number of made-for-television movies that are worth noting.

One of his first roles on American television was as Captain Randolph in the 1982 CBS miniseries, *The Blue and the Gray.* A year later Regehr played the evil Prince Dirk Blackpool in all eight episodes of the short-lived series, *Wizards and Warriors,* which aired on CBS from February 26 to May 14, 1983. This knights-in-shining-armor fantasy co-starred Julia Duffy as Princess Ariel. Ms. Duffy later went on to play a very different type of princess when she replaced Jennifer Holmes as the new maid of the Stratford Inn on *Newhart* (See Entry). "She was a real princess in every way and one of the most professional actresses I have ever worked with," said Regehr.

A year later, Regehr appeared as Charles in the NBC science fiction series, *V* (October 26, 1984–July 5, 1985).

One of Duncan Regehr's favorite roles was Pat Garrett in the Turner Network Television production of *Billy the Kid.*

With the first season of *Zorro* completed, Efrem Zimbalist, Jr. decided to pack it in and not return as Don Alejandro. Some insight and personal observations about this decision was given by Duncan Regehr. "Casting Efrem was a Family Channel choice and he just kind of dived into it without really knowing what he was getting into, I think. It wasn't for him. He didn't want to play the part after a while. He ate something and became very ill for a long period of time—and he missed his home. It's a long haul to be away in a strange country."

In what seems to have become something of a Hollywood tradition of casting actors who have appeared in earlier versions of this popular series, Henry Darrow, who had played Zorro twice before, joined the cast as Don Alejandro de la Vega. Darrow said:

"I was doing the part of Rafael, a mystic magician and the long-lost father of Cruz Castillo (A Martinez) on the NBC daytime soap opera, *Santa Barbara.* As I recall, they originally signed me to a thirteen-week deal and I think I worked on one or two episodes a week. And then the offer for *Zorro* came along. What they had offered me was the part of Montasario for the original pilot for the series that has never been shown. When I turned it down my friend Val De Vargas wound up playing the role. That would have been intriguing, because I would have played the father, the son and the bad guy. It would have been unique, but it was never meant to be. So here I am on *Santa Barbara* and I'm offered the role of Zorro's father, Don Alejandro, on the *Zorro* series. The money was close, but it would have meant leaving the job at NBC's Burbank studios that were just sixteen miles from where I lived, in order to film *Zorro* in Madrid, Spain for five months. So I opted to stay with *Santa Barbara.*

"Unbeknownst to me they cast Efrem [Zimbalist, Jr.]. This had a lot to do with the fact that Efrem had worked for the Family Channel (formerly the Christian Broadcasting Network, CBN), doing things like Bible readings.

"Meanwhile, my contract on *Santa Barbara* had been extended to a year and my part began to grow. They started writing some good stuff for me and there was even talk about writing me into a love story, but that never materialized. In June, a year later, my contract was coming up for renewal and *Zorro* approaches me again. This time my agent asked the producers of *Santa Barbara* if they were going to pick up my option for another year and they said that they didn't know. We then told them that we had this other offer from *Zorro* and they remained very noncommittal.

"I was then invited to lunch at the Polo Lounge by Gary Goodman, the executive producer of *Zorro,* and we discussed the role, the money and the billing—all of which were satisfactory to me. He also agreed to make the role a little more physical for me than it had been for Efrem, which I was very pleased with. I had seen several episodes with Efrem and I liked the quality of the Spanish gentleman Don that he brought to the role, and I said that I would keep that aspect of the character in my interpretation, which was important to me because I have fun doing what I do,"[17] chuckled Darrow.

"Henry fulfills all the requirements for the role perfectly. He makes a fabulous dad. He fell right into the style that we had set on the show. *Zorro* is not a show where you can stand around, take a lot of pregnant pauses and milk a scene. You've got to tell the story in twenty-two minutes, so you've got to make your speeches and get on with it, and Henry does—and he does it well. He comes across like gangbusters. I love his energy.

"Henry takes a lot of time with his scripts. He really looks over his material and he's fabulous at it. Quite often he's got no more than one paragraph in an entire show, but Henry will make it seem like he's been in it from the beginning right to the end. He's just that kind of an actor,"[18] concluded Regehr.

So much for the good guys. The series would get pretty boring if there wasn't anyone for Zorro to thwart—and there was. His name was Luis Ramon, but everyone refers to him as "Alcalde." Taking on the role that was originally offered to Henry Darrow was Michael Tylo, who discusses his views on playing the villain:

"I've always felt that you have to love to hate them. You have to enjoy watching them, you've got to make people want to tune in because they want to see what this idiot is going to do this week, and then you've got to make them interesting. You've got to make them cold, yet comic, yet show a weakness. I think I was lucky with the Alcalde because it was written that way and I was able to exploit it.

"I'm forty-two years old and when I was a kid I used to watch the original Disney *Zorro* series, so I was familiar with it. But my favorite was THE MARK OF ZORRO with Tyrone

---

17. From an exclusive telephone interview with Henry Darrow on January 19, 1991.
18. From an exclusive telephone interview with Duncan Regehr on January 17, 1991.

Power, Basil Rathbone and J. Edward Bromberg as the Alcalde. In fact, it was one of my favorite films and I'm glad they combined the roles of the Alcalde and the Captain from the film and made him one character—it allowed him to have a much broader character.

"When the opportunity came up I was surprised that with the way things are in the industry today, they didn't want to cast a true Hispanic. At the time I went in to read for the part of Captain Luis Ramon, I tried to emulate Basil Rathbone, who is one of my all-time favorite actors. I went through the whole process of several more readings, but didn't have to do a screen test because it was something of a last-minute deal. When they did sign me they said it might be for six episodes . . . it might be for fifteen . . . and then it turned out to be for twenty, because they weren't sure how this character was going to work. They never asked me to review episodes of the old Disney series. Even if they had, I never would have.

"I don't know who I beat out for the role, but I'll tell you this, when I went to audition there were a lot of dark-haired guys, there were a lot of older guys, and when it got down to the wire I was the only blue-eyed blond, though I did have this beard and the attitude. They liked me and they made me the offer.

"When I got over to Madrid everybody was surprised that this blue-eyed blonde was going to be the Alcalde, but my stunt double, who was Spanish, had bluer eyes and blonder hair than me.

"I discussed this with Michael Levine and Gary Goodman and they said that they thought it would be interesting to have the hero, Zorro, have a dark complexion, wear black clothing and ride a black stallion, while the blond-haired blue-eyed villain wore light-colored clothing and rode a white horse, which I thought that was an exceptional casting idea,"[19] he said.

John Gertz expanded on the factors that went into making the difficult casting decision. "The major consideration was that the others auditioning for the part were swarthy, dark actors, while Michael Tylo was quite light. But he performed brilliantly at the audition. We went ahead and cast him as a European-looking Castillian from Spain. Actually, we came to feel that there was a great visual contrast between his blond look and Zorro's blackness."[20]

Yet, as much as Michael Tylo enjoyed the role of the Alcalde, he made the very difficult decision to leave the series.

"It was a tough decision but I was over in Madrid for ten out of twelve months. For the second season my wife and two boys were going to come to Spain with me, and then my wife got a job on *The Bold and the Beautiful* and had to stay in California with our kids. Then my father-in-law passed away and I couldn't go to the funeral. And then my kids brought home the chicken pox and my wife had never had them, and they were all sick, so there was a whole month there of upheaval. I just couldn't take the pressure of being away from them. We just couldn't stand the separation. So, as much fun as it was, I just decided that it wasn't worth being that far away from my family.

"At the time I made the decision, an old friend, Marty [Martin] Sheen, just happened to be in Spain scouting locations [for a movie about bullfighting that never got made]. I talked it over with him and he said, 'I'm with you one hundred percent. If I couldn't take my family with me, the job's not worth it.' My kids are still youngsters and I don't want to miss any part of their growing up, either.

"If they were doing *Zorro* here in California I would not have left—I would still be doing the show, there's no doubt in my mind. It was one of those things that I finally got to do that my kids enjoy seeing, they look forward to watching it," said Tylo.

"My wife, Hunter Tylo, who plays Dr. Taylor Hayes on the CBS soap opera, *The Bold and the Beautiful,* is doing a wonderful job and enjoying her work so much that I just couldn't ask her to leave. So I'd much rather be the flexible one and come back to work here in California or even New York—someplace where I can get home with a lot more frequency,"[21] said Michael Tylo.

Tylo had a first-hand understanding of soap opera work, having previously done three of them himself: *General Hospital, All My Children* and *The Guiding Light.* "On *General Hospital* I played Charlie Prince for about six months. He was Larry Ashton's bastard brother who came and challenged him for the family fortune, which involved a lot of fencing—then *Zorro* came up."

One of Michael Tylo's most outstanding roles was as Dee Boot on the CBS miniseries, *Lonesome Dove,* which aired on February 5–8, 1989.

Like everyone else in the cast, Duncan Regehr was also sorry to see Michael Tylo leave. "I thought he was fantastic—he was wonderful, but if someone doesn't want to stay, you can't force them to stay. But I thought he was just marvelous,"[22] raved Regehr.

Tylo didn't leave, however, without first filming an episode that explained what had happened to his character.

In "The Devil's Fortress," a special hour-long episode that aired on February 24, 1991, Michael Tylo had an opportunity to do a swan dive in what was his swan song in the role of Alcalde Luis Ramon.

The story, set 170 years in the future, is told through flashbacks by Don Diego's great grandson as an old man, played by Regehr in heavy makeup. He has returned to the de la Vega hacienda with his granddaughter to look over the place one last time before it is razed for a new freeway because he can no longer afford to pay the property taxes.

Inside the hidden cave, while the old man is telling his granddaughter about her famous ancestor, they accidentally stumble upon a book written by Don Diego that tells a story of the Devil's Fortress.

Located in Baja California, the Devil's Fortress was said to have been built originally to defend the Spanish empire, but at the end of the eighteenth century it became a prison—a penal colony for those convicted as enemies of the state.

---

19. From an exclusive telephone interview with Michael Tylo on January 21, 1991.
20. From an exclusive telephone interview with John Gertz on December 11, 1991.
21. From an exclusive telephone interview with Michael Tylo on January 21, 1991.
22. From an exclusive telephone interview with Duncan Regehr on January 17, 1991.

Victoria Escalante arrives at the de la Vegas' with a letter from a man, a former prisoner of the fortress, who says that her father is imprisoned there. Both Victoria and Don Alejandro, Alphonse Escalante's best friend, had thought him dead. They believed he had died in Mexico during the revolution.

Diego volunteers to go to the prison to obtain the release of Victoria's father, and this act of courage surprises Don Alejandro greatly. The obvious reason for Diego's offer is to explain his absence, because he knows he will have to go to the fortress as Zorro to free the senior Escalante.

Meanwhile, for unexplained reasons, the Alcalde also sets out for the fortress to help Victoria's father—which is, of course, a lie.

The prison is run by Rosalinda de la Fuente (Jessica Marshall-Gardiner) and at the end of the story she aims a pistol at Zorro from her vantage point on a balcony above the room. The commandante of the prison shouts "Rosalinda, kill him." Then, in an uneven bit of story-telling, the Alcalde appears from out of nowhere echoing the commandante's sentiments "Yes, yes, shoot him." He then gets into an unexplained struggle with Rosalinda during which she is heard shouting, "This is your fault," and then falls to her death to which Zorro exclaims, "The Devil's Fortress has claimed its final victim."

Zorro notices that the door to the Deed Room has been forced open, and since the upper hallway is empty, Zorro deduces that the Alcalde must have tried to escape by going up. Naturally, Zorro is correct and finds the Alcalde clinging precariously on to the wall of the fortress. Zorro approaches him and asks for the stolen document.

ALCALDE: Never!

ZORRO: Never may be sooner than you think. (Playfully poking at the Alcalde's hands with his sword to show the Alcalde the futility of his predicament and get him to turn over the document.)

ALCALDE: All right, all right. Help me and I'll give you the document.

ZORRO: You haven't been paying attention, Alcalde. The document first.

The Alcalde nervously slides his hand into his breast pocket and pulls out the rolled up document. But as Zorro reaches for the paper the Alcalde grabs Zorro and pulls off his hat and mask.

ALCALDE: De la Vega? (losing his footing and beginning to fall) No! (And as he falls to his death he shouts) I should have known!

This was an unsatisfying end to the character who, although a scoundrel at heart, was quite likable and never really did anything terrible enough to deserve this horrible fate.

The document, it turns out, was a deed to the de la Vega property given to Diego's grandfather, Sebastion de la Vega, by King Carlos of Spain. Without the deed, the property would have gone to the state for auction. The Alcalde knew that, which is why he tried to steal it.

At the end of the diary, Diego wrote that, for safe keeping, the document was buried under the bottom left stone of the de la Vegas' fireplace. The old man takes his granddaughter out of the cave to the point where the fireplace had once stood, pries up the previously identified stone. He pulls out the deed and turns it over to the foreman of the construction crew just as they are about to begin bulldozing the property.

This would be the last time we would see the Alcalde alive, but one mustn't forget the episode in which his twin brother appeared. This, of course, leaves open the possibility for a guest appearance by Michael Tylo no matter how remote. But there definitely will be a new Alcalde.

"The new Alcalde will be played by John Hertzler, who is about the same age as Michael Tylo so he will be vigorous and able to pose a threat. They had talked at first about going with someone older, and auditioned some people, but then decided to go with someone of the same age,"[23] said Henry Darrow.

Wisely, "The New Broom," the first episode of the series' third season on the Family Channel, focused on the introduction of the new alcalde.

The story opens with Sergeant Mendoza serving as the pueblo's acting alcalde and given that Victoria and Don Alejandro are screaming at Mendoza, one quickly gets the idea that he is doing a miserable job as alcalde. He himself is not too thrilled with the responsibility and when we finally see him peer out from behind the corner of a building where he has been hiding, Mendoza looks skyward and says, "Your majesty, send us a new alcalde soon. Please!"

The scene dissolves to Madrid, Spain where a confrontation between two men is taking place. One, a fairly handsome man with dark hair, is Don Xavier Miguel Francisco Quiroga. The other, who has cold blue eyes and a shock of white hair, is Don Ignacio DeSoto.

Don Xavier, who has just been appointed by the king to serve as the new alcalde of the Pueblo de Los Angeles, is told by Don Ignacio that *he* came very close to serving in that position.

IGNACIO: There will be a terrible tragedy in your family, making it impossible for you to travel.

XAVIER: Indeed. And what tragedy is that?

IGNACIO: Your death.

Don Ignacio then provokes a fight with Don Xavier by striking him on the face. They draw swords and begin to duel.

23. From an exclusive telephone interview with Henry Darrow on January 19, 1991.

Don Ignacio knocks the sword from his opponent's hand, causing him to concede defeat. Don Xavier is reminded by him that his act of cowardice in the plaza, in full view of the towns-people, will force the king to alter his decision and name Don Ignacio as the new alcalde of Los Angeles.

His plan is to "bend" the good people of Los Angeles to the will of the King and then return to Spain a hero.

When the coach pulls into town, Sergeant Mendoza opens the door to welcome the new alcalde. But instead of the new alcalde, Juan, the coach driver, steps out. It appears that Don Ignacio has taken over at the reins because he was impatient with the slower speed at which Juan drove the coach.

Don Diego recognizes Don Ignacio, who had been a senior at the University of Madrid when he was a freshman. He welcomes his old school chum and shakes his hand warmly. After watching the new alcalde give his garrison a pep talk, Diego exclaims, "We may finally have the right man for the job."

Don Alejandro invites the new alcalde to the de la Vega hacienda for dinner with some of the pueblo's other leading citizens. Don Ignacio graciously accepts the invitation, but at the gathering gets into a heated argument with Don Alejandro when he refers to his predecessor, Alcalde Ramon, as "illustri-ous."

ALEJANDRO: Your predecessor was far from illustrious.

VICTORIA: And it was his own greed that brought about his death at Devil's Fortress.

The guests assembled at the de la Vega hacienda are then informed by Don Ignacio that Alcalde Ramon was obsessed with the capture of the renegade Zorro, who was aided and abetted by those gathered for dinner.

DIEGO: Don't be deluded, Ignacio. You can't just dismiss Zorro so easily.

IGNACIO: We shall see. But in the future, you will address me as 'Don' Ignacio. Our school days are over, senor.

DIEGO: They are indeed.

It is clear from this point on that Don Ignacio DeSoto is not the man for the job, and may prove to be even more ruthless and dangerous than their former alcalde.

In keeping with their original concept, the producers cast John Hertzler in the role of the Alcalde partly because of his light coloring, to keep the same contrast between the Alcalde and Zorro that had already been established.

The one person who was pleased to learn of Michael Tylo's departure from the series was John Gertz, president of Zorro Productions. "I was very happy that Michael Tylo left. Let me explain. He was a terrific alcalde. He is a wonderful, wonderful actor, but I think that you have to refresh villains from time to time. It can get boring watching the same villain from week to week with the same set of motivations. When we went to recast the alcalde we were very careful to give him a different set of motivations, which opens up many new plot ideas. You'll notice that the new alcalde is not as avaricious, but is rather more of a law-and-order freak. In addition to the alcalde, the fourth season of Zorro will also feature some new, exotic and more interesting villains,"[24] explained Gertz.

"John Hertzler's Alcalde DeSoto is a little bit oilier than Michael Tylo's Alcalde Ramon, and I think it's good that they're different," observed Henry Darrow. "He brings a kind of a bluster and bravado to the part. He's excellent to work with and has a marvelous sense of humor—he's a very funny man. There is, however, one thing about John's style of acting. That is, if you don't get your lines in immediately and do a little pause, John will throw in an ad-lib; he usually grunts, growls, huffs and harrumphs, so you have to do your lines quickly—almost in one breath. We call him 'John, pull-the-rug-out-from-under-you Hertzler,'" chuckled Darrow. "And it was that humor that helped him to fit in immediately,"[25] Darrow said.

Serving under the Alcalde was Sergeant Jaime Mendoza, a role that was essentially modeled after the Sergeant Garcia character, as James Victor, the actor who took on the weighty challenge, freely admits.

"I was a big fan of the Disney Zorro. In 1958, when I was right out of high school, I worked in the publicity department at Disney and I adored Zorro and I loved Henry Calvin who played my role—the role that I'm playing now. The only difference is the name has changed, but it's still basically the same character. In the Disney show, for instance, Don Diego's servant was Bernardo, an older man; our Bernardo is Felipe, a young man. Disney's Zorro was filmed in black and white. Our Zorro is filmed in color, but it is basically the same swashbuck-ler that was presented in the 1950s, just with different actors. Watching Zorro as a kid, I never imagined that I would ever wind up playing Henry Calvin's role.

"Working for the Disney publicity department in New York, I did get to meet a lot of the Disney stars and although I never met Henry Calvin, I did meet Guy Williams once. He was a wonderful man. Tall, very good looking and a little shy," Victor recalled. When asked how tall Duncan Regehr is, James Victor responded, "Duncan's about twelve feet."[26]

"I was there when Jimmy [Victor] got the part," recalled John Gertz. "They had brought in Jimmy and a bunch of other actors. Even though Jimmy's audition was brilliant, and well worth the part when judged on its merits, my outspoken attitude that day was to get rid of Jimmy and all the others, since not one of them was overweight. I was completely stuck on the Sergeant Garcia look. I begged the casting agent to call off the audition and come back later with some men of real girth. The

24. From an exclusive telephone interview with John Gertz on December 11, 1991.
25. From an exclusive telephone interview with Henry Darrow on December 13, 1991
26. From an exclusive telephone interview with James Victor on January 11, 1991.

casting agent argued that it would be impossible to find a good actor who was also as fat as Disney's Henry Calvin, since no one nowadays would do that to their body just to get a part. Today Jimmy [Victor] is a good friend of mine, and I love him dearly. But every time we get together for dinner I still try to force a second helping down his throat,''[27] chuckled Gertz.

He went on to explain that the casting of the major roles was achieved by the consensus of a committee of producers that included John Feldtheimer, president, New World Television; Michael Levine, director of Creative Affairs, New World Television; Gary Goodman, Barry Rosen, and the casting director, Barbara Clayman.

James Victor picked up the story from there as he explained how he managed to win the role of Mendoza.

"A friend of mine told me that they were going to do *Zorro* so I called my agent and told him that I had heard they were going to do a new *Zorro* series. He told me that they were already working on it. When they called me in for the audition there were a bunch of fat actors. I'm a husky guy, but I'm not as fat as Henry Calvin and I figured that I wasn't going to get the role because the producers already had it in their minds that they wanted a fat guy like they had seen in the original series. But that wasn't the case. They liked me, they liked my comedy. The only friction we had with New World was that they wanted me to do it without an accent, and I refused to do it without an accent because this man, who was from eighteenth-century Los Angeles, would have an accent. I also felt that it would add to the comedic value if he had some kind of an accent. It's not poking fun at a Spanish accent, it's just that the guy has an accent—and that's how I play it.

"Anyway, after the first two auditions they asked me if I could do it without an accent, and I said, 'I could do it without an accent, I could do it with a British accent, I could do it with an Italian accent, I could do it with no accent, but this man has an accent!' So they said, 'Okay, we'll try it without it.' So I gave them a sample without the accent. But at the final audition for New World Television I just threw the dice. I said if they want me, they're going to want it the way that I'm going to play it. If they want Henry Calvin they're going to have to find a person like Henry Calvin, because I'm not Henry Calvin. And this time it came up roses for me because I got the part.

"One of the sixty or so other actors who were also auditioned for the part was Rene Enriquez, who had played Lieutenant Calletano on *Hill Street Blues*. He was a big fat man and when I saw him I said, he looks like the part. That was my fear—not my acting abilities, just that I didn't think I looked like what I thought they had in mind. But I got the part and it's a dream come true. You work in this industry for years and you're always looking for that role, that particular part that is going to give you some visibility, and this is doing it for me in America and all over Europe.

"When I got the part, John Gertz, the gentleman who owns the rights to Zorro, sent me a tape with about five episodes of the Disney *Zorro* featuring Henry Calvin. And from the beginning I said, 'Hey, I love Mr. Calvin's work and I respect his talent, but you're getting James Victor. I did ask for some of the episodes that featured friends of mine like Perry Lopez and Carlos Rivas, because I would at least have some interest in watching those. But that was the extent of it. I didn't 'study' Henry Calvin. What you see there is what I bring to the role—it's all me.

"Mendoza is not a bad man at all. He is torn between his loyalty to the military and his admiration of Zorro, and really foils everybody's attempts to capture Zorro.

"Of all the acting jobs I've ever had this is the roughest as far as being physically demanding and once in a while something goes wrong. During the filming of one episode for the first season, when I was boxing with the guest star Philip Michael Thomas,[28] he accidentally punched me in the nose,''[29] Victor said.

"I had a great time with Jimmy Victor, who played Sergeant Mendoza. I think that the relationship between the Alcalde and the Sergeant was very, very special and we could feed off of each other very easily. We just loved working together,''[30] said Michael Tylo.

A busy character actor, James Victor has appeared in more than one dozen motion pictures. A few of his more memorable dramatic screen roles include Lopez in ROLLING THUNDER, 1977, and Gil Moreno in BOULEVARD NIGHTS, 1979. He played Mirandez, opposite Charles Bronson's Jeb Maynard, in the 1980 crime drama, BORDERLINE, and Mirandez, Anna's father, in the 1988 Edward James Olmos drama, STAND AND DELIVER.

His extensive work in television includes four episodes of *My Three Sons*. The April 23, 1964 episode, "The Guys and the Dolls," which cast James Victor as Pete Taylor, also featured Victor's longtime friend, Martin Sheen. Twenty-five years later, Victor introduced Sheen to *Zorro* director Ray Austin, which led to guest-starring roles for his son, Ramon and his daughter, Carmen.

Some of James Victor's other appearances on episodic television include four episodes of *Family Affair* and two episodes of *I Married Dora*. James Victor also appeared as Manuel Estebar, the chief of police of Podetera de la Ria, Mexico in the October 1, 1985 episode of *The A-Team*. And in 1986, LA Theatre Center audiences enjoyed him as Buddy Villa, in 265 performances of *I Don't Have to Show You No Stinking Badges*.

In 1983 James Victor co-starred with McLean Stevenson in the ABC situation comedy, *Condo,* in which he played Jose Montoya. And three years later he starred as Victor Valdez in the short-lived ABC sitcom, *Viva Valdez* (May 31 to September 6, 1976), which has the distinction of being the first situation comedy in television to feature an Hispanic family.

---

27. From an exclusive telephone interview with John Gertz on December 11, 1991.
28. Philip Michael Thomas starred as Detective Ricardo Tubbs on NBC's trendy police drama, *Miami Vice* (September 16, 1984–March 17, 1989).
29. From an exclusive telephone interview with James Victor on January 11, 1991.
30. From an exclusive telephone interview with Michael Tylo on January 21, 1991.

"I love the *Zorro* project—I love the show. I wouldn't ever leave the show on my own; whether it goes five or six years, I'll be there. I don't think an actor should leave midstream a show that he's playing an important part in. Why would you leave? Why would you get bored? I don't understand actors getting bored with roles and leaving. Had I been McLean Stevenson I would have done *M*A*S*H* until the end instead of being written out of television,"[31] concluded James Victor.

Zorro, Zorro, Zorro, Zorro, Zorro!

31. From an exclusive telephone interview with James Victor on January 11, 1991.

BIBLIOGRAPHY

Alley, Robert S. & Irby B. Brown. *Love Is All Around: The Making of The Mary Tyler Moore Show*. New York: Delta, 1989.

Allman, Kevin. *TV Turkeys*. New York: Perigee Books, 1987.

Andrews, Bart. *Cheers: The Official Scrapbook*. New York: Signet, 1987.

———. *The "I Love Lucy Book"*. New York: Doubleday, 1985.

——— with Brad Dunning. *The Worst TV Shows Ever*. New York. Dutton, 1980.

Asherman, Allan. *The Star Trek Compendium*. New York: Pocket Books, 1986.

Aylesworth, Thomas G. *Television In America, A Pictorial History*. New York: Exeter Books, 1986.

——— and John S. Bowman. *The World Almanac Who's Who of Film*. New York: World Almanac, 1987.

Beck, Jerry and Will Friedwald. *Looney Tunes and Merrie Melodies A Complete Illustrated Guide to the Warner Bros. Cartoons*. New York. An Owl Book, 1989.

Beck, Ken and Jim Clark. *The Andy Griffith Show Book*. New York: St. Martin's Press, 1985.

Bifulco, Michael. *Superman on Television*. Canoga Park, California: Bifulco Books, 1988.

Bogle, Donald. *Blacks In American Films And Television, An Encyclopedia*. New York: Garland Publishing, Inc., 1988.

Brooks, Tim. *The Complete Directory to Prime Time TV Stars, 1946– Present*. New York: Ballantine, 1987.

Brooks, Tim and Earle Marsh. *The Complete Directory to Prime Time Network TV Shows, 1946–Present*. New York: Ballantine, 1979.

Brown, Les. *Les Brown's Encyclopedia of Television, Your A–Z Guide To The Shows, The People, The History, And the Business of TV!*. New York: New York Zoetrope, 1982.

Collins, Max Allan and John Javna. *The Best of Crime & Detective TV: Perry Mason to Hill Street Blues, The Rockford Files to Murder, She Wrote*. New York: Harmony Books, 1988.

Cox, Stephen. *The Addams Chronicles*. New York: Harper-Collins Publishers. 1991.

Cox, Stephen. *The Beverly Hillbillies*. Chicago: Contemporary Books, 1988.

———. *The Munsters: Television's First Family of Fright*. Chicago: Contemporary Books, 1989.

Davis, Stephen. *Say Kids! What Time Is It?: Notes from the Peanut Gallery*. Boston: Little, Brown & Company, 1987.

Dawidziak, Mark. *The Columbo Phile: A Casebook*. New York: Mysterious Press, 1989.

De Cordova, Fred. *Johnny Came Lately: An Autobiography/by Fred De Cordova*. New York: Simon and Schuster, 1988.

Duke, Patty and Kenneth Turan. *Call Me Anna*. New York: Bantam Books, 1987.

Eisner, Joel. *The Official Batman Batbook*. Chicago: Contemporary Books, Inc. 1986.

Elliott, Bob and Ray Goulding. *From Approximately Coast to Coast. . . It's the Bob and Ray Show*. New York: Atheneum, 1983.

———. *The New! Improved! Bob and Ray Book*. New York: G.P. Putnam's Sons, 1985.

Emory, Cleveland, ed. *Celebrity Register, An Irreverent Compendium of American Quotable Notables*. New York: Harper & Row, Publishers, 1963.

Fireman, Judy, ed. *TV Book, The Ultimate Television Book*. New York: Workman Publishing, 1977.

Fischer, Stuart. *Kids' TV, The First 25 Years*. New York: Facts on File, Inc. New York: 1983.

Forbes, Malcolm with Jeff Bloch. *They Went That-A-Way*. New York: Simon and Schuster, 1988.

Gilford, Denis. *A Pictorial History of Horror Movies*. London: Hamlyn Publishing Group, Limited, 1973.

Glut, Donald, and Jim Harmon. *The Great Television Heroes*. Garden City, N.Y.: Doubleday, 1976.

Goldstein, Fred & Stan Goldstein. *Prime-Time Television, A Pictorial History from Milton Berle to "Falcon Crest"*. New York: An Opus Book, 1983.

Green, Joel. *The Unofficial Gilligan's Island Handbook: A Castaway's Guide to the Longest-Running Shipwreck in Television History*. New York: Warner Books, 1988.

Greenfield, Jeff. *Television The First Fifty Years*. Crescent Books, 1981.

Grossman, Gary H. *Superman: Serial to Cereal*. New York: Big Apple/Popular Library, 1976.

———. *Saturday Morning TV*. New York: Arlington House, 1987.

Halliwell, Leslie. *Halliwell's Filmgoer's companion: incorporating The filmgoer's book of quotes and Halliwell's movie quiz*. New York: Charles Scribner's Sons, 1988. 9th ed.

———. *Halliwell's Film And Video Guide*. New York: Charles Scribner's Sons, 1987. 6th ed.

Harris, Jay S. ed. in association with the Editors of *TV Guide Magazine*. New York: Simon and Schuster, 1978.

Hudson, Peggy. *TV 72*. New York: Scholastic Books, 1971.

Jackson, Carleton. *Hattie, The Life of Hattie McDaniel.* Lanham, Maryland, 1990.

Javna, John. *The Best of Science Fiction TV.* New York: Harmony Books, 1987.

————. *The Best of TV Sitcoms.* New York: Harmony Books, 1988.

————. *Cult TV: A Viewer's Guide to the Shows America Can't Live Without!!.* New York: St. Martin's Press, 1985.

Kaplan, Louis and Scott Michaelsen in harmony with Art Clokey. *Gumby: The Authorized Biography of the World's Favorite Clayboy.* New York: Harmony Books, 1986.

Katz, Ephraim. *The Film Encyclopedia.* New York: Perigee, 1979.

Kelly, Richard. *The Andy Griffith Show.* Winston-Salem, North Carolina: John F. Blair Publisher, 1981.

Koenig, Walter. *Chekov's Enterprise.* New York: Pocket Books, 1980.

Lamparski, Richard. *Whatever Became Of. . . ?* New York: Crown Publishers, Inc., 1967, 1968, 1970, 1973, 1974, 1982, 1985,1986, 1989. Vols. 1, 2, 3, 4, 5, 8, 9, 10, 11.

Levine, Michael. *The New Address Book: How to Reach Anyone Who's Anyone.* New York: Perigee Books, 1986.

Levy, Felice, ed. *Obituaries On File.* New York. Facts On File, Inc. New York: 1979. 2 Vols.

Maltin, Leonard. *Movie Comedy Teams.* New York. Plume, 1985.

————. *Our Gang: The Life and Times of the Little Rascals.* New York: Crown Publishers, 1977.

————. *Leonard Maltin's TV Movies & Video Guide.* New York: Plume/New American Library, 1989. 1989 ed.

Marill, Alvin H. *Movies Made For Television: The Telefeature And The Mini-Series, 1964–1986.* New York. New York Zoetrope/A Baseline Book, 1987.

Marschall, Rick. *The Golden Age of Television.* New York: Exeter Books, 1987.

Marx, Samuel and Joyce Vanderveen. *Deadly Illusions: Jean Harlow and the Murder of Paul Bern.* New York: Random House, 1990.

McCabe, John. *Mr. Laurel and Mr. Hardy.* New York: Signet Books, 1961.

McClelland, Doug. *Eleanor Parker: Woman of a Thousand Faces.* Metuchen, N.J.: Scarecrow Press, 1989.

McClelland, Doug. *Forties Film Talk: Oral Histories of Hollywood, with 120 Lobby Posters.* North Carolina: McFarland & Company, 1992.

McCrohan, Donna. *Archie & Edith, Mike & Gloria: The Tumultuous History of All In The Family.* New York, Workman Publishing, 1987.

————. *The Honeymooners' Companion.* New York: Workman Publishing, 1978.

————. *The Life & Times of Maxwell Smart.* New York: St. Martin's Press, 1988.

McMahon, Ed as told to Carroll Carroll. *The Autobiography of Ed McMahon.* New York. G.P. Putnam's Sons, 1976.

Macnee, Patrick and Marie Cameron. *Blind In One Ear: The Avenger Returns.* San Francisco: Mercury House, Incorporated, 1989.

McNeil, Alex. *Total Television: A Comprehensive Guide to Programming from 1948 to the Present.* New York: Penguin, 1980. 2nd ed., 1984.

Meyers, Ric. *Murder on the Air.* New York: The Mysterious Press, 1989.

Miller, Leo. *The Great Cowboy Stars of Movies & Television.* New York: Arlington House Publishers, 1979.

Mitz, Rick. *The Great TV Sitcom Book.* New York: Richard Marek Publishers, 1980.

Nash, Jay Robert and Stanley Ralph Ross. *The Motion Picture Guide, 1927–1983.* Chicago: Cinebooks, Inc., 1985. 10 vols. 1986, 1987, 1988, 1989, 1990 annuals. The 1991 annual was published in New York by Baseline II, Inc.

Nedaud and Marcello. *Zorro In Old California.* Guerneville, California: Eclipse Books, n.d.

Nimoy, Leonard. *I am not Spock.* New York: Ballantine Books, 1977.

Norback, Craig, T. and Peter G. Norback, and eds. of *TV Guide. TV Guide Almanac.* New York: Ballantine, 1980.

Nowlan, Robert A. and Gwendolyn Wright Nowlan. *Cinema Sequels and Remakes, 1903–1987.* Jefferson, North Carolina: McFarland and Company, 1989.

Packard, William, David Pickering and Charlotte Savidge. *The Facts On File Dictionary of The Theatre.* New York: Facts On File, Inc., 1988.

Parish, James Robert, ed. *The Great Movie Series.* Cranbury, N.J.: A.S. Barnes, 1971.

———— and Michael R. Pitts. *The Great Science Fiction Pictures II.* Metuchen, New Jersey: Scarecrow Press, Inc., 1990.

———— and Vincent Terrace. *The Complete Actors' Television Credits, 1948–1988, Vol. 1: Actors.* Metuchen, New Jersey: Scarecrow Press, Inc., 1989.

———— and Vincent Terrace. *The Complete Actors' Television Credits, 1948–1988, Vol. 2: Actresses.* Metuchen, New Jersey: Scarecrow Press, Inc. 1989.

Pickard, Roy. *Who Played Who On The Screen.* New York: Hippocrene Books, Inc., 1988.

Purcell, Edward L. *Matter of Fact: The Movies.* Stamford, Connecticut: Longmeadow Press, 1988.

Rico, Diana. *Kovacsland: A Biography of Ernie Kovacs.* San Diego: Harcourt, Brace, Jovanovich, 1990.

Roberts, James M., ed. in chief. *Academy Players Directory.* Beverly Hills, California: Academy of Motion Pictures Arts and Sciences, 1989. 4 Vols.

Roddenberry, Gene and Susan Sackett. *Star Trek: The First Twenty-Five Years.* New York: Pocket Books, 1991.

Rogers, Dave. *The Avengers.* London: Independent Television Books Ltd. in association with Michael Joseph, 1983.

Rovin, Jeff. *TV Babylon.* New York: Signet, 1984.

Sackett, Susan. *Prime Time Hits: Television's Most Popular Network Programs, 1950 to the Present.* New York: Billboard Books. 1993.

Schemering, Christopher. *The Soap Opera Encyclopedia.* New York. Ballantine, 1985.

Schwartz, Sherwood. *Inside Gilligan's Island*. Jefferson, North Carolina: McFarland & Company, Inc.

Shulman, Arthur and Roger Youman. *How Sweet It Was, Television: a pictorial commentary with 1435 photographs*. New York: Bonanza Books, 1966.

Smith, Ronald, L. *Sweethearts of '60s TV*. New York: St. Martin's Press, 1989.

Solomon, Charles. *Enchanted Drawings: The History of Animation*. New York: Alfred A. Knopf, 1989.

Sorensen, Jeff. *The Taxi Book*. New York: St. Martin's Press, 1987.

Soukhanov, Anne H., senior ed. *Webster's II New Riverside University Dictionary*. Boston, Massachusetts: The Riverside Publishing Company, 1984.

Stallings, Penny. *Forbidden Channels: The Truth They Hide from TV Guide*. New York: Harper Perennial, 1991.

Steinberg, Cobbett. *TV Facts*. New York. Facts on File, Inc., 1985.

Steinbrunner, Chris and Burt Goldblatt. *Cinema of the Fantastic*. New York: Galahad Books, 1972.

Summers, Neil. *The First Official TV Western Book*. Vienna, West Virginia: Old West Shop Publishing, 1987.

———. *The Official TV Western Book*. Vienna, West Virginia: Old West Shop Publishing, 1989. Vol 2.

———. *The Official TV Western Book*. Vienna, West Virginia: Old West Shop Publishing, 1991. Vol. 3.

Terrace, Vincent. *Encyclopedia of Television: Series, Pilots and Specials (1937–1984)*. New York: New York Zoetrope, 1986. 3 Vols.

Terrace, Vincent. *Television Character and Story Facts: Over 110 details from 1,008 shows, 1945–1992*. North Carolina: McFarland & Company, 1993.

Thomas, Danny with Bill Davidson. *Make Room For Danny*. New York: G.P. Putnam's Sons, 1991.

Thomas, Tony. *The Films of the Forties*. Secaucus, New Jersey: The Citadel Press, 1975.

Thornton, Chuck and David Rothel. *Allan ''Rocky'' Lane, Republic's Action Ace*. Madison, North Carolina: Empire Publishing, Inc., 1990.

Toth, Alex. *The Complete Classic Adventures of Zorro*. Forestville, California: Eclipse Books, 1988. Vols. One and Two.

Trimble, Bjo. *Star Trek Concordance*. New York: Ballantine Books, 1976.

Van Hise, James. *Who Was That Masked Man? The Story of the Lone Ranger*. Las Vegas, Nevada: Pioneer Books, 1990.

Waldron, Vince. *Classic Sitcoms: A Celebration of the Best in Prime-Time Comedy*. New York: Macmillan Publishing Company, 1987.

Weissman, Ginny and Coyne Steven Sanders. *The Dick Van Dyke Show: Anatomy of a Classic*. New York. St. Martin's Press, 1983.

Weldon, Michael. *The Psychotronic Encyclopedia of Film*. New York: Ballantine Books, 1983.

West, Richard. *Television Westerns, Major and Minor Series, 1946–1978*. Jefferson, North Carolina: McFarland & Company, 1987.

White, Patrick J. *The Complete Mission: Impossible Dossier*. New York: Avon Books, 1991.

Whitfield, Stephen E. and Gene Roddenberry. *The Making of Star Trek*. New York: Ballantine Books, 1968.

Who's Who. ed. of Who's Who in America. *The Celebrity Who's Who*. New York: World Almanac, 1986.

Winship, Michael. *Television*. New York. Random House, 1988.

Woolery, George. *Children's Television: The First Thirty-Five Years 1946–1981*. Metuchen, N.J.: Scarecrow Press, Inc., 1983. 2 vols.

Woolery, Lynn, Robert W. Malsbary and Robert G. Strange, Jr. *Warner Bros. Television*. Jefferson, North Carolina: McFarland & Company, 1985.

Yenne, Bill. *The Legend of Zorro*. Greenwich, CT: Bison Group/Brompton Books, Corp. 1991.

INDEX

Entries which are italic bold are the television shows highlighted in this book.

A-Team, The   xvii, *1–6*, 52, 53, 108, 147, 166, 172, 181, 194, 209, 222, 232, 253, 266, 312, 349, 376, 391, 415, 455
a.k.a. Pablo   168, 359
Aaker, Lee   15
Aalda, Mariann   353, 354
Aames, Willie   131, 321, 323
Aaravo, Roger   8
Aaron's Way   239
Abbott, Bruce   106, 107
Abbott, Bud   6
Abbott and Costello   163, 226, 374
ABBOTT AND COSTELLO MEET FRANKENSTEIN   163
Abbott and Costello Show, The   *6*
ABC Movie of the Week   438
ABC Saturday Mystery, The   216
ABE LINCOLN IN ILLINOIS   121
Abel, Walter   214
Abrahms, Jim   231
Absent-Minded Professor, The   108
Acavone, Jay   55
Accidental Family   121
Ace Crawford, Private Eye   372
Acker, Sharon   332, 334
Ackerman, Bettye   56, 77
Act II   423
Adam 12   7
Adam 12   *6–7*, 52, 343
Adamo, Frank   116
Adams, Casey   (See: Max Showalter)
Adams, Don   146, 301
Adams, Harriet   168
Adams, Jane   137
Adams, Joey   425
Adams, Julie   33
ADAM'S RIB   204
Addams, Charles   298
Addams Family, The   *7–9*, 38, 49, 68, 82, 199, 237, 298, 299, 323, 325, 340, 438
ADDAMS FAMILY, THE   9
ADDAMS FAMILY VALUES   9
ADIOS AMIGO   213
Adler, Jerry   321, 324
Adler, William   319
Admiral Presents Five Star Revue   410
Adventures in Odyssey   35
Adventures in Paradise   *9–10*, 414
Adventures of Captain Hartz, The   *10–11*
ADVENTURES OF CAPTAIN MARVEL, THE   367

Adventures of Ellery Queen, The   *11–13*, 363
ADVENTURES OF FRANK AND JESSE JAMES   241
Adventures of Gulliver   155, 156
Adventures of Ozzie & Harriet, The   7, *13–15*, 38, *122, 174, 203, 231, 263, 309, 347*
ADVENTURES OF REX AND RINTY   15
Adventures of Rin Tin Tin, The   *15–16*, 225, 354
Adventures of Robin Hood, The   *16–17*
ADVENTURES OF ROBIN HOOD, THE   16, 444
Adventures of Superboy, The   *17–19*, 24, 269, 421
Adventures of Superman   xiii, xv, xvi, 18, *20–24*, 38, 39, 67, 78, 88, 89, 102, 142, 156, 157, 189, 203, 207, 225, 226, 227, 231, 233, 235, 238, 264, 280, 312, 323, 327, 331, 348, 367, 434, 438, 449, 450
ADVENTURES OF THE WILDERNESS FAMILY   366
AfterM*A*S*H   *24–25*, 126, 259
Ahab the Arab   37
Aherne, Brian   355
Ahn, Philip   218
Aidman, Charles,   211, 437
Ainsley, Paul   401, 402
AIRPLANE!   78, 231, 286, 361
AIRPLANE II: THE SEQUEL   261, 286
Airwolf   181
Akahoshi, Steve   410
Akins, Claude   67, 240, 303
Alan Young Show, The   291
Alann, Lloyd   211
Alasky, Joe   327
Albee, Joshua   227
Alberoni, Sherry   268, 330
Albert, Eddie   161, 406
Albert, Katherine   188
Albertson, Frank   107
Albertson, Jack   97, 98, 121, 258, 289, 292, 400, 410
Albright, Lola   336, 337
Album   214
Alcott, Louisa May   27
Alda, Alan   255, 258
Aldrich Family, The   *25–27*, 279, 293, 405
Alexander, Ben   125, 126
Alexander-Willis, Hope   428, 429
ALF   170, 302, 424
Alfred Hitchcock Hour, The   380
Alfred Hitchcock Presents   149, 153, 214, 412
Alias Smith and Jones   *27–28*, 140, 148, 209, 352
Alice   *28–29*, 147, 270, 279, 343
Alice, Mary   119
ALICE DOESN'T LIVE HERE ANYMORE   28

ALICE'S RESTAURANT 28
ALIEN 209
ALIVE 421
ALL ABOUT EVE 121, 187
All in the Family **29–31,** 52, 65, 102, 161, 165, 171, 180, 204, 209, 211, 228, 239, 247, 275, 276, 302, 323, 324, 325, 330, 341, 356, 373, 392, 397, 399, 410, 425, 447
All My Children 53, 299, 363, 452
ALL QUIET ON THE WESTERN FRONT 173
All That Glitters 304
Allan, Jed 224, 227
Allard, Tom 221, 223
Allen, Chet 73
Allen, Corey 179
Allen, Dayton 191, 192
Allen, Debbie 318
Allen, Don 73, 74
Allen, Elizabeth 84
Allen, Gracie 25
Allen, Irwin 426, 427
Allen, Jonelle 84
Allen, Ricky 307
Allen, Steve 367
Allen, Tim 182
Allen, Woody 41, 247
Allende, Fernando 447
Alley, Kirstie 46, 93, 95, 96
Alley, Robert S. 341
Allman, Elvia 8, 9, 68, 322, 323, 339, 340
Almost Home (See: *The Torkelsons*)
Aloha Paradise 251
Along Fifth Avenue 185
ALONG THE OREGON TRAIL 241
Altay, Derin 52, 53
Altman, Jeff 319, 320
Alvin Show, The 246
Alyn, Kirk 21
Amandes, Tom vii, 417, 419, 420, 421
Amazing Chan and the Chan Clan, The 40
AMAZING DOBERMANS, THE 38
Amazing Spider-Man, The 64
Amazing Stories 81
AMAZING TRANSPARENT MAN, THE 370
Amen 31, 399
AMERICAN GRAFFITI 165, 166
Ames, Florenz 11, 13, 68, 367
Ames, Leon 63, 64, 236, 289, 292
Amini, Alex 391
AMITYVILLE HORROR, THE 127
Amos, John 160, 161, 164, 194, 274, 412
Amos Burke—Secret Agent 83
Amritraj, Vijay 435
Amsterdam, Morey 117
Anders, Merry 188, 281, 412
Anderson, Barbara 206, 207, 284, 285
Anderson, Donna 411, 412
Anderson, Gerry 374, 416
Anderson, Harry 318
Anderson, Herbert 110, 111, 267, 270
Anderson, Jo 54, 55
Anderson, John 233, 234
Anderson, Lew 189, 193
Anderson, Loni 228, 428, 429
Anderson, Pamela Denise 182

Anderson, Richard 332, 333, 334, 444
Anderson, Sara 230
Anderson, Sheila 322
Anderson, Sparky 94
Anderson, Sylvia 374, 416
ANDERSON TAPES, THE 231, 341, 373
Andes, Keith 361
Andrews, Edward 121
Andrews, Julie 263
Andrews, Stanley 39, 40
Andrews, Tige 115
Androcles and the Lion 156, 157
Andy Griffith Show, The 12, **31–38,** 57, 65, 80, 151, 154, 155, 167, 211, 213, 215, 233, 259, 269, 275, 304, 323, 348, 398, 399, 435
Andy's Gang **38–39**
Angel, Jonathan 358
ANGEL IN MY POCKET 36
Angie 274, 327
Angustain, Ira 436
Anholt, Tony 374
ANIMAL HOUSE 9, 434
Ankrum, David 65, 391, 392
Ann Sothern Show, The 36, **40–41,** 64, 148, 263, 308
Anna and the King 172
ANNIE GET YOUR GUN 75, 237
Annie Oakley **39–40**
Annie Oakley and Tagg 39
Anniversary Waltz 263
Another World 53, 149, 299, 336
Ansara, Michael vii, 81, 82, 198
Anything But Love **41–43,** 124, 276, 320
Anywhere U.S.A. 265
Aplon, Boris 376
Applause 187
APPLE DUMPLING GANG, THE 162
Applegate, Christina 271
Applegate, Eddie 331
Apple's Way **43,** 133, 376
Aquaman 155
Aquanauts, The **43,** 195, 347, 360, 361, 393
Archaelogy 421
Archer, Beverly 260
Archie Bunker's Place 30, 102, 275, 373
Arden, Eve 34, 110, 118, 203, 274, 295, 304, 306, 326
Arden, Robert 271
Argenziano, Carmen 216
Ark II 221
ARKADIN, MR. 270
Armetta, Joseph A. 179
Armstrong, Sam 22
Armstrong, Todd 267
Arnall, Curtis 81
Arnaz, Desi 201, 202, 295, 304
Arnaz, Desi Jr. 252
Arnaz, Lucie 201, 252
Arness, James 163
Arnette, Jeannetta 176
Arngrim, Alison 238
Arno, Sig 305, 306
Arnold, Betty 400
Arnold, Roseanne 351
Arnold, Tom 351, 352
AROUND THE WORLD UNDER THE SEA 360
Arrest and Trial 228

ARSENIC AND OLD LACE   121, 215
Art Lamb Show, The   300
ARTHUR   140
Arthur, Beatrice   164, 276
Arthur, Jean   86
Arvan, Jan   445
As the World Turns   66, 148
Ashe, Arthur   286
Asher, William "Bill"   64, 262
Asherman, Alan   17, 380
Ashley, Elizabeth   284
Asimov, Dr. Isaac   228
Askin, Leon   181, 407
Asner, Ed   41, 247, 337, 406
Assignment Danger   274
Assignment Earth   69
Assignment Vienna   146
Astaire, Fred   75
Astin, John   9, 49, 50, 199, 323, 325
Astin, MacKenzie   197, 199
AT THE EARTH'S CORE   328
Atkins, Essence   360
Attenborough, Richard   180, 277
Auberjonois, Rene   57, 58
Austin, Karen   316, 404
Austin, Ray   455
Automan   253, 413
Autry, Gene   39, 339
Avedon, Barbara   85
Avedon, Doe   66
Avengers, The   *43–44,* 285, 345
Averback, Hy   201, 203, 327
Avery, Phyllis   146
Avery, Tol   33, 400
Avramo, Peter   107
Avruch, Frank   73, 76
Awakening Land, The   53
Awdry, The Reverend W.   371
AWFUL TRUTH, THE   266
Aydon, Christopher   46
Aykroyd, Dan   126
Ayres, Leah   78, 79, 80
Ayres, Lew   173
Azarow, Martin   326

B.F.'S DAUGHTER   12
B.J. and the Bear   *66–67*
B.L. Stryker   134, 350
B.S. I LOVE YOU   207
Baa Baa Black Sheep   *45,* 147
Babcock, Barbara   179, 180
BABE RUTH STORY, THE   235
BABES IN TOYLAND   14, 446
Baby Boom   *45*
Baby I'm Back   358
Baby Talk   *46–47,* 103, 113, 165, 406
Bacall, Lauren   187, 188, 298
Bach, Catherine   129
Bachelor Father   *47–48,* 184
BACHELOR PARTY   430
Back to the Future   9
BACK TO THE FUTURE   9, 88
BACK TO THE FUTURE PART II   9, 88
BACK TO THE FUTURE PART III   9, 88

Back to the Streets of San Francisco   386
BACKDRAFT   37
Backes, Alice   47, 48
Backstairs at the White House   234
Backus, Henny   68
Backus, Jim   13, 14, 15, 65, 68, 150, 151, 204
Baddeley, Hermione   275, 276
Badler, Jane   284, 288, 289
Baer, John   398
Baer, Max, Jr.   60, 61
Baer, Parley   33, 37, 38
Bailey, Bill   84
Bailey, Bill "Boom-Boom"   388, 389
Bailey, David   397
Bailey, F. Lee   376
Bailey, Helen   388
Bailey, John Anthony   165, 167
Bailey, Pearl   336, 337
Bailey, Raymond   60
Bailey, William "Willie"   389
Bailey's Comets   149
Bain, Barbara   44, 282, 283, 284, 285, 286, 289, 374
Bain, Conrad   119
Bain, Mary   279
Baio, Scott   46, 47, 90, 165, 166, 244
Baird, Jimmy   143, 144
Bakalyan, Richard "Dick"   51
Baker, Ann   279
Baker, Jo Don   204
Baker, Kenny   109
Balding, Rebecca   246, 247
Baldwin, Bill   230, 232, 278
Baldwin, Judith   149, 150, 151
Baldwin, Peter   157, 447
Baldwin, Walter   33, 37
Balfour, Michael   271
Ball, Lucille   15, 111, 201, 202, 252, 253, 262, 285, 304
Ballard, Kay   295
Ballinger, Art   125, 126
Balmuth, Bernard   179
Balsam, Martin   373
Balson, Allison   238
BAMBI   190
Banacek   1, 89, 256, 399, 436
Bancroft, Anne   127
Bank, Frank   232
Banner, John   xiv
Banyon   40, 53
BAR 20 RIDES AGAIN   186
Barbara Walters Special, The   112
Barbary Coast, The   374
Barbeau, Adrienne   276
Barcroft, Roy   102
Bardette, Trevor   22, 33
Bardolph, Dana   84
Bardolph, Paige   84
BAREFOOT CONTESSA, THE   246
Baretta   *48,* 147
Baretta 690   48
Barker, Lex   393
Barker, Ma   418
Barnaby Jones   *48–49,* 121, 179, 275
Barnes, Ann   67
Barnes, Christopher Daniel   79

Barnes, Joanna   392
Barnes, Paul   182
Barnes, Priscilla   401, 402, 404
Barney Blake, Police Reporter   162
Barney Miller   115, 310, 324, 437, 447
Barnum   282
Barnum, P.T.   388
Baron   382
Barone, Sal   351
Barr, Doug   113
Barr, Roseanne   351
Barrett, Majel   230, 232, 378, 381, 384
Barrie, Barbara   321, 324, 342, 343
Barrier, Edgar   355
Barrier, Michael   377, 379
Barris, Marty   193
Barry, Donald   389, 390
Barry, Gene   82, 83, 100, 233, 234, 312, 326, 327
Barry, John   346
Barry, Robert   26
Barrymore, John   448
Bartlett, Alison   361, 365
Bartlett, Bonnie   238
Bartlett, Sy   413
Barton, Ann   230, 231
Barton, Laura   330
Barton, Peter   82, 83, 342
Barton, Tod   237
Barty, Billy   336, 372
Bar-Yotam   88
Basehart, Richard   238, 239, 427
Basile, Frank   418
Bat Masterson   327, 414
Bateman, Charles   267
Bateman, Jason   423
Bateman, Justine   137
Batman   49–51, 142, 184, 207, 208, 216, 225, 232, 237, 270, 276, 285, 296, 301, 306, 325, 367, 400, 414, 438
BATMAN   49, 51, 141
BATMAN AND ROBIN   51
BATMAN RETURNS   51
Batman/Superman Hour, The   51
Batten, Mary   397
Battimo, Max   358
BATTLE AT APACHE PASS   246
BATTLE HYMN   14, 174
Battlestar Galactica   1, 7, *51–52,* 65, 103, 149, 386
Bauer, Charita   26, 27
Baur, Elizabeth   206, 207
Bavier, Frances   32, 34
Baxley, Barbara   304
Baxter, Anne   187
Baxter-Birney, Meredith   137
Baxters, The   *52–53*
Baywatch   *53–54*, 90, 182
Baywatch: Panic at Malibu Pier   53
Beacon Hill   12, 275
Beaird, Pamela   230, 232
Bear   67
Bearde, Chris   399
Bearse, Amanda   271
Beatles, The   294, 371
Beatty, Warren   267, 269, 421
BEAU GESTE   237, 265

Beauchamp, Richard   447
Beaumont, Hugh   231
BEAUTY AND THE BEAST   229, 406
Beauty and the Beast   *54–55*
Beavers, Louise   58, 59, 262, 263, 276
Beck, Clarence C.   367
Beck, Kimberly   131
Beck, Marilyn   324
Becker, Sandy   90
Becker, Terry   426, 427
Beecher, Janet   444
Beemer, Brace Bell   163, 241
Beery, Noah Jr.   349
Beery, Noah Sr.   350
BEETLEJUICE   449
Bega, Leslie   176
BEGINNING OF THE END, THE   195, 285
Begley, Maggie   96
Behar, Joy   45
Behind Closed Doors   69
Behind the Screen   351
Bell, Bob   74, 76, 77
Bell, Ralph   330
Bellamy, Diana   400
Bellamy, Ralph   vii, 90, 108, 109, 132, 182, 264, 265, 266, 273
Bellem, Leslie   17
Beller, Mary Linn   107
Belli, Melvin   376
Bells Are Ringing, The   157
BELOVED ENEMY   319
Belushi, John   91, 251
Ben Casey   *55–57,* 77, 214
Benaderet, Bea   13, 60, 145, 304, 337, 338, 339, 340
Bench, Johnny   286
Bendetti, Michael   413
Bendix, William   57, 200, 234, 235, 236, 427
BENEATH THE PLANET OF THE APES   311
Benedict, Dirk   xvii, 1, 2, 52
Benedict, Paul   210
BENJI   34
Benji, Zax and the Alien Prince   57
Bennett, Harve   342
Benoit, Patricia   293
Benson   *57–58,* 132
Benson, Anthony   380
Benson, Pat   211, 212
Benson, Robby   54
Berg, Gertrude   152, 153, 154, 155, 237
Bergan, Candice   351
Bergansky, Chuck   275
Bergen, Edgar   190
Bergen, Jerry   387
Bergman, Ingrid   88
Berkley, Elizabeth   358, 359
Berle, Milton   304, 368
Berlin, Irving   77
Berlinger, Warren   279, 280, 326
Berman, Shelley   293
Bernard, Crystal   167
Bernard, Ed   399, 435, 436
Bernard, Jason   435, 436
Bernardi, Herschel   336, 337
Bernsen, Corbin   219
Bernstein, Jay   282

Bernstein, Scott   167
Berra, Yogi   94
Berry, Ken   31, 34, 36
Bert, D'Angelo/Superstar   229
Bertinelli, Valerie   325
Besch, Bibi   379
Bessell, Ted   371, 398
Best, James   128, 129
Best of the Munsters   301, 302
Best Times, The   300
Betty Hutton Show, The   118
Betz, Carl   122
Beulah Show, The   *58–60,* 66, 263
Bevan, Donald   180
Beverly Hillbillies, The   9, 49, ***60–61,*** 64, 145, 151, 204, 232, 237, 275, 326, 339, 340, 342, 398, 407, 408
Beverly Hills 90210   280
Bewitched   xv, 10, 30, ***61–65,*** 128, 199, 250, 300, 302, 303, 323, 352, 363, 392
Beyers, Bill   211
Beyond Westworld   343
Bianculli, David   140
Bickford, Charles   425, 426
BIG CLOCK, THE   126, 261
Big Hawaii   1
Big John, Little John   65
BIG MOUTH, THE   340
Big Show, The   127
BIG SKY, THE   106
BIG STEAL, THE   235
Big Story, The   123
Big Top   388
Big Town   48, ***65–66,*** 406
Big Valley, The   285, 300
Bill Cosby Show, The   59, ***66***
Billingsley, Barbara   21, 80, 231
Billy   (See: *Head of the Class*)
BILLY JACK   100
Billy the Kid   451
Binns, Edward   208
Bionic Showdown: The Six Million Dollar Man and the Bionic Woman, The   373
Bionic Woman, The   133, 333, 361, 373
BIRDMAN OF ALCATRAZ, THE   246
BIRDS, THE   185
Birman, Len   121
Birthday House   270
Bishop, Ed   416
BISHOP'S WIFE, THE   83
Bissell, Whit   47, 48
Bissett, Josie   280
Bivens, Jack   374
Bixby, Bill   103, 167, 300, 434
Black, Karen   141
BLACK BOOK, THE   12
Black Sheep Squadron   7, 45
Blackburn, Norman   191
Blackman, Honor   43, 44
BLACKULA   332
Blair, George   18
Blair, Patricia   106, 348
Blaisdel, Brad   402
Blake, Jean   63
Blake, Madge   232

Blake, Marie   8
Blake, Noah   169
Blake, Robert   10, 48
Blake, Whitney   174, 175
Blake's Seven   67
Blanc, Mel   80, 82, 236, 302
Blanchard, Mari   398
Blanchard, Susan   166
Blankfield, Mark   359
BLAZING SADDLES   164, 397, 412
Blessed Event   83
Bletcher, Billy   241
BLIND ALLEY   109
Bliss, Lela   68
BLOB, THE   38
Blocker, Dan   71, 72, 73
Blocker, Dirk   73
Blondell, Gloria   235, 236
Blondell, Joan   236
Blondie   9, 13, ***67–68,*** 323, 438
Bloodworth-Thomason, Linda   112, 113
Bloom, Annie   329
Bloom, Lindsay   128, 282
Blore, Chuck   430
Blue and the Gray, The   1, 2, 282, 451
Blue Angels, The   ***68–69***
BLUE HAWAII   37
Blue Knight, The   69
BLUE SKIES   304
Blue Thunder   310
Blye, Alan   399
Blyth, Ann   432
Bob   220
Bob and Ray   69, 70
Bob and Ray Show, The   ***69–70,*** 184, 395
Bob and Ray: The Two and Only   70
Bob Crane Show, The   68
Bob Cummings Show, The   15, ***70,*** 149, 268, 306, 307, 342
Bob Newhart Show, The   15, 65, 123, 135, 159, 314, 316, 396
Bob Smith Show, The   193
Bob & Ray & Jane, Laraine & Gilda   70
Bochco, Steven   179, 219
Bochner, Lloyd   10
Bogart, Humphrey   38, 60, 88, 265, 271, 298, 299
Bogle, Donald   168, 324, 399
Bold and the Beautiful, The   452
Bold Ones, The   312
Bold Venture   298
Bolger, Ray   329, 330
Bolling, Angie   57
Bologna, Joseph   425
Bolton, Barbara   109
Bolton, Christopher   197, 200
BOMBSHELL   274
Bonaduce, Danny   330
Bonanza   52, ***70–73,*** 94, 103, 177, 179, 306, 332, 352, 393, 395, 410, 426
Bonanza—The Return   73
Bonanza: The Next Generation   73
Bond, James   103, 216, 217, 266, 267, 278, 337, 345, 346, 355, 416, 437
Bond, Sudie   397
Bond, Ward   57, 430, 431, 432
Bonerz, Peter   159

Bonet, Lisa   119
BONFIRE OF THE VANITIES   168
Bonino   73
Bonner, Frank   429, 430
BONNIE AND CLYDE   18, 269
Bonsall, Brian   382, 385
Boone, Richard   10
Booth, Bill   7
Booth, Shirley   174
Borden, Alice   398, 399
Borden, Lynn   174, 175
BORDERLINE   455
Bordertown   432
Borg, Veda Ann   235, 236
Born, David   165
Born, Steven   165
Bosley, Tom   36, 91, 166, 185, 244, 251, 303
Bosom Buddies   259, 313, 315, 403
Bosson, Barbara   179
Bostock, Barbara   140
Boston Blackie   80
Bostrom, Zachary   170
Bostwick, Jackson   18, 367
Botto, Juan Diego   441, 449
Bottoms, Joseph   222
Bottoms, Sam   222
Bottoms, Timothy   221, 222
Boucher, Sherry   227
BOULEVARD NIGHTS   455
Bourbon Street Beat   173, 390, 413
Bowen, Pamela   185, 186
Bowen, Roger   255
Bower, Antoinette   284
BOWERY BOYS   102, 417
Bowman, Lee   11, 12, 311
Boxleitner, Bruce   31, 89
Boy in the Plastic Bubble, The   131
BOY WITH GREEN HAIR, THE   333
Boyd, William   186
Boyden, Sally   227
Boyett, Bob   423
Boyett, William   7, 126
Boys Against the Girls   117
BOYS FROM BRAZIL, THE   123
BOYS NIGHT OUT   277
Bozo   73–77
Bozo Show, The   76, 77
Bozo the Clown   76
Bozo's Big Top   76
Bozo's Circus   76, 77
Bozo's Place   76
Bozo's Window on the World   76
Bracken, Eddie   14
Bracken's World   23, 77–78, 84
Bradbury, Ray   271
Bradford, Lane   102
Brady Bunch, The   52, 65, 78–80, 86, 109, 151, 268, 340, 409
Brady Bunch Hour, The   78
Brady Bunch Variety Hour, The   78
Brady Girls Get Married, The   78
Brady Kids, The   78
Bradys, The   78
Bramley, Raymond   122, 123

Brand, Jolene   441, 444, 448, 449
Brand, Max   120
Brand, Neville   417, 418, 421
Brand New Life, A   341
Brannum, Hugh "Lumpy"   417
Brant, Eva   393
BRASS BOTTLE, THE   122, 198, 200
Braugher, Andre   216, 217
Brave Eagle   195
Braverman, Bart   322
Braverman, Marvin   322
Bray, Robert   224
Bray, Thom   349
Brazilian Connection, The   356
BREAKFAST CLUB, THE   135
Breck, Peter   200
Brennan, Eileen   117, 228, 313, 342, 343, 396
Brennan, Walter   227, 280, 319
Brenner   208
Bresler, Jerry   185
Brestoff, Richard   326
Bret Maverick   181, 277
Brian Keith Show, The   122, 367
BRIDE OF FRANKENSTEIN   218, 306
BRIDE OF VENGEANCE   149
Bridges, Lloyd   360, 361
Bridges, Todd   119, 159
Bridget Loves Bernie   154
BRIGHT LIGHTS, BIG CITY   157
Brighter Day, The   27
Brill, Marty   30, 31
Brinegar, Paul   233
Bring 'Em Back Alive   89
Bring Me the Head of Dobie Gillis   173, 270
Bringing Up Father   6
Briskin, Mort   370
Britten, Bill   73, 76
Britton, Barbara   117
Britton, Pamela   67, 68, 235
Broadway Jamboree   400
Broadway Open House   183
Brocco, Peter   101, 102
Broderick, Matthew   329
Brodie, Steve   233
Brodkin, Herb   109
Brokaw, Norman   14
BROKEN ARROW   245
Broken Arrow   82, 198
Brolin, James   187, 415
Bromberg, Edward J.   452
Bromfield, John   344, 370
Bromley, Sheila   235
Bronco   97
Bronson, Charles   277, 411, 455
Brooke, Paul   104
Brooke, Walter   13
Brooklyn Bridge   166
Brooks, Avery   58
Brooks, Claude   412
Brooks, Geraldine   71
Brooks, James   396
Brooks, Jim   341
Brooks, Martin E.   373

Brooks, Mel   16, 17, 135, 146, 158
Brooks, Richard   228
Brooks, Roxanne   347
Brooks, Tim   11, 27, 205, 340, 343
Brosnan, Pierce   345
Brosowsky, Ethan   417
Brothers   313, 421
Brothers, The   80
Brothers and Sisters   103
Broughton, Bruce   179
Brown, Charnelle   119
Brown, Christopher J.   326
Brown, Garrett M.   372, 435
Brown, Georg Stanford   179, 350, 351
Brown, Irby   341
Brown, James L.   15, 16
Brown, John   145, 355
Brown, Marie   235, 236
Brown, Olivia   112
Brown, Roscoe Lee   58
Brown, Ted   189, 193
Brown, Vanessa   vii, 303, 305
Browning, Ricou   361
Brubaker, Robert   163, 370
Bruce, Allen   330
Bruce, Carol   428, 429
Bruce, David   58, 59
Brughardt, Arthur   159
Bryan, Arthur Q.   201, 203
Bryan, Zachery Ty   182
Bryant, Clara   177
Bryant, Nana   326, 327
Bryce, Edward   405
Brynner, Yul   172
Buchanan, Edgar   186, 187, 338, 340, 348
Buck, Jerry   255
Buck Rogers in the 25th Century   8, ***80–82,*** 179, 245, 375, 415
Buckely, Betty   131, 132
Buckner, Susan   168
Buckridge, Muriel   405
BUDDY HOLLY STORY, THE   127
Buffalo Bill   127, 316, 398, 415
"Buffalo" Bob Smith   (See: Bob Smith)
Buffalo Soldiers, The   316
Buffo the Clown   182
Bugaloos, The   221
Bula, Tammi   274
Bulifant, Joyce   275
Bull, Richard   240, 426, 427
Bullock, JM J.   406
Bullock, Trevor   107
Bullwinkle   420
Buntrock, Bobby   175
Burghoff, Gary   118, 158, 254, 255, 259, 260, 406
Burke, Chris   234
Burke, Delta   46, 99, 111, 112, 113, 115
Burke, James   271
Burke, Paul   311, 312, 412, 413
Burke's Law   82–83, 327, 340, 347
Burkley, Dennis   356, 357, 358
Burnette, Carol   394, 438
Burnette, Olivia   408
Burnette, Smiley   338, 339

Burns, Allan   341
Burns, Bart   281
Burns, George   145, 248, 291
Burns, Jack   32, 35
Burns, Michael   149, 432
Burns, Stephan   415
Burns and Allen Show, The   (See: *The George Burns and Gracie Allen Show*)
Burr, Raymond   206, 207, 332, 333, 334, 336
Burrell, Maryedith   138, 404
Burroughs, Danton   ix, 392, 393, 394
Burroughs, Edgar Rice   368, 392, 394
Burrows, James   95, 96, 396
Burton, Chris   57
Burton, Levar   383
Burton, Normann   438
Burton, Richard   204
Burton, Robert   68
Burton, Skip   227
Burton, Tim   414
Burtt, Robert M.   374
Buster Brown Gang, The   (See: *Andy's Gang*)
Buster Brown TV Show with Smilin' Ed McConnell and the Busting Loose   398
Butch, Danny   165, 166
BUTCH CASSIDY AND THE SUNDANCE KID   27
Butkus, Dick   310
Butler, Dean   148, 149, 239
Butler, Duke   81, 82
Butler, Lois   109, 110
Butler, Robert   179
Buttons, Red   38
Bye Bye Birdie   117
BYE BYE BIRDIE   302
Byington, Spring   197, 200, 201, 257
Byrnes, Edward "Edd"   366
Byron, Jean   268, 270, 331

C.P.O. Sharkey   84, 447
Cabot, Sebastion   136, 137, 292, 419, 426
Cactus Jim   84
Cady, Frank   33, 34, 35, 338, 340
Caesar, Sid   46, 117
Caesar Presents   193
Caesar's Hour   117
Cafe Americain   325
Cafe Crown   157
Cagney, James   265, 395
Cagney & Lacey   84–86, 200, 219, 247, 436
Caillou, Alan   310
Cain, Dean   20, 24
Calabro, Thomas   280
Calder, King   273
Calderon, Sergio   6
Californians, The   87, 211, 261
Calkins, Dick   81
Call, Brandon   53, 54, 197, 199
Call Me Anna   331
CALL NORTHSIDE 777   109
CALL OF THE PRAIRIE   186, 187
Callahan, James   89
Callan, K   342, 343
Calloway, Northern J.   361, 365

Calvert, Jim 17, 19
Calvin, Henry 116, 118, 441, 445, 446, 448, 454, 455
Cameron, Dean 376
Cameron, JoAnna 207
Cameron, Lyle 349
Camhi, Patrice (See: Patrice Martinez)
Camp, Helen Page 228
Camp Runamuck 86
Campbell, Flora 107
Campbell, Nicholas 436
Campbell, Toni 264
Campo, Angelo 418
Canary, David 71, 72
CANDY 371
Cannell, Stephen J. 45, 54, 194, 255, 335, 349, 389, 409
Cannon, Michael Philip 406
Cannon, William Thomas 406
Canon 245
Canova, Diana 404
Canutt, Yakima 444
Capone, Al 418, 419
Capra, Frank 246, 272
Captain America 27
CAPTAIN BOYCOTT 17
CAPTAIN FROM CASTILE 245
Captain Gallant of the Foreign Legion 86
Captain Hartz and His Pets 10
Captain Kangaroo 417
Captain Nice 34, 339
Captain Scarlet and the Mysterons 374, 416
Captain Video and His Video Rangers xiv, 26, *86–87,* 191, 322, 375, 405
Captain Z-Ro xiv, *87–88*
Car 54, Where Are You? 119, 147, 158, 233, 298, 311
CAR WASH 181
Carballo, Tabare 447
CARBINE WILLIAMS 132
CARDINAL, THE 312
Carey, Macdonald 149
Carey, Michele 282
Caridi, Carmine 341, 373
Carl, Adam 138
Carlin, George 370, 371
Carlson, Richard 332
Carlyle, Richard 105
Carmel, Roger C. 295, 296
Carmichael, Hoagy 223
Carne, Judy 140
Carney, Art 184, 185, 322
Carney, Don (See: Uncle Don)
Carney, Lee 192
Carol, Cindy 148
Carol and Company 350
Carol Burnette Show, The xiv, 36, 147, 260, 438
Caron, Glen Gordon 345
Carpenter, John 276
Carr, Alan 326
Carr, Darleen 387
Carradine, David 217, 218, 237, 306
Carradine, John 218, 298, 305, 306
Carradine, Keith 218
Carradine, Robert 218, 245
Carrere, Tia 4
Carri, Thomas 314

Carrier, Corey 439, 440
Carroll, Beeson 254, 258
Carroll, Bob Jr. 201, 202
Carroll, Diahann 213
Carroll, Leo G. 266, 407
Carroll, Nancy 25, 26
Carroll, Dr. Vincent 187
Carrott, Ric 166
Carson, George 418
Carson, Jack 20
Carson, Johnny 117, 126, 212, 293
CARSON, KIT 241
Carson, Robert 330
Carter, Alan 104, 114
Carter, Conlan 101
Carter, Dixie 112, 113, 118, 120
Carter, Jack 183
Carter, John 48, 49
Carter, Linda 369, 429, 438
Carter, Nell 301
Carter, Thomas 435
Carter Country 239, 275
Cartwright, Angela 261, 263, 349
Cartwright, Veronica 230, 232
Carver, Randall 395, 396
Carvey, Dana 420
CASABLANCA 60, 88
Casablanca *88–89,* 96
CASBAH 363
Case, Randy 34
CASE OF THE BLACK CAT, THE 333
CASE OF THE CURIOUS BRIDE, THE 333
CASE OF THE HOWLING DOG, THE 333
CASE OF THE LUCKY LEGS, THE 333
CASE OF THE STUTTERING BISHOP, THE 333
Case of the Sulky Girl, The 333
CASE OF THE VELVET CLAWS, THE 333
Case of the Velvet Claws, The 332
Casey, Crime Photographer (See: *Crime Photographer*)
Casey, Robert 25, 26
Cash, Johnny 108
Cason, Barbara 391, 392, 397
Cass, Peggy 118
Cassell, Malcolm 236
Cassidy, David 330, 367
Cassidy, Jack 330, 341
Cassidy, Joanna 414, 415
Cassidy, Shaun 168, 169, 323
Cassidy, Ted 8, 9
Cassity, Kraig 326
Castaways on Gilligan's Island, The 149, 151
Castle, Mary 385, 386
Catcher, The 411
Catlett, Mary Jo 119, 120
Caulfield, Joan 177, 179, 303, 304
Cavalcade of Stars 183, 184, 185
Cavanaugh, Michael 194
Cavanaughs, The 25
Cavell, Marc 51
Cavens, Albert 445
Cavens, Fred 445
Cavett, Dick 70
CBS Late Movie, The 44
CBS Playhouse 386

Ceervi, Art   74
Centennial   36
Ceremonies in Dark Old Men   436
Cervera, Jorge Jr.   446
Cezon, Connie   332, 333
Chadwick, June   349
Chalke, Sarah   64, 351
Challenge of the Superheroes, The   142, 367
CHAMPAGNE FOR CAESAR   280
Chamberlain, Richard   120, 121, 205
Chambers, Wheaton   437
Chan, Kim   218
Chandler, George   224, 227
Chandler, Jared   294
Chandler, Jeff   326
Chaney, Lon Jr.   10, 54, 76, 235, 244, 302, 444
Channing, Carol   9
Chao, Rosalind   24
Chaplin, Charlie   306, 330
Chapman, Lyle   418
Chapman, Mark Lindsay   45
Chappell, Jan   67
Chappell, John   24, 25
Charles, Glen   95, 396
Charles, Les   94
Charles in Charge   54, **89–90,** 167, 323, 359
Charlie Hoover   372
Charlie Wild, Private Detective   90
Charlie's Angels   90–93, 160, 205, 250, 282, 318, 370
Charmings, The   93
Charteris, Leslie   355
Charvet, David   53, 54
Chase   99, 207
Chase, Chevy   12, 449
Checkmate   136, 419
Cheech and Chong   282
CHEECH AND CHONG'S NICE DREAMS   282
Cheek, Molly   170
Cheers   93–96, 102, 159
Cherry, Byron   127, 128
Chertok, Jack   241, 244, 307, 373
Chesterfield Soundoff Time   126
Chevy Mystery Show, The   100
Chew, Sam Jr.   326
Cheyenne   89, **96–97,** 277
Chicken Soup   188
Chico and the Man   89, **97–98,** 400
CHILD IS WAITING, A   284
CHILDREN OF A LESSER GOD   345
CHINA SYNDROME, THE   386
Ching, William   327
CHiPS   98–99, 227
Chisolms, The   99, 106, 265
Chris Colby, Space Cadet   405
Christie, Agatha   303
Christie, Howard   432
Christmas in Disneyland   53
Christopher, Gerard   18, 19
Christopher, William   24, 25, 254, 255, 256
Cigliati, Natalia   358, 360
Cimarron City   224
Cimarron Strip   224
CINCINNATI KID, THE   269
Cinderella   285

CINDERFELLA   82
Cindy   168
Cioffi, Charles   146
Circus Boy   51, 294, 337, 350
CITIZEN KANE   164, 333
CITIZEN SAINT   264
City Hospital   123
City of Angels   255
Civil Wars   248
CLAMBAKE   122
Claridge, Frank   7
Claridge, Sharon   7
Clark, Bobby   153
Clark, Dane   214, 299, 332, 334
Clark, Ernest   205
Clark, Fred   145
Clark, Gage   294
Clark, Oliver   359
Clark, Roy   340
Clark, Vernon E.   17
Clarke, Andrew   355, 356
Clarke, Jordan   404
Clary, Robert   180
Clayman, Barbara   455
Clayton, Jan   224, 225, 226
Clayton, Merry   85, 86
Clear, Patrick   420
Clear Horizon, The   375
Cleese, John   16
CLEOPATRA   204
Cleveland, George   224, 225, 226, 227
Cliffhangers   83
Climax   106, 110, 304, 412
Clokey, Art   35
Cloonan, Barney   418
CLOSE CALL FOR ELLERY QUEEN   273
CLOSE ENCOUNTERS OF THE THIRD KIND   131
Clowning Around   389
Clute, Sidney   86, 247
Clyde, Andy   186, 187, 224, 227
Coach   122
Coates, Phyllis   20, 21, 22, 331, 370
Cobb, Julie   89
Cobb, Lee J.   425, 426
Cobler, Jan   400
Coburn, David   170
Coburn, James   277
Coca, Imogene   60, 117, 342, 407
COCOON   37
COCOON II   37
Cocteau, Jean   54
Code Name: Foxfire   415
Coffin, Tristram "Tris"   101, 102
Cohen, Evan   403
Cohn, Mindy   135
Colasanto, Nicholas   93, 94
Colbert, Robert   277, 278
Colby, Barbara   324, 340, 341
Colbys, The   247
Cole, Cassie   169, 170
Cole, Michael   413
Cole, Tina   173, 309
Coleman, Dabney   127, 316, 398, 414
Coleman, Gary   119, 136

Coleman, Kathy   221
Coleman, Ronald   164, 280
Colihan, Patrice   395
Collier, Don   328
Collier, Lois   68
Collins, Joan   286
Collins, Max Allan   48, 171, 180
Collins, Ray   164, 332, 333
Collins, Stephen   140, 272, 303, 395
Collonna, Jerry   387
Collyer, Bud   51
Collyer, June   412
Colt .45   *99–100*
Columbo   94, *100–101,* 312, 356
Colvig, Pinto   75, 76
Colvig, Vance   74, 76
COMA   386
Combat!   *101,* 246, 410
Come Back, Little Sheba   174
Comedy Spot, The   117
COMES A HORSEMAN   245
Comi, Paul   348, 349, 377, 379
COMIC, THE   340
COMMANCHE TERRITORY   38
Commando Cody: Sky Marshal of the Universe   *101–102*
Commish, The   124
CONCORD—AIRPORT '79, THE   436
Condo   255, 455
Condon, Eddie   331
Conflict   96
Conklin, Hal   xv, 87
Conkling, Brandon   46
Conkling, Justin   46
Conn, Didi   58, 371
CONNECTICUT YANKEE IN KING ARTHUR'S COURT, A   235
Connery, Jason   17
Connery, Sean   17, 217, 278, 341, 355, 373, 419, 421
Connolly, Billy   176, 177
Connolly, Joe   300
Connors, Chuck   226, 228, 348, 434
Connors, Michael "Mike"   333
Conrad, Michael   7, 179, 180
Conrad, Robert   45, 173, 437
Conrad, William   37, 81, 163, 245
Considine, Tim   307, 308
Converse, Michael   434
Converse, Peggy   291
Convy, Bert   278
Conway, Gary   82, 83
Conway, Russ   307, 310, 347, 348
Conway, Tim   212, 372
Conway, Tom   270, 355
Coogan, Jackie   8, 9, 330
Coogan, Richard   86, 87
Cook, Nathan   436
Cool Million   89, 436
COOLEY HIGH   436
Coone, Gene   380
Cooney, Joan Ganz   362
Coons, Johnny   374
Cooper, Gary   63, 201, 265, 426
Cooper, Jackie   206
Coopersmith, Jerry   213
Copeland, Maurice   401

Corbett, Glenn   352
Corcoran, Kevin   447
Corcoran, Noreen   47, 48
Corday, Barbara   85
Corey, Wendell   109, 132
Corley, Bob   59
Corman, Roger   154
Cornell, Lydia   406
Corner Bar, The   *102*
Coronet Blue   434
Correll, Richard   232
Corrigan, Lloyd   437
Corsaut, Aneta   33, 38
Cortese, Dan   352
Cortez, Ricardo   333
Cosby   345, 351, 412
Cosby, Bill   66
Cosby Show, The   119, 362
Costello, Lou   6
Costner, Kevin   17, 103, 419
Cotright, Sharleen   397
Cotten, Joseph   100, 140
COTTON CLUB, THE   301
Coughlin, Junior   367
Counterhurst   70
County, Jefferson   (See: Bill Foster)
Court of the Last Resort   154, 232
Courtland, Jerome   292
Courtship of Eddie's Father, The   *102–103,* 213, 393
Coutteure, Ronny   439
Cover, Franklin   210, 211
Cover Up   *103*
Covington Cross   *103–105,* 124, 133, 352
Cowan, Jerome   279, 280, 319
Cowsills, The   330
Cox, Courtney   137
Cox, Ronny   43, 375, 376
Cox, Stephen   198, 298, 299, 302
Cox, Wally   293, 294
Co-Ed Fever   9, 103
Crabbe, Cullen   86
Crabbe, Larry "Buster"   82, 86, 106, 327, 394
Craig, Garrett   142, 367
Craig, Yvonne   268, 270, 438
Cramer, Douglas S.   251, 285, 438
Crane, Bob   xiv, 68
Crane, Norma   293, 294
Crane, Richard   101, 102, 389, 390
Crane, Robert   180, 181
Crawford, Bobby Jr.   223, 224
Crawford, Broderick   98, 267
Crawford, John   342
Crawford, Johnny   224, 348
Crawford, Rachael   391
Crawford, Robert   267
Crazy Like a Fox   406
CRAZY PEOPLE   439
Crean, Patrick   450
CREATURE FROM THE BLACK LAGOON   361
CREATURE WALKS AMONG US, THE   361
Creel, Leanna   359
Crenna, Richard   107
Crime Photographer   *105,* 107, 281, 350
Crime Story   195

Crime Syndicate   153
Crime Time After Prime Time   107
Cristal, Linda   177, 178, 179
Croft, Mary Jane   15, 165, 203, 252, 253
Cromwell, James   239
Cronjager, William H.   179
Crosby, Bing   100, 101, 235
Crosby, Cathy Lee   438
Crosby, Denise   383, 385
Crosby, Kim   392, 394
Crosby, Lou   278
Cross, Dennis   68
CRISS CROSS   299
Crothers, Scatman   88, 89, 98
Croucher, Brian   67
Crowe, Christopher   420, 421
Crowley, Matt   81
Crowley, Patricia   107, 342, 422
Cruikshank, Rufus   16
Cruz, Brandon   103
Crystal, Billy   58
CRY-BABY   280, 414
Culea, Melinda   xvii, 1, 4, 253, 349
Cullen, Brett   99
Cully, Zara   210
Culp, Robert   66, 312, 374
Cummings, Richard Jr.   404
Cummings, Robert "Bob"   70, 268, 306, 307
Cumpsty, Michael   220
Curse of Capistrano, The   444
Curtis, Craig   366
Curtis, Jamie Lee   41, 98
Curtis, Ken   163, 349
Curtis, Tony   259, 393, 394, 396, 402
Cushing, Peter   87
Cutler, Brian   207

D.C. Follies   314
D'Agosta, Joseph   380
D'Andrea, Tom   234, 236
D'Auria, Joey   75, 77
da Vinci, Frank   379
Daddy Dearest   276
Dad's a Dog   414
Daigh, Ralph   367
Dailey, Dan   395
Dalio, Marcel   88, 89
Dallas   13, 53, 103, 141, 199, 204, 232, 352, 373, 423
Dalton, Abby   300
Dalton, Alene   190, 193
Dalton, Timothy   345
Daly, Bill   199, 200
Daly, James   142, 143
Daly, Tyne   85, 86
Damon, Stuart   336
Dana, Bill   447
Dandridge, Ruby   59
Danfield, Bever-Leigh   83
DANIEL BOONE   106
Daniel Boone   40, ***106***, 108, 366
DANIEL BOONE, TRAIL BLAZER   106
Daniels, Carolyn   398, 399
Daniels, Marc   202
Daniels, Ray   179

Daniels, Stan   396
Daniels, William   216
Dannay, Frederick   11, 12
Danner, Blythe   395
Danny and the Mermaid   360
Danny Thomas Show, The   26, 34, 35, 36, 57 (See also: *Make Room for Daddy*)
Dano, Linda   336
Danson, Ted   93, 94, 95, 96, 114, 300
Danza, Tony   46, 47, 165, 396
Dark Justice   ***106–107***, 168
Dark of the Moon   11
DARKMAN   219
Darling, Jennifer   131, 397
Darnell, Linda   271
Darrow, Henry   vii, 9, 16, 17, 170, 171, 177, 178, 179, 206, 342, 441, 446, 447, 448, 449, 451, 452, 453, 454
Darrow, Paul   67
Date with Judy, A   105, ***107***, 279
Date with the Angels   294
Davenport, Bill   14
Davey, John   367
David Frost Review, The   174
Davidson, Bill   128, 251, 262, 328, 438
Davidson, Bret   221, 223
Davis, Ann B.   78, 79, 268
Davis, Bette   121, 187, 333, 372, 432
Davis, Clifton   399
Davis, David   396
Davis, Gail   39
Davis, Howard Lawrence   193
Davis, Jim   386
Davis, Joan   204
Davis, Josie   89
Davis, Phyllis   424
Davis, Roger   27, 28
Davis, Rufe   338, 339
Davis, Stephen   190, 191, 193
Davis, Wendy   428, 429
Davis Rules   ***107***
Davison, Bruce   170, 194
Davy Crockett   40, ***108***
Dawber, Pam   136, 211
Dawson, Richard   180
Dawson, Thelma   191
Day, Clarence Jr.   236
Day, Doris   114, 121, 123, 142, 145, 149, 213, 277, 306
Day, Shannon   223
DAY AT THE RACES, A   241
Day By Day   79, 247
Day in Hollywood/A Night in the Ukrane, A   272
DAY THE EARTH STOOD STILL, THE   12, 34, 39
Days of Our Lives   148, 149
Dayton, June   26
de Beaumont, Mme. Leprince   54
De Forest, Kellam   377
De Mave, Jack   224, 227
De Niro, Robert   395, 419, 422
de Prume, Cathryn   124
De Vargas, Val   449, 451
Deacon, Richard   232, 295, 296
DEAD MAN'S GOLD   234
DEADLINE U.S.A.   38
Dean, Barton   114

Dean, Eddie   273
Dean, Ivor   355
Dean Martin Show   130
Dear Phoebe   27, 414
Death of a Centerfold: The Story of Dorothy Stratten   98
Death Valley Days   40, 386
DEATH WISH   412
DeCamp, Rosemary   234, 235, 337, 339
DeCarlo, Yvonne   296, 297, 298, 299, 300, 301, 446
December Bride   37, 126, 201, 205, 257
Decker, Diana   271
Dee, Sandra   148, 300
Defection of Simas Kudirka, The   17
Defenders, The   57, ***108–109,*** 264, 312
DEFIANT ONES, THE   181
DeFore, Don   vii, 13, 14, 174, 175
DeFore, Marion   ix, 14, 174
DeFore, Pat   175
DeFore, Penny   175
DeFore, Ron   vii, 175
Dehner, John   123, 350, 397, 425, 426
Delgado, Emilio   247
DELIVERANCE   350
Dell, Gabriel   102
DeLorenzo, Michael   176
Delta County U.S.A.   323
Delta House   103, 434
DeLuise, Dom   296, 302
DeLuise, Peter   413, 414
Delvecchio   181, 396
Demarest, William   307, 308
DeMay, Janet   345, 346
DeMille, Cecil B.   299
Demosthenes   (See: George Savalas)
Denier, Lydie   394
Denn, Marie   400
Denning, Glen   375
Denning, Richard   173, 201, 261, 304
Dennis Day Show, The   *109–110*
Dennis O'Keefe Show, The   337
Dennis the Menace   36, ***110–111,*** 120, 189, 270, 279, 303, 372
DENNIS THE MENACE   9, 111
Denver, Bob   33, 65, 150, 206, 267, 268, 269, 270, 340
DePalma, Brian   420
Depp, Johnny   280, 413, 414
Derek, Bo   248, 392
Derek, John   392
Derman, Happy   299
Derryberry, Debi   9
Des Barres, Michael   428, 429
Desert, Alex   141
Designing Women   46, 66, 99, ***111–115,*** 120, 249
Desilu Playhouse   418
DESIRE ME   12
DESTINATION TOKYO   237
Detective School   *115,* 233, 326, 437
Detective School—One Flight Up   115
DETECTIVE STORY   263, 311
Detectives, Starring Robert Taylor, The   *115*
Deuel, Peter   140
Devi, Kamala   198
DEVIL'S BRIGADE, THE   204

Devine, Andy   38, 39
Devine, Loretta   119
DeVito, Danny   51, 396
Devlin, Donald   434
DeVol, Frank   86
Devon, Laura   337
Dewey, Thomas E.   190
DeWitt, Joyce   402, 403
Dexter, Jerry   155, 158
Dey, Susan   112, 219, 220, 247, 248, 249, 252, 330
DIAL M FOR MURDER   137
Diamond, Bobby   143, 144, 305, 331
Diamond, Don   446
Diamond, Dustin   359
Diamond, Peter   450
Diamond, Selma   316, 317, 318
Diamond Head   (See: *Hawaiian Eye*)
Diamond Lil   87
DIAMONDS ARE FOREVER   416
Diary of a Perfect Murder   275
Dibbs, Kem   80, 81
Dick Francis Mysteries   356
Dick Powell Show, The   83
DICK TRACY   269, 421
Dick Van Dyke Show   12, 23, 51, 57, ***116–119,*** 123, 180, 262, 263, 270, 276, 296, 314, 337, 347, 419, 446
Dick Van Dyke Show: Anatomy of a Classic, The   119
Different World, A   *119,* 345
Diff'rent Strokes   ***119–120,*** 135, 136, 159, 313
Dilley, J.C.   325
Dillon, Brendon   29, 31
Dillon, Melinda   170
DiMattia, Victor   110, 111
Dinah Shore Chevy Show, The   100
Dinehart, Mason Alan III   233
Ding Howe of the Flying Tigers   261
Dinner at Eight   291
Dinosaurs   286
DIRTY DANCING   229
DIRTY HARRY   170, 171, 194, 344
Disney, Walt   451, 452, 454, 455
Disney, Walt   76, 222, 311, 389, 441, 447, 449, 450
Dixon, Ivan   180, 181
Dizon, Jesse   326
Dobritch, Sandy   387, 388
Dobson, Kevin   216, 217
Doc   *120,* 372
Doc Corkle   294
Doctors, The   152, 312, 352
Dodson, Jack   36, 165, 166
Doherty, Shannen   240, 280
Dolenz, Micky   294, 295
Domestic Life   53
Don Knotts Show, The   35, 147
DON Q. THE SON OF ZORRO   447
Don Rickles Show, The   *121–122*
Don Rickles Show, The   38
Donaghy, Pip   206
Donahue, Elinor   33, 37, 115
Donahue, Patricia   281
Donahue, Troy   173, 390
Donald, Peter   183
Donna Reed Show, The   *122,* 149, 231, 252, 351, 386
Donnell, Jeff   68, 146

Donner, Robert   136
Donohoe, Amanda   219, 220
Donovan   104
Donovan, King   341, 342
Doogie Howser, M.D.   82, 124, 414
Doohan, James   vii, 209, 378, 380, 381
Dooley, Paul   322
Door with No Name   123
Doorway to Danger   122–123, 264, 280
Doran, Ann   14, 15, 230, 231, 232
Doris Day   342, 344, 424
Doris Day Show, The   123, 161, 213, 215, 251, 350, 424
Dorn, Michael   382, 383
Dortort, David   177
Dotrice, Roy   54
DOUBLE INDEMNITY   307
Double Life of Henry Phyfe, The   38, 145
Double Trouble   324
Douglas, Kirk   106, 204, 263, 386
Douglas, Michael   386
Douglas, Ronalda   207, 322
Douglass, Donna   60, 61
Dow, Tony   231, 349
Down Home   114
Down the Shore   124–125
Downey, Robert Jr.   439
Doyle, David   90, 91, 166
Doyle, Richard   96
Dozier, William   49, 50, 304
DRACULA   446
Draeger, Jason   30, 31
Draeger, Justin   30, 31
Dragnet   7, ***125–127,*** 141, 214, 228, 237, 257, 282, 343
Dragnet '67   126
Dragnet '68   126
Dragnet '69   126
Dragnet '70   126
Drago, Billy   421
Drake, Alice   235
Drake, Larry   219
Drew, Wendy   39, 40
Drexell's Class   127
Driscoll, Patricia   16, 17
Droodles   117
Drugan, Jennifer   221
DRUMS ACROSS THE RIVER   246
Drury, James   27, 425, 426
Dryer, Fred   194, 195
Dr. Demento Show   37
DR. GIGGLES   219
Dr. Kildare   120–121, 132, 143, 173, 204, 220, 233, 300
DR. NO   416
Dr. Simon Locke   121
Dr. Who   67
DR. X   274
Duball, Robert   255
Duboc, Nicole   260
DuBois, Ja'net   160, 161
Dubov, Paul   418
Duddy, Lyn   185
Duel, Peter   27, 28
Duet   46
Duffy, Julia   46, 99, 111, 113, 114, 314, 315, 316
Duggan, Andrew   413

Duggy, Patrick   409
Duke, Anna   330
Duke, Patty   199, 310, 325, 331, 409
Duke, The   20
Dukes, David   372
Dukes of Hazzard, The   120, ***127–130,*** 215, 282
Duke-Pearce, Patty   331
Dulo, Jane   322, 323
Dumas, Alexandre   205
Dumbrille, Douglas   235, 236
Dunbar, Olive   397
Duncan, Archie   16, 17
Duncan, Lee   15
Duncan, Rachel   408
Duncan, Sandy   423, 424
Dunlap, Pamela   402
Dunn, Michael   437
Dunnigan, Tim   1, 108
Dunning, Debbe   182
DURANGO KID, THE   339
Duryea, Dan   349, 350
Duryea, Peter   379
Dusay, Marj   135
Dusty's Trail   340
Dutton, Simon   355, 356
Dye, John   410
Dyer, Jeanne   278
Dykstra, John   52
Dynasty   141, 168, 199, 247
Dynasty, The Reunion   199
Dysart, Richard   219
Dzunda, George   228, 229

EAGLE HAS LANDED, THE   17
EAGLES BROOD, THE   186
*Earth*Star Voyager*   450
East of Eden   141, 222
Eastham, Richard   438
Eastwood, Clint   170, 194, 344
Ebsen, Buddy   49, 60, 61, 204, 275, 301
Ed Sullivan Show, The   153, 362
Eddington, Paul   16, 17
Edelman, Herb   65, 166, 167, 322
Edelman, Louis "Lou" F.   262
Eden, Barbara   121, 127, 188, 196, 197, 198, 199
Edge, The   113
Edge of Night, The   66, 79
Edmiston, Walker   221, 222
EDWARD SCISSORHANDS   414
Edwards, Blake   79, 248, 265, 336, 337
Edwards, Jennifer   337
Edwards, Luke   107
Edwards, Ronnie Claire   409
Edwards, Vince   56, 57
Eggert, Nicole   53, 54, 89, 90
EICHMAN   261
Eight is Enough   79, ***131–132,*** 323, 324, 362
Eight is Enough: A Family Reunion   132
Eikenberry, Jill   219
Einstein, Bob   269
Eischeid   373
Eisley, Anthony   173
Eisner, Joel   49
Eitner, Don   377

Ekberg, Anita   368
Elam, Jack   71, 73
Elcar, Dana   48, 147
Eldridge, John   279, 280
Eleniak, Erika   53, 90
Elenor and Franklin   12
Eleventh Hour, The   109, ***132,*** 264
Elfman, Danny   141
Elizondo, Hector   88
Ellery Queen   12, 273
Ellery Queen   (See also: The Adventures of Ellery Queen)
ELLERY QUEEN, MASTER DETECTIVE   109
Ellery Queen: Don't Look Behind You   11, 12
Ellery Queen: Too Many Suspects   12, 13
Ellington, Duke   190
Elliot, Dick   33, 38
Elliot, Stephen   87, 395
Elliott, Bob   vii, 37, 69, 70, 395
Elliott, Chris   37, 70, 395
Elliott, David   417, 419
Elliott, Ross   230, 232, 233
Elliott, Sam   69, 286, 289
Ellis, Bobby   25, 26, 279
Ellis, Edward   400
Ellis, Herb   125, 126
Ellis, Monie   149
Ellison, Harlan   380
Ellsworth, Whitney   17, 18, 20, 24, 233
Ely, Ron   43, 361, 392, 393, 394
Elyea, Bob   80, 82
Emergency   326, 356
Emerson, Hope   204, 336, 337
EMIL AND THE DETECTIVES   144
Empire   411
Empty Nest   43, ***132–134,*** 320
ENEMY AGENTS MEET ELLERY QUEEN   273
ENEMY MINE   342
Engle, Roy   374, 437
English, Chris   131
English, Diane   248
Engstrom, Jean   411, 412
Enos   128
Enriquez, Rene   455
Entertainment Tonight   133
Epper, Steffi   305
Equalizer, The   413
Erickson, Devon   106
Erickson, Leif   177, 178, 179
ERNEST GOES TO CAMP   326
ERNEST SAVES CHRISTMAS   326
Errickson, Krista   177
Errol, Leon   212
Erwin, Stuart "Stu"   212, 412
ESCAPE FROM NEW YORK   276
Essoe, Gabe   392, 393, 432
Estrada, Erik   98
Estrin, Patricia   110, 111
Eunson, Dale   188
Eure, Wesley   221
Evans, Damon   209, 210, 211
Evans, Linda   300
Evans, Maurice   49, 62
Evans, Mike   30, 209, 211, 399
Evans, Monica   322, 323

Evans, Robin   349
Eve Arden Show, The   34
Evening Shade   ***134,*** 350
Everhard, Nancy   344, 345, 422
Evigan, Greg   67, 310
EXCALIBUR   104
Executive Suite   ***134***
Exile, The   107
EXPERTS, THE   245
EYES OF LAURA MARS   9
Eyes of Texas II, The   349
E/R   399

5,000 FINGERS OF DR. T., THE   226
F.B.I., The   366, 386
F Troop   36, 141, 203
Fabares, Nanette   122, 262
Fabares, Shelly   122
Fabian   122
Facts of Life, The   119, 124, ***135–136,*** 147, 199, 360
Fafara, Stanley   232
Fahey, Myrna   50
Fairbairn, Bruce   350, 351
Fairbanks, Douglas Sr.   444, 445, 447, 450
Fairman, Michael   197, 200
Faison, Frankie   412
Faison, Sandy   41
Falcon Crest   141, 149, 325, 336, 362, 425
FALCON IN HOLLYWOOD, THE   333
FALCON'S BROTHER, THE   271
Falk, Peter   100, 101
Fall Guy, The   120, ***136,*** 448
Fame   313, 362
Fame is the Name of the Game   312
Family   31, 43, 133, 381
Family Affair   ***136–137,*** 167, 213, 253, 278, 281, 331, 371, 419, 426, 455
Family Feud   xiv, 340
Family Ties   5, ***137–138,*** 385, 412
Famous Teddy Z, The   69
Fanelli, Boys, The   237, 314
Fanning, Stephen   280
FANTASTIC VOYAGE   17
Fantasy Island   131, ***139–140,*** 219, 253, 393, 446
FAR AND AWAY   37
Faracy, Stephanie   412
Farentino, Debrah   185, 386
FAREWELL MY LOVELY   83
Farmer's Daughter, The   ***140***
Farnum, Dustin   426
Farr, Felicia   71
Farr, Jamie   24, 25, 116, 118, 158, 254, 259
Farr, Lee   115
Farrell, Mike   xv, 25, 254, 256
Fast Guns, The   (See: *Stories of the Century*)
Fast Times   376
FAST TIMES AT RIDGEMONT HIGH   376
FATAL ATTRACTION   301, 386
Father and Sons   239
Father Dowling Mysteries, The   303
Father Knows Best   37, 40, 122, 231, 366, 385, 386, 412
Father Murphy   239
Father of the Bride   59, 200
Fauci, Dan   114

Faulkner, William   246
Faustino, David   271
Fawcett, William   143, 305
Fawcett-Majors, Farrah   90, 91, 93, 159
Fay   374
Faye, Herbie   313
FBI CODE 98   213
Fedderson, Don   136
Feldon, Barbara   44, 146, 147, 312
Feldtheimer, John   455
Felix the Cat   362
Fell, Norman   401
Felony Squad   126, *140–141*
Fenneman, George   127
Fenton, Mike   420
Ferdin, Pamelyn   68, 227, 321, 323
Ferguson, Frank   224, 227, 305
Ferguson, Jay R.   134
Fernandes, Miguel   7
Fernandez, Abel   417, 418
Fernwood 2-Night   86, 127, 147, 326
Ferrell, Conchata   219, 220
Ferrell, Todd   224, 226
Ferrer, Jose   139, 314, 315
Ferrin, Frank   38, 39
Ferris, Patricia   405
Ferris Bueller   280, 329
FERRIS BUELLER'S DAY OFF   329
Fibber McGee and Molly   59, 146, 270, 437
Field, Sally   67, 142, 147, 148, 149
Field, Sylvia   110
Field, Margaret   148
Fields, Kim   135
FIGHTER SQUADRON   157
Filthy Rich   *141*
Final War of Olly Winter   181
Finder of Lost Loves   251
Fine, Larry   57
Fink, John   408
Finnigan, Joseph   286
Fiorello!   185
Fireball XL-5   375
Firestone, Eddie   418
First Nighter, The   13
Firth, Jonathan   104
Fish   124, 310
Fisher, Gail   207
Fisher, Ham   212
Fisher, Peter S.   303
Fisher, Shug   348, 349
Fisher, Terry Louise   219
Fishman, Michael   351, 352
FISTFULL OF DOLLARS, A   344
FIVE BOLD WOMEN   370
Flamingo Road   90
Flanagan, Bill   310
Flanagan, Markus   319, 320
Flanery, Sean Patrick   439, 440
Flannagan, Maureen   327
Flash, The   23, 78, *141–142*, 268, 367
FLASH GORDON   186, 327
Flash Gordon   405
FLAT TOP   370
Fleischer, Max   192

Fleming, Arthur "Art"   261
Fleming, Eric   260, 344
FLIGHT LIEUTENANT   231
FLIM FLAM MAN, THE   34
Flintstones, The   145, 237, 359
Flip Wilson Show, The   35
Flippen, Lucy Lee   238, 239
FLIPPER   360
Flipper   39, 360
Flo   29, 239
Fluegel, Darlanne   194, 195
FLUFFY   38, 41
Fly Away Home   435
Fly by Night   107
FLY, THE   205
Flying High   251
Flying Nun, The   *142*, 148
Flying Tigers   (See: *Major Dell Conway of the Flying Tigers*)
Flynn, Errol   16, 444, 450
Flynn, Joe   13, 15
FM   245
Foch, Nina   100
FOG, THE   276
Fogel, Jerry   295, 436
Foley, Ellen   316, 318
Foley, Joseph   26, 27, 293
Follett, Charon   401
Follows, Megan   52, 53
Fong, Harold   185
Fontain, Joan   414
Fontana, D.C.   222
FOR A FEW DOLLARS MORE   344
FOR YOUR EYES ONLY   416
Forbes, Kathryn   264
FORBIDDEN PLANET   77, 78, 333, 375, 427
Ford, Glen   285
Ford, Harrison   132, 439, 440
Ford, John   439
Ford, Ruth   105
Ford Theater   265
Foreign Intrigue   *142–143*
Foreign Intrigue: Cross Current   142
Foreign Intrigue: Dateline Europe   142
Foreign Intrigue: Overseas Adventures   142, 143
Foreign Legionnaire   86
Forest, Frederick   413, 414
FOREST RANGERS, THE   16
Forslund, Constance   149, 151
Forster, Brian   329, 330
Forsyth, Rosemary   109
Forsythe, John   47, 48, 90, 184
Forsythe, William   417, 421, 422
Fosse, Bob   60
Foster, Bill   301
Foster, Buddy   32, 37
Foster, Linda   299
Foster, Meg   84, 85, 86
Foster, Melvyn   107
Foster, Phil   228
Foulger, Byron   339
Four Seasons, The   124
Four-in-One   163
Fowley, Douglas V.   233
Fox, Gardner   141

Fox, Michael J. 88, 137, 138, 157, 349, 385
Fox, Nancy 397
Fox, Peter 433, 434
Fox, Sonny 27
Foxx, Redd 345, 353, 354, 356, 357
Frakes, Jonathan 382, 383
Fraley, Oscar 418, 419, 421
Fraley, Pat 9
Franciosa, Anthony "Tony" 312, 361
FRANCIS 289, 291
Francis, Anne 158, 282, 332, 349
Francis, Arlene 121
Francis, Cedric 100
Francis, Genie 336
Francis, Nick 387
Francis, Paul 108
FRANCIS GOES TO THE RACES 291
FRANCIS GOES TO WEST POINT 291
Franciscus, James 311
Frand, Harvey 171
Frank, Charles 99, 277
Frank, Harriet 246
Frank, Howard v, xiv
Frank, Richard 42
Frank Nitti: The Enforcer 419, 421
Franken, Steve 232, 267, 269
Franklin, Bonnie 325, 406
Franklin, Dr. Robert Allen 304
Franklin, Joe 424
Franklin, John 9
Frann, Mary 131, 314
FRANTIC 132
Frawley, William 202, 212, 307, 308
Frazee, Jane 58, 59
Frazer, Dan 217
Free Spirit 79
Freeberg, Stan 76
Freed, Bert 100
Freeman, Devery 41
Freeman, Kathleen 181, 291, 407
Frees, Paul 289
French, Victor 146, 147, 238, 239
Fresco, David 116, 118
Fridays 35
Friel, Tom 418
Frizzel, Lou 71
From Approximately Coast to Coast. . . 70
FROM RUSSIA WITH LOVE 266, 416
Froman, Troy 359
Frontier Circus 246
FRONTIER PHANTOM 234
Fugitive, The 347, 354, 374
Full House 231, 323
Fuller, Robert 224, 431, 432
Fullerton, Scott 222
Fulmer, Ray 174, 175
Funicello, Annette 26, 263
Further Adventures of Ellery Queen, The 11, 12, 13
FURTHER ADVENTURES OF THE WILDERNESS FAMILY—
    PART 2 366
Fury 143, *144,* 285, 305, 331
FURY AT FURNACE CREEK 245
Fusco, Paul 362
F/X 363

G.E. Theater 432
Gabor, Eva 161, 311
Gabor, Zsa Zsa 14
Gabriel, John 151
Galactica 1980 52, 65, 145
Galecki, Johnny 177
Gallant Men, The 27, 410
Gallaudet, John 307, 310
Galloway, Don 207
Gamble, Mason 111
GANTRY, ELMER 231
Gaona, Raul 368
Gardenia, Vincent 29, 30, 31, 399
Gardner, Bill 418
Gardner, Catherine 229
Gardner, Erle Stanley 332, 333, 334, 336
Gardner, Reginald 153
Garfield, Allen (See: Allen Goorwitz)
Garfield, John 363
Gargan, William 11, 273, 274
Garland, Judy 193, 284, 411, 412
Garland, Margaret 405
Garland, Richard 224, 227
Garlund Touch, The 172
Garmon, Pamela 204
Garner, James 121, 146, 277, 278
Garner, Peggy Ann 414
Garrett, Betty 30, 31, 228
Garrett, Jimmy 252
Garrett, Kathleen 428, 429
Garrett, Leif 321, 323
Garrett, Patsy 110, 111
Garrick, Rian 267
Garrison, David xi, 271, 272
Garver, Cathy 136, 137, 330, 331
Garvey, Gerald 401
Garvey, Jerry 11
Gary Shandling Show: 25th Anniversary Special, The 293
Gates, Chief Daryl 7
Gautier, Dick 16, 17
Gauzer, James John 201, 203
Gavin, James 235
Gavin, Robert 221
GAY BLADE, THE 447
Gaye, Lisa 188
Gayle, Tina 98
Gaynor, Mitzi 446
GAZEBO, THE 285
Gazzara, Ben 94, 228
Geary, Paul 246
Gefsky, Harold 157
Gehman, Richard 57
Geisel, Ted 226
Gelbart, Larry 254
Gelbwaks, Jeremy 329, 330
Gelman, Larry 322
Gemini Man, The 206
General Electric Theater 47
General Hospital 40, 179, 299, 336, 452
Generations 124, 351
Genovese, Mike 424, 425
Gent, George 49
Gentle Ben 163, 246
GENTLEMAN'S AGREEMENT 190

Gentry, Heidi   63, 65
Gentry, Laura   63, 65
George, Anthony   417, 418, 419
George, Lynda Day   284, 285, 289
George, Victoria   377, 381
George Burns and Gracie Allen Show, The   26, *145–146,* 202, 248, 291, 306, 339
George Gobel Show, The   37, *146,* 368
Gerald McBoing Boing Show, The   146
Geraldo   200
Gerard, Gill   80, 81, 415
Gerber, Joan   323
Gerrold, David   222
Gertz, John   ix, 448, 449, 452, 454, 455
Gertz, Mitchell   174
Get a Life   37, 70
Get Christie Love!   146
Get Smart Again!   147
Get Smart!   xv, 97, 136, *146–147,* 151, 209, 245, 251, 281, 312, 398, 437
Getting Together   35
GHOST OF FRANKENSTEIN, THE   132
GHOST IN THE INVISIBLE BIKINI, THE   263, 430
GHOST AND MR. CHICKEN, THE   35
GHOST OF ZORRO, THE   241, 444
Ghostley, Alice   32, 34, 65, 322, 323, 397
Giambalvo, Louis   41, 42
Gibbons, Leeza   133
Gibney, Hal   127
Gibson, John   105, 107
Gibson, Mimi   68
Gideon, Bond   326
Gidget   142, *147–149,* 340
GIDGET   148, 173
Gidget Gets Married   149
GIDGET GOES HAWAIIAN   146
Gidget Grows Up   149
Gidget Makes the Wrong Connection   149
Gidget's Summer Reunion   149
Gielgud, John   140
Gilbert, Jody   237
Gilbert, Melissa   238, 239
Gilbert, Sarah   352
Gilbert and Sullivan   446
Gilbreath, Earl   435
Gilford, Gwynne   313
Gillespie, Larrain   268
Gillette, Anita   52, 53, 304
Gilliam, Reg   287
Gilliam, Terry   88
Gilligan's Island   65, 68, *149–152,* 198, 204, 206, 269, 300, 404, 429
Gilligan's Planet   152
Gilliland, Richard   112, 326
Gilman, Kenneth   252
Gilpin, Marc   245
Gilyard, Clarence Jr.   275
Gimme a Break   301
Ginardi, Gina   190, 193
Ging, Jack   1, 3, 4, 349
Girard, Henry   25, 26
Girl From U.N.C.L.E., The   266
GIRL HAPPY   122
Girl with Something Extra, The   148
Girls, The   152

Gitarzan   37
Glass, Ron   321, 324
GLASS BOTTOM BOAT, THE   344
Gleason, Jackie   30, 57, 67, 183, 184, 185, 212, 213, 234, 235, 236, 374
Gleason, James   186, 202, 212, 235, 236
Gleason, Joanna   248
Glenn, Eric   400
Gless, Sharon   84, 85, 86, 188
Glick, Phyllis   252
Glitter   4, 128, 251
Gloria   31
Gobel, Alice   146
Goddard, Mark   115
Goddard, Paulette   149
GODDESS, THE   284
Godfrey, Arthur   388
GODZILLA, KING OF THE MONSTERS   333
Goetz, Peter Michael   24, 25
Going My Way   266
GOLD   355
Goldberg, Leonard   91
Goldberg, Whoopi   42
Goldbergs, The   10, *152–155,* 180, 184, 237
Golden Boy   363
GOLDEN GIRL   446
Golden Girls, The   133, 158, 320
GOLDFINGER   44, 416, 437
Goldie and Kids: Listen to Me   124
Golding, William   313
Goldstein, Jeffrey L.   179
GOLDTOWN GHOST RIDERS   39
Golic, Bob   360
Golonka, Arlene   211, 212, 398
Gomer Pyle, U.S.M.C.   23, 37, *155–158,* 260, 340
Gomez, Thomas   237
Gomez, Vincente   445
GONE WITH THE WIND   59, 100
Gonzalez, Joseph   417
Goober and the Ghost Chasers   158, 330
Goober and the Trucker's Paradise   37
GOOD, THE BAD, AND THE UGLY, THE   344
Good Advice   159
Good Guys, The   65
GOOD INTENTIONS   237
Good Morning, Miss Bliss   (See: *Saved by the Bell*)
Good Morning World   158
GOOD NEIGHBOR SAM   122
Good Sports   159–160
Good Times   *160–161,* 247, 276, 399
Good Times   59, 194, 313
Goodeve, Grant   131
GOODFELLAS   229
Goodman, Dody   274
Goodman, Gary   451, 452, 455
Goodman, John   351
Goodman, Lee   268, 270
Goodwin, Bill   145
Goodwin, Jim   377, 379
Goodwin, Joshua   406
Goodwin, Laurel   377
Goodwyns, Les   76
Goorwitz, Allen   395, 396
Goranson, Lecy   104, 351, 352

Gordon, Barry   299
Gordon, Bruce   418, 421
Gordon, Gale   80, 110, 111, 201, 202, 252, 253, 269, 304, 326
Gordon, Gloria   305
Gordon, Mark   274
Gordon, Virginia   326
GORDON'S WAR   331
Gori, Kathi   149
Gorshin, Frank   49, 50, 51
Gosney, Paige   408
Gosselaarl, Mark-Paul   358, 359
Gossett, Louis Jr.   342
Gough, Michael   51
Gould, Elliott   254, 399
Gould, Harold   166, 375, 376
Gould, Sandra   62, 64
Goulding, Ray   69, 70
Grable, Betty   188
Grabowski, Norman   313
Grade, Sir Lew   355, 376
GRADUATE, THE   216
Grady, Don   308
Graff, Randy   127
Graham, Samaria   229
Grammer, Kelsey   94
Grandpa Goes to Washington   410
Grandy, Fred   250, 251
Granger, Stewart   187, 425, 426
Grant, Bud   201, 202
Grant, Cary   59, 83, 121, 145, 237
Grant, Gil   104
Grant, Kirby   373, 374
GRAPES OF WRATH, THE   306
Graser, Earle W.   241
Grassle, Karen   238
Grauer, Ben   189, 192
GRAVE OF THE VAMPIRE   173
Graves, Peter   143, 144, 282, 283, 284, 285, 286, 287, 305
Graves, Teresa   146
Gray, Billy   39, 40
Gray, Donald   270, 271
Gray, Erin   80, 81, 82
Gray, Gregory   101, 102
Gray, Linda   73, 304
Gray, Michael   367
GREASE   34, 58, 90, 274, 326
GREASE 2   58, 124, 327
GREAT DICTATOR, THE   306
GREAT ESCAPE, THE   180, 181, 277, 412
Great Expectations   54
GREAT GILBERT AND SULLIVAN, THE   17
Greatest American Hero, The   336
Greaza, Walter   273
Green, Bill   235, 236
Green, Joey   150, 151
Green Acres   34, 123, *161–162,* 323, 340, 372, 406, 408
GREEN BERETS, THE   13, 381
Green Bush, Lindsay   238, 240
Green Bush, Sidney   238, 240
GREEN DOLPHIN STREET   12
Green Hornet, The   87, 376, 390
Greene, Gillian   73
Greene, Lorne   52, 70, 71, 72, 73
Greene, Michele   46, 47, 219, 220

Greene, Shecky   101
Greenlee, David   376
Greer, Dabbs   79, 80, 188, 189
Gregg, Hubert   16
Gregg, Julie   282
Gregory, James   115, 153, 436, 437
Gregory, Sylver   354
Greschler, Abby   171
Grey, Brad   160
Grey, Jennifer   229
Grief, Stephen   67
Grifas, Joe   217
Griffin, Merv   192
Griffith, Andy   31, 32, 36, 275
Griffith, Gordon   392
Griffith, James   370
Grimes, Jack   405
Grimes, Jackie   26
Grimes, Tammy   64
Grissom, Gus   197
Groom, Sam   121
Gross, Edward   55
Gross, Michael   137
Grossman, Gary   18, 354, 375
Grover, Edward   48
Growing Paynes, The   162, 185
Guardino, Harry   332, 334
Guastaferro, Vincent   417, 419
Guess Again   376
Guest, Christopher   245
Guest, Nicholas   245
Guiding Light, The   26, 58, 452
Guilbert, Ann Morgan   117, 314
Guillaume, Robert   58, 132, 363
GUN BROTHERS   82
Gun Shy   162, 411
GUNFIGHT AT THE O.K. CORRAL   177
Gunga, the East India Boy   38
GUNN   337
Gunn, Anna   124
Gunn, Moses   160, 161
Gunsmoke   37, 38, 57, 143, 147, 151, 161, ***163,*** 172, 211, 233, 333, 350, 352, 370, 393, 411
Gunty, Morty   117
Guzaldo, Joe   418, 419
Gwenn, Edmund   426
Gwynne, Fred   296, 297, 298, 299, 300, 301, 302, 311, 324
GYPSY   38

H.R. Puffnstuf   221, 314, 371
Hack, Shelly   90, 91, 92, 93, 318
Hackett, Joan   109
Haden, Sara   6
Hagen, Earle   36
Hagen, Jean   261, 262, 263
Hagerthy, Ron   373, 374
Haggerty, H.B.   81, 82
Hagman, Larry   13, 196, 197, 198, 199, 200, 204, 255
Haid, Charles   179
Haiduk, Stacy   19
Haig, Sid   209
Hailey, Arthur   187
Haines, Jacob   46
Hair   210, 330

Hale, Alan Jr.   150, 371
Hale, Barbara   333, 334, 336
Hale, Nancy   39, 40, 435
Haley, Jack   412
Hall, Anthony   377, 379
Hall, Anthony Michael   439
Hall, Cliff   105, 213
Hall, George   439
Hall, Huntz   417
Hall, Kevin Peter   168, 170
Hall, Monty   117
Hallahan, Charles   194
Halliwell, Leslie   205
Halloween That Almost Wasn't, The   301
Halloween with the New Addams Family   7, 8, 9
Halls of Ivy   xiv, **164**
Halop, Billy   102
Halop, Florence   316, 318, 319
Hamel, Veronica   179
Hamer, Rusty   262, 263
Hamill, Mark   131
Hamilton, Alexa   206
Hamilton, Anthony   103
Hamilton, George   447
Hamilton, John   20, 23, 67
Hamilton, Kim   134, 211
Hamilton, Linda   54, 55
Hamilton, Lynn   356
Hamilton, Margaret   8, 9, 68, 340
Hamilton, Richard   277
Hamilton, Ted   250
Hamilton, Tony   284, 286, 287
Hamlet, The   246
Hamlin, Harry   219
Hammond, Earl   81
Hamner, Earl Jr.   433
Hancock, John   167, 168, 220, 247, 248, 318
Hanging In   **164–165,** 358, 412
Hangin' with Mr. Cooper   119
Hank   299
Hanks, Tom   126, 168, 259, 313, 403, 430
Hannah, Daryl   439
Hanna-Barbera   27, 76, 203
Hano, Arnold   136
Hansen, Janis   321
Happy   **165,** 269
Happy Days   35, 36, 47, 54, 91, 115, 147, 161, **165–167**, 185, 228, 244, 246, 261, 272, 275, 303, 223
Happy Days Reunion Special, The   166
Harbor Command   132
HARD DAY'S NIGHT, A   294
Hard Time on Planet Earth   363
Hardcastle & McCormick   **167–168,** 248
Hardin, Ty   49, 96, 97
Hardy, Oliver   331, 446
Hardy Boys and the Mystery of the Applegate Treasure, The 13
Hardy Boys Mysteries, The   **168**
Hargrove, Dean   ix, 334, 335, 336
Harlan, Kenneth   426
Harlem Globetrotters on Gilligan's Island, The   149, 151, 199
Harlow, Jean   274
Harmon, Deborah   316, 318
Harmon, John   348
Harmon, Larry   vii, xiv, 75, 76, 77

Harmon, Mark   345, 414
Harper, Ron   221, 222
Harper, Valerie   166, 423, 424
Harper Valley P.T.A.   127
Harrelson, Woody   93, 95
Harriett, Judy   268
Harrington, Al   172
Harrington, Pat Jr.   117, 262, 263
Harris, Cynthia   219
Harris, Estelle   159
Harris, Jo Ann   115
Harris, Jo Anne   66, 67
Harris, Jonathan   445
Harris, Mark   104, 113, 115, 331
Harris, Neil Patrick   414
Harris, Percy "Bud"   58, 60
Harris, Robert H.   152, 153, 154
Harris, Ross   375, 376
Harris, Sam   389
Harris, Stacy   123
Harris, Susan   132, 320
Harris, Viola   vii, 153, 154
Harrison, Jenilee   401, 404
Harry and the Hendersons   **168–170,** 194
HARRY AND THE HENDERSONS   170
Harryhausen, Ray   311
Harry-O   **170–172,** 179, 206, 217, 256, 347, 446
Hart, Christopher   9
Hart, John   xiii, 240, 241, 243, 244, 245
Hart, Moss   372
Hart, Richard   11, 12
Hart, Trisha   68
Hartline, Mary   387, 388, 389
Hartman, David   425, 426
Hartman, Edmund   304
Hartman, Lisa   65, 391, 392
Harty, Patricia   67, 68
Hartzell, Clarence   84, 401
HARVEY   263
Harvey, John   68, 162
Harvey, Michael   405
Haskins, Dennis   359
Hasse, Rod   141, 367
Hasselhoff, David   53, 216
Hastings, Bob   30, 31, 302
Hat Squad, The   54
Hatch, Richard   52, 386
Hatcher, Teri   20, 24
Hathaway, Noah   51, 52
Hathaway, Samantha   63
Hathaways, The   118
Hausner, Jerry   116, 118
Have Gun-Will Travel   **172–173,** 233, 333
Havoc, June   437
HAWAII   173
Hawaii Five-O   121, **172–173,** 433
Hawaiian Eye   **173,** 347, 389, 390
Hawke   350
Hawkey and the Last of the Mohicans   244
Hawkins, Jimmy   39, 40
Hawkins Falls, Population 6,200   10
Hay, Alexandra   282, 285
Hayden, Russell "Lucky"   273
Hayden, Sterling   370

Hayes, George "Gabby"   186, 187, 189, 192
Hayes, Helen   272
Hayes, Margaret   66
Hayes, Molly "Pitcher"   88
Hayes, Robert   327
Haynes, Bruce   88
Haynes, Lloyd   377, 379
Hays, Kathryn   55
Hayward, Louis   355
Hayward, Susan   12
Hayworth, Vinton   197, 200, 441, 446
Hazel   14, 106, *174–175,* 259
He & She   147
Head of the Class   46, *176–177,* 429
Head of the House   116, 117
Headmaster   36
Healy, David   141
Healy, Myron   233
Hearn, Connie Ann   313
HEART IS A LONELY HUNTER, THE   282
Heart of the City   90
Heasley, Marla   1, 4, 5, 349
Hec Ramsey   94
Hedison, David   58, 427
Hee Haw   35, 37, 340
Heffley, Wayne   426, 427
Heggie, O.P.   218
Heidi   iii
Heinlein, Robert A.   405
Hello Larry   177, 255
Helmond, Katherine   58, 404
Hemblen, David   391
Hemmings, David   108
Hemsley, Sherman   29, 31, 209, 210, 399
Henderson, Chuck   267
Henderson, Florence   78, 79
Henderson, Marcia   26, 27, 414
Hendler, Lauri   313
Henner, Marilu   134
Hennessey   411
Henning, Carol   70
Henning, Linda Kay   338, 340
Henning, Paul   60, 61, 340
Henry, Gloria   110, 111
Henry, Gregg   408
Henry, John   (See: John Harvey)
Henry, Mike   254, 258, 393
Henry Aldrich   26
Henry IV   277
Hensley, Pamela   147, 414, 415
Henson, Jim   231, 362, 363
Hepburn, Katharine   204
Herbert, Don   11
Herd, Richard   88
Here Come the Brides   94
HERE COME THE NELSONS   231
HERE COMES MR. JORDAN   186, 202, 236, 361
Here's Lucy   15, 160, 177, 201, 253 (See also: *The Lucy Show*)
Herbie the Love Bug   68
Herlihy, Ed   189, 192, 193
Herman, Pee-wee   326, 331
Hermann, Edward   12
Herman's Head   372
Herron, Bob   437

Hertford, Chelsea   260
Hertzler, John   441, 453, 454
Heslov, Grant   376
Hesseman, Howard   176, 428, 429, 430
Hewett, Christopher   139
Hexum, John-Erik   103
Hey, Vern, It's Ernest!   326
Hickey, Ralph   51
Hickey, William   46, 47
Hickman, Dwayne   268, 270, 349
Hickox, Harry   341, 342
Hicks, Jack   351
High Chaparral, The   *177–179,* 328
High Jungle   344
High Performance   436
High School, U.S.A.   349
HIGH SIERRA   265
Highway to Heaven   147, 435
Highway Patrol   98, 267, 370
Hiken, Nat   158
Hill, Arthur   328
Hill, Craig   435
Hill, Steven   282, 284
Hill Street Blues   7, 42, *179–180,* 219, 403, 455
Hillebrand, Fred   273
Hines, Connie   291
Hingle, Pat   51
Hirsch, Judd   396
HIS GIRL FRIDAY   83, 109, 266
Hise, James Van   241
Hitchcock, Alfred   153, 185, 231, 285, 373
HITLER GANG, THE   261
Hobbs, Peter   275
Hoblit, Gregory   179
Hodge, Al   86, 87
Hodge, Stephanie   320
Hoffman, Bern   261
Hoffman, Dustin   127
Hoffmann, Cecil   219, 220
Hogan, Robert   269, 325, 326
Hogan Family, The   127, 424
Hogan's Heroes   xiv, 61, *180–182,* 407, 410
Holbrook, Anna   57
Holden, James   9, 10
Holden, Rebecca   216
Holden, William   69, 180
Holdren, Judd   102
Holdridge, Cheryl   232
Holland, Kristina   103
Hollander, David   313
Holliday, Art   436
Holliday, Judy   356
Holliday, Kene   132, 275
Holliday, Polly   28, 29, 342, 343
Holliman, Earl   171
Holloway, Sterling   20, 23, 438
Hollywood Junior Circus   *182*
Hollywood Squares   302
Hollywood Television Theater   167
Holman, Dr. Darren   15
Holmes, Dennis   223, 224
Holmes, Ed   162
Holmes, Jennifer   46, 314, 396, 451
Holt, Charlene   438

HOMBRE   177
Home Improvement 182–183
HOME OF THE BRAVE   361
Honda   37
Honeymooners, The   30, 59, 70, 87, 146, 162, 166, *183–185,* 213, 237, 401
Honeymooners Christmas Special, The   183
Honeymooners Valentine Special, The   183
Hong Kong 185, 398
Hong Kong Phooey   149
Hooker, Richard   (See: Dr. Richard H. Hornberger)
Hooks, Jan   112, 113
Hooks, Robert   135
Hooperman 185–186
HOPALONG CASSIDY   186, 187, 273
Hopalong Cassidy 186–187, 340
Hope, Bob   193, 261
Hopkins, John   14
Hopkins, Telma   313, 321
Hopper, Heather   358
Hopper, Hedda   14, 332
Hopper, William   332, 334
Horan, Hillary   165, 167
Hornberger, Dr. Richard H.   254
Horse, Michael   245, 417, 419
Horta, Samuel   179
Horton, Michael   303
Horton, Robert   393, 431, 432
Hot House   434
Hot l Baltimore   325
Hotchkis, Joan   321, 323
Hotel   24, *187,* 415
HOUSE CALLS   188
House Calls   85, *188,* 410
HOUSE OF FRANKENSTEIN   237
House of Glass, The   153
HOUSE OF WAX   265, 411
HOUSE ON 92ND STREET   273
House on Garibaldi Street, The   44
Houseman, John   157
Hovis, Larry   181
HOW TO MARRY A MILLIONAIRE   188
How to Marry a Millionaire   xiv, *188–189,* 198, 412
Howard, Andrea   147
Howard, Clint   379
Howard, D.D.   316
Howard, Jean   36
Howard, Ken   436
Howard, Leslie   17
Howard, Rance   36
Howard, Ronald   16, 17
Howard, Ronny "Ron"   32, 36, 37, 47, 165, 166
Howard, Sherman   17
Howard, Vince   48, 49
Howard Stern Show, The   79
Howat, Clark   125, 126
Howdy Doody 189–194, 213, 362
Howell, Hoke   33
Howes, Sally Ann   282
Howland, Beth   28, 29
Hoyt, John   379
Hudec, M. Leigh   (See: Majel Barrett)
Hudson, Rock   14, 114, 145, 149, 278, 279
Hughes, Bernard   120, 356

Hughes, John   111
Hugh-Kelly, Daniel   168
Hull, Cynthia   142
Hume, Benita   164
HUNCHBACK OF NOTRE DAME, THE   246
Hunley, Gary   373
Hunt, Gareth   43, 44
Hunt, Marlin   59
Hunter 194–195
Hunter, Jamie   71
Hunter, Jeffrey   377
Hunter, The   43, *195,* 304
Hunter, Timothy   ix, 45, 46, 47, 112, 113, 351, 359
Huntington, Pam   135
Hursey, Sherry   274
Hurst, Rick   128
Hurst, Ryan   359, 360
Husain, Jory   176
Huston, Angelica   9
Huston, Carol   93
Huston, John   9, 281
Hutchins, Will   67, 68
Hutson, Candy   134
Hutton, Gunilla   338, 339, 340
Hutton, Jim   11, 12, 13
Hutton, Paul Andrew   108
Hutton, Timothy   421
Hyde, Bruce   377, 379
Hyde-White, Wilfred   80, 81, 82
Hyland, Jim   88
Hyser, Joyce   220
Hyland, Diana   131

I DISMEMBER MAMA   78
I Don't Have to Show You No Stinking Badges   455
I Dream of Jeannie   196, *197–201,* 204, 255, 259, 328, 410, 427, 446
I Dream of Jeannie: 15 Years Later   196, 198, 199, 255
I'LL SEE YOU IN MY DREAMS   262
I Love Lucy   23, 37, 67, 111, 124, 200, *201–203,* 204, 215, 235, 236, 252, 253, 263, 295, 304, 314, 339, 351
I Love Lucy: the First Show   201, 253, 314
I Married a Dog   414
I Married Dora   455
I Married Joan 204, 305, 337
I'm Dickens—He's Fenster   86, 118, 147, 325
I Remember Mama   (See: *Mama*)
I Spy   66, 103, 180, 204, 312
I Still Dream of Jeannie   199
Iacofano, Tim   420
ICE STATION ZEBRA   274
Ichabod and Me   40
Immortal, The   434
IN SOCIETY   374
In the Beginning   255
In the Heat of the Night 204
IN THE HEAT OF THE NIGHT   204
Incredible Hulk, The   103, 147, 434
INDIANA JONES   234, 439
INDIANA JONES AND THE LAST CRUSADE   421, 439
INDIANA JONES AND THE TEMPLE OF DOOM   176, 439
Inescort, Frieda   279
Infidelities   42
Ingles, Marty   116, 118, 325
INHERIT THE WIND   126

Inner Sanctum 214
Insiders, The 436
International Detective 261
INTERNS CAN'T TAKE MONEY 120
INVASION OF THE BODY SNATCHERS 296
Investigators, The 311
INVISIBLE MAN, THE 205
Invisible Man, The xiv, **205–206,** 374
Invisible Woman, The 206
Ireland, John 73
Iron Mask, The 205
Ironside 147, **206–207,** 213, 334, 399
Irving, Hollis 68
Isenberg, Barbara 400
Isis xiv, **207,** 221
ISLAND OF DESIRE 271
Island Son 121
Islander, The (See: *Hawaiian Eye*)
IT CONQUERED THE WORLD 285
It Takes a Thief 208
It Was a Short Summer, Charlie Brown 323
It's a Great Life 34
It's a Small World 231
IT'S A WONDERFUL LIFE 246, 272
It's About Time 65, 407
It's Always Jan 412
It's Your Move 272
Ivanhoe 16, 355
Ivar, Stan 238, 239
Ivey, Judith 111, 114
Ivins, Molly 114

Jack Paar Show, The 212
Jackee 112, 115, 353, 354
Jackie Gleason Show, The 36, 146
Jackie Gleason and his American Scene Magazine 183, 184, 185
Jackie Gleason Special, The 183
Jackson, David 67
Jackson, Glenda 188
Jackson, Janet 159, 313
Jackson, Jeremy K. 53, 54
Jackson, Kate 31, 45, 89, 90, 91, 93, 408
Jackson, Leonard 362, 365, 370, 371
Jackson, Michael 313
Jackson, Rosemarie 400
Jackson, Selmer 233
Jackson, Sherry 117, 261, 262, 263, 347
Jackson, Stoney 436
Jackson, Tom 370, 371
Jack's Place 220, 395
Jacobs, Christian 30, 31
Jacobson, Art 182
Jacobson, Irving 155
Jacobson, Jill 148
Jaeckel, Richard 53, 54
Jaffe, Sam 55, 56, 57, 77
JAILHOUSE ROCK 193
Jake and the Fatman 124, 245
James, Jeri Lou 268
James, Ken 391
James, Olga 66
James, Patrick 449
James, Sheila 268, 270, 412
James at 15 434

Jameson, House 26
Jamison, Mikki 7
Jane Eyre 26
JANE EYRE 414
Janette, Rhianna 372
Janis, Conrad 211
Jann, Gerald 185
Jansen, Jim 110, 111
Janssen, David 171, 179, 347, 354, 374
Jason, Rick 101
JASON AND THE ARGONAUTS 267
Jason of Star Command 207, **208,** 221, 381, 405
Javna, John 4, 48, 63, 180, 255, 258
Jayne Mansfield Story, The 429
Jean Arthur Show, The 86
Jeffersons, The 31, 52, **209–211,** 325, 399
Jeffries, Adam 412
Jeffries, Anne 407
Jeff's Collie 15, 225 (See also: *Lassie*)
Jenkins, Larry "Flash" 435, 436
Jenkins, Mark 120, 121
Jenner, Bruce 98
Jensen, Pierce A. Jr. 300
Jeopardy 261
Jergens, Diane 70
JERK, THE 164
Jerry Colonna Show, The 110
Jerry Lewis Show, The 48
Jessie 1
Jessup, Paul 46, 165
Jessup, Ryan 46, 165
Jetsons, The 68, 203
JETSONS: THE MOVIE 203
JIGGS AND MAGGIE 6
Jim Nabors Hour, The 158
Jimmy Hughes, Rookie Cop 40, **211**
Joanie Loves Chachi 167
Jocelyn, June 197
Joe Forrester 121, 361
Joe Franklin's First Annual 40th Anniversary Show 424
JOE PALOOKA 212, 412
Joe Palooka Story, The **212,** 236, 261, 306
Joe & Valerie **211–212,** 247, 398
Joey Bishop Show, The 15, **212**
Joe's World 343
Johnny Baretta 48
JOHNNY BE GOOD 439
Johnny Belinda 399
Johnny Carson Show, The 110
Johnny Jupiter xiv, 213, 427
Johnny Ringo 115
JOHNNY TROUBLE 157
Johnson, Ben 70, 73
Johnson, Bob 287
Johnson, Don 281
Johnson, Janet Louise 168, 169
Johnson, Jason 33
Johnson, Nunnally 188
Johnson, Russell 150
Johnston, Christopher 30, 31
JOLSON SINGS AGAIN 333
Jones, Carolyn 9, 438
Jones, David 294, 295, 380
Jones, Ginger 58, 59

Jones, Morgan 68
Jones, Shirley 330, 342
Jones, Stan 370
Jonny Quest 27
Jordan, Bobbi 68
Jordan, Pat 132
Jordan, William 343
Jory, Victor 267
Joseph, Jackie 123
Josie and the Pussycats 156
Journey to the Center of the Earth 406
Joy, Christopher 322
Judd, Ashley 372
Judge Roy Bean 187
JUDGE ROY BEAN 282
Julia 201, **213,** 236, 274
Julia, Raul 9
Jump, Gordon 263, 428, 429, 430
Jurasik, Peter 336
Justice **214,** 237, 334
Juvenile Jury 264

Kahn, Madeline 69
Kalcheim, Harry 117
Kalem, Toni 321, 324
Kalember, Patricia 372
Kalter, Suzy 256
Kamekona, Danny 83
Kanan, Sean 336
Kaplan, Gabe 166, 176
Kaplan, Marvin 268, 270
Kareman, Fred 326
Karen **215–216,** 252, 300, 339
Karen, James 342
Karloff, Boris 121, 205, 237, 263, 298, 356
Karn, Richard 182
Kate Loves a Mystery 127
Katt, William 332, 334, 335, 336
Kaufman, Andy 396
Kaufman, George S. 372
Kauhi, Gilbert 173 (See also: Zulu)
Kavner, Julie 29, 279
Kay, Dianne 131
Kaye, Danny 265
Ke Quan, Jonathan 176
Keach, James vii, 245
Keach, Mary 245
Keach, Stacy 245, 281
Keach, Stacy Sr. 245, 281, 282
Kean, Eddie 192
Kean, Jane 183, 185
Keanan, Staci 310
Keane, Kerrie 334
Kearns, Joseph 21, 110, 111, 188, 189
Kearns, Sandra 89, 90
Keating, Larry 64, 121, 145, 236, 289, 291, 292, 293
Keating, Michael 67
Keaton, Michael 51, 141
Keegan, Chris 389
Keeler, Donald 224
Keen, Malcolm 264
Keenan, Mary Jo 320
Keene, Carolyn (See: Harriet Adams)
Keep Talking 117

Keep the Faith 278
Keeshan, Bob 189, 191, 192, 417
Keith, Brian 136, 137, 167, 281
Keith, Larry 52, 53
Keith, Richard 201, 203
Kelk, Jackie 26, 27
Keller, Mary Page 46
Kellerman, Sally 255
Kelley, DeForest 378, 379, 382
Kellog, Lynn 284
Kelly, Gene 262
Kelly, Grace 137
Kelly, Jack 146, 277
Kelly, Paula 316, 318
Kelly, Richard 35, 36, 37, 38
Kelly, Sheila 219, 220, 221
KELLY'S HEROES 204, 217
Kelsey, Linda 247, 254, 258
Kelton, Pert 183, 184, 185
Kemmer, Ed 375
Kennedy, George 69
Kennedy, Joseph P. 117
Kennedy, Kristina 45
Kennedy, Michelle 45
Kennedy, Mimi 318, 376
Kennedy, Patricia 117
Kenney, Sean 377, 379, 380
Kent, Janice 230, 232
Kentucky Jones 140, 162
Kercheval, Ken 197, 200
Kerr, Jean 342
Kerr, John 156
Kershaw, Whitney 260
Kerwin, Brian 99, 240
Ketcham, Hank 110, 111
Ketchum, Dave 146, 147
Key, Ted 174
KEY LARGO 245
KID, THE 330
Kidnie, James 334
Kiernan, James 341
Killick, Tim 103, 104
Kilpatrick, Eric 435, 436
Kimmel, Bruce 391, 392
King, Alan 102
King, John Reed 374
King, Mike 418
King, Pee Wee 331
King, Perry 349, 408, 409
King, Wright 189, 193, 213, 426, 427
King Leonardo and his Short Subjects 192
KING OF THE BULLWHIP 234
KING OF THE ROCKETMEN 101
KING RAT 267
King's Row 89, 96
Kinison, Sam 372
Kinsella, Walter 273
Kirchner, Claude vii, 387, 388, 389
Kirk, Phyllis 400
Kirkwood, Joe Jr. 212
Kirschenbaum, Alan 124
Kiss and Tell 34
KISS OF THE SPIDER WOMAN 9
Kitaen, Tawny 428, 429

Kitt, Eartha 49, 51
Kleinschmidt, Karl 324
Klemperer, Werner xiv, 60, 61, 181, 311
Kline, Richard 133, 402, 403
Kloer, Phil 255
Klous, Patricia "Pat" 249, 251
Klugman, Jack 53, 321, 322, 324, 334
Klunis, Tom 48
Knight, Christopher 79
Knight, Eric 225
Knight, Felix 14
Knight, Shirley 448
Knight, Ted 90, 227, 407
Knight Rider 53, *216*
Knight Rider 2000 216
Knotts, Don 31, 35, 36, 38, 51, 57, 158, 401, 402, 403, 435
Knotts Landing 5, 260, 351
Knox, Terrance 410
Knyvette, Sally 67
Koch, Howard W. 324
Koenig, Walter vii, 222, 342, 374, 377, 378, 379, 380, 381
Kohner, Frederick 148
Kojak 31, 44, 57, 103, 171, 214, *216–217,* 267, 271, 363
Kojak: The Belarus File 217
Kojak: The Price of Justice 217
Kokomo, Jr. 190
Kolchak: The Night Stalker 105
Kolden, Scott 371
Komak, James 97, 166
Kopell, Bernie 250, 251, 398, 399
Korman, Harvey 438
KOTCH 405
Kout, Wendy 41
Kovas, Dino 294
Kove, Martin 86
Kozoll, Michael 179
Kraft Music Hall, The 35
Kramer, Ross 221, 223
Kramer, Stepfanie 2, 194
KRAMER VS. KRAMER 93
Krofft, Sid and Marty 221, 314, 362, 371
Krofft Supershow, The 167
Krugman, Lou 38, 235
Kruschen, Jack 348, 398
Krystel, Sylvia 147
Kubrick, Stanley 232, 379
Kulky, Henry 426, 427
Kulp, Nancy 60
Kung Fu *217–218,* 237, 239, 306
Kung Fu: The Legend Continues 218
Kurtz, Swoosie 372

L.A. Law 46, 168, *219–221,* 247, 248, 252, 330, 422
La Page, Duane 135
La Rue, Alfred (See: Lash La Rue)
La Rue, Lash 233, 234
Lace 26
Lacy, Tom 446
Ladd, Alan 246
Ladd, Cheryl 90, 91, 92
Ladd, Diane 28, 29, 249, 251
LADY GODIVA RIDES AGAIN 17
Lady Killer 44
Lafayette, Greg 193

Lahart, Marty 418
Lahr, Bert 298
Laire, Judson 264
Lake, Arthur 67, 68
Lakeland, Ben 87
Lamas, Fernando 446
Lamb, Gil 189, 191
Lamparski, Richard 64
Lancaster, Burt 284, 299
Lance, Steven i, ii, xiv, 310
Lancer 207, 233
Land of the Giants 83
Land of the Lost xiv, 207, *221–223,* 381
Landau, Martin 282, 283, 284, 285, 286, 289, 374
Landers, Muriel 237
Landes, Michael 20, 408
Landis, Carole 444
Landon, Leslie 238, 240
Landon, Margaret 172
Landon, Michael 70, 71, 72, 73, 147, 149, 189, 238, 239, 427, 435
Landon, Michael Jr. 70, 73
Lane, Charles 215, 216, 252, 339
Lane, Lauren 194
Langdon, Sue Ane 33, 47, 48, 183, 184, 185
Lange, Ted 250
Langella, Frank 446
Langrick, Margaret 170
Lanier, Monique 234
Lannigan's Rabbi 330, 411
Lansbury, Angela 303
Lansing, Robert 218, 412, 413
Lanteau, William 37
LaPaglia, Anthony 418, 419, 421
LaPlaca, Alison 46
Lara, Joe 392, 393
Laramie *223–224,* 432
Laredo 173
Larkin, John 81, 333, 413
LaRoche, Mary 215
Larroquette, John 318
Larry Harmon Pictures Corporation xii, 76
Larsen, Keith 43, 195, 393
Larsen, Wolf 223, 394
Larson, Jack vii, 20, 22, 23, 155, 156, 157, 225
Lasser, Louise 274
Lassie 23, 57, 90, 135, 149, *224–227,* 341, 438
Lassie Come Home 225
LASSIE COME HOME 225, 226
Lassie's Rescue Rangers 227
Lassie: The New Beginning 227
Last of the Belles, The 121
LAST PICTURE SHOW, THE 222
Last Stagecoach West 386
Lathan, Stan 362
Laughlin, John 436
Laughton, Charles 273, 354
Laugh-In 146, 198, 340
Laurel, Stan 331, 446
Laurel and Hardy 14, 331
Laverne & Shirley *228*
Lavin, Linda 28, 29
Law and Harry McGraw, The 229
Law and Mr. Jones, The 101
LAW VS. BILLY THE KID, THE 370

Law & Order   **228–230**
Lawford, Peter   11, 12, 27, 117, 400, 414
LAWLESS, THE   149
Lawlor, John   135
Lawman, The   209
Lawrence, David   63, 65
Lawrence, Greg   63, 65
Lawson, Bianca   358, 360
Lay, Bernie Jr.   413
Lazenby, George   44, 67, 217, 266
Leach, Nicole   371
Leachman, Cloris   41, 69, 70, 90, 135, 224, 226, 324
Lear, Norman   30, 31, 52, 127, 161, 204, 210, 276, 304, 325, 330, 356
Learned, Michael   300, 434
Leary, Brianne   98
Leave it to Beaver   37, 80, 122, **230–232**, 263, 293, 296, 340, 351, 412
Leavitt, Norman   33
Leavitt, Sharyn   425
LeBlanc, Matt   425
Leckner, Brian   71, 73
Lecornec, Bill   191
Lecourtois, Daniel   86
Lee, Alexondra   372
Lee, Anna   107
Lee, Guy   268, 270
Lee, Manford B.   11, 12
Lee, Marci   xi
Lee, Virginia Ann   39, 40
Lee, Will   361, 363
Leeds, Peter   418
Leeson, Joe   418
Leeves, Jane   404
LeGault, Lance   1, 2
LEGEND OF THE LONE RANGER, THE   9, 244, 245, 396, 419
Legrand, Richard   51
Leichter, Jerry   24, 78, 86, 93, 282, 286, 318
Leiston, Freddie   236
Leisure, David   133
Lembeck, Michael   325
Lemmon, Jack   37, 122, 259, 402, 405
Lenard, Mark   286, 382
Lennon, John   234
Lentin, Chay   395
Lenz, Kay   345
Leonard, Sheldon   35, 36, 37, 117, 262, 263
Leonetti, Tommy   155, 156
Lerman, April   89
LeRoy, Hal   68
Leslie, Bethel   152
Leslie, William   237
Lesser, Sol   393
Lester, Jack   374
Lester, Jerry   183
Leversee, Loretta   26
Levine, Anna   395
Levine, Michael   452
Levinson, Richard   12, 100, 101
Levy, Bob   302
Levy, Weaver   9
Lewis, Al   vii, 296, 297, 298, 299, 300
Lewis, Cathy   305, 306
Lewis, Dan   139
Lewis, Dawnn   119

Lewis, George J.   441, 446
Lewis, Gilbert   331
Lewis, Jerry   82, 319, 340, 421, 446
Lewis, Lightfield   428, 429
Lewis, Richard   41
Lewis, Richard Warren   285
Lidsky, Isaac   359, 360
Lidsville   221, 314, 371
Lieutenant, The   **232,** 269, 380, 406
Life and Legend of Wyatt Earp, The   123, ***233–234,*** 264, 361, 446
Life and Loves of Linda Lovely   69
Life Goes On   46, ***234***
LIFE OF RILEY, THE   235, 236
Life of Riley, The   57, 145, 184, 200, 212, ***234–236,*** 279, 306, 374, 427
LIFE STINKS   158
Life with Father   200, ***236***
LIFE WITH FATHER   236
Life with Lucy   202
Life with Luigi   xiv, ***236–237,*** 306
Life with the Erwins   412
Lights Out   306
Lillie, Beatrice   153
Lincoln, Elmo   392
Linden, Hal   220, 395
Lindgren, Bruce   10
Lindley, Audra   120, 401, 403
Lindley, George   236
Lindsay, Howard   236
Lindsey, George   33, 37
Lineup, The   22, 110, ***237–238,*** 386
Link, William   100, 101
Linville, Larry   254, 255, 257, 258
Liotta, Ray   88
Lipton, Peggy   413
Lithgow, John   170
Little, Cleavon   164, 324, 397, 412
Little, Rich   140
Little House in the Big Woods   239
Little House on the Prairie   80, 147, 149, 172, 189, 231, ***238–240,*** 427, 433
Little House: A New Beginning   214, 239
LITTLE MISS MARKER   271
Little People, The   367
Little Rascals, The   148
LITTLE WOMEN   201
Little Women   27
Littlefield, Lucien   68
Littler, Craig   209
LIVE AND LET DIE   355, 416
LIVES OF A BENGAL LANCER   237
Livingston, Barry   307, 309
Livingston, Robert   241
Livingston, Stanley   308, 309
Li'l Abner   340
Lloyd, Christopher   259, 395, 396
Lobo   67, 99, ***240***
Locane, Amy   280, 376
Locke, Jon   221, 222
Locke, Ned   10, 11
Lockhart, Anne   149
Lockhart, June   224, 225, 226, 227, 337, 339
Lockwood, Gary   232, 286, 377, 379
LODGER, THE   50
Loeb, Philip   152, 153, 154

Loftus, John   217
Logan, Robert   366
Logan's Run   94
Logie, John   362
Lois and Clark: The New Adventures of Superman   24
LOLITA   271
Lombard, Carol   273
Lomond, Britt   441, 446
London, Steve   417   418
Lone Ranger, The   xiii, 102, 149, 163, 227, 235, **240–246,** 273, 280, 281, 307, 327, 355, 373, 376, 419, 434, 444, 446
LONE RANGER, THE   40, 241, 244
LONE RANGER AND THE LOST CITY OF GOLD, THE   246
LONE RANGER RIDES AGAIN, THE   241
LONELY ARE THE BRAVE   204
Lonesome Dove   452
Long, Loretta   362
Long, Richard   111, 390
Long, Shelley   93, 94, 95, 96
Long, Wayne   326
Long Hot Summer, The   **246**
Longstreet   311
Lontoc, Leon   83
LOOK WHO'S TALKING   46, 103, 165, 406
LOOK WHO'S TALKING TOO   46
Lookinland, Mike   79
Lopez, Mario   358, 359
Lopez, Perry   455
Lord, Jack   173, 370
Lord, Marjorie   261, 263
Lord, Philip   10
LORD LOVE A DUCK   269
Lord of the Flies, The   313
Loring, Lisa   7
Lorne, Marion   65
Lorre, Peter   427
LOST ANGELS   280
Lost in Space   115, 226, 263, 445
Lou Grant   133, 179, 180, **246–247,** 258, 312, 399
Lough, James   257
Loughlin, Lori   231
Louise, Tina   149, 151
Love, Montagu   444
Love American Style   iii, 43, 133, 134, 166, 215, 250, 330, 399
Love Boat, The   123, 133, 139, 187, 219, **249–252,** 253, 272, 275, 398
Love Boat I, The   250
Love Boat II, The   250
Love Boat III, The   250
Love Boat: A Valentine Voyage, The   251
LOVE GOD, THE   158
Love Is Hell   248
Love Nest   216
Love of Life, The   66, 211
Love on a Rooftop   140
LOVE STORY   159
Love That Bob   26, 117, 306, 339
Love & War   112, 220, **247–249,** 318, 395
Lovejoy, Frank   264, 265
LOVER COME BACK   115
Loves Me, Loves Me Not   **252**
Lowe, Chad   375, 376
Lowe, Rob   313, 376
Lowell, Tom   246

Lowry, Cynthia   30
Lowry, Robert   51
Loy, Myrna   400
Lu, Lisa   172
Lubin, Arthur   289, 291, 292, 293
Lucas, George   166, 439
Lucas Tanner   52, 399, 426
Lucie Arnaz Show, The   252
Lucille Ball Show, The   252
Lucking, William   1, 3
Lucy Show, The   15, 202, 203, 213, 215, **252–253,** 269
Luft, Lorna   410, 411
Lugosi, Bela   205
Luke, Keye   217, 218
Lumbly, Carl   85, 86
Lumley, Joanna   43, 44
Luna, Barbara   282, 288
Lunghi, Cherie   104
Lupo, Frank   4
LuPone, Patty   46, 234
Lupus, Peter   283, 284, 286, 289
Luttrell, Erica   371
Lutz, Joleen   319
Lux Video Theater   406
LYDIA BAILEY   332
Lynde, Paul   296, 302, 397
Lynn, Cynthia   180, 181
Lynne, Betty   33, 38
Lynne, Staci   xi

M*A*S*H   136, 213, 254
M*A*S*H   xii, xv, 12, 24, 25, 85, 101, 118, 123, 126, 155, 158, 161, 177, 188, 199, 203, 220, 233, 247, **254–260,** 268, 311, 318, 410, 437
McDonough, Mary Elizabeth   434
MacArthur, James   172, 173
MacClosky, Ysabel   62, 64
MacDonald, Blossom   8
MacDonald, Jeannette   8
MacDougall, Alistair   71, 73
MacDuff, Ewen   205
MacGregor, Katherine   240
MacGyver   147
Mack, Gilbert   213
MACKENNA'S GOLD   51
MacKenzie, Robert   18
MacLane, Barton   197, 200, 328
MacLane, Susan   68
MacLeod, Gavin   250, 252, 275
MacMichael, Florence   33, 47, 48, 292
MacMurray, Fred   231, 307, 308, 310, 332, 367
Macnee, Patrick   43, 44, 266, 267
MacRae, Elizabeth   156
MacRae, Gordon   157, 184, 340
MacRae, Meredith   307, 308, 339, 340
MacRae, Sheila   157, 183, 184, 185, 340
Macready, George   312
Macy, Bill   164, 276
Madigan   89, 436
Magder, Ari   371
Maggart, Brandon   313
Maggie   31
Magic Midway   388, 389
Magical World of Disney, The   108
Magnavox Theater   26

MAGNIFICENT SEVEN, THE   411
Magnum, P.I.   45, 439
Magnuson, Ann   41, 42
Maharis, George   352, 353
Maher, Joseph   41, 42
MAHOGANY   436
Mahoney, Jock   148
***Major Dad*   260**
***Major Dell Conway of the Flying Tigers*   212, *260–261,* 344**
Majority Rules   376
Majors, Lee   136, 328, 373, 425, 426
***Make Room for Daddy*   117, *261–263,* 274, 311, 347**
Make Room for Grandaddy   263
Makee, Blaisdell   377, 380
Makin' It   247
Malden, Karl   237, 386
Malibu Run   43, 360
Malina, Judith   9
Malinger, Ross   159
Malone, Mary   26, 27
Maloney, Lauren   325
Maloney, Paige   325
Maloney, Patti   80
MALTESE FALCON, THE   271
Maltese Falcon, The   400
***Mama*   xiv, 204, 237, *263–264,* 265, 280**
Mamakos, Peter   326
Mama's Family   36, 260
Man About the House   44
***Man Against Crime*   ii, 90, 109, 132, 182, *264–266,* 271**
Man and the Challenge   12
Man Called Shenandoah, A   432
Man From Cochise   370
MAN FROM HELL'S RIVER, THE   15
MAN FROM PLANET X, THE   149
Man From U.N.C.L.E., The*   4, 83, 103, 172, 206, 232, *266–267,
    340, 352, 361, 374, 414, 437
Man in the Iron Mask, The   205
Man of La Mancha   9, 155
Man of the People   278
MAN WHO CAME TO DINNER, THE   372
Man Who Never Was, The   413
Man with a Camera   411
MAN WITH THE GOLDEN GUN, THE   139, 416
MAN WITH TWO FACES, THE   280
Man Without a Gun   350
MANCHURIAN CANDIDATE, THE   82
Mancini, Henry   337
Mandan, Robert   58, 404
Mandel, Dennis   165, 166
Mandylor, Louis   124
***Manhunt*   *267,* 271**
Manley, Stephen   217
Mann, Abby   217
Mann, Iris   263, 264
Mann, Larry D.   121
Mann, Rhoda   192, 193
Mannix   172, 207, 211
Manoff, Dinah   133
Mansfield, Sally   47, 48
Mantooth, Randolph   326
Many Happy Returns   115
Many Loves of Dobie Gillis, The*   37, 149, 173, 232, 264, *267–270,
    409, 412

Marais, Jean   355
Marblehead Manor   327
Marcel, Nino   38
March, Frederick   126
March, Hal   76, 145, 305, 306, 414
MARCH OF THE WOODEN SOLDIERS   331, 446
Marchand, Nancy   179
Marcot, Danielle   371
Marcus, Sparky   428, 429
Marcus Welby, M.D.   7, 256, 280, 415
Marcus-Nelson Murders, The   217
Margie   308
Margie   68
Margolin, Stuart   330
Margolis, Mark   229
Marias, Mark   138
Marie, Rose   117, 123
Marill, Alvin   12
Marin, Jason   314
Marion, Richard   326
Maris, Ada   435
MARK OF THE LASH   234
MARK OF ZORRO, THE   177, 444, 446, 447, 451
Mark of Zorro, The   444, 446
Mark Saber*   *270–271
Markham, Monte   53, 54, 141, 332, 334
Marks, Guy   212
Markwell, Terry   284, 286, 287, 288
Marlowe, Hugh   11, 12
Merman, Ethel   193
Marquis, Kenneth   8
Marriage, The   211
***Married . . . With Children*   *271–273,* 359, 376, 425**
MARRYING KIND, THE   356
Mars, Kenneth   135, 136, 146, 147
Marsdan, Jason   296, 302, 408, 409
Marsh, Earle   27, 205, 340
***Marshal of Gunsight Pass, The*   273**
Marshall, A. David   179
Marshall, E.G.   57, 108, 109, 312
Marshall, Gary   166, 322, 323, 324
Marshall, Joan   298, 299
Marshall, Marie   177
Marshall, M.T.   337
Marshall, Penny   228, 321, 324
Marshall, William   331, 332
Marshall-Gardiner, Jessica   453
Martel, K.C.   296, 300
Martha Raye Show, The   279
Martin   320
Martin, Dean   130, 296, 312, 446
Martin, Dewey   106
Martin, Freddy   192
Martin, George R.   55
Martin, Kellie   234
Martin, Melissa   134
Martin, Nan   170
Martin, Pamela Sue   168, 169
Martin, Quinn   229, 418
Martin, Ross   437
Martin, Sharon   372
Martin, Steve   53, 164, 449
Martin, Vince   287
***Martin Kane, Private Eye*   66, 263, *273–274,* 311, 356**

Martinez, A   219, 220, 224, 451
Martinez, Patrice   441, 449, 450
Marx, Carl   182
Marx, Groucho   58, 127, 158
Marx, Marvin   59, 87
Marx Brothers, The   241
Mary Hartline Show, The   389
Mary Hartman, Mary Hartman   127, 147, 274, 358, 386, 429
Mary Noble, Backstage Wife   69, 70
MARY POPPINS   260, 299
Mary Tyler Moore Comedy Hour, The   274, 346
Mary Tyler Moore Show, The   41, 52, 65, 123, 135, 141, 166, 226,
   247, 250, 258, ***274–275,*** 278, 279, 300, 341, 347, 396, 406, 425
Masak, Ron   303
Mask, The   214
Mason, Marlyn   284
Mason, Sydney   305
Masquerade   96
Massey, Raymond   120, 121
Masur, Richard   324, 325
Match Game, The   193
Mathers, Jerry   231
Matheson, Murray   314, 315
Matheson, Tim   372, 425, 426
Matlin, Marlee   345
Matlock   36, 124, ***275,*** 376
Matt Helm   146
Matthau, Walter   111, 188, 322
Matthews, Larry   117
Matthews, Pat   400
Mature, Victor   444
Maude   52, 59, 118, 160, 161, 164, 247, ***275–277,*** 358, 412
Maule, Brad   401
Maverick   146, ***277–278,*** 355, 393
Maxwell, Frank   30, 140, 141
Maxwell, Jeff   254, 258, 260
Maxwell, Lois   416
Maxwell, Marilyn   262
Maxwell, Robert   22, 23, 226
May, Donald   99, 100, 350
Mayberry R.F.D.   32, 34, 36, 37, 65, 167, 212, 278, 398, 408
Mayer, Christopher   127, 128
Mayer, Joseph David   201, 203
Mayer, Michael Lee   201, 203
Mayo, Whitman   356
Mayor of Hollywood   232, ***278***
Mayor of the Town   407
Mazeo, Larry   117 (See also: Larry Matthews)
Mazes, Michael   326
McBain, Diane   390
McCain, Frances Lee   402
McCain, Lee   43
McCalla, Irish   vii, 367, 368, 369, 370, 449
McCallum, David   4, 205, 206, 266, 277
McCallum, Neil   271
McCalman, Macon   408
McCann, John   372
McCann, Sean   52, 53
McCardle, Mickey   291
McCarthy, Nancy   151
McCarthy, Senator Joseph   26, 152
McCartney, Paul   234
McCarty, Mary   410

McCay, Scott   291
McClanahan, Rue   408
McClelland, Doug   xi
McCloud   101, 163, 220, 312, 356, 411
McClure, Doug   328, 361
McClurg, Edie   127
McConnell, James "Ed"   38, 39
McCord, Evan   173
McCord, Kent   7, 51, 52
McCormack, Patricia   403
McCormick, Maureen   78, 79, 80, 109
McCrea, Joel   120, 426
McCrohan, Donna   184, 185
McCulley, Johnston   444, 449
McCullough, Julie   169, 170
McDaniel, Hattie   58, 59, 276
McDonald, Christopher   159
McDonald, Ryan   322
McDonnell, Jo   296, 300
McDonough, Mary Elizabeth   434
McDowall, Roddy   225, 407
McFadden, Gates   382, 383, 384, 385
McFall, Phil   34
McGavin, Darren   105, 281, 328, 349, 351
McGinley, Ted   271, 272
McGiver, John   330, 331
McGlynn, Frank Jr.   187
McGowan, Tom   124
McGrath, Frank   431
McGraw, Charles   88
McGuire, Michael   95
McHale's Navy   15, 31, 256, 302, 398
McHattie, Stephen   55
McIntire, John   57, 311, 425, 426, 430, 431
McIsaac, Marianne   52
McKeon, Nancy   135, 349, 360
McKeon, Philip   28
McKinley, J. Edward   110
McLaughlin, Henry   189
McLaughlin, Rita   331
McLean Stevenson Show, The   255
McLennan, Chuck   330
McLeod, Catherine   47, 48
McLeod, John   425, 426
McIlwraith, David   334
McMahon, Ed   vii, 376, 388, 389
McMahon, Horace   262, 263, 273, 274, 311
McMillan and Wife   101, 147, 152, ***278–279,*** 301, 312, 326, 341,
   356, 400, 412
McNear, Howard   33, 37, 80, 399
McNeil, Alex   168
McNichol, Kristy   43, 132, 133, 134
McNulty, Pat   310
McPherson, Patricia   216
McQuade, Arlene   154
McQuade, John   90
McQueen, Steve   38, 109, 180, 213, 271, 277, 285, 427
McRaney, Gerald   260
McVey, Patrick   65, 66, 267
McWilliams, Caroline   57, 58, 132
Me and Maxx   168
Me and the Chimp   371
Meadows, Audrey   69, 70, 183, 184, 185

Meara, Ann   102, 188
Meat Loaf   318
MEATBALLS   86
Medical Center   144, 214, 386
Meet Corliss Archer   xiv, 26, 235, 264, ***279–280,*** 327, 354
MEET JOHN DOE   201
Meet McGraw   265
Meet Millie   123, ***280,*** 327
Meiser, Edith   203
Melgar, Gabriel   97, 98
Melrose Place   280
Melville, Sam   350
Melvin, Allan   116, 118
Men From Shiloh, The   (See: *The Virginian*)
Menagerie, The   380
Mengatti, John   436
Menkin, Shepard   246
Mercein, Tom   10
Meredith, Burgess   51, 361
Meriwether, Lee   49, 51, 282, 285, 286, 296
Merlin, Jan   405
Merrill, Dina   282, 285
Merrill, Fanny   153
Merrill, Gary   120, 121, 214
Merrily We Roll Along   272
Merrit, Theresa   399
MERRY MONAHANS   173
Metcalf, Laurie   351
Metcalfe, Burt   255
Metchik, Aaron   302, 408
Metzinger, Kraig   275, 276
Meyers, Ari   331
Meyers, Lou   119
Meyers, Ric   12, 126, 171, 337
"Miami Steve"   (See: Steven Van Zandt)
Miami Vice   115, 281, 436, 455
Michael Shayne   173
Michael Shayne, Detective   281
Michael Shayne, Private Detective   281
Michaels, Corinne   238, 239
Michel, Franny   43
Michelman, Ken   436
Mickey Mouse Club, The   13, 192, 224, 232
Mickey Spillane's Mike Hammer   105, 127, 120, ***281–282,*** 336, 350
Middleton, Charles   186
Midgley, Richard   26
Midkiff, Dale   342
Mid-Morning L.A.   340
MIGHTY JOE YOUNG   83
Mighty Mouse   373
Miles, Dallas   57
Miles, Joanna   385
Miles, Sylvia   117
Milland, Ray   117, 137, 261, 264
Miller, Denny   vii, 361, 392, 431, 432
Miller, Hal   362, 363
Miller, Kristine   385, 386
Miller, Leo O.   163, 339
Miller, Mark   342
Miller, Marvin   386
Miller, Scott   (See: Denny Miller)
Miller, Thomas L.   423
Milligan, Spencer   221, 222

Million Dollar Rip-Off, The   97
Millionaire, The   110, 386, 414
Mills, Hayley   359
Mills, Juliet   111
Milmore, Jane   vii, 41, 42, 202, 276, 314, 315, 316, 320
Milner, Martin   6, 7, 352, 353
Minardos, Nico   344
Minelli, Liza   411
Mineo, Sal   171
Mines, Steven   148
Minetti, Larry   45
Mini Munsters, The   302
Minnie's Boys   58
Minor, Mike   340
Minor, Worthington   155
Mintz, Eli   152, 153, 154, 155, 184
Mintz, Hasha   152, 153, 154, 155, 184
MIRACLE OF THE WHITE STALLIONS   311
MIRACLE ON 34TH STREET   137, 190, 202, 241
Miracle on 34th Street   426
Misadventures of Sheriff Lobo, The   67, 240
Miss Stewart, Sir   411
Mission: Impossible   69, 106, 107, 143, 144, 172, 182, 195, 204, 206, 209, 213, 233, ***282–289,*** 374, 419, 424
Mitchell, Cameron   178, 179
Mitchell, Don   207
Mitchell, Jake   45
Mitchell, Keith   162
Mitchell, Shirley   47, 48, 337, 339, 342
Mitchell, Thomas   100
Mitchell-Smith, Ilan   17, 19
Mitchum, Robert   235
Mitz, Rick   29, 64, 145, 161, 164, 202, 210, 255, 264, 276
Mobile One   343
Mobley, Mary Ann   119
Mobley, Roger   144
Mod Squad, The   115, 253, 413
Moger, Stan   15, 16
Mohr, Gerald   142, 143
MOLE PEOPLE, THE   231
Molinaro, Al   146, 147, 165, 167, 321, 322, 323, 324
Moll, Richard   318
MOLLY   154
Molly and Me   152
Molly and Me: The Memoirs of Gertrude Berg   154
Momary, Doug   314
Monahan, Mike   167
Monica, Corbett   212
Monkees, The   294–295, 380
MONKEY BUSINESS   145
Monroe, Marilyn   188, 368, 402
Montalban, Ricardo   139, 140, 379, 446
Montefuscos, The   374
Montgomery, Elizabeth   62, 63
Montgomery, Robert   186
Montoya, Patrick   245
Monty Python's Flying Circus   16, 88
Moody, Lynne   211, 399
Moody, Ralph   348
Moonlighting   345
MOONRAKER   360, 416
MOONTRAP   381
MOON-SPINNERS, THE   359

Moore, Clayton   xiii, 102, 163, 240, 241, 242, 243, 244, 246, 373, 444

Moore, Constance   291

Moore, Del   47, 48

Moore, Dickie   405

Moore, Dudley   248, 439

Moore, Joanna   33

Moore, Mary   (See: Mary Tyler Moore)

Moore, Mary Tyler   117, 118, 263, 274, 347, 438

Moore, Roger   277, 278, 345, 355

Moore, Wilford G.   374

Moorehead, Agnes   62, 100

Mor, Rummel   260

Moran, Erin   36, 47, 166

More Wild, Wild West   437

Moreau, Nathaniel   218

Morgan, Dennis   413

Morgan, Gary   117

Morgan, George   254, 255

Morgan, Harry   viii, xv, 10, 11, 12, 13, 24, 25, 125, 126, 201, 254, 257, 437

Morgan, Robin   263, 264, 279, 280

Morgan, Wesley   234

Moriarity, Michael   228

Morita, Pat   165, 166, 167, 323, 391

Mork & Mindy   107, 136, 205, 211, 228, 437

Moross, Jerome   311

Morris, Greg   182, 283, 284, 286, 289, 424

Morris, Haviland   138

Morris, Howard   102

Morris, Phil   284, 287, 289, 424

Morrison, Brian   275, 276

Morriss, Ann   80

Morrow, Byron   125, 126

Morrow, Don   273

Morrow, Jeff   397

Morrow, Vic   101

Morse, Barry   374

Morshen, Bernie   189, 192

Morton, Howard   296

Moschitta, John Jr.   447

Moses, John   69

Moses, Rick   106

Moses, William R.   332, 335, 336

Mosher, Bob   298, 300

Mosler, Jim   57

Moss, Arnold   379

Mossberg, Julie   366

Most, Donny   166, 167

Mothers-in-Law, The   *295–296*, 327

Mountain, Johnny   74

MOUNTAIN FAMILY ROBINSON   366

Movie of the Week   100

Movin' On   214

Mozee, Phoebe Anne Oakley   39

Mr. Adams and Eve   237

Mr. Belevedere   140

MR. BLANDINGS BUILDS HIS DREAM HOUSE   59

Mr. Dooley   (See: *Hanging In*)

Mr. Dugan   412

Mr. Ed   38, 48, 64, 121, 145, 157, 236, ***289–293,*** 296, 407

Mr. Garlund   172

Mr. Green Jeans   (See: Hugh "Lumpy" Brannum)

Mr. I. Magination   434

Mr. Magoo   204

Mr. Novak   13, 146, 279, 311, 380, 390

Mr. Peepers   27, ***293–294***

Mr. Roberts   97, 157, 366

Mr. T   xvii, 1, 181, 391

Mr. T and Tina   166, 391

Mr. Terrific   331

Mr. Wizard   11

Muir, Jean   26

Muir, Roger   191, 192, 193

Muldaur, Diana   210, 220, 382, 384, 385

Mulgrew, Kate   127

Mulhare, Edward   216

Mull, Martin   147

Mullaney, Jack   306, 307

Mulligan, Richard   43, 58, 132, 320

Mulligan's Stew   330

Mullins, Jim   103

Mumy, Billy   299

Mundy, Meg   109

MUNSTER, GO HOME!   299, 300

Munsters, The   167, ***296–302,*** 303, 306, 311, 324, 354, 371, 446

Munsters Revenge, The   167, 296, 300, 302

Munsters Today, The   301, 302, 414

Murder, She Wrote   67, 111, 131, 220, ***303,*** 411, 435

Murdock, George   435

Murdock, Jack   326

Murphy, Audie   246

Murphy, Ben   27, 28, 206

Murphy, Brittany   408, 409

Murphy, Diane   63, 65, 303

Murphy, Erin   62, 63, 65, 303

Murphy, Mary   96, 251

Murphy Brown   47, 351

Murphy's Law   19

Murray, Bill   91

Murray, Joel   248, 249

Musante, Tony   48

Muse, Clarence   88

MUSIC LOVERS, THE   121

MUSIC MAN, THE   36, 120, 184, 265, 330

MY BLUE HEAVEN   439

My Favorite Husband   179, 195, 201, 201, ***303–305,*** 327

My Favorite Martian   103, 118, 259, 300, 398

MY FAVORITE SPY   261

My Friend Flicka   227, ***305***

My Friend Irma   xiv, 145, 212, ***305–306***

My Living Doll   51, ***306–307***

My Mother the Car   35, 216, 289

My Sister Eileen   117, 162

My Three Sons   48, 64, 166, 173, 213, 299, ***307–310,*** 332, 337, 340, 455

My Two Dads   67, ***310***

My Wicked, Wicked Ways . . . The Legend of Errol Flynn   318, 450

My World and Welcome to It   140, 154, 303

Myers, Carrell   229

Myers, Mike   64

Myers, Nancy   45

Myers, Pauline   134

Myman, Robert   185

Mystery Movie   101

Mystery Wheel of Adventure   356

9 TO 5   127, 343
9 to 5   79
90 Bristol Court   215
A NIGHT TO REMEMBER   146
Nabors, Jim   33, 37, 155, 157
Nader, George   11, 12, 13
Naish, J. Carrol   236, 237
Naked City   147, 180, 204, ***311–312,*** 426, 431
Naked City   413, 426
NAKED GUN, THE   78
Nakia   438
Name of the Game   312, 361
Name Your Adventure   359
Nanasi, Anna Maria   268
NANCY DREW   405
Nancy Drew Mysteries, The   168, 181, 312 (See also: *The Hardy Boy*
    Mysteries)
Nanny and the Professor   111, 213
Nancy Walker Show, The   260, 279
Napier, Alan   51, 225
Napier, Charles   1, 2, 3
Nasser, Edward   292
Nasser, James   292
Nassour, Edward   (See: Edward Nasser)
Nassour, James   (See: James Nasser)
Nation, Terry   67
National Geographic   312
NATIONAL LAMPOON'S ANIMAL HOUSE   103
National Velvet   227
Naud, Melinda   115, 326
Navy Log   69
NBC Mystery Movie, The   163, 312
NBC Sunday Mystery Movie, The   152, 356
NBC Wednesday Mystery Movie, The   89, 436
Needham, Tracey   234
Neher, Susan   166
Neill, Noel   20, 21
Nelkin, Stacey   99
Nelson, Barry   195, 304
Nelson, Craig T.   122
Nelson, David   13, 15
Nelson, Frank   203, 323
Nelson, Harriet   14
Nelson, Kenneth   25, 26
Nelson, Kristin   7
Nelson, Lori   188
Nelson, Ozzie   13, 14, 262, 412
Nelson, Ricky   7, 13, 15, 328
Nelson, Tracy   303
Nemec, Corin   329
Nerman, David   391
Nero Wolf   245
Nesmith, Mike   294, 295
Ness, Eliot   418, 419
Nettleton, Lois   205, 304
NEVADA SMITH   285
NEVER SAY NEVER AGAIN   360, 361
Nevil, Alex   96
Nevins, Francis M. Jr.   13
New Adventures of Charlie Chan, The   237
New Adventures of Ellery Queen, The   12
New Adventures of Flash Gordon, The   373
New Adventures of Gilligan, The   152
New Adventures of Martin Kane, The   274

New Adventures of Perry Mason, The   334
New Adventures of Superboy, The   18
New Adventures of Superman, The   406, 407
New Adventures of Wonder Woman, The   393
New Andy Griffith Show, The   36
New Avengers, The   43, 44
NEW CENTURIANS, THE   282
New Dick Van Dyke Show, The   31
New Doctors, The   109, ***312–313,*** 426
New Family in Town   (See: *Happy Days*)
New Gidget, The   149
New Howdy Doody Show, The   189
New Kind of Family, A   313, 324
New Lassie, The   227
New Leave it to Beaver, The   232, 263
New Love American Style, The   280
New Maverick, The   277
New Monkees, The   294
New Munsters, The   158
New Odd Couple, The   301, 324, 358
New Operation Petticoat, The   325
New People, The   313
New Phil Silvers Show, The   49, ***313***
New Stu Erwin Show, The   412
New Temperature's Rising, The   397
New WKRP in Cincinnati, The   (See: *WKRP in Cincinnati*)
New York Confidential   274
New Zoo Revue, The   314
Newhart   xiv, 42, 46, 113, 124, 132, ***314–316,*** 320, 396, 451
Newhart, Bob   123, 132, 159, 220, 314
Newman, Paul   136
Newman, Robert Connor   194
Newmar, Julie   49, 51, 306, 307
Newton, Helen   423
Newton, John Haymes   17, 18, 19, 419, 421
New! Improved! Bob and Ray Book, The   70
Nguyen, Dustin   413, 414
Nichols, Nichelle   378, 379, 381, 437
Nicholson, Bobby "Nick"   189, 191, 192, 193
Nicholson, Jack   51
Nick & Hillary   (See: *Tattingers*)
Nicoll, Kristina   391
Nielson, Leslie   77, 78
Nigh, Jane   47, 48, 65, 66
Night Court   133, 136, 248, ***316–319***
Night Gallery   253
Night Heat   53
Nightingale, Earl   374
Nimoy, Leonard   102, 181, 282, 286, 378, 379, 381, 382
Nipper, Will   224
Nitti, Frank   419
Niven, David   342, 355
No Time for Sergeants   342
NO TIME FOR SERGEANTS   35
Noah, Peter   41, 42
Noble, James   58
Nolan, Dani   20, 23
Nolan, Jeanette   296
Nolan, Lloyd   126, 273, 274
Nolan, Tom   4, 327, 328
Norby   13, 118
Norell, Henry   110
NORMA RAE   142
Norman, B.G.   236

Norman, Monty   267, 346
Norman, Susan   216
Norris, Christopher   410
Norris, Lee   408
North, Jay   110, 111
North, Sheree   275
North and South   96, 346
NORTH BY NORTHWEST   266, 285
Norton, Cliff   33
Norton-Taylor, Judy   434
Nossen, Bram   xv, 86, 87
Not for Publication   280, ***319***
Noth, Christopher   228, 229
NOTHING BUT A MAN   181
Nouri, Michael   220
Novick, Jill   372
Nowlan, Philip   81
NUDE BOMB, THE   XV, 147
Nurse   434
Nurses   319–320

110 in the Shade   432
O'Brian, Hugh   234, 333, 361
O'Brian, Jack   187
O'Brian, Pat   14
O'Brien, Edmond   246
O'Brien, George   106
O'Brien, Rory   140
O'Byrne, Bryan   68
O'Connor, Brian   371
O'Connor, Carroll   31, 150, 204, 205
O'Connor, Donald   173, 289
O'Connor, Tim   80, 82
O'Donnell, Gene   107
O'Farrel, Conor   386
O'Farrell, Bernadette   16, 17
O'Hanlon, George   201, 203, 234, 236
O'Hara, Paige   54
O'Heaney, Caitlin   93
O'Herlihy, Dan   166, 246, 411
O'Herlihy, Gavin   165, 166, 246
O'Keefe, Dennis   214
O'Keefe, Miles   392
O'Keefe, Paul   331
O'Keefe, Walter   278
O'Kelly, Tim   173
O'Loughlin, Gerald S.   351
O'Malley, J. Pat   116, 118, 276
O'Mara, Teri   250
O'Morrison, Kevin   90
O'Neal, Kevin   313
O'Neal, Ryan   159
O'Neil, Ron   55
O'Neill, Dick   107
O'Neill, Ed   271, 425
O'Neill, Eileen   82, 83
O'Neill, Jennifer   103
O'Sullivan, Maureen   394
Oad-Heim, Gordon   294
Oakes, Randi   98
Oatman, Doney   321, 323
Ober, Philip   197, 200
Oberon, Merle   319
OBJECTIVE BURMA   231

OCTOPUSSY   416
Odd Couple, The   37, 65, 124, 147, 167, 251, ***321–324,*** 325, 341, 358, 405
Odd Couple: Together Again, The   321, 324
Oddball Couple, The   323
Odets, Clifford   363
Off to See the Wizard   344
Ogilvy, Ian   355, 356
Oh Boy, Babies!   366
Oh Kay   389
Oklahoma   407
Old American Barn Dance   84
Oliphant, Peter   116, 118
Oliver   294
OLIVER   371
Oliver, Susan   237
Olivieri, Dennis   313
Ollestad, Norman   373
Olmos, Edward James   455
Olsen, Leila Hee   435
Olsen, Merlen   238, 239
Olsen, Susan   78, 79
Omnibus   143, 332
On Borrowed Time   34
ON HER MAJESTY'S SECRET SERVICE   44, 103, 217, 416
ON MOONLIGHT BAY   306
On the Rocks   30
ON THE TOWN   64
ON THE WATERFRONT   426
Once Upon a Spy   300
One Day at a Time   122, 263, ***324–325,*** 406
One Fella's Family   69
One Life to Live   159
One Man's Family   13, 69, 212
ONE MILLION B.C.   444
Ontkean, Michael   350
Open All Night   228
Openheimer, Alan   165, 167, 373
Operation Neptune   232
Operation Petticoat   9, 41, 115, 323, ***325–326***
Oppenheimer, Jess   201, 202
OPPORTUNITY KNOCKS   420
Orbach, Jerry   228, 229
Oregon Trail, The   2
Orlando, Tony   313
Orman, Roscoe   vii, 362, 363, 364, 365
Orr, William, T.   173, 366
Orsen, Jack   87
Orth, Frank   80
Orville and Wilbur   245
Osterhage, Jeff   125, 127
Osterloh, Robert   418
Othello   420
OUR GANG   405
Our Miss Brooks   83, 110, 111, 118, 146, 202, 203, 293, 304, 306, ***326–327***
Out of the Inkwell   192
Out of this World   327–328
Outer Limits, The   406
Outlaws, The   141, 200, ***328***
Outlaws of the Century   (See: *Stories of the Century*)
Overall, Park   133
Owen, Beverly   296, 299
Owen, Ethel   185

Owen, Reginald   408
Owen Marshall, Counselor at Law   *328,* 426
OX-BOW INCIDENT, THE   126
Oz, Frank   362, 363
Ozzie's Girls   15

P.S. I LUV U   248
Pacino, Al   421
Packer, Doris   232, 267, 269
Padgett, Glenda   268
Padilla, Manuel Jr.   393
Page, LaWanda   358
Paige, Janis   410, 411
Paley, Philip   221, 222
Palin, Michael   88
Pallette, Eugene   444
PALOOKA   212
Pang, Joanna   207
PANIC IN THE STREETS   226
Pantomime Quiz   162, 226
Paradise   234
Paradise Bay   148
Parady, Hersha   238
PARENT TRAP, THE   359
PARENTHOOD   37
Parfitt, Judy   93
Paris   45
Paris, Frank   190
Paris, Jerry   117, 118, 417, 418
Parish, Judy   162
Parker, Bill   367
Parker, Eleanor   77, 263, 300
Parker, Fess   39, 40, 106, 108
Parker, Ginny   128, 129
Parker, Jacob   134
Parker, Maggie   172
Parker, Norman   138
Parker, Penny   261, 263
Parker, Rod   435
Parker Lewis Can't Lose   280, *329*
Parks, Bert   43
Parks, Larry   333
Parnell, Emory   235, 236
Parrish, Helen   230, 232
Parros, Peter   6, 7
Parsons, Fern   400
Parsons, Louella   14
Partners in Crime   429
Parton, Dolly   127, 420
Partridge Family, The   219, 246, 247, 252, *329–330*
Partridge Family: 2200 AD   330
PASSENGER 57   419
Pastene, Robert   80, 81
Pastorelli, Robert   47
Pat Sajak Show, The   225, 226, 227
Patch, Marilyn   190, 194
Pate, Michael   288
PATHFINDER, THE   246
Patrick, Butch   vii, 296, 297, 299, 301, 302, 371
Patrick, Lee   407
Patterson, Lee   390
Patton, Phil   388
Patton, Phillip Bardwell "Bardy"   387, 388
Patty Duke Show, The   149, 199, 240, 270, 310, *330–331,* 409, 414

Paul, Alexandra   53, 54
Paulson, Pat   278
Payne, John   426
PAYOFF, THE   274
Pays, Amanda   141
Pearce, Alice   62, 64
Pearlman, Michael   89
Pearlman, Rhea   93, 94, 95, 96
Peary, Hal   437
Peck, Ed   260, 261
Peck, Gregory   190, 413
Peck's Bad Girls   48, 132
Pee-wee Herman Show, The   331
PEE-WEE'S BIG ADVENTURE   331
Pee-wee's Playhouse   *331–332*
Peldon, Ashley   409
Peldon, Courtney   169, 170
Penghlis, Thaao   282, 286, 287
Penhall, Bruce   98
Pennell, Larry   227, 349
Penny, Don   232
Penny, Joe   349
Penny to a Million   146
Pentagon U.S.A.   270
People's Choice, The   165
Pepito the Clown   182, 201
Peppard, George   xvii, 1, 4, 222, 436
Pepper, Barbara   161, 162
Pepper, Cynthia   307, 308
Pera, Radames   217
Perez, Gary   229
Perez, Joanne   201, 202
Perez, Jose   167
Perlman, Ron   55
Perrine, Valerie   167
Perry, Barbara   116, 118
Perry, John Bennett   414, 415
Perry, Joseph   254, 258
Perry, Miss Zale   361
Perry, Roger   135, 136
Perry, Wolfe   436
Perry Mason   53, 151, 164, 206, 213, 214, 233, 271, 275, *332–336,* 414
Perry Mason Mystery: The Case of the Wicked Wives, A   336
Perry Mason Returns   333, 334
Perry Mason: The Case of the Lethal Lesson   335
Persoff, Nehemiah   437
Pescow, Donna   327
Pete and Gladys   41, 47, 126, 201, 257
Peter Gunn   204, *336–337*
Peter Loves Mary   237
Peters, Art   213
Peters, Brandon   153
Peters, House Jr.   225, 227
Peterson, Chris   52, 53
Peterson, Patty   122
Peterson, Paul   122, 149
Petrie, George O.   230, 232
Petrocelli   106
Petticoat Junction   9, 34, 83, 145, 149, 161, 187, 216, 226, 309, *337–340,* 347, 348
Pettyjohn, Angelique   381
Pevney, Joseph   380
Peyser, Penny   405, 406

Peyton Place 48, 82, 131
Pfeiffer, Michelle 51
Pflug, Jo Ann 136, 326
Phil Silvers Show, The 313
Philbin, Regis 19
Phillips, Barney 125, 125, 140, 141
Phillips, John 325
Phillips, Julianne 372
Phillips, Kathy 109, 110
Phillips, Lee 11, 12
Phillips, MacKenzie 325
Phoenix, River 440
Phyllis 9, 135, 226, 324, *340–341,* 373
PHYNX, THE 246
Picerni, Paul 417, 419
Pickens, Slim 141
Pidgeon, Walter 333, 427
Pierce, Devon 372
Pierce, Jack 54, 76
PIGSKIN PARADE 412
Pike, Mike 179
Pilato, Herbie J. 63, 64
PILLOW TALK 149
Pinchuk, Sheldon 331
Pine, Robert 359
Pinette, John 425
Pink Panther, The 323
Pinky Talks Back 76
Pinter, Harold 69
Piper, Lara 176
Pippin 60
Pistols 'n' Petticoats 233, 246
Pithy, Winsley 355
Pitlik, Noam 356
Pitoniak, Ann 24, 25
Pitt, Norman 355
PLACE IN THE SUN, A 333
Plakson, Suzi 248, 385
Planet of the Apes, The 222
Plante, Carol-Ann 170
Platt, Edward 146, 147, 323
Platt, Howard 356
Play it Again, Charlie Brown 323
PLAY MISTY FOR ME 286
Playhouse 90 36, 412
Plaza, Begona 106, 107
Pleasence, Donald 16, 17, 180, 277
PLEASE DON'T EAT THE DAISIES 201
Please Don't Eat the Daisies 107, 157, 158, *341–342,* 411, 422
Pleshette, Suzanne 217, 311, 316
Plowright, Joan 111
Plumb, Eve 79
Podewell, Buzz 11
Poitier, Sidney 127, 181, 205
Polanski, Roman 123
Polic, Henry II 16
Police Squad! 78
Police Story 179
Police Woman 171, 436
Polinsky, Alexander 89
Pollan, Tracy 137, 138
Pollard, Michael J. 18, 267, 269
Pollock, Bruce 322, 396
Poor Nut, The 34

Popeye Show with Captain Allen Swift, The 192
Popeye the Sailor 308
Porter, Ben 103, 104
Porter, Bobby 221, 223
Porter, Don 40, 41, 148
Post, Markie 120, 136, 316, 318
Post, William Jr. 58, 59
Posten, Tom 314
Potter, Chris 218
Potts, Annie 112, 113, 247, 249
Potts, Cliff 247
Powell, Dick 82, 83, 347
Powell, Jean 254, 258
Powell, Lee 241
Powell, Robert 44
Powell, William 236, 400
Power, Udana 252
Powers, Leona 26
Powers, Mala 106
Powers, Stefanie 266, 408
Powers, Tyrone 444, 445, 446, 448, 450, 451
Powers, Wayne 400
Powers of Matthew Star, The *342,* 381
Poyer, Elizabeth 408
Practice, The 58, 211
Praed, Michael 17
PRAIRIE, THE 245
Prelutsky, Burt 29, 256, 257
Preminger, Otto 49, 50, 51, 180, 312
Prentis, Lou 80, 82
Presby, Archie 38, 39
Prescott, Norm 221, 367, 446, 447
Prescription: Murder 100
Presley, Elvis 37, 122, 167, 193, 370
Press Photographer 105
PRESSURE POINT 299
Preston, Robert 264, 265
Preston, Wayde 99, 100
PRETTY WOMAN 132, 265
Preville, Ann 142, 143
Price, Kirsten 110
Price, Vincent 355
Priest, Ivy Baker 300
Priest, Pat vii, 296, 297, 299, 300, 301, 302, 303
Priestley, Jason 280
Primus 360
Prince, Clayton 107
Prince, Harold 337
Prince, Jonathan 404
Prince, William 214
PRINCE OF THE CITY 229
Princess 239
Princess 411
Pringle, Joan 399, 435, 436
Prinze, Freddie 97, 98
Prinze, Kathy 98
PRIVATE BENJAMIN 103, 117, 342
Private Benjamin 103, 313, *342–343*
Private Secretary 40, 263
PRIZZI'S HONOR 9
Proctor, Philip 400
Professional Father 21
Project Blue Book 343
Project U.F.O. 343

Prosky, Robert   179, 180
Protectors, The   374
Provine, Dorothy   173, 350
Provost, Jonathan "Jon"   224, 225, 226, 227
Prunell, Jessica   395
PSYCHO   373
Public Defender   110
Pugh, Madelyn   201, 202 (Also: Madelyn Davis)
Puppet Playhouse   190
Purl, Linda   275
Purser, Philip   205
Pyle, Denver   128, 215

Quaid, Dennis   245
Quaid, Randy   107, 245
Quantum Leap   88
QUEEN OF OUTER SPACE, THE   344
Quest, The   410
Quillan, Eddie   11
Quincy, M.E.   53, 214
Quinn, Bill   321, 323
Quinn, Glenn   104, 352
Quinn, Martha   79

Rachins, Alan   219
Racket Squad   232
RADAR MEN FROM THE MOON   101
Radditz, Leslie   284, 340
Rae, Charlotte   119, 135
RAIDERS OF THE LOST ARK   421, 439
Rainer, Joe   57
Rainey, Ford   361, 373
Rains, Claude   205, 206
RAISIN IN THE SUN, A   181
Ralph, Sheryl Lee   112
Ramirez, Rick   229
Randall, Stuart   224
Randall, Tony   38, 41, 121, 198, 277, 321, 322, 324, 405
Randolph, Isabel   116, 118, 326, 327
Randolph, Joyce   183, 184, 185
Randolph, Lillian   58, 59, 66
Range Rider, The   39
Rango   212
Rapf, Matthew   57, 217
Rappaport, David   336, 337
Rappaport, Jill   251
Rasche, David   320
Rasey, Jean   168
Rat Patrol, The   410
Rathbone, Basil   444, 452
Ratzenberger, John   93
Raven   359
Ravetch, Irving   246
Rawhide   214, 233, 261, 332, ***344,*** 411, 412
Ray, Aldo   356
Ray, Allan   230, 232
Ray, Connie   408
Ray, James   326
Ray, Marguerite   356, 358
Rayburn, Gene   189, 192, 193
Raye, Martha   278, 279
Raymond, Robin   68
RCA Victor Show, The   109
Rea, Peggy   434

Read, James   346
Reagan, Ronald   40
Real McCoys, The   203, 227, 299
REAR WINDOW   333
Reason, Rex   350
Reasonable Doubts   ***344–345,*** 422
REBECCA OF SUNNYBROOK FARM   109
REBEL WITHOUT A CAUSE   14
Red Badge of Courage, The   433
RED BADGE OF COURAGE, THE   75
Red Channels   152
RED MOUNTAIN   246
Red Skelton Show, The   36, 367
Redd Foxx Comedy Hour, The   358
Redd Foxx Show, The   124, ***345,*** 353
Redeker, Quinn   250
Redfield, William "Billy"   211
Redford, Robert   27, 127
Redgrave, Lynn   85, 188
Redigo   27
Reed, Alan   236, 237
Reed, Albert   207
Reed, Donna   122, 149
Reed, Marshall   20, 22, 237
Reed, Marshall (Michael Reed's twin)   433, 434
Reed, Michael (Marshall Reed's twin)   433, 434
Reed, Ralph   236
Reed, Robert   78, 79, 108, 109, 409
Reed, Shanna   260
Rees, Judson   105, 107
Rees, Lanny   234, 235
Reese, Della   353, 354
Reese, Tom   11, 13
Reeve, Christopher   19, 88
Reeves, George   18, 19, 20, 21, 22, 23, 24, 39, 156, 203
Reeves, Richard   18
Reeves, Steve   291
Regan, Ellen   400
Regan, Margie   281
Regehr, Duncan   vii, 318, 441, 443, 449, 450, 451, 452, 454
Regina, Paul   vii, 211, 212, 418, 421, 422, 441, 447, 448
Regis & Kathie Lee   19, 272
Reid, Tim   428, 429
REIGN OF TERROR   12
Reilly, Hugh   224, 226
Reilly, John   227
Reilly, Tom   98
Reiner, Carl   116, 117, 118, 262
Reiner, Estelle   117
Reiner, Rob   31, 276, 330
Reischl, Geri   78
Reiser, Paul   310
Reisner, Alan   304
Reiss, David   255
Relativity of Icarus   157
Remington Steele   274, ***345–347,*** 362
Rennick, Nancy   140
Reporter, The   214
Reporter Collins   (See: *Not for Publication*)
Repp, Stafford   49, 399, 400
Rescue 8   140
Rescue from Gilligan's Island   149, 150, 151
Rettig, Tommy   224, 225, 226, 227
Return of Ironside, The   207

Return of Maxwell Smart, The   147
Return of the Beverly Hillbillies, The   60, 342
RETURN OF THE LASH   234
Return of the Saint   355
Return of the Six Million Dollar Man and the Bionic Woman, The 373
Return to Fantasy Island   276
Return to Mayberry   31, 32, 33, 34, 35, 38
RETURN TO PEYTON PLACE   269
Return to the Streets of San Francisco   386
Reubens, Paul   331
REVENGE OF THE CREATURE   188, 344, 361
Reyes, Julian   435
Reynolds, Burt   134, 217, 349, 350, 437
Reynolds, Debbie   251, 285
Reynolds, Gene   254
Reynolds, Marjorie   234, 236
Reynolds, William   291
Rhoda   29, 166, 279, 376, 412
Rhodes, Linda   iv, xi
Rhys-Davies, John   417, 419, 421
Riano, Renie   6
Ribisi, Vonnie   107, 108
Ricci, Christina   9
Rice, Gigi   169, 170
Rice, Howard   (See: Uncle Don)
Rich, Adam   162
Rich, Christopher   93
Rich Man, Poor Man—Book I   115
Rich Man, Poor Man—Book II   115
Richard Diamond, Private Detective   xiv, 83, 117, 336, 339, ***347–348,*** 414
Richard Pryor Show, The   319
Richards, Addison   268, 270
Richards, Ann   114
Richards, Beah   66
Richards, Carol   109, 110
Richards, Dick   74
Richards, Grant   123
Richards, Kim   177
Richards, Marc   207
Richardson, Jackie   391
Richardson, Patricia   182
Richie Brockelman, Private Eye   326
Richmond, Caryn   147
Rickles, Don   38, 84, 121, 447
RIDE THE WILD WAVES   122
RIDER OF DEATH VALLEY   26
Ridgely, Robert   393
Ridgeway, Freddy   236
Rieffel, Lisa   132, 134
Rifkin, Ron   325
Rifleman, The   224, 323, ***348,*** 434
Rigg, Diana   43, 44, 285
Righteous Apples, The   181
Riley, Charles Nelson   417
Riley, Jack   135
Riley, Jeannie   337, 340
Riley, John   276
Rin Tin Tin   15, 156
Rin Tin Tin I   15
Rin Tin Tin II   15
Rin Tin Tin III   15
Rin Tin Tin IV   15
Rin Tin Tin K-9 Cop   16

Ringwald, Molly   135
Ringwood, Bob   141
RIO LOBO   177
Ripcord   163, ***348,*** 379
Riptide   4, ***349,*** 389, 409
Rist, Robbie   51, 52, 65
Ritter, Dorothy   14
Ritter, John   133, 185, 402, 403, 433
Ritter, Tex   14
Ritter, Thelma   174
Rivas, Carlos   446, 455
Rivera, Geraldo   xi, 200
Riverboat   105, 134, ***349–350,*** 351
RIVER'S EDGE   104
Road, Mike   27
Roaring 20's, The   xiv, 100, 123, 173, ***350,*** 426
ROARING TWENTIES, THE   265
Roarke, Hayden   198, 311
Roat, Richard   314, 315
Robards, Jason   422
Robbins, Barbara   25, 26
Robbins, Jerome   156
Robbins, Peter   68
Roberge, Sean   394
Roberts, Doris   274, 345, 346
Roberts, Mark   240
Roberts, Mary Ann   18
Roberts, Pernell   71, 73, 410
Roberts, Randolph   165, 166
Roberts, Roy   62, 64
Roberts, Tanya   90, 92, 93, 282, 370
Robertson, Dale   4
ROBIN AND MARIAN   17
ROBIN HOOD   17
Robin Hood   17, 88, 355, 450
ROBIN HOOD, MEN IN TIGHTS   17
ROBIN HOOD DAFFY   16
ROBIN HOOD: PRINCE OF THIEVES   17, 103
Robin of Sherwood   17
Robinson, Charlie   247, 248, 316
Robinson, Dale   332
Robinson, Edward G. Jr.   23, 77, 78, 280
Robinson, Holly   414
Robinson, Jenny   331
Robinson, Larry   152, 154
Robinson, Marc Dakota   169
Robinson, Matt   362, 363
Robinson, Russell Phillip   436
Robin's Nest   44
Robsky, Paul   418, 419
Rocco, Alex   69, 276, 323
Roche, Eugene   102, 318
Rock, Blossom   8
Rock, Clarence W.   8
ROCKETSHIP X-M   361
Rockford Files, The   168, 277, 350
Rockne, Knute   418
Rockwell, John   18, 19
Rockwell, Robert   326, 327
Rocky and His Friends   88, 192, 223, 245, 289, 354
ROCKY III   1
Rod Rocket   405
Rodd, Marcia   276
Roddenberry, Gene   222, 232, 377, 379, 380, 410

Rodgers and Hammerstein 285
Rodman, Howard 170, 172
Rodrigues, Percy 134
Rogers, Ginger 145, 226
Rogers, Kasey 62
Rogers, Melody 359
Rogers, Steven 101
Rogers, Wayne 196, 197, 199, 254, 255, 256, 258
Roker, Roxie 210, 211
Roland, Gilbert 63, 64, 446
Roland, Norma 416
Roll Out 30
Rolle, Esther 160, 161, 275, 276
ROLLER BOOGIE 436
Roller Girls, The 414
ROLLING THUNDER 455
Rollins, Howard 204
Roman Hat Mystery, The 11
ROMANCING THE STONE 386
Romay, Lina 278
Romero, Carlos 448
Romero, Cesar 50, 447
Rookies, The **350–351,** 367
Room 222 149, 213, 367
Room for One More 413
ROOM SERVICE 152
Rooney, Mickey 289, 322
Rooney, Pat 235
Rooten, Luis Van 261
Roots 410
Roots: The Next Generation 433
Ropers, The 403
Roscoe, Burton 407
Rose, Jane 8, 9
Rose, Reginald 109
Rose, Reva 397
Rose, Robin 436
Roseanne 41, 104, 182, **351–352**
Rosen, Barry 455
Rosenberg, Aaron 14, 106
Rosenberg, Arthur 194
Rosenthal, Sharon 217
Rosenzweig, Barney 85, 86
Rosetti and Ryan 332
Ross, Earl 280
Ross, Joe E. 407
Ross, Katherine 374
Ross, Marion 36, 166
Ross, Marty 294
Ross, Mickey 403
Ross, Natanya 177
Ross, Stanley Ralph 444
Roudy, Robert 11
Rough Riders, The 405
Roundtree, Richard 73
Route 66 xiv, 7, **352–353**
Rovin, Jeff 27, 139, 258, 341
Rowan & Martin's Laugh-In 140
Rowe, Misty 16
Rowland, Barber 184
Rowles, Polly 109, 279
ROXIE HART 226
Royal Family, The 345, **353–354**
ROYAL WEDDING 75

Roylance, Pamela 238, 239
Ruben, Aaron 37, 155, 158
Rubenfeld, Paul (See: Pee-wee Herman)
Rubenstein, John 406
Rubinoff, Marla Jeanette 428
Ruck, Alan 329
Rucker, Barbara 397
Rudoy, Joshua 170
Rue, Sarah 351
Ruge, George 448
Ruggles, Charlie 354
Ruggles, The 40, **354**
Ruggles of Red Gap 354
RUGGLES OF RED GAP 354
Ruick, Barbara 109, 110
Ruick, Melville 110, 122, 123
Run, Joe, Run! **354**
RUN SILENT, RUN DEEP 121
Runyon, Jennifer 78, 89
Ruprecht, David 150, 151, 404
Russavage, Bonnie 358, 360
Russell, Jeannie 110
Russell, John 209
Russell, Kurt 411
Russell, Mark 217
Russell, Pee Wee 331
Russell, Rosalind 83
Rust, John 214
Ruth, Kitty 66
Ruttan, Susan 219
Ruysdael, Basil 108
Ryall, David 355
Ryan, Fran 123, 161, 162, 322, 323, 371, 372
Ryan, Irene 60, 61, 342
Ryan, Marisa 260
Ryan, Marla 18
Ryan, Peggy 172, 173

60 Minutes 376
77 Sunset Strip 173, 347, **366–367,** 389, 390, 412
Saber of London 271
Sabin, David 16
Sable 420
Sackett, Susan 379, 380, 382, 384, 385
Sagal, Katey 271
Saint, Eva Marie 81
Saint, The 278, 337, **355–356,** 416
SAINT IN NEW YORK, THE 355
Saint James, Susan 278, 279
Saints and Sinners 413
SAINT'S GIRL FRIDAY, THE 355
Sajak, Pat 226, 227
Sale, Virginia 339, 340
Sales, Clifford 58
Salinger, Matt 108
Salkind, Alexander 18, 24, 421
Salkind, Ilya 18, 24, 421
Sally Jesse Raphael 79
SALOME 299
Saltis, Larry 294
Salvage I 53
Samms, Emma 168
Samuel, Gerhard 157
Sandberg, Carl 421

Sanderford, John   359, 360
Sanders, George   49, 50, 271, 355
Sanders, Hugh   305
Sanders, Lugene   234, 235, 279
Sanders, Richard   429
SANDS OF IWO JIMA   16
Sandy, Gary   428, 429
Sandy Duncan Show, The   122
Sanford   357
Sanford, Isabel   30, 212
Sanford, Ralph   233
Sanford and Son   324, 325, 345, 353, 354, *356–358,* 399, 447
Sanford Arms   84, 345, 358, 399
Santa Barbara   221m 451
Santoni, Reni   328
Santos, Joe   167, 168
Sanz, Carlos   229
Sara, Mia   329
Sargent, Dick   xv, 61, 62, 63, 64, 65, 128, 199
Sargent, Joseph   217
Saroyan, William   235
Satin's School for Girls   91
SATURDAY NIGHT FEVER   211, 247
Saturday Night Live   xiv, 35, 70, 91, 113, 183, 184, 231, 293
Saturday Night Review   183
Satz, Amy   111
Saunders, Gloria   398
Saunders, Lori   338, 340
Saunders, Nicholas   273
Savage, Brad   405
Savalas, George   217
Savalas, Telly   44, 103, 170, 171, 217
Savant, Doug   280
Saved by the Bell   **358–360**
Saved by the Bell: The College Years   360
Saviola, Camille   45
Saxon, John   312
Saxton, Ward   vii, 361, 365, 366
SAY ANYTHING   104, 124
Scandiuzzi, Gian-Carlo   134
Scarecrow and Mrs. King   31, 89, 312
SCARFACE MOB, THE   418
Scene of the Crime   107
Schafer, Natalie   150
Schall, Richard   274
Schaller, Jason   46
Schallert, William   101, 102, 148, 149, 240, 268, 270, 331, 378, 408, 409
Schary, Dore   200
Scheimer, Erica   227
Scheimer, Lane   227
Scheimer, Lou   221, 367, 446, 447
Schell, Ronnie   155, 156, 158
Schiffrin, Lalo   288, 289
Schlatter, Charlie   329
Schmidtke, Ned   419
Schneider, John   127, 128
Schneider, Lew   124
Schreiber, Avery   35
Schuck, John   296, 301, 321, 324
Schuck, Peter   326
Schultz, Dutch   418
Schultz, Dwight   xvii, 1, 4
Schutt, Tasia   372

Schwartz, Lloyd J.   206
Schwartz, Neil J.   165, 167
Schwartz, Sherwood   150, 151, 198, 199, 206
Schwarzkopf, General Norman   200
Science Fiction Theater   386
Scoggin, Nick   387
Scolari, Peter   259, 313, 314, 315, 403
Scooler, Zvee   155
SCOTLAND YARD   237
Scott, Bonnie   398
Scott, Dawan   169
Scott, Devon   405, 406
Scott, Evelyn   47, 48
Scott, George C.   54
Scott, Gordon   393
Scott, Henry   313
Scott, Randolph   99
Scott, Samantha   63
Scott, Simon   410, 411
Scott, Synda   142, 143
Scott, Willard   73
Scotti, Vito   236, 237
Scruples   248
Sea Hunt   43, *360–361,* 393
Seager, Sam   418
Sealtest Big Top   (See: *Super Circus*)
Search   312, *361,* 373
Search for Tomorrow   48, 327, 419
Seaton, George   241
Seay, James   305
Second City TV   245
Second Honeymoon, The   183, 185
Second Hundred Years, The   141
Secrets of Isis, The   (See: *Isis*)
Seeger, Sara   110
Segall, Don   124
Segall, Pamela   124, 345
Selleca, Connie   46, 187
Selleck, Tom   439
Selznick, David O.   100
Sen Yung, Victor   71, 73
SEND ME NO FLOWERS   145
Sennett, Susan   15
Sepe, Michelle   84
Sesame Street   ix, 247, 299, 313, 314, ***361–366,*** 371
Sessons, Almira   23
Seuss, Dr.   226
Seven Year Itch, The   304
Severy, Dick   175
Seymour, Ann   138
Seymour, Dan   88, 89
Shakespeare, William   277, 347
Shamata, Chuck   394
SHAMPOO   269
Shamus   438
Shandling, Gary   293
Shane   100, 118, 237
Sharpe, Karen   200
Shatner, William   108, 213, 286, 307, 374, 377, 396, 437
Shavelson, Melville "Mel"   262
Shaw, George Bernard   421
Shaw, Mel   191
Shaw, Reta   40, 62, 64, 308
Shawlee, Joan   116, 118

Shay, Dorothy   433, 434
Shayne, Bette   ix, 22
Shayne, Robert   vii, 20, 22, 23, 77, 78, 142, 238, 434
Shazam!   xiv, 13, 18, 207, 221, *367*
Shazam! Isis Hour, The   207
SHE DEMONS   370
Shearer, Harry   231
Sheen, Carmen   455
Sheen, Martin   452, 455
Sheen, Ramon   455
SHEENA   91, 93, 282
Sheena, Queen of the Jungle   207, *367–370*, 438, 449
Sheffield, Johnny   394
Sheldon, Gene   441, 445, 446
Shelley, Carole   322, 323
Shephard, Harvey   85
Shepodd, Jon   224, 226
Shera, Mark   49
Sheridan, Liz   64
Sheriff of Cochise, The   163, 344, *370*
Sheriff Who?   340
Sherlock Holmes   17
Sherman, Bobby   35
Sherman, Harry "Pop"   186
Shermit, Hazel   314
She's the Sheriff   327
Shields, Fred   279
Shiloh   (See: *The Virginian*)
SHINING, THE   89
Shining Time Station   *370–371*
Ship, Ron   7
Shipp, John Wesley   141
Shipp, Mary   305
Shirley   342
Shogun   121
Sholdar, Mickey   140
Shore, Dinah   100
Shore, Roberta   425
Shores, Richard   335
Short, Martin   449
Show, Grant   280
Showalter, Max   231
Shroyer, Sonny   127, 128
Shue, Andrew   280
Shuster, Joe   19
Shut Up Kids   127
Shyer, Charles   45
Sid Caesar Invites You   117
Sidney, Sylvia   428
Siegel, Harvey   192, 245
Siegel, Jerry   19
Sierra, Gregory   447
Sierra, Margarita   390
Sigmund and the Sea Monsters   120, 162, 221, 314, *371–372*
SILENCERS, THE   296
Silk Stalkings   107
Silk Stockings   411
Silla, Felix   8, 81, 82, 299
Siller, Jerry   188, 395
Silva, Henry   81, 82
Silver, Johnny   116
Silver, Johnny   416
SILVER CANYON   39
Silver Spoons   82

Silvera, Frank   179
Silverheels, Jay   163, 240, 242, 244, 245, 246
Silverman, Fred   212, 334, 376
Silvers, Cathy   167
Silvers, Jeff   87
Silvers, Phil   167
Simels, Steve   382
Simmons, Richard Lee   201
Simmons, Ronald Lee   201
Simon, Al   291
Simon, Neil   323
Simon, Robert F.   62, 64
Simpsons, The   65
Sinatra, Frank   82
Sinatra, Richard   155, 156, 157
Sinbad   345
Sinbad Show, The   345
Sinclair, Hugh   355
Sinclair, Madge   410
SINFUL DAVEY   9
Singer, Dulcy   364
Singer, Jerry   421
Singer, Raymond   326
Singer, Robert   345
Singer, Stuffy   58, 68
Singer & Sons   425
SINGING IN THE RAIN   262
Singleton, Penny   68
Sinutko, Shane   227
Sirens, The   362
Sirtis, Marina   383, 384
Sissons, Kimber   361
SISTER ACT   42, 303
Sisters   *372–373*
SITTING BULL   237
Six Million Dollar Man, The   136, 167, 328, 333, 361, *373*, 426
Skelton, Red   363
Skerritt, Tom   96
Skinner, Edna   vii, xiv, 38, 289, 290, 291, 292, 293, 407
Skulnik, Menasha   154
Sky King   235, *373–374*, 435
Sky King Theater   374
Skye, Ione   104, 124
Slack, Ben   30
Slade, Mark   178, 179
Slattery, Richard X.   84
Slattery's People   246, 400
Sledge Hammer   320
SLENDER THREAD, THE   127
Slotky, Ann   408
Slow Dance on the Killing Ground   436
Small Wonder   414
Smart, Jean   111, 112, 113, 115
Smart, Ralph   205
SMASH-UP, THE STORY OF A WOMAN   12
Smile Jenny, You're Dead   171
Smilin' Ed McConnell and his Gang   (See: *Andy's Gang*)
Smilin' Ed's Gang   (See: *Andy's Gang*)
Smirnoff, Yakov   435
Smith, Bob   76, 189, 190, 191, 192, 193, 194
Smith, Dick   191
Smith, Hal   33, 34, 35
Smith, Jaclyn   90, 91, 92, 217
Smith, John   223, 224

Smith, Lane   20, 159
Smith, Lois   160
Smith, Reid   99
Smith, Roger   366
Smith, Ronald L.   117, 347
Smith, Stacy Jenel   324
Smith, Taran   182
Smith, William   172, 173
Smith Family, The   36
Smithers, Jan   429
Smitrovich, Bill   234
Smits, Jimmy   219, 248
SMOKEY AND THE BANDIT   67, 350, 360, 437
SMOKEY AND THE BANDIT II   350
Smothers, Dick   123
Smothers Brothers Show, The   123
Smyrl, David L.   362
Smythe, Kit   151
Snipes, Wesley   419
Snoopy   272
Snyders, Sammy   52
Soap   57, 132, 133, 211, 247, 399, 404, 447
Sode, Laura   172
SOLDIER'S STORY, A   168
Solomon, Bruce   330
Solrel, Nancy   124
SOME LIKE IT HOT   259
SOMEBODY UP THERE LIKES ME   154
Somers, Brett   332, 334
Somers, Suzanne   401, 403
SOMEWHERE IN TIME   88
Sommers, Jimmy   107
SON OF LASSIE, THE   226
SON OF ZORRO, THE   447
Sondheim, Stephen   272
SORCERERS, THE   356
Sorel, Louise   307
Sorensen, Jeff   396
Sorenson, Lelani   261, 263
Sorkin, Arleen   336
Soroyan, Lucy   131
Sorvino, Paul   228, 229, 336, 356
Sothern, Ann   40, 263
Sothern, Harry   80, 82
Soubier, Cliff   387, 388
Soul, David   88, 89, 328
SOUND OF FURY, THE   265
SOUND OF MUSIC, THE   263
SOUTH PACIFIC   156
Southside Johnny and the Asbury Jukes   124
Space, Arthur   224, 227
Space Academy   221, 323, 405
Space Explorer   87
Space Patrol   *375,* 386
Space: 1999   *374–375,* 416
SPANISH CAPE MYSTERY, THE   11
Sparks, Don   326
SPARTICUS   154
Spelling, Aaron   91, 106, 187, 251, 252
Spence, Sandra   435
Spencer   280, *375–376*
Spencer, John   219, 220
Spenser for Hire   53
Spicer, George   310

Spielberg, Steven   170, 439
Spillane, Mickey   281
Spilsbury, Klinton   245
Spiner, Brent   382, 383
Spinney, Caroll   362, 363
SPINOUT   122
Spitz, Mark   217
SPLASH   37
SPLENDOR IN THE GRASS   269
SPOOK WHO SAT BY THE DOOR, THE   181
Springsteen, Bruce   124
SPY WHO LOVED ME, THE   416
Square Pegs   448
Stack, Robert   312, 417, 418, 419, 420, 421, 422
Stack, Timothy   329
Stadlen, Lewis J.   57, 58
STAGE DOOR CANTEEN   132
STAGECOACH   306
Stalag 17   153
Stamos, John   231
STAND AND DELIVER   455
Stand By for Crime   *376*
Stander, Arthur   37
Stanley, Florence   310
Stanton, Robert   111
Stanwyck, Barbara   285, 432
Star Search   345, 389
Star Trap   356
Star Trek   18, 37, 67, 69, 82, 87, 88, 95, 96, 102, 109, 140, 143, 149,
   176, 181, 209, 220, 222, 224, 232, 269, 285, 286, 296, 303, 307, 308,
   328, 332, 333, 349, 350, 352, 374, 375, 376, *377–381,* 382, 384, 405,
   410, 413, 416, 437
STAR TREK II: THE WRATH OF KHAN   96, 213, 342, 350, 379,
   446
STAR TREK III: THE SEARCH FOR SPOCK   9, 96, 342, 396
STAR TREK IV: THE VOYAGE HOME   301, 342, 381
STAR TREK V: THE UNDISCOVERED COUNTRY   342
Star Trek: Deep Space Nine   58
STAR TREK: THE MOTION PICTURE   19, 121, 131, 140, 232,
   303, 377, 381, 386, 395
Star Trek: The Next Generation   2, 52, 179, 220, 232, 342, ***382–385***
STAR WARS   51, 52, 87, 103, 131, 149, 386, 439
Starlit Time   162
Starman   327
Starr, Ringo   370, 371
Starrett, Charles   339
Starsky and Hutch   85, 88, 133, 250, 328
States, Chad   354
Steambath   167
Steele, Brian   169
Steffany, Michael   267
Steffens, Roy   88
Steiger, Rod   205, 422
Steinbach, John   222
Steinberg, David   414
Steiner, Fred   335
Stengle, Casey   94
Step by Step   409
Steptoe and Son   356
Sterling, Jack   388
Sterling, Lois   110
Sterling, Robert   407, 427
Stern, David   289
Sternhagen, Frances   375, 376

Steuer, Jon   382
Steve Allen Show, The   314
Steve Canyon   233, 347
Stevens, Connie   173, 270, 366
Stevens, Craig   336, 337
Stevens, Inger   140
Stevens, Julie   65, 66
Stevens, Mark   65, 66, 273, 274, 281
Stevens, Naomi   123, 142, 424
Stevens, Ray   37
Stevens, Rusty   232
Stevens, Stella   315
Stevens, Thomas H. Jr.   179
Stevens, Warren   77, 78
Stevenson, McLean   123, 177, 254, 255, 256, 257, 258, 407, 455, 456
Stevenson, Parker   168, 169
Steward, Charlotte   238
Stewart, French   428
Stewart, James   109, 132, 263, 419, 421
Stewart, Johnny   434
Stewart, Margaret   230, 232
Stewart, Mel   29, 30, 65, 171, 392
Stewart, Patrick   52, 382, 383
Stiers, David Ogden   xv, 254, 257
Stigwood, Robert   326
Stiles, Norman   ix
Stiller and Meara   102, 188
Stilwell, Diane   250
Stingray   374
Stockard Channing Show, The   231
Stockwell, Dean   73
Stockwell, Guy   10
Stockwell, Harry   10
Stoller, Fred   424, 425
Stone, Chris   224
Stone, Dee Wallace   224, 314
Stone, Harold J.   vii, 152, 153, 180
Stone, Jon   299
Stone, Leonard   86
Stone, Martin   190, 213
Stone, Suzanne   84
Stone, Walter   59, 87
Stop Susan Williams   248
Storefront Lawyers   134, 221
Stories of the Century   375, ***385–386***
Storm, Gale   14
Story, Ralph   27
Stowell, Geraldine   163
Straight, Beatrice   438
STRAIGHT TALK   420
Strange, Glen   163
Strange, Robert G. Jr.   366
STRANGE EXPERIMENT   271
Stranger, The   269
Strasberg, Lee   436
STRATEGIC AIR COMMAND   265
Stratemeyer, Edward   168
Stratton, Albert   332, 334
Stratton, Dr. Edward   59
Strauss, Peter   336, 337
Strauss, Robert   153, 180
Streak, The   37
Streets of San Francisco, The   52, 94, 237, 253, ***386–387***
Strickland, Amzie   33, 38

Strickland, Gail   318, 435
Stritch, Elaine   162, 183, 185
Stromberg, Hunt Jr.   298
Stromose, Fred   437
Stroock, Gloria   152
Stroud, Don   126, 127, 281, 282
Struthers, Sally   31
Struycken, Carel   9
Stu Erwin Show, The   7, 212, 412 (See also: *The Trouble with Father*)
Stuart, Barbara   404
Stuart, Patrick   51
Stuart, Roy   vii, 155, 157, 158
Studio One   108
Sturges, John   412
Styles, Henry   116, 118
Styles, Herkie   (See: Henry Styles)
ST. ELMO'S FIRE   313
St. Elsewhere   216
Such Stuff as Dreams Are Made Of   171
Sugarfoot   68, 96
Sullivan, Barry   vii, 333
Sullivan, Danny   420
Sullivan, Kitty   330
Sullivan, Liam   437
Sullivan, Paul   231
Sullivan, Shauna   404
Summer, Cree   119
SUMMER OF '42, THE   103
Summer Smothers Brothers Show, The   278
Summers, Hope   348
Sundstrom, Florence   197, 200, 235, 236
Sunny   184
Sunshine   85
Super Adventure Theater   389
Super Circus   387–389
Super Scary Saturday   301, 302
Superboy   18, 269 (See also: *The Adventures of Superboy*)
Supercar   374
Superfriends   406, 438
SUPERGIRL   17
Superman   (See: *Adventures of Superman*)
SUPERMAN AND THE MOLE MEN   20
SUPERMAN II   xv, 312
SUPERMAN III   xv
SUPERMAN IV: THE QUEST FOR PEACE   xv
SUPERMAN: THE MOVIE   xv, 17, 18, 21, 23, 24, 88
SURE THING, THE   280
SurfSide 6   xiv, 173, ***389–390***
Surprenant, Jennifer   7
Survivors, The   220
Suskind, David   214
Suspicion   214
Sussman, Lorne   46
Sutherland, Donald   254, 280
Sutton, Frank   155, 156, 158
Swaim, Caskey   343
Swamp Fox   233
SWAMP THING   276
Swanson, Jackie   96
Sweating Bullets   107
Sweeney, Bob   80, 145, 303, 304, 327
Swenson, Inga   71, 316
Swenson, Karl   230, 231
Swift, Allen   190, 192

Swit, Loretta 85, 255, 256
Switch 84
Sybil 142
Sydney 325
Sykes, Brenda 15
Symonds, Robert 257

13 East 400
13 Queens Boulevard 228
2001: A SPACE ODYSSEY 232, 379
21 Beacon Street 413
21 Jump Street 413–414
227 354
240-Robert 414–415, 435
26 Men 101
T. and T. 391
T.J. Hooker 131, 399
Tabitha* 30, 65, *391–392
Taggart, Jimmy Medina 394
Takei, George 286, 377, 378, 379, 381
Talbot, Lyle 13, 15, 101
Talbot, Nita 181
Talbot, Stephen 232
Tales of the Apple Dumpling Gang 162
Tales of the Gold Monkey 93, 373, 395
Tales of Wells Fargo 4
Talman, William 332, 333
Talton, Alix 303, 304, 305
Tambor, Jeffrey 403
Tammy Grimes Show, The 64
Tanna, Dan 424
Tannen, William 233
Tanner, Gordon 271
TARANTULA 266
Tartikoff, Brandon 423
Tarzan* 43, 148, 207, 223, 332, 361, 367, *392–394
TARZAN AND THE SHE-DEVIL 333
Tarzan and the Super 7 209
TARZAN AND THE TRAPPERS 393
TARZAN AND THE VALLEY OF GOLD 393
TARZAN FINDS A SON 360
TARZAN OF THE APES 392
Tarzan Takes Manhattan 393
Tarzan the Ape Man 392
TARZAN THE APE MAN 392
TARZAN'S FIGHT FOR LIFE 393
TARZAN'S NEW YORK ADVENTURE 393
Tarzan/Lone Ranger/Zorro Adventure Hour, The 393, 446
Tarzan: Lord of the Jungle 393
Tass, R.C. 221, 223
Tate, Larenz 354
Tate, Sharon 340
***Tattingers* 395**
Taxi* 9, 259, *395–396
TAXI DRIVER 396
TAXI FOR TWO 396
Taxi to Heaven 396
TAXI! 395
Tayback, Vic 28, 29
Taylor, Don 450
Taylor, Elizabeth 204, 225
Taylor, Holland 334
Taylor, Joan 348
Taylor, Josh 423

Taylor, Kent 446
Taylor, Meshach 112, 115
Taylor, Nathaniel 345
Taylor, Robert 115
Taylor, Robert Lewis 411
Taylor, Rod 185
Taylor, Ron 425
Taylor, Ross 51
Taylor, Tom 152
Taylor, Vaughn 213
TEA AND SYMPATHY 156
Tead, Phillips (Phil) (Phipps) 20, 23
Ted Knight Show, The 232, 318, 438 (See also: *Too Close for Comfort*)
Tedrow, Irene 279, 354
Teek, Angela 389
Telfer, Robert 358, 360
Temperature's Rising, The 397, 426
TEN COMMANDMENTS, THE 306
Terrace, Vincent xi
Terrell, Steven 236
Terry, Nigel 104
Terry and the Pirates 398, 435
Terrytoons Circus 388
Tesreau, Krista 336
Tewes, Lauren 249, 250, 251
Texas 149
Thall, Benj 408
Tharp, Richard 344
THAT DARN CAT 359
That Girl* 147, 158, 212, 232, 339, *398–399
That's Life 59
That's My Mama* 211, 250, 362, *399
Thayer, Brynn 275
Theiss, William Ware 380
Then Came Bronson 352
THEY CAME TO CORDURA 63
THEY GAVE HIM A GUN 57
Thibodeaux, Keith 201, 203 (See also: Richard Keith)
THIEF OF BAGDAD, THE 291
Thiessen, Tiffani-Amber 358, 359, 360
THIN MAN, THE 400
Thin Man, The* xiv, 49, 278, 281, *399–400
THIS ISLAND EARTH 350
This Morning 70
This Old House 182
THIS PROPERTY IS CONDEMNED 127
Thomas, Betty 179
Thomas, Danny 117, 211, 262, 263, 274, 311
Thomas, Dave 245
Thomas, Frank 273, 274
Thomas, Frankie 274, 405, 435
Thomas, Gareth 67
Thomas, Jay 95, 220, 248
Thomas, Jonathan Taylor 182
Thomas, Larri 314
Thomas, Margaret (See: Marlo Thomas)
Thomas, Marlo 158, 262, 398
Thomas, Mona 274
Thomas, Philip Michael 455
Thomas, Richard 432, 433, 434
Thomas, Rose Marie 262, 263
Thomas, Rosemarie 103
Thomas, Shirley 14

Thomas, Terre   262
Thomas, Tony   252
Thomas the Tank Engine & Friends   371
Thomason, Harry   112, 113
Thompson, Brian   434
Thompson, Dorrie   326
Thompson, Hilary   326
Thompson, Howard   331
Thompson, Lea   111
Thompson, Sada   30, 31
Thompson, Virgil   156, 157
Thor, Jerome   142
Thorn Birds, The   99, 121
Thornberg, Don   388
Thorndike, Oliver   104
Thorne, Teresa   271
Thorne-Smith, Courtney   280
Thorson, Linda   43, 44
Thorson, Russell   115
Those Endearing Young Charms   84, ***400–401***
Those Two   401
THOUSAND CLOWNS, A   373
THREE AMIGOS, THE   449
Three for Tahiti   269
Three for the Road   323, 374
Three Girls Three   318
THREE MUSKETEERS, THE   121
THREE RING CIRCUS   446
Three's a Crowd   404
Three's Company   36, 44, 120, 133, 185, ***401–404,*** 433, 434
THRILL OF IT ALL   121, 277
Throb   404
Throne, Malachi   49, 208
Through Time and Timbuktu; or The Flight of Prometheus-5   47
THUNDERBALL   416
Thunderbirds, The   374
Thunder-Cloud, Chief   241
Thurber, James   140
Tighe, Kevin   355, 356
TILL WE MEET AGAIN   117
TIME AFTER TIME   88
TIME BANDITS   88
Time for Fun   76
TIME FOR KILLING   267
TIME MACHINE, THE   88
TIME OF YOUR LIFE   235
Time Tunnel, The   88, 278
Timmy and Lassie   (See: *Lassie*)
Tinapp, Barton   111
TO KILL A MOCKINGBIRD   34
To Tell the Truth   xiv
TOBACCO ROAD   431
Tobey, Ken   435
Tobias, George   10, 153
Tobin, Dan   303, 304
TOBY TYLER   446
Todd, Ann   412
Todd, James   164
Tokar, Norman   304
Tolbert, Berlinda   210, 211, 399
Tom, Dick and Mary   269
Tom Corbet, Space Cadet   xiv, ***405,*** 435
Toma   48, 399 (See also: *Baretta*)
Toma, David   48

Toma Starring Robert Blake   48   (See: *Baretta*)
Tomack, Sid   212, 234, 236, 305, 306
Tombstone Territory   438
Tomlinson, David   260
Tone, Franchot   55, 57, 432
Tong, Kam   172
Tong, Sammee   47
Tonight Show   97
Tonight Show Starring Johnny Carson, The   126, 199, 212, 355, 368, 372, 376, 389
Tony Orlando and Dawn   127
Tony Randall Show, The   405–406
Too Close for Comfort   90, ***406–407***
Toomey, Regis   82, 83, 339, 347
TOOTSIE   127
Top Banana   70
Top Cat   270
TOP MAN   173
Top of the Heap   425
Top of the Hill   335
Topper   181, 266, 291, ***407–408,*** 427
TOPPER   408
Topper Returns   407
Tork, Peter   294, 295
Torkelsons, The   240, 302, ***408–410***
TORRENTS OF SPRING   421
Torres, Liz   321, 340, 341
Tors, Ivan   360, 361
Torti, Robert   425
Toth, Alex   444
Tour of Duty   410
Towne, Aline   20, 23, 102
Townsend, Barbara   24, 25
Tracy, Lee   273, 274, 356
Tracy, Spencer   57, 77, 204
Tracy, Steve   240
Tracy, Walter   398
Trainer, Mary Ellen   329
Trapped   306
Trapper John, M.D.   399, ***410–411***
Travanti, Daniel J.   179, 180
Travels of Jamie McPheeters, The   411–412
Travolta, Ellen   89, 90
Travolta, John   46, 47, 131, 211, 245, 447
TREE GROWS IN BROOKLYN, A   273, 414
Treen, Mary   32
Tremayne, Les   11, 12, 13, 367
Tremko, Anne   360
Trendle, George W.   241, 244
Trent, Sue Karen   231, 232
Trevielle, Roger   86
Trials of Rosie O'Neill, The   133
Tripp, Paul   118, 268, 270, 434
Tristan, Dorothy   433, 434
Trotter, Audrey   280
TROUBLE WITH ANGELS, THE   372
Trouble with Father, The   412
TROUBLE WITH HARRY, THE   231
TROUBLEMAN   181
Trout, Dink   13
Truax, Ernest   36, 40, 41
True Colors   164, ***412***
True Colors   304
True Confessions   19

Truman, Bess   25
Truman, Harry S   190
Trumbull, Bobby   87, 88
Trzcinski, Edmund   180
Tucker, Forrest   141
Tucker, Ken   114, 371, 440, 449
Tucker, Michael   219
Tuddenham, Peter   67
Tully, Tom   116, 118, 237
Turan, Kenneth   331
Turman, Glynn   119
Turnbeaugh, Brenda   238, 240
Turnbeaugh, Wendi   238, 240
Turner, George   447
Turner, Jim   205
Turner, Richard   85, 86
Turner, Tim   205
Tuttle, Lurene   110, 197, 200, 236
Tweed, Terry   52, 53
Twelve O'Clock High   312, 410, *412–413*
Twiggy   411
Twigs   31
Twilight Zone, The   67, 106, 211, 214, 276, 306
Twin Peaks   9, 419
Two Faces West   267, 349
Two Girls Named Smith   xiv, *414*
TWO LITTLE BEARS, THE   299
Two of Us, The   376
TYCOON   190
Tycoon, The   280, 319
Tyler, Beverly   66
Tyler, Judy   190, 193
Tyler, Richard   25, 26
Tyler, Tom   367
Tylo, Hunter   452
Tylo, Michael   vii, 336, 441, 449, 451, 452, 453, 454, 455

U.F.O.   *416*
U.S. Marshal   163, 370 (See also: *Sheriff of Cochise*)
Uhnak, Dorothy   217
Ulrich, Kim Johnston   250, 251
Umeki, Miyoshi   103
Uncle Crock's Block   *416–417*
Uncle Don   417
Under One Roof   280, 376
Underdog   294
United States   376
University of Kentucky   21
University of North Carolina   21
Unknown People Part II   21
UNTOUCHABLES, THE   419, 420, 421
Untouchables, The   67, 204, 214, 312, 350, *417–422*
Up and Coming   436
Upsala College   21
Urecal, Minerva   336, 337
Urich, Robert   65

V   451
V: The Series   194, 289
Valdis, Sigrid   180, 181
Valentine, Karen   149, 215, 399
Valentine's Day   118
Valerie   127, *423–424*
Valerie's Family   (See: *Valerie*)

Vallely, Tannis   176
VALLEY OF GWANGI, THE   311
Vampira   298
Van Ark, Joan   397
Van Bergen, Van   420
Van Dyke, Barry   6
Van Dyke, Dick   117, 337, 340, 419
Van Dyke, Hilary   296
Van Dyke, Jerry   150
Van Patten, Dick   16, 131, 132, 250, 322, 324
Van Rooten, Luis   212
Van Zandt, Billy   vii, 41, 42, 124, 201, 202, 276, 314, 315, 320, 324
Van Zandt, Steven   124
Vance, Vivian   15, 200, 202, 252
Vanda, Charlie   388, 389
Varney, Jim   326
Vaughn, Beryl   374
Vaughn, Robert   4, 205, 232, 237, 266, 374
Veasie, Carol   116, 118
Veazie, Carol (See: Carol Veasie)
VEGA$ 65, 123, 142, *424*
VELVET BLUE   307
Verdugo, Elena   280
Verebes, Erno   154
Veritch, Sean de   404
Vernon, Irene   62
Veronica, Betty   10
Very Brady Christmas, A   78, 79
Vesser, Angela   170
Victor, James   vii, 255, 441, 449, 454, 455, 456
VICTOR/VICTORIA   265
VIEW TO A KILL, A   416
Vigoda, Abe   310
Vigran, Herb   203, 235, 236, 312
Vila, Bob   182, 183
Villechaiz, Herve   139, 140
Vincent, Jan Michael   394
Vinnie & Bobby   *424–425*
Virginian, The   27, 232, 234, 299, 328, 340, 361, *425–426*
VIRGINIAN, THE   426
Vise, The   270
VISIT TO A SMALL PLANET   319
Viva Valdez   455
Vives, Viviane   107
Vogel, Mitch   71
Voglin, Jack   8
Voice of the Turtle, The   202
Volz, Nedra   119, 120, 136
Von Zell, Harry   145, 146
Vonnegut, Kurt Jr.   47
Voorhies, Lark   358, 359
VOYAGE TO THE BOTTOM OF THE SEA   37, 426
Voyage to the Bottom of the Sea   *426–427*, 58, 179, 239, 240, 354
Voyagers!   103

Wacked Out   253
Waggoner, Lyle   49, 438
Wagner, Kathy   372
Wagner, Lindsay   328
Wagner, Robert   208
Wagon Train   57, 67, 180, 214, 250, 311, 386, 392, 411, 412, 426, *430–432*
Wagon Train's Thirty and Still Rollin'   432

WAGONMASTER   431
Wakefield, Jack   117
Walberg, Gary   322, 324
Walden, Robert   312
Waldo   23
Waldron, Vince   396
WALK ON THE WILD SIDE   267
Walker, Arnetia   320
Walker, Clint   96, 97, 100, 277
Walker, Jimmy   161
Walker, Nancy   278, 279, 412
Walker, Paul W.   404
Walker, Ray   291
Wallace, George   102
Wallace, Marci   65
Wallace, Marcia   63, 159
Wallace, Mike   376
Wallace, Myron   (See: Mike Wallace)
Wallace, Rick   220
Wallach, Eli   49, 50, 51
Wallas, Ellie Wood   438
Walley, Deborah   148, 295
Walsh, Brigid Conley   412
Walsh, M. Emmet   121, 122
Walsh, Raoul   157
Walt Disney Presents   106, 233, 444
Walter, Jessica   284, 285, 286
Walters, Barbara   112
Walther, Susan   339, 340
Walton, Sunni   406
Waltons, The   12, 136, 162, 300, *432–434*
Wambaugh, Joseph   69
Wanted: Dead or Alive   213, 427
WAR LOVER, THE   271
WAR OF THE WORLDS, THE   327
Ward, Burt   49, 142, 367
Ward, Evelyn   330
Ward, Jonathan   89, 90
Ward, Sela   372
Warden, Jack   408
Warfield, Marlene   275, 276
Warfield, Marsha   316, 319
WARGAMES   127
Warlock, Billy   53, 54
Warner, Jack   174
Warner, Jody   268
Warner Brothers Presents   89
Warren, Elaine   113
Warren, Kiersten   360
Warren, Lesley   284, 285, 289
Warren, Richard Lewis   346
Washbrook, Johnny   305
Washington, Kenneth   180, 181
Watanabe, Gedde   316
Watch Mr. Wizard   11
Waterhouse, Jaryd   46
Waters, Ethel   58, 59
Waters, Harry Jr.   435
Waters, James R.   152
Waters, John   414
Watson, Debbie   215, 300
Watson, Miles   240
Watson, Vernee   119
Watt, Nathan   107

Waxman, Al   197, 200
Wayland, Len   125, 126
Wayne, David   11, 12, 13
Wayne, Ethan   7
Wayne, John   13, 16, 163, 190, 226, 368, 432
WAYNE'S WORLD   64, 104
We Got it Made   194
Weatherly, Shawn   53
Weatherwax, Bob   227
Weatherwax, Ken   8
Weatherwax, Rudd   225, 226, 227
Weaver, Dennis   163
Weaver, Lee   66
Weaver, Tol   215
Webb, Jack   7, 12, 125, 126, 326, 343, 355, 356
Webb, Jane   152, 227
Webster   102, 348, 398
Webster, April   142
WEDDING PRESENT   26
Weddle, Vernon   141
Weil, Jeri   230, 232
Weinberger, Ed   46, 396
Weinraub, Bernard   248
Weintraub, Sy   393
Weismuller, Johnny   392, 394
Weitz, Bruce   41, 42, 179
Welch, Raquel   300
Welcome Back Kotter   90, 97, 161, 166, 176, 447
Weld, Tuesday   268, 269
Welker, Frank   406
Wells, Dawn   150, 198, 300
Wells, H.G.   206
Wells, Mary K.   65, 66
Wells, Orsen   164, 271, 333
Wells, Scott   17
Wendell, Howard   231
Wendt, George   93
Werewolf   *434*
WEREWOLF OF LONDON, THE   201
Wesley   274, *434–435*
Wesley, Richard   362
West, Adam   49, 51, 115, 142, 367
West, Brooks   306
West, John   14
Westmore, Perc   298
Weston, Celia   28, 29
We Got It Made   327
We'll Get By   229
What a Country!   *435*
Whatever Happened to Dobie Gillis?   268
What's Alan Watching?   293
Wheaton, Wil   383
Wheel of Fortune   xiv, 327
Wheeler, Ellen   195
Whelan, Jill   250
Whelchel, Lisa   135
When Michael Calls   386
When the Whistle Blows   168
When Things Were Rotten   16, 17
WHEN WORLDS COLLIDE   145
WHERE ANGELS GO . . . TROUBLE FOLLOWS   372
WHERE DO WE GO FROM HERE?   446
Where No Man Has Gone Before   379
WHERE SHE DANCED   299

WHILE THE SUN SHINES   17
Whiplash   285
Whirlybirds, The   xiv, 40, ***435***
WHISTLING IN THE DARK   363
Whitaker, Johnny   137, 371
Whitcomb, Dennis   310
White, Bernard   125, 127
White, Betty   294, 300
White, David   64
White, De'Voreaux   176
White, Edward H., II   197
White, Jesse   261, 263, 430
White, Karen Maline   119
White, Patrick J.   ix, 284, 286, 289
White, Peter   372
White, Sandra   291
White, Slappy   354
WHITE CHRISTMAS   120
White Shadow, The   399, ***435–436***
Whiting, Arch   354
Whiting, Barbara   374
Whitman, Ernest   59
Whitmore, James   397
Whitney, Bill   448
Whitney, Dwight   136, 333, 334
Whitney, Grace Lee   377
Whitney, Michael   411
Whodunnit?   376
Who's Afraid of Virginia Woolf?   156
Who's the Boss?   376
Wichita Town   121
Wickes, Mary   120, 303, 371, 372
Widdoes, James   89
Widmark, Richard   194, 436
Wightman, Robert   433
Wilcox, Frank   231, 418
Wilcox, Larry   98, 227
Wild, Jack   371
Wild Wild West, The   115, 177, 211, 333, 406, ***436–437***
Wild, Wild West Revisited, The   437
WILD THING   132
Wilder, James   352
Wilder, Laura Ingalls   239
Wilder, Yvonne   326
Wilkes, Donna   177
Wilkof, Lee   315
Willard, Fred   314
Williams, Anson   166, 167
Williams, Barbara   336, 337
Williams, Barry   79
Williams, Bill   418
Williams, Brian   221, 223
Williams, Cindy   228
Williams, Clarence, III   413
Williams, Elmo   76
Williams, Grant   173
Williams, Guy   441, 442, 444, 445, 446, 447, 448, 449, 450, 454
Williams, Hal   356
Williams, John   136, 137
Williams, Liberty   65, 391, 392
Williams, Paul   437
Williams, Robin   107, 136
Williams, Steven   413, 414
Williams, Treat   159

Williams, Van   390
Williams, Vanessa   280
Williamson, Fred   213
Williamson, Mykelti   428, 429
WILLIE DYNAMITE   363
Willis, Bruce   46, 165, 168
Willis, Eric   406
Willis, Jason   406
Willis, Marlene   268
WILLOW   166
Wills, Beverly   204
Wills, Chill   187, 289
Wills, Jerry   448
Willy   ***437–438***
Wilson, Demond   321, 324, 356, 358
Wilson, Dooley   59, 60
Wilson, Harry Leon   354
Wilson, Lanford   124
Wilson, Lewis   51
Wilson, Lois   25, 26
Wilson, Marie   305, 306
Wilson, Patricia   183, 184, 185
Wilson, Sheree   103
Wilson, Terry   431
Wilson, Theodore "Theo"   250, 257, 345, 399
Winant, Ethel   341
Winchell, Paul   323
Winchell, Walter   419
Windom, William   67, 110, 111, 140, 154, 303
Winds of War, The   132
Winfield, Paul   93, 181, 213, 379
Winkleman, Wendy   230, 232
Winkler, Henry   166, 167, 244
Winnie the Pooh   35
Winslow, Paula   326
Winter, Edward   343
Winter, Lynette   148, 339, 340
Winters, Cliff   349
Winters, Gloria   234, 235, 373, 374
Winters, Isabel   68
Winters, Jonathan   107, 437
Winters, Roland   122, 123, 264, 280
Wirth, Sandra   387
Wise, Alfie   416
WISTFUL WIDOW OF WAGON GAP, THE   226
Wait Till Your Father Gets Home   35, 103
WITCHES OF EASTWICK, THE   439
Withers, Bernadette   47, 48
Witt, Paul Junger   252
Wizard, The   337
WIZARD OF OZ, THE   49, 298, 330, 412
Wizards and Warriors   451
WKRP in Cincinnati   176, 263, ***428–430***
WOLF MAN, THE   132, 235, 302, 434
Wolfe, Karen   102, 103
Woliner, Jason   371
Wolpe, Lenny   46, 47
Wonder Woman   181, 207, ***438***
Wonder Years, The   433, 434
Wonderful World of Wilbur Pope   291
Wood, Kelly   330
Wood, Natalie   127
Wood, Peggy   264
Wood, Robert D.   285

Wood, Terri Lynne   52, 53
Woodell, Pat   339, 340
Woods, Donald   333
Wooley, Harold   51
Wooley, Lynn Malsbary   366
Wopat, Tom   127, 128, 129
Working It Out   272
Workman, Jimmy   9
World War III   180
Wren, Sam   340
Wren's Nest   340
Wright, Will   33, 35, 116, 118
Wroe, Trudy   66
WRONG MAN, THE   154
WUTHERING HEIGHTS   266
Wyatt, Jane   385
Wyler, William   265
Wynn, Ed   446
Wynn, Keenan   13, 418
Wynter, Dana   207

X—THE MAN WITH THE X-RAY EYES   154

Yagher, Jeff   414
Yagi, James   268, 270
Yakky Doodle   76
YANKEE BUCCANEER   246
Yarborough, Barton   125, 126
Yarnell, Bruce   328
Yates, Cassie   334
YEARLING, THE   360
YELLOW SKY   245
Yenne, Bill   ix, 444
Yeoman of the Guard, The   446
York, Dick   xv, 61, 62, 63, 64
York, John J.   434
Yothers, Tina   137
You Bet Your Life   127, 158
You Can't Take It With You   327
YOU ONLY LIVE TWICE   416
Young, Alan   291, 292, 293
Young, Carleton G.   230, 232
Young, Chic   68
Young, De De   66
Young, John   197

Young, Julie   63, 65
Young, Loretta   140, 146
Young, Ray   60
Young, Robert   415
Young, Roland   408
Young, Tamar   63, 65
Young and Gay   152
Young and the Restless, The   83, 278, 336
YOUNG DANIEL BOONE   59
Young Dan'l Boone   106
Young Dr. Kildare   121, 214   (See also: *Dr. Kildare*)
YOUNG DR. KILDARE   173
Young Dr. Malone   214
YOUNG FRANKENSTEIN   135
Young Indiana Jones Chronicles, The   **439–440**
Young Lawyers, The   426
Young Maverick   99, 277
Young Mr. Bobbin   27
Young Riders, The   177
YOUNGBLOOD HAWKE   311
Your Hit Parade   156
Your Show of Shows   117

Zachary "Zack" The Wonder Dog Morris   xi
Zada, Ramy   106
Zannuck, Darryl F.   59
Zerbe, Anthony   170, 172
Zimbalist, Efrem Jr.   171, 206, 332, 366, 441, 449, 451
Zimbalist, Stephanie   345
Zippy the Chimp   190, 193, 194
ZOMBIES OF THE STRATOSPHERE   102
Zorba   337
Zorro   xiii, xiv, 64, 90, 118, 171, 179, 200, 206, 234, 237, 255, 336, 342, 355, 366, **441–456**
ZORRO   444, 447
Zorro and Son   16, 206, 237, 447, 448
ZORRO RIDES AGAIN   444
ZORRO'S BLACK WHIP   446
ZORRO'S FIGHTING LEGION   444
Zucker, David   231
Zucker, Jerry   231
Zuckert, Bill   11, 13
Zuconic, Dorothy   191
Zulu   172, 173
Zuniga, Daphne   280

ABOUT THE AUTHOR

Steven Lance is an entertainment industry consultant and author and brings with him expertise from both sides of the camera.

An internationally syndicated columnist, he is also the television critic for *THE HERALD*, Allaire Publishing Company, Allaire, New Jersey.

As an actor, Steven's motion picture roles include an alien being from the planet Vega in Paramount Pictures' science fiction, STAR TREK—THE MOTION PICTURE and the emergency room intern in Woody Allen's semi-autobiographical comedy, STARDUST MEMORIES. He is also the host of *Names in the News with Steven Lance,* a weekly public affairs program simulcast on WHTG's FM 106.3 and AM 1410, which broadcasts from studios located in Eatontown, New Jersey.

He is the founder and executive director of the Silent Running Society, a nonprofit organization dedicated to the preservation of the planet through conservation, communication and reforestation.

When he is not writing, Steven enjoys fencing, horseback riding and, of course, watching television.